Archaeology & Tradition

(Prof. D. N. Tripathi Felicitation volume)

Archaeology & Tradition

(Prof. D. N. Tripathi Felicitation volume)

Volume – I

Editors

B.R. Mani

I.D. Dwivedi

Vimal Tiwari

AGAM

Agam Kala Prakashan

DELHI

First Published 2016

ISBN : 978-81-7320-169-1

Published by :
Dr. Agam Prasad, M.A., Ph.D., Diploma in Museology
for **Agam Kala Prakashan**
34, Central Market, Ashok Vihar, Delhi-110052
Ph. : 27212195, 65688806-7
Fax : 91-11-27212195
E-mail : agambooks@gmail.com, agambook@yahoo.com
Website : www.agamkala.com

Composed by :
Elegant Printographics
Delhi-110085

Printed by :
Chawla Offset
Ashok Vihar, Delhi-110 052

Printed in India.

Prof. D.N. Tripathi

Mrs. and Prof. Tripathi at their grand daughter's Marriage on 20 Nov. 2011

Contents

Editor's Note xi

Bibliographical Sketch xxvii

List of Contributors xxxix

List of Plates xlv

Tributes & Reminiscences

1	Colin Renfrew	Tribute to Professor Daya Nath Tripathi	l
2	अजय कुमार पाण्डेय	परम्परा के संवाहक परमाचार्य प्रोफेसर दयानाथ जी	li
3	कुवॅर बहादुर कौशिक	पुरातत्व के प्रमाता (प्रो0 दयानाथ त्रिपाठी)	liii
4	Devesh N Tripathi	An Untold Saga of My Papaji & Tribute (poem)	lv
5	देवेश नाथ त्रिपाठी	पिता–पुत्र	lxi
5	Sibesh Bhattacharya	My Friend Daya Nath, Indian Archeology --- Some Nostalgia, Some Rambling Thoughts	lxii
6	सुरेन्द्र दुबे	बहुस्तरीय संचरना का उत्कृष्ट व्यक्तित्व	lxv
7	ईश्वर शरण विश्वकर्मा	आचार्य–परम्परा के एक बहुआयामी व्यक्तित्व : मेरे गुरूवर्य	lxviii
8	राकेश तिवारी	सोहगौरा से सोहगौरा : प्रोफेसर दया नाथ त्रिपाठी	lxxi
9	Y Sudarshan Rao	Message	lxxiii
10	उमेश नाथ त्रिपाठी	आचार्य दयानाथ त्रिपाठीः मेरे पिता एवं प्रेरणा	lxxv
11	अंजुला शुक्ला	गर्व है पुत्री होने का	lxxvii
12	Irfan Habib	Professor D.N. Tripathi	lxxix

Volume - I

Section I : Archaeology

1 An Evolutionary Perspective on the Development of Human Culture 1
– *Colin Renfrew*

2 Evolution of Society and Culture in Rajasthan 6
– *V. N. Misra*

3 Over-view of the Mesolithic Culture of the Vindhya-Ganga Region 15
– *Radhakant Verma*

4 The Iron Age Society of India: Pattern of Technology Adaptation and Culture Change 23
– *Vibha Tripathi*

5 Archaeology of Kausambi: Review of a City Site of the Lower Ganga-Yamuna Doab 45
– *J N Pal*

6 Early Agro-pastoral Cultures of India 56
– *Vasant Shinde*

7 Pakkākot: Transition from Rural to Urban Settlment: An Archaeological Study 64
– *Sitaram Dubey & Santosh Kumar Singh*

8 Dwarka: Traditions and Excavations 80
– *Alok Tripathi*

9 Climate, Environment and the Break-up of the Indus-Sarasvati Civilization 85
– *Michel Danino*

10 Jalore-Elana (Irina) and Swarnagiri: A Study 93
– *K S Shukla*

11 River Saraswati— The Cradle of Indian Civilization 96
– *Rajesh Purohit*

12 Archaeological Investigations along the Ancient Pilgrimage Route from Ayodhya to Sravasti 103
– *Indudhar Dwivedi, Vimal Tiwari* and *Abha Dwivedi*

13 सरस्वती नदी का प्रवाह तंत्र एवं तीर्थ (पुरातत्त्व के संदर्भ में) 119
– *रत्नेश कुमार त्रिपाठी*

14 विन्ध्य क्षेत्र की मध्यपाषाणिक संस्कृति में जीवन–निर्वाह के साक्ष्य 136
– *रमाकांत सिंह*

15 Archaeology of Bhrigu Kshetra (with special reference of Waina) 146
– *Santosh Kumar Singh*

16 Neolithic Culture of Saryupar Region 165
– *Shitala Prasad Singh*

17. Evolution of Early Farming Culture in Middle Ganga Plain 173
– *Neelesh Kumar Pandey*

18 Palaeolithic Tools from Shekhawati Region: A Preliminary Study 179
– *Vineet Godhal*

19. New Appearance of Beads in NBPW Culture in the Middle Ganga Plain 187
– *Shanker Jaikishan*

20. Excavations at Peetnagar 192
– *D.K. Mathur*

Section II : Epigraphy & Numismatics

21 A Study of Inscriptions: History and Administration 195
– *T. P. Verma*

22 The Allahabad Museum Copperplate grant of Raṇabhañjadeva-I 221
– *G. C. Tripathi*

23 Fragmentary Stone Inscription of the Kachchhapaghāta Ratnapāla: V.S. 1165 230
– *Arvind K. Singh*

24 The Tradition of Shaiva Ascetics and their Significance (with special reference of early Medieval Inscriptions) 235
– Rajesh Kumar Dhar Dubey
25 Seals and Sealings from Sanchankot 238
– D P Tewari
26 हिन्द–यवन शासकों की मुद्राओं पर अंकित 'गज' प्रतीक : एक विवेचन 243
– विपुला दुबे
27 Stylistics of Kalachuri Coinage in Chhattisgarh 247
– Vishi Upadhyay
Plates 257

Volume – II

Section III : Art, Iconography & Architecture

28 Invocation of Sārasvatī Power in Jainism 289
– M N P Tiwari & S S Sinha
29 Śaivism of *Tattvaprakāśa* and Parallels in the Śaiva images in *Samarāngaṇsūtradhāra* 296
– Susmita Pandey
30 पूर्व मध्यकालीन जैन वास्तु में भेद अभेद के तत्व 301
– दिवाकर प्रसाद तिवारी
31 A Note on the Newly Discovered Brick Temple and it's Site at Pipri, District Siddharthnagar, U.P. 304
– Praveen Kumar Mishra
32 Yaksha Iconography: Thematic Variation and its Implications 309
– Namrata Singh
33 Depiction of Brahma's Life through the Vaishnava Sculptures of Udayagiri Caves, Vidisa: A Proportionate Blend of Iconography and Philosophy 320
– Pooja Saxena & Apurva Sinha
34 Sculptural Art of Trans-Ghaghara Region 323
– Neetu Tiwari
35 Transformation of West Asian and Greco-Roman Elements in Indian Art 329
– Vinay Kumar
36 खम्भात में अर्द्धकीमती पत्थर के मनके बनाने की पारम्परिक तकनीक 333
– राजेश कुमार मीणा
37 Newly Discovered Painted Rock Shelters of Chandauli District, Uttar Pradesh 340
– Prabhakar Upadhyay & Om Prakash Kumar
38 चम्पानेर–पावागढ के जैन बावनढेरी मंदिर के श्वेताम्बर मूर्तियों की पहचान एवं विवेचना 347
– बृजेश रावत एवं अनुपमा सिंह
39 Earliest Human Bronze Image from Middle Ganga Plain and its Iconic Representation in the Rock Art of Kaimur region, India 353
– Sachin Kumar Tiwary
40 Brahmanical Figures on the Terracotta-Art of Bihar 355
– Anantashutosh Dwivedi

Section IV : Religion

41 The Human Stratum of the Rāma Story 362
– S R Goyal

42 The Four *Varnas*: A Vedic Concept of Division of Society 376
– *Shashi Tiwari*

43 A Note on the Origin of the Āśrama Institution 381
– *Rajawant Rao*

44 The Nāynārs & Āḷvārs and their contribution to the Bhakti Movement in South India 385
– *Shankar Goyal*

45 The Living Saura Traditions of Gujarat 396
– *Atul Tripathi*

46 इक्ष्वाकु परम्परा एवं संस्कृति 405
– *ईश्वर शरण विश्वकर्मा*

47 राम चरित मानस का धर्मशास्त्रीय अध्ययन : परहित सरिस धरम नहिं भाई परपीड़ा सम नहिं अधमाई 412
– *संचिता घोष*

48 Athena Pallas : The Greek Goddess 417
– *Rekha Chaturvedi*

49. Deepaawali : Celebrations & A Message 423
– *R.C. Tripathi*

50 ऋग्वेद में मानव एवं मानवीय मूल्य 428
– *दिग्विजयनाथ*

51 The Concept of Mandal in Tantric Form of Mahayan Buddhism 433
– *Kamlesh Kumar Gautam*

52 पांचरात्र आगम में वैष्णवी दीक्षा 437
– *रामप्यारे मिश्र*

53 पांचरात्र संहिताओं में नृ–सिंह का स्वरूप 445
– *ध्यानेन्द्र नारायण दूबे*

Section V : Historiography

54 Purusha, Purana and Itihasa: History and Spiritual Understanding 450
– *Ramashray Roy*

55 The account of nearchos' voyage: an appraisal 466
– *U.P. Arora*

56 Lalitaditya Muktapida : The First Indian Antiquary 473
– *J. N. Pandey*

57 वेद–व्याख्या के नैरुक्त प्रस्थान में इतिहास की भूमिका 475
– *मुरली मनोहर पाठक*

58 यूनानी इतिहास–दर्शन : एक सर्वेक्षण 478
–*कुवॅर बहादुर कौशिक*

59 भारतीय इतिहास की सनातन परम्परा 485
–*अजय कुमार पाण्डेय*

Section VI : General

60 Ancient Indian Ideals and Modern Realities 494
– *K. Paddayya*

61 The Indo-European Problem: A New Paradigm, A complete re-look 503
– *Mohan Gupta*
62 A Cultural-Psychological Orientation to Self-Understanding 518
– *Girishwar Misra*
63 A study of Human Evolution and Migration on the basis of Analysis of Deoxyribonucleic Acid (DNA) 526
– *Ram Rudra Shukla*
64. On Our History, Our Tradition and Astronomy 530
– *Krisnanand Sinha*
65 Ganesh Shankar Vidyarthi and his Crusade Against Communalism (1915-1931) 533
– *P.K. Shukla*
66 The Aesthetics of Sanskrit Theatre and the Structure of Sanskrit Drama 540
– *Kamalesdatta Tripathi*
67 Shorapur: A Palace City of Late-Medieval Southern Deccan 550
– *S. K. Aruni*
68 Water Resources and their Management in Ancient India 555
– *Pragya Chaturvedi*
69 Lumbini: The Birthplace of Lord Buddha 560
– *Gitu Giri*
70 प्रयाग और भरद्वाज 565
– *राजेश मिश्र*
71 Power and Imagination : Representation of India in European Cartography 569
– *Deepak Kumar* and *Ravindra Kumar*
72 "पूर्व वैदिक काल में स्त्रियों की स्थिति: एक ऐतिहासिक विमर्श" 578
– *संगीता सिंह*
73 Banking in Ancient India 582
– *Praveen Kumar Sharma*
Plates 585

Editor's Note

It was the month of April 2014 when the idea of this felicitation volume came in the mind of pupils and well wishers of Professor D.N. Tripathi to felicitate him for his contribution to the subject. The theme of this volume titled 'Archaeology and Tradition' was chosen as this is the favourite subject of Professor Tripathi and most of his research was oriented to this topic.

Indology and archaeology represent faces of the same coin in an ideal combination. In most other countries with an ancient past like West Asia, China and Egypt, terms like Assyriologist, Sinologist or Egyptologist signify 'an expert in the study of human antiquities of the respective country, focusing on evidences drawn from archaeological excavations.' However, the term Indology has been defined as 'the study of literature and history of India.' The reason for this anomaly may be that an Indologist, in Indian parlance, has come to mean one who is not an archaeologist and is, therefore, not aware of the importance of the study of pottery and of modern dating methods. The situation is changing now. In post- independence India much of the writing of history is based upon the synthesis of archaeology and tradition. Archaeological cultural sequence for a given region is a paradigm with which the traditional culture-framework of the same region (as from Puranic data) will have to be compared. The resultant congruency will have to be taken as the best fitting restoration of the past. Traditional data in India does not necessarily lack authenticity of occurrence, but mainly lack chronological consistency or cohesion. Archaeological data provide this invaluable correction.

The answer of these problems could be found in its analysis on the basis of the data available to us both from Archaeology and Tradition. The history of ancient civilizations cannot be written correctly without the help of both. Schliemann was probably the first archaeologist who tried to identify the Greek traditions in its archaeological remains. With his complete faith in the historicity of Homer's Iliad, he started his search for the city of Troy and Mycenae. In 1872 he identified the "Palace of Priam" and "Priam's Treasure" which included two diadems, six bracelets, sixty ear-rings, 8,700 rings, buttons and ornaments of gold, an electrum vase and others of silver and bronze, and many bronze weapons. In spite of scholastic jeers of the contemporary academics, Schliemann continued his search, and in 1876, while excavating the Shaft Graves at Mycenae, he not only identified the 'Golden Mycenae' of Homer but also had a 'gaze upon the face of Agamemnon!' And then digging by Schliemann in Greece and Evans (1900) in Crete at Knossos, 'the Palace of Minos', and Sir Leonard Wooley (1926) at Ur—'Royal Tombs of Ur'— and many other excavations in Lebanon, Palestine and Syria with a view to locating the Bible cities or sites, have yielded good results.

In India, scholars turned to archaeology for the verification of the Epic stories quite late. B.P. Sinha may be correct in thinking that "this was partly because the earlier archaeologists from Cunningham onwards were very much concerned with Buddhist sites about which there were Chinese accounts and datable Buddhist and Jain literary texts". In the second decade of the last century, when archaeologists came to know of the Indus civilization accidentally, much of the energy and resources of the Archaeological Survey of India was invested in the study of this civilization. It was left to B.B. Lal to "embark on the adventure of testing Indian traditions in the crucible of archaeology", although Pargiter, a great proponent of the value of historical traditions, had asserted as early as 1922 that "the general trustworthiness of the tradition is the fact demonstrated, whenever it has been possible to test tradition by results of discoveries and excavations." In any case, the process once started by Lal in the field has been carried on by other historians and archaeologists in India and *Puratattva* No. 8 is largely devoted to the discussion of the theme 'Archaeology and Tradition'. The present position in India is that, whereas some scholars believe that the traditions contain some real truth, and that they refer to genuine historical traditions, scholars like D.C. Sircar think that the Indian traditions as stored in the Puranas and Epics and corroborative additional information gleaned from the vast Vedic literature are imaginary and provide no base for sober history. M.C. Joshi is of the opinion that the Indian tradition, Vedic or Puranic, is not "likely to help much in the interpretation of archaeological data" as they are "unhistoric and coloured". Tradition and archaeology should not be mixed together in any form at least as far as Indian protohistory is concerned. Romila Thapar also considers that "in the absence of contemporary written record or deciphered scripts, any attempt to correlate archaeological material with traditional accounts of the past becomes a venture into speculation." Despite these doubts, there are many historians and archaeologists in India who are trying to identify the tradition with archaeology. R.S. Sharma is of the view that the Painted Grey Ware phase of Indian archaeology is "comparable on many counts to the material culture of the later Vedic texts". Sankalia has been consistently arguing the case of identification of various Chalcolithic and Neolithic cultures of India with the Vedic and Puranic tribes. Malati J. Shendge may be right in saying that:

> It is possible to verify the literary tradition through archaeological findings and the literary tradition may also be used to throw light on the archaeological remains without which they may be best described as artefacts which do not seem to breathe life on their own ... if a coherent picture is to be drawn, both literary and archaeological evidence have to go hand in hand.

We all know that Lal, after having worked on the archaeology of Mahabharata, also worked on the national project of the 'Archaeology of Ramayana Sites'. Sānkalia and Gupta have also done work on the two great epics. Recognizing the importance of this subject, the Advisory Board of the Archaeological Survey of India, in its meeting held in November 1974, approved this project out of the list of twenty five problem-oriented national projects, which were required to be undertaken during the Fifth Five Year Plan (1974-79). Sinha may be right in admitting that the archaeology and literary traditions are the "twain that do not meet" today. Still we feel that in the near future we will strive and strive with success to make Archaeology and Tradition meet since all our traditions cannot be fully false. But in this effort the approach has to be "contextual rather than textual" and one will have to bear always in mind the caution given by Ghosh that ". . . It is indeed tempting to utilize archaeological evidence for substantiating tradition, but the pitfalls in the way should be guarded against, and the caution is necessary that fancy does not fly ahead of facts."

Traditional evidence yielded by literary texts and archaeological evidences can perhaps meet only at certain points. This perhaps may be possible by "undertaking a total structural study of society and the major trends of societal change in terms of both archaeology and literary tradition." Sankalia also holds the same opinion. He thinks "Our literary data are preserved in the Vedic and Puranic literature ... something about the political, social, religious and economic conditions, however, may be gathered to putting together the scraps of evidence from these sources."

Earlier attempts to correlate archaeology and the literary sources have, in the main, focused on the question of identifying the Aryans. Studies made on the basis of linguistic paleontology became acceptable to scholars only after the excavation of Boghazkeui by the German archaeologist, Hugo Winckler, in 1906-1908. About ten thousand inscriptions in cuneiform script were unearthed. When the Czech linguist, Freidrich Hrozny, read them in 1924, several issues concerning the Aryan problem seemed to have been solved. Ever since then the authority of the Vedic literature for interpreting the Aryan culture has been accepted by the scholars. Jean Deshayes in the beginning of the present century had identified the Aryan race on the basis of their copper and bronze tools found from Danube to the Ganga valley.

D.N. Tripathi became interested in the problem of tracing the material artifacts of the Aryan people who were surely the first users of copper and bronze artifacts on an industrial scale after his studies on the copper and bronze artifacts of the Mainland Greece (2600 B.C.-1450 B.C.). He has published several articles in his book *Archaeology and Tradition* which deals with this problem in detail.

New trends in Indian historiography since independence gained a new momentum and have been enriched by a variety of archaeological approaches. This has spurred scholars and students alike to have an archaeological look at the Aryan problem. The myth of a parent Indo-European language, the myth of an Aryan race speaking this language, the myth of a homeland for them in Central Asia or some region outside India, the myth of their invasion on India, and the myth of Arya-Dasa, Arya-Harappan or Aryan-Dravidian confrontation are completely exploded now. Prof. B.B. Lal (*Saraswati Flows on*, 2002) has first exploded the myth of Aryan invasion and only recently Michel Danino has quite convincingly discussed this problem in his book *The Lost River-on the trails of the Saraswati* (Penguin Books, 2010).

The origin of the Indus civilization is now dated in the fifth millennium BC (*Pre-Kot Dijian deposits at Harappa*: R.H. Meadow and Mark Kenoyer). Early Harappan phase now goes back to 3300 B.C.-3100 BC. A 4-meter deposit of the so-called early Harappans or Kot Dijian levels, Pre-Early Harappans or Pre-Kot-Dijian levels at Dholavira, and G.F. Dale's excavations at Bala Kot suggest that the early levels may go back to the 4th millennium BC. The Harappan civilization could easily now be placed along with Mesopotamian civilisation insofar as antiquities of both the civilisations are concerned. Vedic people were not the primitive nomadic pastoralists, as once Max Muller thought, but they were, in fact, fully aware of the craft specialisations of the urban culture. Since there is no other pre-600 B.C. urban culture in India except the Harappans, there is no way out but to accept the proposition that the Harappans and the Vedic were neither two different culture-complexes, nor the earlier proceeded the later. The Myth of Aryan invasion of the Harappan town was exploded long ago and the theory of non-presence of true domesticated horse at Harappan sites is no longer substantiated (cf. Mohenjodaro, Kalibangan, Ropar, Surkotda, etc.).

More than 30,000 miniature sculptures of clay, marble, bone, copper and gold from some 3000 sites of the Neolithic and Chalcolithic era in South Eastern Europe along with enormous models of temples and actual temples have been reported in recent years. Marija Gimbutas of California has identified various cosmogonical and cosmological images of moon, bull, snake, fish and primordial Egg in them. These archaeological images are well dated on the basis of the radio-carbon analysis and their calibration with dendochronology in circa 6500 to 3500 B.C.

The cosmogonical and cosmological images could be better explained and appreciated on the basis of the study of Vedic literature and Puranas which have a long tradition. Much has been written on the date of various works of the Vedic literature. While some scholars have attached a label of high antiquity to them, others have placed them not much farther from the historical period of written records. H. Jacobi and Shankar Balakrishna Dixit have fixed the date of the Satapath Brahmana in 3000 B.C. on the basis of the astrological calculation of a verse in it. Winternitz too 'agreed with them when he placed the beginning of the Brahman tradition in 2000 or 3000 B.C. On the basis of the date of the Brahmanas the date of Samhitas may be placed in the tenth to sixth millennium B.C.

We would like to draw the attention to the fact that the well dated proto-Indo-European images of southeastern Europe are really the material manifestations of the Vedic mythological concepts and legendary ideographs. None will doubt the fact that the Vedic literature is the first written record of the human race consisting the best thinking regarding the origin of universe, religion and philosophy carrying traditions of thousands of years.

The exact parallels of the Vedic legendary concepts are found in these archaeological records and, as such, it would not be incorrect to place the beginnings of the Vedic tradition in the sixth millennium BC rather than in the third millennium BC. The parallels drawn from the Proto-Indo-European art motifs, the Vedic ideograms and mythological concepts will certainly justify such an assumption.

The origin of this great civilisation lies in Indian soil. The birth of no civilisation lies in any single place or single factor because civilisation is a process and not an event. It took around 1000 years to integrate all the cultural elements of Pre-Harappan sites of Baluchistan through Harayana into an urban 'process the components of which were villages and townships interacting with each other and supporting the growth of Harappan civilisation. Effective long-distance trade with West Asia was the outcome of urbanization in India and not vice-versa.

On the basis of a detailed study of the representation of Primeval Water, Primordial Egg, Snake and Fish in the Proto-Indo-European and Indo-European art forms of circa 7000 BC to 4000 BC. Marija Gimbutas has rightly concluded that these representations are definitely associated with the cosmological myths of the Indo-European people. The parallels drawn from the Vedic literature and Avesta regarding the creation of the universe simply confirms the cosmogonical and cosmological associations of the above art motifs in the Indo-European contexts. A further study of the animals, plants and trees, both in the Indo-European art and Vedic literature, reconfirms the above parallelisms. It would, therefore, be not a mere fancy to conclude that the antiquity of the Vedas would go further in the past. Since no artistic representations similar to those found in the Old Europe of seventh and fifth millennium BC is available in India, the Vedic cosmogony and cosmology could not be archaeologically attested. But, in the light of the proto-Indo-European and Indo-European art representations discussed here it would not be unfair to rethink about the antiquity and geographical expanse of the Vedic literature. Stephen Knapp's book –*Proof of Vedic Culture's Global Existence* (Lexington, KY, USA, 2010) - clearly demonstrates the Vedic influence and proof of its existence found in such countries as Greece, China, Egypt, Middle East and Africa and its link with other ancient cultures, such as the Sumerians, Persians, Egyptians, Romans, Greeks, etc. He further asserts that "*the origins of world languages and literature are found in India and Sanskrit*".

Two areas for future research in the ancient history of India have been summarized in the above paragraphs, which involve matters of global interest and within each of which a number of interesting problems can be formulated which deserve further investigation on a fairly broad interdisciplinary basis. The prospects of such studies are fairly tremendous in India.

The present felicitation volume contain total 73 articles on different aspects of History, Culture, Archaeology, Epigraphy, Numismatics, Art & Iconography, Philosophy, Tradition, Historiography and other related subjects in the honour of Professor Tripathi. Out of 73 articles, 15 are in Hindi and 58 are in English language and divided into six sections i.e. Archaeology; Epigraphy & Numismatics; Art, Iconography & Architecture; Religion & Tradition; Historiography and General. Apart from article the volume also contains 12 tributes to Professor Tripathi. Section wise summary of the papers are as follows:

Section I – Archaeology

This section contains 20 articles. The first paper by Colin Renfrew titled 'An Evolutionary Perspective on the Development of Human Culture' recognizes the aspiration that the story of human cultural development over the past 100,000 years, and more especially over the past 10,000 years, be encompassed within the broad explanatory framework of Darwinian evolution.

V.N. Misra' paper titled 'Evolution of Society and Culture in Rajasthan' deals with the archaeological antiquity of the region and followed by the continuity of the components of different cultures in present days. Several parts of Rajasthan were inhabited during the Stone Age which has been divided in lower, middle and upper Palaeolithic and Mesolithic. After Stone Age, Protohistoric cultures i.e. Harappan, Chalcolithic, OCP and PGW and early historic cultures were developed in this region. The paper reviews main components of above mentioned cultures in the first part of the paper and in the second part it deals with the several features in the form of ceramics, structures, metal technology, agriculture products, decorations, ornaments, etc. which are still surviving in this region.

Paper of Radha Kant Verma titled 'Over-view of the Mesolithic Culture of the Vindhya-Ganga Region' is focused on the Mesolithic culture of this region. The term Mesolithic was used to denote a group of industries supposed to be transitional between the Palaeolithic and the Neolithic cultures. Three stages of Mesolithic culture have been noticed in this region i.e. Epi-Palaeolithic, early Mesolithic and advanced Mesolithic. This paper deals with the material culture of Mesolithic culture on the basis of the important excavated sites located in the Vindhyan region and Ganga valley.

Paper titled 'The Iron Age Society of India: Pattern of technology adaptation and culture change' by Vibha Tripathi is focused on the developmental stages of iron technology and its role in socio-economic changes that took place in ancient India especially in the Ganga plain. The copper was used for fashioning hunting and war weapons for several centuries after emergence of iron. Qualitative and quantitative improvement in iron objects was done during the middle Iron Age and the iron metallurgy attains greater heights during the late Iron Age i.e. opening centuries of Common Era. It took a long time to perfect the metallurgy of iron to produce good quality tools and implements superior to copper- bronze that was used prior to advent of iron. The metallurgy had to attain a status of efficiency to produce cheaper and affordable objects that too in sufficient quantity to be socially adaptable and effective.

J.N. Pal's paper titled 'Archaeology of Kausambi: Review of a City Site of the Lower Ganga-Yamuna Doab' is focused on the literary references of Kausambi in ancient literatures and archaeological investigations carried out at the site. The ancient site of Kausambi is located on the left bank of river Yamuna in district Kausambi of U.P. and was the capital of Vats Mahajanapada. This ancient city was one of the fortified cities of Northern India and has been frequently mentioned in various ancient literatures. The site was identified by A. Cunningham in the year 1861 and the Archaeological Survey of India under N.G. Majumdar excavated it in 1937-38 but the large scale excavations were only carried out by the University of Allahabad under G.R. Sharma between 1949 and 1965. The paper also deals with the several issues associated with the archaeology of the site.

Vasant Shinde presented a clear picture of Indian agro-pastoral cultures in his article on 'Early Agro-Pastoral Cultures of India'. Beginning of agriculture was an important phase of human history and before that the food economy of man was based on the wild plants and hunting. During last few decades several sites related with early farming have been explored and excavated. The paper reviews the evidences of early farming from the various sites of different regions of India i.e. Ganga valley, Western India, Deccan, South India, North-East India, etc. The paper also provides scope for future work for the study of origin and development of agro-pastoral societies.

Joint Paper of Sita Ram Dubey and Santosh Kumar Singh titled 'Pakkakot: Transition from Rural to Urban Settlement: An Archaeological Study' is basically a summary of the excavation carried out by the authors at the ancient site Pakkakot. The site is located in Ballia district on the ancient bed of Chhoti Saryu (*Tons*) river. The excavation had brought to light a six-fold cultural sequence ranging from Neolithic to Medieval periods without any break. The paper includes details of each period along with important findings.

The ancient city of Dwarka is mentioned in several ancient Indian texts and is of great religious significance for Hindus. Alok Tripathi's paper titled 'Dwarka: Traditions and Excavations' is based on the excavations conducted by him in the search of the city. The paper is divided in to two parts and the first part provides literary references of Dwaraka and previous attempts which were conducted by different institutions to locate the site. The second part of the paper demonstrates the preparation and process of underwater excavations carried out by him in collaboration with the Indian Navy.

Several studies have been carried out to solve the problem of downfall of Indus-Saraswati civilization. Michel Danino's paper titled 'Climate, Environment and the Break-up of the Indus-Sarasvati Civilization' is focused on climatic and environmental studies carried out by various scholars to solve this problem.

K.S. Shukla tried to identify the present town of Jalore, village Elana and Suvarnagiri hills with the literary evidences in his paper titled 'Jalore-Elana (Irina) and Swarnagiri: A Study'. Jalore is an important town and Elana is a small village and archaeological site in the district Jalore of Rajasthan. Suvarnagiri hill ranges are located in the same district and find mention in ancient literatures.

The river Saraswati and its tributaries gave birth to a mighty civilization presently termed as Indus-Saraswati civilization in the north-western part of Indian subcontinent around 3rd millennium B.C. Rajesh Purohit's paper on 'River Saraswati- The Cradle of Indian Civilization' is based on the human colonization in this region as exemplified by the archaeological sites and materials. The paper provides detail of literary references of river Saraswati available in various ancient works. The Rig-Veda mentions Saraswati as *Ambitame*, (the best among the mothers), *Naditame,* (the best among the rivers) and *Devitame*, (the best among the goddesses). A large number of habitational sites have been discovered along the palaeo-channels of river Saraswati in Haryana, Rajasthan and Gujarat. Discussion on the major sites of Harayana along these palaeo-channels has been made in this paper.

Paper of Indu Dhar Dwivedi and others titled 'Archaeological Investigations along the Ancient Pilgrimage route from Ayodhya to Sravasti' is based on the explorations carried out by the team of Lucknow Circle of ASI under the project titled 'Anctient Pilgrimage route from Kaushambi to Kapilvastu'. Ayodhya and Sravasti were politically as well as religiously very much important during different periods and were the capitals of ancient Kosala kingdom. The paper deals with the outcome of the exploration conducted between these two pilgrimage centers. Total 44 sites, 30 in Gonda district, 11 in Balrampur district and 3 in Sravasti district were located. These sites are associated with different cultural periods ranging from pre-NBP to late Medieval. Two routes are proposed from Ayodhya to Sravasti i.e. 1. via Nawabganj, Wazirganj, Gonda, Itiathok and Balrampur, 2. Nawabganj, Mankapur, Utraula and Balrampur. On the basis of the results of exploration, it is proposed that the first route was more popular during NBPW period. In later periods, both routes were used for travelling from Ayodhya to Sravasti.

Sarasvati was a gigantic river system that originated from Himalaya, entered the plains and flowed in southwesterly direction through present day Haryana, Punjab, Rajasthan and Gujarat before joining the Arabian sea. Ancient Civilization flourished along its banks and important cities flourished along this mighty river. It was a lifeline of northwestern and western India. Paper of Ratnesh Kumar Tripathi titled 'Saraswati Nadi ka Pravaah Tantra evam Teerth' deals with the river Saraswati and is divided in to two sections. The first section illustrates the water system of river Sraraswati from the Himalaya to the Gulf of Kachchh. The second section deals with the pilgrimage centers on the river Saraswati which were visited by lord Balrama, brother of lord Krishna.

The Vindhyan region of India is one of the oldest regions where remains of prehistoric settlements have been found. A large number of sites related with Mesolithic culture are reported from this region. These sites are located in either open areas or in the rock shelters. Excavation of some sites named Morahna Pahad, Bagahikhor, Lekhahia and Chopanimando have been carried out. Paper of Ramakant Singh titled 'Vindhya Kshetra kee Madhyapashanik Sanskriti me Jeevan Nirvaah ke Sakshya' is the review of subsistence pattern of Mesolithic culture of Vindhyan region on the basis of material evidence.

Paper of Santosh Kumar Singh titled 'Archaeology of Bhrigu Kshetra' is basically a report of excavation carried out at the ancient site Waina, located in Bhrighu ksetra (Ballia district of U.P.) on the confluence of rivers Ganga, *chhoti* Saryu and Magai. The site of Waina was excavated by Purushottam Singh of Banaras Hindu University in the nineties of last century. The first part of the paper comprises geographical scenario, water resources, historical background and archaeological scenario of the area. The second part of the paper comprises details of excavation carried out at the site. The site was first occupied for habitation during Neolithic period and was continued upto post Gupta period. The author has described important potteries and other antiquities in detail. He has also given details of structural, faunal, botanical and other important remains in his paper.

Saryupar region of middle Ganga plain is one of the most important regions where evidences of early farming have been found. Paper of Shitala Prasad Singh is based on the excavated remains of Neolithic culture of this region which titled 'Neolithic Culture of Saryupar Region'. He has provided details of all three excavated sites related to Neolithic named Sohgaura, Imlidih Khurd and Lahuradewa in his paper. Apart from Saryupar, he has also given a list of Neolithic sites in middle Ganga plain.

Paper of Neelesh K Pandey titled 'Evolution of early farming culture in middle Ganga plain' deals with the beginning of agriculture in middle Ganga plain. He has given details of crops identified during excavations at the sites of middle Ganga plain and their original habitats from where they probably transported to this region. He has divided the crops into three major groups on the basis of their origin i.e. Indian, Mediterranean and African.

Vineet Godhal's paper titled 'Palaeolithic Tools from Shekhawati Region: A Preliminary Study' is the study of explored sites and materials found by him during explorations in Shekhawati region of Rajasthan. He located 8 lower Palaeolithic [Sohanpura, Bheetaro, Reedh Ka Tila, Peer Baba Ki Bani (Badalwas), Udaipurwati (Kot), Salahadipura, Shobh (Chaneja Ki Dhani) and Gopalpura], 03 middle Palaeolithic [Bageshwar, Burja Ki Dhani, Laloda] and 01 upper Palaeolithic [Deoli Ki Dhani] sites in this region. He has also made the typological study of explored materials in his paper.

Paper of Shankar Jaikishan titled 'New Appearance of Beads in NBPW Culture in the Middle Ganga Plain' is based on the review of beads found during excavations from different NBPW sites of middle Ganga plain. He has given details of several sites of middle Ganga plain where excavations have been conducted and beads of different materials and shapes have been found. According to his paper some new materials like amethyst, basalt, coral, crystal, granite, lapis-lazuli, lime-stone, onyx, oyster, quartz, sardonyx, glass, ivory, paste, etc. were used for the first time for bead manufacturing during the NBPW period.

Last paper of this section titled 'Excavation at Peetnagar' by D K Mathur deals with the outcome of the excavation carried out at Peetnagar. The site is located on the left bank of the river Narmada in tehsil Badwaha of district Khargaon in Madhya Pradesh and the earliest level of the site is associated with the Ahar culture.

Section II - Epigraphy and Numismatics

It contains seven papers. T.P. Verma's paper titled 'A Study of Inscriptions: History and Administration' is a detailed work on the inscriptions. Inscriptions are considered as the most reliable source of Indian history. The earliest known inscriptions are found at the sites of Indus-Saraswati civilization but the script is still to be deciphered. Asoka's inscriptions are considered as the oldest inscriptions of India but some scholars claimed a pre-Asokan date for the inscriptions found at Sohgaura, Piprahwa and Mahasthan. Epigraphic records are classified into two groups: 1) those issued by the ruling authority, and 2) those issued by individuals or organizations. Being contemporary records these inscriptions provide welcome glimpses of social, religious, fiscal and administrative aspects which are otherwise unknown. The paper discussed important features of inscriptions like language, Prashastis, types of Raja-Shasana, process of writing on copperplate, etc. The paper also discussed the process of issuing land grants; offices and officers involved in this process; number of addressees in the copperplates, taxes, and many more related issues.

Rulers of Bhanja dynasty ruled over different parts of Orissa from the 5th-6th century onwards. Paper of G.C. Tripathi titled 'The Allahabad Museum Copperplate of Ranabhanjadeva-I' is based on the inscription of Ranabhanjadeva-I of the western Bhanja family who ruled in the second half of 10th century A.D. The paper is divided into two parts; the first is related with the history of Bhanjas while the second part is related with the copperplate grant. There are two copper plates and they contain total 23 lines; 12 on first and 11 on second. The inscription records the grant of a village by the king Ranabhanjadeva to a prominent Shivaite ascetic Shikhadeva for the purpose of establishing a monastery of his sect. The grant was issued in the 50th regnal year of the king and the inscription was written by Devachandra and was incised by Kulaputraka Divakara. According to the author this copper plate grant is a testimony to the fact that the Bhanja kings not only adopted Shaivaism as their personal and state religion but were also keen to propagate it throughout their empire by inviting learned Acharyas and scholars of Shaiva philosophy.

Paper of Arvind Kumar Singh titled 'Fragmentary Stone Inscription of the Kachchhapaghata Ratnapala: V.S. 1165' is a firsthand work on the inscription which was found at Gwalior fort and presently housed at Lucknow Museum, Lucknow. It consists of twenty-five lines and the language of the inscription is Sanskrit and the script is developed Nagari. The inscription is a eulogy and commences with the description of Krishna and Samkarshana followed by the description of the Kachchhapaghata rulers. The object of the present inscription is to record the construction of a temple of the Balarama on the top of the Gopa hill or Gwalior fort by Kulhana who was the 'lord of the entire army' and the 'chief minister' of the king. The last line of the inscription records that at the request of Ratnapala the *prashasti* was composed by Ananda who was the son of Manikantha. The date of the inscription is Samvat 1165 as given at the very end of the inscription. The paper also includes text of the inscription at the end.

Inscriptions are one of the very important sources of religious activities of the ancient India. Rajesh Kumar Dhar Dubey has tried to use the references of early medieval inscriptions for his paper titled 'The tradition of Shaiva Ascetics and their Significance'. References of Bilhari, Chirva, Abu, Achalesvara, Bheraghat and several other inscriptions are quoted by him in his paper which shows that the Shaiva sect was very popular in early medieval India and the Shaiva teachers and their pupils continued their tradition. They played very important role in society and politics of early medieval period. Some very learned teachers like Aghorshiva and Shrikumar composed many works related with Shaiva philosophy.

Seals and sealings are one of the most important antiquities recovered during excavations which provide information about the different aspects of the society/culture. The paper of D.P. Tewari titled 'Seals and Sealings from Sanchankot' is focused on the seals and sealings found during the excavations carried out by him in different field seasons at Sanchankot which is located on the Sai river in district Unnao of Uttar Pradesh. Most of the seals and sealings found from the site are associated with religious activities which throw sufficient light on the fact that Sanchankot was a great center of Shaivism.

The Greco-Bactrian king Demetrius I invaded India in the first quarter of second century BC and founded the Indo-Greek kingdom in northwestern part of Indian subcontinent. Near about 30 kings of this dynasty ruled and most of them are known only by their coins. The paper titled 'Hind-Yavana Shasakon kee Mudraon par ankit Gaja Prateek: Ek Vivechan' by Vipula Dubey is the study of elephant symbols especially with Zeus on the coins of Indo-Greek rulers.

Paper of Vishi Upadhyay titled 'Stylistics of Kalachuri Coinage in Chhattisgarh' is the study of coins of Kalachuri dynasty who ruled between 10th and 13th century A.D. with their capital at Ratanpur in Chhattisgarh. These coins were minted on three metals- gold, silver and copper with higher and lower denominations with a large number of motifs i.e. deities (Lakṣmi, Viṣṇu, Hanumna), Fauna (Lion and elephant), mythical animals (Gajashardula) and few mint marks. She included study of metallurgy, metrology, script, artistic features, mint marks, etc. in her paper. She also used line drawings, tables, charts, etc. as supporting instruments.

Section III - Art, Iconography and Architecture

This section contains 13 papers. Paper of M.N.P. Tewari and Shanti Swaroop Sinha titled 'Invocation of Sarasvat Power in Jainism' is focused on the status of Saraswati in Jainism. Their study reveals that the worship and rendering of Sarasvati in Jaina tradition and art, popular from the Kushan period through the centuries, had the dynamics of rapid evolution from being the goddess of wisdom to the presiding goddess of music and fine-arts. She has been invoked mainly as benevolent goddess granting power of knowledge to the worshippers but in tantric invocation she has also been conceived in gruesome form with attributes like goad, noose and having such appellations as Kali, Kapalini, Kauli, Trilochana, etc. She was also given a status equal to the Jinas, as is evident from an image of Sarasvati from Deogarh depicting her with two Jinas on the same pedestal and in same composition and size.

Shaivism was the most popular sect between 9th and 12th century A.D. in the central India. Paramara king Bhoja was the great follower of Shiva. His two works named Samarangana Sutradhara and Tattva Prakash provides very useful information regarding philosophical as well as iconographical aspects of Shaivism. Shiva is called the upadana of all the elements. Paper of Sushmita Pande titled 'Śaivism of *Tattvaprakāsa* and Parallels in the Śaiva images in *Samarānganṣūtradhāra*' is based on the study of these two important works of Bhoja.

The architectural remains of Jaina are found in the form of caves, stupas, viharas and temples. Diwakar P Tewari's paper titled 'Purva Madhyakaaleen Jaina Vastu me Bhed Abhed ke Tatva' is an analysis between the Jaina religion and the architecture related with the Jaina tradition.

Praveen Kumar Mishra's Paper Titled 'A Note on the Newly Discovered Brick Temple and It's Site at Pipri, District- Siddharthnagar, U.P.' provides a firsthand information of the exposed brick temple. The site of Pipri is a centrally protected site under the Archaeological Survey of India and yielded several small and large mounds. Scientific clearance work was initiated by the Lucknow Circle under the guidance of the author between December 2013 and February 2014 at one of the small mound. The exposed brick temple is a *pancha ratha* temple having three projections in each lateral side.

Yakshas have occupied an important place in Indian art and iconography through the ages. They were accepted within Buddhist, Jaina and Brahminical theology and assigned a subordinate status. The *Yaksha* sculptures are the earliest known anthropomorphic representation of any deity in stone in India and as such they have evoked considerable interest among scholars. Namrata Singh's paper on 'Yaksha Iconography' is the study of thematic variation in *Yaksha* iconography over space and time. She has grouped the *Yaksha* sculptures available from ancient India into four regional groups in accordance with the locations at which they have been found - Northern region, the Eastern region, the Western region and the Central region. She concluded in her paper that the most popular themes in *Yaksha* iconography have little correspondence with what the text tells us about the cult and it would be prudent if *Yaksha* iconography would be used as a source to study the *Yaksha* cult as well, instead of the sole reliance on textual sources and the *Yaksha* iconography also indicates that there were regional manifestations of the *Yaksha* cult at different places and time periods in ancient India.

Joint paper of Pooja Saxena and Apurva Sinha titled 'Depiction of Brahma's Life through the Vaishnava sculptures of Udayagiri caves, Vidisa: A Proportionate Blend of Iconography and Philosophy' is a deep study of iconography and literature. The Udaygiri caves at Vidisha are famous for the sculptures of Sheshshayee Vishnu and Varaha incarnation of Vishnu of Gupta period. The philosophical aspects of the iconography based on the puranic references have been explained by the authors in this paper.

Paper of Neetu Tiwari titled 'Sculptural Art of Trans-Ghaghara Region' is based on the primary and secondary sources. She has made explorations in district Deoria & Gorakhpur and taken references of sculptures found in this region. The region is located in the north-eastern part of the Uttar Pradesh covering 11 districts. After dealing the historical background and archaeological investigations carried out in this region, she discussed the concept and antiquity of image worship in India. She has incorporated several sculptures found in this region and related to the Maurya, Sunga, Kusana, Gupta, late Gupta and early Medieval periods.

Vinay Kumar's paper on 'Transmission of West Asian & Greco-Roman Elements in Indian Art' is the study of West Asian and Hellenistic elements which were adopted by the Indian Artisans with or without modifications during Mauryan, Sunga and Kusana periods. Beads are one of the important ornaments which are in use since ancient times.

The paper titled 'Khambhat me Ardhkeemti Patthar ke Manke banane kee Paramparik Takaneek' by Rajesh Kumar Meena is a documentation work of manufacturing technique of semiprecious stone beads presently under practice in Khambhat region of Gujarat.

Paper of Prabhakar Upadhyaya and Om Prakash Kumar titled 'Newly Discovered Painted Rock Shelters of Chandauli District, Uttar Pradesh' is focused on the painted rock shelters brought to light in course of explorations in southeastern parts of Chandauli district Uttar Pradesh and adjacent parts of Kaimur district, Bihar at Arjikalan, Nasopur, Kaurihar Khas, Ghurahupur, Tala, Tenui, in Chandauli district and at Diha, Basaha, Kharauli, Patesar and Ratanpurva in Kaimur district. The paintings executed in the rock shelters show superimpositions attempted by the artists right up to the historical period as clearly evinced by the subject matter of the paintings. The paintings depict day-to-day life-scenes of people. According to the authors, these paintings may be assignable to Upper Palaeolithc, Mesolithic, Chalcolithic and early historical periods.

Champaner and Pavagarh is located in the Godhara district of Gujarat and is a world heritage site. Antiquity of this place goes back to the prehistoric period. It was an important seat of Gujarat during the Medieval period and was came under the control of Kichchhi branch of Chahmaan Rajputs around 1300 AD. Later on, in 1484, it was conquered by the Mahmood Begda, the Sultan of Gujarat. Several Hindu, Jain and Muslim monuments are located at this place. Paper of Brajesh Chandra Rawat and Anupama Singh titled 'Champaner-Pavagarh ke Jaina Bavandheri Mandir ke Shwetambar Moortiyon kee Pahchan evam Vivechana' is focused on the documentation of Bavandheri temple which was constructed around 13th century AD. The paper illustrates nine sculptures which were identified by them.

Sachin Kumar Tiwary's paper titled 'Earliest Human Bronze images from Middle Ganga Plain and its Iconic Representation in the Rock art of Kaimur Region, India' is the study of similarities between the earliest bronze image of a male found from Chechar, Bihar during excavation and pictographs found in the Kaimur ranges.

Terracotta is considered as the most powerful and ancient mode for the artistic representation of human's emotion. Paper of Anantashutosh Dwivedi 'Brahmanical Figures on the Terracotta-Art of Bihar' is based on the terracotta having brahmanical figures over it found from the sites of Bihar. He has selected several specimens of terracotta in the form of seals, sealings and plaques found from the sites of Nalanda, Basarh, Bulandibagh and Chausa. He discussed the iconographic features of the brahmanical deities i.e. Brahma, Shiva, Ganesha, Ganeshini, Varaha, Narsimha, Duraga, Abhishek Lakshmi, Garuda, Chamunda, Harihara, Surya depicted on these terracotta remains along with Ramayana scenes. He has also included the inscriptional records engraved over these modes in his paper.

Section IV - Religion

Section IV contains 13 papers. S.R. Goyal's paper titled 'The Human Stratum of Rama Story' deals with the evolution of Ramayana. According to the author, the story of Ramayana acquired the shape of a Mahakavya in four stages. Its evolution began with the composition of stray gathas composed by unknown sutas who portray the character of Rama as a human hero and his story as a human story of a great king who has strength as well as weakness of a man. The final stage portrays Rama as an incarnation of Vishnu and a sole object of devotion. The paper also deals with several other aspects of Ramayana i.e. Dasaratha's promise of bride's price, two boons of Kaikeyi, nomination of the successor by Dasaratha, Rama's relation with his brothers. The outcome of the paper shows that Rama had no legitimate claim to the throne of Ayodhya and the atmosphere of the royal family of Ayodhya was full of factional intrigues, suspicion and hatred even before the question of Dasharatha's successor arose. Apparently Rama and Bharata both had a purely pragmatic approach to this problem.

Shashi Tiwari's paper on 'The Four Varnas: A Vedic concept of division of Society' throws light on the Vedic concept of four *Varna*. According to her the idea of classification of society into four groups is originally of Vedic Seers having intention to highlight inner quality based work- structure in the society. Nothing like caste was determined by birth. Duties of a person appear to have been based on activities rather than heredity. Undoubtedly it may be assumed that later developed caste system has its root in the *Varna* system of Vedic period.

The ancient Indian social life was divided into four stages termed as *Ashrama dharama* namely *Brahmacharya Ashrama, Grahastha Ashrama, Vanaprastha Ashrama* and *Sanyasa Ashrama*. The paper titled 'A Note on the origin of the Ashrama Institution' by Rajawant Rao shows that the scheme of the four Ashrama of life originated in eastern region during the post-Vedic period as a result of the conflict and comingle of the Shramana and Brahmana traditions. According to the author a clear reference to the of the Ashrama system is found in Jabalopanishad, which describes in sequence the four stages of an individuals' life, i.e., Brahmacharya, Grihastha, Vanaprastha and Sanyasa and the Jabalopanishad is definitely post-Buddhist.

The paper of Shankar Goyal titled 'The Nayanars and Aalvars and Their Contribution to the Bhakti Movement in South India' is based on the works of Nayanars and Aalvars for the revival and development of Vaisnava and Shaiva sect in South India. In South India till about the fifth century A.D. harmony and tolerance characterized the relations between the different religious sects. But thereafter a great change came about particularly in the Tamil region and people began to entertain fears of the whole land being converted to Jainism and Buddhism. Devotees of Vishnu and Shiva under the leadership of saints called the Alavars (Vaishnavas) and Nayanars (Shaivas) began to traverse the country through their ways. Sun worship has a very long tradition. The primitive men witnessed the miraculous power of Sun as the chief source of light, warmth and fertility. Its unique qualities aroused a deep sense of reverential emotions in the minds of primitive people.

The paper titled 'The Living Saura Tradition of Gujarat' by Atul Tripathi is the study of Sun worship in Gujarat. Gujarat lies closer to the area where the artistic activity of the *Saura* sect had first started and the region is still in possession of a sufficient number of sun temples roughly ranging from the 8th century to the 12th century CE presenting almost a continuous artistic, iconographic and architectural development for five centuries. Saurașhțra was an epicenter of the sun worshippers. In the Puranas and other religious texts Surya is shown attached to this region as his wife Sanjana Devi (locally known as Ravi Randal Devi or Ranna Devi) and father-in-law Vishwakarma were from the Prabhas Patan. The artisans and craftsmen of the region who consider themselves the descendants of Vishwakarma recognize her as their *phoi* (aunt). In any auspicious occasion they worship her and the folklore related to her marriage and married life having Vedic and Puranic backgrounds are parts of their cultural life. Many legends were also added and adopted by the society which later became part of the rituals and other ceremonies. The paper discusses in detail of those living Saura traditions which are part of the Ravi Randal worship and also of Saura festival Uttarayaṇa and focuses on the social persuasion and developments in this regard.

Paper of Ishwar Sharan Vishwakarma titled 'Ikshvaku Parampara evam Sanskriti' is focused especially on the tradition and culture of Iksvaku dynasty of Ayodhya. Although the other branches of this dynasty ruled over the Mithila and South Kosala. The genealogy of the Iksavakus of Ayodhya begins from Manu Vaivasvata. Iksavaku was the second, Mandhata was ninetieth, Purukutsa was twentieth and Dasaratha was sixtieth king of this race. The famous Iksavaku king Rama appears in the 61st generation while Vrihadabala of the same dynasty, who fought against the *Pandavas* in the Mahabharata war, was the 76th king. Sumitra was the last king of the Kosalan Empire.

Ramcharitmanas by Tulsidas is an epic dedicated to the life of lord Rama. It consists seven kands namely Bal, Ayodhya, Aranya, Kishkindha, Sundar, Lanka and Uttar Kand. Paper of Sanchita Sharma titled 'Ramcharitmanas ka Dharmashastriya Adhyayan' explains the role of Ramacharitamanasa in the society as a Dharma Shahstra.

Rekha Chaturvedi's paper titled 'Athena Pallas: The Greek Goddess' deals with the character of Athena who was the goddess of wisdom, war, polity and industrial art, etc. Athena Pallas is mostly shown on the coins Parthian king Andragoras, Apollodotus II, Menander, Dionysius, Zoilus, Apollophanes, Amyntas, Ranjabala, Azes, Azilises, Spalhores with Vinones, Spalagadames, Gondophares and Demitrious II. Author has given details of legends of Athena's origin, her attributes, epithets and her status among the goddesses. She also compared Athena with the Indian deity Saraswati in her paper.

Deepawali is an important festival which is celebrated on the Kartika amavasya every year. Paper of R.C. Tripathi 'Deepaawali: Celebrations & A Message' is focused on the celebration of Deepawali which is associated with the victorious return of Lord Rama and with the Nirvana of the Jaina thirankar, Sri Mahavira. Deepawali is a full five-day long festival, each day having specific worship and rituals. For this reason, it is also called "Pancha-raatra" mahotsava or celebrations and each of the five days has traditional / Puranic stories linked to its significance.

The Rigveda is the oldest in four Vedas and is a collection of 1017 hymns and about 10600 verses, organized in ten mandalas. Paper of Digvijayanath titled 'Rigveda me Manava aur Manviaya Moolya' is focused on the various aspects of human and human values in the Rigveda.

Paper titled 'The Concept of Mandal in Tantric Form of Mahayan Buddhism' by Kamlesh Kumar Gautam describes the origin and development of mandal in Buddhism which represents panch dhyani Buddhas named Vajrasattava in center, Vairocana in east, Ratnasambhava in south, Amitabh in west and Amoghsiddhi in north side. The intermediate directions are symbolized by four goddesses named Lochana, Mamaki, Pandaravasini and Tarini. Each goddesses represents one of the four elements – earth, water, fire, air respectively. Paanchraatra Aagam is one of the oldest sects of Vaishnavism.

Paper of R.P. Mishra titled 'Paanchratra Aagam me Vaishnavi Deeksha' is the focused on the different aspects of Deeksha or initiation mentioned in the various literatures of this sect.

Paper of Dhyanendra Narayan Dubey titled 'Panchratra Samhitaon me Nr-Singh ka Swaroop' is focused on the various types of worship of God Nr-Singh as mentioned in various Samhitas i.e. Sanatkumar, Jayakhya, Saatvat, Ishwar, etc. Lord Vishnu had taken his fourth incarnation as Nr-Singh to kill the demon Hiranyakshipu who was the father of Prahlad, a great devotee of him.

Section V - Historiography

Section V titled 'Historiography' contains 6 papers. 'Purush, Puran and Itihas: History and Spiritual Understanding' by Ramashray Roy is focused on historiography which can be broadly divided into two categories: secular and sacred. Sacred history belongs to the type of symbolic speculation that found its culmination not only in the Old Bible and writers such as Saint Augustine, Joachim of Fiora and others who used Christian symbolism in constructing the history of the world. It is also reflected in ancient historical writings, especially the *Puranas*. The purpose of the *Puranas* is not simply to describe in a neutral way what really happened in the mist of time but also to evoke in the people the need for adopting the most appropriate mode of living an exemplary life in conformity with the spirit of what had happened. History has three very distinct but important stages which can be symbolically identified as *Purusha, Purana and itihas.* These three symbols constitute the essence of history as the mode of describing man's participation in the flux of divine reality. Aim of the paper is to revive the link between *Purusha, Purana and Itihas* not only for apprehending reality better and presenting a realistic and holistic account of it but also for making man aware of his proper place in the cosmos so that he may not be affected by *pleonexisa* or *hybris*.

U.P. Arora's paper titled 'The Account of Nearchos' Voyage: An Appraisal' is a detailed exploration of references of Nearchos' expedition from the mouth of the Indus to the head of the Persian gulf available in different literary sources i.e. Arrian's *Indika*, and *Anabasis*, Strabo's *Geography* and Pliny's *Natural History*, etc. Nearchos was the admiral of Alexander's army who was selected by him for this expedition. Nearchos has given a long list of places on the coast lines, races, the number of stades sailed each day, the navigational facilities, climatic condition and some hints on the maritime trade. According to the literary records, he was deputed not to navigate the ocean, but to investigate the coast lying on the ocean, and the inhabitants of the coast, and its anchorages, and its water supplies, and the manners and customs of the inhabitants and what part of the coast was fertile, and what part was not.

Lalitaditya Muktapida was the ruler of Karkota dynasty of Kashmir who ruled between 724 and 760 A.D. Owing to his remarkable achievements, Lalitaditya became a halo of popular stories in the tradition of Kashmir. The paper of J N Pandey titled 'Lalitaditya Muktapida: The First Indian Antiquary' is focused on one of these stories mention by Kalhan in his work Rajatarangini regarding the king's initiative to expose two temples.

Murli Manohar Pathak's paper 'Veda-Vyakhya ke Nairukt Prasthan me Itihas kee Bhumika' deals with the knowledge of history to describe the verses of Vedas. To know the real meaning and pure pronunciation of Vedas, Vedangs were created. Shiksha, Kalpa, Vyakarana, Nirukta, Chhandas and Jyotisha are six Vedangas and out of these Nirukta is most important. To know the fundamental meaning of Vedas knowledge of Nirukta is necessary. It is also important to know the history and historical events to describe the verses of Vedas.

Kuar Bahadur Kaushik's paper 'Yunani Itihas Darshan: Ek Sarvekshan' and Ajay Kumar Pandey's paper 'Bhartiya Itihas ki Sanatan Parampara' deals with the Greek Historiography and Indian Historiography respectively.

Section VI - General

This section contains 14 papers on various aspects. India is a country of values and customs and these are continuing in the society since very ancient times. In other words, the past continues and lives into the present. The paper titled 'Ancient Indian Ideals and Modern Realities' by K.

Paddayya aim to explore certain dimensions of this connectedness or relationship between the past and the present.

The paper of Mohan Gupta titled 'The Indo-European Problem: A New Paradigm, A Complete Re-look' is a wonderful paper which is focused on the origin and mainland of the Aryans and traces the facts on the basis of four lanes viz. 1. Archaeology, 2. Archaeo-astronomy, 3. Cosmology and cosmogony, Linguistic paleontology, theology etc. and 4. the literary history, starting from Rigveda down to the Mahabharata. He concluded in his paper that the Vedic period extends from 9th millennium B.C. to 2000 B.C. and the Sapta Sindhu or the Brahmavarta is the homeland of Proto-Indo-European language and this language is none other than the Proto-Vedic Sanskrit. The Aryan migration or Aryan invasion theory is completely baseless. There is no indication in the entire vast Indian literature of any foreign origin or any reminiscence of a foreign land. The ancient Rigvedic Aryans in 7th, 4th and 2nd millennium B.C. were the carriers of Proto Vedic Sanskrit in the distant lands of Crete, Greece, Anatolia, Sumer, Egypt and Babylonia because they ruled these countries during various periods.

The paper titled 'A Cultural-Psychological Orientation to Self-Understanding' by Girishwar Misra is focused on the thoughts on the notion of selfhood. The notion of self may be characterized as a multifaceted, dynamic system that emerges in socio-cultural processes and subsequently regulates and mediates behavior at individual and group levels. It acts as an anchor and affords and constraints our behavior, perceptions, feelings, values and meanings held by the people.

DNA is the chemical basis of life for all living organisms, including humans. It is the blue-print of life, growth and differentiation as the information stored in its sequence is specific to every organism. Ram Rudra Shukla's paper titled 'A study of human evolution and migration on the basis of analysis of Deoxyribonucleic acid (DNA)' is based on the review of molecular biology methods used in predicting human evolution and migration.

Krishnanand Sinha's paper titled 'On Our History, Our Traditions and Astronomy' is focused on the astronomical facts recorded in ancient texts to establish our tradition. On the basis of astronomical references available in Valmiki Ramayana, dates related with the important events of lord Ram's life have been calculated by different scholars.

Ganesh Shankar Vidyarthi was born on 26 October 1890 and was assassinated on 25 March, 1931 in the wake of the Kanpur riot. He was a dedicated and prominent Congress leader, and one of the leading literary figures of India. Ganesh Shankar Vidyarthi was associated with the 'Pratap' newspaper. He wrote extensively against communal frenzy. The article of P K Shukla titled 'Ganesh Shankar Vidyarthi and His Crusade Against Communalism (1915-1931)' is based on Ganesh Shankar Vidyarthi's writings which discusses his crusade against the rising tide of communalism, and also focuses on his perception of India as nation, his concern for the distortions of India's past history in the writings of the imperialist historians.

Tradition of theatre is a very old practice in India. Bharata Muni is regarded as the preceptor of Drama and Theatre (Natya). His work Natyashastra is an encyclopaedic compendium of ancient Indian Theatre. Paper of Kamaleshdutta Tripathi titled 'The Aesthetics of Sanskrit Theatre and the Structure of Sanskrit Drama' deals with the practice of Sanskrit theatre in India.

Several capital cities and urban centers were established during the Medieval period in Karnataka. The paper of S.K. Aruni titled 'Shorapur: A Palace City of Late-Medieval Southern Deccan' is focused on the setup of the city of Shorapur located in the present day district of Yadgir in Karnataka. The city was founded by Raja Pid Nayaka-II around 1710 who divided the city into 14 quarters and assigned them to various classes of the society. The paper presents the details of the fort, palaces, temples, space arrangement of city, etc.

Water is one of the essential elements for the existence and no one can survive without it. Pragya Chaturvedi's paper on 'Water resources and their management in Ancient India' presents a variety of data for water and water resources in ancient India. She used literary references like Rigveda, Atharvaveda, Mahabhasya, Arthashastra, etc. and archaeological evidences from different sites and periods for water, water resources and water management for her paper and shown that these evidences reflect the ingenuity and wisdom of our ancestors who made water and its management an integral part of the native culture and community life. This water-wisdom at all levels of society ensured adequate availability of water for all, which in turn, formed the basis of all-round development and prosperity.

Lumbini is considered as one of the great centers of Buddhism as lord Buddha was born here. It is located in the Rupandei district of Nepal near the Indo-Nepal border. The paper of Gitu Giri titled 'Lumbini: The Birth Place of Lord Buddha' presents a wide range of information regarding Lumbini and its importance. The site was visited by King Asoka in his 20th year of kingship and an inscribed stone pillar was installed here. A large number of artifacts of the Mauryan, Sunga, Kushana and Gupta periods were recovered in course of various excavations. Due to its outstanding universal value it was inscribed in the World Heritage list in the year 1997.

Rajesh Mishra pointed out the importance of Allahabad (Prayaga) and its association with the sage Bharadwaja in his paper titled 'Prayaga and Bharadwaja'. Greatness of Prayaga is mentioned in various Indian texts i.e. Vedas, Brahmans, Epics, Puranas, etc. Bharadwaja was a great sage who lived on the bank of river Ganga at Prayaga. An archaeological site named Bharadwaj Ashrama is located in Allahabad city. Before the establishment of a city called Allahabad by the Akbar in 1575 AD, Prayaga was known as a great religious center.

Maps are temporal frozen frame that are devoid of dynamic landscape processes but they do reveal themselves as a site of theater where ethnocentricity, racism and other biases play. The recent trends in the historiography of cartography are a step away from writing cartobibliography and viewing maps as simplistic representation of space. Paper of Deepak Kumar and Ravindra Kumar titled 'Power of Imagination: Representation of India in European Cartography' is an attempt to explore history of cartography in India to study maps and marginalia constructed by Europeans reflecting Imperial agendas, social stereotypes and other biases.

Paper of Sangeeta Singh titled 'Poorva Vedic Kaal me Mahilaon ki Sthiti: Ek Aitihasik Vimarsh' is focused on the role and condition of ladies during the early Vedic age as cited in the Vedic literatures i.e. Vedas, Upanishadas, Brahmanas, etc. During this period male and female have the same status and rights in the family and the society.

Praveen Kumar Sharma's paper titled 'Banking in Ancient India' describes the role of temples as banking centers in ancient India. The religious centers like temples were safe places for the protection of money and other valuable things. The temples in ancient India used to give loans to various customers from its own treasury with the stipulation that the fixed interest on the loan should be paid regularly into the treasury of the temple. The paper also discussed the terms and conditions of the loans which were disbursed by the temples.

Acknowledgement

We are thankful to all the contributors for their papers and tributes. We are also thankful to Dr. Agam Prasad of Agam Kala Prakashan, Delhi who has taken keen interest in the publication of this volume.

Bibliographical Sketch

Prof. Daya Nath Tripathi is one of those renowned academicians who don't need any introduction. His vast academic and research experience in the field of Archaeology and Ancient History shows his excellence, love and affection for the subject. He was born on 13th June 1938 as the eldest son of Smt. Krishna Devi and Pandit Ram Kishor Sharma of Jairam Purwa located in the Meja tehsil of district Allahabad (U.P.). He completed his primary education at Modern School, Allahabad and passed High School from Seva Samiti Vidya Mandir, Allahabad. After passing Intermediate from Government Inter College, Allahabad, he joined Allahabad University for Graduation. He has completed his Post Graduation from the department of Ancient History, Culture & Archaeology, Allahabad University, Allahabad in the year 1958. At the age of 19 year, he was married to Smt. Leela Tripathi. He joined Ancient History department of Gorakhpur University, Gorakhpur as Lecturer in 1958. He was promoted as Reader in the year 1979 and as Professor in the year 1989. Professor Tripathi has taken the charge of Head of the Department in the year 1994 and was retired from University in 1998. He received a lot of love and respect from teachers, students, administrative officers and employees during his about 40 years long teaching carrier. In addition, he possessed administrative responsibilities of Chief Proctor (1980-84) and Director of Rahul Peetha (1994-98) in the same University.

During his service at Gorakhpur University, he also served as the General Secretary of Gorakhpur University Teachers' Association between 1961 and 1964; Hon. Bn. Comdt. of U.P. Home Guards between 1963 and 1970; President of Gorakhpur University Teachers' Association between 1977 and 1979; Chief Proctor and Special Executive Magistrate of Gorakhpur University between 1980 and 1983; General Secretary of Federation of U.P. Residential Universities Teachers' Association, between 1985 and 1987 and President of Federation of U.P. Residential Universities Teachers' Association during 1987 and 1989. He was also deputed as the authorized Controller of Kishan Post Graduate College, Basti, U.P. in 1994 and continued till 1998.

Professor Tripathi has been awarded Greek Government Scholarship (1971-74), British Council Scholar (1974-76) and Studentship of British School of Archaeology at Athens, Rome, Ankara and Tehran (1971-76) and received Diploma in Greek language from Athens University in 1972 and awarded Ph.D. in 1976 by Southampton University (U.K.) under the guidance of Lord Colin Renfrew for his masterly work titled 'Bronze work of Greece'.

He has participated in the excavation at Kaushambi under the direction of Professor G.R. Sharma during his post graduation in 1957-58; at Sohgaura, an important Neolithic site, under the supervision of Prof. S.N. Chaturvedi between 1961 & 63; at Ahar, a well known Chalcolithic site of Rajasthan, under the supervision of late Prof. H.D. Sankalia in 1963-64. He was the co-director of excavation at Fazilnagar, district Kushinagar and was the director of excavation at Usmanpur Dih both in district Kushinagar. The first site was excavated in 1978-79 and the later was in 1997-98. Apart from the above, Prof. Tripathi was involved in finding new archaeological sites and between 1994 and 1998 more than 200 sites were explored by him in Gorakhpur division, located in Saryupar region. Apart from India, he has contributed in the excavations at Meneleon under the supervision of Dr. H.W. Catling, Director, British School at Athens in the year 1973-74 and at Pylos under supervision of Prof. G.S. Korres of Athens University in the year 1974-75. The above sites are located near Sparta in Greece.

Professor Tripathi received the chance to study the copper and bronze objects of the Aegean World kept in the museums of the Mainland Greece, The Cyclades, Dodecanese and Crete between 1971 and 1974. He also studied all the Pre and Protohistoric materials in the museums of Yugoslavia (Belgrade), France (Louvre), Germany (Munich, Bonn and Frankfurt), Italy (Rome), U.K. (Ashmolean, Cambridge, Southampton and London (British Museum), Egypt (Cairo), Turkey (Istambul and Ankara), and Iran (Tehran) between 1975 and 1977.

After his retirement from Gorakhpur University, he was the visiting Professor in Allahabad University in 1998-99, fellow of Indian Institute of Advance Study, Shimla between 1999 and 2002, visiting Professor at British Academy, London, U.K. in 2003. He was appointed a member of Indian Council of Historical Research (ICHR), New Delhi in 1998 and continued till 2004. In the year 2004 he was appointed as the Chairman of the same institution and completed his tenure in 2007. He was the member of cultural delegation of ICCR, Government of India to Indo-Greek festival in 1988; ICHR delegate to XXXVIth ICAANAS conference at Canada in 2000 and ICHR delegate to XIVth UISPP conference at Liege (Belgium) in 2001.

During his vast academic carrier Professor Tripathi completed several major research projects, attended and organized National and International conferences, chaired more than 50 academic sessions in National and International seminars held in India and abroad, delivered academic lectures in India and abroad and reviewed books. He has published several books and more than 50 research papers in prestigious National and International Journals and Felicitation volumes. 'Archaeology and Tradition' of University Grant Commission, New Delhi; 'Archaeolinguistics' of Indian Council of Historical Research, New Delhi; 'Hinduism & Hellenism' of Indian Institute of Advance Study, Shimla are the numerous projects which have been completed by him. More than half dozen students have received Doctorate and D.Litt. degree under his supervision.

Prof. Tripathi is a life member of Indian Society for Greeco-Roman Studies, Indian Archaeological Society, Indian History & Culture Society and Indian Society for Prehistoric & Quaternary studies. He is holding post of member of Madhya Pradesh Heritage Development Council, Bhopal and Allahabad Museum Society and its Governing Council, Allahabad at present.

Professor Tripathi has two daughters and two sons. The eldest daughter Smt. Aparna Shukla is a housewife and residing in Virginia, USA with her husband Dr. Ram Rudra Shukla. His second daughter Dr. Anjula Shukla is married to Shri Ashok Shuka and working as Associate Professor in B.Ed. Department of Buddha P. G. College, Kushinagar, U.P.. Dr. Umesh Nath Tripathi is the eldest son and working in the Department of Chemistry, DDU Gorakhpur University as Associate Professor and is married to Smt. Usha Tripathi. Dr. Devesh Nath Tripathi is working in the Defence Institute of Psychological Research, New Delhi as Scientist and is married to Smt. Jyoti Tripathi. Professor Daya Nath Tripathi is residing in Gorakhpur with his wife at present.

Books by Professor Tripathi

1. 2013. *India and Central Asia*- Indo-Russian Seminar Proceedings, ICHR & Aryan Books International, New Delhi.
2. 2012. *A Golden Chain of Civilizations: Indic, Iranic, Semitic and Hellenic from c. 600 BC to A.D. 600,* Vol. 1, Part 5 of the PHISPC, New Delhi.
3. 2007. *A Golden Chain of Civilizations: Indic, Iranic, Semitic and Hellenic up to c. 600 BC,* Vol. 1, Part 4 of the PHISPC, New Delhi.
4. 2005. *A Discourse on Indo European Languages and Culture*, ICHR, New Delhi.

5. 2004. *Hinduism and Hellenism,* Indian Institute of Advanced Study, Shimla.
6. 1996. *Cultural Interactions Between India and Greece,* K.P. Jayaswal Research Institute, Patna.
7. 1994. *Puratattva Paribhasha Kosha,* CSTT, Ministry of HRD, Govt. of India.
8. 1988. *Archaeology and Tradition,* Ramanand Prakashan, Delhi.
9. 1987. *Bronzework of Mainland Greece from 2600BC to 1450 BC.*, Studies in Mediterranean Art Archaeology Series, Vol.69, Gottenburg University, Sweden.
10. *Rock Art of India and France*, Indo-French Seminar Proceedings, ICHR, New Delhi (In Press)

Published Articles of Professor Tripathi

1. 2015. "Art and Religion" in *Early India: Historical Probings*, S.R. Goyal Felicitation volume, Kusumanjali Prakashan, Jodhpur, pp. 1-7.
2. 2015. "Foreword" in *Mani-Sushma: Archaeology and Heritage*, Felicitation volume of Dr. B. R. Mani, B.R. Publishing Corporation, Delhi.
3. 2015. Tribute to Prof. V.S. Pathak in *Probings into Indian Culture: Prof. Pathak as a Historian*, Pratibha Prakashan, Delhi.
4. 2015. A Tribute to my friend Ramesh Chandra Tripathi in *Indian Culture and Art: Continuty and Change* (Shri R C Tripathi Felicitation Volume), pp. xvii-xx, Swati Publication, Delhi.
5. 2015. "Trading during the Prehistoric and Protohistoric periods: Perspectives from the Ancient Civilizations" in *Man and Environment Vol. XL(1)*, pp.94-104.
6. 2014. "Rewriting History: Archaeology and Tradition" in *Prachyabodha: Indian Archaeology and Tradition (Professor T.P. Verma Festschrift)*, B.R. Publishing Corporation, Delhi.
7. 2014. "Indian Archaeology and Tradition: A Historical Perspective" in *Itihas Darpana,* Vol.XIX (2), pp.209-217.
8. 2014. "Ethics & Civilization" in *Aitihya,* Journal of Ancient History, Culture & Archeology vol-5, pp.42-63 edited by A.K. Sinha, Anamika Publishers & Distributers Private Limited, Delhi.
9. 2014. "Art and Religion" in *Kala evam Purushartha*, Allahabad Museum, Allahabad.
10. 2013. "Preface" in *India, Central Asia and Russia: Three Millennia of Contacts*, ICHR and Aryan Books International, New Delhi.
11. 2013. "India and Western Asian Cultural Contacts" in *Itihas Darpana,* Vol. XVIII (2), pp.267-286.
12. 2013. "Dimensions of Indian Art, Heritage and Contributions of Buddhism" in History of Science, Philosophy and Culture in Indian Civilization, vol. VII, part 9 entitled *Buddhism*, Ed. by G.C. Pande, PHISPC, Centre of Studies in Civilization, New Delhi, pp. 791-818.
13. 2013. "Dimensions of Indian Art Heritage and Contributions of Jainism" in History of Science, Philosophy and Culture in Indian Civilization, Vol. VII, part 4 entitled *Jainism* edited by G.C. Pande, PHISPC, Centre of Studies in Civilization, New Delhi, pp. 503-36.
14. 2013. "Central Asia and Indo-Aryans" in *India, Central Asia and Russia: Three Millennia of Contacts*, ICHR and Aryan Books International, New Delhi.
15. 2013. "Archaeology and the date of Buddha" in History of Science, Philosophy and Culture in Indian Civilization, vol. VII, part 9 entitled *Buddhism*, Ed. by G.C. Pande, PHISPC, Centre of Studies in Civilization, New Delhi, pp. 3-40.
16. 2012. "Itihaas Lekhan me Greek-Roman Parampara" in *Itihaas Lekhan ki Vibhinn Drishtiyan*, ed. by P.K. Shukla, Granth Shilpi, Delhi, pp. 46-84.

17. 2012. "Brahman Samaj: Kal, Aaj aur Kal" in *Sarayu Chetana*, ed. by Harish Mishra, Noida, pp. 65-69.
18. 2011. "Philosophy of History and Indian Historiography" in *Bharti*, vol. 35, Bulletin of the Department of Ancient Indian History, Culture & Archaeology, B.H.U., Varanasi, pp. 1-16.
19. 2011. "Cultural Interaction between South India and South East Asia" in *Aitihya,* Journal of Ancient History, Culture& Archeology , Vol.2, pp.37-64 edited by A.K. Sinha, Anamika publishers &distributers private limited, Delhi.
20. 2010. Presidential Address entitled "Vedic Roots of Hinduism and Hellenism" published in the souvenir of the National Seminar on '*Vedic Foundations of Indian and Hellenic Cultures*' held at Maharshi Panini Sanskrit Vishwavidyalaya, Ujjain, on 16-18 August, 2010.
21. 2009. "Vedic Roots of Hinduism and Hellenism" in *Vikramshila Journal of Social Sciences*, vol. 6, no. 2, ed. by Panchanand Mishra, Vikramshila Research Institute, Bhagalpur, pp. 5-52.
22. 2009. "History and Historiography: Some issues" in *Approaches to History, Culture, Art Archeology: Essays in honour of Prof Om Prakash* edited by A K sinha, pp.61-78, Anamika Publishers & Distributer Private Limited, Delhi.
23. 2008. "Greeco-Roman Historiography and Writing of Ancient Indian History" in *Papers from the Aligarh Historian Society*, ed. by Irfan Habib.
24. 2007. "Trail of Proto-Indi-Europeans: Archaeological Evidence" in History of Science, Philosophy and Culture in Indian Civilization, Vol. I, part 4 entitled *A Golden Chain of Civilizations: Indic, Iranic, Semitic and Hellenic up to 600 B.C.* edited by G.C. Pande & D.N. Tripathi, PHISPC, Centre of Studies in Civilization, New Delhi, pp. 3-28.
25. 2007. "The Problem of the Aryan People and their Language" in History of Science, Philosophy and Culture in Indian Civilization, Vol. I, part 4 entitled *A Golden Chain of Civilizations: Indic, Iranic, Semitic and Hellenic up to 600 B.C.* edited by G.C. Pande & D.N. Tripathi, PHISPC, Centre of Studies in Civilization, New Delhi, pp. 29-65.
26. 2007. "Cosmogonic Myths of Indo-Europeans" in History of Science, Philosophy and Culture in Indian Civilization, Vol. I, part 4 entitled *A Golden Chain of Civilizations: Indic, Iranic, Semitic and Hellenic up to 600 B.C.* edited by G.C. Pande & D.N. Tripathi, PHISPC, Centre of Studies in Civilization, New Delhi, pp. 477-98.
27. 2007. "1857 ka Itihaas Vimarsh" in *Anbhai Sancha (Shaitya aur Sanskriti ki Traimasik Patrika)*, ed. by Dwarika Prasad Charumitra, Rohini, Delhi, pp. 49-57.
28. 2006. "Cellular Jail in Freedom Struggle" in Newsletter, vol.6, no.1 Indian Council of Historical Research, New Delhi, pp. 1-2.
29. 2005. "The Indo-European Homeland: An Indian Perspective" in *A Discourse on Indo-European Languages and Culture*, edited by D.N. Tripathi, ICHR & Manak Publications Pvt. Ltd., Delhi, pp. 21-41.
30. 2005. "Editorial" in *A Discourse on Indo-European Languages and Culture*, edited by D.N. Tripathi, ICHR & Manak Publications Pvt. Ltd., Delhi, pp. 1-20.
31. 2004. "The Concept of Man and Hinduism" in Tripathi, D.N. *Hellenism and Hinduism*, Indian Institute of Advance Study, Rashtrapati Nivas, Shimla, pp. 14-40.
32. 2004. "Origin and Evolution of Indo-European Languages" in Tripathi, D.N. *Hellenism and Hinduism*, Indian Institute of Advance Study, Rashtrapati Nivas, Shimla, pp. 14-40.
33. 2004. "Indian and Western sian Cultural Contacts" in *Studies in Humanities and Social Sciences*, vol. XI, no. 1, ed. by. R.N. Misra, IIAS, Shimla, pp. 1-28.
34. 2004. "Hellenism and Hinduism: An Archaeological and Historical Study" in Tripathi, D.N. *Hellenism and Hinduism*, Indian Institute of Advance Study, Rashtrapati Nivas, Shimla, pp. 1-13.

35. 2004. "Cosmogony and Cosmology" in Tripathi, D.N. *Hellenism and Hinduism*, Indian Institute of Advance Study, Rashtrapati Nivas, Shimla, pp. 41-81.
36. 2004. "Concept of Justice, Social Justice and Ethics" in Tripathi, D.N. *Hellenism and Hinduism*, Indian Institute of Advance Study, Rashtrapati Nivas, Shimla, pp. 82-110.
37. 2000. "New Archaeology and Vedic Cosmogony" in Man and Environment, vol. XXV (1), Journal of Indian Society for Prehistoric and Quaternary Studies, Pune, pp. 1-17.
38. 1998. "Saraswat Samskriti ki Puratatvika Anveshna" in *Facets of Indian Culture, Gustav Roth Felicitation Volume,* Bihar Puravid Parishad, Patna (India), pp.526-53.
39. 1994. "Pit-Dwellings: An Archaeological and Literary Study", Proceedings of the National Seminar on '*Rural Life and Folk Culture in Ancient India*', Department of Ancient History, Archaeology and Culture, Allahabad University, Allahabad, February, 1994.
40. 1994. "Emergence of Bhakti Cult and Indian Society" in the Proceedings of the National Seminar on '*The Bhakti-Cult and Indian Society through Ages*' at BHU, Varanasi, 7-9 April, 1994.
41. 1994. "Diffusion Vs. Evolution" in the Proceedings of the National Seminar on '*Models in Archaeology*', Allahabad Museum, Allahabad, 13 March, 1994.
42. 1994. "Chalcolithic Cultures and Indo-Aryan Problem", Proceedings of the National Seminar at Patna Museum, Patna, 14-15 May, 1994.
43. 1993. "Trade and Urban Centres", Proceedings of the National Seminar, BHU, Varanasi, 1 March, 1993.
44. 1993. "*Place names of Western Asia*" in the Felicitation Volume of Prof. V.S.Pathak, Gorakhpur University.
45. 1993. *"Metallurgy and the Emergence of Aegean Civilization",* Commemorative Volume of the Greek Pundit Galanos, Department of Ancient History, Culture and Archaeology, MJP Rhilkhand University, Bareilly.
46. 1993. "Indo-European Goddesses and Gods and the Indo-European Problem" in the National Seminar of Bharatiya Itihas Samskriti Sankalan Yojana on '*Dating in Archaeology*' at Mysore, 19-21 December,1993.
47. 1993. "Historical Geography of Madhyadesa", Proceedings of the National Seminar, Allahabad Museum, Allahabad, 22 March, 1993.
48. 1993. "Evolution of Symbols in Ancient Indian Art Tradition" Proceedings of the National Seminar , Allahabad Museum, Allahabad, 25-26 Feb. 1993.
49. 1992. Presidential Address on "History, Archaeology and Ecology", Proceedings of the National Seminar on the same subject held at HRPG College, Khalilabad, Sant Kabir Nagar (U.P.), 20 Nov. 1992.
50. 1992. "*Vedic Vajra*" in the Felicitation Volume of Prof. G.C. Pande, Allahabad University, Allahabad.
51. 1992. "*Archaeology and Tradition*" in the Felicitation Volume of Prof. Lallanlji Gopal, BHU, Varanasi.
52. 1991. "Swami Ramtirtha: His Socio-Cultural Contributions", Proceedings of the National Seminar on '*Indian Nationalism*' held at Hindi Sahitya Sammelan, Allahabad, August, 1991.
53. 1991. "Middle Helladic Bronzework", Proceedings of the International Seminar of Indian Society for Graeco-Roman Studies at MJP Rohilkhand University, Bareilly, 29-30 Nov. 1991.
54. 1991. "Ayas in Rigveda", Proceedings of the National Seminar on '*Archaeometallurgy*', BHU, Varanasi, 3-4 Oct.1991.
55. 1991. "Archaeology of Feudalism", Proceedings of the National Seminar on "*India in the Seventh Century A.D.*", Centre of the Advance Studies in Indology and Museology, Bhopal, 25-26 February, 1991.

56. 1991. "Archaeology and Indo-Iranian Language", Proceedings of the National Seminar on '*Aryan- A Myth or Reality?*' at APS University, Rewa, 6-8 Dec.,1991.
57. 1990. "Protohistory of Upper Ganga Valley", Proceedings of the National Seminar on "*Panchal through Ages*", MJP Rohilkhand University, Bareilly, 21-22 March,1990.
58. 1989. "*Archaeology and Language*" in the Felicitation Volume of Dr. Sampurnanand, Sanskrit University Varanasi.
59. 1988. "Vedic Vajra" in Tripathi, D.N. *Archaeology and Tradition* (The Heritage of India no. XV), Ramanand Vidya Bhavan, New Delhi, pp. 1-6.
60. 1988. "Tin in Ancient World: A Literary Study" in Tripathi, D.N. *Archaeology and Tradition* (The Heritage of India no. XV), Ramanand Vidya Bhavan, New Delhi, pp. 18-25.
61. 1988. "Prehistoric and Protohistoric Indi-Greek Cultural Interactions: An Archaeological Study" in Tripathi, D.N. *Archaeology and Tradition* (The Heritage of India no. XV), Ramanand Vidya Bhavan, New Delhi, pp. 46-55.
62. 1988. "Preface" in Tripathi, D.N. *Archaeology and Tradition* (The Heritage of India no. XV), Ramanand Vidya Bhavan, New Delhi, pp. vi-x.
63. 1988. "Pit-Dwelling: An Archaeological and Literary Study" in Tripathi, D.N. *Archaeology and Tradition* (The Heritage of India no. XV), Ramanand Vidya Bhavan, New Delhi, pp. 26-34.
64. 1988. "Original Indo-Iranian Sources of Vajra" in Tripathi, D.N. *Archaeology and Tradition* (The Heritage of India no. XV), Ramanand Vidya Bhavan, New Delhi, pp. 66-91.
65. 1988. "Metallurgy and Emergence of Aegean Civilization" in Tripathi, D.N. *Archaeology and Tradition* (The Heritage of India no. XV), Ramanand Vidya Bhavan, New Delhi, pp. 35-45.
66. 1988. "Indo-Aryan Sources on Ayas" in Tripathi, D.N. *Archaeology and Tradition* (The Heritage of India no. XV), Ramanand Vidya Bhavan, New Delhi, pp. 92-100.
67. 1988. "Copper in Ancient World: A Literary Study" in Tripathi, D.N. *Archaeology and Tradition* (The Heritage of India no. XV), Ramanand Vidya Bhavan, New Delhi, pp. 11-17.
68. 1988. "Ayas in the Rigveda" in Tripathi, D.N. *Archaeology and Tradition* (The Heritage of India no. XV), Ramanand Vidya Bhavan, New Delhi, pp. 7-10.
69. 1988. "A Study of Some Indo-Aryan Personal Names of Ancient Western Asia" in Tripathi, D.N. *Archaeology and Tradition* (The Heritage of India no. XV), Ramanand Vidya Bhavan, New Delhi, pp. 56-65.
70. 1987. "*A Parallel to OC-EO (Cambodia) Seal from Sunet*", Journal of the Numismatic Society of India, Vol. XLIX, Patrs I&2, pp. 68-69.
71. 1987 "*Copper Harpoons- their possible use*" K.D. Bajpayi Felicitation Volume, State Museum, Gauhati, Assam.
72. 1986. "A Study of the Indo-Aryan Personal Names of Ancient Western Asia", Proceedings of the National Seminar on '*The Cultural Contexts of Personal Names in India up to 12th century A.D*", University of Gorakhpur, 22-24 Feb.1986.
73. 1984. "A Study of the Social-ecology of the Professions in Ancient India", Proceedings of the National Seminar on the '*Sociology of Professions*', Department of Sociology, Jodhpur University, Jodhpur, 13-16 Oct. 1984.
74. 1983. "Copper and Tin in Ancient World", Proceedings of the International Seminar on '*Recent Advances in Indian Archaeology*', Deccan College, Pune, 13-14 December, 1983.

Addresses, Lectures, Radio Talks, Paper presentations, etc. by Professor D.N. Tripathi

1. 2015. Presidential Address at the National Seminar on *Indo-Greek Relations* held at Allahabad Museum, Allahabad on 13-14 February, 2015.

2. 2015. Key-note address entitled "Language and Archaeology", during the Centenary Year celebration of the BHU and National Seminar on *Recent Field Researches in Indian Archaeology and Literature* (24-26 April, 2015), Centre of Advanced Study, Department of A.I.H.C. & Archaeology, BHU, Varanasi.
3. 2014. Key-note address entitled "Sir Alexander Cunningham and the Indo-Greek Art" at the International Seminar on '*Sir Alexander Cunningham and the Art Heritage of India*', Department of History of Art, Banaras Hindu University, Varanasi, February 20-22, 2014.
4. 2014. Inaugural Address in the National Seminar on *The Archaeology of Ancient Capital Cities in India* at Allahabad Museum, Allahabad on 5-6 February 2014.
5. 2014. Inaugural Address at the UGC sponsored National Seminar on "Technological Basis of Cultures of Vindhya-Ganga Region" held at the Centre of Advanced Study, Department of AIHC & Archaeology, BHU, Varanasi on 3-4 March, 2014.
6. 2014. Inaugural Address at the National Seminar on "Samskriti, Kala evam Darshana: Bhartiyata ke Pariprekshya me", Mahila Mahavidyalaya, Banaras Hindu University, Varanasi, March14-15, 2014.
7. 2014. Addressed the Inaugural function of the 10th Refresher Course on "New Dimensions in the Study of History, Culture & Archaeology" in the Department of Ancient History, Archaeology & Culture, DDU Gorakhpur University, Gorakhpur on 6th September 2014.
8. 2014. Acharya Vishambhar Sharan Pathak Memorial Lecture titled Indian Culture: New Perspective delivered in the Department of Ancient History, Archaeology & Culture, DDU Gorakhpur University on 19.12.2014.
9. 2014. "Concept of Humanism in Ancient Indian Tradition" lecture delivered at the UGC-Academic Staff College, DDU Gorakhpur University, Gorakhpur on 31 January 2014.
10. 2013. Valedictory Address in the National Seminar on *Rationality, Science and Theology*, organized by Department of Philosophy, DDU, Gorakhpur University, Gorakhpur on 22-24 December 2013.
11. 2013. Presidential address at the Refresher's Course on "The Concept of Bhakti and its Role in the Formation of Indian Culture", Department of Ancient History, Archaeology and Culture, DDU Gorakhpur University, Oct.4,2013.
12. 2013. Presidential Address at the Inaugural Session of the National Seminar on "*Kala aur Purushartha*", Allahabad Museum, Allahabad, March 16-17,2013.
13. 2013. Paper presented on the occasion of the 74th Indian History Congress at the Ravenshaw University Cuttack under the aegis of Aligarh Historian's Society's Panel on Merchant, Trade and Commerce, entitled "Commerce in Early Civilization" on 29th December, 2013.
14. 2013. Address at the UGC sponsored National Seminar on *Archaeology and Culture of Bundelkhand* organized by JRH University, Chitrakoot on 7-8 December 2013.
15. 2012. Inaugural Address of the National Seminar on Cultural Heritage of Buddhism , Buddha Study Centre, Buddha P.G.College, Kushinagar (U.P.), March 1-2,2012.
16. 2012. Addressed the Inaugural Session of the National Seminar on "Indian View of History: A Critical Investigation" as Chief Guest held on March 13-14,2012, at the HRPG College, Khalilabad, Sant Kabir Nagar, U.P.
17. 2011. Inaugural Address at the National Seminar on *R.Shamasastry: New Dimensions in Indian History*, Nov.8-10, 2011.
18. 2011. Chief Guest's Address in the National Conference on *Environment in Buddhist Literature* held on 23-24 February, 2011 at HRPG College, Khalilabad, Sant Kabir Nagar, U.P.

19. 2010. Presidential Address entitled *"Vedic Roots of Hinduism and Hellenism"* published in the souvenir of the National Seminar on 'Vedic Foundations of Indian and Hellenic Cultures' held at Maharshi Panini Sanskrit Vishwavidyalaya, Ujjain, on 16-18August, 2010.
20. 2009. Lecture on "Value Education: Humanism and Human Rights", Department of Education, DDU, Gorakhpur University, 27 March, 2009.
21. 2009. Lecture on "Indo-Greek Art", Allahabad National Museum, Allahabad, 15 February, 2009.
22. 2008. Presidential lecture at the ICPR's National Seminar on "Ethics and Epics: Reflections on Indian Ethos", held in the Department of Philosophy, DDU Gorakhpur University, 05 January, 2008.
23. 2008. Paper entitled "Cultural Interactions between South India and South East Asia" presented at the International Seminar held at the Allahabad National Museum, 11-13 January, 2008.
24. 2008. Lectures on "Dimension of Indian Art Heritage and Contributions of Jainism and Buddhism", Parshwanath Vidyapeeth, Varanasi, 17-19 October, 2008.
25. 2008. Inaugural Address at the National Seminar on *Bhartiya Samskriti ka Jeevan Mulya Ahimsa tatha Vartmaan Vaishvik Paridrishya me iski Prasangikta* held on 22-23 February 2008 at Chandrakanti Ramawati PG College, Gorakhpur.
26. 2008. A Lecture on "Graeco-Roman Historiographic Tradition", Indian Council of Historical Research, New Delhi, February, 2008.
27. 2007. Press interview titled 'Kam Nahi ho Sakti Itihaas ki Prasangikta' published in Hindustan Bhagalpur edition on 29.01.2007 at page 6.
28. 2007. Lecture as a Chief Guest on *"Meaning and Process of History: Socio-Economic Interpretations"* at the National Seminar in the Department of Ancient History, Archaeology and Culture, DDU Gorakhpur University, 18 January, 2007.
29. 2007. A Lecture on "History, Philosophy of History & Research Methodology" in Refreshers Course of the Department of Education, DDU Gorakhpur University, 01 October, 2007.
30. 2006. Professor R. Sathianathier Endowment Lecture titled *"South India and South-East Asia"* at the University of Madras, Department of History, Nov.10, 2006.
31. 2006. Press interview titled 'Arya Bahar se Nahi Aaye' published in Panchjanya on 16.07.2006 on page 5.
32. 2006. Presidential Address of the International Seminar on *"Reason and Tolerance in Indian History"* on the occasion of the 4th Centenary of Emperor Akbar's Death on 28th November 2006 at India International Centre (IIC) New Delhi.
33. 2006. Presented paper at the National Seminar on "Evolution of India's Composite Culture" on the occasion of the Indian History Congress at Vishwa Bharati Shanti Niketan. 28-30 January, 2006.
34. 2006. Lecture on '*Rewriting History, Archaeology and Tradition*' organized by the School of Historical Studies, Madurai Kamraj University on 13.11.2006.
35. 2006. Lecture on '*Philosophy of History*' at the National Institute of Advanced Study, JRD Tata Auditorium, Bangalore on 21.06.2006.
36. 2006. Lecture at the ICHR's National Seminar on the "Historiography of 1857: Debates in the Past and the present state of knowledge" at India International Centre, New Delhi, 9-10 December, 2006.
37. 2006. Lecture at the 3 Day International Seminar on "Identity, Emotion and Culture: Language of the Subcontinent, c.1900-1971" at Indian International Centre, New Delhi, 21-24 December, 2006.

38. 2006. Key-note Address at the Seminar organized by Kerleeyan Smarak Samiti, Malabar Institute for Research and Development on "*Nationalism, Peasantry and All India Kisan Sabha*" held at Calicut (Kerala) on 16-17, September, 2006.
39. 2006. Inaugural Address of the Seminar on '*Gender Equality*' at Kaktiya University, Warangal on 20.01.2006.
40. 2006. Inaugural Address of the ICHR Seminar entitled "*From Orality to Writing: Understanding Hundred Years of Change in Mizoram*", held at the Department of History, Mizoram University, Aizwal, on 2-4 May, 2006.
41. 2006. Inaugural Address of the 10th Annual Congress of the Rock Art Society of India (RASI) at Institute of Archaeology, ASI, Delhi on 11-12 February 2006.
42. 2006. Inaugural address at the ICHR National Seminar on "*The Tribe, Peasants and Modern Identity in Northeastern India (c,1800-2000 A.D.*", held at the Department of History, Tripura University on 5-7 April, 2006.
43. 2006. Golden Jubilee Year Lecture in the Department of Ancient History, Culture and Archaeology, Allahabad University On "Middle East and Indo-European Languages: Problems and Issues", 9 January, 2006.
44. 2006. General Presidential Address at the 43rd Annual Conference of the Institute of Historical Studies at Bhubaneshwar, 13-15 October, 2006.
45. 2006. Chief Guest's Lecture on "Recent Trends in the writing of Indian History" at the C.P.Ramaswamy Foundation, Madras, Nov.10, 2006.
46. 2006. Chief Guest's lecture on '*Jawaharlal Nehru and International Diplomacy*' delivered under the auspices of the Centre for Nehru Studies, Bharathidasan University, Tiruchirappalli on 14.11.2006.
47. 2006. Chairman's Address at the International Seminar on "*Reason and Tolerance in Indian History*" at India International Centre, New Delhi, on 28 October,2006.
48. 2006. Addressed one day symposium on "Gandhi: His Relevance in the Present Scenario" at Centre for Gandhian Studies (UGC Programme), Department of History, Chaudhary Charan Singh University, Meerut. 22 Dec. 2006.
49. 2006. Addressed as a Chief-Guest on the occasion of the releasing ceremony of the *Special Issue* on the "*1857 First War of Independence*" at N.A.S.P.G. College, Meerut, 14 September, 2006.
50. 2006. A Lecture on "Language and Archaeology" organized jointly by the U.P. State Archaeology Department and the Department of Ancient Indian History and Archaeology, Lucknow University at Lucknow on 17 April, 2006.
51. 2005. Lecture on "*Vraja Samskriti ki Vaidik Prishthabhumi*" in Dr. Ramdas Gupta Memorial Lecture at Vrindavan Shodh Samsthan, Vrindavan, 6 Dec. 2005.
52. 2005. Key-note Address of the Ancient Section of the Joint Indo-Turkish International Seminar (under the cultural exchange programme) on "Turkish and Indian Studies: An Appraisal" organized by the Indian Council of Historical Research, New Delhi. 9 February, 2005.
53. 2005. Inaugural Address of the Two-day Conference of the 6th Bihar History Conference at Langat Singh Postgraduate College, Muzaffarpur, Bihar, 29-30 July, 2005.
54. 2005. Inaugural Address of the National Seminar on "Literature, Art and Secular Thought in Medieval India", Aligarh Muslim University, Aligarh. April 5-7, 2005.
55. 2005. Inaugural Address at the Three-Day National Research Conference on "Rashtriya Chetana ke vikas tatha swadhinata aandolan me kaviyitri Srimati Subhadra Kumari Chauhan ka Yogadana" at Jabalpur University, Jabalpur (M.P.) on 28 Sept. 2005.

56. 2005. Inaugural Address at the Joint Conference of Indian Archaeological Society, Indian Society for Prehistoric and Quaternary Studies and Indian History and Culture Society at Bangalore, 15 Dec. 2005.
57. 2005. Chief Guest's Lecture at the 5th National Seminar on "The Jats: Their Role and Contribution to the Socio-Economic Life and Polity of North & North-West India", organized by Surajmal Memorial Education Society, New Delhi, April 30-May 1, 2005.
58. 2004. Special Guest's Lecture at the National Seminar on "Professor Vasudeva Sharan Agrawal and his contributions to Indian Art and Culture" organized by the Department of History of Art in Senate Hall of Swatantrata Bhavan, BHU, Varanasi, 28-30 November, 2004.
59. 2004. Paper presented at the National Seminar on "Indian Identity and Cultural continuity", organizes by the Indian Institute of Advance Study, Shimla at Delhi University Guest House, Delhi, 4-5 May, 2004.
60. 2004. Paper presented at the National Seminar on "India and Asia: Glimpses of the Aesthetic Discourse", Sponsored by India International Centre, Centre for the Study of Civilizations, Indian Council of Historical Research, New Delhi and Indian Institute of Advanced Study, Shimla, held at India International Centre , 26-27 April, 2004.
61. 2003. Paper presented at the International seminar on "Cultural Interface of India with South, Southeast and east Asia (Religion, art and architecture) at Indian Institute of Advanced Study, Shimla, 6-10 March, 2003.
62. 2002. Address at the National Seminar on "The Homeland of Indo-European Languages and Culture" Convened by the Indian Council of Historical Research, New Delhi at India International Centre, Conference Room No.II, IIC, New Delhi on 7-9 January, 2002. Paper presented at the National Seminar on "Historiography of Indian Culture: Language and Culture, at Indian Institute of Advanced Study, Shimla, 9-11 October, 2002.
63. 2001. Lecture on "Social Justice and Traditional Indian Thinking" at the Indian Institute of Advanced Studies, Shimla, 28 Sept., 2001.
64. 2000. Paper entitled "Indian Religious Traditions and Humanism" presented at the National Seminar on 'Indian Religious Traditions in their Interdisciplinary Profile' held at the Indian Institute of Advanced Study, on 7-9 May, 2000.
65. 2000. Paper entitled "Hèllenism and Hinduism" presented at the International Seminar on 'Relevance of Ancient Classics in the New Millennium' held at the Department of Ancient History and Culture, M.J.P. Rohilkhand University, Bareilly on 5-8 February, 2000.
66. 1994. Video lectures of the U.G.C. "On the Original Homeland of Aryans and Vedic Language and Literature", New Delhi, 22-23 January, 1994.
67. 1994. Two lectures "On Second Urbanization of Mid-Ganga Valley" at the UGC Refresher's Course held at the Allahabad University, 26 February, 1994.
68. 1994. Two lectures "On Historical Geography of Mid-Ganga Valley" at the UGC Refresher's Course held at the Allahabad University, 26 February, 1994.
69. 1994. Presidential Address on "Identification of Kapilvastu", Kapilvastu Mahotsava, Siddharthnagar (U.P.), 30 March 1994.
70. 1994. Presidential Address in the Lecture Series of U.P. Government Buddhist Museum, Gorakhpur on "Decline of Buddhism" 28 Jan. 1994.
71. 1994. Four U.G.C.'s Extension Lectures on "The Aryan Problem and Research Methodology" at Kurukshetra University, Kurukshetra, Harayana on 12-13 Feb., 1994.
72. 1994. Delivered two lectures "On the evolution of political society in Ancient India" at the UGC Refresher's Course held at the Sampurnanad Sanskrit University, Varanasi, 27 February, 1994.
73. 1994. A Lecture on "Rahul and Buddhism" at the U.P. Government Buddha Museum, Gorakhpur, 31 May.1994.

74. 1993. Valedictory Lecture on "Facets of Indian Nationalism", M.J.P. Rohilkhand University, Bareilly, 15 Jan, 1993.
75. 1993. Two lectures on "New Archaeology" at the UGC'S Refreshers Course at DDU Gorakhpur University on 25 Nov. & 2 Dec. 1993.
76. 1993. A Lecture on "Prehistoric Art of Greece" at the U.P. Government Buddhist Museum, Gorakhpur on 29 Sept. 1993.
77. 1993. A Lecture on "Archaeology of Mid-Ganga Valley" at the Academic Staff College, Allahabad University, 3-4, Sept.1993.
78. 1993. "Archaeology and Indo-European Languages', in the Annual Conference of the IAS, IPQS,& IHCS, Bhopal, 16-19 Dec., 1991.
79. 1992. Two Lectures on "Historical Research Methodology" at the Academic Staff College of Allahabad University, 19 October, 1992.
80. 1992. A Lecture on "Minoan Religion and Art" at the Allahabad National Museum, Allahabad on 1 March, 1992.
81. 1992. A Lecture on "Archaeology and Tradition" at the Birla Museum, Bhopal , February, 1992.
82. 1991. Valedictory Lecture in the National Seminar on "India in the 7th century A.D." at Prachya Niketan, Barakatullah University, Bhopal, Feb. 1991.
83. 1991. Two Lectures on "Minoan-Mycenaean Art" at the National Human Resource Research Institute, Varanasi, 6 June, 1991.
84. 1991. Presidential Address in the National Seminar on "Archaeological Evidence of Religious Tolerance in Bundelkhand Region", Banda, 19-25 Nov.1991.
85. 1990. Presidential Lecture at the National Seminar on "Panchal through Ages" held at M.J.P. Rohilkhand University, Bareilly, 22 March, 1990.
86. 1990. "Archaeological Models for the Study of Rural Development", at the National Seminar on 'Rural Development: Problems and Prospects', Jodhpur University, Jodhpur, Rajasthan, 17-19 March, 1990.
87. 1984. Two U.G.C. Extension lectures on "Indo-Greek Relations through Ages" at the Jodhpur University, Jodhpur, 13-15 Oct. 1984.
88. 1984. A series of three lectures on "Theory and Methods in Archaeology" delivered at the U.G.C. Workshop in Higher Education, Gorakhpur University, Gorakhpur, on 20 Nov. & 9 Dec.1984.
89. 1984. "*Bharat ki Navapashanakalin Sanskritian*", A radio-talk, published in AIR Journal. Broadcast on 16 April, 1984 at 9.16 p.m.
90. 1983. A series of two lectures delivered On "Wonder that was Greece" at Saint Andrews Post-Graduate College, Gorakhpur under U.G.C. Scheme.

International Conferences attended by Professor Tripathi

1. 2015. 3rd International Dharma and Dhamma Conference, Indore (M.P.), Oct.24-26, 2015.
2. 2011. Indo-Turkish Seminar of ICHR at New Delhi.
3. 2008. 18th Vedanta Conference at Dartmouth, Massachusetts, USA, August 2008.
4. 2001. XIVth UISPP conference, Liege (Belgium), Sept. 2001
5. 2001. World Samskrit Conference, New Delhi, 4-8 April, 2001.
6. 2000. XXXVI ICAANAS Conference, Montreal (Canada), August 2000.
7. 1994. World Archaeological Congress, New Delhi, December, 1994.
8. 1991. IInd Congress International Di Micenologia, University of Rome and Naples, "Cultural Interactions between India and the Aegean World" 14-20 Oct. 1991.
9. 1990. International Seminar on "New Archaeology and India", New Delhi, January 1990.

10. 1989. World Archaeological Inter-Congress, South Dakota, U.S.A., "Sati Burial-A Myth or Reality" August 5-10, 1989.
11. 1987. International Colloqueum in Agean Prehistory, Athens, (through a paper). August 29-Sept. 7, 1987.
12. 1986. XXXIII, ICAANAS conference, Hamburg, Germany, "Vajra-An Archaological and Literary Study" August 25-30, 1986
13. 1986. World Archaeological Congress, Southampton-London, "The Origins of Middle Helladic Metallury" and "The Origins of the Early Hellladic Metallurgy" Sept. 1-7, 1986.
14. 1986. International Seminar on Recent advances in Pre- and Protohistoric Studies in India, National Museum, New Delhi, January 3-6, 1986.
15. 1984. Indo-Greek Symposium, Delphi, Greece, "Prehistoric and Protohistoric Indo-Greek Cultural Interactions: An Archaeological Study" June 8-14, 1984.

Membership of Academic Bodies

1. Member, Board of Studies, Greek and Latin, Sampurnananda Sanskrit University, Varanasi (1979-82).
2. Academic Member of the Indian Delegation of the Ministry of External Affairs, Government of India at the Greek Festival in Athens and Delphi, Greece, June 1984.
3. Chancellor's Nominee in the Syndicate of Rajasthan University, Jaipur (1986-1989).
4. Chancellor's Nominee in the Executive Council of R. M. L. Awadh University, Faizabad (U.P.) (1992-1994).
5. Member of the Executive Committee of the Indian Archaeological Society, New Delhi, (1986-88), Indian History and Culture Society, New Delhi (1984-86), and Indian Society for Prehistoric and Quaternary Studies, Pune (1995-98).
6. Member Editorial Board of *Summerhill,* IIAS Review, Indian Institute of Advanced Study, Shimla. (1999-2002).
7. Member, Inquiry Committee, NCERT, New Delhi. (2003-2004).
8. Member CABA, Ministry of Culture, New Delhi (2004-2007).
9. Member, Governing Body, IIAS, Shimla. (2004-2007).
10. Member CBSE, Ministry of HRD, New Delhi. (2004-2007).
11. General Secretary, Indian Society for Graeco-Roman Studies, Bareilly.

List of Contributors

Abha Dwivedi
Depts of A.I.H. & Archaeology,
University of Lucknow,
Lucknow.
E-mail: jaydra.ad@gmail.com

Ajay Kumar Pandey
Principal
Hiralal Ramniwas P.G. College
Khalilabad,
Sant Kabir Nagar-272175(U.P.)

Alok Tripathi
Director
Centre for Archaeology and Museology
Department of History
Assam University, Silchar
Email: alok.asi@gmail.com

Anantashutosh Dwivedi
Bihar Heritage Development Society,
Patna, Bihar
E-mail:- adwivedi195@gmail.com

Anjula Shukla
Associate Professor
Buddha P.G. College, Kushinagar (U.P)

Anupama Singh
Asstt. Archaeologist
Archaeological Survey of India, Vadodara

Apoorva Sinha
98, Sindhu Nagar, P.O Manas Nagar,
Lucknow-226023
Email: apurvasinha3@gmail.com

Arvin K. Singh
Professor Depts. Of AIHC
and Archaeology, Jiwaji University,
Gwalior-474011 (M.P.)
E-mail: aks_archju@yahoo.co.in;

Atul Tripathi
Professor, Depts. of the History of Art,
Faculty of Arts,
BHU, Varanasi-221005

B.R. Mani
Former Additional Director General,
Archeological Survey of India
Janpath
New Delhi

Brijesh Rawat
Asstt. Professor Depts. Of History
Dr. Shakuntala Mishra Rehabilitation
University,
Lucknow (U.P.)

Colin Renfrew
Former Director
Mcdonald Institute of Archaeology
Cambridge University,
Cambridge (U.K.)

D.P. Tewari
Professor Depts of A.I.H. & Archaeology,
University of Lucknow,
Lucknow
E-mail : tewaridplu@gmail.com

Deepak Kumar
Research Scholar,
Depts of AIHC and Archaeology,
Gurukul Kangari University,
Haridwar
E-mail : deepakmeluha@gmail.com

D.K.Mathur
Former Director,
V.S.Wakanker Research Institute
State Museum Compounds
Shymla Hills,
Bhopal

Devesh N. Tripathi
Scientist
Defence Institute of Psychological Research,
New Delhi

Dhyanendra Narayan Dubey
Asstt. Professor Deptt. of AHA and Culture
DDU Gorakhpur University,
Gorakhpur

Digvijaynath
Associate Professor,
DDU Gorakhpur University, Gorakhpur

Diwakar Prasad Tiwari
Retd. Principal
D.N. Pandey State Girls College
Deoria, (U.P.)
5/444, Deoria Ramnath West,
C.C. Road, Deoria (U.P.)

Gaya Charan Tripathi
Director, B.L. Institute of Indology
Vijay Vallabh Jain Mandir,
G.T. Karnal Road, P.O. Alipur, Delhi-36
E-mail : gctripathi235@gmail.com,

Girishwar Mishra
Vice-chancellor
Mahatma Gandhi Antarrastriya
Hindi Vishwavidyalaya,
Wardha (Maharashtra)

Gitu Giri
Tribhuwan University,
Nepal

Indudhar Dwivedi
Superintending Archaeologist (Retd.)
Archaeological Survey of India,
Janpath, New Delhi
E-mail : indidhardwivedi@gmail.com

Irfan Habib
Prof. (Retd.)Depts. of History
Aligarh Muslim University,
Aligarh (U.P.)

Ishwar Sharan Vishwakarma
DDU Gorakhpur University,
Gorakhpur
E-mail: isvishwakarma@gmail.com

J.N. Pal
Department of AHC and Archaeology
University of Allahabad
Allahabad 211 002 (U.P.)
E-mail : Jnpal@hotmail.com

J.N. Pandey
Former Professor & Head
Depts of AHC and Archaeology
Central University of Allahabad,
Allahabad.

K.D. Tripathi
Advisor
IGNCA, Eastern Regional Centre
Ravindrapuri Extension
Varanasi-221005

K.K. Paddayya
Former Director and Emeritus Professor of Archaeology
Deccan College (Deemed University)
Pune 411 006

K.S. Shukla
36, Shuklana
Bangarmau, Unnao (UP) 209868
E-mail : ksshukla50@rediffmail.com

Kamlesh Kumar Gautam
Dept. of Ancient History
DDU Gorakhpur University,
Gorakhpur

Kunwar Bahadur Kaushik
Vivekpuram,
Taramandal,
Gorakhpur, U.P.

Maruti Nandan Pd. Tiwari
Deptt. of History of Art
Banaras Hindu University,
Varanasi-221005
Email- mnptiwari@rediffmail.com

Michel Danino
Guest Professor
IIT Gandhinagar (Gujarat)
E-mail: micheldanino@gmail.com

Mohan Gupta
Former Vice Chancellor
Maharshi Panini Sanskrit evam
Vedic Vishwavidyalaya
Ujjain, M.P.

Murli Manohar Pathak
DDU Gorakhpur University
Gorakhpur-273009

Namrata Singh
Assistant Professor
University of Delhi, Delhi

Neelesh Kumar Pandey
C/o B.K. Pandey, A-206,
Indraprastha Villa,
Sector-61, Noida
Gautam Buddha Nagar, U.P.
E-mail : nileshpandey21@gmail.com

Neetu Tiwari
Independent Archaeologist
163/P, L.I.C. Colony
Patel Nagar, GONDA, U.P.
E-mail : neetudivedi@gmail.com

Om Prakash Kumar
Senior Research Fellow,
Department of AIHC & Archaeology,
Banaras Hindu University,
Varanasi-221005

P.K. Shukla
Former Member Secretary, ICHR and
Fellow, NMM & Library,
New Delhi

Pooja Saxena
HIG- 71, Shankaracharya Nagar,
Bagh Sewania, Bhopal (M.P.)
E-mail: poojabpl@yahoo.com

Prabhakar Upadhyay
Assistant Professor,
Depts. of AIHC & Archaeology,
Banaras Hindu University,
Varanasi-221005

Pragya Chaturvedi
Associate Professor
Depts. of AHA & Culture
D.D.U. Gorakhpur University
Gorakhpur

Praveen K. Sharma
Research Scholar
Depts. of History, Archaeology & Culture
DDU Gorakhpur University,
Gorakhpur

Praveen Kumar Mishra
Superintending Archaeologist
Archaeological Survey of India,
Patna Circle,
Patna (Bihar)
Email: pkmgkp@gmail.com

Radhakant Varma
Former Chairman
Allahabad Museum Society,
Allahabad (U.P.)

Rajawant Rao
Professor
Depts. of AHA and Culture
DDU Gorakhpur University,
Gorakhpur

Rajesh Kumar Dhar Dubey
Ex-Post Doctoral Fellow,
ICHR, 35, Firozshah Road,
New Delhi,

Rajesh Kumar Meena
Asstt. Archaeologist
Archaeological Survey of India
Jaipur Circle,
Jaipur

Rajesh Mishra,
Allahabad Museum,
Allahabad

Rajesh Purohit
Director,
Allahabad Museum,
Allahabad.

Rakesh Tewari
Director General
Archaeological Survey of India
New Delhi

Ram Rudra Shukla
46494 Cedarhurst Drive,
Sterling, VA 20165, USA
E-mail : shuklarr@yahoo.com

Ramakant Singh
Associate Professor and HOD
Department of History,
Nagric P. G. College Janghai,
Jaunpur U.P.

Ramashray Roy
Former Director and Emeritus Fellow
Centre for the Study of
Developing Societies (CSDS),
Delhi (India)

Rampyare Mishra
Asstt. Professor
Depts. of AHA and Culture
DDU Gorakhpur University,
Gorakhpur

R.C.Tripathi
Former Secratery General Rajaya Sabha,
A-1055,Girja Bhavan,
Lekhraj Marg, Indira Nagar,
Lucknow-226016

Ratnesh Kumar Tripathi
Asstt. Prof. (Guest), History Deptt.,
B.N.C. College, Delhi University,
Research Associate, Indian Old Study
Organisation
(Madhav Sanskriti Nyas), New Delhi

Ravindra Kumar
Associate Professor,
DIHRM, Qutub Institutional Area
18/A, Satsang Vihar,
New Delhi.
E-mail : ravindrakumar1101@gmail.com

Rekha Chaturvedi
Depts. of Anc. History and Culture
DDU Gorakhpur University
Gorakhpur

S R Goyal
Former Professor, Depts. of History,
JN Vyas University,
Jodhpur, Rajasthan

S.K. Aruni
Member Secretary
ICHR, 35, Firozshah Road, New Delhi
E-mail : skaruni@gmail.com

Sachin Kumar Tiwary
Assistant Archaeologist,
Archaeological Survey of India,
Sarnath Circle, Sarnath,
Varanasi-221007, UP.
E-mail : sachintiwary@rocketmail.com

Sanchita Ghosh
Associate Professor,
Deptt. of Ancient History
D.A.V. College,
Kanpur (U.P.)

Sangeeta Singh
11, Jai Nagar Colony,
Gilat Bazaar, Shivpur,
Varanasi-221002

Santosh Kumar Singh
Depts. of A.I.H.C. & Archaeology
Banaras Hindu University,
Varanasi-221005
E-mail: sksingh1169@gmail.com

Shankar Goyal
Department of History
Jai Narain Vyas University
Jodhpur (Rajasthan)

Shankar Jai Kishan,
Curatorial Associate
Bihar Museum, Patna
E-mail : jaikishan5183@gmail.com

Shanti Swaroop Sinha
Deptt. of History of Art
Banaras Hindu University,
Varanasi-221005
E-mail : sssbhu@gmail.com

Shashi Tiwari
Former Professor, Sanskrit,
University of Delhi & Secretary General,
WAVES, New Delhi
Resi : 54, Saakshara Apartments,
A-3, Paschim Vihar, New Delhi

Shitala Prasad Singh
Associate Professor
Depts. of AHA & Culture
D.D.U. Gorakhpur University,
Gorakhpur
Email : dr.shitalaprasadsingh@gmail.com

Sibesh Bhattacharya
Professor (Retd.)
Deptt. of Ancient History
University of Allahabad,
Allahabad

Sita Ram Dubey
Department of A.I.H.C. & Archaeology
Banaras Hindu University,
Varanasi-221005
Email: dr.sitaramdubey@yahoo.co.in

Surendra Dubey
Dean, Faculty of Arts
DDU Gorakhpur University,
Gorakhpur

Susmita Pande
Former Professor & Head
Depts. of AIHC& Archaeology
Vikram University,
Ujjain

T. P. Verma
397-A, Ganga Pradushan
C, Road, Bhagwanpur,
Varanasi-221 005

Umesh Nath Tripathi
Associate Professor
Department of Chemistry
DDU Gorakhpur University,
Gorakhpur

U.P. Arora
Former Emeritus Professor
of Greek Studies
Jawahar Lal Nehru University,
New Delhi

V.N. Misra
G-2, B Wing, Ganga Park,
Mundhawa Road,
Pune 411036
Email: vnmisra1935@gmail.com

Vasant Shinde
Vice Chancellor
Deccan College Post-Graduate and
Research Institute (Deemed University)
Pune, Maharashtra

Vibha Tripathi
Senior Academic Fellow
Indian Council of Historical Research
35, Firozshah Road,
New Delhi

Vimal Tiwari
Curator
Maharajadhiraj Lakshmishwar Singh
Museum
Darbhanga, Bihar
Email : vimal311@gmail.com

Vinay Kumar
Assistant Professor,
Department of AIHC & Archaeology,
Indira Gandhi National Tribal University,
Amarkantak, M.P.
E-mail : vinaykumar166@yahoo.com

Vineet Godhal
Agrasena Colony,
Near Power House, Kotputli,
District Jaipur (Rajasthan)
E-mail: vineetgodhal@gmail.com

Vipula Dubey
Professor, Depts. Of AIHC& Archaeology
DDU Gorakhpur University,
Gorakhpur

Vishi Upadhyay
Curatorial Associate, Bihar Museum,
Patna (Bihar).
E-mail : vishi.arch@gmail.com

Y. Sudarshan Rao
Chairperson
Indian Council of Historical Research
35, Firozshah Road,
New Delhi

List of Plates

Plate 3.1 : Main Section Belan Valley
Plate 3.2 : Distribution of Sites in the Vindhyas
Plate 3.3 : Mesolithic Settlements of the Ganga Valley
Plate 3.4 (a) : Epi-palaeolithic Tools
Plate 3.4 (b) : Tools - Non Geometric Tools
Plate 3.4 (c) : Tools - Non Geometric Tools
Plate 3.5 : Stratigraphy of Damdama
Plate 3.6 : Four Burials Sarai Nahar Rai-Couples
Plate 3.7 : Couple Burial Mahadaha
Plate 3.8 : Burils and Hearths of different periods
Plate 3.9 : Pit Hearth, Damdama
Plate 3.10 : Antler, Ornaments, Mahadaha
Plate 3.11 : Ornaments in the Manufacturing Stage
Plate 3.12 : Male Skeleton With ear rings
Plate 3.13 : Rock Painting; A group of Boars
Plate 3.14 (a) : General view of Ronp Shelter
Plate 3.14 (b) : Rock Art of Northern Vindhyan Region : Evolution in Styles
Plate 5.1 : King and queen in low relief, Manhai, Kausambi
Plate 5.2 : Nativity scene, Kausambi.
Plate 5.3 : Palm leaf capital, Manhai, Kausambi.
Plate 5.4 : Buddha in Bhumisparsha Mudra, Kausambi.
Plate 5.5 : Bodhisattva, Kausambi.
Plate 5.6 : Bodhisattva, Kausambi.
Plate 5.7 : Unfinished Sculpture, Kausambi.
Plate 5.8 : Gajalakshmi, Kausambi.
Plate 8.1 : Dwarka: Diving near Samudra Narayan temple (photo: UAW)
Plate 8.2 : Dwarka: A submerged structural remain after cleaning (photo: UAW)
Plate 8.3 : Dwarka: Excavations in Dwarkadheesh temple complex (photo: UAW)
Plate 8.4 : Dwarka: Partly broken circular structure in intertidal zone (photo: UAW)
Plate 15.1 : General View of the Mound, Waina, Ballia
Plate 15.2 : Microliths of Waina, District Ballia (U.P.).
Plate 15.3 : Bone Points of Plate IB & II, Waina, Ballia.
Plate 15.4 : Terracotta Beads of Plate IB, II & III, Waina, Ballia.
Plate 15.5 : Antlers of Plate II & III, Mound, Waina, Ballia.
Plate 15.6 : Occupation floor with Post-holes Plate III, Mound, Waina, Ballia.
Plate 18.1 : Lower Palaeolithic tools from Sohanpura
Plate 18.2 : Lower Palaeolithic tools from Sohanpura

Plate 18.3 : Lower Palaeolithic tools from Bheetaro
Plate 18.4 : Lower Palaeolithic tools from Bheetaro
Plate 18.5 : Lower Palaeolithic Handaxe from Reedh Ka Tila
Plate 18.6 : Lower Palaeolithic Handaxe from Reedh Ka Tila
Plate 18.7 : Lower Palaeolithic tools from Peer Baba Ki Bani
Plate 18.8 : Lower Palaeolithic tools from Peer Baba Ki Bani
Plate 18.9 : Lower Palaeolithic tools from Shobh
Plate 18.10 : Lower Palaeolithic tools from Shobh
Plate 18.11 : Middle Palaeolithic tools from Bageshwar
Plate 18.12 : Middle Palaeolithic tools from Bageshwar
Plate 18.13 : Middle Palaeolithic tools from Laloda
Plate 18.14 : Middle Palaeolithic tools from Laloda
Plate 18.15 : Upper Palaeolithic tools from Deoli Ki Dhani
Plate 18.16 : Upper Palaeolithic tools from Deoli Ki Dhani
Plate 20.1 : A cylindrical neck & collared mouth Chalcolithic Pot
Plate 20.2 : Fragmentary remains of Chalcolithic Earthen Pots
Plate 20.3 : Precious and Semi-precious stone bead excavated from Peetnagar
Plate 20.4 : Terracotta Beads
Plate 20.5 : Painted thin fragments of Lota & thick Globular Vessel
Plate 20.6 : Painted fragmentary pieces of Stand Bowls and Vessels
Plate 23.1 : Fragmentary Stone Inscription of Kachchhapaghāta Ratnapāla: V.S. 1165
Plate 23.2 : Close up of the upper left portion of the Stone Inscription of Ratnapāla
Plate 23.3 : Close up of the upper right portion of the Stone Inscription of Ratnapāla
Plate 23.4 : Close up of the lower right portion of the Stone Inscription of Ratnapāla
Plate 23.5 : Close up of the lower right portion of the Stone Inscription of Ratnapāla
Plate 25.1 (A) : General view of the mound with its highest elevation
Plate 25.1 (B) : General view of mound on the bank of river Sai
Plate 25.2 : Terracotta Seals and Sealings
Plate 25.3 : Seals and Sealings from Sanchankot.
Plate 25.4 : Seals and Sealings from Sanchankot.
फलक 26.1 : गजमस्तक का शिरस्त्राण धारी डिमेट्रियस
फलक 26.2 : डिमेट्रियस की मुद्रा पर अंकित गज का शिरोभाग एवं अंकुश
फलक 26.3 : एण्टियालकिड्स की मुद्रा पर अंकित गज का शिरोभाग
फलक 26.4 : एण्टियालकिड्स की मुद्रा पर अंकित गज का शिरोभाग
Plate 27.1 : Gold coin of Prithvideva obverse (in collection of Kamal Vaid)
Plate 27.2 : Silver coin of Prithvideva Reverse (in collection of Prshant kulkarni)
Plate 27.3 : Copper coin of Prithavideva Reverse (in collection of L.P. Pandey)
Plate 27.4 : Gold coin of Ratandeva obverse (in collection of Kamal Vaid) copy
Plate 27.5 : Silver coin of Ratandeva, Reverse (in collection of Prashant kulkarni)
Plate 27.6 : Copper coin of Ratandeva obverse (in collection of Pushparaj Victor)
Plate 27.7 : Gold coin of Jajalladeva obverse (in collection of Kamal Vaid)
Plate 27.8 : Copper coin of Jajalladeva (in collection of Bhanupratap singh)
Plate 27.9 : Silver coin of Jagpaladeva obverse
Plate 27.10 : Copper coin of Pratapmalladeva
Plate 27.11 : Gold coin of Pratapmalladeva

Plate 28.1 : Tritîrthî – showing Sarasvatî with two Jinas, Jaina Dharmashala Museum, Deogarh (Lalitpur, U.P.), 11th century CE.
Plate 28.2 : Six-armed Sarasvatî, southern adhiṣṭāna rathikā, Pārśvanātha temple, Khajurāho (Chhatarpur, M.P.), c. 950-70 CE.
Plate 28.3 : Sarasvatî, Pañcakūṭa Bastî, (Shimoga, Karnataka), 11th century CE.
Plate 28.4 : Sarasvatî joined by dancing divine figures, corridor ceilings, Vimala-Vasahî (Sirohi, Rajasthan), c. 1150 CE.
Plate 28.5 : Sarasvatî, Pallū (Bikaner, Rajasthan), now in National Museum, New Delhi, c.11th CE.
Plate 31.1 : View of Temple from North-eastern side
Plate 31.2 : View of Temple from Northern side
Plate 31.3 : View of the Temple from Southern side
Plate 32.1 : Patna - Yaksha - Mauryan Period
Plate 32.2 : Besnagar - Yakshi (2nd century BC)
Plate 32.3 : Parkham - Yaksha - Post Mauryan
Plate 32.4 : Atlantes - Yaksha - Sanchi
Plate 32.5 : Bowl Suporting Yaksha - Pitalkhora (2nd century BC)
Plate 32.6 : Moggarapani Yaksha - Satavahana period
Plate 32.7 : Kuber - Ahichhatra Kushan (2nd century AD)
Plate 32.8 : Yakshi - Sanchi (1st century BC)
Plate 33.1 : Udaygiri Hill, Vidisha
Plate 33.2 : Shehshayi Vishnu, Cave No. 13, Udaygiri Hills, Vidisha
Plate 33.3 : Mutilated figure of Brahma seated on lotus, Cave No. 13, Udaygiri Hills, Vidisha
Plate 33.4 : Nrivaraha, Cave No. 5, Udaygiri Hills , Vidisha
Plate 34.1 : Monolithic Pillar, Mauryan Period.
Plate 34.2 : Lion Capital, Mauryan Period.
Plate 34.3 : Yakshi, Sunga Period.
Plate 34.4 : Kuber, Kushan Period.
Plate 34.5 : Head of Bodhisattva, Kushan Period.
Plate 34.6 : Buddha, Kushan Period.
Plate 34.7 : Surya, Gupta Period.
Plate 34.8 : Rishabhnath, Gupta Period.
Plate 34.9 : Jaina Pillar with images of Teerthanakas, Gupta Period.
Plate 34.10 : Jaina Pillar with images of Teerthanakas, Gupta Period.
Plate 34.11 : Buddha in declining posture, Gupta Period.
Plate 34.12 : Image of Teerthankar, Gupta Period.
Plate 34.13 : Ekmukhlinga, Gupta Period.
Plate 34.14 : Navagrah Panel, Early Medieval Period.
Plate 34.15 : Uma-Maheshwar, Early Medieval Period.
Plate 34.16 : Mahishamardini, Early Medieval Period.
Plate 34.17 : Jeevant Swami, Early Medieval Period.
Plate 34.18 : Agni, Early Medieval Period.
Plate 34.19 : Neminath, Early Medieval Period.
Plate 34.20 : Vishnu, Pala Period.
Plate 34.21 : Agni, Early Medieval Period.
Plate 34.22 : Buddha, Early Medieval Period.

Plate 34.23 : Head of Bodhisattva, Early Medieval Period
Plate 35.1 : Horse on the abacus of Sarnath Lion Capital
Plate 35.2 : Lady of Auxerre in Daedalic style
Plate 35.3 : Tanagra Terracotta figures, about 250 B.C.
Plate 35.4 : Dancing girl, Patna Museum, Mauryan Period
Plate 35.5 : Open mouth of the lion in West Asian art
Plate 35.6 : Open mouth of the lion in Mauryan art
Plate 35.7 : So-called shrine of the Double headed Eagle at Sirkap.
फलक 36.1 : धूप में नमी को सुखाने के लिए रखा कच्चा माल
फलक 36.2 : प्रथम हीटिंग का दृश्य
फलक 36.3 : प्रथम चिपिंग के लिए प्रयोग किया जाने वाला लकड़ी का हथौड़ा
फलक 36.4 : प्रथम चिपिंग के लिए लोहे की पतली नोंक वाली छड़
फलक 36.5 : प्रथम एवं द्वितीय चिपिंग के लिए प्रयोग किये जाने वाले भैंस के सींग से बने हथौड़े
फलक 36.6 : मनकों की प्रथम चिपिंग
फलक 36.7 : मनकों में द्वितीय चिपिंग
फलक 36.8 : मनकों की घिसाई एवं पॉलिश के लिए प्रयुक्त एमरी व्हील्स
फलक 36.9 : मनकों की घिसाई
फलक 36.10 : मनकों की एमरी व्हील द्वारा पॉलिश
फलक 36.11 : छिद्र के लिए प्रयोग किये जाने वाले औजार
फलक 36.12 : मनकों में छिद्र प्रक्रिया
फलक 36.13 : मनकों को गर्म करने के लिए तैयार की गई भट्टी
फलक 36.14 : लकड़ी के बुरादे से भरी गई भट्टी
फलक 36.15 : भट्टी में आग का दृश्य
फलक 36.16 : अगले दिन सुबह भट्टी का दृश्य
फलक 36.17 : भट्टी में परिवर्तित हुए कार्नेलियन के मनकों का चित्र
Plate 37.1 : Map of the area under the discussion
Plate 37.2 : Rock Shalter Kaurihar Khas
Plate 37.3 : Hunter, Animale and Loade Carrier, Ghurahupur
Plate 37.4 : Humped Bull, Ghurahupur
Plate 37.5 : Depications of Budha, Stupa and female Dancer, Ghurahupur
Plate 37.6 : Painting Belongs to Deference Period, Tanui
Plate 37.7 : A bull shown with roap around in its neck Kharauli
Plate 37.8 : Mesolithic Rock Paintings, Ratanpurawa
फलक 38.1 : त्रिभंग शांतिदेवी, जैन बावनढेरी, चाम्पानेर–पावागढ़, गुजरात
फलक 38.2 : आसनस्थ सरस्वती, जैन बावन ढेरी, चाम्पानेर–पावागढ़, गुजरात
फलक 38.3 : त्रिभंग इन्द्राणी, जैन बावन ढेरी, चाम्पानेर – पावागढ़, गुजरात
Plate 39.1 : Earliest evidence of excavated bronze object from Chechar. (Photograph courtesy ASI, Patna Circle)
Plate 39.2 : Polychrome Pictographs of human executed on the wall of the shelter very much similar to the bronze image, Chand Block of Kaimur district, Bihar
Plate 39.3 : Pictographs of human holding hammer or stick like object on left hand and rope or symbolic form of an un-iconic form holding on right hand executed on the wall of the cave also very much similar to the bronze image, Chand Block of Kaimur district, Bihar

Plate 45.1 : Rāndala Mātā with Chāyā, a photograph commoly seen during worship in households in the Saurāṣṭra Region

Plate 45.2 : Mānat at Ravi Rāndala Mātā Temple, Daḷavā (Bhavṇagar) : For the ailments of the bodyparts devotees offer either small wooden replicas of the whole body or the part(s) which is/are affected; displayed on the left side here are the wooden replicas at a shop for sale. On the right side are the photographs of the new born children being put up after their mānat of childbirth is fulfilled.

Plate 45.3 : Diaspora of Ravi Rāndala Mātā : Rituals being performed by Non Resident Gujaraties outside a Hindu Temple at Leister in England.

Plate 45.4 : A scene of the celebrations during the inauguration of the International Kite Festival, Ahmedabad.

Plate 45.5 : A large number of domestic as well as foreign kite enthusiasts flying their kites at a vanue during the International Kite Festival at Ahmedabad.

TRIBUTE TO PROFESSOR DAYA NATH TRIPATHI

It is a pleasure and an honour to pay tribute to my friend (and former student) Daya Tripathi, for whom I had the privilege of acting in the formal capacity of supervisor during his years as a doctoral student at the University of Southampton, where I was at the time Head of the Department of Archaeology. In reality there was little "supervision", since Daya Tripathi, then as now, was a formidable scholar, and his time of research in Athens and then in Southampton had been well spent. His impressive doctoral dissertation was of course accepted and welcomed by the examiners, and was subsequently published (in Paul Åström's *Studies in Mediterranean Archaeology* series (SIMA)) with the title: *Bronzework of Mainland Greece from c. 2600 BC to c. 1450 BC*. It is a significant contribution to Aegean prehistory.

It is a great pleasure to contribute to this Felicitation Volume with a recent paper 'An evolutionary perspective on the development of human culture', which will fall within his wide range of interests. Among these is the still not fully resolved problem of the origin of the Indo-European languages, on which I would have wished to present a paper for the Felicitation Volume. But several chapters of the new *Cambridge World Prehistory*, written in collaboration with my colleague Paul Heggarty, have recently addressed this theme, so that I hope the 'evolutionary perspective' will be found acceptable.

It is my great please to offer warm felicitations and congratulations to Daya Tripathi, with every good wish for a long and happy retirement.

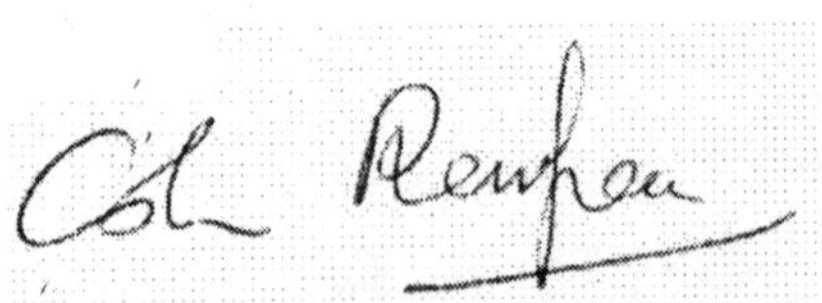

Colin Renfrew
(Lord Renfrew of Kaimsthorn)

परम्परा के संवाहक परमाचार्य प्रोफेसर दयानाथ जी

अजय कुमार पाण्डेय

प्रयाग के पवित्र भूमि के स्थित जयरामपुर पत्रालय दोहरिया के स्वर्गीय राम किशोर शर्मा तथा स्वर्गीय श्रीमती कृष्णा शर्मा का सम्पूर्ण परिवार भारत की सनातन हिन्दू परम्परा में संस्कारित था। इसी संस्कारित परिवार में गुरूवर प्रो0 दयानाथ त्रिपाठी उत्पन्न हुए, संस्कारित और दीक्षित हुए, जिसका प्रभाव उनके परम्परागत मानस में अद्यावधि विद्यमान है।

परम्परागत शिक्षा

ममतामयी माँ एवं पूजनीय पिता की छत्रछाया में गुरूवर त्रिपाठी को माता–पिता के संस्कार प्राप्त हुए। प्रो0 त्रिपाठी के पिताश्री स्वर्गीय पं0 राम किशोर शर्मा सर्वाय इण्टर कालेज, इलाहाबाद के प्रधानाचार्य थे और वे सनातन धर्मी थे। गुरूवर त्रिपाठी के पिताश्री और स्वर्गीय महिमामयी माँ दोनों हिन्दू धर्म के देवताओं की उपासना और पूजा करने के पश्चात ही प्रातः काल जलग्रहण करते थे। अल्पाहार के पश्चात रामायण, गीता और रामचरितमानस का पाठ करने के पश्चात ही विद्यालय प्रस्थान करते थे। प्रो0 त्रिपाठी माता–पिता के पूजा सामग्री, फल–फूल तथा हवन सामग्री आदि एकत्रित कर स्वयं माता–पिता के साथ कुछ समय पूजा करने बैठ जाते थे। पुत्र प्रो0 दयानाथ के इस पूजा रूचि को देखकर उनके प्रारम्भिक शिक्षा–दीक्षा को सनातन धर्म का संस्कार प्रदान किया। जो उनके जीवन का अंग बन गया।

अध्ययन–अध्यापन में परम्परा पालन– अपने प्रारम्भिक शिक्षाकार इलाहाबाद विश्वविद्यालय के प्राचीन इतिहास, संस्कृति और पुरातत्व विषय में प्रथम श्रेणी प्राप्त करने के अवधि में भी गुरूवर त्रिपाठी इलाहाबाद के हनुमान मंदिर का दर्शन करने जाते थे, लड्डू चढ़ाते थे, प्रसाद प्राप्त करते थे और अपने आवास पर लौट आते थे। अध्ययन अवधि में उनके अनेक सहपाठी उनका अनुकरण करते हुए हनुमान जी के मूर्ति के सम्मुख उपस्थित होकर हनुमत वंदना करते हुए प्रसाद प्राप्त कर अपने आवास पर लौट आते थे। विशेष ध्यातत्य तथ्य यह है कि प्रो0 त्रिपाठी के अध्ययन कक्ष में विभिन्न हिन्दू देवी–देवताओं के चित्रों के साथ हनुमान जी का सबसे बड़ा चित्र लगा रहता था और उस पर माला चढ़ाया गया होता था। क्रमशः हिन्दू परम्परा को मानते हुए हनुमान जी के प्रति उनके निष्ठा बढ़ती गई। गुरूवर का यह मानना था कि हनुमान जी की कृपा से ही उन्होंने एक अच्छे विद्यार्थी के रूप में अपनी पहचान बना ली।

इष्टदेव हनुमान

मैं दीनदयाल उपाध्याय गोरखपुर विश्वविद्यालय के प्राचीन इतिहास पुरातत्व एवं संस्कृति विभाग का विद्यार्थी था और गुरूवर प्रो0 त्रिपाठी की मुझपर पर्याप्त कृपा बनी रहती थी। प्रो0 त्रिपाठी जी प्रति मंगलवार को बेतियाहाता में स्थित हनुमान मंदिर पहुँचकर हनुमान जी का दर्शन करते और कुछ समय तक खड़े रहकर हनुमान जी की पूजा करते रहते थे। कभी–कभी मैं भी गुरूवर के साथ हनुमान मंदिर जाता था और उनके साथ पूजा भी करने लगा। राह चलते चर्चा में गुरूवर प्रो0 त्रिपाठी जी कहते थे कि मेरे इष्टदेव हनुमान जी हैं। मैं प्रतिदिन प्रातःकाल एक घण्टा हनुमान जी की पूजा करता हूँ और हनुमान जी की कृपा से ही मैं दीनदयाल उपाध्याय गोरखपुर विश्वविद्यालय के नियंता पद को स्वीकार कर विश्वविद्यालय में शांति व्यवस्था स्थापित करने में सफल हो पाया। उनका यह विश्वास रहा कि हनुमान जी कृपा से ही उन्हें निरन्तर उन्नति प्राप्त होती गई।

बहन से रक्षा बन्धन

गुरूवर दयानाथ त्रिपाठी भारतीय परम्परा से इतने अधिक आबद्ध हैं कि वे भारत के किसी भी भू–भाग में रहते हुए भी 'रक्षाबन्धन' के अवसर पर अपनी बहन (श्रीमती–शुक्ला) से अवश्य ही रक्षा बंधवाने के लिए उपस्थित हो जाते हैं। यदि गुरूवर विदेश में रहते हैं तो वही से अपनी बहन के रक्षा बन्धन हेतु द्रव्य प्रेषित करते हैं कि रक्षा बन्धन के एक दिन पूर्व बहन को निश्चित रूप से प्राप्त हो जाता है। परम्परा के प्रति इतनी अधिक घनिष्ठता और मान्यता प्रदान करने वाले व्यक्ति को मैं सदा प्रणाम करता हूँ। उनकी बहन भी रक्षा बन्धन के अवसर पर इस प्रत्याशा में निश्चित रहती है कि उनके भाई प्रो0 त्रिपाठी का कुशल क्षेम प्राप्त होगा और वह भाई के आरती के लिए दीपक और मिष्ठान की तैयारी पहले से ही कर लेती हैं।

पत्नी का परम्परा में सहयोग

आचार्य प्रवर प्रो0 दयानाथ त्रिपाठी का प्रिय शिष्य होने के कारण माता तुल्य श्रीमती (त्रिपाठी) का निरन्तर सहयोग गुरूवर को प्राप्त होता रहता है। गुरूमाता उनके पूजा, स्थल, पूजापीठ, पूजा सामाग्री के पात्र आदि की व्यवस्था पूजा प्रारम्भ के पूर्व ही कर देती हैं। गुरूमाता अस्वस्थता और स्वस्थता की स्थिति में भी गुरूवर के धर्माचरी के होने का पूर्ण दायित्व निभाती हैं। कभी–कभी पूजा सामग्री लाने का सौभाग्य मुझे भी प्राप्त हुआ है। यह मेरा परम सौभाग्य है कि गुरू, गुरूमाता तथा देव प्रतिमाओं के प्रति अपनी श्रद्धा समर्पित करने का अवसर सौभाग्य से प्राप्त होता रहा है।

मेरे शोध निर्देशक

मैं अत्यधिक भाग्यशाली हूँ कि ऐसे सनातन पुरूष और परम्परा के संवाहक मुझे एम0ए0 (प्राचीन इतिहास पुरातत्व एवं संस्कृति) विषय में शिक्षा प्रदान किया। मेरे पी–एच0डी0 के निर्देशक रहे तथा डी0लिट् के परामर्शी रूप में उनके वैश्विक पुरातत्व के अगाध ज्ञान का परिचय मुझे प्राप्त हुआ। मेरे डी0लिट् करने की अवधि में उत्पन्न बाधाओं का क्षणैक में समाधान प्रस्तुत करने वाले गुरूवरज्ञय के प्रति सदा नमित हूँ। मेरे अनुसंधान अवधि में अपनी सनातन परम्पराओं के परिपालन तथा विश्वविद्यालय के पूर्वायतन के आचार्य एवं अध्यक्ष के कार्य दायित्व का निर्वाह करते हुए भी मेरे अनुसंधान विषय पर लिखे जाने वाले प्रत्येक पृष्ठों का स्वयं अवलोकन करते हुए त्रुटियों का संशोधन एवं समाधान प्रस्तुत करने का समय निकाल लेते थे।

तीर्थयात्रा के तपस्वी

प्रो0 दयानाथ त्रिपाठी के जीवन चारिका की यह विशेषता यह रही है कि भारत के प्रमुख तीर्थो की यात्रा करते रहते हैं। यात्रा का प्रमुख उद्देश्य ऐतिहासिक संस्थानों, स्थानों, संग्रहालयों का निकट से अध्ययन एवं अवलोकन करना रहता था। परन्तु इस अध्ययन अनुसंधान यात्रा केन्द्रों के निकट स्थित राजगृह से लेकर जरासंध का अखाड़ा, नालन्दा विश्वविद्यालय के खण्डहरों, एवं विक्रमशिला विश्वविद्यालय के अवशेषों के साथ ही साथ बिहार के धर्म स्थलों का अध्ययन करते हुए काश्मीर से कन्याकुमारी तक धार्मिक स्थलों की यात्रा उनकी अत्यधिक अभिरूचि रही है। प्रत्येक मंदिरों में स्थापित देव मूर्तियों के तदानुकूल दर्शन एवं प्रसाद समर्पण का कार्य करते रहे। आज भी वे एक जीवन्त पुराविद् एवं परम्परा के संवाहक रूप में निरन्तर चारिका करते रहते हैं।

प्राचार्य
हीरालाल रामनिवास स्नातकोत्तर महाविद्यालय
खलीलाबाद, संत कबीर नगर, उ0प्र0

पुरातत्व के प्रमाता
(प्रो0 दयानाथ त्रिपाठी)

कुँवर बहादुर कौशिक

प्रयाग की प्रशस्त भूमि में प्रस्थित् इलाहाबाद विश्वविद्यालय के प्रख्यात पुरातत्ववेत्ता प्रो0 गोवर्धन राय शर्मा के सनिध्य में पुरातत्व की विभिन्न विधाओं का अध्ययन किया। कौशाम्बी उत्खनन में गुरूवर त्रिपाठी ने अपनी सक्रिय सहभागिता प्रस्तुत करते हुए पुरातत्व एवं परम्परा का प्रौढ़ ज्ञान प्राप्त किया। इलाहाबाद विश्वविद्यालय के प्राचीन इतिहास, संस्कृति एवं पुरातत्व विषय में स्नातकोत्तर उपाधि अर्जित करने के पश्चात ही दीनदयाल उपाध्याय, गोरखपुर विश्वविद्यालय के स्थापना उपरांत 1958 से ही 'प्राचीन इतिहास, पुरातत्व एवं संस्कृति' विभाग में प्रवक्ता, प्रवाचक एवं आचार्य–अध्यक्ष के रूप में 40 वर्षो तक निर्बाध पूर्वायतन की सेवा में संलग्न रहे। प्रवक्ता काल में ही आचार्य त्रिपाठी अपने कर्त्तव्यनिष्ठा के कारण विश्वविद्यालय के प्रमुख नियंता (1980–84) पद पर आसीन रहे तथा विभिन्न बाधाओं में सफलता–पूर्वक अपने कार्यकुशलता से विद्यार्थियों–अध्यापकों में अधिक लोकप्रियता प्राप्त की।

अनुसंधित्सु

पूर्वायतन् में इनके अध्यापन का मुख्य विषय पुरातत्व, प्राग इतिहास एवं पुरैतिहास रहा है। गुरुवर त्रिपाठी ने वर्ष 1971 से 1974 तक ग्रीक स्कालरशिप तथा 1974 से 1976 तक ब्रिटिश काउंसिल स्कॉलरशिप प्राप्त की तथा अपनी उपलब्धियों से यूरोपीय पुरातत्व के क्षेत्र में महत्वपूर्ण स्थान स्थापित किया। आचार्य त्रिपाठी को एथेंस विश्वविद्यालय से यूनानी भाषा की उपाधि 1972 में प्राप्त हुयी। विश्व प्रसिद्ध पुरातत्ववेत्ता लार्ड कोलिन रेनफ्रियू के निर्देशन में प्रो0 त्रिपाठी को 'साउथसेम्पटन विश्वविद्यालय, यूनाइटेड किंगडम' से पी–एच0डी0 की उपाधि 'ब्रान्ज वर्क ऑफ ग्रीस' नामक शोध प्रबन्ध पर प्रदान किया गया।

शोध–यात्रा

गुरूवर त्रिपाठी ने अपने यूनान के अध्ययन में ही ग्रीस, फ्रांस, जर्मनी, इटली, यूनाइटेड किंगडम, इजिप्ट तथा ईरान आदि देशों में प्रसिद्ध संग्रहालयों में संरक्षित पुरावशेषों का प्रत्यक्ष दर्शन करते हुए पुरातत्व विषय में अपनी पुरातत्व विषयक विधाओं का अध्ययन किया तथा भारत के संग्रहालयों में स्थित प्रमुख संग्रहालय– राष्ट्रीय संग्रहालय, नई दिल्ली, भारतीय संग्रहालय, कलकत्ता; इलाहाबाद संग्रहालय तथा मध्य प्रदेश, उत्तर प्रदेश, बिहार, राजस्थान के राज्य संग्रहालयों का पूर्ण अध्ययन एवं अवलोकन किया। अपने अध्ययन के आधार पर गुरूवर त्रिपाठी जी यूरोपीय देशों तथा भारतीय विश्वविद्यालयों में पुरातत्व विषयक शोध–पत्रों का वाचन और सम्बोधन करते हुए एक लब्ध प्रतिष्ठित पुराविद् के रूप में विख्यात हो गये।

यूरोपीय देशों में विशेषकर यूनान के पुरातत्व का गहरा अध्ययन करके आचार्य प्रवर – त्रिपाठी जी ने दीनदयाल उपाध्याय गोरखपुर विश्वविद्यालय में क्रमशः पूर्वायतन् के आचार्य एवं अध्यक्ष पद को सुशोभित करते हुए विभिन्न शैक्षिक संस्थानों इलाहाबाद विश्वविद्यालय, 1998–1999, इंडियन इंस्टीट्यूट ऑफ एडवांस स्टडीज शिमला के अनसंधित्सु (1999–2002) तथा ब्रिटिश एकाडमी, लंदन 2003 के विजिटिंग प्रोफेसर के रूप में प्रसिद्धि प्राप्त की।

अनुसंधान–परिषद के अध्यक्ष

आचार्य प्रवर प्रोफेसर दयानाथ त्रिपाठी पुरातत्व के साथ ही साथ परम्परा की सहचारिता के समर्थक विद्वान थे। वे भारतीय इतिहास अनुसंधान परिषद के सदस्य रूप में 1998–2004 तक महत्वपूर्ण स्थान भारतीय इतिहास एवं पुरातत्व के क्षेत्र में प्राप्त कर चुके थे। अखिल भारतीय स्तर पर प्रो0 त्रिपाठी की महत्ता का अनुभव प्रशासनिक क्षेत्रों में भी व्याप्त हुआ। इसी कारण प्रो0 त्रिपाठी को भारतीय इतिहास अनुसंधान परिषद, नई दिल्ली के अध्यक्ष पद पर वर्ष 2004 में नियुक्त किया गया जिसका सफलतापूर्वक निर्वहन उन्होंने अपनी कार्यावधि में किया। भारतीय इतिहास अनुसंधान परिषद के सदस्य के रूप में आचार्य प्रो0 त्रिपाठी की अध्यक्षता में एक अन्तर्राष्ट्रीय गोष्ठी का आयोजन

07–09 जनवरी, 2002 तक भारतीय अन्तर्राष्ट्रीय केन्द्र, नई दिल्ली में “A DISCOURSE ON INDOEUROPEAN LANGUAGES AND CULTURE” विषय पर कियागया जिसमें पुरातत्व, पुराभाषा, भाषिक पुरातत्व एवं संस्कृति विषय के अन्तर्राष्ट्रीय विद्वानों ने अपने शोध–पत्र प्रस्तुत किये। तीन दिनों तक इस विषय के विद्वानों ने प्रस्तावित विषय पर गम्भीर विचार – मंथन किया। परामाचार्य गुरूवरज्ञ प्रो0 त्रिपाठी की कृपा से मुझे भी इस अन्तर्राष्ट्रीय गोष्ठी अपना शोध पत्र हिन्दी भाषा में प्रस्तुत करने का सुअवसर प्राप्त हुआ।

पुरावशेषों के उत्खाता

गुरूवर त्रिपाठी जी ने सोहगौरा (बाँसगाँव–गोरखपुर) के त्रिपाठी परिवार से अपने सम्बन्ध को उद्घाटित करते हुए सोहगौरा के उत्खनन की एक योजना तत्कालीन आचार्य एवं अध्यक्ष प्रो0 विश्वम्भर शरण पाठक के सम्मुख प्रस्तुत किया। विभाग के वरीयता क्रम में गुरूवर त्रिपाठी का तीसरा स्थान था। इसीलिए द्वितीय स्थान के प्रवाचक प्रो0 शैलनाथ चतुर्वेदी को सोहगौरा के उत्खनन का दायित्व प्रदान किया गया। भारत के अहाड़ तथा यूनान के मेनीलियोन और पिलोस के उत्खनन का अनुभव होने के कारण सोहगौरा उत्खनन में अपना सक्रिय सहयोग प्रदान कर प्रो0 त्रिपाठी ने सोहगौरा के पुरावशेषों को भारतीय पुरातत्व के क्षितिज पर प्रतिष्ठापित किया। गोरखपुर परिक्षेत्र के फाजिलनगर और उस्मानपुर डीह (कुशीनगर) के उत्खनन का कार्य सम्पन्न किया। पुरातत्व के प्रमाता के रूप में लगभग 200 प्रमेय स्थलों को पुरातत्व का प्रमाण आधुनिक इतिहास के वस्तुनिष्ठता के लिए एक अनिवार्य तत्व के रूप में स्वीकार किया जाने लगा। इस दृष्टि से उन्होंने शताधिक राष्ट्रीय एवं अन्तर्राष्ट्रीय संगोष्ठियों में भाग लिया तथा उनके लगभग 50 शोध–पत्रों को प्रतिष्ठित राष्ट्रीय एवं अन्तर्राष्ट्रीय पत्रिकाओं में स्थान प्राप्त हुआ। गुरूवर त्रिपाठी ने विभिन्न राष्ट्रीय तथा अन्तर्राष्ट्रीय पुरातत्व, इतिहास एवं संस्कृति संगोष्ठियों की अध्यक्षता की तथा नई दिल्ली, शिमला एवं गोरखपुर में अनेक संगोष्ठियों का आयोजन करने का श्रेय उन्हें प्राप्त है।

शोध प्रकल्पों के प्रणिधि

आचार्य प्रो0 दयानाथ त्रिपाठी का व्यक्तित्व निरन्तर अध्ययन–अध्यवसाय में अद्यावधि व्यस्त रहता है। अपने व्यस्त क्षणों में भी विश्वविद्यालय अनुदान आयोग के वृहद प्रकल्प के रूप में 'आर्कियोलाजी इन ट्रेडीसन' विषय पर महत्वपूर्ण ग्रंथ प्रस्तुत किया और इस ग्रन्थ में उन्होंने पुरातत्व एवं परम्परा को सहचर रूप में प्रस्तुत करने का श्लाघनीय प्रयास किया है। प्रो0 त्रिपाठी ने भारतीय इतिहास शोध परिषद के पुरातत्वीय अनुसंधित्सु के रूप में 'हिन्दूइज्म एवं हेलनिज्म' शोध प्रकल्प में अपने इस शोध–पत्र के द्वारा अन्तर्राष्ट्रीय जगत में एक नवीन आयाम प्रस्तुत किया है। उनके निर्देशन में लगभग दसाधिक शोध छात्रों ने पी0एच–डी0 और डी0 लिट्0 की उपाधियाँ प्राप्त की। उनके शिष्य लोक सेवा आयोग, दिल्ली और उत्तर प्रदेश के अतिरिक्त विश्वविद्यालयों तथा उच्च शैक्षिक संस्थानों में कार्यरत हैं।

कृतित्व

पुरातत्व के व्याख्याता आचार्यवर त्रिपाठी ने 1987 में 'ब्रांज वर्क ऑफ मेन लैंड ग्रीस' (2600 ई0पू0–1450 ई0पू0) तक के यूनानी कांस्य सभ्यता पर अपना शोध ग्रन्थ लिखा है। 1988 ई0 में उन्होंने 'पुरातत्व एवं परम्परा' ग्रन्थ का प्रणयन किया, 'पुरातत्व–भाषा–कोष' का सम्पादन 1994 में किया, 1996 ई0 में 'कल्चरल इंटरएक्शन इंडियन ग्रीस' का प्रणयन किया, 2004 ई0 में 'हिन्दूइज्म एवं हेलेनिज्म' शोध निबन्ध प्रस्तुत किया, 2005 ई0 में 'ए डिस्कोर्स आन इंडो–यूरोपियन लंग्वेज एण्ड कल्चर' विषय पर आयोजित गोष्ठी में प्रस्तुत शोध पत्रों का सम्पादन किया, ए गोल्डेन चेन ऑफ सिविलाइजेशंस : इंडिक, ईरानिक, सेमेटिक एण्ड हेलेनिक', प्रथम भाग, 600 बी0सी0 तक विवरण इस ग्रंथ में प्रस्तुत है। 'ए गोल्डेन चेन फार सिविलाइजेशनः इंडिक, ईरानिक, सेमेटिक एण्ड हेलेनिक', 600बी0सी0 भाग दो का संपादन वर्ष 2012 में तथा वर्ष 2013 में इंडियन सेन्ट्रल एशिया – इंडो–रशियन सेमिनार की कार्यवाही में शोध प्रस्तुत किया।

व्यक्तित्व

पुरातत्व के प्रमाता गुरूश्रेष्ठ प्रो0 दयानाथ त्रिपाठी का विराट व्यक्तित्व पुरातत्व के प्रमेयों (पुरावशेषों) के अभिज्ञान तथा परम्परागत भारतीय लोक जीवन में प्रचलित शाब्दी परम्परा के सहचर की अन्वेषणा करने में सदा संलग्न रहा है। व्यक्तित्व की विराटता का अभिज्ञान उनके कृतित्व के साथ ही साथ समकालीन ऐतिहासिक, पुरातात्विक तथा सांस्कृतिक क्षेत्र की श्रेष्ठ संस्थाओं से अपनी सम्बद्धता सदा बनाये रखे है। प्रो0 त्रिपाठी ग्रीको–रोमन स्टडीज के भारतीय समिति के आजीवन सदस्य के रूप में, भारतीय पुरातत्व समिति, भारतीय इतिहास एवं संस्कृति समिति तथा प्री हिस्टोरिक एवं क्वाटर्नरी स्टडीज के आजीवन सदस्य रूप में अपना अमूल्य योगदान प्रदान करते रहते है। प्रो0 त्रिपाठी मध्य प्रदेश हेरीटेज़ डेवलपमेंट काउंसिल, भोपाल तथा इलाहाबाद संग्रहालय समिति के प्रशासकीय परिषद के पदाधिकारी रूप में पुरातत्व के क्षेत्र में अनवरत सहयोग, सम्मति परामर्श और निर्देशन के जीवंत साक्षी हैं। इस प्रकार पुरातत्व के प्रमाता के रूप में पुरावशेषों के प्रमेय एवं प्रमाण के सिद्ध पुरूष हैं। मैं उनका अन्तेवासी रहकर गुरूवर त्रिपाठी से अधिकाधिक प्राचीन भारतीय इतिहास, पुरातत्व एवं संस्कृति में ज्ञान प्राप्त करने का सौभाग्यशाली अध्येता हूँ।

AN UNTOLD SAGA OF MY PAPAJI

Devesh N Tripathi

Prologue

I am extremely happy to find the invitation to contribute something to Papaji's felicitation volume. "तेरा ज़िक्र हैया कि इत्र है, जब भी होता है महक जाता हूँ मैं : A M Turaz" (*It is your mention or perfume; whenever it happens I become fragrant*). I am addressing Professor D.N.Tripathi as 'Papaji' frequently in this paper because I am going to write something straight from my heart, as a proud son of this giant personality. Believe me, for past 20 years as a student and learner of psychology, I have a firm belief that no single test of personality in psychology can ever map Papaji's personality. At this juncture, few lines of Qateel Shifai sahib are worth mentioning, "आसमान जो शख्स है सबकी नज़र में उसको छू लेने की जुर्रत कर रहा हूँ मैं" (*I am daring to touch that individual who is a sky in everybody's eye*). He is far beyond the words as expressed in most of his vitae.

Though it's quite true that others can only perceive the overt personality however to build up this overt persona there are always many covert facets. When we refer about knowledge too, there is an explicit aspect that can be seen by everyone but the tacit aspect is always hidden and explicit knowledge is basically an offshoot of this tacit knowledge. Whatever is written in the vitae of any individual are basically his/her achievements in the worldly view. If we ever ask about it personally, we shall be enlightened that whatever world perceives to be as 'achievement' is basically nonentity in that person's view. Products take front stage; however, the process backstage also is equally important and interesting.

Life is not a destination rather it's a journey. When we start the journey, destinations are never seen but mere presence of them in our psyche drives ourselves towards them and we are so engrossed in thinking about these mirage destinations that at times, we forget to enjoy the pleasures of journey.

The Journey

To start this ever interesting journey of my father's untold, unknown, hidden aspect of personality, let me humbly accept this truth in few of these lines: "समंदर को समझना है तो उसकी तह में टहल कर, ये तो साहिल है यहाँ मछलियाँ कपड़े बदलती हैं।" (*To understand sea one has to go deep down at the base, this is the seashore only futile things happen here*). What Bashir Badr sahib has written in the aforesaid lines, I thought it was about my father and, I ponder whether Papaji ever met him? Also I am amazed because for few days I firmly believed that Badr Sahib had written these lines especially for my father. Later, in-depth evaluation of this ode made me realize that this was true for most of us in this dynamic and ever changing society.

Always I have felt that Papaji has been most talked and referred but least understood. He always presents tougher side of his persona to everyone he meets. Even if someone stubborn like me always clings to him then also he never reveals, especially his earlier struggles and sorrows. One has to understand him; he never divulges. He is alike sacred book which neither opens its pages to anybody nor asks others to read it, rather who so ever is interested can readily access him and if one is wise enough s/he will be able to understand that he is like a coconut. Who shall get the nectar of this coconut is basically dependent upon the desire, wish and striving of the person who wants to obtain it.

It is such a Herculean task to come up with a sketch of Papaji because of his multifaceted personality. Earlier life of Papaji reveals that as an individual he too has been a proud son of an honest and hence poor School Principal. In material sense Papaji was deprived yet an emperor. He didn't possess ever enough money but there were lot of values, ethics, culture, dedication, determination and confidence to prove his mettle. He always has been a go-getter type of person who never says die. Throughout his life he has been a true fighter to achieve whatever was justice. He is resolutely grounded yet elite minded. Most positive aspect of his personality has always been his non-compromising nature with life's struggle. No problems of life have ever deterred his ambitions to attain whatever is righteous. Like me, readers might be amazed to see the paradoxical nature of his personality.

It might be a revelation for many that Papaji is very emotional for everyone be it his parents, wife, Gurus, sons, daughters, students, down trodden persons or anyone whom he has known, yet he is very firm. In any context, emotionality seldom overshadows his decision making. Papaji is so successful because of his ability to take decisions, be it wrong at times, and is bold and firmly ever ready to face the consequences of the decisions so taken. In his whole life, his resilient nature has made him bounce back. The tougher the conditions life has offered him the stronger he emerges from that problem and has never complained about it to anyone. Even though suffering with various types of diseases he has been ever contended and satisfied with his life conditions. He always believes that, *"Whenever you feel depressed; keep this in mind, things are yet to happen, life is yet to go; this is just a bend not the end"*.

Any person evolves into such a multifarious personality because some habits become lifestyle of that individual. Lifestyle of Papaji is interwoven in few of these habits such as 'Paan', 'Puja', 'Paper', 'Paidal', 'Padhai' and 'Pehnawa'.

Anyone who has met him can never overlook his face especially his mouth filled with *paan*. Papaji without *paan* will be synonymous to sun without warmth. In the worldly affair, he knows and understands that it is not a good habit for health. Many a times he has attempted to quit this habit and often tells us too that never imitate this habit of mine but HABITS DIE HARD.

Another habit of Papaji is *puja*. Come what may, he never misses it. He is a firm believer of God especially Bajrang Bali. He believes, "मेरा मुहाफ़िज़ मेरा खुदा है, यही बहुत है; चिराग आंधी में जल रहा है यही बहुत है।" (*This is enough that lamp is lit in storm, his saviour is God).*He always has an unshakeable belief on his 'Karma' and 'Tail of Bajrang Bali'. Often he narrates that whatever has been portrayed as his achievements is basically blessings of Prabhu Hanumaan. He is resolute believer in the fact; "हानि लाभ जीवन मरण यश अपयश बिधि हाथ।" (*Loss, gain, birth, death, fame and ill repute are controlled by God).*In our memory, without fail, for past 40 years Papaji has been visiting to Hanuman Mandir preferably Betiahata Gorakhpur on every Tuesday. He incessantly prays to Almighty; "जेहिं बिधि होंहि नाथ हित मेरा करहुँ सो बेगि दास मैं तोरा।" *(O Lord! I am your servant, find a way out in what so ever manner my goodwill happens*).

For the past 50 years, he has a daily habit of reading at least three newspapers and penning down all his routine activities in his small diary: *'Geeta-Dainandini'*. Mornings start with green tea and newspaper. He considers newspapers are basically mirror of this society. After reading these papers often he is very disgusted to find perishing value system of this society. Alone retired professor attempts to reconnect himself with the happenings of the society. At times, he is so happy with any of the article/poetry published in any paper that immediately it is scribbled at any corner of paper, later to be sent to persons whom he feels they can appreciate the essence of it.

Another habit of Papaji is walking a few miles which I have listed as *paidal*. Despite of being diagnosed with osteoarthritis he is in a habit of walking daily in the evening. He makes it a point to collect his 'Paan' himself. Seeing my pumpkin shaped body he always passes on to me the famous quote of Mahakavi Kalidas, "शरीर माध्यम् खलु धर्म साधनम्।" (*The body is the means of fulfillment of Dharma).* In his age he is so disciplined about his body that he rarely misses yoga, exercises and walking, now with the help of a cane stick. When the sun sets and birds return to their nest no one can ever miss this lonely archaeologist walking silently, chanting Gayatri Mantra in the busy shrieking lanes of Bilandpur, Gorakhpur.

'Padhai' or reading has always enthralled Papaji. Few persons can ever beat him in reading. I believe reading habit is very close to his heart. He is not a bookworm but can hardly resist *padhai* for less than 3 to 10 hour/day. The library he possesses is worth watching. In addition to his favourite subjects– culture, linguistics, archaeology and tradition – it is stacked with archives of many historical accounts, literary and philosophical books along with dictionaries of many languages. He seems to be totally engrossed and happy, whenever he is dusting them. He is such a quick learner that with the technological revolution these days he is adept in reading e-books but still enjoys reading printed books.

Last of the habits of Papaji's *'Pehnawa'*. He is very cautious about the dress he wears. His wardrobe is always packed with different types of matching dresses and perfumes for various occasions. Also he never ever misses to take out sometime to get rid of budding hairs on his chin. I always felt that with such a magnetic personality whatever he wears will suit him but he never presents himself ill-dressed to anyone. This habit of him, I believe, is rooted in his British training. Moreover, he is of an era when being a university teacher he was supposed to be a role model to his students and other members of society.

Every individual seems to be composite of HABITS and various ROLES s/he plays during entire lifetime. How truly and effectively do we play our roles fundamentally indicates the significance of our being in this mortal world. In our complete chapters of life we are assigned various roles by The Supreme Playwright: The Almighty. We simply dance like a buffoon on the tunes of that rhythmic composer. Further, Papaji's untold saga encapsulates his dutiful personality for various roles to which he had been passionately committed.

As a son, Papaji, being the eldest child of his parents, assumed responsibilities in quite an early age. His parents lovingly called him *'Bachau'*. He joined Gorakhpur University in 1958 at the tender age of 21. He very efficiently delivered all his responsibilities as a son, and as an elder brother he even got his single sister married. Also he supported his younger brothers in the best way he could. He did his best of efforts to support his parents. He was quite fearful of my Grandfather and was very attached to his mother. His parents have been a whole world for him. Words of his parents behold Gospel for Papaji. I saw his eyes full of sea when my Grandfather, then Grandma and again when one of my uncle bid adieu to this world, in a very short span of time. As a souvenir Papaji has preserved letters written to him by my Grandfather. Even today anyone can find his parents' portrait in his *puja room,* next to God. As a son Papaji seems to be humming couplet of Manzar Bhopali sahib, "इसी से अज़मत की मंज़िलों का पतामिलेगा, ये जो बुजुर्गों की ख़ाक़–ए–पा है, यही बहुत है।" (*Services of one's parents is sufficient enough to understand the path of ultimate reality*).

As a loving husband, my father holds a lot of respect for my mother. He understands Mummy better than her. Always together they have shared their good and bad days. In his earlier struggling days, he had very less time for the household chores and children. The saying *'Behind every successful man there is a woman'* seems to be relevant in his life too. Till date, Papaji admires her dual responsibility both as father/mother. He often refers that it was she who took the pains of upbringing us. They share a very friendly and cordial relation. A lot of times it is amusing to find both of them affectionately teasing each other. They are made for each other and these days it seems to be a vacuum for them, if anyone of them is far. For these and many other reasons Papaji forever refers my mummy as *"Deviji"*.

I think words fall short when I have to elaborate the role of Papaji as a father. According to his basic personality he never expressed his true feelings of love, compassion and emotion to his children; but we as his progeny may probably express our feelings through these lines by Azm shakiri, "धूप में जल रहा था बदन, पाँव बांधे हुए थी थकन; तेरी बाँहों में आकर लगा ज़िंदगी ताज़ा दम हो गई।" (*My body was burning under sun, I was too tired, when I came into your lap I felt rejuvenated*). Papaji has ever been solution to the problems we face. The values, ethics, morality, character, straight forwardness, impartiality, fearlessness, discipline, punctuality, respect for elders, and courage to say *no,* are all his personality traits that has been imbibed by all of us. Due to our parents' effort we all are well settled and well placed at our respective places. If ever we had desired for anything in life, those have been silently fulfilled by them. At times in his role as father Papaji has been strict, but as a punishment for himself he missed his supper that day. Papaji has always been friends of his children and has always expected and did open communication on varied issues of life. Today we all have become parents and realize how much pain and sacrifice they did for us. I have heard this from my mother that due to our joint family he always put himself out of sight and steal a look to see my eldest sister playing and if ever he could be in the lone company of my sister he would shower all his love on her. Similarly, he has been attached to each one of us but never displays it before public. He has always respected others' individuality and never intervenes until it is very pertinent to do so. He has always taught us, "ज़िंदगी को हमेशा ज़रूरतों में रखो, ख़्वाहिशों की तरफ न ले जाओ; क्योंकि ज़रूरत फ़कीरों की भी पूरी हो जाती है और ख़्वाहिशें बादशाहों की भी अधूरी रह जाती हैं।" (*Keep yourself limited within necessities, don't ever desire too much because necessities of everyone is fulfilled; however desires of even emperors remain unfulfilled*).

About modern days Bashir Badr Sahib has stated very aptly: "कोई हाथ भी न मिलायेगा जो गले मिलोगो तपाक से, ये नये मिज़ाज़ का शहर है जरा फ़ासले से मिला करो।" (*In this materialistic world keep a distance while interacting, as no one will even shake hands if you are ever ready to embrace them*). These lines hold true when I think about Papaji as Friend. He is very cautious in selecting friends however he has always been a very devoted and loyal friend to those who are his real friends. He had many acquaintances but very few friends. These friends lovingly called him *'Panditji'*. In friendship he believes "शर्तें लगाई नहीं जाती दोस्ती के साथ, कीजिये मुझे कुबूल मेरी हर कमी के साथ।" (*one has to accept friends with all their negativities as you cannot lay a wager in friendship*). For his friends Papaji has been most dependable person on this earth and they would vouch for him in extreme conditions. Also this holds true about Papaji as he too would look forward towards them in his happiness and sorrow alike. As written by Goswami Tulsi Dassji, "धीरज धर्म मित्र अरु नारी, आपद् काल परिखिहहुं चारी।" (*Patience, Dharma, friends and wife are well tested during testing times*). He and his friends were time tested and even preferred to sacrifice their lives for each other.

At times seeing his immaculate tactical prowess and anger many of his acquaintances called him *Chanakya*– the strategist and others termed him *Durvasa*– the angry man, but for a friend who truly understands him Papaji is *Daya Nath*– Master of Kindness. I think across time and era no one can ever be equated with any other person in this universe. Each individual is unique and this forms the basis of psychology. One of the behavioural manifestations of kindness is forgiveness. Papaji has always believed "अपराध क्षमा गुर्वीणाम्" (*forgiveness has an edge over crime*) especially in the context of friendship. He has forgiven everyone even those foe and friend who at times have attempted to demean or even be-head him. Papaji seems to be articulating Munnavar Rana sahib's thought, "मुझे दुश्मनों से भी खुद्दारी की उम्मीद रहती है, सिर किसी का भी हो कदमों में अच्छा नहीं लगता।" (*I expect self-respect even from my enemies as I am never delighted to see a surrendered self before other human being*). His philosophy of friendship and enmity may be summarized through this couplet of Bashir Badr sahib, "दुश्मनी जम कर करो, लेकिन ये गुंजाइश रहे, कि जब हम दोस्त बनें तो शर्मिंदा ना हों।" (*Even do enmity with lot of determination but always keep a chance that if ever again we be friends we are not ashamed*).

Above elucidated roles were performed by Papaji at personal level. At the professional level too, as a student Papaji is so attached with his teachers that in his office cum reading room photographs of both the *Gurus* Lord Colin Renfrew and Prof. G.C. Pande are easily traceable. It seems, he feels that till date whatever knowledge he acquires is bestowed upon him by these teachers. He has faced a lot of hardships to attain the position, he has. His relentless pursuit for knowledge and assiduous character as a student made him a success to overcome all the challenges life has ever posed before him. His multilingual ability, clarity of thought and clear goals in combination with the blessings of Almighty, his parents and *Gurus* made him a highly successful student who could further become a teacher, a role model for many students.

As a teacher, without fail Papaji made a point to complete the curriculum assigned to him. Despite of being busy in various activities he never missed his classes. He has always been a very methodical, well prepared, strict and punctual teacher. Papaji believes that life is a learning process and to be effective teacher one has to a continuous learner and student. Morality, character and ethics were the driving forces of this disciplined teacher and I think that who so ever possesses these qualities, people become fearful of him. I shall again refer to Manzar Bhopali Saheb, "मैं मुत्मइन हूँ कुफ़्र की आंधियों में मंज़र, चिराग–ए–ईमान जल रहा है, यही बहुत है।" (*I am contended even under the thunders of 'Kufra: Refuting the existence of Almighty'; this is enough for me that my character is intact hence attached to Almighty*).

As a teacher, Papaji never compromised with the values of this noble profession and had to face lot of anguish of his students but never subdued to anyone's unethical demands. As a teacher, he believed in himself and was very tenacious for what he believed as correct. For these reasons I can easily state about Papaji's role as a teacher through this poetry of Dr Kumar Vinod,

देखिये उस पेड़ को तन कर खड़ा है आज भी
आंधियों का काम चलना है, चलीं तो क्या हुआ?
कम से कम तुम तो करो खुद पर यकीं ऐ दोस्तों
गर ज़माने का नहीं तुम पर यकीं तो क्या हुआ?

(*Till date see that unwavering standing tree even if there were many storms, who cares? At least have the self-confidence, my friends! Who cares if the society does not believe you?*)

Papaji has always been a guide, mentor and motivator to many students. Even though he has always believed that one should not express his opinions regarding any problem unless sought but unobtrusively he never misses to indicate the correct path. "वो जब भी देते हैं मायूसी के लम्हों में जरा सा हौसला, हम कागज़ की कश्ती में ही समंदर में उतर जाते हैं।" (*Whenever I am depressed small motivation provided by him is enough for me to jump into the sea with a paper boat:* Anonymous). He has always been a true motivator, by his words and deeds. As a motivator and guide he exemplifies to think big, face challenges bravely without losing self-confidence. Many a times, by his speech and actions it seems he wants to reverberate the couplet of Rahat Indori sahib, "तूफ़ानों से आँख मिलाओ सैलाबों पर वार करो, मल्लाहों का चक्कर छोड़ो तैर के दरिया पार करो।" (*Face the adversaries, attack the enemy fleet, abstain from the expectation of any help, and just do self-efforts to swim across the sea*).

As an academician, Papaji's contributions are well known to the learned readers. I am reminded about the international conference organized single-handedly by him as Head of the Department, Ancient History and Archaeology, Gorakhpur University. All the scholars around the globe, in addition to the people of Gorakhpur marvelled at the organizing ability of Papaji at such a small place with meagre funds. It was his honest incessant effort and academic acumen that many well-known figures of the city, though poles apart in personal life came forward to contribute in this historical event. Also as an administrator and leader Papaji has been very successful. He held various positions with integrity throughout his career. As an administrator he believed to keep distance from the persons sitting at top, if there was no genuine reason of doing so. He had to face many obstacles, untoward incidences and opposition during enforcement of rules, regulations and discipline. I often thought, "ज़माना क्यूँ ख़िलाफ़त करता है हर बात में उसकी, हक़ीक़त में मुझे वो शख़्स तो खुद्दार लगता है।" (*Why he is always opposed by the society; in reality I feel that he is a person of integrity*). During his administrative regime whenever he and his Webley Scott .32 revolvers roared no other person even dared to perform any misconduct. Papaji has always been a fearless and risk taking individual for truth. When his bosom friends would advise him to refrain from such risky situations he seems to be saying in words of Shahid,

दुनिया उलझ रही है तो सुलझा रहा हूँ मैं
आँधी से कुछ तो सोच कर टकरा रहा हूँ मैं।
मुझ पर हंसो न तुम मेरी हिम्मत को दाद दो
ज़र्रा हूँ..... और पहाड़ से टकरा रहा हूँ मैं।
जारी रहेगी जंग हवाओं से सुबह तक
ये किसने कह दिया कि बुझा जा रहा हूँ मैं।

(With certain faith I am opposing the thunders as I am attempting to solve the puzzles of this life. Don't laugh at me rather compliment my courage as being a miniscule I am fighting the mountain. Till the dawn, fight with adversaries shall keep on going, who says that I am lit off?)

Papaji's tenure as Head of flying squad, President of FUPRUTA (Federation of Uttar Pradesh Residential Teachers Association) and as Chief Proctor, to name a few, can hardly be forgotten by people of that period. During these days too, he was so sagacious and sympathetic that he provided employment to many persons. As a leader, Papaji always gave importance to the tasks at hand but never overlooked his companions.

Epilogue

I am quite dissatisfied hence sad with myself that despite of my best efforts I was not able to convert my feelings and Papaji's accurate personality into words. Believe me, whatever has been experienced in this brief journey put in my words is just tip of an iceberg. May be, if you permit still I can say that Papaji possesses a magnetic personality. Papaji is versatile; utmost honest; man of character, integrity, ethics and values; astute; he hates lies; loves truth; straight forward; a true philosopher; methodical archaeologist; avid reader; prolific researcher; lover of semi classical music; precisely – a person who believes in no-nonsense; compassionate; magnanimous; impartial; uncompromising, etc. He is a true follower of simple living and high thinking. Papaji had never been part of minute rat races. He has always been a satisfied person with whatever has been provided to him by the Almighty. Manzar Bhopali sahib has truly stated, "मुझे फलक की बुलंदियों की हवस नहीं है, जो मेरे रब ने मुझे दिया है, यही बहुत है।" *(I don't have lust for top positions I am contended with whatever has been given to me by my Lord).*

Papaji is a person who enjoys discussing ideas not persons, for him work is worship and he understands that even if you give yourself to others, in this materialistic world once the chair is gone everyone will disown. Wrinkles of his face in a strong and echoic voice often communicate this verse to me, "टूट कर रोज़–रोज भी मुकम्मल खड़ा हूँ मैं, जिंदगी देख तुझसे कितना बड़ा हूँ मैं।" *(Though many hardships have been presented to me at various fronts still I am intact and bigger than life).*

पिता–पुत्र

देवेशनाथ त्रिपाठी

हमारा सम्बंध
पहले से स्थापित
नहीं हुआ कभी परिभाषित।
मैं देवदारु,
तुम हिमालय
मैं पत्थर
तुम शिवालय।
आधुनिकता ग्रसती जा रही है
सभी सम्बंधों को।
आज के पिता–पुत्र सम्बंधों को
देखिये अगर गौर से
तो मिलेगा
पिता अग्नि है
पुत्र धुंआ
पिता सागर है, तो
पुत्र कुंआ।
पिता स्वयं जलता है
और उसी से
पुत्र की उत्पत्ति होती है।
छोड़ देता है पिता
पुत्र को सहज ही
अपना आकाश टटोलने के लिए
और पुत्र भी बढ़ चलता है
असीमित ऊँचाइयाँ पाने के लिए
अपने पिता से दूर ....
यहाँ पिता जलता रहता है
और पुत्र
आकाश में जाकर
न जाने कहाँ
अपना अस्तित्व खो देता है
और पिता सिर्फ उसकी राह देखता
इंतज़ार करता रहता है
अपने पुत्र के लौट आने का।
हमारा सम्बंध तो
जस का तस है
मैं देवदारु
आपकी ही गोद में
अपनी जड़ें और मजबूत करता
बढ़ रहा हूँ
उन्हीं असीमित
ऊँचाइयों को पाने के लिए,
जो आधुनिक पुत्र
अपनी जड़ें खोकर पाते हैं।
मैं पत्थर ही सही मगर
खुश हूँ कि
मेरे पास शिवालय तो है।
मैं देवदारु सा
एकांतिक अकेला वृक्ष ही सही
बहुत खुश हूँ कि
मेरे पास हिमालय तो है।

My Friend Daya Nath, Indian Archeology --- Some Nostalgia, Some Rambling Thoughts

Sibesh Bhattacharya

Although we were batch mates in our postgraduate final class --- MA in Ancient History, Culture and Archaeology at Allahabad University, 1958 --- we were not very close then. My intimacy with Daya Nath developed later. There was no natural common platform for regular interaction during our earlier career. While Daya Nath joined Gorakhpur University as a teacher, I was fortunate to get an appointment in my alma mater itself. During postgraduate days our syllabus did not offer scope for choice or specialization; every student had to take same sets of papers. So area specialization could begin only at the research stage. I personally don't think it was such a disaster. Again speaking in purely personal vein, I don't think I had then the maturity and equipment to independently decide upon an area of specialization. In fact, my research topic was chosen more by my teachers, the research committee members of the department, than by me and for that I remain eternally grateful to them. It was in that manner that I was initiated into the area of socio-economic history of early India. I do not know the story of how Daya Nath came to the field of archaeology. I should assume that it must not have been very different from my own.

It was exciting time. The Freedom of the country still had freshness about it; the air of expectation had not yet taken flight. New ideas were arising or coming from outside. If there was clearly discernible enthusiasm for many of these ideas, there was an equal measure of unease and confusion about them. Meanwhile, important, even momentous, changes were taking place in the political, social and economic fabric of the country. Universal adult franchise had recently been introduced and two elections were already successfully conducted on that basis. Zamindari was abolished. States were being reorganized on linguistic basis and other local factors. Five Year Plans for channelized economic development had been launched. However, everything was not just positive; there was ample measure of negative things to worry about as well. The scar of partition had not fully healed and 'refugee' problem was not fully solved. The country was in the throe of food shortage and had to depend on foreign aids on that front. These led to considerable restrictions in trade and consumption, the 'ration' regime and 'license permit raj' breeding corruption. And then there was the shadow of the 'cold war' and the two contending ideologies. It was not that the everyday life of a young man in Allahabad or Gorakhpur was directly affected by all these, but the universities were sensitive places prone to reflect even distant issues. The intellectual discourse in the country naturally could not remain unaffected by the changes.

Among the various developments taking place --- all of them not always mutually harmonious or coherent --- two proved significant for moulding the thought world of the country. There was a growing sensitivity and appreciation of the problems of poverty. It was natural therefore that the deprived and the marginalized received considerable intellectual and academic attention besides that of the politicians and planners. Poverty and deprivation have of course remained a perennial milch cow for politicians of all hue and they perhaps account for a great deal of the depravity found in our public life. Our main interest here, however, is the thought-environment in which our generation grew and not so much the public life and politics directly. The growing sensitivity about poverty and deprivation and the urge for economic development led to a greater, deeper and a more critical interest in the roots of our civilizational history. Unfortunately, the 'critical interest' later in the hands of excessively ideologically oriented scholars became a synonym for the rejection of everything lock stock and barrel of early Indian heritage -- a clear case of pouring the baby out with the bath water. In the beginning, however, this sensitivity gave a fillip to the expansion and diversification of focus in the study of our early past. This was particularly true of archaeology. There was an upsurge of interest and a welcome expansion in archaeological studies of early India. The ground for that expansion to some extent was already laid by Wheeler when he invited universities to take up archaeological field works on equal footing with the Archaeological Survey. The University of Allahabad was among the first ones to respond to the call. Gorakhpur university too followed suit after it was opened. The career of Daya Nath very largely coincides with this happy phase of Indian archaeology.

The other development that I mentioned was the rising assertion of regional identities. This came to be described in the contemporary intellectual parley in various terms: regionalism, regional nationalism, sub-nationalism, multiculturalism, pluralism, and so on. It's most aggressive early expressions were in the North Eastern India and a slightly less aggressive one was the assertion of Dravidian identity. Our concern here, however, is not with the politics of the development, but with its impact on academic and intellectual field, particularly on the study of archaeology and early history of India. The expansion of archaeological work, with new areas coming under archaeologist's spade and exploration, universities contributing substantially towards it, was revealing distinct regional traits within a broad common pattern of development. These had two interesting characteristics: (a) emergence of certain common features that could be loosely described as 'Indian', and (b) within the rubric of the Indian, pluralistic trends. The cumulative effect of the new and expanding archaeological studies within the country was the emergence of a culture-profile that had three simultaneous strands interacting with each other. These three can be likened to three concentric circles: the local, the Indian, the global. While the general pattern more or less conformed to the universal sequence of human development, within it there was a distinctive Indian flavor and then even within that there were regional and local features.

Some ideas that held sway came to be challenged and some of the accepted neat divisions tended to become hazy or obliterated by the emerging new archaeological evidence; the pre-Aryan Aryan divide, for example. Inconsistency of the theory of the wanton total destruction of the pre-Vedic urban Drāvidian high Harappan culture by the nomadic barbarian Aryan invading hordes became more and more evident; like its origin the end of Harappan culture too appeared to have been gradual. It never seemed to have died; it rather seemed to have merged into succeeding sequences providing the stimuli for the growth of a new phase of urban development in the Ganga valley and eastern India. The space for the purely nomadic/ pastoral Vedic culture, untouched by urbanism of any sort tended to dry up. All these necessitated re-looking at the overall development sequence during early India.

We may mention in passing another thing. The new archaeological methods and techniques appeared to make archaeology an autonomous subject. It seemed it was not necessary any longer (unlike the earlier phase when epigraphy, numismatics and study of monuments dominated archaeology, particularly in India) to correlate it to literary evidence. However, the narrowing gap between the waning of the Harappan and the subsequent urban development seem to be bringing back the issue of the relevance of the correlation of the archaeological and the literary evidence to the fore. Archaeology seemed in fact to be preparing a case and offering the ground for reexamining the relative chronology of the Harappan and Vedic, of the Samhita, Brahmana, Aranyakas and Upanishads, of the Vedic and the Puranas. The theory that the four classes of Vedic literature originated in four succeeding periods has been stoutly contested by Anirvana, for example. And, the general archaeological picture seems to point out that the profile of India right from the very beginning was predominantly pluralistic. It was pluralistic not only in regional cultural manifestations but equally strongly in patterns of living and economy as well; within the same region and within same period urban and rural, agricultural and pastoral, even hunting and gathering economy and way of life could and did coexist without too much frictions. While there could be a magnificent urban establishment at Kausambi, for example, not far from it, the

Vindhyan/ Mirzapur area continued to remain in hunting gathering state. This is also the general picture that we get from literature.

Daya Nath was well equipped to deal with the emerging challenges of Indian archaeology. He had close familiarity with the Bronze Age material of Greece and had done an important book on it. We have noted above that a good deal of the emerging problems of Indian archaeology actually related to the 'Bronze Age' phase and the knowledge of the Greek material surely was an advantage. His association with Renfrew gave him a vantage point in the interesting area of the archaeology of language. He had conducted significant archaeological explorations of the Rapti valley. He was also among the pioneers to attempt to relate Indian archaeology to tradition. In his later life, Daya Nath began moving from field work based archaeology towards comparative history, comparing Hinduism and Hellenism. Perhaps he was making a statement through this transition: value of archaeology ultimately lies in shedding light on the less illumined aspects of human past.

A few words on the human qualities of Daya Nath may not be out of place here. He is a friend par excellence. His loyalty as a friend has always touched me most. I would always remember those misty early dawns during winter months when I would get down from the train from Allahabad at Gorakhpur Station, the twilight had hardly broken, and Daya Nath would be there with his warm welcome smile to receive me. Those days I was a frequent visitor to Gorakhpur University and Daya Nath would be present every time without fail at the station to receive me. And then we would first go to the platform-teashop and have tea before proceeding towards the University Guest House. The sun was still hidden below the eastern horizon. Many a times Daya Nath would make me stay with him at his house. His hospitality has always been extremely warm and generous. I would also always remember the numerous meetings of various committees we attended together, the number of viva voce examinations we conducted together. I always found him ever conscientious and totally committed never sharking work or responsibility. On the occasions of viva voce examinations of PG classes, on the concluding days of the examinations, the filling of the mark sheet and the completion of the required formalities would take us almost into midnight! I don't remember Daya Nath ever betraying any sign of annoyance or impatience for this. Among the fondest memories of our long association of well over half a century are the days we spent together at Shimla at the Indian Institute of Advanced Study. I will treasure these memories for ever.

बहुस्तरीय संचरना का उत्कृष्ट व्यक्तित्व

सुरेन्द्र दुबे

आचार्य दयानाथ त्रिपाठी मेरे लिए गुरु कल्प आदरणीय सहयोगी और संरक्षक की भूमिका में रहे हैं। मेरे ऊपर सदैव उनका स्नेह और विश्वास रहा है। वे जहाँ एक ओर अपने विषय ख्यात आचार्य रहे हैं, वहीं दूसरी ओर उनकी प्रशासनिक क्षमता भी अद्वितीय रही हैं। विद्वान और प्रशासक के बीच उनकी तीसरी विशेषता है उनकी अद्भुत संगठन और नेतृत्व क्षमता। विद्वान, प्रशासक और नेता की यह त्रिवेणी ही उन्हें अपने समकालीन अन्यों से विरल बनाती है।

दीनदयाल उपाध्याय गोरखपुर विश्वविद्यालय, गोरखपुर के इतिहास का विलक्षण काल–खण्ड। परिसर–शिक्षण और आवासीय में अजीब दहशत का माहौल जारी था। जाड़े की रात–समय होगा कोई 7:30 से 8:00 बजे बीच का। एक वरिष्ठ आचार्य आवासीय परिसर की सड़कों पर टहल रहे थे कि अचानक किसी ओर से चोरों की तरह आकर कुछ गुण्डों ने उन पर आक्रमण कर दिया। एक निर्दोष व्यक्ति पर अकारण किया गया यह हमला सबको विचलित और हमप्रभ कर देने वाला था। खैर, उन्हें लेकर लोग सिविल अस्पताल गए। प्रारम्भिक जाँच और हल्की सुश्रुषा के बाद उन्हें छोड़ दिया गया। मैं उन दिनों शिक्षक संघ का महामंत्री था। अनेक शिक्षक साथियों के साथ अस्पताल से परिसर तक हमलोग चक्कर काटते रहे। उस दिन के बाद रात में पहरा देने का कार्यक्रम भी चला। दहशत इतनी कि लोग दिन ढलते ही अपने घरौदों में कैद हो जाते थे। इस कायरतापूर्ण हमले को अखबारों ने प्रमुखता से छापा। परिणाम वही हुआ जो होना था–हीरापुरी कॉलोनी के मुख्य द्वार पर पहला बंगला सुबह से ही आने जाने वालों से भर गया। लोग आते, हालचाल पूछते, अफसोस जाहिर करते और चले जाते। जाड़े का समय, चोटिल आचार्य धूप में अपने आंगन में लेटे थे। लोग चर्चा करते–हमले का कारण क्या है? क्या यह हमला एक कठोर अनुशासन लागू करने वाले आचार्य पर है? विश्वविद्यालय से लेकर प्रदेश स्तर तक शिक्षक राजनीति में अपने नेतृत्व कौशल और सक्रिय जीवन संघर्ष से एक स्थायी पहचान बनाने वाले शिक्षक नेता पर है? या ....अनेक तरह की खुसुर–फुसुर चलती रही। दोपहर ढल रही थी। शाम धीरे–धीरे आँगन में उतरने लगी। श्वेत वस्त्र और केश दाढ़ी वाले एक सज्जन चोटिल आचार्य जी के पास आते हैं। लोगों को लगता है कि आचार्य जी उनसे रात की घटना के विषय में कुछ महत्त्वपूर्ण सूचना देंगे या लेंगे। पर, यह क्या? ....इस दशा में भी आचार्य जी अपने किसी लेख के विषय में उनसे बात कर रहे हैं। ऐसे हैं आचार्य श्रेष्ठ प्रो. दयानाथ त्रिपाठी। यह देखकर वहाँ स्थित हम शिक्षकों को लगा कि इस व्यक्ति को अपने शरीर से ज्यादा अपने विषय से प्रेम है।

दीनदयाल उपाध्याय गोरखपुर विश्वविद्यालय के मजीठिया भवन का कमरा नं. 113। कुलपति श्री जी.सी. चतुर्वेदी का विदाई समारोह। इस समारोह के पहले तक हम लोगों को यह भरोसा था कि चतुर्वेदी जी को एक टर्म और मिल जाएगा। चतुर्वेदी जी ने विश्वविद्यालय के कीचड़ को स्वच्छ कर उसमें ज्ञान का कमल खिलाने का सार्थक प्रयत्न किया था। एक घनघोर अराजक माहौल से विश्वविद्यालय को मुक्ति दिलाई थी। संस्था को अराजक, अव्यवस्था और गुण्डई से मुक्त कर एक स्वस्थ वातावरण दिया था। विदाई समारोह में चतुर्वेदी जी की इन्हीं बातों की प्रशंसा हो रही थी। प्रशंसा जायज थी। शिक्षक के रूप में हमलोगों ने पहली बार पठन–पाठन का माहौल पाया

था। चतुर्वेदी जी ने जब अपनी बात कहने के लिए माइक सँभाला तो उन्होंने कहा–'मैंने जो किया, आप सबके सहयोग से किया। हाँ, मुझे एक जादू की छड़ी मिल गई थी। वह भी यहीं से। वह जादू की छड़ी थी–डॉ. दयानाथ त्रिपाठी। मैं इनके भरोसे बहुत कुछ कर सका। डॉ. त्रिपाठी उस समय मुख्य नियन्ता थे। यह थी उनकी अनुशासनिक और प्रशासनिक क्षमता। मुझे स्मरण है, उस समय विश्वविद्यालय में से अभी जौनपुर अलग नहीं हुआ था। जौनपुर और काशी विद्यापीठ का बहुत–सा हिस्सा गोरखपुर विश्वविद्यालय परिक्षेत्र में ही आता था। विश्वविद्यालय परिसर के साथ–साथ उसके परिक्षेत्र में आने वाले सभी महाविद्यालयों को नकल विहीन परीक्षा का वरदान देने वालों में डॉ. त्रिपाठी महत्त्वपूर्ण रहे हैं। डॉ. माहेश्वर मिश्र, डॉ. दयानाथ त्रिपाठी और डॉ. करुणाकर त्रिपाठी की इस तिकड़ी ने विश्वविद्यालय का जो कायाकल्प किया उसका मीठा फल, आज भी बिना किसी अतिरिक्त श्रम के हम खा रहे हैं। नब्बे के दशक के बाद की पीढ़ी के शिक्षकों को तो शायद यह बोध भी नहीं होगा नकल रोकने और विश्वविद्यालय में पठन–पाठन का अनुकूल वातावरण बनाने के लिए हमारे पुरखों ने किस तरह का जोखिम उठाया और आपने को दाँव पर लगाया था? इस संदर्भ में आज स्मरण में अनेक घटनाएं उमड़ घुमड़ रही हैं किन्तु आजमगढ़ की घटना तो अलग खड़ी आज भी स्मृति में जीवन्त है। ऐसी अनेक घटनाओं की कोख से निकला था डॉ. त्रिपाठी का कठोर अनुशासक व्यक्तित्व। इलाहाबाद विश्वविद्यालय के टॉपर और गोरखपुर विश्वविद्यालय के इस अत्यन्त तेजस्वी और लोकप्रिय शिक्षक ने शिक्षा के मंदिर को स्वच्छ करने के लिए अपने व्यक्तित्व को एक इतर रूप दिया था, जो विश्वविद्यालय के इतिहास में सदैव के लिए दर्ज रहेगा।

प्रो. त्रिपाठी ने अपनी उत्कृष्ट नेतृत्व और संगठन क्षमता का परिचय देते हुए विश्वविद्यालय शिक्षक संघ में सक्रिय भूमिका के निर्वहन के साथ ही आगे चलकर उ.प्र. आवासीय विश्वविद्यालय शिक्षक महा संघ के अध्यक्ष तक की लम्बी यात्रा तय की थी। महासंघ के गठन और उसके सुदृढ़ीकरण में जिन लोगों का उत्कृष्ट योगदान रहा है उसमें त्रिपाठी जी का महत्त्व उल्लेखनीय है। मुझे याद है 1983 का वह लम्बा आन्दोलन जिसने विश्वविद्यालय शिक्षकों को प्रोन्नति का अवसर सुलभ कराया। पहले विश्वविद्यालय के विभागों में रीडर और प्रोफेसर के बमुश्किल क्रमशः 3 से 4 और 1 से 2 पद हुआ करते थे। अनेक अपने विषय के ख्यातिलब्ध आचार्य प्रवक्ता पद से ही सेवानिवृत्त हो जाया करते थे। हताशा और कुण्ठा के उस दौर से शिक्षक समुदाय को उबारने में इस प्रोन्नति योजना ने बड़ी मदद की। इतना ही नहीं कैडर पद पर नियुक्ति के लालच में शिक्षकों का जिस तरह शोषण होता है वह अपने आपमें एक कटु अनुभव था। कभी–कभी बिना किसी प्रयत्न के मिली हुई सहज और सरल जीवनोपलब्धि हमें उसकी नींव के पत्थरों की याद ही नहीं दिलाती है। लगता है कि यह सब जो हमें मिल रहा है, वह मेरा पैतृक अधिकार है, जबकि ऐसा है नहीं। इस अधिकार को पाने के लिए और इसके रक्षण–पोषण के लिए कितने लोगों ने अपने को खपाया है जरा, उसे भी हमें स्मरण कर लेना चाहिए। प्रो. त्रिपाठी पर बात करते हुए मुझे वे दिन स्पष्ट आईने की तरह दिख रहे हैं, जब इन लोगों ने अपनी संघर्ष क्षमता से हमें यह सुखद अवसर उपलब्ध कराया। आज बिना किसी कठोर परिश्रम के मिली हुई यह उपलब्धि हमारे भीतर अकर्मण्यता और अक्षमता भी भर रही है। हम शोषण से मुक्त हो गए, प्रोन्नति के अवसर भी सुलभ हो गए, किन्तु हमारी अकादमिक उपलब्धियाँ आज कहाँ हैं? विषय और विभागों के प्रति दायित्वबोध एवं समर्पण कहाँ है? त्रिपाठी जी के बहाने अपने शिक्षक बंधुओं से प्रार्थना है कि जो सुअवसर हमें मिला है उसका हम सदुपयोग करें। अपने को माँज कर और अधिक तैयार करें। कहीं ऐसा न हो कि यह सुअवसर हमें जड़ बना दे। इस विषय पर मेरी प्रो. त्रिपाठी से कभी बात तो नहीं हुई है, किन्तु मुझे लगता है कि वे हमारी पीढ़ी की कर्तव्य–विमुखता को देखकर निश्चित ही पछताते होंगे। उन्हें लगता होगा कि किनके लिए हम लोगों ने संघर्ष किया? क्यों किया? उच्च शिक्षा की गुणवत्ता की अभिवृद्धि के लिए जिन लोगों ने अपना सब कुछ खपाया है ऐसे त्रिपाठी जी का स्नेह उन शिक्षकों के लिए निरन्तर मिलता रहता है जो अन्य प्रशासनिक या शिक्षक राजनीति में कुछ करते हुए भी अपने विषय में अपना सर्वोत्तम योगदान कर रहे हैं, क्योंकि उन्होंने स्वयं यही किया है।

प्रो. त्रिपाठी इलाहाबाद विश्वविद्यालय से स्नातकोत्तर उपाधि प्राप्त करने के बाद हमारे विश्वविद्यालय में प्रवक्ता पद पर नियुक्त हुए थे। उसी विभाग में प्रवक्ता, उपाचार्य और आचार्य पद पर कार्य करते हुए अध्यक्ष पद से

1998 में सेवानिवृत्त हुए। इस बीच ग्रीक सरकार की अध्येतावृत्ति (1971–74) लेकर ग्रीक भाषा में, डिप्लोमा तथा कालान्तर में ब्रिटिश काउंसिल की अध्येतावृत्ति के साथ पी–एच.डी. उपाधि प्राप्त की। सैकड़ों शोधपत्रों, संगोष्ठियों और कार्यशालाओं में अपने व्याख्यानों द्वारा पुरातत्त्व और प्राचीन इतिहास के क्षेत्र में अपना उल्लेखनीय योगदान किया। यह हमलोगें के लिए गौरव की बात है कि कौशाम्बी, सोहागौरा, फाजिलनगर, उस्मानपुर डीहा (कुशीनगर) की खुदाई आपकी देखरेख में ही सम्पन्न हुई। ये सब ऐसी बातें हैं, जिनकी चर्चा मात्र इसलिए कर रहा हूँ कि मेरी दृष्टि में ऐसे कई शिक्षक हैं, जो अच्छे प्रशासक रहे या अच्छे शिक्षक नेता रहे हैं, किन्तु यह सब रहते हुए भी अपने विषय में उत्कृष्ट योगदान करना निश्चित ही एक बहुमुखी प्रतिभा और बहुस्तरीय मनोसंरचना के व्यक्तित्व द्वारा ही संभव है। पुरातत्त्व और इतिहास को जीने वाले त्रिपाठी जी कालान्तर में भारतीय इतिहास अनुसंधान परिषद के अध्यक्ष बने। किसी भी इतिहासविद् के लिए यह सर्वोच्च उपलब्धि है।

आज प्रो. त्रिपाठी विश्वविद्यालय परिसर से जा चुके हैं। सेवानिवृत्ति के बाद किसी संगोष्ठी, पुनश्चर्या या किसी शैक्षणिक कार्यक्रमों में सादर आमंत्रित करने पर निश्चित ही आते हैं और अपनी ज्ञानराशि के अशेष पुंज को श्रोताओं पर लुटाना चाहते हैं, पर दुःख है कि हमारी और हमारे बाद की पीढ़ी के पात्र बहुत छोटे हैं। कुछ सुबुद्धजन दो–चार दिन उसकी चर्चा करके शान्त हो जाते हैं। काश, कुछ ऐसे जिज्ञासु और सुपात्र विद्यार्थी आते जो इस ज्ञानगंगा से कुछ बूँद चुरा लेते तो उनका जीवन भी धन्य हो जाता। हम बड़भागी हैं कि हमें त्रिपाठी जी की सन्निधि प्राप्त हुई थी, उनके व्यक्तित्व की सुगन्ध आज भी स्मृतियों में महक उठती है।

अधिष्ठाता कला संकाय
दीनदयाल उपाध्याय गोरखपुर विश्वविद्यालय
गोरखपुर

आचार्य–परम्परा के एक बहुआयामी व्यक्तित्व : मेरे गुरूवर्य

ईश्वर शरण विश्वकर्मा[1]

भारतीय मनीषा आचार्यतत्व से आलोकित हुई है। इसीलिए इसकी सुदीर्घ आचार्य–परम्परा विश्व संस्कृति में समादृत एवं आचरणीय रही है। यह श्लाघनीय परम्परा आचार्य (गुरू) के प्रति सदैव श्रद्धेय, सम्पूज्य एवं श्रेष्ठ भाव व्यक्त करती रही है क्योंकि यही परम्परा शिष्यों को 'आचार' या चारित्रय की शिक्षा प्रदान करता था। इसीलिए आचार्य यास्क ने निरूक्त में कहा है कि ''आचार्यः कस्यात्।'' आचार्य आचारं ग्राहयति'' अर्थात् आचरण या विशुद्ध चारित्रय की शिक्षा ही आचार्य का उद्देश्य एवं जीवन है। महर्षि व्यास ने इसे और व्यापक तथा स्पष्ट किया है कि ''आचार्य वह था जिसमें वेदों के प्रति उत्सर्ग की भावना हो, उत्तम परिवार का हो, श्रोत्रिय हो, शुचि हो, वैदिक भाषा का अध्ययन किया हो तथा जो आलसी न हो''

वेदैकनिष्ठं धर्मज्ञं कुलीनं श्रोत्रियं शुचीम्।
स्वाभाषाज्ञमनालस्य विप्रं कर्तारभीप्सतम्।।

महर्षि व्यास ने भारतीय आचार्यो के जिन गुणों का वर्णन किया है वही आचार्यत्व की आर्ष कसौटी है। मेरे गुरूवर्य प्रो. दयानाथ त्रिपाठी पर आचार्य यास्क और महर्षि व्यास की दोनों ही व्याख्याएँ ठीक बैठती है। उनके व्यक्तित्व के निरूपण तथा शिष्यों के प्रति भाव के लिए आचार्य परम्परा का निकष ही चरितार्थ होता है। एक पुरातत्त्ववेत्ता होने के साथ ही वैदिक परम्परा के प्रति उनकी आसक्ति सदैव बनी रही। 'आर्क्यालाजी एण्ड ट्रेडिशन–(1988) नामक प्रकाशित ग्रंथ तथा 'अयस् इन दि ऋग्वेद' शोध लेख उनकी इसी भावना को व्यक्त करते है। इसी प्रकार 'हिन्दुइज्म एण्ड हेलेनिज्म' (2004) नामक वृहत्प्रकल्प पर शोधकृति में इस भावना का वैश्विक विस्तार होता है। गुरूवर्य का सम्पूर्ण जीवन एक आचार्य की भाँति शुचितापूर्ण, सात्विकता से ओतप्रोत तथा सत्यपरक रहा है।

गुरूवर्य के बहुआयामी व्यक्तित्व में उनका उत्तम कुल में जन्म एवं श्रेष्ठ माता–पिता के वे संस्कार भी थे जिन्होंने उनमें आचरण, चरित्र, कर्मठता, अनुशासन तथा दया भावना का बीजारोपण कर उनको शिक्षा क्षेत्र में प्रस्तुत किया। मेरा यह सौभाग्य रहा है कि उनके पूज्य पिता स्वर्गीय पं. एम किशोर शर्मा तथा पूज्यामाता स्वर्गीया श्रीमती कृष्णाशर्मा का आर्शीवाद तथा सान्निध्य प्राप्त हुआ था। उनके पूज्यपिता एक आदर्श शिक्षक तथा स्वाधीनता आंदोलन के एक ऐसे सेनानी भी थे जिन्होने सेना की नौकरी छोड़कर इलाहाबाद के रामबाग मुहल्ले में स्थित सेवा समिति विद्या मंदिर इंटर कॉलेज में अध्यापक बने तथा बाद में सरयूपारीण इंटर कॉलेज, रामभवन, चौराहा, बहादुरगंज के प्रधानाचार्य पर से अपनी सेवापूर्ण की थी। इसी प्रकार उनकी पूज्यामाता जी परमसात्विक कुल से सम्बन्धित थी। वृन्दावन के स्वामी अखंडानन्द सरस्वती उनके संबन्धी थे तथा माधवानन्द सरस्वती उनके भतीजे थे। इस प्रकार गुरूवर्य के व्यक्तित्व के विकास में उच्च श्रोत्रिय कुल के संस्कार तथा उनकी कुल परम्परा के वंशानुगत लक्षणों का बड़ा योगदान रहा है।

यह एक उल्लेखनीय तथ्य है कि गुरूवर्य मूलतः गोरखपुर जनपद के कौड़ीराम के समीप स्थित प्रागैतिहासिक ग्राम सोहगौरा के निवासी रहे हैं। छः पीढ़ी पूर्ण पं. जयराम तिवारी ने सोहगौरा से जाकर इलाहाबाद मे बसना स्वीकार किया। मेजा तहसील में डोहरिया के पास का ग्राम अभी भी ''जयरामपुरवा'' कहा जाता है।

---

[1] आचार्य, प्राचीन इतिहास, पुरातत्व एवं संस्कृति विभाग, दीनदयाल उपाध्याय गोरखपुर विश्वविद्यालय, गोरखपुर (उ.प्र.)–273009

इसीलिए गुरूवर्य के व्यक्तित्व में सनातनता पाण्डित्य तथा पूर्वजों के प्रति अनन्य श्रद्धाभक्ति का भाव मानों मोतियों की तरह सजे हैं।

यह गोरखपुर विश्वविद्यालय का सौभाग्य रहा है कि गुरूदेव प्रो. दयानाथ त्रिपाठी जैसा आचार्य व्यक्तित्व शिक्षक के रूप में मिला। 1958 में इलाहाबाद विश्वविद्यालय से एम.ए. करने के पश्चात् वे गोरखपुर विश्वविद्यालय के प्राचीन इतिहास विभाग में प्रवक्ता नियुक्त हुए। तब से लगातार चालीस वर्षो तक (1958 से 1998) इस विश्वविद्यालय की अविस्मरणीय सेवा अर्पित की। इस चारदशक की सेवा अवधि में उन्होंने विषम परिस्थितियों में अपनी उच्च शैक्षणिक अध्येतावृत्ति को बाधित नहीं होने दिया। अध्यापकीय जीवन में ही पीएच.डी. शोध हेतु उन्हें इन्डो–ग्रीक फेलो स्कॉलरशिप (1971–74), ब्रिटिश कौंसिल स्कॉलरशिप (1974–76), एथेंस में ब्रिटिश स्कूल ऑफ आर्क्यालाजी की अध्येतावृत्ति के साथ रोम, अंकारा, तेहरान में कार्य करते हुए यूनानी भाषा में डिप्लोमा (1972) तथा साउथस्पटन विश्वविद्यालय (यू.के.) से प्रख्यात पुराविद लार्ड कॉलिन रेनफ्र्यू के शोध निर्देशन में ब्रान्ज वर्क ऑफ मेनलैण्ड ग्रीस (2600 बी.सी.–1450 वी.सी.) विषय पर पीएच.डी. उपाधि प्राप्त कर विषय, विधा, विश्वविद्यालय तथा क्षेत्र को गौरवान्वित किया। गुरुवर्य सही अर्थों में प्राच्यविधा के महामनीषी हैं। भारतीय–यूनानी संस्कृतियों के समन्वय को उन्होंने अपने जीवन तथा अनुसंधान में व्यक्त किया है।

गुरूवर्य प्रो. त्रिपाठी के व्यक्तित्व में पुरातनता, पुरातत्व तथा पारम्परिकता का अद्भुत समन्वय है। पुरातत्व के प्रति उनके मन में अनुराग महज संयोग नहीं है। वे एक ऐसे ग्राम (सोहगौरा) के मूलनिवासी है जो भारत का प्राचीनतम ग्राम है और पिछले पांच हजार वर्षो से निरन्तर आवासित है। इसीलिए गोरखपुर विश्वविद्यालय के प्राचीन इतिहास विभाग ने प्रो. शैलनाथ चतुर्वेदी के निर्देशन तथा विभागीय सहयोगियों के कुशल नेतृत्व में 1962–65 में इसका पुरातात्विक उत्खनन कराया। इस नवपाषाणकालीन ग्राम ने राप्तीघाटी की संस्कृति को एक नई पहचान दी। इस प्रकार अपने प्राचीन ग्राम के इतिवृत्त तथा पुरातत्व के साथ गुरूवर्य सदैव जीवन्त रहते हैं तथा गर्वानुभूति का दृष्टान्त देते हैं। इसी पृष्ठभूमि ने आपको भारत तथा यूनान के अनेक पुरातात्विक स्थलों पर पुरातात्विक सर्वेक्षण तथा उत्खनन का सुअवसर प्रदान किया।

गुरूवर्य का "शिक्षक–व्यक्तित्व" सदैव प्रेरणास्पद, अनुकरणीय तथा आचारणीय रहा है। मुझे स्नातक एवं स्नाकोत्तर दोनों ही कक्षाओं में 1974 से 1978 तक (जब वे भारत में थे) शिष्य के रूप में उनका स्नेहिल सान्निध्य मिला है। वे विश्व की प्राचीन सभ्यताओं तथा विश्व प्रागितिहास के कुशल अध्येता, अध्यापक तथा आचार्य रहे हैं। यह विषय का ही प्रभाव था कि उनके व्यक्तित्व में विश्व की श्रेष्ठ सांस्कृतिक विरासत समन्वित होकर शिक्षण में सहयोगी रहती थी। यही कारण था कि उनके शिष्य के रूप में मुझे सदैव गर्व की अनुभूति होती है। महाकवि कालीदास ने गुरू–शिष्य के पारस्परिक सम्बन्ध को 'गुरूवो गुरूप्रियम्' कहा है। मेरे लिए उनकी गुरुता सदैव वन्दनीय तथा प्रंशसनीय रही है। वे सहज ही शिष्यों के विद्यानुराग से प्रभावित हो जाते थे तथा उन्हें 'शिष्य–पुत्र' बना लेते थे। यही घाती उनके व्यक्तित्व की विशालता का एक आधार है। एक श्रेष्ठ गुरू के रूप मे वे कुशल थे क्योंकि सदाचारी, प्रतिभावान और सुयोग्य शिष्य को चुनना गुरू की कुशलता कही गई है। वे ऐसे शिष्यों को सदैव अपने सानिध्य से योग्यतम बनाने के लिए सद्भाव रखते रहे हैं।

वर्ष 1998 में गोरखपुर विश्वविद्यालय से सेवानिवृत्त होने के पश्चात् वे निरन्तर अकादमिक सक्रियता के सद्गुण को संरक्षित किए है। सेवानिवृत्त होने के पश्चात् वे इलाहाबाद विश्वविद्यालय के प्राचीन इतिहास, संस्कृति एवं पुरातत्व विभाग में विजिटिंग फेलो (1998–99), भारतीय उच्च अध्ययन संस्थान, राष्ट्रपति निवास, शिमला के फेलो (1999–2002), विजिटिंग फेलो, ब्रिटिश एकेडमी, लन्दन (2003), भारतीय इतिहास अनुसंधान परिषद, भारत सरकार, नई दिल्ली के सदस्य (1998–2004), तथा परिषद के अध्यक्ष (2004–2007) के गौरवमय पदों को सुशोभित कर अघावधी अपनी अध्येतावृत्ति के साथ सक्रिय हैं। उन्होंने तीन वृहतशोध प्रकल्पों को पूर्ण कर अपनी शोधपरक पहचान बनायी है। इस दृष्टि से विश्वविद्यालय अनुदान आयोग इस स्वीकृत 'आर्क्योलॉजी एण्ड ट्रेडीशन' भारतीय इतिहास अनुसंधान परिषद द्वारा स्वीकृत "आर्कियो लिंग्विस्टिक्स" तथा भारतीय उच्च अध्ययन संस्थान शिमला द्वारा स्वीकृत "हिन्दुइज्म एण्ड हेलेनिज्म" विद्वत्वर्ग में समाहृत एवं प्रशंसित है।

गुरूवर्य के व्यक्तित्व का एक अनुकरणीय पक्ष उनका अनुशासन प्रिय होना रहा है। वे बचपन से (जैसा कि उनके पूज्य पिता एवं पूज्यामाता जी से सुना है) ही कठोर, अनुशासन प्रिय तथा विद्या के प्रति अनुसक्त रहे हैं। शैक्षणिक व्यवस्था तथा शिक्षा–परिसरों को अनुशासित बनाने में उनकी दृष्टि पारम्परिक रही है। वर्ष 1980–84 तक वे गोरखपुर विश्वविद्यालय के मुख्य नियंता एवं दंडाधिकारी रहे हैं जिसमें उनका परिसर की सुचिता, व्यवस्था आज भी स्मणीय है। इसी क्रम में गोरखपुर विश्वविद्यालय शिक्षकसंघ तथा उत्तरप्रदेश आवासीय विश्वविद्यालय शिक्षक महासंघ के अध्यक्ष रहे हैं जिसमें विश्वविद्यालयों के शिक्षकों के लिए अनेक उल्लेखनीय कार्य किया।

गुरूवर्य के व्यक्तित्व में स्पष्ट वादिता तथा सत्यनिष्ठता का अनुपम योग रहा है। वे निर्भीक, स्पष्टवादी तथा सत्यनिष्ठ रहे हैं। उनकी इस लाक्षणिकता से उनके शिष्य–मित्र परिचित हैं। उनकी इसी पहचान ने शिक्षा, राजनीति, प्रशासन, समाज आदि विविध क्षेत्रों में उनके प्रशंसकों की लम्बी पंक्ति खड़ी कर दी है। वे एक राजनीतिक सूझ–बूझ के धनी तथा समाज–कार्य में कुशल समाज–चितंक रहे है। उनकी शिष्य परम्परा में समाज के प्रत्येक क्षेत्र, वर्ग तथा श्रेणी के लोग सम्मिलित हैं। उनकी स्पष्टवादिता तथा सत्यपरकता ने शिष्यों तथा मित्रों को एक जीवन शैली दी है जिसका स्मरण कर उनके व्यक्तित्व को नमन् किया जाता है।

अपने गुरूजनों के प्रति असीम श्रद्धा तथा पूज्यभाव गुरूदेव के व्यक्तित्व का सबसे सुन्दर पक्ष है। अपने अध्ययन कक्ष, पुस्तकालय तथा कार्यालय आदि में वे भारती विद्या के महान आचार्य प्रो. गोविन्द चन्द पांडे तथा इंग्लैंड के गुरू लार्ड कॉलिन रेन्फ्यु को अपना प्रेरणास्त्रोत मानते है। यह भाव उनके जीवन में पाश्चात्य एवं पुरातत्व विद्या परम्परा के प्रति आदरभाव का प्रत्यक्ष दर्शन कराता हैं। यही कारण है कि गुरूवर्य के व्यक्तित्व में परम्परा एवं पुरातत्व का अनुपम योग है। भारतीय दर्शन, परम्परा, संस्कृति, कला तथा पाश्चात्य कला संस्कृति के समन्वय को वे अनुभव करते थे। ऐसा बहुआयामी व्यक्तित्व दुर्लभ होता है। ऐसे अभिनन्दनीय व्यक्तित्व को नमन्।।

आचार्यत्व के निकष पर निकषित व्यक्तित्व की एक बड़ी विशेषता उसका विद्यानुराग तथा विषयगत अध्ययन, अध्यापन एवं अनुसंधान है। गुरूवर्य एक विद्यानुरागी माँ शारदा के वरदपुत्र तथा गहन अध्येता एक पुरातत्व मनीषी आचार्य हैं। वे विश्व पुरातत्व के अध्येता रहे हैं। विश्व पुरातत्व परिषद (वर्ल्ड आक्योलाजिकल कांग्रेस), इण्डियन सोसाइटी फार ग्रीको – रोमन स्टडीज, इण्डियन आर्क्यालाजीकल सोसाइटी नई दिल्ली, इण्डियन हिस्ट्री एण्ड कल्चर सोसाइटी, नई दिल्ली, इण्डियन सोसाइटी फार प्री हिस्ट्री एण्ड क्वार्टर्नरी स्टडीज, पूना, मध्यप्रदेश धरोहर विकास परिषद, भोपाल तथा इलाहाबाद राष्ट्रीय संग्रहालय, इलाहाबाद के आजीवन सदस्य, पदाधिकारी तथा अध्येता रहे हैं।

एक पुरातत्वविद् के रूप में उन्होंने न केवल विषय को जिया अपितु क्षेत्रीय पुरातत्व को अपने पुरातात्विक सर्वेक्षणों, उत्खननों एवं विश्लेषणों से समृद्ध किया। गोरखपुर विश्वविद्यालय द्वारा उत्खनित पुरास्थल सोहगौरा, फाजिलनगर (उस्मान (डीह)) एवं वीरमाटीपुर के उत्खनन से प्रत्यक्ष सम्बद्ध रहे हैं। उन्होंने अपने विश्वविद्यालयी सेवा के अंतिम चरण में वीरभारी के उत्खनन का निर्देशन कर विभागीय पुरातत्व संग्रहालय को अमूल्य पुरावशेषों का धरोहर देकर उपकृत किया है। इतना ही नहीं उन्होंने यूनान प्रवास के समय मेनेलियॉन तथा पीलॉस जैसे पुरास्थलों के पुरातात्विक उत्खनन में महत्वपूर्ण योगदान दिया है। उनके द्वारा सर्वेक्षित पूर्वी उत्तरप्रदेश के लगभग 150 पुरास्थल भावी उत्खननों के दिशा प्रदर्शक हैं।

'चरैवेति चरैवेति' गुरूवर्य के जीवन का मंत्र रहा है। वे ऐसे पथ के पथिक हैं जहां चरणशीलता आचरण में है। अथक परिश्रमी, उद्यमी एवं पुरूषार्थी व्यक्तित्व के धनी हैं। प्रातः काल ब्राह्ममुहूर्त से प्रारम्भ दिनचर्चा मध्यरात्रि में विश्राम लेती रही है। चारिका, चंक्रमण एवं चर्चा की भांति वे अपनी गतिविधियों से विषय को समृद्ध करते रहते है। शांत, गंभीर, सौम्य, मितभाषी एवं मृदुभाषी जैसे सदगुणों से गुरूवर्य का व्यक्तित्व निरूपित हुआ है। पांडित्यपूर्ण जीवन की ये विधाएँ कठिन साधना तथा अध्यवसाय से प्राप्त होती हैं। गुरूवर्य को ये सौभाग्य मिला भी है, उपार्जित भी है। इसीलिए वे 'दयानाथ' है तथा उनके दो अनुज क्रमशः कृपानाथ (पं. कृपानाथ त्रिपाठी अधिवक्ता, इलाहाबाद) तथा स्व. शिवानाथ (स्व. शिवानाथ त्रिपाठी, पूर्व पुलिस उपाधीक्षक, मध्यप्रदेश विशेष सशस्त्र दल) सही अर्थों में नाम को चरितार्थ करने वाले हैं।

गुरूवर्य के बहुआयामी व्यक्तित्व की विनिर्मिति में अपना सम्पूर्ण जीवन अर्पित करने वाली उनकी धर्मपत्नी पूज्या अम्मा श्रीमति लीला त्रिपाठी का महत्वपूर्ण योगदान है। आज भी दोनों ऋषि परम्परा का जीवन व्यतीत करते हुए विद्या की साधना में लीन हैं। वे साक्षात देवी हैं। उनके चरणों में कोटिशः नमन है। वे प्रत्यक्ष अन्नपूर्णा हैं जिनका घर शिष्यों के लिए, विद्यार्थियों के लिए सदैव आश्रमवत खुला रहता है। मुझ जैसे शिष्य को उन्होने इसी परम्परा में शिक्षित कर विद्या के क्षेत्र में अग्रेसित किया।

ऐसे आचार्य मनीषी विद्वत्ता एवं वात्सल्य के पूर्ण मेरे गुरूदेव सदैव अभिनन्दनीय एवं श्रद्धा–स्पद भाव के साथ प्रणम्य हैं। उनका बहुआयामी व्यक्तित्व, छात्रों, अध्यापकों, अनुसंधित्सुओं सभी के लिए प्रेरणास्त्रोत तथा पाथेयपरक रहेगा। गोरखपुर के इन्द्रानगर मुहल्ले का उनका आवास'लीलानिलयम' सदैव एक आश्रम की भाँति प्रणम्य एवं गमनीय है। अंत में इस अभिनन्दन के अवसर पर अपने गुरूवर्य के श्री चरणों में प्रणाम निवेदित करते हुये उनके चिर यशस्वी वैदुष्यपूर्ण जीवन की कामना तथा ईश्वर से प्रार्थना करता हूँ कि वे "शतायुर्वे पुरुषाः" की परम्परा में अपने आचार्यत्व से विषय, समाज तथा राष्ट्र को समृद्ध करें। "तस्मै श्री गुरवे नम :"।।

सोहगौरा से सोहगौरा : प्रोफेसर दया नाथ त्रिपाठी

राकेश तिवारी

प्रोफेसर त्रिपाठी का नाम तो बड़े–बड़कवों से एक जमाने से सुनते रहे लेकिन पहली बार उनके दर्शन का संयोग बना 1997 में जब देश की आज़ादी की पचासवीं सालगिरह के मौके पर पिछले पाँच दशकों में हुई पुरातात्विक गतिविधियों से नफे–नुकसान का हिसाब बैठाने के इरादे से लखनऊ में पुराविद–संतों की जुटान में भागीदारी के लिए हमारा आमंत्रण स्वीकार कर पधारे।

मज़बूत कद काटी, प्रभावशाली गोल चेहरा, चौड़ा माथा, गहरी प्रभावशाली ऐसी आँखें कि जब चढ़ा कर बोले तो उनसे आँखें मिला कर बात करना सबके बस का ना रहे, मज़बूत कद काठी, एक बड़े विद्वान और मल्ल एक में मिला दिए जाएं तो उनका व्यक्तित्व बन जाए।

सेमीनार के दौरान जब सौहगौरा की चर्चा चली तो बेलौस बोले। राप्ती और आमी नदियों के संगम पर बसे इस गाँव का नाम 1962–63 में वहाँ लगाई गई छोटी सी खन्ती की गहराई से उभर कर पुराविदों के आकश में देदीप्यामान हुआ। इस खन्ती में उतर कर धरती की परतों में दबी पुरासम्पदा का महत्ता आंकने वालों में गोरखपुर विश्वविद्यालय में उस समय प्राचीन भारतीय इतिहास की कमान संभाल रहे प्रोफेसर गोविन्द चन्द्र पांडे की टोली में डॉक्टर शैल नाथ चतुर्वेदी के साथ वे भी शामिल रहे।

सोहगौरा के शोध से ऐसे साक्ष्य सामने आए जो आगे सरयूपार सहित पूरे पूर्वी उत्तर प्रदेश में मानव आवास के प्रारम्भ का काल दूसरी सहस्त्राब्दी ईसा पूर्व से भी पहले ले जाने के अनुमानों के आधार बने। प्राचीन आवासीय गतिविधियों की अटूट कड़ी ने सिद्ध कर दिया कि यह गाँव लगभग 4000 वर्ष से भी अधिक समय से उसी जगह आबाद रहा है। इस गाँव की चर्चा यहाँ से मिले एक ताम्र–पत्र पर अंकित लेख के लिए भी होती रही है जिसकी गिनती देश के सबसे पुराने लेखों में की जाती है।

सरवरिया ब्राह्मणों में सोहगौरा के तिवारियों या त्रिपाठियों का बड़ा मान रहा है, इतना ऊँचा कि किसी ज़माने में और काफी हद तक आज भी खेती–बारी, धन सम्पदा हो ना हो सोहगौरा का तिवारी होना ही अच्छे वर के चयन के लिए पर्याप्त रहा। कालान्तर में मालूम हुआ कि इलाहाबाद जिले में गंगा–पार के शुकुलपुरा गाँव के जिस पुरवे के वे मूल निवासी हैं उसका नाम 'सोहगौरन का पुरवा' पड़ने का कारण उनके पुरखों के किसी समय गोरखपुर के सोहगौरा गाँव से आ कर वहाँ बसने के कारण पड़ा। यह भी एक कारण रहा उनका सोहगौरा से विशेष लगाव रखने का।

उनका जन्म 1938 में इलाहाबाद में हुआ, वहीं पले–बढ़े पढ़ते हुए 1958 में इलाहाबाद विश्वविद्यालय से प्राचीन भारतीय इतिहास, संस्कृति एवं पुरातत्त्व विषय में स्नातकोत्तर की डिग्री हासिल करते ही अपनी मेधा के चलते उसी वर्ष गोरखपुर विश्वविद्यालय में लेक्चर के पद पर सुशोभित हो कर सोहगौरा की मूल धारा से जुड़ गए। उसके बाद 1971–74 के बीच ग्रीक सरकार की स्कालरशिप पा कर एथेंस यूनिवर्सिटी से ग्रीक भाषा में डिप्लोमा किया। 1974–76 में ब्रिटिश कौंसिल स्कॉलरशिप प्राप्त कर के 'ब्रॉन्ज़ वर्क ऑफ़ ग्रीस' विषय पर 'साउथेम्पटन यूनिवर्सिटी' (यू.के.) से प्रोफेसर कॉलिन रेनफ्रिउ के पर्यवेक्षण में, पी–एच. डी. की डिग्री पाने के सिलसिले में एथेंस, रोम, अंकारा और तेहरान की शोध–यात्राओं के अनुभव बटोरा। फिर, गोरखपुर विश्वविद्यालय में 1979 में रीडर और 1989–1998 तक प्रोफेसर के पदों को सुशोभित करते हुए सतत मुक्त हस्त विद्यादान में डूबे रहे। 1998–99 में अपनी मातृ–संस्था, इलाहाबाद यूनिवर्सिटी में विज़िटिंग प्रोफेसर रहे।

लगभग चार दशक पठन–पाठन में खपा कर भी विद्या–व्यसन से मुक्त नहीं हुए। विश्वविद्यालय से निकले तो 1999–2002 तक इंडियन इंस्टिट्यूट ऑफ एडवांस इंस्टिट्यूट, शिमला और 2003 में ब्रिटिश अकादमी, लन्दन के फेलो, और फिर, 2004–2007 तक इंडियन कौंसिल ऑफ हिस्टोरिकल रिसर्च के अध्यक्ष रहे। व्यक्तित्व के अनुरूप

1980–1984 तक गोरखपुर विश्वविद्यालय के चीफ प्रॉक्टर और 1997–1998 तक किसान पोस्ट ग्रेजुएट कॉलेज, बस्ती के अधिकृत नियंत्रक के प्रशासकीय पदों पर दायित्व सम्भाला। उनके विश्वविद्यालयों और शोध–संस्थाओं तथा उनकी विभिन्न कमेटियों के सदस्य एवं अन्य पदों को सुशोभित करते हुए महत्त्वपूर्ण योगदान किया।

भारतीय इतिहास, संस्कृति और पुरातत्व जगत में उनका नाम खूब जाना गया। शोध और अध्ययन के साथ साथ क्रमशः प्रोफेसर गोवर्धन राय शर्मा, प्रोफेसर शैल नाथ चतुर्वेदी तथा प्रोफेसर एच. डी. सांकलिया के पर्यवेक्षण में कौशाम्बी (1957–58), सोहगौरा (1961–63), और अहाड़ (1963–64) के अतिरिक्त क्रमशः डॉ. एच. डब्लू. कैटलिंग तथा प्रोफेसर जी.एस. कोर्रेस के पर्यवेक्षण में ग्रीस में स्पार्टा के निकट मेनेलिओन (1973–74) और पाइलोस (1974–75) के पुरातात्त्विकउत्खनन में भाग लेने का अनुभव प्राप्त किया। 1978–79 में फाजिलनगर (कुशीनगर) के उत्खनन का सह–निदेशन और 1997–98 में उस्मानपुर डीहा (कुशीनगर) के उत्खनन का निदेशन किया। इतना ही नहीं उनके दिशा–निर्देशन में 1994–1998 के बीच संपादित सर्वेक्षण से लगभग 200 पुरास्थल भी प्रकाश में आए।

अपने शोध सिलसिले में उन्होंने ग्रीस, युगोस्लाविया, फ्रांस, जर्मनी, इटली, यू.के., मिस्त्र, टर्की और ईरान तथा भारत के संग्रहालयों में संग्रहीत 'प्री एंड प्रोटो स्टिोरिक' पुरा सामग्री का अध्ययन किया। 'पुरातत्त्व और परंपरा' (1995–99) तथा 'हिंदुइज़म और हेलेनिज़म' (1999–2002) विषयों पर संपादित शोध आधारित प्रकाशन विशेष महत्त्वपूर्ण हैं। उनके निर्देशन में लगभग आधा दर्जन शोध प्रबंध प्रस्तुत हुए।

ताजिंदगी ज्ञान की पताका लहराते देश–विदेश के सौ से अधिक राष्ट्रीय–अंतर्राष्ट्रीय सेमिनारों में भारत और इंगलैण्ड, ग्रीस, इटली, जर्मनी, बेल्जियम, अमरीका और कनाडा के सभागृहों में डंका बजाते घूमते रहे और आज भी घूम रहे हैं। विशेषज्ञों को आमंत्रित कर उनके विचारों से लाभान्वित होने और विचार विमर्श के अवसर जुटाने के लिए उन्होंने समय–समय पर अनेक कॉन्फ्रेंस, सेमीनार, पाठ्यक्रम आयोजि कराए। 'ग्रीस–भारत सम्बन्ध', 'पुरातत्त्व और परम्परा', 'इंडो–यूरोपियन भाषा और संस्कृति', 'भारत और मध्य एशिया', 'पश्चिम एशिया से सांस्कृतिक सम्बन्ध' उनके प्रिय विषय रहे हैं जिन पर उनकी 9 किताबें और 50 से अधिक शोध–पत्र एवं समीक्षाएं प्रकाशित हैं। आज भी वे गहन अध्ययन–मनन में लगे रह कर इस कोष को भरते ही जा रहे हैं। प्राचीन अवशेषों से डी एन ए निकाल कर मॉलिक्यूलर पापुलेशन जेनेटिक तकनीक (आर्किओजेनेटिक्स) के माध्यमसे मानव, पशुओं और वनस्पतियों की विभिन्न प्रजातियों के इतिहास और उनकी आनुवंशिक परम्परा का अध्ययनउनका परम रुचिकर विषय बन गया है।

एक बार उनके पुरखों ने इलाहाबाद जा कर सोहगौरन का पुरवा बसाया था। लेकिन उन्होंने इलाहाबाद से गोरखपुर आ कर वापस लौटने से बेहतर अपनी सोर से जुड़ कर अपने मूल निवास प्राचीन 'सोहगौरा' ग्राम के निकटतम गोरखपुर में ही बसना पसंद किया। वे जहाँ रहते हैं वहाँ प्राचीन भारतीय इतिहास व उससे जुड़े विषयों के अध्येताओं का जमावड़ा लगा रहता है।

एक अवसर मिला था हमें खलीलाबाद (जिला संत कबीर नगर) के पोस्ट ग्रेजुएट कॉलेज में आयोजित समारोह में उनके एक और रूप से साक्षात्कार पाने का। वे वहाँ मुख्य अतिथि के रूप में आमंत्रित थे। खचाखच भरे सभागार में हम सब अपनी अपनी कुर्सियों पर बैठे उनके आने की प्रतीक्षा कर रहे थे। थोड़ी देर बाद मुख्यद्वार पर हलचल के साथ सभी लोग खड़े हो कर उधर ही देखने लगे। हमने देखा, सबसे आगे आगे अपनी विशिष्ट प्रभावशाली मुद्रा में एक सम्राट के समान माथा उठाए, 'रेड कार्पेट' पर धीरे–धीरे पग धरते बढ़ते प्रोफेसर दया नाथ त्रिपाठी, पीछे–पीछे उन पर फूल बरसाते जयकारा लगाते आयोजक। उनके अभिनन्दन में पढ़े गए व्यक्तव्य में परम वरेण्य जैसे अनेक संस्कृतनिष्ठ विशेषणों से परिपूर्ण माला ने गोरखपुर क्षेत्र की विशिष्ट शैली और त्रिपाठी जी के प्रति उद्‌गारों ने अभिभूत कर दिया। हम कामना करते हैं कि उनकी यह आन–बान–शान यूं ही बनी रहे और वे इससे भी ऊंची ऊंचाइयों पर आसनस्थ रहें।

महानिदेशक
भारतीय पुरातत्त्व सर्वेक्षण
जनपथ, नई दिल्ली

INDIAN COUNCIL OF HISTORICAL RESEARCH
(AN AUTONOMOUS ORGANTSATTON)
MINISTRY OF HUMAN RESOURCE DEVELOPMENT GOVT. OF INDIA
35. Ferozeshah Road, New Delhi-110 001

Y. Sudershan Rao
Chairperson

Phone : 23387 877, 23386033, 23382321, 23386973
23389021, 23388857, 23388747, 23384829
Fax : 23383421, 23387829
E-mail : ms_ichr@rediffmail.com,
support@ichrindia.org
Website : www.ichrindia.org

19 August 2014

It gives me great pleasure to hear that a Felicitation Volume is being brought out, titled 'Archaeology and Tradition', in honour of Prof. Daya Nath Tripathi. Prof. D. N. Tripathi is a renowned archaeologist and respected academician. His area of research was not just limited to a micro-area. The scope of his research covered India, Greece and England. He had also worked on linguistic parlances of early civilizations of the ancient world. Since I do not belong to this area of specialisation, I am not fortunate enough to give any critical assessment of his work but my recent interests fall in the ancient historical tradition of India's remote past, I have great appreciation for his contribution to our knowledge of the ancient world.

Unlike other countries, Indian culture is not based on material culture alone. Indian culture is basically evolved from Shastras formulated from the Vedic thought by the Rishis. Indian polity, social customs, traditions, faiths and material cultures are the developments out of meditation (single pointed attention), *Tapas* (wait for the result) and intellectual exercise (to make it comprehendable to others) of the ancient rishis. Archeology has helped us in tracing our ancient history from the past providing us material artefacts from about two centuries. The new trends in archeology are also stepping forward to consider the collective memory of generations as sources of history which are still available in form of tribal lore, folklore and Vedic-lore in form of Orature as sources for history. This would help us bridging-up the missing link between known and unknown worlds of the remote Indian past. Hope the historical researches in the coming years would address this problem to improve our understanding of ancient past.

I know Dr D N Tripathi for more than a decade as we were both members of ICHR in 2002. I developed a great regard for him for his positive outlook on Indian past. I wish him a long life and good health. May his scholarship and experience guide the succeeding generations of archaeologists to look at India's ancient past in a proper perspective and let our Indian historical tradition getneeded support from the 'new' archaeological explorations.

Warangal

Telangana State

Y.Sudershan Rao

आचार्य दयानाथ त्रिपाठी: मेरे पिता एवं प्रेरणा

उमेश नाथ त्रिपाठी

मैं अभिभूत हूँ और साथ ही साथ असमंजस में भी हूँ कि मुझे पापाजी के सम्मान में प्रकाशित होने वाले ग्रंथ में कुछ लिखना है। अभिभूत इसलिए हूँ कि मेरे पिता, जिन पर हमें लगता था कि उनका पुत्र होने के कारण, केवल हमारा अधिकार है, उनको चाहने और उनका सम्मान करने वाले दुनिया में और कितने लोग हैं? असमंजस में इसलिए कि जिन्होंने सब कुछ दिया उनके उपर क्या लिखूँ? मेरा नाम, मेरा पद, मेरी प्रतिष्ठा, मेरा परिवार, मेरा सब कुछ तो उन्हीं का दिया हुआ है। शायद अब यह बात समझ में आने लगी है कि क्यों संस्कृत के श्लोक में यह लिखा है –

त्वमेव माता च पिता त्वमेव, त्वमेव बन्धुश्च सखा त्वमेव।
त्वमेव विद्या द्रविणम् त्वमेव, त्वमेव सर्वम् मम देव देव।।

ईश्वर से सबका साक्षात्कार सम्भव नहीं है, इसीलिए ईश्वर माता – पिता के रुप में आकर अपनी संतानों का पालन पोषण करते हैं।

क्या लिखूँ, कहां तक लिखूँ, विज्ञान विधा का विद्यार्थी होने के कारण भाषा तथा अपने भावों की अभिव्यक्ति हमेशा से मेरे लिए कठिन कार्य रहा है। अनुसंधान मेरे लिए प्रयोगों से प्राप्त आंकड़े की विवेचना तक ही सीमित रहा है। वो व्यक्ति जिसका पूरा जीवन, अपने आदर्शों तथा दर्शन पर आधारित रहा है, उसकी विवेचना करना मेरे इस रसायनशास्त्रीय बुद्धि तथा विवेक से अतिरिक्त वस्तु है। परन्तु जो आपने (पापाजी ने) सिखाया आपको ही समर्पित करने की कोशिश कर रहा हूँ, मेरा इसमें लेशमात्र भी अपना कोई योगदान नहीं है।

हमेशा से सूरज पकड़ने की चाहत लिये मैं जब भी क्षितिज तक पहुँचता हूँ तब पता चलता है कि सूरज तो बहुत दूर है और मैं फिर बढ़ चलता हूँ, सूरज की किरण पकड़ते हुए।

मैं और मेरे पिता जी दोनों अपने पिता जी के सबसे बड़े लड़के हैं, पापाजी अध्यापक थे, मैं भी हूँ, ध्यातव्य है कि मेरे पितामह भी अध्यापक थे, पापाजी ने घर परिवार छोड़कर विदेश से शोधकार्य पूर्ण किया, उन्हीं के लिखने पर मैने भी महान रसायनज्ञ प्रो0 आर0सी0 महरोत्रा के साथ हास्टल में रहकर शोधकार्य किया। पापाजी गोरखपुर विश्वविद्यालय में थे, मैं भी अंततः यहाँ आ ही गया। अपने सेवा काल के दौरान विश्वविद्यालय की परीक्षाओं को सुधारने के लिए उन्होंने उड़ाका दल का नेतृत्व किया, कालंतर में मैंने भी वह दायित्व निभाया। पापाजी हीरापुरी कालोनी में रहे, मैं भी वहां रह रहा हूँ। पापाजी ने दयनीय स्थिति में पहुँच चुकी अनुशासन व्यवस्था को विश्वविद्यालय के मुख्य नियंता के रुप में ठीक किया, मैं भी नियंता मण्डल में अनेकों बार रहा। पापाजी ने विश्वविद्यालय तथा उत्तर प्रदेश विश्वविद्यालय शिक्षक संघ का नेतृत्व किया, मैं भी उनका अनुकरण करते हुए गोरखपुर विश्वविद्यालय शिक्षक संघ का अध्यक्ष बना।

हमेशा से पापाजी की परछाई पकड़ने की कोशिश करता रहा लेकिन जो कुछ उन्होंने किया, वो मैं क्या मुझे पूरा विश्वास है कि, कोई भी नहीं कर सकता है। कहावत है कि–

बाढ़ै पूत पिता के धर्मे, और खेती उपजै अपने कर्मे।

हम सभी उनके पुत्र तथा अनुयायी उनके ही पुण्य प्रताप का फल हैं। आज अनुभव हो रहा है कि जो कुछ भी हमने किया, जानते हुए या अंजाने में, प्रेरणा तो पापाजी ही रहे।

पापाजी ने अपने समय के जिन मूल्यों को जिया, तत्कालीन परिस्थितियों में भी उनका निवर्हन कठिन था। आज के समय में तो लगता है जैसे कि असम्भव है। आज की वर्तमान विश्वविद्यालयीय परिस्थितियों तथा पिता जी के समय के विश्वविद्यालयीय मूल्यों की विवेचना करना सवर्था उपयुक्त विषय है क्योंकि मूल्यों पर आधारित शिक्षा व्यवस्था पापाजी का सर्वाधिक प्रिय विषय रहा है।

मूल्यों की बात करना मेरे इस वैज्ञानिक बुद्धि के लिए अतिरेक तो होगा पर आचार्य प्रो0 दयानाथ त्रिपाठी (पापाजी) के जीवन को जितना देखा है, उसे ही आधार मानकर लिखने की कोशिश कर रहा हूँ।

बहुत बचपन का तो नहीं पर पांच या छः वर्ष की वय से पापाजी को देखने समझने का प्रयास कर रहा हूँ। मेरे अनुज डॉ0 देवेशनाथ त्रिपाठी के जन्म के सवा महीने पर होने वाली पूजा के पश्चात् पापाजी शोधकार्य करने हेतु यूनान चले गये और हम सब अपने पितामह के साथ रहने इलाहाबाद आ गये। हमारी ज्यादातर यादें तभी की हैं। हम सभी उस समय पापाजी के लिए हींग और मसाले पार्सल द्वारा यूनान भेजते थे जिसका पापाजी हमेशा विदेश में इंतजार करते थे। ऐसा उनके द्वारा लिखे पत्रों से ज्ञात होता था। उनके पत्र हमेशा ही अपने पिता जी के लिए और मेरी माता जी के लिए आते थे। उनके द्वारा अपने पिता जी को लिखे पत्रों से ज्ञात होता था कि उनका जीवन दर्शन अपने पिता जी द्वारा ही प्राप्त था। इस संदर्भ में एक बात का स्मरण आता है कि भारत में आपातकाल की घोषणा के बाद विदेश में रह रहे भारतीय छात्रों की छात्रवृत्ति भारत सरकार द्वारा बंद कर दी गई थी। पापाजी भी उस समय इंग्लैण्ड में अपने शोध निर्देशक के साथ ही थे। धनाभाव के कारण जीवन कितना कठिन हो जाता है, इसकी कल्पना अपने देश में ही रहने पर बहुत कठिन है, ऐसे में जो अपनों से दूर विदेश में हो उसकी कठिनाई का अनुमान लगाना भी आसान नहीं है। बहुत कठिनाई का सामना करते हुए जब समस्याएं बढ़ गई तो पापाजी को इंग्लैण्ड में रह रहे भारतीय समाज द्वारा धार्मिक उपदेश देने का कार्य दिया गया। उस समय शायद एक व्याख्यान का 25 पाउण्ड पारिश्रमिक तय किया गया। अपनी माता जी (मेरी पितामही स्वर्गीय कृष्णा शर्मा) द्वारा वर्णित धार्मिक कथाओं में पुरोहित कर्म को निंदनीय समझते हुए, उनका मन विचलित हो गया। इस संदर्भ में आपने अपने पिता जी से निर्देश मांगा। उनके द्वारा अनुमति मिलने पर ही आपने साप्ताहिक धार्मिक उपदेश द्वारा धनं लेना स्वीकार किया। इसी तरह मैंने अपने बाल्यकाल से ही पापाजी को धनाभाव की चिन्ता न करते हुए अपने जीवन मूल्यों की रक्षा करते हुए पाया है। आज तो अध्यापक किसी कोचिंग संस्था में अपनी सेवायें धन के लिए आसानी से देने को तैयार हैं, और जरूरत पड़ने पर मूल्यांकन को भी प्रभावित करते हैं। कर्त्तव्य परायणता उनके जीवन मूल्यों में एक महत्वपूर्ण स्थान रखता है। इस संदर्भ में मुझे पापाजी के सेवाकाल से एक उदाहरण स्वरुप घटना आप सब सुधि पाठक के समक्ष रखने की इच्छा हो रही है। यह घटना उस समय की है जब गोरखपुर विश्वविद्यालय अराजकता की चरम पर था, सम्भवतः 1980–83 का समय था, प्रो0 जी0सी0 चतुर्वेदी जी कुलपति थे, एवं पापाजी मुख्य नियन्ता, विश्वविद्यालय परीक्षा को सुधारने हेतु उड़ाका दल का गठन पहली बार किया गया। उसमें तत्कालीन सभी संकायाध्यक्ष, प्रति कुलपति तथा मुख्य नियन्ता को सम्मिलित किया गया। रक्षा अध्ययन विभाग में परीक्षा चल रही थी, अराजकता के माहौल में कुलपति द्वारा निरीक्षण करने के बाद इसका निर्णय लिया गया कि उस दिन की परीक्षा को निरस्त कर दिया जाय। इस निर्णय के पश्चात आन्दोलन होना ही था। इस आंदोलन तथा विश्वविद्यालय की अन्य अराजकताओं में दोषी छात्र नेताओं को विश्वविद्यालय नियन्ता द्वारा काली सूची में डाला गया। उल्लेखनीय है इस सूची में हमारे कुछ रिश्तेदार तथा पापाजी के परम् मित्र श्री रविप्रताप सिंह जी (लल्लू चाचा) के रिश्तेदार भी सम्मिलित थे। समाज तथा मित्रों के दबाव के बावजूद इन लोगों का नाम उस काली सूची से निकाला नहीं गया। कुछ दिनों पश्चात पापाजी से मैंने पूछा तो उन्होंने कहा मुख्य नियन्ता का कार्य विश्वविद्यालय की अनुशासन व्यवस्था को सुधारना है न कि अपने रिश्तेदारों की मदद करना।

अपने कर्त्तव्य परायणता के लिए ही पापाजी एवं हमारे आवास पर तीन बार पूरी ताकत के साथ अराजक तत्वों ने हमला किया। इन घटनाओं में से पहली घटना के समय मैं नवीं कक्षा का छात्र था। बाहर लगभग हजार की संख्या में अराजक तत्वों ने हमारे आवास (20 हीरापुरी कालोनी) को घेर कर देशी तमंचों से गोली एवं देशी बम द्वारा प्रहार किया था। पापाजी ने भी लाइसेंसी रिवाल्वर द्वारा हवा में गोली चलाकर उन अराजक तत्वों को घर में प्रवेश करने से रोका तथा मुझे कहा कि कैन्ट थाने पर जाकर प्रथम सूचना रिपोर्ट पहुंचा दो। फिर मुझसे पूछा तुम्हें डर तो नहीं लग रहा है? यदि लग रहा है तो हनुमान जी का नाम लेते रहना। मेरे द्वारा प्रथम सूचना रिपोर्ट पर भी पुलिस प्रशासन द्वारा कार्यवाही नहीं होते देख, मैं पापाजी के उन्हीं मित्र श्री रविप्रताप सिंह जी के आवास पर गया, वो तुरन्त मेरे साथ ही उसी समय रिक्शे से हमारे घर आ गये। आज उस घटना के स्मरण मात्र से डर लगता है, परन्तु उस घटना से यह सबक मिलता है कि कर्त्तव्य परायणता के लिए पापाजी ने न केवल अपना, अपने सबसे प्रिय पुत्र तथा परिवार की भी चिन्ता नहीं की और शायद इसी कर्त्तव्य परायणता के कारण पूरा समाज उनका सम्मान करता है।

अन्ततः परिवर्तित होते हुए इस आधुनिक समाज में भी मूल्यों को संजोये और गुरू–शिष्य परम्परा का निर्वहन करते हुए सभी सम्पादकों को मैं साधुवाद देना चाहता हूँ, जिनके प्रयासों के फलस्वरुप पापाजी जैसे बहुमुखी प्रतिभा के व्यक्तित्व, जिसने अनेक कठिनाईयों के बाद भी कभी अपने आदर्शों एवं मूल्यों से समझौता नहीं किया, आज सुधिजनों के समक्ष आ सका।

डॉ0 उमेशनाथ त्रिपाठी
रसायनशास्त्र विभाग
दी0द0उ0 गोरखपुर विश्वविद्यालय, गोरखपुर

गर्व है पुत्री होने का

अंजुला शुक्ला

कक्षा में शिक्षण कार्य समाप्त कर जैसे ही विभाग में बैठी एक अन्जान नम्बर से मोबाइल की घंटी बजती है, मैडम आप डॉ0 अन्जुला शुक्ला बोल रही हैं। हाँ मैं बोल रही हूँ। मैडम मैं विमल तिवारी बोल रहा हूँ। मैं गुरूजी के ऊपर एक किताब प्रकाशित कर रहा हूँ, चाहता हूँ आप कुछ लिखें।

इतना सुनते ही मेरे मुख से निकला 'मुझे गर्व है उनकी पुत्री होने का'। शायद ही कोई इतना भाग्यशाली होगा जितना हम भाई–बहन हैं। प्राचीन इतिहास के विद्यार्थी ही नहीं अपितु भारतीय इतिहास, संस्कृति एवं पुरातत्व के सभी जानने वाले पापा पर गर्व करते हैं। बात उस समय की है जब सन् 1962 में चीन ने भारत पर आक्रमण किया था। दुर्भाग्यवश उसमें भारत को हार का मुंह देखना पड़ा था। ऐसे आपातकालीन समय में भारत सरकार ने देश के सभी नागरिकों से मदद की अपील की थी कि वे देश की सुरक्षा के लिए आगे आए। विश्वविद्यालयों में भी इसके लिए नाम मांगे गए और पापा ने देश सेवा के लिए सहर्ष अपना नाम आगे दिया था। इसी के निमित्त उन्हें जनवरी 1963 में केन्द्रीय आपात राहत प्रशिक्षण संस्थान, नागपुर में प्रशिक्षण के लिए भेजा गया। उसी समय मेरा जन्म 30 जनवरी 1963 को मेरे पैतृक आवास मुट्ठीगंज, इलाहाबाद मे हुआ। मेरे जन्म होने के साथ ही पूरे माहौल मे मायूसी सी छा गई क्योंकि मेरी एक बड़ी बहन पहले से ही थी। लोग कहने लगे, "लो फिर बेटी आ गई, यह तो मनतोरा अर्थात मन को तोड़ने वाली आ गई। पापा जब मार्च 1963 में अपना प्रशिक्षण पूरा करके लौटे और जब सुना कि लोग ऐसा कह रहे हैं, तो उन्होंने कहा यह मनतोरा नहीं मेरी मनबोधा अर्थात मन को भाने वाली है। तदुपरांत पापा ने मार्च 1963 से लेकर अपने शोध कार्य के लिए 30 नवम्बर 1971 में यूनान जाने के पूर्व तक गोरखपुर में होमगार्ड के डिप्टी कमांडेंट का अतिरिक्त पद भी संभाला और देश के लिए अपनी सेवाएं समर्पित की। यह घटना पापा के बेटियों के प्रति धनात्मक दृष्टिकोण और उनके बहुमुखी व्यक्तित्व की पहचान कराता है।

पापा उपर से जितने कठोर दिखते हैं, उतने ही अन्दर से मृदु हैं। हमारा जरा भी कष्ट उन्हें बर्दाश्त नहीं होता है। उन्होंने कभी भी लड़के और लड़की में भेद नहीं किया। हम जो विषय लेना चाहे, जैसा पढ़ना चाहे, उन्होंने पूरी स्वतन्त्रता दी। परन्तु अनुशासनहीनता उन्हें जरा भी नहीं पसन्द थी। हम सबको उन्होंने कठोर अनुशासन में पाला। जिसका स्पष्ट प्रमाण हम भाई–बहनों में दिखता है। उनके द्वारा दिया गया संस्कार आज इतनी विपरीत परिस्थितियों में भी हमें सही रास्ते पर चलना सिखाता है।

पापा जब विश्वविद्यालय में मुख्य नियन्ता पद पर थे, उन्होंने गोरखपुर विश्वविद्यालय में नकलमुक्त परीक्षा कराने में जितना साहस दिखाया वह सामान्यतः आज असम्भव है। उनके उपर गोली चली, आवास पर बम फेका गया परन्तु पापा ने साहस नहीं खोया और दृढ़ संकल्प के साथ अपने कार्य को सम्पादित किया। उनके इस पुनीत कार्य का प्रतिफल आज भी है कि, गोरखपुर विश्वविद्यालय नकलमुक्त परीक्षा करा रहा है। पापा से जुड़ी उनकी बहुत सी बातें प्रेरणादायक हैं। किन–किन का उल्लेख करूँ। घर और बाहर अपने विचारों को रखने की पूरी स्वतन्त्रता हमें दी और हमेशा शिक्षक का सम्मान करने की शिक्षा दी।

आज मैं जहाँ हूँ पापा एवं माँ के दिये संस्कारों के कारण सफलता पूर्वक अपने कर्तव्यों का निर्वहन कर रही हूँ। कक्षा में समय से जाना, अपने विषयवस्तु की तैयारी के साथ कक्षा में विद्यार्थियों के साथ सामन्जस्यपूर्ण व्यवहार करना, यह सब पापा के दिखाये मार्ग से ही सम्भव है।

विश्वविद्यालय शिक्षक नेता के रूप में भी पापा ने एक आदर्श शिक्षक अध्यक्ष के रूप में गोरखपुर विश्वविद्यालय एवं उत्तर प्रदेश आवासीय विश्वविद्यालय संघ में कार्य किया। गलत बातों को स्वीकार न करना, शिक्षकहितों के लिए संघर्ष करना यह सब उन्हीं से सीखा है। आज मुझसे लोग कहते हैं यह वह समय नहीं है परन्तु मैं कहती हूँ मुझसे गलत बात बर्दाश्त नहीं होगी क्योंकि मेरे अन्दर जिसका खून है वह व्यक्तित्व प्रो0 दयानाथ त्रिपाठी हैं। आज सामाजिक सम्बन्धों में एक संक्रमण सा हो गया है। व्यक्ति नितांत स्वार्थी होकर जी रहा है। परन्तु आज भी समाज में कुछ अच्छे लोग है जो 'बहुजन हिताय–बहुजन सुखाय' की भावना से प्रेरित होकर स्वयं के साथ दूसरों का भी जीवन सुखमय बना रहे हैं। मेरा मानना है कि यह समाज इन्हीं लोगों की वजह से चल रहा है। यद्यपि ऐसे लोग बहुत कम रह गये हैं परन्तु मैं गर्व से कह सकती हूं कि पापा उनमें से एक है। पापा की एक बात और प्रेरणादायक है कि वह उस व्यक्ति (शिक्षक) को अच्छा नहीं मानते हैं जो अपने विषय में कार्य न कर अन्य क्षेत्रों में कार्य करता है। उनका कहना है कि तुम जिस विषय के हो तुम्हारा प्रथम दायित्व है कि तुम अपने विषय को पढ़ो, समझो और उसमें कुछ नया करो। समकालीन समय में शिक्षक के रूप में उच्च शिक्षा के द्वारा एक तरफ जहाँ हमें अपने भविष्य निर्माताओं को तैयार करना है वहीं पर साथ ही साथ हमें इस बात का का ध्यान भी रखना है कि हमारा व्यक्तित्व गुण कर्म स्वभाव को परिष्कृत करने वाला हो। न केवल वैयक्तिक समृद्धि एवं सुख शान्ति के लिए वरन् सामाजिक सुव्यवस्था एवं प्रगति के लिए भी पापा जैसे ही परिष्कृत व्यक्ति की आवश्यकता है। ईश्वर से प्रार्थना है कि पापा स्वस्थ एवं दीर्घायु हों, जिससे हम लोगों को उचित मार्ग दर्शन मिलता रहे। उनके इतना तो आज करना मुश्किल लगता है परन्तु कुछ कर सकूँ यही ईश्वर से प्रार्थना है।

डॉ0 अंजुला शुक्ला
उपाचार्य, बी0एड0 विभाग
बुद्ध पी0जी0 कालेज, कुशीनगर

Professor D.N. Tripathi

Irfan Habib

Professor Daya Nath Tripathi (b. 1938) is a historian of eminence who has combined much work in archaeology with work in an area in which few Indian historians have ventured, viz. Hellenic studies. He has had the rare privilege of his Ph.D. work on Bronze work of Greece (Southampton University) supervised by anarchaeologist of the status of Lord Colin Renfrew. Besides this thesis which was published in the prestigious Mediterranean Archaeology series of the University of Gottenhurg, Sweden (1987), he has published widely on India's relations with Greece, notably *Cultural Interaction between India and Grece* (1996) and *Hinduism and Hellenism,* (2004). These and his other publications constitute substantive contributions to both History and Archaeology.

Professor D.N. Tripathi had an eventful term as Chairman, Indian Council of Historical Research (2004-07). He was able to bring together historians of all persuasions in fruitful collaboration and revived such important projects of archival importance as "Towards Freedom" (1937-47), "Epigraphical Dictionary" and "Economic History documentation". The volumes that were published or prepared during this term have won wide acclaim.

I cannot end this note without a reference to my personal experience. I always found him immensely considerate to friends and colleagues, always cheerfully dealing with the differences of opinion that are a natural part of the discipine of History. As he passes theage of seventy-six, I as a still older man, hasten to wish him a long life and further attainments.

1

AN EVOLUTIONARY PERSPECTIVE ON THE DEVELOPMENT OF HUMAN CULTURE

Colin Renfrew

Summary

While the notion of evolution in the Darwinian sense has offered an informative framework for the evolution of species including the human species *Homo sapiens*, it has proved less effective in offering insights or understanding of the trajectories of development subsequently followed by human societies, or human "cultures", to use the prevalent archaeological term. The distinction is drawn here between the "speciation phase" and the "tectonic phase" of human development. It is argued also that the proposed evolutionary mechanism, the "meme" or "cultural virus", does not seem to offer many valid insights for cultural developments. Symbolic behaviour, dependent on the formulation of culturally accepted institutional facts, has not yet been modelled successfully within a Darwinian framework. Such modelling would be highly welcome but has yet to emerge.

1. Introduction

This short paper recognizes the aspiration that the story of human cultural development over the past 100,000 years, and more especially over the past 10,000 years, be encompassed within the broad explanatory framework of Darwinian evolution. It recognizes progress towards this aspiration, exemplified by the work of Leslie White (1959) or of Cavalli Sforza and Feldman (1981), and more recently of Stephen Shennan (2002). But while considerable work has been undertaken in expressing or translating potential explanations of culture process into a broadly Darwinian terminology (e.g. Durham 1991), few insights have yet emerged that are helpful to the archaeologist or cultural anthropologist. The notion of adaptive advantage over the several million years duration of the Palaeolithic era, when evolutionary processes led from *Australopithecus* to *Homo* sapiens has been well explored (Boyd and Richerson 1985; Mithen 1996). But such arguments have been less successful when applied to the much more striking changes visible in the human story over the past ten to fifteen thousand years (Renfrew 2007). My critique is not of the aspiration: I share the wish to deal with the human story within a broadly "scientific" framework, and admire the success of the Darwinian approach in placing the emergence of humankind within the broader framework of the evolution of species. My concern is that this approach has so far been less rewarding than one might have expected with the human story since the emergence of our species.

2. The "speciation" and "tectonic" phases of human evolution

It is now widely recognized that the emergence of our species, *Homo sapiens*, had been accomplished, in Africa, more than 100,000 years ago. The molecular genetic record supports this conclusion, and offers quite a detailed scenario for the out of Africa dispersal of our species around 60,000 years ago (Forster 2004).

The interesting observation which follows is that in evolutionary terms, thinking specifically about the genetic basis for humankind, namely the sequence of bases composing the human genome, this was established by that time. Certainly the basic Darwinian processes of variation and natural selection did not end 100,000 years ago and are still operational today. However a baby born today is not very different genetically from one born 100,000 years ago. The variation between now and then is not significantly different in scale from the variation between living members of our species today.

It is certainly the case that we do not yet understand very well the evolutionary processes which led over the past 5 million years or so from *Australopithecus* to *Homo sapiens*. That they involved the participation of human material culture — man the toolmaker — with adaptive advantages operating selectively upon the genome, is altogether likely. That is what is sometimes implied by the term coevolution. But the process was in some senses accomplished well before the out-of Africa dispersal episode of 60,000 years ago. This is what may be termed the speciation phase in the development of our species, and it was accomplished 100,000 years ago.

From then on the human story is one primarily of cultural development. Of course the processes of mutation and genetic drift did not cease. But the differences which were visible in the different cultures of the globe some 500 years ago, before the colonization processes of the second millennium AD, are not to be ascribed to differences in the DNA of their bearers.

With the human dispersal of some 60,000 years ago the picture changes. The Momentum we see in cultural evolution after that point, and in particular after the agricultural and sedentary revolutions in different parts of the world, is no longer genetically based. Cultural innovation and cultural transmission have now become the dominant mechanisms. We may refer to this phase of development, where change in the genome is no longer significant, as the tectonic phase, laying the emphasis upon the notion of the construction of human culture (Renfrew 2007, 97).

The *Oxford English Dictionary* defines tectonics as "the constructive arts in general". This phase is characterized by new forms of engagement with the material world, and the name refers to the construction of the cultural world in which we live. The distinction now is that in the tectonic phase the genotype is broadly fixed. Within the tectonic phase the evolution that is taking place is essentially cultural evolution.

3. Evolution and culture

It is worth returning for a moment at this point to reconsider what is implied by the term "evolution". Darwin's position, at its most concise, has been summarized (Szthamáry 2006): "Units of evolution must multiply, have heredity and possess variability: and among the heritable traits, some must affect survival and/or reproduction. If these criteria are met, evolution by natural selection is possible in a population of such entities".

When we are talking of the human speciation phase, that long period of hominin development over perhaps 5 million years leading to the emergence in Africa between 200,000 and 100,000 years ago of our own species *Homo sapiens*, the processes involved may be subsumed under the term "natural selection", as so defined. It is, however, necessary to observe that "horizontal transmission" — the borrowing of cultural features between contemporaries who may not be closely related genetically — becomes increasingly important (Cavalli-Sforza and Feldman 1981).

The term coevolution, commonly used in biology to refer to the interaction of competing species, predators and prey, hosts and parasites etc. (Slatkin and Maynard Smith 1979), has been appropriated in discussions of human evolution to refer to the interacting evolutionary processes of human genes and human culture (Lumsden and Wilson 1981, 237; Mace 2005, 4). But while it is an attractive term it may carry with it problems at the more detailed explanatory level. For the mechanisms of genetic evolution are increasingly well understood, following the elucidation of the structure of DNA, and it is not clear how the horizontal transmission process implicit in this use of the term "coevolution" operates within such a framework. At the same time, however, the insights of Darwin and of Mendel have in general been upheld in the light of molecular genetics, although they could have no detailed knowledge of its mechanisms at the molecular level.

The same might be claimed for the term "meme", conceived as the cultural equivalent of the gene, and introduced into the discussion by Richard Dawkins (1976). It has been enthusiastically adopted by several authors (e.g. Mace 2005, 4). However it carries with it implications about mechanism, indeed mechanistic implications, which may be highly dubious. It is a term which Shennan (2002) generally avoids, despite the title of his book.

One criticism of the term "meme" is that it regards the units of cultural information as single atomistic particles, perhaps traveling independently. It is the case, however, that most major innovations involve complexes of related innovations, for which the structure of the recipient society must be "ready", or "pre-adapted". Single units or members do not seem an appropriate mechanism. This being said, however, the validity of the term in some cases must be respected. It is notable, for instance, how the innovation of alphabetic script was readily adopted, after its inception in the Levant of Egypt, on a widespread basis. In some areas it replaced pre-existing (usually syllabic) systems of writing. In other areas it proved apt for the introduction of writing as a novel recording system. The inception of the alphabetic, as single, coherent system, can perhaps be modelled in this way.

That human learned behaviour, or "culture" frequently does behave in a gradual way, aptly described by the term "evolution", was noted by several archaeologists in the years following the publication of Darwin's *On the Origins of Species*. Among them were General Pitt Rivers and Oscar Montelius. The evolution of languages, following Darwin's insights, was modelled in tree-like form by Augustus Schleicher (1863) and has since continued to prove amenable to phylogenetic analysis (Forster and Renfrew 2006; Gray, Drummond and Greenhill 2009). That this is so may perhaps be explained by the considerable degree to which language transfer is indeed by inheritance between generations, indeed usually from the parents. It is in those cases where horizontal transfer by "borrowing" is particularly marked that the reconstruction of linguistic trees by standard phylogenetic methods becomes more dubious (Heggarty 2006).

4. Emergent properties in human culture and society

Following the out-of-Africa dispersals of *Homo sapiens* some 60,000 years ago, human populations gradually became dispersed about the various continents. It is easy to characterize the subsequent histories of regional populations on these various continents as trajectories through time of the different cultures or culture systems. And it is tempting to make a comparison or analogy between the emerging cultural diversities of these groups and the emerging differences between plant or animal species as studied by Darwin. Splitting of populations, isolation, and genetic drift are processes which can lead to the differentiation into new species.

So, at a very general level the differentiation into different cultures (as defined archaeologically) of the human populations along their trajectories of development might be compared with the development of new varieties and species among plant and animal populations.

These patterns, however, are not simply those of increasing diversity. There are emergent features, which might be described as of increasing complexity (Flannery 1972). Moreover, analogous events may be noted along different and apparently independent cultural trajectories. Among these may be noted:

- The use of the bow and arrow

- The construction of boats for marine travel
- The development of formalized burial practices for the ritual disposal of the dead
- The sedentary revolution, implying also the development of farming to sustain the settled villages which developed, along with a series of cultural traits including the making of pottery, the practice of weaving etc.
- The development of figurative representation (or art)
- The development of pyrotechnological skills (cooking, pottery, metallurgy, glass)
- The development of systems of trade and exchange
- The development of ritual practices which often involved the veneration of postulated beings or deities
- The emergence of urban centres or cities
- The development of systems of ownership and inheritance of property
- The emergence of commodities esteemed to be of high value (gold, feathers, jade etc.)
- The emergence of writing systems
- The emergence of formalized exchange systems involving units of value (money).

Most of these are innovations which occurred independently along several trajectories of development, on several continents. And it is major developments such as these which one would like to see developed in evolutionary terms. They can of course be described in what approximate to evolutionary terms, and most narratives in the relatively new discipline of world prehistory take such a form (Clark 1961; Renfrew 2007).

Several problems arise in their analysis. And of course it must be recognized that several in the list are relatively simple technical innovations (bow and arrow, sea-going boat) while others are much more complex. In the first place, it must be questioned in what sense the different instances in various locations, as listed, may be regarded as the "same" innovation. Agriculture in different parts of the world relies upon different species, and the domestication of one plant food is not the same as that of another.

It is tempting, however, to see an analogy here with Darwinian evolution among animal species. A major cultural development, such as the inception of metallurgy or the phenomenon of urbanization might be compared with a major innovation, archived independently by some species along different lineages. Such, for instance, would be the phenomenon of flight. The flight of birds may first have been achieved by an ancestor of all bird species today. But the flight of a mammal, such as the bat, is believed to have a different ancestry. And that of flying insects is different again. The archaeologist and anthropologist may have much to learn from the evolutionary analysis of evolutionary advances along different trajectories which may in some sense be considered comparable.

5. The cognitive dimension

Many of the advances exemplified above, and others like them are firmly rooted in the cognitive dimension. They are, moreover, the result of the experience of humans with the material world. They are emergent properties which involve the simultaneous engagement of the brain and the body (Malafouris 2004; Renfrew2004). In this respect they cannot be modelled in molecular genetic terms, and a different approach is needed which involves certain fundamental concepts.

Among these are notions of measurement, for instance the concept of weight. There is also the notion of value, as ascribed to a commodity. These come together in a nexus which is the basis of the commercial systems which form the basis for much of the social and economic life of the modern world. The notion of the "meme" here seems, at any right at first sight, too atomistic to model the phenomenon.

For many of the properties involved are examples of what the philosopher John Searle would call "institutional facts" (Searle 1995). They depend upon a consensus in understanding among humans in a group. They are not "brute facts" about properties of the material world, but rather accepted conventions operating within the social world of the society in question. It is these novel and emergent features which are difficult to model using the available tools of evolutionary theory.

References

Boyd R., Richerson P. J., 1985, *Culture and the Evolutionary Process*, Chicago: University of Chicago Press.

Cavalli-Sforza L. L., Feldman M. W., 1981, *Cultural Transmission and Evolution, A Quantitative Approach*, Princeton: Princeton University Press.

Clark G., 1961, *World Prehistory: An Outline*, Cambridge: Cambridge University Press.

Dawkins R., 1976, *The Selfish Gene*, Oxford: Oxford University Press.

Durham W. H., 1991, *Coevolution: Genes, Culture and Human Diversity*, Stanford: Stanford University Press.

Flannery K. V., 1972, "The cultural evolution of civilisations", *Annual Review of Ecology ad Systematics* 3: 399–425.

Forster P., 2004, "Ice ages and the mitochondrial DNA chronology of human dispersals: a review", *Philosophical Transactions of the Royal Society*, Series B 359: 255– 64.

Forster P., Renfrew C. (eds.), 2006, *Phylogenetic Methods and the Prehistory of Languages*, Cambridge: McDonald Institute for Archaeological Research.

Gray R. D., Drummond A. J., Greenhill S. J., 2009, "Language phylogenies reveal expansion pulses and pauses in Pacific settlement", *Science* 323: 479–83.

Heggarty P., 2006, "Interdisciplinary indiscipline? Can phylogenetic methods meaningfully be applied to language data – and to dating languages?", in Forster P., Renfrew

C. (eds.), *Phylogenetic Methods and the Prehistory of Languages*, Cambridge: McDonald Institute, 183–94.

Lumsden C. J., Wilson E. O., 1981, *Genes, Mind and Culture: The Coevolutionary Process*, Cambridge, Mass.: Harvard University Press.

Mace R., 2005, "Introduction: a phylogenetic approach to the evolution of cultural diversity", in Mace R., Holden C. J., Shennan S. (eds.), *The Evolution of Cultural Diversity: A Phylogenetic Approach*, Walnut Creek, Cal.: Left Coast Press, 1–10.

Malafouris L., 2004, "The cognitive basis of material engagement: where brain, body and culture conflate", in DeMarrais E., Gosden C., Renfrew C. (eds.), *Rethinking Materiality,the Engagement of Mind with the Material World*, Cambridge: McDonald Institute, 53–62

Mithen S., 1996, *The Prehistory of the Mind*, London: Thames & Hudson.

Renfrew C. 2004, "Towards a theory of material engagement", in DeMarrais E., Gosden C., Renfrew C. (eds.), *Rethinking Materiality: The Engagement of Mind with the Material World.* Cambridge, McDonald Institute, 23-32.

Renfrew C., 2007, *Prehistory: The Making of the Human Mind*, London: Weidenfeld & Nicolson

Schleiicher A., 1863, *Die DarwinischeTheorie und die Sprachwissenschaft*, Weimar: H. Boehlau.

Searle J., 1995, *The Construction of Social Reality*, Harmondsworth: Penguin.

Shennan S., 2002, *Genes, Memes and Human History*, London: Thames & Hudson.

Slatkin M., Maynard Smith J., 1979, "Models of coevolution", *Quarterly Review of Biology* 54: 233–63.

Szthamáry E., 2006, "Darwin for all season", *Science* 313: 306–7.

White L., 1959, *The Evolution of Culture*, New York: McGraw-Hill.

2

EVOLUTION OF SOCIETY AND CULTURE IN RAJASTHAN

V.N. Misra

From the archaeological and ethnographic data available from Rajasthan it is possible to get a glimpse of the society and culture of the State that was emerging from at least half-a-million years ago. The State came to be inhabited by the humans at the end of Early Pleistocene, and continued to be continuously inhabited thereafter, without any break. We will briefly summarize salient features of the ethnographic scene before examining the archaeological evidence of how some of the main aspects of the living society of Rajasthan came into existence.

Ethnographic Scene

Like almost all States of the Indian Union, barring Jammu and Kashmir and the northeast outside the Brahmaputra valley, majority of the population of Rajasthan consists of Hindus. Most of the Muslims, Christians and Sikhs are converts from Hinduism, and, therefore, the core of their culture is also essentially Hindu. The Hindu population can be broadly classified into upper castes, middle castes, lower castes, and Scheduled Castes. Though members of all these groups practise agriculture in some measure, it is the middle castes for whom agriculture is the main occupation and who make the best cultivators.

The major upper castes are Brahmins, Rajputs and Mahajans. The Brahmins are in teaching profession, priesthood and service in government and public and private industrial organizations. The Rajputs are rich landowners but, except the poor ones, rarely cultivate the land themselves because they consider manual work demeaning. The Mahajans are businessmen and traders and almost all of them are engaged in trade-related activities. A sizeable section of them are followers of Jainism, and they, as well as Hindu Mahajans, are almost all vegetarians. In fact, except for some Rajputs, lower castes and tribal people, majority of the people of the State are vegetarians. This is probably due in large measure to the strong influence of Jainism. The upper caste as well as some of the middle caste people, like the Jats and Gujars, are tall, well-built and fair-complexioned.

Among the middle castes the more important are Jats, Dangis, Kalbis (Patels) and Malis. They are the principal agricultural communities, are extremely hard working, and are economically much better off than most other castes, barring Mahajans. All over the State plant cultivation is supported by animal husbandry and all farming families own some livestock. However, in the semi-arid and arid western part pastoralism is the main economic mode, plant cultivation either playing a subsidiary role or being totally absent. Certain castes like the Garis and Rabaris live entirely on livestock, the former keeping sheep and goats, and the latter mainly camels and goats.

About 17% population of the State consists of Scheduled Castes, which were, before the promulgation of the constitution of the Indian Republic, included among the lower and untouchable castes. They are found all over the State but their share in the total population is much higher in areas which consist of alluvial plains, have fertile soils, receive good rainfall and have irrigation facilities. These areas are favourable for intensive agriculture and are, therefore, densely populated. Why it is so, we will discuss a little later.

Among the Scheduled Castes, Chamars, Meghwals, Balais, and Khatiks are most numerous. Members of these castes are engaged mainly in activities related to sale of animal and bird flesh, processing of, and working in, leather, scavenging, cloth weaving (Balai, Koli, Salvi), comb making (Gavaria), basket making (Gancha), bow and arrow making (Tirgar), making of brushes used for sizing of cotton yarn, and weaving of cotton cloth (Koochband), entertaining people with music and dance (Dom, Kalbelia, Nat, Dholi, Rawal, Bhand, Kamad, Badi, and Bazigar), and crime (Bawaria, Bagri, Sansi, Kanjar and Bedia).

The religion of the Scheduled Castes as well as of the other lower castes mainly consists of the worship of Mataji (Mother goddess), Bhairon, (a variant of Shiva), Dharmaraj or Takhoji, represented by snake and a number of minor deities, and ancestral spirits (Purvaj) (Erskine 1908, 1909; Mathur 1969, 1983; Nagar 1974).

Archaeological Background

The earliest inhabitants of the State were stone age people. Their economy consisted entirely of hunting and plant food gathering. Stone age consists of two main stages: (1) Palaeolithic, and (2) Mesolithic. Palaeolithic, in turn, is divisible into three stages: Lower, Middle and Upper. Among these Lower Palaeolithic is the best known.

Lower Palaeolithic

Evidence of the Lower Palaeolithic is found on both sides of the Aravalli mountains and consists of stone tools which lie buried in the alluvial sediments of the rivers or exposed on hill slopes or on plain ground.

Early Acheulian

In Eastern Rajsthan these tools are found abrivers and their tributaries and sub-tributaries like the Manasi, Bandi, Khari, Berach, Gambhiri, Kothari, Wagan and Kadmali. These artefacts belong to a culture stage known as the Early Acheulian, and comprise choppers, chopping tools, handaxes, cleavers, scrapers and flakes. They were made on quartz and quartzite and were used for skinning dead animals, butchering carcasses, cutting them into slices of meat, and for digging roots and tubers.

Western Rajasthan

In the western part of the State there is no perennially flowing river. The only river of any consequence is the Luni, which, rising in the Aravallis, near Ajmer, flows in a southwest direction for a long distance, and eventually gets lost in the marshes of the Rann of Kutch/Kachh. A few km. west of Pachapadra, near the town of Balotra in Barmer district, the river takes an abrupt turn towards the south. Its right bank consists of a several metres high cliff. Its bed here has an awesome width and depth. Even in its upper reaches, west of Luni town, relatively lower cliffs along its banks, have preserved deposits of consolidated hard gravel. All these features are quite disproportionate to the meagre amount of rain water the river carries in its wide bed. They are witnesses of a time when the rainfall was considerably higher and was able to fill its wide and deep bed. Even today during periods of unusually heavy rain the river breaches its banks, turns a vast region into a continuous sheet of water and carries away a large number of villages and livestock coming in its way.

Late Acheulian

Stone artefacts of Late or Evolved Acheulian are found scattered on the sandy beds of these streams or lie buried in cemented sandy-pebbly gravel deposits along the banks of its several tributaries and sub-tributaries like the Jojri, Bandi, Khari, three Sukris, Lilri, and Reria. Where the deposit has been eroded by flash floods, the artefacts are found strewn on sandy beds of the river. They are made of fine-grained chert, jasper, chalcedony and volcanic rocks like rhyolite and feldspar porphyry and comprise small, but symmetrical and well-made handaxes, cleavers, unifacial and bifacial knives, scrapers, points, flakes and blades.

North of Jodhpur where there is no flowing river, stone artefacts are found only in calcareous loam quarries and at the bottom and sides of the tanks dug in calcareous loam. Between Jodhpur and Ladnun Middle and Upper Palaeolithic artefacts have been found at several localities like Jenana, Lakshmipura and Shyampura, providing tell-tale proof that in the past there was flowing water over an extensive region where no surface water is seen today; instead. only cultivated land and low sand dunes are seen on the land surface.

Middle Palaeolithic

Middle Palaeolithic tools are found from 66 sites in the alluvial deposits of the Chambal, Berach, Wagan and Kadmali rivers in Eastern Rajasthan, and limestone formation at Sojat, alluvial deposits and beds of Luni and its tributaries like the Jojri and Reria, and calcareous loam quarries at Jenana, Lakshmipura, Baklia, and Shyampura in western Rajasthan. They are made of chert, jasper and chalcedony and comprise various types of scrapers, knives, points, borers and slender Levallois flakes.

Upper Palaeolithic assemblages are found at only eight localities, all of them in western Rajasthan, and comprise blades in addition to tools of the Middle Palaeolithic type but smaller and lighter in size than the latter. Both these cultural periods fall in the geological Upper or Late Pleistocene. The climate during this period was hyper-arid. There was limited rainfall for short periods, and temperatures were very high. Both vegetation and animal life were scarce, and consequently the density of human population was very low.

Upper Palaeolithic artefact assemblages have been collected from the surface of the lake shore dunes at Budha Pushkar, limestone outcrop at Sojat, and excavated profile of the buried fossil dune at 16 R locality on the Bangur Canal near Didwana in Nagaur District. The 20 m. deep profile at 16R produced a climatic and archaeological history of nearly 400,000 years. The profile was dated by Carbon 14, Thermoluminiscence (TL) and Uranium/Thorium Decay Series. The Upper Palaeolithic assemblage of 16R is dated by C-14 to c.26,000 B.P. The existence of only eight Upper Palaeolithic sites in contrast to 66 Middle Palaeolithic and 86 Lower Palaeolithic sites is evidence that the human population had drastically declined during this hyper-arid period. Presence of three handaxes in the Upper Palaeolithic assemblage at this late date is evidence that the older technology continued to persist right up to the Mesolithic in the cultural backwater of the Thar Desert. Human population drastically declined during the hyper-arid Terminal Pleistocene. The steadily increasing aridity had reduced the once well-watered region of the Thar to a cultural backwater where handaxe technology survived long after it had become obsolete and gone out of use everywhere in the country.

Mesolithic

The richest evidence of stone age comes from the Mesolithic period. It is not only the best in Rajasthan, but one of the best in the whole country. Mesolithic culture flourished when the Upper Pleistocene aridity had come to end, rainfall had begun to increase, and consequently vegetation had begun to regenerate and fauna subsisting on it had begun to increase. As a result, human population, which had drastically declined during the Upper Palaeolithic, as attested by the only eight sites of this period, began to revive at a fast rate.

As against only eight sites of the Upper Palaeolithic, there are as many as 160 sites of the Mesolithic. This number is bigger than that of the sites of all the three phases of the Palaeolithic.

Only two sites of this period, namely Tilwara and Bagor, have been horizontally excavated. Tilwara is located on a low dune, along the left bank of the Luni river in Barmer district, and has a deposit of only about 80 cms. It was excavated by me in 1967 and has produced evidence of two phases of the Mesolithic culture. In phase I, there is only stone industry. This is made mainly of fine-grained chert which was heat-treated to produce a good conchoidal fracture. The industry consists of large blades and bladelets. These are very symmetrical and sharp-edged. In addition, there are geometric microliths comprising blunted back blades, crescents, triangles, trapezes and transverse arrowheads, besides several types of scrapers, points and borers. There is also a small quantity of animal bone fragments.

In phase II, besides stone tools, there are a few bits of iron and wheel-made red and grey pottery. Iron and pottery were obviously obtained in exchange for hunted flesh, animal skins, honey, etc. There is no known Iron Age site in the immediate neighbourhood of Tilwara but there are such sites towards the north in Jaipur, Sikar, Ganganagar and Hanumangarh districts. The earliest of them belongs to the Painted Grey Ware (PGW) culture, dated to the end of the second millennium or the beginning of the first millennium BC. However, as Tilwara is several hundred kilometres away from all these sites and the pottery from here is much inferior to PGW, iron here must be much later than 1000 BC, probably of the Early Historic period, i.e, second half of the first millennium BC or even later. This is not surprising considering Tilwara's location in the very heart of the Thar desert and far away from early Iron Age sites.

There are no C-14 dates from the site. Hence its dating has to be done only on the basis of archaeological evidence. Iron in western Rajasthan appeared around 1000 BC in association with the Painted Grey Ware. So at Tilwara it could, at the earliest, have reached around this date.

The second horizontally excavated site, Bagor is located on a low dune along the left bank of the Kothari river, a tributary of the Banas, in Bhilwara district. The site, excavated by me during 1968-70, has a deposit of 1.80 m., divided into three phases. In phase I, the cultural material consists of an exceptionally rich microlithic industry, equally rich animal bones, and one extended human burial of an adult female. Two C-14 dates, obtained from charred bone were, 5200 and 4800 BC.

In Phase II the microlithic industry and animal bones slightly declined but this was compensated by the appearance of copper objects and pottery. Three human burials, all laid in a crouched position, were found in this phase. They had offerings of clay pots, copper objects, and beads of semi-precious stones and bone. In one case, the beads were arranged around the neck of the buried person in the form of a necklace while in other cases they were found loose. The pots, comprised handis with globular body and wide mouth. One of them had a sharply carinated body, recalling a shape natural to metal. One skeleton had a large animal bone, near its feet, originally no doubt placed as a chunk of meat for the dead person's journey to the other world. Two C14 dates from this phase were 2800 and 2100 BC.

In Phase III, the microlithic industry further declined but iron tools appeared. They are represented by two arrowheads. One of them is tanged and the other socketed. Besides, there are some small bits of this metal.

The offerings made to the dead in the form of pottery, copper objects and beads, could not have been produced by the Mesolithic inhabitants of Bagor as they did not possess the requisite technology. They were obviously obtained in exchange for the flesh and skins of hunted animals, honey and other vegetable, animal and mineral products. The clay pots were obviously acquired from the potters of the neighbouring settlements of the Chalcolithic farmers. The copper objects and beads were probably acquired from the itinerant traders who also catered to the needs of the contemporary Harappan communities of the ancient Sarasvati (present day) Ghaggar Valley. They must have also supplied them to the people of the succeeding OCP and Ganeshwar-Jodhpura cultures.

The sites of this culture are mainly concentrated in Sikar district but a few are also found in Jhunjhunu, Jaipur and Bharatpur districts. Our knowledge of this culture is very limited as it is based on the small excavation of only two sites, namely Ganeshwar and Jodhpura. The people of this culture lived in small settlements and in very modest houses with walls of undressed stone blocks or of mud.

The main ceramic of the Ganeshwar people was a thin dull red ware with paintings in black with white strokes, but they also used a sturdy red-slipped ware, which is partly handmade and partly wheel-made. The main decoration on this pottery consists of a variety of incised designs. The pottery from Jodhpura is turned on wheel, is coated with a thick slip, and is orange to deep red in colour. The common shapes are bowl, vase, knobbed lid and dish-on-stand, and are mainly decorated with incised designs.

Very little is known about the economy of these people. Recovery of animal bones from Ganeshwar shows that they kept livestock and also hunted wild animals. The evidence for agriculture is indirect in the form of saddle querns and grinders. Other items of material culture comprise stone, terracotta and bone beads, querns, mullers, pestles, a bone spike and a round terracotta cake.

Introduction of Iron Technology and the beginning of Historical Period

Ganeshwar-Jodhpura culture was succeeded by the Black-and-Red Ware (BRW) culture. The authors of this culture introduced the use of iron for making tools and weapons. As only two sites of this culture, namely Noh and Jodhpura, have been excavated on a very small scale, we know very little about the way of life of its authors except that, in addition to iron, they were using black-and-red ware which lacked decoration and was technologically inferior to its predecessor of the Chalcolithic Ahar culture. The only other items known from this culture are a ghata (vase) shaped terracotta bead and a bone spike from Noh. At Jodhpura a floor made of mud lumps was found. The BRW culture is dated to the later half of the second millennium B.C.

The BRW culture was succeeded by the Painted Grey Ware (PGW) culture which is the principal early iron age culture of north-west India. In Rajasthan the PGW culture is found only in the Ghaggar valley in Hanumangarh-Ganganagar districts and in the northeastern part of the State bordering western Uttar Pradesh. Our knowledge of this culture too is limited because of the small size of excavation at only three sites, namely Jodhpura, Noh, and Sunari. However, from other excavated sites of this culture in the upper Yamuna-Ganga doab, we can get some idea of the way of life of the PGW people.

PGW or Painted Grey Ware users were the first people to use iron on a large scale for making a wide range of weapons and tools. Sunari in Jhunjhunu district and Atranjikhera in Etah district of U.P. have yielded evidence of furnaces for smelting of iron ore and forging of iron objects. With the help of iron tools the PGW people cleared the primeval vegetation and brought about the first large-scale human colonization of the upper Ganga plain and the Indo-Gangetic Divide. Besides iron tools they also used bone tools. The PGW people cultivated wheat, barley, rice and several legumes, and raised cattle, buffalo, sheep, goat, pig and horse. The ornaments of these people consisted of beads of semiprecious stones, including etched ones, and ghata (vase) shaped ones of terracotta, and bangles and rings of copper. Other items of their material culture comprised copper rings, terracotta gamesmen, sling-balls, and weights, bone spikes, terracotta discs with incised designs, bone styluses, terracotta figurines, ivory hairpins, and ear-studs of semi-precious stones.

PGW people lived in small houses made of wattle-and-daub and mud-bricks. Their pottery, the Painted Grey Ware, after which the culture and the people are named, was wheel-made and technologically of a very high quality, and comprised mainly deep bowl with straight or convex sides, and large dish with convex sides and sagger base, and less commonly a small jug (lota) or vase. The vessels were decorated with painted, mostly geometric, motifs in black pigment.

While in northeast Rajasthan there is a continuity of habitation from the Chalcolithic Ganeshwar-Jodhpura culture to the Iron Age PGW, in the Ghaggar valley there is a clear discontinuity between the Harappan and the PGW. However, at most PGW sites there is a continuity of habitation till at least the Kushana period and in some cases even beyond.

The protohistoric PGW culture was succeeded from fifth century B.C. onwards by the emergence of historical times proper when political entities in the form of republics emerged and names of kings, ministers, generals, religious leaders, etc. are known and can be verified from different sources. There is a considerable increase in the number of settlements. A number of sites of this period like Sambhar (Sahani 1936). Bairat (Sahani 1936), Rairh (Puri n.d.), Nagar (Carlleyle 1878), Nagari (Bhandarkar 1920), Noh, Sunari and Jodhpura (Agrawala and Kumar 1982), Ahar (Sankalia et al. 1969) and Balathal (Misra 1997) have been excavated on varying scales, and provide us a good picture of the industries, crafts, dress, ornaments, and other aspects of the material culture, social organization and religion of the people.

Hunter-gatherers, who continued to be omnivorous and were considered as living an unclean life, were assigned ritually impure tasks, and placed outside the system, as untouchables.

Many features of the present-day life in Rajasthan, particularly in rural areas, can be traced to the Ahar Chalcolithic culture, Harappan culture of the Ghaggar valley, and subsequent protohistoric and early historic cultures. In Mewar villages the houses are still built of undressed stones, set in mud mortar, mud, and sometimes mud-bricks, as they were made during the Chalcolithic period. The Chalcolithic people cultivated wheat, barley, panicum millet, green gram, black gram, common pea, Italian millet, Indian jujube, and safflower. During the later part of the Chalcolithic period, African crops like jowar, bajra and ragi were introduced. Bajra continues to be a major food crop in the semi-arid and arid-zones of Rajasthan. In addition, the Early Historic people cultivated rice, kodo millet, and Bengal gram. All these crops are being grown and consumed to this day. The only major new cereal introduced a few centuries ago is maize, and it has become a staple food in the Mewar region.

Many of the vessel forms used today for storage of water, milk, pulses, etc, as well as for cooking, eating and drinking, and for use in rituals are the same as used by the Chalcolithic and later people. Single or double unit earthen ovens (chulhas) in use in village homes today are identical to those found at Ahar and Balathal. The earthen tawa used for baking bread and the bowl-on-stand used for offering incense to the deities in the local shrines (devras) in Mewar are identical to Chalcolithic forms. The dish with incurved sides and the lota, the two most distinctive shapes of the PGW, are also found in the succeeding NBPW culture and the early historic period at Balathal, and are commonly used all over northwest India though now they are produced in metal. The use of these Chalcolithic and early historic vessel types shows a continuity of tradition over 5000 years.

The methods of making clay pots have also not changed much. The same techniques of preparing a small proto-type of the large jar, first on the wheel, and then expanding it by the use of dabber and mallet, used by the Chalcolithic potters, are being followed by today's potters. The practice of profusely decorating pots with painted designs seems to be derived from the Chalcolithic period, and many of the painted designs, used during the Chalcolithic and Early Historic periods, are still in use.

The printed designs on the *ghaghra* (skirt) and *odhni* (cloth for covering the upper part of the body) worn by the women in Mewar, indeed all over Rajasthan, are not only identical to those seen in Chalcolithic black-and-red ware but are also printed in white over a black background for women's *odhnis* and men's *pagadis* (turbans) all over Rajasthan (Nagar 1969).

Though there is an apparent cultural discontinuity after the Harappan period in Rajasthan, yet, as noted by A. Ghosh (1952), Hanna Rydh (1959) and B.B. Lal (2002), many features of the Harappan culture have survived into the present. Lal (2002:82-135) has meticulously documented a whole range of such Harappan cultural traits found at Kalibangan and several other Harapan sites. These include the wearing by women of spiral bangles all over the arms, a conical ornament on the head, vermillion (*sindur*) in the medial parting of the hair (*mang*), an hour-glass (*damaru*) -shaped ornament on the wrist, girdle (*kardhani*) around the waist, (*payal*) around the ankle; use of wooden (now more in plastic) comb with teeth on opposite sides, nail-pairer, three-in-one toiletry gadget and (kajal) collyrium by both men and women; and of terracotta hop-scotches, found at almost all Chalcolithic and later sites, and toy animals by children. A number of features relating to house construction at Harappan Kalibangan are seen in the villages around the site today. Harappan houses were made of mud-bricks laid in header and stretcher fashion, had roofs made of horizontal wooden beams covered with thatching material and mud, and floors made of a layer of broken terracotta nodules and covered with clay. Many houses had small platforms (*chabutaras*) on both sides of the entrance on which family members and visitors could sit and chitchat. Courtyards of the houses were provided with *tandurs* for cooking. These methods of house construction and the provision of sitting platforms and *tandurs* are still in use in the villages around Kalibangan. The *tandur* in fact is widely used not only in Rajasthan but in all the areas in northwest India formerly occupied by the Harappan people.

To revert to metallurgy, metalsmiths of the Harappan and Chalcolithic periods used a variety of techniques like 'sinking', 'raising', 'cold working', 'annealing', 'lapping', 'closed casting' and 'lost wax' or *cire perdu* for making copper objects, and they are continuing to be used till today. In fact, the poor and lower caste women of Rajasthan even today wear bangles, bracelets and anklets of copper and its alloys made by local craftsmen by lost wax method. However, due to rising incomes and new fashion trends, more and more women have taken to wearing glass bangles and silver armlets and anklets, and the profession of producing ornaments of copper and its alloys is fast dying.

All the ancient communities from the Chalcolithic period onwards were using and many of them producing beads of semi-precious stones, copper, shell, steatite, faience and terracotta for making necklaces, and bangles of shell, terracotta and copper. The early historic town of Nagar near Tonk was a major centre of bead production as testified by the large quantity of beads found in various stages of production on the mound locally known as *jawahiri* bazar or jewellery market. This tradition of producing high quality gold and diamond jewellery continues to this day, and Jaipur is one of the most important centres of jewellery making and export in the country.

Both Chalcolithic and Harappan people used carts for transport similar to those in use at present. The Harappan carts had solid as well as spoked wheels. This is shown by the discovery of terracotta toy cart frames and wheels at several sites and of cart tracks at Gilund. Among household goods Kalibangan has yielded a terracotta toy cot covered with a bed sheet having a printed design of dots, semi-circles and cross-hatchings. In respect of religion, mention has already been made earlier of the discovery of a terracotta *linga* and *yoni* at Kalibangan, identical to those worshipped by the Hindus all over the country.

Hanna Rydh (1959) has noted remarkable similarities between the Rang Mahal culture of the early centuries of the Christian era and the life style in the present-day Rang Mahal and other villages in the area. The dwelling houses are built of mud and sun-dried bricks and occasionally painted as they were built and decorated during the Kushana period. Many present-day forms of clay vessels are strikingly like the old ones and the painted patterns are as common as they were in earlier times and are very similar to them. The quality of Rang Mahal pottery is, however, much superior to that of the present day. The same similarity is seen in terracotta toys. The livestock and the crops grown are also identical between the ancient and modern times. There is a possibility that the people ate beef but they certainly ate buffalo meat because the bones of this animal have clear traces of gnawing by human teeth. They also consumed meat of sheep and goat as well as of wild animals like gazelle and wild boar and birds. The main difference is that the villagers of "Rang Mahal time" lived under far more favourable conditions than do those of today. The decline in the economy and quality of life has been due to the increasing aridity and desertification of the landscape.

We have very little knowledge of the physical appearance of the ancient inhabitants of Rajasthan. No human skeletal remains have been found from any of the Palaeolithic sites. Remains of five individuals were found at the Mesolithic site of Bagor. Of these the one from Phase I or Mesolithic, was an adult female. Of the three skeletons from Phase II (Chalcolithic) one was a child and the other two an adult male and an adult female. However, the bones are too poorly preserved to draw any inferences about the physical features of the individuals.

The thirteen skeletons recovered from the Mature Harappan cemetery at Kalibangan have not yet been described for their physical features. The only information we have about them is that some of them had suffered from certain diseases.

Except some of the tribal people like the Bhils and the Van Vagris, who generally tend to be short and dark, people of almost all the communities of Rajasthan are tall, well-built and fair-complexioned like the other people of northwest India and regions further to the west. Their physical features must have evolved much earlier during the Palaeolithic and Mesolithic periods. There is no evidence of any large scale immigration of outside people into the region during protohistoric times. Some Greeks from the west and Sakas, Kushanas and Hunas from the north came as invaders during the early historic times and they were all biologically and culturally assimilated into the indigenous population. The bulk of the population must have developed autochthonously over a very long period of time.

On the basis of recent studies of human biological remains from several Harappan sites, particularly Harappa, which lay emphasis on adaptation to ecological factors, diet, pathological features, etc. rather than on outdated racial classification, K.A.R. Kennedy (2000: 306-07) observes that Harappan populations were marked by considerable regional biological diversity. According to him, "the participants in the mature phase of the Harappan civilization were not a mysterious people of unknown biological origins, or migrants from centres of high culture in western Asia, but were descendants of populations identified with the pre-Harappan cultures of the northwestern sector of the subcontinent". This indigenous origin and evolution must be true of the majority of the population of Rajasthan as well.

References

Agrawala, R.C. and V. Kumar 1982. Ganeshwar-Jodhpura Culture: New Traits in Indian Archaeology, In, *Harappan Civilization A Contemporary Perspective* (G.L. Possehl Ed.) 125-134. New Delhi:

Bhandarkar, D.R. 1920. *The Archaeological Remains and Excavations at Nagari.* Calcutta

Carlleyle, A.C.L.1878. *Report of a Tour in Eastern Rajputana in 1871-72 and 1872-73*, Archaeological Survey of India, Report VI:107-108, 160-61.

Dalal, K.F. 1981. RD 89, : A New Hakra Ware Site ? *Man and Environment* V:77-86.

Erskine, Major, K. D. 1908. *Rajputana Gazetteers*, Vol. II A. The Mewar Residency. Ajmer: Scottish Mission.

Erskine, Major, K. D. 1909. *Rajputana Gazetters*, Vol.III A. The Western Rajputana States Residency and the Bikaner Agency. Allahabad: Pioneer Press.

Ghosh A. 1952. The Rajputana Desert: Its Archaeological Aspects, *Bulletin of the National Institute of Sciences of India* I: 37-42.

Kennedy, K.A.R. 2000. *God-Apes and Fossil Men: The Palaeoanthropology in South Asia*: Ann Arbor: Michigan University Press.

Kenoyer, J.M. 1998. *Ancient Cities of the Indus Valley Civilization.* Karachi : O.U.P.

La Touche, T.H.D. 1902. Geology of Western Rajputana, *Geological Survey of India, Memoir* 35: 1-116.

Lal, B.B. 1997. *The Earliest Civilization of South Asia* (Rise, Maturity and Decline). New Delhi: Aryan Books International.

Mathur, U.B.1969. *Ethnographic Atlas of Rajasthan* (with Reference to Scheduled Castes and Scheduled Tribes). Delhi: Government of India.

Mathur, U.B.1986. *Pathways in Rajasthan.* Jaipur: The Folklorists.

Meena, B.R. and Alok Tripathi. 2000. Excavations at Ojiyana. *Puratattva* 30: 67-73.

Meena, B.R. and Alok Tripathi. 2001. Excavations at Ojiyana. *Puratattva* 31: 73-78.

Misra, V.N. 1971. Two Late Mesolithic Settlements in Rajasthan: A Brief Review of Investigations. *Poona University Journal* 35: 59-89.

Misra, V.N. 1973. Bagor, A Late Mesolithic Settlements in North-West India, *World Archaeology* 5 (1): 92-110.

Misra, V.N. 1976. Evidence of Culture Contact between Terminal Stone Age Hunter-Gatherers and Contemporary Farmers. In, U.V. Singh (Ed.). *Archaeological Congress and Seminar: 1972*, pp. 151-161. Kurukshetra: Kurukshetra University.

Misra, V.N. 1990. The Van Vagris, "Lost Hunters of the Thar Desert. *Man and Environment* XV(2): 89-108.

Misra, V.N. 1990. Balathal: A Chalcolithic Settlement in Mewar, Rajasthan, India: Results of First Three Seasons Excavation, *South Asian Studies* 13: 251-273.

Misra, V.N. and S.N. Rajaguru. 1989. Palaeoenvironment of the Thar Desert, Rajasthan, India, In, Karen Frifelt and Per Sorensen (Eds.), *South Asian Archaeology* 1985, pp. 296-320. Copenhagen: Scandinavian Institute of Asian Studies.

Nagar, M. 1969. Clues to Aharian Prehistory in contemporary Village Life, *Eastern Anthropologist* 22 : 55-73.

Nagar, M. 1974. Folk Religion in Mewar. *Journal of the University of Poona (Humanities Section)* 41: 75-93.

Nagar, M. and V.N. Misra.1989. Hunter-gatherers in an Agrarian Setting: The Nineteenth Century Situation in the Ganga Plains. *Man and Environment* XIII : 65-78.

Nagar, M. and V.N. Misra.1993. The Pardhis: A Hunting Community of Central and Western India, *Man and Environment* XVIII (1): 115-140.

Puri, K.N. *Excavations at Rairh during Samvat 1995-96* (1138-1139 A.D. Jaipur: State Archaeology Department.

Rydh, Hanna. 1959. *Rang Mahal, The Swedish Archaeological Expedition to India*, 1952-54. Gleerup Verlag and the New Book Company.

Sahani, D. R. *Archaeological Remains and Excavations at Bairat* (1936-37 and 1937-38). Jaipur: Publication Scheme (Reprinted 1999)

Sahani, D. R. *Archaeological Remains and Excavations at Sambhar* (1937-38 and 1938-398). Jaipur: Publication Scheme reprinted 1999)

Sankalia, H. D., Deo, S.B and Ansari, Z.D. 1969. *Excavations at Ahar (Tambavati) 1961-62.* Poona: Deccan College.

Singh, G., R.D. Joshi, S.K. Chopra, and A.B. Singh. 1974. Late Quaternary History of Vegetation and Climate of Rajasthan Desert. *Philosophical Transactions of the Royal Society*. London 257 (889): 467-501

Thaomash, J.V., A. Kar, A.J. Kailath, N.Juyal, S.N. Rajaguru and A.K. Singhvi. 1999. Late Pleistocene-Holocene History of Eolian Accumulation in the Thar Desert of India, *Zeitschrift fuer Geomorphologie (N.F.)* Supplement Band, 116: 181-194.

3

OVER-VIEW OF THE MESOLITHIC CULTURE OF THE VINDHYA-GANGA REGION

Radhakant Varma

The end of the Pleistocene marked the end of the extreme climatic conditions worldwide. The glaciers started shrinking and the watery landscape started drying up. The changed environmental conditions not only changed the face of the earth but it marks a definite stage in the history of mankind. It ushers in a new era of all round development. In most of the regions the earth attained its present form. Milder climate was more congenial for the growth of grassy lands, scrub jungles and dense forests in suitable ecological zones. It gradually increased the fertility of the soil many folds, as a result, new types of grasses ancestor to the modern grains started sprouting at suitable places.

The climatic change and the ecology affected the man and the fauna also. In order to cope with the changed conditions man creates non-biological solutions to environment challenges. This potentially reduces the need to evolve genetic responses to the challenges. But, normally, among the animals the changed environmental conditions, natural selection, operating on random mutations, causes evolution. In other words, the population's gene pool is altered as a result of adapting to a new environment. The great mammoths and their cousins were replaced by cattle, deer sheep, goat etc., which survived mainly on scrub and grasses.

This change was a long drawn process. It is very well reflected in the behavior of the rivers - their erosional and depositional activities and tool- technology and subsistence pattern of the people living in the region towards the south of the Ganga on both sides of the Vindhyan escarpment in the valleys of Belan, Son and their tributaries.

With the onset of the milder climate the hitherto inaccessible region became accessible and gradually became inhabited. It seems that there was a spurt in human population. The mesolithic sites are many times more than all the other sites taken together. Moreover the sites have been located in diverse ecological zones with their own characteristic features. They have been located in almost all such places where raw material for making tools, animals, edible flora was available. Even such places were also inhabited by the Mesolithic man where stone for the manufacture of tools was not locally available. There was a lot of regional diversity depending upon the ecological pattern of the region.

The term Mesolithic was first used by Hodder M. Westropp in 1866 (Wilkins 1969. 130) to denote a group of industries supposed to be transitional between the Palaeolithic and the Neolithic cultures. But the stratigraphic position was finally settled only after the excavation of Mas-de-Azil in France in 1895. In India the position remained fluid for a long time because in the beginning it was not certain whether the microlithic industries of the Mesolithic had developed from the blade-flake-scraper tradition of Middle Stone Age on African pattern or it had developed from the Upper Palaeolithic industries on the pattern of Europe.

The explorations and excavations in the Vindhyan tract which were started in the mid fifties and early sixties of the last century (IA-Review from 1957 onwards) under the general supervision of Prof. G.R.Sharma by the present author and V.D.Misra is still continuing by their students. From time to time a number of teams from Indian and foreign Universities have participated in the explorations and excavations. We can, without hesitation say that at present it is one of the most thoroughly explored and studied regions of India. The work done within the last nearly six seven decades has filled up most of the gaps in the evolution of culture of Man right from the earliest times up to the Early Historical period. In the present paper an overview of the Mesolithic has been given.

The stratigraphic position of the Upper Palaeolithic industries in India had remained doubtful due to want of evidence till the Belan section was reported and accepted by the scholars in the Symposium on C14 and Indian Archaeology organised by TIFR at Bombay in 1971. It was only after 1971 that this term was accepted by all. It replaced the term Late Stone Age completely which was adopted in the First Asian Congress on Archaeology held in New Delhi in 1961 on the suggestion of Late Prof. Subba Rao.

The Belan river sections provided the stratigraphic evidence (Sharma, G.R. 1971; Varma, R.K. 1999). It was observed that the Upper Palaeolithic deposits over lie the Middle Palaeolithic deposits and underlie the deposits yielding microliths. In the Belan section Gravel III which is not very consolidated and at places is loose has yielded Upper Palaeolithic tools. It has an average thickness of 1.21m. The overlying deposit - layer 3 composed of mottled clay and calcium carbonate yielded along with Upper Palaeolithic tools non geometric microliths. It had an average thickness 1.48m. This layer was followed by layer (2) composed of Kanker and stone chips. Its average thickness was 2.43m. It yielded geometric microliths and pottery. Overlying is the topmost layer grey in color and full of calcium carbonate, lateritic pallets and stone chips. This sequence of industries was confirmed by the stratigraphic sequence obtained in the middle Son Valley where the upper member of the Baghore formation yielded the Upper Palaeolithic Tools and from the overlying Khetauni deposit were obtained the microliths of the Mesolithic period.

Cumulative evidence from the explored and excavated sites in the region studied so far make it clear that the Mesolithic industries in India like its European counterpart evolved from the Upper Palaeolithic blade industries and it precedes the Neolithic. The technological change from the Upper Palaeolithic to Mesolithic was a gradual one. At least three stages have been marked between the Upper Palaeolithic to the Mesolithic transition known from their type site –Amaradan, Patwadh and Murwa (Varma and Pal 1997). It has been observed that backed and truncated blades make their first appearance in the second stage of the transition (Varma and Pal 1997). It marks the beginning of blunting technique which was commonly used during the Mesolithic for making tools. In the third stage of transition from Upper Palaeolithic to Mesolithic blades become smaller, narrower and the section thinner. Lunates appear for the first time but they are much larger and broader than their Mesolithic counter parts. Their width is more than half the length of the tool. During the Mesolithic period both the length and breadth decrease but the decrease in respect to width is more in relation to length (Varma and Pal 1997; Varma, R.K. 1985; Varma, R.K. 1986.).The final transitional phase between the Upper Palaeolithic and the Mesolithic has been named as epi- palaeolithic.

The microliths of the Mesolithic period are made on tiny flakes or blades taken out generally from tiny fluted cores through indirect percussion and pressure technique. Manufacture of each tool requires special care and precision. All the tools are made by retouching. A slight change of place and method of retouch changes a tiny blade into a blunted back blade or a truncated blade, a lunate, a trapeze or triangle etc.(Varma R.K. 2002). Besides microliths bone tools were also made .Where stone was not available alternate remedy was devised. For example in Ganga valley stone was not locally available, hence it was imported from the Vindhyan region and utmost economy was resorted. Technology came to the rescue of culture. The Ganga valley microliths are very diminutive. The number of bone tools increases and the stone tools decreses as we go up. The cores were completely exhausted. As an alternative to stone bone tools were made. Other perishable material such as hardened wood might have also been utilized but we have no evidence for the same in the study area. It is again interesting to note that with the increasing use of vegetal food new types of stone tools such as quern and mullers, ringstone etc were needed for processing vegetal food. Stone for the manufacture of these tools were again imported from their home land that is the Vindhyan region.

Generally the Mesolithic sites are located on the top surfaces of river sections, nalas, low hillocks, elevated plain surfaces within and outside the rock shelters etc.. Where ever the topsoil was eroded by rain water microlithic tools and debitage could be seen in very large numbers.

It was observed that the microlithic assemblages of the mesolithic period were found at least in three contexts. It was the position elsewhere in India also (Varma, R.K. 1985; 1986).

1. Non-geometric microliths without pottery.
2. Geometric microliths without pottery.
3. Geometric microliths with pottery.

In order to ascertain their actual position excavations were undertaken in the rock-shelter and open-air sites of Morahana Pahar (Varma,R.K.1964;1977;1981-83), Baghahi Khor (Varma, R.K.1964;1977;1981-83) and Lekhahia (Misra,V.D.1977) and Chopani-Mando (Sharma et.al. 1980:36-37) in the Belan Valley. These excavations proved very important because they for the first time threw light on the evolutionary sequence within the mesolithic.

The following sequence was obtained:

1. The earliest phase is represented by non-geometric tools made purely of impure cherty-flinty material.
2. In the second phase geometric shapes appear but they were still unassociated with pottery. Triangle precedes the emergence of Trapeze.
3. In third phase pottery makes its appearance.
4. In the fourth stage the microliths tend to become smaller and the geometric shapes are made with precision.

Excavation on the Chopanimando site was on a fairly large scale. The habitation deposit of 1.55m has been divided into three phases.

1. Phase I, is Epi-Palaeolithic,
2. Phase II is Early Mesolithic. It has further been divided into two sub-phases that is IIA and IIB. Phase IIA yielded non-geometric microliths and IIB yielded Geometric Microliths un associated with pottery.
3. Phase III is Advanced Mesolithic (Proto Neolithic). This phase is characterized by the emergence of fragile handmade pottery and some new tool types such as quern and mullers, ring stone, sling balls etc. Examination of the pottery brought to light husk of wild rice. It seems that rice had become an important item of their subsistence economy. A large number of hutments, pit hearths, storage bins etc. were also located. The population had increased many folds.

In the limited area plans of atleast thirty huts were recognized in the last phase of Chopanimando. The large number of the Mesolithic sites in the Vindhyan region and the extensive settlement at the site of Chopanimando reveals that the population had increased many folds.

Ganga Valley (Sharma, G.R. 1973; Varma, R.K. 1985; 1989; 1994 Kennedy, K.A.R 1984; 1986) Human activity, in this part of the Ganga valley, seems to have started when Mesolithic settlements were being formed in the Vindhyan region. The trough between the Himalayan foothills and the Vindhyan-Rohtasgarh, Chotanagpur plateau in the south which is termed as Ganga valley attained its present form during the post tertiary period. With the onset of the Holocene and the growing aridity, the marshy land and water locked Ganga alluvium gradually turned into vegetation friendly land, especially near the horse shoe lakes made by the meandering Ganga, where grasses and seed bearing plants sprouted. A few soil samples collected and examined from the vicinity of Mahadaha (Pant and Pant 1980:

229) and horseshoe lake of Nevari (25^{0}31' 30" E) (Gupta 1976: 109-19) near Sarai Nahar Rai suggested a green land vegetation during the period under consideration.

The leftover meanders of the Ganga turned into vast horseshoe lakes some of which collected enough water to last throughout the year. These lakes with vegetation all round and aquatic fauna could support a good number of both men and animal alike. Such lakes can be seen and located even now on the northern side of the Ganga though a number of them have silted.

The chance discovery of the Mesolithic site of Sarai Nahar Rai (25^{0}40' 0" N Long. 81^{0}51' 0") in the year 1969 was instrumental. It prompted us to start intensive explorations in the middle Ganga Valley within the districts of Allahabad, Pratapgarh, Sultanpur, Jaunpur and Varanasi. As a result two scores of sites ranging from the Epi-Palaeolithic stage to full fledged semi sedentary Mesolithic settlements on the banks of old horseshoe lakes of the Ganga were located (Sharma *et. al* 1980: 123-131).

On the evidence of the located sites we can surmise that the man from the Vindhyan region though first entered into the Ganga Valley when he was in the Epi-Palaeolithic stage but large scale settlement started only during the third phase of the Mesolithic when Geometric shapes had evolved.

On the basis of the analysis of the artifacts collected from the sites, they are divisible into the following groups:

1. Epi-Palaeolithic- Transitional between Upper Palaeolithic and Mesolithic.
2. Early Mesolithic- Characterised by non-geometric microlithic tools.
3. Mesolithic- Characterised by geometric microlithic tools.

Sites of the first two categories are represented by a few microlithic tools which are slightly bigger, broader and thicker than the Mesolithic and smaller, narrower and thinner than the upper Palaeolithic tools.

The sites of the third category, can further be subdivided into three groups: A B C The sites belonging to group A are represented by a few microliths only and are devoid of any habitation deposit. The sites of group B and C have habitation deposit and are represented by burials and hearths. These sites are invariably located on the banks of horseshoe lakes on a relatively higher ground beyond the flood level of the lakes. The sites of group B do not have deposit of more than one or two periods. Thick deposits of fairly long duration of time represent the sites of group C. None of the sites reported so far are associated with pottery. The microlithic assemblage belongs to the geometric stage. The industry may be described as pre-pottery and geometric in character. It is comparable with the second phase of the Mesolithic of the Vindhyas (Varma, R.K. 1986) and the IIB phase of Chopani-Mando (Sharma *et.al* 1980).

Why and how they left their original habitat in the Vindhyas for an entirely new place with completely different environment and ecological setup is an important question which needs investigation. The new habitat was completely devoid of the raw material with which the Mesolithic people made their hunting equipment. The entirely new ecological setup demanded a change in the life style also.

At least three possibilities may be sighted which prompted these people to adopt the new habitat. The first and the foremost reason seems to be environmental change, the second spurt in population and the third innate adventurous spirit of man with a longing to see new places and face new challenges. We have already stated that the drier conditions of the Holocene probably created water scarcity on account of which man and animal opted for the river valleys to the north of the Vindhyan hillocks beyond the medial ridge.

Water scarcity is a regular phenomenon during the summer months in the Vindhyan region even during the present time. It forces shifting of population to the north of the Vindhyan regions into the Ganga Valley. The dry climatic conditions which made the Vindyhan region inhospitable created better living condition in the Ganga Valley.

The man in the Vindhyan region, wandering in search of food, fodder and water descended down from the hills to settle near the horseshoe lakes with greenery all around abounding in vegetal food aquatic fauna, small game and birds. The theory of seasonal migration of Prof. Sharma may be taken as only partially correct. In the beginning it might have been a seasonal affair only. But it seems more probable that later (during the Geometric phase of the Mesolithic) the people who came in the Ganga Valley continued to stay on.

There is no habitation deposit at any of the Epi-Palaeolithic and non geometric Mesolithic sites so for discovered in the Ganga Valley. Out of the excavated sites of the Ganga Valley only at Sarai Nahar Rai there is evidence of only one period of burial activity (Pal, J.N. 2002). Study of the skeletal remains indiated that there the population consisted of adults only. Damdama and Mahadaha continued to be inhabitated for a long time where male female young children and old lived together. The thick habitation deposit of 1.5 m. at Damdama is divisible into ten layers and eight phases of burial activity with corresponding floor levels. This condition further finds support from the fact that the lithic material-microliths gradually decrease in member in the upper levels and are replaced by bone tools. It means that there was no regular supply of raw material. Had the people been coming seasonally the number of microlithic tools would not have decreased progressively. Moreover utmost economy was practiced in the manufacture of microliths.

Material Culture of the Mesolithic of the Vindhya-Ganga region

The material culture of the Vindhya Ganga Valley presents a very interesting picture of cultural evolution and technological development. We have already discussed how the man coped with the changing environment by changing the tool kit and subsistence economy. The evolution of microliths and the fabrication of composite tools there from was the result of the gradual modification of his extra corporeal equipment. The composition of composite tools achieved their greatest perfection during the mesolithic. The popular use of bow and arrow, the sickle made by inserting a number of tiny microliths in a slotted hardened wood or bone, tiny scrapers, exquisitely made triangles and trapeze may be regarded as of revolutionary importance. The new weapons added to the striking power and the speed of man who was physically weaker than most of the other contemporary animals. Besides microliths Quern and mullers, ring stones and pottery were also added as part of their cultural equipment in due course of time.

By the second phase of the Mesolithic the hunter gatherers gradually became gatherer hunters. Their dependence on hunting decreased and gathering increased. It also prompted the man to make semi sedentary bases. It is evident from the excavation at the site of Chopani-Mando (Sharma,G.R.et al 1980)in the Vindhyan region where habitation deposit of 1.55m and in the Ganga Valley Damdama where a deposit of 1.5m and Mahadaha where a deposit of 65 cm was unearthed. There is sufficient evidence to demonstrate that by the last phase of Chopanimando vegetal food was abundantly used Quern and mullers were used to process the vegetal food and the people had started semi sedentary way of life. The large number of huts (30), circular pit hearths (11) support the contention stated above. In the Ganga Valley also the same picture is obtained. The cultural deposit of 1.5m composed of ten layers has revealed burial activity in almost from the beginning to end. These people preferred to make stable bases rather than moving from place to place. The heavy dependence on vegetal food, the heavy food processing tools and easy availability of aquatic fauna in the lake nearby bound them with the soil. Vegetal resources were abundant and easily available. From these bases these people operated unto a distance of safe return within a day because the vegetal food had to be processed at the base station only on account of food processing equipments being there. In case of hunters it was not necessary to come back to the base camp for food processing. There is also evidence to suggest that they had now surplus food. A number of pits with plastered walls and unburned interior have been brought to light in the excavations at Mahadaha and Damdama. This in all probability served as storage pits.

As a corollary to the dependence on vegetal food the formation of smaller units within a larger group of persons followed. It's a well-known fact that hunting, especially large-scale hunting is a social event but the same may not be true for gathering and processing of vegetal food. A large number of small hearths have been located on each site. Construction of small hutment and small pit hearths at may be taken as evidence of formation of smaller units in the big social setup. Here reference to Couple burials which have been marked at the excavated sites of the Ganga Valley is most noteworthy. Couple or multiple couple burials (Varma, R.K. 1997: 29-34 in Joshi J.P. (ed.) 1997) have been excavated at each of the sites in which pairs of males and females were buried side by side or in two tiers in a set pattern. In each grave female was put to the left of the male. There are however three exceptions. In two cases the females were placed to the right of male and in one case both the skeleton are in the opposite directions. There was no time gap between the placement of the first and the second body.

Here again some explanations are needed. Did the male and female die together by accident, disease or the man died and the female was killed and buried together? There is no evidence to prove or disprove any of the above options.

On the basis of couple burials it is not improper to postulate the thesis that some sort of family unit of male and female and children had formed in the Mesolithic itself and a new social order was emerging in which the concept of ownership of individual hut, hearth, family and surplus food was being recognized. It may also suggest division of labour within a male female unit. It is true that men and women are equally effective foragers but mothers carrying dependent children are not effective hunters. A perusal of the rock paintings shows that women did not participate in big game hunting. They must thus depend on male hunters for meat and other provisions. This favors a system in which males have exclusive sexual access to females, and females can predict that their sexual partner will provide food for them and their children.

In conjunction with the subsistence strategies these people developed important socio-ritual traditions. The Mesolithic folk buried their dead with meticulous care generally in west east direction, within their living space. The excavations in the Baghahi Khor rock shelter revealed one burial and in Lekhahia shelter no1 at least 17 human burials belonging to eight different periods were located.

The meticulous way in which graves were prepared in west-east orientation represents the performance of a ritual belief on a group level. There are a few exceptions only. In case of one couple burial the orientation is north south and south north. These people were not simply concerned with the problem of existence and were thinking about life beyond death and supernatural. They were not simply disposing of the dead but were immortalizing them by making elaborate burial in a set pattern within the habitation area. Evidence from Damdama suggests that some sort of fire ritual was performed in the grave itself before burying the dead. The placement of grave goods in the form of microliths, bones, fresh water molluscs, bone and antler ornaments etc. further confirms the above hypothesis. The west east or east west orientation of the graves must have been guided by the position of the sun. The life giving sun must have attracted them. The beginning of sun worship may be traced from these Mesolithic folk.

Artistic Activities

In the Vindhyan hills a very large number of shelters have been located that are profusely painted with animal figures by the mesolithic hunter gatherers. In some of these shelters they camped, buried their dead, made their tools also. There is no doubt about the authorship of the paintings as they all have revealed cultural deposit of the Mesolithic people only. A study of the superposition of the paintings has revealed a cyclic development from naturalistic>stylistic>symbolic and back to naturalistic form.

This Aesthetic sense further developed into self awareness and self beautification. In the Vindhyan region in the LKH-1 a cylindrical bead made from tubular bone and a stone bead from layer 2A of Chopani-Mando, Phase III (Last Phase) was discovered. Excavation in the Ganga Valley revealed a variety of ornaments made of antler bone.

Earrings and necklaces have been recovered from the graves at Mahadaha (Sharma *et.al* 1980: 108-109). Two male individuals (Skl. V and VII) were buried adorned with necklace made from rings, carved from antlers, the presence of unfinished antler ornaments at Mahadaha indicate that the ornaments were manufactured locally. At Damdama in grave VII was found a carved ivory pendant and two bone arrowheads (Varma *et.al* 1985: 64). The carved pendent had two circles or eyes at either end.

The discoveries of these items of adornment raise some important issues. The first and the foremost question is whether these ornaments were indicative of social status or position of authority? At this stage of our knowledge it is difficult to answer but we can safely presume they were meant to signify both. Such a large settlement necessarily requires an authority to manage social issues.

The skeletal remains of the male members of the Mesolithic folk of the Vindhyan region (Lekhahia) and the Ganga Valley people (SNR, MDH and DDM) is not much different. "The only male for which stature could be estimated (LKH-5) resulted in a value of 177.4 cm. but the mean stature was

161.7 cm" (John Lukacks and V.D.Mishra 2002 p.276ff.). The mean stature of Lekhahia females is much below that of plains females. The Ganga Valley people were relatively tall with the stature of males being approximately 173.93 cm to 192.08 cm (Kennedy 1984: 37). Kennedy who had studied the skeletal remains of Sarai Nahar Rai states 'we recognize here an ancient population which was extremely successful in its adaptation to the hunting and gathering way of life carried out in an ecological setting of abundant food resources. Only in this way we may explain the physical responses of this population towards a high realization of their ontogenetic growth potentials and the low incidence of disease related to nutritional stress' (Kennedy KAR *et.al* 1986 p. 40-41). It is further supported by the fact that here we find people living up to 40 to 60 years of age which is exceptionally high for any Mesolithic society.

How these flourishing pre agricultural settlements were deserted is a question which needs proper explanation. At none of these sites we find any evidence of settlement after the desertion of the site by the Mesolithic folk. The sites remained unoccupied till 100 years ago. That is why these are so well preserved.

The Mesolithic people though dependent heavily on vegetal food could not start cultivation. Probably because the stage was not set yet for the same. Gradually the catchment area became depleted of resources and could not support the steadily growing population. Hence, they had no option but to shift to more congenial location.

There seems to be a strong possibility that these people returned back to the Vindhyan region from where they had come. By this time pottery had been introduced there. These people probably introduced quern and mullers there. We have evidence from Chopani-Mando that during the advance Mesolithic phase rice was being exploited in the Belan Valley. Rice husk has been found in the pottery and burnt rice has been obtained through excavation. We have evidence form Koldihwa that the transformation from gathering to cultivation took place by 6000 BC and the first grain to be cultivated in that region was rice.

The Antiquity

There are a number of C14 dates available to fix the antiquity of the Mesolithic of the Vindhya-Ganga region.

From the Lekhahia Rock-shelter (Vindhyan region, Bhainsore group) we have four Carbon dates belonging to the Phase III of the Vindhyan Mesolithic. The dates are:

TF-417: 3560 ± 110 BP (1710±110 BC)
TF-419: 4240 ± 115 BP (2410±115BC)

Beside there are two more C 14 dates, by accelerator mass spectrometry from human bone apatite were obtained. These dates are based upon thorough pre-treatment and sample preparation methods suggest that the skeletons from Lekhahia may have an antiquity two times greater than previously believed:

Geochron 8,370 ± 75 BP (Skl.IV)
Geochron 8,000 ± 75 BP (Skl.XIII, XV)

These are not isolated dates. There are confirmatory dates from the Belan, Son and Ganga Valley sites.

The Upper Palaeolithic horizon (Gravel III) in the Belan Valley has given two C14 dates reading 23840 BC (PRL 86) and 17765 BC (TF 1245). Another date reading 18000 BP has been obtained from the Upper Palaeolithic horizon (Clark and Williams : 1990 : Prehistoric Ecology etc. .Man and Environment XV (i);13-24).

The Epi-Palaeolithic horizon (Gravel IV) in the Belan section has yielded five dates (Varma 1981-83; Possehl and Rissman 1992) reading 13740+400/-380 BP (PRL 603); 11550±180 BP (BS 130); 10980±190 BP (PRL602); 9830±160 BP (BS 131) and 9740 ± 115 BP (SVA 1421).

Baghor II a Mesolithic settlement (Geometric microliths unassociated with pottery) in the Son Valley has yielded one C14 date reading 6380±220 BC (PRL 715) Clark and Williams 1990).

Similar early dates have been obtained from the Mesolithic settlements of the Ganga Valley (Mesolithic Phase II of the Vindhyan region). There is one date from Sarai Nahar Rai TF 1104; 8365± 110 BC and one TL date 5000-7000 BC and two AMS C14 dates reading 6670± 65 BC and 6915± 69 BC.

On the basis of the above discussion the Epi-Palaeolithic may be placed within a time bracket of 14,000-13,000 BC to 10,000-9,000 BC and the Mesolithic between 12,000-11,000 BC to 2,000-1500 BC. The dates for the beginning of the Mesolithic is still flexible because we do not have any date from the Ist phase of the Vindhyan Mesolithic. All the dates are from Phase II and III only. Thus there is all possibilities that the dates will be pushed back further with the availability of new data.

References

1. John Lukacks and V.D. Mishra 2002 Human Skeletons in Lekhahia in Misra,V.D and Pal, J.N (Ed) Mesolithic India. Publishrd by Department of AHC&Arch, University of Allahabad.
2. Kennedy, Kenneth A.R.et al. 1986. *Mesolithic Human Remains from the Gangetic Plain: Sarai Nahar Rai.* South Asia Occasional Papers and Thesis No. 10 Cornell
3. Misra,V.D. 1977 Some Aspects of Indian Archaeology
4. Misra, V.N. and M.S. Mate, 1965. *Indian Prehistory 1964.*
5. Pal, J.N. 1985 Some New Light Universityon the Mesolithic Burial Pracices. Of the Ganga Valley, Evidence from Mahadaha. *Man and Environment* IX.
6. Pal, J.N. 2002 Mesolithic Gangetic Plain in Misra,V.D. and Pal, J.N. (Ed) Mesolithic India. Publishrd by Department of AHC & Arch, University of Allahabad.
7. Pant, D.D. and R. Pant 1980. Preliminary observations on pollen flora of Chopani-mando (Vindhyas) and Mahadaha (Ganga Valley). In *Beginnings of Agriculture* edited by G.R. Sharma, V.D. Misra, D. Mandal, B.B. Misra and J.N. Pal, Allahabad. Abinash Prakashan.
8. Sharma, G.R. 1973. Stone Age in the Vindhyas and the Ganga Valley, in *Radiocarbon and Indian Archaeology,* (D.P. Agrawal and A. Ghosh eds.), Mumbai: TIFR,.
9. Sharma, G.R. 1973. Mesolithic lake cultures in the Ganga Valley, India. *Proceedings of the Prehistoric Society* 39: 129-146.
10. Sharma, G.R. 1975. Seasonal Migrations and Mesolithic Lake Cultures of the Ganga Valley. *In Chattopadhyaya memorial volume* G.R. Sharma (ed.).
11. Sharma, G.R., V.D. Misra, D. Mandal, B.B. Misra, and J.N. Pal 1980. *Beginnings of Agriculture*, Department of Ancient History, Culture and Archaeology, University of Allahabad, Allahabad.
12. Sharma, G.R. and J.D. Clark, 1983, *Palaeoenvironment and Prehistory in the Middle Son Valley*, University of Allahabad, Allahabad.
13. Varma, R.K. 1981-83. The Mesolithic Culture of India, *Purattava* No. 13-14.
14. Varma, R.K. 1985a. *Unique couple burials of the Ganga Valley.* Paper read at Gauhati Conference IAS and ISPQUS and in Facets of Indian Civilization (ed.) by J.P. Joshi: 1997, Varma, R.K. p. 29-34.
15. Varma, R.K. 1985b. A preliminary report of the excavation at Damdama (1982-84). *Man and Environment IX.*
16. Varma, R.K. 1986. *The Mesolithic Age in Mirzapur.* Allahabad. Paramjyoti Prakashan.
17. Varma, R.K. 1989. Pre Agricultural Mesolithic Society of the Ganga Valley. p. 55-85 in old Problems and New Perspectives in the Archaeology of South Asia in *Old Problems and New Perspective in the Archaeology of South Asia* Edited by J.M.Kenoyer, Wisconsin Archaeological Reports Vol.2
18. Varma, R.K. and J.N. Pal, 1997, The Upper Palaeolithic Culture of the Vindhyan Region, pp. 94-102, In V.D. Misra and J.N. Pal (Ed.) *Indian Prehistory 1980*, University of Allahabad, Allahabad.
19. Varma, R.K. 1999. Emergence of Culture in the Vindhya-Ganga Region with Special Reference to Old Stone Age, in *The Dawn of Indian Civilization (upto c. 600 BC)* (G.C.
20. Pandey (Ed.), pp. 175-204. *History of Science, Philosophy and Culture in Indian Civilization* Vol. I, Part 1 General Editor D.P. Chattopadhyaya. New Delhi: Project of History of Indian Science, Philosophy and Culture, Centre for studies in Civilizations.
21. Varma.R.K. 2002 Mesolithic technology in Misra,V.D and Pal,J.N(Ed) Mesolithic India. Publishrd by Department of AHC&Arch,University of Allahabad.
22. Varma, R.K. 2011. Changing Pattern of Lower Palaeolithic in South Asia and Recent Researches in Belan valley (U.P.) and Mid-Son Valley (M.P.), *Puratattva* 41: 49-70.

4

THE IRON AGE SOCIETY OF INDIA: PATTERN OF TECHNOLOGY ADAPTATION AND CULTURE CHANGE

Vibha Tripathi

Iron metallurgy represented a new technological configuration being different from all the earlier technologies and was also the most significant innovation of its age. Human civilization received a great impetus with application of iron and steel which is a utilitarian metal. Steel still continues to be the most sought after metals in almost every possible sector of activity. The present discussion is focused primarily on the developmental stages of iron technology and its role in socio-economic changes that took place in ancient India. Iron technology was slow to develop as it had to undergo through a long period of trial and error because it was entirely different from earlier metallurgies known to the metalworkers of copper-bronze age. It may also be noted here that iron at its earliest level, as reported on the basis of some available records of ancient world civilizations was five times more expensive than gold (Gurney 1961:20, 83). Generally, composite tools like an ornamental stone studded handle and an iron blade or a bronze dagger inlaid with iron buttons to embellish the handle are reported from Bronze Age cultures of centres of ancient civilizations (for detail see Tripathi 2001). We hardly have a comparable evidence of status of iron in India. At the most an uncertain status of metallurgical development may be discerned at sites like Noh where we come across tiny indeterminate bits of (metallic?) iron in the Pre- Painted Grey Ware (PGW, henceforth) cultural horizon using Black and Red Ware (BRW, now on). In some of the megalithic burials, composite tools using both copper/bronze and iron have been found, indicating a scarcity or importance of iron. While it will give us an idea about the stages through which the metallurgical processes underwent, it will also throw light on the level and pattern of utilization and adoption of the newly discovered technological know-how. The researches conducted so far suggest that iron metallurgy took a long time to evolve to attain a level of maturity to be truly effective. In our attempt to do so, we are faced with questions like: How and when did iron technology achieve this status? How many stages of growth of the metallurgy are perceptible in archaeological material? What was the pattern of its adaptation in the early cultures? Is there an interrelationship between level of technological skill and its social acceptance? In what way is this fact reflected in the material milieu? Why did it take centuries for iron technology to be effective enough to leave its imprint on the culture? Has its gradual adaptation got something to do inherently in iron metallurgy itself? Or alternatively, is it the conservative and slow pace of social temper which may be held responsible for the delayed adaptation of a technological product? A comparative assessment of quality and quantity of iron objects and status of material culture at a particular age may provide a cue to the degree of impact of technology on society. These are the issues we propose to address in the present paper. This is being attempted here in the context of cultures of the Ganga Plain which became the 'area of attraction' with emerging Iron Age cities after the decline of the Bronze Age urban civilization. The significance and context of high antiquity of iron as indicated by recent radiocarbon dates may also be examined here, especially with a view point of its impact on cultural development. Before we proceed further, let's compare the metallurgical processes and relative advantages of the copper –bronze vis-a-vis iron technology, at least at the early stages of its development.

I. Interfacing Copper-Bronze with Iron

In archaeological parlance, however, we find that even after centuries of advent of iron, copper- bronze continues to be in use for variety of purposes. As the evidence stand today, we notice that at Early Iron Age metallic iron makes a slow appearance in an otherwise Chalcolithic milieu. It is commonly assumed that metallic iron is superior in strength, sharpness, malleability and ductility compared to copper-bronze, especially as utilitarian metal. But iron fails to exert any perceptible impact on material culture for centuries after its emergence. It may, therefore be worthwhile taking a close look at this anomalous situation. A delayed adoption of iron is attributed to the complexity of metallurgical process involved in production of iron. Significantly enough, experts doubt about superiority of iron over copper bronze at least at the early stage of beginning of use of iron. In comparison to wrought iron which was initially produced, copper bronze is supposed to have definite advantage. Firstly, copper is easier to smelt that too at much lower temperature in simpler furnaces and can be produced on larger scale in moulds if required. It is also a myth that copper-bronze is inferior to iron in strength. Any bronze even with ten per cent tin alloying has superior strength than wrought iron having no carbon content in the matrix of metal. Talking about change over from bronze to iron in the Chinese context Taylor and Shell (1988:205-221) remarked, "Two misunderstandings regarding the change over from bronze to iron plague archaeological literature... they are that iron is better than bronze and that the difficulty in smelting iron lies in the high temperature required. In fact it is only steel that is consistently stronger than bronze... Furthermore, a usable bloom, or molten iron, if it contains a large amount of carbon or other impurities can be produced at temperatures close to or even below those needed to melt copper or gold... the difficulty with iron lay not in obtaining high temperatures but in developing the new techniques necessary to hot forge the bloom..." Thus iron required a new kind of technological configuration to be evolved that necessitated a long process of experimentation through trial and error. The nature and quality of early iron objects remain uncertain and scarce. This resulted into a slow production of iron that too on a considerable scale for a long duration of time. If the nature and type of iron objects at early Iron Age is a guide, we find that there is a very gradual change in pattern of utilization of metal objects. Copper-bronze remains a favoured medium for fashioning not only toiletries and ornaments but even war and hunting tools. Was it a compulsion or a choice made by the Copper-bronze using societies which actually first explored the possibilities of use of metallic iron?

To answer this, we need to examine the circumstances of emergence of iron in the Indian context. Metallic iron, in view of R.F. Tylecote (1962: 211) was discovered by some copper using communities which were not well adept in copper-bronze metallurgy. This has been further argued that for a long time it is the same metal worker who produced copper and later experimented with an alternative material, which is iron. This fact has been corroborated by other studies also. For instance, according to Maxwell Hyslop (1974), 'black smithy and bronze smithy were not yet strictly separated, a fact which is also suggested by analysis of certain objects'. An iron sword from Luristan (7th century BC) and an 8th century implement from Khorsabad show that the technology employed in their manufacturing were more apt for bronze than iron. In the opinion of Waldbaum (1980: 90-91) this resulted into a lack of "complete control over the special technique for producing high quality iron." This must be cause of 'rather a halting adaption of iron and the continued production of bronze utilitarian implements".

These observations are true about most of the early Iron Age cultures including India. At most of the Proto-historic-Early historic sites in India, almost up to the early centuries of the first millennium

BCE, we come across copper being used for fashioning hunting and war weapons for several centuries after emergence of iron. Copper-bronze arrowheads, spearheads and axes continue to be used for a long time. An example in the case is the PGW culture at Hastinapur dated by the excavator between circa 1100 to 600 BCE (Lal 1954-55). The evidence of Pandurajar Dhibi in district Burdwan (West Bengal) is also noteworthy in this regard. A dish shaped object was recovered from Period II dated to 800-700 BCE by the excavator. On analysis, it has been described as a 'dark brown object with yellowish tinge that could easily be confused with copper based object as work of a copper smith who accidentally seems to have worked it' (De and Chattopadhyay 1989:34). They further observed that it is very hard and 'could not be sliced with a hacksaw blade. EPMA revealed cobalt, oxygen, ruthenium, alumina and silica. It clearly appears to be work of the Chalcolithic metal workers The Chalcolithic cultures of eastern India, especially the Ganga Plain show a scarcity of copper objects, at times being just a couple of objects that too tiny ones like fish-hooks, wires, ornaments or toiletries. Some of them have been found to be alloyed with tin but the number of such objects is very small. It may be assumed that such objects were exclusive and confined to the privileged class of the social structure. It is reasonable to assume, therefore, that the introduction of iron proceeded to fill in a void, a scarcity of metal in daily life in metal starved early Indian Chalcolithic cultures albeit very gradually. At the earliest stage, iron is used to manufacture arrow heads, spearheads, rods, nails, chisels etc. most of which could have been used effectively as weapons of offence and defence as well as for hunting and carpentry though copper remained in use even for these purposes. It will be worth taking a close look at the status of metallurgy in the early cultures of the region under study.

II Status of Iron Metallurgy

We need to examine the status of iron metallurgy at different cultural phases to see whether there is any correspondence between metallurgical know – how and type and number of tools utilized therein. And also to examine the problem as to why it takes so long for iron to have any perceptible impact on cultural make up despite an early appearance of iron, sometimes appearing as early as the first quarter of second millennium BCE at several sites of the Vindhya-Ganga Plain which happens to be the focal point of the present study. This assessment may be done at the three stages of development of Iron Age cultures.

II.1. Early Iron Age, the Age of Commencement

It may only be reiterated here that between the period of last quarter of the 2nd millennium B.C. and the beginning of the 1st millennium B.C. iron comes to be used, albeit in small quantities at several sites in different parts of India. The Early Iron Age cultures have been classified as zones A to F because of the ecological and geographical specificities of the Indian sub-continent (Tripathi 2001; 2008, Fig. 1). These are: (a) the North-western region with cairn burials (b) the PGW culture (c) the pre-NBP culture with BRW-BSW pottery tradition (d) Madhya Pradesh with continuous Chalcolithic and Early Iron culture (e) Megalithic culture of Vidarbh (f) Megalithic culture of peninsular India. We have good number of Early Iron Age sites like Noh, Jodhpura in Rajasthan, Atranjikhera, Jakhera, Alamgirpur etc. in Uttar Pradesh (belonging to PGW cultural phase (1100-600 BCE) in Indo-Gangetic divide; Prakash, Bahal in Deccan and Kaytha, Eran, Nagda etc. in M.P. (Chalcolithic level); Chirand, in Bihar; Dadupur, Raja Nal-ka-Tila, Malhar, Raipura, Koldihwa, Kausambi, Jhusi, Rajghat, Narthan etc. in Uttar Pradesh, (18/1700-600 BCE); Hatigra, Mangalkot, Mahaisdal, Pandurajar Dhibi (1200-600 BCE) in West Bengal; Naikund, Takalghat-Khapa, Mahurjhari, Hallur, Tadkanhalli, Komaranhalli (1400-6/500 BCE) etc. in Vidarbh and Tamil Nadu. However, for an in – depth examination the present discussion is focused more on the Iron Age cultures of the Ganga Plain and the adjacent Vindhya-Kaimur hilly tracts which are not only rich in iron ore deposits but are potentially significant to production and distribution of iron to the early cultures situated in the nearby alluvial plains. This region incidentally, holds a special position in Post-Harappan archaeology of India. It is here that the next genre of cities developed after the decline of the copper-bronze age Harappan civilization. Besides, in recent decades, sites in the Vindhya-Kaimur hilly terrain bordering the middle Ganga Plain have yielded considerably early radiometric dates from iron bearing strata. They have pushed back the antiquity of iron in India to the first quarter of the second millennium BCE.

The analytical examination of iron objects from the early levels indicates that the metallurgy of iron was quite elementary in nature. Bloomery iron that could be produced at much lower temperature was the norm; slag inclusions are commonly found in the matrix of iron. The analysed objects of Hatigra dated to 1100-1000 BCE (Ghosh and Chattopadhyay 1987 : 88) had Widmanstaatten structure due to prolonged exposure at a temperature of about 1200^{0}C followed by a slow cooling. It is said to be a 'low carbon hypereutectoid steel'. The concentration of carbon on the edges of analysed samples seen in some of the micrographs suggests knowledge of carburization. It is not unlikely that carburization at the early stages was incidental due to the technique of repeated heating and hammering in contact with charcoal. This imparted some carbon to the matrix of metal adding to its strength. The furnaces at this stage were not efficient enough to generate sufficient temperature. The specimens from Hatigra, Pandurajar Dhibi in district Burdwan (West Bengal), as noted above has yielded iron in second phase of Chalcolithic culture which Chattopadhyay (De and Dhattopadhyay 1989) prefers to call ferro-chalcolithic (Period II, B) datable to 2940±55 BP (1048 B.C.) and 2870 ± 30 BP. 970 B.C. Period III is dated to 2580 BP (630 B.C.). Chattopadhyay has analysed two objects belonging to Period II and and III as well as slag from both these periods (De and Chattopadhya, op.cit. Pl. VII, Table 6). Both chemical and microscopic observations were made providing information about metallurgy in this region.

There are important iron-yielding sites that indicate evolutionary stages in iron metallurgy within this stage of Early Iron. There are both qualitative and quantitative improvement in iron technology within this stage as borne out by the phase-wise distribution of metals is available for Early Iron Age (E.I.A Tables 1, 2). The more westerly sites of the Painted Grey Ware (PGW) culture have failed to yield iron objects. Within a short span stray shapeless bits and pieces of iron appear at sites like Noh; finished objects or iron appear in small number at most of the sites of the Gangetic Doab. Atranjikhera (Gaur 1983) has yielded Painted Grey Ware (PGW, henceforth) in a thick deposit of up to 2.50m. The period has been divided into three sub-periods. The lowermost phase has yielded only seven objects and a lump and does not contain even the most elementary types like arrowheads and spearheads. These hunting tools appear in the mid-PGW phase which has a total of 44 objects and two lumps (slag?) making it 46 in number. The upper phase has yielded 81 objects thus indicating a gradual rise in use of number of iron objects. Iron here comes to be used for variety of purposes over a period of half a millennium (11/1000 B.C. to 600 B.C. of span of PGW culture). Jakhera another site situated nearby has yielded an iron ploughshare along with pieces of slag and iron bloom in the Black and Red Ware (BRW) and the succeeding proto-PGW phase. It is followed by a regular use of iron from the beginning of PGW yielding hoe, sickle, spearhead, arrow-head, dagger, chopper, chisel, axe, nails, rods etc. (Sahi 1994). At Hastinapur and Almgirpur in Meerut district iron appears for the first time during the PGW cultural period. At this period Hastinapur yielded four objects and slag pieces. Alamgirpur (with 137 cm. thick deposit) yields iron right from the earliest levels, spearheads, a barbed arrow-head, nail and pins being the main objects, (see Tripathi 2001, fig. 12). A somewhat similar evidence comes forth from the site of Mangalkot in West Bengal in an otherwise Chalcolithic cultural milieu dominated by Black and red ware. It has been dated to 1300 BCE (Dutta 1992).

The richest iron tool repertoire at EIA is that of the megalithic burials of southern India. Swords, spikes, tridents, horse's bits and also utensils are found along with usually used shapes found at this period, i.e. arrow-head, spearhead, chisel, axe, fish hook and bangles. Even the metallurgy appears to be quite developed as indicated by high carbon steel found on analysis of megalithic tools from Mahurjhari (Despande, 2010).

Iron objects from Tadkanhalli, a megalithic site dated by T.L. to 14th-13th B.C. have been analysed (Hari Narain et.al. 1998). Though the micrographs are stated to show presence of pearlite along with slag inclusion in the matrix on metal, Bhanu Prakash of Department of Metallurgical Engineering, Banaras Hindu University expressed doubts about the evidence of steeling therein (Personal communication). So far the samples analysed from E.I.R. indicate a solid state reduction at a low temperature in elementary furnaces.

The metallurgy generally indicates an elementary level of skill at this stage. The ferrite structure indicates a solid state reduction. The iron samples analysed from the site of Hatigra dated 1100-1000 B.C. as noted earlier had Widmanstaatten structure due to prolonged exposure at low temperature producing a 'hypo-eutectoid steel'. The concentration of carbon on the edges visible in the metallograph indicates carburization (Ghosh and Chattopadhyay 1987).

The dish shaped object from Pandu Rajar Dhibi mentioned earlier was also analysed. It was a dark brown object with a yellowish surface colour that could easily be confused for copper-based object. "The specimen could not be sliced with a hacksaw blade as it is extremely hard ad at the same time brittle" (De and Chattopadhyay 1989 op.cit., 34 see Table 6). The chemical analysis (wet method) revealed only silicon and iron qualitatively. The EPMA analysis given above shows it to be iron with high amount of silicon that led to brittleness. Fayalite in large quantity suggests the elementary stage of metallurgy. No carbide or pearlite structure could be detected on etching. High potassium content indicates use of charcoal as fuel. Thus, it may be suggested that though the metallurgy was not well developed yet the method of forging imparted it sufficient strength compared to copper objects that were used though rare at this stage. Analysis of an iron object from Tadkanhalli dated to 13/1400 BCE by TL method shows elementary metallurgical know-how with plenty of slag inclusion (Fig. 2).

To sum up, we may state that the scarcity of iron objects and the primarily elementary nature of hunting-fishing tools is suggestive of the fact that iron at this level is a product of solid state reduction. Most of the analysed specimens show slag inclusion due to low temperature (1100^0 to 1300^0 C) and inefficient metallurgical skill.

Iron thus produced has little advantage over a good quality bronze having 11% tin that will have the Brinnel hardness of 60,000 per sq. inch (P.S.I.). As mentioned earlier, the hardness increases to 120,000 P.S.I. after cold working. Wrought iron, on the other hand has the hardness of only 40,000 P.S.I. Repeated hammering and heating in contact with charcoal raises its hardness up to 100,000 P.S.I. This may also explain the reason of late adoption of iron for purposes other than weaponry or carpentry at the earliest level.

II.2. Middle Iron Age, the Age of Florescence

The Northern Black Polished Ware (NBPW) culture takes over the major part of North India by 9/800 BCE. At certain sites it was contemporaneous with the late phase of Painted Grey Ware culture on the one hand and the Megalithic cultures on the other. This was a period of consolidation of iron technology with traces of steeling and case hardening or carburization. A relative increase is recorded in the number and types of iron object. (Table 2; Fig.5.B, also see Tripathi 2001, Figs. 20-24) There is thus a qualitative and quantitative improvement in iron objects. We come across more sophisticated weapons like javelin, lances, daggers, blades, and elephant goads along with the earlier types. Agricultural implements, which were rarely reported earlier at the previous state, and were found only from a few sites (Jakhera yielded sickle and ploughshare, and Atranjikhera an axe), become relatively frequent now.

Though solid-state reduction of iron continues to be the norm of smelting, improvisation in metallurgical technique is clearly perceptible; steeling of objects become more common. Whether carbon in the matrix of iron was accidental is uncertain as two samples pertaining to the same period from several sites like and Rajghat and Prakash show different conditions (Bhardwaj 1979; Thapar 1965, PI, 20-21). While sample No. 29 (fig. 21A at Prakash) indicates a low metalloid content indicating solid state reduction, sample No. 30 (21. B) shows presence of equiaxed ferrite grains with small amount of pearlite at the grain boundaries and presence of streaks of iron oxide and slag. The chemical composition shows steeling. In a broader framework, the results have been corroborated by samples from Rajghat (Tripathi 2001, figs. 19 A, B; 20, A). A total of six iron samples from Rajghat belonging to 600-400 BCE levels were analysed. All of them are found to be wrought iron having slag inclusion. Evidence of carburization has been attested to (Bharadwaj op.cit.). Sample No. 6 of Rajghat has 1.4% carbon. It is difficult to ascertain whether carburization was deliberate as only one sample shows carburization. It is worth mentioning here that humid climate of this region is detrimental to the preservation of evidence of carburization as the upper layers of iron objects are almost invariably lost due to corrosion. It is also worth mentioning here about the state of preservation of iron artefacts. Generally, a thick layer of corroded iron comes off due to moisture in soil and only the core of iron objects remains available. It is difficult to detect traces of carburization from deep core of such corroded objects. It is also possible that carburization was practised selectively according to the function and nature of objects.

An iron sickle belonging to period III, of Pandurajar Dhibi was analysed (NBP phase, Fig.3). At this stage though solid state reduction of iron continues to be the basic technique of iron smelting, there was improvisation in metallurgical techniques; steeling of iron became more frequent during this stage raising the efficacy of iron artefacts. The result is noteworthy. It is observed, "Electron micrograph obtained at a magnification of 100 X clearly represents its tempered martensitic structure". It shows non-uniform structure and retained acicularity at certain places, especially around large patches of ferrite areas. It was forged at a significantly high temperature to extricate the slag particles giving the metal a more homogenized structure. Carburization was done during smithy in course of heating and forging of objects at the subsequent stage. Inside the core, the carbon content that is retained is only 0.22%. But the high level of corrosion that took place over the time must have caused depletion of carbon. There is also an uneven distribution of carbon concentration. It indicates that carbon was more than 0.4% initially.' There are indications of quenching and tempering of this specimen (De and Chattopdhya 1989: 37, Fig. 4.C).

Analysis of iron objects from Senuwar in Dist. Rohtas, Chirand, (Dist. Saran) and Taradih in Bihar and Narhan in U.P. demonstrate relatively better know how of metallurgy (Singh, et.al. 2001; Tripathi 2001, Fig. 24). These analyses confirm fairly good knowledge of carburzation including use of lamination technique (see Tripathi 20001, 11, 11a, Figs. 25 A, B).

The metallographs belonging to the NBPW phase of Narhan (Tripathi 2001, PL.X.C, Figs. 24C, and D) are typical of this period. A spearhead has 0.3% carbon as pearlite in the matrix of X grains alternating with coarser ferrite grains has been detected. Forging is indicated in elongated grains. Sample 24 D from the same site is badly corroded with equi-axed grains, a small amount of pearlite but no case hardening. The sample from Taradih (Tripathi 2001, Figs. 24A, and B) has 0.7% carbon and X grains of size 8-9. The surface indicates some decarburization at extreme outer edges where the grains were ragged and considerably larger. A sample from Chirand, from NBP phase was taken from a knife (Tripathi 2001, Fig. 25 C.D) and a scraper. Samples are highly mineralized but relic carbide could be located. Hot forging is indicated. Lamination technique was also in practice at this time (Sringverpur, Fig. 23 A). The results of analysis at Senuwar and other sites in the region like at Narhan, Chirand and Taradih indicate knowledge of such technique (Tripathi, 2008:pp. 83-88).

The use of titaniferous ores with apatite complex is also found in Singhbhum (Jharkhand) and Mayurbhanj (Orissa). Forging and repeated hammering and heating imparted some carbon to the objects. Whether carbon was accidental in the matrix of iron is uncertain as two samples pertaining to the same period from Prakash show distinct structures.

II.3. Late Iron, the Age of Culmination

At stage III, starting from the opening centuries of Common Era, there is not only a proliferation in tool types (figs. 3 B, C and table 2), but iron metallurgy attains greater heights. Techniques like lamination and quenching become common as it is evidenced in several artefacts. Taxila has yielded rich iron tool repertoire, including some armour grade weapons of high carbon steel. Hadfield (1913-14 had analysed some Taxila iron objects. he noticed that in composition these compare closely with iron produced by ethnic smelters of India who were actively engaged in iron production at that time. Sisupalgarh in Orissa (datable to 2th -6th C.E, Lal. 1949: 95, Fig. 10.32) yielded a caltrop, a weapon to be used in the battlefield to curb speed of elephants. Some iron samples of this period have been analysed. Hari Narain at NRLC, Lucknow analysed five objects from Sringverpur (Hari Narain et.al., 1998, Figs. 23 A). It has been observed that different techniques were applied on separate categories of objects, for example, a spoon had a lower hardness than that of an axe. The carbon content varied from 0.1% to 0.6%. There was also evidence of rapid cooling and Widmanstaatten structure with ferrite and pearlite. Edges were found to be carburized further, giving them greater hardness and strength. This high carbon zone is restricted to deeper areas and had low slag inclusion too. Most of Sringverpur objects belong to

Sunga-Kusana level may be categorised as mild steel having clear evidence of cementite in the matrix of iron. Lamination technique was employed especially on sharp edged artefacts like knife blades and axes. It is well attested that the ancient Indian smiths at this stage had a thorough knowledge of carbon alloying, case hardening and tempering. However, these techniques seem to have been used judiciously wherever necessary. For instance, a nail differs in composition from a knife or a dagger. This shows a selective use of carburization or quenching. These technical skills must have been acquired over a long period before the craftsmen could have ventured to take up challenging jobs of manufacturing a 7 ton iron pillar with a high corrosion resistant property. That must have required skill of high order. The Delhi Iron Pillar dated to 4th – 5th century C.E. is a unique example of such a metallurgical skill. Scholars have expressed differing view on the technique of its production, corrosion resistance and many other technical aspects of this iron pillar. A number of hypotheses have been put forward and many corrosion studies have been carried out on Delhi Iron Pillar (Bardget 1963; Ghosh, 1963; Lahiri, 1963; for details see Balasubramaniam, 2001, 2008). The Iron Pillar is an excellent quality wrought iron product about 7375 mm in diameter at the bottom and 304 mm at the top. It is estimated to weigh more than 6096 kg. It was built by seamlessly forge-welding large pieces of high purity (99%) wrought iron. The quality of iron is such that even after standing in the open for more than two thousand years it still maintains its anticorrosive property.

The study of objects of shows that by this stage ironsmiths had attained mastery over cementing and forge-welding small rods of iron and strongly forging them to shape such large objects. It also indicates that the ancient craftsman had mastered the operation and technique of control over temperature in furnaces to produce iron of uniform composition on such a large scale. For example, for the manufacture of the Delhi Iron pillar at least 7000 Kg of iron must have been used, and as per published records the largest iron-making furnace on Nagpur a pre-industrial iron working furnace dated to 17th century) could produce about 40 Kg of iron, per heat. Thus, at least 200 furnaces would have operated simultaneously or the same furnace would have to be used repeatedly to produce iron of such uniform property consistently. The iron produced from each heat was hot forged to squeeze out the slag and then shaped into rods of 15 to 20 mm cross-section. In the absence of any documentation of the type of forging anvil, hammer and the hot metal handling tools used in the manufacture of such large objects, one can only offer conjectures to reconstruct the details of the manufacturing technique (Prakash and Tripathi 1986). This exhibits expertise in construction of such colossal structures that has drawn attention of modern metallurgists. Suffice it to say here, on the basis of the above survey that the ancient Indian iron workers had acquired a thorough knowledge of the importance of carbon alloying and also of hardening and tempering by 3rd-4th C.E. These technical skills must have been acquired over a long period before the craftsmen could have ventured to take up such a challenging job of so efficiently putting together a victory pillar weighing several tons. Thus we find a consistent improvement in iron metallurgy over the centuries. The simple wrought iron was replaced by high carbon steel by Late Iron age. In southern India, a special metallurgical skill was developed which comes to be known as wootz steel after the Telugu word *Ukku* for steel. This was produced in crucibles. It produced beautiful watering pattern on steel. Exquisite looking swords and daggers were being fashioned with crucible steel and sold into the world market by Arab traders during the early medieval-medieval period as Damascus steel in the world marke at high profit. Researches are still going on production of wootz steel all over the world.

With this brief survey on iron and steel production in India we are now faced with the question: in what way does the metallurgical advancement reflect itself in the material culture, if at all? To look into this, we need to take a quick look at the Iron Age Cultures with a view to underline the salient features of cultures which reflect growth and the pattern of utilization of iron objects at respective cultural stages. Some of the parameters selected here for comparative assessment are settlements system, especially structural activity, economic development reflected in agriculture and trade, art and craft production, area of cultural interaction, social organization etc. as seen in archaeological remains at respective periods.

III. Pattern of Adaptation and culture change

III.1 Stage I- the Age of Commencement

Early Iron settlements are of a simple nature with moderate sized habitations. The house plans are rarely available but for traces of post-holes and plastered reads which indicate the common use of thatched wattle and daub structures. Mud-brick houses must have also been in use. At sites like Kausambi (Sharma 1960) and Hasinapura (Lal 1954-55) sun dried mud bricks were traced during excavations. Towards the end to this period, roads have been located; at Rajghat, kaccha (mud rammed) street from early NBPW period is reported. But it is more as an exception; a few baked bricks have also been noticed (Narain and Roy 1976). Protective bunds and embankments or moats have been found at Atranjikhera, Jakhera, Kausambi, Sonkh and Eran. It suggests an organized socio-political system coming into the picture by 9th-8th century BCE. The megalithic burials, however, show massive stone slabs hewn into diverse shapes. We may surmise application of good quality iron implements in their manufacturing, a fact which is substantiated by iron tool repertoire of the megalithic culture (Fig.4; 5.A)

2. Economy

Hunting and agricultural activity and animal husbandry were the props of economy at this stage. Atranjikhera has shown the use of wheat and barley along with rice. Lack of agricultural implements suggests a low priority and resultant low yield of agricultural produce. It must have been substituted by hunting and animal husbandry; the domesticated animals include cow, buffalo, goat, sheep, pig and dog (the remains of the last reported from Atranjikhera). Cattle must have been of great significance to these people as among the animal figurines bulls are the most common type. The common occurrence of bull figurines both in red and grey colour may also be suggestive of some kind of ritualistic importance of the animal, perhaps due to its indispensability to the economy. The toy carts which are found in excavations point to use of bull as draft animal. In the near absence of iron ploughshare (Jakhera yielded iron ploughshare as an exception). We do not know whether the bulls were used for ploughing fields even if they were wooden ones. The later Vedic texts attest to such plough shares being in vogue. The soils in the region of the habitation were easily pliable with a wooden ploughs. Since the sites under study are situated on river banks, there is every possibility that the above mode of agriculture was being adopted even at the earliest stage of settlement. This fast is further corroborated by occurrence of variety of grains collected in excavations of these levels (Saraswat, 2010).

We do not come across coinage of any kind in the Early Iron Age. Exchange must have been possible by simple barter system. Small weights of chert and jasper have been found at Hastinapur which implies some sort of commerce but what merchandise required such weights is not clear (Ghosh 1973: 10).

Minor antiquities of this stage are beads of terracotta and objects like points, styli, beads and bangles, stone balls, ivory shell and horn objects. Glass is used for the first time at PGW level, beads and bangles are fashioned with glass.

Both copper and iron technology were in practice albeit on a restricted scale. Copper was still used for fashioning objects of offence like arrowheads, spearheads and axe but more commonly for toiletries and ornaments. Iron was used primarily for manufacturing hunting tools like arrowheads and spear-heads found at each and every site enumerated above. Leaf shaped points, socketed tang (Noh) and blades are reported from a few sites suggesting supremacy of war weapons at these sites. Elephant goad was found at Sravasti at early NBP level (Sinha 1967). Agricultural implements are absent except for the stray occurrence of cutting tools like sickle and axe. The ploughshare at Jakhera (Sahi 1994) mentioned earlier is more of an exception that may suggest knowledge of regular ploughing using an iron share instead of the wooden one which was common in the earlier days.

Objects classified as building material like rods, pins, nails, etc. might as well been used in chariots and carts which were the mode of transport as well as part of war machinery of the period as frequently referred to in Vedic literature.

That iron was being smelted locally at most of early Iron Age sites in U.P. is proved by the presence of slag and furnaces and forges at sites like Jakhera, Atrajikhera, Noh, Jodhpura (both the latter in Rajasthan close to the U.P. Rajasthan border) and belong to PGW culture. The context is BRW-BSW and Grey Ware pertaining to the first quarter of the second millennium BCE. In the Vindhyan foothills (in southern UP) excavations were conducted at Malhar, Raja Nal Ka Tila, Musa Khand etc. (Tewari, et.al. 1999-2000) on River Karamnasa and Raipura (Tripathi and Upadhyay 2013; Tripathi, 2014). Extensive iron smelting was evidenced at these sites in the Vindhya-Kaimur region. Comparatively richer sites are located at frequent and regular intervals in the Ganga valley, at least from NBP level onwards.

The cultures of Vindhya-Ganga Plain having a hoary antiquity going back to Stone Age cultures were abode of man from Pre-historic period. However, the present discussion is limited only to iron yielding cultures of the region - both in the alluvial plains and in the adjacent hilly zone that is rich in mineral deposits. A Chalcolithic culture marked by Black and Red Ware, Black-Slipped Ware, Red Ware both of plain and painted varieties precedes iron yielding phase in the region. In the Upper Ganga Plain the Black Wares are generally plain, except for the PGW which is the deluxe ware of the period. In the mid Ganga plain we come across a different type of BRW pottery having linear paintings like stokes, bands etc. mostly on the inner surface of the pots. During the succeeding period, a new pottery culture characterized by Northern Black Polished Ware (NBPW) takes over the entire plain extending over thousands of kilometres.

III.2 Stage II: Middle Iron Age, the Age of Florescence

The entire Gangetic Plains and the areas around this come to be occupied by a ceramic culture known as Northern Black Polished Ware (NBPW). This has a distribution extending from Texila and Charsadda in Pakistan in the North to Brahmagiri and Ter in south. It has been found even at Anuradhpur in Sri Lanka. It has been found from Prabhas Patan in Saurastra, in the west to Mahasthan in Bangladesh, in the east. Culturally NBP overlaps with the upper phase of PGW on the one hand and the Sunga period on the other. In peninsular India it overlaps with the Megalithic culture. This was generally, dated between 7/600to 200BC, earlier. But in recent years radiometric dates have pushed back the antiquity of this culture further down to 1000 BC if not earlier (from a good number of sites there are ^{14}C dates ranging between to 1200-900 BC).

The habitations were still mostly close to river banks, though some NBP settlements did start to show up on lakes and tanks. NBP sites have also been found outside the river plains, closer to raw material locations in Madhya Pradesh and Deccan. Not only many new settlements were occupied during this period, comparatively larger area came under occupation during the NBP period. This suggests a growth in population, an intensification of building activity and a comparative sophistication of settlement system (Fig.7). Although at the early level of NBP culture mud houses or structures of mud-brick are normally found; regular use of backed bricks begins at a relatively later stage of the culture. The earlier technique of fashioning structures with plastered reeds and clay for floors continue to be in practice mud mud-bricks are used along with baked ones. At bigger and more important sites like Hastinapur and Kausambi, remains of larger houses have been unearthed. Kausambi had a double storied house measuring 28' x 15' and 16 steps, while in Hastinapur, a long wall has been traced. Lined and unlined drainage system and ring wells have been introduced. Protective embankments and bunds were constructed encircling the settlements. At those sites where they were already in existence earlier, such as at Atranjikhera and Kausambi, they were further reinforced and enlarged. Rajghat excavations also revealed a road made by ramming potsherds gravel and mud clods which had a thickness of 33.1 cm. (Roy 1983: 138, at the late NBP level). Pataliputra yields a pillared hall with colossal stone pillars, fortification, and drains etc. at the relatively later phase of this period. The Asokan pillars with glossy finish and elegant capital-heads also belong to this period (300 BCE) use of excellent quality iron implements in carving these sculptural pieces is inevitable and of significant to the present discussion. In a nutshell the urbanization of the Ganga Plain takes place during the NBPW culture.

2. Economy

We get evidence of double crop arrangement. Pulses like back gram appear for the first time in this period as attested by excavations like Narhan (Singh 1994) brought forth kodo millet, black gram, green gram, peas, khesari, sesame, goose berry and *anwala*. Agricultural activity intensifies as attested by number of granaries (Atranjikhera) and large sized storage jars. Rajghat has yielded evidence of animal husbandry of both varieties – draught and milch animals.

The sophistication in pyrotechnology reached a high standard – the ceramic art specially evolved in the form of NBP Ware with its typical surface treatment. We have unearthed kilns for brick and tile making at sites like Anai (District Varanasi, Tripathi and Upadhyay 2013) and Khairadih (District Ballia), (Tipathi`1994), respectively. The latter shows a double chamber perhaps used for variety of purposes like producing grey/black pottery under reducing condition in the same kiln (Figs. 9, 9 – Brick kilk and potterykiln, respectively). Terracotta figures of a large variety and beautiful subject treatment again hint at a specialist class involved in their manufacture. Glass objects are used more freely now though terracotta beads continue to be in use. The art of figurine making has also improved a lot with a richer variety and a larger number.

Beads of semi-precious stones occur in large quantities. At Atranjikhera, twelve beads were reported in the previous period (Stage I) and forty-three in the next stage. The occurrence of topaz and crystal beads suggests long distance trade. A bead making workshop was discovered at Agiabir, near Varanasi. Ivory working shows sophistication, a beautiful dice with finely marked dots for numbers indicate use of fine implements in its fashioning.

Copper was continued to be used for hunting tools even though in small numbers. Copper arrowheads and axe have been found at sites like Hastinapur. Other copper objects used during this period are: hooks, chisels, borers, and antimony rods. Toiletries like nails, pliers, ornaments, pins, pendants, bangles, rings, and rarely ear ornaments show up. The number of copper objects is quite small and hints at the scarcity of use of metal either because of non-availability of ore in the vicinity or due to a high cost and low demand. Coins as noted above appear for the first time at this stage. Both punch marked and un-inscribed cast coins were in use. Silver and copper coins are reported from its later phases. Sealing also appears for the first time during this period.

Weaponry during iron stage II undergoes a comparative improvisation, in addition to the earlier arrowheads and spearheads, double or single tang, javelins, spears, lances, dagger blades, elephant goad, etc. are in the use. Iron chisels have been reported form almost every site indicating thereby a proficiency in carpentry and masonry. Iron objects are more profuse and of better quality at this stage. The building material also appears in a greater variety. Objects like door hooks, chains, clamps, a large number of nails, sockets, ring fasteners etc. are frequently found.

The culture of this period is thus associated with several innovations besides the beautiful sophisticated NBPW, a pottery industry that has been designated the deluxe ware of the period. Iron technology attained greater heights during this period. Both, the metallurgy as well as ceramic technology of this period shows mastery of skill. The culmination of pyrotechnology is closely interlinked demanding a total control and manipulation of temperature in a closed atmosphere of the kiln-furnace. It may not be too far-fetched to suggest that the metal and ceramic technologies derived from each other.

The urbanization of the Ganga Plain was knocking on the door during this period. It was at this stage that features like coinage, writing, fortification, baked brick structures appear for the first time. By the mid-phase of NBPW culture we come across evidence of sanitary arrangements using ring wells and pukka drains (Agiabir shows use of wedge shaped bricks and pottery drain attached with it as a sanitary arrangement, Fig10). It is during this period that a political system consolidated itself in India. The rise of Mahajanpadas coincides with this cultural stage. The fall of Nandas and rise of the Mauryan dynasty synchronizes with this period. Needless to state that political organization played a role in shaping the socio-cultural life of people but the role of technology in the economic affluence cannot be under played either. Rise of Buddhism and Jainism must have played a key role in bringing about changes not only in religio-spiritual life but also in setting fresh

norms in conducting life. This period, in brief is thus a witness to multi-dimensional growth and the beginning of historical age in India.

III.3. Stage III: Late Iron Age BC 2/100 to 5/600 C.E., the Age of Culmination

Iron was commonly used by this stage and in every walk of life. The technological levels had attained a higher standard now. The typology proliferation is noticeable as perceptible in iron tool types from Taxila and Khairadih (Figs.6. A, B).

The settlement pattern shows the emergence of full-fledged towns, for example Taxila, Kausambi, Hastinapura, Sonkh, Mathura, Rajghat, Khairadih, Atranjikhera, etc. Building activity attains a boost at most of the sites, many of them must have been capitals of Mahajanapadas and later, or imperial powers. The Buddhist pilgrim centres with exquisitely carved stupas and monastic settlements across the subcontinent bear testimony not only to the spiritual wealth but also to material prosperity and artistic acumen. The stone sculptures of exquisite beauty found at these sites amply testify this. Especially noteworthy are Gandhara, Mathura and Sarnath centres of art. Towards the later part of this period temple architecture starts evolving. The masonry and intricate stone carving indicates mastery in sculpting and carving but that could be possible only with the availability of fine quality iron tools and implements.

Potters' art at this level tends towards standardization. Moulded terracotta statues are fashioned beautifully. Luxury goods like beads of semi-precious stones are found in large number. Rajghat was the centre of manufacture of such beads where unfinished beads have been found. Glass objects in different colours were fashioned. Gold and ivory were also in use. Inscribed coins of local rulers have been found. Copper utensils, toiletries and ornaments are more common. The beautiful copper chariot with spoked wheels coming come from the Sunga-Kusana period from Khairadih is an example of metal art of this period (Fig. 11).

2. Economy

A large number and variety of agricultural implements indicate the shift of emphasis on technology-exploitation. Spade, ploughshare, hoe, etc., are commonly found at most of the sites mentioned earlier The crops must have been the same as today as the Ganga valley is not supposed to have had any major climatic changes since then. But production must have grown with application of better technology necessary to meet the demand of the specialist class which was growing in number. The wootz steel which was being produced mostly in southern part of the country had drawn attention of the world with its beautiful watering pattern on the surface of steel. There grew a great demand for it in the world market. Indian steel became a valuable commodity. It created a niche for itself in the world market.

Thus there appears to be an upward movement in the economy as perceived in the archaeological data discussed earlier. At this juncture we are faced with the issue of an interconnection between growth of technology and economic development. The factors of change need to be brought to the fore to resolve the issue at hand.

The technique developed further to the highest degree of sophistication under the state patronage of the mighty Guptas. This period has been designated by historians as the Golden period of Indian history. After the decline of the Mauryan Empire, the Sunga-Kusana rulers assumed power in most of the Northern India, and parts of Deccan. It was an era vibrant with life and activities marked with India diplomatic and cultural relations with outside world. Greco-Roman trade with India was at its peak. There was an exchange of scholars with neighbouring countries who seriously deliberated on spiritual and scientific issues. Literary works of high standard were being composed. Indian mathematics and science was attracting world attention. Suffice it to state here that this was an era of overall growth and prosperity. It is during this period (5th century C.E.) that the 7 ton iron pillar at Mehrauli now standing in the Qutab complex was manufactured. Much has been written about its metallurgical aspects (Balasubraniam 2002; 2008) to give further details about techno-economic aspect of the age here.

IV. Discussion

A gradual Technological Development and Slow adaptation of Iron

At the end, we must examine the oft repeated question about the efficacy of iron technology as an agent of change. The questions that we are confronted with are: Did iron really play a role in socio-cultural upsurgence? Whether iron was indeed a superior metal capable of bringing about economic change? If so, why was the adaptation of iron so slow? Was there ascarcity of raw material for exploitation? There is sufficient evidence of availability of ore and local production of iron around the Ganga plain where the future urban centres were to develop. Why did the metal workers take so long to take up the challenge of higher production? The evidence suggest that the iron workers struggled with production of iron for too long. Only tiny non-descript objects that too in small numbers could be fashioned at first (such as at Noh). Excavations at Hastinapur yielded only 4 objects. Rajghat is reported to have yielded pieces of slag at the upper level of period I.A. Kausambi yielded a couple of objects at Period I with BRW. However, at Malhar, nails, sickle (?) knife, bangle, bracelet, chisel and 'khurpi' are reported from the lower levels (Tewari, et.al. 1999-2000). In the next level more evolved tools and implements like ploughshare, sickle, clamp, awl, spearhead, arrowhead, flat bar, sword etc. have been found. In comparison with the number of iron objects only six copper objects have been reported. Copper is rather rare at sites in the Vindhya-Kaimur area. At Raipura in District Sonbhadra, no copper was found at the earliest level which possesses an otherwise Chalcolithic character. (Tripathi and Upadhyay, 2013 and Tripathi 2014). It may be noted that this region is rich in iron ore while copper ore is found only in small pockets at a few places. We have come cross iron smelting furnaces and forges along with iron objects in Period II at Pre-NBPW period at Raipura. Iron ingot belonging to NBPW period is a noteworthy finding reiterating that the site was an iron production centre. But these production sites give the impression of impoverished villages inhabited by artisan class who manufactured and supplied their ware to the nearby emerging settlements in the alluvial plain.

This area of Vindhya-Kaimur hilly belt had a congenial environment for iron working. There are rich iron ore deposits. Nodules of iron are found scattered all around. This may be handpicked even without regular mining of the deposits. The forests provide charcoal which was the main source of energy of iron smelting. The river Karamnasa, a tributary of Ganga flows nearby. This could not only sustain the cultures on its bank but also provide a passage for communication to the sites located in the Ganga Plain. In spite of these facts when we look at the pattern of use of iron in the plains, the number and types of tools are almost scantly at the pattern of use of iron in the plains, the number and types of tools are almost scantly at the early level. The answer to this anomalous situation perhaps lies with iron metallurgy itself.

As noted earlier, it took a long time to perfect the metallurgy of iron to produce good quality tools and implements superior to copper- bronze that was used prior to advent of iron. But the cultures of the Ganga Plain suffer from scarcity of copper-bronze. Real utilization of metal in this region begins with iron only. The metallurgy had to attain a status of efficiency to produce cheaper and affordable objects that too in sufficient quantity to be socially adaptable and effective. But the difficulty, as commented by Taylor and Shell (op. cit.), 'lay in developing the new techniques necessary to hot forge the bloom...'

Bloomery iron production prevalent in most of the early world civilizations, including India is a labour intensive metallurgical process. The production is also uncertain unless the technique has been fully mastered. Our own experimental work to review iron production with a group of Agarias who have abandoned smelting several decades back resulted into zero yield after hours of attempt to smelt iron. During an experimental smelting by the Agarias who had abandoned iron working a generation back and having only a memory of the smelting process, we discovered that at the end of 5 hours of hard work of pumping the foot bellows virtually nothing came out of the charge. It took them several attempts of produce a small bloom of about 2kg. of refined iron. On analysis, it proved to be steely iron but showed slag inclusion. It this can happen to those iron worker claim to have observed iron working of their fore elders we can visualize the situation that must have existed in the antiquity by the first timers having no prior experience trying to produce a new metal. It confirms the uncertain nature of iron production at the early stages of its emergence. The early metal workers naturally had no experience of the metallurgical

technique or behaviour of the material in course of smelting-forging at all? In view of such uncertainty of iron production coupled with the low quality of the newly produced wrought iron, it should not at all surprise us that the adoption of iron by early communities was slow. In such case, the impact of iron on economy is bound to be minimal. It took several centuries of experiment and experience for the artisans followed by acquainting people with the newly discovered metal and its efficiency. It is only at such a stage that iron was adopted by first millennium BCE society that too slowly and staggeringly. There might have been long gaps between supply and demand for obvious reasons as discussed above. Economic prosperity is proportionately dependent on technology in-put. To be effective the technological out-put had to achieve a higher level and rise up to expectation and demand of society. The society itself had to be in a state of readiness to adopt the new inventions and adapt to innovations taking place.

Table 1 : Distribution of Iron objects (Stage 1) from PGW at Atrankikhera

Sl. No.	Objects	Lower	Middle	Upper	Total
1.	Arrow-head	-	7	14	21
2.	Spear-head	-	3	5	8
3.	shaft	2	5	3	10
4.	Tongs	-	-	1	1
5.	Clamp	-	10	11	21
6.	Nail	2	4	14	20
7.	Bar/Rod	-	2	5	7
8.	Hook	-	2	5	7
9.	Borer	1	2	3	6
10.	Chisel	-	4	2	6
11.	Needle	-	-	1	1
12.	Axe	-	-	1	1
13.	Knife	-	1	2	3
14.	Bangle	-	1	1	2
15.	Indeterminate	2	3	9	14
	Grand Total	7	**44+ 2 lumps=46**	**77+4 lumps=81**	**128/135**

Table 2 : Relative Position of Iron Objects at Different Cultural Periods

TOOL TYPE	NAME OF TOOL	EARLY STAGE	MIDDILE STAGE	LATE STAGE
Hunting Tool	Spear heads	*	*	*
	Arrow heads	*	*	*
	Points	*	o	o
	Socketed tangs	*	o	o
	Blades	*	*	o
	Spear lances	o	*	o
	Dagger	o	*	*
	Sword	o	*	*
	Elephant goad	o	*	*
	Lances	×	×	*
	Armour	×	×	*
	Helmet	×	×	*
	Horse bits	×	×	*
	Caltrop	o	o	*
Agricultural Tools	Axes	*	*	*
	Sickles	*	*	*
	Spade	×	*	o
	Ploughshare	×	*	o
	Hoe	×	*	*
	Pick	o	o	*

Household objects	Knives	*	*	*
	Tongs	*	o	o
	Discs	×	*	o
	Rings	×	*	o
	Spoons	×	*	*
	Sieve	×	×	*
	Cauldron	×	×	*
	Bowls	×	×	*
	Dishes	×	×	*
Structural and craft tools	Rods	*	o	o
	Pins	*	o	o
	Nails	*	*	*
	Clamps	*	*	*
	Chisel	×	*	*
	Pipes	×	*	o
	Sockets	×	*	o
	Plump bob	×	*	o
	Chains	×	*	*
	Door hooks	×	*	*
	Door handle	×	×	*
	Hinges	×	×	*
	Spikes	×	×	*
	Tweezers	×	×	*
	Anvils	×	×	*
	Hammers	×	×	*
	Scissors	×	×	*
	Saw	×	×	*

* Definite existence o Confirmed data not available × Non-existence

References

1. Balasubramaniam R. 2002 *'Delhi Iron Pillar – New Insights.* Shimla: Indian institute of Advanced Studies and New Delhi : Aryan Books International.
2. Balasubramaniam R. 2008 *Marvels of Indian Iron Through the Ages*, Infinity Foundation Series, New Delhi Rupa & Co.
3. Bardget, W.E. & J.F. Stanner, 1963, 'The Delhi iron Pillar: A Study of the Corrosion Aspects', Journal of Iron and Steel Institute, p. 201.
4. Bhardwaj, H.C. 1979 *'Aspects of Indian Technology'* Varanasi & New Delhi, Motilal Banarasidass,
5. De, S. & P.K. Chattopadhaya 1989 'Iron Objects from Pandurajar Dhibi: Archaeometallurgical Studies', *Steel India*; a Biannual Technical Journal for the Iron and Steel Industry, Vol. 2 No., pp. 33-41.
6. Deshpande, P.P, R.K.Mohanti and V.S. Shinde. 2010, Metallographical Study of a Chisel Found at Mahurjhari, Vidarbha, Maharashtra. *Current Science*, 99 (5): 636-6-39
7. Dutta, A. 1992 'Early Stages of Iron Technology and Development of Regional Pattern in India' in *Man and his Culture*: A Resurgence. Peter Bellwood (ed.) New Delhi, Books and Books. 293-308
8. Gaur, R.C. 1983 Excavations at Atranjikhera. Delhi, Motilal Banarasidass
9. Ghosh, A. 1973 The City in Early Historical India, Indian Institute of Advanced Study, Shimla.
10. Ghosh M.K. 1963 'The Delhi Iron Pillar and Its Iron,' *National Mineral Lab. Technical Journal,* No.5 (1), pp.31 – 45.
11. Ghosh, N.C. & P.K. Chattopathyay. 1978 'The Archaeological Background and an Iron Sample from Hatigra,' *Puratattva* No. 18: 21 – 27.
12. Gurney, G.R. 1961 *The Hittites*, Pelican Books. (First Published 1952).
13. Hadfield, R. 1913-14 Archaological Survey Annual Report -1913-14, in *Taxila*, Sir John Marshall Delhi, Motilal Banarasidass (Reprint 1975): 534-535
14. Hari Narain, Jai Prakash, O.P. Agrawal and M.V. Nair, 1998, 'Metallographic Studies of Iron Artifiacts of Domestic Use, Tools and Weapons from Sringverpur (250 B.C. – 100 A.D., Uttar Pradesh,' *Archaeometallurgy in India*, Vibha Tripathi (ed.), pp. 44 – 53.

15. Lahiri, A.K. 1963 'Some Observations on Corrosion Resistance of Ancient Delhi iron Pillar and Present time Adivasi Iron Made by Primitive Method, '*National Mineral lab. Technical Journal*, No.3 (1), pp. 46 – 54.
16. Lal, B.B. 1954-55 Excavations at Hastinapur and Other Explorations in Ganga-Satluj Basin(1950-52) *Ancient India* no. 10-11 Delhi, Archaeological Survey of India.
17. Lal, B.B. 1949 Excavations at Sisupalgarh, *Ancient India* No. 5: 62-105
18. Maxwell Hyslop, K.R. 1974, 'Assyrian source of iron: Preliminary Survey of Historical and Geographical Evidence' Iraq 36:139 – 154.
19. Narain, A.K. and T.N. Roy 1976. *Excavations at Rajghat*, Banaras Hindu University, Varanasi
20. Prakash, B. &Tripathi, V. 1986 'Iron Technology in Ancient India, '*Metals News* 12 (1), pp. 568-579
21. Roy, T.N. 1983 *The Ganges Civilization.* Delhi, Ramanand Vidyasagar: 1– 6.
22. Sahi, M.D.N. 1994 *Aspects of Indian Archaeology*, Jaipur Publication Scheme, Jaipur.
23. Saraswat, K.S. 2010 'Agricultural Background of the Early Farming Communities in the Middle Ganga Plain; *Archaeology of the Ganga Basin: Paradigm Shift* (vol.I), (ed.) Vibha Tripathi and P. Upadhyay, Delhi, Sharada Publishing House: 155-193
24. Sharma, G.R. 1960 *Excavations at Kausambi* (1957-59) The Defences and the Shyenachiti of Purushmedha, Allahabad University, Allahabad
25. Singh, P. 1994 *Excavation of Narhan* (1984-89), Varanasi, Banaras Hindu University
26. Singh, R.N. & J.R. Merkel 2001-02. A Study of Iron Objects from Chirand and Taradih, *Pragdhara,* 11 Jl. of U.P. State Archaeology Department: 135-142
27. Sinha, K.K. 1967. *Excavations at Sravasti*-1959. Varanasi, BHU
28. Tewari, R. R.K. Srivastava, K.S. Saraswat, K.K. Singh, 1999-2000, 'Excavation at Malhar, Dist (Chanauli (U.P.): A preliminary Report' *Pragdhara* 10: 69 – 98. Jl. of U.P. State Archaeology Department
29. Tayor, S.J. & C.A. Shell 1988. 'Social and Historical implications of early Chinese Iron Technology, *Proceedings of BUMA II – 1986* R. Maddin (ed.) MIT, USA: 205 – 221.
30. Thapar, B.K. 19665 "Excavations at Prakash – 1995, A Chalcolithic site, *Ancient India* No. 20 – 21. ASI, New Delhi.
31. Tripathi V. and S. K. Singh 1994. 'Excavations at Khairadih 1996-97', Varanasi, *Bharati*, Bulletin of Department of A.I.H.C. Arch. BHU, No. 28 : 1-69
32. Tripathi V. 2001.*The Age of Iron in South Asia: Legacy and Tradition.* Delhi, Aryan Books International
33. Tripathi V. 2008. '*History of Iron Technology in India (From Beginning to Pre – Modern Times*), New Delhi, Rupa & Co. Pp. 83 – 88; 93 – 94.
34. Tipathi V. and P. Upadhyay 2013 A *Rural Site of Ancient Varanasi (Excavations at Anai*) Delhi, Sharada Publishing House
35. Tipathi V. and P. Upadhyay 2013. 'Raipura: An Early Iron Age Site in Vindhya-Kaimur Region', *Puratattva*, No.34, Delhi , Jl. of Indian Archaeological Society:149-157
36. Tripathi V. 2014. 'Recently Discovered Iron Smelting Site in Vindhya-Kaimur Region, India', *Iron and Steel Inst. of Japan, International* Vol.54 (2014) No.5:1010-1016
37. Tylecote, R.F. 1962. *Metallurgy in Archaeology*, London, Edward Arnold: 211.
38. Waldbaum J.C. 1980, 'The First Archaeological Appearance of Iron and the Transition to the Iron Age'. in *Coming of the Age of Iron* (T.A.Wertime7 James D. Muly, New Haven, London, Yale University Press, 69-98.

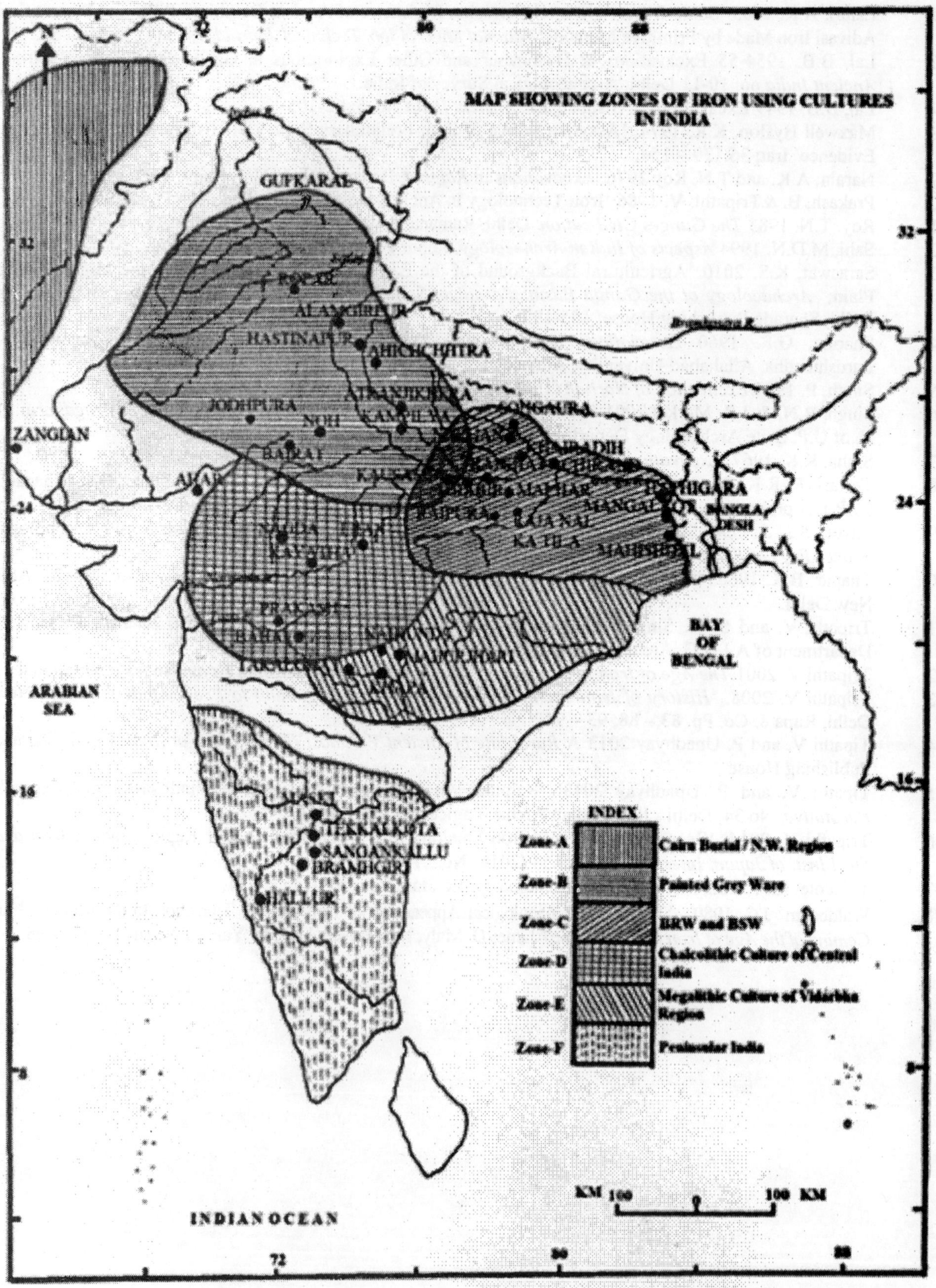

Fig. 1 : Map showing zones of Iron Age Cultures of India

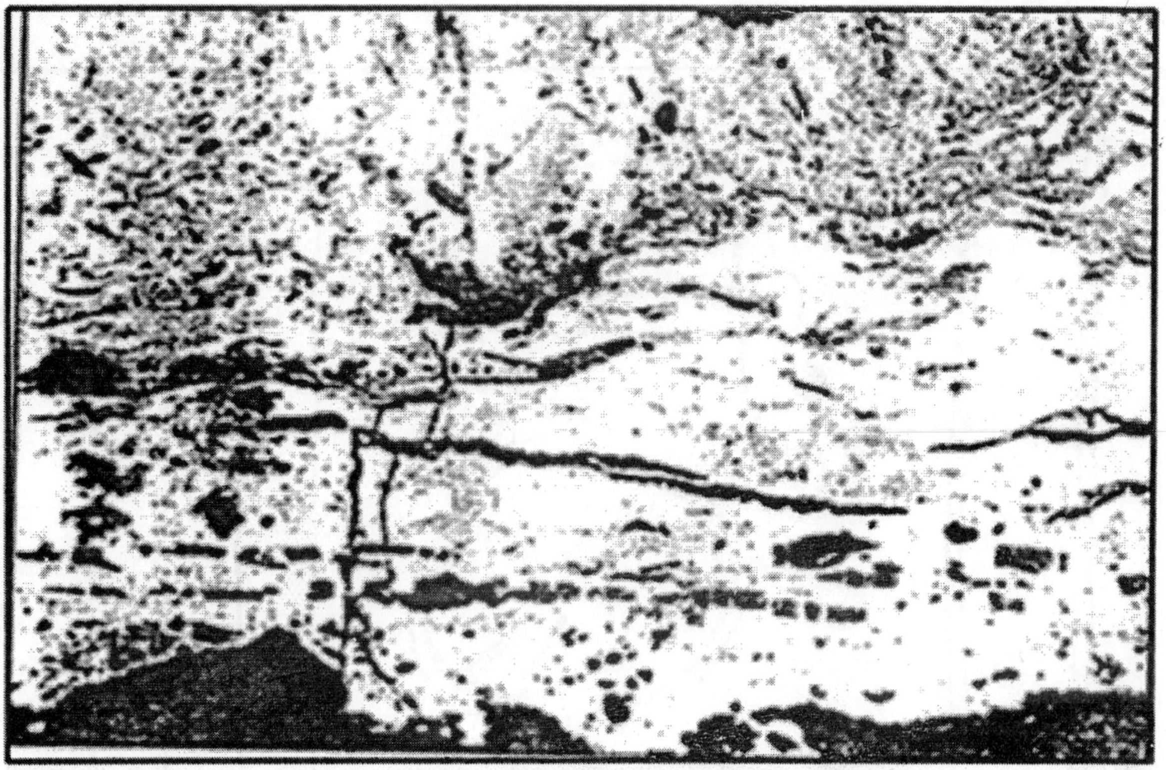

Fig. 2 : Electron micrograph of celt, Tadkanhalli

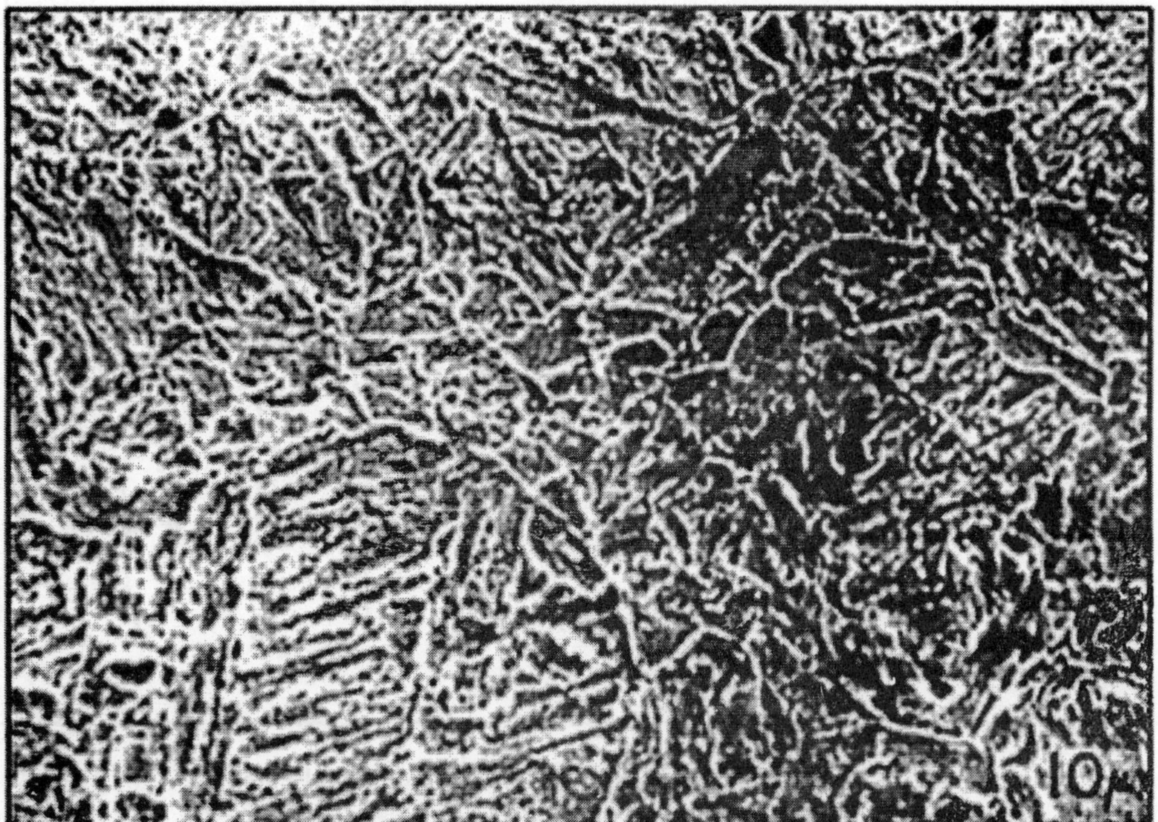

Fig. 3 : Tempered martensitic structure of sickle, Pandurajar Dhibi 1000X 15 KV.

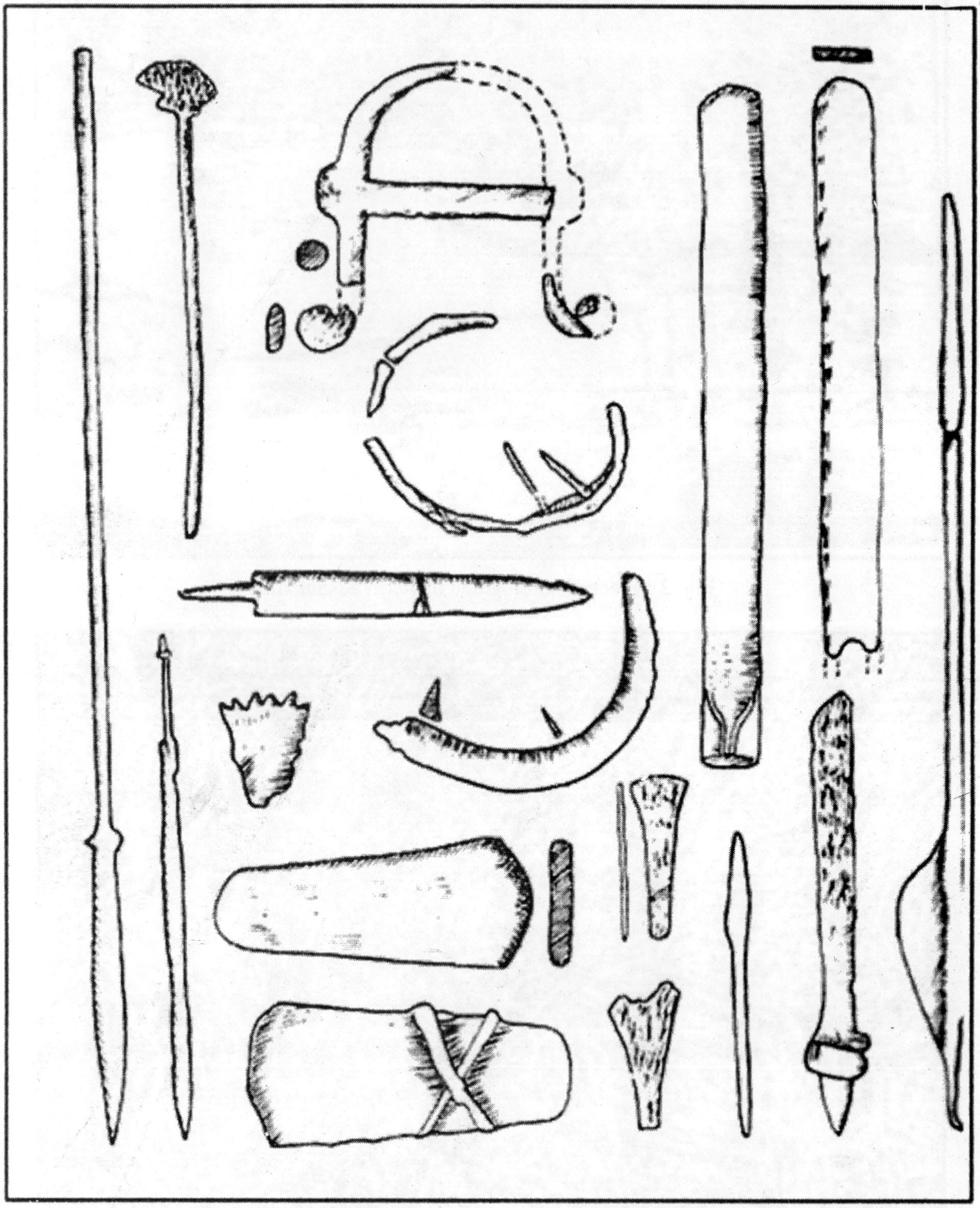

Fig 4 : Iron Objects from Megalithic Burials (Vidarbh Region)

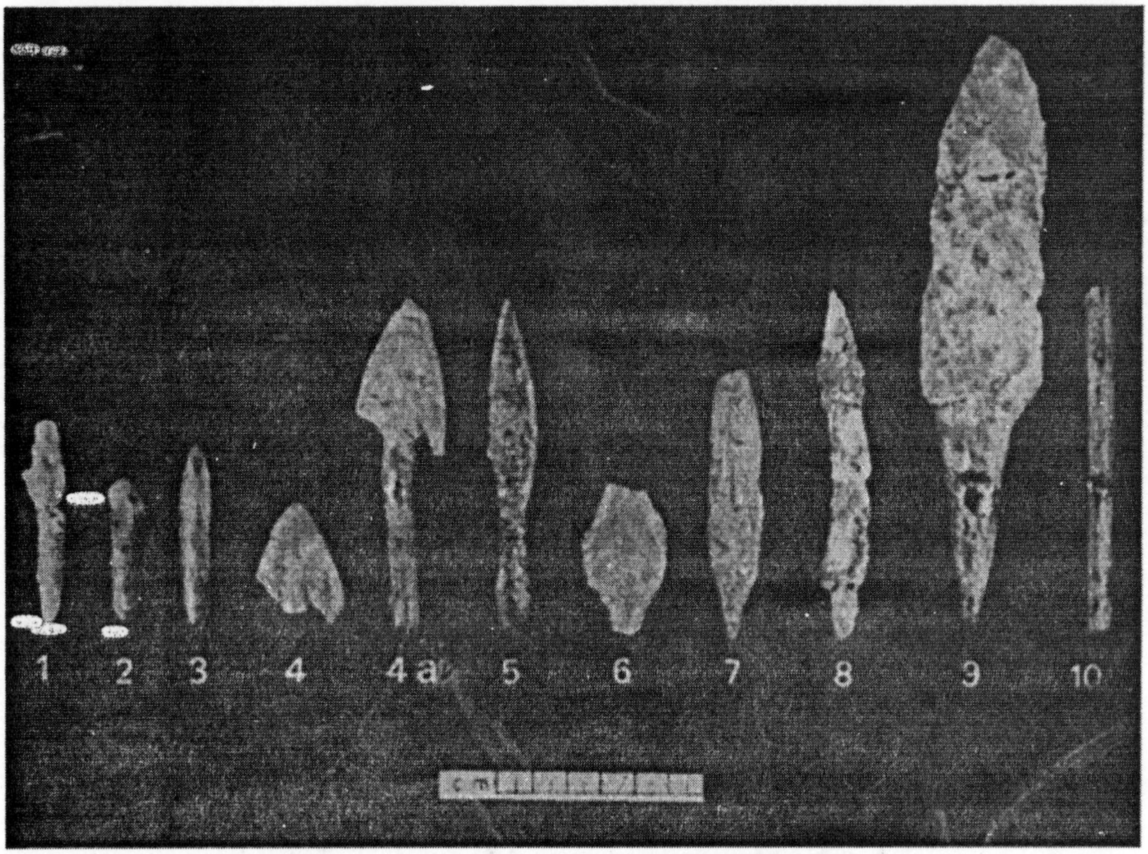

Fig. 5 A : Iron objects PGW (Stage I, Atranjikhera)

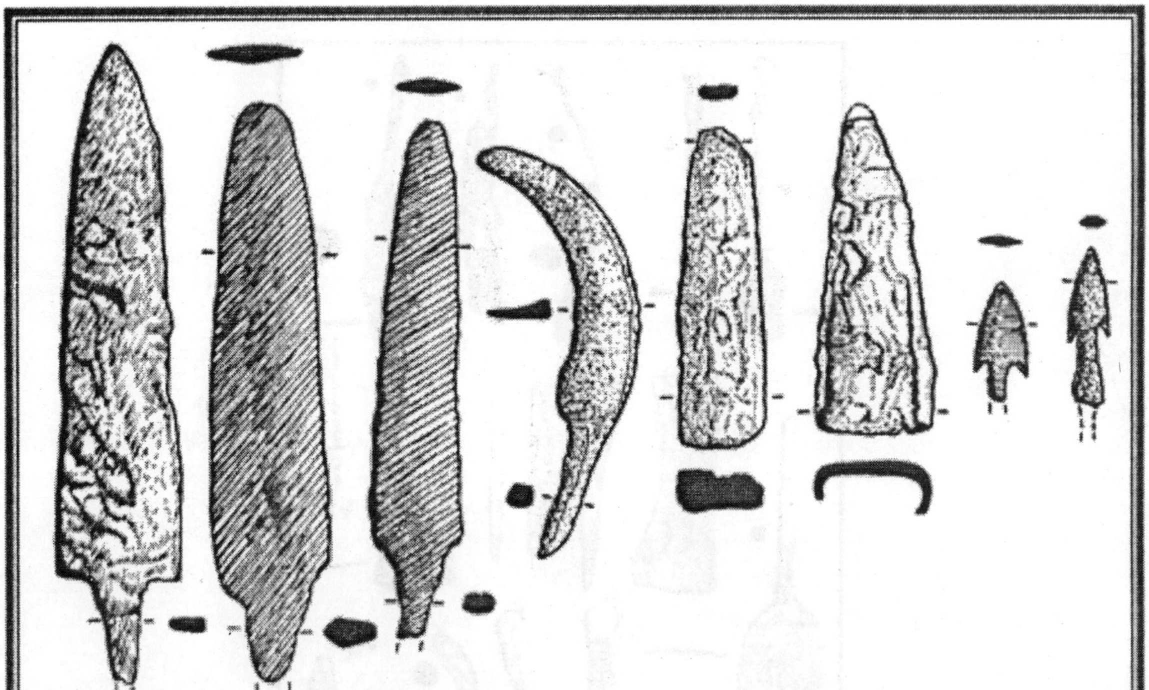

Fig. 5 B : Iron objects NBPW (Stage II, Atranjikhera)

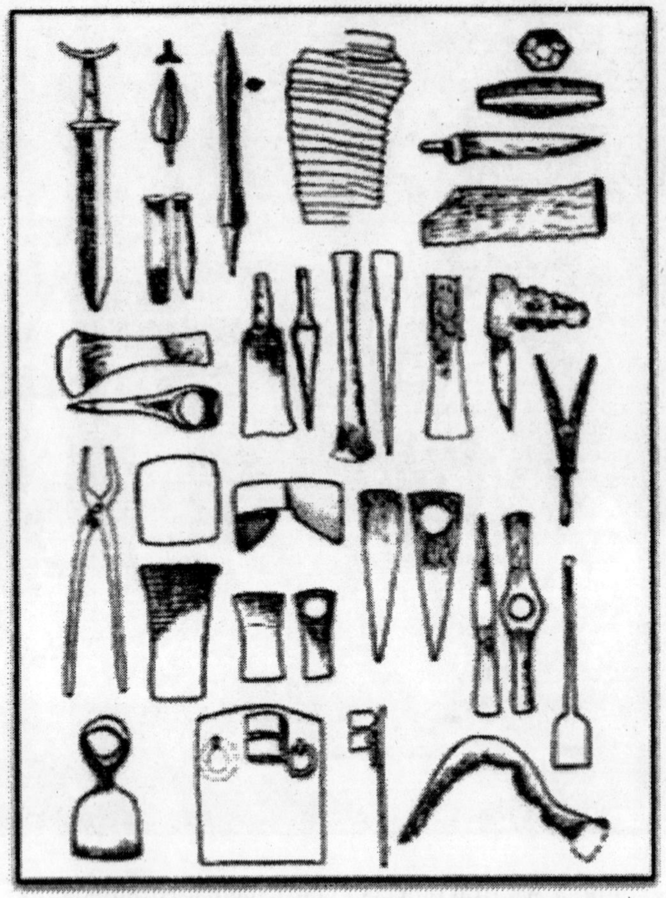

Fig. 6 A : Iron objects (Stage III) Taxila

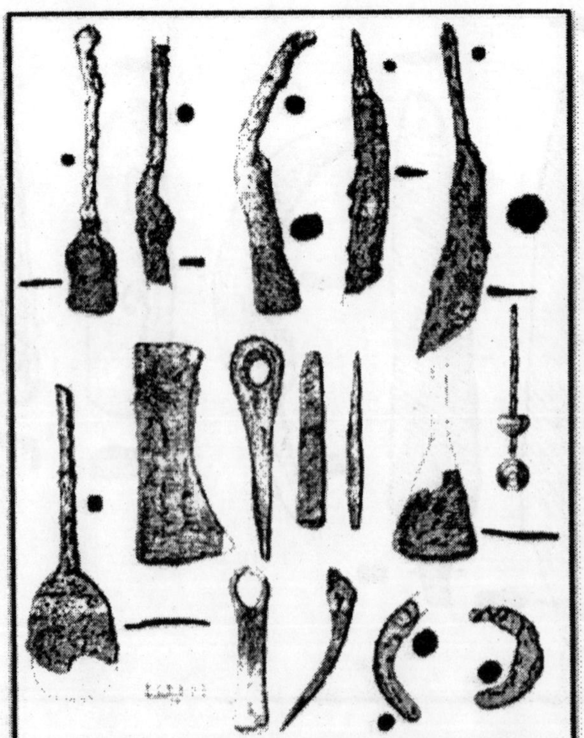

Fig. 6 B : Iron objects (Stage III) (Khairadih, UP)

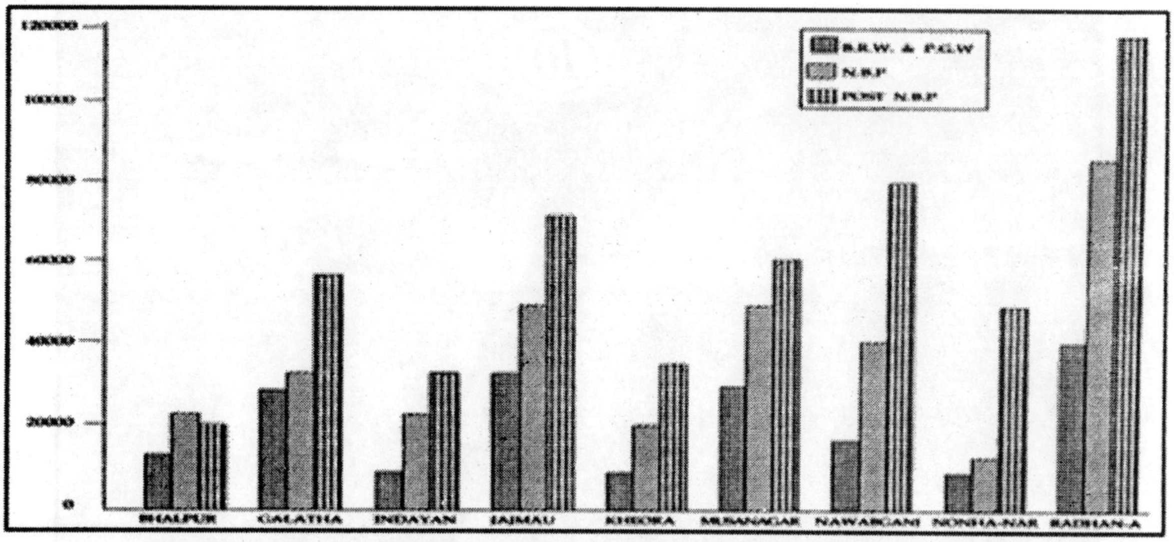

Fig. 7 : Relative Position of Settlement Size at Different Cultural Stages in the Ganga Plain

Fig. 8 : Brick Kiln, Anai (NBPW)

Fig. 9 : Pottery/Tile Kiln, Khairadih (Late NBPW)

Fig. 10 : A Terracotta drain connected with a brick lined drain , Agiabir (NBPW)

Fig. 11 : Copper Chariot with spoked wheel found from Sunga-Kusana level- Khairadih, Ballia.

5

ARCHAEOLOGY OF KAUSAMBI: REVIEW OF A CITY SITE OF THE LOWER GANGA-YAMUNA DOAB[1]

J.N. Pal

The lower Ganga-Yamuna doab is the south eastern part of the Upper Gangetic plain (Singh 1971:51, which having rich alluvial soil of the plain has been centre of attraction for the people right from the hoary past. The archaeological investigations in the districts right from Kanpur in the west to Allahabad in the east in the doab region have revealed a good number of sites from early historical period to the medieval period. The rich availability of natural resources was one of the reasons for this richness of the archaeological sites and also for a densely settled area. The existence of a variety of wild flora-fauna even in 16th-17th centuries has been mentioned by Spate and Learmonth (1967: 94) when 'wild elephants, buffaloes, bison, rhinoceros, lions and tigers were hunted in the Ganga-Yamuna doab.' The distribution of archaeological sites as revealed by explorations in Kanpur and Kanpur Dehat (Lal 1984), Fatehpur (Pal 2006, Bahadur 2012), Kausambi (Gupta 2014) and Allahabad districts (Misra 2000, Erdosy 1988) shows richness of human settlement in the past going back to pre-NBPW period. Among the excavated sites of the area mention may be made of Jajmau, Kausambi, Shringverpura, Jhusi and Hetapatti. Among such excavated sites Kausambi was the first which was put to excavation. Considering significance of archaeological significance, a brief history of archaeology of Kausambi is presented here.

Kausambi (Lat. 25^0 20' 30" N, Long. 81^0 23' 12" E) situated on a meander, on the left bank of the river Yamuna in Manjhanpur sub-division of Kausambi district at a distance of 51.2 km from Allahabad in south-westerly direction has been famous in ancient Indian literature as the capital city of Vats Mahajanapada. The site, is characterized by high mounds of different dimensions and elevations, is so prominent and towering that viewed from a distance it gives the impression of imposing hillocks. Encircled by imposing rampart and a moat on three sides, west, north and east its southern extremity is bounded by the Yamuna (Sharma 1958, 1968). As the present topography shows, it is one of the largest and biggest fortified city-sites of northern India (Fig. 1). The rampart at present has an average height of 9 to 10 metres from the surrounding field-level (Sharma 1969). There are towers or bastions, at regular intervals, those in the north-western and north-eastern corners are as high as 21.33 metres. The fortified city forms a irregular oblong on the plan.

---

1 It is a paper based on one of the most significant archaeological investigations of Prof. G.R. Sharma in north India. Prof. D.N. Tripathi has been fortunate to be one of the bright students of Prof. Sharma.

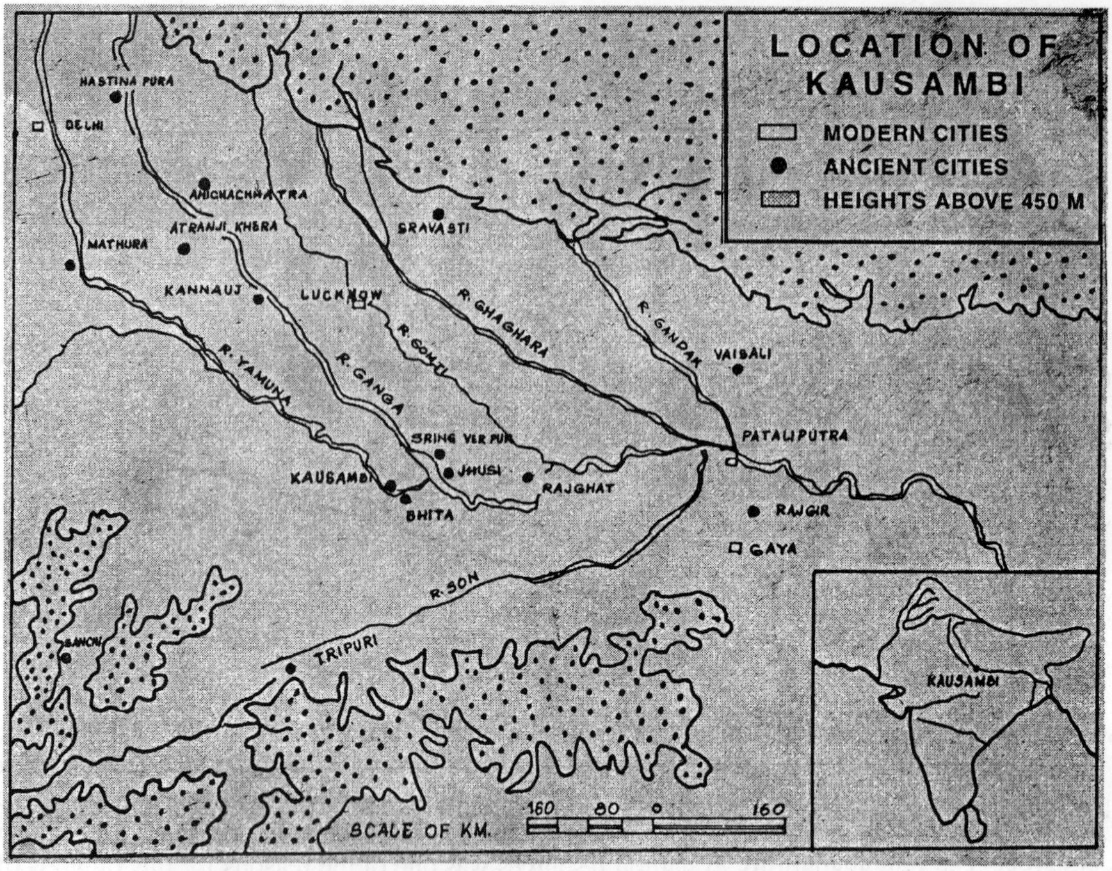

Fig. 1 : Location map of Kausambi

The site is now represented by modern Kosam, Garhwa and other neighbouring villages. Archaeologically it can be termed as a key site of the Gangetic plain, yielding wide range of cultural relics going back at least to the Chalcolithic period. For the last five decades it was a key site for cultural sequence of the central Ganga valley.

The extension of the site (Fig. 2) can well be guessed by the length of fortification, having a peripheral circuit of about 6.45 km. The length of the different faces of the fortress is: north - 1560 metre, south - 1794 metre, east - 1767 metre and west - 1230 metre. The city was fortified with brick revetment and it was provided with five main and six subsidiary gates on the three sides - east, west and north. At places the gates are provided with curtain-walls on the outside, the same being best illustrated on the eastern gate (Sharma 1980a).The city was encircled on three sides by a moat. There was probably double moat on the northern side. The defences at Kausambi betray an advanced knowledge of fortification.

Being one of the oldest cities of early historic India, Kausambi is hallowed by innumerable tales, myths and legends. It has been frequently referred to in various traditions of ancient literature (Law 1939). Kausambi was the capital of Vatsa Janapada, one of the prominent janapadas of the Later Vedic times, figuring prominently in the *Brahmanas* and *Upanisads*. The *Aitareya Brahmana* (VIII. 14) mentions the Vatsas of Kausambi along with the Kuru-Panchalas and Usinaras. The *Gopatha Brahmana* (1. 2. 9) and. *Kausitaki Upanisad* (IV) also mention the Vatsas in association with the Kuru-Panchalas, Usinaras, etc. Kausambi, famous in literature as the capital of the Vatsas, possibly, existed at the time of Janaka (Raychaudhuri 1972). The *Satapatha Brahmana* mentions Proti Kausurubindi, a pupil of Uddalaka Aruni, the coptemporary of Janaka, as 'Kausambeya', which according to Hariswamin, means a native of Kausambi. It is, therefore, fairly plausible to say that the city of Kausambi existed in the period of the *Brahmanas* and *Upanisads.* If Raychaudhuri's (1972: 44) view that Nichakshu was a contemporary of Janaka, is correct, it further strengthens the argument that Kausambi existed in the period of Janaka and was the seat of the Vatsas who figure prominently in the *Brahmana* literature.

SKETCH PLAN OF KAUSAMBI SHOWING EXCAVATED AREAS

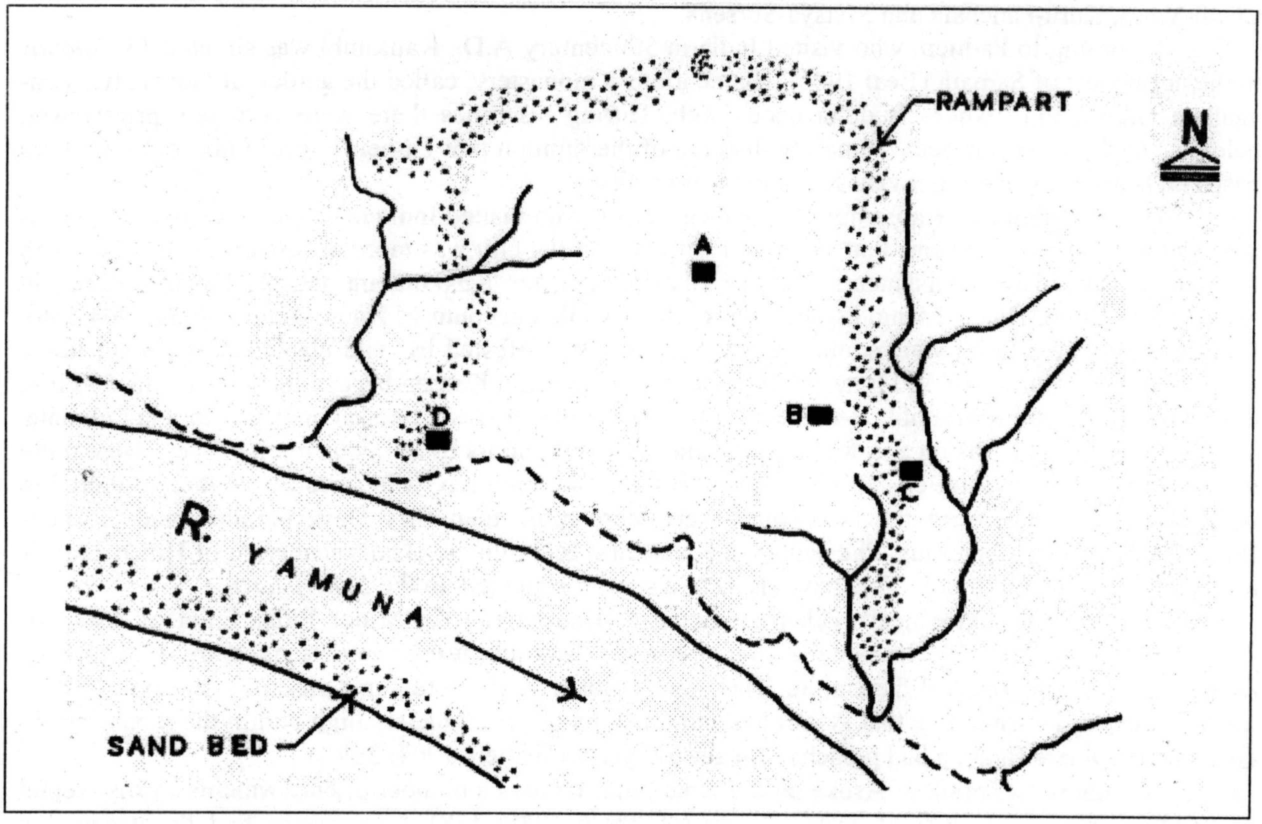

Fig. 2 : Extension of site showing excavated areas.

According to the Puranas, Nichakshu, the sixth in line from Parikshita transferred his capital from Hastinapura to Kausambi, as Hastinapura was ravaged by flood of the Ganga, invasion of locusts and the internal upheavals in the Kuru family itself (Raychaudhuri 1972).

During the time of Nichkshu, Kausambi had already grown into a settlement of sufficient importance to attract his attention and induce him to make it his capital (Sharma 1969: 5). The city of Kausambi, therefore must have come into being not later than the *Mahabharata*-time if not earlier. According to the *Mahabharata* the city was founded by prince Kusamba, the third son of the Chedi King Uparichara Vasu. The *Ramayana,* on the other hand, says that prince Kusamba, a son of Kusa was the founder of Kausambi. The tradition of the foundation of Kausambi by Kusamba is corroborated by the *Kasika* which, while illustrating a grammatical rule of *Astadhyayi* of Panini, mentions that Kausambi was founded by Kusamba. The legend, thus corroborates the antiquity of the city as recorded in the *Ramayana, Mahabharata* and *Puranas.*

Pramatthajyotika, the commentary on the *Sutta-Nipata,* records that Kausambi was the hermitage of the sage Kusamba after whom it came to be known by that name. Buddhaghosa says that Kausambi was so named because a large number of Kusamba-trees were uprooted while founding the city. According to the Jaina *Vividha-Tirtha-Kalpa,* Kausambi was so called because it abounded in Kusamba trees.

There are clear references in the Buddhist tradition that Kausambi was an important centre on the principal trade routes in north India: (i) South to North-East and (it) East to West (David 1903: 103ff). As referred to by the *Mahaparinibban-Sutt* Kausambi alongwith Champa, Rajgriha, Sravasti, Saket and Varanasi were the most important cities of north India in the time of Buddha. The Buddhist literature corroborates and supplements the picture of the Vatsas and their capital, Kausambi, as depicted in the Vedic sources. The Vatsas continued to be powerful even during the time of Buddha. The *Anguttara Nikaya* mentions that the land of the Vatsas was rich and prosperous and abounded in seven kinds of gems.

The *Janavasabha-Suttanta* of *Digha Nikaya* couples the Vatsas with the Chedis and includes them amongst the prominent groups of the people then ruling in India *viz.,* Kasi-Kosala. Vajji-Malla, Chedi-Vatsa, Kuru-Panchala and Matsya-Sursena.

According to Fa-hien, who visited India in 5th century A.D., Kausambi was situated 13 *Yojanas* to the north-west of Sarnath (Beal 1906). He mentions a monastery, called the garden of Govisa (Govisa-vana or Ghositaram), where Buddha once dwelt. During his times there were very few priests who belonged to the Hinayana sect. Some scholars are of the opinion that Fa-hein's record about the site was based on hearsay as he did not visit Kausambi personally.

The next notice of Kausambi is by Hiuen-Tsang, who visited India during 629-45 A.D. From his description of the city it seems that at the time of his visit the city was more or less on the decline, with the famous Buddhist establishments, like the Ghoshitaram, the Kukkutaram and the Pavaria garden in ruins (Beals 1906). Hiuen-Tsang, however, has left a detailed account of Kausambi (Watters 1904:366). From Prayaga the pilgrim went south-west through a forest infested by wild elephants and other fierce animals. After a journey of 500 li he reached the 'Kai-Shang-mi' (Kausambi) country which was 600 li in circuit and its capital Kausambi, more than 30 li in perimeter. It was a fertile country with a hot climate. The people were enterprising and fond of arts, and were cultivators of religious merits. There were more than ten Buddhist monasteries but all in utter ruins, and the brethren, who were above three hundred in numbers were adherents of the Hinayana. There were more than fifty Deva temples, and the non-Buddhists were very numerous. The people of Kausambi, according to Beal's rendering of Hiuen Tsang's account, were hard and rough. This reminds us of a similar statement in the *Lalitvistara.*

The earliest epigraphical evidence relating to Kausambi is in Minor Pillar Edict of Asoka at Allahabad (Sirkar 1965: 70). During the time of Asoka, Kausambi was an important centre, probably the head quarter of a province of the empire. That Asoka took a keen interest in Kausarnbi is also proved by the statement of Hiuen-Tsang that Asoka had built a stupa about 60 metres high within the monastery of Ghositarama where Buddha had preached for several years (Watters 1904: 369).

Another inscription of Asoka on the same pillar records a number of endowments by his second queen, Karuvaki, the mother of prince Tivara (Hultzsch 1925: 158). This proves that the queen was likewise interested in Kausambi. A number of inscriptions of subsequent period have been recovered during the excavations at Kausambi. Among these most important is the Ayagapatta from Ghositarama monastery bearing the name of Ghositarama Vihar.

The Bodhisattva image inscription of Buddhamitra (of the years 2 and 3(?) of Kaniska (Goswami 1937-38: 210 ff) and the sealing of Kaniska (Sharma 1969: 19) furnished the evidence of the Kusana conquest of Kausambi. A fragmentary stone inscription of Vasiska, proves that Kausambi remained a Kusana centre even during the reign of Vasiska.The pillar which bears the Asokan inscriptions contains the most important record of the Gupta period, the *prasasti* of Samudragupta (Sirkar 1965: 262-63). The city of Kausambi remained in the Gupta dominions upto the time of Budhagupta (Sharma 1969: 10). A seal of Huna king Tormana, recovered from the site, shows that Kausambi had to face an invasion of Tormana (Sharma 1969: 19). After this, nothing is known epigraphically about Kausambi till the veil is lifted by the Kara inscription of the Pratihara King Yasapala *(circa* A.D. 1027 -1036). The inscription mentions the grant of the village of Payatara (modern Pras or Parsiha) in the Kausambi *mandala* to Mathura Vikata of Prabhasa (Pabhosa). From this inscription, as well as from the Jhusi Copper Plate inscription of Trilocanpala, N.N. Ghosh (1936: 93) infers that Kausambi was in the 11th Century an administrative sub-division of the Pratihara Kings of Kanauj in the 11th century.

A small inscription in Nagari on a pillar at Kausambi mentions 'Mogal Patisah Akbar Patisah Gaji' (Sharma 1969: 11). Another inscription on the same pillar is dated *samvat* 1621 or A.D. 1564 and records the prayers of five leading goldsmiths together with thirteen of their employees to Ganesa and Siva Bhairava to bestow favour on the goldsmiths of Kausambi town. The large number of coins of pre-Mughal kings collected by B.M. Vyas from Kausambi also indicates that Kausambi had some political importance during this period.

The inscribed cast coins from Kausambi are also useful source for the reconstruction of early history of the city. The earliest inscribed coins e.g. those of Brhaspatimitra I and Sudeva are connected with the uninscribed cast coins from the site in style type and date. On grounds of palaeography these coins have been assigned to the second century B.C. (Sharma 1969: 9). The struck coins of Asvaghosa (Allan 1936: XCVI) and Parvata are perhaps the earliest of this series, with those of Brahaspatimitra II, Agnimitra and Jyesthamitra belonging to next group. Allan (1936: 108) has assigned them to the end of the second century or the beginning of the first century B.C.

New kings, altogether unknown from any other source, such as Rajamitra, Rajanimitra, Prajapatimitra, etc., have come to light from Altekar's examination of the Mitra coins collected by B.M. Vyas (Sharma 1969: 9). The excavations have brought to light a large number of copper coins of Kusana rulers - Kaniska, Huviska and Vasudeva (Sharma and Negi 1968: 51).

The Puranas speak of nine kings of the Magha dynasty, who succeeded the Kusanas at Kausambi. So far we know of only eight Magha kings of Kausambi from inscriptions and coins (Sharma 1969: 10). The information about the Maghas is derived mainly from the coins collected by Vyas from Kausambi. According to Altekar (1942), the Maghas were succeeded by king Nava. He has also identified a coin of king Purvasri whom he places in the middle of the fourth century A.D. The successor of this ruler was, ousted by Samudragupta (Majumdar and Altekar 1967: 83).

Alexander Cunningham (1871: 301-12) was the first to identify the ruins of Kosam with Kausambi as early as 1861. He prepared a site map of Kausambi and also published some sculpture pieces, inscriptions and coins (Cunningham 1880: Plate II) recovered from the site (Fig. 3 and 4). The Archaeological Survey of India, under the direction of N.G. Majumdar, excavated in 1937-38 a large portion near the Asokan Pillar area and laid bare walls and rooms of a living complex. No detailed excavation report of this excavation could be published by the Archaeological Survey of India. University of Allahabad excavated at Kausambi from 1949 to 1965 under the guidance of G.R. Sharma. The excavations at the site brought to light valuable materials not only about ancient Kausambi but also helped to fix the archaeological sequence of the Gangetic plain.

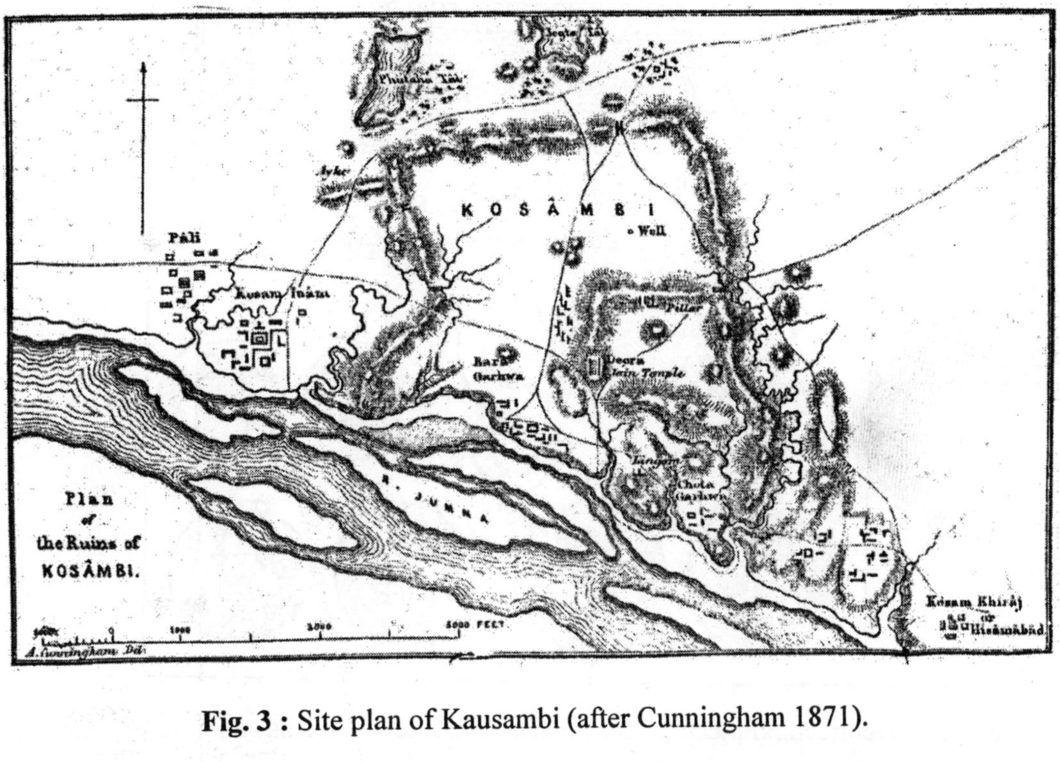

Fig. 3 : Site plan of Kausambi (after Cunningham 1871).

The major excavations at Kausambi have been conducted in the following four areas:

1. Near the Asokan Pillar which laid bare a part of city (1949-50);
2. The Ghositarama monastery (1954-1957);
3. The Defences near the eastern gateway and the tower at the north-eastern corner (1957-59)
4. The Palace Area (1961-64)

University of Allahabad under the supervision of G.R. Sharma started excavations in 1949 near the Asokan Pillar adjacent to the area excavated by the Archaeological Survey of India in 1937-38. The excavations revealed for the first time the plan of public residential area of an ancient Indian township. According to the available evidence, this area of the city, had a continuous settlement from the middle of 8th century B.C. to the middle of fourth century A.D. (Sharma 1980a: 60). The Asokan Pillar stood at the junction of the road and the principal thoroughfare connecting various parts of the city. The houses were aligned with roads and lanes and generally maintained correct orientation with the cardinal points.

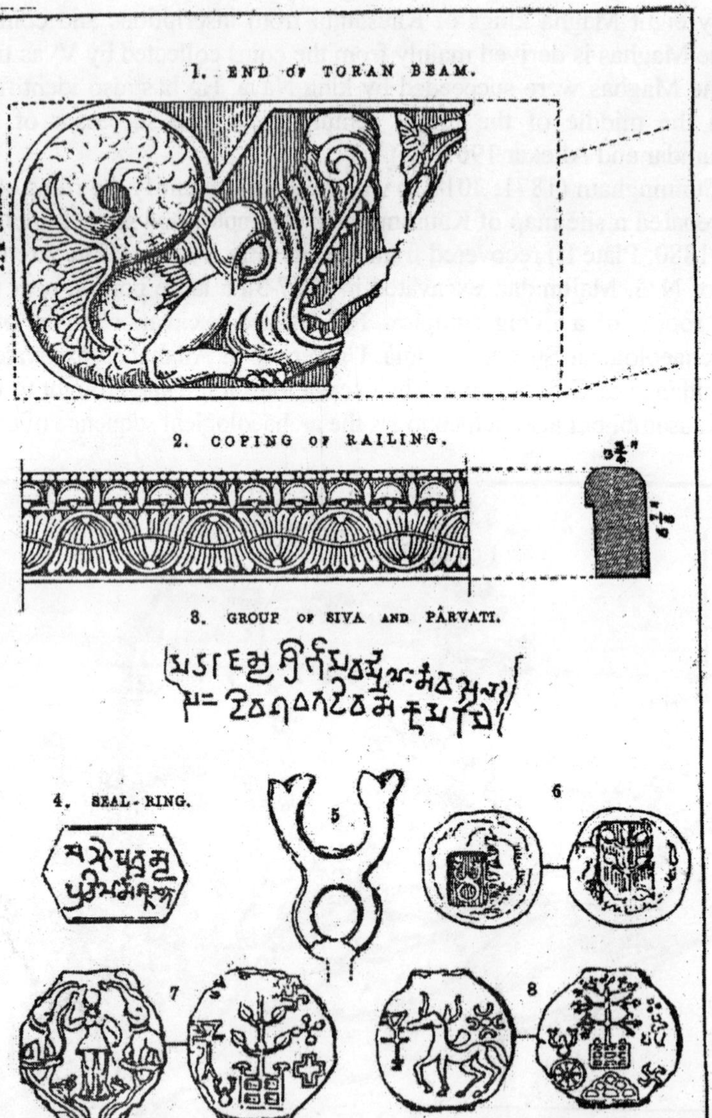

Fig. 4 : Decorated architectural pieces, inscriptions, coins, etc. from Kausambi (after Cunningham 1880)

The excavations have thrown valuable light on the drainage system prevalent in the Gangetic plain. Ring-wells, soakage jars, terracotta pipes, open brick drains, covered brick drains and brick tanks were the main drainage devices. Excavations yielded a number of seals, including a unique sealing of king Kaniska, a large number of coins, four coin-hoards containing coins and cowries, terracotta figurines of which the Saka-Parthian ones constituted a unique group, sculptures, iron objects used in agriculture, etc.

The Ghositarama monastery, frequently mentioned in early Buddhist literature, was built by Ghosita, a leading banker of Kausambi and treasurer of king Udayana. During his frequent visits to Kausambi the Buddha stayed at the monastery. Numerous incidents are mentioned in the *Tripitaka* in connection with his visits. The Ghositarama monastery was well-known all over the Buddhist world. A number of inscriptions have been discovered from the excavations in the monastery, including satdal lotus lamp inscription, sealing of Ghoshitaram and Ayagpatta inscription below the foot print of the Buddha (Sharma 1980a).

The Ghositarama monastery was a combined chaitya-cum-vihar. In it a number of small chapels, with verandahs on the inner sides and pillars resting on stone bases, enclosed a huge courtyard which was dominated by a massive stupa. The stupa, due to later enlargements, was square on plan with recesses at the corners. The courtyard of the monastery had structures in the eastern part and open space in the western part (Sharma 1980a: 11-14). The open space was reserved for congregation. The eastern side with the main chaitya, *pradakasinapatha* and two smaller stupas yielded relics in earthen pots. At the entrance there was the shrine of Hariti. The terracotta images of Gajalaksami, Hariti and Kubera, the consort of Hariti, are the significant finds from the shrine.

The most important structure in this part of the monastery was the main chaitya. Votive offerings were made to the chaitya, is suggested by the discovery of more than 250 sealings with Buddhist text *'ye dharma hetu prabhavah'*. Smaller stupas, generally rectangular on plan, were also erected. The successive floors built one upon another and the walls and stupas erected on earlier foundations provide a convincing sequence and the large number of inscriptions, some of them belonging to the Mitra, Kusana, Magha, Huna and the post-Huna kings, together with numismatic evidence, show very close dating of the various occupational periods. The C-14 dates obtained from the monastic area indicate that it was in existence from circa 5th century B.C. to the 6th century A.D

The earliest phase of the settlement at Kausambi had no evidence of defence (Sharma 1960: 26). The excavations have brought to light two pre-defence sub-periods. The first rampart and its revetment was encircled by a moat. The roads helped in determining the stratification and the relative chronology of the moat. Another significant addition to the defence complex was the construction of an underground tunnel built on the principle of corbelled arch which was possibly a passage. The next major stage in the evolution of the defence system was the construction of the tower and guard rooms at the top of the rampart and flank walls ranging from top to the toe which played the same role as the revetment and bastions had played in earlier times. These additions in the defence system have been dated to 3rd century B.C. By these constructions the defence reached in its final shape. Invasion by Menander, proved disastrous for the defences. When the Greeks were overthrown, the defences were rebuilt. These defences were finally destroyed by Huna king Tormana (Sharma 1960: 18).

In the south-western corner of the ancient walled city of Kausambi the palace area is clearly marked out from the rest of the site by its well defined contours. On the Yamuna two small mounds covering an overall area of almost 75m x 45m were included within this complex. A strongly built tower still stands in utter defiance of the formidable currents of the Yamuna, especially during the rainy season.

A massive stone fortress towards south-west on the Yamuna measuring 320m x 150m has been exposed. Its northern and southern sides are parallel and the eastern and western curvilinear. At the north-eastern, north-western and south-eastern ends three circular towers were also exposed. The considerable part of the palace complex has been washed away by the river. Four main stages in the architectural evolution of the palace have been worked out.

The palace was destroyed by Menander sometime in the 2nd century B.C., the stone boundary walls and towers were razed to the ground (Sharma 1980a: 21-22). There is also evidence of conflagration. The debris covering the ruins of wall have yielded sherds of Northern Black Polished Ware, a sealing bearing an inscription in the Brahmi script of c. 2nd century B.C. Double-tanged arrowheads ascribed to the Indo-Greeks also have been found. The discovery of inscription of Menander at Reh on the left bank of the Yamuna in Fatehpur district also indicates devastating campaigns of Menander into the heart of north India in the second century B.C. (Sharma 1980b: 99).

The chronology of the four main phases in the construction of the palace, on the basis of the stratigraphy, pottery and other finds, as worked out by G.R. Sharma (1980a: 22) is as follows:

1. The first stage of undressed stone wall was built not later that c. 8th century B.C.- 6th century B.C
2. The second stage of dressed stone wall may be dated between c. 6th century B.C. and 2nd century B.C.
3. The third stage ranges between c. 2nd century B.C. and 1st century A.D.
4. The last stage ranges between c. 1st century A.D. and 2nd century A.D. (Kusana period).

The ceramic assemblage from the earliest levels of Kausambi (pre PGW phase) is divisible in two groups. The first group, comparable to Kakoria group of pottery of the Vindhyas, consists of sturdy red, coarse black-and-red, crude grey and ochre coloured wares. The functional types in this group include dish-on-stand, lid-cum-bowl, beaker, high necked jar, dish of dish-on-stand, convex sided dish, large sized bowl-cum-basin and cooking vessel. Graffiti marks, channel like depressions and cord impressed designs are the decorative motifs. The pottery of second group, comparable to Koldihwa group of pottery of the Vindhyas, consists of red, black-and-red, black slipped and grey wares, the shapes represented by bowl, dish, lid-cum-bowl, dish of dish-on-stand, bowl-on-stand, large sized hemispherical bowl, beaker, storage jar, medium sized vase, cooking vessel or *handi*, straight sided trough or basin, etc. The pottery, occasionally is decorated with paintings and incised or appliqué patterns. The painting is executed in black or creamy pigment on red or black-and-red ware (Sharma 1980a: 7; Pal 1986: 142-144).

The PGW phase at Kausambi is marked by sherds of Painted Grey, red, black-and-red and black slipped wares. The types are globular bowls, convex sided dishes, basins, some with thickened or collared rim, lipped basin, footed and perforated basins, medium sized vases with concave or straight neck, storage jars, rimless cooking vessels with short constricted neck, miniature and small vases, etc. Painted motifs are horizontal band or zonal designs, groups of horizontal bands, strokes, some times emanating from rim band or circle, groups of dots or dashes, concentric semi-circle or arched designs formed by loops or dots, groups of sigma and loops, triangular pattern, loop emanating from circle, trident like motifs, etc.

The NBPW phase at Kausambi is marked by NBPW of different shades – steel-grey, black, chocolate, orange, golden, appears in profusion. Some of the earliest specimen are painted with bands on the rim and oblique lines, arches, triangles and a complex motif in chocolate. The bowl, dish, lid, vase and carinated *handi* are the common shapes. The other associated wares are – thick plain grey ware, red ware and black-and-red ware. The red ware is mostly of medium fabric containing sand particles, husk and straw in the paste, usually treated with ocherous red slip.

Evidence of early art at Kausambi have their close parallel in Bharhut and Sanchi and deal with events and scenes in Buddha's life. They are in low relief and the treatment on the whole is archaic (Plate 5.1). The nativity scene on a plaque is one of the earliest depictions of Buddha's birth in Indian art (Plate 5.2). There are two other examples, both of them on railing pillars on which Maya is shown standing on a lotus holding the branch of a tree.

The sculptures from Manhai out side the walled city of Kausambi in the north-east are also significant. The bell shaped capitals represent the continuation of Mauryan art in shape and in general design as well as in polish. Palm leaf capital with lustrous polish is one of such examples (Plate 5.3). On an abacus are shown a seated double-humped camel surrounded by four lions in different postures (Sharma 1980a).

The Kausambi images, especially of Gupta period (Misra 1994, Pal 1994) are characterized by a broad forehead, curved eye-brows, and half closed bird-like eyes. The images also display full cheeks, broad chin and elongated ears. The artist of Kausambi school of art has shown his predilection to facial symmetry and serene expression (Plate 5.4). A rich variety of coiffure may be seen in the figures of devotees. The figures of Bodhisattvas (Plates 5.5, 5.6) also have elaborate head-dress. Bodhisattvas are richly ornamented with crown or head-dress, necklace of beads with central gem, two-stringed long pendant of beads hanging up to the knee, elaborate armlets and anklets and girdle with a rectangular gem below the navel. These sculptures were manufactured within the monastery from local sand stone brought from the hills south of Kausambi across the Yamuna or from Pabhosa hill to the west of Kausambi is clear from unfinished images (Plate 5.7).

The plastic art of terracotta at Kausambi has also a long history of local development. Large sized terracotta figurines of Hariti, Gajalakshmi (Plate 5.8) and Kubera recovered during excavation of temple of Hariti in Ghoshitarama monastery have great significance in the history of terracotta art of the Gangetic plain.

The art of Kausambi has greatly influenced the art activity of the reason lying to the east and south of Kausambi and there is ample evidence to put the art activity of this great centre under Kausambi School of Art (Misra 1978: 311-316).

The excavations brought to light a total of about 16.83 m of habitational deposit. divided into 25 structural periods of which two are pre-defence, twenty-two are coeval with five building periods of the rampart and the last one stands over the ruins of the last defence-phase of the city. On the basis of ceramics, the structural periods, represented by the remnants of walls and floors, lying over one another, were divided into four major cultural periods which were named and dated as Kausambi I (First Four Structural Periods), *circa* 1265 to *circa* 885 B.C.; Kausambi II (Structural Periods 5 to 8), circa 885 B.C. to circa 605 B.C.; Kausambi III (Structural Periods 9 to 16), *circa* 605 B.C. to *circa* 45 B.C. and Kausambi IV (Structural Periods 17 to 25), *circa* 55 B.C. to 580 A.D. (Sharma 1960: 17-19). According to the excavator the pottery of first phase has similarity with those of the post-Harappan sites of Kathiawar and the early defences, built of hard rammed clay having bastions at regular intervals and baked brick rivetment are the copy of Harappan pattern of defences. However archaeologists like Wheeler (1959: 129) have expressed doubt 'whether across the many intervening centuries a significant structural tradition had been preserved'. The ceramic industry of this phase actually is closer to the ceramic tradition of Chalcolithic culture of the middle Ganga plain.

The second cultural period is marked by the presence of Painted Grey Ware, black slipped and black-and-red ware The Painted Grey Ware of Kausambi is late and degenerate in comparison to those of upper Gangetic plain. Ceramic industry of this phase may be equated with the pre NBPW with iron phase of the middle Ganga plain. The rampart, however, continued throughout this period. The third phase witnessed the appearance of NBP alongwith PGW and black-and-red ware. Ramparts 2 and 3 also came into existence. The inscribed cast coins of Mitra kings, lanky bull type, and silver and copper punched marked coins alongwith terracotta figurines, were also found in the period. The last period is devoid of NBPW. With this phase the occupation comes to an end at the site. There are evidence of repair and raising of the rampart and construction of walls and floors in this phase.

In the palace area there are three cultural phases. Phase I, yielded pottery-types like the dish-on-stand with a corrugated stem. The other forms resemble with the Chalcolithic sites of western and central India. Phase II, was associated with the NBPW. The last phase, was dated to *circa* first-second century A.D. (Sharma 1960: 58)

Kausambi, as the above description shows, has a continuous history of more than two thousand years beginning from Chalcolithic periods till the time of Harshavardhana, and, in all probability, down to the end of the Pratihara rule, if not till the time of Akbar (Sharma 1969: 12).

There has been much disagreement of opinion among the Indian archaeologists (Ghosh: 1973, Sinha 1973) unfortunately some after the passing away of the excavator, specially about the antiquity of defences and its relation with Harappans (Lal 1982, 1982a) antiquity of ceramics (Dikshit 1982), and structures (Soundararajan 1982). According to B.B. Lal (1982, 1982a) there is nothing Harappan about the Kausambi defences. On the basis of the analysis and comparison of pottery types K.N. Diskshit (1982) has opined that so called Harappan pottery from Kausambi has no similarity with Harappan pottery. The antiquity of palace like that of defences has also been questioned. K.V. Soundararajan (1982) on the basis of analysis of available data has disagreed with G.R. Sharma regarding the antiquity of the palace.

Questions raised on the antiquity of ceramics, structures and chronology of the sites need some clarification in the light of new evidences obtained from the subsequent investigations in the neighbouring areas of Kausambi. The area was colonized in Mesolithic period much before the Harappan civilazation area was colonized. Myth of dense forest is now no more valid and there is evidence of continuous human settlement in the Gangetic plain right from the Epipalaeolithic/Mesolithic to modern times (Tewari 2004, Lal 1986, Erdosy 1985). When Harappan or even pre Harappan cultures came in existence in the north-west, the Gangetic plain had already witnessed the advent of Mesolithic, Neolithic and Chalcolithic cultures. The physical anthropologists having studies the Mesolithic human skeletal remains of the Ganga plain and the Harappan people have opined that both belong to the same human physical type. Now we are getting though still very sparse that both the areas were in contact to each other. The Harappan elephant, ecologically, was more native to the Gangetic plain than the North-west India. The scholars now have looked common elements of the cultures of both the regions (Sahi 2004-05).

Recent investigations in the deep rain-gullies at Kausambi have revealed handmade early pottery having similarity with the Neolithic ceramics. Conclusions of G.R. Sharma in most of the cases have been confirmed and his foresight has been proved correct.

In the light of present archaeological picture revealed from recent excavations of Jhusi and Hetapatti the antiquity of settled cultures in the lower Ganga-Yamuna doab has been pushed back to the Neolithic period. In the surrounding regions of Kausambi Mesolithic sites have been located. The site needs fresh and extensive horizontal excavation which may throw new light on the process of development of human cultures, process and development of urbanization in the central Ganga valley and cultural contact from Lower and Upper Ganga valley on the one hand and from the Vindhyan plateau on the other.

References

1. Allan. J. 1936. *Catalogue of the Coins in the British Museum, Ancient India.* British Museum, London
2. Altekar, A.S. 1942. The New Kings and Interesting Coin Types from Kausambi, *Journal of Numismatic Society of India,* Volume IV.
3. Bahadur, Amar 2012. Archaeology of Lower Doab with special reference to fatehpur District, D.Phil. Thesis of Allahabad University, Allahabad
4. Beal S., 1906. *Buddhist Records of Western World,* 1. K. Paul, Trench, Trubner & Co. Ltd., London.
5. Cunningham. A. 1871. *Archaeological Survey of India, Four Reports Made During the Years 1862-63-64-65,* volume I. Superintendent of Government Printing, Calcutta.
6. Cunningham. A. 1880. *Archaeological Survey of India, Reports Volume X.* Superintendent of Government Printing, Calcutta.
7. David, Rhys, 1903. *Buddhist India,* London
8. Erdosy, George 1985. Settlement Archaeology of the Kausambi Region. *Man and Environment* IX: 66-79.
9. Erdosy, George 1988. *Urbanization in Early Historic India,* B.A.R. International Series, Oxford.
10. Ghosh, A., 1973, The *City in Early Historical India,* Indian Institute of Advanced Study, Simla
11. Ghosh, N.N. 1936. *The Early History of Kausambi.* Law Journal Press, Allahabad
12. Goswami,. K.G. 1937-38. *Epigraphia Indica.* XXIV. Archaeological Survey of India, New Delhi.
13. Hultzsch. E. 1925. *Corpus Inscriptionum Indicarum, Volume I Inscriptions of Asoka.* Clarendon Press, Oxford.
14. Lal, B.B. 1982, Are the Defences of Kausambi Really as old as 1025 B.C. ? *Puratattva* No. 11. pp. 88-95.
15. Lal. B.B. 1982a. West was West and East was East, But when and how did the Twin Meet? The Role of Bhagwanpura as a Bridge between Certain Stages of the Indus and Ganges Civilization, in *Harappan Civilization-A Contemporary Perspective,* (G.L. Possehl Ed.), pp. 395-398. American Institute of Indian Studies and Oxford & IBH Publishing Corporation Ltd. Delhi.
16. Lal, M. 1986. Iron Tools, Forest Clearance and Urbanization in the Gangetic Plain. *Man and Environment* X: 83-90..
17. Lal, M. 1984. *Settlement History and Rise of Civilization in the Ganga-Yamuna Doab from 1500 B.C.-300 A.D.*, B.R. Publishing Corporation, New Delhi.
18. Law, B.C. 1939, *'Kausambi in Ancient Literature, Memoirs of* the *Archaeological Survey of India. No. 60,* Archaeological Survey of India. Delhi.
19. Majumdar, R.C. and A.S. Altekar 1967. *The Vakataka-Gupta Age.* Motilal Banarsidas, Delhi.
20. Mishra, R. N. 1978, *Bhartiya Murtikala Ka Itihas.* Granthashilpi, Delhi.
21. Misra V.D. 1969, Pottery of Kausambi, in *Potteries in Ancient India,* (B. P. Sinha Ed.), pp 203-222, Patna University, Patna.
22. Misra V.D. 1994. Gupta Sculptures from Kausambi, *Indian Art and Culture* (Ed. G.C. Pande), pp. 173-177. Raka Prakashan, Allahabad.
23. Pal, Gyanendra 2006. *Art and Archaeology of Fatehpur District* A Ph.D. Thesis of HNB University, Shrinagar, Garhwall.
24. Pal, J.N. 1986. *Archaeology of Southern Uttar Pradesh: Ceramic Industries of Northern Vindhyas.* Swabha Prakashan, Allahabad.

25. Pal, J.N. 1994. Some Masterpieces of Kausambi School of Art of Gupta Period, *Indian Art and Culture* (Ed. G.C. Pande), pp. 102-104. Raka Prakashan, Allahabad.
26. Raychaudhuri. H.C. 1972, *Political History of Ancient India.* University of Calcutta, Calcutta.
27. Sahi, M.D.N. 2004-2005. Early Interactions between the Culturs of the Mid-Ganga Valley and Western India. *Pragdhara* 15: 91-108.
28. Sharma G.R. 1958, in *Annual Bibliography of Indian Archaeology.* Kern Institute, Leyden, Vol. XVI, PP. XXXVI-XLV.
29. Sharma, G.R. 1960. *The Excavations at Kausambi (1957-59): The Defences and the Syenciti of the Purusamedha.* University of Allahabad, Allahabad.
30. Sharma, G.R. 1968, *Kushana Studies.* University of Allahabad, Allahabad.
31. Sharma, G.R. 1969, *Excavations at Kausambi, 1949.50, Memoirs of the Archaeological Survey of India No. 74,* Delhi.
32. Sharma, G.R. 1980a. *History to Prehistoy,* University of Allahabad, Allahabad.
33. Sharma, G.R. 1980b. *Inscription of Menander and the Indo-Greek invasion of the Ganga Valley.* Abinash Prakashan, Allahabad.
34. Sharma. G.R. and J.S., Negl. 1968, The Saka-Kusanas in the Central Ganga Valley in G.R. Sharma (ed.) *Kusana Studies,* pp, 43-73. University of Allahabad, Allahabad.
35. Sinha, K.K. 1973, Stratigraphy and Chronology of Early Kausambi, in *Radiocarbon* and *Indian Archaeology.* (D.P. Agrawal and A. Ghosh Eds.), pp. 231-238, Tata Institute of Fundamental Research, Bombay.
36. Sircar, D.C., 1965, *Select Inscriptions,* Vol. I. University of Calcutta, Calcutta
37. Soundara Rajan. K.V. 1982, The Use of Arch in the Kushan Palace at Kausambt, *Puratattva* No. 11, pp. 98-102.
38. Spate, O.H.K. and A.T.A. Learmonth 1967. *India and Pakistan: A General and Regional Geography.* Methuen & Co Ltd. London.
39. Tewari, R. 2004. The Myth of Dense Forest and Human Occupation in the Ganga Plain. *Man and Environment* XXIX (2): 102-16.
40. Watters, T. 1904, *On Yuan Chwang's travel in India,* Volume1. Royal Asiatic Society, London.

6

EARLY AGRO-PASTORAL CULTURES OF INDIA

Vasant Shinde

Indian Archaeology has made considerable progress in the post-Independence period with many significant discoveries such as taking back the antiquity of Stone Age man to 2 million years and the beginning of agriculture to the seventh millenium and so on. The earlier hypothesis of nuclear zone of origin of agriculture and settled life has been discarded and there has been a very evidence of the multiple-zone of origin of agriculture and village life coming from different parts of the country.

The beginning of farming is the first important revolution in human history. As Gordon Childe says, man was a parasite on nature, but when he started producing his own food, he became its partner. He was not prepared to do it willingly, but was forced to do so. Man had started selecting animals for food from the Middle Palaeolithic, particularly those he knew intimately, as for instance deer, and in the Upper Palaeolithic he kept their herds. In the Mesolithic there was a heavy reliance on wild sheep and goat in West Asia. Animals in the herd was man's stored food which could come in handy in times of need. The availability of food with little effort afforded some leisure to the Mesolithic man who could enjoy settled life at least seasonally. This led to domestication of plants and animals such as sheep and goat, followed by cattle and pig.

The question that then arises naturally is: Why did foragers become farmers? The answer appears to be largely climate change. Graeme Barker (2006) says: "At the global scale a key factor of the subsistence change was clearly climate change." Mark Cohen (1975) has analysed various factors and has succinctly demonstrated that drastic climatic shift towards aridity was the main factor. The situation in West Asia was not different, and in India too the onset of aridity has been established on the basis of palynological data (Gurdip Singh 1971). The favourabale environment during the Mesolithic afforded leisure to man which resulted in population growth for which available food supply was not adequate. It was therefore necessary to procure food by some other means. This led to domestication of plants and animals in which women played a key role.

The change was first noticed at Jericho (Israel) during 10,000-8000 when it was occupied by sedentary hunter-gatherers. Later domesticated plants and wild animals occur between 8500-7300 whereas domesticated sheep and goat appear during 7300-7000. The Kebaran people 20,000 years ago relied heavily on animal food, but later the Natufians ate more plant food. Ain Mallaha (Jordan) was a settlement of incipient agriculturists in 11000-9000 when the people lived in round huts and cereal cultivation started at Abu Hureyra by 8500 BCE. Maintenance of herds of cattle forced man to stay at one place for some time in a year, hence building huts became necessary for which carpentry tools were required and pottery for storage. All the stages of this development have been traced in West Asia and Europe by employing scientific tests of Molecular Biology, more particularly DNA studies.

In the Indian sub-continent also the antiquity of food production now goes back to 8000-10000 years as the evidence from Mehrgadh and Lahuradeva shows and it is therefore possible that the processes of domestication of plants and animals as also population histories can be traced by new techniques. The transition from Mesoliithic to Neolithic/ Chalcolithic can be detected at a few sites, as for instance, Gilund in Mewar part of Rajasthan. The excavated evidence from Adamgarh in Madhya Pradesh is interesting because of the occurrence of animal bones, both wild and domesticated species (Joshi 1978). It appears that the people were in the transitional stage when animal domestication had begun. Palynological data indicates that the environment was quite favourable some thirteen thousand years ago when rainfall was high and the lakes were full, resulting in good vegetation cover which is why there are such a large number of Mesolithic sites in Rajasthan assignable to the sixth millennium BCE.

Mid-Ganga valley

The mid-Ganga valley is slowly emerging as an independent centre of rice cultivation. Explorations in the Belan valley in the Vindhyan region (U.P.) have brought to light not only rich palaeolithic sites but also early agricultural settlements a few of which viz. Koldihwa, Mahagara, Sarai Nahar Rai and Panchoh have been excavated. They can be dated to the 6th-5th millennium on the basis of radiometric assays. Although the Neolithic settlement at Mehrgarh can be said to have West Asian inspiration, the same cannot be said about the mid-Ganga Plain as both the regions, Baluchistan and eastern Uttar Pradesh, are far removed from each other and there is no evidence to suggest any contact between them. On the other hand there are microlithic sites in the Belan valley which were occupied by herders leading a semi-nomadic existence. They may have been the forebears of the early farming communities. The land of the Ganga Plains is among the most fertile in the country. It is located close to the flood plain and hence rice could be cultivated without any irrigation facility or manuring. Floods bring fresh silt every year which is spread along the flanks of the river.. Besides, the region being hilly, the habitation could be located on the ridges which afforded protection from floods.

Lahuradeva

In recent years significant evidence has become available from some sites in the mid-Ganga Plain which has stretched back the beginning of settled life to the eighth millennium (Tewari 2007). The excavations at Lahuradeva and Jhusi (U.P) have yielded evidence of food production which is as early as that from Baluchistan. It has been observed that the presence of micro-charcoal in the lake sediments at Lahuradeva, dated by radiocarbon determinations, indicates that human activities continued in that area from about 10000-11000 years B.P. (Tewari et al 2002-03). It is therefore clear that there was another agricultural centre in the mid-Ganga basin where rice, both wild and cultivated, could be grown. The Neolithic habitation at Lahuradeva has been divided into two phases of which Phase IA (8th-4th millennium) is marked by sedantary existence of people living in flimsy huts with reed and grass walls, plastered with mud, and subsisting on wild and cultivated rice (*Oryza rufipoga* and *sativa*) besides low millets. Their diet was supplemented by fishes, tortoise etc. and their hearths were also exposed. Their microlithic implements have been found at Jhusi. This phase lasted for some four thousand years when a change is noticed in Phase IB (end of 4th millennium to the beginning of the second millennium). The people cultivated rice, used Black and Red pottery, a corded ware and bone tools. In the latter half of the third millennium barley and wheat and dish-on-stand occur. These, along with steatite beads, indicate Harappan contact.

It is somewhat difficult to understand the division of the earliest cultural period into IA (8th – 4th millennium) and IB (end of 4th to the beginning of 2nd millennium). It is likely that there is a huge hiatus of two millennia between the two phases because Phase IB appears to be related more to Period II (Ca. 2200-1700 BCE) which has all the elements of IB, and in addition has painted pottery, Black and Red, red and black wares as also barley and wheat which may be due to Harappan contact.

Evidence for human habitation during the Neolithic period has been obtained from excavations in this region. Animal bones include those of wild cattle, antelope, wild boar, tortoise, fish and even horse of the non-wild variety. Wild sheep and goat have been reported from the advance Mesolithic phase at Chopani Mando and those of wild boar from Neolithic levels of Mahagara. The faunal collection suggests that the region was well wooded; the pollen analylsis, however, indicates grassland vegetation. These are rich sites which can be expected to shed light not only on the transition from foraging to farming but also on the socio-economic aspects of the communities.

Origins and Development of Village Life in Western India

The introduction and origin of the Chalcolithic cultures in western India was once attributed to Harappan influence, which was itself the result of the continued development begun at Mehrgarh around 7000 BC. However, in the last decade the first hint of indigenous development of village life in western India has been found in Saurashtra, North Gujarat and at the site of Balathal going back to the middle of 4th millennium BC and hence based on the evidence from Bagor it has been hypothesized that this area could be another primary zone where domestication and village life may have evolved.

The recent evidence from North Gujarat, Saurashtra and Balathal in Mewar region of Rajasthan suggests that the Chalcolithic village community came into being much before the Harappan period. It is obvious therefore that the Harappans did not play any significant role in the origin of the Chalcolithic village cultures in Gujarat and Central India. The beginnings of the village life in these regions go back to the last quarter of the fourth millennium B.C. as the radio carbon dates from the sites of Loteshwar in North Gujarat, Padri in Saurashtra and Balathal in Mewar region would indicate. The Chalcolithic culture here, in fact are contemporary with the Pre/Early Harappan culture of Northern and Western Rajasthan, Sind and northwestern Indian Subcontinent.

The region of Gujarat though indicates local evolution of the village society it seems to have been influenced from the Sind region especially on the basis of its similar Black-on-Red ceramic type. Small excavation carried out at Loteshwar, 17 km north-east of Shankheshwar in Mehasana district of Gujarat, has produced interesting evidence of the beginning of settled life that is earlier than the Harappan period. The Chalcolithic deposit overlies the Mesolithic material. The thin habitation deposit has revealed numerous large pits, some of which could have been even pit-dwellings, were found filled in with pottery the Black-on-Red type (Gritty Red ware), animal bones, clay lumps, etc. The other material equipment associated with the Chalcolithic culture includes micro steatite beads, microlithic tools and some crudely made shell bangles and beads. The site of Padri in Saurashtra also shows the moorings of a village community with Black-on-Red pottery indicating influences from the Sind region which is not impossible as the pastoral groups from very early days might have known the rich pastures of North Gujarat and Saurashtra.

The excavations at Balathal (Udaipur District, Rajasthan) roughly 42 km northeast of Udaipur city, have produced evidence in respect to the origin of the early farming community of central India. The evidence from this site is particularly interesting as the pottery is unique both the incised ware and the Black-and-Red ware, with an earlier date for the former from the site of Bagor. A considerable thick deposit at the base of the settlement (Phase A) at Balathal (around 1 meter) has produced evidence of the origin of the Chalcolithic culture and a gradual development of the village community in the ascending order. Excavation to the natural level in a limited area has demonstrated a gradual growth of the settlement from the modest beginning at the site. The people who established settlement on the bedrock constructed mud and wattle-and-daub structures with well-made floor plastered with cow dung. Some of the characteristic Chalcolithic wares of this region such as thick and thin incised Red, Black-and-Red were introduced right from the beginning. However, they are coarse, thick in section, inadequately fired and the majority of vessels are handmade. Shapes such as wide-mouthed deep carinated bowls, small narrow-mouthed jars and storage jars with beaded rim, the fossil types of the Chalcolithic phase in this region, are present right from the beginning. A gradual development is seen in these different wares in terms of technology and quality of vessels from the early to Mature Chalcolithic.

The earliest phase at Nagwada in North Gujarat has been identified as part of the Amri-Nal-Kot Diji complex with Gritty red ware and the typical Amri pottery from the burials (Sonawane and Ajit Prasad, 1994) on the basis of pottery. This indicates that sometime after the village life was introduced, the region came under the sphere of influence from northwest part of Indian subcontinent. Similar evidence also has been reported from the site of Padri near the Gulf of Cambay and Prabhas Patan near Somnath in Gujarat (Dhavalikar and Possehl, 1991). In the basal levels at Padri dated to 3300 BC is found the evidence of rectangular mud structures with well made floors plastered with cow dung and having low mud walls, coarse handmade Black-on-Red painted pottery and there is evidence of semi-precious stone bead and copper tool manufacture technology. A gradual development is seen in the material culture and towards the end the overall development around 2500 BC results in the culture attaining full maturity. The culture at the basal levels at Prabhas Patan dated to 2900 BC and termed as Pre-Prabhas, is characterized by the presence of plain Black-and-Red and painted Black on Red pottery. We have very limited information available for this culture, as the excavation carried out at the site was very small in nature.

The excavations at Balathal and Gilund in Rajasthan and Padri in Gujarat have demonstrated a gradual development and prosperity in the material culture of the Chalcolithic people from 3000 BC and by 2500 BC there was a drastic change in the life-style of the people. The cause for this change is both internal development as a result of agricultural maximization and external influence from the developed Harappans who were in constant contact with the Chalcolithic people for their requirements of varied raw materials. This contact resulted in several shared cultural characteristics especially visible in the Chalcolithic cultural pattern and reflects not a single cultural developmental continuum, but they do indicate interaction. At about 2500 BC there is a rapid transformation at Balathal and Gilund, and they become well-planned settlements. At Balathal structural complexes of stone and mud-brick are organized along a central road and subsidiary lane; Gilund gives the impression of a citadel and lower town plan with outer fortifications, public structures and large residential complexes indicating a socially stratified and politically organized society. Though there is no evidence of a planned settlement at Padri, it develops into an important settlement specializing in salt manufacture around 2500 BC. The site played a significant role in the economic organization that time. Thus, there is evidence in western India for a gradual development of technology, the circular huts were replaced by rectangular dwellings of mud or occasionally mud bricks and the coarse handmade pottery was replaced by fine and wheel made pottery. By 2500 BC the Chalcolithic settlement is fully transformed, with prosperous and well-developed trade mechanism, craft specialization and external contact and the beginnings of an urban veneer due to internal and external trade contacts. Around this time we also see the development of the Harappan culture into a flourishing civilization in western and northwestern India and Pakistan. As the climatic data is sketchy and contradictory, we are not sure about its role in the development of village-based cultures into semi/proto or fully urban and developed societies around 2500 BC. There were certainly a number of other factors apart from the climate, which contributed to the cultural process.

OCP-Copper Hoards

The OCP and Copper Hoards occur in north India in a large area which covers parts of Western U.P, Haryana, Punjab and Rajasthan. They are found in what can be called a flood deposit and it is difficult to trace the remains of their houses and other material equipment but there is clearly Harappan influence on the OCP. Although a number of radiocarbon dates are available, a majority of them fall in the 2200-1600 time brackets. The hoards appear to have been buried in times of trouble like a great flood. It has been averred that the people who buried them were Harappan refugees (Piggott 1952).

The Ganga Plain

The degeneration that set in from about 2200-2000 BCE was gradually increasing, and the environment became more and more arid. Almost the entire country was dotted by agro-pastoral village communities which never achieved the urban status and vanished from the scene towards the close of the second millennium.

A number of Chalcolithic sites have been discovered in the mid-Ganga basin. They are all rural settlements characterized by mud architecture, painted pottery, stone and bone tools and restricted use of copper. In their cultural equipment there is discernible Harappan influence. These communities can be divided into two phases: I – Neolithic (2200-1950) and II – Chalcolithic (1950-1300) with a brief break in between. In Period II new grains are introduced viz. barley *(Sorghum vulgare)* and wheat (*T.aestivum*) which, according to palaeo-botanists, are the same as those cultivated by the Harappans (Singh 2004:605-608). The Harappan influence is noticed at several sites such as Chirand, Taradih, Senuwar and others. (Saran and Sant 1994). It includes underground ovens *(tandoor*), pottery forms such as dish-on-stand, pointed base goblet etc. One artifact deserves a special mention: a bone object with holes and parallel cut marks along with central hair lines. It appears to be an angle measure which is exactly similar to that from Kalibangan (IAR 1962-63:Pl.LXI-B).

Deccan

The same story is repeated in the Deccan where the Late Jorwe people lived in small huts, subsisted on barley, and *jowar* and hunted small game, particular deer and bustard. They became sheep/goat pastoralists, staying in villages during the rainy season and moving from October to May as the present day Dhangars do. The Dhangars worship their god at Inamgaon, represented by a huge chunk of rock at the ancient site, which they are told is their ancestral deity. But after 900 BCE the chalcolithic inhabitants abandoned their settlements and became foragers.

South India

Agricultural communities appear in South India from about the beginning of the third millennium in the Maski-Watgal region and spread a little later at several sites particularly in the southern Deccan. They come in contact with the chalcolithic folk of northern Deccan in the mid-second millennium, but vanish from the scene at the end of the second millennium when the megalith builders dominate the region.

A most vexing issue in South Indian archaeology is that of ash mounds. Over a hundred ash mounds have so far been discovered so far, mostly in the Krishna-Tungabhadra valleys and a few have been excavated. They consist of huge heaps of burnt cattle dung. In a way they are garbage dumps which, on excavation, have been found to contain Neolithic implements, pottery and other objects of daily use of the inhabitants. Robert Bruce Foote, who first discovered them, suggested that they were heaps of cattle dung and his view was confirmed by the scientific analysis of the ash. F.R. Allchin (1963) argued that they were burnt intentionally and were a part of Neolithic fire cult aimed at cattle fertility. Paddayya (1991-92, 2011) does not agree with these theories; he employs the symbolic approach to interpret it. To him, they are monuments from garbage disposal, and that every ash mound is a Neolithic settlement.

The Ash Mounds can be divided into two groups: those associated with habitation sites (e.g. Kupgal and Gadignur), and those without (Kudatini and Utnoor). It can be inferred that the isolated ash mounds appear to be early in point of time, assignable to the first half of the third millennium when transition from hunting-gathering to incipient agriculture was taking place. Such isolated ash mounds may represent cattle camps where wild cattle were herded for taming and dung heaps were kept burning for protecting them from wild animals as also for the young men staying in the camp.

Eastern and Northeastern India

The eastern part of the subcontinent seems to show two evolutionary processes; the extreme east has links with eastern Asia especially China as can be seen in the ceramic and rice cultivation while the Ganga basin has independent evolution as is now evident from the site like Jhusi and Lahuradeva with the beginnings going back to 5500 BCE. Below is presented a summary of the salient features of the Neolithic and Chalcolithic cultures of different regions in Eastern and Northeast India:

Orissa

Excavations at a few sites like Golabai Sasan, Kuchai, Hikudi, Deoposh, Gopalpur, Sankerjung, and Kuanr have provided evidence of different aspects of the life ways of the people of Neolithic-Chalcolithic period. The occurrence of pointed-butt celts and cord-impressed pottery from Kuchai and the bone tool industry, circular and rectangular wattle-and-daub structures, hand and wheel made pottery and stone celts from Golabai Sasan indicate the life ways of Neolithic people. The Neolithic culture of Orissa is characterised by ground and polished stone tools including axe, adze, stone hammer, wedge grinder, shoulder celts, chisel, ring stone and fabricator in which axes are the dominant types. Excavated Neolithic pottery has been classified by Dash (2000) into four categories: (i) thick to medium variety of pottery and coarse variety of micaceous red ware found at Baidyapur and Kuchai respectively, (ii) Corded ware, Grey and Brown ware, (iii) Black ware having resemblance with outside Indian pottery such as Thailand, (iv) bigger round vessel with small round face and dull brown colour. The crops recovered from these sites include rice, horse gram, pigeon pea, *mung* and *urad*.

With regard to the Chalcolithic period in Orissa, sites like Sankerjang, Golbai Sasan, Gopalpur, Kameswaripali, Kuanr are of considerable importance. The Chalcolithic period at Golbai Sasan is marked by a well developed ceramic industry, tools made of bone, stone and copper, domestication of plants and animals and hunting-fishing economy. The pottery types include Red burnished slip ware, Chocolate burnished slip ware, Black slipped or black burnished slip ware, Black and Red ware, Chocolate and red ware, Blackish grey and Grey ware, Buff ware, Buffish Red ware and dull Red ware. A variety of copper objects like ring and bangle and a furnace and a number of crucibles suggests onsite production of copper items.

West Bengal

A clear Neolithic stage in West Bengal cannot be identified and therefore the early farming sites could be classified as Neolithic/Chalcolithic in this part of the country. Datta (1992) discussed in details the Neolithic artefacts and rice-husk tempered crude pottery of West Bengal excavated at several sites including Bharatpur, Haraipur, Pandu Rajar Dhibi, Tamluk, etc. However, the sporadic evidence is not considered as traits of a separate Neolithic cultural phase in this part of Eastern India. Datta (2004-05: 59) believes that there is no clear cut sub-stratum of Neolithic culture below the Chalcolithic level as none of the excavated sites have yielded any prominent evidence and the stray occurrence of Neolithic tools in the context of Chalcolithic does not suggest a Neolithic economy.

The Chalcolithic sites are widespread in West Bengal with a major concentration in the Ajay-Damodar river valleys covering the districts of Burdwan and Birbhum. Some of the important excavated sites in the state are Mahisdol, Bharatpur, Haraipur, Dihar, Mangalkot, Pandu Rajar Dhibi, Tamluk, Baneshwardanga, and Pakhanna. The Chalcolithic pottery is represented by a wide variety of types and shapes including dish on stand, tulip shaped bowl, beaker, bowl with stand, channel spouted bowl, and flower vases. Black and red ware is the most diagnostic type of pottery in West Bengal besides Black slipped ware, Red ware and Grey ware. Due to wide and profuse distribution of Black and Red ware during this period in western plains of Bengal, the Chalcolithic phase is also known as Black and Red ware culture. The Chalcolithic pottery has elaborate painting either in black or white. The site of Pandu Rajar Dhibi has yielded rich bone tool industry and a variety of copper artefacts include ring, spiral bangle, bangle, bead, and fish hook. Radiometric dates suggest a time bracket of 1450 to 700 BCE for the Chalcolithic stage in the region (Datta 2004-05).

Northeast India

It was the pioneer efforts of late T.C. Sharma in association with late M.C. Goswami who established the Neolithic phase in stratigraphic context at the site of Daojali Hading in the North Cachar hill district of Assam during 1961 and 1963 (Goswami and Sharma 1963). The artefacts from excavation comprised edged tool, grinding stones, querns, mullers, and quartzite pebbles made of locally available shale, sandstone, quartzite and fossil wood. Shale was used for making edged tools and so also fossil wood; sandstone for grinding stones whetstones, and querns (Sharma 1966). The pottery is classified into three varieties, *i.e.* Cord-impressed, Stamped dull red and brick Red variety. Majority of the potsherds are heavily weathered and broken into small fragments which prevent in identifying the shapes and forms of the vessels. The Cord-impressed coarse grey ware is made of coarse and unevenly mixed clay, heavily tempered with large quartz particles. These vessels were prepared by the coil-building method (Sharma 1967). After establishing the characteristic features of the Neolithic tradition in Northeast India, data from a number of sites such as Parsi-Parlo in Arunachal Pradesh (Ashraf 1990), Sarutaru and Marakdola in Assam (Rao 1973), Nongpok Keithelmanbi and Napachik in Manipur (Singh 1993), Selbalgiri 2 (*IAR* 1966-67 and 1967-68) and Pynthorlangtein in Meghalaya (*IAR* 1992-93) have enabled reconstruction of various features and regional variations present during the Neolithic phase. The stone industry of Sarutaru includes ground stone celts made of grey to black coloured slate and cream to buff coloured sandstone. Pottery from the excavations at the site of Nongpok Keithelmanbi is mostly Corded ware overlying the Hoabinhian stratum in the cultural sequence (Dikshit and Hazarika 2012; Mishra and Hazarika in press). This ill-fired and handmade pottery is heavily weathered and in many cases the corded surface is also eroded. The cord-marks are found in the form of linear and criss-cross patterns. The pottery is made of fine clay and tempered with sand and a few quartz particles. The site of Napachik yielded potsherds decorated with cord-marks and tripod legs in association with pebble and flake tools as well as ground celts. The cord-marks are similar to the ones found at the site of Phunan. The Tripod wares characterize the ceramic industry of the Napachik site of Manipur. Among the tripod legs, there is a solid flat leg that resembles the ring tripod type of the late Neolithic of South China (Mishra and Hazarika in press).

Northeast India is situated in the crossroads between two important regions which have yielded the evidences of early rice agriculture, *i.e.* Gangatic valley of India and Yangtze river basin of China. Considering the presence of wild, intermediate and domestic varieties of rice species in this region, and on the basis of recent archaeological, genetic and ethnographic data, Hazarika (2006) suggests that this region must have contributed to the process of early domestication of rice. Rice, the most important crops of the Neolithic period of Northeast India has shaped the culture and has contributed in the historical development in the region (Hazarika 2011). Due to lack of sufficient number of C14 dates, the Eastern Indian Neolithic/ Chalcolithic is not yet put in proper chronological framework in relation to other regions of the country.

Future wok

The misleading understanding about the origin and development of agro-pastoral societies in the country is mainly because of biased research strategies we have adopted. There are numerous pockets of the country which need proper survey and attention of archaeologists. The north Gujarat is a promising area to understand this issue but the work initiated there could not be taken to logical conclusion. More work is required in Mewar and Eastern part of the country. Combined efforts of archaeologists and archaeological scientists is the need of the hour. We need to generate enough data on the climatic conditions of the early Holocene period to assess its impact on the origin and development of agro- pastoral societies in the country.

Bibliography

Alllchin, F.R. (1968) *Neolithic Cattle-keepers of South India – A* Study *of the Deccan Ash Mounds*, Cambridge : Univ. Press.

Barker, Graeme (2006) *Agricultural Revolution in Prehistory*. Oxford : Univ. Press.

Burgess, C. (1989) Volcanes, Catastrophe and the Global Crisis of the Late Second Millennium BC. *Current Archaeology* 5:325-29.

Cohen, Mark (1975) Population Pressure and Origins of Agriculture :An Archaeological Example from the Coast of Peru. In Steven Polgeer (ed), *Population, Ecology and Social Evolution*. 79-121. The Hague : Mouton.

Dikshit, K.N. (2009) The Decline of Harappan Civilization, *Ancient India*, N.S. No.1 : 125-78.

Gurdip Singh (1971) Indus Valley Culture seen in the context of Post-Glacial, Climatic and Ecological Studies in North-western India, *Archaeology and Physical Anthropology in Oceania*, 6:177-88.

IAR – Indian Archaeology : A Review.

Joshi, J.P. (1993) *Excavations at Bhagwanpura and other Explorations in Haryana, Jammu & Kashmir and Punjab.* New Delhi: ASI.

Joshi, R.V. (1978) *Stone Age Cultures of Central India.* Pune:Deccam College.

Kosambi, D.D.(2002) *Combined Methods in Indology.* New Delhi : Oxford Univ.Press.

Mashkour, Marjani (ed), (2006) *Equids in Time and Space – Papers in Honour of Vera Eisenmann.* Oxford : Oxbow Books.

Masica, Colin P. (1978) Aryan and Non-Aryan Elements in North Indian Agriculture. In M.M.Deshpande and P.Hook (ed), *The Aryan and Non-Aryan in India*, 55-151. Ann Arbor,Mich: Univ.of Michigan.

Mehta, R.N. and V.S.Sonavane (1993) Some Rural Harappan Settlements in Gujara. In G.L.Possehl (ed*), Harappan Civilization – A Recent Perspective, 167-74. New Delhi : Oxford-IBH.*

Misra, V.N. (1973) Bagor – A Late Mesolithic Settlement in Northern India. *World Archaeology* 5(1):92-110.

Paddayya, K. (1991-92) The Ash Mounds of South India:Fresh Evidence and Possible Implications. *BDCRI* 51-2:573-626.

(2011) Newer Perspectives in the Investigation of the Agro-Pastoral Cultures of India. *Man and Environment* 36(2):1-19.

Parpola, Asko (1988) The Coming of the Aryans to Iran and India and the Culture of the Ethnic Entity of the Dasas, *International Jr of Dravidian Linlguistics*, 17(2) : 85-229.

Piggot, Stuart (1952*) Prehistoric India.* Harmondsworth :Penguin.

Saran, S.C.and U.S.Sant (1994) Harappan Elements in the Neolithic-Chalcolithic Contexts of the Middle Ganga Plain.Paper read at the *III World Archaeology Congress.*

Saraswat, K.S. (1995) Ancient Crop Economy of Harappans from Rohira (Punjab) (Ca.2000-1700 BC). *The Palaeobotanist* 40:514-45.

Singh, B. (1995-96) Transformation of Cultures in the Middle Ganga Plains:A Case Study of Senuwar. *Pragdhara* 6:179-93.

(2004) *Early Farming Communities of Kaimur (Excavations at Senuear 1986-87; 1989-90*). 2 Vols. Jaipur : Publicaion Scheme.

Sonawane, V.S. (2002) Post-urban Harappan Culture in Gujarat. In S.and Ravikori Settar, Protohistory – Archaeology of the Harapan Civilization, 158-72. New Delhi : Manohar.

Tewari, Rakesh, et al (2002-03) Preliminary Report of the Excavation at Lahuradeva, Dist.Sant Kabir Nagar,U.P. *Pragdhara* 13:37-68.

Warren, B.A. (1987) Ancient and Mediaeval Records of the Monsoon Winds and Currents of the Indian Ocean. In J.S.Fein and P.Stephens (ed), *Monsoon,* 137-58. New York : John Willey.

Weber, S.A. (1991) *Plants and Harappan Subsistence.* New Delhi : Oxford-IBH.

Zimmer, Stephen (1990), On Indo-Europeanization. *Jr. of Indo-European Studies* 18:140-55.

Dash (2000) Hararika (2006) Datta (1992) Hararika (2011) Goswami and Sharma (1963) Childe (1939) Sharma (1966) Yasuda (2000) Sharma (1967) Shinde (2006) Ashraf (1990) Tewari (2007) Rao (1973) Shinde (2000) Singh (1998) Shinde (2001) Dikshit and Hazarika (2012) Shinde (1998) Shinde (2002)

7

PAKKĀKOT: TRANSITION FROM RURAL TO URBAN SETTLMENT: AN ARCHAEOLOGICAL STUDY

Sitaram Dubey, Santosh Kumar Singh

The problem of transition from rural to urban settlement is a vexed one. There are very few archaeological sites which delineate this transition effectively. Of all the sites excavated in Uttar Pradesh and Bihar, Pakkākot is the only site which presents a continuous occupation from Neolithic down to the medieval Period. At other important sites of Uttar Pradesh and Bihar ,e.g., Kausambi, Sravasti, Rajghat, Agiabeir, Jhusi, Nindaur, Nahush-Ka-Tila, Khairadih, Pataliputra, Champa, Rajgir, Vaisali, Chirand and Sonepur and many others, habitation starts later and in most of the cases, except Pataliputra, Champa and Chirand, the sites were deserted earlier, than those of Pakkākot. The excavations conducted at Pakkākot (2010-11, 2011-12 and 2012-13) help us in discerning how a rural settlement gradually developed into an urban settlement.

The ancient settlement of Pakkākot (Lat 25°45'10" N, Long. 84°0'30"E) is located on the ancient bed of Chhoti Saryu (*Tons*) river in Ballia district of eastern Uttar Pradesh. Ballia district, the eastern most part of the state of Uttar Pradesh, lies between 25° 33" and 26° 11" North latitude and 83° 38" and 84° 39'' East longitudes. Total geographical area of the district is 2981 sq. km. The district was recognized as an independent administrative unit on Nov. 1st, 1879 in eastern Uttar Pradesh. The District headquarter is Ballia containing six Tehsils namely Ballia Sadar, Bansdih, Rasara, Belthara, Bairia and Sikanderpur. Blocks in the district are seventeen in number. Ballia is served by the North-Eastern Railway. It lies on the main line of the Chhapra-Varanasi section of the North-Eastern Railway passing through Aurihar, Ghazipur, Phephana and Ballia. A branch line runs from Phephana (Ballia district) **(Fig.1)** to Shahganj (Jaunpur district).

The first archaeological investigation in the area was carried out by A.C.L. Carlleyle who explored a few sites of archaeological importance in 1874-75 under the guidance of Alexander Cunningham. In 1891 A. Fuhrer did archaeological investigation in this area and subsequently the Department of Ancient Indian History, Culture and Archaeology, Banaras Hindu University, in early sixties and in 1994-95 (*IAR*. 1963-64: 43; Singh & Singh. 1994-95: 21-36).Black-and-red wares were reported from Bhimapurdih, Bijalipur, Godabirgadha, Lovika-Ka-Tapa, Khairadih, Pakkākot and Waina. The same department has conducted archaeological excavations at Khairadih, situated on the right bank of the Ghaghara in the north-western part of the district during 1980-86 and subsequently in 1996-97 (Singh. 1989: 28-34, 1990-91: 78-86; Tripathi and Singh. 2004: 1-69). The archaeological excavations reveal deposits of Chalcolithic to Kushana Period.

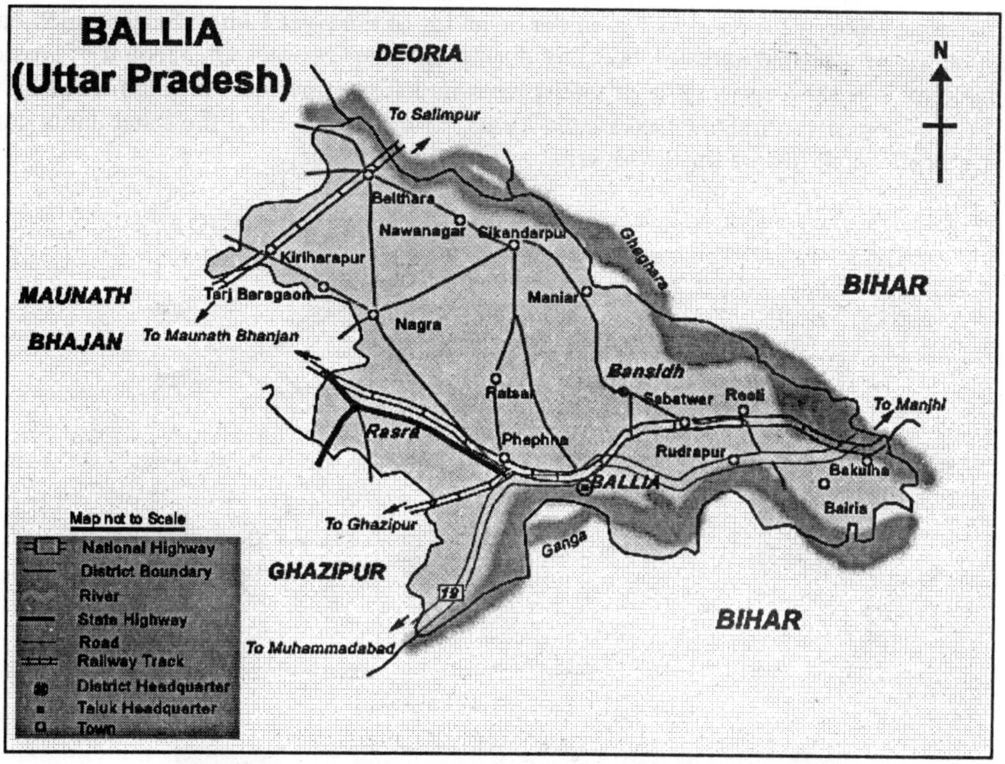

Fig. 1: Location of Ballia district (Utter Pradesh).

Previous Archaeological Work in region

An ancient settlement named Lakhaneshwardih located on the left bank of the Chhoti Saryu in district Ballia was excavated in 1956-57 by a team of the State Museum, Lucknow, yielding NBPW, stone pestles, terracotta figurines etc. (*IAR*. 1956-57: 24). An extensive village to village survey was conducted by the Department of AIHC & Archaeology, Banaras Hindu University, in 1993-94 (Singh *et al.* 1994-95: 21-36) and the sites reported are : Janwan, Bhunadih, Alam Ka Tola, Zimi Chak, Chhatarsand, Karsanar, Isar, Pithapatti, Halpur, Deorhi, Muryari, Chandayar (all located in Tehsil Bansdih), Waina situated on Ballia-Ghazipur Road, Sihpur and Kurmipur in Ballia Tehsil, Pakkākot, Jagdishpur and Hajauli located on Ballia-Rasara Road, and Tikka Deori, Unai, Lakhaneshwardih and Surwaradih on Ballia-Mau Road. All these sites were reported to be Chalcolithic, NBPW and later periods.

P. Singh and his team had reported Pakkākot as ranging in date from NBPW to medieval period (Singh *et al.*1994-95:21-36). Dilip Chakrabarti and R.N. Singh had also reported Pakkākot as a NBPW site. Further, they also mentioned a small BRW settlement to the east of Pakkākot situated on the Buḍhi nālā (Chakrabarti and Singh.1998:108). Actually, it was the extension of the same site. The present team visited the site in the month of July, 2010 and observed that the site belongs to Neolithic to medieval period (Dubey *et al.* 2010 : 200-204), which was well supported by the result of excavations done in the months of Feb.-May, 2011, 2012 and 2013 (Dubey *et al.* 2012 : 198-205).

The newly discovered Urban Settlement of Pakkākot

The ancient settlement of Pakkākot (Lat 25°45'10" N, Long. 84°0'30"E) is located on the ancient bed of Chhoti Saryu (*Tons*) river in Ballia district of eastern Uttar Pradesh (**Fig. 2, 3 & 4**). This site was excavated in the months of February to May, 2010-11, 2011-12 and April to Jun 2012-13 (Dubey, *et al.* 2012) by the Department of Ancient Indian History, Culture and Archaeology, Banaras Hindu University. The mound is extended in a wide area, about 2 km square and located on at least four different mounds (1-4) at Pakkākot.

During excavation, we tried to ascertain the behavior of the river Chhoti Saryu which had played a vital role in the life of the inhabitants of Pakkākot during different periods. On account of erosion by the river, the inhabitants were forced to settle at safer places in different periods. It is indicated by the flood deposits in the sections of the trenches excavated by us. In the later period the inhabitants constructed fortification wall and watch towers for the security against river erosion.

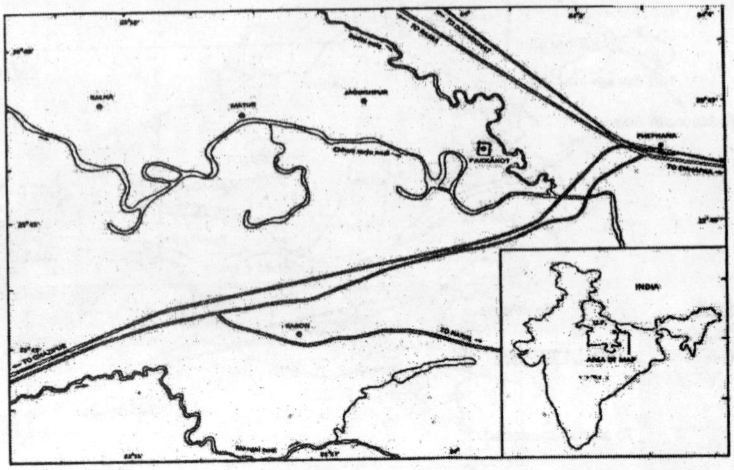

Fig. 2 : Location of Pakkākot.

Fig. 3 : Pakkākot- Mound 2, Google Image.

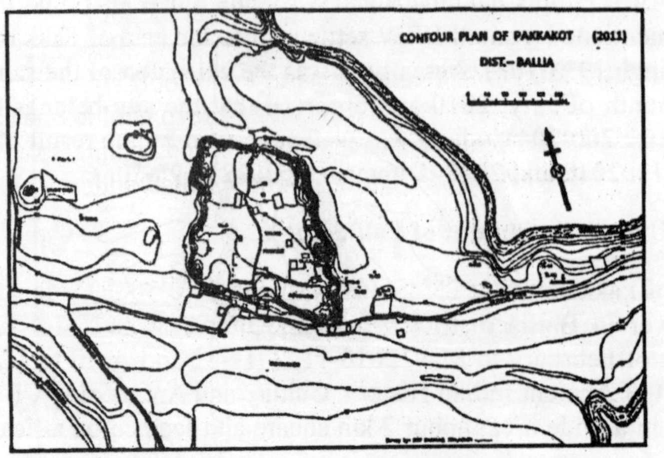

Fig. 4 : Contour Plan of Pakkākot.

The limited excavations on mounds 1-4 had brought to light a six-fold cultural sequence ranging in approximately date from 5000 BC to 15th century AD without any break in its continuity between all of them. All the six periods were characterized by their typical ceramic industry and other antiquities. The features of these periods are described below:

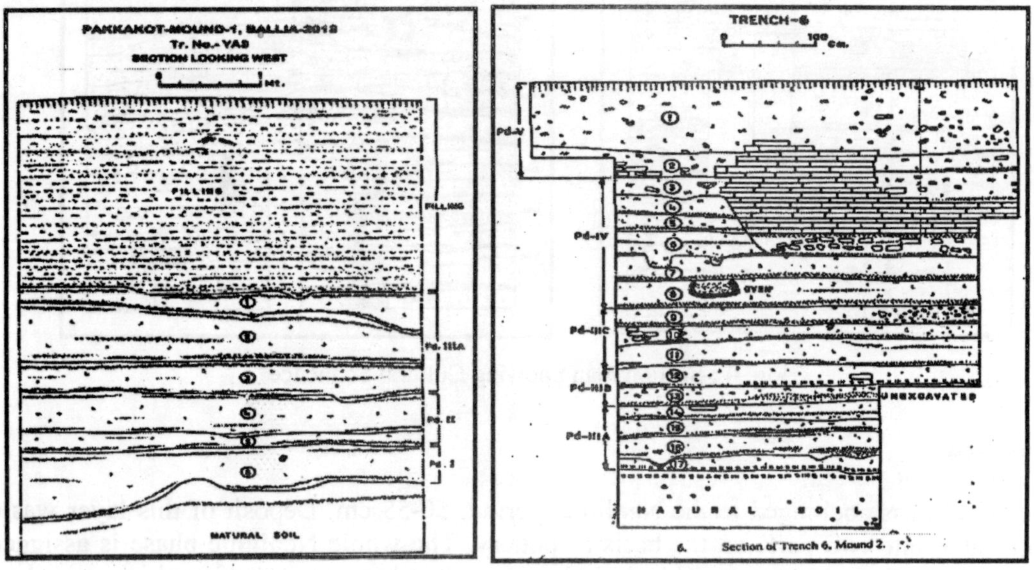

Fig. 5 : Section Plan showing Cultural Sequence

Periods	Settlements	Approximately Dates
I	Neolithic	5000 BCE -2000 BCE
II	Chalcolithic	1500 BCE -900 BCE
III	Northern Black Polished Ware	900BCE-200 BCE
III-A	NBPW	900BCE-600 BCE
III-B	NBPW	600BCE-450 BCE
III-C	NBPW	450BCE-200 BCE
IV	Śuṅga-Kuṣāṇa	200 BCE - 300 CE
V	Gupta and Post- Gupta	300 CE - 700 CE
VI	Early Medieval - Medieval Periods	700 CE- 1500 CE

The ancient settlement of Pakkākot is located on the ancient bed of chhoti Saryu (*Tons*) river in Ballia district of eastern Uttar Pradesh. The rivers thus provided the perennial source of water to the earliest settlers and induced them to settle here. There were other geographical considerations also which attracted habitation here. The rivers facilitated the easy movement of material through rivers in the beginning and later on gave growth to mercantile activities. Besides, the deposit of alluvial soil made Neolithic farming easier. The rivers also solved the problem of food to some extent. Due to heavy rainfall in the area there was luxuriant growth of vegetation. There were other advantages also which made Neolithic settlement possible here. There was plenty of bamboo, reed and other wood in the area, which could be used as building material. The animals who roamed in forests provided hunting as livelihood and their bones were used for making tools. Thus the possibility of mixed economy at the site was one of the most important factors for the development of Neolithic settlement at Pakkākot. The excavations of the site brought to light six distinct cultural levels, the first four of which are continuous but there is some gap between the five and six cultural levels (**Fig. 5 & 6**).

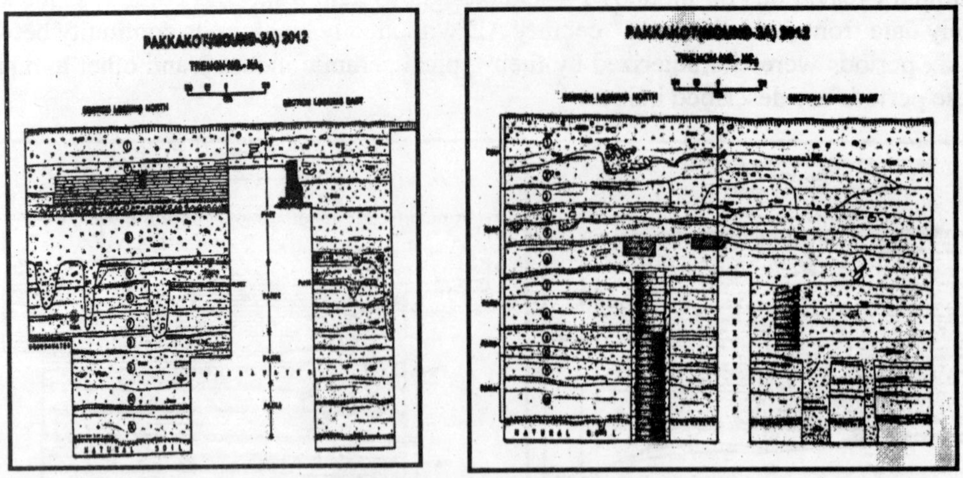

Fig. 6 : Section Plan Showing Cultural Sequence

Neolithic period

The first cultural phase belonged to the Neolithic period. 50-55 cm. Deposit of this layer was exposed which is divisible into two parts on the basis of pottery. The whole Neolithic phase is assigned a date range of C. 5000 B.C. to 1500 A.D. This period was marked by ceramics of cord-impressed red ware, rusticated ware and red ware which were made on slow wheel. Some of the potsherds are handmade. Rice husk is used as degraissant, which is seen both on the surface and on the core of potsherds which are thick in fabric. The pots of medium quality are also found. Generally the pots are ill-fired and the clay used in the ceramics is not well levigated. Shapes are limited in comparison to wares of the overlying Chalcolithic Culture. They include bowls, including pedestalled bowls, medium sized vases, *martbans*, footed vessels and a few spouted vessels. The inhabitants of Neolithic period used several methods to decorate the pottery. The first method comprises post-firing scratching by a sharp instrument which includes geometrical patterns. Such designs have already been reported from Imlidih Khurd-I, Lahuradeva-I and Bhunadih-I. The second method of decorating was appliqué. Types of rope and chain pattern were executed on the ceramics of this period.

The main feature of this phase is absence of metals and the use of stone and bone tools. The Neolithic economy was based on hunting, fishing and limited cultivation. During the early Neolithic phase people lived in underground floors which had roofs above but later on they began to live on the ground level itself. Gradually they developed some architectural designs also. The huts were circular in shape and made of bamboo, wattle and daub. Due to limited excavations, no precise nature of structures was traced. Fragments of reed marks and burnt clay lumps suggest that the inhabitants used to live in wattle-and-daub houses. The walls were plastered with clay. This becomes clear from the discovery of a circular paved floor. Outside this floor there were post-holes at regular intervals to support poles. There was provision of hearths and oblong ovens in the huts.

A good quantity of animal bones and archaeo-botanical remains were recovered. These were analyzed by P.P. Joglekar, Anubha Pathak and R.N. Singh respectively.

Table – 1

Serial no.	*Archaeological Context*	*Depth in cm.*	*Result*
1.	PKT-1, 14 (3)	265-270cm	*Nigella sp* , *Brassica sp* (Mustard), *Lens culinaris* (Lentil), *Triticum sp* (Wheat), *Hordeum sp*(Barley)., *Chenopodium album* (pigweed), .*Trigonella occulta*.

2.	PKT-1, 14 (3)	270-280cm.	*Chenopodium album* (pigweed), *Trienthema sp*, *Triticum sp* (wheat), *Pisum sativum (*Matar*)?*, *Lens culinaris (*Lentil*)*, *Hordeum sp (*Barley)., *Dolichus biflorus (*bean*)*.
3.	PKT-1, 14 (4)	310-315cm.	*Dolichus biflorus (*bean*)*., *Vigna sp.*, *Oryza sativa (*Rice*)*, *Chenopodium album (*pigweed*)*, *Brassica compestris (*Mustard*)*, *Hordeum sp (*Barley*)*, *Argemone maxicana?*, *Trienthema sp*, *Pisum sativum?*.
4.	PKT-1, 14 (4)	315-325cm	*Lens culinaris (*Lentil*)*, *Lathyrus sp (*wild pea., *Vicia sp.?*, *Hordeum vulgare (*barley*)*, *Triticum aestivum* (Wheat), *Chenopodium album*, *Oryza sativa (*Rice).
5.	PKT-1, 14 (4)	325-330cm	*Oryza sativa (*Rice*)*, *Lens culinaris (*Lentil*)*, *Chenopodium album (*Pigweed*)*, 1 seed unidentified.
6.	PKT-1, 14 (4)	335-340cm	*Triticum aestivum. (*Wheat*)*, *Hordeum vulgare (*Barley*)*, *Chenopodium album (*Pigweed*)*, *Brassica sp. (*Mustard*)*, *Lathurus sp. (*Wild pea), *Nigella sp.*, *Pisum sp (*Matar*)*., 1 unidentified
7.	PKT-1, 14 (4)	345-350cm	*Oryza sativa(*Rice*)*, *Brassica sp (*Mustard*)*, *Vigna sp.*, *Triticum aestivum (*Wheat*)*, *Triticum sphaerococcum*, *Dolichus biflorus (*Bean*)*, *Lens culinaris (*Lentil), *Hordeum sp. (*Barley*)*, *Chenopodium album (*Pigweed*)*.

The faunal remains are cattle, buffalo, and goat.

Fig. 7 : Floral Remain

Table – 2 Number of Identified Specimens (NISP) at Pakkākot

Period	**I**	**II**		**IIIA**	**IIIB**		**IIIC**			**IV**		
Trench	9	9	6	9	2	7	7-8	6	6	7	7	7-8
Layer	(4)	(4)	(8)	(3)	5	(5-6)	(3)	(9)	(11)	(1)	(2)	(1-2)
Bos indicus	5	0	0	2	0	1	3	0	0	1	0	2
Bos/Bubalus	4	0	0	9	0	6	12	0	0	0	0	9
Bubalus bubalis	2	0	0	0	0	0	0	0	0	0	0	1
Capra hircus	3	0	0	0	0	0	0	0	2	0	0	1
Capra/Ovis	0	0	0	0	0	1	4	0	0	0	0	12
Sus domesticus	0	0	0	0	0	0	0	0	0	0	0	2
B. tragocamelus	1	0	0	0	0	0	0	0	0	0	0	1
T. quadricornis	0	0	0	0	0	0	1	0	0	0	0	0
A. cervicapra	0	0	0	0	0	0	0	0	2	1	0	1
Axis axis	1	0	0	0	1	0	2	1	0	0	0	3
Cervus unicolor	0	0	3	0	0	0	0	1	0	0	2	0
Sus scrofa	1	0	0	0	0	1	4	0	0	0	0	3
Lepus nigricollis	1	0	0	0	0	0	0	0	0	0	0	1
Pavo cristatus	0	0	0	0	0	0	0	0	0	0	0	1
Grus antigone	0	0	0	0	0	1	0	0	0	0	0	0
Trionyx gangeticus	0	0	0	1	0	0	0	0	0	0	0	0
Kachuga tecta	1	0	0	0	0	0	0	0	0	0	0	0
Sperata seenghala	0	1	0	0	0	0	0	0	0	0	0	0
Lamellidens sp.	0	0	0	0	0	0	1	0	0	0	0	0
NISP total	19	1	3	12	1	10	27	2	4	2	2	37

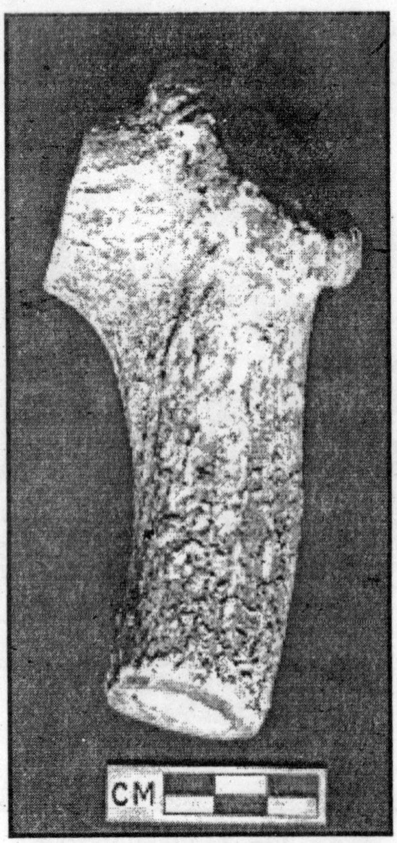

Fig. 8: Faunal Remains

The economy to the people was based on limited cultivation, domestication of cattle and different types of arts and crafts. The evidence for the cultivation of rice is supplied by the discovery of charred rice and paddy husk. For hunting, cultivation, storage of grains, food and for cooking purposes the people needed tools, implements and vases. Therefore, they learnt the art of making bone and stone tools, pottery and different types of crafts. One of the most important crafts of the Neolithic settlers of Pakkākot was the making of tools of stone and bone. The bones of antler, deer, elephant, buffalo, ox, stag, tortoise etc are discovered.

Chalcolithic Period

Period II belongs to the Chalcolithic Culture and was traced on Mound-1 only from trench nos. 9, 14 and 23. The layers are light yellowish and ashy in colour. They measure 60 cm in thickness. Ceramics of black-and-red ware, black slipped ware, red slipped ware and red ware were recovered. The potteries are wheel made and ranges from fine to coarse variety. Important types are bowls, spouted vessels, vases, large sized basins and footed bowls. Ceramic industry and pottery types associated with this phase may be compared with potteries of sites like Checher-Kutubpur, Senuwar and Chirand, all located in Bihar; Waina, Bhunadih, Lahuradeva, Narhan, Khairadih, Agiabir, Jhusi, Tokwa, Raja-Nala Ka Tila and Malhar in Uttar Pradesh.

Apart from ceramic assemblage, antiquities recovered include terracotta beads, bone points and arrowheads, gamesman and pottery discs. Wheat and barley along with rice was firmly established in the economy at the site.

Northern Black Polished Ware Period

Period III of Pakkākot has been termed as the N.B.P. phase, extending from C. 900 B.C. to 2nd century B.C. This phase marked the beginning of "Early Historic Urbanization" in India. The extensive use of iron implements in agriculture brought in surplus production, diversification of arts and crafts, the growth of trade and commerce facilitated by the use of coins, monumental buildings, art of writing and consequently the re – emergence of cities in northern India (Childe, 1965 and Singh, 2010). At Pakkākot also some of the traits of urbanization are noticed. Thus it can be said that the NBP phase at Pakkākot marks the beginning of the city life (Singh, 2012: 47-49 and Singh, 2014: 89-100). In the beginning, the structures in this phase were also built of perishable materials like reed, bamboo but later on brick structures appear. The use of baked bricks in structures definitely points to the economic prosperity of the people. Special mention may be made of a wharf is the most striking structural feature at Pakkākot , signs of brick floors and two ring - wells (**Fig.9**) belonging to the late NBP phase were noticed during the latest excavation of the site.

Fig. 9 : Ring well, Period IIIC

The wharf was found in the north boundary of the site close to a water logged deposit (Lakda Nala / Chhoti Saryu). The part of the Wharf that could be excavated was a huge structure measuring 20m of 18 courses of Mauryan bricks where the vessels moored alongside to load or unload or to lie at rest (Fig. 10 & 11). This wall was buttressed as to strengthen it. The size of the bricks used in this wall measuring 52 x 26 x 12 cm. This type of wharf is not reported from any other site of Middle Ganga plain. To strengthen this wall another mud-wall was made of clay and concrete.

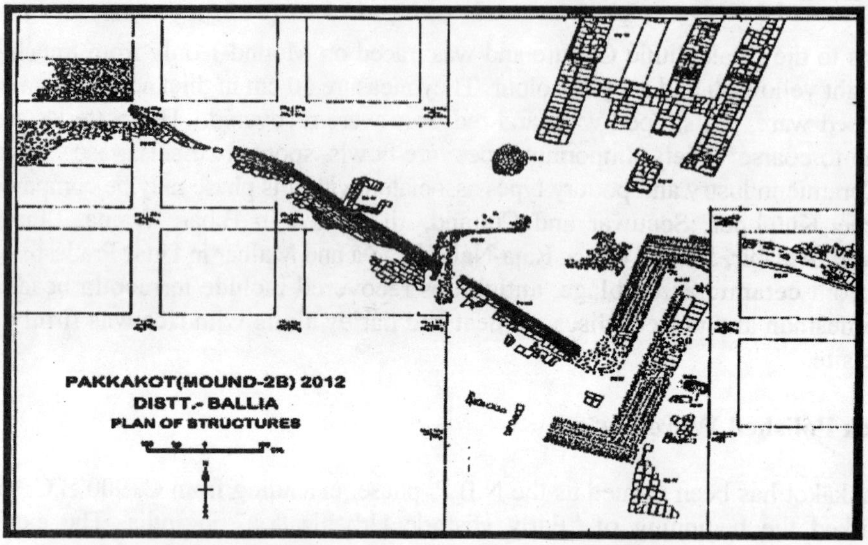

Fig. 10 : Plan of Wharf, Period IIIC

Fig. 11 : Structure of Wharf, Period IIIC

A rare discovery is a figurine of dancing girl made of a silver sheet which was found from the pre-Mauryan level (**Fig. 12**). This type of figurine is not reported from any other site of Ganga plain in this context. Although Ghosh has reported a golden figurine from Lauria Nandangadh (Bihar) in his book *An Encyclopaedia of Indian Archaeology* but its photograph is not published and its present status is unknown (Ghosh. 1989 : 326-327).

Fig. 12 : Silver Figurine of Pre-Mauryan Period

This silver female figurine measuring 10.75 cm long is a masterpiece of art recovered along with a punch-marked coin. It was made by cutting the silver sheet. Headdress is shown by incised lines, design of dots is shown below the headdress. Hair is well combed and parted in the middle. Locks of hair are shown on both sides of the cheeks. High eyebrows and flat nose represent archaic features. Right ear is broken while an ear ring is worn in the left ear. A necklace is shown by wide strips. Head of the figurine is broken and seems to be attached separately. Incised lines are shown from neck to the waist on both obverse and reverse sides. Rounded breasts seem to be uncovered. Incised lines are also shown on both hands and on both sides from shoulder to below the elbow which may have been made to show bangles. There are four bangles on each wrists. Fingers of both hands are found slightly broken. Left hand is broken from the elbow. The upper portion of the body is conical-shaped; the waist is very thin while the hips are very large and heavy. This type of hip is named *pṛthuśroṇi* in *Abhijñānaśākuntalam.* The term *vṛhad śroṇi* is used by V.S. Agrawala for this type of hip. He has opined that large hips of females are helpful for easy delivery. A button type design within a circle is shown in the middle of the hip. Two parallel lines with dots are also shown on both sides of the hip. The large genital organ is beautifully carved. An anklet is shown in the right leg by four incised lines. Fingers of the right leg are slightly raised upwards. It seems that the figurine is in *tribhaṅgamudrā*. C. Margabandhu has observed that a terracotta figurine recovered from Champa (Bhagalpur, Bihar) has the same type of features while B.R. Mani opines that except the archaic features the figurine is very much similar to the dancing girl from Mohenjodaro. K. Paddayya of Deccan College, Pune, also suggested in his review of our first season's report entitled *Pakkākoṭ-some new archaeological dimensions of mid-Ganga Plain* published in *Man and Environment*, vol. xxxvii (i)-2012 that it shows the depiction of a dancing girl. Left leg of the figurine is broken. This is a unique discovery of Pakkākot excavation and is helpful in establishing the site to be a city. The antiquity, artistic features and the metal used in making the figurine not only prove its importance but also suggest that it was brought here by traders.

The excavation at Pakkākot yielded 415 stone and bone beads. Among the stone beads glass, carnelian and agate are most prolific, as they account 52, 25 and 11 specimens respectively. Quartz and chart come next in order of frequency of 8 specimens each respectively. Crystal accounts for 7 specimens and were distributed in Periods III C and IV. Amethyst, topaz and faience were the other semi-precious stones used for making beads with 02 and 01 specimen respectively. Ivory and bone are the other popular material accounting for 8 and 10 specimens respectively. A single bead of stone was recovered from

Period IV while two broken beads were found from Period V. Aforesaid beads are diverse in shapes. They are circular square, spherical, hexagonal and long barrel cylindrical in shape. Some beads have etched bands and some have natural colour.

In many parts of the world, beads are used for symbolic purposes, for example:

- Used as rosary beads
- Used as anti-tension devices
- Used for gaming
- Used as currency.

Here at Pakkākot a large number of beads were recovered from NBPW to Gupta/post-Gupta periods. Stone and bone beads account for 415 specimens while the terracotta beads are 381in number. The large concentration of semi-precious stone beads has been seen in the last phase of NBPW and Sunga-Kushana periods. It shows that in these periods the site was fully developed as a city site. Less number of these beads in Gupta/post-Gupta periods was due to high disturbance in the levels of these periods. Materials used for making these beads i.e. agate, quartz, amethyst, carnelian etc. were not found on the site and its vicinity. It seems that these materials were imported from Vindhyan ranges. (Fig.13).

Table 3 : Period wise distribution of Stone and Bone beads and Pendants

Material	Period							
	I	II	III A	III B	III C	IV	V	Total
Agate	-	-	01	02	06	10	01	20
Amythyst	-	-	01			01	01	03
Carnelian	-	-	03	07	16	14	02	42
Crystal	-	-	-		06	05	01	12
Glass	-	-	07	08	20	28	05	68
Ivory	-	-	03	02	11	06	01	23
Faience	-	-	-	-	-	-	01	01
Topaz	-	-	-	-	-	01	-	01
Stone	-	-	-	-	-	01	-	01
Bone	-	-	-	03	06	01	-	10
Chert	-	-	-	01	03	04	-	08
Indeterminate	-	-	-	-	-	-	02	02
Jasper	-	-	01	-	01	-	-	02
Quartz	-	-	-	01	04	03	-	08
Pendant	-	-	01	-	-	-	-	01

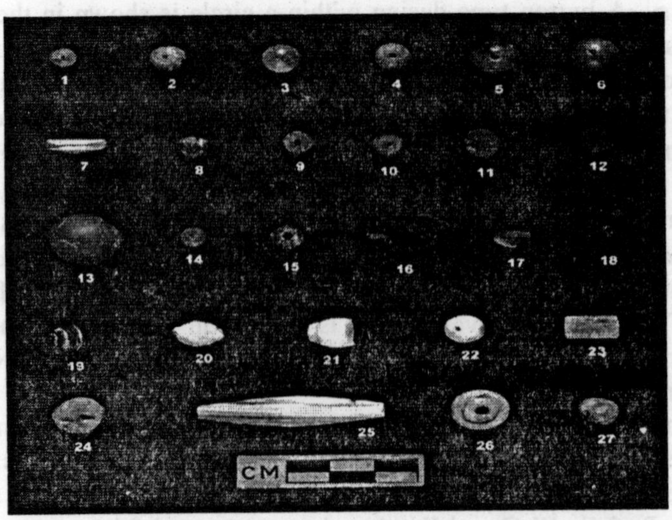

Fig. 13 : Beads of semi precious stones, Period IV.

Other important findings of this period include beads of semi-precious stones and terracotta, iron and copper objects, a large quantity of bone points and arrowheads, terracotta and pottery discs and skin rubbers, balls and pestles of clay. Excavation yielded a total no. of ten copper coins of which six are Punch-marked while four are cast category.

In the excavations at Pakkākot, we have found nineteen seals and one hundred eighteen sealings. Seals are made of copper, bone and terracotta while sealings are made of terracotta only. Of these, one hundred fifteen came from various trenches and one was found from surface. Some of the seals and sealings are oval and some of them are circular in shape. Most of them bear legend while a few bear both legend and device and very few bear symbols only. The sealings recovered from the site belong to a special category because some of them have five impressions on it. Legends of these sealings throw light on the names of a few kings like *Revatimita, Dhandeva, Rāmadāsas, Rāmadatta* etc.

A unique sealing depicted on the chariot that is possibly covering a '*Shivaliṅga*' on the chariot by umbrella. Legend as '*Śivasa*' in Brāhmī script of Fist century A.D. (**Fig.14**).

Fig. 14 : Sealings of Period IV, with the legend "Sivasa" in Brahmi script

Table 4 : Period and material wise distribution of seals

Type & Material	I	II	III A	III B	III C	IV	V	Total
A. Copper	-	-	-	-	-	01	-	01
B. Bone	-	-	-	-	-	01	-	01
C. Terracotta	-	-	-	-	08	37	3	48
Total	-	-	-	-	08	39	3	50

Table 5 : Period and material wise distribution of sealings

Type & Material	I	II	III A	III B	III C	IV	V	UNS	Total
Terracotta	-	-	-	05	17	70	19	01	115
Total	-	-	-	05	17	70	19	01	115

The history of seals and sealings goes back to the Saindhava Period. But after that its discontinued till fourth century BC. From Mauryan period it has a continuous history till date. The seals and sealings have important role in history writing and determination of archaeological stratifications.

The above description shows that the seals and sealings of Pakkākot belong to Periods III A to VI dated to 4th century BC to 15th century AD. Regarding their use, it is clear that they had been used for sending materials for trade. It is noteworthy that Pakkākot lies on an important trade route between

Pataliputra to Kapilvastu *via* Buxar. The trader's used to cross Ganges near Buxar and proceeded towards Kapilvastu through Pakkākot. The discovery of a number of seals and sealings from the limited excavation proves that the traders of Pakkākot were taking active part in the riverine trade.

Coins also make their appearance from the site of Pakkākot during Sunga- Kushana period. Punch - marked coins as well as cast copper coins have been unearthed from this level. These coins also were found from the upper level or the late NBP phase, suggesting thereby that the site had grown into an urban settlement by the Maurya - Sunga period. This was possible because the geographical situation of Pakkākot made it possible for its inhabitants to have commercial links with other contemporary towns and cities of Uttar Pradesh and Bihar like Kausambi, Nahush-Ka-Tila , Khairadih, Sravasti, Rajghat, Agiabir, Jhusi, Nindaur, Pataliputra, Champa, Rajgir, Vaisali, Chirand and Sonepur. By the Sunga-Kushana period Pakkākot had developed into full fledged urban centre. All these sites appear as urban settlements in the NBP phase.

With the changing economic set – up now the use of metals (copper, Iron) becomes more prominent than those of bone and stone which hence forth was used only in making house–hold implements and ornaments. The tools and implements to be used in agriculture and crafts were made of metals only. Copper was mainly used for making antimony rods. Iron objects like blades, spade, nails, daggers etc. have been found. Considerable progress was made in the field of ceramic industry. This period is mainly characterized by the use of NBPW.

Sunga-Kushan Period

The economic transformation became more distinct at Pakkākot during the IV stage (200 B.C. – 300 A. D.). We notice a full–fledged urban culture at Pakkākot during this phase. It suggests increased density of population. We may form some idea about the town–planning of the period, though the evidences are not plenty (Singh, 2010). The houses were built in a planned manner. Burnt bricks become the - chief building material **(Fig.15A & B).** Both religious and secular structures have been brought to light from this period; the exposed residential complex is of fairly large size. To strengthen this wall another mud-wall was made of clay and concrete. Besides, remains of other structures (Walls) of the Kushan period were exposed. For the purposes of defense the houses were fortified. The discovery of the pieces of terracotta tiles indicates that the roof – tops of the houses were tiled.

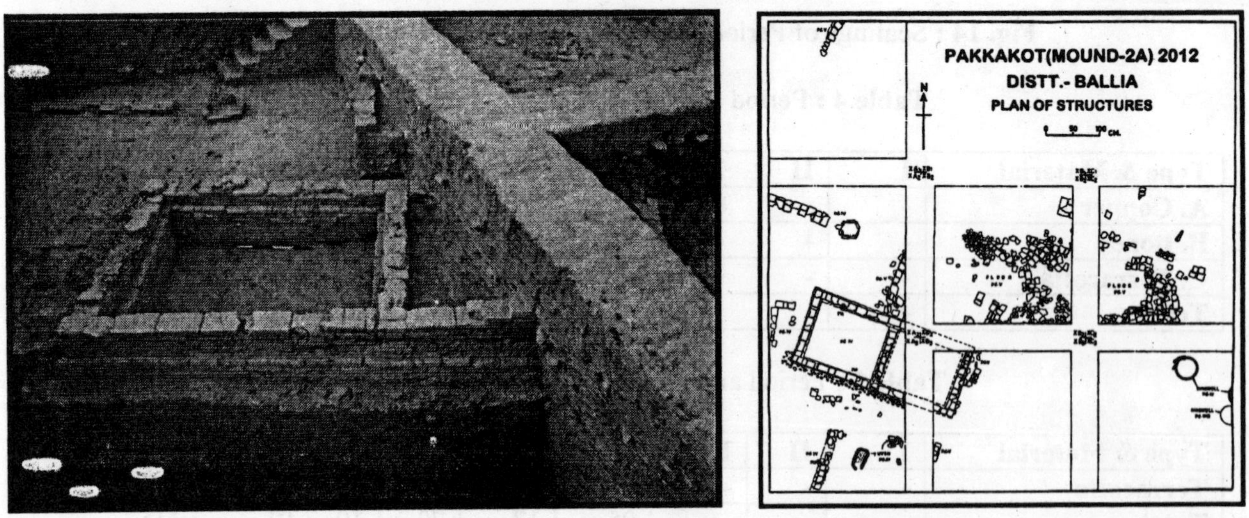

A B

Fig. 15A & B : Plan of burnt brick structure, Period IV

The material remains exhumed from the IV stage at Pakkākot indicate the existence of many crafts and industries, but surprisingly no agricultural implement has come to light from this level. This may be taken to suggest that during this phase the site had developed into a full grown township. Its economy was based on crafts and commerce. There is evidence to suggest the existence of crafts like pottery, terracotta, bricks, and beads of semi–precious stones, ornaments, vessels and house -hold objects, bone and ivory ornaments, metallurgy, etc. Although these crafts flourished in the earlier period also, but we notice marked improvement in these crafts, except pottery and terracotta figurines.

With the changing economic set – up now the use of metals (copper, iron) becomes more prominent than those of bone and stone which hence forth was used only in making house–hold implements and ornaments. The tools and implements to be used in agriculture and crafts were made of metals only. Copper was mainly used for making antimony rods. Iron objects like blades, spade, nails, daggers etc. have been found. The terracotta art and bead making also flourished. The terracotta figurines of the period throw interesting light on contemporary socio–cultural life of the people. The best specimen is represented by the figurine of a dancing girl who is wearing a flanked skirt, a special type of head–dress and *nupur*.

We may form some idea about the artistic activities of the people also. A large number of terracotta decorative pieces, which might have been hung on walls for beautification, have been found. Clay toys and skin – rubbers of varied size and shapes are also important. Some of the terracotta human figurines are shown wearing peaked - head dresses which became prevalent in the Kushan period. The use of sprinklers is another novelty of this period. The discovery of sprinklers at Pakkākot clearly suggests commercial activity. Another evidence for trade and commerce is supplied by the use of raw materials like copper and iron and numerous varieties of semi – precious stones which must have been imported from outside. The discovery of large number of Kushana coins also supports the idea of trade. Its geographical location helped considerably in fostering commercial activity. Pakkākot was well connected with other important commercial and urban centers of the period through land and river routes.

Gupta and Post Gupta Period

In the Gupta and Post Gupta Period the importance of Pakkākot began to decline. This is clearly demonstrated by the material remains of the succeeding layers. The Gupta and Post Gupta remains at Pakkākot are negligible as neither structures nor antiquities belonging to the Gupta and Post Gupta period has come to light. Most probably on account of political instability and its economic repercussions in northern India, Pakkākot like many other contemporary urban centers witnessed a rough weather. It might have led to its desertion. That's why we do not find any sign of habitation in the Gupta and Post Gupta period for many centuries to come.

A stone slab with circular top and the head of *Śiva* emerging from it was found from a pit of Period V **(Fig.16)** .The left portion of the head and portion below the chin are broken. The right portion of slab is also damaged. The back portion of slab is flat and unadorned. The god wears circular pearl rings in elongated ear lobes and an elegant *ja□āju□a* with circular bun secured by a fillet of which the string bifurcates the hair into two halves on the lower section and ends in a circular amulet in the middle on the forehead. The face of the god shows an expression of bliss and repose with closed lips; the drooping eyes have narrow eyelids with marked pupils; the nose is sharply cut; and the third eye is incised with pupil.

Early Medieval - Medieval Period

The site was also inhabited during the medieval period as shown by glazed ware recovered from the surface. Mention may be made of several ponds and wells made of *lakhauri* bricks which are still present nearby the Pakkākot mound. The deposits of this period no longer exist.

Emerging Picture

As far as the site of Pakkākot is concerned, it is also a fortified city extended in about more than 8 hectares of area. Pakkākot, excavations brought to light a six-fold cultural sequence ranging in date from 5000 BC -1500 AD without any break in between all of them. All the six periods were characterized by their typical ceramic industries and other objects. Continuation of the settlement is observed even in the medieval period by glazed ceramics, and ponds and wells made of *lakhauri* bricks.

Fig. 16 : Head of *Śiva* Period V

While copper was in use in *circa* 1900 B.C., the properties of iron as the principal metal of daily use were truly understood by the people around 1300 B.C. Agriculture was the mainstay of the economy of our area and the concept of cultivating two crops in a year had already come in to practice even in the Neolithic period datable to 5000 B.C. Cultivation of rice, wheat, barley, various types of millets, several types of pulses and oil seeds were done in the Neolithic stage.

Thus if we go by Childe's criteria of urbanization, we may safely conclude that by the NBPW Period III B Pakkākot had developed into a full - fledged urban centre.

The beginning of urbanization at Pakkākot is witnessed in Period III B which is marked by the use of NBPW. It is observed that during this period river Chhoti Saryu used to flow nearby the site. Because of the threat of recurring flood people occupied the main mound and built fortification but when population increased people migrated to other mounds.The geographical situation of Pakkākot made it possible for its inhabitants to have commercial links with other contemporary towns and cities like *Pataliputra, Rajghat* and *Vaisali*. The archaeological evidences show that by the Sunga-Kushan period Pakkākot had developed into a full-fledged urban centre.

Thus the excavation of Pakkākot indicates how a settlement changed from rural to urban settlement. Political, economic and religious factors were mainly responsible for this transformation. The evidence from Pakkākot conforms to the general pattern of growth and decline of cities in northern India.

A figurine of dancing girl of silver is a rare discovery of this site which was found from the pre-Mauryan level. This type of figurine is not reported from any site of Ganga plain. Although Ghosh has reported about a golden figurine in his book *An Encyclopaedia of Indian Archaeology* recovered from Lauria Nandangaḍh (Bihar) but its photograph is not published and its present status is unknown.

References

Childe, V. Gordon, The Urban Revolution, *Town Planning Review*, Vol. 21, 1950, pp. 3-17.

Chakrabarti, D.K. (2001), *Archaeological Geography of the Ganga Plain: The Lower and the Middle Ganga*, Permanent Black, Delhi.

Childe, V., Gordon (1950), The Urban Revolution, *Town Planning Review*, Vol. 21, pp. 3-17, Reprinted in *Ancient Cities of the Indus*, (ed. Possehl G.L.), New Delhi, 1979.

Dubey, S.R., *et al* (2012) *Pakkākot: Some New Dimensions of Mid-Ganga Plain*, Rishi Publications, New Delhi.

Dubey, S.R., *et al* (2010), Archaeological Investigation in Ballia District with Special Reference to Pakkākot *Puratattva*, No. 40, pp. 200-204.

Ghosh, A., (ed.) (1989), *An Encyclopaedia of Indian Archaeology,* Munshiram Manoharlal, New Delhi.

Indian Archaeological 1956-57: A Review

Indian Archaeological 1963-64: A Review.

Singh, P. (1994), *Excavations at Narhan 1984-89,* Banaras Hindu University and B.R. Publishing Corporations, New Delhi.

Singh, S.K. (2010), *Urbanization of the Middle Ganga Plain: An Archaeological Perspective,* Rishi Publication, Delhi.

Singh, S.K. (2012), *Settlement Pattern Urban Growth and Craft Technology in North India: An Archaeological Perspective,* Research India Press, New Delhi.

Singh, S.K. (2014), Pakkākot: Super Trade and Urban Center of the Middle Ganga plain, *ICON* Journal of Archaeology and Culture, Vol. I, pp.89-100.Wakankar Rock Art and Heritage Welfare Society, Bhopal, Research India Press, New Delhi.

Singh, S.K. (2009), Settlement Pattern and Environment in Middle Ganga Plain (with Special reference to Chirand) *Monograph* of the Department of AIHC & Archaeology, B.H.U. Varanasi, No.21, pp.77-84.

Singh, S.K. (2004-05), Emergence of Cities in Middle Ganga plain-New Archaeological Evidence, *Pragdhara,* No 15, pp. 119-126.

Singh, B.P. (1989). Khairadih: A Chalcolithic Settlement, *Puratattva,* 18.

Singh, B.P. (1990-91), Excavations at Khairadih, *Journal of Bihar Puravid Parishad,* Vols. IX-X, pp. 78-86.

Singh, P. *et al.* (1994-95), Proto-historic Investigations in Ballia District, *Pragdhara,* No. 5.

Singh, P., *et al* (1995-96), Excavations at Waina, District Ballia (U.P.), *Pragdhara,* No. 6, pp. 41 – 61.

Tripathi, V. and S.K. Singh (2003-2004), Excavations at Khairadih (1996-97), *Bharati* No. 28, pp.1-69.

Verma B.S., (1970-71) Excavation at Chirand New Light on Indian Neolithic culture Complex' *Puratattva,* Vol. 4, pp. 19-22.

8

DWARKA: TRADITIONS AND EXCAVATIONS

Alok Tripathi

Introduction

Dwarka (22^{0}14' N., 68^{0}57' E.) in district Jamnagar is a famous religious as well as archaeological site. Traditionally the place is identified with the legendry city *Dvaraka*, which finds mention in several ancient Indian texts, e.g. *Mahabharata*, *Puranas*, Buddhist and Jain texts. Besides archaeology and literature, it is also of great religious significance for Hindus, being one of the four *Dhams*. It is the only *dham* which is also included in *sapta puries*, seven sacred cities. Since 8th century, its religious importance further enhanced when Adi Shankara established one of the four *peethas* here and many famous Vaishnav saints visited Dwarka.

This ancient town located on the promontory was an important port on the western coast of India. Natural harbors to the north and south would have made it a favourable port for ships sailing across the Arabian Sea. There are no clear evidence to trace the antiquity of the port but there are indications being it active port since antiquity. Okhamandal area was a group of islands during ancient period. It is also identified with the island of *Barake* mentioned in the *Periplus Maris Erythraei*. A variety of stone anchors found on the floor of the sea suggest its links with ports across the Arabian Sea. The port was active until the reign of Gaekwad of Baroda when Sayajirao had built a *ghat* and a dock along the Gomati to facilitate anchoring of ships.

Although famous for centuries, this town attracted scholars and historians about a century back. While translating the *Markandeya Purana* F.E. Pargiter (1904: 289) identified this place with legendry *Dvaraka*. He discussed about the location of mount *Raivataka* near *Dvaraka* (Pargiter 1904: 289) and also mentioned its construction on the remains of an earlier city, *Kusasthali* (Pargiter 1922: 98). Since then, several attempts were made by various scholars to search reliable evidence and establish the antiquity of the site.

A.S. Altekar (1925: 25), while writing on ancient cities of Saurashtra, accepted that it had been submerged, as mentioned in some ancient texts. A.D. Pusalkar (1943: 111-127; 1945: 218-224) in his article identified it with the *Dvaravati* of the *Mahabharata*. However these attempts were mainly based on local traditions and descriptions given in ancient literature but traditional identification of modern Dwarka with legendry *Dvaraka* was generally accepted. Careful reading of previous works make it clear that at times scholars had interpreted selected descriptions in literature to suit their hypothesis.

In the twentieth century several attempts were made to enquire in long standing traditions. Several historians also tried to identify ancient places with those mentioned in literature. Besides literary sources, these approaches also adopted scientific and advance techniques to understand and establish the authenticity of such traditions. In the second half of the last century archaeologists also tried to use excavations not only to confirm identification but also to establish their antiquity. Theoretically it could have been done easily by searching material evidence and analyzing them.

Based on the literary references, archaeological excavations were conducted. Works of famous archaeologists H.D. Sankalia of Deccan College and Research Institute, Pune followed by S.R. Rao of the Archaeological Survey of India on this site drew attention of all. Although a great interest was generated amongst scholars and general public alike, but their findings and results varied considerably. To settle the issue and to take it to some logical conclusion another archaeological excavation had to be conducted by the Underwater Archaeology Wing (UAW) of the Archaeological Survey of India (ASI).

First excavation was conducted in 1963, in a very limited area near temple of Dwarkadheesh. This archaeological excavation, which was conducted by Deccan College, Pune in association with the Department of Archaeology, Government of Gujarat, revealed remains of earlier settlements dating back to the beginning of the Common Era. This excavation provided evidence that the site was under occupation for about last 2000 years. In the report of the excavation Sankalia also wrote that "... from this step we have to go further backwards in time in search of still earlier Dwarkas, which may lie hidden, in the vicinity of the present Dwarka or elsewhere ... " (Ansari and Mate 1966: viii).

In 1979, the Archaeological Survey of India excavated four trenches in the forecourt of Dwarkadheesh temple. About 10 m. thick cultural deposit was noticed in one of the trench. However the report of this excavation has not been published, but a review mentions about finding of the remains of earlier temples and pottery datable to mid 2nd millennium BCE (*IAR* 1979-80: 25-29). Lack of analytical approach and willingness to accept "the earliest" amongst archaeologists overlooked that certain things were imagined and speculated without any material evidence. Since the conclusions drawn by excavator matched with popular tradition it was easily accepted and widely spread.

Inspired by the outcome of second excavation, the National Institute of Oceanography started search for the legendary sunken city in the Arabian Sea. Beginning from 1981, these expeditions were carried out for about two decades. Based on these marine archaeological explorations claims were made of finding remains of a large well planned submerged city–structural remains of temples, palaces, gates, bastions, fortification walls, etc. Artifacts such as bronze or brass objects, pieces of stone sculptures, other metal objects, iron anchors, a copper *lota*, a bell, a metal plate, some pieces of marble statues, wooden parts of boats, etc. belonging to different periods were also found (Rao 1984: 16-26; 1985: 22-40; 1987; 1988a: 82-86; 1988b: 47-53; 1988c: 231-253; 1989: 54-68; 1990: 59-98; 1991: 51-59; 1995: 119-131; 1995-1996: 64; Nayak and Rao 1992; Sila and Gaur 1992: 506; Rao et al. 1994: 115; Gaur et al. 1994: 167).

While going through the reports and articles published time to time, one could easily notice several glaring discrepancies. Several wild speculations were made without any material evidence hence the authenticity of these claims was questioned by the scholars (Kenny 1993: 95-100: Tripathi 1996: 49-58; 2001: 360-365) on several grounds.

Perhaps, as a corrective measure to the erroneous claims made earlier, further marine archaeological work were carried out from 1998 to 2001. Results of these investigations in phase II varied considerably from earlier claims (Desa et al. 2001). Contrary views by same authors in subsequent publications raised serious doubts about the works carried out here (Gaur, Sundaresh and Sila 2004: 1259-1260; 2005: 56-71; Sundares et al. 2005: 31). These contrary views now generated serious doubts about the authenticity of finds and antiquity of the site.

Since its establishment, in 2001, the Underwater Archaeology Wing is known for scientific underwater archaeological researches of high standard based on established archaeological principals. In 2005, UAW was assigned the task to investigate the antiquity of the site scientifically. There are a number of places, which have been identified with *Dvaraka*, by various scholars. To confirm the veracity of earlier claims and for systematic study of archaeological remains it was necessary to start investigations afresh and reexamine all such sites in the state of Gujarat.

Exploration conducted during January–February 2006, started from Dwarka in district Jamnagar. Study of ancient monuments and archaeological remains in and around the town and in intertidal zone revealed structural remains, ancient sculptures, stone anchors, etc. Results of this fieldwork provided valuable information about nature and construction of coastal structures (Tripathi 2013a: 101-124).

In Beyt Shankhodhar, an island also known as Bet Dwarka, four important areas were identified in coastal explorations. Archaeological remains noticed during the study include structural remains, late Harappan and historical pottery, shell debitage, sling balls, hopscotch, shell bangles, copper coins, etc. Finding artifacts of different periods together makes it clear that it has been transported and deposited by the waves. Small excavation along a cliff revealed evidence of structure made of undressed stones set in mud mortar, industrial activities and shell working.

Several sculptures and remains of ancient temples were noticed around ancient temple at Mul-Dwarka, in district Junagarh. Several temples at Visawada, in district Porbandar, suggest its religious importance and association with Ranchhodrayji. This place is also known as Mul Dwarka. Another village having a small temple of Krishna, in district Rajkot is known as Panch Dwarka. Madhavpur, in district Porbandar, has an ancient mound and ancient temple close to the coast.

Area around Girnar, in district Junagarh, is strewn with several ancient monuments archaeological sites and remains. Satellite imagery of the area showed a prominent rectangular structure. Exploration in forested areas was a difficult task but attempts were made to locate the remains. Ancient mounds and remains of structures in the forest need to be studied in detail.

Apart from these sites which have been traditionally associated with Krishna, an area in great Rann of Kachchh was also explored where a large feature appearing like a submerged fortified town was noticed in the satellite imagery.

Among these sites, Girnar and Dwarka deserve special attention. From the archaeological point of view, Girnar emerges as the most probable site but the area still needs to be explored extensively. Traditionally Dwarka has been identified with *Dvaraka*. Scientists and archaeologists had also claimed of finding remains of a submerged city here. It warranted a scientific study of the area.

To understand the nature of the seabed near Dwarka a detailed hydrographic survey was carried out. Survey ship of the Indian Navy equipped with state-of-the-art survey equipments and well trained and committed team of hydrographers, and technicians surveyed 2 x 1 nm area in October-November 2006. Bathymetric survey was conducted close to shore using multi-beam echo-sounder, digital side scan sonar, acoustic doppler current profiler, motion sensor, DGPS, etc. Enormous data was generated and simultaneously analysed in well equipped facilities on *INS Nirdeshak*. Test diving were also conducted during the survey to examine significant features.

Based on detailed bathymetric map and three-dimensional Digital Terrine Model (DTM) underwater excavation in the area was planned. Selected area south of Samudra Narayana temple was very close to shore and shallow. Inflatable rubber-boats and a large mechanised wooden boat *Dharamraj*, were used for storing the equipments and conducting diving.

Divers from ASI, Western Naval Command, and *INS Dwarka* successfully conducted underwater archaeological operations (Plate 8.1) such as systematic searches, laying of grids, documentation, controlled digging, packaging, retrieval and transportation of the remains, etc.

Diving operations started in the area 100 m. from the shore. Architectural remains on seabed were searched and marked by the divers. Underwater archaeologist examined every feature and confirmed features were duly marked. After exploring an area of about 200 x 200 m. detailed investigations were conducted in western part measuring 50 x 50 m.

Selected area was duly marked by buoys and divided in four meter square grids. To indicate directions underwater lines of different colours were used. Laying straight parallel lines running east - west and north - south was a difficult task. Though the visibility was generally good, but covering a 4 m. square grid in a single frame was difficult. Optical considerations forced us to reduce the size of the grids to three square meters, marked by thicker ropes.

Rocks and stone blocks were covered under a thick sheet of seaweeds. Vegetation and calcareous incrustations were removed manually. Once the area was cleaned stone blocks scattered on the seabed became clearly visible. All these remains were studied and documented in detail. Digital and conventional underwater cameras were used for photo-documentation. Besides photography, drawings were also prepared. Excavation around these structural remains (Plate 8.2) revealed that they are not *in situ.* Lying over loose sand and stones they might have been moved by currents and waves.

Systematic underwater excavation helped in understanding the nature of submerged remains, but it was not possible to date them in absence of datable material and stratified deposits. Archaeological evidence to establish the antiquity of site could be gathered from thick cultural deposits on land.

High mound on which stands Dwarkadheesh temple was subjected to excavations in 1963 and again in 1979. There is hardly any open space available on the top of the mound as the area around the temple is thickly populated. In 2005, ASI demolished parts of a building which created some open space close to the northern gate of the temple. Two trenches, measuring 5 x 5 m., were laid for conducting archaeological excavation (Plate 8.3). One of the trenches was soon entirely covered with structures of different periods.

It was only in the second trench some space was available to go down to natural rock. This trench encompasses the area excavated in 1979. It not only helped in excavation but also to compare findings of these two excavations. The entire excavation was conducted by students systematically as a result most antiquities were recovered from their original context. Excavation progressed very slowly and meticulous documentation was carried out.

Cultural deposit of 9.51 m. was divided in 25 layers. Besides antiquities and pottery, botanical remains and soil samples were recovered from all the layers. Total 553 artifacts recorded during excavation include objects of gold, silver, copper, brass, iron, shell, stone, terracotta, glass, etc. (Tripathi 2013b: 53-55). Among 2,74,276 pottery pieces, 60,700 were pieces of tiles. Pottery was broadly classified according to the wares. Pottery was cleaned carefully as a result shoot-marks were observed on a number of cooking vessels.

Vast intertidal zone was also investigated to relate findings on land as well as underwater. The area is strewn with a variety of archaeological and structural remains. Among these circular structures were of great interest. Covered under sand it was difficult to expose them in conventional way as the time between tides was too short. After several experiments six courses of one circular structure could be exposed.

Another partly broken circular structure was cleaned thoroughly (Plate 8.4). This structure had three courses of stone and its lowest course was made of wood. As the wood can be dated, it in turn could provide the date of the structure. It may also help to date other similar structural remains lying scattered in intertidal zone as well as underwater.

Conclusion

All the excavations conducted so far have been limited to a very small area due to the constraint of open space on the mound. These excavations could provide chronology of the site and it is now clear that the area, where excavations were conducted, was inhabited for about two millennia. Heavy concentration of successive structures also indicates towards the importance of the site. Platforms, floors and walls with postholes suggest that the superstructure of these structures could have been made of perishable materials. Large number of iron nails and fittings also seems supporting the view. It is likely that some of these structures might have been occupied seasonally.

Tradition about the location of *Dvaraka* also vary. According to earlier tradition the city was located near the hill, while later sources mention it being close to sea. Underwater excavations conducted by the Underwater Archaeology Wing has established it beyond doubt that the structural remains reported lying submerged are not *in situ*. They could have been transported by the waves and strong currents. Cyclones and natural disasters could have destroyed coastal structures and their parts are now lying on the bottom close to shore. Their close resemblance with those still standing onshore also suggests that they are the fallen superstructures of the coastal structures. Since no datable material was found earlier they could not be dated directly. Recovery of wooden course from a circular coastal structure can now establish the age of these structures. Once these structures are dated long debates on the submerged structures and their antiquity would be settled, once for all, authentically.

Bibliography

1. Altekar, A.S. (1925) A History of Important Ancient Towns and Cities in Gujrat and Kathiawad, *The Indian Antiquary*, 54.
2. Ansari, Z.D. and Mate, M.S. (1966) *Excavations at Dwarka: 1963*, Deccan College Postgraduate and Research Institute, Poona.

3. Desa, E., Vora, K.H., Sundaresh, and Gaur, A.S. (2001) *Marine Archaeological Explorations Off Dwarka, Bet Dwarka and Somnath, Gujarat, Phase II, Final Report (1998-2001)*, Department of Ocean Development, New Delhi, and National Institute of Oceanography, Goa.
4. Gaur, A.S., Sundaresh and Sila, T. (2004) An Ancient Harbour at Dwarka : Study Based on the Recent Underwater Explorations, *Current Science*, 86 (9).
5. Gaur, A.S., Sundaresh and Sila, T. (2005) Ancient Dwarka: Study Based on Recent Underwater Investigations, *Migration and Diffusion*, 6 (21).
6. Gaur, A.S., Sundaresh, Gudigar, P. and Sila, T. (1994) Protohistoric Ceramics of Dwarka and Bet Dwarka, In: S.R. Rao (ed.), *The Role of Universities and Research Institutes in Marine Archaeology*, Society for Marine Archaeology, Dona-Paula.
7. *Indian Archaeology 1979-80 - A Review*, Archaeological Survey of India, New Delhi.
8. Kenny, L.B. (1993) Archaeology of Krsna's Dvaraka, *Journal of the Asiatic Society of Bombay*, Bombay.
9. Nayak, B.U. and Rao, S.R. (1992) Existence and Location of Dvaraka city of Mahabharata Era and its Submergence – A Reality or a Myth?, In: B.U. Nayak and N.C. Ghosh (ed.), *New Trends in Indian Art and Archaeology*, Aditya Prakashan, Delhi.
10. Pargiter, F.E. (1904) *The Markandeya Purana* (Eng. tr.) The Asiatic Society, Calcutta.
11. Pargiter, F.E. (1922) *Ancient Indian Historical Tradition*, (reprint) Motilal Banarasi Das, Delhi.
12. Pusalkar, A.D. (1943) Historicity of Krishna, In: K.M. Munshi (ed.), *The Glory That was Gurjaradesa*, Bharatiya Vidya Bhavan, Bombay.
13. Pusalkar, A.D. (1945) Dvaraka, In: D.R. Bhandarkar, K.A. Nilkantha Sastri, B.M. Barua, B.K. Ghosh and P.K. Gode (ed.), *B.C. Law Volume*, pt. I, The Indian Research Institute, Calcutta.
14. Rao, S.R. (1984) Submergence of Dwarka is a Fact, In: S.R. Rao (ed.), *Jnan Jyothi*, Sri Jaya Satya Pramoda Nidhi Trust, Bangalore.
15. Rao, S.R. (1985) Marine Archaeological Investigations in Indian Waters and Discovery of Dvaraka, In: S. Shastri and H.G. Ramchandra Rao (ed.), *Manjusha* Gyanjyothi Kala Mandir, Bangalore.
16. Rao, S.R. (1987) *Progress and Prospects of Marine Archaeology in India*, First Indian Conference on Marine Archaeology of Indian Ocean Countries, Goa.
17. Rao, S.R. (1988a) Protohistoric Inscription from the Sea near Bet Dvaraka, *Journal of the Epigraphical Society of India*, 15.
18. Rao, S.R. (1988b) Excavation of Submerged Ports - Dwarka: A Case Study, *Marine Archaeology of Indian Ocean Countries*, In: S.R. Rao (ed.), National Institute of Oceanography, Dona-Paula.
19. Rao, S.R. (1988c) Marine Archaeology Research in India, *40 Years of Research - A CSIR Overview*, Council of Scientific and Industrial Research, New Delhi.
20. Rao, S.R. (1989) The Quest for Dvaraka, *The India Magazine* (October), New Delhi.
21. Rao, S.R. (1990) Excavation of the Legendary City of Dwarka in the Arabian Sea, *Journal of Marine Archaeology*, 1.
22. Rao, S.R. (1991) Further Excavations of the Submerged City of Dwarka and Bet Dwarka, In: S.R. Rao (ed.), *Recent Advances in Marine Archaeology*, Society for Marine Archaeology, Dona-Paula.
23. Rao, S.R. (1995) The Quest for Krishna's Dwarka, *Manthan* 15 (4)-16 (1).
24. Rao, S.R. (1995-1996) From Dwarka to Kurukshetra, *Journal of Marine Archaeology*, 5-6.
25. Rao, S.R., Sila, T., Gaur, A.S., Gudigar, P., Sundaresh and Vora, K.H. (1994) Underwater Archaeological Exploration of Dwarka and Somnath – Results of 1992 Survey and Problems to Attend, In: S.R. Rao (ed.), *Role of Universities and Research Institutes in Marine Archaeology*, Society for Marine Archaeology, Dona-Paula.
26. Sila, T. and Gaur, A.S. (1992) Search for Dwarka, In: B.U. Nayak and N.C. Ghosh (ed.), *New Trends in Indian Art and Archaeology*, Aditya Prakashan, Delhi.
27. Sundaresh, Gaur, A.S., Vora, K.H., Sila, T. and Bandokar, S.N. (2005) Some New Thoughts on the Discovery of Ancient Dwarka, In: R.K. Sharma and Devendra Handa (ed.), *Revealing India's Past : Recent Trends in Art and Archaeology*, Aryan Books International, Delhi.
28. Tripathi, Alok (1996) Dvaraka in Literature and Archaeology, *Man and Environment*, 21 (2).
29. Tripathi, Alok (2001) Dvaraka of Mahabharat: Rethinking about its Identification and Archaeology, In: Sitakant Mahapatra, H.C. Das and Abhiram Biswal (ed.), *Rethinking Indian Culture: Challenges and Responses*, Institute of Oriental and Orissan Studies, Cuttack.
30. Tripathi, Alok (2013a) Excavations at Dwarka - 2007, In: Alok Tripathi (ed.), *Maritime Heritage of Indian Ocean*, Organizing Committee of ISMA and Sharada Publishing House, Delhi.
31. Tripathi, Alok (2013b) *Excavations at Dwarka – 2007: An Interim Report*, Organizing Committee of ISMA and Sharada Publishing House, Delhi.

9

CLIMATE, ENVIRONMENT AND THE BREAK-UP OF THE INDUS-SARASVATI CIVILIZATION

Michel Danino*

Much ink has flowed over the decline and disappearance of the Indus-Sarasvati Civilization in its urban form around 1900 BCE. Barbarian invasions having been firmly ruled out as a potential cause, the main alternatives remain political, socioeconomic or environmental factors. The first two are very hard to test in view of the paucity of evidence; the opposite is true of the last: in recent decades, considerable data has been accumulating regarding the environmental and climatic conditions of the northwest of the Indian subcontinent before, during and after the Harappan age.

Although some archaeologists have warned against the pitfall of attributing disruptions in the course of ancient civilizations and cultures to "environmental determinism," the impact of environment and climate can no longer be ignored either. The prolonged drought that affected, in 2200-2100 BCE, large parts of Africa,[1] China,[2] North America,[3] Near and Middle East,[4] probably causing the collapse of the Akkadian empire,[5] is a case in point. The case of the Indus-Sarasvati civilization remains complex, partly because of apparently conflicting views on what kind climate and environment prevailed in its Mature or urban phase. Although John Marshall remarked in 1931 that the extensive use of fired bricks at Mohenjo-daro pointed to a wetter environment,[6] later archaeologists disagreed and found little or no evidence for a climate significantly different from today's. As the late Gregory Possehl wrote in 2002, "The climate of this region [Greater Indus Valley] was not markedly different in the third millennium BC from the one we have today."[7]

Can we today decide who was right? In a recent paper,[8] I presented seven studies coming in support of each side. I will briefly list them here and add a few recent ones as well as a discussion on the collapse of the Sarasvati system.

---

* Michel Danino, a long-time student of Indian civilization, is the author of *The Lost River: On the Trail of the Sarasvati* (Penguin India, 2010); he lives near Coimbatore and is currently guest professor at IIT Gandhinagar, where he is assisting the setting up of an Archaeological Sciences Centre. Email: micheldanino@gmail.com.

Was the Harappan Climate as Dry as Today's?

Among the studies leading to the conclusion that the Harappan climate and environment were hardly different from today's in the same regions, let us list:

- Gurdip Singh's 1971 palynological study of three lakes of Rajasthan.[9]
- R.A. Bryson's and A.M. Swain's 1981 study of lakes of Rajasthan.[10]
- M.B. McKean's 1983 study of pollen and sediments around Balakot.[11]
- The 1983–85 Indo-French mission exploring the Ghaggar in Haryana and Rajasthan.[12]
- M.A. Geyh's and D. Ploethner's 1995 isotopic study of palaeowaters in a section of the Hakra's floodplain in Cholistan.[13]
- S.M. Rao's and K.M. Kulkarni's 1997 isotope study of well waters in western Rajasthan.[14]
- Y. Enzel et al.'s 1999 study of sediments from Rajasthan's Lunkaransar lake.[15]

Or Was It Wetter than Today?

Other studies, generally more recent ones, point to the opposite conclusion, including a more intense monsoon in Mature Harappan times:

- R.J. Wasson et al.'s 1983 study of Rajasthan's Didwana lake.[16]
- P.D. Naidu's 1996 study of planktonic foraminifers from the Arabian Sea.[17]
- Ulrich von Rad et al.'s 1999 study of sediments in the Arabian Sea off Karachi.[18]
- Netajirao Phadtare's 2000 study of pollen and peat in the Garhwal Himalaya.[19]
- M. Staubwasser et al.'s 2003 planktonic oxygen isotope ratios off the Indus delta.[20]
- Anil K. Gupta et al.'s 2006 survey of current research on the monsoon and other climatic inputs from many sources including their own.[21]
- A 2008 study by Rita Wright, Reid A. Bryson and Joseph Schuldenrein used archaeoclimatology models to plot the intensity of the monsoon and river flow in the region of Harappa.[22]

More studies have been quoted on both sides.[23] It is understandable that focusing on different regions and using different approaches (sediments, pollen, plankton, palaeowaters, etc.) should lead to apparently diverging results. Nevertheless, the trend of most recent studies has been to observe "a decrease in the strength of the Southwest monsoon about 4000 cal yr BP,"[24] that is, towards the end of the urban Harappan phase. For example, Dorian Q. Fuller, while cautioning against hasty conclusions,[25] points to a series of "marked events of sudden aridity,"[26] with the last one taking place around 2200 BCE, the severe worldwide drought I mentioned above:

> A climatic event cannot be blamed simplistically for [Harappan] collapse and de-urbanisation, but Quaternary science data make it clear that we cannot accept a view of climatic and environmental stability since the mid-Holocene in the region (as promoted by Possehl ...).[27]

In the last few years, more studies have sought to answer the above questions. I will mention five of them here:

- In 2010, Prasanta Sanyal and R. Sinha synthesized a large number of studies of the Indian Summer Monsoon across north India over long ages; commenting on the records of lakes in the Thar Desert, they observed that "Didwana and Lunkaransar playas were completely desiccated at 3–4 ka."[28]
- An international team led by Liviu Giosan studied in 2012 the climatic as well as fluvial conditions before, during and after Harappan times. They confirmed the now dominant view that "precipitation from both monsoon and westerly sources that feed rivers of the western Indo-Gangetic Plain decreased since approximately 5,000 y ago, and was at its lowest after approximately 4,000 y BP. ... as aridity intensified, monsoon-augmented floods became less frequent and/or less intense."[29]
- Also in 2012, M. Berkelhammer led an international team to study variations in the oxygen isotopes of a stalagmite from a cave in Meghalaya. They observed a "dramatic event ... ~ 4000 years ago when, over the course of approximately a decade, isotopic values abruptly rose above

any seen during the early to mid-Holocene and remained at this anomalous state for almost two centuries." This suggested either "a shift toward an earlier Indian Summer Monsoon withdrawal or a general decline in the total amount of monsoon precipitation." The study's "tight age constraints of the record show with a high degree of certainty that much of the documented deurbanization of the Indus Valley at 3.9 kyr B.P. occurred after multiple decades of a shift in the monsoon's character...."[30]

- A 2013 study by Anjum Farooqui, A.S. Gaur and Vandana Prasad of the palaeoenvironment at two sites of southern Saurashtra showed "low precipitation and arid climatic conditions ~ 2000 BC. During this period the dominance of evergreen and moist deciduous arboreals from both the sites do not show equilibrium with the prevailing dry/arid climate and therefore, the pollen assemblage here represents the remnants of wetter middle Holocene vegetation in the region. ... The moister climatic conditions and comparatively rich forest cover around the Saurashtra coast was one of the main attractive reasons for the expansion and settlement of Harappans...."[31]
- In 2014, Yama Dixit, David A. Hodell and Cameron A. Petrie, studying the sediments of a palaeolake in Haryana (at Kotla Dahar), detected "ca. 4.1 ka marking a peak in the evaporation/precipitation ratio in the lake catchment related to weakening of the ISM [Indian Summer Monsoon] ..., suggesting that climate may have played a role in the Indus cultural transformation. ... Taken together, the records from Kotla Dahar, Mawmuluh [in northeast India], and the Arabian Sea provide strong evidence for a widespread weakening of the ISM across large parts of India at ca. 4.2–4.0 ka. The monsoon recovered to the modern-day conditions after 4.0 k.y. ago, and the event lasted for ~200 yr (ca. 4.2–4.0 ka) in this region."[32]

This may be regarded as the current broad consensus among experts, quite in tune with the worldwide drought noted at the start of this paper. Although we cannot yet point to a precise chain of events, it is now clear that this prolonged period of sharply reduced rainfall must have considerably strained the Harappans' monsoon- and flood-dependent agricultural production.

Circumstantial Evidence

Early archaeologists pointed to the extensive use of baked bricks at Mohenjo-daro, Chanhu-daro and Harappa as a clue that climate was wetter; it was answered (by Mortimer Wheeler,[33] for instance) that baked bricks were more likely a flood-mitigating device. The depictions on Indus seals of animals like the elephant, the tiger, the rhinoceros or the water buffalo were seen as so many clues to a moister and greener environment; it was objected in reply that the depiction of a particular animal did not prove its existence at the site, and that the above-mentioned animals were still seen in parts of the Indus valley till recent decades or centuries.

However, positive evidence emerged at Kalibangan in the form of bone remains of the elephant, the one-horned rhinoceros (recently confirmed at Karanpura, also in Rajasthan[34]), the water buffalo and the river turtle. In Bhola Nath's opinion, "the remains of these animals show that the climate at that time was more humid than the arid climate of present day."[35] The presence of the rhinoceros, in particular, "strengthens the geological evidence that the desert conditions of this area are of recent origin."[36] Similar evidence came from Gujarat, where P.K. Thomas observed that the animal is identified from a large number of Harappan and Chalcolithic sites ... [and] inhabited a major part of the Gujarat plains in the protohistoric period. ... The identification of large herbivores like rhinoceros, wild buffalo and probably wild cattle at many of the Gujarat Harappan sites suggests that the ecological conditions were more congenial for animal life during the protohistoric period in Gujarat.[37]

These considerations, together with the last twelve studies listed above, do point to a greener environment during the urban phase. If so, could human activities have played a part in its degradation? Mortimer Wheeler suggested that the Harappans were "wearing out [the] landscape"[38] by overexploitation of their natural resources, particularly forests, for their brick, pottery, bronze and seal-making industries; intensive agriculture for the consumption of the city dwellers combined with overgrazing by numerous herds of cattle and goats would have added to the pressure on an already strained environment. Walter

Fairservis attempted a calculation of the amount of fodder consumed by the cattle used by Mohenjo-daro both as a source of food (dairy products and meat) and for ploughing. His conclusion was:

> The inhabitants of the mature period at Mohenjodaro would have grown only about one-fourth of their fodder needs. It follows that the remaining three-quarters had to be obtained by foraging in the surrounding forests and grasslands. This formidable assault on the indigenous flora most certainly affected the ecology and had an adverse effect on the land and aided the spread of the active floodplain.[39]

The Sarasvati

One major and fairly unambiguous environmental change is the desiccation of the Ghaggar-Hakra system in the eastern domain of the Indus-Sarasvati civilization, which was home to some 360 sites of the Mature Harappan period,[40] the best known of which include (from east to west) Farmana, Rakhigarhi, Banawali, Bhirrana, Kalibangan and Ganweriwala. This river system located in the Yamuna-Sutlej interfluve, and identified since the mid-nineteenth century by generations of geographers, geologists, Indologists and archaeologists with the Sarasvati River of the Rig-Veda, dried up in stages, probably owing to a tectonic uplift of its basin, which deprived it of contributions from the Sutlej and the Yamuna, leaving only seasonal streams in its upper reaches.[41] As V.N. Misra put it, "The large number of protohistoric settlements, dating from *c.* 4000 BC to 1500 BC, could have flourished along this river only if it was flowing perennially."[42]

Studies of settlement patterns have showed that between 2000 and 1900 BCE, the central basin of the Ghaggar basin was deserted by the Mature Harappans (Kalibangan is a well-known case, with no Late phase). A crowding of Late Harappan settlements took place in following centuries along the Shivaliks' foothills, besides migrations eastward into the Ganges Valley and possibly southward to the Aravallis and the Vindhyas.

Recent geological studies have broadly confirmed this scenario sketched in the early 1980s.[43] In 2009, H.S. Saini et al. studied buried channels in the northwestern Haryana Plains and documented "the existence of channel activity during the mid-Holocene ... in a part of the Haryana plains"; by mid-Holocene is meant a "second fluvial phase ... represented by a palaeochannel segment whose signatures are dated between ~ 6.0 and ~ 2.9 Ka,"[44] after which a depleted Ghaggar was left. The dates bracket the Indus civilization.

The same year, reviewing findings on the Ghaggar-Hakra, Peter Clift concluded, "Provisional age data now show that between 2000 and 3000 BCE, flow along a presently dried-up course known as the Ghaggur-Hakkra River ceased, probably driven by the weakening monsoon and possibly also because of headwater capture into the adjacent Yamuna and Sutlej Rivers."[45]

I mentioned above the 2012 study led by Liviu Giosan (of which Clift is a co-author). Apart from confirming a steep decline in the summer monsoon circa 2000 BCE, it observed, "The most spectacular case of climate-controlled landscape transformation is the Ghaggar-Hakra system, which became ephemeral and was largely abandoned."[46] In a later comment on their paper, Giosan et al. clarified, "Our research points to a perennial monsoonal-fed Sarasvati river system with benign floods along its course."[47]

There is thus a broad consensus here too, although these last two studies have cast doubt on the existence of glacial sources for the Ghaggar in Mature Harappan times, reducing it to a rain-fed river. This was strongly refuted in 2013 by K.S. Valdiya[48] and further defended by Giosan et al.,[49] but as the issue ultimately makes little difference to the existence of a perennial river during Harappan times — albeit one already on the decline and of modest dimensions — we may leave this debate out of the present discussion.

Regionwise Discussion

As far back as in 1968, Wheeler wrote presciently, "The decline and fall of an immense, evolved and, on any showing, long-lived civilization as that of the Indus valley archaeological are inevitably a tangled and contentious problem. ... For a civilization so widely distributed as that of the Indus no uniform ending need be postulated."[50] More recently, Yama Dixit et al. put it thus: "The Indus settlements spanned a diverse range of environmental and ecological zones; therefore, correlation of evidence for climate change and the decline of Indus urbanism requires a comprehensive assessment of the relationship between settlement and climate across a substantial area."[51]

This should be warning enough against proposing a single environmental mechanism — reduction of the monsoon or the loss of the Sarasvati — for the final break-up of the Harappan urban order. Yet it is tempting to propose the following regionwise possibilities, at least as an exercise:

- In the eastern region, the desiccation of the central Sarasvati basin accelerated towards 2000 BCE, leading to its almost complete abandonment and à concentration of Late sites at the foot of the Shivalik Hills, in the Ganga-Yamuna Doab, and in Cholistan.[52] This loss of one of the two major lifelines of this civilization must have been a major factor in its deurbanization. As Dilip Chakrabarti puts it, "To a considerable extent the process [of weakening of the political fabric of the Indus civilization] must have been linked to the hydrographic changes in the Sarasvati-Drishadvati system."[53] Whether or not the loss of the river system was caused by a long drought, the two phenomena together certainly compounded the severity of the situation, as might have an overuse of natural resources.
- The Indus basin suffered no such loss, perhaps in fact more destructive floods if, as has been assumed, the part of the Sutlej that flowed into the Sarasvati shifted to the Beas, eventually swelling the Indus's waters: "An increase in water and sediment discharge of that magnitude [provoked by the westward shift of the Sutlej] would have had dramatic effects downstream in the Lower Indus Basin,"[54] according to Louis Flam. This might help explain the near complete absence of Late Harappan sites in this region: they may have been either washed away or buried under sediments.
- On the Makran coast, Harappan outposts like Sutkagen-dor and Balakot are now over 50 km inland. G.F. Dales, who excavated Balakot, suggested that "a sudden rise in the Arabian Sea coastline of West Pakistan apparently took place sometime around the middle of the second millennium. This resulted in a disastrous increase in the already serious floods in the major river valleys...."[55] There is independent geomorphologic evidence of relatively rapid uplifts of the Makran coast,[56] which perhaps left these Harappan ports high and dry, disrupting their trading functions.
- The Rann of Kachchh has an ecological history of its own. Home to several sites including Dholavira, its northern border may have been part of the Sarasvati's estuary (the present Nara channel). There is independent evidence that the Rann was, in Mature Harappan times, a "shallow arm of the sea,"[57] and therefore navigable (Greek records suggest that it was still partly so in the first century BCE[58]). Precisely when it ceased to be so and how far the Sarasvati's break-up was responsible for it is unclear; a gradual tectonic uplift is a more likely cause, as is sedimentation. Be that as it may, if at some point the "metropolis" and major trading centre that Dholavira was found itself cut off from the sea route, its very survival as a city must have been challenged.
- Similarly, satellite photography and sedimental studies have shown that the sea level near Lothal was higher in the third millennium than it is today, lending strong support to the interpretation of the site's huge basin as a "dockyard."[59] A receding shoreline may have spelt doom for the town's maritime function.
- The rest of the Gujarat domain of the Indus-Sarasvati civilization, together with northern Maharashtra, was not affected by changes in the Sarasvati and the Indus basins, or by the retreat of the Arabian Sea, but would have felt the impact of the 2200 BCE drought. More so, it would have been affected by the disruption of the trade networks in the other regions.

Other possible contributing factors include disruptions in commercial exchanges with the Iranian plateau, Magan, Dilmun, Mesopotamia and BMAC, socioeconomic tensions, sheer geographical overstretch, and a falling apart of the various Harappan regions.[60]

Whether one of these factors started off a chain reaction, or whether several of them converged about the same time, current evidence does not allow us to conclude. Clearly, however, climatic and environmental disruptions played a major part in the break-up of the Indus civilization. Environmentalists have been warning that Ganga may turn into a seasonal river in the 21st century; we must hope that, despite current trends, wisdom will prevail and all mitigating steps will be taken to make sure that the twenty-first century CE does not turn out to be a repetition — of course on a much larger scale — of the twenty-first century BCE.

References & Notes

1. Thompson, L.G., et al. 2002. "Kilimanjaro Ice Core Records: evidence of Holocene climate change in Tropical Africa," *Science* 298, pp. 589–593.
2. An, Cheng-Bang, et al. 2005. "Climate change and cultural response around 4000 cal yr B.P. in the western part of Chinese Loess Plateau," *Quaternary Research* 63, pp. 347–352.
3. Booth, R.K., et al. 2005. "A severe centennial-scale drought in midcontinental North America 4200 years ago and apparent global linkages," *The Holocene* 15, pp. 321–328.
4. Gupta, Anil K., et al. 2006. "Adaptation and human migration, and evidence of agriculture coincident with changes in the Indian summer monsoon during the Holocene," *Current Science*, vol. 90, no. 8, pp. 1082–1090.
5. Weiss, H., et al. 1993. "The genesis and collapse of third millennium north Mesopotamian civilization," *Science* 261–5124, pp. 995–1004. Also Kerr, R.A. 1998. "Sea-floor dust shows drought felled Akkadian Empire," *Science* 279, pp. 325–326.
6. Marshall, John. 1931. *Mohenjo-daro and the Indus Civilization*, Arthur Probsthain, London, vol. 1, p. 2.
7. Possehl, Gregory L. 2002. *The Indus Civilization: A Contemporary Perspective,* Altamira Press, Oxford, p. 13.
8. Danino, Michel. 2014. "Climate and Environment in the Indus-Sarasvati Civilization," in Banerjee, Arundhati, (ed.), *Ratnasri: Gleanings from Indian Archaeology, Art History and Indology* (Papers Presented in Memory of Dr. N.R. Banerjee), Kaveri Books, New Delhi, pp. 39–47. (This paper was written in 2010.)
9. Singh, Gurdip. 1971. "The Indus Valley Culture seen in the context of post-glacial climate and ecological studies in north-west India," *Archaeology and Physical Anthropology in Oceania,* 6(2), pp. 177–189. Gurdip Singh's dates actually pointed to a wetter climate, but led to the opposite conclusion after recalibration by Shaffer, Jim G. & Diane A. Lichtenstein. 1989. "Ethnicity and Change in the Indus Valley Cultural Tradition," in Kenoyer, Jonathan Mark, (ed.), *Old Problems and New Perspectives in the Archaeology of South Asia*, University of Wisconsin, Wisconsin, pp. 117–126.
10. Bryson, R.A. & A.M. Swain. 1981. "Holocene variations of monsoon rainfall in Rajasthan," *Quaternary Research,* vol. 16, pp. 135–145. As in Gurdip Singh's case, this is after recalibration by Madella, Marco, & Dorian Q. Fuller. 2006. "Palaeoecology and the Harappan Civilisation of South Asia: a reconsideration," *Quaternary Science Reviews* 25, p. 1297.
11. McKean, M.B. 1983. *The palynology of Balakot, a pre-Harappan and Harappan age site in Las Bela, Pakistan*, Ph.D. thesis, Southern Methodist University, Dallas, quoted in Madella, Marco, & Dorian Q. Fuller. 2006. "Palaeoecology and the Harappan Civilisation of South Asia: a reconsideration," op. cit., p. 1292.
12. Courty, Marie-Agnès. 1989. "Integration of sediment and soil information in the reconstruction of protohistoric and historic landscapes of the Ghaggar Plain (North-West India)" in Frifelt, Karen, & Per Sorensen, (eds), *South Asian Archaeology 1985,* Scandinavian Institute of Asian Studies, Occasional Papers No. 4, Curzon Press, London, p. 259. See also Courty, Marie-Agnès. 1986. "Geoarchaeological Approach of Holocene Paleoenvironments in the Ghaggar Plain," *Man and Environment*, vol. X, pp. 111–115; Francfort, Henri-Paul. 1992. "Evidence for Harappan Irrigation System in Haryana and Rajasthan," *The Eastern Anthropologist,* vol. 45, pp. 87–103.
13. Geyh, M.A. & D. Ploethner. 1995. "An applied palaeohydrological study of Cholistan, Thar Desert, Pakistan," in Adar, E.M., & C. Leibundgut, (eds), *Applications of Tracers in Arid Zone Hydrology,* International Association of Hydrological Sciences, Vienna, publ. no. 232, pp. 119–127. Quoted by Valdiya, K.S. 2002. *Saraswati, the River that Disappeared,* Indian Space Research Organization & Universities Press, Hyderabad, p. 31.
14. Rao, S.M., & K.M. Kulkarni. 1997. "Isotope hydrology studies on water resources in Western Rajasthan," *Current Science*, 72(1), pp. 55–61.
15. Enzel, Y., et al. 1999. "High-Resolution Holocene Environmental Changes in the Thar Desert, Northwestern India," *Science*, vol. 284, pp. 125–128.
16. Wasson, R.J., et al. 1983. "Geomorphology, Late Quaternary Stratigraphy and Palaeoclimatology of the Thar Dune Field," in *Zeitschrift für Geomorphologie*, N.F. Supplementband 45, pp. 117–151, partly reproduced in Radhakrishnan, B.P. & S.S. Merh, (eds). 1999. *Vedic Sarasvati: Evolutionary History of a Lost River of Northwestern India,* Geological Society of India, Bangalore, p. 222.

17. Naidu, P.D. 1996. "Onset of an arid climate at 3.5 ka in the tropics: evidence from monsoon upwelling record," *Current Science* 71, pp. 715–718.

18. Von Rad, Ulrichn et al. 1999. "A 5000-yr Record of Climate Change in Varved Sediments from the Oxygen Minimum Zone off Pakistan, Northeastern Arabian Sea," *Quaternary Research*, vol. 51, pp. 39–53.

19. Phadtare, Netajirao R. 2000. "Sharp Decrease in Summer Monsoon Strength 4000–3500 cal yr B.P. in the Central Higher Himalaya of India Based on Pollen Evidence from Alpine Peat," *Quaternary Research,* vol. 53, pp. 122–129.

20. Staubwasser, M., et al. 2003. "Climate change at the 4.2 ka BP termination of the Indus valley civilization and Holocene south Asian monsoon variability," *Geophysical Research Letters* 30(8), p. 1425.

21. Gupta, Anil K., et al. 2006. "Adaptation and human migration, and evidence of agriculture coincident with changes in the Indian summer monsoon during the Holocene," *Current Science* 90(8), pp. 1082–1090.

22. Wright, Rita P., Reid A. Bryson & Joseph Schuldenrein. 2008. "Water supply and history: Harappa and the Beas regional survey," *Antiquity,* vol. 82, pp. 37–48.

23. For recent reviews, see those discussed in Madella, Marco, & Dorian Q. Fuller. 2006. "Palaeoecology and the Harappan Civilisation of South Asia: a reconsideration," op. cit.; Fuller, Dorian Q., & Marco Madella. 2000. "Issues in Harappan Archaeobotany: Retrospect and Prospect," in Settar, S., & Ravi Korisettar, (eds), *Indian Archaeology in Retrospect*, vol. 2: *Protohistory, Archaeology of the Harappan Civilization*, Manohar & Indian Council of Historical Research, New Delhi, pp. 317–390; Korisettar, Ravi & R. Ramesh. 2002. "The Indian Monsoon: Roots, Relations and Relevance," in Settar, S., & Ravi Korisettar, (eds), *Indian Archaeology in Retrospect*, vol. 3: *Archaeology and Interactive Disciplines*, Manohar & Indian Council of Historical Research, New Delhi, pp. 23–59.

24. Phadtare, Netajirao R. 2000. "Sharp Decrease in Summer Monsoon Strength 4000–3500 cal yr B.P. in the Central Higher Himalaya of India Based on Pollen Evidence from Alpine Peat," *Quaternary Research,* vol. 53, pp. 122–129.

25. Fuller, Dorian Q., & Marco Madella. 2000. "Issues in Harappan Archaeobotany: Retrospect and Prospect," op. cit., pp. 363 & 366.

26. Fuller, Dorian Q. 2008. "Neolithic Cultures," in Pearsall, Deborah M., (ed.), *Encyclopedia of Archaeology*, Academic Press, New York, pp. 756–768.

27. Madella, Marco, & Dorian Q. Fuller. 2006. "Palaeoecology and the Harappan Civilisation of South Asia: a reconsideration," op. cit., p. 1283.

28. Sanyal, Prasanta, & R. Sinha. 2010. "Evolution of the Indian summer monsoon: synthesis of continental records", in Clift, P.D., R. Tada & H. Zheng, (eds), *Monsoon Evolution and Tectonics–Climate Linkage in Asia*, Geological Society, London, Special Publications, 342, pp. 153–183.

29. Giosan, Liviu, et al. 2012. "Fluvial landscapes of the Harappan civilization", *PNAS*, E1688–E1694 (published online May 29, 2012).

30. Berkelhammer, M., A. Sinha, L. Stott, H. Cheng, F. S. R. Pausata, & K. Yoshimura. 2012. "An Abrupt Shift in the Indian Monsoon 4000 Years Ago", in Giosan, Liviu, et al., (eds), *Climates, Landscapes, and Civilizations,* Geophysical Monograph Series 198, American Geophysical Union, Washington DC, pp. 75–87.

31. Farooqui, Anjum, et al. 2013. "Climate, vegetation and ecology during Harappan period: excavations at Kanjetar and Kaj, mid-Saurashtra coast, Gujarat," *Journal of Archaeological Science*, no. 40, pp. 2631–2647.

32. Dixit, Yama, D.A. Hodell & C.A. Petrie. 2014. "Abrupt weakening of the summer monsoon in northwest India ~ 4100 yr ago," *Geology,* 42(4), pp. 339-342.

33. Wheeler, Mortimer. 1968. *The Indus Civilization,* Cambridge University Press, Cambridge, 3rd edn, p. 8.

34. Prabhakar, V.N. 2014. Personal communication.

35. Nath, Bhola. 1969. "The Role of Animal Remains in the Early Prehistoric Cultures of India," *Indian Museum Bulletin,* Calcutta, p. 107; quoted by Jagat Pati Joshi in Lal, B.B., et al. 2003. *Excavations at Kalibangan*, Archaeological Survey of India, New Delhi, vol. 1, p. 19.

36. Banerjee, S., & S. Chakraborty. 1973. "Remains of the great one-horned Rhinoceros, *Rhinoceros unicornis*, Linnacus from Rajasthan," *Science and Culture*, vol. 39, Calcutta, pp. 430–431, quoted by Jagat Pati Joshi in Lal, B.B., et al. 2003. *Excavations at Kalibangan*, op. cit., p. 18.

37. Thomas, P.K., "Investigations into the Archaeofauna of Harappan Sites in Western India," in Settar, S., & Ravi Korisettar, (eds), *Indian Archaeology in Retrospect*, vol. 2: *Protohistory, Archaeology of the Harappan Civilization*, op. cit., pp. 414 & 417.

38. Wheeler, Mortimer. 1968. *The Indus Civilization,* op. cit., p. 127.

39. Fairservis, Walter A. 1967. "The Origin, Character and Decline of an Early Civilization," *Novitates*, 1967, 2302:1–48, partly reproduced in Lahiri, Nayanjot, (ed.). 2000. *The Decline and Fall of the Indus*, Permanent Black, New Delhi, p. 261.

40. Danino, Michel. 2010. *The Lost River: On the Trail of the Sarasvati,* Penguin, New Delhi, p. 139.
41. On the Sarasvati River, see (chronologically): Misra, V.N., "Climate, a Factor in the Rise and Fall of the Indus Civilization: Evidence from Rajasthan and Beyond" in Lal, B.B. & S.P. Gupta, (eds). 1984. *Frontiers of the Indus Civilization,* Books and Books, New Delhi, pp. 461–89; Misra, V.N., "Indus Civilization and the Rgvedic Sarasvati," in Parpola, Asko & Petteri Koskikallio, (eds). 1994. *South Asian Archaeology 1993,* Suomalainen Tiedeakatemia, Helsinki, vol. II, pp. 511–525; Radhakrishnan, B.P. & S.S. Merh, (eds). 1999. *Vedic Sarasvati: Evolutionary History of a Lost River of Northwestern India,* Geological Society of India, Bangalore, especially for Herbert Wilhelmy, "The Ancient River Valley on the Eastern Border of the Indus Plain and the Sarasvati Problem," pp. 95–111; Valdiya, K.S. 2002. *Saraswati, the River that Disappeared,* Indian Space Research Organization & Universities Press, Hyderabad; Lal, B.B. 2002. *The Sarasvati Flows On: The Continuity of Indian Culture,* Aryan Books International, New Delhi; Kalyanaraman, S., (ed.). 2008. *Vedic River Sarasvati and Hindu Civilization,* Aryan Books International, New Delhi, & Sarasvati Research and Education Trust, Chennai; Chakrabarti, Dilip K. & Sukhdev Saini. 2009. *The Problem of the Sarasvati River and Notes on the Archaeological Geography of Haryana and Indian Panjab,* Aryan Books International, New Delhi. For an attempted synthesis: Danino, Michel. 2010. *The Lost River: On the Trail of the Sarasvati,* Penguin, New Delhi.
42. Misra, V.N. 1994. "Indus Civilization and the Rgvedic Sarasvati," op. cit., p. 515.
43. Joshi, J.P., Madhu Bala & Jassu Ram. 1984. "The Indus Civilization: A Reconsideration on the Basis of Distribution Maps," in Lal, B.B. & S.P. Gupta, (eds). 1984. *Frontiers of the Indus Civilization,* op. cit., pp. 511–530.
44. Saini, H.S., S.K. Tandon, S.A.I. Mujtaba, N.C. Pant and R. K. Khorana. 2009. "Reconstruction of buried channel-floodplain systems of the northwestern Haryana Plains and their relation to the 'Vedic' Saraswati," *Current Science,* 97(11), pp. 1634–43.
45. Clift, Peter. 2009. "Harappan Collapse", *Geoscientist,* 19(9), pp. 18–22.
46. Giosan, Liviu, et al. 2012. "Fluvial landscapes of the Harappan civilization", *PNAS,* E1688–E1694 (published online May 29, 2012).
47. Giosan, Liviu, Peter D. Clift, Mark G. Macklin, Dorian Q. Fuller. 2013. "Sarasvati II," *Current Science,* 105(7), pp. 888–810.
48. Valdiya, K.S. 2013. "The River Saraswati was a Himalayan-born river," *Current Science,* 104(1), pp. 42–54.
49. Giosan, Liviu, Peter D. Clift, Mark G. Macklin, Dorian Q. Fuller. 2013. "Sarasvati II," op. cit.
50. Wheeler, Mortimer. 1968. *The Indus Civilization,* op. cit., p. 126.
51. Dixit, Yama, D.A. Hodell & C.A. Petrie. 2014. Abrupt weakening of the summer monsoon in northwest India ~ 4100 yr ago, *Geology* (published online 24 February 2014).
52. See references in endnote no. 41 above.
53. Chakrabarti, Dilip K. 1997. *The Archaeology of Ancient Indian Cities,* Oxford University Press, New Delhi, p. 140.
54. Flam, Louis. 1999. "The Prehistoric Indus River System and the Indus Civilization in Sindh," *Man and Environment,* 24(2), p. 55.
55. Dales, George F. 1964. "The Mythical Massacre at Mohenjodaro," *Expedition* 6(3), pp. 36–43, reproduced in Lahiri, Nayanjot, (ed.). 2000. *The Decline and Fall of the Indus,* op. cit., p. 81.
56. Snead, Rodman E. 1967. "Recent Morphological Changes along the Coast of West Pakistan," *Annals of the Association of American Geographers,* 57(3), pp. 550–565. (My thanks to Prof. R.N. Iyengar for drawing my attention to this paper.)
57. Mathur, U.B. 2002. "Chronology of Harappan Port Towns of Gujarat in the Light of Sea Level Changes during the Holocene," *Man and Environment,* 27(2), p. 64.
58. *Periplus of the Erythrean Sea,* see quotation and discussion in Iyengar, R.N. & B.P. Radhakrishna. 2007. "Geographical Location of Vedic Irina in Southern Rajasthan," *Journal of the Geological Society of India,* vol. 70, pp. 699–705.
59. Khadkikar, A.S., et al. 2004. "Palaeogeography around the Harappan port of Lothal, Gujarat, western India," *Antiquity,* 78 (302), pp. 896–903.
60. Useful discussions of possible causes of the end of the urban Harappan phase can be found in Lal, B.B. 1997. *The Earliest Civilization of South Asia,* Aryan Books International, New Delhi, ch. 14; Possehl, Gregory L. 2002. *The Indus Civilization: A Contemporary Perspective,* op. cit., ch. 13; Chakrabarti, Dilip K. 2006. *The Oxford Companion to Indian Archaeology: The Archaeological Foundations of Ancient India,* Oxford University Press, New Delhi, ch. 11; Lahiri, Nayanjot, (ed.). 2000. *The Decline and Fall of the Indus,* op. cit.

10

JALORE-ELANA (IRINA) AND SWARNAGIRI: A STUDY

K.S. Shukla

A study of Jalore Elana and Swarangiri is a great desideratum for the proper understanding of Indian proto-history and archaeology. For this purpose we are obliged to take resourse to literary as well as archaeological evidences along with the traditional accounts prevalent among the masses.

Geology and geography also play a dominant part to unravel the past history and prehistory of the region. A study of place-names is also of great help in collaborating the geological and geographical landscape with the arhaeological remains and traditional accounts.

Location : (24°36'50"NW to 25°45'37"N and 71°71"E) Jalore is an important town and archaeological site in the district of the same name, in Sindhu Sauvir region of the ancient Arbud Mandal that is now known as Mt. Abu. It is virtually an oasis along the Swarnagiri and Sureshwar hills. It is surrounded by Badmer district in NW, Pali district in NE, Sirohi district in SE and Banaskantha and the Rann of Kachchha on the southern border. For some distance its border, in Badmer district, meets with that of Pakistan. Thus, Jalore is situated on a very strategic point where five rivers viz. Luni, Javai, Khari, Sukadi and Nadi form their watershed. In the long past, the Saraswati river passed through it. It is now completely dried up due to seismic upheavals. Only the Luni river flows about 460 km. from its original point in Puskar hills and ultimately, falls into Rann of Kachchha, and loses her identity (Patni 2002). All the above mentioned rivers make this region fertile and proseperous with their flowing waters; and, consequently, this fertile land earns its fair renown as a `bowl of grain' in the local parlance.

Hill Ranges : The famous hill ranges of this region are as follows :

1. Jirapatti Hill Ranges
2. Suganjhadri Hill Ranges
3. Swarnagiri Hill Ranges
4. Mt. Abu Hill Ranges

The Desert : Jalore is situated at such an strategic point that the 60 yojana long and wide spread desert has to be crossed before one reaches Sindh through this tiresome route - `satthi yojanākam maru kāantārram (Vimānvatthu Attakathā). According to the `Mahamayuri', Jambuka yaksha protected the 'sarthvahas' from the parching heat and hurricanes as well as pillagers on the trade-route to Sindh. The present-day Mohenjodaro was called 'Vittamayapattan' in the past. We also find the description of this desert in the Junagarh inscription of Rudradaman.

Identity of Jalore : According to the old tradition, Jalore is identified with the great Vedic seer Jābāli, who is said to have practised penances in the prehistoric caves of Swarnagiri hills. Etymologically, Jalore appears to have derived its name from jalodha i.e. the deluge. It appears that in the prehistoric period the water of the Rann of Kachchha flooded this area upto the foothills of this region.

Geology of Jalore : Geologically, the strip of Jalore region is very important in Rajasthan. It mainly consists of the basin of the river Luni. Earlier, it was watered by the river Saraswati after the Tethis had receded. Certain words or linguistic terms are very significant to the proper understanding of its geology. These are given below:

1. Meru - This term is used for high mountain region.
2. Maru - It indicates the desert area which includes the dry and sandy region west of Aravalli ranges.
3. Māl - The lower plateau, which is rocky and wavy in formation along the plains, is called Māl.

All these three geological terms are aptly applicable to the geography of the Jalore region. Right from the border of Sirohi to the Sivānā ranges, the whole region is called Meru. The highest point of the Swarnagiri is called `Kanchameru Peak'. The western portion of this Meru region or sandy desert, is called Maru. The plains and plateau beyond the Sivānā town is called Māl and the fertile region is known as `malāni' or 'malanchal' (Patni 2002). It is very interesting to note here that an inscribed Harappan seal with bull as field symbol had been discovered during excavation at tell Jokha (Umma) in Sumer by Langdan, the excavator of the site. It was bronght to India by Dr. V.S.Vakankar (Rahi 1983). It bears seven signs. Dr. Vakankar deciphered them as `marumālā', and six numeral dots with a trident were left undeciphered. It appears to me that the four signs of this sealing represent the old *Brahmi* and were correctly deciphered as `marumālā' by Dr. Vakankar, but the other three signs belong to the Indus script and may be deciphered as 'anchani'. Thus, the whole biscriptual inscription (Shukla 2005-06) can be read as "Marumālānchani" i.e. the region of Marumālā, which was probably nowhere else but in the Jalore region, which is well-known as 'Marumālānchal'. The remnants of cotton cloth-impressions suggest some valuable item or commodity being parcelled to Jokha (Umma) in 2800 B.C. from Jalore, which was itself a flourishing trading centre, and the ancient trade-route to Sindh passed through that town, India appears to be the first cotton fabric producing country in the world.

Geologically speaking, Jalore justifies all the three geographical terms viz. Maru, Māl and 'Meru' in its geophysical formations. The geological formation of Jalore area is nothing but the extension of the hill ranges of Mt. Abu. The desert-based hill ranges of Jalore region were ruined due to neo-tectonic movement in oceanosphere. The height of southern hill-ranges is only 150 meters in the Luni basin, but in Jasvantpura region it is about 975 meters. The formation of the plateau of the Swarnagiri is also the result of the same oceanic tumult i.e. neo-tectonic movements. The slope of the hills of Jalore is towards west. The palaeo-channel of dried-up Saraswati river in the desert still contains sweet potable water in its great depth.

Literary evidences : In the ancient period the Rann-of-Kachchha was known as Irina. The Rigveda speaks of a special type of topography of a place known as `Irina'. Irinya is one of the many names of lord Shiva (Taittariya Samhita 4.5.9.). There is an archaeologically important village in the Jalore district. It is called Elana village (एलाना गांव). The word appears to have its derivation from Irinā-Erinā-Ilanā-Elanā. This is mainly a Harappan site. In the Vedic literature Ilinā is associated with Nirrti, the deity of disaster, and the south-east (SE) direction. According to the Mahabharata, `Irinā' was formed by the recession of the sea. It is assumed to be situated slighty north of the present day Rann-of-Kachchha. (lyengar Radha Krishna: 2007)

The word Erinam occurs in the Rigveda (I-106-9) and speaks of the sparkling arrows of the Marutas capable of flooding the desert and making it fertile. Here `erinam' means barren soil or unfertile or fallow land or desert. In the hymn (VIII.87.4) also `erinan and `gaur' i.e. (wild-bull) are mentioned.

What is quite interesting is the association of wild-bull with the barren land i.e. `Erinā' or Elanā'. In English language the word `arena' appears to have the same sound and meaning i.e. sandy place (Chamber's Dictionary). If this interpretation is accepted, the Elanā village in Jalore District justifies its name in respect of its geographical position in the Rann-of Kachchha.

As regards the presence of `gaur' (wild bull) in the region, we may refer to a mythological story (legend) connected with the nearby Mt. Abu region where Lord Siva's mount, a bull, (named Nandi) was rescued from, a chasm or a fire-pit by Arbud, a powerful serpent. This indicates the geographical nearness of Erinā or `Elanā' with Arbud i.e. Mt. Abu. Again, it was close to the sea and also close to Aravalli mountain ranges.

Another Vedic reference needs to be given due consideration and credence. Indra is said to have cut down the head of Arbud (RV.II.14.4). Indra is the god of rain. It appears that at some point of time Indra (द्युलोकस्य अग्नि) i.e. the sun had melted by its fiery rays the snow capped peak of Mt. Abu and cut it to the present size. This hymn equates Indra with the highest god and also mentions his above deeds as most anicent (Radhakrishna et. al. 2008). According to Radhakrishna, `This could have happened at an unknown period in 4th 5th millennium B.C.'(Radhakrishna et. al. 2008).

Now, I am tempted, to cite a reference from the epic Ramayana of Rishi Valmiki to make the above mentioned episode more tangible and explicit. In the Yuddha Kand (22.6-12, 32, 36) Rama's arrow at the request of the sea-deity of Lanka, fell on the mountain region near `(Vi) drum-Kulya' sea, in the north of Lanka. Consequently, the whole region turned into a 'maru-kāntāra' i.e. sandy desert-cum-hilly forest:

तेन तन्मरूकान्तारं पृथिव्या किल विश्रुतं।
निपातित शरोयत्र वज्रा शनि समप्रभः।।

(Ramayana, Yuddha 22.36)

Moreover, the near-by sea also dried up. Then, Lord Rama bestowed on this gulf (zr) his grace and blessesd it with the gift of eternal prosperity and healthy climate bearing fruits, cereals and medicial aromatic plants.

शोषयित्वा तु तं कुक्षिं रामो दशरथात्मजः।
वरं तस्मै ददौ विद्वान मखेऽमर विक्रमः।।

(Ramayana, Yuddha, 22.40)

पशवश्चाल्परोगश्च फल–मूल रसायुक्तः।
वहुस्नेहो वहुक्षीरः सुगन्धि विविधौषधिः।।

(Ramayana, Yuddha, 22.42)

As stated above, this episode of natural disaster had probably taken place in 4th 5th millennium B.C. which is supposed to be appropriate time of Rama's incarnation on this land (Bohra 2002:78-91). Even the geologists are also of the view that this region of Rajasthan was not a sandy desert and was watered by the mighty rivers like Saraswati in those days. Many scientists and scholars have given different reasons of the drying up of river Saraswati, but one valid reason given by Dr. Patni is that Indra had destroyed the Rohini glacier, the soure of the Saraswati river, and caused the seven rivers to flow freely. (RV.II.12.12). Consequently, the Saraswati dried up in due course, but Jalore, Elena and Swamagiri stand mute witness to the whole geological, geographical and protohistorical event.

References

1. Patni, S.L.2002: *Jalore evam Swarnagiri Durg Ka Sanskritik Itihasa*, Hindusan Printing House, Jodhpur, p. 3.
2. Rigveda I 186.9
3. Rahi, I.C. 1982. *Lekhan Kala Ka Itihasa*, Vol. I. Pl. 27, p. 71.
4. Iyngar, R.N., RadhaKrishna, B.P. and S.S. Mishra. 2008. Vedic Irina and the Rann-of kutch, *Puratattva* 38, p. 170-180.
5. Shukla, K.S. 2006. A.Bi-Scriptual Seal Identified, *Pragdhara*, 16, pp.264-66.
6. Gupta & Patni. 2008. Cotton : A probe into Archlaeological Erdences, *Puratattva* 38, pp. 136-47
7. Bohra, M.L. 2002. Rama's Birth Chart in Valmiki Ramayana, *Panchal* new no.2, pp.78-90.

11

RIVER SARASWATI— THE CRADLE OF INDIAN CIVILIZATION

Rajesh Purohit

Although the river Saraswati has sunk into oblivion as a physical entity, it has left behind its cultural legacy and signatures on the Indo-Gangetic plains in such a way that it hardly can vanish from the fabric of Indian culture. This very river and its tributaries gave birth to a mighty civilization, sustained a perennial culture, and conceived an incredible literature and philosophy, be it Vedic, Vedantic or the Puranic. The tangible finds as have been unearthed from archaeological excavations and the intangible legacy in the form of a living tradition and customs of the people who dwelled on the lost banks of a 1600-km-long river, that used to flow from the Himalayas to the Arabian Sea, are valuable sources that unfold the saga of the age-old Indian civilization. The signatures of the lost river which have been revealed in the forms of palaeo channels are seen from the imageries of high resolutions taken from the remote-sensing satellites. These images suggest the existence of a mighty river underneath the soil. The buried material of the civilization that was nourished by the water of the river has also been unearthed by archaeological excavations carried out right on the banks of the lost river. Both the palaeo channels of the lost river and the archaeological findings unfold the story of the Indian civilization from its genesis to the contemporary times.

The term 'civilization' comes from the Latin word *civis,* meaning 'citizen' or 'townsman.' Therefore, 'civilization' literally means a complex society. However, archaeologically speaking, the presence of agriculture and urban settlement, which is a consequence of the Neolithic Revolution, is identified as civilization. A 'civilized' way of life is ultimately linked to conditions coming forth almost exclusively from intensive agriculture manifesting the signs of transformation of incipient agriculture to sedentary agriculture and domestication of animals. Gordon Childe described the development of civilization as the result of two successive revolutions: the Neolithic Revolution, triggering the development of settled communities, and the Urban Revolution that enhanced tendencies towards dense settlements, specialized occupational groups, social classes, exploitation of surpluses, monumental public buildings and tool-making, which permits the development of intensive agricultural techniques, such as the use of human power, crop rotation, and irrigation. This has enabled farmers to produce a surplus of food beyond what is necessary for their own subsistence.

Geographically speaking, the Fertile Crescent is the most cited example of the possible locations for the emergence of a civilization. It is usually applied to the Chalcolithic culture of Lower Egypt, the

Levant, Mesopotamia, Anatolia, and the Persian Plateau, and the Indian subcontinent or the region of *Sapta Sindhu* or the seven streams of rivers which are considered to be the cradle of civilizations.

Interestingly, the geomorphology and geography responsible for the emergence of fertile crescents of all major civilizations have something in common. For instance, all of them had a desert alongside them (Egypt has African desert, Mesopotamia has Arabian desert, China has Gobi desert, and India has Thar or great Indian desert), and they were all nourished by twin rivers (the Blue and the White Nile of Egypt, the Euphrates and the Tigris of Mesopotamia, the Yellow rivers of China and the Indus and the Saraswati of India). Again, climatically speaking, they were located in a semi arid zone.

The stone tool users of prehistoric times, who were used to hunting and food gathering as their subsistence economy, gradually with the change of environment and games, adopted new subsistence economy in which they used to hunt fast-running animals like deer, etc, for which they needed finer and smaller tools like the microliths during the Mesolithic period. Subsequently, with further changes in climatic conditions in the late Pleistocene period, flora and fauna started changing as a result of which the people across the world initially started adapting to incipient agricultural economy during the transition between Mesolithic and Neolithic periods itself. Eventually in the Neolithic period they settled permanently on the banks of fertile rivers as these were conducive to farming and fishing.

It was the first interglacial period in Holocene marking the break-up of glaciers and release of the pent-up waters that flowed out in seven mighty river channels referred to as the '*Sapta Sindhu*', i.e. Saraswati, Shatadru [Sutlej], Vipasa [Beas], Asikni [Chenab], Parosni [Ravi], Vitasta [Jhelum] and Sindhu [Indus] in the *Rig-Veda*, traced from east to west. Therefore sequentially, the easternmost stream among the seven Sindhus (etymologically, the word *Sindhu* in Sanskrit means a stream) is called the seventh stream Saraswati and the westernmost is called Sindhu. The Indian civilization flourished between these two rivers.

The *Rig-Veda* (7.36.6) says 'May the seventh (stream), Sarasvati, the mother of the Sindhu and those rivers that flow copious and fertilizing, bestowing abundance of food, and nourishing (the people) by their waters, come at once together'.

Saraswati has also been referred to as *Prāchi* (east) or the easterly flowing river. Prithudak or the present Pehawa in Kurukshetra, Haryana is considered the sacred most place located on the bank of Saraswati. Anang, the grandfather of Prithu after whom the *tirtha* (place of pilgrimage) Prithudak has been named, happened to be the first king of India.

Geological record indicates that during late Pleistocene glaciating waters of the Himalayas were frozen and that in place of rivers there were only glaciers, masses of solid ice. At the outset of Holocene, say about ten thousand years from now, as the warm period began the climate became warmer and the glaciers began to melt and the frozen water held by them surged forth in great floods, inundating the alluvial plains. The release of pent-up water gave birth to a number of rivers such as Sindhu on the west and Saraswati on the east along with five other tributaries which were flowing through the plains. As the frozen river started melting, people started moving towards the riverside areas in search of suitable places where they could settle and practice agriculture, fishing and horticultural activities. So, they settled on the banks of seven rives in the subcontinent. Among those seven, the Saraswati and the Sindhu were major rivers that flowed from the mountains right up to the sea. It is the hub of one of the largest and the longest living civilization which is more than 6,000 years old.

Between the eastern (Saraswati) and western (Sindhu) rivers; or in cities where agriculture was practised, the non-food producers settled permanently. In archaeological term, this was the first sign of an early civilization. Thus early human settlements were built mostly in river valleys where the land was fertile and suitable for agriculture. Easy access to a river or a sea was important, not only for food (fishing) or irrigation for agricu lture, but also for transportation and trade.

According to the *Shukla Yajurveda* (34- 19), 'Among these, the Saraswati and the Sindhu were major rivers that flowed from the mountain right up to the sea. Five rivers converge in Saraswati along with their streams. The Saraswati becoming fivefold in that region becomes a vast river.'

The material evidences and signatures of the Indian civilization found invariably in every archaeological site of the Saraswati and Indus valley are indicative of the birth and growth of a civilization that spread over an area of almost one million sq. km in the Indian subcontinent, starting from the northernmost site in Kashmir called 'Manda' to Daimabad (Maharashtra) in the south, Sutkagendor (Pakistan) in the west to almost Alamgirpur and Hulas (Uttar Pradesh) and the recently discovered site Sanauli (Uttar pradesh) in the east.

The cardinal traits distinctively seen as signatures of the Indus-Saraswati civilization in all the sites pertaining to Saraswati valley are: elaborate grid pattern town planning, monumental architecture, standardized bricks 1:2:3 and 1:2:4, 'S' shaped Jar, seals, terracotta cakes, terracotta bangles, perforated jar, copper, double-sided chalcedony blade and burial.

No civilization would ever have been born without the perennial source of a river and ours is no exception. The river in India is considered as mother who feeds her children for nourishment, protects them from enemies, diseases and other natural and unnatural onslaughts. Therefore we find the following prayer in the *Rig-Veda* (1.164.49): 'Oh Saraswati, offer that breast of yours for our nourishment here which is on your body, which spreads happiness by which you nourish (those who praise you) with all the choicest things, the one which holds all the beautiful things, which knows the enemies wealth and which offers good gifts.'

The Saraswati as the mother of the civilization has been eulogized in the *Rig-Veda* (2.41.16) as *Ambitame* (the best among the mothers), *Naditame* (the best among the rivers) and *Devitame*, (the best among the goddesses).

The saga of Indian culture has been unfolded through scientific archaeological excavations on the banks of the lost bed of Saraswati, Drishadvati, Apaya or Apaga, Indus, Ravi, Sutlej, Beas, Ghaggar, Yamuna and Ganga. The explorations and excavations in the post-independence era have revealed astounding evidences pertaining specially to the river Saraswati and its tributaries. Rakhigarhi (Hissar, Haryana) on Drishadvati, Bhirrana, Kunal and Banawali (Fatehabad, Haryana) on the ancient Saraswati or Ghaggar reveal adequate evidences pertaining to the pre, mature, and post-Harappan civilization from 5500 BC to 1700 BC. The data also indicate how the birth of a civilization took place in the newly discovered sites on the bank of Saraswati in Haryana such as Bhirrana, and Kunal which are contemporaneous with the cultural assemblages and findings of Baluchistan valley.There are many archaeological sites of immense historical and cultural importance within the Kurukshetra region such as Balu[1] (Kaithal), a Pre-Indus-Saraswati site (C.2900-1700 BC) on the bank of river Apaya or Apaga, a tributary of Saraswati, Bhagwanpura[2] (Kurukshetra), a unique site showing the interlocking phase of Indus and Painted Grey Ware culture identified as the culture of the *Mahābhārata* period on the right bank of river Saraswati (C.1700-1300 BC), Daulatpur[3] (Kurukshetra), a site yielding the antiquity from Late Indus to Medieval period, Mirzapur[4] (Kurukshetra) another Late Indus site along with the historical deposits from Kushan and Medieval period, Raja Karna Ka Qila[5] (Kurukshetra) represented by Northern Black Polished Ware to Medieval times, and Thanesar[6] (Kurukshetra), the ancient capital of Harshavardhana of the Pushyabhutis, bearing antiquity uninterruptedly from the Pre-Kushana to Late Medieval period. The scientific excavations of these sites have revealed the story of Kurukshetra, the cradle of Indian civilization. The artifacts, broken earthen ware, ruins of buildings, stone sculptures, temples and murals reported from various *tirtha-s* and archaeological sites throw eloquent light on the cultural heritage of the regions from its earliest time to the modern period. Throughout its history it has been an important centre of art, culture, and religion. The excavations also show how slowly the civilization reached its highest water-mark and these declined due to desiccation of the Saraswati and eventually ushering in a new Gangetic civilization on the banks of the Indus, the Yamuna and the Gangetic valley.

The prayer in the *Rig-Veda* (10.75.5) thus says: 'Oh Ganga, Yamuna, Sarasvati, Sutudri with Parshi, Marudvridha with Asikni; Arjikiya with Vitasta and Sushnoma hear this praise'.

The findings of Bhagawanpura in Kurukshetra are important because it is one of the rarest sites that yielded late Harappan antiquities along with Painted Grey Ware culture, indicating the emergence of PGW in the late Harappan time. This phenomenon can also be interpreted environmentally as well. It shows how with the passage of time, with the decline of major sources of glacier waters, the river either lost its course or was captured by later river systems such as Indus, Sutlej and Yamuna which could be the causes that led to the vanishing of the river Saraswati. Newer civilization emerged and flourished on the banks of Ganga and Yamuna (erstwhile Chambal) which is a tributary of the Ganga. It is believed that it captured the Saraswati source at Paontasaheb (the site is known as a Sikh shrine in Himachal Pradesh). Owing to rivercapturing, Saraswati was deprived of its perennial source of molten glaciers from the Himalayas. As the river started drying up, people slowly started migrating eastward towards the Ganga-Yamuna *doab* or westward towards Indus and Sutlej. Many scholars opine that Saraswati was a river independent of Shatadru. In the *Rig-Veda*, it has been described as a mighty river and nowhere has been stated that Shatadru had ever joined Saraswati. It neither met Shatadru, nor did it flow along the Hakra-Nara course. Oldham (1886) was himself not much convinced, and in his map the connection has been shown with broken lines. Saraswati, according toscholars, took a southwesterly swing near Anupgar in Rajasthan.

The modern search for Saraswati on the ground level started in 1893 by C F Oldham, an engineer, when he was riding his horse along the dry bed of a seasonal Rajasthani river called the Ghaggar. He was of the opinion that the bulk of the water of ancient Saraswati was contributed by Sutlej which later changed its course and become a tributary of the Indus. Most geoscientists believe that neotectonism and river-capturing or piracy caused the eastward diversion of the water of Saraswati and the westward drifting of Sutlej to become a tributary of Indus. This has been substantiated by archaeological findings in the region of Indus and Yamuna during the so-called Mature Harappan period in the Indus and its tributaries and later during the Harappan and PGW periods at the recently excavated sites such as Sanauli and Daksha Khera on Yamuna. This could be further justified by the behaviour of the river and phenomena of capturing and drifting of rivers. It is seen today that Sindhu (Indus) and Chenab are met by Sutlej. Ravi joins Chenab and so does Jhelum. Beas meets Sutlej in its upper course. Earlier Sutlej, whose dry bed today is seen at Hakra and Eastern Nara, flowed directly to the sea. Beas was earlier flowing as an independent river parallel to the then flowing Sutlej and this old course of Beas was obliterated after it was captured by Sutlej near Harike north and north-east of Ferozepur. The older Beas (Vipasa) prior to its capture by Sutlej flowed for a distance of around 300-400 km through Bahawalpur and met Shatadru near Derawar.

The satellite images of the palaeo channels, geological and sediment data and ground water surveys and the presence of thousands of archaeological sites revealing human antiquity of more than 5,000 years have significantly contributed to our knowledge about the existence of a mighty river which for a considerable time, had been considered as a mythical river. The satellite data precisely on the topo-sheets of Haryana, Rajasthan and Gujarat along the track of the lost Saraswati indicates many archaeological sites of historical and cultural importance showing the signature of river Saraswati and Drishadvati right from Siwaliks to Bhatner desert and further joining at the confluence of the Arabian Sea in Gujarat.

Kurukshetra

The present paper is a discussion on the major sites of Haryana along the lost rivers of Saraswati, Drishadvati and Apaga rivers. The findings are virtually unfolding the story of the lost Saraswati and its contribution to the Indian civilization. The place par excellence on the banks of Apaga, Drishadvati and Saraswati is Kurukshetra, the land of the *Mahābhārata* and the *Bhagavad-Gītā*. The earliest reference to Kurukshetra has been found in the *Taittiriya âranyaka* of *KrishnaYajurveda*[7] and *Satapatha Bràhmana*[8]. In the text of the *Mahābhārata*, Kurukshetra has been identified as 'Samantpanchaka' consisting of a land spread over twenty yojanas[9] and lying between river Saraswati on the north and Drishadvati on the south bounded by four door-keepers or *yaksha-s* at four cardinal corners viz., *Ratnuk Yaksha* at Bid Pipli (Kurukshetra) on the north-east, *Arantuk Yaksha* at Behar Jakh (between Patiala and Kaithal) on the north-west, *Kapil Yaksha* at Pokhar Kheri (Jind) on the southwest and *Machakruk Yaksha* at Sinkh (Panipat) on the south-east, as has been identified by Sir Alexander Cunningham. The antiquity of Kurukshetra dates back to the time of Indus Saraswati civilization (C.3200-1700 BC). *The Rig-Veda* (3.23.4) declares: 'Oh Agni, you were placed on the earth on an auspicious day on the best of the places on the earth. Blaze with wealth among the men (on the banks of) Drishadvati, Apaga and Saraswati.'

Let us now undertake a journey along the lost rivers—Saraswati, Apaga, and Drishadvati—starting from its point where it merged with the desert to the point where itdescends on the plains in the foothills of Siwalik or the Himalayas. The journey area is none other than the epic land of Kurukshetra, that not only witnessed the saints who chanted the Vedas but also the great battle of *Mahàbhàrata* and heard the song celestial *Bhagavad-Gītā.*

The *Rig-Veda* (7.95.1) again observes that 'This Saraswati, firm as a city made of *Ayas* (copper) flows rapidly with all-sustaining water, sweeping away in its might all other waters as a charioteer (clears the road).' Or, '(Saraswati is) like a great fortified town. With her, fertilizing stream the Saraswati comes forth. (She is to us) a stronghold, an iron gate'.

The Incredible heritage of Saraswati river in Haryana shows traces of cities with fortified structures and houses which were built on almost identical plans of well laid out streets, elaborate drainage systems, public baths, differentiated residential areas, flat-roofed brick houses, and fortified administrative- cum-religious centres enclosing meeting halls, standardized weights and measures. Distinctive engraved stamp seals were used, perhaps to identify property. Cotton was spun, woven, and dyed for clothing by the Indus-Saraswati people as also by their successors. Wheat, rice, and other crops were cultivated and a variety of animals domesticated.

The earliest among the sites on the lost bank of Saraswati in Haryana is of course Bhirrana in the district of Fatehabad. The excavation at Bhirrana on Ghaggar or Saraswati bed is considered to be the earliest among the sites excavated so far in India after the partition. The dates of the findings from Bhirrana goes back to 4565 BC (fifth millennium BC).

The early inhabitants here used to live in dwelling pits which are supposed to be the early village settlement on the dried up bed of Saraswati. These pits are circular in shape having occasional brick lining having superstructure without any signs of postholes on the floor and are mud-plastered. The average diameter of the pit is 2.30 metres. The tradition of pit-dwelling, especially in the early Harappan period was in vogue at Mitathal, Hissar district, and Kunal, Fatehabad of Haryana. The distinguishing ceramic of the period is the bichrome ware where the outlines of the motifs are painted in black and the space within is painted in evanescent white. In the transitional period, there was a phenomenal change in the settlement pattern. The entire site was occupied and the town appears to have been fortified. People started dwelling in houses made of sundried bricks of pink and buff colour which conformed to the ratio of 3:2:1 of Mature Harappan period. Besides, a few rectangular mud brick platforms with circular fire pits and hearths were unearthed by the excavators. 'Apart from the fortification wall, drainage system and pit-houses, various copper objects, carnelian, chert and lapis lazuli beads, seals made of steatite, weapons like axes and spearheads and a highly stylized animal head with horns, which seems like a ritualistic object, have been found so far.'

The excavation at Kunal (29.38N- 75.43E) on Ghagar Saraswati bed has revealed that the antiquity of the civilization in this region dates back to 3200 BC. The site has yielded pit-dwelling settlement, pottery resembling that of the Baluchistan region, bead manufacturing centre, two royal silver crowns of Harappan period and many more.

The excavation at Banawali (29.36N- 75.25E) on Ghagar Saraswati bed in the same Fatehabad district has unearthed antiquities belonging to the early and mature Indus civilization which includes typical Harappan settlement of grid pattern, wells, terracotta plough, micro weights and many more.

These apart, the excavations at Bhagwanpura, Joganakhera, Daulatpur— all in and around Kurukshetra—have revealed the story of Kurukshetra from 4000 BC to contemporary times without any significant gap.

The epic city of Kurukshetra on the bank of Saraswati instantly reminds us of the epic battle of the *Mahābhārata*. The war started at Kurukshetra. The vast sea of soldiers from either side were striking each other like two mighty tidal waves. The whole battlefield became so dusty as if ravaged by a desert storm. The noise of the war cries, blowing of conches, beating of drums, call of elephants and neighing of horses were horrifying. It was no small battle, it was the *Mahābhārata.* Amidst such horrified moments the land witnessed the battle of righteousness and heard the song celestial of the *Bhagavad-Gitā.* Both the event and the song have been immortalized over the years. Every moment of the myths and realities of civilization flourishing on the banks of Saraswati has been encoded in myriads of tangible and intangible heritage.

The land has not changed much. The dust reminds the battle. The water of sacred tanks of *Brahma Sarovar* and *Sannehit Sarovar* has remained as sacred as it was in the days of the *Mahābhārata* when the Pandavas visited the Dwaitavana in Kurukshetra during their exile. Kurukshetra as a pilgrimage destination has been in the limelight ever since the days of the *Mahābhārata*.

It is here that the *Rigvedic* sage Dadhichi gave up his life for the sake of Indra, the God of the Thunder. The *Bhāgavata Purāna* mentions that at this place, on the day of solar eclipse, Krishna met the Gopis and other kinsmen who came here from Braja. Krishna along with his family came from Dwārkā to participate in the fair of solar eclipse at Kurukshetra. During the fair, there was an interesting dialogue between the Gopis and Krishna. Krishna told the Gopis that he is the beginning and the end of all mortal beings and he permeates every being just as the five elements or *Panchbhuta-s*—ether, earth, water, fire and air—are present in all created things. The created objects are pervaded by these elements but the soul is untouched by these elements and is enshrined in the body.

The river Saraswati had witnessed Buddha while he was giving sermons to the people of Kurukshetra. This fact has been corroborated by the findings of Buddhist stupa at Thanesar, the capital of Vardhana dynasty, Stupa at Channeti of the time of Asoka and Stupa and Vihāras at Adibadri and Assandh of the time of the Kushanas and the Shungas. The archaeological findings have also been corroborated by the Buddhist literature like *Digha* and *Majjhima Nikāyas*. It is probable that Buddha preached and converted a considerably large portion of the population of ancient 'Kurudesha' or Kurukshetra. The Buddhist remains in the form of stupa, vihàra and sculptures found from Haryana are testimony to the fact that Buddhism flourished on the banks of Saraswati, Apaga and Drishadvati rivers.

Yet another significant dimension of the land of Saraswati at Kurukshetra is that it attracted spiritual gurus, mystic Sufi saints, thinkers, travellers and chroniclers. Kurukshetra was visited by Buddha, Baba Farid the Sufi saint, Dara Shikoh, Akbar, Alberuni, and Huen Tsang. Again, a learned Sanskrit scholar of the time of Akbar called Hazi Sultan who was one of the two translators of the *Mahābhārata* into Persian called '*Razm nama*', lived here. This virtually shows how the spiritual land of Saraswati even after its desiccation spread its resonance of knowledge to everyone who dwelled on its banks. The Tomb, Mosque, Stupa and Gurudwaras are integral parts of the tangible heritage and its intangible segments are seen in its fairs like solar eclipse, Shravan mela, Somavati amāvasyā, Pehowa mela, Phalgu mela and, off late, the Kurukshetra Utsava Gita, Jayanti held every year on the lost bank of Saraswati.

The river-bed of the lost river Saraswati was only seen at some places at Kurukshetra along with the sacred ghats and bridges belonging to the Mughal and British periods. However, what is there beneath the river was never traced before the discovery of an archaeological site on the bank of the lost river at Kurukshetra. The sensational archaeological finding of an ancient river-bed on the north of Kurukshetra has been traced by the author after a meticulous survey and study of palaeo channels of Haryana. The river-bed has been found adjacent to an archaeological site known as Bhore Saidan, 13 km from Kurukshetra on Pehowa Road. It has an alluvial deposit of great antiquity. G. E. Pilgrim had presumed long time back and had published a landmark paper drawing attention to an alluvial deposit of great antiquity found stretching all the way from the Himalayan foothills to the Sindh gulf. Pilgrim imagined that the deposit must have been laid by a primitive river which he named Siwalik. But this Siwalik is none other than Saraswati.

The cynosure of all eyes is on a huge river-bed displaying a clear-cut section of a river-bed. It has been confirmed from the palaeo channel furnished by ISRO, Jodhpur, that a buried channel runs beneath Bhore Saidana. A large number of images of the palaeo channels, buried rivers, old alluvial soils have been mapped on toposheets from the satellite which also shows distinct channels below the archaeological sites of Haryana yielding antiquities dated back to fourth and third Millennium BC. Bhore Saidana, a multicultural site, starting from PGW period to Mughal period furnishes evidences at a depth of about 30 feet in a rain gulley of the mound, antiquities of the lost river along with archaeological materials such as pottery, stone image of Pratihāra period and structure of Gupta period. The river-bed has seven layers alternatively carrying riverine sand and an alluvial clay deposits.

The search for Saraswati eventually unraveled not only an incredible heritage but also the wealth of ground water in the form of palaeo channels, most precious among the human needs especially in the drought-prone and arid zones like Rajasthan, Haryana and Gujarat. The existence of palaeo channels and groundwater resources within a depth of 30 to 60 meters below offers a possibility of constructing one million sustainable tube wells in the central Saraswati river basin alone to augment the water resources of the region.

The revival of the Saraswati river therefore will benefit the country in every way.

References

1. Balu (Kaithal) is an excavated site. Its pottery sequence starts with early Siswal, Siswal, mature Harappa and late Harappa. Early Harappa or Kalibangan I-2900-2700 BC: *An Encyclopedia of Indian Archaeology*, Vol. 2, edited by A. Ghosh, p. 40; for Balu, p. 414; for Siswal and p. 194 for Kalibangan.
2. Bhagwanpura (Kurukshetra) on the right bank of the Saraswati. It has revealed a twofold sequence of cultures viz, period I A and I B with interlocking of late Harappa with PGW. Period is comparable with late Harappa types of Bara, Bahadrabad, Siswal II B, Mitathal II B, Daulatpur and Raja Karna ka Qila: Ibid. p. 64.
3. The excavations at Daulatpur has revealed that the late Harappan culture can be bracketed with Sanghol I B, Mitathal 2 B, Mirzapur, Bhagwanpura I A and Banawali III followed by period II yielding remains of PGW, followed by period III bearing the antiquities of early historical remains (C. 500 BC to 500 AD): Ibid., pp. 117-18 Ghosh, pp. 117-18.
4. Mirzapur (Kurukshetra) pottery of period I (late Harappa) resembles to those from Bara, Sanghol, Chandigarh, Mitathal II B, Daulatpur, Bhagwanpura and also Kalibangan I. The period II yields early historical antiquities followed by period III bearing late medieval deposits. Ibid.p. 289.
5. Raja Karna ka Qila (Kurukshetra) reveals a continuous sequence of six periods of cultures from Northern Black Polished Ware to Medieval times. (C. 800 BC to 1600 AD). Ibid pp. 58-59.
6. Raja Karna ka Qila (Kurukshetra) reveals a continuous sequence of six periods of cultures from Northern Black Polished Ware to Medieval times. (C. 800 BC to 1600 AD). Ibid pp. 58-59.
7. *Taittiriya âranyaka*, V. 1.1.
8. *Satapatha Bràhmana*, IV, 1.5.13; *Sacred Books of the East*, p. 275.
9. Datta V. N. and Phadke H. A., *History of Kurukshetra*, p. 11.
10. Rao, L.S. 2004. Unearthing Harappan Settlement of Bhirrana; Puratattva : no. 34.

12

ARCHAELOGICAL INVESTIGATIONS ALONG THE ANCIENT PILGRIMAGE ROUTE FROM AYODHYA TO SRAVASTI

Indudhar Dwivedi, Vimal Tiwari, Abha Dwivedi

PILGRIMAGE?

The word *tirthayatra* is the synonyms of Pilgrimage in Indian context which means 'undertaking a journey to river fords or visit of sacred places known as *tirthas'*. Pilgrimage, one of the religious and cultural phenomena most common to human society, is an important feature of the world's major religions. A pilgrimage has been defined as, ''A journey resulting from religious causes, externally to a holy site, and internally for spiritual purposes and internal understanding''. (Barber 1993:1) The pilgrimage denote four connotations: a route, riverbank, sacred site and religious territory related to divine activities (Singh, 2006). A majority of pilgrim centers in India are closely associated with nature, their locations being near flowing water, mountaintops and forest.

The main objective of the pilgrim is to see the Divine. He wants to see holy environment of the *tirtha* and to see the images abiding in the ancient sanctums. The pilgrim also wants to be seen by the God, to reveal himself, uncover himself, stand before the God and be known to Him. *Darshana* is the essence of every pilgrim's journey, the rationale, the inner and outer goal.

In the wider Hindu tradition, these places, particularly those associated with waters, are often called *tirthas*, and pilgrimage to these *tirthas* is one of the oldest and still one of the most prominent features of Indian religious life. A *tirtha* is a "crossing place," a "ford," where one may cross over to the far shore of a river or to the far shore of the worlds of heaven. Hence, *tirtha* has come to refer to these places of pilgrimage, where the crossing might be safely made. (Eck 1981:323-44)

In Vedic times, the word may have concerned only those sacred places associated with water, but by the time of the Mahabharata, *tirtha* had come to denote any holy place, be it a lake, mountain, forest, or cave. The *Mahabharata,* in the *Tirthayatra* section, lists hundreds of holy destinations. Sage Pulastya describes to Bhishma a tour circumambulating all of India in a clockwise fashion, beginning from Pushkara in Rajasthan, then to Somnath and Dwarka in the West, to the Himalayas, across the top of India through Varanasi and Gaya to the mouth of the Ganges in the East, then southward to Kanyakumari, back up the western side of India to Gokarna in Karnataka, and ultimately returning to Pushkara. The existence of this pilgrimage route in ancient times proves that undivided India was a one culture unified by a one religion. (http://www.hinduismtoday.com/pdf_downloads/what_is_hinduism/Sec4/WIH_Sec4_Chapter35.pdf)
Mahabharata and Puranas rate pilgrimage more significant and rewarding than *yajnas*. Vanaparva

(82.13.17) comparing_*Devayajnas* and *tirthayatras* or pilgrimage says that the virtues gained through pilgrimage are greater than those obtained by performing *Yajna*.

There are references to the pilgrimage in ancient Buddhist texts also. The Buddhacharita (ii.37; vii.40) states that purification from sin may be achieved by living or bathing at sacred places and such places are "ladders to heaven". The same text says: "those who bathe and offer worship in the sacred river and holds high regard to the *chaitya*, become bodhisattvas and mahasattvas, and reach *nirvana*. (Buddhacharita x.2, xv.78)

The Buddha himself promulgated the sacred character of pilgrimage centers and stated that, "There are four places which the follower should visit with feelings of respect and awe: the place where Tathagata was born; the place where Tathagata attained supreme bodhi; the place where Tathagata set foot making the spot into a kingdom of dhamma and the place where Tathagata passed away. (Mahaparinivana Sutta, v.16-22)

Introduction

The Lucknow Circle of Archaeological Survey of India has taken a project titled 'Ancient Pilgrimage route from Kaushambi to Kapilvastu' in the session 2007-08 under the directorship of the first author who was the Superintending Archaeologist of the Circle at that time. The aim of the project was to locate ancient settlements and religious centers along the route and to highlight the importance in different cultural periods. The present paper is a part of that project which covers the area between Ayodhya and Sravasti.

The area under reference covers Gonda and Balrampur districts of Uttar Pradesh and bounded on the north by Nepal *tarai*, on the south by the Ghaghara river, on the east by Basti and Siddharthnagar districts and on the west by Bahraich and Sravasti districts. The area is drained by several rivers including Ghaghara, Rapti and Kuwano. Topographically the area is divisible into three broad divisions viz. *Tarai*, *Uprahar* and *Kachhar*.

The ancient settlements of Ayodhya and Sravasti were politically as well as religiously very much important during different periods and were the capitals of ancient Kosala kingdom. Ayodhya was the capital of South Kosala whereas Sravasti was the capital of North Kosala.

Sravasti was located at the meeting point of three important trade routes of India. One of these lay to the south-west from Sravasti, with a destination, the countries Alka (Mulaka) and Assaka via Saket, Kausambi, Vana, Vidisha Gonaddhya, Ujjayini, Mahishmati and Pratishthan on the Godavari. Another trade route led to the south-east ultimately reaching the Rajgraha via Setavya, Kapilvastu, Kushinara, Pava, Bhognagar and Vaishali. The third proceeded to the north-west from Sravasti towards Gandhara and Taxila in Uttarapatha via Mathura across the desert of Rajputana.

The city of Ayodhya was situated on the trade route from Sravasti to Pratisthan and was next to the Sravasti. Most of the religious places related to the different sects were located on these routes and for such reasons these routes played an important role in the development of pilgrimage.

Ayodhya in Literature and Archaeology

The city of Ayodhya (Lat.26^{0}48'N; Long.82^{0}14'E) is located on the right bank of river Saryu/Ghaghara in district Faizabad, U.P. It is one of the seven holy places of the Hindus and was the capital of Ikshvaku (*Brahmandapurana* IV, 40, 91), birth place of lord Rama and first and fourth Tirthatikaras (*Aavassaka Nirjjuti*, 382). On the basis of the genealogical tables of the *Puranas* and other relevant ancient literatures, Vishuddhanand Pathak (1963) proposed that about one hundred and two kings of the solar race ruled up to one or two generations later to the Buddha. The genealogy of the Iksavakus of Ayodhya begins from Manu Vaivasvata. Iksavaku was the second, Mandhata was ninetieth, Purukutsa was twentieth and Dasaratha was sixtieth king of this race. The famous Iksavaku king Rama appears in the 61st generation while Vrihadabala of the same dynasty, who fought against the *Pandavas* in the Mahabharata war, was the 76th king. Sumitra was the last king of the Kosalan Empire. The Bhagavata Purana (IX, 8.19) refers to it as a city. According to the Skanda Purana (Chap. 1, 64-65) Ayodhya looks like a fish. In the Buddhist period Kosala was divided into north and south. The capital of the southern Kosala was Ayodhya and Northern Kosala was Sravasti.

B.C. Law (1967: 76-78) mentioned in his book that there are several references in the Ramayana regarding Ayodhya and according to which, Ayodhya was a city, full of wealth and granaries of paddy. It had spacious streets and roads, well-watered and decorated with flowers. It had lofty gates furnished with doors and bolts. It was fully protected. It was the home of skilful artisans and craftsmen. It contained palatial buildings, green bowers and mango-groves. The city was rendered impregnable being surrounded by a deep ditch filled with water. A large number of pinnacled houses and lofty seven-storied buildings existed there. It was a crowded city and frequently resounded by musical instruments. This city had Kamboja horses and mighty elephants. In the Mahabharata, it is called '*punyalaksana*' that is, endowed with auspicious signs. It was a delightful spot on earths. According to the Ramayana there were four grades of social order at Ayodhya, e.g., the Brahmanas, the Ksatriyas, the Vaisyas and the Sudras. They had to fulfill their respective duties and obligations.

Ayodhya is also a sacred place for Buddhists. It is said that Buddha bit a branch of the nettle-tree and planted it in the ground, where it grew to the height of the seven feet, and never increased or diminished in size. This event has been mentioned by Chinese pilgrims Fa Hian & Heun Tsang in their travel accounts. According to the Ceylonese books, Vishakha, a great follower of Buddha, constructed Purvarama monastery for Buddha at Sravasti and Saketa (Ayodhya). According to the Ceylonese annals, Buddha spent 16 years in the *Pubbarama* monastery at Saketapura, whereas Heun Tsang mentioned in his travel account that Buddha spend his 6 years at Vishakha which has been identified by Cunningham (1979: 338-43) with Ayodhya.

Ayodhya was included in the kingdom of Pushyamitra Sunga who ruled after the downfall of Mauryan Empire. An inscription of Dhandeva, who was sixth from him and was the son of Phalgudeva, found from here mentions that Pushyamitra performed two *asvamedha yajna* during his reign. (E.I., XX: 57)

Archaeological investigations were first carried out at Ayodhya by Major General A. Cunningham who explored it in the year 1862-63 (ASIR vol. I). The excavations were carried out by the Banaras Hindu University in the session 1969-70 by A.K. Narain (IAR 1969-70: 40-41). The earliest period which was encountered during excavation was related with the N.B.P.W. culture. Later on B.B. Lal carried out excavations at Ayodhya under the project 'Archaeology of the Ramayana Sites' (IAR 1976-77: 52-53). The excavations were carried out at Ram Janma Bhumi mound, in the open area to the west of Hanuman Garhi and at Sita-ki-Rasoi. At the lowest levels Northern Black Polished Ware, few sherds of grey ware, painted with fugitive bands in black pigment, were found. In the earlier stages, the houses were of wattle-and-daub or mud, followed by those of baked bricks.

The excavation yielded a rich crop of antiquities which include seals, coins and terracotta figurines. The most noteworthy among them are a terracotta sealing of king Vasudeva of the second century B.C., a coin of Muladeva of the same period and a grey terracotta figurine of a person (Jaina Kevalin?) with bald head, distended ear-lobes and in *kqyotsarga* pose datable to *circa* fourth century B.C. One of the most significant discoveries, pertaining to the early historic stage, was the occurrence of sherds of the Rouletted Ware in levels assignable to the first-second century A.D. This phenomenon may well be regarded as signifying large-scale trade and commerce at Ayodhya in the early centuries of the Christian era. After the early historic deposits, there is a break in occupation, with considerable debris and pit formations before the site was again occupied around the eleventh century A.D. Recently, the Archaeological Survey of India has also conducted excavations in the session 2002-03 at the Ram Janma Bhoomi site, Ayodhya.

Sravasti in Literature & Archaeology

The ancient city of Sravasti has been identified with the ruin of Sahet-Mahet, Orajhar, Penahiajhar and Kharahuajhar (Lat. 27^0 31' N. and Long. 82^0 02' E) located in the newly created district of Sravasti on the border of Balrampur district of Uttar Pradesh.

Sravasti finds mention in the Ramayana and Mahabharata as a prosperous city in the kingdom of Kosala. In the Puranas it is described as the capital of North Kosala. According to the Vishnupurana (II,

4) the city was founded by the legendary king Shravasta of Solar race. In the Matsya and Brahma Puranas (XII, 29-30; VII, 53) Shravasta is mentioned as the son of Yuvanasva. The Mahabharata represents Shravastaka as the son of Shrava and the grandson of Yuvanasva (Vanaparva, 201, 3-4). Vayu Purana (88.200) and Ramayana (VII; 108.5) mention Sravasti as the capital of Lava, the son of Rama. Saravasti is mentioned in the Buddhist literature as the capital of Kosala, which was stood on a high road. The material prosperity of Sravasti was due to the fact that it was a meeting place of three main trade routes and a great centre of trade.

Sravasti was not only the capital of a powerful kingdom and a great emporium of Indian trade but also the home of philosophical speculations, where a number of schools of thought had already established themselves before the advent of Buddha. Mahavira, the twenty fourth and last Jaina Tirthankara, gathered here a great following particularly among wealthy merchants and bankers (Kalpasutra 103,105,106). Prasenajit too was initially one of his a votaries. Enjoying royal patronage, Mahavira built a stronghold for his faith. Sravasti was also the birth-place of two other Tirthankaras, Sambhavanatha and Chandraprabha, facts which added to its attraction for the Jainas (Jaina Harivanshpurana, p.717).

Prasenajit was the king of Sravasti at the time of Buddha. Sudatta, a wealthy merchant of Sravasti and popularly known as Anathapindika invited Buddha to Sravasti and purchased the royal garden of Jeta, son of king Prasenjit, and built a retreat for Buddha's stay at Sravasti. A pictorial representation of this purchase was found in the bas relief at Bharhut.

Buddha performed here the Great Miracle on account of which and other less famous occurrences Sravasti became one of the eight holy places of Buddhist pilgrimage, the other seven places being Lumbini, the place of his birth; Bodh Gaya, the place of the Enlightenment; Sarnath, the place of the First Preaching of the Law; Rajagriha, where he tamed a mad elephant; Vaishali, where a monkey offered honey to him; Sankasya, where he descended from heaven; and Kusinagara, where he passed away.

In the third rainy season after his enlightenment Buddha visited Jetavana, and since then he regularly made his stay to the monastery spending there twenty-four rainy seasons in all. Presenajit visited Buddha at Jetavana and heard a sermon which led to his conversion.

The pious lady Visakha, also known as Migaramata, who had nursed Prasenajit through a severe illness, built for the use of Buddha a magnificent monastery to the east of Jetavana, hence call Purvarama. Both Fa-hien and Hiuen Tsang refer to it, and, from all accounts, it was only second to Jetavana in extent, having been erected in wood and stone.

According to Divyavadana, Emperor Ashoka visited Jetavana and Sravasti when he undertook a country-wide pilgrimage to the holy spots of Buddhism, at each of which he left some monument to signify his attachment to the religion. Hiuen Tsang states that Asoka erected two pillars, each 21 m high, on the left and right sides of the eastern gate of Jetavana. One was surmounted by a wheel and the other by a bull.

Buddhism became a popular religion with royal support during the reign of Kusanas. The buildings of Jetavana were revived; new stupas and shrines were added and images of Buddha were installed. An image of Bodhisattva which was found from here was the gift of two Kshatriya brothers. Another image of Bodhisattva was installed by one Bhikshu Bala, who was well versed in the Tripitaka. All the statues bear inscriptions recording the respective donations.

The Buddhist establishments at Sravasti were flourished during Gupta age which is confirmed by the fact that almost all the present ruined structures show the style and ornamentation of the Gupta period. Further, in nearly every building have been found some vestiges of the Gupta period, among which clay sealing and tablets inscribed with the Buddhist creed were numerous.

The Buddhist establishments survived at Sravasti down to the middle of the twelfth century. This was mainly due to the patronage of the Gahadavala kings of Kanauj, Madanapala and his son Govindachandra. Inscriptions of their reigns were found in Jetavana, in a monastery dated samvat 1176 (A.D. 1119), records that the king's minister Vidyadhara, forsaking the Śaiva religion, devoted his wealth to the foundation of a vihara at Jetavana. The other record, of the reign of Govindachandra (A.D.1129-30), conveys the royal gift of six villages around Sravasti to Buddhabhattaraka and other monks of Jetavana-mahavihara.

Archaeological works were initiated at the fortified site of ancient Sravasti by Cunningham in the year 1862-63 who identified it and carried out excavations (ASIR I: 330-48; ASIR XI: 78-99). Later on the site was again excavated between 1907 and 1910 by J.Ph. Vogel, Daya Ram Sahni and J.H. Marshall. (ASIAR 1907-08: 81-131; ASIAR 1910-11: 1-24)

In the year 1959, a small-scale excavation was carried out K. K. Sinha on behalf of Archaeological Survey of India. Period I was represented by the presence of a few sherds of the Painted Grey Ware, N. B. P. Ware, black-slipped, black-and-red, thin grey, and plain red wares. Period II was marked by the coming up of a mud-rampart, red and thick grey wares, with shapes commonly found in the Sunga period. Period III was represented by typical early medieval pottery.

The site was again excavated by the Archaeological Survey of India several times between 1987 and 2003 and total eight periods were encountered. The earliest deposit was associated with the Pre-NBPW period followed by NBPW period, Maurya & Sunga period, Kushana period, Gupta period, Post-Gupta period, Early Medieval period and Late Medieval period. (IAR 1987-88: 106-08; IAR 1988-89: 82-84; IAR 1991-92: 102-04; IAR 1992-93: 91-92; IAR 1993-94: 104-105; IAR 1995-96: 76-81; IAR 1996-97: 171-76; IAR 1997-98: 186-97; IAR 2000-01: 140-52; Takahashi, et.al. 2000)

A wide range of terracotta objects including animal, human and bird figurines, besides beads of semiprecious stones mainly of agate and carnelian; discs, hopscotch, wheel, ball, gamesman of different varieties were collected. The iron objects are represented by razor, spear-head, arrow-head, chisel, nail, knives, blade and iron slag, seal, sealings, etc. Some seals and sealings bearing script in Kushan Brahmi characters were also recovered. Mention may be made of, a terracotta sealing with inscription of *'Sivadevasa'* in Kushan Brahmi characters. The copper objects include: coins, both circular and rectangular, antimony rod; bangle; ring, etc. Mention may also be made of a beautiful copper sprinkler with handle. Other finds include, glass bangles of different colours, ivory comb, stone pestle and sandstone quern.

Routes from Ayodhya to Sravasti

There are two main routes for Sravasti from Ayodhya. The first route is via Nawabganj, Wazirganj, Gonda, Itiathok and Balrampur. The second route is via Nawabganj, Mankapur, Utraula and Balrampur. Mention may be made of several link routes which are existed at present namely Gonda to Utraula and Itiyathok to Sravasti via Khargupur. Explorations have been carried out along the above mentioned routes to locate ancient settlements.

Archaeological Investigations

1. **Baijpur, tehsil- Gonda (Lat. $27^0$13'33" N; Long. 82^0 03'10" E)**- The site is situated about 22 km from Gonda via Alawal Deoria on Utraula road. The site extends in an area of about 6 acres and is about 2 mt high from the surrounding area. The site is partly occupied for residential purpose. The western part of the site is used as Muslim graveyard. Bricks sized 26+? x 29 x 6 and 34+? x 26 x 7 have also been noticed at the site during exploration. The site yielded red ware in medium fabric along with few specimens of black slipped ware. The shapes include high necked vessels, water vessels, bowl, bowl with inturned rim, basin. On the basis of the remains found during exploration it may be suggested that the site was inhabited between Kusana and early Medieval periods.
2. **Basati, tehsil- Gonda (Lat. $27^0$15'22" N; Long. 82^0 03'40" E)**- The site is situated about 22 km from Gonda; 17 km on Balrampur road till Parasarai then 5 km towards east. The site extends in an area of about 10 acres and is about 2 mt high from the surrounding area. Primary and Junior High School buildings are constructed on the site and new construction is in progress. The peripheral area of the mound is covered with shrubs. The site yielded red ware and black ware in medium fabric along with few specimens of red slipped ware. The shapes include bowl, bowl with inturned rim, carinated handi, basin, water vessel. On the basis of the remains found during exploration it may be suggested that the site was inhabited between Kusana and post Gupta periods.
3. **Belawan, tehsil- Gonda (Lat. 27^0 08' 33" N; Long. 82^0 06' 53" E)**- The site is situated about 20 km from Gonda on Utraula road; 12 km on Utraula road then 8 km to the east. The site extends in an area

of about 4 acres and is about 1.5 mtr high from the surrounding area. The site is fully intact and full of trees and shrubs. *Dargaah* of Bashir is built on the top of the site. The site is presently used for Muslim graveyard. The site yielded red ware in medium fabric and the shapes include bowl, bowl with inturned rim, water vessel, inkpot type lid. On the basis of the remains found during exploration it may be suggested that the site was inhabited during Kusana period.

4. **Bhatpi, tehsil- Gonda (Lat. 27⁰ 19' 40" N; Long. 81⁰ 59' 43" E)-** The site is situated at a distance of about 27 km from Gonda; 18 km on Balrampur road till Itiyathok then 7 km on Khargupur road then 2 km on Aryanagar road. The site extends in an area of about 15 acres and is about 4 mt high from the surrounding area. A big Saryu canal passes from the centre of the site and divided it into two parts. The site is partly used for agriculture purpose. Large numbers of brickbats are lying at the site. The residents of nearby villages excavated the site to find the brickbats. The site yielded red ware in medium and coarse fabric, black ware and black slipped ware, grey ware and red slipped ware. The shapes include carinated handi, bowl, bowl with inturned rim, knife edge bowl, water vessel, handled pot/pan, basin, lid, inkpot type lid, storage pot. On the basis of the remains found during exploration it may be suggested that the site was inhabited between Kusana and early Mediaeval periods.
5. **Binduli Deeh, tehsil- Gonda (Lat. 27⁰ 19' 10" N; Long. 82⁰ 01' 15" E)-** The site is situated at a distance of about 24 km from Gonda on Khargupur road via Itiyathok. The site extends in an area of about 16 acres and is about 4 mt high from the surrounding area. Primary and Junior High School buildings and few houses are built over the site. The mound is full of trees and shrubs. The site yielded Northern Black Polished ware, black slipped ware, grey ware, black ware, red slipped ware and red ware. The shapes include bowl, bowl with inturned rim, water vessel, high necked vessel, basin, storage pot, miniature vase, lid, button knobbed lid, spouted pot. On the basis of the remains found during exploration it may be suggested that the site was inhabited between NBPW and Early Medieval periods.
6. **Bishunpur Bairia, tehsil- Gonda (Lat. 27⁰ 09' 53" N; Long. 82⁰ 03' 03" E)-** The site is situated about 11 km from Gonda on Utraula road via Salpur. The site extends in an area of about 5 acres and is about 1.5 mt high from the surrounding area. Few houses, mango orchard and a tube well are built over the site. The site is partly under cultivation. The site yielded red ware in medium and coarse fabric along with few specimens of red slipped ware. The shapes include bowl, bowl with inturned rim, high necked vessel, water vessel, inkpot type lid, spouted pot, basin, knife edge bowl. On the basis of the remains found during exploration it may be suggested that the site was inhabited during Kusana and early Medieval periods.
7. **Buknapur, tehsil- Mankapur (Lat. 27⁰ 01' 28" N; Long. 82⁰ 15' 08" E)-** The site is situated about 33 km from Gonda via Mankapur. The site is located to the east of the village. It extends in an area of about 3 acres and slightly raised from the surrounding area. The site presently occupied for agriculture purpose. The site yielded only red ware and the shapes include water vessel, carinated handi and lid. On the basis of the remains found during exploration it may be suggested that the site was inhabited during late Medieval period.
8. **Dinara, tehsil- Gonda (Lat. 27⁰ 08' 24" N; Long. 82⁰ 10' 48" E)-** The site is situated about 32 km from Gonda via Kahoba and Motiganj on Kahoba- Datauli road. The site is located to the south-west of the village. It extends in an area of about 12 acres and is about 1.5 mt high from the surrounding area. Two houses and a tube well are built over the site. The site is presently occupied for agriculture purpose. The site yielded red ware in medium and coarse fabric and the shapes include water vessel, carinated handi, basin, trough, lid, storage pot, bowl, bowl with inturned rim, miniature pot. On the basis of the remains found during exploration it may be suggested that the site was inhabited between Kusana and early Medieval periods.
9. **Dumariadeeh, tehsil- Tarabganj (Lat. 27⁰ 01' 58" N; Long. 82⁰ 04' 23" E)-** The site of Dumaria Deeh is situated about 18 kms from Gonda on Gonda-Faizabad road. A Police chowki, Primary school and Intermediate collage is built over the site. There is a Sthan of Samay Mai on the top of the mound. The site is situated near an ancient water channel. The site extends in an area of about 9 acres and its height is about 2.5 mtr from the surrounding area. It is partly used for agriculture. The site yielded red ware, black slipped ware, black ware & black and red ware and the shapes include bowl,

bowl with inturned rim, water vessel, basin, storage pot. On the basis of the remains found during exploration it may be suggested that the site was inhabited between Kusana and Early Medieval periods.

10. **Itahia Tiwaripurwa, tehsil- Gonda (Lat. 27⁰ 08' 58" N; Long. 82⁰ 13' 22" E)-** The site is situated about 44 km from Gonda; 30 km on Utraula road till Dhanepur then 14 km on Kurasan road. The site is situated to the north of the village and a primary school building is built on the north-east side of the site. There is a pond to the south-east of the site. The site extends in an area of about 4 acres and is about 1 mt high from the surrounding area. Brick bats have also been noticed during exploration. The site yielded red ware in medium and coarse fabric & red slipped ware and the shapes include bowl, bowl with inturned rim, water vessel, carinated handi, storage pot. On the basis of the remains found during exploration it may be suggested that the site was inhabited during Kusana period.
11. **Karamdeeh Belwa, tehsil- Gonda (Lat. 27⁰ 19' 37" N; Long. 82⁰ 02' 12" E)-** The site is about 24 km from Gonda on Balrampur road; 22 km on Balrampur road then 2 km in west direction. The site is located to the south-west of the village at a distance of about 500 mt and extends in an area of about 8 acres and is about 1 mt high from the surrounding area. A modern Shiva temple is constructed over the site which houses Shivalinga. Some ancient sculptures made of black basalt in weathered condition are stored outside the temple. The site yielded red ware in medium and coarse fabric and black ware in medium fabric. The shapes include bowl, water vessel, storage pot, carinated handi. On the basis of the remains found during exploration it may be suggested that the site was inhabited between Gupta and early Medieval periods.
12. **Karohanath, tehsil- Mankapur (Lat. 27⁰ 5' 22" N; Long. 82⁰ 15' 44" E)-** The site is about 38 km from Gonda on Sadullanagar road via Mankapur to the south-east of Machhali Bazar, a small town. The site extends in an area of about 12 acres and is about 1 mt high from the surrounding area. A shiva temple, Primary school, houses and talab are built on the site. According to the stone placed on the entrance of the temple, it is 700 years old and it was renovated by Maharaja Raghuraj Singh in vikram samvat 1963. The site is covered with mango trees. The site yielded Northern Black Polished ware, black slipped ware, grey ware all in fine fabric and red ware in fine, medium and coarse fabric. The shapes in NBPW and black slipped ware include dish and bowl; in red ware high necked vessel, bowl, bowl with inturned rim, water vessel, handled pot/pan, carinated handi. On the basis of the ceramics and shapes found during exploration it may be suggested that the site was inhabited between NBPW and Early Medieval periods.
13. **Kazi Dewar, tehsil- Gonda (Lat. 27⁰ 04' 16" N, Long. 82⁰ 04' 28" E)-** The site is about 16 km from Gonda on Mankapur road via Darjikuwan. The site extends in an area of about 15 acres and is about 2.5 mt high from the surrounding area. More than half portion of the site is occupied for cultivation while rest of the area is used for residential purpose by the villagers. As told by the villagers foundations of the brick structures have been found earlier during agriculture and residential activities. Bricks sized 28+? x 27 x 5-6 cm. have also been noticed during exploration along with brick bats. The site yielded red ware in medium and coarse fabric, grey ware & black slipped ware and the shapes include water vessel, carinated handi, bowl, bowl with inturned rim, basin, and storage pot. On the basis of the remains found during exploration it may be suggested that the site was inhabited between Sunga-Kusana and early Medieval periods.
14. **Koiripur, tehsil- Gonda (Lat. 27⁰11'28" N; Long. 82⁰11'32"E)-** The site of Koiripur is situated about 30 km; 22 km on Utraula road then 8 km on Kurasan road. The site is to the north-east of the village. The site extends in an area of about 8 acres and is about 1.5 mt high from the surrounding area. There is a canal in the eastern side of the site. The site is partly under cultivation. There is a mango orchard over the site. Brick bats have also been noticed during exploration. The site yielded red ware in fine, medium and coarse fabric, black slipped ware and grey ware in fine and medium fabric. The shapes include bowl, bowl with inturned rim, high necked vessel, water vessel, storage pot. On the basis of the remains found during exploration the site seems to be inhabited between NBPW and Kusana periods.
15. **Kongawan, tehsil- Gonda (Lat. 27⁰ 14' 14" N; Long. 81⁰ 58' 44" E)-** The site is situated about 14 km from Gonda on Balrampur road; 12 km till Gilauli on Balrampur road then 2 km in west direction. The

site extends in an area of about 15 acres and is about 3 mt high from the surrounding area. A Primary school building and few houses are built on the site. It is also used for agriculture purpose. Brick bats have also been noticed at the site. The site yielded red ware in medium and coarse fabric. The shapes include bowl, knife edge bowl, carinated handi, water vessel, and basin. On the basis of the remains found during exploration the site seems to be inhabited during early Medieval period.

16. **Kopa, tehsil- Gonda (Lat. 27^{0} 07' 06" N; Long. 82^{0} 12' 37" E)**- The site is situated about 41 km from Gonda via Mankapur on Mankapur-Utraula road; 10 km on Utraula road then 3 km to the west. The site extends in an area of about 30 acres and is about 2 mt high from the surrounding area. A large canal cuts the mound in the eastern side. Brick bats have also been noticed during exploration. The site yielded red ware in fine, medium and coarse fabric, black slipped ware in medium fabric, grey ware in fine fabric along with red slipped ware. The shapes include high necked vessel, water vessel, bowl, bowl with inturned rim, carinated handi, basin, handled pot. On the basis of the remains found during exploration it may be suggested that the site was inhabited between late phase of NBPW and Kusana period.
17. **Marauncha, tehsil- Mankapur (Lat. 27^{0} 06' 25" N; Long. 82^{0} 13' 58" E)**- The site is situated about 37 km from Gonda via Mankapur on Mankapur-Utraula road; 09 km on Utraula road. The site extends in an area of about 5 acres and is about 1.5 mt high from the surrounding area. The site is presently occupied for cultivation. The site yielded red ware and the shapes include water vessel. On the basis of the ceramic and shapes it may be suggested that the site was inhabited during early Medieval period.
18. **Mihian, tehsil- Tarabganj (Lat. 27^{0} 02' 38" N; Long. 82^{0} 07' 52" E)**- The site is about 35 km from Gonda; 25 km from Gonda on Faizabad road upto Wazirganj then 10 km on Jhilahi road. More than half portion of the site is occupied by the villagers for residential purpose while rest of the area is under cultivation. The site extends in an area of about 7 acres and its height is about 1 mtr from the surrounding area. The site yielded red ware in medium and coarse fabric and the shapes include bowl, bowl with inturned rim, basin, water vessel, carinated handi. On the basis of the ceramic and shapes it may be suggested that the site was inhabited between Kusana and early Medieval periods.
19. **Mudadeeh, tehsil- Gonda (Lat. 27^{0} 09' 01" N; Long. 82^{0} 04' 12" E)**- The site is situated about 14 km from Gonda on Utraula road; 10 km till Salpur and then 4 km to the east. More than half portion of the site is occupied by the villagers for residential purpose while rest of the area is under cultivation. The site extends in an area of about 8 acres and its height is about 2.5 mtr from the surrounding area. The site yielded NBP ware, black slipped ware, grey ware, black-and-red ware, corded red ware and plain red ware. The shapes include bowl, dish, bowl with inturned rim, water vessel and vase. On the basis of the remains found during exploration it may be suggested that the site was inhabited between Pre-NBPW and Kusana periods.
20. **Parasarai, tehsil- Gonda (Lat. 27^{0} 15' 51" N; Long. 82^{0} 01' 25" E)**- The site is situated at a distance of about 17 km from Gonda on Balrampur road. The site is fully occupied by the villagers for residential purpose. It extends in an area of about 12 acres and the highest part is about 3 mt high from the surrounding area. Most of the site is fully occupied while some area is exposed. It is believed that this place is *taposthali* of Maharshi Parashar who lived at this place and this village got its name from him. There are two modern temples inside the village named 'Bhagwan Chaturbhuj Mandir' and 'Pareswar nath' which houses sculptures and shivalinga. In the sanctum of 'Bhagwan Chaturbhuj temple', which is constructed at a height of about 3 mt, image of Vishnu is installed which is in broken condition. In the *mandapa* of this temple many broken sculptures and architectural members are stored. The 'Pareswar nath' temple is also constructed over a fallen ancient bricks mound at a height of about 2.5 mt and houses a shivalinga made of black basalt. There is ancient well made of bricks near this temple. At a distance of about 100 mt from the village in southern direction there is a place called 'Dhuria Baba' where a shivalinga made of black basalt is installed. The site yielded red ware in medium fabric and the shapes include water vessel and carinated handi. On the basis of the remains found during exploration it may be suggested that the site was inhabited during early Medieval period.
21. **Patijiya, tehsil- Mankapur (Lat. 26^{0} 58' 30" N; Long. 82^{0} 24' 39" E)**- The site is situated about 49 km from Gonda on Babhnan road via Mankapur and Chhapia. The site is located on the western side

of a large talab and covered with mango and teak trees. It extends in an area of about 9 acres and its height is about 1.5 mtr from the surrounding area. Janta Inter Collage and few houses are built over the site. Brick bats have also been noticed during exploration. The site yielded red ware, red slipped ware and black slipped ware and the shapes include water vessel, carinated handi, bowl, bowl with inturned rim, spouted pot. On the basis of the ceramic and shapes it may be suggested that the site was inhabited between Kusana and Gupta periods.

22. **Prithvinath, Tehsil- Gonda (Lat. 27^0 22' 45" N; 81^0 57' 26" E)-** The site is situated about 33 km from Gonda via Itiyathok and Khargupur. The temple is located about 4 km west to the Khargupur town. The site is spread over an area of about 100x100 m and the main site where the temple is located is about 4 mt. high from the surrounding area. The temple houses a highly ornamented sivalinga made of black basalt. According to the local belief, this shivalinga was installed by Bhima during Mahabharata period. This temple is a centrally protected monument under the Archaeological Survey of India. The temple belongs to Early Medieval period.
23. **Purani Payer, tehsil- Mankapur (Lat. 26^0 57' 09" N; Long. 82^0 20' 15" E)-** The site is situated about 56 km from Gonda via Mankapur and Chhapia on the border of Gonda and Basti districts. The site is located on the north-east of a large talab and extends in an area of about 25 acres. The site is about 3 mtr high from the surrounding area. The site is presently occupied for residential as well as agriculture purposes. As told by the villagers, brick wells were found at the site during agriculture works. Bricks sized about 20+? x 24 x 6 cm. have also been noticed during exploration. The site yielded red ware, black and red ware, grey ware and red slipped ware and the shapes include water vessel, high necked vessel, bowl, bowl with inturned rim, basin, storage pot, miniature pot, carinated handi, knife edge bowl. On the basis of the ceramic and shapes it may be suggested that the site was inhabited between Sunga-Kusana and early Medieval periods.
24. **Ramapur, tehsil- Tarabganj (Lat. 26^0 53' 44" N; Long. 82^0 13' 49" E)-** The site is situated about 48 km from Gonda via Nawabganj and Tikri. A large lake is situated on the east side of the village at a distance of about one km which forms the border between Gonda and Basti districts. The site extends in an area of about 8 acres and slightly raised from the surrounding area. The central part of the site is about 3 mtr high which extends in an area of 50x50 mt. The site is presently occupied for residential as well as agriculture purposes. Brick bats have also been noticed during exploration. The site yielded only red ware and the shapes include water vessel, carinated handi, bowl and basin. On the basis of the remains found during exploration it may be suggested that the site was inhabited during early Medieval period.
25. **Sadasiva Dihwa, tehsil- Gonda (Lat. 27^0 16' 48" N; Long. 82^0 05' 56" E)-** The site is situated at a distance of about 26 km from Gonda; 18 km on Balrampur road till Itiyathok then 8 km on Babaganj road. The site extends in an area of about 10 acres and is about 1.5 mt high from the surrounding area. A school named 'Sadasiva Higher Secondary School', a recently constructed Primary Health Centre, a shiva temple and few houses are built over the site. Rest of the site is under agriculture use. Mango, Bel and teak trees are also planted over the site. Bricks sized 23+? x 22 x 6 cm are also noticed at the site. The site yielded red ware and red slipped ware and the shapes include water vessel, bowl, bowl with inturned rim, carinated handi, storage pot, knobbed lid, knife edge bowl. On the basis of the remains found during exploration it may be suggested that the site was inhabited between Kusana and early Medieval periods.
26. **Saidani, tehsil- Tarabganj (Lat. 26^0 54' 36" N; Long. 82^0 07' 40" E)-** The site is situated on Gonda-Faizabad road at a distance of about 32 km from Gonda. The site is presently occupied by the villagers for residential and agricultural purposes. Parvati lake is situated on the eastern side of the site. A mosque and three *majars* are built over the site. The site extends in an area of about 4 acres and is almost level plain. The site yielded only red ware and the shapes include bowl, water vessel. On the basis of the remains found during exploration it may be suggested that the site was inhabited during early Medieval period.

27. **Subhagpur, tehsil- Gonda (Lat. 27^0 12' 23" N; Long. 81^0 59' 28" E)-** The site is situated about 10 km from Gonda on Balrampur road. The site is located to the north-east of the village and on the bank

of a lake. The site extends in an area of about 17 acres and is about 5 mt high from the surrounding area. As told by the villagers during ancient time this place was known as Saubhagyapur and Chyawan muni lived at this place. A Primary school building is built over the site. Presently soil digging work is continuing at this site. The site yielded red ware in medium and coarse fabric. The shapes include bowl, bowl with inturned rim, high necked vessel, water vessel, carinated handi, button knobbed lid, storage jar, basin. On the basis of the remains found during exploration it may be suggested that the site was inhabited between Kusana and Gupta periods.

28. **Tikia Ashokpur, tehsil- Tarabganj (Lat. 26^0 59' 36" N; Long. 82^0 06' 22" E)-** The site is situated on Gonda-Faizabad road at a distance of about 23 km from Gonda. A Primary school is built over the site. The site extends in an area of about 4 acres and its height is about 0.5 mt from the surrounding area. Soil digging for the manufacture of bricks is continuing at the site. The site yielded red ware in medium and coarse fabric and black ware. The shapes include water vessel, carinated handi, knife edge bowl, bowl, storage pot. On the basis of the remains found during exploration it may be suggested that the site was inhabited between Gupta and early Medieval periods.
29. **Tilharwa, tehsil- Mankapur (Lat. 27^0 05' 17" N; Long. 82^0 09' 46" E)-** The site is situated about 30 km from Gonda on Mankapur road via Jhilahi. It is about 5 km from Jhilahi on the north-west direction. The site is located on the north side of the village and extends in an area of about 5 acres. It is about 1 mtr high from the surrounding area. Primary and Junior high school buildings are built over the site. There is a *talab* to the east of the site. Brick bats have also been noticed during exploration. The site yielded red ware in medium and coarse fabric, black slipped ware in medium fabric and grey ware in fine fabric along with few specimens of red slipped and chocolate slipped ware. The shapes include bowl, bowl with inturned rim, knife edge bowl, carinated handi, water vessel, lid. On the basis of the remains found during exploration it may be suggested that the site was inhabited between Kusana and early Medieval periods.
30. **Tilyani, tehsil- Gonda (Lat. 27^0 12' 57" N; Long. 82^0 00' 31" E)-** The site is situated about 14 km from Gonda on Balrampur road; 10 km on Balrampur road then 4 km towards north-east. The site extends in an area of about 5 acres and is about 1 mt high from the surrounding area. This site is presently used for cultivation and residential purposes. The site yielded red ware, black slipped ware, black and red ware and red slipped ware. The shapes include bowl, lid, water vessel, basin, carinated handi. On the basis of the remains found during exploration it may be suggested that the site was inhabited between Sunga-Kusana and Gupta periods.
31. **Amarhwa, tehsil- Balrampur (Lat. 27^0 21' 38" N; Long. 82^0 10' 24" E)-** The site is situated about 10 km from Balrampur on Birahimpur road via Ajabnagar. The site extends in an area of about 8 acres and slightly raised from the surrounding area. Primary and Junior High School buildings, Gram Panchayat building, Govt. Tubewell building, Samay Mai ka Sthan and few houses are built over the site. An ancient well is also noticed at the site. Brickbats have also found during exploration. The site yielded only red ware of medium and coarse fabric. The shapes include bowl, bowl with inturned rim, miniature bowl, high necked vessels, water vessels, handled pot/pan, carinated handi. On the basis of the remains found during exploration it may be suggested that the site was inhabited during Kusana period.
32. **Banrahwa deeh, tehsil- Utraula (Lat. 27^0 18' 58" N; Long. 82^0 20' 03" E)-** The site is about 36 km from Balrampur and 8 km from Utraula via Chamrupur on Utraula-Gonda road. The site extends in an area of about 300x300 mt and is about 2 mt high from the surrounding area. A *majar* dedicated to Malangshah baba is built on the south-eastern side of the site. The site is presently used for agriculture. The site yielded Northern Black Polished ware, black slipped ware, grey ware, corded ware and red ware. The shapes include dish, bowl, water vessel, carinated handi, high necked vessel, bowl with inturned rim. On the basis of the remains found during exploration it may be suggested that the site was inhabited between NBPW and Gupta periods.
33. **Bansedila, tehsil- Balrampur (Lat. 27^0 24' 07" N; Long. 82^0 16' 45" N)-** The site is about 20 km from Balrampur; 18 km on Utraula road till Katia and then 2 km on Siria road. The site extends in an area of about 700x500 mt and is about 2-3 mt high from the surrounding area. Most of the site has been converted into agriculture field. At present soil digging work is in progress and lots of ancient bricks and brick bats have been collected on the site. A government tube well is built over the site. The site yielded red ware in medium and coarse fabric and the shapes include water vessel, storage

pot, carinated handi, bowl, bowl with intuened rim, lota, spouted pot, basin, knife edge bowl. On the basis of the remains found during exploration it may be suggested that the site was inhabited between Kusana and early Medieval periods.

34. **Chakwa, tehsil- Balrampur (Lat.27⁰ 29' 22" N; Long. 82⁰ 05' 02" E)-** The site is situated about 13 km from Balrampur on Bahraich road to the left side of the road. Most of the site has been removed for agriculture and presently extends in an area of about 4 acres. It is slightly raised from the surrounding area. The site is located to the west of the village and a house is built in the northern side. The site yielded only red ware and the shapes include water vessel, bowl, bowl with inturned rim, carinated handi and knife edge bowl. On the basis of the remains found during exploration it may be suggested that the site was inhabited during Kusana and early Medieval periods.
35. **Kalandarpur, tehsil- Balrampur (Lat. 27⁰ 29' 14" N; Long. 82⁰ 08' 48" E)-** The site is about 8 km from Balrampur; 5 km on Bahraich road till Hariharganj then 3 km in north direction on Lalia road. The site is situated to the east of the village and presently used for agriculture. The site extends in an area of about 5 acres and is slightly raised from the surrounding area. An ancient well is located on the site. The site yielded red ware & red slipped ware and the shapes include water vessel, bowl, bowl with inturned rim. On the basis of the remains found during exploration it may be suggested that the site was inhabited during Kusana period.
36. **Panahia deeh, tehsil- Balrampur (Lat. 27⁰ 28' 11" N; Long. 82⁰ 09' 56" E)-** The site is situated about 8 km from Balrampur; 3 km on Bahraich road till Sekhui Kalan then 5 km in north direction. The site extends in an area of about 3 acres and is slightly raised from the surrounding area. The site is presently occupied for agriculture purpose. The site yielded red ware and red slipped ware and the shapes include carinated handi, bowl, inkpot type lid, water vessel. On the basis of the remains found during exploration it may be suggested that the site was inhabited during Kusana and early Medieval periods.
37. **Pehar Bharia, tehsil- Utraula (Lat. 27⁰ 15' 50" N; Long. 82⁰ 19' 35" E)-** The site is about 14 km from Utraula. The site is approachable first 12 km to Pehar market on Mankapur road then 2 km in north-west direction. The site extends in an area of about 400x300 mt and is about 3 mt high from the surrounding area. A government tube well is built over the site. The site is presently used for agriculture. The site yielded red ware in medium and coarse fabric and the shapes include bowl, bowl with inturned rim, water vessel, carinated handi, basin, storage pot. On the basis of the remains found during exploration it may be suggested that the site was inhabited between Kusana and early Medieval periods.
38. **Prithvideeh, tehsil- Utraula (Lat.27⁰ 15' 05" N; Long. 82⁰ 19' 23" E)-** The site is about 13 km from Utraula on Mankapur road. The site extends in an area of about 500x400 mt and is about 1 mt high from the surrounding area. The central part of the site is covered with teak trees while the remaining part is used for agriculture. There is a sthan of Samay mai on the site. The site yielded red ware in medium and coarse fabric and red slipped ware. The shapes include water vessel, bowl, bowl with inturned rim, storage pot, carinated pot, miniature vase. On the basis of the remains found during exploration it may be suggested that the site was inhabited during Kusana period.
39. **Srinagar, tehsil- Balrampur (Lat.27⁰ 21' 33" N; Long. 82⁰ 13' 45" E)-** The site is about 12 km from Balrampur on Utraula road via Maheshbhari. The site extends in an area of about 250x100 mt. and is about 1 mt high from the surrounding area. A primary school, Police chouki and Sahkari Bank building are built over the site. The site is located on the western bank of a large pond. The site yielded NBP ware, black slipped ware, grey ware and red ware and the shapes include dish, bowl, bowl with inturned rim, basin, lid, water vessel, storage pot. On the basis of the remains found during exploration it may be suggested that the site was inhabited during NBPW and Kusana periods.
40. **Tendua, tehsil- Balrampur (Lat.27⁰ 29' 50" N; Long. 82⁰ 04' 54" E)-** The site is situated about 14 km from Balrampur on Bahraich road to the right side of the road at a distance of about 500 mt. The site yielded only red ware and the shapes include water vessel, carinated handi, bowl, lamp, lid, miniature pot. On the basis of the remains found during exploration it may be suggested that the site was inhabited during Gupta and early Medieval periods.
41. **Turab, tehsil- Utraula (Lat.27⁰ 17' 38" N; Long. 82⁰ 22' 12" E)-** The site is about 36 km from Balrampur and 8 km from Utraula via Sahiapur on Utraula-Gonda road. The site is located on the

southern bank of a horse-shoe lake and extends in an area of about 200x150 mt and is about 1 mt high from the surrounding area. An Idgaah is built over the site. The site is presently used for agriculture. The site yielded red ware in medium and coarse fabric and the shapes include bowl, bowl with inturned rim, water vessel, basin, high necked vessel. On the basis of the remains found during exploration it may be suggested that the site was inhabited during Kusana period.

42. **Banjarhi, tehsil- Ikauna (Lat. 27^{0} 27' 31" N; Long. 82^{0} 01' 14" E)**- The site is about 13 km from Ikauna via Katra on Khargupur road. The site has been damaged by the Saryu canal which runs through the northern part of the site. The site extends in an area of about 250x200 mt and is about 2 mt high. The site is presently used for agriculture. The site yielded red ware in medium and coarse fabric grey ware in medium fabric and red slipped ware. The shapes include bowl, bowl with inturned rim, knife edge bowl, handled pot, carinated handi, water vessel. On the basis of the ceramic and shapes it may be suggested that the site was inhabited between Kusana and early Medieval periods.
43. **Kalyanpur, tehsil- Ikauna (Lat. 27^{0} 28' 47" N; Long. 82^{0} 00' 49" E)**- The site is about 9 km from Ikauna via Katra on Khargupur road. The Saryu canal passes through the southern side of the site. The site extends in an area of about 250x150 mt and is about 1 mt high from the surrounding area. The site yielded red ware in medium and coarse fabric and the shapes include bowl, carinated handi, water vessel, storage pot. On the basis of the ceramic and shapes found during exploration it may be suggested that the site was inhabited between Gupta and early Medieval periods.
44. **Srijot, tehsil- Ikauna (Lat. 27^{0} 29' 57" N; Long. 82^{0} 00' 56" E)**- The site is about 7 km from Ikauna on Balrampur road. The site is approachable first 6 km on Balrampur road then 1 km in right side. The site extends in an area of about 200x150 mt and is about 1 mt high from the surrounding area. A minor canal passes on the eastern side of the site. The site yielded red ware in medium and coarse fabric and the shapes include bowl, carinated handi, water vessel, and lid. On the basis of the ceramic and shapes it may be suggested that the site was inhabited between Gupta and early Medieval periods.

Concluding Remarks

As stated above the site of Sravasti and Ayodhya were excavated several times and the results suggest that the site of Sravasti was inhabited before Buddha during pre-NBPW period and the site of Ayodhya was during NBPW period. Both of the sites are associated with Brahmanism, Buddhism and Jainism.

Total 44 sites were explored along the main and link routes between Ayodhya and Sravasti (see Map). Of these 30 sites are located in Gonda district, 11 sites are in Balrampur district and 3 sites are in Sravasti district.

Out of these, Pre-NBPW remains were found at 01 site, NBPW remains at 07 sites, Sunga-Kusana remains at 32 sites, Gupta remains at 26 sites, early Medieval remains at 29 sites and Medieval/late Medieval remains at 01 site.

Pre-NBPW remains were found at 01 site named Mudadih in Gonda district and the occupation at this site continued upto Sunga-Kusana period.

06 sites came into existence during NBPW period. 03 of them showed occupation upto Sunga-Kusana period, 01 upto Gupta period whereas at 02 sites habitation continued upto early Medieval period.

25 sites were first inhabited during Sunga-Kusana period. 03 of them showed occupation upto Gupta period while at 16 sites habitation continued up to early Medieval period. 06 sites are single culture site.

05 sites came into existence during Gupta period and continued up to early Medieval period. 06 sites were first inhabited during early Medieval period and continued only in same period. 01 site named Buknapur came into existence in late Medieval period.

On the basis of the explorations conducted between these two major sites, it may be said that during NBP period the route from Ayodhya to Sravasti via Nawabganj, Mankapur, Utraula and Balrampur was more popular as most of the sites are located on this route. In later periods, both routes were used for travelling from Ayodhya to Sravasti as exemplified by the emergence of new settlements on both the routes.

Acknowledgement

The project was carried out under the auspices of Lucknow Circle of Archaeological Survey of India under the direction of first author. I am grateful to the Director General, Archaeological Survey of India for granting license to this project. Thanks to all the staff of Lucknow Circle of ASI including Navratna Kumar Pathak, Praveen Kumar Mishra, Indu Prakash (now Superintending Archaeologists), Om Dutt Shukla (Retd. Deputy Superintending Archaeologist), Rajeev Dwivedi & Anil Kumar Tiwari (now Assistant Superintending Archaeologists), Mohan Chandra Joshi, Rajendra Yadav, Sanjay Kumar Singh, Nikita Chandra & Deepti Trivedi (Assistant Archaeologists), Shyam Bihari Shukla (Retd. Senior Surveyor), Surendra Kumar Arora (Senior Photographer), Kamlesh Kumar Pangty & Ravi Shankar Saxena (Draughtsmans) who has taken deep interest in the project and completed the field work. I am also thankful to C.B. Mishra, who has taken charge of the Superintending Archaeologist of Lucknow Circle after my transfer in April 2010, for continuing the project in the session 2010-11.

Appendix : Explored Sites in District Gonda

Sl. No.	Site name	Location	Tehsil	Ceramics	Period
1.	Baijpur	Lat. 27^{0}13'33" N Long.82^0 03'10" E	Gonda	Red ware, Black slipped ware.	Kusana to Early Medieval period.
2.	Basati	Lat. 27^{0}15'22" N Long.82^0 03'40" E	Gonda	Red ware, Black ware, Red slipped ware.	Kusana to post Gupta period.
3.	Belawan	Lat. 27^0 08' 33" N Long.82^0 06' 53" E	Gonda	Red ware.	Kusana period.
4.	Bhatpi	Lat. 27^0 19' 40" N Long.81^0 59' 43" E	Gonda	Red ware, Black ware, Black slipped ware, Grey ware and Red slipped ware.	Kusana to Early Medieval period.
5.	Binduli Deeh	Lat. 27^0 19' 10" N Long. 82^0 01' 15" E	Gonda	NBPW, Black slipped ware, Grey ware, Black ware, Red slipped ware and Red ware.	NBPW to Early Medieval period.
6.	Bishunpur Bairia	Lat. 27^0 09' 53" N Long. 82^0 03' 03" E	Gonda	Red ware and Red slipped ware.	Kusana and Early Medieval period.
7.	Buknapur	Lat. 27^0 01' 28" N Long. 82^0 15' 08" E	Mankapur	Red ware	Late Medieval period.
8.	Dinara	Lat. 27^0 08' 24" N Long. 82^0 10' 48" E	Gonda	Red ware.	Kusana to Early Medieval period.
9.	Dumariadih	Lat. 27^0 01' 58" N Long. 82^0 04' 23" E	Tarabganj	Red ware, Black slipped ware, Black ware & Black and red ware.	Kusana to Early Medieval period.
10.	Itahia Tiwaripurwa	Lat. 27^0 08' 58" N Long. 82^0 13' 22" E	Gonda	Red ware, Red slipped ware.	Kusana period.
11.	Karamdeeh Belwa	Lat. 27^0 19' 37" N Long. 82^0 02' 12" E	Gonda	Red ware, Black ware.	Gupta to Early Medieval period.
12.	Karohanath	Lat. 27^0 5' 22" N Long. 82^0 15' 44" E	Mankapur	Northern Black Polished ware, Black slipped ware, Grey ware & Red ware.	NBPW to Early Medieval period.
13.	Kazi Dewar	Lat. 27^0 04' 16" N Long. 82^0 04' 28" E	Gonda	Red ware, Grey ware & Black slipped ware.	Sunga-Kusana to Early Medieval period.
14.	Koiripur	Lat. 27^{0}11'28" N Long. 82^{0}11'32"E	Gonda	Red ware, Black slipped ware and Grey ware.	NBPW to Kusana period.
15.	Kongawan	Lat. 27^0 14' 14" N Long. 81^0 58' 44" E	Gonda	Red ware	Early Medieval period.
16.	Kopa	Lat. 27^0 07' 06" N Long. 82^0 12' 37" E	Gonda	Red ware, Black slipped ware, Grey ware and Red slipped ware.	NBPW to Kusana period.

17.	Marauncha	Lat. 27^{0} 06' 25" N Long. 82^{0} 13' 58" E	Mankapur	Red ware.	Early Medieval period.
18.	Mihian	Lat. 27^{0} 02' 38" N Long. 82^{0} 07' 52" E	Tarabganj	Red ware.	Kusana to Early Medieval period.
19.	Mudadeeh	Lat. 27^{0} 09' 01" N Long. 82^{0} 04' 12" E	Gonda	NBPW, Black slipped ware, Grey ware, Black-and-red ware, Corded ware and Red ware.	Pre-NBPW to Kusana periods.
20.	Parasarai	Lat. 27^{0} 15' 51" N Long. 82^{0} 01' 25" E	Gonda	Red ware.	Early Medieval period.
21.	Patijiya	Lat. 26^{0} 58' 30" N Long. 82^{0} 24' 39" E	Mankapur	Red ware, Red slipped ware and Black slipped ware.	Kusana to Gupta period.
22.	Prithvinath	Lat. 27^{0} 22' 45" N; Long. 81^{0} 57' 26" E	Gonda	Temple with sivalinga of black basalt.	Early Medieval Period
23.	Purani Payer	Lat. 26^{0} 57' 09" N Long. 82^{0} 20' 15" E	Mankapur	Red ware, Black and red ware, Grey ware and Red slipped ware.	Sunga-Kusana to Early Medieval period.
24.	Ramapur	Lat. 26^{0} 53' 44" N Long. 82^{0} 13' 49" E	Tarabganj	Red ware.	Early Medieval period.
25.	Sadasiva Dihwa	Lat. 27^{0} 16' 48" N Long. 82^{0} 05' 56" E	Gonda	Red ware and Red slipped ware.	Kusana to Early Medieval periods.
26.	Saidani	Lat. 26^{0} 54' 36" N Long. 82^{0} 07' 40" E	Tarabganj	Red ware.	Early Medieval period.
27.	Subhagpur	Lat. 27^{0} 12' 23" N Long. 81^{0} 59' 28" E	Gonda	Red ware.	Kusana and Gupta periods.
28.	Tikia Ashokpur	Lat. 26^{0} 59' 36" N Long. 82^{0} 06' 22" E	Tarabganj	Red ware and Black ware.	Gupta and early Medieval periods.
29.	Tilharwa	Lat. 27^{0} 05' 17" N Long. 82^{0} 09' 46" E	Mankapur	Red ware, Black slipped ware, Grey ware, Red slipped ware and Chocolate slipped ware.	Kusana to Early Medieval periods.
30.	Tilyani	Lat. 27^{0} 12' 57" N Long. 82^{0} 00' 31" E	Gonda	Red ware, Black slipped ware, Black and red ware and Red slipped ware.	Sunga-Kusana and Gupta periods.

Explored Sites in District Balrampur

Sl. No.	Site name	Location	Tehsil	Findings	Period
31.	Amarhwa	Lat. 27^{0} 21' 38" N Long. 82^{0} 10' 24" E	Balrampur	Red ware.	Kusana period.
32.	Banrahwa deeh	Lat. 27^{0} 18' 58" N Long. 82^{0} 20' 03" E	Utraula	NBPW, Black slipped ware, Grey ware, Corded ware and Red ware.	NBPW to Gupta period.
33.	Bansedila	Lat. 27^{0} 24' 07" N Long. 82^{0} 16' 45" N	Balrampur	Red ware.	Kusana to Early Medieval period.
34.	Chakwa	Lat.27^{0} 29' 22" N Long. 82^{0} 05' 02" E	Balrampur	Red ware.	Kusana and Early Medieval periods.
35.	Kalandarpur	Lat. 27^{0} 29' 14" N Long. 82^{0} 08' 48" E	Balrampur	Red ware & Red slipped ware.	Kusana period.
36.	Panahia deeh	Lat. 27^{0} 28' 11" N Long. 82^{0} 09' 56" E	Balrampur	Red ware & Red slipped ware.	Kusana and Early Medieval periods.
37.	Pehar Bharia	Lat. 27^{0} 15' 50" N Long. 82^{0} 19' 35" E	Utraula	Red ware.	Kusana to Early Medieval periods.

38.	Prithvideeh	Lat.27^0 15' 05" N Long. 82^0 19' 23" E	Utraula	Red ware and Red slipped ware.	Kusana period.
39.	Srinagar	Lat.27^0 21' 33" N Long. 82^0 13' 45" E	Balrampur	NBPW, Black slipped ware, Grey ware and Red ware.	NBPW and Kusana periods.
40.	Tendua	Lat.27^0 29' 50" N Long. 82^0 04' 54" E	Balrampur	Red ware.	Gupta and Early Medieval periods.
41.	Turab	Lat.27^0 17' 38" N Long. 82^0 22' 12" E	Utraula	Red ware.	Kusana period

Explored Sites in District Sravasti

Sl. No.	Site name	Location	Tehsil	Findings	Period
42.	Banjarhi	Lat. 27^0 27' 31" N Long. 82^0 01' 14" E	Ikauna	Red ware, Grey ware and Red slipped ware.	Kusana to Early Medieval period.
43.	Kalyanpur	27^0 28' 47" N 82^0 00' 49" E	Ikauna	Red ware.	Gupta and Early Medieval period.
44.	Srijot	27^0 29' 57" N 82^0 00' 56" E	Ikauna	Red ware.	Gupta and Early Medieval period.

References

- *Aavassaka Nirjjuti*
- *Bhagvata Purana*
- *Brahma Purana*
- *Brahmanda Purana*
- *Buddhacharita*
- *Divyavadana*
- *Jain Harivamsapurana*
- *Kalpasutra*
- *Mahabharata*
- *Mahaparinirvana Sutta*
- *Matsya Purana*
- *Skanda Purana*
- *Valyamiki Ramayana*
- *Vayu Purana*
- *Vishnu Purana*
- ASIAR- *A.S.I. Annual Reports*
- ASIR- *ASI Reports*
- IAR- *Indian Archaeology: A Review*
- EI- Epigraphica Indica
- *Sravasti,* Guide Book published by Archaeological Survey of India, New Delhi.
- Barber, R. 1993. *Pilgrimages*. London: The Boydell Press.
- Cunningham, A. 1979. *The Ancient Geography of India*, Varanasi.
- Eck, Diana L. 1981. India's "Tirthas": "Crossings" in Sacred Geography. In *History of Religion*, vol. 20, No.4, Chicago.
- Ghosh, A. 1989. *An Encyclopaedia of Indian Archaeology*, volume Two, New Delhi.
- Law, Bimala Churn. 1967. *Historical Geography of India*, Paris.
- Mitra, D., 1971, *Buddhist Monuments,* Calcutta.
- Pande, Kailash Narain (Ed.). 1989. *Uttar Pradesh District Gazetteers- Gonda*, Lucknow.
- Pathak, Vishuddhanand. 1963. *History of Kosala*. Delhi.

- Singh, R. 2006. Pilgrimage in Hinduism: Historical Context and Modern Perspectives. In D. J. Timothy, & D. H. Olsen (Eds.), *Tourism, Religion, and Spiritual Journeys* (pp. 220–236). London: Routledge.
- Sinha, K.K. 1967. *Excavations at Sravasti-1959*, Varanasi.
- Takahashi, Takahiro, Taizo Yamaoka, Fumitaka Yondea and Akinori Uesugi. 2000. The Ancient City of Sravasti: It's Significance on the Urbanisation of North India, *Puratattva* 30, pp. 74-92.

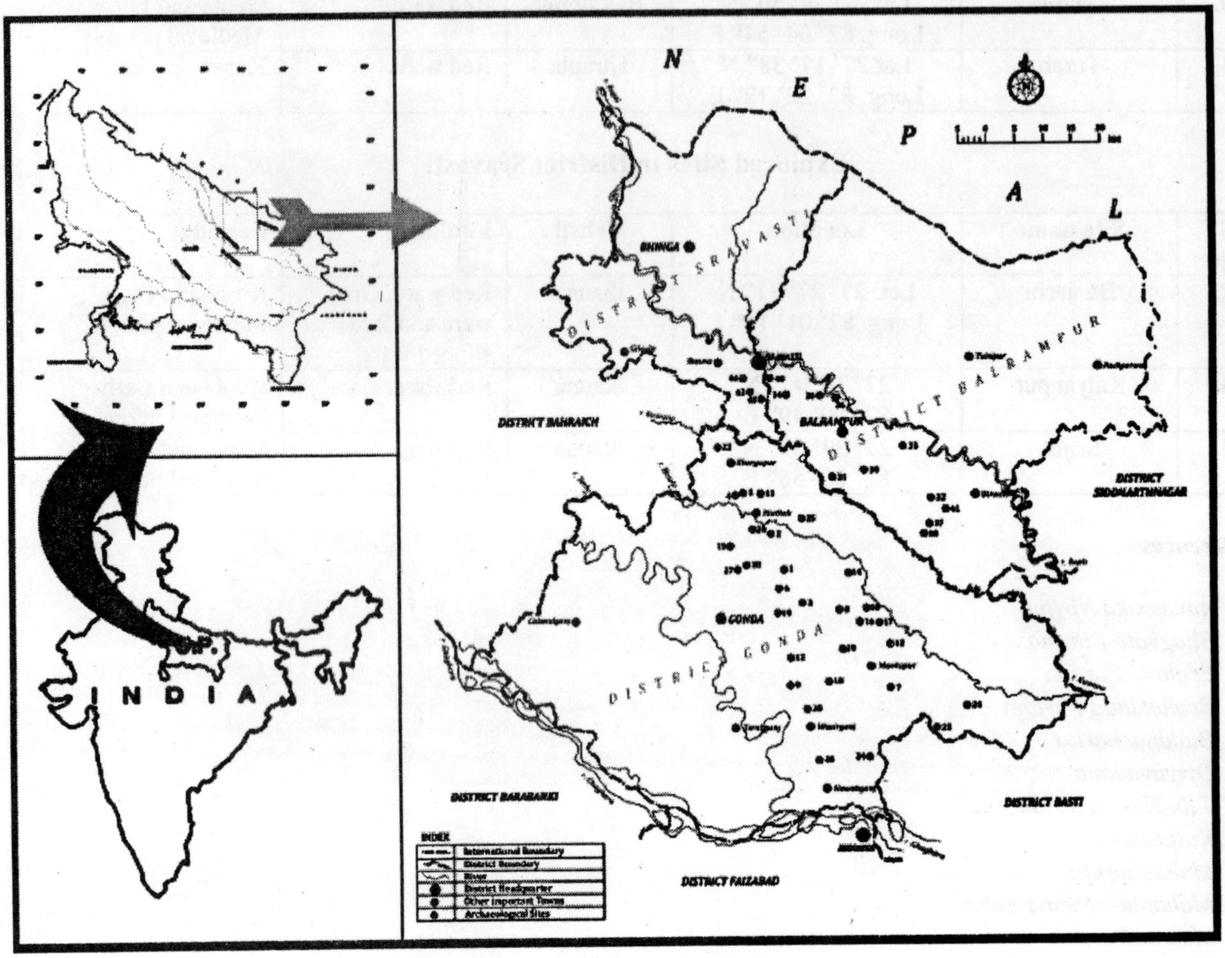

13

सरस्वती नदी का प्रवाह तंत्र एवं तीर्थ (पुरातत्त्व के संदर्भ में)

रत्नेश कुमार त्रिपाठी

यूँ तो वर्तमान में नासा व इसरो के उपग्रह चित्रों ने सदियों के मिथक को तोड़ते हुए साहित्य में वर्णित सरस्वती नदी का प्रमाण दे दिया है तथा वर्तमान में विभिन्न शोध संस्थानों द्वारा इस पर व्यापक शोध व निष्कर्ष ने सरस्वती नदी के मार्ग को पूरी तरह उद्घाटित कर दिया है। सरस्वती नदी के प्रवाह मार्ग का वर्णन करते हुए डॉ० देवेन्द्र सिंह चौहान ने अपनी पुस्तक "पुण्य सलिला सरस्वती नदी" में स्पष्ट करते हुए वर्णित किया है कि सरस्वती नदी के सम्भावित पुरामार्गों को विभिन्न विद्वानों ने अलग–अलग रुप में दिखाया है। इनमें डॉ० विष्णु श्रीधर वाकणकर (1986) द्वारा चिन्हित किये गये सरस्वती नदी प्रवाह मार्ग, जो मोटे रुप में अधिकांश विद्वानों द्वारा दिखाये गये पुरामार्गों से समानता दर्शाते हैं, समुचित लगते हैं। पूर्व से पश्चिम तक फैले ये पुरामार्ग हैं– आदिबद्री, पेहोवा, सिरसा, हनुमानगढ़, सूरतगढ़, अनूपगढ़, मरोट, किशनगढ़, तनोट, घोटारु, शाहगढ़ इनके आस–पास के पाकिस्तान का बहावलपुर सिन्ध प्रदेश व कच्छ का रन। उपर्युक्त प्रवाह जो भारत के जैसलमेर के पश्चिम भाग और पाकिस्तान के बहावलपुर सिन्ध प्रदेश में पड़ता है, ही सरस्वती नदी का मूल प्रवाह था, जिसका सरस्वती नदी वैदिक काल से महाभारत काल (10,000 वर्ष से 5000 वर्ष) तक अनुसरण कर सिन्धु सागर में समाहित होती थी। इस प्रवाह को हम आज घग्घर–हाकरा–नारा प्रवाह के रुप में जानते हैं (आर.डी. ओल्डेहम 1886, सी.एफ. ओल्डेहम 1893, स्टैन 1942, विल्हेमी 1969, यशपाल एवं सहयोगी 1980, मिश्रा 1995)। इस प्रवाह मार्ग में अनेक प्राक् हड़प्पीय व हड़प्पीय पुरास्थल संकेन्द्रित मिलते हैं, जो उपर्युक्त कथन का समर्थन करते हैं।[1]

उपर्युक्त उल्लेखित पुरानदी मार्ग, मूलरुप से वैदिक सरस्वती प्रवाह मार्ग था। इसकी सत्यता सिद्ध करने के लिए मरुस्थल के जैसलमेर भाग का विस्तार से अध्ययन किया गया। भू–उपग्रह छाया चित्रों के आधार पर इस क्षेत्र के पुरानदी मार्गों को चिन्हित किया गया। भूभौतिकी के आधार पर इस क्षेत्र में पाये जाने वाले पुरानदी मार्गों से संचित भूजल की सम्भावना का पता लगाया गया। इन पुरामार्गों से जुड़े हुए किशनगढ़ से लेकर शाहगढ़ तक के क्षेत्र में खोदे गये 17 नलकूपों से ज्ञात हुआ कि इन पुरानदी मार्गों में पाये जाने वाले नदीजनित अवसाद के दो स्तरों में पर्याप्त मीठा जल उपलब्ध है। ये वैज्ञानिक तथ्य उस कथन का समर्थन करते हैं कि वैदिक सरस्वती का मूल प्रवाह इसी क्षेत्र में था।[2] सुदूर संवेदनशील विद्या द्वारा इस क्षेत्र में किया गया नवीनतम अध्ययन भी इन्ही पुरानदी मार्ग को सरस्वती नदी का मूल प्रवाह बतलाते हैं (गुप्ता एवं सहयोगी 2003)।[3]

वैज्ञानिक यशपाल, बलदेव सहाय, आर०के० सूद तथा डी०पी० अग्रवाल ने उपग्रह द्वारा इस क्षेत्र की तस्वीरों के आधार पर कुछ निष्कर्ष प्रस्तुत किये। जो इस प्रकार है :– पटियाला (पंजाब) से लगभग 25 कि०मी० दक्षिण में

घग्घर (सरस्वती) नदी के पाट की चौड़ाई में अचानक वृद्धि हो जाती है। इस अचानक वृद्धि का कारण यह समझ आ जाता है कि इस स्थान पर कोई एक महान सहायक नदी घग्घर में मिलती होगी। उपग्रह के भू–चित्र में इस स्थान एक महान नदी का घग्घर में मिलना नजर आता है। अतः उन्होंने निष्कर्ष निकाला कि प्राचीन काल में किसी समय सतलज घग्घर नदी में मिलती थी।[4]

वैदिक सरस्वती नदी के प्रवाह मार्ग सुनिश्चित करने में नदीवेदिका अवसाद अध्ययन बहुत उपयोगी सिद्ध हुए हैं। ये वर्तमान में टोंस नदी प्रवाह मार्ग में स्थित गरीबनाथ और उसके लगे आदिबद्री के उत्तर में शिवालिक पहाड़ी क्षेत्र में स्थित सुदानवाला व दो विपरीत दिशाओं मे बहने वाली बाटा नदी व मार्कण्डा नदी प्रवाह मार्ग में मिलने वाले बहुत उपयोगी लगते हैं **(चित्र 1)**। यहाँ यह बतलाना उचित होगा कि बाटा एक छोटी सी नदी है जो हिमालय प्रदेश के शिवालिक मे स्थित राम और जलमूस संरक्षित वनों के मध्य स्थित जलमूस खोल नाड़ी से प्रकट होती है। पहले यह पूर्व दिशा में और बाद में दक्षिणपूर्व दिशा में बहकर बाटामान के निकट यमुना से मिलती है। मार्कण्डा ऊपरी शिवालिक से उदित होकर पहले पश्चिम में और बाद में वाह्य शिवालिक को काटती हुई दक्षिण–पश्चिम में बहकर घग्घर से मिलती है **(चित्र 1.1)**।[5]

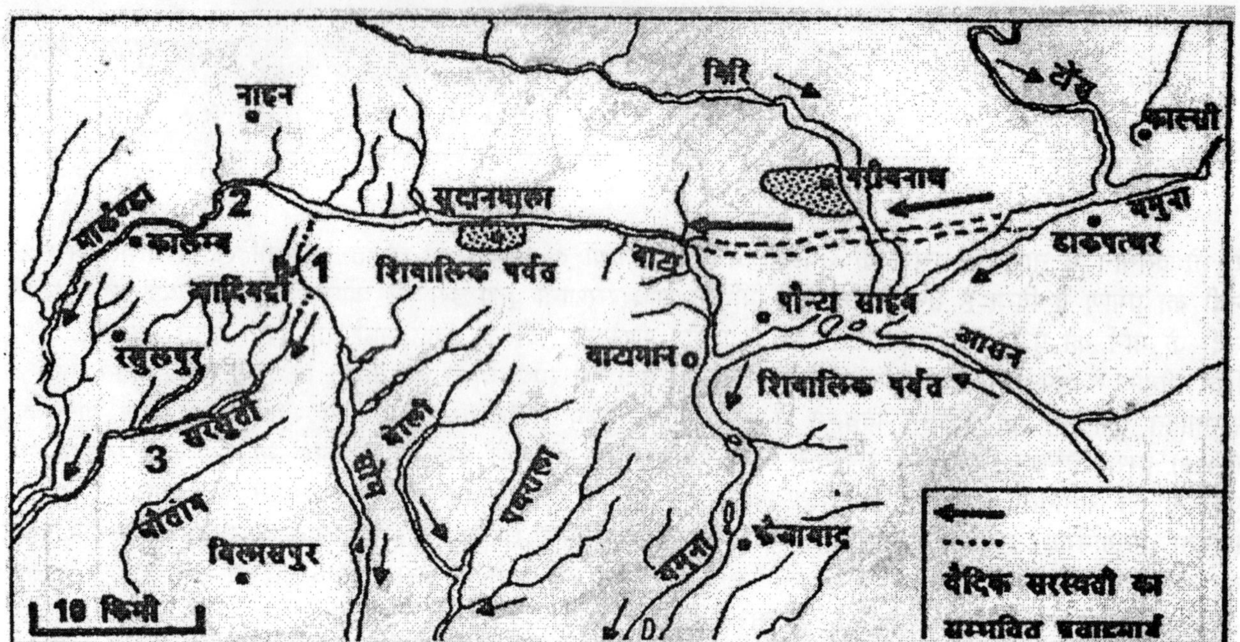

चित्र 1 : सरस्वती नदी के विभिन्न ऊपरी प्रवाहमार्ग : 1. सरस्वती का वैदिक–महाभारतकालीन प्रवाहमार्ग–टोंस–बाटा–ऊपरी मार्कण्डा–ऊपरी सोम व सरसुती नाड़ी का अनुसरण करते हुह आदिबद्री से दक्षिण–पश्चिम दिशा में बहना 2. सरस्वती का पौराणिक प्रवाहमार्ग – मार्कण्डा के रूप में प्रवाहित होना 3. सरस्वती का वर्तमान स्वरूप – वर्षा आधारित सरसुती नाड़ी के रूप में भवानीपुर और पहोवा के मध्य अल्प–अस्थाई प्रवाह। देखें ! टोंस नदी को पश्चिम दिशा में बाटा–मार्कण्डा का अनुसरण कर प्रवाहित करने वाले मार्ग को चिन्हित करने वाली गरीबनाथ व सुदानवाला के निकट स्थित नदीवेदिकाएँ। (आधार – वालदिया 2002)

उपर्युक्त नदिवेदिकाओं की अवसादी रचना बतलाती है कि इनका निचला भाग अधिकांशतः उच्चतर (गढ़वाल) हिमालय में पाये जाने वाले क्वार्टजाइट व कायान्तरित शैल खण्डजों के बने हुए है और ऊपरी भाग अधिकतर शिवालिक बलुए पत्थर व अन्य शैलखण्डजों के। इस प्रकार की नदिवेदिका अवसाद रचना यह संकेत करती है कि उच्चतर हिमालय क्षेत्र से लेकर जहाँ तक ये पायी जाती हैं, वहाँ तक प्रभावी जल प्रवाह था, जिसने इस उच्चतर हिमालय में पाये जाने वाले विशिष्ट कायान्तरित शैल खण्डजों को यहाँ तक बहाकर जमा किया होगा। इसके अनुसार वैदिक सरस्वती का प्रवाह मार्ग उच्चतर हिमालय में नैतवार, जिसे प्लक्षप्रस्रवण कह सकते हैं, से आरम्भ होता है। वहाँ से वह 40 कि०मी० दक्षिण–पश्चिम दिशा में बहकर विशाल स्वरुप ग्रहण करती है। आगे अपनी सहायक पब्बर को साथ ले दक्षिण दिशा मे 100 कि०मी० बढ़कर पौन्तदून में प्रवेश करती है, जहाँ उसमें गिरि

नदी भी आकर मिलती है। यहाँ तक का सरस्वती प्रवाह मार्ग वर्तमान की टोंस नदी प्रवाह मार्ग का ही था। पर पौन्तदून में पहुँचकर उसके प्रवाह मार्ग में विशेष परिवर्तन दिखाई देता है। कालसी के दक्षिण में पहुँचकर वह गरीबनाथ, पौन्त व बाटा–मार्कण्डा घाटी में प्रवेश हेतु पश्चिम से दक्षिण–पश्चिम दिशा मे मुड़कर बहने लगती है।[6]

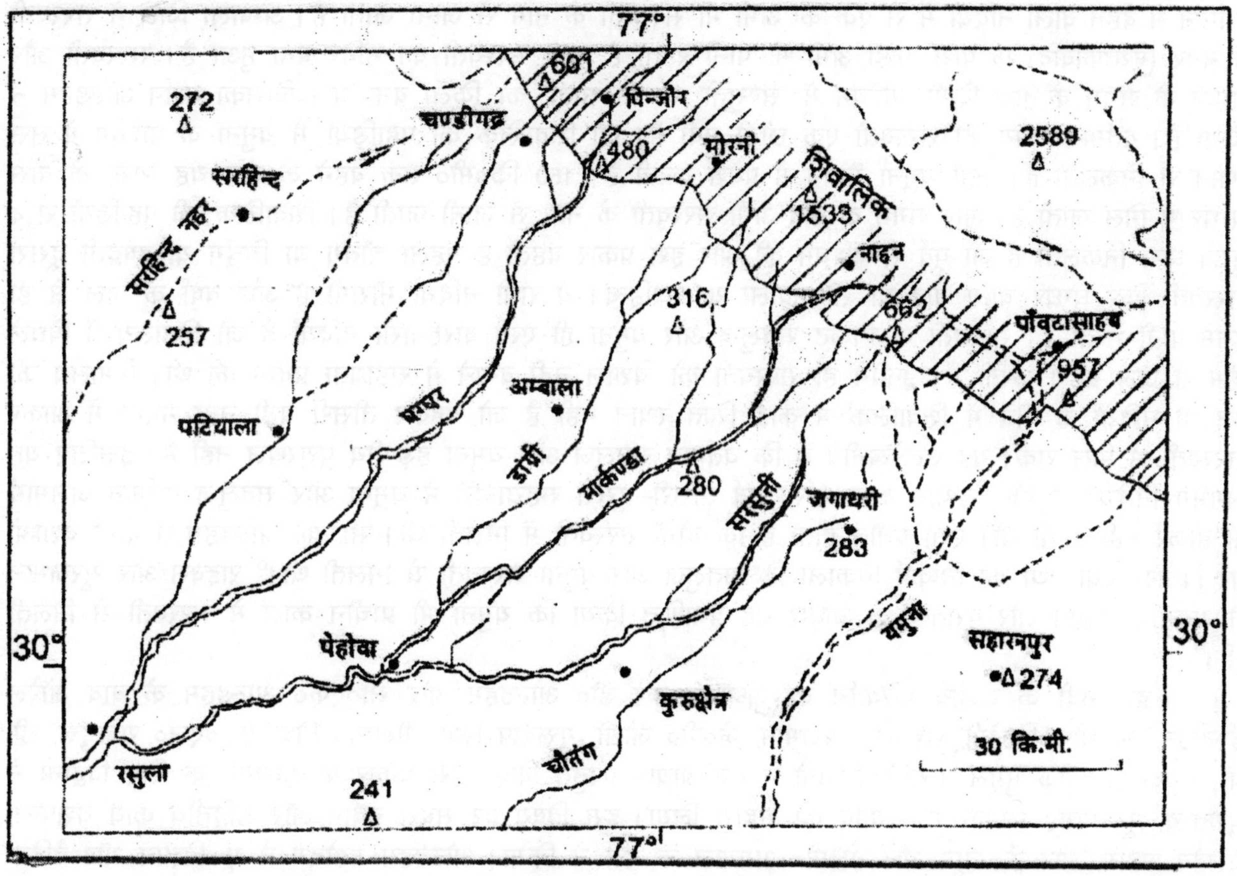

चित्र 1.1 : शिवालिक के पहाड़ी अंचल से निकलकर चौड़े पाट वाली मार्कण्डा नदी तलहटी में उपजी 'सरसुती' सरिता से मिलती है। रसुला में सरसुती घग्घर नदी से जा मिलती है। शतराना के पास रोपड़ से आने वाला चौड़े पाट वाला नाला मिलता है, जिसमें आज सरहिन्दी नहर बनी हुई है। (आधार – वाल्दिया 2010)

बाटा, मार्कण्डा नदियाँ यद्यपि देखने में छोटी लगती हैं, पर वे वर्तमान में बड़ी घाटियों से प्रवाहित हो रही हैं, जिनमें पर्याप्त नदी जनित अवसाद भरा हुआ है। यह तथ्य प्रतिपादित करता है कि इस नदी घाटियों का निर्माण पूर्व में उनके मार्गो से बहने वाली किसी विशाल नदी नें किया होगा। हम जब बाटा–मार्कण्डा नदी घाटी और आदिबद्री के मध्य स्थित शिवालिक को देखते हैं तो हमे ज्ञात होता है कि, पूर्वी भैरव खोल संरक्षित वन में स्थित एक अवसाद युक्त सुप्तनदी घाटी, जो उत्तर में बाटा मार्कण्डा घाटी से जुड़ी हुई है और दक्षिण में आदिबद्री से। वर्तमान में इस घाटी में भैरव खोल वन के दक्षिण से भैरव खोल नाड़ी निकलती है, जो आदिबद्री में पहुँचकर सोमनदी के रुप में मैदान में प्रवेश करती हुई दिखाई देती है। इसी के कुछ दूर दक्षिण में भवानीपुर के निकट पुरानदी मार्ग से सरस्वती नाड़ी निकलती हुई दिखाई देती है। इससे प्रतीत होता है कि वैदिक सरस्वती पौन्त तक पहुँचकर बाटा–मार्कण्डा घाटी में प्रवेश करती थी, जहाँ से आज भैरव खोल नाड़ी प्रकट होती है, इस नाड़ी का अनुसरण कर वैदिक सरस्वती आदिबद्री पहुँच कर मैदान में प्रवेश करती थी। आगे दक्षिण–पश्चिम दिशा में आज के सरस्वती नाड़ी मार्ग द्वारा कुरुक्षेत्र और उसके आगे घग्घर–हाकरा–नारा मार्ग द्वारा राजस्थान, पाकिस्तान के बहावलपुर, सिन्ध व गुजरात में कच्छ के रन में प्रवेश कर सिन्धु सागर में प्रवाहित होती थी। यहाँ यह ध्यान देने योग्य है कि हाल ही के पुरातात्त्विक उत्खनन से आदिबद्री में वैसे ही नदीजनित अवसाद मिल रहे हैं जैसे गरीबनाथ, सुदानवाला आदि में मिलते है। इन नदीजनित अवसाद में सेन्ट्रल क्रिस्टलाई व जुटोग समूह के

कायान्तरित शैल खण्डज पाये जाते हैं। जैसा पूर्व में कहा, ये अवसाद उच्चतर हिमालय से बहाकर वैदिक सरस्वती ने यहाँ आदिबद्री में लाकर जमा किये होगें, ऐसा प्रतीत होता है। (डॉ.वी.एम.के.पुरी 3003)।[7]

पुराणों मे वर्णित सरस्वती तथा वर्तमान में शोध के निष्कर्ष यह प्रमाणित करते हैं कि सरस्वती गिरि से मिलकर समुद्र में मिलती है। सरस्वती और दृषद्वती के मध्य का क्षेत्र कुरुक्षेत्र कहलाता है। शिवालिक से निकलकर वर्तमान में बहने वाली नदियों में से एक को अभी भी सरस्वती के नाम से जाना जाता है। अम्बाला जिले में सरस्वती में नगर (मुस्तफाबाद) के पास, जहाँ अभी भी पानी रहता है, देवी सरस्वती का मंदिर बना हुआ है। सरस्वती और घग्घर के संगम के 100 किमी. पश्चिम में 'सरसूती' या 'सरस्वती' का किला बना था। जिसका वर्णन ओल्डहम ने किया है। वर्तमान समय की सरस्वती एक छोटी नदी है। जो शिवालिक की पहाड़ियों से यमुना के पश्चिम में उस स्थान से निकलती है। जहाँ यमुना मैदान में प्रवेश करती है। 150 कि०मी० तक बहने के बाद यह 'रासू' के पास घग्घर में मिल जाती है। और संगम के बाद अभी सरस्वती के नाम से जानी जाती है। शिवालिक की पहाड़ियों से 4 मुख्य धारा निकलती है जो पूर्व से पश्चिम की ओर इस प्रकार बहती है पहला चौतंग या चित्रुंग या हषद्वती दूसरा सरस्वती फिर घग्घर चौथा वाह या सोनमवाला या सरहिन्द। ये सभी नदियाँ मौसमी हैं और वर्षा के जल से ही इनमें पानी भरता है। सरस्वती के निकट सतलुज और यमुना ही ऐसी बारहमासी नदियाँ हैं जो हिमालय में पिघले हिम से जल ग्रहण करती हैं। इन्होंने ही सरस्वती को विशाल नदी बनाने में सहायता प्रदान की थी। हिमालय की इन दो नदियों के बीच में शिवालिक में कोई रिक्त स्थान नहीं है जो बहकर तीसरी बड़ी नदी मैदान में आकर सरस्वती से मिल सके। यह उल्लेखनीय है कि वर्तमान सतलुज और यमुना हड़प्पीय पुरास्थल नहीं है। इसलिए यह लगभग निश्चित है कि हड़प्पीय काल (ईसा पूर्व तीसरी–दूसरी सहस्राब्दी) में यमुना और सतलुज वर्तमान जलमार्ग से होकर नहीं बहती थीं। ऐसा प्रतीत होता है कि दोनों सरस्वती में मिलती थी। सी.एफ. ओल्डहम ने दोनों दशाओं पर विचार किया तथा यह निष्कर्ष निकाला कि सतलुज और यमुना सरस्वती से मिलती थी।[8] राइक्स और सूरजभान ने अवसाद विज्ञान और पुरातत्व के आधार यह प्रमाणित किया कि यमुना भी प्राचीन काल में सरस्वती से मिलती थी।[9]

इस नदी के जलीय परिवर्तन का अध्ययन कर डी० ओल्डहम और सी०एफ० ओल्डहम के बाद ऑरेल ईस्टाइन, ए० घोष, बिल्हेमी, राईक्स, सूरजभान, जे०पी० जोशी, गुरूदीप सिंह, वी०एन० मिश्र, एस०एल० राजगुरू, डी. पी. अग्रवाल, रफीक मुगल इत्यादि विद्वानों ने नए आयाम प्रस्तुत किए। इस प्रकार के अध्ययन के लिए विद्वानों ने पुरातत्त्व, भू–उपग्रह छायाचित्रों इत्यादि का सहारा लिया। इस विषय पर सबसे नवीन और अद्वितीय कार्य यशपाल, बलदेव सहाय, आर०के० सूद और डी०पी० अग्रवाल के दल ने किया। ओल्डहम महोदय ने भू–विज्ञान और वैदिक महाकाव्य परम्पराओं के आधार पर जो निष्कर्ष निकाले उनमें से कुछ इस प्रकार हैं –

1. सतलुज व्यास संगम के बाद भी यह नदी सतलुज नाम से ही जानी जाती है। यह नाम हिन्दू–मुसलमानों के प्राचीन लेखों में नहीं देखने को मिलता। क्योंकि यह इसका आधुनिक नाम है। इस संयुक्त धारा को विपासा, व्यास, एवं व्ययः नाम से भी जाना जाता है। तात्पर्य यह है कि इसका वास्तविक नाम व्यास था ना कि सतलुज।

2. प्राचीन परम्पराओं (वेद और महाभारत) के आधार पर इन्होंने यह निष्कर्ष निकाला कि यमुना नदी सरस्वती से नहीं मिलती थी। और सतलुज ही इसकी मुख्य सहायक नदी थी। यद्यपि किन्हीं स्थानों पर ऐसा होने की भी चर्चा है।

3. बहुत से प्राचीन जलमार्ग (पूर्व से पश्चिम वाह, नाईवाल, पश्चिमी नाईवाल तथा दो अतिरिक्त जलपथ जो वर्तमान सतलुज के लगभग सटे से हैं) जो मिलकर हाकरा बनाते हैं, सतलुज से इतनी कम दूरी पर मिले हैं, जिससे यह अनुमान लगाया जा सकता है कि वे इनके अतिरिक्त किसी अन्य नदी का भाग नही होगें।

4. हाकरा नदी के सभी प्राचीन जलपथ रोपड़ नगर से दक्षिण पश्चिम दिशा में मुड़ जाते हैं। यह उस स्थान पर होता हैं जहां सतलुज मैदान में प्रवेश करती है। इन तटों पर विशाल नगर थे जिनके ध्वंसावशेष अभी देखने को मिलते है।

5. सरस्वती रासू के पास घग्घर में मिलती है।[10]

जर्मन विद्वान विल्हेमी ने भी नदी के जलपथ में परिवर्तन का वैज्ञानिक दृष्टिकोण से अध्ययन किया है। इस कार्य में उन्होंने भूविज्ञान और भू–आकृति विज्ञान का सहारा लिया। उन्होने यह निष्कर्ष निकाला कि सरस्वती जो सिन्धु की प्रमुख सहायक नदी थी विकसित हड़प्पा काल के अन्त में लुप्त हो गयी। इनके अनुसार जल की मात्रा

कालिक सकुंचन के कारण नदी तथा अविरत बहाव रेगिस्तानी क्षेत्रों में कायम न रख सकी और इसके कारण वह हाकरा के माध्यम से न तो समुद्र तक ही पहुँच सकी और न सिन्धु से मिल सकी। यह तभी सम्भव था जब इसकी सहायक नदियों ने इसका साथ छोड़ दिया हो और उनका किसी दूसरी विशाल नदी नें हिमालय में अपने प्रवाह क्षेत्र में (**catchment area**) अधिग्रहण कर लिया हो। ऐसा प्रतीत होता है कि सरस्वती पूर्णरुपेण यमुना द्वारा अधिकृत कर ली गयी होगी।[11] राइक्स महोदय ने भू–आकृति विज्ञान और अवसाद विज्ञान के आधार पर यह सिद्ध किया है कि यमुना हड़प्पीय काल में घग्घर से मिलती थी। भू–आकृति विज्ञान के अनुसार विभ्रमणित (**Meandering**) यमुना के जलपथ का प्रव्रजन (**Migration**) 10–15 कि.मी. चौड़े मैदानी क्षेत्र में हुआ है। यह मैदान पश्चिम में सिन्धु की ओर थोड़ा ढ़लान लिये हुए है। वर्तमान समय में पश्चिमी यमुना नहर अधिकांशतः इसके ही प्राचीन जलपथ से होकर बहती है।[12] कालीबंगा से निकट घग्घर तल से (वर्तमान जलाप्लावित मैदान के 11 मीटर नीचे से) बोरिंग करके मिट्टी के कुछ नमूने पता किये गये हैं जिनका अवसाद वैज्ञानिकों ने अध्ययन किया है। इनके अनुसार यहाँ से प्राप्त अपरिष्कृत धूसर बालू की खनिज संरचना वर्तमान यमुना तल में प्राप्त बालू की खनिज संरचना के समान है। इस गहराई के ऊपर प्राप्त चिकनी मिट्टी और गाद मिट्टी घग्घर की वर्तमान जलप्लावित क्षेत्र से प्राप्त मिट्टियों के समान है। राइक्स महोदय ने अवसादन की गति, घग्घर घाटी में पुरास्थलों की अवस्थित और इन स्थानों में जमाव के मोटाई के आधार पर यह निष्कर्ष निकाला कि घग्घर बारी–बारी से सिन्धु तन्त्र और गंगा तंत्र द्वारा अधिगृहीत कर ली गयी थी। वास्तव में ये घटनाएं यमुना द्वारा अधिग्रहण एवं परित्याग की सूचक हैं।

यशपाल, बलदेव सहाय, आर०के० सूद और डी०पी० अग्रवाल ने भू–उपग्रह द्वारा लिये गये छाया चित्रों का विभिन्न वैज्ञानिक पद्धतियों से अध्ययन किया और यह निकर्ष निकाला कि यमुना और सतलुज दोनों ही नदियाँ किसी समय सरस्वती से मिलती थीं। इस दल नें यमुना और सतलुज की कई प्राचीन जलधाराओं को चित्रित कर अपने मानचित्र में दिखाया है। इनके अनुसार सतलुज और यमुना के मध्य घग्घर, सरस्वती, मार्कण्डा व चौतंग जैसी केवल चार मौसमी नदियाँ हैं जो वर्तमान समय में न तो समुद्र तक पहुँचती हैं न ही किसी बड़ी नदी में मिलती हैं। इन्होने उपग्रह छाया चित्रों के अध्ययन से सतलुज तंत्र और यमुना तंत्र पर अपने जो निष्कर्ष निकाले हैं वे इस प्रकार हैं :–

सतलुज तंत्र

1. सतलुज नदी का पश्चिम की ओर जो समकोण बनाता हुआ मोड़ है वह इस मत को व्यक्त करता है कि प्राचीन काल में इसका विपथन हुआ था। ऐसे स्थानों पर जहाँ से नदी का अभिग्रहण या नदी का विपथन हुआ हो, तो इसी प्रकार के कोण बन जाया करते हैं। यहाँ से किसी भी भौतिक रुकावट का पता नही चला है, जिसमें इसका विपथन हुआ हो।

2. पटियाला नगर के 25 कि०मी० दक्षिण में घग्घर अकस्मात् चौड़ी हो जाती है। इस आकस्मिक चौड़ाई का अर्थ है कि यहाँ इसकी कोई सहायक नदी आकर मिलती थी। छाया चित्रों से पता चलता है कि कोई पुरानदी पथ यहाँ घग्घर से मिलता है। यह पथ सतलुज का ही हो सकता था। इन्होने सतलुज के विपथन के तीन कारण बताये हैं :– भू–विवर्तन (**Tectonic**), व्यास की सहायक द्वारा सतलुज का अभिग्रहण और भ्रंश की उपस्थिति जिससे होकर इसका विपथन हुआ।

घग्घर तंत्र

1. पंजाब में सतराना से लेकर पाकिस्तान के मरोट तक घग्घर के प्राचीन काल की चौड़ाई 6–8 किमी. की है।

2. मार्कण्डा के दक्षिण पूर्व में एक स्पष्ट पुरानदी पथ है जो सतराना के निकट घग्घर के प्राचीन तल से मिलता है। वर्तमान सरस्वती इसी पथ से होकर बहती है।

3. नदी पथ जो वर्तमान चौतंग से मेल खाता है, सूरतगढ़ के पास घग्घर से मिलता है।

4. अनूपगढ़ के पास घग्घर का यह प्राचीन तल विभाजित होकर अचानक ही समाप्त हो जाता है। ऊपरी पुरानदी पथ का मरोट के पास तथा निचले का बेरीवाला के पास अन्त हो जाता है।

इसके अनुसार घग्घर के दोनो नदी पथ एक गर्त में लुप्त हो जाते हैं। इसका ज्ञान हमें उस स्थान से प्राप्त लवण पपड़ी व भू–आकृति से भी हो जाता है। ऐसे किसी प्राचीन नदी पथ का पता नही चलता जो घग्घर को सिन्धु या लूनी से जोड़े।[13]

सरस्वती पुरानदी मार्ग

वैदिक सरस्वती के यथार्थ स्वरुप को स्थापित करने में सुदूर संवेदनशील विद्या द्वारा निर्मित भू–उपग्रह छाया चित्रों में अंकित पुरानदी मार्ग अध्ययन बहुत उपयोगी सिद्ध हुए। इसके अनुसार घग्घर नदी प्रवाह सतराना से मरोट तक लगातार 6 से 8 किमी. चौड़े दिखाई देते हैं। वर्तमान में सरहिन्द नहर द्वारा चिन्हित उत्तर में रोपड़ से आरम्भ होकर दक्षिण में सतराना तक फैला सतलज पुरामार्ग घग्घर में मिलता हुआ दिखाई देता है। इसी प्रकार से उत्तर पूर्व दिशा से आरम्भ होकर यमुना पुरामार्ग वर्तमान के चौतांग शुष्क प्रवाह के रुप में सूरतगढ़ के निकट घग्घर में मिलता हुआ प्रतीत होता है। यही प्रवाह अतीत की दृषद्वती नदी थी, जिसके और सरस्वती के मध्य के क्षेत्र को महाभारत काल में कुरुक्षेत्र कहा जाता था। (चित्र 1.2, 1.3) इस प्रकार वैदिक काल में शुतुद्री और दृषद्वती ने वर्षा आधारित सरस्वती को उसकी सहयोगिनि बनाकर, वर्ष पर्यन्त बहने वाली विशाल नदी का स्वरुप प्रदान किया, ऐसा माना जाने लगा (सी०एफ० ओल्डेहम 1893, कृष्णनन् 1960, यशपाल एवं सहयोगी 1980, मिश्रा 1995)।[14]

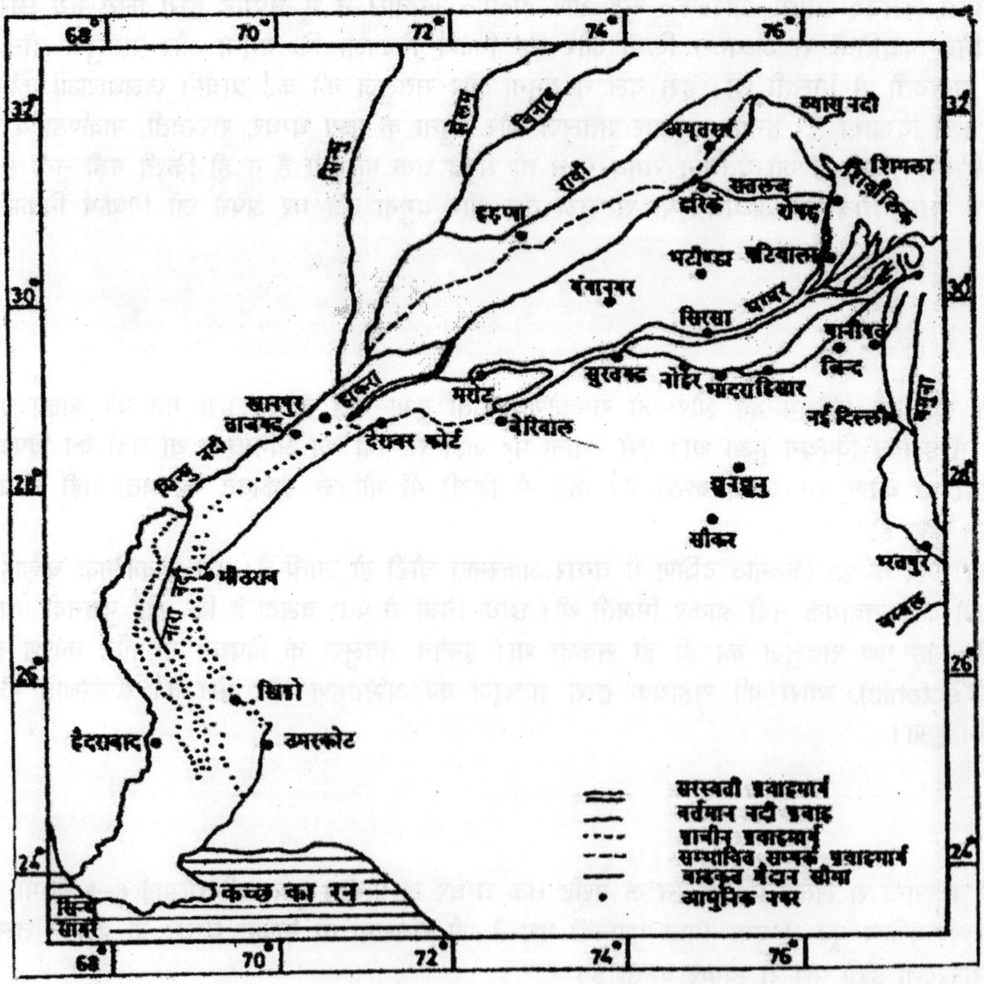

चित्र 1.2 : शिवालिक से कच्छ के रन तक सरस्वती प्रवाहमार्ग – सरसुती, घग्घर व नारा के रूप में। देखें ! नारा, सिन्धु से स्वतंत्र धारा के रूप में सरस्वती का निचला प्रवाह चिन्हित करती है। (आधार – यशपाल एवं सहयोगी 1980)

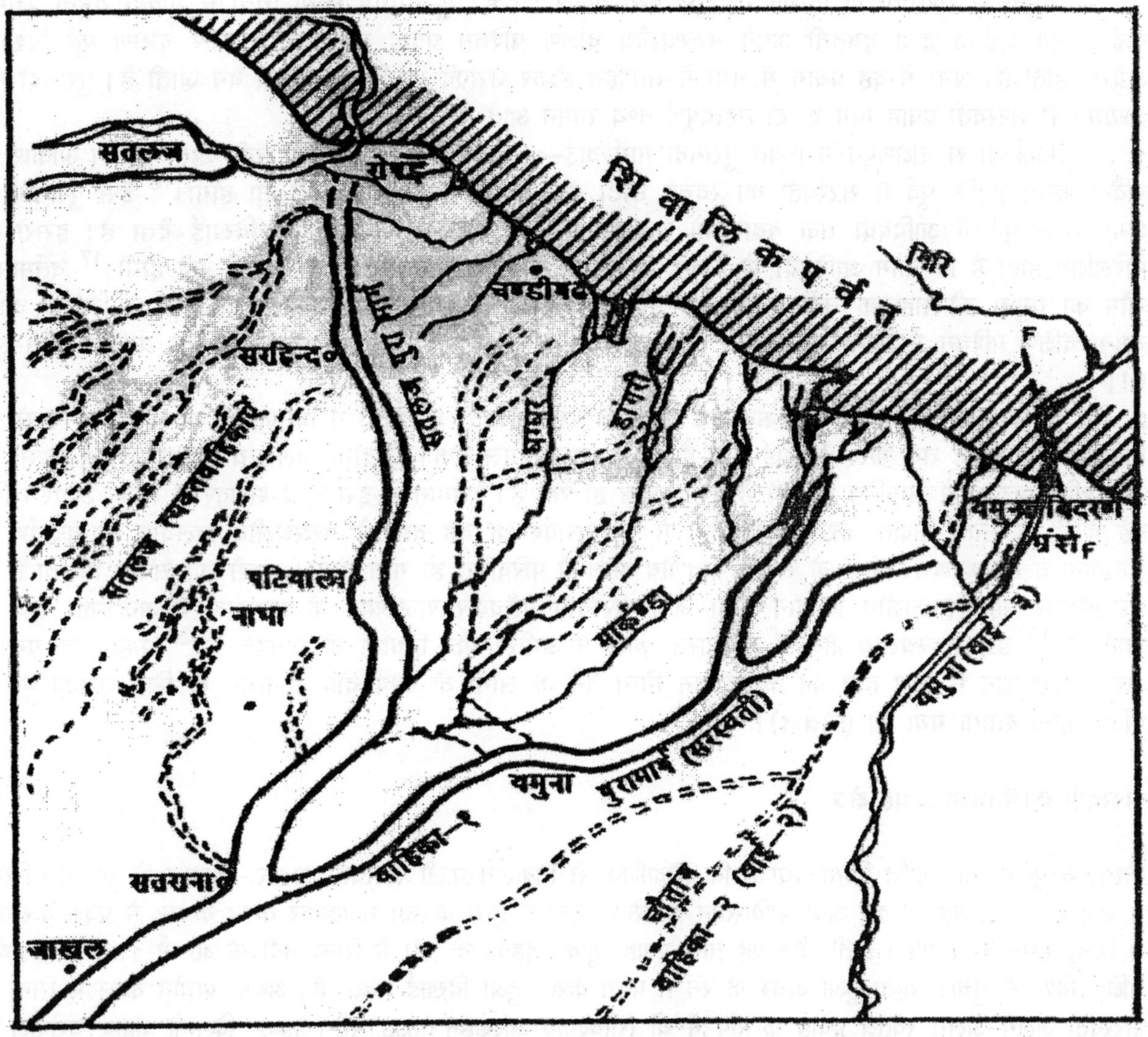

चित्र 1.3 : सतलज, घग्घर, डाँगरी, मार्कण्डा, सरसुती व यमुना और उनके पुरा प्रवाहमार्ग, जो इंगित करते हैं कि अतीत में इन सबके सम्मिलित होने से उत्तर–पश्चिम भारत में वैदिक सरस्वती नामक विषालतम नदी बहती थी। आगे चलकर यमुना व सतलज सरस्वती से विलग हो गई जिससे सरस्वती में जलभराव हो गया और वह वर्षा आधारित लघु सरसुती नाड़ी बन गई। (आधार – यशपाल एवं सहयोगी 1980)

आगे सतलज एवं यमुना के अधिकांश पुरामार्गों को स्पष्ट अंकित किया गया, जिसमें प्रवाहित होकर इन दोनों नदियों ने सरस्वती से विलग होकर वर्तमान स्थिति प्राप्त की। शिवालिक को विदीर्ण कर दक्षिण दिशा में बहने वाली सतलज सरहिन्द नाड़ी के पश्चिम में स्थित, पूर्वमध्य एवं पश्चिमी नैइवाल और अन्य अनेक पुरामार्गों को शनैः शनैः पार कर पश्चिमगामी बन जाती है। इसके फलस्वरुप सतलज रोपड़ से समकोण पर मुड़कर पश्चिमी दिशा में बहकर हरिके निकट व्यास को अपने में समाहित करके मुल्तान के दक्षिण में पहुँचकर सिन्धु की सहचरी बन जाती है। व्यास नदी के पुरामार्ग अध्ययन से ज्ञात होता है कि पूर्व में वह सतलज से नही मिलती थी। अर्थात् व्यास अकेले ही दक्षिण–पश्चिम दिशा में बहकर सिन्धु से मिलती थी। इस कारण समन्वित सतलज–व्यास को उस क्षेत्र के लोग पहले व्यास नाम से ही पुकारते थे।[15] महाभारत में उद्धृत आख्यान बताता है कि एक बार वशिष्ट खिन्न होकर आत्महत्या की मनसा से शुतुद्रि में कूद पड़े। उनको बचाने के लिए नदी अनेक धाराओं में विभक्त हो गयी। इससे संकेत मिलता है कि शुतुद्रि का सरस्वती से विछोह महाभारत काल में आरम्भ हो गया था।

यमुना से सरस्वती के विछोह भी कुछ इसी प्रकार का है। भू–उपग्रह छाया चित्रों में अंकित यमुना पुरामार्ग वाई–2 एवं वाई–3 द्वारा दृषद्वती अपने मरुस्थलीय दक्षिण पश्चिम प्रवाह मार्ग को छोड़कर दक्षिण पूर्व दिशा में अग्रेसर होती है। अन्त में वह प्रयाग में गंगा में समाहित होकर उसकी महती सहयोगिनी बन जाती है। पुरानदी मार्ग अध्ययन से सरस्वती प्रवाह मार्ग के दो महत्वपूर्ण तथ्य सामने आते हैं :–

1. मार्कण्डा से दक्षिणपूर्व में स्थित पुरानदी मार्ग वाई–1 जिसमें वर्तमान सुरसती नदी बहती है, का आकार यह संकेत करता है कि पूर्व में सरस्वती का स्वरुप छोटी नदी का न होकर बड़ी नदी सा होगा।[16] इस पुरामार्ग को अगर उत्तर पूर्व में आदिबद्री तक बढ़ाएं तो यह वर्तमान की सोम से जुड़ता हुआ दिखाई देता है। इससे यह परिलक्षित होता है कि सोम आदिबद्री के निकट शिवालिक से निकलने वाली सरस्वती नदी रही होगी।[17] वर्तमान में सोम का यमुना की सहायक नदी बनना, नदी विपथन की उन भू–वैज्ञानिक प्रक्रमों से संबंधित है जिसके कारण यमुना दक्षिण पश्चिम में स्थित मरुस्थलीय मार्ग को छोड़कर उत्तर पूर्व दिशा में प्रयाग की ओर प्रवाहित होने लगी थी।

2. घग्घर जलशून्य प्रवाह मार्ग अनूपगढ़ के पश्चिम में पहुँचकर दो भागों में विभक्त हो जाता है। इनमें से एक पाकिस्तान के मरोट तक फैला दिखाई देता है, तो दूसरा वैरीवाल तक। ये दोनों जलशून्य वहिकाएँ मानो किसी बड़े जल रहित सरोवर में समाहित हो रहीं हैं ऐसा प्रतीत हो रही है। वर्तमान में इस सूखे सरोवर में लवण आवरण मिल रहे हैं।[18] ये लवण संकेत करते हैं कि पूर्व में जो सरोवर था वह बाद में मरुस्थलीय जलवायु के पदार्पण से, डीडवाना व लूणकरणसर झील के समान, लवणीय झील मे परिवर्तित हो गया होगा। इससे यह संकेत मिलता है कि यह सरोवर महाभारतकालीन विनशन होगा जहाँ सरस्वती पहुँचकर राजस्थान के मरुस्थल में अकस्मात लुप्त हो जाती है।[19] इस मरुस्थलीय क्षेत्र में महाभारत काल में अभीरों और निषादों के जनपद थे।[20] महाभारत ग्रन्थ में सरस्वती विनशन मे लुप्त होने का कारण उन निम्न वर्ग के लोगों के स्पर्ष दोष से बचने के लिए उसका भूमि में प्रविष्ट होना बताया गया है। **(चित्र 1)**।

सरस्वती का निचला प्रवाह क्षेत्र

जैसा कि पूर्व में यह वर्णित किया गया है कि शिवालिक से निकलने वाली सरस्वती, घग्घर– हाकरा के रुप में हरियाणा व राजस्थान मे प्रवाहित होकर आगे पाकिस्तान के सिन्ध प्रान्त में नारा के रुप में बहकर कच्छ के रन मे प्रवेश कर अन्त में सिन्धु सागर में समाहित होती थी। यह नारा प्रवाह, शुष्क वहिका के रुप में सिन्धु नदी के 40 से 110 किमी. पूर्व में दक्षिण दिशा में सुचारु रहता हुआ कच्छ के रन में प्रवेश करता हुआ दिखाई पड़ता है। अर्थात् प्राचीन काल में सिन्धु एवं सरस्वती अलग–अलग स्वतंत्र प्रवाह के रुप में थीं (सी०एफ० ओल्डेहम 1893, स्टैन 1942, विल्हेमी 1969, यशपाल एवं सहयोगी 1980)। ऋग्वेद में सरस्वती का सम्बोधन सिन्धुमाता, सप्तस्वासा– सात बहनों वाली, सप्तथी– सातवीं नदी आदि यह प्रकट करता है कि सिन्धु एवं उसकी पाँच सहायक नदियाँ अवश्य रही होगी।[21] परन्तु यजुर्वेदिक काल में पूर्व सिन्धु का सरस्वती से विछोह हो गया होगा, जैसा यजुर्वेद मंत्र से जानकारी प्राप्त होती है। इस मंत्र में **"पंच नद्य सरस्वतीमपी यन्ति सस्त्रोतस"**[22]– पाँच समयश्वी नदियाँ सरस्वती में मिलती थीं, से ज्ञात होता है। अर्थात् यजुर्वेदकाल में सरस्वती और सिन्धु दो स्वतंत्र प्रवाह के रुप में रही होंगी।[23] सिन्धु का भू–वैज्ञानिक अध्ययन बताता है कि वह पिछले 5000 वर्षों में 160 किमी. पश्चिम दिशा में चली गयी है।[24] यह तथ्य भी संकेत करता है कि सिन्धु व सरस्वती– जिसे नारा प्रवाह के रुप में जाना जाता है। किसी समय दोनों एक साथ रही होगी।

सरस्वती नदी के ऊपरी प्रवाह

पूर्व वर्णित तथ्यों से यह ज्ञात होता है कि वैदिक सरस्वती नदी शिवालिक से उदित होने वाली एक बरसाती नदी रही होगी। उसका विशाल सदानीरा स्वरुप तो उसे उसकी वर्षपर्यन्त बहने वाली सहयोगिनी दृषद्वती एवं शुतुद्री से प्राप्त हुआ होगा। परन्तु यह तथ्य ऋग्वेद में वर्णित सरस्वती नदी से मेल नही खाता। ऐसा होता तो वैदिक ऋषि उसे 'नदीतमे' अर्थात् महानदी न कहते। इस विषय में अनेक विद्वानों का मत है कि सरस्वती नदी शिवालिक से निकलने वाली बरसाती नदी नहीं हो सकती। उसे तो मुख्य हिमालय से उदित होने वाली सदानीरा नदी होनी चाहिये (वालदिया 1996, 2002, पुरी एवं वर्मा 1998, चौहान 1999, 2001)। हिमनद विज्ञान और भू–आकृति–भूविज्ञान

पर आधारित वैदिक सरस्वती का अध्ययन अत्यन्त रोचक और महत्व का लगता है।[25] इस अध्ययन से ज्ञात होता है कि आज के पश्चिमी गढ़वाल हिमालय से निकलने वाली यमुना नदी की प्रमुख सहायक टोंस नदी ही मूल रुप से वैदिक सरस्वती नदी थी। यह नदी वर्तमान में बन्दरपूँछ हिमनद, जो 9 कि.मी. लम्बा है, के मुख से प्रकट होती है। यह पहले 75 किमी. दक्षिण–पश्चिम दिशा में बहकर अपनी सहायक पब्बर नदी को साथ ले, फिर दक्षिण दिशा में बहती है। आगे यह काल्सी में पहुँचकर यमुना नदी में मिल जाती है। टोंस नदी जलसंग्रहण पात्र में लगभग 152.19 वर्ग किमी क्षेत्र में फैले अन्य हिमनद भी है, जिनसे इसे लगातार जल उपलब्ध होता रहता है। इस कारण टोंस नदी का नित्यजल प्रवाह आज भी यमुना और उसकी अन्य सहायक नदियों से कहीं अधिक है। अर्थात् यमुना को आज अधिकांश जल टोंस नदी से ही उपलब्ध हो रहा है। जबकि यमुना हिमजल स्रोत, जमनोत्री समाप्त हो चुका है। इससे संकेत मिलता है कि टोंस नदी, सरस्वती के रुप में यमुना से भी बड़ी नदी रही होगी। पुरी एवं वर्मा (1998) के टोंस नदी संग्रहण पात्र उसके वर्तमान एवं पुराप्रवाह मार्ग एवं उनमें स्थित नदी वेदिका अवसाद के गहन अध्ययन से वैदिक सरस्वती का मुख्य हिमालय के एक विशाल हिमनद से प्रकट होने का पर्याप्त प्रमाण उपलब्ध हुए हैं। कुछ महत्वपूर्ण तथ्य जो दृष्टिगत होते हैं निम्न हैं :–

1. वैदिक सरस्वती का उदय पश्चिम गढ़वाल हिमालय के टोंस नदी संग्रहण प्रात्र में स्थित सरस्वती नामक हिमनद से हुआ। जो 58.8 किमी. लम्बा, 3.5 किमी. चौडा और 205.8 वर्ग किमी. क्षेत्र में फैला था।

2. टोंस नदी जल संग्रहण पात्र में और भी अनेक हिमनद विद्यमान थे, जिन्हे आज के संदर्भ में रुपिन हिमनद, सुपिन हिमनद, जमादार हिमनद कहा जाता है। सरस्वती हिमनद समेत इन सारे हिमनदों का प्रवाह आँज जिस नैतवर कहते हैं, पर केन्द्रित था। वहाँ से सरस्वती नदीरुप धारण कर प्रवाहित होना आरम्भ करती थी। इसलिए नैतवर को हम प्लक्षप्रस्रवण कह सकते हैं, जहाँ से सरस्वती वैदिक काल में उदित होती थी।

3. प्लाईस्टोसीन काल (17 लाख से 10 हजार वर्ष पूर्व तक) में टोंस नदी संग्रहण पात्रा का 1713.13 वर्ग कि०मी० क्षेत्र हिमाच्छादित था। तदनुसार उसके 35.1 प्रतिशत भाग पर हिमनद स्थित थे। प्रतिवर्ष के वर्षा और हिम से जल प्राप्ति को ध्यान में रखकर हम अनुमान लगाएं तो उन हिमनद से 24840 करोड़ घन मीटर जल उपलब्ध हो सकता है।

4. वर्तमान में टोंस नदी संग्रहण पात्र का 3.12 प्रतिशत क्षेत्र ही हिमाच्छादित रह गया। अर्थात् इसके 32 प्रतिशत क्षेत्र से पिछले लम्बे उष्ण काल के प्रभाव से हिम पिघल कर लुप्त हो गया, जिससे 22625 करोड़ घन मीटर जल उपलब्ध हुआ होगा।

5. वह जल वैदिक काल में अधिकांशतः सरस्वती में ही प्रवाहित होता रहा होगा। इससे संकेत मिलता है कि, जैसा वेदों में वर्णित है, सरस्वती अथाह जल प्रवाह वाली महानदी रही होगी, न की आज दृष्टिगोचर होने वाली 'सरस्वती नदी'।[26]

मरुस्थल में सरस्वती नदी का मूल प्रवाह

सरस्वती के पुरानदी मार्ग की सत्यता सिद्ध करने के लिए जैसलमेर भाग का विस्तार से अध्ययन किया गया। भू–उपग्रह छाया चित्रों द्वारा इस क्षेत्र में पुरानदी मार्गों को चिन्हित किया गया। भू–भौतिकी के आधार पर इस क्षेत्र में पाये जाने वाले पुरानदी मार्गों मे संचित भू–जल की संभावना का पता लगाया गया। इन पुरामार्गों से जुड़े हुए किशनगढ़ से लेकर शाहगढ़ तक के क्षेत्र में खोदे गये 17 नलकूपों से ज्ञात किया कि इन पुरानदी मार्गों में पाये जाने वाले नदीजनित अवसाद के दो स्तरों से पर्याप्त मीठा जल उपलब्ध है। इसके विपरीत इन पुरामार्गों से दूर के कुँओं में खारा पानी मिलता है।[27] कार्बन 14 कालगणना अध्ययन से ज्ञात हुआ है कि ऊपरी 30 मीटर तक के अवसाद स्तर मे पाये जाने वाले भूजल की आयु 5000 वर्ष से 1800 वर्ष की है, और निचले 60 मीटर से कुछ गहरे कुओं में पाये जाने वाले अवसाद स्तर से प्राप्त होने वाले भूजल की आयु 22000 वर्ष से 6000 वर्ष की है। ये वैज्ञानिक तथ्य उपर्युक्त कथन का समर्थन करते हैं कि वैदिक सरस्वती का मूल प्रवाह इसी क्षेत्र में था।[28] सुदूर संवेदनशील विद्या द्वारा इस क्षेत्र में किया जाने वाला नवीनतम अध्ययन भी इन्ही पुरानदी मार्ग को सरस्वती का मूल प्रवाह बतलाते हैं।[29]

गुजरात में सरस्वती प्रवाह (समुद्र संगम)

वैदिक काल (10 हजार से 8 हजार वर्ष पूर्व) में उत्तर पश्चिमी हिमालय व पश्चिमी हिमालय अरावली से उदित होने वाली सारी नदियाँ आज के कच्छ के रन तक ही नही अपितु कच्छ के मुख्य भूमि तक फैले सिन्धु सागर मे समाहित होती थीं।[30] वे नदियाँ सिन्धु नदी तंत्र, सरस्वती नदी तंत्र व लवणावती (लूनी) नदी तंत्र के रुप में जानी जाती थीं। मध्य वैदिक काल में वे नदियाँ आज के कच्छ के रन स्थल में अपना-अपना स्वतंत्र डेल्टा बनाती थीं। उनमें से सरस्वती डेल्टा विशालतम था। जैसा कि विदित है सरस्वती यजुर्वेदकाल में पाँच धाराओं में विभक्त होकर सागर में समाहित होती थीं।[31] वे पाँच धाराएँ, स्कन्द पुराण के अनुसार हरिणी, विज्रिणी, न्यंकु, कपिला व सरस्वती थी।[32] उत्तर वैदिक काल में उपर्युक्त तीनों नदियों द्वारा लाये गये अवसाद से वृद्धि प्राप्त करने वाले उनके डेल्टाओं के प्रभाव से और उस काल मे हुए नवविवर्तनिक परिवर्तनों से कच्छ का रन क्षेत्र ऊपर उठने से सागर छिछला होता गया। उसके फलस्वरुप एक ओर सिन्धु सागर दक्षिण दिशा में खिसककर आज की स्थिति प्राप्त करने लगा तो दूसरी ओर सरस्वती की मुख्य धारा पूर्व की ओर स्थानान्तरित होने लगी। महाभारत काल में वह खादिर द्वीप के निकट से विशाल कच्छ का रन लांघ कर नानु रन होते हुए **प्रभास (सोमनाथ)** में पहुँचकर सागर में समाहित होती थी। यहीं से बलराम जी ने सरस्वती के तीर्थों की यात्रा प्रारम्भ की थी। उत्तर महाभारतकाल में हुए नवविवर्तनिक परिवर्तनों के कारण सौराष्ट्र क्षेत्र ऊपर उठा, जिससे सरस्वती का प्रभास समुद्र संगम समाप्त हो गया। तब वह नानू रन से होते हुए नलसरोवर मार्ग द्वारा लोथल के निकट खम्बात की खाड़ी में पहुँचकर समुद्र में समाहित होने लगी। सरस्वती का मध्य हड़प्पीय काल में यह यह प्रमुख प्रवाह मार्ग रहा था।[33] इसी सरस्वती प्रवाह मार्ग पर खादिर द्वीप के निकट धौलावीरा व आगे सुरकोटदा प्रमुख हड़प्पीय नगर थे। लोथल उस समय का प्राचीनतम् बन्दरगाह था।[34]

सरस्वती प्रवाह मार्ग आदिबद्री से समुद्र संगम तक

वैदिक सरस्वती प्रवाहमार्ग सुनिश्चित करने में नदीवेदिका अवसाद अध्ययन बहुत उपयोगी सिद्ध हुए हैं। ये वर्तमान में टोंस नदी प्रवाह मार्ग में स्थित गरीबनाथ और उसके लगे आदिबद्री के उत्तर में शिवालिक पठारी क्षेत्र में स्थित सुदानवाला व दो विपरीत दिशाओं में बहने वाली बाटा नदी व मार्कण्डा नदी प्रवाह मार्ग में मिलने वाले बहुत उपयोगी लगते हैं। यहाँ पर बतलाना उचित होगा कि बाटा एक छोटी सी नदी है जो हिमांचल प्रदेश के शिवालिक में स्थित राम व जलमूस खोल नाड़ी से प्रकट होती है। पहले यह पूर्व दिशा में और बाद में दक्षिण पूर्व दिशा में बहकर बाटामान के निकट यमुना से मिलती है। मार्कण्डा ऊपरी शिवालिक से उदित होकर पहले पश्चिम में और बाद में वाह्य शिवालिक को काटती हुई दक्षिण-दक्षिण पश्चिम में बहकर घग्घर में मिलती है। इन नदी वेदिकाओं की अवसादी रचना बतलाती है कि इनका निचला भाग अधिकांशतः उच्चतर (गढ़वाल) हिमालय में पाये जाने वाले क्वार्टजाइट व कायान्तरित शैल खण्डजों के बने हुए हैं। और ऊपरी भाग अधिकतर शिवालिक सैण्डस्टोन व अन्य शैल खण्डजों की उच्चतर हिमालय क्षेत्र से लेकर जहाँ तक ये पायी जाती है, वहाँ तक कोई प्रभावी जलप्रवाह था, जिसने इन उच्चतर हिमालय में पाये जाने वाले विशिष्ट कायान्तरित शैल खण्डजों को यहाँ तक बहाकर जमा किया होगा। इसके अनुसार वैदिक सरस्वती का प्रवाह मार्ग उच्चत्तर हिमालय में नैतवार, जिसे प्लक्षप्रस्रवण कह सकते हैं, से आरम्भ होता है। वहाँ से 40 किमी. दक्षिण-पश्चिम दिशा में बहकर विशाल स्वरुप ग्रहण करती है। आगे अपनी सहायक पब्बर को साथ लेकर दक्षिण दिशा मे 100 किमी. बढ़कर पौन्तदून में प्रवेश करती है, जहाँ उसमे गिरि नदी भी आकर मिलती है। यहाँ तक का सरस्वती प्रवाह मार्ग वर्तमान की टोंस नदी का प्रवाह मार्ग का ही था, पर पौन्तदून तक पहुँचकर उसके प्रवाह मार्ग में विशेष परिवर्तन दिखाई देता है। काल्सी के दक्षिण में पहुँचकर वह गरीबनाथ, पौन्त व बाटा-मार्कण्डा घाटी में प्रवेश हेतु पश्चिम से दक्षिण-पश्चिम दिशा में मुड़कर बहने लगती है।

बाटा-मार्कण्डा नदियाँ यद्यपि देखने में छोटी लगती है, पर वे वर्तमान में बड़ी घाटियों में प्रवाहित हो रही हैं, जिनमें पर्याप्त नदीजनित अवसाद भरा हुआ है। यह तथ्य प्रतिपादित करता है कि इन नदी घाटियों का निर्माण पूर्व में उनके मार्गों से बहने वाली किसी विशाल नदी ने किया होगा। जब हम बाटा-मार्कण्डा के नदीघाटी और आदिबद्री के मध्य स्थित शिवालिक की स्थिति को देखते हैं तो हमे ज्ञात होता है कि, पूर्वी भैरव खोल संरक्षित वन में स्थित एक अवसाद युक्त सुप्तनदी घाटी, जो उत्तर में बाटा-मार्कण्डा घाटी से जुड़ी हुई है और दक्षिण में आदिबद्री से। वर्तमान में इस घाटी में भैरव खोल वन के दक्षिण से भैरव खोल नदी निकलती है, जो आदिबद्री में

पहुँचकर सोम नदी के रुप में मैदान में प्रवेश करती हुई दिखाई देती है। इसी के कुछ दूर दक्षिण में भवानीपुर के निकट पुरानदी मार्ग से सरस्वती नदी निकलती हुई दिखाई देती है। इससे यह प्रतीत होता है कि वैदिक सरस्वती पौन्त तक पहुँचकर बाटा–मार्कण्डा घाटी में प्रवेश करती थी। आगे दक्षिण–पश्चिम दिशा में आज के सरस्वती नदी मार्ग द्वारा कुरुक्षेत्र और उसके आगे घग्घर–हाकरा–नारा मार्ग द्वारा राजस्थान, पाकिस्तान के बहावलपुर, सिन्ध व गुजरात में कच्छ के रन मे प्रवेश कर सिन्धु सागर में समाहित होती थी।

यहाँ यह बताना उपयुक्त होगा कि हाल ही के पुरातात्त्विक उत्खनन से आदिबद्री में वैसे ही नदीजनित अवसाद मिल रहे हैं जैसे गरीबनाथ, सुदानवाला आदि में मिलते हैं। इन नदीजनित अवसाद में सेन्ट्रल क्रिस्टलाई व जुटोग समूह के कायान्तरित शैल खण्डज पाये जाते हैं। जैसा कि पूर्व में यह वर्णित है कि, ये अवसाद, उच्चतर हिमालय से बहा कर वैदिक सरस्वती ने यहाँ आदिबद्री में लाकर जमा किये होगें, ऐसा प्रतीत होता है।

ऐसा प्रचलित है कि उत्तर महाभारत काल में वाह्य शिवालिक के ऊपर उठने से सरस्वती का आदिबद्री वाला प्रवाह मार्ग धीरे–धीरे अवरुद्ध होने लगा। उसके फलस्वरुप सरस्वती का जल बाटा–मार्कण्डा मार्ग से, मार्कण्डा नदी के रुप में प्रवाहित होने लगा। सरस्वती के मार्कण्डा रुप को, मार्कण्डेय ऋषि ने सर्वप्रथम ज्ञात किया होगा, इसलिए उसे मार्कण्डा नदी के नाम से पुकारा जाने लगा। अतः पौराणिक काल में सरस्वती मार्कण्डा मार्ग से प्रवाहित हो कर मार्कण्डा कहलायी।[35]

वेदों में इसका उद्गम हिमालय माना है। जहाँ से यह आदिबद्री के मैदानी क्षेत्र में शिवालिक पर्वतमाला को पार कर प्रवेश करती थी। इसका पात्र क्षितिज तक फैला हुआ था, जिसे नंगी आखों से देख पाना असम्भव था। कालान्तर में सात नदियों की जलराशि को अपने साथ लेकर यह प्रबल वेग वाली नदी अरावली पर्वत श्रृंगों को कमलनाल के समान तोड़ डालती रही होगी। ऋग्वेद काल में यद्यपि सरस्वती के सूखने का उल्लेख नहीं है, परन्तु इसके जल को लेकर युद्ध अवश्य प्रारम्भ हो गये थे, ऐसा लगता है। यथा सरस्वती की उपत्यिका में हुआ इन्द्र वृत्र युद्ध, सतलज व्यास की उपत्यिका में हुआ जमदग्नि वाणासुर युद्ध, सरस्वती सिन्धु की उपत्यिका में हुआ दिवोदास–सुदास का दाशराज्ञ युद्ध, पर्वतीय क्षेत्र में हुआ शम्बर–इन्द्र एवं दिवोदास युद्ध, यमुना एवं सरस्वती की उपत्यिका में वृहदाश्व के पुत्र कुवलाश्व एवं मधुकैटभ के पुत्र धुन्ध के युद्ध, सम्राट सगर का तालजंघ, यवन, शकश्हैहय एवं कपिल मुनि के साथ युद्ध, अंशुमान मान का कपिल के साथ युद्ध इस बात का प्रमाण देता है। ऐसा लगता है कि दाशराज्ञ युद्ध के उपरान्त परशुराम के साथ क्षत्रिय राजाओं का संघर्ष–ब्राह्मण बस्तियों, ऋषि आश्रमों की पुर्नस्थापना के कारण हुआ। क्योंकि आज भी भारतवर्ष का सम्पूर्ण ब्राह्मण समाज परशुराम को अपना पूर्वज मानता है।

भारतीय जनमान्यता के अनुसार पहले भारतवर्ष की दो प्रमुख नदियाँ ही थीं जिन्हें ब्रह्मपुत्री एवं ब्रह्मपुत्र नाम से सम्बोधित किया गया। ये दोनों ही मानसरोवर के हिम क्षेत्र की नदियाँ रहीं। यद्यपि यह तथ्य आज लोगों को स्वीकार्य न हो परन्तु वांग्मयी संकेत यह बताते हैं कि जमदग्नि काल में हिमालय क्षेत्र में भयंकर भूचाल आया और कैलाश की स्थिति उत्तर से दक्षिण हो गयी। इस प्रक्रिया में मानसरोवर के हिम क्षेत्र से तीन नदियों का प्रवाह हुआ। जिसमें ब्रह्मपुत्र तो आज अपने स्वरुप में है, सतलज ने वाणासुर के प्रयत्न से बने मार्ग का अनुसरण किया और तीसरी नदी सिन्धु थी। अतः मूल सरस्वती में प्रथम खण्ड इसी काल में आया।

यदि शिवालिक के ऊपरी क्षेत्र में यमुना एवं सतलज के मध्य की घाटी का अध्ययन करें तो यह स्पष्ट प्रतीत होता है कि यह क्षेत्र किसी प्रबल नदी का मार्ग रहा होगा। यह सिरमौर शिवालिक पहाड़ों के पाद क्षेत्र में पाये जाने वाले शैलखण्डों से स्पष्ट होता है। अधिकतर विद्वानों की यह मान्यता बनती जा रही है कि सरस्वती के पानी का अपहरण यमुना, एवं सतलज (शतुद्रि) ने ही किया है। जबकि सिन्ध की ओर किसी का ध्यान ही नही गया।

इस स्थिति के लिए सम्राट सगर से लेकर भगीरथ तक के प्रयत्नों को भी अनदेखा नही किया जा सकता। वर्तमान बद्रीनाथ के उत्तर में स्थित माणाग्राम के निकट एक अत्यन्त वेगवान नदी प्रवाह अलकनन्दा में आकर मिलती है, जिसे स्थानीय लोग सरस्वती कहते हैं। यह सरस्वती का मूल स्रोत है इसमें सन्देह है, क्योंकि अलकनन्दा एवं उसकी सभी सहायक नदियाँ चौखम्भा, शिखर के पूर्वी पार्श्व से निकलती है। अतः इस स्थिति में सरस्वती का प्रवाह पश्चिम की ओर नही हो सकता। इस क्षेत्र में सेनाधिकारियों का भी मानना है कि इस क्षेत्र में किसी नदी के प्रवाह को बदलने के प्रयत्न दिखाई पड़ते हैं।

आदिबद्री जहाँ से सरस्वती मैदान में आती है वहाँ पत्थरों की कटान को देखते हुए भी यह स्पष्ट लगता है कि यह किसी हिमनदी के द्वारा निर्मित होना चाहिए। स्वर्गीय डॉ० वाकणकर ने अपने सरस्वती नदी शोध अभियान के बाद अपने निष्कर्षों मे बताया है कि उत्तर–दक्षिण वाहिनी सरस्वती जो आदिबद्री (यमुना नगर से हरियाणा) बूढ़ी यमुना, डीडवाना एवं लूणी के वर्तमान प्रवाहमार्ग से 25000 वर्ष पूर्व तक और उसमें 5 लाख वर्ष पूर्व तक बहती रही। यहीं से कच्छ के रन के रास्ते सीधे वर्तमान में खम्भात की खाड़ी से दक्षिण समुद्र को मिलती थी। खम्भात के मुहाने पर हुए जमाव एवं भूगर्भिक परिवर्तनों के कारण कालान्तर में इसका दक्षिण प्रवाह क्षीण हो गया एवं पश्चिम में द्वारिका वाला प्रबल प्रवाह रहा होगा।[36]

क्षेत्रीय अध्ययन में यह देखने में आया कि उत्तर गुजरात की सरस्वती का उद्‌गम स्थान कोटेश्वर के निकट विन्ध्य की पहाड़ी का है। यहाँ दो छोटी पहाड़ियों के बीच 10–12 फुट मार्ग की गहराई में जाने पर यह ज्ञात हुआ कि वहाँ एक झरना है जिसे अल्पत्य प्रमाण में पानी आता है। जो प्रथम कुण्ड में से द्वितीय कुण्ड में आकर नीचे की ओर आगे बढ़ता है। सिद्धपुर के दक्षिण भाग में यह मोड़ लेता है, जहाँ यह बड़ी और चौड़ी होती है। आगे पश्चिम की ओर जाकर कच्छ के छोटे रण में विलीन होती है। एक दूसरी नदी छोटी रण, कच्छ के अखांत के मूल पर आती है। जो मेवाड़ मे से नाथद्वारा के पास उत्तर में बहती बाँये जाकर दक्षिण गामिनी बनती है और उत्तर गुजरात के उत्तरवर्ती बड़े रण में विलीन हो जाती है। गुजरात में इसे 'बनास सरस्वती' कहते हैं। उत्तरी गुजरात का बड़ा रण और छोटा रण किसी भी नदी के मुख हैं। बनास सरस्वती और कोटेश्वर वाली सरस्वती नदियाँ लघु और लघुत्तर मार्गीय नदियाँ हैं। मूल कोई बड़ी नदी के अदर्शन के बाद इन दोनों का महत्व हुआ होगा। वास्तविकता में ये दोनों नदियाँ किसी बड़ी की शाखा नदियाँ हैं। सुदूर संवेदनशील उपग्रह प्रणाली से प्राप्त चित्रों के आधार पर भी लुप्त सरस्वती के शुष्क मार्गों की पहचान की गई है। उसका मार्ग भी कच्छ के दोनों रणों की पूर्वीय सीमा, जहाँ उत्तर गुजरात की पश्चिमी सीमा है, वहीं कोई बड़ी नदी का प्रवाह मार्ग था। उस प्रवाह के बायें भाग के दो मुखों का पहिला प्रवेश द्वार बड़ा रण है, और दूसरा प्रवेश द्वार छोटा रण है। बड़े प्रवाह का मार्ग यहाँ पूर्ण न होकर सौराष्ट्र की पूर्वी सीमा और गुजरात की पश्चिमी सीमा को सन्धि रुप बनाकर उस सन्धि भू–भाग की निम्न सपाट वाली जमीन पर से आगे दक्षिण में अहमदाबाद के पश्चिम सीमावर्ती वीरमगाम (जंक्शन) के पश्चिम से निम्न सपाट वाले भू–भाग से दक्षिण में स्थित नल सरोवर के रुप में आज भी स्पष्ट रुप से दीख पड़ती है। नल सरोवर की सपाट भूमि पर दो–तीन फुट पानी हमेशा रहता है। इसकी लम्बाई–चौड़ाई दर्शनीय है। यहाँ से अग्निकोण की ओर निम्न सपाट भू–भाग है। जो लोथल नगर तक जाता है। यह स्थान उत्तर सिन्धु संस्कृति के काल का है। यहाँ से खम्भात का अखात प्रारम्भ होता है।

इन स्थानों को देखने से स्पष्ट प्रतीत होता है कि यह प्राचीन काल की किसी बड़ी नदी का मार्ग है। इसी खम्भात के अखात के आगे जाकर साबरमती प्रवेश करती है। अतः खम्भात का अखात ही सरस्वती का समुद्र संगम स्थल है।[37]

पुरास्थल वितरण के आधार पर सरस्वती प्रवाह मार्ग

पूर्व पुरापाषाण युग के पुरास्थल प्राचीन सरस्वती व लवणावती परिक्षेत्र में चारों ओर बिखरे दिखाई देते हैं। इन 1400 पुरास्थलों में से 1097 पुरास्थल पाकिस्तान के चोलिस्तान क्षेत्र के बहावलपुर जिले से लेकर राजस्थान के हनुमानगढ़ व गंगानगर और हरियाणा, पंजाब व पश्चिमी उत्तर प्रदेश तक दक्षिण–पश्चिम से उत्तर–पूर्व दिशा में फैले पाये जाते हैं। इन पुरास्थलों के संकेन्द्रण इन्हीं नदी घाटियों में दिखाई देते हैं जो तत्कालिक सभ्यता का इस क्षेत्र में विस्तार प्रदर्शित करते हैं। ये पुरास्थल वैदिक सरस्वती के प्रायः अदृश्य प्रवाह मार्ग अर्थात् घग्घर–हाकरा–नारा को चिन्हित करते हैं।[38]

प्राक्–हड़प्पीय, पूर्व हड़प्पीय व मध्य हड़प्पीय पुरास्थल घग्घर–हाकरा, शुष्क प्रवाह मार्ग पर संकेन्द्रित मिलते हैं। केवल 44 पुरास्थल ही सिन्धु नदी क्षेत्र में पाये गये है। विगत कुछ वर्षों में एक महत्वपूर्ण तथ्य यह भी उजागर हुआ है कि जिसे हम अब तक सैन्धव सभ्यता के नाम से जानते रहे हैं वह वस्तुतः सारस्वत सभ्यता अर्थात् सरस्वती घाटी सभ्यता है। उल्लेखनीय है कि यह प्राचीनतम् सभ्यता है। उल्लेखनीय है कि इस प्राचीनतम् सभ्यता के जितने स्थल सैन्धव घाटी से मिले हैं उससे छः गुने से भी अधिक स्थल सरस्वती घाटी (घग्घर–हाकरा नारा) में प्राप्त हुए हैं। केवल स्थलों का आधिक्य ही नहीं, बल्कि कई अन्य प्रमाणों से भी इस बात की पुष्टि होती है कि इस सभ्यता

का उद्‌भव सारस्वत क्षेत्र में ही हुआ था जहाँ से यह सभ्यता प्रथमतः सैन्धव घाटी के निचले इलाकों और तदुपरान्त अन्य भू–भागों में विस्तृत हुई। इस नवीन तथ्य के प्रकाश में अधिकांश विद्वान अब इसे **'सरस्वती सिन्धु सभ्यता'** नाम से अभिहित करते हैं।[39]

पश्चिमी पंजाब व उससे जुड़े राजस्थान के गंगानगर जिले में वर्तमान में कोई नदी नहीं मिलती है। परन्तु रोपड़ के ठीक दक्षिण में उत्तर से दक्षिण दिशा में फैले शुष्क वाहिकाओं के रूप में सरहिन्द व नइवाल दिखाई देते हैं। उपर्युक्त शुष्क वाहिकाओं के साथ–साथ पूर्व हड़प्पीय व मध्य हड़प्पीय पुरास्थलों से ऐसा प्रतीत होता है कि पूर्ववर्ती काल में सतलज उत्तर से दक्षिण दिशा में बहती थी। अतः अनुमान लगाया जाता है कि सतलज सरस्वती की सहायक नदी रही होगी। भू–उपग्रह छाया चित्र से ज्ञात होता है कि सतराना के निकट उत्तर से आने वाला पुरानदी मार्ग, घग्घर शुष्क प्रवाह से मिलता है। चौहान के अनुसार स्थल शुतुद्रि–सरस्वती संगम रहा होगा, जहाँ वर्तमान में शुष्क नदी घाटी 20 किमी0 चौड़ा दिखाई देता है।[40] इसी प्रकार हरियाणा के जीन्द व हिसार जिले व इनसे जुड़े राजस्थान के हनुमानगढ़ जिले में सघन रूप से पाये जाने वाले हड़प्पीय पुरास्थल से ऐसा प्रतीत होता है कि यमुना इस क्षेत्र में दक्षिण–पश्चिमी दिशा में दृषद्वती के रूप में प्रवाहित होती थी, जो आज चौतांग शुष्क प्रवाह के रूप में जानी जाती है।[41]

आज के यमुना प्रवाह मार्ग में चित्रित धूसर पुरास्थलों (2800–2400 वर्ष पूर्व) का अधिक संख्या में पाया जाना यह प्रतिपादित करता है कि हड़प्पीय काल में यमुना दृषद्वती के रूप में दक्षिण पश्चिम दिशा में बहकर सरस्वती से मिलती थी। लगभग 3700 वर्ष पहले यमुना विदारण भ्रंश क्रियाशील होने लगा, जिसने दक्षिण पश्चिमी दिशा में बहने वाली सरस्वती की सहायक दृषद्वती को आगे चलकर दक्षिण–पूर्व में बहने वाली गंगा की सहचरी यमुना बना दिया। यही नहीं उस विवर्तनिक परिवर्तन के कारण यमुना ने सरस्वती का सारा जल अधिग्रहित कर वर्तमान प्रवाह मार्ग का निर्माण किया। इस प्रकार प्रयाग में गंगा से मिलकर गंगा–यमुना–सरस्वती की त्रिवेणी बना दी।[42]

उत्तर हड़प्पीय काल में सरस्वती का निचला प्रवाह अर्थात् गुजरात व राजस्थान का प्रवाह सूख चुका था। इस काल में सरस्वती नदी वर्षा पर निर्भर रहने वाली लघु सरस्वती बन गयी थी जिसके कारण सारस्वत सभ्यता का विस्तार उत्तर–पूर्वी हरियाणा उससे जुड़े उत्तरी पंजाब व पश्चिमी उत्तर प्रदेश में हुआ। उल्लेखनीय है कि उत्तर हड़प्पीय पुरास्थलों की अधिक संख्या उपर्युक्त क्षेत्रों से प्राप्त हुई है।[43] गुजरात में पाये जाने वाले अनेक मध्य हड़प्पीय पुरास्थलों जैसे– धौलावीरा, सुरकोटड़ा, रंगपुर, लोथल आदि के उत्खनन से यह प्रतीत होता है कि सरस्वती का प्रवाह दक्षिण दिशा में सागर पर्यन्त था।[44]

नदी मार्गों के पुरातात्विक एवं उपग्रह फोटोग्राफी से प्राप्त साक्ष्यों के आधार पर हम कह सकते हैं कि ऋग्वैदिक युग में सरस्वती एक महानदी थी जिसमें यमुना और सतलज की धाराएँ मिलती थीं और जो हरियाणा और राजस्थान पार कर समुद्र में गिरती थी। किन्तु कालान्तर में यमुना और सतलज की धाराएँ पलट कर गंगा और सिन्धु में गिरने लगी। कालान्तर में यह अन्तःसलिला होकर मरूस्थल में लुप्त हो गयी।

बलराम जी की सरस्वती नदी के तीर्थों की यात्रा (नदी प्रवाह व तीर्थ)

महाभारत में बलराम जी की सरस्वती की उत्सर्पिणी प्रदक्षिणा का वर्णन बड़े ही विस्तृत रुप में मिलता है। श्रीकृष्ण के इस निर्णय से कि वे युद्ध में पाण्डवों का साथ देगें, बलराम जी प्रसन्न नहीं थे, इसलिए उन्होंने युद्ध में भाग न लेकर तीर्थ यात्रा करना ज्यादा श्रेयस्कर समझा। बलराम जी ने द्वारिका से यात्रा आरम्भ की। उस समय पुष्य नक्षत्र था। उन्हे इस यात्रा को पूरा करने में 42 दिन लगे। उनकी यात्रा श्रवण नक्षत्र में पूरी हुई। बलराम जी ने यात्रा आरम्भ करने से पूर्व अपने सेवकों को आदेश दिये। द्वारिका से पवित्र अग्नि व प्रमुख पुरोहितों को साथ लेवें। खाद्य सामग्री, वस्त्र, रत्न, सोने–चाँदी के आभूषण एवं मुद्राएँ विपुल मात्रा में लेवें। इन सभी को ले जाने के लिए हाथी, घोड़े, ऊँट और रथ लेवें। अच्छी श्रेणी की गाय भी साथ लेवें।

सरस्वती के तट पर बने हुए प्रमुख तीर्थों की उन्होने यात्रा की। हर स्थान पर उन तीर्थों के महत्व के अनुसार बलराम जी ने पूजा–अर्चना की और सभी वर्ग के वृद्ध लोगों को आवश्यक सामग्री का वितरण किया। उन्होनें ब्राह्मणों को विपुल धन एवं गौवें दान की।[45]

प्रभास तीर्थ – अपनी यात्रा के प्रथम चरण में बलराम जी प्रभासपाटन पहुँचे, जहाँ सरस्वती का समुद्र संगम है। "सरस्वती पुण्य वहा–समुद्र महावेगा"[46] अर्थात् सरस्वती का पुण्य प्रवाह तीव्रवेग से समुद्र में समाहित हो रहा है। इससे संकेत मिलता है कि बलराम जी ने अपनी यात्रा वर्षाऋतु के अन्त में प्रभास तीर्थ से प्रारम्भ की होगी, जिससे सरस्वती को उसके सौराष्ट्र जलसंग्रहण पात्र से पर्याप्त जल प्राप्त हो सका होगा। प्रभास तीर्थ वह स्थान है जहाँ चन्द्रमा ने सरस्वती में स्नान कर अपना खोया हुआ कान्ति युक्त जीवन पुनः प्राप्त किया था। ऐसा कहते हैं कि चन्द्रमा ने दक्ष प्रजापति की 27 कन्याओं से विवाह किया। परन्तु वे उनमें से एक रोहिणी से ही प्रेम करते थे। शेष कन्याओं ने अपने पिता से शिकायत की कि उनका पति, पतिधर्म नहीं निभा रहा है। इस पर दक्षप्रजापति नें चन्द्रमा को शाप दिया कि वह अपनी कान्ति खोकर नष्ट हो जाये। तब चन्द्रमा ने दक्षप्रजापति से क्षमा याचना की। उसे स्वीकार कर दक्षप्रजापति नें चन्द्रमा को प्रभासतीर्थ में सरस्वती में स्नान करने को कहा। स्नान करने से चन्द्रमा को हर 15 दिन बाद अपना खोया हुआ कान्ति–युक्त जीवन पुनः प्राप्त होने लगा।

आगे बलराम जी **चमसोद्भेद, नागोभेद, शिवोभेद** होते हुए **विनशन** पहुँचते हैं। इन स्थानों के मध्य वाले क्षेत्र में सरस्वती प्रायः सूख चुकी थी। केवल उसका अन्तःसलिला रुप बना रहा होगा। सरस्वती के जलशून्य प्रवाहमार्ग में जहाँ–जहाँ भू–जल स्तर, नदी अपर्दन से भू–जल स्तर, नदी अपर्दन से भूसतह पर प्रकट होता, उन स्थलों पर भू–जल स्रोत बन गये होगें। इन भू–जल स्रोतों ने कहीं–कहीं लघु सरोवरों का भी निर्माण किया होगा। चमसोभेद, नागोभेद एवं शिवोभेद ऐसे ही भूजल संग्रहण स्थल रहे होंगे। बलराम जी यात्रा के अगले चरण में **उदपान तीर्थ** पहुँचे। वहाँ सूखी नदी के तट पर कुँए विद्यमान थे, जिनमें पर्याप्त जल उपलब्ध था।

विनशन : राजस्थान के मरुस्थल में ऐसा स्थान माना जाता है, जहाँ पहुँचकर सरस्वती लुप्त हो गई। अर्थात् विनशन के बाद सरस्वती का निचला प्रवाह पूर्णरुप से सूख गया था। जैसा निम्नलिखित श्लोक से ज्ञात होता है –

ततो विनशनम् गच्छेन्नियतो अशनः गच्छतियन्तर हितयातरा मरुपृष्ठे।
सरस्वति चमसोभेद शिवोभेद नागोभेदेच दृष्यते ।।[47]

अर्थात् "तब बलरामजी विनशन पहुँचे है जहाँ सरस्वती अदृश्य हो गयी परन्तु चमसोभेद, शिवोभेद और नागोभेद मे पुनः प्रकट होती हुई दिखाई दी।" इससे यह ज्ञात होता है कि बलरामजी के यात्रा के समय सरस्वती ने विनशन के आगे अपना प्रवाह स्वरुप छोड़ कर अन्तःसलिला बन गयी।

महाभारत में विनशन की उत्पत्ति के अनेक आख्यान मिलते हैं।

ततो विनशनम् राजन् जगामाथहलायुधः।
शुद्राभिरान् प्रतिद्वेषाद् यत्रा नष्टा सरस्वती ।।[48]

'राजा बलराम विनशन पहुँचे जहाँ शूद्रों व अभीरों के प्रति द्वेष प्रकट करने के लिए सरस्वती नष्ट हो गयी।'

द्वारम् निशाद राष्ट्रस्य येषाम् दोषात् सरस्वती।
प्रविष्ठा पृथ्वीम् वीर या निषादाहि मां विदुः ।।[49]

'निषाद राज्य के द्वार पर पहुँचकर सरस्वती उनके स्पर्श दोष से बचने के लिए पृथ्वी में प्रविष्ट हो गयी।'

यहाँ यह बताना उचित होगा कि सिन्धु नदी के पश्चिम तट की ओर मरुस्थल में अभीरों, निषादों एवं शूद्रों के छोटे–छोटे जनपद थे।[50] सरस्वती वहाँ तक प्रवाहित होकर, भू–वैज्ञानिक परिवर्तनों के कारण अकस्मात् लुप्त हो गयी होगी। उस स्थान को जहाँ पर सरस्वती लुप्त हो गयी, विनशन नाम से पुकारा जाता होगा।

विनशन से स्नान करके बलराम जी **सुभूमिक तीर्थ** पहुँचे। वहाँ उन्होने सरस्वती को बहते हुए देखा, जिसके तट पर फूलों से लदी हुई लताएं थीं और वहाँ अप्सराओं के निवास थे। इसी कारण वह रमणीक स्थान सुभूमिक कहलाता था। बलराम जी वहाँ स्नान करके और दान–पुण्य करके आगे बढ़े। वे **गंधर्व तीर्थ** तथा **गंगस्रोत तीर्थ** गये। आगे चलकर **शंख तीर्थ** पहुँचे, जहाँ उन्होंने मेरु पर्वत के समान बहुत ऊँचे– ऊँचे महाशंख वृक्ष देखे। बलराम जी ने वहाँ बलवान यक्ष एवं रक्षकों को देखा जो पिशाच भाषा में संवाद करते थे। वहाँ से वे **द्वैत सरोवर** पहुँचे जहाँ अनेक प्रकार के वेशधारी योगी स्नान कर रहे थे। बलराम जी सरस्वती के दक्षिण तट पर आगे बढ़ते हुए **नागधन्वा तीर्थ** पहुँचे यह नागों की नगरी थी, जहाँ नागराज वासुकी का देवताओं ने अभिषेक किया था। इसके बाद वे पूर्व दिशा मे आगे बढ़े। उन्होने आश्चर्य से देखा कि सरस्वती जो पश्चिम दिशा मे बहनी चाहिए, पूर्व दिशा में प्रवाहित हो रही थी। वहाँ से वे **नैमिषारण्य तीर्थ** पहुँचे, जहाँ सरस्वती तट के आस–पास के अरण्यों हजारों ऋषि निवास कर रहे थे।

उसके पश्चात् बलराम जी **सप्तसारस्वत तीर्थ** पहुँचे जहाँ मार्कण्डेय ऋषि ने तपश्चर्या की थी। ऋषि वैशम्पायनजी राजा जनमेजय को कहते हैं– उस सप्त सारस्वत तीर्थ में सात सरस्वती धाराओं का संगम होता है। ये

सरस्वती की सात धाराएं अथवा सात सरस्वतियाँ विभिन्न तपस्वी ऋषियों और देवताओं के आह्वान पर प्रकट हुई, ऐसा माना जाता है। इसलिए इसके संगम स्थल को **सप्तसारस्वत तीर्थ** कहते हैं। ये सात सरस्वतियाँ हैं, ब्रह्मा जी द्वारा आहुत **पुष्कर** की सुप्रभा, सत्रायाजि मुनि द्वारा आहुत नैमिषारण्य की कांचनाक्षी, गया की विशाला (राजा गय), उत्तर कौशल की मनोरमा (उद्दालक ऋषि), कुरुक्षेत्र की ओघवती (वसिष्ठ ऋषि), कुरुक्षेत्र ऋषभद्वीप की सुरेणु (राजा कुरु) और हिमालय की विमलोदका (ब्रह्मा जी)।

आगे बलराम जी **औशनस तीर्थ** पहुँचे, इसे **कपाल मोचन तीर्थ** भी कहते हैं। यहाँ सरस्वती में स्नान करके भगवान शंकर को ब्रह्महत्या से मुक्ति मिली थी। भगवान राम ने यहाँ एक राक्षस को मारकर उसका सिर दूर फेंका था, वह सिर (कपाल) महोदर मुनि की जाँघ में जा लगा था वहीं पर उस मुनि ने मुक्ति पायी थी। इसी स्थान पर शुक्राचार्य जी ने तप किया था। जिससे उन्हें नीतिशास्त्र की रचना करने की प्रेरणा मिली थी। दशम गुरु, गुरु गोविन्द सिंह जी ने भी यहाँ आराधना की थी। आज भी यहाँ कार्तिक पूर्णिमा को विशाल मेला लगता है।

इसके पश्चात् बलराम जी **पृथूदक तीर्थ** गये। इस तीर्थ को वर्तमान में **पेहोवा** कहते हैं। यहाँ राजा पृथुवैन्य ने तपस्या की। यहीं से उन्हे कृषि का अविष्कार करने की दृष्टि प्राप्त हुई। आगे चलकर बलराम जी सरस्वती के ऐसे स्थान पर पहुँचे जहाँ ब्रह्मा जी ने सृष्टि निर्माण के लिए तपस्या की। उन्होने **लोकालोक पर्वत** की यहाँ स्थापना की। इसी स्थान पर ऋषि आर्ष्टिषेण, सिन्धुद्वीप, देवापि तथा विश्वामित्र ने घोर तपस्या कर ब्रह्मर्षि पद प्राप्त किया। वहाँ से वह **ययात तीर्थ** पहुँचे जहाँ राजा ययाति, जो यादवों और कौरवों के पितामह थे, ने अनेक यज्ञ किये। इसके उपरान्त वे **वसिष्टपवाह तीर्थ** गये जहाँ सरस्वती वेग से प्रवाहित हो रही थी। तत्पश्चात् बलराम जी **स्थाणु तीर्थ** पहुँचते हैं। यहाँ सरस्वती के पूर्व तट पर वशिष्ट आश्रम था और पश्चिम तट पर विश्वामित्र आश्रम। इसी तीर्थ में कार्तिकेय को देवता का सेनापति घोषित किया गया था। यहाँ पर अरुणा नदी सरस्वती से मिलती थी। वर्तमान में अरुणा मार्कण्डा की सहायक नदी है। इससे प्रतीत होता है कि उत्तर महाभारत काल में मार्कण्डा ही सरस्वती नाम से जानी जाती थी। महाभारत में विश्वामित्र और वशिष्ठ की आपसी शत्रुता का वर्णन मिलता है। एक बार विश्वामित्र ने सरस्वती से वशिष्ठ को अपने पास उपस्थित करने का आदेश दिया। सरस्वती वशिष्ठ को विश्वामित्र के समीप लाती हैं। वशिष्ठ को अपने समीप पाकर विश्वामित्र उनकी हत्या करने के लिए अग्रेसर होते हैं। सरस्वती समझ गयी उसे ब्रह्म हत्या का दोष लगने वाला है। उसने तुरन्त वशिष्ठ को बचाते हुए सुरक्षित स्थान पर पहुँचा दिया। इसपर विश्वामित्र क्रोधित होकर सरस्वती को श्राप देते हैं कि उसका जल एक वर्ष के लिए रक्तमय हो जाये। वसिष्ठ सरस्वती के इस उपकार को नहीं भूले। उन्होंने सरस्वती को श्राप से मुक्त कराने के लिए वरुण देवता से प्रार्थना की और अपना ध्यान, धरती पर दो बिन्दुओं पर केन्द्रित किया। एक बिन्दु से पवित्र होकर अरुणा के रुप में सरस्वती प्रकट होती है, और दूसरे विन्दु से साम्ब्रमती। इस साम्ब्रमती को वर्तमान में सोम कहा जाता है।[51]

उपर्युक्त से संकेत मिलता है कि अरुणा और सोम का उदय महाभारत काल मे ही हुआ होगा। ये दोनों सरस्वती तंत्र की नदियाँ होनी चाहिए। सोम बाद में भू–वैज्ञानिक परिवर्तनों के कारण दक्षिणपूर्वी दिशा में बहकर यमुना की सहायक बन जाती है। तदन्तर बलराम जी **सोमतीर्थ** गये, जहाँ राजा सोम नें राजसूय यज्ञ किया। इसी स्थान पर वरुण देवता का अभिषेक किया गया था। आगे चलकर बलराम जी **कुबेर तीर्थ** पहुँचे। यहाँ कुबेर यक्षों के यक्षों के राजा और धन के देवता बने। आगे वे **यमुना तीर्थ** पहुँचे जहाँ भगवान विष्णु ने मधु और कैटभ राक्षसों का वध किया। यहाँ से बलराम जी **सारस्वतमुनि** के आश्रम में गये। ऐसा कहा जाता है कि जब इस क्षेत्र में 12 वर्ष से अधिक समय तक अकाल रहा, तब सारस्वतमुनि ने यहाँ रहकर उत्तम कुल के ब्राह्मणों को वेदों की शिक्षा दी। स्पष्ट है उत्तर महाभारत काल में इस क्षेत्र मे अकाल के कारण वर्षा का आभाव रहा होगा। जिसमें सरस्वती का प्रवाह क्षीण हो गया होगा। तदन्तर बलराम जी कुरुक्षेत्र में स्थित **समन्तपंचक तीर्थ** पहुँचे। यह स्थान ब्रह्मा जी की तपोभूमि कहलाता है। वर्तमान में इसे ब्रह्मसर कहते हैं। यहाँ पर पहुँचकर बलराम जी ऋषियों से महाभारत के युद्ध की जानकारी प्राप्त करते हैं। आगे चलकर वे **रामसरोवर** पहुँचे जहाँ परशुराम जी ने तपस्या की थी। उसके बाद बलराम जी ने हिमवन्त (हिमालय) की यात्रा प्रारम्भ की। हिमवन्त को प्रणाम कर वे सरस्वती के उद्गम स्थल प्लक्षप्रस्रवण पहुँचे। इस स्थान पर वे सरस्वती के दर्शन कर वे बहुत प्रसन्न हुए। इसके आगे वे यमुना के उद्गम स्थल **कारपवन तीर्थ** गये। वहाँ वे यमुना जी के पापनाशक जल में स्नान करके प्रफुल्लित होते हैं। वहीं पर बलराम जी को नारद मुनि से ज्ञात हुआ कि महाभारत के युद्ध मे भीष्मपितामह, द्रोणाचार्य, कर्ण आदि योद्धा वीरगति को प्राप्त हो चुके थे और दुर्योधन भीम से युद्ध को तत्पर था। यह जानकर वे अपने सेवकों से द्वारिका लौटने का आदेश देते हैं। तत्पश्चात् वे पवित्र हिमवन्त के **तीर्थ प्लक्षप्रस्रवण** से नीचे उतरने की यात्रा प्रारम्भ करते हैं। वहाँ पर संतो द्वारा

सरस्वती के किनारे पर स्थित सभी पवित्र तीर्थों के महात्म्य को सुनकर बलराम जी उनके मध्य सरस्वती की इस प्रकार स्तुति करते हैं–

सरस्वतीवससमा कुतो रतिः, सरस्वतीवास समाः कुतो गणाः।
सरस्वती सर्वनदीषु पुण्या, सरस्वती लोक सुखावहा सदा ।।
सरस्वतीं प्राप्त जनाः सुदुष्कृताः, सदा न सोचयन्ति परत्र चेहच ।।

"सरस्वती के समीप रहने से जो सुख प्राप्त होता है वैसा सुख और कहाँ? सरस्वती के समीप रहने से जो श्रेष्ठता प्राप्त होती है वैसी अन्यत्रा कहाँ? ऐसी सरस्वती नदियों में पवित्रतम नदी है। सरस्वती मनुष्यों को परम सुख प्रदान करने वाली है। सरस्वती से विनय करने पर मनुष्यों को इहलोक एवं परलोक में दुःखी नही होना पड़ता है।" अन्त में सरस्वती के बार–बार दर्शन कर प्रफुल्लित हो बलराम जी उत्तम घोड़ों वाले रथ पर आरुढ़ होकर धर्मक्षेत्र कुरुक्षेत्र के लिए प्रस्थान करते हैं।

उपर्युक्त वर्णित सरस्वती नदी प्रवाह मार्ग व तीर्थों का पुरातात्त्विक भौगोलिक और ऐतिहासिक वर्णन के साथ बलराम जी की सरस्वती प्रदक्षिणा से ज्ञात होता है कि सरस्वती का उदगम स्थल प्लक्षप्रस्रवण, हिमालय में स्थित था, तथा उनका गन्तव्य स्थल प्रभासपाटन, आज के सोमनाथ के समीप सिन्धु सागर था। सरस्वती और यमुना के उदगम स्थल क्रमशः प्लक्षप्रस्रवण व कारपवन, हिमालय में ही आस–पास स्थित थे। बलराम जी प्लक्षप्रस्रवण के दर्शन करते हैं और कारप वन में स्नान करते हैं। इससे संकेत मिलता है कि प्लक्षप्रस्रवण में पर्याप्त जल उपलब्ध नही था। अर्थात् सरस्वती का उच्चत्तर हिमालय से प्राप्त होने वाला हिमजल स्रोत समाप्त हो गया था। सप्तसारस्वत तीर्थ जहाँ सात सरस्वती अथवा उसकी सात धाराएँ मिलती थीं, वे सात धाराएँ कहीं आज की चौतांग, सोम, सरस्वती, मार्कण्डा, डाँगरी, घग्घर वाली, पटियाली वाली तो नही थीं? अर्थात् बलराम जी की यात्रा के समय सरस्वती का हिमालय में स्थित स्रोत पूर्णरुपेण अवरुद्ध हो गया। इसके फलस्वरुप सरस्वती नें शिवालिक से निकलने वाली वर्षा आधारित वर्तमान की उपर्युक्त नदियों का रुप धारण तो नही कर लिया? सबसे महत्वपूर्ण बात यह है कि सरस्वती के तट पर स्थित जिन तीर्थों की यात्रा बलराम जी ने की, उनमे से अधिकांश आज भी विद्यमान हैं। जैसे प्रभासपाटन, सिद्धपुर, पेहोवा, कपालमोचन, ब्रह्मसर, स्थानेश्वर व्यास तथा पुष्कर आदि। यह इस बात को प्रमाणित करता है कि सरस्वती भारत में ही विद्यमान थी, अन्यत्र नही अतः बलराम जी की यात्रा सरस्वती के प्रवाह मार्ग और उसके तटों पर आने वाले तीर्थों को यथार्थ रुप मे चिन्हित करती है।[52]

संदर्भ

1. डॉ० देवेन्द्र सिंह चौहान : 2004, पुण्य सलिला सरस्वती नदी, वैदिक सरस्वती नदी शोध संस्थान, जोधपुर, बाबा साहेब आप्टे स्मारक समिति, बंगलौर
2. ए०आर० नैयर, एस०वी० नवाडा एण्ड एस०आर० राव : 1999, 'आइसोटोप स्टडी टू इन्वेस्टिगेट दि ओरिजिनल एण्ड ऐज ऑफ ग्राउंड वाटर, अलोंग पेलियोचेनल्स इन जैसलमेर एण्ड गंगानगर डिस्ट्रीक्ट ऑफ, राजस्थान, जियोलोजिकल सोसाइटी ऑफ इण्डिया, बेंगलोर, मेमॉयर 42, पृष्ठ 315–319
3. ए०के० गुप्ता, जे०आर० शर्मा, जी श्रीनिवास एण्ड के०एस० श्रीवास्तव : 2003, 'न्यू फाइंडिंग्स ऑफ दि कोर्स ऑफ रिवर सरस्वती' जनरल रिमोट सेनसिंग सोसायिटी ऑफ इण्डिया, देहरादून
4. यशपाल, बलदेव सहाय, आर०के० सूद तथा डी०पी० अग्रवाल 'रिमोट सेंसिग ऑफ दी लास्ट सरस्वती रिवर', प्रोसिडिंग्स ऑफ दी इडियन एकेडमी ऑफ साइन्सेज, जिल्द 89, नं. 3, नवम्बर 1980, पृष्ठ 317
5. देवेन्द्र सिंह चौहान, पूर्वोक्त, पृष्ठ संख्या 78–79
6. वही
7. वही
8. डॉ० अरुण केसरवानी : 1998, इतिहास दर्पण, अंक 4, भाग 2, अखिल भारतीय इतिहास संकलन योजना, नई दिल्ली
9. सूरजभान : 1972, 'चेन्जेज इन दी कोर्स ऑफ यमुना एण्ड देयर वेयरिंग आन प्रोटोहिस्टारिकल चेन्ज ऑफ हरियाणा', सम्पादक– एस. वी. देव, नागपुर विश्वविद्यालय, पृष्ठ संख्या– 124–128
10. डॉ. अरुण केसरवानी, पूर्वोक्त, पृष्ठ संख्या– 79
11. ब्रिगेट आलचिन : 1984, 'दि हडप्पन इन्वाइरमेन्ट', फ्रन्टियर ऑफ दी इण्डस सिविलाइजेशन, सम्पादक– बी.बी. लाल एण्ड एस. पी. गुप्त, पृष्ठ संख्या– 445–454
12. आर.एल. राइक्स : 1968, 'कालीबंगन : डेथ फ्राम नेचुरल काजेज', एन्टिक्वीटी, पृष्ठ संख्या– 286–291
13. यशपाल तथा अन्य, पूर्वोक्त, 1989
14. देवेन्द्र सिंह चौहान, पूवोक्त
15. सी०एफ० ओल्डेहम : 1893, 'दी सरस्वती एण्ड दी लास्ट रिवर ऑफ दी इण्डियन डेजर्ट', जनरल रोमर सोसाइटी, वाल्यूम 34, पृष्ठ संख्या 49–76

16. यशपाल एवं सहयोगी : 1980, 'रिमोट सेंसिंग ऑफ दी लोस्ट सरस्वती रिवर', प्रोसिडिंग ऑफ इण्डियन एकेडमी ऑफ साइन्स (अर्थ एण्ड प्लेनेटरी साइंस) वाल्यूम 89, पृष्ठ संख्या– 317–337
17. वाकणकर : 1986, 'वैदिक सरस्वती नदी शोध अभियान की उपलब्धियाँ' हिन्दू चेतना, वर्ष–5, अंक 5, पृष्ठ संख्या 9–10
18. यशपाल एवं सहयोगी, पूर्वोक्त
19. देवेन्द्र सिंह चौहान, पूर्वोक्त
20. अली : 1973 'दि जियोग्राफी ऑफ पुरानाज' पीपल्स पब्लिशिंग हाऊस, नई दिल्ली, पृष्ठ संख्या 233
21. ऋग्वेद 6/61/10–12, 7/36/6
22. यजुर्वेद 3/11
23. देवेन्द्र सिंह चौहान, पूर्वोक्त, पृष्ठ संख्या– 75
24. ए०के० स्नेलग्रोव : 1979, 'माइग्रेशन ऑफ दी इण्डस, पाकिस्तान इन रिस्पोन्स टू प्लेट टेक्टॉनिक मोशन्स' जनरल जियोलोजिकल सोसाइटी ऑफ इण्डिया, वाल्यूम 20, पृष्ठ संख्या 392–403
25. वी०एम०के० पुरी एण्ड वी०सी० वर्मा : 1998, 'ग्लेशियोलोजिकल एण्ड जियोलोजिकल सोर्स ऑफ सरस्वती इन दी हिमालयाज', इतिहास दर्पण, अंक 4 भाग 2, भारतीय इतिहास संकलन योजना समिति, दिल्ली द्वारा प्रकाशित, पृष्ठ संख्या 7–36
26. देवेन्द्र सिंह चौहान, पूर्वोक्त, पृष्ठ संख्या 79
27. वही, पृष्ठ संख्या 80
28. शशीन्द्र विश्ववन्धु : 1995 'सरस्वती नदी के वांग्मयी संदर्भों में अध्ययन', सम्पादक प्रो0 देवेन्द्र सिंह चौहान, शशीन्द्र विश्ववन्धु, वैदिक सरस्वती शोध संस्थान, डॉ. हेडगेवार भवन, जोधपुर
29. पद्मश्री डॉ. केशवराम का. शास्त्री : 1995 'नदीतमा सरस्वती का समुद्र संगम', सम्पादक प्रो0 देवेन्द्र सिंह चौहान, शशीन्द्र विश्ववन्धु, वैदिक सरस्वती शोध संस्थान, डॉ. हेडगेवार भवन, जोधपुर
30. महाभारत 5/35/16–22
31. अली, पूर्वोक्त
32. ओ०पी० भारद्वाज : 1991, 'दि वैदिक सरस्वती इन' सम्पादक– ओ.पी. भारतद्वाज, एशियन्ट कुरुक्षेत्र स्टडीज इन हिस्टोरिकल एण्ड कल्चरल जियोग्राफी, न्यू देलही, पृष्ठ संख्या 22–44
33. देवेन्द्र सिंह चौहान, पूर्वोक्त पृष्ठ संख्या 38–46
34. बी०बी०लाल : 1998 'इण्डिया एड्स न्यू डायमेन्सन टू दी इण्डस सिविलाइजेशन इन रिविजिटिंग इण्डस सरस्वती एज एण्ड एन्शिएन्ट इण्डिया', सम्पादक– भूदेव शर्मा एण्ड नवरुन घोष, उर्वशी प्रेस, मेरठ, पृष्ठ 1–21
35. विमल सोनी : 1995, 'राजस्थान मे सरस्वती नदी के पुरामार्ग' अंतस्सलिला सरस्वती में, सम्पादक– देवेन्द्र सिंह चौहान, शशीन्द्र विश्ववन्धु, वैदिक सरस्वती नदी शोध संस्थान, जोधपुर प्रान्त पृष्ठ संख्या– 53–54
36. ए०आर० नैयर, एस०वी० नवाडा एण्ड एस०आर०. राव : 1999 'आइसोटोप स्टडी टू इन्वेस्टिगेट दि ओरिजन एण्ड ऐज ऑफ ग्राउण्ड वाटर अलोंग पेलियोचैनल्स इन जैसलमेर, एण्ड गंगानगर डिस्ट्रिक्ट ऑफ राजस्थान', जियोलोजिकल सोसाइटी ऑफ इण्डिया, बेगलौर, मेमोयर 42, पृष्ठ संख्या 315–319
37. ए०के० गुप्ता, जे०आर० शर्मा, जी० श्रीनिवासन एण्ड के०एस० श्रीवास्तव : 2003, 'न्यू फाइडिंग्स आन दी कोर्स ऑफ रिवर सरस्वती', जनरल रिमोट सेंसिंग सोसाइटी ऑफ इण्डिया, देहरादून
38. देवेन्द्र सिंह चौहान, पूर्वोक्त, पृष्ठ संख्या– 108–109
39. वही, पृष्ठ संख्या 109, प्रो. शिवाजी सिंह : मई 2004 'ऋग्वैदिक आर्य एवं सिन्धु सभ्यता', भारतीय इतिहास संकलन समिति, वाराणसी आमुख 3
40. देवेन्द्र सिंह चौहान, पूर्वोक्त, पृष्ठ संख्या 111
41. वही
42. वही
43. वही
44. ऋग्वेद 8/24/27
45. जे०एन० मलिक, एस०एस० मेर एण्ड वी श्रीधर : 1999, 'पेलियोडेल्टा कॉप्लेक्स ऑफ वैदिक सरस्वती एण्ड अदर एन्सिएण्ट रिवर्स ऑफ नार्थ वेस्टर्न इण्डिया', जियोलोजिकल सोसाइटी ऑफ इण्डिया, बेंगलोर, मेमायर 42, पृष्ठ संख्या 163–174
46. महाभारत 3/80/27
47. महाभारत 3/80/118
48. महाभारत 3/36/1
49. महाभारत 3/30/4
50. यजुर्वेद 1803
51. दोमोदर झा : 1995, 'वैदिक एवं पुराणिक सरस्वती', अन्तस्सलिला सरस्वती में, सम्पादक– देवेन्द्र सिंह चौहान, शशीन्द्र विश्व वन्धु, पृष्ठ संख्या– 21–24
52. एम०एल० भार्गव : 1964, 'दि जियोग्राफी ऑफ ऋग्वैदिक इण्डिया', दि अप्पर इण्डिया पब्लिशिंग हाऊस, लखनऊ, पृष्ठ संख्या– 157.

14

विन्ध्य क्षेत्र की मध्यपाषाणिक संस्कृति में जीवन–निर्वाह के साक्ष्य

रमाकान्त सिंह

विन्ध्य क्षेत्र का परिचय : भारत एक विशाल देश है। भौगोलिक विविधता के कारण यह अनेक परिस्थितिकी क्षेत्रों में विभक्त है जिनमें मानव के उद्भव और विकास की दृष्टि से विन्ध्य क्षेत्र विशेष रूप से महत्वपूर्ण है। विगत चार दशकों में सम्पादित प्रागैतिहासिक अनुसंधानों से स्पष्ट हुआ है कि यह क्षेत्र मानव–जीवन के उषाकाल से ही अनेक संस्कृतियों के उद्भव और विकास का साक्षी रहा है। भौगोलिक विविधता वाला यह भू–क्षेत्र दकन तथा उत्तरी भारत के मध्य एक अन्तस्थ क्षेत्र की तरह स्थित है (वाडिया 1973; 121–131)। प्राकृतिक सम्पदा तथा आर्थिक दृष्टि से समृद्ध यह भूक्षेत्र ऐतिहासिक तथा सांस्कृतिक दृष्टि से भी अत्यन्त महत्पूर्ण है। प्रागैतिहासिक शिलाचित्र के लिए प्रसिद्ध भीमबैठका नामक पुरास्थल इसी क्षेत्र में स्थित है। यहाँ पर नृजातीय तथा सांस्कृतिक विविधता वाली अनेक जनजातियां भी निवास करती हैं जिनके अध्ययन से हम अतीत के पुननिर्माण के लिए कुछ महत्वपूर्ण संकेत पा सकते हैं।

भारतीय पुरातात्विक अनुसंधान की दृष्टि से विन्ध्य क्षेत्र विशेष रूप से उल्लेखनीय है, जहाँ प्राचीन मानव के विकास की गौरव गाथा अनेक भूतात्विक तथा पुरातात्विक जमावों में संरक्षित पायी गयी है। इस क्षेत्र का जो भू–भाग प्रस्तुत अध्ययन क्षेत्र में सम्मिलित है, वह वस्तुतः उत्तरमध्य भारत का पठारी क्षेत्र है, जिसे हम उत्तरी विन्ध्यक्षेत्र की संज्ञा से भी अभिहित कर सकते हैं। गंगा तथा यमुना नदियाँ इस क्षेत्र की उत्तरी सीमा का निर्धारण करती हैं तथा दक्षिण में यह विन्ध्य की पहाड़ियों से घिरा हुआ है। इसकी पश्चिमी सीमा पर भिण्ड, ग्वालियर, दतिया, शिवपुरी (म0 प्र0) जिले स्थित हैं तथा दक्षिणी सीमा को मध्य प्रदेश के सागर, गुना, टीकमगढ़, छतरपुर, पन्ना, सतना, रीवा, सीधी और अम्बिकापुर जिले निर्धारित करते हैं। बिहार के शाहाबाद और पलामू जिले इस क्षेत्र की पूर्वी सीमा पर स्थित हैं। सोन, कर्मनाशा, चन्द्रप्रभा, बेलन, टोंस, पयस्विनी, केन, चम्बल तथा इनके सहायक नदी–नाले इस क्षेत्र के अपवाह तंत्र को नियंत्रित करते हैं।

यह सम्पूर्ण भूक्षेत्र प्रायः पहाड़ी तथा सीढ़ीनुमा भू–आकृति से युक्त है जिसका ढ़लान दक्षिण–पश्चिम से उत्तर–पूर्व की ओर है (तिवारी 1971; 102)। इस क्षेत्र में पायी जाने वाली चट्टानों में ग्रेनाइट, नीस, बलुआ पत्थर, क्वार्ट्ज और शेल विशेष रूप से उल्लेखनीय है। विन्ध्य क्षेत्र का सम्पूर्ण क्षेत्र अर्धमरुस्थलीय वनस्पति के क्षेत्र में आता है। यहाँ वर्षा का औसत लगभग 100 सेमी0 रहता है। भूगर्भीय दृष्टि से यह क्षेत्र काफी धनी है क्योंकि यहाँ प्री–कैम्ब्रियन युग से तृतीयक काल तक के सभी युगों के जमाव दिखायी पड़ते हैं (पन्त)। चतुर्थक काल का दर्शन यहाँ भूतात्विक जमाव के रूप में होता है। इस क्षेत्र के नदी–अनुभाग भी चतुर्थक कालीन जमान का निदर्शन करते हैं। विन्ध्य क्षेत्र में इस तरह के अनेक जमाव विधिवत देखे जा सकते हैं।

इसमें दो राय नहीं कि इस क्षेत्र में पाये जाने वाले प्राकृतिक संसाधनों (उपजाऊ मिट्टी, फ्लोरा–फौना, विविध चट्टानों) ने इस क्षेत्र में मानव–जीवन के विकास को समुचित गति प्रदान की। सत्य भी है क्योंकि इस क्षेत्र

में हमें निम्न पुरापाषाणकाल से नवपाषाण काल तक बिना व्यतिक्रम या सांस्कृतिक अन्तराल के मानव जीवन के विकास में सातत्यता दिखायी देती है।

इलाहाबाद विश्वविद्यालय के प्राचीन इतिहास, संस्कृति एवं पुरातत्व विभाग, जियोलॉजिकल सर्वे ऑफ इण्डिया और संयुक्त राज्य अमेरिका के बर्कले स्थित कैलिफोर्निया के विश्वविद्यालय, मानवशास्त्र विभाग के संयुक्त प्रयास के विन्ध्य क्षेत्र में स्थित टोंस की सहायक बेलन तथा गंगा की सहायक सोन नदियों की घाटियों में सम्पादित अनुसंधान ने न केवल भारतीय पाषाण युगीन संस्कृति के अध्ययन में एक नये अध्याय को जोड़ा है अपितु इस अध्ययन के फलस्वरूप विन्ध्य क्षेत्र में मध्यप्रातिनूतन काल से लेकर आरम्भिक नूतन काल तक के मानव जीवन की क्रमबद्ध कहानी का उद्‌घाटन हुआ है।

उपर्युक्त अनुसंधानों के फलस्वरूप बेलन नदी घाटी (मिश्रा, 1977; 30–31) में 18 मी0 तथा सोन नदी घाटी (विलियम 1983; 9–21) में 30मी0 मोटे प्रातिनूतन कालीन तथा आरम्भिक नूतन कालीन अनुभाग प्रकाश में आये हैं जिनमें निम्नपुरापाषाण काल से लेकर मध्य पाषाण काल तक की संस्कृति का लम्बवत् रिकार्ड सुरक्षित है। नवपाषाण के साक्ष्य स्वतंत्र रूप से धरातल पर प्राप्त किये गये है। इन जमावों में पाषाण उपकरणों के अतिरिक्त पशुओं के जीवाश्म भी भारी मात्रा में मिले हैं, जिनमें गाय बैल, भैंसा, घोड़ा, दरियाई घोड़ा, गैंडा, हाथी, हिरण, घड़ियाल तथा पशुओं के जीवाश्म उल्लेखनीय हैं। (आलूर, 1980) प्रसिद्ध विद्वान एच0 डी0 सांकलिया (1974 : 172) बेलन नदी–अनुभाग को देखकर बड़े प्रभावित हुए तथा उन्होंने इसे टेक्स्ट बुक सेक्शन की संज्ञा प्रदान की[8] (रेखाचित्र 1,2)।

भारत में मध्यपाषाणिक संस्कृति की खोज का इतिहास – पाषाण युगीन संस्कृतियों के उद्‌भव और विकास के क्रम में मध्य पाषाण काल, पुरापाषाणकाल और नवपाषाण के मध्य एक संक्रमणात्मक अवस्था का अभिद्योतन करता है। इस काल में मानव–जीवन विधा में नवीन परिवर्तनों के कारण सांस्कृतिक विकास की प्रक्रिया में महत्वपूर्ण परिवर्तन हुए। सांस्कृतिक विकास की इस अवस्था में कुछ विशेष सांस्कृतिक तत्व उद्भूत हुए जिन्होंने समयान्तराल में नवपाषाणिक संस्कृति के विकास में अपना महत्वपूर्ण योगदान दिया (मिश्रा एवं पाल 2002)।

प्रागैतिहासिक अनुसंधान की शैशवावस्था में पुराविदों का विचार था कि पुरापाषाण तथा नवपाषाण युगीन संस्कृतियों के मध्य एक लम्बा अन्तराल था। परन्तु कालान्तर में जो अनुसंधान हुए उनसे यह ज्ञात हुआ कि इन दोनों कालों के मध्य एक संक्रमणात्मक अवस्था थी जो दोनों को आबद्ध करके संयोजित करती थी। इस संदर्भ में 1887 में फ्रांस की "मास द एजिल" (Mas D Azil) नामक गुफा के उत्खनन से प्राप्त साक्ष्य विशेष महत्व रखते हैं। कालान्तर में विद्वानों ने इस संक्रान्ति अवस्था को मध्यपाषाण काल का नाम दिया। भारतीय उपमहाद्वीप में मध्यपाषाणिक सांस्कृति के अध्ययन के संदर्भ में विवेच्य है कि प्रारम्भ में यहाँ "लघुपाषाणोपकरण" केवल भूतल से प्रतिवेदित थे, स्वरित जमानव से नहीं मिले थे। अतः प्रायः ऐसी धारणा थी कि यहाँ पर भी लघुपाषाण उद्योग का विकास अफ्रीका के अनुरूप मध्य पुरापाषाणिक उद्योगों से हुआ होगा। लेकिन बीसवीं शताब्दी ई0 के साठ एवं सत्तर के दशकों में भीमबैठका, रेणुगुण्टा, मध्य सोनघाटी (शर्मा एवं क्लार्क 1983 : 161–96), बेलन घाटी (शर्मा एवं मिश्रा 1980) तथा भारत के अन्य क्षेत्रों में पुराविदों द्वारा किये गये उत्खननों के फलस्वरूप ऐसे साक्ष्य प्रकाश में आये हैं, जिनसे यह बात स्पष्ट हो गयी कि भारत में लघु पाषाण उद्योग का विकास उच्च पुरापाषाणिक ब्लेड उद्योग से हुआ। भारत में मध्य पाषाणिक अनुसंधान 100–वर्ष से अधिक पुराना है। सन् 1867 में ए0 सी0 एल0 कार्लाइल ने विन्ध्य क्षेत्र से ही लधुपाषाण उपकरणों को प्रविवेदित किया था। (मिश्रा 1965; 57–58) उस समय से लेकर आज तक भारत के विभिन्न भागों से लघुपाषाण उपकरण प्रतिवर्ष होते रहे हैं जिससे भारतीय मध्यपाषाणिक संस्कृति के संदर्भ में हमारा ज्ञानवर्धन हुआ है।

विन्ध्य क्षेत्र में मध्यपाषाणिक संस्कृतिः सामान्य विशेषाताएं – विगत दशकों में सम्पादित प्रागैतिहासिक अनुसंधान के फलस्वरूप विन्ध्यक्षेत्र मानव के उद्‌भव एवं विकास के मूल केन्द्र के रूप में प्रकाश में आया है। भारत में मध्यपाषाणिक संस्कृति के अध्ययन की दृष्टि से यह क्षेत्र विशेष रूप से महत्वपूर्ण है। इस क्षेत्र में स्थित बेलन, अदवा तथा सोन नदी घाटियाँ प्रारम्भ से ही मानव संस्कृति के विकास में सहायक रही हैं। इलाहाबाद विश्वविद्यालय के प्राचीन इतिहास, संस्कृति एवं पुरातत्व विभाग द्वारा सम्पादित अनुसंधान से इस क्षेत्र की नदियों के भूतातत्विक जमावों से तो मध्यपाषाणिक उपकरण मिले ही हैं साथ ही इस क्षेत्र से अनेक पुरास्थल भी प्रकाश में आये हैं जिनमें ज्यादातर खुले स्थान में नदियों के तटवर्ती ऊँचे स्थान में, पहाड़ियों की तलहटी, ढलानों या उनके ऊपरी भाग में स्थित हैं। दूसरी स्थिति में ये शिलाश्रय या गुफाओं के रूप में प्रकाशित हैं। इस क्षेत्र के प्रमुख मध्यपाषाणिक पुरास्थलों में चन्दौली जिले में कर्मनाशा नदी घाटी में स्थित लतीफशाह, कौड़िहार और चन्दौली जिले में ही चन्द्रप्रभा नदी की घाटी में बैरा–दोमुहवा, कपिशहा, सोनवर्सा, पंचपेड़िया, राजा बाबा की पहाड़ी, भैंसहवा और कुसुम्हार का उल्लेख किया जा सकता है। (मिश्रा 1977 : 52) मिर्जापुर और सोनभद्र जिलों से भी पचास से अधिक मध्यपाषाणिक

पुरास्थल प्रकाशित है। प्रो0 आर0 के0 वर्मा ने इस क्षेत्र से 32 खुले स्थान में स्थित पुरास्थल तथा 27 शिलाश्रयों की खोज की थी। (वर्मा 1986 : 9–14) इन पुरास्थलों में लेखहिया, मोरहना तथा बगहीखोर विशेष रूप से उल्लेखनीय हैं। ये शिलाश्रय बेलन घाटी में ऊँचे स्थान में कैमूर की पहाड़ियों में स्थित हैं। बेलन घाटी में स्थित अन्य पुरास्थलों में चोपनी–माण्डो, कुण्डीडीह, लोनामाटी, कपासी कला, बदउआ कला, मझगवाँ और महुली है। अनुसंधानों के फलस्वरूप सोन नदी घाटी में भी जिनमें बाघोर II, घघरिया शिलाश्रय I, कुनझुन II, में मेढ़ौली और बांकी अनेक मध्यपाषाणिक पुरास्थल प्रकाशित हैं जिनमें शिलाश्रय विशेष रूप से उल्लेखनीय है (वर्मा 1986 : 9)। इसके अतिरिक्त चित्रकूट जनपद में लालापुर, भौरी, ऐंचवारा और पहारा नामक स्थलों से भी लघुपाषाणोपकरण प्रतिवेदित हैं। विन्ध्यक्षेत्र के अन्य जिलों यथा–महोबा, हमीरपुर, झाँसी तथा ललितपुर से भी उक्त संस्कृति के साक्ष्य प्रकाशित हुये हैं। इस प्रकार से हम देखते हैं कि मध्यपाषाणिक मानव ने विन्ध्यक्षेत्र के एक बड़े भू–भाग को आबाद किया था।

विन्ध्यक्षेत्र में यद्यपि अनेक मध्यपाषाणिक पुरास्थल हैं लेकिन अद्यतन उत्खनित पुरास्थलों की संख्या बहुत सीमित है। प्रमुख उत्खनित पुरास्थलों में विन्ध्य क्षेत्र की महत्वपूर्ण नदी बेलन की घाटी में स्थित उच्च कैमूर में मोरहना पहाड़, बगहीखोर, लखहिया नामक शिलाश्रय तथा चोपनीमाण्डो नामक महत्वपूर्ण मध्यपाषाणिक पुरास्थल विशेष रूप से उल्लेखनीय है। इसी प्रकार मध्य प्रदेश के सीधी जिले में स्थिर बाघोर II, मेढ़ौली, बाँकी, कुनझुन II तथा घघरिया नामक शिलाश्रय का भी उत्खनन किया गया है।

मोरहना पहाड़ बगहीखोर तथा लेखहिया शिलाश्रय मिर्जापुर जिले में भैंसोर ग्राम से लगभग पाँच किमी दूरी पर मिर्जापुर से दक्षिण की ओर जाने वाली रोड पर स्थित है। इलाहाबाद विश्वविद्यालय के प्राचीन इतिहास, संस्कृति एवं पुरातत्व विभाग के निर्देशन में सन् 1962–63 तथा 1963–64 के बीच इनका उत्खनन सम्पादित कराया गया।

मोरहना पहाड़ :– यह पुरास्थल भैंसोर ग्राम के पश्चिम में लगभग 5 किमी की दूरी पर स्थित है। यहाँ के शिलाश्रय संख्या–4 के अन्दर तथा शिलाश्रय संख्या – 1 के बाहर स्थित खुले क्षेत्र में एक–एक खत्तियाँ प्रो0 आर0 के0 वर्मा द्वारा डाली गयी। शिलाश्रय संख्या–4 के अन्दर उत्खनन से 55 सेमी मोटा मध्य पाषाणिक जमाव प्रकाश में आया जिसे चार स्तरों में विभाजित किया गया। यहाँ सभी स्तरों से ज्यामितीय लघुपाषाण उपकरण तथा मिट्टी के बर्तन के टुकड़े प्राप्त किये गये। यहाँ पर स्तर 2 तथा स्तर 1 से प्राप्त लघुपाषाण उपकरण अपेक्षाकृत लघु आकार के हैं। (वर्मा 1986 : 24) मोरहना पहाड़ के शिलाश्रय संख्या–1 के बाहर जो खन्ती डाली गयी, उसमें 1.15 मीटर मोटा सांस्कृतिक निक्षेप मिला जिसे 6 स्तरों में विभाजित किया गया। छठां स्तर अपघटित शिला का ही भाग है, जिससे किसी प्रकार के कोई पुरावशेष नहीं मिले हैं। इसके ऊपर के स्तर 5 से अज्यामितीय लघुपाघाण उपकरण नहीं मिले हैं। चौथे स्तर से अज्यामितीय तथा ज्यामितीय दोनों प्रकार के लघुपाषाण उपकरण प्राप्त हुए हैं। लघुपाषाण उपकरणों के अतिरिक्त इस स्तर से हस्तनिर्मित मृदभाण्ड के कुछ टुकड़े भी मिले हैं जो अत्यन्त क्षणभंगुर है। स्तर 3 से सबसे अधिक संख्या में लघुपाषण उपकरण मिले हैं। इस स्तर से प्राप्त मृदभाण्ड स्तर 4 से प्राप्त मृदभाण्डों की ही तरह हैं। स्तर 2 तथा स्तर 1 से हस्तनिर्मित मदृभाण्डों के टुकड़ों के साथ लघुतर आकार के मध्यपाषाणिक उपकरण प्राप्त हैं। ऊपरी सतह के लगभग एक इंच नीचे चतुर्भुजाकार क्रास अनुभाग का लौह निर्मित एक बाणग्र भी प्राप्त है।

बगहीखोर : यह पुरास्थल मोरहना पहाड़ के पूर्व में एक किलोमीटर की दूरी पर स्थित है। यहाँ पर शिलाश्रय संख्या–1 में प्रो0 आर0 के0 वर्मा ने उत्खनन कराया था जिसके फलस्वरूप 55 सेमी मोटा मध्यपाषाणिक जमाव प्रकाश में आया है। यह जमाव चार स्तरों में विभाजित है (वर्मा 1986 : 25)। बघहीखोर के उत्खनन से भी मोरहना पहाड़ के उत्खनन के परिणामों से मिलता–जुलता लघुपाषाणोपकरणों का विकासात्मक क्रम ज्ञात हुआ है। यहाँ पर सबरो निचले चतुर्थ स्तर से केवल अज्यामितिक प्रकार के लघुपाषाणोपकरण मिले हैं। तीसरे स्तर से भी अजयामितिक प्रकार के लघुपाषाणोपकरण मिले हैं। इस स्तर से मृदभाण्ड के टुकड़े भी मिले हैं। दूसरे स्तर से अज्यामितीय तथा ज्यामितीय लघुपाषाण उपकरण प्राप्त हुए हैं जो आकार में अपेक्षाकृत छोटे हैं। मिट्टी के बर्तनों के नमूनों की संख्या भी इस स्तर में बढ़ जाती है। स्तर 2ए से लेयर 3 और 4 को काटते हुये एक गढ्ढा आधारशिला को काटकर बनाया गया था। इस गढ्ढे में एक विस्तीर्ण शवाधान मिला है। कब्र में मानव ककाल परिश्रम की ओर सिर तथा पूर्व दिशा की ओर पैर करके दफनाया हुआ मिला है। प्रथम स्तर से जो लघुपाषाण उपकरण मिले हैं वे आकार में अपेक्षाकृत छोटे हैं। मिट्टी के बर्तनों के नमूनों की संख्या भी इस स्तर में बढ़ जाती है। सबसे ऊपरी प्रथम स्तर से लोहे के बने हुये दो बाण तथा लोहे का एक टुकड़ा भी प्राप्त हुआ है (वर्मा 1986 : 28)।

लेखहिया : यह पुरास्थल भैंसोरे ग्राम से पूर्व में लगभग 3 किमी की दूरी पर स्थित है। यहाँ पाँच शिलाश्रय स्थित हैं, जिनमें से चार चित्रकारी युक्त हैं। इस पुरास्थल का उत्खनन इलाहाबाद विश्वविद्यालय के प्रो0 जी0 आर0 शर्मा के निर्देशन में वी0 डी0 मिश्र ने कराया था। शिलाश्रय संख्या 1 तथा 2 का चयन उत्खनन के लिए किया गया। शिलाश्रय संख्या 1 में उत्खनन के फलस्वरूप 48 सेमी0 मोटा मध्यपाषाणिक जमाव प्राप्त हुआ जिसे चार स्तरों में विभाजित किया। शिलाश्रय संख्या 2 के बाहर खुले हुए क्षेत्र में उत्खनन के फलस्वरूप 1.10 मी0 मोटा जमाव

मिला। जमाव की संरचना तथा रंग के आधार पर इसे 9 स्तरों में विभाजित किया गया। इनमें से ऊपरी आठ स्तरों से लघुपाषाण उपकरण प्राप्त हुये हैं जिन्हें नीचे से ऊपर की ओर चार श्रेणियों में विभाजित किया गया है, जो लघुपाषाण उपकरणों के क्रमिक विकास का अभिद्योतन करते हैं (मिश्रा 2007) –

1- अज्यामितीय मृदभाण्ड–रहित लघुपाषाण उपकरण
2- ज्यामितीय मृदभाण्ड–रहित लघुपाषाण उपकरण
3- ज्यामितीय मृदभाण्ड–सहित लघुपाषाण उपकरण
4- लघुतर ज्यामितीय मृदभाण्ड–सहित लघुपाषाण उपकरण

लेखहिया शिलाश्रय संख्या–1 एक से मध्य पाषाणिक लघुपाषाण उपकरणों के अतिरिक्त 17 मानव कंकाल भी प्राप्त हुए हैं। स्तरीकरण के आधार पर 14 कंकालों को आठ कालखण्डों में विभाजित किया गया है। अधिकांश विस्तीर्ण शवाधान हैं। कंकाल II और XII को छोड़कर शेष सभी का विस्थापन पश्चिम पूर्व की ओर था, जो मध्यपाषाणिक मानव द्वारा सूर्य–उपासना का संकेत माना जा सकता है (मिश्रा 2002 : 231)। अमेरिका के ऑरेगान विश्वविद्यालय के जॉन0 आर0 लुकास (1993) के अनुसार लेखहिया में कुल 27 मानव कंकालों की हड्डियाँ मिली हैं। पूर्णतः निर्मित तथा अर्धनिर्मित लघुपाषाण उपकरण बहुत बड़ी संख्या में कंकालो के साथ प्राप्त हुए हैं। कंकाल संख्या II तथा V के साथ अन्त्येष्टि सामग्री के भी प्रमाण मिले हैं। कंकाल II के साथ किसी पशु के जबड़े का एक हिस्सा, हिरण के दो सींग तथा एक घोंघा रखा हुआ मिला है। कंकाल V के साथ भैंस की एक पसली मिली है।

चोपनी–माण्डो – यह मध्यपाषाणिक पुरास्थल इलाहाबाद जिले की कोरांव तहसील में इलाहाबाद से दक्षिणपूर्व की दिशा में 77 किमी और देवघाट से पूर्व दिशा में लगभग 3 किमी0 की दूरी पर बूढी बेलन के बायें तट पर स्थित है। यह पुरास्थल लगभग 1500 वर्गमीटर क्षेत्र में विस्तृत है। इस पुरास्थल पर सर्वप्रथम 1967 में वी0 डी0 मिश्रा ने जी0 आर0 शर्मा के निर्देशन में उत्खनन किया था जिसके द्वारा इस पुरास्थल का कालक्रम निर्धारित हुआ। तत्पश्चात 1978–79 से 1981–82 के बीच अपेक्षाकृत बड़े पैमाने पर जी0 आर0 शर्मा के निर्देशन में वी0 डी0 मिश्रा ने चोपनी–माण्डों का उत्खनन कराया। भूतल से लगभग 30–35 सेमी की गहराई तक जाने के बाद अधिकांश खन्तियों में उत्खनन रोक दिया गया। सन् 1967 में अंशतः उत्खनित एन0 एच0 I (NHI) नामक खन्ती में आधार शिला तक उत्खनन किया गया। इस खन्ती में उत्खनन के फलस्वरूप 1.55 मी0 मोटा सांस्कृतिक जमाव प्रकाश में आया (रेखाचित्र 5)। इस जमाव को 10 स्तरों तथा चार सांस्कृतिक कालों में विभाजित किया गया है। (शर्मा एवं मिश्रा 1980)

1- अनुपुरापाषाणकाल (Epi-Palaeolithic)
2- आरम्भिक मध्यपाषाण काल 'अ' (Early Mesolthic-A)
3- प्रारम्भिक मध्यपाषाण काल 'ब' (Early Mesolthic-B)
4- विकसित मध्य पाषाणकाल अथवा आद्य नव पाषाण काल (Advance Mesolthic or Proto Mesolithic)

अनु–पुरापाषाण काल नामक प्रथम उपकाल चोपनी–माण्डो के 20 सेमी0 मोटे दसवें अन्तिम स्तर से सम्बन्धित है। इस उपकाल के पाषाण उपकरण परवर्ती उपकालों के पाषाण उपकरणों की तुलना में बड़े आकार के हैं। इसलिए उसको उच्च पुरापाषाण काल तथा मध्यपाषाण काल के बीच की संक्रमणात्मक अवस्था का द्योतक माना गया है। चोपनी–माण्डो के नवें तथा आठवें स्तर आरम्भिक मध्य पाषाण काल 'अ' का द्योतन करते हैं। इससे अज्यामितीय प्रकार के उपकरण मिलते हैं जो अधिकांशतः चर्ट पर निर्मित हैं। इस उपकाल के प्रमुख उपकरणों में इस काल के समानान्तर पार्श्व वाले ब्लेड, कुण्ठित ब्लेड, बेधक, खुरचनी आदि उल्लेखनीय है। सम्बन्धित 3.80 मी0 व्यास की दो गोलाकार झोपड़ियों के साक्ष्य भी प्रकाश में आये हैं। प्रारम्भिक मध्य पाषाणकाल 'ब' का सम्बन्ध सांस्कृतिक जमाव के सातवें स्तर से लेकर चौथे स्तर तक है। इस जमाव से ज्यामितीय लघु पाषाण उपकरण प्राप्त हुये हैं। जिनका आकार अपेक्षाकृत छोटा है। प्रमुख उपकरणों में विभिन्न प्रकार के ब्लेड, त्रिभुज, चतुर्भुज, दांतेदार ब्लेड आदि उल्लेखनीय हैं। इस उपकाल से सम्बन्धित गोलाकार पांच झोपड़ियों के साक्ष्य मिले हैं। इनमें से तीन झोपड़ियां सातवें स्तर से और दो झोपड़ियां छठवें स्तर से सम्बन्धित है। झोपड़ियों के फर्श से बहुसंख्यक लघुपाषाणोपकरण तथा छोटे–छोटे पत्थरों के टुकड़े बिखरे हुए मिले हैं। इनके अतिरिक्त पत्थर की निहाई, हथौड़े आदि के टूटे हुए टुकड़े मिले हैं। विकसित मध्य पाषाण काल नाम चोपनी–माण्डो का तीसरा उपकाल तीसरे से लेकर प्रथम स्तर तक सम्बन्धित है। इस उपकाल से ज्यामितीय उपकरणों के साथ–साथ हस्तनिर्मित मृद्भाण्ड भी मिले हैं। इस उपकाल से त्रिभुज तथा ट्रांचेट नाम कुछ नये प्रकार के उपकरण मिले हैं।

चोपनी–माण्डो के इस तीसरे उपकाल से 13 गोलाकार/अण्डाकार झोपड़ियाँ तथा चार गर्त चूल्हों के प्रमाण भी मिले हैं। झोपड़ियों के फर्श पर लघुपाषाण उपकरण, निहाई, विविध आकार प्रकार के हथौड़े, सिल–लोढ़े, गदाशीर्ष आदि भी मिले थे। सात तथा आठ नम्बर के फर्श पर दो विशालकाय निहाईयां भी मिली थी। यहाँ के गर्त चूल्हों में राखयुक्त मिट्टी, हड्डी के टुकड़े, कोयले आदि मिले थे (मिश्रा 2002 ; 222)।

बाघोर II – यह पुरास्थल मध्य प्रदेश के सीधी जिले की सिहावल तहसील में सिहावल टाउन से 8 किमी पूर्व सोन नदी के सहायक कुढ़ोरी नाला के बायें तट पर स्थित है। इस पुरास्थल का उत्खनन इलाहाबाद विश्वविद्यालय के प्रो0 जी0 आर0 शर्मा तथा कैलीफोर्निया स्थित बर्कले विश्वविद्यालय के जे0 डी0 क्लार्क के संयुक्त निर्देशन में 1980–81 और 1981–82 के दो सत्रों में सम्पादित किया गया (शर्मा एवं क्लार्क, 1983 : 161–96)। पुरास्थल पर परीक्षण खन्ती में लगभग 2 मीटर गहराई तक उत्खनन के बाद उत्खनन समाप्त कर दिया गया क्योंकि इसके नीचे पुरावशेष विद्यमान नहीं थे। समयाभाव के कारण मुख्य ग्रिड में भी 30 सेमी0 की गहराई तक ही उत्खनन किया जा सका। उत्खनन के फलस्वरूप सात स्तर पहचाने गये। स्तर 1 से चल्सिडनी तथा अगेट के अनेक तरह के पिण्ड और टुकड़े प्राप्त हुए। स्तर 2 ए से भारी मात्रा में तथा स्तर 2 बी से अपेक्षाकृत कम मात्रा में लघुपाषाण उपकरण प्रतिवेदित हुए। स्तर 3 से एकाकी चर्ट निर्मित ब्लेडलेट मिला। स्तर 4, 5 तथा 6 से कोई पुरावशेष प्रतिवेदित नहीं हुए। उत्खनन के परिणाम स्वरूप लेयर 2 बी से अर्धगोलाकार/चतुर्भजाकार पांच या छह झोपिड़ियों के साक्ष्य प्रकाश में आये। इन झोपड़ियां के फर्श पर पत्थर के टुकड़े, निहाइयाँ, हैमरस्टोन, सिल–लोढे, रबरस्टोन, विभिन्न अवस्थाओं में निर्मित लघुपाषाण उपकरण, चर्ट, चल्सिडनी और क्वार्ट्ज पत्थर के टुकड़े मिले। इस पुरास्थल के लयर 1 से कुछ मृदभाण्ड के टुकड़े भी मिले थे जिनकी समता चोपनी–माण्डों के विकसित मध्य पाषाण अवस्था के मृदभाण्डों से की जा सकती है। बाघोर II से एक रेडियो कार्बन तिथि भी उपलब्ध है जो इस पुरास्थल को मध्य पाषाण काल के प्रारम्भिक आर–24ए चरण में रखती है। इस तिथि का मान 8330 ± 220 BP है।

घघरिया शिलाश्रय I – यह पुरास्थल मध्य प्रदेश के सीधी जिले में सिहावल से उत्तर–पूर्व की दिशा में 20 किमी की दूरी पर कैमूर श्रृंखला में स्थित है। यहाँ पर चार शिलाश्रय हैं जिनमें शिलाश्रय संख्या–1 का उत्खनन 1980 में इलाहाबाद विश्वविद्यालय तथा बर्कले विश्वविद्यालय की संयुक्त टीम ने सम्पादित कराया था (मिश्रा एवं क्लार्क 1983 : 251–259)। उत्खनन के परिणामस्वरूप 0.58 मी0 मोटा सांस्कृतिक जमाव प्रकाशित हुआ। जिसे चार स्तरों तथा दो संस्कृतिक कालो में विभाजित किया गया। इस पुरास्थल के सबसे ऊपरी स्तर 1 से भारी मात्रा में प्रस्तर–फलक, सिल–लोढ़े के टुकड़े, मृदभाण्ड, प्रस्तर पर निर्मित एक मनका कुछ जीवाश्म तथा चारकोल मिला है। दूसरे स्तर से आभूषण को छोड़कर, स्तर 1 के समान ही पुरावेशष प्राप्त हुए। तीसरे स्तर से अपेक्षाकृत कम मात्रा में पुरावेशष प्राप्त हैं तथा जीवाश्म और मृदभाण्ड नदारत हैं। स्तर 4 से मात्र कुछ प्रस्तर–फलक ही प्रतिवेदित हैं। इस पुरास्थल के द्वितीय सांस्कृतिक काल से (स्तर–1–2) हड्डियों के 150 टुकड़े और दो दांत भी उत्खनन में मिले थे। शिलाश्रय के उत्खनन से लगभग 17988 लघुपाषाण उपकरण तथा हड्डी के दो प्वाइंट भी प्राप्त हैं। लघुपाषाण उपकरण आकार में छोटे हैं तथा अच्छी तरह तैयार समपाश्विक, क्रोड से निपीड पद्धति से निकाले गये ब्लेड पर बने हैं। बाघोर II की तरह यहाँ से भी सिल–लोढ़े, रिंग स्टोन, बर्निसर्स आदि अन्य प्रस्तर निर्मित उपकरण प्राप्त किये गये। इस पुरास्थल के दूसरे सांस्कृतिक काल से हस्तनिर्मित बर्तन के 246 टुकड़े भी प्राप्त हैं जिनका सम्बन्ध विकसित मध्य पाषाणिक, नवपाषाणिक तथा परवर्ती लौहयुगीन अवस्था से था (मिश्रा 2002 : 247)।

कुनझुन II : यह पुरास्थल मध्य प्रदेश के सीधी जिले में सिंहावल से 10 किमी दक्षिण–पश्चिम दिशा में सोन नदी के दाहिने तट पर स्थित है। यह नवपाषाणिक पुरास्थल कुनझुन I से 500 मीटर की दूरी पर पश्चिम दिशा में वेदिका 1 और वेदिका 2 के मध्य में स्थित है (क्लार्क एवं विलियम 1990)। वेदिका 2 को ही खुटेली जमाव की संज्ञा दी गयी है। प्रो0 जी0 आर0 शर्मा तथा प्रो0 जे0 डी0 क्लार्क के निर्देशन में सम्पादित उत्खनन के फलस्वरूप यहाँ पर 8 स्तरों से सम्बन्धित दो सांस्कृतिक कालों की पहचान की गयी। इस पुरास्थल के सभी स्तरों से बड़ी संख्या में लघु पाषाण उपकरण, चर्ट, अगेट और चल्सिडनी के हीटट्रीटेड टुकड़े, जानवरों की हड्डियाँ, कई आकार के बलुआ पत्थर के टुकड़े, हैमरस्टोन, सिल, बनिर्सस आदि बिखरे हुए मिले थे नीचे के स्तरों की अपेक्षा उपरी स्तरों से अपेक्षाकृत ज्यादा संख्या में उपकरण प्राप्त होते हैं। कुनझुन II के सबसे ऊपरी स्तर 1 से हस्तनिर्मित मृदभाण्ड का एक टुकड़ा मिला है। इस पुरास्थल के सभी स्तरों से सन्तोषजनक मात्रा में जानवरों की हड्डियाँ मिली हैं। कुछ हड्डियों पर कटने के निशान भी मिले हैं, जिससे संकेतित होता है कि इस पुरास्थल के मध्य पाषाणिक लोगों के जीवन में शिकार की महत्वपूर्ण भूमिका थी। पुरावशेषों के स्वरूप और चरित्र के आधार पर यह पुरास्थल मध्य पाषाणिक संस्कृति के परवर्ती चरण का अभिद्योतन करता है (क्लार्क एवं खन्ना 1989; 29–46)। इस पुरास्थल पर

शिल्प–तथ्यों के वितरण से स्पष्ट है कि ' ओवन' का उपयोग अच्छे फलक निकालने तथा शिकार से प्राप्त मांस को भूनने में किया गया होगा।

मेढ़ौली : यह पुरास्थल मध्य प्रदेश के सीधी जिले की सिहावल तहसील में कुढेरी नाला के दाहिने तट पर उत्खनित मध्य पाषाणिक पुरास्थल बाघोर II के विपरीत दिशा में स्थित है (आई.ए.आर. 1982–83 : 57–58)। यह पुरास्थल लगभग 9600 मीटर क्षेत्र में विस्तृत है। 1982–83 में इलाहाबाद विश्वविद्यालय के प्राचीन इतिहास विभाग द्वारा उत्खनित इस पुरास्थल के ऊपरी धरातल पर विभिन्न आकार के बलुए पत्थर के टुकड़े, विभिन्न कालों में निर्मित लघुपाषाण उपकरण, चर्ट, चल्सिडनी, अगेट पत्थर के टुकड़े, कुछ निहाई, हैमरस्टोन, रबरस्टोन तथा सिल–लोढ़े के टुकड़े प्राप्त किये गये हैं। इस पुरास्थल पर एक परीक्षण खन्ती में 1.05 मी0 गहराई तक उत्खनन किया गया तथा 6 स्तरों की पहचान की गयी।

इस पुरास्थल के उत्खनन से प्राप्त उपकरण अपने विकासात्मक क्रम का अभिद्योतन करते हैं। इस पुरास्थल पर अन्तिम उत्खनित स्तर 5 पुरा पाषाणकाल और मध्य पाषाण काल के बीच की संकमणात्मक अवस्था का अभिद्योतन करता है। इस स्तर से प्राप्त उपकरण, उच्चपुरापाषणिक उपकरणों से छोटे तथा मध्य पाषाणिक उपकरणों से आकार में बड़े हैं। ये बहुतायत चर्ट पर निर्मित हैं। स्तर 4 और स्तर 3 से अनेक प्रकार के ब्लेड, प्वाइंट, बोरर, स्क्रेपर और त्रिभुज मिले हैं जिनका आकार स्तर 5 से प्राप्त उपकरणों से छोटा दिखायी देता है। इस काल के निर्माण में नानपर्टी मटेरियल बढ़ जाता है। स्तर 3 से स्तर 1 तक मिले उपकरणों में निपीड पद्धति से निर्मित ब्लेड बहुतायत हैं। अन्य उपकरणों में बोरर, लुनेट्स, विषमबाहु तथा समद्विबाहु त्रिभुज, ट्रैपेज, स्क्रैपर, ट्रॉचेट, ब्यूरिन आदि मिले हैं। उपकरण नये और आकार में छोटे हैं। उपकरणों के निर्माण में चल्सिडनी, चर्ट, अगेट, कार्नेलियन का प्रयोग किया गया है। उत्खनन में मिट्टी के बर्तन के साक्ष्य नदारत हैं। अन्य उपकरणों में सिल–लोढ़े और हैमरस्टोन के टुकड़े भी इस स्तर से प्राप्त हैं।

बांकी : यह मध्य पाषाणिक पुरास्थल मध्य प्रदेश के सीधी जिले के सिहावल से 2 किलोमीटर उत्तर की दिशा में कुढ़ेरी नाले के बायें तट पर स्थित है (आई. ए. आर. 1982–83 : 57)। यह पुरास्थल उत्तर से दक्षिण 114 मीटर तथा पूर्व में पश्चिम 100 मीटर के आकार में 2 मीटर ऊँचे टीले के रूप में स्थित हैं। इस पुरास्थल की खोज इलाहाबाद विश्वविद्यालय के प्राचीन इतिहास विभाग ने की थी। पुरास्थल के ऊपरी धरातल पर अनेक मध्य पाषाणिक उपकरण बिखरे हुए मिले थे। मध्यपाषाणिक उपकरणों के पुरातात्त्विक संदर्भ की जानकारी के लिए सन् 1982–83 में एक परीक्षण खन्ती में 1.8 मीटर की गहराई तक उत्खनन किया गया। बाद में 1992 में पुरास्थल पर मध्यपाषाणिक संस्कृति के विभिन्न पक्षों की जानकारी के लिए व्यवस्थित उत्खनन किया गया। उत्खनन के परिणामस्वरूप 1.17 मी0 मोटा सांस्कृतिक जमाव प्रकाश में आया जिसे पाँच स्तरों में विभाजित किया गया। सबसे ऊपरी स्तर 1 से जो पुरावशेष मिले उनमें माइक्रोलिथ, प्रयुक्त नोडुल्स, अपशिष्ट आदि उल्लेखनीय हैं। दूसरा स्तर 2 ए और 2 बी नामक दो उपस्तरों में विभाजित है। इन दोनों स्तरों से चर्ट, चल्सिडनी, अगेट, कार्नेलियन पर निर्मित अनेक प्रकार के ब्लेड, त्रिभुज, लुनेट्स, प्वाइंट बोरर और स्क्रेपर प्राप्त हुए। स्तर 3 से प्राप्त उपकरणों में हल्की वृद्धि दिखायी देती है। स्तर 4 से प्राप्त उपकरण इस श्रृंखला में सबसे बड़े आकार के हैं। जिनकी तुलना बाघोर III तथा चोपनी–माण्डो के फेज 1 से प्राप्त उपकरणों से की सकती है।

इस पुरास्थल पर स्तर 2 के फर्श 2 ए और फर्श 2 बी के उद्घाटन के बाद मुख्य ग्रिड में उत्खनन स्थगित कर दिया गया। इन दोनों फर्शों पर बलुये पत्थर के टुकड़े, सिल–लोढ़े, विभिन्न अवस्थाओं में निर्मित उपकरण आदि बिखरी हुयी अवस्था में प्राप्त हुये। ग्रिड के उत्तर–पश्चिम और दक्षिण–पूर्व भाग में भारी मात्रा में एकत्रित पत्थर प्राप्त हुए हैं। इन दोनों फर्शों पर बलुए पत्थर के छोटे तथा गोलाकार अनेक पेवमेंट भी प्राप्त किय गये हैं। बहुत संभव है कि इनका उपयोग स्टोरेज बिन के आधार के रूप में किया जाता रहा हो। (मिश्रा 2002 : 255) इन दोनों ही फर्शों पर हाईकंसेन्ट्रटेड जोन के बीच बिन के आधार के रूप में किया जाता रहा हो। इन दोनों ही फर्शों पर हाईकंसेन्ट्रेटेड जोन के बीच बलुए पत्थर के रबर्स, सिल, लोढ़े, हैमरस्टोन, निहाई, चर्ट, चल्सिडनी, अगेट के टुकड़े अर्धनिर्मित उपकरण रिंगस्टोन के टुकड़े भारी संख्या में मिले हैं। जो पुरास्थल पर उपकरणों के निर्माण और फूडप्रोसेसिंग के संकेत माने जा सकते हैं। (मिश्रा एवं क्लार्क 1983 : 251–59) इस पुरास्थल के फर्श 2 बी से बाघोर II तथा चोपनी–माण्डों की तरह अर्धवृत्ताकार या वृत्ताकार झोपड़ियों के स्तम्भगर्त भी मिले हैं।

इस पुरास्थल से प्राप्त मध्य पाषाणिक उपकरणों में एक विकासात्मक क्रम भी परिलक्षित होता है। इस पुरास्थल के स्तर 4 से प्राप्त उपकरण आकार में बड़े हैं जो अधिकांश चर्ट पर बने हैं (आई.ए.आर. 1966–67 : 38)। स्तर 3 से प्राप्त उपकरण भी अधिकांशतया चर्ट पर ही बने हैं, लेकिन इनका आकार अपेक्षाकृत छोटा हो जाता है। इस पुरास्थल के स्तर 2 व स्तर 1 से प्राप्त उपकरण मध्य पाषाण काल की प्रारम्भिक अवस्था से ही सम्बन्धित

दिखायी पड़ते हैं। लेकिन स्तर 4 से स्तर 1 तक उपकरण आकार में क्रमशः छोटे होते जाते हैं तथा उपकरणों के निर्माण में प्रयुक्त चर्ट पत्थर का प्रतिशत कम होता जाता है। इस प्रकार इस पुरास्थल के उत्खनन से उच्चपुरापाषाणिक संस्कृति में मध्य पाषाणिक संस्कृति के परिवर्तित होने की प्रक्रिया पर स्पष्ट प्रकाश पड़ा है।

उद्‌भव और तिथिक्रम : बेलन तथा सोन नदियों के भूतात्विक जमाव तथा चोपनी–माण्डो, लेखहिया, बाघोर II और बांकी नामक पुरास्थलों के उत्खनन से न केवल मध्यपाषाणिक संस्कृति के विभिन्न चरण प्रकाशित हुए हैं बल्कि इस संस्कृति के उद्‌भव और कालानुक्रम पर भी महत्वपूर्ण प्रकाश पड़ा है।

उपलब्ध साक्ष्यों के आलोक में हम कह सकते हैं कि विन्ध्य क्षेत्र में मध्य पाषाणिक संस्कृति का विकास एक लम्बी और सतत् विकास प्रक्रिया थी। हमारे पास पर्याप्त आधार हैं जिनके आलोक में हम यह कह सकते हैं कि विन्ध्य क्षेत्र की मध्य पाषाणिक संस्कृति का विकास इसी क्षेत्र की पूर्ववर्ती उच्चपुरापाषाणिक संस्कृति से हुआ (मिश्रा 2002 : 447–64)। बेलन नदी अनुभाग 10 इकाइयों में विभाजित है। इस भूतात्विक जमाव में निम्न पुरापाषाण काल से लेकर मध्य पाषाण काल तक संस्कृतियों का क्रमिक विकास दिखायी पड़ता है। बेलन के II स्तर 1 ग्रेवेल से उच्च पुरापाषाणिक उपकरण प्राप्त होते हैं। III ग्रेवेल के ऊपरी जमाव के उच्च पुरापाषाण काल के ब्लेड तथा मध्यपाषाण काल के अज्यामितीय उपकरण प्राप्त हुए हैं। अर्थात् यह जमाव उच्च पुरापाषाण काल और मध्यपाषाण काल के बीच एक संक्रमणात्मक अवस्था का द्योतन करता है। इस जमाव के ऊपर के दो मिट्‌टी के जमावों से भी मध्य पाषाणिक उपकरण प्राप्त हुए हैं, जो उक्त संस्कृति के क्रमिक विकास को दर्शाते हैं। सोन के भूतात्विक जमाव से प्राप्त साक्ष्य भी उपरोक्त बातों का समर्थन करते हैं। सोन के भूतात्विक जमाव बागोर के निचले रूक्ष वर्ग से उच्चपुरापाषाणिक उपकरण मिलते हैं जबकि ऊपरी महीन वर्ग अनुपुरापाषाणिक तथा मध्य पाषाणिक उपकरणों का प्रतिनिधित्व करता है। इस प्रकार यहाँ भी बिना किसी व्यवधान के उच्च पुरापाषाण काल तथा मध्य पाषाण काल के बीच विकास का सतत् अनुक्रम दिखायी पड़ता है।

नदियों के भूतात्विक जमावों से इस क्षेत्र की मध्य पाषाणिक संस्कृति के उद्‌भव एवं विकास सम्बन्धी प्राप्त जानकारी का समर्थन इस क्षेत्र के महत्वपूर्ण पुरास्थल चोपनी–माण्डो, लेखहिया, बाघोर II और बाँकी के उत्खनन से भी होता है। यहाँ पर मध्य पाषाणिक उद्योग परम्परा में एक विकास क्रम परिलक्षित होता है। उपकरण आकार में क्रमशः छोटे होते जाते हैं। उपकरणों के निर्माण की तकनीक, प्रकार तथा इनके निर्माण में प्रयुक्त सामग्री में भी विकासात्मक क्रम परिलक्षित होता हैं। इन पुरास्थलों के अन्तिम धरातल से प्राप्त उपकरण उच्च पुरापाषाण काल और मध्य पाषाण काल के बीच की संक्रमणात्मक अवस्था का अभिद्योतन करते हैं। उदाहरणार्थ : चोपनी–माण्डो (फेज–1) बगहीखोर (लेयर 4), लेखहिया के ओपेन एयर साइट के सबसे नीचे की लेयर से प्राप्त उपकरण, ग्रेवेल जमाव IV बेलन नदी अनुभाग, बाघोर II लेयर 3, मेढ़ौली लेयर 5 और बाँकी लेयर 5 से प्राप्त उपकरण विशेष रूप से उल्लेखनीय हैं। इन स्तरों में प्राप्त उपकरणों के निर्माण में अधिकांशतया चर्ट पत्थर प्रयुक्त हैं। लेकिन इनके ऊपरी स्तरों में प्राप्त लघु पाषाण उपकरणों के निर्माण में नानचर्टी मेटेरियल यथा–अगेट, चल्सिडनी, कार्नेलियन आदि का प्रतिशत बढ़ने लगता है।

बेलन नदी अनुभाग में लघुपाषाण तृतीय ग्रेवेल के ऊपरी जमाव से सोन के बाघोर जमाव के ऊपरी महीन वर्ग से सतना जिले के मैहर (मिश्रा एवं पाण्डेय 1977) से अन्तिम भूतात्विक जमाव से प्राप्त हुए हैं जो इस क्षेत्र की मध्य पाषाणिक संस्कृति के कालानुक्रम को काफी पीछे ले जाने को विवश करते हैं। पुरास्थलों के उत्खनन से प्राप्त साक्ष्य भी इस क्षेत्र की मध्य पाषाणिक संस्कृति के दीर्घ जीवन का संकेत करते हैं।

विन्ध्य क्षेत्र की मध्यपाषाणिक संस्कृति के कालक्रम के निर्धारणार्थ तीन तिथियाँ हमारा ध्यानाकर्षण करती हैं। सोन घाटी के बाघोर II से एक रेडियाकार्बन तिथि प्राप्त है जिसका समयामान 6380 $\pm$ 200 है (पॉषेल एवं रिजमैन 1992)। मिर्जापुर जिले के लेखहिया शिलाश्रय 1 से दो ए0एम0एस0 रेडियोकार्बन तिथियाँ भी प्राप्त हैं जिनका समयमान क्रमशः 6420 $\pm$ 75 ई0पू0 और 6050 $\pm$ 75 ई0पू0 है। (लुकास एवं अन्य 1996) इन तिथियों के आलोक में हम कह सकते हैं कि इस क्षेत्र में मध्य पाषाणिक संस्कृति का उद्‌भव नूतनकाल के पहले चरण में हुआ।

आजीविका के साधन : प्रागैतिहासिक संस्कृतियों के विकास के क्रम में मध्यपाषाणिक मानव का जीवन और अर्थव्यवस्था एक ऐसे विशिष्ट तथा संक्रमणात्क अवस्था का प्रतिनिधित्व करती है जब मानव आखेट और संग्रह का जीवन यापन करते हुये एक ऐसी अवस्था में पहुँच गया था जहाँ से एक उत्पादनपरक अर्थव्यवस्था का उदय होता है। इसमें कोई दो राय नहीं कि कृषि और पशुपालन पहली बार मध्यपाषाण काल में ही शुरू हुए जो आगे चलकर नवपाषाणिक मानव की आजीविका से स्थायी रूप से जुड़ जाते हैं (थामस एवं अन्य 1995)।

मध्यपाषाणिक मानव की आजीविका के निर्माणक साक्ष्य (जीव–जन्तुओं तथा वनस्पतियों के अवशेष) विन्ध्य क्षेत्र से यद्यपि बहुत ही सीमित मात्रा में उपलब्ध हुए हैं फिर भी इस क्षेत्र में स्थित पुरास्थलों के सर्वेक्षण तथा

उत्खनन से जो साक्ष्य उपलब्ध हैं उनके समवेत आलोक से स्पष्ट होता है कि विन्ध्य क्षेत्र के मध्यपाषाणिक मानव के जीवन में जंगली पशुओं के शिकार तथा जंगली फलों, कन्दमूल तथा अन्य वनस्पतियों के संग्रह की महत्वपूर्ण भूमिका थी। इस क्षेत्र में स्थित मध्यपाषाणिक पुरास्थलों में मोरहना पहाड़, बगहीखोर, लेखहिया, चोपनी–माण्डो (बेलनघाटी), बाघोर II, घघरिया शिलाश्रय I, कुनझुन II, मेढ़ौली और बाँकी (सोनघाटी) के उत्खनन से जो जीव–जन्तुओं तथा वनस्पतियों के जीवाश्म, लघुपाषाण उपकरण, खाद्योत्पादक उपकरण, अन्य प्रस्तर–उपकरण, मिट्टी के बर्तन, गुफाचित्र आदि मिले हैं उनके विश्लेषण तथा संश्लेषण से हम विन्ध्य क्षेत्र के मानव की आजीविका का अनुमान लगा सकते हैं। विन्ध्यक्षेत्र में लेखहिया शिलाश्रय 1 के उत्खनन में प्रो0 वी0डी0 मिश्रा को हड्डी निर्मित प्वाइन्टस तथा जानवरों की हड्डियों के टुकड़े प्राप्त हुये थे जिन पर काटने तथा प्रयोग के निशान विद्यमान हैं। इसी प्रकार प्रो0 बी0बी0 मिश्रा ने चोपनी–मण्डो के फेज II बी से झोपड़ियों के फर्श पर बिखरे हड्डी के कुछ टुकड़े को प्रतिवेदित किया था।[40] साथ ही साथ चोपनी–माण्डो के फेज III से गर्त चूल्हों में भी भारी मात्रा में हड्डियों के टुकड़े मिले हैं जो विन्ध्य क्षेत्र के मानव के जीवन में आखेट की भूमिका को रेखांकित करते हैं। सोनघाटी में स्थित पुरास्थलों में केवल कुनझुन II से जानवरों की हड्डियाँ मिली हैं जिनमें विशेष प्रकार का फ्रैक्चर है। ऐसा प्रतीत होता है कि इन्हें फाड़–चीरकर मज्जा निकाल लिया गया है। जिन जानवरों की पहचान की गयी है उसमें जंगली मवेशी, हिरण तथा चौसिंगा है। यहाँ से प्राप्त कुछ हड्डियों मे कटे के निशान भी हैं। इनसे संकेत मिलता है कि इस पुरास्थल से सम्बन्धित मध्य पाषाणिक मानव की आजीविका में जंगली पशुओं के शिकार की महत्वपूर्ण भूमिका थी। उपरोक्त पुरास्थलों भारी मात्रा में लघुपाषाण उपकरण प्रतिवेदित हैं जिनका उपयोग संयुक्त उपकरण बनाकर किया जाता था। इस काल के महत्वपूर्ण उपकरण धनुषबाण, बरछे अथवा भाले और हंसिया थे। लघुपाषाण उपकरणों की भारी मात्रा में उपस्थिति भी अप्रत्यक्ष रूप से इनके जीवन में आखेट की महत्वपूर्ण भूमिका को दर्शाते हैं।

चूँकि शिकार करना एक खतरे का काम था; इसलिए उन क्षेत्रों में जहाँ जंगली फल–फूल विद्यमान थे, मध्यपाषाणिक मानव की निर्भरता उन पर बढ़ती गयी। यह विश्वास किया जाता है कि जंगली फल–फूलों की सहज उपलब्धता ने लोगों को स्थायी–जीवन की ओर प्रेरित किया। इस संदर्भ में विन्ध्यक्षेत्र के चोपनी–माण्डो नामक पुरास्थल का उल्लेख आवश्यक है। इस पुरास्थल पर मध्यपाषाणिक मानव काफी पहले से ही स्थायी जीवन शुरू कर देता है। इस बात का संकेत इस पुरास्थल से प्राप्त अण्डाकार तथा गोलाकार झोपड़ियों, चूल्हों, स्टोरेज पिट, स्टोरेज विन्स तथा भारी मात्रा में प्राप्त प्रस्तर निर्मित रिंगस्टोन, सिल–लोढ़े आदि की उपस्थिति से होता है। खाद्य–संग्रह के साक्ष्य के संदर्भ में चोपनी–माण्डो विशेष रूप से उल्लेखनीय है क्योंकि इस पुरास्थल के फेज III से जहाँ एक ओर पकी मिट्टी के टुकड़ों में चावल की भूसी/दाने मिले हैं वही दूसरी ओर मध्य गंगाघाटी की तरह (दमदमा) स्टोरेज पिट तथा झोपड़ियों के समीप कुछ गोलाकार/अण्डकार संरचनायें भी मिली हैं। ऐसा प्रतीत होता है कि ये सम्भवतः बाँस तथा मिट्टी से बने संग्रह–पात्रों के आधार थे। इस प्रकार यहाँ से प्राप्त साक्ष्य इंगित करते हैं कि यहाँ के मध्यपाषाणिक मानव के जीवन में जंगली खाद्यान्न (चावल, ओरिजा, निवारा, ओरिजारफिगोना), फलों तथा वनस्पतियों ने अपनी महत्वपूर्ण भूमिका अदा की। यहाँ के फेज 3 से प्राप्त जंगली चावल तथा मृदभाण्ड के साक्ष्यों से यहाँ के मध्यपाषाणिक मानव की अर्थव्यवस्था अधिक सुरक्षित तथा विकसित दिखायी पड़ती है।

विन्ध्य क्षेत्र के विभिन्न पुरास्थलों से लघुपाषाण उपकरणों के साथ कुछ खाद्योत्पादक उपकरण भी प्राप्त हैं जो अप्रत्यक्ष रूप से यहाँ के लोगों की खाद्य–संग्राहक अर्थव्यवस्था की ओर संकेत करते हैं। इन उपकरणों में मुख्यतः सिल–लोढ़े उल्लेखनीय हैं जिनका उपयोग संग्रहीत अनाज, जड़ों तथा कंद आदि को कूटने और पीसने के लिए किया गया होगा। इन पुरास्थलों से जो सिल–लोढ़े प्राप्त हैं उन पर प्रयोग के निशान स्पष्टतः देखे जा सकते हैं। इन पुरास्थलों से रिंग–स्टोन, स्लिंग बाल, हैमर–स्टोन, आदि पत्थर के औजार प्रकाशित हैं जिनकी भूमिका शायद मानव की आजीविका से ही सम्बन्धित रही होगी। उक्त साक्ष्यों के आलोक में हम यह कहने की स्थिति में है कि आखेट के साथ–साथ जंगली धान्य तथा फलों के संग्रह ने भी मध्यपाषाणिक मानव की आजीविका में अपना महत्वपूर्ण योगदान दिया।

मध्यपाषाणिक मानव की आजीविका के साक्ष्य विन्ध्यक्षेत्र में स्थित अनेक शिलाश्रयों से भी प्राप्त हैं। इन शिलाश्रयों के कतिपय चित्रों के वर्ण्यविषय मध्यपाषाणिक मानव की आजीविका से सम्बन्धित है। शैलचित्र मुख्यतः पशुवर्ग से सम्बन्धित हैं जिनमें अधिकांशतया उन पशुओं का चित्रण किया गया है जिनका वे शिकार करते रहे होंगे। पशुओं के अतिरिक्त उनके दैनिक जीवन से सम्बन्धित झांकी भी शैलचित्रों में दिखायी पड़ती है। इन चित्रों में आखेट के विविध दृश्य, मधुसंग्रह तथा नृत्य के दृश्य विशेष रूप से उल्लेखनीय हैं। विन्ध्य क्षेत्र में स्थित शिलाश्रयों से प्राप्त चित्रों का अध्ययन इलाहाबाद विश्वविद्यालय के प्राचीन इतिहास विभाग ने किया है। ये शिलाचित्र पाँच वर्गों में विभाजित हैं जिनमें से प्रथम से लेकर चौथे स्तर तक के सम्बन्धित शिलाचित्र मध्यपाषाण काल से सम्बन्धित है। इनका सूक्ष्म विश्लेषण भी मध्यपाषाणिक मानव की आखेट और खाद्य संग्राहक अर्थव्यवस्था को प्रमाणित करता है।

इस हाल के कुछ वर्षों में प्रस्तर–निर्मित पुरावशेषों की माइक्रोवीयर स्टडी आधारित प्रागैतिहासिक संस्कृतियों का अध्ययन काफी लोकप्रिय हो रहा है। इस संदर्भ में उल्लेखनीय है कि आरेगान विश्वविद्यालय के नृतत्व शास्त्र विभाग ने विन्ध्यक्षेत्र (लेखहिया) तथा गंगाघाटी से प्राप्त लघुपाषाण उपकरणों की माइक्रोवीयर स्टडी की है।

माइक्रोवीयर एनालिसिस के लिए जो माइक्रोस्कोप प्रयोग में लाया जाता है वह उपकरण के स्वरूप को 50 गुणा सम्वर्धित कर देता है जिससे उपकरणों के कार्यांग के क्षतिग्रस्त होने, रेखांकन (Striation) उनके प्रयोग के दिग्(विन्यास, कार्योगों के गोलमटोल एवं तीक्ष्ण होने तथा इनके ऊपर भी पालिश को स्पष्ट रूप से देखा जा सकता है। विन्ध्य क्षेत्र तथा गंगाघाटी के मध्यपाषाणिक लघुपाषाण उपकरणों के माइक्रोवीयर एनालसिस से ज्ञात होता है कि इनका उपयोग खुरचने, चीरने, काटने, छिद्र करने तथा खाँचा बनाने में किया गया था। इन उपकरणों की एनालसिस से उन पदार्थों की भी जानकारी प्राप्त की गयी है जिन पर इनका प्रयोग किया गया था। इस अध्ययन से भी विन्ध्य क्षेत्र के मध्य पाषाणिक मानव की आजीविका शिकार तथा वन्य खाद्य के संग्रह पर आधारित दिखायी पड़ती है जैसा कि अन्य पुरातात्विक अवशेषों तथा जैव पुरातत्वीय अध्ययन से स्पष्ट है।

उपसंहार : इस प्रकार हम देखते हैं कि विन्ध्यक्षेत्र की प्राकृतिक पृष्ठभूमि में अनेक जंगली जानवर यथा–हिरण, चौसिंगा, नीलगाय, खरगोश आदि तथा वन्यखाद्य यथा मीठे फल, कन्द, जड़ें तथा अनाज मौजूद थे जिनके शिकार तथा संग्रह पर आधारित एक स्वस्थ जीवन यापन करते हुए मध्यपाषाणिक मानव ने इस क्षेत्र की नवपाषाणिक संस्कृति के उदभव एवं विकास के लिए एक मजबूत एवं प्रशस्त पृष्ठभूमि तैयार की।

संदर्भ

1. वाडिया डी0एन0, 1973, द विन्ध्यन सिस्टम, जियोलॉजी आफ इण्डिया, नई दिल्ली।
2. तिवारी, ए0 आर0, 1971, जियोग्राफी ऑफ उत्तर प्रदेश, नई दिल्ली।
3. पन्त, पी0 सी0, प्रीहिस्टारिक उत्तर प्रदेश, दिल्ली।
4. सिंह, के0 ए0 सदर्न अपलैण्ड ऑफ यू0 पी0 ए स्टडी इन लैण्डफार्म एण्ड लैण्ड सेटलमेंट डिस्ट्रीपुलेशन, पीएच0 डी0 शोधग्रन्थ (अप्रकाशित), बी0 एच0 यू0 वाराणसी।
5. मिश्रा, वी0डी0, 1977, प्री हिस्ट्री इन उत्तर प्रदेश, सम आसपेक्टस ऑफ इण्डियन आर्क्यालॉजी, प्रभात प्रकाशन, इलाहाबाद।
6. विलियम, एम0 ए0 जे0 एण्ड के0 रास, 1983, एल्यूवियल हिस्ट्री ऑफ मिडिल सोन वैली, नार्थ सेन्ट्रल इण्डिया, जी0 आर0 शर्मा एण्ड जे0 डी0 क्लार्क (सम्पादक), पेलियो इन्वायरमेन्ट एण्ड प्री हिस्ट्री इन मिडिल सोन वैली, पृष्ठ 9–21, अविनाश प्रकाशन, इलाहाबाद।
7. आलूर के0 आर0, 1980 फॉनल रिमेन्स फ्राम विन्ध्याज एण्ड द गंगा वैली, जी0 आर0 शर्मा और अन्य द्वारा लिखित, विगनिंग्स ऑफ एग्रीकल्चर, प्राचीन इतिहास संस्कृति एवं पुरातत्व विभाग इलाहाबाद विश्वविद्यालय इलाहाबाद।
8. सांकलिया, एच0 डी0, 1974, प्रीहिस्ट्री एण्ड प्रोटोहिस्ट्री ऑफ इण्डिया एण्ड पाकिस्तान, डकन कालेज, पूना।
9. मिश्रा, वी0 डी0 और जे0 एन0 पाल (सम्पादक), 2002 मेसोलिथिक इण्डिया, प्राचीन इतिहास, संस्कृति एवं पुरातत्व विभाग इलाहाबाद विश्वविद्यालय इलाहाबाद।
10. शर्मा0 जी0 आर0 और जे0 डी0 क्लार्क (सम्पादक), 1983, पेलियो इन्वायरमेंट एण्ड प्रीहिस्ट्री इन मिडिल सोन वैली, इलाहाबाद।
11. शर्मा जी0 आर0 और वी0 बी0 मिश्रा, 1980, एक्सकेवेशन एण्ट चोपनी–माण्डो (बेलन वैली), 1977–79, इलाहाबाद, प्राचीन इतिहास संस्कृति एवं पुरातत्व विभाग इलाहाबाद विश्वविद्यालय, इलाहाबाद।
12. मिश्रा, वी0 एन0, 1965, मेसोलिथिक, इन द प्रीहिस्ट्री ऑफ इण्डिया, इण्डियन फेज प्रीहिस्ट्री 1964, (वी0 एन0 मिश्रा और एम0 एस0 माटे, सम्पादक), पूना, डकन कालेज।
13. मिश्रा, वी0 डी0 1977, प्रीहिस्ट्री इन उत्तर प्रदेश, सम असपेक्टस ऑफ इण्डियन आर्क्यालॉजी, पेज–52, प्रभात प्रकाशन, दिल्ली।
14. वर्मा, आर0 के0, 1986 द मेसोलिथिक एज इन मिर्जापुर, पेज 9–14 परमज्योति प्रकाशन, इलाहाबाद।
15. मिश्रा, वी0 डी0, 2007, स्टोन एज कल्चर्स, देयर क्रोनोलॉजी एण्ड बिगनिंग ऑफ एग्रीकल्चर इन द नार्थ सेन्ट्रल इण्डिया, मैन एण्ड इन्वायरमेन्ट, नं0 32 पेज 1–14
16. मिश्रा, बी0 बी0, 2000, मेसोलिथिक कल्चर ऑफ बेलन बैली, इन मेसोलिथिक इण्डिया, (वी0 डी0 मिश्रा और जे0 एन0 पाल, सम्पादक), प्राचीन इतिहास संस्कृति एवं पुरातत्व विभाग, इलाहाबाद विश्वविद्यालय, इलाहाबाद।
17. लुकास, जे0 आर0 और जे0 एन0 पाल, 1993, मेसोलिथिक सबसिस्टेंस इन नार्थ इण्डिया इन्फेरेन्स फ्राम डेन्टल एट्रीब्यूट्स, करेंट एन्थ्रोलॉजी नं0 34 (5) पेज 745–765।
18. मिश्रा, वी0 बी0 एण्ड जे0 डी0 क्लार्क, 1983, कन्टेम्पोरेरी, एबान्डोन्ड सेटलर्स एण्ड टेम्पोरेरी कैम्पसः सम इम्प्लीकेशन्स फॉर एथनो–आर्क्योलॉजिकल इन्टरप्रटेशन, इन पेलियो इन्वायरमेन्ट एण्ड प्रीहिस्ट्री इन द मिडिल सोन वैली (मध्य प्रदेश, नार्थ सेन्ट्रल इण्डिया), जी0 आर0 शर्मा एण्ड जे डी0 क्लार्क सम्पादक, पृष्ठ 251–259, अविनाश प्रकाशन, इलाहाबाद।
19. क्लार्क, जे0 डी0 और एम0 ए0 जे0 विलियम, 1990 प्रीहिस्टारिक इकोलॉजी, रिसोर्स स्ट्रेटजीज एण्ड कल्चर चेन्ज इन द सोन वैली, नार्दन मध्य प्रदेश, सेन्ट्रल इण्डिया, मैन एण्ड इन्वायरमेन्ट XII (I): पेज 13–17
20. क्लार्क जे0 डी0 एण्ड जी0 एस0 खन्ना, 1989, द साइट आफ कुनझुन II मिडिल सोन वैली एण्ड इट्स रिलिवेन्स फार द नियोलिथिक ऑफ सेन्ट्रल इण्डिया, इन ओल्ड प्राब्लम्स एण्ड न्यू पर्सपेक्टिव्स इन द आर्कियोलॉजी ऑफ साउथ एशिया, (जे0 एम0 केन्वायर सम्पादक), पेज 29–46, विसकान्सिन आर्कियोलॉजिकल रिपोर्ट नं0 – 2, माडिसन एफ0 एण्ड एच0 प्रिटिंग कम्पनी।

21. मिश्रा, वी0 डी0, 2002, ओरिजिन क्रोनोलॉजी एण्ड ट्रांसफारमेशन आफ द मेसोलिथिक कल्चर इन इण्डिया, इन मेसोलिथिक इण्डिया वी0 डी0 मिश्रा और जे0 एन0 पाल, (सम्पादक), पेज 447–64, प्राचीन इतिहास, संस्कृति एवं पुरातत्व विभाग, इलाहाबाद विश्वविद्यालय, इलाहाबाद।
22. मिश्रा, वी0 डी0 एण्ड जे0 एन0 पाण्डेय, 1977 माइक्रोलिथ इण्डस्ट्री ऑफ मैहर, सतना, मध्य प्रदेश, मैन एण्ड इन्वायरमेन्ट, पेज 61–631
23. पॉशेल, जी0 एल0 और रिजमैन, 1992, द क्रोनोलॉजी ऑफ द प्रीहिस्टारिक इण्डिया फ्राम अर्लिस्ट टाइम टू द आयरन एज, इन क्रोनोलॉजी इन ओल्ड वर्ल्ड आर्कियोलॉजी, (आर0 डब्लू एरिच, सम्पादक) पेज–447–66, शिकागो।
24. लुकास, जे0 आर, वी0 डी0 मिश्रा और जे0 एन0 पाल, 1996, क्रोनोलॉजी एण्ड डाइट इन मेसोलिथिक नार्थ इण्डिया, ए प्रीमिलिनरी रिपोर्ट ऑफ न्यू AMSCI14 डेट्स एस–सी[13] आइसोटोप वैल्यूज एण्ड देयर सिग्नीफिकेन्स इन वायोआर्क्यालॉजी आफ मेसोलिथिक इण्डियाः एन इन्ट्रेगल एप्रोच, कोलोक्वियम, XXXIII आफ द इण्टरनेशनल यूनियन ऑफ प्रीहिस्टारिक एण्ड प्रोटोहिस्टारिक साइंसेस, जे0 आर0 लुकास और एम0 तोषी सम्पादक, पेज 301–311,फोर्लीः ABACO एडिजियोनी।
25. थामस पी0 के0, पी0 पी0 जोगलेकर, वी0 डी0 मिश्राा, जे0 एन0 पाण्डेय एण्ड जे0 एन0 पाल, 1995, ए प्रीमिलिनरी रिपोर्ट आफ द फानेल रिमेन्स फ्राम द दमदमा, मैन एण्ड इन्वायरमेन्ट XX(I) पेज–29–36।
26. लुकास, जे0 आर0, और वी0 डी0 मिश्रा, 1997, द पीपुल आफ लेखहिया बायोआर्कियोजालिकल एनालिसिस आफ लेट मेसोलिथिक हन्टर फोरेजर्स आफ नार्थ इण्डिया, इन साउथ एशियन आर्कियोलॉजी, (बी0 अल्चिन सम्पादक), पेज 873–889, न्यू देहली, आक्सफोर्डः आई बी0 एच0 पब्लिशर्स।
27. पाल, जे0 एन0, 1996–97, माइक्रोवीयर स्टडीज ऑफ माइक्रोलिथ्स ऑफ द मेसोलिथिक नार्थ इण्डिया, प्रीलिमिनरी रिपोर्ट आन मेथड्स एण्ड रिजल्ट्स, प्राग्धारा 7, पेज 1–9।
28. थामस, पी0 के0, पी0 पी0 जोगलेकर, वी0 डी0 मिश्रा, जे0 एन0 पाण्डेय एण्ड जे0 एन0 पाल, 1996 फौनेल रिमेन्स फार द मेसोलिथिक फूड इकोनॉमी आफ द गंगेटिक प्लेन विद स्पेशल रिफरेन्स टू दमदमा इन बायोआर्कियोलाजी आफ मेसोलिथिक इण्डियाः एन इंटेग्रेल एप्रोच, कोलोक्वियम ग्ग्प्प आफ द इन्टरनेशनल यूनियन आफ प्रीहिस्ट्रारिक एण्ड प्रोटोहिस्टारिक साइसेंज, पेज 255–256, फोर्ली ए0वी0ए0सी0ओ, एडिजियोनि।

15

ARCHAEOLOGY OF BHRIGU KSHETRA
(With special reference of Waina)

Santosh Kumar Singh

Introduction

Bhrigu Kshetra, presently known as Ballia is the eastern most part of Uttar Pradesh which lies between 25^0 33" and 26^0 11" North latitude and 83^0 38" and 84^0 39'' East longitudes. In ancient times the region covered by the present district of Ballia lay in the kingdom of Kosala. It is probable that the river *Ganga*, in its sweep towards the north-east of present town of Ballia, formed the boundary of Kosala which included the whole of the present Ballia district as far as the junction of the *Sadanira* and the Great *Gandak* (Pathak. 1963: 19). The back-strewn mounds and fragmentary remains of structural character, which evoke memories not only of mythology but also of history, are found at a number of places in the district.

Ballia was recognized as a district on Nov. 1st, 1879 in eastern Uttar Pradesh. Total geographical area of the district is 2981 sq. km. The District headquarter is Ballia containing six Tehsils namely Ballia Sadar, Bansdih, Rasara, Belthara, Bairia and Sikanderpur. Blocks in the district are seventeen in number. Ballia is served by the North-Eastern Railway. It lies on the main line of the Chhapra-Varanasi section of the North-Eastern Railway passing through Aurihar, Ghazipur, Phephana and Ballia. A branch line runs from Phephana (Ballia district) to Shahganj (Jaunpur district). The north-western part of the district is served by the Bhatni-Aurihar-Allhabad section passing through Indara, Mau, Aurihar, Varanasi and Madho Singh. Metalled roads connect Ballia with Ghosi, Mau and Ghazipur.

Geographical scenario

Bhrigu Kshetra comprises an irregularly shaped tract extending westward from the confluence of the *Ganga* and the *Ghaghara*, the former separating it from Bihar in the south and the latter from Deoria and Bihar in the north and east respectively (Singh. 1973: 20). The boundary between the region and Bihar is determined by the deep streams of these two rivers. It is bounded on the west by Azamgarh, on the north by Deoria, on the north-east and south-east by Bihar and on the south-west by Ghazipur (Singh. 1973: 24). Physiographic-ally, the area can be divided into two units:

(i) Central uplands region, and

(ii) Lower land tract along the river *Ganga* and the *Ghaghara* (Singh. 1965: 165).

The uplands comprise the eastern half of the district comprising almost the whole of Rasra tehsil and a small strip of country extending eastwards into Bansdih and Ballia tehsils. They extend in the south-west up to the river *Saryu*. In the interior, the level is only broken by scattered depressions. The low-land tract comprises the rest of the district. The surface of the lowland is often very uneven, being scored in every direction by irregular depressions. Main source of irrigation in the district is through ground water irrigation and canals. For drinking water supply pipe line schemes and hand pumps exist in the district.

Water resources

The chief rivers of the district are the *Ganga*, the *Ghaghara* and the *Saryu.* The *Ghaghara* and the *Ganga* cause extensive floods in the district causing loss of life, property and standing crops (Singh. 1973: 27). The tributaries of the *Ghaghara* are small and of an insignificant character. The chief tributary of the *Ganga* is the *Saryu,* which for several miles separate Ballia from Ghazipur (Singh. 1986: 345). Lakes and tanks are fairly common, the most important being the *Suraha Tal* because of its size (8,500 acres). Among other lakes of considerable importance are *Taleji Tal, Goka Tal, Dah Mundiari, Dah Reoti* etc.

Agriculture

Agriculture was the mainstay of the economy of our research area and the concept of cultivating two crops in a year had already come in practice even in the Neolithic period datable to 5000 BC. Cultivation of rice, wheat, barley, various types of millets, several types of pulses and oil seeds was done in the Neolithic stage. Agriculture had taken deep roots in the middle Ganga plain by about 2000 BC. This resulted into the production of adequate surplus which could sustain different categories of artisans, so essential for the growth of a city.

Metal

The technological advancement of the second millennium BC was also impressive. While copper was in use in circa 1900 BC, the properties of iron as the principal metal of daily use were truly understood by the people around 1300 BC. These two factors helped in the growth of large villages, a few of them had the potential of becoming small towns.

Historical Background

The early political history of this region is complex. According to the Puranic tradition the solar dynasty of Kṣatriyas, founded by one Manu, was the earliest known dynasty which gave Kosala a systematic form of government and of which Ikṣvāku, the eldest son of Manu, famed in Vedic tradition, was the first ruler. The line that descended from Ikṣvāku produced a number of illustrious kings till the accession of Rama who was the greatest ruler of this dynasty. Lakhneswardih, in tehsil Rasra, is named after Lakshmana, the brother of Rama, who is said to have visited this place and built a temple at this spot in honour of Lord Shiva. The remains of an ancient town are still to be seen on the high band of the river in the form of immense piles of ruins, from which numerous pieces of sculptures have been, obtained from time to time which bear testimony to the fact that even in those early times it was a settled abode with a flourishing population. This site was excavated in 1956-57 by K. M. Nagar, Director, State Museum, Lucknow, which yielded NBPW, terracotta figurines, stone pestles etc. (*IAR.* 1956-57:29). Lakshmana's son Chandraketu, entitled Malla (valiant) in the Ramayana, established a kingdom known as the Malla state, of which some portion of this district formed a part. It is probable that the territories of the Mallas touched those of Kashi in the south, Magadha in the south-east and Kosala in the south-west, of which an area of the present day Ballia district then formed a part. It came to be the biggest and the most important of the autonomous states of Kosala in respect of territorial extent and political influence.

Ballia itself is supposed to have derived its name by the eruption of the name Valmiki, that of the great sage who is said to have had his hermitage or to have dwelt here for some time. It is also associated with Bhrigu, another renowned sage who, according to a local legend, came and dwelt here because of the sacredness of the place. Other *Ṛṣi* like Garga, Parasar, Vashishtha and Atri are traditionally believed to have visited the neighbourhood of Ballia attesting to the sacredness of its environs extending to a circuit of about 16 km. According to tradition, Hansnagar (town of swans), a village 9.6 km east of Ballia, is said to taken its name from the legend that a swan turned into a man and a crow into a swan by drinking the water of the holy river *Ganga* at this place. At a distance of about 137 km from Ballia there is an ancient tank named *Dharmāranava* Pokhara where an excavation is said to have revealed that thousands of *Ṛṣi* practiced austerities there and that to the north and east of it there were traces of the previous existence of an ancient forest, probably a remnant of the ancient *aranya*. Some other places of this district are also associated with the Vedic sages. Bhalsand (in tehsil Ballia) is said to have derived its name from Bhardwaja who resided there for sometime and Dhuband (also in tehsil Ballia) to be a corrupt of *Durvasa-āśrama*, signifying the abode of *Durvasa*, a celebrated *Ṛṣi*.

The ruins in the neighbourhood of Brahmain and Hanumanganj, consisting of a large mound called Mira Dih, covered with brick-bats and pottery of a dark hue, are probably the remains of an ancient city. Khairadih, near Turtipar in tehsil Rasra, is also a ruined site of a very ancient city named *Bhargavapur*. It is presumed to have been the place where the *Ṛṣi* Jamadagni lived. The explorations carried out under the auspices of the Banaras Hindu University, Varanasi, have brought to light relics of the black-and-red ware culture (1450-1200 BC) at various sites such as Bhumapardih, Bijulipur, Godabirgaḍh, Lovika-ka-topa, Mira Dih, Pakkākot and Waina, indicating that the tract enjoyed settled life and civilization from this early time.

Popular legends also bear witness to the antiquity of these sites, one such being that of the village of Karon, in tehsil Ballia, its name being considered to be a corruption of the word Kam-anaunya. The legend is that Lord Shiva, being enraged at the attempts of Kamdeo (the god of love) to beguile him from his meditations, burnt him to ashes at this spot (Mishra. 1988: 19).

In the sixth century BC, Kosala came to be known as one of the sixteen Mahajanapadas. At that time it was ruled by the powerful king Mahakosala. His son, Prasenjit the last great monarch of the solar dynasty of Kosala, was an important figure of his time. During his reign the kingdom attained great glory and prosperity. The Malla kingdom also figured as one of the sixteen Mahajanapadas with an independent entity and status equal to that of Kosala itself. Its chief, Bandhula, was a close ally of Prasenjit as well as of Mahali, the Lichchhavi prince of Vaisali. They were deeply influenced by the teachings of two great religious exponents-Mahavira and Buddha and both sramanic sects found many followers among the Mallas. The period gave rise to a different culture, that of the Northern Black Polished ware, as has been revealed by explorations conducted at Ajaneragaḍha, Bhimapurdih, Bijulipur, Godabirgaḍha and Masumpur. After Prasenjit, the kingdom of Kosala began to decline rapidly and the history of this area is shrouded in obscurity.

The existence of numerous ruined forts and other remains in the district connected with the Bhars and the Cherus in legend and folklore point to the fact that they might have held domination over the major part of the region at that time. The Bhars were the occupants of the western part of the region. According to local legend, the heaps of earthen brick-bats in the parganas of Lakhneswar, Bhadaon and Sikandarpur belong to the time of the Bhars. The Cherus probably ruled over the eastern half of the district. Kopachit in tehsil Rasra is believed to have been the western limit of the Cheru dominion. Tradition states that Bansdih lay in the heart of the Cheru country. Though no remains attributable to the group are found in Bansdih itself, the remnants of a fort are in the neighbouring and now almost deserted village of Deorhi. A number of places in the Ballia tehsil are also associated with this group. Karnai is believed to have been originally owned by the Cherus. Garwar is alleged to have been founded by them and a small mound near the village and a large brick mound at Zirabasti are presumed to be the debris of Cheru strongholds. Extensive ruins at Pakkākot are also said to be the debris of a fort and other buildings dating back to the time when the Cherus ruled the district. According to tradition the large inland lake, the *Surha Tal* at Basantpur, was constructed by the Cherus but no traces are found of any artificial construction. The significance of the tradition implies how completely the power of the Cherus has been impressed upon the imagination of the people.

About the middle of the 4th century BC the realm of Kosala was brought to an end by Mahapadma Nanda, who has been described in the Purāṇas as the exterminator of the Kshatriya race and who, by uprooting the Kosalans, extended his empire over the major part of this region. He was the first great historical emperor of northern India. But a part of the district under the Mallas did not come under the domination of this emperor as they saved their authority and existence by merely accepting the supremacy of the Nandas. The Nandas were supplanted by the Mauryas under Chandragupta (324-300 BC) who ruled over a vast empire and the district became a part of the Maurya dominion except for the portion under the Mallas, which remained independent. Kautilya, who took a leading part in this revolution, mentions in his *Arthaśāstra* that this republic was a *Saṁgha*, or a state in a federation. He enjoins upon Chandragupta Maurya to cultivate friendship with the Mallas: *"It is better to have a Samgha on your side than to acquire an army or to secure an ally."* The most illustrious king of this dynasty was Asoka (273-236 BC), Chandragupta's grandson, who became a Buddhist and combined in himself the zeal of a monk with the wisdom of a king. The explorations show the possibility of remains of a stūpa at Matahi, Ballia, and the ruins of Buddhist monasteries here and at Brahmain. The latter has remains of old walls and very large bricks measuring about 45× 23× 11 cm and many carved and ornamental specimens.

With the fall of the Mauryas a new dynasty that of the Sungas, came into power under Pushyamitra (187-151 BC) whose dominion covered only the central portion of the Maurya empire. The fact is confirmed by an inscription found at Ayodhya, describing him as the lord of Kosala. As he uprooted the Malla republic, the whole of the area covered by the district came under his sway. During his reign, the Greeks of Bactria invaded India and it is likely that the district also suffered the effects of the invasion of Menander, who carried his arms for Madhyamika, Saketa and Pataliputra. The history of the district in the era immediately following the fall of the Sungas is shrouded in obscurity till the advent of the Kushanas. That the region became a part of the Kushana dominion is undoubted as evinced by the finding of a large number of coins, mostly of this period, in the ruins of Khairadih. The large bricks (measuring 60× 45× 13 cm) found in the ruins are a witness to the antiquity and the prosperity of the place.

After the dismemberment of the Kushana empire, the history of the region is mostly enveloped in darkness, but a glimpse of the history of the area is provided by a number of inscribed coins found at the ancient city of Ayodhya of certain rulers such as Satyamitra, Ayumitra (or Aryamitra), Sanghamitra, Vijayamitra, Devamitra, Ajavarman and Kumudasena, who appear to have flourished, after the end of the Kushana rule, in what is now eastern Uttar Pradeṣh, including the area then covered by district Ballia. Of these, Kumudasena alone was called a raja. It is surmised that the Guptas, probably Samudragupta, conquered this region and annexed it to the empire in the fourth century AD. During the reign of his son, Chandragupta II (380-413), the celebrated Chinese pilgrim Fa-hien (400-411) came to India to pay homage to the holy places of Buddhism. He mentions that on his way from Kashi to Pataliputra, he came across a Buddhist monastery and a Buddhist temple (in Ballia) which bore the name of 'the vast solitude.' The Indian name is not given but the literal translation of the term used is *Vrihadāraṇya* or *Bidaran*. The decline of the Gupta Empire was precipitated by the assumption of independence by its feudatories. About the beginning of the second quarter of the sixth century, Yashodharman of Malwa overran the whole of northern India and the region seems to have come under his meteoric sovereignty after which it passed under the rule of the Maukharis of Kannauj. They established an empire comprising the whole of modern Uttar Pradesh in addition to a large part of Magadha. Thus the glory of Magadha was eclipsed with the rising power of Kannauj. The Maukharis were succeeded by Harshavardhana (606-647) who established an extensive empire, and the region became a part of the Vardhana empire. During his reign Hiuen-tsang (629-644), another famous Chinese pilgrim, came from China and passed through this district on his way from Varanasi to Nepal. He describes the Buddhist monastery of *Aviddhakarba* which he calls *A-pi-te-ka-la-na saṁgharama* (the monastery of the brethren with unpierced ears) situated close to the town of present Ballia. According to him, this monastery had been built for the use of Buddhist pilgrims. From there he went to the temple of Nārāyaṇa, which he describes as being of two storied with halls and terraces beautifully adorned with the most marvellous sculptures in stone in the highest style of art. Carlleyle identified the ruins of an ancient temple at Narainpur (in tehsil Ballia) with the remains of the temple mentioned above.

After the death of Harsha his empire broke up and anarchy and confusion prevailed for about half a century. The history of Bhrigu region during the interval between Harsha's death and the rise of Yashovarman, nearly three-quarters of a century, is again obscure. He must have reigned in the latter part of the seventh and the first part of the eighth century AD and the region is likely to have formed an integral part of his dominion. After Yashovarman the kingdom of Kannauj (which included modern Uttar Pradesh) was a dependency of the empire of Dharmpala of Bengal, who nominated Chakrayudha as the ruler of Kannauj but who was to be directly subordinate to him. In the first part of the ninth century, probably soon after the capture of Kannauj by Nagbhatta II, it came under the sway of the rising power of the Gurjar Pratiharas among whom Bhoja was the strongest ruler in northern India. He maintained peace in his kingdom and defended it against external dangers but the power of the Gurjara Pratiharas began to decline in the latter half of the tenth century and was brought to an end by Mahmud Ghajni's invasion in 1018 AD. The downfall of the Gurjara Pratiharas was followed by a period of chaos which came to an end only in the last decade of the 11th century by the establishment of the Gahaḍvāla dynasty at Kannauj under Chandradeva. The only reference of this suzerainty is that he was the protector of the holy places of Kashi, Kusika (Kannauj), Uttarakosala (Ayodhya) and the city of Indra (Ancient Delhi). It will thus be seen that Chandradeva's jurisdiction comprised almost the whole of what is now Uttar Pradesh. Therefore, it may be presumed that the present district of Ballia was also under his control. Reference to a Rajput raja of Haldi, Ramdeo, who was installed in the 11th and 12th centuries AD, shows that some parts of the district were subjugated by local chiefs.

Archaeological scenario

Archaeological relics of Bhrigu region push back the permanent settlements of human habitation from Neolithic to medieval period. In spite of rich archaeological wealth and hoary past, the region didn't receive adequate attention of archaeologists. Archaeological investigations in the area were carried out for the first time by A.C.L. Carlleyle who explored a few sites of archaeological importance in 1874-75 under the guidance of Alexander Cunningham. After that A. Fuhrer has done archaeological investigation in the region in 1891 (Fuhrer: 1891) and subsequently by the Department of Ancient Indian History, Culture and Archaeology, Banaras Hindu University, in early sixties and in 1994-95 (*IAR*. 1963-64: 43. Singh and Singh, 1994-95: 21-36). In this connection Black-and-red wares were reported from Bhimapurdih, Bijalipur, Godabirgaḍha, Lovika-Ka-Tapa, Khairadih, Pakkākot and Waina. The same university conducted archaeological excavations at Khairadih, situated on the right bank of the *Ghaghara* in the north-western part of the district during 1980-86 and subsequently in the year 1996-97 (Singh. 1987-88: 28-34. 1990-91: 78-86; Tripathi and Singh. 2003-04: 1-70). The archaeological excavations resulted the deposits of Chalcolithic period to Kushana period.

An ancient settlement named Lakhneshwardih was excavated in 1956-57 by a team of State museum, Lucknow, yielding NBPW, stone pestles, terracotta figurines etc. (*IAR*. 1956-57: 24). An extensive village to village survey was conducted by the Banaras Hindu University in 1993-94 (Singh *et al.* 1994-95: 21-36) and the sites reported were : Janwan, Bhunadih, Alam Ka Tola, Zimi Chak, Chhatarsand, Karsanar, Isar, Pithapatti, Halpur, Deorhi, Muryari, Chandayar (all located in tehsil Bansdih), Waina situated on Ballia-Ghazipur Road, Sihpur and Kurmipur in Ballia Tehsil, Pakkākot, Jagdishpur and Hajauli located on Ballia-Rasara Road, and Tikka Deori, Unai, Lakhaneshwardih and Surwaradih on Ballia-Mau Road. All these sites were reported to be Chalcolithic, NBPW and of historical periods. Among aforesaid sites Waina (1995) and Bhunadih (1996) were excavated. The proto-historic settlement of Waina is situated on the ancient bed of the Chhoti Saryu River. The archaeological excavations conducted in 1994-95 resulted the deposits of Neolithic period to Post-Gupta period ranging in date from pre-second millennium BC to 700 AD (Singh *et al.* 1995-96: 41-61). The archaeological excavation at Bhunadih was conducted in 1996. It is located two km east of Janwan on the right bank of *Bahera Nala*, about 28 km north of Ballia town on the Ballia-Sikanderpur Road. The excavation resulted into two fold cultural sequence from Neolithic to Chalcolithic culture ranging in date from pre-second millennium BC to first millennium BC (Singh *et al.* 1997-98: 11-29).

Waina: archaeological background

The ancient settlement of Waina lies between Ghazipur-Ballia metalled road and the railway line (NER) between Phephna and Ballia. The small railway station of Sagarpali is located about 1.5 km east of Waina. The ancient settlement is spread over an area of 20 acres and the height of the mound from the surrounding plain is about 8 meters. The present-day village of Waina covers a portion of the mound and is located to the north-east of the main site **(Plate 15.1 & Fig.1).**

The excavations at this site were conducted by Purushottam Singh of the Banaras Hindu University during 1994-1995. Fortunately, I was also associated with the excavation for entire season which provided me an occasion to broaden my vision in proto and early historic archaeology. The primary objective of this excavation was to ascertain the culture-sequence at this site and to locate Pre-Narhan and Narhan assemblages, if present (Singh, *et. al.* 1995-96; 41-61).

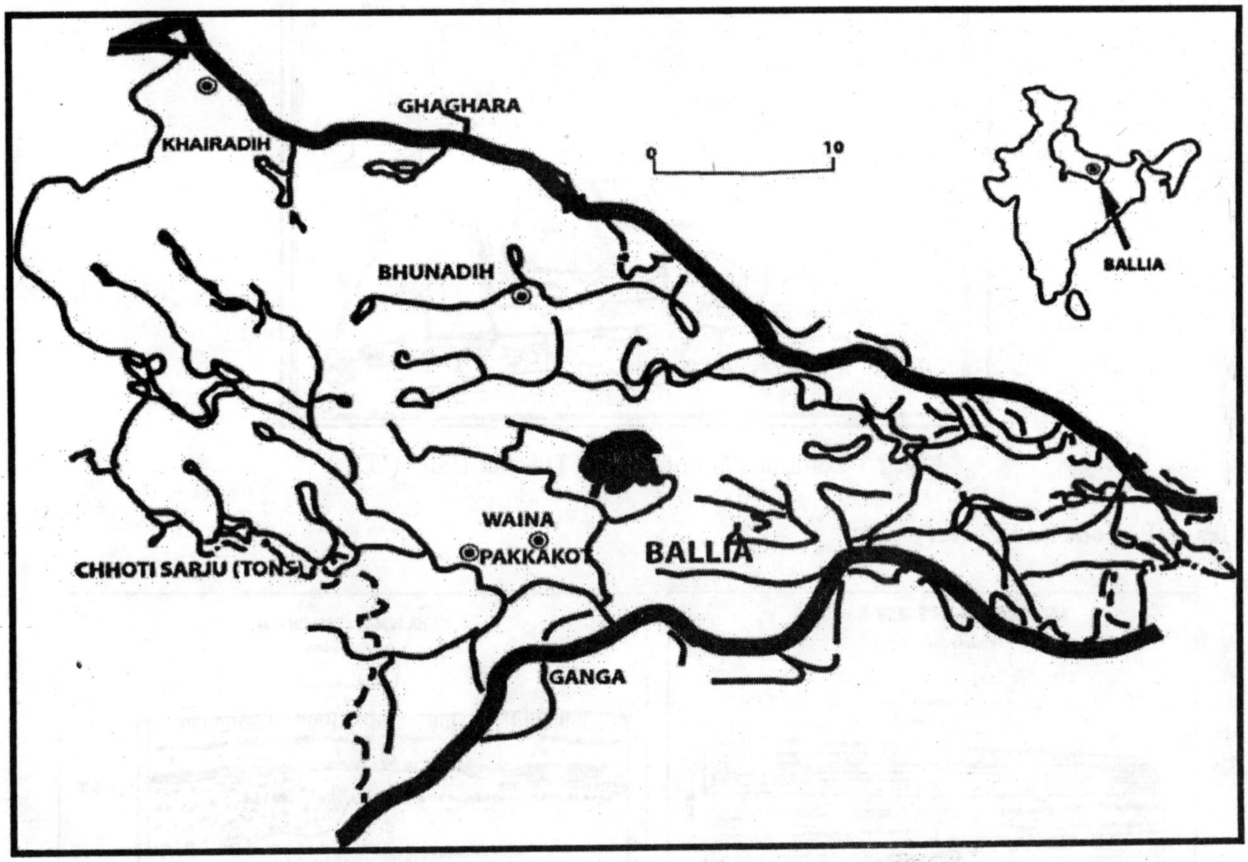

Fig. 1 : Location Map of Waina, District Ballia (U.P.)

The Digging

Vertical digging was conducted at nine places in various parts of the mound as indicated in contour plan **(Fig.2)**. The primary objective of this excavation was to ascertain the culture- sequence at this site and to locate Pre Narhan & Narhan assemblages if present. Of these, one 5 m. × 5 m. trench (tr. AD4) located on the highest part of the mound was dug up-to the natural soil (Fig.2). Besides, five trenches measuring 3m. × 3m. × 3m. each was excavated up-to natural soil on the western periphery of the mound.

The total cultural deposit ranges between 2.5 m to 8 m. A comparative study of stratigraphy of different trenches has revealed the existence of four periods, some of which are further subdivided as follows:

Periods	Settlements	Approximately Dates
Period IA	Neolithic/Pre-Narhan culture	2500BCE-1300BCE
Period IB	Chalcolithic/Narhan Culture	1300BCE-600BCE
Period II	NBPW Culture	600BCE-200BCE
Period III	Sunga-Kushana Period	200BCE-300CE
Period IV	Gupta and post Gupta deposit	300CE-700CE

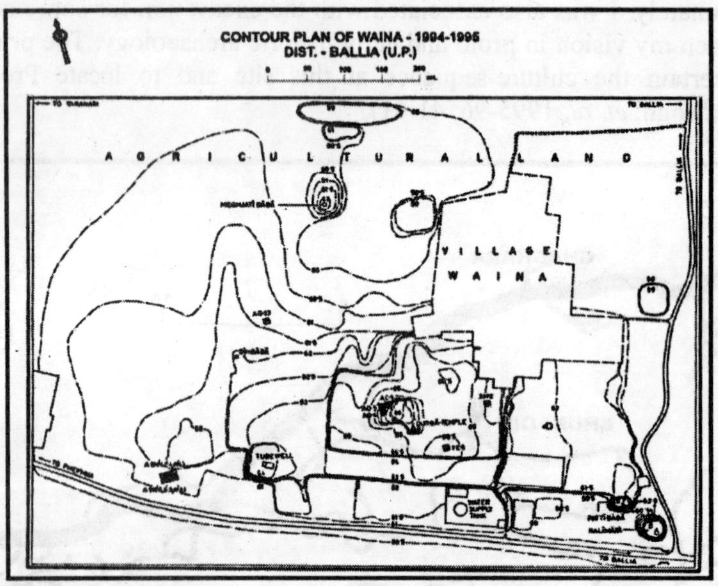

Fig. 2 : Contour Plan of Waina, District Balla (U.P.).

Strata, Periods and Pottery

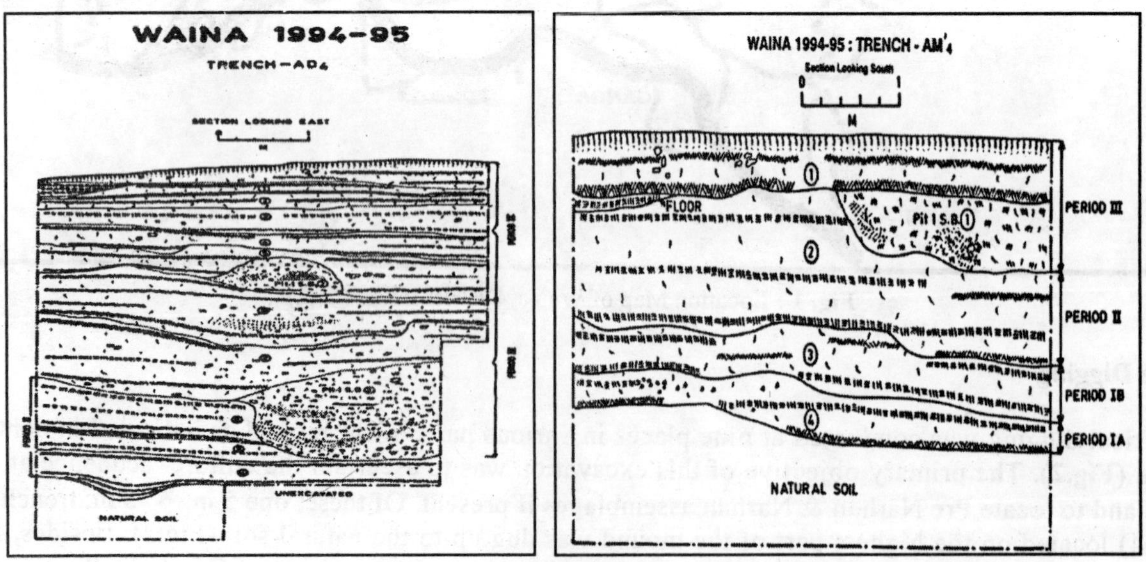

Fig. 3 & 4 : Waina, Section Plan

Period IA

The settlement of this period was found on the south-west corner of the mound. Four 5 m. x 5 m. trenches were excavated in this area which resulted into the identification of two sub-periods, distinguished mainly on the basis of ceramic evidence. Period IA is represented by cord-impressed red ware with spouted vessels, bowls and vases as the principal types. The principal shapes in this ware are straight sided jars with a short spout (*Martban*) and *Lota* shaped vessel. This pottery assemblage is comparable with Pre-Narhan pottery found at Iimlidih khurd located on the left bank of the Kuwana, tributary of the Ghaghara in district Gorakhpur. This sub-period can be tentatively date 2500 B.C. The important shapes are illustrated below: (Singh, 2000-2001:105-107).

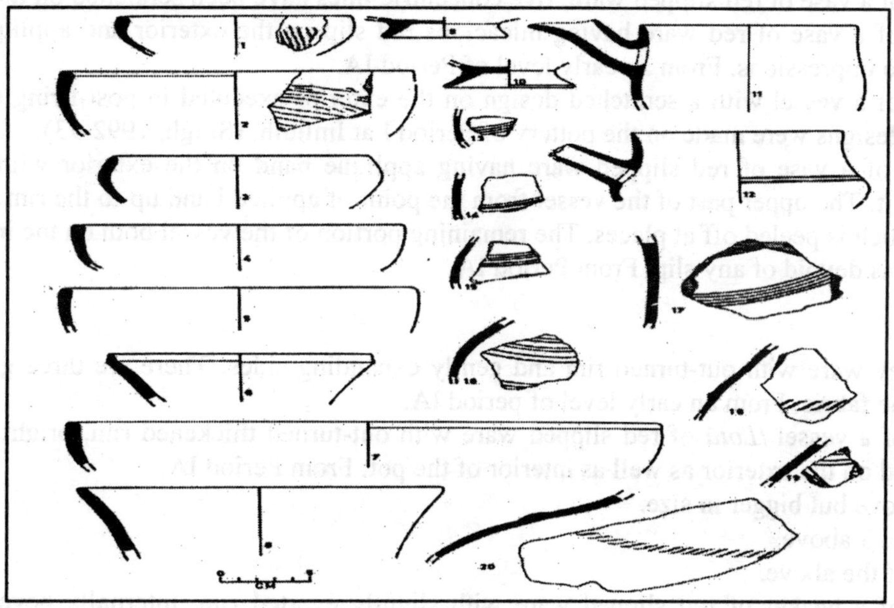

Fig. 5 : Pottery of Period IA

Fig. 5

1. **Bowl of red ware with internally thickened rim, cord-impressions on the exterior, coarse fabric. From an early level of Period IA.**
2. **Fragment of bowl of red ware with incurved internally thickened rim, cord-impressions on the exterior. The section has smoky grey colour. From an early level of Period IA.**
3. **Same as above but the cord-impression is confined to the rim portion of the exterior. From an early level of Period IA.**
4. **Bowl of red ware with featureless rim, drooping sides, coarse fabric. From mid level of Period IA.**
5. **Deep bowl of red ware with vertical internally sharpened rim, medium fabric. The red slip on both sides has peeled off at places. From an early level of Period IA.**
6. **Bowl of burnished red ware with a sharpened rim and tapering sides, fine fabric. It bears luster on account of burnishing. A similar shape occurs in Black-and-red ware from the same site (Fig.6, No.11). From an early level of Period IA.**
7. **Bowl of red ware with featureless rim, coarse fabric. From mid level of Period IA.**
8. **Vase of red slipped ware with rounded flaring rim. It bears a thick red slip on both surfaces, medium fabric. From an early level of Period IA.**
9. **Lower portion of a pedestal led bowl of red slipped ware. The interior portion of this vessel bears a bright red slip which is peeled off at places. From an early level of Period IA. A similar shape of red slipped ware has been recovered from Pre- Narhan phase at Imlidih, district Gorakhpur (UP.).**
10. **Same as above but the slip is more preserved. From an early level of Period IA.**

11. A spouted vessel (*Martbān*) of red burnished ware with gently expanding body. It has a smooth surface and has been burnished on the exterior only. The tubular spout has been luted just below the neck to facilitate the controlled flow of liquid. From an early level of Period IA.
12. A spouted vessel / *Lotā* of red slipped ware, two grooves on the exterior at the waist of the pot, smooth surface. A bright red slip has been applied on both sides. From an early level of Period IA.
13. Fragment of a vase of red ware having convex waist. Four concentric lines have been scratched on the waist of the vessel.
14. Same as above but the bright red slip is prominent.
15. Same as No. 13 above.
16. Same as above.
17. Fragment of a vase of red slipped ware, five concentric lines have been scratched on the exterior.
18. Fragment of a vase of red ware having micacious red slip on the exterior and appliqué band with typical rope impressions. From an early level of Period IA.
19. Fragment of a vessel with a scratched design on the exterior executed in post-firing stage. Similar scratched designs were made on the pottery of Period I at Imlidih, (Singh, 1992-93).
20. Fragment of a vase of red slipped ware having appliqué band on the exterior with rope pattern incised on it. The upper part of the vessel from the point of applied band up-to the rim bears a bright red slip which is peeled off at places. The remaining portion of the vessel both on the interior as well as exterior is devoid of any slip. From Period IA.

Fig. 6

1. Vase of grey ware with out-turned rim and gently expanding sides. There are three grooves on the exterior, fine fabric. From an early level of period IA.
2. Fragment of a vessel /*Lotā* of red slipped ware with out-turned thickened rim, bright red slip have been applied on the exterior as well as interior of the pot. From Period IA.
3. Same as above but bigger in size.
4. Same as No. 3 above.
5. A variant of the above.
6. Fragment of a beaker of red slipped ware with slightly everted rim, internally beveled rim From Period IA.
7. Fragment of a *Lotā* of red slipped ware without turned rim. From Period IA.
8. Same as above No. 5.
9. A variant of the above.
10. Fragment of a vase with out-turned rim, two grooves on the exterior, fine fabric. From Period IA.
11. Similar to No. 8 above.
12. Miniature vase of red slipped ware with flaring rim, constricted neck. From Period IA.
13. Same as above but bigger in size.
14. Vase of red ware with flaring rim concave neck and progressively expanding body. From Period IA.
15. A miniature vase of red slipped ware with internally incurved rim and expanding body. From Period IA.
16. Vase of red slipped ware with out-going internally sharpened rim, medium fabric. From Period IA.
17. Same as above with thickened rim, medium fabric. There is a bright red slip both in the interior as well as exterior of the pot. From Period IA.
18. Same as above.
19. Vase of red slipped ware without turned rim and gently expanding sides, medium fabric. From Period IA.
20. Same as above.
21. Vase of red slipped ware with splayed out thickened rim and expanding sides. This vessel has bright red slip on the interior and exterior which is peeled-off at places. From Period IA.
22. Vase of red ware with flaring rim thickened at the middle, carinated neck, bulging sides, coarse fabric. From Period IA.
23. Same as above but gently expanding sides. From Period IA.

24. Vase of red ware with flaring rim progressively thickened at the neck which is carinated. Coarse fabric. From Period IA.
25. Same as above.
26. Vase with splayed out and internally thickened rim, carinated neck, coarse fabric. From Period IA.

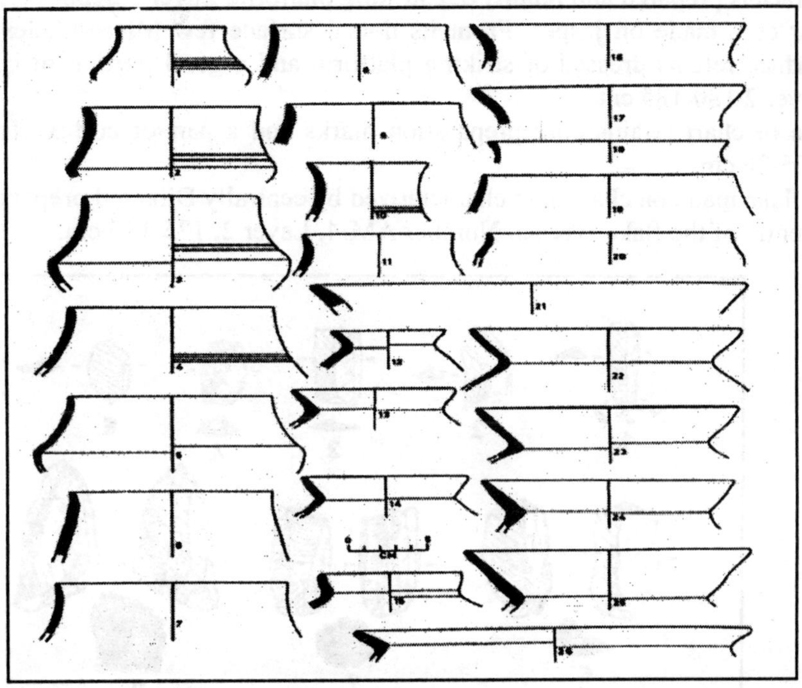

Fig. 6 : Pottery of Period I A.

The Lithic Industry

The lithic component which has been excavated from period IA at Waina comprises among the excavated materials a sizeable collection of waste chips, flakes and cores was obtained from sub-period IA. A study of this lithic material is presented below.

Though a good collection of stone beads has been recovered from the excavations at Waina, this is not included in the present note. The remaining collection includes chips, flakes, cores and microliths. Besides, some nodules of stones were also found. This group is significant as it suggests impart of raw material. It may be mentioned that these were not available locally in this region. Though, these nodules do not come under the category of artifacts, yet they are important as to suggest chipping of stone, tools and beads of the site. Two specimens of this category have been illustrated (**Fig. 7, Pl. 15.2**). Both of the illustrated examples are small flat lumps of agate. Besides agate, charts, chalcedony and jasper were the other stones used for making tools and beads at Waina.

All the representative types have been illustrated and are described below:

Fig. 7

1. Microlith made on banded agate. It has been retouched at high angle at the bottom of left and right edges. Trench number AM-3. Layer 1 depth 15-20 cm.
2. This trapeze of chalcedony is small specimen with one long sharp edge and three small.
3. Broken micro-blade on jasper, Trench No. AM-4. Layer 2 135-140 cm.
4. Small dressing chip of agate. Trench No. AM-3. Layer 1 30-35 cm.
5. Small dressing chip of chalcedony. Trench No. AM-3. Layer 2 30-35 cm.

6. This flake converted into core is made of banded agate. Small Flakes were detached from the top and side at the ventral surface. A micro-blade was also detached from the same surface. Trench Number A-E-4. Layer 9; 535-540 cm.
7. Flattened core made on banded agate, micro blades have been detached from dorsal surface and under surface is prepared and retains flat striking platform. Layer 1 depth 1-15 cm.
8. Triangular core made on jasper. From its dorsal surface few Micro-blades have been detached. Under surface retains dressed-of striking platform and a good portion of cortex. Trench number AK-3, Layer 2 180-185 cm.
9. This flake of chart retains core preparation marks and a part of cortex. Trench Number AM-3. Layer 1, 25-30 cm.
10. Dressing flake made on chart. It is characterized by centrally Directed preparation scats with form a ridge in centre of the flake. Trench Number AM-4. Layer 2, 125-130 cm.

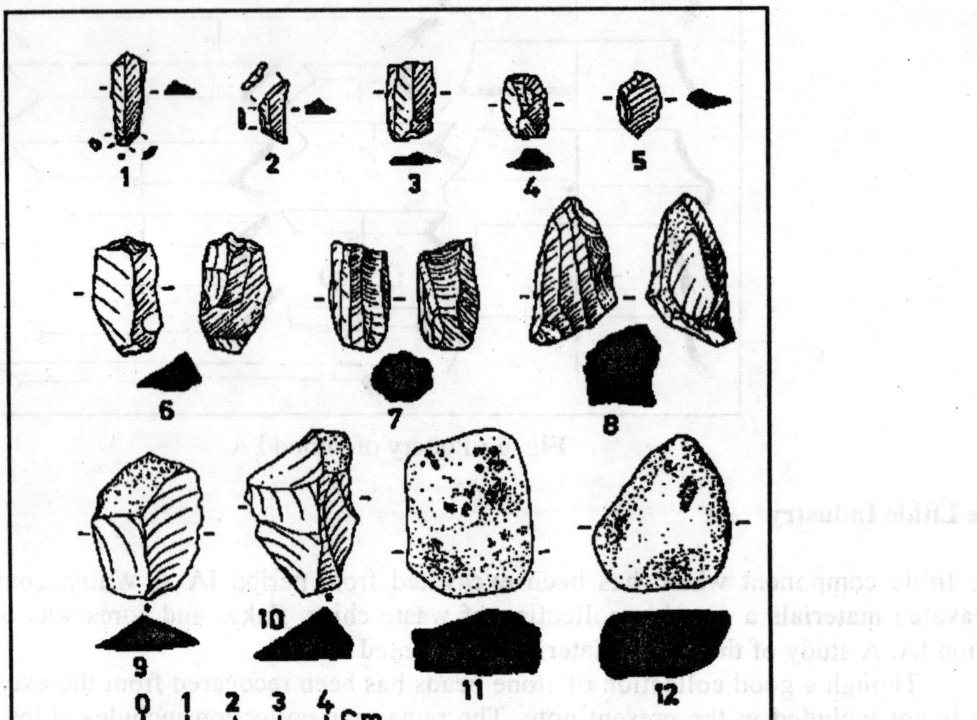

Fig. 7 : Microliths of Waina, District Ballia (U.P.).

Period IB

This sub-period is marked by the pottery assemblage of Narhan culture which in now well documented. The principal wares comprise Black-and-red ware, black slipped ware and plain red ware. The shapes in Black-and-red ware are mainly bowls, basins and vases. Dishes in Black-and-red ware are not reported from this site. This feature is noted from other sites as well like Chirand, Narhan, and Imlidih from these strata. The Black-and-red ware pottery is made essentially on a fast wheel except for the large storage jars which are hand-made. Few sherds of burnished Black-and-red ware were also recovered.

The settlers of this period lived in wattle-and-daub houses. Remains of post-holes, ovens and storage pits were found. A good quantity of archaeobotanical remains was recovered by flotation technique by K.S. Saraswat of Birbal Sahni Institute of Palaeo-botany, Lucknow. Although the people of this period practiced agriculture; meat was an important component of their diet as is evidenced form the presence of a large number of charred animal bones and antlers. The important antiquates comprise bone points, beads of terracotta and semi-precious stones and pottery discs.

The important pottery shapes are illustrated below:

Fig. 8

1. Deep bowl of Black-and-red ware with featureless rim and tapering profile, medium fabric. From mid level of Period IB.
2. Deep bowl of Black-and-red ware with splayed out rim, convex sides, several grooves on the exterior at the waist, medium fabric, shining slip. From mid level of Period IB.
3. Same as above with featureless rim and convex sides, medium fabric. From an early level of Period IB.
4. Beaker of Black-and-red ware with vertical featureless rim, medium fabric. From mid level of Period IB.
5. Deep bowl of Black-and-red ware with internally sharpened rim, medium fabric. From mid level of period IB.
6. Lower portion of a pedestal-led bowl of Black-and- red ware with uneven thickness of the walls. From mid level of Period IB.
7. Same as above but the base is rounded.
8. Globular vessel/vase with vertical, sharpened rim and globular body. From mid level of Period IB.
9. Vase of Black-and-red ware with flaring rim, carinated neck, coarse fabric. From mid level of Period IB.
10. Vase with flaring and thickened rim, carinated neck, globular body, coarse fabric. From mid level of Period IB.
11. Same as above but internally sharpened rim, carinated neck, coarse fabric. From an early level of Period IB.
12. Fragment of a vase with splayed out rim, constricted neck and expanding body, medium fabric. From mid level of Period IB.
13. Vase with splayed out thickened and drooping rim, medium fabric. From an early level of Period IB.
14. A large sized basin/vase with interned collared rim and convex sides, incised designs on the exterior, medium fabric. From mid level of Period IB.

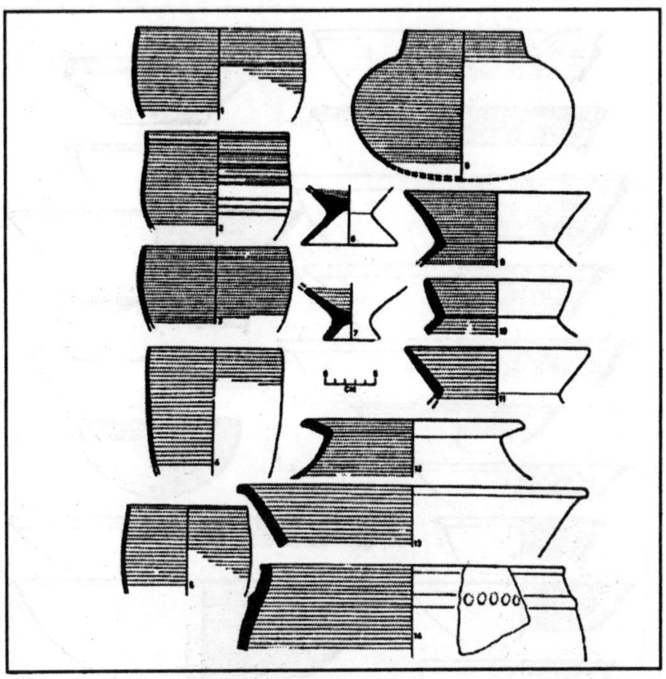

Fig. 8 : Pottery of Period I B.

Fig. 9

1. Bowl of Black-and-red ware with externally beveled rim and convex sides. Cord impressions have been made on the exterior below the neck, medium fabric. From an early level of Period IB.
2. Bowl of Black-and-red ware with everted rim and smooth convex sides, medium fabric, cord-impressions on the exterior. From an early level of Period IB.
3. Same as above. From an early level of Period IB.
4. Upper portion of a pedestal bowl (?) with flaring externally thickened rim and tapering sides. From mid level of Period IB.
5. Same as above but externally beveled rim. From an early level of Period IB.
6. Bowl with internally thickened rim, rounded sides, medium fabric. From an early level of Period IB.
7. Deep bowl with a flaring flattened rim, convex sides, fine fabric. From an early level of Period IB.
8. Same as above but less convex sides, medium fabric, from an early level of Period IB.
9. Bowl with everted rim flattened from the top, tapering sides,-medium fabric. From an early level of Period IB.
10. Bowl with internally thickened everted rim, rounded sides, medium fabric. From an early level of Period IB.
11. Bowl with a sharpened rim and tapering sides, fine fabric and flat base. It has a prominent ridge on the waist. From an early level of Period IB. A variant of the same type occurs in Period I at Narhan (Fig. 27, Nos. 9 -12).
12. Bowl with a sharpened everted rim, medium fabric. From mid level of Period IB.
13. Bowl with featureless rim and rounded sides, medium fabric. From an early level of Period IB.
14. Bowl with vertical sharpened rim, a ridge on the rim portion of the exterior, fine fabric. From an early level of Period IB.
15. Same as above. It bears a luster on account of burnishing, fine fabric. From an early level of Period IB.
16. Miniature bowl of Black-and-red ware with vertical featureless rim and tapering sides. From an early level of Period IB.
17. Upper portion of a pedestal led bowl (?), tapering sides, coarse fabric. From an early level of Period IB.
18. Upper portion of a pedestal led bowl (?) with flaring flattened rim, medium fabric. From an early level of Period IB.

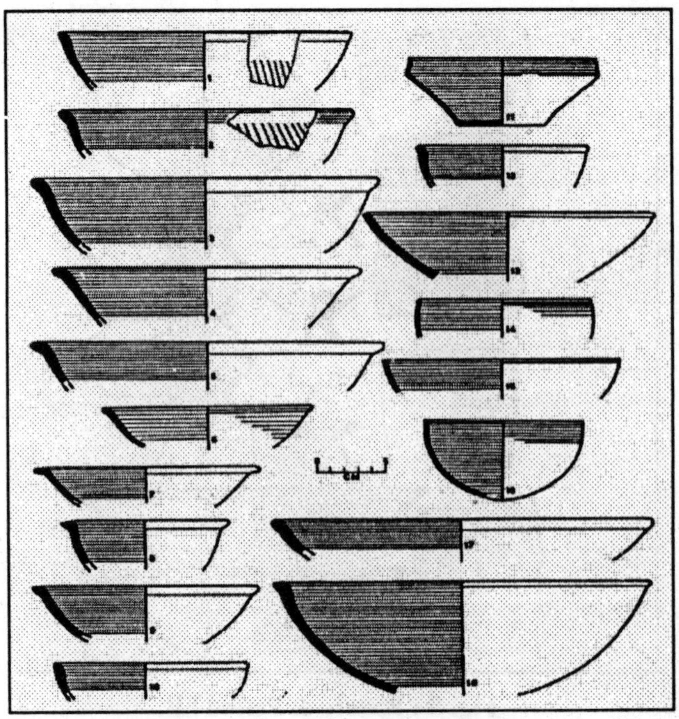

Fig. 9 : Pottery of Period I B.

Period II

This period is represented by dishes, straight sided beakers and bowls of black slipped ware, vases and lipped basins of red slipped ware and plain red ware. Among the NBP associated wares, dishes with incurved rim are the principal type. The structural activity of this period comprises of postholes, wattle-and-daub huts and mud walls in the limited excavations the use of burnt bricks as building material was not attested. The small finds comprise iron objects, bone points and arrow-heads, beads of terracotta and semi-precious stone, terracotta balls and terracotta discs (**Pl. 15.3, 15.4 & 15.5**).

The important shapes are illustrated below:

Fig. 10

1. Bowl of black slipped ware with featureless rim notched from the exterior, convex sides. From period II.
2. Deep bowl of black slipped ware with internally sharpened rim and convex sides, medium fabric. From Period II.
3. Bowl with everted rounded rim and straight sides, fabric. From Period II.
4. Similar to No. 2 above but with thicker section, medium fabric. From Period II.
5. Fragment of a basin/plate of black slipped ware with rounded, thickened rim and bulging body, medium fabric. From Period II.
6. Fragment of a base portion of a bowl of black slipped ware having five grooves on the exterior, medium fabric, From Period II.
7. Bowl of grey ware with featureless rim, convex sides, fine fabric, From Period II.
8. Deep bowl of red ware with externally thickened rim, convex sides, and medium fabric. From Period II.
9. Dish of black slipped ware with an in-turned internally bevelled rim, medium fabric. From Period II.
10. Dish of black slipped ware with a vertical featureless rim, tapering sides and a prominent sagger base, medium fabric. From Period II.
11. Dish of black slipped ware with featureless rim, convex sides. From Period II.
12. Dish of grey ware with externally thickened rim, medium fabric. From Period II.
13. Bowl of Red Slipped Ware with rounded splayed out rim and a sagger base, medium fabric. From Period II.
14. A complete beaker deep bowl of Red ware with vertical externally bevelled rim, medium fabric. From Period II.
15. Same as above but with externally thickened rim. From Period II.
16. Basin of red slipped ware with externally thickened rim and sharp carination at the neck, convex side. The red slip on both sides has peeled off at places. From Period II.
17. Same as above but bigger in size. From Period II.

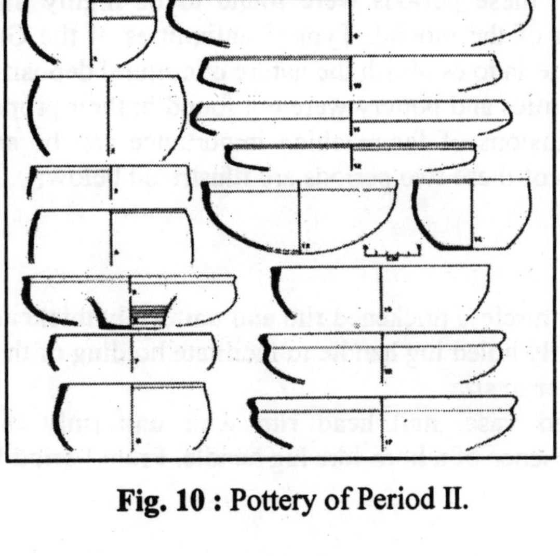

Fig. 10 : Pottery of Period II.

The Archaeo-botanical remains

Archaeo-botanical samples from this period of the site were collected stage by stage by K.S. Saraswat. His preliminary observations show that an advanced agriculture was enjoyed by the settlers at Waina. They were well acquainted with the rotation of crops and grew cereals, pulses and oilseeds in the summer and winter seasons. A preliminary examination of the crops remains during the course of collection of the samples from different horizons of cultural deposits from 1300 B.C. to 600 B.C. revealed the presence of rice (*Oryza sativa*), bariey (*Hordeum vulgare*), wheat (*Triticum aestivum*), mung (*Vigna radiate*), lentil (*Lens culinaris*), field pea (*Pisum arvense*), grass-pea or Khesari (*Lathyrus sativus*), gram (*Cicer arietinum*), field-branssica (*Brassica juncea*) and til/seasame (*Sesamum indicum*). A good number of weeds and other wild seeds have also been found which on detailed examination will certainly throw light of the ecological surrounding of the settlement.

Period III

This period is marked by Sunga-Kushana pottery with sprinkler of red ware as the diagnostic type, burnt brick structures which have been largely robbed by present-day inhabitant of Waina village **(Pl. 15.6, Fig. 11)**. The noteworthy antiquities of this period are terracotta human and animal figurines, terracotta balls, beads and pestles, bone points, antlers iron and copper objects **(Pl. 15.3, 15.4 & 15.5)**.

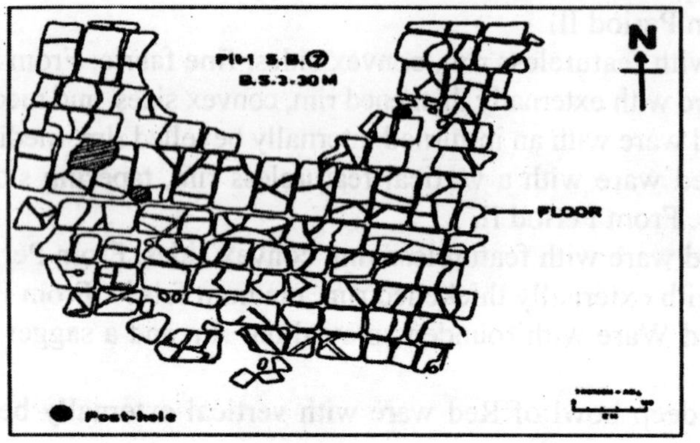

Fig. 11 : Occupation floor with Post-holes Plate III, Mound, Waina, Ballia.

Period IV

The mound was inhabited during the Gupta period as also for a few centuries during the post-Gupta times. However, strata belonging to these periods were found to be highly disturbed in the three trenches excavated on the highest part of the mound. Typical antiquities of the Gupta period and characteristic pottery shapes are the only criteria to establish the nature of cultural deposits of these periods. However, it may be added that such antiquities and pottery were not found in their proper archaeological context with the result that no vital conclusions of far reaching importance can be arrived at regarding these two periods. The important shapes of these two periods are illustrated below:

Fig. 12

1. Fragment of *Karãhi*, featureless thickened rim and uniformly thickened sides. It is distinguished by the presence of a centrally holed lug handle to facilitate holding of the vessel. From Period IV.
2. Same as above but bigger in size.
3. Fragment of a handled vase, nail head rim with uniformly thickened convex sides. It is distinguished by the presence of a horn-like lug handle. From Period IV.

4. Pan or *Karãhi* having a featureless rim and thickened convex sides, the handle of the pot is decorated by punching straight lines. From Period III.
5. Same as No. 3 above but smaller in size. From Period IV.
6. Fragment of upper part of sprinkler with obliquely cut flanged rim. It has been treated with a bright red slip. From Period III.
7. Miniature bowl of grey ware with an everted featureless rim and a solid pedestal base, it is devoid of any wash or slip, medium fabric. From an unstraitified level.
8. Fragment of a bowl with featureless thickened falnged rim, uniformly thinner sides and a saggar base. From Period IV.
9. Fragment of a lid with splayed out rim, less pronounced thickend knob, flattish thickened base. From Period IV.
10. Same as above.
11. Complete specimen of a lid with horizontally splayed out rim having a depression on the top. From Period IV.
12. Lid of red ware with flared rim, having a flattish base. From Period IV.
13. An almost complete specimen of a lid with flared flat waist, vase shaped central depression and a sagger. From Period IV.
14. Basin of red ware with externally thickened rim with rounded base From Period IV.

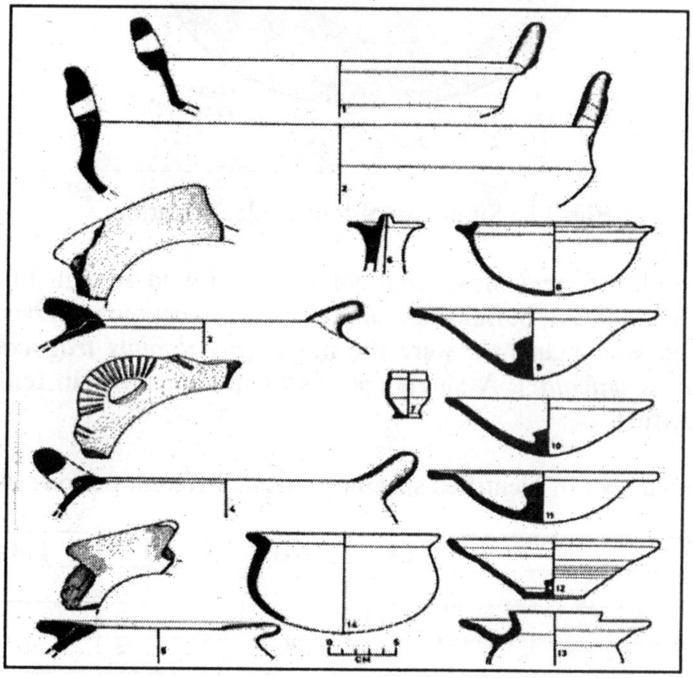

Fig. 12 : Pottery of Period III and IV.

The faunal remains

A good quantity of animal bones was collected in the process of excavation, particularly from the large refuge pits cut into the natural soil. Faunal remains of the site were studied by P.P. Joglekar, Deccan College, Pune. Faunal material from a single trench (AK3) belonging to periods IA, IB and II was available for analysis. Each bone fragment was thoroughly examined to find out the impact of both pre- and post-depositional factors. Bone modification includes intentional fractures (Sadek-Kooros. 1975:139-150) as well as accidental breakage in the past and after their recovery during the excavation process. A total of 197 fragments were examined. Of these it was possible to identify 156 (79.19%) fragments (Table 1, **Fig.13**). This high proportion of identifiable fragments is due to excellent preservation of the skeletal elements.

Table 1 : Summary of faunal identification at Waina

Layer	Cultural period	NISP	Unidentifiable			UF	TF
			UF-S	UF-M	UF-L		
2	NBP	39	5	4	6	15	54
3	Narhan culture	73	3	6	8	17	90
4	Pre-Narhan culture	44	6	2	1	9	53
Total		156	14	12	15		197

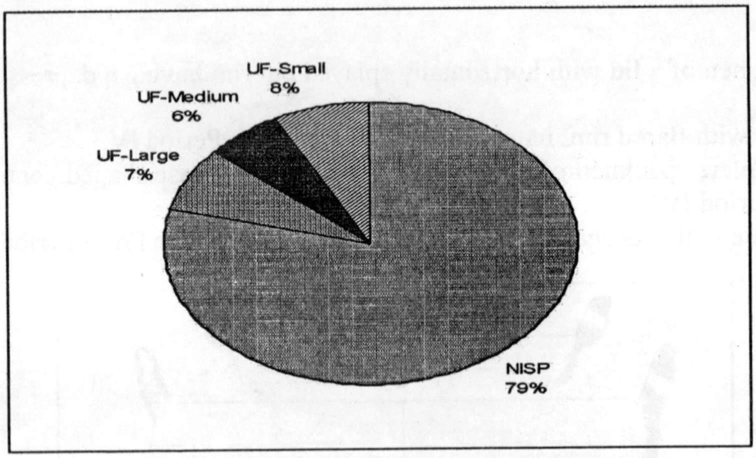

Fig. 13 : Summary of faunal identification

It was possible to identify remains of both domestic and wild animals (Table: 2). The domestic species were the cattle (*Bos indicus*), buffalo (*Bubalus bubalis*), sheep/goats (*Ovis/Capra*), and domestic pig (*Sus domesticus*). The wild mammals were the nilgai (*Boselaphus tragocamelus*), wild pig (*Sus scrofa*) and sambar (*Cervus unicolor*). A single species of non-mammalian remains in form of turtle (*Kachuga tecta*) was identified.

Table 2 : Number of identified specimens from different periods at Waina

	IA	IB	II	Total	%NISP
Bos indicus	18	24	23	65	41.7
Bos/Bubalus	17	43	10	70	44.9
Bubalus bubalis	0	6	5	11	7.05
Ovis/Capra	3	0	0	3	1.92
Sus domesticus	2	0	0	2	1.28
Boselaphus tragocamelus	1	0	0	1	0.64
Cervus unicolor	0	0	1	1	0.64
Sus scrofa	2	0	0	2	1.28
Kachuga tecta	1	0	0	1	0.64
Total	44	73	39	156	100

The quantity of bones available from Waina is not adequate to comments on animal-based economy. Since the excavation was vertical and on a trial basis, no quantitative statements about relative importance of wild or domestic species be made. However, the measurements and observations could be used in future to talk about animal-based subsistence in the Proto-historic period in Ganga Plain. Hence, study of this small material is a significant step towards our understanding of faunal background of archaeological sites in Ganga Plain at a general level.

Emerging facts

The excavations at Waina have brought to light following facts:

The site is located at place which has permanent water source on the confluence rivers Ganga, Chhoti Saryu *(Tons)* and Magai. The largest cities and towns are situated along major river systems and coastal areas where people could control the movement of goods and raw materials along the 314 trade routes. Built on enormous mud-built platforms high above the flood waters, the cities had advantage point from which to view the surrounding plains. Watch towers built along the city walls could provide lookouts to signal the approach of river boats and caravans.

Waina is located on the old bed of the Choti Sarayu, tributary of the Ganga river in the Ballia district and it has given a similar culture deposit as the above noted site. The occurrence of a few microliths in the lowest level of this site, a solitary polished stone axe (celt) from Narhan and vestiges of a Neolithic deposit at Sohagaura demonstrate that these site were vested by Neolithic people, presumably around 2500 BC and since then permanent human settlements flourished in the valleys of Ghaghara, Kuwana and Choti Sarju.

The lithic collection brings out the fact that Waina was involved in lithic craft for two purposes: (1) for the production of stone beads, (2) for production of microliths. It is interesting to note that for both categories of artifacts similar groups of stones, where used. Raw material was transported to the site in natural form.

The presence of limited number of microliths at Waina is an important component. It may be noted that although beads were manufactured at Narhan, microliths are totally absent on all sites of the Sarayupar plains. In the mid-Ganga plain; traces of Neolithic culture were found at Sohgaura in the early sixties of the last century. In recent years Neolithic artifacts comprising a limited number of microliths and the characteristic cord-impressed, hand-made pottery have been found from more than a dozen sites. Of these, Imlidih Khurd and Lahuradeva have been excavated. Microlithic tools have been picked up from Susipar and Gerar in Sant Kabir Nagar district as also from the excavated site of Waina in district Ballia. The radio carbon dates of Neolithic levels at Lahurdeva put it to 6290 ±160 B.C.

The practice of rotation of crops was pursued by the Chalcolithic culture people. Rice, bajra, Kodon-millet, horse-gram, green-gram, moth-bean and black-gram were grown in warm-rainy season, while wheat, barley, gram, khesari, lentil and field-pea were the winter crops. Pulses constitute a group of the Legume family which, with the help of bacteria in their root nodules, fix atmospheric nitrogen and improve soil fertility. Their ability to thrive under a wide range of soil and climatic conditions resulted pulse crops finding an important place in the agricultural economy at Narhan and surrounding area. Kharif crops of horse-gram (*Kulthi*), moth-bean, green-gram (*mung*) and black-gram (*urd*) serve as a good cover crop under a taller growing associated crop of millets like jowar and bajra. It may reasonably be presumed that the Narhan settlers may have practiced the mixed cultivation of cereals and pulses, during the summer-rainy seasons (Saraswat, 1992-93).

People of the Neolithic culture were the first to make effective colonization at Waina. The ceramic industries show striking similarity both in fabric and forms with those recovered from Imlidih Khurd, Pakkākot, Bhunadih, Senuwar, Lahuradewa and Chirand. Agriculture was the mainstay of the economy of our area and the concept of cultivating two crops in a year had already come into practice even in the Neolithic period datable to 2500 B.C. to 1300 B.C. Cultivation of rice, wheat, barley, various types of millets, several types of pulses and oil seeds were done in the Neolithic stage. Chalcolithic Period was rural.

As stated above, agriculture was the mainstay of the economy of these cultures and the concept of cultivating two crops a year (summer as well as winter) had already come in practice even in the Neolithic culture datable to the first half of the second half millennium B.C. Cultivation of rice, wheat, barley, various types of millets, several types of pulses and oil-seeds was done in the Neolithic stage.

Acknowledgements

This research Paper was supervised by Prof. Purushottam Singh, who not only provided academic guidance but also encouraged me at every stage of its preparation. I express by gratefulness and thanks to him. Prof. Vidula Jayaswal has helped me in classifying Lithic material and guided me in course of this study. My grateful thanks are due to her. The tool and Pottery drawing was done by Sri Shiv Kumar, Draughtsman of the Department. I thank him for this help.

References

Chakrabarti, D.K. and R.N. Singh. (1998), Archaeology between Ballia and Robertsganj in Uttar Pradesh: Notes on Some Early Historic Routes of the Area. *South Asian Studies*, 14.

Chakrabarti, D.K. (2001), *Archaeological Geography of the Ganga Plain*: *The Lower and the Middle Ganga,* Permanent Black, Delhi.

Dubey, S.R., *et al* (2012) *Pakkākot: Some New Dimensions of Mid-Ganga Plain*, Rishi Publications, New Delhi.

Indian Archaeological 1956-57: A Review.

Indian Archaeological 1963-64: A Review.

Joglekar, P. P., P. Singh, and A.K. Singh (2012-2013), Faunal Remains ,From Waina, District Ballia, Uttar Pradesh, *Bharati* No. 37, pp.38-44.

Pathak, V. (1963) *History of Kosala upto the Rise of Mauryas*, Varanasi, Motilal Banarasidas.

Singh, B.P. (1990-91), Excavations at Khairadih, *Journal of Bihar Puravid Parishad*, Vols. IX-X, pp. 78-86.

Singh, B.P. (1989). Khairadih: A Chalcolithic Settlement, *Puratattva*, 18.

Singh, S.C. (1973), *Changes in the Courses of Rivers and their Effects on Urban Settlements in the Middle Ganga plain*, National Geographical Society of India, Varanasi, pp. 15 – 18.

Singh, S.C. (1965), Delimitation of the Middle Ganga plain. *The National Geographical Journal of India*, Vol. XI, part 2, June, Banaras Hindu University, Varanasi, pp. 79 ff.

Singh, P. (1994), *Excavations at Narhan 1984-89*, Banaras Hindu University and B.R. Publishing Corporations, New Delhi.

Singh, P. *et al*. (1994-95). Proto-historic Investigations in Ballia District, *Pragdhara,* No. 5.

Singh, P. and A.K. Singh (1995-96), Excavations at Waina, District Ballia (U.P.), *Pragdhara*, No. 6, pp. 41 – 61.

Singh, P. and A.K. Singh (1997-98), Trial Excavations at Bhunadih, *Pragdhara*, No. 8, pp 12-29.

Singh, R.L. (1971), *India: A Regional Geography*, Banaras Hindu University, National Geographical Society of India, Varanasi, pp. 191 – 192.

Singh, S.K. (2000-2001), Lithic Industry of Waina, District–Ballia (UP), *Pragdhara*, No. 11, pp. 105-107.

Singh, S.K. (2010), *Urbanization of the Middle Ganga Plain: An Archaeological Perspective*, Rishi Publication, Delhi.

Singh, S.K. (2012), *Settlement Pattern Urban Growth and Craft Technology in North India: An Archaeological Perspective,* Research India Press, New Delhi.

Singh, S.K. (2014), Pakkākot: Super Trade and Urban Center of the Middle Ganga plain, *ICON* Journal of Archaeology and Culture, Vol. I, pp.89-100.Wakankar Rock Art and Heritage Welfare Society, Bhopal, Research India Press, New Delhi.

Saraswat, K.S., (1993), Seed and Fruit Remains of Imlidih Khurd, Gorakhpur, A Preliminary Report, *Pragdhara*, No. 3, pp. 37-42.

Tripathi, V. and S.K. Singh (2003-2004), Excavations at Khairadih (1996-97), *Bharati* No. 28, pp. 1-69.

16

NEOLITHIC CULTURE OF SARYUPAR REGION

Shitala Prasad Singh

Saryupar plain lies between latitudes 26^0 5' and 28^0 30' North and longitudes 80^0 57' and 84^0 29' East and basically it is situated on the foothills of the Himalayan ranges in the middle of the Ganga basin. Its Western boundary is delimited from Ghaghra (Saryu) River and Eastern boundary is demarcated by Gandak River and from east to east it has maximum length of 260 km while width of 160 km from north to south. It covers the administrative districts of Bahraich, Shravasti, Balrampur, Gonda, Basti, Sidhartha Nagar, Maharajganj, Kushinagar, Gorakhpur & Deoria. It touches International boundary of Nepal in the north, Bihar in the east. The western and southern sword shape rim is delimited by the river Saryu (Ghaghra) a major tributary of the Ganga river. The region is made of alluvium deposits of river Ghaghra, Rapti and their tributaries. The area is watered by Ghaghra, Manwar, Kuwana, Rapti, Ami and chhoti Gandak.

The Saryupar plain partakes of similar geographical features as the vast Ganga plains. The region has been classified into three broad divisions viz., (i) The Tarai (ii) The Bhangar or the upland and (iii) The Kachhar or the flood-prone low land. Terai region is extended in narrow belt in width of 25 to 30 km parallel to International boundary of Nepal in length of 400 km. This is region of unmanaged drainage system and often affected from flood. The changes in river course in this region are very common. Khadar region if flood plain, which is extended parallel to Ghaghra River in width of 15 to 25 km besides this is also lies parallel to Rapti river from Basti in west to Barhaj in east. This is region of severe flood which determines the land use pattern, population distribution and settlement pattern as well as socio-economic development. The Bhangar region lies in major portion of the Saryupar plain between Terai and Khadar. The slope gradient in this region is from north-west to south-east. This is region of high density of population and settlements characterized by ancient alluvial soil. Moreover this is region of highly fertile soil and intensive agricultural attractive for human settlement.

Rivers, Lakes & other water sources

The area is drained by several rivers including Ghaghra, Rapti, Rohini, Terhi, Suwan, Manwar, Bhurhi Rapti,Aami, Kuwano, Gurra, Tons, Kunhra, Ghonghi, Banganga, Saryu, Gandak, Little Gandak, Banarsi, Bakela etc. Apart from rivers, lakes and Tals like Kakarahwa, Anarkali, Majhghawa, Koharagaddi, Chura Tal, Pathri Tal, Kondar Tal, Parsia Tal, Parbati Tal, Bakhira Tal, Komar Tal, Chillua Tal, Likhia Tal, Chando Tal, Ramgarh Tal, Narhi Tal, Nador Tal etc. are the other water sources of the region.

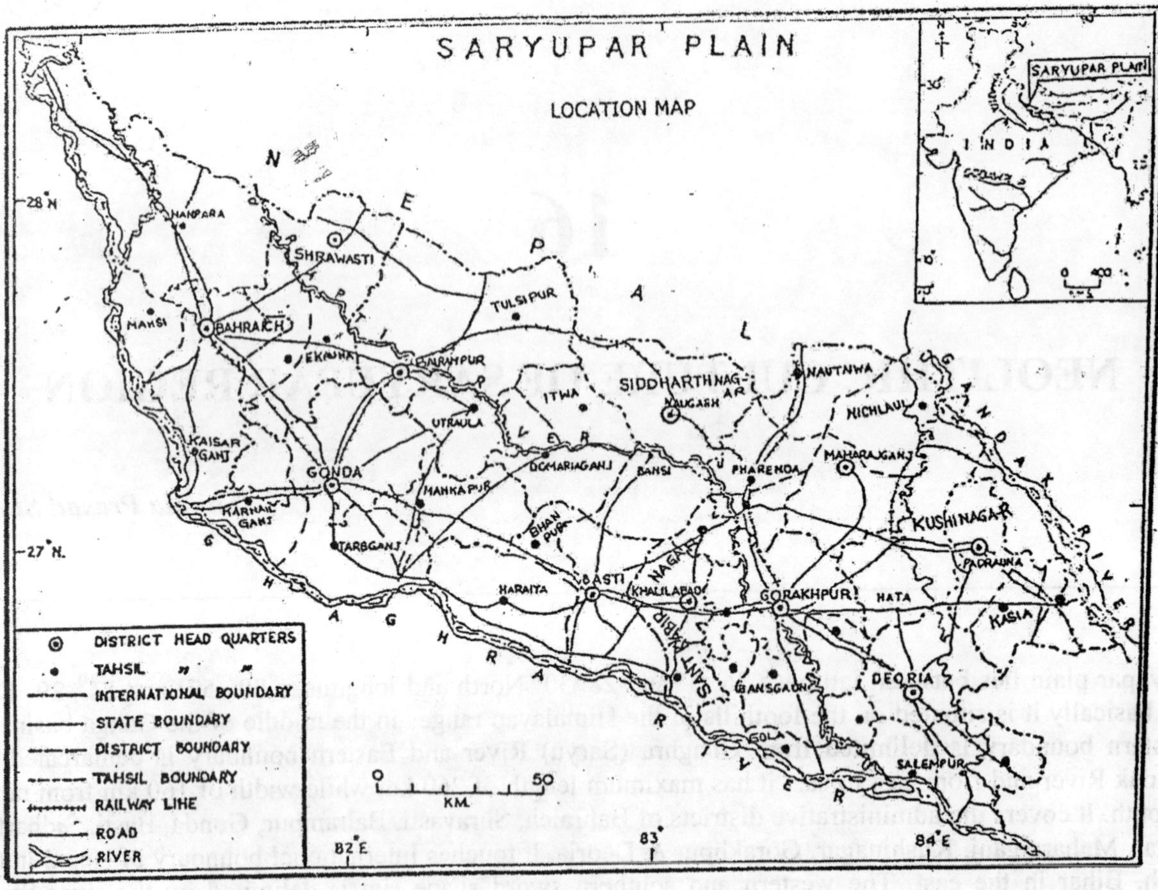

Climate

The climate of the region is sub humid tropical where monsoon is predominant. The climate is characterized with surplus/deficiency, uncertainity and variability of rainfall, extreme temperatures showing diurnal and seasonal variations and low humidity during the drier months.

Rainfall

The average rainfall of the region is 120 cm. About 85% of the total rainfall occurred in the rainy season. Retreating monsoon also causes a few amount of rainfall during the months of October and November. March, April and May are the driest months receiving only a negligible amount of rainfall mainly by local storms followed by lightning and hails. The rainfall decreases from north-east to south-west. The north-eastern part of the region receives average annual rainfall more than 140 cm. The central part of the region receives 120 to 140 cm. rainfall while the southern part of the region receives rainfall between 100 and 120 cm.

In the early Vedic literature there is only casual reference to this region, but by the late Vedic period it had become an important administrative unit due to the formation of the Kosala and Videha kingdoms. The region is first mentioned in the Satapatha Brahmana (1.4, 1.14-20), a text that relates to the spread of the Aryan culture. In this text we read about Videgha Mathava, the king of Videhas. Accompanied by the priest Gotama Ragugana, he carried the sacrificial fire from the bank of the Saraswati river eastwards across Kosala and the Sadanira and established a settlement known as Videha after the tribal name of Mathava. During the lifetime of the Buddha several small kingdoms flourished in this region, e.g. the Mallas of Pawa and Kusinara and the Sakyas. In the Gahadavala inscriptions this region has been mentioned as Saryupar.

The archaeological study began for the first time by A. Cunningham (AR I: 330-48) who identified the ancient city of Sravasti with the remains of Sahet-Mahet. Later on A. C. L. Carlleyle explored some area in the Saryupar region under the guidance of Alexander Cunningham during 1874-76(AR XIII). In 1890, A. Fuhrer explored this area. In February 1897 Vincent A. Smith suspected that Piprahwa might represent the ancient stupa. In the subsequent year W. C. Peppe (Mukherjee 1901: 4) excavated and found the famous Piprahwa vase containing Buddha's relics, beads, crystals, gold ornaments, cut stars etc.

The excavations and explorations conducted during the last three decades by Banaras Hindu University, Deen Dayal Upadhyaya University Gorakhpur, University of Lucknow, U.P. State Archaeology Department and Patna circle of the Archaeological Survey of India pushed back the antiquity of the Sarypar region. Now it is accepted that the region was first inhabited during the Neolithic phase. Recent excavations have thrown new light on the early farming culture of the area. Excavations conducted at Sohgaura, Narhan, Imlidih Khurd, Dhuriapar, Lahuradeva, Sravasti, etc. have thrown welcome light on the corpus of cereals having been cultivated by the people in the mid Saryu region.

The following sites related with Neolithic culture have been excavated in this area:

Sohgaura (IAR 1961-62:56; Chaturvedi 1985)

The ancient settlement of Sohgaura (Lat. 26^0 30' 30" N; Long. 83^0 15' 25" E.) is situated at the confluence of the Rapti and Ami rivers in a district Gorakhpur. The site was excavated by G. C. Pandey in 1961-62 and re-excavated by S. N. Chaturvedi of Gorakhpur University in 1974-75. The excavation yielded five fold cultural periods:-

Period I: Handmade pottery with matt impressed

Period II: Plain and Painted Black Slipped ware, Plain and Painted Black and Red ware, Grey and Red ware.

Period III: NBPW

Period IV: Kushan

Period V: Medival

Imlidih Khurd (Singh 1993; 1994)

The ancient settlement of Imlidih (Lat. $26^0$30'30"; Long. 83^0 12' 5") is an inconspicuous, featureless mound located on the left bank of Kuwano, a tributary of Ghaghara river. It was excavated during 1992 and 1993 by Purushottam Singh of Banaras Hindu University. The deposit of the site is divided into 3 periods.

Period I: Pre-Narhan culture. The ceramics include crude Red Ware, some with cord impression. The bones of sheep/goat, cattle, pig, deer, wolf, fresh water turtle, fish and fresh water mollusca have been found, this indicates that people were engaged in animal domestication, as well as in hunting and fishing. Circular pits with a diameter of 19.5 m. are reported within the huts. It indicates that these were used to store surplus grains for future consumption. The cereals include rice, barley, wheat, jowar, bajra, lentil, green gram, field pea, til and mustard oil seeds. It indicates that farming was also in practice.

Period II: It is Narhan culture and is placed between c.1300-800 B.C. Main potteries are white painted Black and Red Ware, Coarse Black and Red Ware, etc. The bones of cattle, goat, sheep, bear, deer, chital and barhasingha have been recovered. They indicate that hunting was still in practice alongwith animal domestication. Shell of mollusca are found.

Period III: It is comparable to period II of Narhan dated to 800-400 B.C. The ceramic industries include Black and Red Ware, Red Ware, Grey Ware and NBPW.

Lahuradeva (Tewari *et.al.* 2003; 2006; 2008)

It is located near a lake in district Sant Kabir Nagar. It is connected with Katnahia river, a tributary of Kuwano river which ultimately meets the Ghaghra river. The cultural remains are divisible into five periods.

Period I: Early Farming phase

Period II: Developed Farming phase

Period III: Advanced Farming/Early Iron Age

Period IV: NBPW phase

Period V: Early Historic (Early centuries BC/AD).

The rice cultivation and cord impressed pottery are interlinked to each other, having greater antiquity in the Neolithic in a wide area. The cord impressed ware associated with the Neolithic culture (rice cultivation) has been found in south eastern coastal China, in the Yangtze valley, southern China, Japan, Indo-China, Gangetic Plain, Vindhyas, eastern and north-eastern India and in the Himalayas. Recent excavations of the early farming culture sites in the Gangetic Plain have revealed interesting evidence of a center of early origin of agriculture in India. The excavations at Lahuradewa in Sant Kabir Nagar district and at Jhusi in Allahabad district have revealed a Neolithic Culture characterized by mostly handmade ceramic industry, bone tools, beads of semi-precious stone, micro disc-beads of steatite, circular hut floors, cultivated and wild cereals and domesticated and wild animal bones.

The Neolithic settlements have been located on the bank of rivers or nalas, generally above the flood plain. In the selection of sites for settlements the main consideration was the availability of land for cultivation, water resource and animals and wild plants in surrounding areas. They cultivated plants and domesticated animals. As the evidence shows the Neolithic people were not dependent on agriculture and domestication alone for their subsistence. They exploited wild plants available in forests, rich in woodland and grassland vegetations. The rivers and nalas not only provided suitable land for agriculture, they also provided food in the form of aquatic animals like fish, tortoise and snails etc.

The Neolithic culture of the Saryupar region is marked by a rich and varied ceramic industry. The available evidence indicates that in the early stage of the culture, as indicated at Imlidih khurd and Lahuradewa, people were using hand-made pottery subsequently the slow wheel appears to have been used for the purpose. The ceramic assemblage includes cord impressed ware, ordinary red ware, lustrous red ware, burnished ware (red, black and grey), rusticated ware and crude black and red ware and the clay used for manufacturing the pots is not well levigated. It contains grits, husks and chaff as degraissant. Pots are generally ill fired and have blackish grey core. Pottery types including bowls with varying profile, vases, vessels, basins, miniature jars, handis, etc. suggest that these were used for storing, cooking and also as kitchen wares. A large number of vases with rustication and soot mark on outer surface indicate that these were for cooking, possibly for boiling rice. Bowls, basins and vases also have sometimes spouts, suggesting consumption of liquid or semi-liquid food. The Neolithic pottery is represented by four wares called cord-impressed, rusticated, burnished red and burnished black, all hand-made and ill-fired.

The explorations conducted in the part of the Saryupar plain during the last four decades have resulted in identification of several Neolithic settlements. The important excavations sites in Uttar Pradesh outside Saryupar region are Jhusi (Misra *et.al.*2000) and Hetapatti (Pal and Gupta 2005) Allahabad, Bhunadih (Singh *et.al.* 1998) and Waina (Singh *et.al.* 1996) in Ballia (Singh et.al.1994-45),

Sohgaura and Imlidih Khurd in Gorakhpur, Lahuradewa in Sant Kabir Nagar district, while Chirand (IAR 1981-82:13-14 Verma 1971, Sinha 1994) in Saran, Checher Kutubpur (IAR1977-78:17-18) in Vaishali, Pran (Dr.Bijoy Kumar Chaudhary: personal communication), Taradih (IAR 1984-85:9-10; IAR 1984-85:9-10; IAR 1986-87:23-24; IAR 1987-88:9-11) in Gaya, Maner (IAR 1985-86:11-12; IAR 1986-87:25-26; IAR 1987-88:11-12; IAR 1988-89:7-8) in Patna and Senuwar (Singh 1997) in Rohtas district in Bihar. Most of these excavated sites are multi-cultural sites having yielded archaeological relics ranging from Neolithic to early historical periods (Misra 2007).

Table : Neolithic Sites in the Middle Ganga Plain

Name of the Site	Location	Excavated by	Thickness	Reference
Jhusi (Lat 25⁰ 26' 10" N Long 81⁰ 54' 30" E)	Allahabad, U.P., on the confluence of the Ganga and Yamuna	University of Allahabad	1.5m	Misra *et al.* 2000
Hetapatti (Lat 25⁰ 29' 0" N. Long 81⁰ 55' 31" E)	Allahabad, U.P., on the left bank of the Ganga.	University of Allahabad	60 cm	Pal and Gupta 2005
Bhunadih (Lat 25⁰ 19' 10" N Long 84⁰ 5' 11" E)	Ballia, U.P., on the right bank of Bahera nala, a tributary of Ghaghara.	Banaras Hindu University	About 50 cm	Singh *et.al.* 1998
Waina (Lat 25⁰ 45' 5" N Long 84⁰ 5" E)	Ballia, U.P. on the left bank of old bed of Chhoti Sarju (Tons), a tributary of the Ganga.	Banaras Hindu University	About 40 cm	Singh *et.al.* 1996
Lahuradewa (Lat 26⁰ 46' N Long 82⁰ 57' E)	Sant Kabir Nagar, U.P. on a horseshoe lake.	State Archaeology, U.P.	45 cm	Tewari *et.al.* 2003; 2006; 2008
Sohgaura (Lat 26⁰ 30' 30" N; Long 83⁰ 15' 25" E)	Gorakhpur, U.P., on the confluence of Ami and Rapti.	Gorakhpur University	60 cm	Chaturvedi 1985
Imlidih (Lat 26⁰ 30' 30" N, Long 83⁰ 12' 5" E)	Gorakhpur, U.P., on the left bank of the Kuwano river, a tributary of the Ghaghara.	Banaras Hindu University	50-60 cm	Singh 1993; 1994
Chirand (Lat 25⁰ 45' 5" N Long 84⁰ 50' E)	Saran, Bihar, on the confluence of the Ghaghara and Ganga.	State Archaeology, Bihar and Patna University.	3.5m	Verma 1971
Chechan-Kutubpur (Lat 25⁰ 30' 10" N, Long 85⁰ 30' 45" E)	Vaishali, Bihar, on the left bank of the Ganga.	ASI, Patna Circle		IAR 1977-78 17-18
Taradih (Lat 24⁰ 42' N Long 85⁰ 0' E)	Gaya, Bihar, South-west of Mahabodhi temple.	State Archaeology, Bihar	70 cm	IAR 1984-85 9-10, IAR 1986-87 23-24, IAR 1987-88 9-11
Maner (Lat 25⁰ 30' 45" N Long 84⁰ 45'25" E)	Patna, Bihar, on the bank of the Ganga.	Patna University	3.45	IAR 1985-86 11-12, 1986-

N Long 84^0 45'25" E)	of the Ganga.			87, 25-26, IAR 1987-88, 11-12, IAR 1988-89, 7-8.
Senuwar (Lat 24^0 56" N Long 83" 56' E)	Rohtas, Bihar, Right bank of Kudra river.	Banaras Hindu University.	1.50m	Singh 1997

Table: Showing the Main Ceramics, Shapes and Painting Traditions of Neolithic Stage in middle Ganga Plain

Sites	Cultural Periods	Ceramics
Sohgaura	Pd. I	Corded ware, Rusti-cated ware and small quantity of Red ware
Chirand	Pd. I	Red ware, Grey ware (in less quantity), Black, Black & Red ware (largely hand- made and rarely made by turn-table method.
Imlidih Khurd	Pd. I	Corded ware and plain Red ware.
Lahuradeva	Pd. I A	Mainly course variety of Red ware, Black and Red ware which includes hand and wheel turned (slow wheel) varieties
	Pd. I B	Course variety of Red ware, Black and Red ware with few sherds of Grey ware and Black were.
Senuwar	Pd. IA	Red ware and Burnished Red ware, Burnished Grey ware,Cord-impressed and Rusticated ware, crude Black and Red ware. All these have been distinguished mainly on the basis of surface treatment and other techno- logical details. All these are mainly wheel made, although hand-made are also found.
	Pd. IB	All the preceding (IA) ceramics and common shapes are continue with improvement of surface treatment.
Jhusi	Pd. I	Cord impressed ware, Rusticated ware, Burnished Red ware, Burnished black ware and crude Black and Red ware. The first three may considered as sub groups of Red ware. Pots are thick to medium in fabric and ill fired. Core of the pots are blackish, Grayish and occasionally reddish. Clay used for making pots is not well levigated and uneven surface of pots ware indicating that these pots are handmade.
Hetapatti	Pd. I	Handmade pottery characterised by the Cord-impressed ware, Rusticated ware, ordinary Red ware and occasionally Burnished Red ware.

Settlement Pattern

All the excavated sites are located on the banks of rivers, generally on the confluence of two rivers near meander above the flood plain or on horse-shoe lakes (as in the case of Lahuradewa). Easy availability of water, cultivable land and also easy availability of food in the form of suitable vegetation, animals and aquatic creatures was the prime consideration for selecting a site for settlement.

Subsistence

The Neolithic people of the Saryupar region as those of the Vindhayas were farming and pastrol communities is attested by the cultivated variety of rice, barley, wheat, field pea, lentil, green gram, etc, recovered from the excavated sites. However, the botanical evidence obtained from Senuwar and Jhusi in mid Ganga valley read with its counterpart of Tokwa in the Vindhayas suggests that in the early phase only rice and some primitive millets were being cultivated.

Chronology

Four excavated Neolithic sites of the mid Ganga Plain have furnished C-14dates also, on the basis of which a reliable chronology of the culture can be worked out. The sites in question are Chirand, Senuwar, Lahuradewa and Jhusi. Two dates obtained from Chirand read 1760±150 B.C. and 1680±135 B.C. These dates push the beginning of the Neolithic culture at the site around 2000 B.C. From the overlap phase (Neolithic and Chalcolithic) of Senuwar four dates reading 1770±120 B.C.,1660±120 B.C.,1500±110 B.C. and 1400±110 B.C. have been obtained.

The earliest date obtained from the site would put the beginning of the Neolithic culture of the site in the 8th millennium B.C. From Lahuradewa (Tewari *et.al.*2003:55-56), a multi cultural site in Sant Kabir Nagar, two C^{14} dates read 5320±90 B.P.(Cal B.C.4220, 4196 and 4161) and 6290±160 B.P. (Cal B.C. 5298). An AMS C^{14} date for carbonized domesticated rice would push the antiquity of the Neolithic culture at the site to the 7th millennium B.C. From the Neolithic horizon of Jhusi three C^{14} dates have been obtained. These dates when calibrated, read 7477 B.C. (BS-2526), 5837 BC (BS-254) and 6196 BC (BS-2525). The earliest date obtained from the site would put the beginning of the Neolithic culture of the site in 8th millennium BCE. In the Ganga Plain Neolithic culture and Neolithic way of life lasted for a long time starting from 8th-7th miliennium BCE to 3rd-2nd millennium BCE.

Acknowledgement

I express my gratitude to Prof. J. N. Pal for his encouragement and discussions on the various aspects of this paper.

References

Allchin, B. and R. Allchin 1997. *Origin of a civilization: The Prehistory and Early archaeology of South Asia*, New Delhi : Viking Penguin India.

AR- Cunningham's Archaeological Report, ASI, New Delhi.

Binford, Leuis 1968, Post-Pleistocene Adaptations, in S.R. Binford and L.R. Binford (Eds.) *New Perspectives in Archaeology* pp. 313-41. Chicago : Aldine.

Chaturvedi, S.N. 1985. Advance of Vindhyan Neolithic and Chalcolithic Cultures to the Himalayan Tarai – Excavation and explorations is Saryupar region of U.P., *Man and Environment* IX: 101-108.

Clark, J. Desmond and Gurucharan S. Khanna. 1989. The site of Kunjhun II, Middle Son Valley, and its Relevance for the Neolithic of Central India, in J.M. Kenoyer (Ed.) *old problems and New Perspectives in the Archaeology of South Asia,* Wis consin Archaeological Reports Vol. 2. pp 29-46 Madison: Department of Anthropology, University of Wisconsin.

Cockburn, J. 1879 notes on Stone Age Implements from Khasi Hills and the Banda and Vellore Districts, *Journals of the Asiatic Society of Bengal XLVIII*, pt. 2.

Harvey, E.L., D. Fuller, J.N. Pal and M.C. Gupta 2005. Early Agriculture of the Neolithic Vindhyas (North-Central India). *South Asian Archaeology* 2003 ate Franke Vogt and Hans-Joachim Weisshaar (Eds.), pp. 329-334. Aachen: Linden Soft Verlog E.K.

IAR- Indian Archaeology: A Review

Joglekar, P.P., J. N. Pal, V.D. Misra and M.C. Gupta 2008 Faunal Remains Recovered from the Neolithic Phase at Jhusi District Allahabad, Uttar Pradesh. *Puratattva* 38:251-259.

Mishra, V.D., J.N. Pal, M.C. Gupta. 2000. Further excavations at Jhusi, *Pragdhara* 10: 23-30.

Misra, V.D. 2002. Origin, chronology and transformation of the Mesolithic Culture in India. In V.D. Misra and J.N. Pal (Eds.) *Mesolithic India*, pp 447-464. Allahabad: Department of Ancient History, culture and Archaeology University of Allahabad.

Misra, V.D. 2007. Stone Age cultures, their chronology and Beginnings of Agriculture in the North-Central India, *Man and Environment* 32 (1) : 1-14.

Misra, V.D., J.N. Pal and M.C. Gupta 2004. Signifance of Recent Excavations at Tokwa in the Vindhya and Jhusi in the Gangetic Plain. *Journal of Interdisciplinary Studies in History and Archaeology* 1(1) : pp. 120-127.

Mukharjee, P. C. 1901. *Antiquities of Kapilvastu, Tarai of Nepal*, Archaeological Survey of India Report.

Pal, J.N. 1977. 'Bhartiya Nava Pashanik Sanskritiyan (Hindi). In '*Bhartiya Pragaitihasik Sanskritiyan* (Hindi) R.K. Verma pp. 272-282. Allahabad : Paramjyoti Prakashan.

Pal. J.N. and M.C. Gupta 2005. Excavations at Hetapatti (Allahabad District). Some Preliminary observation, *Journal of Interdisciplinary Studies in History and Archaeology* 2(1) (Summer 2005): 163-168.

Pandey, J.N. 2012. Aspects of Urbanization in the upper Ganga Plain: A Review, *Man and Environment*, vol. XXXVII, No. 2, Pune.

Pokharia, A.K., J.N. Pal and Alka Srivastava 2009. Plant macro remains from Neolithic Jhusi in Ganga Plain : evidence for grain-based agriculture, *Current Science*, Vol. 97, No. 4, 25 August 2009, pp. 564-572.

Possehl, G.L. 1988. Radio-carbon dates from South Asia, *Man and Environment* Vol. XII, pp. 169-196.

Singh, B.P. 1997. Neolithic and Chalcolithic Pottery of Middle Ganga Plain: A case study of Senuwar, in P.C. Pant and Vidula Jayaswal (Eds.) *Ancient Ceramics (Historical Enquiries and Scientific Approaches)*, pp.3-33. New Delhi: Agam Kala Prakashan.

Singh, P and A.K. Singh. 1998. Trial excavations at Bhunadih, District Ballia (U.P.) *Pragdhara* 8, pp.11-29.

Singh, P. 1994. Further Excavations at Imlidih Khurd-1993, *Pragdhara* 4, pp.41-48.

Singh, P. and A.K. Singh. 1996. Trial Excavations at Waina, District Ballia (U.P.), *Pragdhara*: 4, pp.41-61.

Singh, Purushottam, Ashok K. Singh. 1998. Trial Excavations at Bhunadin, Distt. Ballia, U.P., *Pragdhara* 8, pp.11-30.

Singh, Purushottam. 1993. 'Archaeological Excavations at Imlidih-Khurd-1992', *Pragdhara* 3, pp.22- 35.

Singh, Shitala Prasad. 1996. *Palaeo-Environment and Prehistoric Cultures in the Adwa Valley*, Allahabad.

Sinha, H.P. 1994. *Archaeological and Cultural History of Bihar, (with special reference to Neolithic Chirand)*, New Delhi : Ramanand Vidya Bhawan.

Tewari, Rakesh, R.K. Srivastava and K.K. Singh. 2002. Excavations at Lahuradewa, District Sant Kabirnagar, *Puratattva* 32, pp.54-62.

Tewari, Rakesh, R.K. Srivastava, K.K. Singh, K.S. Saraswat and I.B. Singh 2002-2003. Preliminary Report of the Excavations at Lahuradewa, District Sant Kabirnagar, U.P. 2001-2002: wider Archaeological Implications. *Pragdhara* 13, pp.37-68.

Tewari, R., R.K. Srivastava, K.K. Singh, K.S. Saraswat, I.B. Singh, M.S. Chauhan, A.K. Pokharia, A. Saxena, V. Prasad, M. Sharma. 2006. 'Second Preliminary Report of the Excavations at Lahuradewa, district Sant Kabir Nagar 2002-2003-2004 & 2005-06', *Pragdhara* 16, pp.35-68.

Tewari, Rakesh, R.K. Srivastava, K.S. Saraswat, I.B. Singh, K.K. Singh. 2008. Early farming at Lahuradewa, *Pragdhara* 18, pp.348-373.

Thapar, B.K. 1965, Neolithic Problem in India, in V.N. Misra and M.S. Mate (Eds.) *Indian Prehistory: 1964* pp. 87-112. Poona.

Verma, B.S. 1971. Excavation at Chirand: New Light on the Neolithic Culture Complex, *Puratattva* 4: 19-23.

Verma, R.K. 1989, Pre- Agricultural Mesolithic society of the Ganga Valley, P. 55-58 in *old problems and New perspectives in the Archaeology of South Asia*.

17

EVOLUTION OF EARLY FARMING CULTURE IN MIDDLE GANGA PLAIN

Neelesh Kumar Pandey

The Ganga, the river par excellence is the heart of India. It is the life source the very nerve of the land through which it flows. The Ganga plain has played major role in origin and development of agricultural in India. The ecosystem and the land divide the Gangetic plains into several subdivisions. The plain with its non-homogeneous nature is roughly divided into three divisions Upper Ganga plain, Middle Ganga plain and Lower Ganga plain. Middle Ganga plain has the maximum length of approximately 600 Km from west to east and the width to about 330 Km. The middle Ganga Plain Covers the States of eastern Uttar Pradesh and western Bihar lying on either side of Ganga and Saryu (Ghaghara) with the Himalyan and Peninsular ramparts on the north and south respectively. The rich fertile soil of the region and a network of river communication sustained and supported ever expanding needs of growing civilizations. It is believed that the fertile alluvium and favorable climate system has always been the centre for origin of agriculture and domestication in India. The archeological excavations and investigation reveals long cultural history of the region.

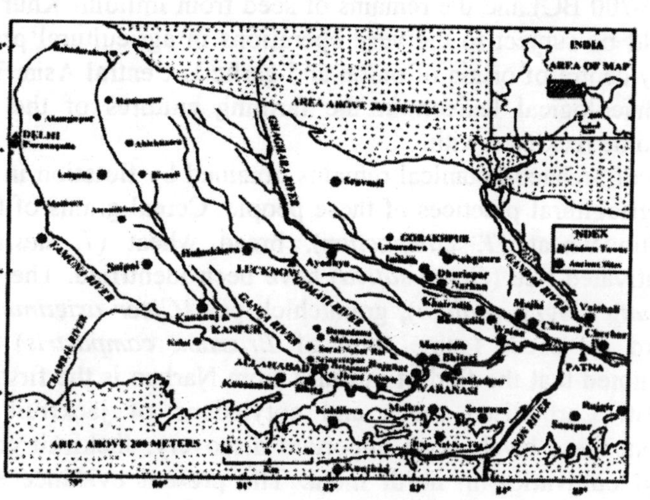

Fig. 1 : Archeological Sites in the Ganga Plain

The region of Middle Ganga Plain receive loans of a large number of crops of almost all kinds, cultivated in the present times, and seem to have been exploited apparently in the same way but in different technological circumstances of early cultural groups. In view of the ecological requirements of particular crops, the technological complexities would have inevitably directly concerned with the early agricultural pattern. One group, of which rice is most important, has its wild relatives in India and can be assumed to have been domesticated indigenously. Other than rice (*Oryza Sativa*), crops in this category include the remains of kodon-millet (*Paspalum scrobiculatum*), horse-gram (*Macrotyloma uniflorum*), green-gram (*Vigna radiate*), black-gram (*Vigna mungo*), moth-bean (*Vigna aconitifilia*), field-brassica (*Brassica juncea*), and sem (*Lablabpurpureus*). The second is major group of crop related to their wild relatives in the Mediterranean zone. These crops in the archaeological record, include the remains of barley (*Hordeum vulgare*), dwarf-wheat (*Triticum sphaerococcum*), bread-wheat (*Triticum aestivum*), lentil (*Lens culinaris*), field-pea (*Pisum arvense*), grass-pea (*Lathyrus sativus*), chick-pea (*Cicer arietinum*), linseed (*Linum usitatissimum*), safflower (*Carthamus tinctorius*) etc.

Another group of crop of African origin, encountered in the archaeological record of Middle Ganga Plain comprise ragi-millet (*Eleusine Coracana*), jowar-millet (*Sorghum bicolor*), pearl-millet (*Pennisetum glaucumsyn P. typhoides*) and cow-pea/lobiya (*Vigna unguiculata*). The areas of the origin of the sesame (*Sesamum indicum*) and castor (*Ricinus communis*) appear unresolved, some authors favouring Africa, others India.

Castor is reported to run in wild state in the scrubby jungles/plants of the outer Himalayas, East and North Africa, the Yemen, as well suggestive of its origin in India. On archaeological ground, its presence from Badarian culture of Egypt during the first half of 4th millennium B. C. is much earlier to the ancient records in India, during second-first millennia B. C. Presence of castor in the archaeological record from the Middle Ganga Plain is recorded by its wood charcoals. Phut/Kheera (*Cucumis melo*) and watermelon (*Citrullus lanatus*), recorded in the crop assemblage, are also decidedly African domesticates. *Cucumis melo* is truly wild in eastern tropical Africa and exploded into numerous cultivars in India. *Citrullus lanatus* is reported to be feral in the warmer regions but it is truly wild or native only in sandy and dry areas of South Africa, mainly in Kalahari Desert. These were also grown, for their luscious fruits, in the Middle Ganga Plain.

Cotton was grown by early farming communities in the region of Middle Ganga Plain. The genus comprises thirty tropical and subtropical species in the old world. *Gossypium herbaceum*- race *africanum*, distributed in the savanna vegetation of South Africa was probably first cultivated in Arabia and Syria before finding its way to the Indian subcontinent where *G. arboretum* had differentiated under cultivation in north-western India and Pakistan. (Phillip 1976: 196-200)

In the advancing state of our knowledge on the field-crops, onion (*Allium cepa*) seeds have also been encountered. The evidence of onion from Waina (1600-800 BC) and Raja-Nala-Ka-Tila (Tewari et.al. 1997: 77-96) (1300-700 BC) and the remains of seed from Imlidih- Khurd (Singh et.al. 1992: 120-22) (1300-800BC), would be subject to the very operations in agricultural practice which characterize horticulture. The primary centre of origin of onion and garlic is Central Asia. The introduction of onion encountered in the archaeological lexicon in the farming cultures of the Middle Ganga Plain, is considerably gratifying to be reckoned with.

A good quantity of archaeo-botanical remains obtained by flotation in Narhan (Singh 1994: 15) give a fair idea of the agricultural practices of these people. Cereal grains of hulled and six-row barley (*Hordeum vulgare*), club wheat (*T. campactum*), bread wheat (*T. aestivum*), dwarf wheat (*T. sphaerococcum*) and cultivated rice (*Oryza sativa*) have been identified. The pulse include pea (*Pisum sativum*), green gram/*mung* (*Vigna radiata*), gram/chick pea (*Cicer arietinum*) and *khesari* (*Lathyrus sativus*) besides mustard oil seeds (some form of *Brassica campastris*) and flax/linseed (*Linum usitatissium*). It may be noted that the find of mustard from Narhan is the first record of this oil-seed in the Indian sub-continent. Carbonised seeds and cotyledons of jackfruit or katahal (*Artocarpus heterophyllus*) found from these levels is an important discovery. Jackfruit grows wild in the Western Ghats and was taken to cultivation in north India. The present evidence suggests that the Narhan inhabitants cultivated it for its fruit.

An important advancement in crop economy of Chalcolithic site of Senuwar (Singh 2001: 109-18) can be seen by cultivation of *til* (*Sesanum indicum*), field- brassica/ brown mustard (*Brassica iuncea*), soft flower/ *kusum* (*Carthamus tinctorius*), linseed/*alsi* (*Linum usitattssimum*) and caster (*Ricinus communis*). The above evidence will show in what measure the Chalcolithic communities of Senuwar contributed to the advancement of the crop economy of the early agricultural communities. Besides, the find of watermelon seeds is unprecedented one. Orchard husbandry began to be practiced. Mango and jackfruit tree/ *Katahal* charcoals provide testimony to this effect. *Deodar* (*Cedrus desdara*) wood is also important to suggest that during this stage the quality of timbers of Himalayan forests became of considerable demand.

The record of crop remains shows that even the simple and unpretentious people in the initial non-metallic phases of occupations practiced persistently self-sustaining arable agricultural system characterized by the rotation of crops. Cultivation of rice is obvious as the region is one of the hearths of the domestication of this most staple crop in south–east Asia. Rotation of crops becomes remarkably apparent from Senuwar (Pd IA), Imlidih Khurd (Pd I) that the formers could successfully exploit the land resources for the sufficient means of agriculture, regardless of the use of any metallic tools. I feel no surprise to state that the agriculture in the metal-free stage of Neolithic set the desired foundation of economic base for the Chalcolithic and iron using cultures which were to follow, simply to upgrade the economy by the larger selection of crops. The expansion of agriculture facilitated by the copper and iron tools apparently provided only an additional "techno-environment efficiency", as put forward by Harris (1975).

A crucial point in the social organization of Chalcolithic and Iron Age farming societies would have been in commercial manner in which goods were exchanged, for without exchange of some kind of craft specialization was impossible to come up. This inclination in trade is spasmodically reflected by the presence of some cherished and imported items, such as grapes (raisins), dates, *chiraunji*, *jaiphal* (nutmeg), sandal wood, etc. in the Chalcolithic and Iron using cultures at Narhan and Khairadih, datable from 1300-200 B. C. (Saraswat 1992). These finds, on botanical ground, affirm the well knit organization of commerce and trade in the farming communities of Middle Ganga Plain.

Most of us are familiar that wheat, barley, lentil, field-pea, chick-pea (gram), jowar-millet, ragi-millet, Italian-millet, etc. are the main components of farming of the Harappan culture-complexes in the north-western regions of India, during 3rd-2nd millennia B.C. Earlier, these crops in the Ganga Plain were recorded later than their occurrence in Harappan times. The sign of crucial economic change in the dietary of rice-growing Neolithic-Chalcolithic occupants at Lahuradeva in Sant Kabir Nagar District in Middle Ganga Plain has become strikingly noticeable by the presence of barley. (Saraswat et.al. 2004)

The region of Middle Ganga Plain has at one times or other been considered as a part of early hearths of rice domestication and cultivation. The aggregate consensus aroused on botanical, phytogeographical, genetical, ecological, palaeoclimatological and philological grounds is that the *Oryza sativa* evolved from annual putative progenitor (supposedly *Oryza nivara*) over a broad belt extended from Ganga Plains below the foothills of Himalayas, across Myanmar (Burma), northern Thailand and Laos, to northern Vietnam and South China.

Domestication could have occurred independently and concurrently in different regions, inside and bordering the vast expanse from India to South China (Chang 1976; 1976b; 1985). The evolutionary sequence leading to the development of early annual forms of rice to the state of crop is very complex because of the gaps or deficiencies in evidence outside the botanical disciplines, as well as the state of fluidity that still faces the biosystematics of the wild species in the genus *Oryza*. The studies in the specialty areas have largely been discipline oriented, and do not provide an overall view. The palaeogeographers and geneticists have often taken option to conjectural reconstructions of South-East Asian prehistory to support hypothetical models of the evolutionary history of rice crop.

The rice cultivation in ancient Ganga Valley has long been a subject of debate and discussion in archaeology. Regretfully, the terms "cultivated" and "domesticated" rice have often been interchangeably used in archaeological records. Ambiguity may, it focuses attention upon the plant morphology rather than man and plant relationship, with which archaeologists are concerned. Identification is solely based on readily comprehensible botanical classification, characterizing the feature between the grains of morphologically cultivated and morphologically wild species of rice.

Archaeologists may also keep in mind that the grains and seeds of rice and many other plants of food value, which do not differ in any way from those of modern wild forms in our botanical classification, may have, however, been in a close relationship with prehistoric man, similar or indeed in some cases identical to consanguinity within the range of crop plants we now regard as cultivated. This standpoint has recently been elaborated in the plant economy from Senuwar. The terms cultivation and domestication refer to the two very different processes, with neither of them depending on the other. It is possible to cultivate non-domesticated (primordially) plants, while it is also conceivable to have domesticated plants without raising them in formal agricultural system. Domestication basically represents a process of genetic rather than environmental manipulation. It is not different from genetic change in nature except that the man is important selective factor for bringing out genetic change in plants. Domestication, according to Helbaek (1969), calls for conscious effort in the way, starting from the cultivation of wild species, of selection, nursing and propagation of crop plant, creating a reciprocal dependency between plant and man. A vast literature is produced by a number of workers on the domestication of cereal crops.

Oryza sativa is an important variety of rice found in Middle Ganga Plain. I want to discuss some Chalcolithic sites of Middle Ganga Plain which give evidences of *Oryza sativa* and some other varieties of rice.

Certain technological innovations for the food-production in early cultural development during the 6th-5th millennium B.C. at Lahuradewa (Tewari et.al. 2003), are deduced by the presence of a few grains of rice corresponding to *Oryza sativa*, cultivated all over the regions in south-east Asia. The evidence of rice circumscribed to its morphological characteristics, furnishes beyond doubt that some form of agriculture was in operation at and in the region of Lahuradewa site. As agriculture was being carried out within the habitats of wild forms of rice comparable to *Oryza rufipogon* have also been found. Wild forms of rice still occur predominantly all over the region, and also harvested for consumption exclusively or along with the rice crop.

The presence of cultivated rice at Lahuradewa during 6th-5th millennium B.C. is very significant. It may be mentioned that early dates for the cultivation of rice of about 7th-6th millennium B.C. were proposed by G. R. Sharma (et.al. 1980) from the well known site Koldihwa, district Allahabad, located on the right bank of the Belan River in Vindhyan Hills. But currently it has been found that dates (7th millennium B.C.) for wild and cultivated rice of Lahuradewa is earliest. Evidences of rice have been also found in Narhan, Waina, Senuwar etc.

Evidence of the early stages of plant manipulation in post-glacial times is understandably very vague. Sickle blades are found with a sheen, which is supposed to be produced in the course of cutting of reeds and grass stems. These generalized stone tools could be used for many purposes by non-agricultural communities. Plant remains elude us at this time range. Nothing is very conclusive. Food procurement is regarded to have been focused on harvesting the grains and seeds of wild grasses and other herbaceous plants. This system would have functioned as the beginning of pathway to agriculture in some of the areas where it was practiced, but certainly not all over.

There are five harvesting methods with which early cereal cultivators were, in all probability, familiar. Beating the ripe spike lets applied in a single or in multiple passes; use of sickles or other cutting equipments-for near-ripe or unripe crops; uprooting of plants, with near-ripe or unripe grains; plucking or hand-striping; and burning. The feasibility of each of these methods is attested by ethnographic studies of recent wild grass-seed foragers, including hunter-gatherers and farmers who supplement their domestic yield. Field experiments and observations of number of scientists (Wilke et.al. 1972) and by experiments at archaeo-agricultural research centers suggest that when exposed to these different methods (Reynolds 1981; Anderson 1988), the wild type of crops would be domesticated only if harvested by sickle-reaping or uprooting, while the grains are partially ripe or near-ripe (Hillman et.al. 1990).

What is most pertinent and crucial to note that the crops of wheat, barley, lentil, Field-pea, African millets, etc., which were mainstay in the agricultural prosperity of advanced Harappans in the north-western regions, made a bulwark in the agriculture of Neolithic-Chalcolithic rural communities up to the regions in Bihar. On the other hand, the rice from the region of Ganga Plain spread and held ranking in the agriculture of Early and Mature phases of Harappan civilization in the regions of Haryana. The problem of diffusion of agricultural traits in strict cultural apprehension, having established the spatial expression of crop plants in two-way avenues between the culturally and environmentally contrasting regions during third millennium B.C., does not appear to be so simple. This aspect came up to be initially discussed recently in the archaeological background of the Middle Ganga Plain (Saraswat 2004). A botanist may not be so much concerned with the diverse cultural complexes diffused over a wide zone, as with those of crop remains that act as indicators of agricultural expansion. Our main concern of discussion is of crop dispersal, which has drawn our attention to the long distance migration of crops and agricultural systems, during much ancient times i.e. 3rd millennium B.C. It presents a problem to archaeological research which will surely attract attention in future. In the present context it is relevant to remark that agro-economic zones crossed climatic and vegetational territories and became fully established between the Harappans in the north-western India and the peoples of Neolithic-Chalcolithic culture in the Middle Ganga Plain.

Some archaeological consideration will not be out of place here. It is sometimes possible to find incontrovertible proof of contact on archaeological grounds, when and where it occurs. The discovery of particular type of pottery and other artifacts brought with it, could give some inescapable conclusion that some trans-regional contact had existed. Yet, even when contacts between two regions did not in fact occur, it is logically impossible to prove the point. No conceivable find can ever show that contact did not take place. All that can be said is that the absence of evidence to the contrary makes the assumption tenable, which is not a conclusive statement. This being so, the task of the proof must always be on those arguing contact as a significant factor in initiating cultural or agricultural change. Quite clearly we do not have all the convincing answers as to time, motivation, dispersal, routes of direct or indirect diffusion in the archaeological lexicon of northern India, and equally clearly the waters have been considerably muddled in the archaeology, especially by inventiveness of spanning the cultural spread on the grounds of ceramic typology. Corridors are two-way avenues and there is no reason to suppose that the corridors of agricultural diffusion of which we are speaking, were not operative in much earlier times during 3rd millennium B.C. The question must next be faced as how this process of gradual diffusion unfolded and how farming and its correlates spread between apparently independent cultural zones of north-western India and Middle Ganga Plain. Not only the distance was great, but the geographical barriers were major, whether gatherers or farmers, slowly from one region to another and generation after generation, took the high bridle-path across the vast zone.

References

Anderson Gerfaud, P.C. 1988. Using prehistoric stone tools to harvest cultivated wild cereals: Preliminary observation of tracts and impact. In Beyries, (Ed.)- *Industries Lithiques, Traceologieet Technologic:* 175-195. British Archaeological Reports, Oxford.

Chang, T.T. 1976. *The rice cultures.* Phill. Trans. R. Soc. Lond. B. 275:143-147

1976b. The origin, evolution, cultivation, dissemination and Diversification of Asian and African rice, *Euphytica,* 25: 425-441.

1985. Crop history and genetic conservation: Rice- A case study, *IOWA State Journal of Research,* 59(4): 425-455;

Harris, M. 1975. *Culture, people, nature: an introduction to general anthropology.* Crowell, New York.

Helbeak, H. 1969. Plant collection, dry- farming and irrigation agriculture in prehistoric Dehluran. In: Hole, F., KV. Flannery and J.A. Neely (Eds.)-*Prehistory and human ecology of the Deh Luran Plain:* 383-426. Ann Arbor: Univ. of Michigan. Neely

Hillman, G.C. and M. Stuart Davies, 1990. Measured domestication rates in wild wheats and barley under primitive cultivation, and their archaeological implication. *Journal of World Prehistory, 4(2):* 157-222.

Phillips, L.L. 1976. Cotton: Gossypium (Malvaceae). In Simmonds, N.W. (Ed.)- *Evolution of crop plants,* 196-200. Longman: London and New York.

Reynolds, P. 1981. Deadstock and livestock. In: Mercer, R.(Ed.)- *Farming practice in British Prehistory:* 97-122. Edinburgh University Press, Edinburgh

Saraswat, K.S. 2004. Plant Economy in Ancient Malhar, *Pragdhara* no 14, Lucknow, pp. 137-72.

Saraswat, K.S. 2004. Plant Economy in Ancient Malhar, *Pragdhara* no 14, Lucknow, pp. 137-72.

Saraswat, K.S. and Anil K. Pokharia 2004. Plant economy at Lahuradeva: A preliminary contemplation. Abstract: Proc. Joint Annual Conference of IAS, ISPQS. and IHCS and National Seminar on the Archaeology of the Middle Ganga Plain:46-47. U.P. State Archaeology Dept., Lucknow.

Sharma, G.R., V.D. Misra, D. Mandal, B.B. Misra, J.N. Pal, 1980. *Beginning of Agriculture,* Abhinav Prakashan, Allahabad.

Singh, B.P. 2001. 'Stages of culture development in the Middle Ganga Plain: A case Study of Senuwar, *Pragdhara* no. 11, Lucknow. pp. 109- 118.

Singh, P. 1994. *Excavations at Narhan (1984-89),* New Delhi.

Singh. P., Ashok K. Singh and Indrajeet Singh. 1992. Excavation at Imlidih Khurd. *Puratattva* No. 22, p. 120-122.

Tewari, R. & R.K. Srivastava. 1997. Excavations at Raja Nal-ka-tila (1995-96), District Sonbhadra (U.P.): Preliminary Observations, *Pragdhara* no. 7, pp.77-96.

Tiwari, Rakesh. R.K. Srivastava, K.K. Singh, K.S. Saraswat and I.B. Singh. 2003. Preliminary report of the excavation at Lahuradeva, Distt. Sant Kabir Nagar, U. P. 2001-2002: Wider Archaeological Implications, *Pragdhara* no. 13, Lucknow, pp.37-68.

Wilke, P. J. Robert Bettinger, Thomas F. King, James F. O 'Connel. 1972. Harvest selection and domestication in seed plants. *Antiquity*, 46:203-209.

18

PALAEOLITHIC TOOLS FROM SHEKHAWATI REGION: A PRELIMINARY STUDY

Vineet Godhal

Rajasthan has been a centre of human's activities since prehistoric period, evidenced by the collection of lower Palaeolithic tools from all over the parts of the state. Since the last decade of 20th century, not a single prehistoric site was reported from Shekhawati region. The region encompasses the administrative units of Sikar, Jhunjhunu and Churu districts. However, some parts of Nagaur district are also considered in this region. Some of the researchers also considered Kotputli of Jaipur district in the same region. In recent survey of the Shekhawati, 8 lower Paleolithic, 3 middle Paleolithic and one upper Paleolithic sites had been located which throw light on the prehistoric archaeology of the specified area.

Study area

Shekhawati is a semi-arid historical region located in the northeast part of Rajasthan, bounded on the north-west by *Jangaldesh* region, on the north-east by Haryana, on the east by Mewat, on the south-east by *Dhundhar*, on the south by Ajmer, on the south-west by Marwar region and covers the area of 13,784 square kilometers. The inhabitants of the region are considered brave, sacrificing and hard working people which provide the highest number of persons to the Indian Army. This region is also known as Scotland of India because of its brave, sacrificing and painstaking Rajput people.

The word "Shekhawati" was first mentioned in the book '*Bankidas ri khyat*'. Col. W.S. Gardener was contemporary of Bankidas, who used the word Shekhawati in the year 1803. Later Col James Tod wrote the first history of Shekhawati. The term Shekhawati was used frequently in '*vamsh bhaskar*'. This suggests that the term Shekhawati came in use about two and half centuries ago. Shekhawati derives its name from the Rajput Kachhwaha chieftain Rao Shekha Ji. The descendants of Rao Shekha Ji, the ruling clan is called Shekhawat. Shekhawati means Garden of Shekha or Land of Shekhawat Rulers.

Most of the prehistoric sites are located in the hilly area of Shekhawati region. The major part of the land seems to have witnessed a storm in the ocean which washed the area and left its marks in the shape of sand layers visible everywhere. The Geology of the zone is obscured by the wind blown over-burden. Most of the area is a semi-desert which formed the bed of an ocean extending from the present shore of the sea to the line of Aravalli range. The south and south-eastern part of the region is occupied by loamy soil and hills of the Aravalli range. The rock exposed in the area belongs exclusively to the Delhi group of meta-sediments which are separated from the older Aravallis by a conspicuous unconformity.

The prominent rock exposures of the Delhi group are seen in the Neem Ka Thana hill situated in the south and south-eastern part of the Shekhawati region, along the continuation of the Khetri copper belt upto Sangarwa and from Bajor to Roopgarh. Delhi super group further been subdivided into two groups: an older Alwar group and a younger Ajabgarh Group.

Alwar Group is characterized by the dominance of arenaceous rocks consisting of quartzite of various types with sub-ordinate proportion of argillaceous. These rock types are seen in the eastern part of the Sikar district along the continuation of the Khetri belt upto Roopgarh in the south-central part. Besides these, many isolated out-crops of the rocks of the Alwar formation are present in Salhadipura, Sevli, Khandela, and Kotri. In the Salhadipura area, the major anticline exposes the amphibole quartzite, marble and schist. Along the eastern and northern part of the Salhadipura and Khandela anticline, well developed doubly plunging folds are noticed in Kotri hills.

Ajabgarh group is characterized by large portion of calcareous as compared to Alwar formation. The main rock types are marble, calc-gneisses, calc-silicate rocks, phyllites and mica schist. The rock types comprise mainly grey soft quartz mica schist with subordinate proportion of intercalated quartzite and mica schist. Igneous intrusive both of basic and acidic rock types are exposed throughout the region. The basic intrusive include epidiorites and amphibolites in the form of veins and sheets. These are fine grained, massive and melanochroic. Metamorphism in this region has a complex history of overprinting and meta-somatic activities. A prograde regional metamorphism, broadly coeval with regional deformation episode is the major metamorphic event of this region.

This paper deals with the settlement pattern of Palaeolithic man in Shekhawati region. The site belongs to the lower Palaeolithic tools are Sohanpura, Bheetaro, Reedh Ka Tila, Peer Baba Ki Bani (Badalwas), Udaipurwati (Kot), Salahadipura, Shobh (Chaneja Ki Dhani) and Gopalpura while middle Palaeolithic artifacts are collected from Bageshwar, Burja Ki Dhani, Laloda and from Udaipurwati (Kot) also. Upper Palaeolithic artifacts in a limited number are recovered from only one site called as Deoli Ki Dhani.

Lower Palaeolithic

Sohanpura

The village of **Sohanpura** is located 30 kilometres away from Kotputli in western direction, which is located 165 kilometres from Delhi and 105 kilometres from Jaipur on NH-8. Sohanpura village is 5 kilometres away from Patan, located on Kotputli-Dabla road. The nearest railway station is Dabla (10 kilometres away from Sohanpura) and Neem Ka Thana (25 kilometres from Sohanpura). Sohanpura is an important site from the archaeological point of view (Sharma 1997, Sharma *et al.* 2006, 2009), a type rock art site of Ganeshwar-Jodhpura Culture. The hill located in north-east of the village, called as "Payga", situated one kilometre away from the village; is a single hill in this area formed of sand stone, consist 14 rock shelters of different sizes and depth. Only 5 shelters bear rock paintings. In recent surveys, Palaeolithic artifacts made on quartzite have been collected from this archaeological site. Probably, it was a depression between the hills where water was accumulated in ancient period before the shelters.

From Sohanpura, total four lower Palaeolithic tools are recovered consisted 3 handaxes and one discoid tool (**Plate 18.1 & 18.2**). All of these tools are prepared on core of quartzite stone. The handaxes recovered from Sohanpura are as similar as the handaxe culture of south Rajasthan. One of the handaxe is prepared on a thick core of brownish quartzite stone having the size of 12 cm length, 9.5 cm wide and 3.3 cm thickness. This tool has been totally flaked. Dorsal face has comparatively large scars with deep negative bulb of percussion on the edges. Working end portion of the tool has been broken. Striking platform may be easily observed on the both sides of the tool. Marks of stepped flaking are also observed. Another handxae is made on the quartzite stone of light bluish colour having the length of 12.7 cm, 7.7 cm width and 3.5 cm thickness. Dorsal face has bigger and deep flake scars. Right side of the dorsal face has bigger flake scars compare the left portion of the tool. Ventral face is flaked only from one side. Third handaxe is made on the quartzite stone having the length of 10.7 cm, 8.5 cm width and 2.7 cm thickness. Two mini flake scars are observed on the working end of the tool, with cortex on the dorsal face. Ventral face is more flaked with stepping technique than dorsal face. Striking platform is easily observed on the ventral face also. Working area has wideness with some round corners. During the exploration, only one discoid tool was collected, made on quartzite stone of light brownish colour. This tool has the length of 9.8 cm, 7.8 cm wide and 3.7 cm thickness. Patination may be easily observed on the tool. A major part of the cortex is easily observed on the dorsal and ventral part of the tool.

Bheetaro

The village of Bheetaro is located about 15 kilometres away from Sohanpura on Neem Ka Thana road. The site is 4 kilometre away in north-west direction of Dokan village on the road of Sohanpura-Patan-Neem Ka Thana, in the vicinity of Ganeshwar, having scattered copper slag in all over area. Actually the site is located between the hills and inside area so it is called as "Bheetaro" means situated in inner area. The river of Kansawati flows in the eastern side of the village. There are four shelters in this group in which only one bears painting. Three handaxes made on quartzite stone are collected from Bheetaro **(Plate 18.3 & 18.4)**. First handaxe is made on dark brownish quartzite stone having the length of 14.5 cm, 8.6 cm wide and 3.8 cm thickness. This tool made on roundish pebble stone having some patination on the dorsal face. Flaking has been done in different stages. Flake scars may be easily seen on the dorsal and ventral face of the tool. Original cortex may be seen on the both of the dorsal as well as ventral face. This tool has a shape of almond, may be put in the developed Acheulian culture. Another handaxe is prepared on the quartzite stone of cream colour, with the length of 11.2 cm, width 7.5 cm and 3.7 cm thickness. Dorsal face is more flaked against the ventral face. Striking platform is easily observed on the same part. Third handaxe is made on the light brownish colour of quartzite stone, have the length of 10.8 cm, wide 6.8 cm and 3.6 cm thickness. This tool is made on the core. Cortex may be seen on ventral face. Deep flake scars may be easily observed on the edges of the dorsal as well as ventral face.

Tyonda-Rampura

The villages of Tyonda and Rampura are located approximately 25 kilometers away from the Khetri sub-division in the east of the same, in the district of Jhunjhunu. Between both of the villages ancient mound called as "Reedh Ka Teeela" by local people, is located. The mound is spread approximately in the area of one square kilometer. Iron and copper slag is scattered on the mound which reflects the smelting activities of ancient past. In the north-west part of the mound, a Paleolithic artifact **(Plate 18.5 & 18.6)** is collected, probably in secondary context. This handaxe tool is prepared on quartzite sandstone, but due to the flow in water, it has been rolled. This tool has the length of 14.9 cm, wide 9.2 cm and 4 cm thickness prepared on core. Patination may be seen on the ventral part of the tool. This tool may be placed in the category to bifacial tools. Both of the parts of the tools are flaked by the using of stone hammer with limited stroke. The flake scars are comparatively deep.

Badalwas (Peer Baba Ki Bani)

The site of the Badalwas or Peer Baba Ki Bani is located approximately 20 kilometers away from office headquarter of the Khetri subdivision. The village is located 0.5 km away from Tyonda and at same distance from Badalwas in opposite direction. During the exploration total 5 tools have been recovered consisted one handaxe and four cleavers **(Plate 18.7 & 18.8)**. These tools may be placed in the developed Acheulian culture. The first handaxe is prepared on the milky quartzite stone having length of 15 cm, wideness 9 cm and thickness 5 cm, prepared on a thick core. The dorsal part of the tool is made sloppy. Big flake scars are detached from the edges of the tool. Positive bulb of percussion and striking platform may be easily observed on the dorsal face. Both face dorsal as well as ventral having cortex. Butt end of the tool is of 'U' shape. Four cleaver tools are collected during the exploration from this site. One of the cleaver of light brownish color of quartzite stone having length of 13.2 cm, 8 cm wideness and 4 cm thickness, prepared on the Levallois flake of middle size. But due to the effect of time, the tool has been rolled with some patination on the surface. Striking platform may be easily seen on the dorsal face. The butt end is of 'V' shape which has its maximum wideness on the working end of the tool. Another cleaver is made on quartzite stone of light brownish colour having length of 7.3 cm, width 7 cm and thickness 2.2 cm, made on flake. Total three flakes are detached from the dorsal portion of the tool. The third cleaver is comparatively a developed tool compare to other artifacts, may be put in the developed Acheulian culture. Working end of this tool has a wide end. It has 14 cm length, 9 cm wideness and 4.3 cm thickness. Positive bulb of percussion may be seen in the centre of the tool. This tool is totally flaked from both of the sides. Butt end has 'V' shape. The fourth cleaver recovered from this site made on quartzite stone of light brownish colour. It has 12.8 cm length, 7.5 cm wideness and 4.7 cm thickness. Control flaking technique has been used for preparation of this tool. Striking platform may be easily observed. Butt end portion of this tool is in shape of 'U'.

Kot

The village of Kot is located approximately 5 km away from Udaipurwati tehsil headquarter. A dam called as Kot Bandh is also located here. A fortified structure is located in the outside hilly area of the village. Most of the artifacts made on quartzite stone are collected from here, consisted the three series of the Paleolithic industry. Total four lower Paleolithic tools and three middle Paleolithic tools have been recovered from here. Lower Paleolithic tool comprised three cleavers while one belongs to scraper. One of the cleavers is made on quartzite stone of light brownish colour. The working end has some broken part also. Size of this tool is 14 cm x 9.5 cm x 3.6 cm. Shallow flake scars are detached from working part of the tool. Mini flakes are also detached from ventral face. Second cleaver from this site is also prepared on the quartzite stone of light brownish colour, having length of 9.8 cm, wideness 11.5 cm and thickness of 3.8 cm. On the dorsal face, cortex may be easily observed. Working end has also deep and sloppy flake scars. The third cleaver from this site also made on light brownish colour of quartzite stone having length of 15.3 cm, 5.2 cm thickness and 12.8 cm wideness. This tool has no proper flaking. Stepped flaking technique is used for the preparation of the tool. Only one scraper is found from this site made on dark brownish quartzite stone, having length of 10 cm, wideness 9 cm and thickness of 5.1 cm. All of the types of flakes are detached from the tool. Dorsal face has comparatively more flaked the ventral face.

Salhadipura

The village of Salhadipura is located in the district of Sikar. The name of the village is based on the name of Salhadi Singh, who constructed a dam on the origin of the source of river Kantli at here. One kilometer away from Salhadipura in the western direction, the temple of Omal-Somal is located. On the basis of the architectural specialties this temple may be placed in the period of 9th-10th century AD. No image of deity is placed inside the *Garbhagriha*. Total three tools were picked from here in which one is discoid while two are handaxes. Discoid tool from Salhadipura is made on light brownish quartzite stone, having 12.4 cm length 4.3 cm thickness and 11 cm wideness. Working end is made as sloppy. Cortex may be observed in the lower part of the tool. From the edges, minor flakes are detached while cortex is also present in ventral face. One of the handaxe is prepared on quartzite stone of light brownish colour, having length of 14 cm, thickness of 5.5 cm and wideness of 10.8 cm. Block on block technique is used for preparation of this tool. Cortex is absent in this tool. The second handaxe recovered from this site, is made on the core of light brownish colour, having length of 14.8 cm, thickness of 4.3 cm and wideness of 10.3 cm. Cortex is present at both of the dorsal as well as ventral face. Deep and bigger flake scars may be easily observed on both of the faces.

Shobh

The village of Shobh is located 25 km north-east of the district headquarter of Sikar. From the hilly and sandy area of the region, Paleolithic artifacts made on quartzite stone are collected. These tools are comparatively larger than other tools recovered from the sites of the same region. Scraper, handaxes and discoid tools are collected from here. Total nine tools are picked which consist two scrapers, five handaxes and two discoid tools (**Plate 18.9 & 18.10**). One of the scrapers is made on core, having length of 18.5 cm, wideness of 10.5 cm and 9 cm thick. Flake scars have been removed from the edges of the tool. Ventral face has been more flaked. One of the handaxe is made on quartzite stone of light white color with the length of 15.5 cm, 4 cm thickness and 12 cm wideness. This tool is made upon a slim flake detached from the core, the main part of a broken stone. Working end is not so good of this tool. Signs of the flake scar may be easily observed. Another scraper is made on quartzite stone of colour of light white with the length of 13 cm, 4.5 cm thickness and 8.5 cm wideness. Working end may be easily observed. Dorsal face as well as ventral face has a good signs of irregular flake scars. Other handaxe recovered from this site is prepared on quartzite stone of creamy white colour with the length of 18 cm, 10.5 cm wideness and 3.5 cm thickness. Deep flake scars may be easily seen on the ventral and dorsal face of the tool. Another handaxe is prepared on the quartzite stone of light white colour. The nature of this stone is comparatively good to other tools. This tool has the length of 13 cm, thickness of 3 cm, and wideness of 7.2 cm. The tool is in shape of almond. Working end of this tool is quite in better condition. Discoid tool recovered from this site is made on quartzite stone of light brownish colour. Dorsal face has a similarity in the flake scars of all of the edges of the tool. This tool has the length of 13.4 cm, 10.3 cm wideness and 5.8 cm thickness. Original cortex is not available on the dorsal face while ventral face has original cortex. Deep and big flake scar may be seen in the ventral face of the tool. Another handaxe is made on quartzite stone of light cream colour with the length of 11.1 cm, 5cm thickness and 11 cm wideness. The length and wideness shows the similarity of both. Deep and big flake scars may be easily seen on the dorsal face of the tool. Another handaxe is prepared on quartzite stone of light creamy colour having the length of 14 cm, 4 cm thickness and 9 cm wideness. It seems that this tool is made on a core. Cortex may be observed on the dorsal face of the tool. Striking platform is also seen on the upper part of the dorsal face. Other discoid tool is made on quartzite stone of light white colour having length of 12 cm, width of 11cm and 4 cm thickness. This tool has the shape of ovate. Original cortex is present on the dorsal face of the tool. Irregular shaped flakes are detached from the edges of all sides. The reason behind the detaching of the flake scars was probably to make the tool similar dorsal as well as ventral.

Dungar Balaji

Dungar Balaji (Gopalpura) is located in the district of Churu, the first Paleolithic site in the same district, approximately 13 km away from headquarter of Surajgarh tehsil. A temple of Bhairun Baba is located one kilometer away from Dungar Balaji. Some lower Paleolithic handaxes and cleavers were also collected during the exploratory work. Blades and flakes made on chert are also collected from nearby field. Finding of a hammer stone has its importance also. The village of Deedwana is located 23 kilometers away from here where V.N. Misra did a pioneer work on prehistory of Rajasthan. More than 15 lower Paleolithic artifacts are collected from here but only four tools which consists 2 handaxes and two cleavers are described here. One of the handaxe is made on flake of quartzite of light red colour, having the length of 14.3 cm, 4 cm thickness and 6 cm width. The working end of the tool has been broken. Left portion of the dorsal face has a deep flake scar. The tool is divided into two equal parts by a natural line on the tool. Cortex is available only on ventral part of the tool. Another handaxe made on quartzite stone of light white colour having length of 17 cm, 5 cm thickness and 10.5 cm wideness. The nature of stone is not good. Minor flakes were removed from the edges of the tool. There is no cortex on the tool. One cleaver tool is made on quartzite stone of light brownish colour having length of 16.3 cm, thickness of 4.3 cm and wideness of 13.4 cm. Deep flakes are removed from the right edge of the tool. Different sized flakes have been removed from the butt end portion of the tool. On the dorsal face, cortex may be observed. Another cleaver made on light brownish colour of quartzite stone also recovered from this area. Cortex may be seen on the dorsal and ventral face of the tool. The tool has the length of 6.8 cm, thickness of 3.2 cm and wideness of 8 cm. This tool is made on flake.

Middle Palaeolithic

Bageshwar

The village of Bageshwar is located in the Tehsil of Neem Ka Thana of Sikar district; 15 km north of same tehsil headquarter on Neem Ka Thana-Patan road. Three small sized handaxes are collected from here (**Plate 18.11 & 18.12**). One of the middle Paleolithic handaxe is prepared on quartzite stone of light brownish colour having length of 12.9 cm, width of 10 cm and thickness of 4.3 cm. This tool has a look of almond. Edges are flaked by the use of hammer stone. Dorsal face has cortex also. Another handaxe is also prepared on the quartzite stone of light brownish colour having length of 9 cm, wideness of 6.5 cm and thickness of 2.8 cm. It seems that this tool was prepared on the ovate pebble. The working end of the dorsal face is broken. Different sized flake scars are observed on the dorsal face. Cortex is also available on the dorsal face. It seems that wooden hammer was used in preparation of this tool. Another handaxe is made on mica mixed quartzite stone having length of 15.2 cm, wideness of 8.2 cm and 4.2 cm thickness. This stone has not n good nature. Dorsal and ventral face of the tool has been totally rolled. The tool has the shape of amygdaloid. Butt end portion of the tool has 'U' shape. Cortex may be seen on ventral face.

Burja ki Dhani

Burja Ki Dhani is located 40 kilometers away from Srimadhopur, tehsil headquarter in the district of Sikar. Two specimens, one handaxe and one scraper, are describing here. Handaxe tool is made on flake having 10 cm length, 6.2 cm width and 3.5 cm thickness. On the basis of size this tool may be placed in the middle Palaeolithic tools. Control flaking technique was used in making this tool. Striking platform is also present on the dorsal face of the tool. Flake scars are removed from the edges of the tool. Butt end portion is comparatively thick against the working end. Another tool is unifacial scraper which was collected from this area during the exploration, having the length of 7.8 cm, 5.3 cm width and 2 cm thickness. It is made on quartzite stone of light brownish colour. Striking platform is easily observed on the dorsal face of the tool. This tool is made on flake.

Laloda

The site of Laloda is located on Khetri-Neem Ka Thana road, approximately 15 km away from Khetri. The local people called this village as Maid. two small sized handaxes are recovered from this size (**Plate 18.13 & 18.14**). These tools are prepared on quartzite stone. On the basis of technique of preparation and typology, these tools may be placed in middle Paleolithic period. The first handaxe is prepared on the flake of quartzite stone of dark brownish colour having length of 12.3 cm, 6.7 cm wideness and 3.2 cm thickness. Dorsal and ventral face of the tool is totally flaked. Sloppy flakes are detached from the edges of the tool. Striking platform may be seen on the upper part of the ventral face of the tool. Butt end portion of the tool is flat. Another handaxe is prepared on the quartzite stone of light green colour having length of 10.3 cm, 6.3 cm wide and 2.5 cm thick. Working end portion of the tool has some wideness also. Flakes are detached from the edges of the tool. Butt end portion has 'U' shape. Ventral part has some flatness also. Both of the arms of the tools are parallel.

Upper Palaeolithic

Deoli Ki Dhani

The village of Deoli Ki Dhani is located 20 km away from Khandela, a subdivision in Sikar district. The region is disturbed by the seasonal rivulets. Till recent survey, only from this place upper Palaeolithic (**Plate 18.15 & 18.16**) artifacts are recovered.

Discussion

The Palaeolithic man lived when the climate of the earth was much more fierce than it is now; there were long periods of severe cold and snow-fall in the high altitudes; they were followed by equally severe dry and warm spells. In the adjoining plains there were corresponding periods of heavy rainfall and desiccation. All these resulted in immense changes in the face of the earth and configuration of the land. Palaeoliths are found generally on the old terraces of rivers, on the deserted river beds, in the deposits of boulders and gravels in the sections of rivers and in caves. In recent years, there has been a spurt in Palaeolithic exploration and research in the country, as a result of which hundreds of tool-bearing deposits have been found in the sections and terraces of many rivers in Rajasthan. The discovery of palaeoliths in the region has pushed back the antiquity of this region a hundred thousand years ago. The significance of archaeological work in the prehistoric period can be better appreciated if the natural, geological, orographical and vegetation features of Rajasthan are properly understood. The study of the archaeological materials in the above pages reveals an interesting image of the primitive man in Shekhawati region. It shows that during the prehistoric period the region was also inhabited by primitive man. We may now try to see how the prehistoric culture was developed through the lower to upper Paleolithic in the specified region and also in nearby area. While doing so we shall constantly keep in mind Graham Clark's caution about "Conclusion being drawn from distribution patterns which reflect no more than the contemporary state of prehistoric research" (Clark 1960).

The early Stone Age represented by the early Acheulian culture is known from the district of Sikar, Jhunjhunu and Churu. Total 33 Lower Palaeolithic tools are collected from the region of Shekhawati in which 17 handaxe, 9 cleavers, 4 disoids and 3 scrapers. Maximum 9 no. of tools are collected from Shobh have the percentage of 27.27 and minimum one tool was recovered from Reedh Ka Tila (Table:1, Table:2). The lack of palaeontological evidences from any of the sites precludes the establishment of a relative chronology on the basis of the comparative study of the tools recovered from the different parts of the country. Typologically, there is homogeneity among the tools all of the sites. Even we did not picked more than 15 tools from any of the site but on the basis of the recovered material we can assume that this area was also suitable region for primitive man in ancient period. We have not seen any of the river section in the area. Spatially the Acheulian culture is better known in the eastern part of the Berach basin. The main concentration of tools lies near Hajiakheri in the Wagan and near Chittorgarh in the case of the Berach and Gambhiri. Most of the lower Paleolithic tools have been recovered from the district of Sikar and Jhunjhunu. The territory lying to the north of the Kantli river basin has yielded very little evidence of the early Stone Age.

All the artifacts are made of quartzite of which two varieties are discerned. Those from the Sikar and jhunjhunu districts are of a good conchoidal fracture, compare to Churu district. The artifacts of both of these districts have deep flake scars. It produces good conchoidal fracture and is suited for tool manufacture. The artifacts recovered from Churu district have flattish scars. Evidences of three techniques are seen in the Shekhawati industry called as, stone hammer, wood hammer and Levallois. The stone hammer technique is seen in the manufacture of a small number of handaxes, a majority of cleavers and in core scrapers and large flakes. All these exhibits deep, large scars, irregular outlines and uneven surfaces. The use of cylinder hammer technique is seen in a majority of handaxes, some cleavers and in secondary work on flakes. It has produced small, shallow scars, regular outlines, thin section and even surfaces.

There is no evidence of the use of heavy stone hammer seen in the large, thick flakes of the early Stone Age. In the preparation of tools in upper Paleolithic period, all the flakes were detached either by a light stone hammer or a wood or bone hammer. The same technique was mostly employed in the preparation of core tools. Prepared core technique is more common in this culture than in the lower and middle Paleolithic period. Flake scrapers and points bear very fine retouch on their margins. This could have been produced by the use of a sharp, pointed instrument, possibly of bone or tooth.

Raw material has its own importance in the life of human being. Quartzite stone was the first priority of lower Paleolithic man for making the tools. Scrapers, handaxes and cleavers are the main tool of the primitive man. In the middle Paleolithic period, the continuity of handaxes may be observed with the variation in sizes on the same raw material. Small sized handaxes are of middle Paleolithic period. The lower Paleolithic industry was based on core tools while middle Paleolithic tools are made on flakes. Upper Paleolithic industry is totally based on flakes. Upper Paleolithic tools consisted flake choppers, burins, flake blades etc. All of the upper Paleolithic tools are made on quartzite stone in Shekhawati region while in southern Rajasthan most of the upper Paleolithic tools are made of chert stone.

On the basis of the comparative survey with Banas-Berach basin, it may be said that although we have no more sites belonging to Paleolithic period in the Shekhawati region as compare to southern Rajasthan; it seems that the Acheulian man did not avoid the hilly and thickly forested country of the foothills and the Aravallis proper.

References

Clark, J.G.D. 1960. Comments on J.G.D. Clark's article "Human Ecology during Pleistocene and Later times in Africa South of Sahara", *Current Anthropology*, Vol. I, No. 4: 321.

Sharma, Murari lal.1997. Rock Art of Northern Rajasthan. *Purakala* 8 (1-2):25-35.

Sharma, Murari Lal, Madan Lal Meena, Krishna Gopal Sharma and Vineet Godhal. 2006. Copper age Remains from Sohanpura Rock Art Site and nearby (North-East Rajasthan). *Nucleus* VI (2): 53-62.

Sharma, Murari Lal, Madan Lal Meena, Krishna Gopal Sharma and Vineet Godhal. 2009. Chalcolithic Antiquities from Sohanpura and nearby Region in North-East Rajasthan. *Puratattva* 39: 58-67.

Table 1

Name of the Site	Number of Tools
Sohanpura	4
Bheetaro	3
Reedh Ka Tila	1
Peer Baba Ki Bani (Badalwass)	5
Kot (Udaipurwati)	4
Salhadipura	3
Shobh	9
Balaji Ki dungari	4
Total	33

Table 2

Name of the Site	Handaxe	Discoid	Cleaver	Scraper	Total
Sohanpura	3	1	----------		4
Bheetaro	3	----------			3
Reedh Ka Tila	1	----------			1
Peer Baba Ki Bani (Badalwass)	1		4		5
Kot (Udaipurwati)	----------		3	1	4
Salhadipura	2	1			3
Shobh	5	2		2	9
Balaji Ki Dungari	2		2	----------	4
Total	17	4	9	3	33

19

NEW APPEARANCE OF BEADS IN NBPW CULTURE IN THE MIDDLE GANGA PLAIN

Shankar Jaikishan

The N.B.P.W. period was noticeable by noteworthy changes- introduction of coinage which facilitated trade, highways which promoted long-distance communication and commerce, extensive use of iron, structure of kiln-burnt brick, virtually forgotten after the Harappan culture, and above all the origin of cities, many of them strongly fortified, some at the time of their very establishment and others later on. The oft-repeated list of sixteen maha-janapadas mentioned in the early Buddhist literature comprises a few oligarchical (sometimes called republican) principalities as well in the tarais, the capitals are identifiable and include such important city sites as CHAMPA (the capital of Anga), VAISALI (the Licchavis), RAJGIR (Magadh) RAJGHAT (Kasi), SRAVASTI (Kosala), and all are comes under the boundary of this region.

The diagnostic pottery of the first part of the period is the NBPW, which overlaps with the last phase of the PGW; though distinctive in hue, indicative of a different kind of slip and condition in the kiln, its shapes are practically identical with the PGW ones; there is also similarity in some of the red wares associated with the two. With its origin in east Uttar Pradesh and west Bihar and thus having a more e. origin than the PGW, it nevertheless indicates a sort of continuity in the ceramic tradition. The NBPW spread practically all over India, though the diffusion must have been gradual and dependent on the distance from the epicenter. It has been variously conjectured that the expansion followed in the wake of Mauryan imperialism or of iron from Bihar or of Buddhism. The fact probably is that being the distinctive ceramic competent such as terracottas, provides yet another evidence of a semblance of cultural uniformity over large parts of the country in the initial part of the period. (Ghosh 1989: 131)

Beads of NBPW Culture

Beads were profusely used in a variety of mediums during this phase. Mediums like clay, stone and bone must have been adopted by common man while semi precious stones were used by comparatively higher class. It is also likely that diverse usages depending on different purposes were other causes of different types of materials for bead manufacturing.

Chirand is located on the confluence of river Ganga and Gandak and revealed beads of chalcedony, blue glass, green glass, black glass, carnelian, soap stone, grey stone, crystal, amethyst, oyster, ivory, steatite, agate, jasper and faience in various shapes like long cylindrical, short barrel, long barrel, button shaped, hexagonal, rectangular, short truncated barrel, oval shaped, long elliptical, tubular, hemispherical, long tubular, drum and disc at the level of Period-III (800B.C.-200B.C.).(Verma 2007: 213-221). Sonpur, located in the Gaya district of Bihar, revealed the evidence of Agate, amethyst, bone, ivory, carnelian, chalcedony, shell, copper, crystal, glass, jasper, soap-stone and terracotta beads in various shapes like long truncated barrel, long convex hexagonal, long barrel circular, spherical, conical, pentagonal truncated, half moon (Semi-circular), cornerless square, oval shaped, short tricone, triangular, animal shaped, elliptical, long collared, lion faced scorpion body and ghata shaped beads from period II Northern Black Polished Ware period. (Sinha and Verma 1956 and 1959-62: 6, 101-113). Agiabir (Lat.25°13'52"N; 82°38'41"E) is located on the left bank of the Ganga on the border of Mirzapur and Bhadohi district. Here a bead manufacturing workshop has been discovered along with finished and unfinished materials of beads. (Puratattva-29: 117). From period-III (600B.C.-200B.C.) beads of agate, carnelian, chert, jasper, quartz, ivory, faience, glass, bone, shell, ghata shaped and arecanut shaped terracotta beads have been found (Singh and Singh: 2004: 72-74). Terracotta conical beads are reported from N.B.P.W. level at Apsad (IAR 1983-84: 14). Beads of semi-precious stones are recovered from period-I N.B.P.W (second century B.C. to second century A.D.) at Balirajgarh (IAR 1974-75: p. 10). From period-II N.B.P.W, beads of semi-precious stones have been unearthed at Buxar (charittarvan) (IAR: 1963-64: 8). Semi-precious stones, glass and terracotta beads have been found from period-I Late N.B.P.W. at Champa (IAR: 1971-72: 5; 1974-75: 9). Period-I N.B.P.W (second century B.C. to First century A.D.) of Chandadih, revealed beads of carnelian, jasper, agate, rock-crystal, bone and ghata-shaped terracotta (IAR: 1977-78:15). Beads of terracotta, glass, ivory, crystal, agate and bone have been unearthed from period-II at Checher-Kutubpur (IAR: 1988-89, p. 9). Terracotta, glass, carnelian, onyx, faience and sardonyx beads have been found from period-I (circa 8th - 6th century B.C.) of Ganwaria/Piprahwa (Srivastava: 1996: 167-173). Period-IVA of Jakhera belonging to a co-occurence of PGW and NBPW revealed beads of semi-precious stone (IAR: 1986-87: 78). Beads of terracotta and semi-precious stones are reported from Period-V (N.B.P.W.) at Jhusi (IAR: 1997-98:167; 1994-95:71). Terracotta beads from period-II N.B.P.W have been unearthed at Juafardih (Puratattva 38: 59-73). Semi-precious stone beads have been unearthed from Period-I (N.B.P.W.) at Katragarh (IAR: 1976-77: p.12). From period-IV marked by N.B.P.W., numerous steatite disc-shaped beads are recovered at the site of Lahuradeva (IAR: 2002-2003:296-297). Period-III belonging to N.B.P.W at Maner, beads of terracotta and semi-precious stone have been found. (IAR: 1984-85:12) From period IB appearance of NBPW, beads of terracotta have been revealed at Masaon (IAR: 1965-66:51; 1967-68:46-47). Beads of glass, terracotta and semi-precious stones have been found from period-II belonging to NBPW at Oriup. (IAR: 1966-67: p-6) Period-II belonging to NBPW at Panr, beads of carnelian, crystal, jasper, chalcedony, agate, coral, steatite and ivory are reported. (Prajna-Bharti Vol.-XI: 84) Beads of chalcedony in hexagonal shape, bone in apple shape, white stone in spherical shape and terracotta in vase, circular and pear shaped have been unearthed from period I (c.600 B.C. to 150 B.C.) at Patliputra (Sinha and Narain: 1970: 54). Beads are reported from NBPW level at Prahladpur (IAR: 1962-63:41). Period III NBPW culture (700-200 B.C.), beads of terracotta have been revealed at Raja-Nal-ka-Tila. (IAR: 1995-96:106; 1996-97:171) Beads of agate, amethyst, bone, carnelian, chalcedony, chert, copper, coral, crystal, faience, glass, ivory, jasper, lapis lazuli, paste, terracotta and topaz in various shapes like long barrel circular, long cylinder circular, short cylinder circular, standard cylinder, globular (plain), long cylinder square, tapering lenticular and spacer bead are recovered from period IB circa 600 B.C. to 400 B.C. at Rajghat (Narain and Singh: 1977: 21-23). Banded agate and terracotta beads have been revealed from period-I (3rd – 2nd century B.C.) at Rajgir (IAR: 1974-75:11). From period III NBPW, beads of terracotta, carnelian and other semi-precious stones have been unearthed at Ramchaura. (IAR: 1995-96:6; 1996-97:9; 1997-98:18) Semi-precious stone beads are reported from period-IB NBPW at Sarai-Mohana. (IAR: 1967-68:49). Beads of semi-precious stones are recovered from period IV c.7th-6th century B.C. to c.5th-4th century B.C at Senuwar (IAR: 1986-87: 27-28). Beads of carnelian, crystal, agate, and terracotta are reported from period-III at Sohgaura. (IAR: 1974-75:47) From period-IV, beads of semi-precious stones, terracotta, copper and steatite have been revealed at Taradih (IAR: 1981-82:11; 1983-84:13; 1985-86:8; 1986-87:24;). Agate, amethyst, horn, red coral, carnelian, chalcedony, vitreous material, shell, copper, crystal, glass, jasper, soap-stone and terracotta beads in various shapes truncated standard barrel circular, small hexagonal, long convex circular, double-holed semi-circular flat, circular flat, peculiar shape, convex flat, spherical, pentagonal truncated, long cylinder circular, rectangular, disc cylinder circular, short cylinder circular, long barrel circular, and ghata shaped beads from period II (600 B.C. to 200 B.C.) have been unearthed at Vaisali (Sinha and Roy : 1969 : 172-190). From period-II of Black slipped ware, red slipped ware and plain red ware among the NBP associated wares at Waina, beads of terracotta and semi-precious stones are recovered (IAR: 1994-95:72-73).

New Appearance in beads

On the basis of above discussion agate, carnelian, chalcedony, jasper, chert, faience, slate-stone, soap-stone and steatite are also continue for bead manufacture in lapidaries of N.B.P.W. culture, while a few new stones were introduced like amethyst, basalt, coral, crystal, granite, lapis-lazuli, lime-stone, onyx, oyster, quartz, sardonyx and other material like glass, ivory and paste also used for manufacture beads in this period.

Agate and carnelian retained their popularity on top in also N.B.P.W. culture. Unfinished agate beads were collected from Sravasti. This indicates towards its local manufacture.

The most popular shape of bead were spherical and long barrel, which were practiced in most of the materials at almost every sites of this culture. Spherical bead of crystal are reported from Rajghat, Sravasti and Vaisali. The Rajghat specimens were grounded and polished to such a degree that shapes like spherical and long convex circular has been achieved with remarkable precision.

There is one long cylinder circular bead at Sonpur which was made with banded agate and carnelian. Only a few bead of lapis-lazuli were recovered from the N.B.P.W. sites, which indicate that India's trade relation with Central Asia was maintained during this period, which is attested by Rajghat.

Similar is the case with faience beads. They were also very meager in N.B.P.W. culture. The popular shape of terracotta beads '*amalaka*' was represented by one bead of faience at Rajghat (Niharika: 1993:256-257). Circular, hexagonal, barrel, bicone, cylinder, disc, rectangular, spherical shapes were continued in this culture too.

Discussion

Evidence of the use of beads in India comes from the Mesolithic and runs through all the subsequent periods. Early evidences of beads in India reported from Langhnaj in Gujarat and Bagor in Rajasthan. Beads of dentalium shell from the Mesolithic/Neolithic site of Langhnaj and stone beads have been reported from phase-I (c. 5000 to 2000 B.C.) of Bagor. Though it is suspected that they might really belong to a subsequent phase dated between c. 2800 and 600 B.C. (Ghosh: 1989: 216).

Among the Neolithic and Chalcolithic sites only a few yielded stone beads. Only nine types of stones were used in Neolithic and Chalcolithic cultures for manufacturing. Among them the commonly used stones were agate, carnelian, chalcedony, jasper and steatite. Beads of bone, conch, copper, ivory, shell and terracotta also occurred from these cultures.

Agate was most popular material for this art than carnelian and steatite, that's why the number of agate beads is reported maximum in quantity. Carnelian and steatite was represented by a few beads, but both are also popular for bead manufacturing and these are from Agiabir, Bhunadih, Chirand, Imlidih-khurd, Lahuradeva, Oriup, Ramchaura, Sohgaura and Taradih respectively. Only one bead of each slate-stone, shell and conch were reported from Chirand, Agiabir and Taradih.

In the comparison to the previous culture, the lapidaries of NBPW culture used limited variety of stones for bead manufacture. The use of previous material was not dropped by the artisans of this culture, while new materials were introduced like amethyst, basalt, coral, glass, ivory, lapis-lazuli, onyx, oyster, paste, quartz, sardonyx and topaz.

The settlements of entire middle Gangetic plains come under immigration. The settlement pattern at this stage shows advancement on the previous stages. While most of the settlements of middle Gangetic plain lie on the river banks, the other sources of water were also exploited. So, the people of this culture have got new raw materials for bead within the boundary of middle Gangetic plain. Some material was obviously having been imported from other regions also, as they locally not available in view of its natural resources.

Such changes refer to the rising affluence in settlement and change the socio-economic life of the occupants of the Gangetic plains which is gradually leading them towards the phase. The variety and typology in bead manufacturing during the period was more advanced in due emergence of the life style into the urban or city settlement and contact therein to each other's and even far beyond their political jurisdiction. This possibility was only made in due trading communications and cultural exchanges made similar role to producing the objects like beads.

References

Excavation at Panr, Prajna-Bharti, Vol.-XI, p-84.

Ghosh, A. 1989. *An Encyclopaedia of Indian Archaeology*, Munshiram Manoharlal Publishers Pvt. Ltd, New Delhi, p. 131.

Ghosh, A.; 1989: *An Encyclopaedia of Indian Archaeology*, Munshiram Manoharlal Publishers Pvt. Ltd, New Delhi, p. 216.

IAR: Indian Archaeology: A Review.

Narain, A.K. and Singh, P.; 1977: *Excavation at Rajghat (1957-58; 1960-65)*, Varanasi, pp-21-23.

Niharika., 1993. *A Study of Stone Beads in Ancient India*, Bhartiya kala prakashan, Delhi, pp 256-257.

Sigh, Purushotam and Singh, A.K.; 2004: *Excavation at Agiabir*, Aryans Books International, New Delhi, pp. 72-74.

Singh, Purushotam and Singh, A.K.; 1999: "Agiabir-1999: A preliminary report", *Puratattva*-29. Bulletin of the Indian Archaeological Society, New Delhi, p.117.

Sinha, B.P. and Narain Lala Aditya.; 1970: *Pataliputra Excavation (1955-56)*, the Directorate of Archaeology and Museums, Bihar, Patna, p-54.

Sinha, B.P. and Roy, S.R.; 1969: *Vaisali Excavations (1958-1962)*, The Directorate of Archaeology and Museums, Bihar, Patna, pp-172-190.

Sinha, B.P. and Verma, B.S., *Sonpur Excavation:1956 and 1959-62*, Directorate of Archaeology and Museums, Govt. of Bihar, Patna, pp. 6 & 101-113.

Srivastava, K.M., 1996, *Excavation at Piprahwa and Ganwaria*, Archaeological Survey of India, Delhi, pp-167-173.

Verma, V.S.;2007: *Chirand: Excavation Report, 1961-64 and 1967-70*, Directorate of Archaeology, Department of Youth, Art and Culture, Govt. of Bihar, pp. 213-221.

Name of the Sites	Materials																									
	Agate	Amethyst	Basalt	Bone	Carnelian	Chalcedony	Chert	Copper	Coral	Faience	Glass	Ivory	Jasper	Lapis-Lazuli	Onyx	Oyster	Paste	Quartz	Sardonix	Shell	Soap-Stone	Topaz	Steatite	Terracotta	Remarks
Agiabir	Y				Y		Y			Y	Y	Y	Y					Y		Y				Y	
Apsad																								Y	
Balirajgarh																									SPS
Buxar																									SPS
Champa																								Y	SPS
Chandadih	Y			Y	Y								Y												
Checher-Kutubpur	Y			Y							Y	Y												Y	
Chirand	Y	Y			Y	Y					Y	Y	Y			Y					Y				SPS
Ganwaria/ Piprahwa					Y					Y	Y				Y				Y					Y	
Jakhera																									SPS
Jhusi																								Y	SPS
Juafardih																								Y	
Katragarh																									SPS
Kumrahar	Y																								
Lahuradeva																							Y	Y	SPS
Maner																								Y	SPS
Masaon																								Y	
Oriup											Y													Y	SPS
Panr	Y				Y	Y			Y			Y	Y										Y		
Pataliputra				Y		Y																		Y	SPS
Prahladpur																									SPS
Rajgir	Y																							Y	
Raja-Nal-ka-Tila																								Y	SPS
Rajghat	Y	Y		Y	Y	Y	Y	Y	Y	Y	Y	Y	Y	Y			Y					Y		Y	
Ramchaura					Y																			Y	SPS
Sarai-Mohana																									SPS
Senuwar																									SPS
Sohgaura	Y				Y																			Y	
Sonpur	Y	Y		Y	Y	Y		Y			Y	Y	Y							Y	Y			Y	
Taradih								Y															Y	Y	SPS
Vaisali	Y	Y			Y	Y			Y		Y		Y					Y		Y	Y		Y		
Waina																								Y	SPS

<Y for Yes> & <SPS for Semiprecious Stone>

20

EXCAVATIONS AT PEETNAGAR

D.K. Mathur

The ancient site Peetnagar (Lat. 22°11' 22" N and Long. 75° 57' 30" E) is situated on the left bank of the river Narmada, beside the upper part of the present village Peetnagar, and about 14 kms from Sanabad towards north-west direction in Tehsil Badwaha of district Khargaon in Madhya Pradesh. The nearest railway station is Omkareshwar on the Indore – Khandwa meter gauge line. The circular shaped mound is lie on the top and upper side of the village. It measures about 60 meters in length and 50 meters in width, and has a height of about 25 metres; its northern part is very much destroyed due to the digging by the villagers. The river Narmada flows here in serpentail form taking a turn on the other side of the mound. Near the trench, there is stone structure of Paramara period which was placed on the top of the mound.

Cultural Potentiality of Petnagar Excavations

Aiming at vertical digging off, two Trenches viz. : PTR-I and PTR-II were dug out in the year of 1998-1999, and 1999-2000 respectively. Most of the area of mound was found eroded by the illegal digging by the villagers in making their own houses, near the mound. Two Trenches were taken at different levels. The thickness of the habitational deposit were noticed in this mound are 4.72 metres and 4.40 metres in the Trench no. PTR.I and PTR.II respectively. The stratification of the mound was marked by seventeen layers and thirteen layers in Trench PTR.I, PTR.II respectively. The size of the Trenches was 8x7 metres in PTR.I and 5x5 metres in PTR.II.

Period-I – Ahar Culture 2000-1500 B.C.

The site was first occupied by the people of Ahar Culture, which is identified on the basis of the finding of well refined blades and cores, along with beautifully painted potteries. Other important finding includes-incised potteries, carinated necked vessels, high necked pots, dishes on the stand, steatite beads, stone ball, pestles, shell bangles and storage jars. The thickness of the habitation deposit of this period was 35 centimeters in the PTR.I and 10 centimetres in the PTR.II. The soil of this stratum was blackish brown in colour. This is the earliest layer constituted as the first settlement over the virgin soil. The stratum of this period yielded the following implements and materials.

Pottery : The peculiar pottery are Painted Black and Red Ware, Painted Black on Red Ware, these pottery are of two types thick and thin coarse. Some potsherds posses white graffiti marking over the neck and shoulder part of the eartnen pots.

Associated materials : The cultural assemblage of this period also include microliths, stone pestles, stone balls, stone blades, terracotta beads, stone beads, terracota toy, terracotta stopper, discs, terracotta wheel; etc.

Period-II – Malwa Chalcolithic Culture (1500-1000 B.C).

The second culture of Peetnagar habitants may be assessed to be the prominent Chalcolithic Culture of Malwa. This era was found to spread through out the whole part of Central India specially, Malwa. This period are recognized by a excavated distinct pottery like – Black on Red ware as well as Red on Red ware, very few sherds of Red on Red ware was found, but its percentage is least, in compare to the Black on Red ware. The ceramic industy of this period denote various sized vessels, basins, bowls and dish on stands with paintings either on exterior or interior. Different designs viz., straight, curved, zig-zag, criss-cross, check matted lines are reported over the pottery. In this period a remarkable earthern pot having cylindrical neck and collared mouth were excavated in different fragmentary form as well as in full shaped, such types of pot are similar to the potteries excavated in Navdatoli.

Associated Materials :

Cultural assembldage of this period also includes stone discs, fragment of a glass bangle; terracotta discs, beads, stoppers and miniature pots, iron tools, shell bangle pieces, ivory bangle pieces, antimony rod; microliths bone points, bone implements, steatite beads, ivory beads, etc.

Early Historic Culture

In early historic period P.M.C., shell bangle pieces, terracotta beads, Ear lobes, beads of precious and semi precious stone were found in PTR.I and II. Pottery of this period is mostly Micaceous in texture. Black and Red Ware, undressed Stone structure along with incurved Bowls and Vessels were reported. Some potsherds having incised marking on the shoulder part of globular structure. A fine variety of Red Polished and Stamped Ware abundantly noticed from this period. On the basis of finding this period is grouped in three phases : The first phase yielded Punch marked coins as well as Northern Black Polished Ware along with Shell Bangle, Terracotta Beads, Earlobes, Disc, Stopper, Stone Disc and Miniature pots. This strata revealed Mauryan phase. Second phase of it, yielded number of Red and Black pottery along with Iron, Shell Bangle fragments, T.C. Bead, T.C. Stopper, Copper object and Stone Lid. In this strata Micaceous Pottery were also continuously noticed. Satavahan Coins/cast Coins revealed this phase as Sunga period. Last phase of it yielded Polished Red Pottery, Stamped Pottery was also continuously excavated. The strata revealed Gupta and post Gupta period.

Period-III – Maurya

This Cultural phase is differentiate from the previous Cultural phase by the occurrence of Punch-marked coins, inferior NBP, Iron implements, Bone point, Glass as well as Shell bangle, ivory objects and other antiquities like – Steatite beads, Miniature pots, Stone and terracotta beads usually found in other contemporary.

Period-IV – Sunga/Satavahana

Copper coins of Satavahana kingdom and punch marked coins are reported in this period along with other important antiquities usually recorded are continued in this period e.g. bone bangle piece and bone point, Copper objects also continue in this strata, large number of glass bangle pieces were excavated in this period. Some antiquities of shell are recorded in the form of bangle piece, kaurri, ring while steatite bead are also an important finding of this strata. Stone made implements excavated in this period are Ball, Disc, Lid, Toy. A huge number of antiquities, made of terracotta are T.C. Ear lobes, T.C. Ball, T.C. Beads, T.C. Disc., T.C. Pendants, T.C. Stoppers and T.C. Toys are recorded in abundantly.

Period-V – Gupta

In this period large number of Terracotta figurines, decorated bangles of terracotta, glass and shell were excavated. Iron objects are abundantly found, Shell bangles were reported secondly in this era, while different other object like – Antimony rod, Bone points, Glass Beads, shell cowries, Stone Ball, Bead, Disc, Toy are excavated in stratigraphy of this period.

Period-VI – Paramara

This period is differentiate with other findings by the presence of early medieval pottery, which posses a predominancfe of Coarse Grey Ware over Red Ware. Few stone structural evidences were reported from the surface of this mound very near to the village in surrounding area of the trenches no. PTR.I.

Period-VII – Mardha / Muslim

Structure of large stone grevals over the mound was noticed. Thick black Ware are dominantly recorded in this strata. Muslim Grey coloured pottery along with Mughal coins were reported in this stratum. This period is also marked by the destruction of the site during Muslim invasions. The structures of Parmara period later on, were brought down.

21

A STUDY OF INSCRIPTIONS : HISTORY AND ADMINISTRATION

T.P. Verma

Preamble

Inscriptions are considered the most reliable source for history of India. There is a long continuous tradition of inscribing on lithic, metal and other objects since Asoka created a new script in the middle of the third century BCE to write edicts on stone in the local dialect of Magadha. (Verma, 2013: 47-53). In due course of time this script replaced all the eighteen existing scripts, mentioned in the Jain *Samavayangsutt* of 300 BCE and became so popular that almost every community of the society, royal and laity adopted it. As a result the number of inscriptions in Indian subcontinent during past two and half a millennia have excelled hundred thousands. D. C. Sircar (1965 A: 2) broadly classifies epigraphic records into two groups: 1) those engraved by or on behalf of the ruling authority, and 2) those incised on behalf of private individuals or organizations. Being contemporary records these inscriptions provide welcome glimpses of social, religious, fiscal and administrative aspects which are otherwise unknown. Study of epigraphical material reveals many such aspects of Indian social and political set up that has never been visualised so far. It can confidently be confessed that inscriptions supplement the literary traditions and complete the picture which is most gratifying. Here is an attempt on these lines. To understand this it will be helpful to know a brief account of westward shifting of the centre of political gravity in north India as a background of history.

Ascendency of Kanauj

The political history of north India after the collapse of the Imperial Guptas has been overshadowed by the lope sided glorification of Harsha. It were the Imperial Maukharis who established Kanauj as imperial seat in north India in the middle of the sixth century on the ruins of the Gupta empire. Since then Kanauj as a centre of imperial power continued for six and a half centuries till the end of twelfth century when the power of the Gahadavalas collapsed due to Muslim onslaughts and Delhi became the epicenter of imperial power. This continues till date. It is very interesting to watch a gradual eastward shift of the centre of imperial power from Magadha to Kanauj, then to Delhi. Sometime in the sixth century BCE Magadha became the center of imperial power in North India with its capital at Pataliputra. With the assassination of the last

Maurya king Brihadratha Pushyamitra Shung shifted his capital to Ayodhya that remained so till the end of the Imperial Gupta dynasty (Verma 2001:45-79). The Maukharis stepped in the shoes of the Imperial Guptas and remained imperial power till 750 when the Maukhari empire collapsed after the defeat of the last great Maukhari king Yashovarma by Lalitaditya of Kashmir; he died shortly after it. The epigraphic records reveal that in the beginning the Maukhari empire was extended over whole of North India covering almost the whole Gupta empire. Their rule extended up to Asirgadh in south and up to Kullu in Kangra district in Himachala Pradesh and Assam in the North-east. The Later Guptas till Mahasenagupta, the Aulikaras of Mandsor, the Pushyabhutis of Thaneshvara, the Bhauma kings of Assam and Shashanak of Gaud were Maukhari feudatories. The Maukhari dynasty continued from Ishanvarma to Yashovarma, a total of sixteen kings, except for a short inter-regnum of Harsh for about four decades. Harsh, a relative and Maukhari feudatory from Thaneshvara, used the army and resources of the Maukhari empire to aggrandize himself and eclipsed the glory of his imperial overlord. R. S. Tripathi (1964: 77) notes "Thus beginning with a modest guardianship or regency, Harsha's imposition of his authority over Kanauj was a sort of quite usurpation in which the people acquiesced owing to the chaotic conditions rampant in the kingdom after Grahavarman's assassination. This dexterous stepping into the shoes of the Maukharis places the entire resources of Kanauj at the disposal of Harsha."

That the Maukhari dynasty continued after Harsh is proved by epigraphic records. A total number of at least sixteen kings are known to have ruled from Kanauj till 750. Epigraphic records also tell that during his regency Harsh had installed his friend and relation, Madhavagupta of Malwa as king in the Magadha area whose descendents were called 'Later Guptas' by Fleet. He (1963: 14, Introduction) erroneously claimed 'that the family is an offshoot of the original Gupta stock'. After some time these Guptas of Magadha proved menace for the Imperial Maukharis and Jivitagupta II of the dynasty, ruling over Magadha and Gauda was defeated and killed for his unruly behaviour at Gomatikottaka in the heart of Maukhari Empire (Sircar 1983: 50).

After the Maukharis, in the middle of the eighth century the Gurjara Pratiharas of Malwa and Rajasthan established their empire with capital at Kanauj. At the same time the Rashtrakutas of Manyakhet and the Palas of Magadha and Vanga also were vying for supremacy over Kanauj. The Muslim forces from north-west also continued their onslaughts on Kanauj. By the last quarter of eleventh century the Gahadavalas of Varanasi conquered Kanauj and ruled till the end of twelfth century. After them the Muslim Sultans established them with capital at Delhi. Thus ends the supremacy of Kanauj as centre of imperial power that remained as the most coveted seat for more than six centuries.

The Post Classical Period

India, in the middle of sixth century, after the decline of the Imperial Guptas, enters in a new age of post-classical or, we can say, a mature-classical era. In this period we see an all round expansion in every field of life, may be literature, economy and trade, art and architecture, and even sciences. The state craft also saw an elaboration in administration because kingdoms acquired more and more power of taxation and provided protection to learning through granting tax-free properties to religious institutions and to individual Brahmanas of different Vedic schools. The age of large empires, like that of the Guptas, has gone and comparatively smaller kingdoms took its place. But activities in different fields continued. After Kalidas in Gupta period literature continued to enriched by scholars like Dandin, Bhasa, Banabhatta and many others. In the field of astronomy and astrology the tradition of Aryabhata and Varah Mihir was carried forward by a long galaxy of scholars. All the three styles of the temple styles of Nagar, Besar and Dravid reached their culmination during this period. The temples of Bhubaneshwar, Khajuraho, Rajasthan and Gujarat are the classical examples of Nagar style while those of Thanjavur and Halibid and many other places represent Dravida style. In the field of trade and commerce India dominated the oceans and land routes. Muslim chroniclers attest the enormous wealth of the country when they describe the onslaughts of Islamic invaders and their plunders. It is also be noted that the dynasties of this period did not feel the necessity of coining money because of affluence. These aspects of India's civilization have not been properly assessed and there exists a general belief that it declined in every field during this period.

Politically, during this period a large number of dynasties ruled over India and left their epigraphic records from which we can derive many inferences about the society; fiscal and political administration and many other aspects. Some of the major dynasties of the north were the Chandelas in Bundelkhand, the Tomars in Delhi, the Chahmanas in Shakumbhari- Ajmer, the Paramaras in Malwa, the Chaulukyas in Gujrat-Saurashtra, the Kalachuris in Tripuri in west, Ratanpur in east and Gorakhpur in north, etc. In South India also several dynasties issued a large number of inscriptions.

Introducing Epigraphs

Study of epigraphs in India was initiated by Western scholars who not only rescued long forgotten Brahmi and Kharoshthi scripts but also took keen interest in discovering, deciphering and editing inscriptions written various forms of writings and languages throughout the subcontinent. They put in so much diligence and showed intelligence and insight in their studies that many of them were regarded as infallible as ancient *rishis*. But, in spite of all sympathy and straightforwardness in their studies they could not understand Hindu rituals, customs and beliefs and therefore made blunders in their writings. Many Indian scholars also have failed to look at these epigraphs in Indian context. Undoubtedly their pioneer work forms base for our discussion. In ensuing pages we have tried to see the things in a fresh light of social, religious and literary contexts.

Some Important Features of Inscriptions

Language : The credit to begin the tradition of engraving epigraphs on lithic objects goes to the Maurya king Asoka who devised a new script to propagate his famous sermon delivered at Sarnath at the culmination of his 256 night-halts pilgrimage (*dhamma-yata*) in his twelfth regnal year. (Verma 2013). Ignoring the existing eighteen scripts during his reign, as stated in the Jain *Samavayangsutt* dated in c. 300 BCE by Buhler, Asoka decided to create a new and simpler script to promulgate his speech throughout his empire. The reason behind this drastic decision seems to be that he wanted to write this in the language spoken the Magadha region. This script was so simple and easy that it became the principal script of India since his times. But for about three centuries only Prakrit languages were written in this script to which Buhler gave the name Brahmi. There is a wrong notion among the scholars who believe that the language of the Asoka's administration was Magadhi. This is not true. Magadhi was the language of his edicts and Sanskrit was the language of literature and administration. Its thrust was so great that very soon, within three centuries or so the script of Asoka was adopted to the Sanskrit language.

Sircar (1965 A: 38), however, perceives the issue the other way and writes "Originally the epigraphic language of the whole of India was mainly Prakrit and Sanskrit is first noticed in the inscriptions of North India from about the second half of the 1st century B.C. Sanskrit gradually ousted Prakrit from the field of Indian epigraphy in all parts of the country. In North India, the establishment of Sanskrit in place of Prakrit in inscriptions was merely complete by the end of 3rd century A.D. But the suppression of Prakrit in epigraphs of South India took place as late as the second half if the 4th century.' Obviously this reflects the perception prevailing from the colonial times.

The number of inscriptions during first two centuries after Asoka diminished because it took time to adopt this new script, and these are very short in Prakrit language by persons coming from general population. However, the royalty in India also followed Asoka for few centuries. The Hathigumpha inscription of Kharavela and the Satavahanas used Prakrit for their royal proclamations but the Saka dynasties, believed to be of foreign origin, preferred Sanskrit for writing. Some inscriptions of the time of Saka Kshatrapa Sodasa, first quarter of the first century CE, from Mathura are written in Sanskrit language. Some stanzas are composed in Classical Sanskrit in ornate meters like *Shardulavikridita* and

Bhujangavijrimbhita. The Junagarh rock inscription of Rudradaman (150 CE) of Kardamaka family is an excellent piece of Sanskrit prose composed in Classical *kavya* style. It appears that while early indigenous dynasties were adhering to the tradition of Asoka to issue royal charters in local Prakrits but there was no such tradition before the Sakas. However, in inscriptions from Mathura there is gradual shift from Prakrit to Sanskrit because many of these epigraphs are written in an admixture of both languages. By the time of the imperial Guptas Sanskrit replaced Prakrit completely. In India Prakrit was running side by side with Sanskrit since Vedic period. The *Taittiriyasamhita* discloses that in the beginning Prakrit was spoken by all and Indra was requested to codify the language which he did with the help of Vayu. Thus Prakrit was spoken in homes in informal talks and Sanskrit became the language of the books and literature. It is not that Sanskrit was altogether ousted from the field of inscriptions. There are some mediaeval Jain inscriptions that are written in Prakrit. The Ghatiyala inscription of Kakkuka of the Pratihar dynasty, dated in 862 CE is composed in chaste Prakrit. The Dhar inscription of Bhoja Paramara (c. 1000-55 CE) contains the text of the Prakrit poem entitled *Kurmashataka* composed by the king himself. An inscription written in characters resembling those of Bhoja also quotes several kinds of Prakrit speech.

One is confronted with a distorted picture when one hears from a scholar of the eminence of Sircar (Id. :42) that "The Sanskrit language as used in the early inscriptions shows that the influence of the grammar of Panini was not fully established even in the central part of India, which was the home of its great commentator, Patanjali (2nd century B.C.) of Gonarda (between Ujjayini and Vidisha) as late as the 3rd century A.D." There are many anomalies in above statement because we see no conflict of existence between the two. The sphere of operation of both the languages was well defined. Panini's grammar was well established by the time Kautilya composed his *Arthashastra*. We have stated above that the court language of the Mauryas was Sanskrit and Magadhi Prakrit was Asoka's mother language which he used to dictate his edicts. All these edicts are in first person that prove our contention. Prakrits in different parts of the country continued as living languages in homes and literature even after the epigraphs switched over to Sanskrit language. The Jain works continued it in their Agama literature. Secondly, Patanjali was the contemporary of Pushyamitra Shung for whom he performed sacrifices in Ayodhya where he shifted his capital after the assassination the Brihadratha. We have pointed it out earlier. Gonarda of Patanjali has been identified by us with Gonda, head quarter of a district in eastern U. P. which is on the northern side of the river Sarayu or Gahaghara while Ayodhya is situated on its southern bank. The Ayodhya inscription of Dhana(deva), the sixth descendant of Pushyamitra, is in Sanskrit. This may be regarded as Patanjali's influence if one wants to believe.

These inscriptions and land grants were composed by Sanskrit scholars of high ability. It is not that they necessarily were Brahmanas. Most of the composers of land grants belonged to the Kayastha community who claim to be scholars of highest grade. One, Vijayadasa, composer of Basahi and Banaras grants of Govindachandra claims to be the son of *pandita Kuke*. Here pandita is intended to be a Sanskrit scholar. Many of the *prashastis* (eulogy) or *kavyas* are compositions of poets of very high order. Some of the composers of *prashastis* are known only from their inscriptions and no other work of them have survived. Harishena, the writer of the Allahabad prashasti of Samudragupta is well known. From the Gahadavala inscriptions names of three poets, Kunda, Udain and Manoratha are known. Kunda, the composer of the Sarnath stone inscription of Kumaradevi describes himself as a poet of eight languages and a well known friend of the king of Vanga. He calls this eulogy a *prashasti* composed in beautifully woven letters, i.e. words. Udain composed the Sahet-Mahet stone inscription of Vidyadhara while Manorath, the son of Sri Sida, was the composer of a Buddhist inscription of Bodh-Gaya. He claimed to be the swan of the Kayastha family (*Kayasthavamshahamsa*). Many more poets are known to have composed eulogies known from inscriptions. Among them are Ravikirti of the Aihole inscription of Pulakeshin II (636 CE), Chittapa of the Bhilsa inscription (c. 1050 CE), Vachaspati of the Bhubaneswara inscription of Bhavadeva, minister of Harivarman (1090-1110), and Umapatidhara of the Deopada inscription of Vijayasena (c. 1096-1159 CE) are known for their poetic skill, to name the few. No other composition of these poets has come to us and they are known only from these lithic or metallic inscriptions, but the literary merit of these are very high.

It is true that most of the inscriptions were composed by well versed and skilled poets and some of these may be regarded as best literary creations but at the same time some of the epigraphs were written by unskilled poets with many mistakes. Sircar (Id. 4) notes that 'private records were often composed by people of indifferent education and generally contain numerous errors of orthography and language. But epigraphs like Chhoti Sadri inscription of Gauri and Vasantgadh inscription of Purnapala show that even the Pandits at the kings' courts possessed very poor knowledge of the Sanskrit language.' In this list we can add the Nalanda and the Gaya copperplate inscriptions of Samudragupta, dated respectively in his 5th and 9th regnal years. These are relegated as spurious by Fleet and Sircar on account of faulty language. However, it can be argued that these two copperplates were drafted by local pundits of eastern UP employed by the king in his early career. Goyal including present writer believe that the Guptas hailed from this part of the country had their capital at Ayodhya. Of course, 'There are many instances of indifferently drafted and badly engraved records even among royal charters, particularly those issued by minor ruling families.'

Other Languages used in Inscriptions

Asoka, responsible for beginning the tradition of writing inscriptions, used Magadhi Prakrit for majority of his inscriptions, the scripts being Brahmi and Kharoshthi. For his Yavana and Kamboja subjects he used Aramaic and Greek for his Minor Rock Edicts that were discovered from Afghanistan. As we have discussed above earlier Prakrit and later Sanskrit became languages for epigraphs. Among the regional languages Sircar names following ten languages that were used in writing inscriptions. These are 1) Tamil, Kannada, 2) Telugu, 3) Malayalam and Tulu, 4) Marathi, 5) Hindi and allied languages, 6) Gujarati, 7) Kashmiri and allied dialects, 8) Oriya, 9) Bengali and Maithili, 10) Assamese. He gives examples of epigraphs in these languages but we do not intend to in details.

Prashastis

It is not that only *prashastis* and royal charters are engraved on lithic and copperplates, some literary works such as poems and dramas are also engraved on these materials. For example the Udaipur Rajasmudra inscription, called *Rajaprashasti*, is a *kavya* written in 24 cantos by an Andhra poet named Ranachoda. It was composed on the occasion of the excavation of a tank by Rana Rajasimha of Mewar and is engraved on not less that 24 slabs. These slabs were fixed into the embankment of the said tank. Similarly Rana Kumbha's *prashasti* was found written on five stone slabs and were fixed in the Kumbhasvamin, also called Mahadeva temple at Kumbhalgadh. The Paramara king Bhoja's Prakrit poem entitled *Kurmashataka* and the *Parijatamanjari* or *Vijayasrinatika* of Madana, written on stone can also be mentioned in this context. Two drama works are also found engraved on stone. The *Lalitavigraharaja* composed by Someshvara, the court poet of the Chahamana king Vigraharaja IV of Ajmer is a lithic inscription. King Vigraharaja's drama, known as *Harakelinataka*, also was engraved on stone slabs. It is important to note that a work on musical notations also was inscribed in the characters of seventh century was discovered from Kudumiyamalai in Pudukottai of Tamilnadu. Similarly a Digambara Jain work called *Unnatashikhara Purana*, composed in 1170 CE, was inscribed on the flat surface of a rock at Bijolia in the Bhilwada district of the Udaipur division of Rajasthan.

Copperplates also were used for engraving important poetic or other compositions. Hiuen Tsang records a tradition that Kanishk caused the Buddhist texts engraved on copperplates and deposited in a stupa. The Kasia copperplate contains the Buddhist *Nidanasutra* in Sanskrit which was deposited in the *Nirvanachaitya* there. There is a story that Sayana's commentary on the Vedas was engraved on copperplates. Some copperplates are now deposited at Tirupati that contain a Telugu work known as Tallapakamvari.

These *prashastis* on stone and copperplates provide us with valuable information about kings and dynasties that were not known otherwise. It is interesting to note an example from an inscription of the so-called Later Guptas of Bihar which has been avoided, following Fleet, by early historians like Sircar and many others. The Aphsad stone inscription from Gaya in Bihar of Aditysena (660-75 CE) furnishes us with a connected account of his seven ancestors since the time they were petty rulers in Malava and perhaps feudatories of the Maukharis. Their history has been analysed by S. R. Goyal and by us (Verma 2006-7) that sheds new light on the history of the period. Here is a brief account of new history of imperial Maukharis of Kanauj as revealed from this inscription of Adityasena. Krishnagupta is said to be the first ruler of this dynasty. His son was Harshagupta from whom sprang Jivitagupta I. From the names of these early kings it was inferred by historians that they had matrimonial relations with the Maukharis of Kanauj as deduced by the names of the queens of latter dynasty. Then it appears that a conflict begins between two families. It is said that Kumaragupta, the son of Jivitagupta churned the army of the Maukhari king Ishanavarma (c. 550-75 CE) but had to commit suicide at Prayaga (Allahabad) by entering a funeral pyre of cow-dung. His suicide at Allahabad in the heart of the Maukhari empire shows that Kumaragupta rebelled against Ishanavarma and was defeated in some battle. But Dr. Sircar holds (1983: 44) that 'Kumaragupta defeated [Maukhari] Ishanavarma and advanced as far as Prayaga where he committed religious suicide.' It is also described in this inscription that Kumaragupta's son 'Damodaragupta broke up the proudly stepping array of mighty elephants, belonging to the Maukhari king, which had previously thrown aloft in battle the troops of the Hunas in order to trample them to death, but became unconscious on the battle-field and expired.' (Id.). An analysis of these two verses of the Aphsad inscription shows that earlier historians, under the influence of Fleet who first edited this inscription and declared the descendents of Adityasena as successors of the Imperial Guptas, twisted and translated to suit their preconceived idea of these Later Guptas being the adversaries of Maukhari empire. It shows that Kumaragupta and his son took part in the battle against the Hunas as feudatories of Ishanavarına Maukhari and there Damodaragupta was killed and aggrieved father Kumaragupta committed suicide at Prayaga. It will be out of place here to go into details of these verses for want of space. The son of Damodaragupta was Mahasenagupta whose fame 'marked with the honour of victory over Susthitavarmana [of Pragjyotisha] was still sung on the banks of the Lauhitya (Brahmaputra). Here again the Maukhari emperor comes in the picture on whose behalf a petty ruler of Malawa fought this battle against the Pragjyotish king. In this battle two sons of Susthitavarman, Supratishthitavarman and Bhaskaravarman, were captured and kept as prisoners in Gauda. Bewildered historians vainly search this king of Gauda in Shashanka, but as we have shown, it was the Maukhari king whose kingdom spread over the region. After this Mahasenagupta is never heard of, perhaps his kingdom was captured by his scion and his two sons, Kumara and Madhavagupta, took shelter with their relation Pushyabhutis of Thaneshvara. This Madhavagupta was the father of Adityasena and was installed as king in Magadha and Gauda. The composer of this eulogy was Sukshmashiva of Gauda. This justifies our identification of Jivtagupta II, the great-grand-son of Adityasena, with king of Gauda of the Prakrit epic *Gaudavaho*, who was killed by the last great Maukhari king Yashovarma. Thus the new analysis of the Aphsad inscription of Adityasena leads us to unknown realm of the Maukhari history which remains neglected due to initial error of identification of Malava Guptas by Fleet as successors of the Imperial Guptas.

In later period the practice of writing *prashastis* on lithic and metal objects was replaced by copperplate grants. The kings used their land grants on copperplates to eulogize them and their ancestors. Dr. Sircar is critical of connecting these kings with the epic and puranic heroes. He (Id. 24) notes "A tendency is often noticed in ruling families from the early mediaeval age to *fabricate* a respectable genealogy on the basis of the *gotra* name of the royal family. The Pallavas of Kanchi claimed to have belonged to the Bharadvaja-gotra which offered them the opportunity to trace their descent, through a number of *mythical and imaginary personages*, from the sage Bharadvaja, famous in the epics and the

Puranas, and through him to the god Brahman, the creator. ... *Many of the rulers claiming such respectable descent belonged really to aboriginal families.*" (emphasis by us). He cites another case and writes "... in the later records of the family, including inscriptions belonging to the later years of Anantavarman Chodaganga himself, the origin of the family is traced to the god Vishnu through his navel-born son Brahman, his mind-born son Atri, his eye-born son Chandra (the Moon), his son Budha, his descendents Pururavas, Ayus, Nahus, Yayati and Turvasu-- all known from epics and Puranic literature, and a host of apparently *imaginary personages* standing between Turvasu and Gunarnava who was the progenitor of the family according to the earlier account, but is here represented as Gunarnava II." He is also sour about this king changing loyalty from Siva to Vishnu. He writes "The genealogy was fabricated on the basis of *gotra* claimed by the Eastern Gangas; but it also exhibits their eagerness to claim descent from the lunar dynasty and some connection with the god Visnu, to whom Ananatavaraman Chodaganga transferred his allegiance from Siva during later part of his career."

Here Sircar cannot be singled out for expressing such views that were promoted by colonial rulers whom they are following literally; it was the order of the day and regarded a sign of scholarship. Any resentment was destined to de-recognition as a scholar. To some extent this mode of thinking continues even after six decades of independence. For the Hindus the heroes of epics and puranas were not mythical personages as they are still real historical persons whose stories are popular among the common man. They believe them to be ancestors. No king of this land was aboriginal and he cannot be disbelieved if traces his ancestry from solar or lunar races. Similarly, sectarian antagonism was not so blood-thirsty as it was in Europe and common man was, and still is, being taught tolerance of other sects (this profusely reflects in devotional songs every day). The kings were especially trained since childhood to respect other religious sects. Asoka talks of the welfare of brahmana and sramana in his edicts. It pains a sensitive historian when he reads someone saying that 'in spite of being a follower of this or that sect he helped or worked for the other sect. If Anantavarman Chodaganga cannot be blamed for change of faith if he traces his descent from Visnu in some early inscription and professes devotion to Siva in some later one.

Types of Raja-shasana

A majority of inscriptions are royal charters called *raja-shasanas*. These known by many names. For example the Kakatiya ruler Ganapati (1244-45 A.D.) names his Motupalli inscription '*abhaya-shasana*, i.e. 'charter of assurance'. In this it is said that "Formarly kings used to take away by force the whole cargo, viz. gold, elephants, horses, gems, etc. carried by ships and vessels which, after they had started from one country for another, were attacked by storms, wrecked and thrown on shore. But we, our of mercy, for the sake of glory and merit, are granting everything besides the fixed duty (klipta-shulka) to those who have incurred the great risk of sea voyage with the thought that wealth is more valuable than even life." (Id. 109). Sircar writes that 'the fixed duties are enumerated an the records and stone pillar bearing the document is styled a *shasana-stambha*. A stone inscription of 1531 A.D. of the Vijayanagara king Achyutaraya from the Vishnupada temple at Gaya is called '*dharma-shasana*' where the king performed the *shraddha* ceremony of his ancestors. Sircar holds that 'although it is called an edict for religion (i.e. religious merit), it is not a *shasana* in the real sense of the term.' Sircar cites another inscription of 1521 A.D. of Krishnadevaraya which calls itself *vijaya-shasana* (a document relating to victory) although this vijaya can only be regarded as *dharma-vijaya*, i.e. success relating to religion or religious merit. An example of *kraya-shasana* comes from the Madras Museum plates (10th century) of the time of king Narendradhavala of Orissa. This records a sale deed of a village by a king and is called *kraya-shasana*. Sircar holds that 'A private deed of purchase or sale has been called a *kraya-chiraka* in the Mangraon inscription and a kraya-lekhya in Brihaspati's work while *chirika* and *chilika* are both used in the sense of a private document in *Lekhapaddhati*.' It can be added here that in some parts of the country the word *chittha* is used for piece of such papers. Another kind of *shasana*, called *kara-shasana*, is known from the early epigraphs of Orissa and Andhra Pradesh. Sircar notes that 'In the Bengal Asiatic

Society's plate of Gayadatunga, we have : '*Toro-gram* is made a *kara-sasana* at nine *palas* of silver, while the Talcher plate of the same king speaks of the fixation of *trinodaka* for the gift land at four *palas* of silver without using the word *kara* or *kara-sasana* in the context.'

The Chakravarti-kshetra

It is necessary to emphasise that culturally the entire subcontinent was one unit. Until tenth century Afghanistan, with the Hindu Shahis, also was included in this geographical unit. Asoka in his thirteenth Rock Edict claims Yavana-Kamboj as 'his provinces'. The Mehrauli Iron pillar inscription of 'Chandra' of Gupta dynasty also claims to have conquered Vahlika after crossing the seven mouths of Indus (Sircar 1965 B.: 283). The Hindu Shahis also ruled in Afghanistan till tenth century where in Mazar-e-Sharif their inscription was found (Mohan 2003:162-63). This is not all, it was considered within the ideal *chakravarti-kshetra* of Hindu kingship. In an eleventh century inscription of Paramaras, Lakshamanavarman (c. 1087-97) claims to have conquered Turushkas (Mohammadans) on the banks of Vankshu (Oxus). It is another question if his claims can be believed or not but it certainly shows that in the Hindu psyche Bahlika was included within the *Chakravrti-kshetra.* (Sircar 1965 A. :28-29 and also 351). There are other such instances as well. The Pala king Devapala (812-50) in his Nalanda copperplate inscription claims to have 'triumphantly marched over the Vindhyas and from there to the Kamboja country and ruled the whole region from Himalayas to Rama's Bridge and from the abode of Varuna to that of Lakshmi (i.e. from Eastern to Western Sea, i.e. from the Bay of Bengal to to the Arabian Sea).' (Sircar 1983:71). This was the *chakravarti-kshetra*. One thing is unique in this Chakravarti-kshetra that though there were innumerable states or kingdoms in the entire region but all were governed by a single constitution, i.e. the Code of Manu. Principles of kingship and rules of governance (*rajadharma*) are prescribed in its seventh chapter. A study of inscriptions reveals that kings used to collect revenue in accordance with the rules prescribed by Manu throughout the region. Their personal conduct, ideals of kingship and inter-state relations were also regulated by the Code of Manu.

Writing on a Copperplate

Most of the copperplates are actually land grants issued as certificates for revenue-free lands granted by the king. These are not original documents but copy of the raja-sasana or royal charter, the original of which were kept in the office of the Akshapatalika, the officer in-charge of the revenue records. A copy of the revenue record with the order of the king, with his personal identification, was engraved on a piece of copper or on several pieces, and issued to the donee as a lasting certificate of registration that could be preserved for generations. Such donations were for ever and ordinarily could not be taken back or confiscated by future kings. A donation to the Brahmanas or to the religious establishments like a temple or a *matha*, was called *brahma-deya* or *brahma-daya*, also *deva-deya* or *deva-daya*, and was given for the period till endure the Sun and Moon. In some epigraphs these are also called *sasana-patra*, *tamra-patra* or *dana-patra*, etc.

D. C. Sircar (1965 A: 103) holds: "The word *patra* in these compounds suggests that the records were written on *bhurja-patra* (birch-bark sheets) or *tala-patra* (Palmyra leaves) and only some of them were later engraved on copperplates." It may be cleared here that all the documents written on these materials cannot come in the category of revenue records while the copperplates generally are land grants issued by the king. Therefore a copperplate declaring a land grant is necessarily a copy of the the original document preserved in the revenue office of the kingdom or of the Akshapatalika. We have no knowledge about the material used for maintaining revenue registers in ancient India; the use of paper cannot be excluded. About the process of writing a land-grant *Sabdakalpadruma* quotes Vyasa as follows: "It should first be written with chalk on tablet (*phalak*) or ground (earth) and after correcting errors be written on *patra*." Here *patra* may be taken as to mean a piece of paper, *tala-patra, bhurja-patra* or even a *tamra-patra*.

There was a prescribed procedure to create a land grant. D. C. Sircar (1965-A: 104) notes that according to Vishnu, "[The king] should grant land to Brahmanas. For the information of future kings, he should also give the donee of the grant a charter written on cloth or copper-plate endowed with his own seal and with a description of the boundaries of the land, of his own ancestors and of the measurement of the area. He should not confiscate land granted by others... The king should kill persons who prepare spurious charters, and also those preparing spurious documents." Then he quotes Yajnavalkya as saying "After granting land or making a *nibandha*, the lord of the soil (i.e. the king) should have a document prepared for the information of noble kings of the future. He would then cause the preparation of a lasting charter written on cloth or copper-plate, adorned with his own seal on the outer side, with his own signature and date and with a description of himself and his ancestors and the amount of the gift and the boundaries of the gift land." Here *nibandha* should be taken in the sense of 'registration' that necessarily points out towards a regular office of revenue department.

Sircar sums up the information drawn from the above sources as follows: (1) After making a grant of land, etc., the king caused the preparation of a *lekhya* or document for the guidance of future kings of the land. (2) It was then written on a piece of cloth or engraved on copper-plates or a copper tablet, and thus was made a permanent charter. (3) It contained a description of the king and three of his immediate predecessors and of the land granted together with its boundaries and measurement; it was also endowed with the king's seal, signature and date. (4) There is no explicit statement regarding the donee by Yajnavalkya, though it is supposed that the donee is implied in his language and that his name should also be written in the charter. (5) A high official was entrusted with the drafting of a document according to *Mitakshara*. (Id, 105-06).

Administrative Setup

The above noted procedure of writing land grants and issuing of copperplates does not speak of the revenue administration in ancient India. But on the other hand a study of these inscriptions provide us with a fair idea about the administrative set up of the revenue records in the whole country. Inscriptions on copperplates are only a perceptible part or the net result of a comprehensive and lasting network of revenue system in ancient India that remained undisturbed by political changes like making or unmaking of empires. Perhaps the system evolved during centuries and continued through the ages. The revenue offices of the British government, as we will see, were more or less organized on the same pattern. We can say that the revenue system based on the land survey and office-noting was not less developed and complicated than those followed in the modern revenue offices. These copperplate inscriptions recording the land grants can be compared with the registration of land transactions in modern revenue offices. The word *patta* still continues for such registration which is an abbreviation of *patta* or *tamra-patta*.

The two Satavahana inscriptions incised on the cave walls in Nasik (Sircar 1965 B: Bk. II. Nos. 83, 84) were initially land-grants on copperplates. Some terms in these inscriptions reveal that there was a well established procedure to keep the revenue records and oral orders of the king were first required to be registered in the office of the Book-Keeper (*Pustapala*) and the donee was provided only with a copy of the order to keep as a certificate. In this case it was later engraved on the wall of the cave by some *bhikshu* as a more enduring and irremovable document that could be used by the mendicants of future generations. Some technical terms used in the first record (No. 83) with explanation are as follows. 1. *Bhukti*: The land granted to the Buddhist saints was earlier a *bhukti* of Ushavadat , the defeated Kshaharata governor and it came to the king Gautamiputra Satakarni after victory over the region. Other phrases are: 2. Register this (*etha nibadhapehi*). 3. Orally ordered (*aviyena anatam*). 4. Written by the minister Shivagupta (*amacena Sivgupten chato*). 5. Inspected by the King (*Mahasamiehi uparakhito*). 6. The plate was issued to the donee on first day of second half-month of the Rainy Season (*data patika savachare 10+8 vasapakhe 2 divase 1*). 7. The plate was engraved by Tapasa (*Tapasena kata*).

The second cited epigraph (Sircar: No. 84) is more interesting as it records the donation of land orally granted by the Queen of Gautamiputra Satakarni; not by the King. This also has the status of a royal charter and is addressed to Samaka, the governor of Govardhan directly by the Queen. This was the 'oral order' (*ukten ajnptam*) of the Queen; and she ordered it to 'be registered' (in the Revenue Books) (*atra nibandhayat*). Here it is significant to note that this inscription was 'written by the (female) Pratihara Lota' and 'engraved by Sujivina', another female officer in service of the Queen. This shows that in Satavahana administration the queens enjoyed constitutional right to issue such orders and also maintained a staff to execute it. But, of course, she was to followed the procedure to inform the office of the Revenue Department and register her 'Oral Order' there. There are some other things to be noted. 1. There are two dates given in the epigraph. The 'Order' was first registered on the 10th day of the second *paksha* of the Summer of the year 24, and, then it was executed, a few months later, on 5th day of the 4th *paksha* of the Rainy Season of the same year. The epigraph informs at the end of the 7th line that the 'registration' (of the Order) was 'registered' on the 10th day of the year 24 in 2nd half of the month (*nibadho nibadho savchre 24 gimhan pakhe 2 divase 10*). According to Sircar "(the first) '*nibadho*' seems to be engraved twice owing to the engraver's inadvertence." Obviously he failed to understand the purport of using twice the word '*nibadho*'; the first being a noun and second a verb. This specifically notes that the entry of the order was executed in the Revenue Register. 2. The order for registration was already given in the line six. This is also noteworthy that there is no mention of 'inspection' by the king in this case.

To sum up, it can be said that the land was a government property or king's *bhukti* that automatically stands transferred to the victorious king. The King and Queen followed the procedure of executing their oral order through the governor (*amacha*) of Govardhana. The order was first to be entered in the revenue records and then it was written and engraved on copperplate by the staff of the king/queen. In case of the first grant the entry in the Revenue Register was checked by the King (*mahasamiyehi uparakhito*).

Some of the copperplates are found to have word 'seen' (*drishtam*) in the margin which shows that the king has seen and signed the Revenue Register. Many land-grants of Vakataka copperplates contain the word '*drishtam*' (seen) usually on the left margin of the text (Sircar: 1965 B: Bk. III, Nos. 59, 60, 62 & C). In Prakrit or Prakrit-influenced-Sanskrit inscriptions the word '*ditham*' or '*dittham*' is used to denote the same sense. (Id, Nos. 64, 65). According to D. C. Sircar this indicates 'that the original of the document on the plate had been examined by the proper authorities who found it alright'(1965 A: 127, fn 2). We beg to differ. To examine or tally 'the original of the document on the plate' cannot be the work of higher authorities, that could be done by some subordinate officer or clerk. In our opinion the remark *drishtam* denotes that the King or highest authority has seen and signed on the Revenue Register and confirmed that the donation is in accordance with it. We have seen that the Nasik cave inscription of Gautamiputra Satakarni (yr. 18) contains the the word '*upalakshitam*' (seen) by the king (*mahasvamiyehi*). This is the proper procedure.

On some copperplates the name of the king's signature is also copied because there appear the words '*svahasto mam*' i.e. my signature. The Banskhera copperplate of Harsh ends with beautifully engraved words "*svahasto mam maharajadhiraja sriharshasya*". I have seen some books reproducing this as the specimen signature of king Harsh. Obviously this is a wrong claim. This copperplate is written in a highly ornamental script; and so is the signature. Similarly the recently acquired Kurukshetra-Jnana Pravah copperplate of Harsh also contains these words at the end (*Jnana Pravah Bulletin* No. 5, 2001-02: 225 ff). But the calligraphy of both copperplates differ. Therefore, the idea of specimen signature on copperplates is a misconception. On the other hand this certainly indicates that the king has authenticated and confirmed his order of donation by signing on the Revenue Register.

These features of copperplate inscriptions have never been discussed by epigraphists. We will point out some more facts for the first time in order to present a clear and complete picture of the administrative setup and land management in ancient India. It is noted earlier that the content of the first Nasik epigraph of Satavahanas shows that the oral order for the land-grant was given by the King

Gautamiputra Satakarni from a victorious army-camp at Govardhana after defeating the Kshaharata governor Ushavadata. This land was a *bhukti* (king's land) enjoyed by the defeated king and after his defeat it now became the property of the victorious king. The word *bhukti,* in some form or the other is found in inscriptions from every region and in every period. From this it can be inferred that there was a tradition of *bhukti* lands in the entire country which were enjoyed by the ruling king/s. Later some provinces or other administrative unites were also named after such *bhuktis*. In other words such *bhukti* lands were traditionally used as king's personal land or state lands. We will have occasion to discuss the issue but here it is sufficient to mention that the roots of this tradition go deep in antiquity. The king was granted some privileges for protecting the people. He was equipped with the privilege in the form of *bhaga, bhoga, kara/ hiranya*. The purpose of these privileges will be explained under the section 'Revenue System'. These three types of taxes covered every section of the society. There were eight types of *bhoga*. One type of *bhoga* (tax) was in the form of several kinds of things offered to the king that were used or collected by the non-agriculturist or non-trader section of the people in general. This was a huge amount of things that needed a big staff. Other form of the *bhoga* was in the form of land enjoyed by the king as personal property usually called *bhukti* in inscriptions. Though Hindu kings were known as Lord of the Earth (*Bhupati* or *Prithivipati*) he had no rights to confiscate the land of the common man. In principle he was paid in the form of these privileges to protect the people. A *bhukti* needed special attention of the king and in course of time became a centre of administration; the adjoining regions came to be known by that name. A town or region or sometimes the entire province was named after a *bhukti* but it never meant that the whole region was king's personal property or land. This explains the Pundravardhana Bhukti during the Gupta period.

Returning to the revenue records we find an officer in inscriptions called *Pustapala*, the keeper of the books pertaining to land measurement, ownership and revenue collection. Though every kingdom was supposed to maintain a revenue office, it seems that at the lowest or village level the system was traditionally maintained in the entire country that remained undisturbed by political changes. No doubt some adjustments were done by each individual kingdom, such as number of staff and names of officers, but essence of the system remained undisturbed by individual king. In essence the institution of revenue collection and keeping of revenue records had acquired the shape of ever lasting nature that continued from generation to generation. It continued from the village level to higher unites of administration and perhaps there was a well established system of distribution of shares between the subordinate kingdoms, i.e. feudatories and the overlord. But we have no clear picture of particulars of this hierarchy. We have reasons to believe that the system continued till the British period. Our study shows that the Muslim sultanates could not establish a reliable and peaceful system of revenue collection and they had to depend on an imposed hierarchy of *jagirdars* and *mansabdars* which adopted the practice of revenue collection by seasonal/occasional raids.

The Adhikarana or the Office

About administrative offices of Indian kingdoms A. K. Majumdar (1956: 212) writes "For the purpose of administration the government seems to have been divided into several '*karanas*' or 'secretariats' that is departments. The work *Lekhapaddhati*, which is a collection of model documents, begins with a verse in which the names of the following *karanas* are found." Then he names and describes 32 *karanas* or offices from that book and obviously this list seems to be a model because all of them may not be required by all the kingdoms. This work is a collection of documents and 'that in the dated documents in the work, the dates range from VS 802 to VS 1483 and the manuscript at present available was copied in the 16th century AD.' According to Majumdar 'all the documents are related to Gujarat'. In copperplate inscriptions these *karanas* are called '*adhikaranas*' and these offices were modeled after the local requirements of the kingdom and the regional practices. But one thing is certain, that the practice of keeping records of mensuration of cultivable and uncultivable land along with the revenue assessment was widespread in the entire country. A study of copperplate inscriptions shows that in early times the state craft was simple but as the time passed and resources of the governments enhanced these offices became more and more complex.

Some Gupta period copperplates reveal that there was a well established system where the records were properly kept in administrative offices and every public transaction was processed in accordance with a set procedure. An enduring certificate in the form of copperplate was issued to the applicant in which the process of transactions also was recorded. The application was submitted in the main office (*adhikarana*) of the *vishaya* (district) or the village and it was forwarded to the office of the *Pustapala* (Revenue record keeper) for enquiry and remarks. One or two or more officers were deputed to check the records and return with their note of validity of the claim. And then the copperplate was issued. In the Domodrapur copperplate of the time of [Vishnu]gupta year 224 the word '*tamrapattikritya*' is used for the finalization of the registration. In modern India also, where the practice of issuing *tamra* is no more in vogue, the term used for land transaction and registration is *patta*.

The offices were called *adhikarana* or *karana.* The word *adhisthanadhikarana* was used for administrative offices at the level of *bhukti, vishaya, or vithi*. There were offices at the village (*grama*) level also. The Damodarpur copperplate inscription of the time of Kumargupta I mentions the *Adhisthanadhikarana* of the *Kumaramatya* Vetravarma of Kotivarsha *vishaya*. This was perhaps the highest governing and superintending office of the *vishaya* (administrative unit). Four members of the governing body are named as 1) *Nagarasreshthi* Dhritipala, 2) *Sarthavaha* Vandhumitra, 3) *Prathama-kulika* Dhritimitra, and 4) *Prathama-kayastha* Shambapala. Of course this *adhikarana* was headed by the *Kumaramatya* Vetravarma. Prof. D. C. Sircar does not include Vetravarma in this board. He notes (1965 B: 291, fn. 8): "*Adhisthana*=city; *Adhikarana*= office of administration. Note that the governor was helped in the administration by a Panchayat Board of 4 member ... The Board seems to have worked like the West Indian Chauthia (Chaturjataka) of which the chairman is the Nagar-seth (Nagara-sreshthin) and the Patel (village headman) and Patwari (accountant-scribe=Kayastha) are members."

Thus Sircar reduced the status of the Governing Council of Kumaramatya of the Kotivarsha Vishaya to a City Administrative office and compared it with a village Panchayat. He is also not very clear about the status of Kumaramatya. According to him (1965 A: 358) "The *Kumaramatya* was probably an *Amatya* enjoying the status of a prince of the royal blood." This is no better than defining the word *kumara*+ *amatya* etymologically that leads nowhere. He has profusely cited references to the office of Kumaramatya in inscriptions but nowhere he offers a discussion on his status. We know that the Kumaramatya of Kotivarsha *vishaya* was appointed by the Uparika of Pundravardhana-bhukti. But a Kumaramatya was very high officer is evident from the Vaigram copperplate inscription where the Kumaramatya Kulavriddhi issued a land-grant from Panchanagari directly meditating on the feet of *Parama-bhattarak,* with out mentioning the Uparika. A Kumaramatya's office cannot be a petty city administrative board is evident from the fact that many a high officials directly serving the sovereign are designated Kumaramatya. A Kumaramatya could hold the highest offices in the empire. Harishena, the author of the Allahabad pillar inscription of Samudragupta was a *Kumaramatya* besides being *Sandhivgrahiaka* and *Mahadandanayaka*. However, in our estimation the Adhishthanadhikarana of these land-grants was the highest governing office of a vishaya which was in some cases an administrative unit of a *bhukti* under the Uparika.

Perhaps the administrative office of a cluster of villages or a smaller administrative unit like a district or a tehsil was called *Ashtakuladhikarana*. The Damodarpur copperplate inscription of the time of Budhagupta mentions the *Ashtakuladhikarana* of the town-place ? named Palashavrinda. This office of the *ashtakula* was headed by the *Mahattara* Savishvasa. We know that Mahattara was a village head and addressed as such in a large number of land-grants. This office of Ashtakula addresses the village family-heads, Brahmanas and other petty family-heads of the village Chandagrama and announces the application of the villager Nabhaka for purchase of a land for some Brahman families. The meaning of Ashtakula is not clear. According to Dr. Sircar (1965 A: 359) *ashtakuladhikarana* is administrative board consisting of members from eight communities. At another place (1965 B: 288, fn. 4) he notes "Ashtakula, like Panchamandali (mod. Panchayata) may indicate the Panchayata Board. Adhikarana= court of justice and office of administration. The passage thus seems to mean 'the office of the Panchayata Board of the village'. Ashtakula=eight families representatives of eight (or more) families forming the board of administration." It is interesting to note that the Sanchi stone inscription of Chandragupta II also mentions 'Panchamandali' to which Dr. Sircar has referred in the above quotation.

The Damodarpur copperplate inscription of the time of Kumaragupta I (year 124) also mentions the *Prathama Kulika* Dhritimitra who was a member of the *Adhishthanadhikarana* headed by the Kumaramatya Vetravarman. It is possible that he was elected/selected from some body of eight *Kulikas*.

However, here *Ashtakuladhikarana* may mean the 'administrative office' governed by eight noble families of a village or a region. The Dhanaidaha copperplate inscription of the time of Kumaragupta I mentions the *Gramashtakuladhikarana* which certainly was a village office. These inscriptions show that revenue records and records of land measurement of every of the villages were properly maintained in these offices.

Here it may be noted that for Manu (VII. 119) '*kula*' is a measurement of land. Head of ten villages gets one '*kula*' land and that of twenty villages is authorized to cultivate five '*kula*' of land for maintenance. According to Kullukabhatta the land cultivated by 12 *halas*, i.e. ploughs is equal to one *kula*.

Pustapala

The office of the *Pustapala* was of somewhat a different nature. *Adhishthanadhikaranas* were the administrative offices from where final orders were passed or files were sent to the office of *Pustapala* for verification because all the records of mensuration of land and collection of revenue were maintained there. This can be compared to the modern Lekhapalas (Patawaris) under a Kanungo of a pargana, converging in a tehsil under a Tehsildar. The structure of these administrative divisions is not clear from inscriptions.

These copperplates from the Gupta period show that when an application was filed by a party with the office (*adhikarana*) of the authority it was forwarded to the office of *Pustapala* for verification and report. After verification the *Pustapala* returned the application with the note that it was verified with the office records and is in accordance with the local practice, and that the application may be accepted. He also used to put a note that 'there is no objection and it will give the ruling king one sixth of the *dharma* or *punya*.

The number of deputed *pustapalas* may differ in accordance to the need. While only one *pustapala* is deputed in the Damodarapura copperplate of the time of Budhagupta, year 163 there are two, three, four or even more number of *pustapalas* in other copperplate inscriptions discovered from Damodarpur. The Pahadapura copperplate inscription of the year 159 (there is no mention of the King) mentions as many as seven *pustapalas* including one *Prathama Pustapala*. This was perhaps due to the fact that the purchased and donated land was situated under the domain of different *pustapalas*. This is why the committee was headed by the *Prathama pustapala*.

There is one interesting term '*darvikarma*' in the Vaigram copperplate inscription of the time of Kumaragupta I, year 128. This is used in the sense of measurement of land. Therefore it is not unlikely that mensuration of land for assessment of crops and fixation of revenue to the exchequer was done in very orderly manner in every locality. There are some inscriptions that provide the amount of annual revenue collection from a village which points out that land was thoroughly measured and classified to assess the annual collection. The Madanapada (Faridpur District of Bangladesh) copperplate inscription of Suryasena (1210-15 CE) and Vishvarupasena (1206-22 CE) (Sircar 1983: 131) records the annual revenue of the donated village in terms of *puranas* or *curnis* (coins) to calculate the loss to the donee and to compensate it. This practice of estimation of revenue of every locality and region might have been in vogue in the whole country. Thus it is not out of place to assume that there was prevalent some sort of traditional institution of revenue assessment and collection that remained unaffected by the changing borders of the kingdoms due to victories and defeats of kings. Taxes of different nature were fixed and there was judicious method of sharing these right from the petty local ruler to different strata of overlords. *Bhaga, bhoga, kara* and/or *hiranya* were the four types of main taxes that involved every section of the society. The subject has been dealt with here after. But it will not be proper that the kingdom has no control over these traditional offices. Some officers like Mahakshapatalika are mentioned to control the whole network of field survey and revenue collection without changing the staff which, most probably was traditional. They automatically were adjusted with the changing governments.

Office of the Mahakshapatalika

According to Roma Niyogi (1959: 152) the office of the *akshapatalika* is generally taken to be 'an officer in the revenue department, one in charge of the receipts of the royal treasury ... He may be compared to the accounts officer or more correctly the accountant-general.' Dr. Sircar (1965 A: 366) is more specific when he notes "The Mahakshapatalika was the keeper of records according to some but the chief accountant according to others, though he seems to have acted in both the capacities." But, however, these definitions do not give an accurate idea about the office of *akshapatalika*.

His office was very old, perhaps older than the Maurya period because Kautiya (*Arthashastra*, II. 7) deals with the subject under the heading of a chapter called the 'Office of Accounts under Akshapatala' (*akshapatale gananikyadhikara*). Here he prescribes that the 'accounts register-books' (*nibandha pustastham karayet*) should be kept under seven heads. Thus it was called the office of *akshapatala*. This department must have continued since long before his times. It was so common that he thought it unnecessary to talk about the essential nature of their work, i.e. mensuration. From general references in inscriptions and etymological analysis of the words '*aksha*' and '*patala*' it is possible to speculate about its nature. To our assessment the office of the *akshapatalika* was originally associated with the land survey and fixation of revenue accordingly. This practice started so early and became so common that we seldom find any reference to it.

Monier-Williams (3) besides many other meanings, defines '*aksha*', as "terrestrial latitude", and '*aksha-drik-karman*' as "operation or calculation for latitude", '*aksha-bhaga*' as "degree of latitude", '*akshansa*' as "a degree of latitude". He also defines it as "name of a measure (=104 *angula*). For him the term 'aksha-pata' means "an arena, a wrestling ground, place of contest" and 'aksha-patala' means "court of law; depository of legal documents". Thus the meaning of *aksha-patala*, given above, seems to be derivative of the original word when the revenue office of the Akshapatalika had become well established and (land) litigations were heard and settled there. As regards the 'depository of legal documents', Kautilya prescribes revenue registers of seven departments to be kept in his office. Undoubtedly the word seems to be associated with the land survey and the land revenue. Kautilya's *Arthashastra* and the inscriptions never mention of land measurement and revenue assessment. Perhaps by Kautilya's time this had become so common to be mentioned. It relates with the origin of state in India. It has already been pointed out that in the Vaigram copperplate inscription of Gupta period a word '*darvikarma*' occurs in the sense of measurement of land. It is also interesting to mention here the testimony of the *Shatapathabrahmana* (1.2.5.2) where measurement of land is said to be done by bull-hide. Here it may be taken to mean the tape made of hide.

Monier-Williams (373) explains the term '*gramakshapatalika*', as meaning "a village archivist", equal to modern '*Lekhapala*' or '*Patavari*' who is in charge of a group of villages under a 'Kanungo'. Here the word '*pata*' in '*Patavari*' is significant because this officer is related with land mensuration and surveying along with keeping a record of the revenue of the villages under his charge. It is relevant to mention here that Banabhatta in his *Harshacharita* (Ch. VII) also mentions a *gramakshapatalika* who appears before the King along with all his office-staff while the latter assumed kingship and was camping on the bank of the river Sarasvati. He offers a gold seal with bull emblem embossed with king's name and requests him to start issuing land-grants from this auspicious day. An officer called *gramakshapatalika* also finds mention two copperplate inscriptions of the Gupta emperor Samudragupta. His Nalanda and Gaya copperplates, dated respectively in his regnal years 5 and 9 name '*Gramakshapataladhikrita* Gopasvami'. It is, however, difficult to agree with Dr. D. C. Sircar (1965:272-74), who, following Fleet, has declared both the documents as spurious. Disagreeing with him we have advocated (Verma 2011: 147-54) that these are genuine Gupta grants; though composed in faulty language. Without going into the details of other arguments we can conclude that Sircar's theory of 'copying lost copperplates' cannot be upheld because two copyists, separated in time by one or two centuries, cannot commit same faults in two separate documents that are dated in different regnal years of the same king.' How these two copyists, centuries apart, can commonly dream of an officer called '*Gramakshapataladhikrita* Gopasvamai' to have existed and worked under Samudragupta. However, there can be no doubt that there existed the office of '*Akshapataladhikarana*' in the 4th century CE in the Gupta empire.

In the middle of the sixth century an officer with this designation was working under the Maukhari emperor Ishanavarma. His Devakali copperplate inscription (Verma 2008-09: 272; and also Thaplyal & Srivastava 1988: 85 ff) mentions this officer. In seventh century all the three copperplates inscriptions of Harsha, referred to above, were written by officers called '*Mahakshapataladhikaranadhikrita*'; though the personal names naturally differ. This goes to prove the authenticity of Banabhatta's *Gramakshapatalika*.

Office of the *Mahakshapatalika* was maintained by almost all the major dynasties in north India. Many of them have mentioned in their copperplates. But it is doubtful if all the officers called akshapataladhikrita were assigned similar type of duty in all these dynasties. The Pandukesvara CP inscription of Lalitasura (854 CE) declares *Mahadanakshapataladhikrta* Piuka was the *dutaka* of the grant while the record was prepared by *Mahasandhivigrahaksha-pataladhikrita* Aryata (Sircar 1965 A: 271). Thus one officers called *akshapataladhikrita* was looking after the department of donations while the other was given the charge of *sandhivigrahika*.

However Sircar (Id. 99) notes about this office as follows. "The originals of the grants from which the plates were prepared, probably written on perishable material, must have been preserved in the records office of the kings. As we have seen, an officer called *Akshapatalika*, very often mentioned in inscriptions, is regarded by some as an Accountant and by some others as a Record-keeper, though he may have served in both the capacities. The store-room of the original grants in a king's Akshapatala department is probably called the phalaka-vara (literally, 'the store-house of plates') in a Nasik inscription of the second century A.D." He further writes (Id. 86) that "According to Kalhana's *Rajatarangini*, the officer-in-charge of the preparation of documents at the Kashmirian court was called *Pattopadhyaya* (i.e., a professional teacher in charge of the preparation of title-deeds), who belonged to the *Akshapatala* department which Stein understands as Accountant General's office and Buhler as the Record office or the Daftar or court of Rolls."

Such observations about the office of the *Akshapatalika* are based on European understanding of the term, not on the study of different terms with various combinations of *aksha* and *patala* used in inscriptions. Here, it will be out of place to go in details but his office can neither be equated with that of 'Accountant General' nor 'the Record office or Daftar or court of Rolls'. It must be seen as that of the 'Land-records and Revenue' combined.

Some land-grants of the Gahadavalas were written by an officer called *karanika* who usually held the rank of Thakkura. *Karana* or *adhikarana* is used for office and *karanika* is one who holds an office or works in an office as clerk. It also may mean writer, scribe or accountant. These offices of writers and accountants were controlled by an officer called Mahakshapatalika at the highest level. In the Gahadavala inscriptions about 23 writers of land-grants are mentioned and most of them call themselves 'Karanika' and/or 'Kayastha'. They seem to hold very high office in the empire because many of them endowed with the title of 'Thakkura'. There are reasons to assume that there was a network of *akshapatalikas* right from the village level up to highest officer. Most of them could claim to be *kraranika* but there is no information about other classes of these workers. It can be assumed that right from a village up to the office of the Mahakshapatalika a large number of clerks were employed. A perusal of copperplate inscriptions shows that the office of the Kayastha, like that of a Purohita, was an obligatory in every kingdom because revenue and accountancy was an important department of the state.

Announcement of Land-grant

It has already been mentioned that according to Dharmasastras kings were asked to grant land to the Brahmanas and issue a charter written on *'pata'* or *'tamra-pata'* endowed with his own seal and with a description of the boundaries of the land, of his own ancestors and of the measurement of the area for the information of future kings because such donations cannot be taken back or confiscated. It was also prescribed that the king should address in the land-grant right from the Brahmanas, (State) officers, families (of villagers), Kayastha, duta, Vaidya, Mahattaras (village officer) up to (the lowest strata of society like) Mlechha and Chandala. Sircar (1965 A: 105, fn. 2) quotes original text from *Krityakalpataru.* This prescription was literally followed in almost all land-grants from earliest times till twelfth-thirteenth centuries throughout the country. The later land-grants are more and more elaborate than earlier ones.

Number of Addressees in Copperplates

In later times the number of addressees increased. The reason may be seen in enhancement of resources and complications in administration. Fondness for aggrandizement may also be responsible to some extent. The word *maha-* is prefixed to many designations. The number of officers also swelled. There seems no relation between the size of the kingdom and the number of officials addressed in a copperplate. The nature of duties assigned to an officer also could vary. Sircar (Id. 354) points out that 'in later times official designations did not always indicate the same responsibility and may have indicated merely a rank in many cases is suggested by the mention of the *Dandanayaka* and *Mahadandanayaka* in the mediaeval records of the Kannada area. Often he is the governor of a territory and, in some cases, the collector of a particular taxes. In many cases, he enjoyed several other official designations at the same time, ... It is not known whether the different responsibilities associated with particular designations were held by an officer at the same time; but it will be seen that a distinction is sometimes made between the *Dandanayaka* and the commander of the army (*sena, sainya*), the latter officer being often mentioned in these records as the *Senapati, Sainyadhikarin, Sainyapala, Camupati, Dala-adhikarin, Dalavay*, etc.'

The Nalanda and Gaya copperplate inscriptions of Samudragupta, 4th century, are the earliest in north India and here only the Brahmanas and village families are addressed. But in South Indian inscriptions of the same period a big number of officials and other village people were addressed. Sircar (Id. 356) notes that "The earliest copper-plate grant giving such a list of officers is the Hirahadagalli plates of Pallava Sivaskandavarman. The royal order in respect of a grant of land was addressed in this case to the following categories of the king's subordinates: *Rajakumara, Senapati, Rashtrika, Mandapika, Desadhikrita, Gramagramabhojaka, Vallava, Govallava, Amatya, Arakshadhikrita, Gaulmika, Tairthika, Naiyogika* and other servants like *Sancharika* and *Bhatamanushya*."

The Kavi plates of the Gurjara king Jatabhata III (737 CE) of West India cites a small number of addressees like *Rajan, Samanta, Bhogika, Vishayapati* and *Rashtragrama-mahattara* while in Deccan the Elora plates of Dantidurga (742 EC) are addressed to the *Rajan, Samanta, Bhogika, Vishayapati, Rashtrakuta, Mahattara* and *Adhikarika.* Similarly the Sanjan plates of Amoghavarsha I (871 CE) were addressed to the *Rashtrapati, Visahayapati, Gramakuta, Yuktaka*, or *Ayuktaka, Niyukta, Adhikarika* and *Mahattara.* Sircar (Id. 363) notes that 'from about the 8th century A.D., the list of addresses was fairly big in the charters of rulers of the North India'. He cites the names of as many as 26 officers in the Khalimpur plates of the Pala ruler Dharmapala. However, he notes that the 'addressees in the grants of Harsha (606-47 A.D.) are not too many. The Deo-Barnark inscription of Jivitagupta II (about the second quarter of 8th century A.D.) is one of the earliest records containing a big list which the Palas appear to have imitated.'

Sircar presents a list of as many as 42 addressees from the Manahali plate of Madanapala (c. 1143-61 A.D.) who was one of the latest rulers of the Pala family. But largest lists of addressees come from the carters of Lalitasura (middle of 9th century) (50+12 addressees) and the Padmata (middle of the 10th century) (52 + 12 addressees). But, however, Dr. Sircar (Id. 372) holds that 'one of the biggest such lists comes from the charter of a small chief of Dhekkari in North Bengal. Mahamandalika Ishvaraghosha, who flourished about the 12th century, has the following list in his Ramganja plate:' Then he lists as many as 59 officers from this plate.

Thus there seems little relation between the number of addressees and the size and the prestige of the kingdom. We have, on the other hand, no reason to disbelieve in these lists. These officers appear to be real howsoever long these lists are. The Bhatpar copperplate inscription of Kirtipala (VS 1167, 1111 CE) (Verma 2011: 759 ff) furnishes the names of the addressees along with their offices. This leaves no doubt about that these were real offices.

Here I wish to draw attention to a peculiarity in these lists that have never been noticed. These land-grants, as indicated in Dharmashastric injunction, are to be announced before officers of the kingdom and all the inhabitants of the village concerned. Thus these addressees are always mentioned in two sections and they are supposed to be present in the announcement. Take the example of the Khalimpur CP inscription of Dharmapala (775-812 CE). Here all the addressees are mentioned in two sections: in first category there are 24 officers who directly earn their livelihood from the state (*rajapadopajivinah*). In the second category are the workers like *Chata*, *Bhata*, *Jyeshthakayastha*, *Mahamahattara*, *Mahattara*, *Dashagramika* etc., *Vishaya-vyavaharinah*, *Karanas*, and all residents of the region and the Brahmanas. Sircar (1983: 64) is not specific on the topic when he summarizes this second portion as "... and other dependents of the king such as Chatas, Bhatas etc. ..." This is not the whole truth. In the inscription they are called '*yathakaladhyasinah*' which means 'officers posted at respective places for the time being'. Many of these posts were hereditary. This category might belonged to the traditional infrastructure about which we have already discussed. They were not required to be specifically appointed every time with the change of the regime and were not removed from their posts after the change of the king. They enjoyed royal favour through the officers of the first category. The first category of officers were personally appointed by the sovereign and were required to attend the duties assigned by him.

Officers of Kingdom

As enjoined by the Dharmashastras the king was required to address all the inhabitants of the area right from the Brahmanas up to Chandala, the lowest in social status including all the officers of the state and the petty village officers. It was customary that he should ask their welfare and then declare the land grant. Here it is important to note that though king was known to be 'lord of the earth' in reality he was not the owner of all land. The king had no authority to gift the land held by cultivators or the inhabitants of his kingdom. He could only exempt his share of taxes in the form of *bhaga, bhoga* and *kara* and ask his subjects to pay these dues to the donee. The announcement was aimed at informing every one in the village that the officials of the state are prohibited to enter the area for collection of these dues. This was the purpose of public announcement of the land grant and address all concerned including king and his officers.

King, Queen and Crown-prince

The list of addressee officers usually begins with the king, queen and the crown prince because these constitutionally three are included among the salaried officers of the state. After these come other officers of the central administration. Some scholars are of the opinion that the first three addressees refer to the feudatory chiefs and their families or to the provincial governors and their families. But a careful perusal of the lists of officers it appears that all of them belong to the 'central government' that issued the charter. Here one may ask as to why the issuing authority, the king, should be included in the list because all the orders are promulgated in his name. In this respect the attention may be drawn to the fact that the Gorakhpur CP inscription of Ramapala, the son of Kirtipala, gives the personal names of these officers. Interestingly, names of the Queen and of the Maharajaputra are given but not of the king. This may be explained by the fact that his name appears in the beginning of the record. But the Pala and the Gahadavala land-grants begin with Rajan.

Reason for this is not clear we can speculate on this. We believe that all the dignitaries in these lists, including the king, are constitutionally (according to Dharmashastra) the officers of the state. Though it was the king in whose name the grants were issued, with the intention of increase of the merit of his own and his mother and father, he was paid for his services in the form of taxes, as discussed above. So were the (Chief) Queen and the Crown-prince. They are ceremoniously anointed and become the part of the administration in that capacity. All the queens and princes could not claim these offices. From the Gahadavala inscriptions we gather that Govindachandra had two Chief Queens anointed one after the other. The first *Pattamahadevi* Nayankelidevi issued the Daravali grant along with the king in VS 1176 (Verma 2011: 530). Here she is said to be 'endowed with all the royal prerogatives' ((*samasta-raja-prakriyopeta*). After her death Govindachandra's second senior Queen Gosaladevi was appointed as '*patta-mahadevi*' who also issued the Banagava land-grant along with her husband in VS 1208. She also is describe to be 'endowed with all royal prerogatives' (Id. p. 640).

In the same way the Crown-prince also was duly consecrated and was entitled to issue land-grants. The *Yuvaraja* Asphotachandra issued the Bhadaini CP grant in the year 1201 and he also is said to be 'endowed with all the royal prerogatives' and 'consecrated as *yuvaraja*' like the *Patta-mahadevis* mentioned above. But in the case of two land-grants issued by the *Maharajaputra* Rajyapaladeva, respectively in the years VS 1201 and 1203 these words are not used. This means that the posts of *Patta-mahadevi* and *Yuvaraja* were constitutionally recognised and they enjoyed certain rights in administration. It is for this reason that the Queen and the Crown-prince are included in the list of addressees. In some land-grants Rajakumara or Maharajakumara are mentioned and it is not unlikely that they also held some office.

Same was the case with the king also who was duly consecrated and endowed with constitutional powers. The king was the head of the state but never enjoyed unlimited powers as often alluded to by Western scholars and repeated by many native ones. R. S. Tripathi (1969: 337) writes:

> At the head of the state was the king, whose office was hereditary. He exercised despotic powers, and except his immediate advisers the people in general had hardly any share in the determination of his policy in peace and war.

The intention behind this jargon is not pious. That the 'office of the king was hereditary' is an universal truth. But the statement that, i) 'he exercised despotic powers' and ii) 'except his immediate advisers the people in general had hardly any share in administration of his policy in peace and war', is based on biased thinking and aimed at showing Hindu kings as despots. A Hindu king can never be a despot, except in exceptional cases; and these are exemplarily cases as denounced by all scriptures. A Hindu king was bound by the rules of *dharmashastras* and was considered fit for disapprobation if he deviates. The *dharmashastras* emphasise much on the personal merits and character of the king in spite of advocating his divinity; but it was aimed at preventing chaos and giving good and judicious government in the state. The probability of a Hindu king being despot was properly taken care of in the *dharmashastras* and the *smritis*. It is important to note that the Hindu kings, including those of the foreign origin like the Kshaharatas and the Kardamakas of Western India, in their epigraphs, have always claimed to be most benevolent and devout followers of varnashrama-dharma and depict themselves engaged in public welfare; no sign of despotism is seen from their claims and behaviour. We have demonstrated above that a king is required to announce his intention of donating a tax free land to the lowest person in the village. No despot can be expected to do that. Regarding the divine position of a king U. N. Ghoshal writes:

> The climax of this principle of the king's divine creation to the old Smriti conception of the co-ordination between taxation and protection. The king, we read, having the aspect of a master was ordained by Brahma for the service (*dasyatva*) of the people with his own share of the produce as his fee (*bhriti*) for the purpose of of their consistent protection.

Thus, according to the *dharmashastras* king was in essence a public servant, i. e. official, who was paid in form of taxes for protection and to maintain law and order. To perform this duty he was equipped with some privileges. Therefore, the practice of including king among the addressees of a land-grant, though may seem paradoxical, is not unjustified.

Other Officers

There is large number of officers mentioned in land-grants and there are several variations in some of these names. The list is so long and varied that it is perplexing to discuss all of them. At present we have absolutely no information about the nature of the work of these officers except to speculate from the etymological analysis of these names. It is also a fact that the nature of the work of same/similar name-bearing officer also varied in different regions, periods or kingdoms. Therefore it is not very safe to speculate much from these names. Here we will deal only with a limited number of officers and analyse in historical prospective. Our main guide in this respect is Dr. D. C. Sircar who has done spectacular in the field of epigraphy.

In north Indian inscriptions there seems big variation in the name and number of state officers. The Gahadavala CP inscriptions refer to, besides *Raja*, *Rajni* and *Yuvaraja*, the officers like *Mantrin*, *Purohita*, *Pratihara*, *Bhandagarika*, *Akshapatalika*, *Bhishak*, *Naimittika*, *Antahpurika* and *Duta* besides heads of six departments looking after *kari*, *turaga*, *pattana*, *akara*, *sthana*, and *gokula*. (Verma 2011: 306) But in Bengal CP inscriptions the list is entirely different. For example the Khalimpur CP inscription of Dharmapala (775-812 CE) mentions 26 officers including "*Rajan*, *Rajanaka*, *Rajaputra*, *Rajamatya*, *Senapati*, *Vishayapati*, *Bhogapati*, *Shashthadhikrita*, *Dandashakti*, *Dandapashika*, *Chauroddharanika*, *Dauhsadhasadhanika*, *Duta*, *Khola*, *Gamagamika*, *Abhatvaramana*, *Hastasvagomahishajavikadhyaksha*, *Naukadhyaksha*, *Baladhyaksha*, *Tarika*, *Saulkika*, *Gaulmika*, *Tadayuktaka*, *Vinyuktaka*, *Chata* and *Bhata* as well as the district officers like *Jyeshthakayastha*, *Mahamhattara*, *Mahattara*, *Dashagramika* and *Vishayavyavaharin* whose Karanas are specifically mentioned." (Sircar 1965 A: 363-64). The Manahali CP inscription of Madanapala (1143-61 CE), who was one of the latest rulers of the Pala family, mentions as many as 42 officers. (Id. 366). The new officers are *Mahasandhivgrahika*, *Mahakumaramatya*, *Rajasthaniya* and *Uparika*, *Dandika*, *Shaunika*, *Kshetrapala*, *Prantapala*, *Kottapala*, *Angaraksha*, *Tadayukta*, *Kishoravadavada-gomahishajavikadhyaksha*, *Preshanika* and *Gramapati*. Apart from these *Gauda*, *Malava*, *Choda*, *Khasa*, *Huna*, *Lulika*, *Karnata* are also mentioned among addressees.

Among the Pala officers four, i.e. *Rajan*, *Rajanaka*, *Rajaputra* and *Rajamatya* have the word *raja* prefixed with them. D. C. Sircar (Id. 364) seems right when he notes 'The *Rajanaka* was apparently a smaller feudatory than *Rajan*. *Rajaputra* is the same as *Rajakumara* of the Hirahadagalli plates, although the intention here may be to refer to the sons of the feudatories since the following *Rajamatya* possibly indicates the ministers or administrators of the subordinate rulers.'

But this a partial view of the picture. To understand this it is required to have a full view of Hindu political system. *Rajan* undoubtedly is the donor king and the Rajanaka is the subordinate king of the region or the village. In ancient India there were innumerable petty kings and kingdoms of different sizes and potentialities in every part of the country. They enjoyed the privileges and prestige of a king in their kingdoms. They usually accept the suzerainty of a superior power and attend his court. Most of offices of the central power, like Pratihar etc., were enjoyed by them. Such smaller kings are called Rajanaka. In some copperplates the suzerain claims to be '*samasta-raja-chakra-sansevita-charana*'; this raja-chakra or circle of kings is formed by these petty kings. So far as *Rajaputra* is concerned, he may be 'the same as *Rajakumara* of the Hirahadagalli plates' but he cannot be 'the sons of the feudatories as Sircar asserts. We do not intend to discuss here other officers in copperplate inscriptions but wish to point out some interesting office names that linger up to modern times.

Chauroddharanika now continues in Indian society as *chaudhari* or *chaudhury*. This has become a family title and is used by different strata of the society. According to Sircar he 'was a police officer responsible for collecting fines for theft.' We beg to differ. The word is composed of *chaura* and *uddharanika* which means an officer who rescued stolen material from the thieves. The *Smritis* prescribe that king should restore and return the stolen things to the aggrieved persons. However this title is used by the families of higher classes as well as by other people. This shows that there was a hierarchy among the holders of this office.

Dusadha: At present *dusadhas* are considered backward or scheduled caste. It seems an abbreviated form of the officers called 'Daussdhyasadhanika. Sircar holds that he 'seems to have been a leader of expeditionary forces requisitioned on occasions of emergency.' He may be the head of the regular troupe responsible for preparing or constructing roads and bridges to facilitate the march of the army. They appear to have formed a caste that degenerated to the scheduled category.

Mehatar or *Mahattara*: In the present society Mehatar is a caste who follow the profession of cleaning human excreta. Mahattara was an officer who worked right from the village level. A large number of copperplate inscriptions mention this office who seems to be the most important officer of the village. The Khalimpur plate of Dharmapala addresses the officers called *Mahamahattara* and *Mahattara*. On this Sircar writes 'Since *Mahattara* was the head of a village or community and the member of a Panchayat, the *Mahamahattara* appears to have been head of a group of villages or the chairman of its council of administration,...' Another interesting fact is that the term *Mahato* is still used for an important person of a village which might be a corrupt form of *mahattara*. But the question is how a caste, called Mehatara, came into being who undertook the profession of cleaning human excreta. Most probably they were forced to adopt this profession. In Muslim onslaughts a large number of villagers were captured and they were reduced to slavery and sold as such. This might be one reason. The first generation might have resisted but from the next they adopted this as wish of the providence. A good number of these captured slaves may have been village mahattaras and hence this name for this caste. They are also known as *bhangi*, i.e. broken or of 'broken pride' (*mana-bhangi*). This is a painful aspect of history from inscriptions.

Revenue Administration

The question of revenue system is related with the ownership of land in Indian economic setup. Almost all synonyms for the king unambiguously show that he was the lord of the land. The *smriti* literature also is unanimous on the point. But at the same time, it also lays down that the peasant is the owner of his fold and his rights cannot be violated. Accordingly, the convention and the tradition both are right. Modern historians have expressed divergent opinions on the issue and made it complicated. It is true that our knowledge of the system or systems of land-tenure is extremely vague and incomplete. It is also true that to a modern educated man with the knowledge of world fiscal system, it may appear intriguing. For a Marxist historian it is hierarchical control over the land created by large-scale feudalization to give rise to graded type of landlords, who not only shared but controlled the agricultural surplus and reduced the peasant to serfdom. All the Indian thinkers on these lines are knowledgeable persons but do not seem equippred or ready to utilize their personal knowledge of conventional land practices in villages of land revenue system in the pre-British India or in the native states. The colonial British rulers are guilty of systematically destroying the traditional village setup. Earlier, the Sultans of Delhi could evolve, as described above, no revenue system of their own and often used brute force for revenue collection. But the could not penetrate the traditional village setup and consequently damage it as the British have done.

It is not a dilemma that in India the king was the lord of the land and the peasant was the proprietor of his land. Lallanji Gopal writes:

> When Medhatithi speaks of the King as the master of the soil and of the soil as belonging to the peasant, he does not mean to lay down the legal status of the King as the owner of of all cultivable land in the state, but only points out the sovereignty of the King implying a general lordship of the King over all things in his kingdom.

The whole epigraphic wealth of India, issued mostly by kings, is witness that the king had no right to confiscate the agricultural land of a peasant until he pays dues. Even issuing the land-grant was not a private business between the king and the donee; it had to be officially notified and announced among all in the kingdom right from the king to the man of lowest strata, the Chandala.

The kings, in mediaeval period, have gathered more and more power and prestige because the governance had become more complicated with several types of officials and departments, as noted above, that made the system of taxation complex and elaborate. But the guiding principles remained more or less the same. All were governed by the Dharmashastras, with some variations according to local situations and requirements of governance. The guiding principle was that the taxes were paid to the king ion lieu of his protecting the subjects. U. N. Ghoshal has note that "Save and expect the legal taxes the king was not authorized to take the property for his own use from the inhabitants of his realm." The taxes were regarded as 'pay' received by the king for protecting his subjects. It amounted to one-sixth (of their income and spiritual merit).

Sukra advises the king to collect his revenue in such a way as the cultivators are not destroyed; he should do it like garland-maker, who does not destroy the flower plant, and not like the charcoal-maker who destroys the tree. The tax collection should not destroy the prosperity of the subjects. Sukra prescribes that proper survey and measurement of the land should be done, followed by careful classification in matter of variety and produce for the purpose of revenue assessment. It is also prescribed that no tax be collected by persons who improve the land by irrigation, until they have earned twice their cost of production including state revenue. Tax was collected on produce, not on area of land in possession.

No ambiguity was left in land-grants. The gift of tax-free land and exemption in certain taxes by the king should not be seen in the light of making a new class of permanent landlords or feudatory as intermediaries between the peasant and the king. Its purpose was, besides increase in religious merit and fame, to maintain the education, especially Vedic. It was the need of the society and state had to fulfill it.

On the revenue governance in 19th century Mewar (Rajasthan) Mahabir Prasad Jain (2007) has given a vivid account which can be regarded as the remnant of ancient revenue practices in the region. Some of his observations seem relevant to us. He writes:

> The ancient revenue was in vogue in Mewar till the last years of the 19th century A.D. ... Here revenue was the part of the product of the land, not on the land. A family might have had any amount of land but it was not liable to pay tax on it. A peasant was not bound to cultivate the whole area; and he was liable to pay on the basis of produce of the crop. Revenue was paid in the form of *banta* and *bighodi* which were called *bhoga.*

He writes under the title 'Bhusvamitva' which seems a glimpse of ancient village administration:

> To understand the revenue system it is necessary to know the nature of ownership of land. In Mewar whole village community had a right on all the land within the boundary of the village. This included pasture and forest land. Agricultural land was the property of individual family. All the peasant families were considered to be the successors of those who initially brought the land under agriculture. They had common right on the

community land such as pasture, forest land, tanks, river and bed of the tank, etc. as a member of the village community. The village community used to protect its right on the community land. The surplus of the land of the village was the collective property of the village and reserved for future common use. All the peasant families were entitled to prepare new agricultural land if necessary. Generally no recompense for it was charged. In some *paraganas* there was a custom of paying a nominal charge.

Jain gives some more information about the revenue collection and concessions to certain communities. An abstract follows. Rates of revenue collection were very flexible. Banta bhoga varied from one half of the produce to 1/4, 1/5, 1/6, 1/7, 1/8 or 1/9 as per convention of the locality and quality of the land as well as the produce of the crop. It may vary in the same village. For higher castes like Brahmanas, Kshatriyas and Mahajanas, concessions were provided. Service providers of the village, such as barber, potter, washer-man, and persons engaged in other services like artisans, iron-smith, etc. were often given concessions in revenue. Those who developed land for cultivation were given concession for certain period. There were definite and well established conventions about revenue and the state usually had to follow it. Thus cultivator and the state authorities were sure about their share.

In the light of these established conventions, there was not much scope for new dynasty and empire to meddle with the revenue. The whole hierarchy of kingship (*raja-chakra*), which the modern historians fondly call the 'feudal system' had its definite share in the villsage revenue which was called *bhaga*, *bhoga*, *kara* and *hiranya* in copperplate inscriptions.

The Gahadavala land-grants state that 'all other offerings to me' and all other things under or out of the soil as well as what so ever produced by earth, should go to the king'. All the offerings to the king are called *daya*, or '*adaya*'. Roma Niyogi (1959:167) holds that the 'inscriptions of the contemporary kings also attempt a similar distinction between taxes and royal rights and other sources of revenue'. She further writes "The epigraphic evidence of the dynasty shows that generally the taxes were divided into two broad classes -- regular (*nity-adaya* or *niyat-adaya*) and irregular (*anity-adaya* or *aniyata-adaya*)."

In the contemporary land-grants a large number of taxes are enumerated from which the grantee was exempted. But it should be kept in the mind that all of these taxes were neither levied everywhere nor it should be presumed that all the villagers were expected to to pay all these. R. S. Sharma (2003: 14) is right when he observes that "The utmost that we can say is that all these taxes may not have been imposed on the same person, traders and craftsmen paying taxes different from those paid by peasants."

Bhaga, Bhoga, Kara/Hiranya

The number of taxes is too large to discuss here. Here we will like to deal with the three basic taxes which were almost universal to ancient India and seem to be related with the origin of kingship and state. We can go back into old primeval days when population was very scanty and far between. People, in general, were victims of rowdy people living on the wealth of others. This is described as '*matsya-nyaya*' situation where big fish lives at the cost of weaker fishes. People needed protection. It was agreed that they will contribute towards all the needs of some brave and just person in lieu of the protection. The agriculturist will pay a 'portion' (say, one-sixth) of their produce. This was known as '*Bhaga*'. The other section of the society was of those who were earning their livelihood through some crafts and collecting forest products or by any other means will share certain 'portion' of their earnings. This was (mostly) in kind and comes under the '*siddhi*' type of '*Bhoga*'. The third section of the society was those of traders. They were neither engaged in trade and commerce. They were required to pay certain amount of money or cash from their profit. This was known as '*Kara*' or '*Hiranya*'. Though there were certain variations in '*kara*' and '*hiranya*' in some inscriptions, but these term are more or less synonyms. Thus in these three types of taxes almost the entire society, called '*visha*', was involved. But this was not all. There were certain other facilities enjoyed by the king under the term '*bhoga*' which are of eight types and we will discuss later.

All these facilities were provided to the 'King' to live in comfort and maintain an office as well as an army for protection and management. Besides this king was the lord of all natural resources and he was designated as the 'Lord of the earth'. This is a broad outline of the origin of kingship and the state in ancient India. As we have seen above that 'the king was ordained by Brahma for the service (*dasyatva*) of the people with his own share of the produce as his fee (*bhriti*) for the purpose of of their consistent protection'. The Dharmashstras have prescribed several restrictions on kingship and these were literally followed. Inscriptions show that the kings, even of foreign origin, were eager to follow the *dharmashastric* injunctions in every respect. There is no scope here to go into details of the issue.

Bhaga

There seems no dispute about '*bhaga*' which was the main part of the original share of the king in all agricultural products including the good and bad merit of the people. It was one-sixth but often varied according to the quality of the land. In his Lumbini pillar inscription Asoka exempted this village from taxes (*ubalike kate*) in which he specifies that the 'eighth part' (*atha bhagiye cha*) was exempted.

From inscriptions we gather that some small and subordinate kingdoms also issued land-grants exempting from the *bhaga-bhoga-kara* etc. This is an intriguing situation as the supreme sovereign also gives exemptions in these taxes. We do not know what system was followed to share these taxes between the higher and subordinate kings. But we can cite one example. The Gahadavala kings of Kanauj as well as their subordinate, the Khadirpala kings of Japil, have issued land-grants giving exemptions in these taxes. Not only this, the Khadirpala king Pratapadhavala issued an injunction prohibiting his descendents to not to accept a spurious Gahadavala land-grant which was obtained by the Brahamanas of a certain village by bribing an officer of the king of Kanauj. He asked his successors to realize all the taxes from these grantees. This shows that the subordinate king had to forego his share of these taxes at the bid of his suzerain.

Bhoga

There seems some ambiguity about this term in the mind of modern historians and epigraphists. According to scholars like Ghoshal boga is a periodical supply of fruits, fire-wood, flower, etc. by the peasants to the king. D. C. Sircar, on the other hand, has rendered the term as *jagir* throughout his book, *Indian Epigraphy*. Perhaps he had in his mind terms like bhukti of the Gupta records, derived from *bhoga*, for administrative units and officers like *bhogika*, *bhogapatika* etc. occurring in inscriptions. It is strange that scholars like R. S. Sharma take *bhukti* in the literal sense of the term that suits the ideology he professed. According to him (2003: 14),

> Literally the term *bhukti* means something intended for enjoyment, for the idea of rulers enjoying the earth was fairly current during this period. So it is likely that as a territorial unit the *bhukti* may have been meant for enjoyment of the governor under whose charge it was placed.

It is not that the scholar was not conversant with the Indian history but this sectarian interpretation is an instance of twisting history to support some ideology. In fact, his whole book, *Indian Feudalism*, is full of such perverted statements and twisting of facts. But Sircar also cannot be supported that *bhoga* was a *jagir* (fief) allotted by the king to someone as the Sultans and the Mughal kings used to do.

A. K. Majumdar (1956: 248) informs about eight types of bhoga in mediaeval period.

> The next part of the formula, namely, *sa-hiranya-bhaga-bhoga* presents some difficulties, for *bhoga* is certainly the *ashta-bhoga* mentioned in some texts and inscriptions. These

> eight *bhogas* were the following: (1) *nidhi*, treasure trove; (2) *nikshepa*, unclaimed property deposited on the soil; (3) *pashana*, mines etc.; (4) *siddha*, lands yielding produce on which improvements have been made; (5) *Sadhya*, produce from such lands after improvement have been made; (6) *jala*, water; (7) *akshini*, present privileges; (8) *agami*, future profits. Of these eight *bhogas*, with the exception of of first three the rest must be held to be part of legal formula while *jala* is a repetition. About unclaimed property left on the soil we have no information but mines and treasure trove have been considered by *sastras* to be property of the king.

This classification of *bhoga* in some texts is exhaustive and may be accepted as belonging to the period when states had developed extensive governing structure and power to control over all the natural resources of the kingdom. We have reasons to believe that initially *bhoga* was of two types. Most likely, one kind of *bhoga* was in the form of sustenance of the king of his daily requirements like food, fuel, oil, ghee, honey etc. which the villagers used for themselves. In due course of time it took the form of convention and regular source of income to the state. Certainly this was so huge that it required the state to evolve an elaborate system for collection and preservation of these items and deposition in the state store-house. Such arrangements beginning from a single village and then to the clusters of ten and hundred villages till it was controlled by the officers in the capital. Such officers are called *Bhandagarika* in inscriptions. Most likely this class of *bhoga* can be identified with the fourth category '*the Siddha*' of the texts described above. In such a case we have differ from Majumdar who defines it as 'lands yielding produce on which improvements have been made'. Obviously such lands are known as "bhumi-chhidra nyaya" in inscriptions and were considered the property of the peasant who developed it and was liable to exemption from taxes. On the other hand '*siddha*' means besides accomplished, fulfilled and acquired etc. prepared, cooked (as food), also 'ready for payment'. Thus our interpretation may more probable. Besides, the term '*ahara*', originally meaning 'food' is used in the sense of 'region of operation' in Asoka's Sarnath pillar inscription. This is suffixed to some cities and towns in inscriptions.

The other class of *bhoga* was in the form of some agricultural land reserved for the king. Some times cities and towns are also mentioned as *bhukti* or *bhoga*. Certainly these are traditional and cannot be regarded as the creation of some king. These must have traditionally been considered as such. Here are some examples.

The Eran stone pillar inscription of Samudragupta (Sircar 1965 B: 270) calls the city of Airikina as his *sva-bhoga-nagar*. Most likely this was not created a *bhoga-nagar* by Samudragupta. Similarly the all the six Damodarpur copperplate inscriptions of the Gupta period were issued from Pundravardhana-bhukti. We do not know if this *bhukti* was the creation of the Gupta emperors. Most likely this also was a traditional *bhukti*. It is also possible that initially only the city of Pundravardhana, being a bhukti, became the center of administration and the capital of the province, hence the whole region acquired that name.

Another example of bhukti land comes from Gahadavala inscriptions (Verma 2011: 338). 'In Rein copperplate inscription of Govindachandra, *dasa-hala* (ten plough) land was granted by the king from his 'own land' (*svake-bhumih*). ... this land of ten-plough (of the king or state) was traditionally enjoyed by the donee and it seems to have been only renewed by the king; thus the village got its name 'Dosahali'.' This came under the Gahadavalas by conquest. It is possible that the *bhoga* land of the village Dosahali changed many hands before them. Thus there seems some sort of permanent arrangement of *bhoga-lands* and *bhoga-nagaras* was made throughout the country. We are inclined to put such lands under the '*Sadhya*' category of text quoted above which means 'to be subdued or mastered or won or managed, or conquerable, amenable'. Thus Majumdar's contention can be ignored which defines it as 'produce from such lands after improvement have been made'. Besides *bhoga* there are many variants of the word such as *bhoja* and *bhojaka*, etc. This word later became synonym of king. In Mahabharata King Yayati is said to have deprived his son Druhyu of kingship and cursed him to the status of Bhoja. This is the earliest literary reference to the word.

Remaining six types of bhoga belong to natural resources and can be attested belonging to king as the Lord of the Soil (*Bhupati* or *Bhumi-pati*).

Kara/Hiranya

Kara is often synonym of *Hiranya* that means cash. In some inscriptions these two words appear separately denoting some other variety. It is levied on businessmen or on those who are involved in any kind of production. These formed a category different from agriculturists and other professionals. By involving this class through *kara* the whole society came to contribute it share towards the king or the state for the protection by it. The number of taxes too exhaustive and varied according to the professions and to the regions to be discussed here.

The Formula Sajala-thala, etc.

We cannot close the discussion on inscriptions without commenting on the epigraphic formula of land-grants. The inscriptions introduce the granted land with the formula 'with its water and dry land, with its mines of iron and salt, with and including its groves of *madhuka* and mango trees, enclosed gardens, bushes, grass and pasture land, with its ravines and saline waters, with what is above and below, defined as to its four abuttals, up to its proper boundaries', etc. This is one of the most elaborate version of the formula quoted from the Bengal Asiatic Society copperplate inscription of the Chandradeva and Madanapala, VS 1154 (CE 1077). Land-grants of other dynasties also more or less quote it with some variations. It is, however, to be noted that most of the items related in these phrases are not really part of the donation. It is also unlikely that these are found in every locality. It is not possible that 'mines of iron and salt' or and 'ravines and saline waters' are found in everywhere. Therefore, the whole phrase should be considered a set formula to be quoted in every land donation.

The real purport of this formula was often misunderstood and scholars usually explain it on the basis of literal meaning of terms used. For example, let us quote Roma Niyogi (1956: 185) who holds:

> A perusal of the common series of inscriptions reveals that generally the royal right extended over different parts of the villages excluding the land inhibited and cultivated; it, thus extended over *jala-sthala, loha-lavanakara, matsya, gartta-oshara* and *madhuk-amra-vana-vatika-trinayuti-gochara*. The first term *jala-sthala*, may have meant either marshy land or plain land and water reservoir; these reservoirs probably included *vapi* (well with flights of steps), *kupa* (ordinary well), *tadaka* (tanks) and probably all the gardens on the bank of the reservoirs (*kaccharama*).

Then she goes on describing *akara, matsya-akara*, and *gartt-oshara* as royal property and observes "Sometimes the *madhuka* and the *amra* gardens were also considered royal property". Again,

> *Triniyuti* and *gochara* are almost synonymous terms, the former meaning grass-plots and the latter grazing grounds. *Triniyuti* has been explained sometimes as inadequately fertile plots, which were allowed to lie uncultivated for a year or two by turns. As such, however, *trinayuti* certainly was the private property of the the cultivator and the king's right to provide posture grounds in the uncultivated land and probably the villagers were allowed to use these grounds on payment of a tax to meet the initial expense and the cost of upkeep.

Some scholars go one step further and suggest that these and other similar expressions show that the ordinary tenants enjoyed none of these rights and the king or state owned everything. But such assumptions are forced derivations on the basis of literary interpretation of the phrase. These lead to wrong interpretation about the rights of the state mediaeval period.

Dr. A. K. Majumdar (1956: 248) is more specific on the issue. He rightly observes:

> From this formula it should not be concluded that all the trees, woods, grass and water in the kingdom belonged to the king. This recital was necessary to make the gift valid, it is learnt that even when a house was sold it was necessary to recite a part of this formula. Similarly in the time of Marathas, when land or villages were granted, it was usual to put in such words as '*jala-taru-trina-kashtha-pashana-nidi-nikshepa*', and it was decided by the British Indian courts that these words conferred on the grantee ownership in the soil itself, and that in the absence of these words it is possible to hold that the grant was only of the royal share of the revenue and not the soil.

Thus speculations about king's authority over the things enumerated in the formula is unwarranted.

Bibliography

Elliot, H. M. and John Dowson (1999, LPP Reprint). *The History of India as told by its own historians*, Volume I, Delhi

Fleet, J. F. 1963 (reprint). *Corpus Inscriptionum Indicarum*, Vol. III, Delhi.

Jain, Mahabir Prasad 2007. 'Mewar men paramparagata Gram-vyastha aur British arthika tatha prashasanika nitiyan' (Hindi) in *Smarika* issued on the occasion of National Seminar, February, 24-25, 2007, by Bharatiya Itihasa Sankalana Samiti, Jaipur.

Majumdar, A. K. 1956. *Chaulukyas of Gujarat*, Bombay.

Mohan, R. T. 2003. *Afghanistan Revisited*, New Delhi.

Monier-Williams, M. *Sanskrit English Dictionary*, 1999 edition, New Delhi.

Niyogi, Roma 1959. *The History of the Gahadavala Dynasty*, Calcutta.

Sharma, B. N. 1972. *Social and Cultural History of Northern India*, New Delhi.

Sharma, R. S. 2003. *Indian Feudalism, c. A.D. 300-1200*, 2nd edition, New Delhi.

Sircar, D. C. 1965 A. *Indian Epigraphy*, Motilal Banarasidas.

Sircar, D. C. 1965 B. *Select Inscriptions*, bearing on Indian history and civilization, Volume I, Calcutta.

Sircar, D. C. 1983. *Select Inscriptions*, bearing on Indian history and civilization, Volume II. Delhi.

Srinivasan, Doris M. (edited) 1989. *Mathura: The Cultural Heritage*, New Delhi.

Tripathi, R. S. 1969 (reprint). *History of Kanauj to the Moslem Conquest*, Delhi.

Thaplyal, K. K. and V. N. Srivastava 1988. 'Maukhari Naresha Ishanavarma ka Devakali tamrapatra-lekh' (Hindi), *Bulletin of Museums and Archaeology in U.P.*, Nos. 41-42, June-Dec. 1988, pp. 77-86.

Verma, T. P. 2001. *Ayodhya ka itihasa evam puratattva* (Hindi), New Delhi.

Verma, T. P. 2006-07. *Pragdhara*, Journal of the U.P. State Archaeology Department, Lucknow, No. 17, 2006-2007.

Verma, T. P. 2013. "Writing in the Vedic Age, Harappan and Asokan writing", *Itihas Darpan*, No. 18 (1).

22

THE ALLAHABAD MUSEUM COPPERPLATE GRANT OF RAṆABHAÑJADEVA-I

G. C. Tripathi

In the year 1987 when I was Principal of the Ganganatha Jha Research Institute at Allahabad, an antiquity dealer of Delhi personally contacted me at my residence and showed me a set of two copperplates which he had procured from somewhere in Orissa (from where, he did not tell me). He wanted to know the approximate date of the plates and their content so that he may price them accordingly. I kept the plates for two days with me and noted down its text. The plates, as I learnt later, were sold to the Allahabad Museum where they must still be there, I presume.

The plates record the grant of an unspecified 'village', or a relatively large piece of land lying between the outer boundaries of the village known as '*Svalpakirāsara'*, and the river Mahanadi, by the *'parama-māheśvara'* king **Raṇabhañjadeva (I)** out of his crown land to a prominent Shivaite ascetic **Shikhādeva** hailing from **Terambi,** obviously for the purpose of establishing a monastery of his sect. It is a known fact in the religious history that major Mutts were always keen to establish their branches elsewhere, and even in distant lands, to propagate their faith. On the other hand, there is an uninterrupted tradition all along the history of Orissa (and Bengal) of rulers inviting learned scholars and religious teachers to their land, especially from the *Madhyadesh,* for cultural and intellectual enrichment of their region[1].

The plates are still unpublished and not even the recently published monumental work of Ms. Snigdha Tripathy ("*Descriptive Topographical Catalogue of Orissan Inscriptions*", Delhi 2010) enlisting all the known Orissa-related inscriptions till date, makes a mention of it, hence I want to draw the attention of the epigraphists, historians and scholars working on Orissan religious sects of medieval ages towards it.

This set of twin plates is joined by a round ring which contains the royal seal of the donor **Raṇabhañjadeva** (I) of the **Bhañja** dynasty containing a small image of crouchant bull and the name of the king. The grant has been issued from the capital city of **Dhritipur**. This town has not yet been properly identified; however as most of the inscriptions of this king have been discovered from the Sonepur-Baudh-Daspalla region of the north-western Orissa, it is likely to have been located there. The town seems to have been situated either on the bank of, or at least not too far off from the southern bank of the river Mahanadi which often finds mention in his land-grants.

The Bhañjas

The Bhañjas are the people whose branches have ruled over different parts of Orissa, from the 5th-6th century onward for about 1500 years, right down to the merger of their states in Indian Union, a rare record indeed.

They were originally tribal people living in and around the area of Mayurbhanj, adjacent to the eastern boundaries of what is now Jharkhand. Different branches of these people ruled over various tracts of Northern, Western and Southern parts of Orissa, covering the area which is today marked by the districts of Mayurbhanj, Keonjhar, Baudh, Daspalla, Sonepur and Ganjam etc.. Even the state of Bastar in the South-Eastern part of Madhya Pradesh (now Chhattisgarh) was under the rule of the Bhañjas and its ruler Pravinachandra Bhanjadeva was very popular with his subject in the fifties and sixties of the previous century.

The Bhañjas very soon cast aside their tribal character and became great promoters of Art, Culture and Literature in Orissa[2]. They invited learned scholars, ritual experts and religious personalities from all over Midland and Andhra and settled them in their territory granting them lands. The entire Volume VI of the *'Inscriptions of Orissa'* compiled and edited by Ms. Snigdha Tripathy (State Museum, Bhubaneswar, 1976) is devoted to such grants and contains around 50 inscriptions of the Bhañjas. Upendra, a scion of the royal family of Ghumsur, who is considered to be the greatest poet of the medieval Oriya literature, was also a Bhañja. The basic core of the library of the State Museum in Orissa is formed by the books coming from the Palace library of Mayurbhanj. The rulers of Mayurbhanj also donated a chair of Sanskrit to the Benares Hindu University which is still in existence.

The Bhañjas believed that their Progenitor 'Ādibhañja' *alias* **'Gaṇadaṇḍa-Vīrabhadra'** slipped out of the broken (Sans. *'bhanj'*) egg of a peahen *(mayurī)* in the hermitage of the sage Vasishtha which was known as *'Koṭyāshrama'*, and that he was brought up and educated by the same sage. A number of CP grants mention this fact in the very beginning of the text of grants (with many variant readings !) :

āsīt koṭyâśramākhya-mahātapovanâdhiṣṭhāne,
māyūrāṇḍam bhittvā, gaṇadaṇḍo vīrabhadrâkhyah /
pratipakṣinidhanadakṣo, vasiṣṭha-munipālito nṛpatiḥ //

It is very likely that these earliest Bhañjas, originally called themselves actually as *'Mayūra-bhañjas'*, shortened later into the clan name *'bhañja'* only. The royal seat of the earliest Bhañjas was **'Khijjing [-koṭa]'** which is identical with the historical town of *'Khiching'* lying in the Mayurbhanj district of the Northern Orissa. From the North of Orissa split-groups of the Bhañjas spread towards South, South-west and occupied the area which is today marked by the districts of Keonjhar, Daspalla, Baudh right upto Sonepur, where they ruled till the end of 11th century when they were driven out of that region by the **Somavanshi** kings coming from the West, i.e. from the Sirpur-Raipur region of Chhattisgarh. That the town of Sonepur bordering on today's Chhattisgarh was under their control, is proved by the fact that king Raṇabhañjadeva-I has been referred to as "enjoying the grace of the goddess Stambheshvarī" (*'stambheśvarī-labdha-vara-prasādaḥ'*) whose famous temple is situated in that city.

The capital of this Western branch of *the* Bhañjas is mentioned as **Dhrtipura** which according to Snigdha Tripathy[3] seems to have been situated in the present Baudh-Khondmal region. The area which they occupied is referred to as **'Khiñjali-maṇḍala'**, in which the word 'Khinjali' seems to have been formed by adding the diminutive *la/li* to 'Khijjing' meaning 'Small Khijjing', 'New Khijjing' or the like. This Khiñjali-maṇḍala was divided into two parts – Western and Eastern, or as some scholars believe, the Northern and Southern parts of the kingdom with the river Mahanadi as the dividing line between the two. The rule of Raṇabhañjadeva-I extended over the both, as in six of his earlier inscriptions he calls himself *'Ubhaya-khiñjalyadhipatiḥ'*[4]

Of the, *Ādi–Bhañjas* ruling over the Northern region of Mayurbhanj-Keonjhar, their original habitat, 11 copper plates have been discovered till now. They have been issued from the *'Khijjing-koṭa'*. On the basis of these we know the names of 15 rulers of this dynasty. The South-Western dynasty which concurrently ruled in the 9th-10th century gave rise to the following four great rulers, all of whom had twin names, i.e. besides their tribal names (which sometimes appear in Sanskrit translation), also 'royal' appellatives and titles (cf. Snigdha Tripathy : 1976, Introduction):

1. Angadi *alias* Śilābhañja-deva
2. Gandhāṭa *alias* Śatrubhañja-deva
3. Yathāsukha *alias* Raṇabhañja-deva - I (our donor)
4. Pallagambhīra *alias* Digbhañja (or Diśābhañja) - deva

Since in the opening verses of the grants of these kings each ruler mentions himself as the legitimate heir and successor of his predecessor, it may be presumed that they belonged to the same family and the same line. Of these the rule of Raṇabhañjadeva-I lasted probably longest, roughly from the year 950 to 1000 of the current era. After being attacked by **Mahashivagupta Yayāti** of *Somavaṁśa*, the ruler of Mahakosala region, and getting ousted from the Baudh-Daspalla-Khondmal-Sonepur region, they (perhaps under Digbhañja-deva) migrated towards extreme South of Orissa, to the forest and hilly track of Ganjam, and established their new capital at **Vañjulavāk** from where again a number of grants have been issued. Later the line of **Ghumsur** became more important; it not only produced important rulers but also excellent literary figures including such a 'poet-king' as **Upendrabhañja-deva**. Over the period, especially in the late medieval ages (17th-18th C.), the southern Bhañjas got split up in many houses and ruled peacefully till the advent of British. They even extended their sway upto Bastar (now in Chhattisgarh), as already stated, where the popular king Pravinachandra Bhanjadeva successfully ruled till the merger of his state in the Indian Union, but who later was eliminated – as is commonly believed— by his powerful, political adversaries of the newly formed state of Madhya Pradesh.

The 'Ādibhañjas' of Mayurbhanj-Keonjhar region also had to face tough times when Orissa was conquered by **Anantavarman Choḍagangadeva** in the year 1112 CE. The Gangas did not tolerate the independent nature of the Bhañjas of Mayurbhanj and Keonjhar. They also had to secure their Northern borders against the rulers of Bengal. Wars with the Bhañjas were therefore inevitable. According to the Chronicle of the Jagann'tha temple known as the *Mādalā Pāñji* (*Prachi edition* of Prof. A.B. Mohanty) the Gangas, in the early years of their conquest of Orissa, caused great havoc in the land of the Bhañjas leading to heavy losses of their men and resources. Three of such attacks by the Gangas on the Bhañjas of Keonjhar-Mayurabhanj and of Sonepur by Anaṇgabhīmadeva, Pratāpa-Narasiṃhadeva and Kali-Bhānudeva respectively have been explicitly mentioned in the *Mādalā Pāñji*. All three, according to this text, ended with the defeat of the Bhañjas. Whereas the second of the above-named Gangas ransacked Keonjhar and controlled it for long, the third one according to *Mādalā Pāñji* is said to have defeated and 'cut off the heads of several Bhañjas of Sonepur and brought them to his capital'. It appears, however, that later a truce was worked out and these decimated 'Ādi'-Bhañjas could survive in their land as vassals of the Gangas due to political arrangements with this supreme central power of Cuttack.

As already mentioned, the grant under reference was issued by **Raṇabhañjadeva I** (first) of the Western Bhañja family ruling over *Khiñjali-maṇḍala* in the 9th-10th C. The period of the long rule of Raṇabhañjadeva appears to have been approximately from 950 to 1000 CE, starting a few years earlier or ending a few years later. His son Digbhañjadeva also ruled over the territory from the same city (Dhritipur) but, as mentioned above, it was probably he, who in the last years of his rule was displaced and ousted from this region by the inroads of the Somavanshins.

Although the Bhañjas were basically Shaivas/ Shāktas which is proved by the benedictory verses occurring in their royal charters, yet in some of his grants king Raṇabhañjadeva (See No. 17, 18, 19 of the *Inscriptions of Orissa*., Vol.VI) describes himself as '*parama-vaiṣṇava*' as well due to 'political' reasons. But in these grants also the benedictory verses relate to Shiva and not to Vishnu. The most frequently occurring first verse in many of his charters is as follows:

Saṃhāra-kāla-hutabhug-vikarāla-ghora-
sambhrānta-kiṅkara-kṛitānta-nitānta-bhinnam /
bhinnândhâkasura-mahā-gahanâtapatram
tad bhairavam hara-vapur bhavataḥ punātu/prapātu //

It is also significant that in the early years of his rule, at least for the first 26 years, the king Raṇabhañjadeva refers to himself simply as '*rāṇaka*', and much later as '*mahārāja*'. It seems that though originally perhaps a vassal under the **Bhaumakara** rulers, he gradually increased his political power and stature to become an independent king, and thereafter assumed the title of '*mahārāja*'. Our's is a unique record in which he calls himself '*Mahārājādhirāja*'.

The Plates

The length and the breadth of the Copper-plates are ca. 20cm (7.25") X 13 cm (5") respectively. They have a thickness of some 3 mm. each and the total weight of the plates along with the seal is approximately 1600 grams. The seal has a squire base of 6.0 centimeters. The height of the seal is 2.7 cm and its form resembles that of a folded bud of *campaka* – a highly fragrant flower of yellowish – orange colour commonly found in the hilly tracts of Orissa and very popular with the village girls as hair decoration. The lowermost square part of the seal bears the characters "*Śrī raṇabha = ñjadevasya*" in two lines.

The plates are inscribed only on one side although the thickness of the plate would have easily allowed incision on the other side as well. The inscribed surfaces are placed face to face and the joined with a metallic ring containing the royal seal. The first plate on the back (*verso*) has only the letters "*Oṃ svasti /srīḥ*" incised at the top left in the same style and form as on the front (*recto*), and the rest is left blank. It appears that the plate was initially meant to be used for some other inscription, or, may be, for the same inscription, but with a different beginning. No *maṅgalācaraṇa* verse appears in the beginning which is very unusual because Bhañjas (including our Donor) are known to start their grants not only with benedictory verses but also with reverential references to their forefathers, or at least to their progenitor, the Ādibhañja (Gaṇadaṇḍa-Vīrabhadra). A short genealogy of the immediate forefathers of the donor king usually also appears. Very often these matters occupy one full plate and the actual grant starts from the second plate. Since in a number of grants, this first plate appears to have been inscribed by a different hand, it may be presumed that such "first plates" were kept handy in the stock and were appended to the grants as and when required. If this is true, it is possible that the grant originally consisted of *three* plates and that the upper plate was willfully and cleverly removed at some stage (to be sold separately?!). The open unwelded ends of the round ring holding the remaining two plates also lend support to this supposition.

The text of the first plate runs into 12 lines whereas the second plate has 11 lines inscribed on it. A fair distribution of the text in two almost equal parts is thus achieved. Each line contains approximately 25 characters which are more or less of equal size. The text of the grant is composed throughout in grammatically flawed, and often defective, Sanskrit prose—except for the usual precatory verses at the end of the grant beseeching the future rulers to 'protect' the grant and condemning the person who takes away the grant from the donees.

Of these two traditional verses the first one praises in general terms the merit accruing out of 'protection' (*rakṣaṇa)* of the grant of a previous ruler to a donee and his successors, i.e. of honouring and recognizing the title of the grant, and the other casts a spell for being condemned in hell on the ruler who takes away the granted land from the donee or his successors.

The prose text thus contains only the functional or the operational part of the grant. The flawed Sanskrit of the text leaves out many conjugational and declensional endings. The tribal rulers of the Bhañja clan perhaps did not have good Pandits in their court. However, the vocabulary used is proper and precise, the administrative terms are correct and the draft of the grant, in general, follows the previous grants of the Bhañjas.

The Text of the Plates

Plate –I

१. [ॐ][१] परममाहेश्वरो मातापितृपदानुध्यातो महाराजाधिराज

२. श्री रणभञ्जदेव[:] कुशली। धृतिपुर-स(सं)निकृष्टग्रामसम्प्रवारके ब्राह्म-

३. णां[न्] सम्पूज्य तत्प्रतिनिवासिकुटुम्बिन[:] ससामन्ता[न्] समाहर्तृसन्निधातृ-प्र-

४. मुखां[-खान्] सर्व्वराजपुरुषां[-षान्] समाज्ञापयति। विदितमस्तु भवतां। यदा(द)स्मा-

५. भिरयं ग्रामः राजस्वौवारिकः (राजस्ववारितः?) स[कल][२] लोकविज्ञप्तिकया सनिधिः सोपनिधिः

६. सर्वकरादानसमेत[:], सर्व्वपीडाविवज्जि[र्जि]तः निषिद्धचाट-भटप्र-

७. वेश[:] चतु[:] सीमानिबद्ध उत्तरेण महानदी पर्यवसानः।
८. पश्चिमेन वृक्षपिम्पलं यावत् । ततः प्रगुणमेव(वं) चामुण्डा-
९. भर्तरि कामाडि[दि]त्य तडागं ततः ऊर्ध्व(र्वं) दक्षिणेन स्वल्पकिरासरग्राम-
१०. सीमासन्धिं। एवं अ[आ]ग्नेयां दिशि बोबूलडा सीमां यावत्। पू-
११. र्व्वेणापि श्रीधरस्य वापिं पूर्व्वभागं गृह्य। एवं ऐशान्यां दिशि
१२. हं(?)[३]सक्रमतडागं यावत्। माता पित्रोरात्मनश्च पुण्यव(वि)वृद्धये श्री

Plate – II

१. तेरम्बीविनिर्ग्गतायार्य (आचार्य?) शिखादेवपादां (-दान् ?) ब्रह्मचर्योपस्थितः [ϒा]=शै[वो][४] पा-
२. ख्यदर्शनसिद्धान्तस्थितिप्रपादक। तस्य सन्ततिना(तीनाम् ?) उदकपूर्व्वक(कं) कृ-
त्या(त्वा आ)चन्द्रार्कसमकालं समुपभोगार्थं ताम्ब्रशासनेनाकरत्वेन [प्रतिपादितः] [तदियं दत्तिः?] समुचि-
४. तभोगभागाधि(दि)कम(मु)पनयद्भिः सुखं पालनीयेति। भाविभिश्च
५. भूपालैरस्मत् उपरोधात् दत्तिरियं पालनीयं(या)। मा भूदफ-
६. लशङ्का वः परदत्तेति पार्थिवा[:]। स्वदत्तात्फलमानन्त्यं परद-
७. त्तानुपालने। स्वदत्तां परदत्तां वा यो हरेत्(त) वसुन्धरा[म्]। स विष्ठा-
८. यां कृमिर्भूत्वा पितृभिः सह पच्यते। इति कमलदलाम्बुबिम्ब(न्दु)लोलाम्
९. शृयां(श्रिय) मनुचिन्त्य मनुष्यजीवितञ्च। सकलमिदमुदाहृतं हि बुध्वा(द्ध्वा) न हिः (हि)
१०. पुरुषैः परकीर्तयो व(वि)लोप्याः इति ।। सम्वत् π^{0} (५०)[५] माघवदि ३
११. उत्कीर्णं कुलपुत्रदिवाकरेण लाञ्छितं च देवचन्द्रेणेति ।।

---

1. Expressed with a conventional symbol.
2. Omitted in the plate. Supplied by the editor on the basis of similar text in other plates.
3. This first letter is illegibly blurred except the Anusvāra; *haṃ* - is my conjecture (haṃsa=duck).
4. This letter which I read as *śai* could also be a symbol denoting Mattamayūra/Pāśupata sect.
5. The number of the year has been denoted by a symbol (ϒ) which looks very similar to the Greek letter π (pi). According to the chart supplied by G. H. Ojha in his classical work **प्राचीन भारतीय लिपिमाला**, it refers to the number 5.

Translation

(Since the language is grammatically not perfect*, only a free translation is being given)*

'Highly devoted to Lord Shiva and constantly meditating upon the feet of his mother and father, the great king Raṇabhañjadeva is hale and hearty [due to their blessings]'.

'After having revered (i.e. having paid his respect to) the Brahmins in a royal camp erected in the rural area near the outskirts of **Dhritipur,** he makes announcement [as a royal decree] in the assembly of the people consisting of the inhabitants of the village, in the presence of his feudatories as well as his court officers, especially the Revenue Collector and the Treasurer, as following':

"Let it be known to the honorable audience here that we have proclaimed this village as exempt from paying [all kinds of] revenue to the royal treasury. This has [also] been made known by public announcements [to the accompaniment of drum beats]. This exemption is valid on all main and subsidiary produces of the village. The village is [however] empowered to collect taxes [from its residents for its own maintenance]"

"We have prohibited all kinds of interference and pressure from outside [by royal officers] and have also prohibited the entry of policemen and soldiers of the army into the village"

"We have made over this village for the sake of the enhancement of the merit of our mother, father and our own self with a vow [solemnly] spoken with water in hand, and confirmed by a royal charter engraved on copper plates, to the venerable Preceptor **Shikhādeva** hailing from **Terambi**, who is a lifelong celibate and a propagator of the philosophy of the ***Shaiva-siddhānta,*** as well as to his [future] chain of successors [*santati=progeny,* meant are disciples].

"Let them [therefore] enjoy it happily and undisturbed for all times to come (lit. 'till the Sun and the Moon exist') after keeping aside and distributing appropriate shares for all who have stake in it (i.e. temple deities, priests, tenants, servants of the monastery etc.).

"Now the limits of the grant are as follows: Towards the North, up to the river Mahanadi; towards the West, up to the Pipal (banyan) tree *(ficus religiosa),* and proceeding from that point in straight line (lit. 'following the line of thread', *praguṇam*) upto the temple of Chamuṇḍā / Chāmuṇḍeshvara (in the South-West), including the tank called *'kāmāditya'*; then moving towards South up to the subsidiary settlement of the village *Kirāsara;* proceeding in the same manner towards South-East up to the fringes of the village *Bobulaḍā;* further towards East up to the fringe of the step-well of Shridhara and likewise towards North-East up to the tank known as *(Ha ?)ṃ sakrama* [or '*Sakra-*]*taḍāga*'."

"We also earnestly request the future kings to honour this grant"

[The grant is followed by three traditional verses]

'Let there be no doubt, O kings, about earning merit by protecting the grant of the previous rulers. Immeasurable more merit accrues to the person who protects the grant given by an earlier doner, than when he himself makes a grant'. 'One who takes away the grant given by some previous ruler, or takes back the grant given by his own self, is tormented in the fire of hell along with his forefathers and is then reborn as a worm in human waste.' 'The riches as well as the human-life are as fickle and as unsteady as a drop of water on a lotus-leaf. Keeping all this and such other wise sayings in mind, one should not wipe out the traces of the [meritorious] acts performed by foregone persons to perpetuate their name through the posterity'

'[Issued on] the 3rd day of the dark fortnight of [the month of] Māgha in the 50th [regnal] year [of the king]. Marked (= written) [on the plate] by Devachandra [and] incised by Kulaputraka-Divākara.'

Remarks on the Contents of the Plate

It is difficult to locate exactly the spot where the land was granted to Acharya Shikadeva and his disciples for establishment of a monastery. The grant simply speaks of the donation of 'a village' (*ayaṃ gramaḥ* = this village), but the name of the village occurs nowhere. It was perhaps still only an open site for establishment of a mutt and for maintenance of the mutt through farming and produce of orchards etc. It appears to be quite a fertile land adjacent to the river Mahanadi with ample water-bodies all around, somewhere along the track of Mahanadi between Sonepur and Baudh since it is only in this region that the Mahanadi flows in a straight line West to East so that the site might have existed on its southern side, not too far from its right bank. After Baudh, the river takes a slanting turn towards South-East so that Mahanadi cannot be said to have existed on the northern side of the village

It is striking that whereas the CP grants of Raṇabhañjadeva mention the year of the issue of the charter usually in words, this one uses a special symbol i.e. a chronogram (π^{o}) which poses some difficulty of decipherment. A similar chronogram appears in the CP grants of certain North Indian rulers of the 5th to 8th centuries which according to the numerical tables given as appendices by G. H. Ojha in his *Prāchīn Bhāratīya Lipimālā* (2nd. Ed., Ajmer 1918) represents the number 5 which, combined with the clearly visible small circle on the right, gives the number 50 which I accept. Although there is also some similarity with the chronogram representing 10 in the table No. 73 of the above work, yet I rule it out because our plate refers to the king as '*Mahārājādhirāja*' whereas we know that at least till the 26th year of his rule (*vide* Grant No. 19 in Vol. VI of the *Inscriptions of Orissa*) Raṇabhañjadeva-I refers to himself only as a 'small king', a *rāṇaka*. One more chronogram for 40 in the same table also bears a fair amount of similarity with the symbol engraved on our plate. I therefore leave it open whether it denotes the year 40 or 50, but am more in favour of the latter because the royal title in our plate goes better with the title of '*mahārāja*' that appears in the grants of 54th and 56th year (*ibid*, No. 20,21) as well.

This one is thus among the grants issued by the king in the last years of his rule. There are only two grants which are later than this, both from the district of Baud (No.21 & 22 of the Vol. VI of the *Inscriptions of Orissa*), issued to Shubhadāma of Shravasti and Devadhara of 'Madhyadesh', in the years

54th and 58th of his rule respectively. It is rare for a king to enjoy such a long period of rule, but not impossible. One may also consider the possibility that the year mentioned here is counted according to '*Ankiya*' reckoning which is typical of Orissa. According to this system the years having the number 6 or 0 (except 10) are left out, the first year starts with 2 and it changes not on the anniversary of coronation, but on the following *Vāmana-dvādaśī* day (the 12th day of the bright fortnight of the month Bhādrapada, known as *Sūniyā* in Orissa [*śūnya* = 0]). Counting with that system the present year could actually be the 40th year of his rule which corresponds to the 50th of the Añka-wise calculation. However since the numeral of zero does not figure in the *Añka* system, there are only two possibilities, either the number given is actually the year of rule of the king (which is more probable), or some other system of reckoning the regnal years was in force at that time.

It is really remarkable that the king refers to himself in this grant as '*Mahārājādhirāja*', a presumptuous title which he has never used in any of the grants known so far. In his earlier grants, at least upto his 26th regnal year, he mentions himself humbly as a '*Rāṇaka*', i.e. a smaller king., a vassal to some greater king, may be one of the Bhaumakaras, although he is already the '*adhipati*' of both the sections of the Khinjali region. After that the next grant is the present one in which he is already a '*Mahārājādhirāja*' ("king of the kings"). However, in his grants issued later in the 54th and 56th years respectively (No. 20 & 21 of the *Inscription of Orissa, Vol. VI*), he again becomes humbler and refers to himself only as '*Mahārājā*'. It is not improbable that between his 26th and 50th regnal years, he annexed a couple of neighboring territories, made himself independent and has assumed the title of '*Mahārājā*' or '*Mahārājādhirāja*. Whether the latter was an officially assumed title or just 'conferred' upon him by some sycophant courtier who drafted the text of the grant, is difficult to say.

Further, though he mostly refers to himself as '*parama-māheśvara*', yet he seems to have been favorably disposed towards other religious sects also. He has granted land, for example, to the Vaishnavas as well in which he assumes the title '*parama-vaiśṇava*' in his charters (cf. No. 16, 17 and 18 of the Vol. *VI* of the *I.o.O.*). But also in the grants in which he describes himself as a 'devout Vishnuite', the *maṅgalācaraṇa* verses are devoted to Shiva and not to Vishnu.

Contents of the Grant

The town of **Terambi**, where the present donee, a Saivite preceptor, is said to have come from, has been rightly identified by Prof. R.N. Misra[5] with the town known today as ***Tirāhi*** and the same is located in the Shivapuri district of Madhya Pradesh. A cluster of dilapidated and deserted religious monuments still exist at this spot in the midst of a forest. Prof. Misra who has personally visited the spot and has closely examined the religious complex, informs that the most prominent among the edifices standing in a quasi ruined state at this spot are a [Shaivite] monastery and two temples belonging to the 9th and 11th centuries respectively. According to him, it was a distinguished centre of ***Siddhānta*** Shaiva ascetics. Our donee in the present inscription is also referred to as "[*shaivo*]*pākhya-siddhānta-sthiti-pratipādaka*", i.e. 'the one who propagates the *siddhānta* philosophy of Shaivism'. This Shaiva-siddhānta seems to be different from the *Shivādvaita* of Kashmir but probably a precursor of the Shaivite philosophy of the same name widely prevalent in South India.

The particular strain of the Shaiva ascetics based at Tirahi was known as the **Mattamayūra** sect of the Pāshupata Shaivas and the name of the founder Acharya of this very influential sect is mentioned as **Gaganashiva** in a number of inscriptions and grants. *Tirahi* had a number of sister-monasteries over a large part of Central India and even down South in Andhra Pradesh. The existence of a monastery of this sect is also reported from Ranipur-Jharial in Orissa.

The present grant testifies the existence of such a monastery in the Baudh-Daspalla region of North-Western Orissa. It may be presumed that since the Bhañjas were basically Shaivas and they traced their origin from the egg of a pea-hen (*mayūra*), they showed special favour towards the sect of *Matta-mayūra* ('ecstatic peacocks'), invited its followers and established Mutts for them in the area of their influence.

However, Terambi was not the original centre of the Siddhānta-Shaivism. This itself was a branch of the 'mother-monastery' located originally at ***Kadambaguhā,*** a penance grove of the Shaivaite Siddhas, which was later named as '*Mattamayūrapur'*. It is difficult to say whether the term 'mattamayūra' has some esoteric meaning referring to the spiritual practices of these ascetics, or simply a word denoting those sylvanic surroundings, full of dancing peacocks, amidst which the first monastery was situated. But the term came to stay and the ascetics belonging to this monastery and its later branches, were referred to as 'the *mattamayūra* Shaivas' and their sect came also to be known as such.

Kadambaguhā is identical with the small settlement known as ***Kadvahā*** today. Its first occupation, according to Prof. R.N. Misra, goes back at least upto 675 CE from which time onward we can uninterruptedly trace its history. We do not know the actual name of its founder Acharya. He is simply referred to in the later inscriptions as '*Kadamba-guhā-vāsī*' ("the occupant of the cave lying amidst the cluster of Kadamba trees"). Not mentioning ones Guru by name is a time honored and well established practice in India[6]. With the passage of time, the 'cave' gave way to a full fledged monastery and the monastery grew in terms of its population and influence, several branches of this 'Kadambaguh'' *alias* 'Mattamayūrapur' came into being in and around the nearby regions. At least five of these were quite prominent and are known from various epigraphic records. They were located at '*Araṇipadra'* (now called 'Ranod'), *Madhumatī* (now 'Mahua'), *Sarasvatī-pattan* (now 'Sarvaya', the monastery here was known as '*Shankhama-hikā'*) and ,*mardaka* (now 'Amrol', lying near Gwalior).

Of these sister monasteries, the one at Ranod was the first to come into prominence. Its chief Acharya *Purandara* migrated to Kadambaguhā in 825 CE – which probably did not have any senior Acharya there at this time, let himself be anointed as its chief Abbot, and renamed the place as *Mattamayūrapur*. He commanded such a great respect by virtue of his learning and spirituality that the [Western] Chalukya king Anantavarman became his disciple, donated his kingdom to him and ruled in his name as regent.[7]

Madhumati was highly patronized by a number of Kalachuri kings who invited a number of Munis from the monastery to their kingdom and granted them land to establish their monasteries in the Eastern part of Madhya Pradesh. Influence of Āmardaka, established in 775 CE, reached as far as Rajasthan, Maharashtra and Karnataka where branches of this monastery existed for long.

The seat of Terambi came into being sometime between 725 to 750 CE and soon developed into a distinguished centre of Siddhanta Shaivism. We do not know the name of its founder who is again simply referred to as *'Terambīpāla'* in the inscriptions. The corrupt reading in our inscription *('terambī-vinirgatāya ārya shikhādevapādāṃ brahmacaryôpasthitaḥ shai... pākhya-darshanasiddhānta-sthiti-pratipādaka tasya santatinā ...')* does not let us determine unambiguously whether the grant is meant for ***'Ārya Shikhādeva'*** or someone of his disciples who has successfully passed his novitiate under him and has been ordained by him in the order of the *Siddhānta* Shaivas. But that the proposed monastery in this North-Western part of Orissa, was meant to be a sister monastery of the Terambi line is evident and it is interesting to note that the Terambi is now extending its religious influence further eastward right upto Orissa.

The Mother monastery Terambi had witnessed a fierce battle between the forces of the Rashtrakutas and the Gurjara-Pratihāras on the bank of the river Madhuveni in 923 CE, not too far back than this grant, in which the *koṭapāla* (protector of the fort) of Terambi named Chaṇḍian lost his life. Why he participated in this strife between two political forces is not clear. But it is significant to note that the monasteries in those days were well protected with a surrounding wall, much like a fort, and perhaps also maintained a small force, just like all major Christian monasteries in medieval Europe.

The region of Orissa has been a stronghold of Śaivism and Shakti-worship. Viṣṇuism enters late into Orissa, may be, earliest with the Conquest of this region by the Viṣṇavite Gupta rulers in the 5th Century, and remains confined only to the Puruṣottama kṣetra and the surroundings. It is later strengthened by penetration of Gauḍīya Viṣṇuism from the 1500 CE. onwards. Even the king Choḍagangadeva who is credited to have initiated the construction of the present temple of Jagannātha was basically, Śivite in his personal conviction. In Bhubaneswar which is situated at a distance of less than 50 Km. from Puri, there are traces of near-about 500 Śiva temples built over the past one and a thousand years.

The text of the present c.p. grant is a testimony to the fact that the tribal Bhañja kings not only adopted Śivaism as their personal and state religion but were also keen to propagate it throughout their empire by inviting learned Ācharyas and scholars of Śaiva philosophy, especially from Northern strain of Śivaism owing to which it has set firm roots in Orissa which is not the case with the southern one (Śaiva-siddhānta).*

References

1. See in this context *'The Ritual of Founding a Brahmin Village'*, Delhi 1981, (GDK Publications) by the present Author.
2. G. C. Tripathi, The *Transformation of a Tribal State into a Centre of Regional Culture* in H. Kulke & G. Berkemer "Centres out There ? : Facets of Sub-regional Identities in Orissa", Manohar Books, Delhi 2011, Pp. 85-110.
3. Tripathy, S., *Inscriptions of Orissa, Vol. VI*, Orissa State Museum, Bhubaneswar 1974, Introd., p. 3 & 15.
4. Vide Pp. 67, 73, 79, 87, 92, 94, 98, 100 of *Inscriptions of Orissa*, Vol. VI
5. Misra, R.N. (2005) *"Beginning of ˜aiva Siddh'nta and its expanding space in Central India"* in Das, Sadanand and Furlinger, Ernst (eds): ***Sāmarasya*** : Studies in Indian Arts, Philosophy and Inter religious dialogue – in honour of Battina Bäumer, New Delhi : D.K. Printworld (P.) Ltd., pp . 275-306.
6. *ātmanāma guror nāma, nāmâtikripaṇasya ca |*
   śreyaskāmo na gṛhṇīyāt jyeṣṭha-putra-kalatrayoḥ ||
7. *Vide Chandreha Inscription of 973 CE,* published in Mirashi, V.V. (1955) Inscriptions of the Kalachuri-Chedi Era, **Corpus Inscriptionum Indicarum**, Vol. IV, Pt. 1. Ootacamund; pp. 198-204, also Misra, R. N. *ibid*, fn. 105.

---

* I am highly indebted to Prof. R. N. Mishra, Lucknow who has supplied me very-valuable information about the Shaiva sect of the *Mattamayuras* and from mutual discussion with whom I have profited a lot during his stay at the Indian Institute of Advanced Studies, Shimla.

23

FRAGMENTARY STONE INSCRIPTION OF THE KACHCHHAPAGHĀTA RATNAPĀLA: V.S. 1165

Arvind K. Singh

The inscription under discussion was discovered from Gwalior fort and now preserved in the reserve collection of Lucknow Museum. It is not published yet and was only noticed by some scholars. The inscription is edited here from the original stone and photographs made available by Dr. Yashwant Singh Rathore.

The stone is well prepared for writing the inscription, and its bulgy borders edge formation is possibly to protect the letters. It consists of twenty-five lines, of which twenty-four on the surface of the stone and last line on the bulgy lower border portion that is extended to the right border portion to cover the details of the date. The language of the inscription is Sanskrit and the script is Nāgarī. As for the palaeographic features, most of the alphabets are in developed Nāgarī form. However, initial *i*, letters *cha*, *dha*, *ja*, *pha*, *bha*, and *śa* are in transitional phase. The medial sign *e* is of two varieties depicted by a leftward vertical line form as well as in top-stroke form. In ligatures, the subscript *chha* did not complete their developmental path.

The inscription is badly effaced, mostly in the middle part, and now it became difficult to decipher the entire portion of the inscription. However, an attempt has been made here to read the legible portion looking into the importance of the inscription. It is the first known dated inscription of Ratnapāla, a successor of the Kachchhapaghāta ruler Mahīpāla. An inscription of V.S. 1161 is already known to us but in that inscription the name of the successor of Mahīpāla is damaged hence not mentioned by the editor (Hultzsch 1886: 201-203). Another Fragmentary inscription of Ratnapāla was edited by the author but its date portion with other details is now broken (Singh 1994: 113-116).

There are dissimilar opinions about the original place and content of this inscription. For example, according to one view this is the inscription which was discovered by Cunningham from a Jain temple at Gwalior fort, likely it was originally placed in the Jain temple. Other view is that it was brought from some other place and put in the Jain temple. In the same way, the content of the inscription is related with the construction of the Jain temple, or the content is linked with the construction of the Balarāma temple, and after the destruction of the Balarāma temple the Jain temple was constructed on its ruins at that place.

In fact, Cunningham had discovered a Jain temple in 1844 C.E. placed against the eastern wall of the Gwalior fort just mid-way between the Hathiyā-paura and Padmanātha (Sās-bahū) temples. The excavation of the temple yielded several Digambara Jain images and a stone inscription dated in V.S. 1165 (C.E. 1108). On the basis of the findings Cunningham (1862-65: 362-363) considered them the remains of a Jain temple and on the ground of the inscription stated its construction in C.E. 1108. The facsimiles of this inscription marked as No. IX with other inscriptions were sent to Rajendralal Mitra by Cunningham who returned it cited 'not decipherable' because of its badly damaged condition (Cunningham 1862-65: 363). On the other hand, it was noticed by Hiranand Sastri, the then Curator of the Lucknow Museum, as E 17 in the Catalogue which states that it is a stone inscription from Gwalior in 25 lines of writing which is badly effaced in most places and the inscription records the erection of a Jain temple. Later on, after examination of the impression, N. P. Chakravarti (1936-37: 93-94.) argues against the opinion of Sastri and confirmed that it has no connection with a Jain temple. However, he believed that it is the same inscription referred to by Cunningham as being found in a Jain temple and which was returned to him by Rajendralal Mitra as 'not decipherable'. Chakravarti also believed that if the inscription is found *in situ* by Cunningham this must have been the site of the original temple of Saṁkarshaṇa which was later on converted into a Jain temple, probably after its destruction by the Muhammadans. Further, he also presumes that it is not unlikely that it had been brought from elsewhere and preserved in the Jain temple. In fact, the contents of the inscription under discussion is absolutely unrelated with Jain temple whereas another fragmentary inscription of the time of Ratnapāla, known from Gwalior fort, begins with the obeisance of eighth Tīrthaṅkara Chandraprabha, followed by the description of rock-cut Jina image and of Mūla-saṁgha (Singh 1994: 113-116).

The inscription is a eulogy as recorded in the beginning of the last line. It commences with the description of Kṛishṇa and Saṁkarshaṇa followed by the description of the Kachchhapaghāta rulers. Unfortunately due to the badly damaged nature of the inscription it is not easy to determine the precise relations among the kings as well as the role and achievements of all the rulers of the house. The first name mentioned in the fourth line of the inscription is that of Lakshamaṇarāja. After him, only the name of Sūryapāla might be comprehend in the preserved portion of the line seven. The line nine of the inscription consist the name of Sūryapāla's wife but from the fragmentary nature of the inscription it is difficult to ascertain whether her name was Lakshmī or she is only compared to the goddess of fortune. Mahīpāla, the son of Sūryapāla found mention in the line 10. Mahīpāla is described as the forehead-mark of the rulers of the earth and seems to have distributed his weight in gold. From line 14, it is fairly obvious that Mahīpāla's son, born of Rannadevī, was Ratnapāla which is, therefore a new name in the Kachchhapaghāta genealogy. He is so far known only from another fragmentary inscription and believed that his name was engraved in the damaged portion of the inscription of V.S. 1161. The latest date of the Mahīpāla is found in the Padmanātha temple inscription of V.S. 1150 (Kielhorn 1886: 33-46.). The epigraph under consideration being an evidence for the Gwalior inscription of V.S. 1161 belonging to Mahīpāla's successor should also be ascribed to this Ratnapāla. On this basis it could be surmise that Mahīpāla must have died sometime before V.S. 1161 and succeeded by Ratnapāla.

The object of the present inscription is to record the construction of a temple of the Balarāma (Chhīrapāṇi) on the top of the Gopa hill or Gwalior fort by Kulhaṇa who was the 'lord of the entire army' and the 'chief minister' of the king. Kulhaṇa was the son of Sāhani. The name of his grandfather is lost however the name of his great-grandfather was Madhumathana, who was a Brahmin belonging to Śāṇḍilya-gotra. The last line of the inscription records that at the request of Ratnapāla the *praśasti* was composed by Ānanda, the son of Maṇikaṇṭha. It is fascinating to observe in this connection that the Padmanātha temple inscription of Mahīpāla was composed by his father, Maṇikaṇṭha himself. This indicates the continuity of the profession in the family. The name of the writer is not visible. The date of the inscription, as given at the very end, is actually *Saṁvat* 1165 *Phālguna-sudi* 8, however, Chakravarti (1936-37: 94.) mention it as 1167 due to mistake or it might be the printing error.

Only six inscriptions of the Kachchhapaghāta rulers of Suhāniyā-Gwalior branch are known until now. Of these, Padmanātha temple inscription of V.S. 1150 is more understandable and offer thoroughly the achievements of the Kachchhapghāta rulers, is mainly devoted to the construction of the Padmanātha temple and grants given to the temple and Brahmins. It records that after the first king Lakshmaṇa his son Vajradāman became the ruler, who defeated the ruler of Gādhinagara and conquered the fort of Gwalior. His name is also cited in the Suhaniyā Jain image inscription of V.S. 1034 with the title '*Mahārājādhirāja*' (Mitra 1862: 411.). His follower Maṅgalarāja was succeeded by Kīrtirāja, who defeated the prince of Mālava and built a temple of Śiva in the town of Suhāniyā, that is identified as the Kakanamaṭha temple. The minor inscription recording the date V.S. 1044 (C.E. 987) and engraved on the outer back wall of the sanctum sanctorum of the Kakanamaṭha temple confirm that its builder Kīrtirāja was ruling before that date (Singh 2009: 113-121). His son and successor, Mūladeva was also known as Bhuvanapāla and Trailokyamalla. His son with the wife Devavratā was Devapāla. Devapāla's son and successor Padmapāla started the construction of the temple but due to his untimely sad demise the completion of the temple and other arrangements was done by Mahīpāla, the son of Sūryapāla. The Gwalior fragmentary stone inscription of V.S. 1161, which is now preserved in the Lucknow Museum, records the construction of a Śiva temple by Āśāchandra and mentions the names of Kachchhapaghāta rulers Bhuvanapāla, Devapāla, Padmapāla and Mahīpāla while the name of the successor of Mahīpāla was not reported due to the damage in the portion. On the other hand, the inscription under consideration and another Gwalior fragmentary inscription made it clear that Ratnapāla was the successor of Mahīpāla in Kachchhapaghāta dynasty. Even, the other fragmentary inscription of Gwalior fort also records the name of Ratnapāla's successor but due to the damage in the inscription it is not certain that his name was Īśāna or he was compared with Īśāna (Śiva).

TEXT

1. Oṁ namaḥ Saṁkarshaṇāyā yasyodyadbhuja-hastasīmti-vilaṭhanvun= nālanīlotpala-kroḍabhrāṁta-madhuvrata śriyamadhād=govardhanasyādharaḥ / niḥ pratyūha-maharṇṇiśaṁdiśatusa śreyāṁsi bhūyāṁ sivaḥ

2. Kṛishṇod=ṛipūdanūtanūjataruṇīva .... cha dodasaḥ // puñjībhūyāti ·Kṛishnerd=dinakara-duhituḥ sīrambhutyāgravarttī yasyovāha pravāhaḥ kshaṇamatvimalinaḥ sphāraphālānukāraṁ kṛichchhaṁ-Saṁkarshaṇova-

3. ḥ sa-suchirama-chiroddhṛita sa .... narendro vidrāṇāriḥ sasāṁdva-draḍhimabhujayugaḥ saṁ-

4. yugā saktachittaḥ / rājyaṁ yasyodāridbhudda .... pat=rājjāṁ Lakshmaṇarāja ityabhūdabhūrnbhiyāṁ bhūmi-bhujaṅga-puṁ-

5. gavaḥ / sayonutetānaya varo yatrana .... bhuvata sūnurabhūna-vikramas=trivikramāṁdi praṇati-pravī-

6. ṇedhīḥ // tasyāḥ sūnura-bhava-pravala .... vṛidhadṛidva-rājyaḥ // tasmādvismāpitadvidbhaṭaraṇarabha-

7. saḥ Sūryapālaḥ sakālaḥ pratyarthikshma .... ṇāśa ...... tāpa .... nasthirātarishaktrenaṁ sudhīrapyadhita giraṁmṛitāmatrayaḥ sarvvadai-

8. va // dhairyaṁ yasyā pradiyamimalaṁdhṛibhu .... nirvvyājānyopakṛiti-rasadṛidvaravaha .... kiṁ vapotyatsnadamabhidadhedhūta śrī Shairamapatyaktvotkarshaḥ pratikathamapi-dveshibhirya-

9. dguṇānām // dayitā tribhuvanadadhī .... vadṛi .... tīva purllakshmīḥ / siṁdhushi ..... tabhuradyo satīshvasya // tasyāttasmāda-bhūda-cyuta-charaṇa-dṛiḍhā-rādhanādhyasta-chittaḥ kṛittāśesha-

10. risaṁ-kshitipati-tilakaḥ / Śrī Mahīpāla .... styāgebhāra .... pa ..... na ...... ragra-lekhāṁlebheṇasva-dvitīrṇṇadbhuta-kanakatulāpūrushaḥ purukīrttiḥ // niryan=nānā-viṭapidha-

11. ḍatībhidbhi-nāgānisarpatsuptāraṇa-ratāda-mahipasūkāra .... rā ... chchhatikara-latālaparatha // vanīniprauḍhaṁ yasya prakaṭamaṁgadandorvvaladvidyurāṇi // valāda-kośanyaka-

12. ragrahaṁ vyadhātrāṁmitra .... puratu-sūnīra ... gaḥ ... / na ..... sahe guṇidṛiḍha ...... // kanibhṛitaṁ yasyaṁ cha mūśvakrena tata dharābhujaṅgahanaṁ / vidhṛitāmalataravāri-

13. ḥ śaradivaśarabhāsha .... bhujaṅgahaeḥ // sāvitrīvrataḥ ... tasya ... ha cha kāmadvisho gaurīvāmvudhijeva kaiṭabhajitastvāshdīvarirmmadyuta .... syedhdhītasya nitānta-sundara-vadhuḥ Śrī

14. Rannadevī-prabhoḥ // .... raṇotavveḥ sharivṛiḍhasyaśonana-śrīrabhūt // tasyāttabhū-nṛipāda-jāyata jagatkalyāṇakāri-kriyaḥ krauñchārātirivaśarād= giribhuvi Śrī Ratnapālābhidhaḥ /

15. yaḥ kaumārabhūda .... rdhanāḥ prathamaḥ parākramavatāmagre-sarastyāginām / nirākurvvangarvvonmṛidita vinayānprauḍhitmabhūtaḥ pratikshoṇī-bharttṛitpu-

16. ra parighavāhu .... smṛiti ...... rdditi-sadonnataḥ sthānāmvārātkatikatina-gāṇḍīva-dhanushaḥ // yasya Śrī Ramalā-tanoḥ pariṇatirtvādhīma vā ggocharaḥ saṁ-

17. raṁbhaḥ samarājisa .... rātravve ...... śārddviṇi-nirvvaṇā-praṇayini-prītiḥ sphuṭānāṁ-kulā-tushṭiḥ satpathavarttini pratihatopādhirgganityādṛitiḥ / yaste-

18. jasā-jagatidīpa Ra[tna]pālo-bhuyadvāmasī ..... bhaḥ / vīrograṇīrdvihita-nitya-kavi-prasādaḥ // samvarddhitonmūdita kaṁṭakaviprasādaḥ // yasyā vālyādgurushu sakalevva-

19. pya nāptāpadād=āchārasyārchchitihahi-vinayaja .... ritu-punarnnitya-luptāntarā yastā dṛigyārdṛigjagati samantaṁdvānaga Rāghavasya // vivekaṁsyārjatya kshitipa-sutalabhyasya

20. sapituḥ prasādasyakshoṇī-ramaṇaṁ-sujaṭasyāṁhi-mahataḥ / dala-prabhu ...... ripu-saṁhāraṁ rabhasorasātpūrtta śreyasya dhitadhiyamudyama-hṛidayaḥ // yaḥ prakhyātaḥ kulodcha prabhava śuchitarāchāra Śā-

21. ṇḍiṁlya-gotra vrahma-śreshṭhasya-dhīmāniha Madhumathanāhvasya sākshāt= prapautra ...... rāyatyasya pravaravarametaryaḥ sutaḥ Sānhināmnaḥ sosyāsīt= Kulhaṇākhyo nikhila-valapatirm=maṁtrimukhyaḥ suhṛichcha-

22. nprāpurmmārnnālatannuchchhidurataramidaṁ śrīriyaṁ kumbhi-karṇṇa-prāntaikānta-praśāda .... chiravibhā-bhaṅguro-sauvilāsaḥ / tenāṁlochyai-vameratadanusa-vidushā Gopāśailasya-mūrddhni-prāsādaṁ subhra-

23. mabhraṁlihamihatarasāchīkara-Chchhirapāṇeḥ // dhrurva-Śrī-Ratnapālasya-bhavva .... Śeshāvatāraḥ kundendu-visado-darśitaḥ svakaḥ // Kūrmmendrochchhrita-pṛishṭhakaṁ-rparatale-tishṭhatyasaumedinīyā-

24. dadyāvadiyaṁ vibhartti-bhagavatyaṁbhāṁsi Bhāgīrathī-valoyāvadayaṁ vilaṁghayati ....nīvallabhastāvan=maṁdirametadastu vigatopāyaṁmuradreshiṇaḥ // Vāgdevyās=padakaṇṭhasya-maṇikaṇṭhasya-nirmmage /

25. praśastirnnadaneneyam=Ānandenaṁ-vipaśchito // Śrī Ratnapālena kṛitoparodhaḥ sudārayā Śrī Maṇikaṇṭhasvareḥ / ale(ne)ka-bhāshā-sukavirllilekha pa .... saṁvat 1165 Phālguna sudi 8

References

Chakravarti, N. P. 1936-37. Collection and Decipherment of Inscriptions. *Archaeological Survey of India Annual Report 1936-37*: 93-94.

Cunningham, A. 1862-65. *Archaeological Survey of India Reports*, 2: 362-363.

Hultzsch, A. 1886. A Gwalior Inscription of V.S. 1161. *Indian Antiquary*, 15: 201-203.

Kielhorn, F. 1886. The Sasbahu Temple Inscription of Mahipala: V.S. 1150. *Indian Antiquary*, 15: 33-46.

Mitra, Rajendralal 1862. Vestiges of the Kings of Gwalior. *Journal of the Asiatic Society of Bengal*, 31: 411.

Singh, A. K. 1994. A Kachchhapaghata Inscription from Gwalior. *Bharati*, 20: 113-116.

Singh, Arvind K. 2009. Kirtiraja and Kakanamatha Temple of Suhaniya. *Journal of the Asiatic Society of Mumbai*, 82: 113-121.

24

THE TRADITION OF SHAIVA ASCETICS AND THEIR SIGNIFICANCE

(With special reference of early Medieval Inscriptions)

Rajesh Kumar Dhar Dubey

The Shaiva Sect was very popular in early medieval India. In this contest the role of Shaiva ascetics were very positive and progressive for not only the religious and philosophical point of view, but they had have a lot of impact and interference in the society and politics in that time. We have found ample information about the Shaiva Ascetic traditions in early medieval inscriptions.

The Bilehari inscription[1] shows that Lakshaman Raj continued his father's patronage of the Shaiva ascetics. We have told that this line of ascetics emigrated from Kadambguha, an object of veneration found of this sage was of Rudrashambhu, his disciple was Mattmayuranatha, his disciple's disciple was Madhumateya. His disciple was Hridayashiv who still further increased the renown spread ever the illustrious Madhumateya lineage. Hridayashiv's disciple was Aghorshiva, which he gave one Matha of Nohaleswar[2]. In Udaipur Inscription found from Shiva temple[3], state about the donation of Umarattha village to the God Vaidyanath. In the line 20-21 of the inscription state that the donation was received by a Shiava ascetic Neelkantha Swamin on behalf of the God.

The Chirva inscription[4] describe about the great Pashupata ascetic chief Shivarashi. In the Abu inscription[5] of the time of Parmara Dharavarsha mentioned the Shaiva ascetics *Vikalrashi, Jyeshtharashi, Yogeswararashi, Mounirashi,* and *Kedarrashi*. In the Achaleswara inscription[6] of 1285 A.D., found from Abu, it is mentioned that Samar Singh the pupil of Shaiva ascetic Bhāvshankar, built a Matha ornamented with gold flag. The tradition of Shaiva teachers is also described in this inscription, like the chief of the Matha Bhavagni and his disciple Bhavashankar and his disciple also. Cintra stone inscription[7] speak about the importance of Shiava teachers in the state, in one line (14-39) it described the spiritual family of the Lakuleesha pashupata ascetic Tripurantaka the benefactor of the teertha of Somanatha. Verses 40-46 informs us that Tripurantaka built temples and dedicated five lingas and erected a Torana at Somanath. Verses 47-72 enumerate the benefactions which Tripurantaka made in order to provide for the service of his temples, and rule regarding the worship, at the end of the word used *linga pratishtha Mahotsava.* It is interesting to note that the roles of the chiefs of the Matha's like Tripurantaka were very important for not only the management of the temples but they ruled over worshiping and other ceremonies regarding the temples.

The Shaiva ascetic Tripurantaka claims to have visited many temples from Kedarnath in the Garhwal hills in the North to Rameswaram in the South. Latter he came and settled at Devapattan where the chief temple priest Ganda Brihaspati made him Ārya and Mahattar. A. K. Majumdar gives detail about the meaning of Ārya and Mahattar[8]. Bhavā Brhaspati received the same titles from Siddharaj about a century earlier, and in an inscription of G.E. 61, the Saiva ascetic Uditachanya is called an Ārya[9]. D. R. Bhandarakar following the Abhidhanachintamani translated Ārya as 'owner' and was of the opinion that Mahattar denoted an office. But the Cintra prasasti definitely states that "the illustrious Ganda Brihaspat visibly the husband of Umā, having made him (Tripurantaka) an Ārya, appointed him sixth Mahattara" (V. 31) D.R. Bhandarkar thought that, as Tripurantaka was the owner of five temples, Arya of this verse could be appropriately rendered as 'owner' but it is difficult to see how Ganda Brihaspati could have 'appointed' Tripurantaka as an owner[10]. It cannot be said that Brihaspati had paid the cost of the temples, for the inscription records that all expenses were met by Tripurantaka out of his own earnings. Moreover, in the Somanatha pattan Prashasti of Bhāva Brahaspati[11], it is stated that, Brihaspati was appointed a Mahattra by the King, and that "when he (Brihaspati) settled his boundary in order, in order to renovate the (sacred) place he made the number of five hundred and five Āryas (Pañchettaram Panchsatim Āryanam) full". Buhler suggested that the verse refer to a settlement of new inhabitants, but, it seems obvious that Brihaspati was appointing a clans of temple officials, and that he was the first or the chief mahattra while Tripurantaka was the sixth. Hence it seems that Ārya like Mahattra and Ganda were ranks in the hierarchy of the Shaiva priests[12]. The suggestions of A.K. Majumdar are obviously true due to course of evidences. Meanwhile I like to say that the position of these Shaiva ascetics of the period of Choulukyas of Gujrat were very strong and the rulers appointed the senior Shaiva ascetic as the temple chiefs called Mahattar.

The Tradition of Mahattar's were continued in further days, in the Veraval grant it is state that in the time of Solanki ruler Arjundeva, the order of the Panchakula of Somanatha city, Mahant Abhya Singh, the pariparswik of Mahattar Gand Sri Parveerbhadra the great teacher of Pashupatas, a part of the field given for the erection of a Masjid. This passage of the veraval grant inform us that in that time the Shaiva teachers were also the member of important Panchkula of the city administration.

In Some inscriptions of the region of Gujrat we find the existence of Saiva monasteries. One of these monasteries was at Mandali and was in charge of one Vedagarbhrasi, who is called sthanpati. One of the inscription mentions vedgarbhrāshi's son called *Someshvra*[13], which show that superiors of monasteries in those days did not have to observe celibacy. The other monastery was at Arbuda under a Siva ascetic called Kedararāsi[14]. The most remarkable fact about this monastery was that a women could be its spiritual head, for one of the spiritual ancestors of Kedararāsi, mentioned in the inscription, is a female ascetic named yāgeshvari (tapaswini vijayini yageshvari) or yogesvari. The sister of Kedarrāsi, Moksheshvari, an ascetic (Brahmacharya parayanā) herself had constructed a temple of shiva[15].

The importance of Shaiva ascetics were really very much in the society, it is also reveal from Bheraghat inscription[16] where it is told that kings mother Alahandevi invites Pashupat Shaiva teacher Rudararashi from Lata country and for him she built the temple of Vaidyanath (shiva), a hall and a garden on the bank of the river Narmada. The term Vamdevapadanudhyata, were used many times in the Kalchuri inscriptions, this Vamdeva was not the member of the tripuri branch of the Kalchuris but was the chief Shaiva teacher of the Golaki Matha[17].

South Indian inscriptions also reveal the importance of Shaiva ascetics. South Indian Ruler Rajraj was also a great devotee of Shiva, in 1003 the nineteenth year of his reign. Rajraj began construction of an imperial temple in the capital. By the time of the construction six or so years later, the Rajrajeswara stood as the most massive temple in India, granite toward of fourteen stories 190 feet high with a base 96 feet square, set in a rectangular courtyard 500 feet by 250 feet. The primary icon of the temple was a colossal Shiva linga, probably the largest such linga in existence. It is important to say that priests (āchāryas) were brought in from all parts of the subcontinent to execute the liturgical program[18]. One inscription details the provision made for them, each year roughly forty five hundred bushels of paddy were to be supplied for the head priest Sarvashivapandita his worthy students and his students 'student who were natives of Aryadesh (North India), Madhyadesha (The Deccan) and Gaudadesha (Bengal)[19].

The Shaiva teachers were the demonstrator of Shaiva teachings and philosophy. The traditions of these are very old. The sources of knowledge of Shaiva Sidhanta were Āgama's. The knowledge of Āgama's were reach the ears of human, a monumentous event. The first human creditors of one Āgama's are always Rishis, sages portrayed as the most highly accomplished of all human. The traditions of these teachers were continue in the twelfth century. Many Shaiva teachers were composed the Shaiva Sidhantas and their students also followed and proceeds their philosophies and ideas. Aghorshiva the twelfth century South Indian author of many Shaiva Sidhanta works, serves as an apt exemplar of this 'stem' with many widely spreading branches[20]. At the conclusion of his kriyakarmadyotikas he specified his lineage of twelve Saiva preceptors reaching back to the legendary sage Durvāsas[21]. Among his predecessors, he lists Uttungshiva, a Gujrati leaving in Kalyananagari and *Brahamashiva*, also hailing from Gujrat, *Puranashiva* and Vidyantshiva, who served as royal preceptors in Varanasi; Sarvatmashiva, who was received hospitably by the ruler of great Puri, in the northern konkan near present day Bombay; and Srikanthashiva 'a bull among the Bangalies', Aghorshiva's own preceptor came from Bengal, apparently travelling South to Tamilnad, several others in the succession lived and taught in the chola dominions of South India.

In the above-mentioned epigraphical and literary records, we have found that the Shaiva teachers and their pupils have continued their tradition. They played very important role in society and politics on those days. In these teachers, some were very learned like Aghorshiva and Shrikumar, they proceed the Shaiva philosophical ideas and composed many of works related with Shaiva philosophy.

References

1. Edited by Kielhorn, EI, I, 254, Also Seem, corpus, volume:4,45,PP 204-24
2. Ibid, verse-58, Swikrityapi munirbhooyo matham sri nouhalleshwaram|
   Aghorshiva shisyasya sadhuvrittsya Duttawan ||
3. Edited by Kilhorn, IA, Volume, XVIII, P. 344,
4. Viena oriental Journal, Volume, 21, p. 155-162, AE, Volume , 27, pp. 285-95.
5. Ojha, G.H., Dungarpur Rayya Ka itihas.
6. Bhavanagar Inscriptions, 5, pp. 83-87.
7. Edited by Buhler, EI, 1892, Vol. I, pp. 271-87. The record is sometimes known as Veraval Inscription, See EI, Vol. XX, Appendix, p. 87, No. 611.
8. Majumdar A.K., Chalukyas of Gujrat, p. 291.
9. WZKM, Also known as Vienna oriental Journal, III, I. Mathura pillar Inscription of Chandragupta II, EI, XXI,
10. Majumdar, A.K., ibid, p. 291.
11. WZKM, III, I.
12. Majumdar, A.K., Choulukya of Gujrat, p. 291.
13. Vedagarbharashi is mentioned in Kadi Grant, Nos. 5, 6 and 7 (I. A, VI, 199-204). His son Someshvara is mentioned in Kadi Grant No. 7.
14. IA, XI, 200.
15. Majumdar A.K. Choulukyas of Gujrat, p. 292.
16. Corpus Inscription Indicarum, Vol. 4, p. 317, verse 27-31, "Latanvyah Pashupat-stapsvi Sri Rudrarashir virgadhi vadwidvattam."
17. Shastri Anyaya Mitra, Tripuri Ke Kalchuri, Kalchuri Rajvansh aur unka Yug (Hindi), p. 67.
18. Richard H. Devis, ritual in Oscillating universe, p. 5. Princeton newzersy.
19. Ibid, p. 6.
20. As a tenth century inscription from Madhya Pradesh refer to one important Saiva Siddhanta branch the Matimayura. F. Kielhorn "A Stone Inscription from Ranod (Narad), EI, (1892), 351-6.
21. Ibid, p. 15.

25

SEALS AND SEALINGS FROM SANCHANKOT[1]

D.P.Tewari

Sanchankot (Lat. 26°59'10''N and Long. 80°19'50'' E) (**Plate 25.1 a-b**) is a common and well known name of a revenue village Ramkot located in Tehsil Safipur of Unnao district of Uttar Pradesh. It is approachable from Lucknow by rail and road up to Sandila a tehsil headquarters of Hardoi district and from there by Sandila-Bangarmau metalled road which passes through the mound. It is 19 km from Sandila and about 80 km from Lucknow, the capital city of Uttar Pradesh. The mound is about 16 meter high from the surrounding ground level and is surrounded by two sides by the river Sai, ancient Syandika, a tributary of Gomati (Fig.1). The geologists are of the opinion that it is a river of Ganga plain which is older even to Ganga. The travel accounts of Fa-Hien (Beat : XLIII) (399 – 414 A.D.) indicate that it was located on the ancient route of Kannauj to Ayodhya (Fuhrer : 318; ASIR 1899 : 275). The place was a center of Buddhism where Buddha came and preached and Ashoka built a brick stupa in his honor on the site (Shukla 1986 : 34). Some scholars had suggested (Dutta and others 1956 : 7) that the mound should represent ancient city of Saket mentioned in Buddhist literature as one of the six great cities of that time (Digha II : 16). Traditionally it is believed that military forces of Rama halted on the mound and it was the southern post of Kuru king Shantanu and is known now days as Ramkot and Sanchankot consequently.

The author of this paper made an effort to excavate its different parts in field seasons of 2004-5, 2007-08, 2008-09 and 2009-10. About hundred of trenches were excavated and thousands of antiquities were collected from these excavations which include some interesting terracotta seals and sealings throwing light on the different aspects of the then society especially on religious condition, administrative system and political authorities. A short description of these is here as under:

1. A terracotta seal-die, (Accession no 1988/85) circular in shape having a round knob on its top to handle was recovered from a trench T-4, out of a pit deposit sealed by layer 1 at the depth of 85 cm below surface which stratigraphically belongs to Gupta period. The diameter of its bottom is 5.8 cm and height is 3.2 cm. which is almost well preserved (**Plate 25.2 a**). It has few figures and legend in *Brahmi* alphabet in negative which are clearly visible (**Plate 25.2 b**). In the upper portion of seal-die in center is symbol of *shivalinga* and *trishul* in left and *chhatra* on its right. A wavy line and eight dots in horizontal in second row separates the pictures and legend engraved on it (**Plate 25.2 c**). Prof K.K.Thaplyal (Dec. 2006 : 451-56) deciphered this legend as *KalanjarVa* (?) *ta* which means like Kalanjar. The contents of this seal-die clearly indicates that there was a temple of Shiva at Sanchankot on the bank of river Sai and which was equally important like Kalanjar shrine of Bundelkhand.

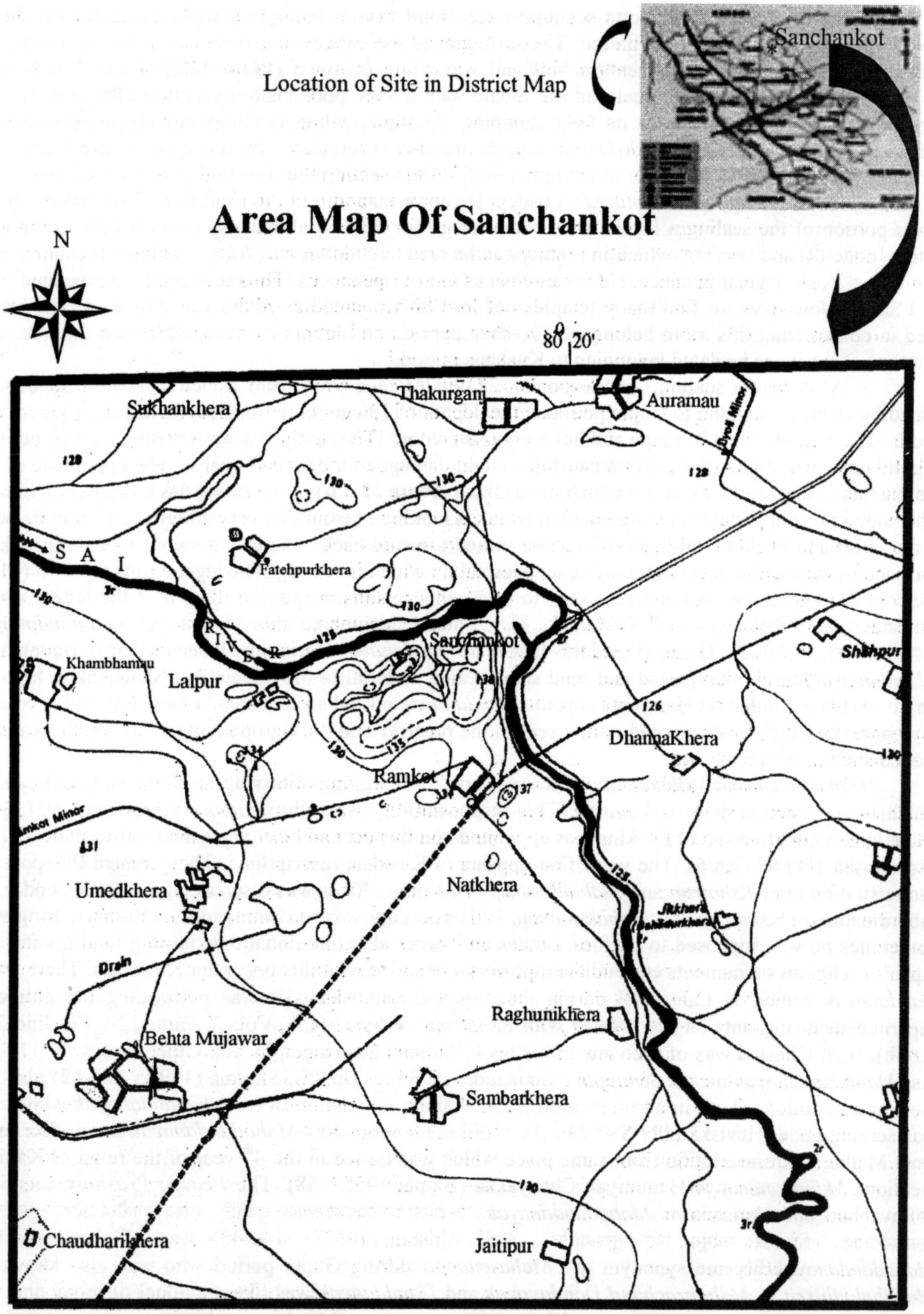

Fig. 1 : Location of site, topographic features and other archaeological mounds in the area

2. Seven pieces of terracotta sealings were found from a temple complex excavated at Jalesar mound, a part of Sanchankot habitation. These fragments were recovered from a small room from ashy deposit. One of it clearly represents a bull and wavy line below it (**Plate 25.2 d**) while others are representing the outer mark of seal and the theme with a very poor visibility (**Plate 25.2 e & f**). The depictions are not visible due to its light stamping. Another sealing is comparatively intact and well preserved (**Plate 25.3 a**). The motifs and legends are also very clear. The scene is departed in to two compartments by a horizontal line. In the upper half of the sealing there is a bull with a prominent hump in sitting posture facing to a *shivalinga.* A trident is shown standing in the right to the *shivalinga.* In the lower portion of the sealing a legend runs comprising four *Brahmi* alphabets. Two of it are compound letters 'ddhe'(द्धे) and 'sva'(श्व) which in totality can be read as Siddhesvar (सिद्धेश्वर). Hindus recognize lord Shiva as a Yogi or great penance. He is famous as God of penances. Thus the legend is associated with lord Shiva. Nowadays we find many temples of lord Shiva named as Siddhesvar temple. As the bricks used in constructing this room belongs to Kushana period and letters also resembles with the letters of that time. Thus it can be dated belonging to Kushana period.

3. A terracotta sealing (Accession no. 2129/226) recovered from trench T-4 from pit deposit sealed by layer 1 belonging to Gupta period at the depth of 130 cm below surface. Its length is 4.6 cm and width is 3.3 cm. It is oval in shape and has a grayish colour. The sealing is almost well preserved but it is slightly damaged in its lower portion causing a slight damage to the legend over it. The upper side of the sealing has a clear mark of rope on which it was fixed (**Plate 25.3 b**). The sealing has a figure of a lion on other side in its upper part in sitting position which is looking in front in a very attentive posture. Its body is muscular and healthy and hairs are shown turned towards back. There is a sword like weapon kept horizontally beneath its feet but it may be a pedestal on which it is sitting. The legend runs below it (**Plate 25.3 c**). The letters are bold and very near to each other. Nails are seen on the top of the letters which indicates that it belongs to 3rd CAD. Dr. K.S. Shukla deciphered this legend as *Mahādaṇdanāyak* (महादण्डनायक). Prof. K.K. Thaplyal read this legend as *Dandanayak* Harigupta. It seems that Harigupta was a *Dandanayak* during that period and send some sealed material to the officials of Sanchankot. In other way it is also possible that Harigupta was the *Dandanayak* posted at Sanchankot and he used his seal on any parcel which by chance could not be sent to the receiver and during opening of the bundle seal was broken and thrown on the site.

Dandanayak and *Mahadandanayak* was a post discharging military duties in the army of any king which is not mentioned in *Arthshastra.* This responsibility was with *Senapati* (Arthasastra : 2133/3). Sometimes a qualified son of the king was appointed on this post and discharges their duties under *Nayak* (Arinasasha 10/9/9; 10/6/6). The word first appears in Kushana inscriptions. They created this post for administration after *Kshatrap* and *Mahakshatrap.* This new officer was discharging his duties under the subordination of *Kshatrap* and *Mahakshatrap.* His basic duty was to command the military during war. Sometimes he was supposed to perform other civil works also like donations, issuing land grants, and repair of religious monuments etc. Judicial powers were added with this post after Kushanas. There was a *Dandanayak* named as Lala (लल) during the reign of Kanishka who was performing the duties of superintendent of grants (अनुदान अधीक्षक) with *Kshatrap* Veshyasi (CII, Vol. 2, Part 1, No. 76 line 2-3) (वेश्यसि). U.N. Ghoshal was of the view in his book 'Indian Historiography and Other essays (P. 177-79) that *Mahadandanayak* means *Senapati,* Commander of force. Dr R.S. Sharma (1990 : 288-89) also has the similar opinion. There in an inscription from Mathura is mention of a *Mahadandanayak* whose son was serving under Huviska (JRAS 1924 : 2). Valin is mentioned as *Mahadandanayak* in an inscription from Mathura. An inscription from same place which was issued in the 4th year of the reign of Kaniska mentions *Mahadandnayak* Hummiyak Chanyakka (Bajpai 1958 : 68). The *Prayag Prashasti* mentions Dhruvabhuti and Harisena as *Mahadandanayak* "खाद्यकोटि महादण्डनायक ध्रुवभूति पुत्रस्य सांधिविग्रहिक कुमारामात्य महादण्डनायक हरिषेणस्य सर्वभूत हित सुखायास्ति". A.S. Altekar (2033 : 144-45) was of the view that *Mahadandanayak* became synonym of *Mahasenapati* during Gupta period who was also known as *Mahabaladhikrit* or *Mahaprachand Dandanayak* and *Dandanayak* was like a colonel of today and was commander in charge of military posted in different states. D.C. Sircar (1942) took it granted for Commander of forces who was also called *Khadyakutpadik* (खाद्यकूटपादिक). Any way *Mahadandanayak* became an important executive officer in this period. He was the master of a good number of soldiers. On the basis of the seals found from Bhita (ASIAR 1911-12 : 54-55) and Vaishali (ASIAR 1911-12 : 109) R.S. Sharma (1990 : 317) has opined that this post was common in administration in the region of U.P. and Bihar. He was the master of his other military subordinates like *Mahasvapati*, *Mahapilupati* and *Pilupati*. We do not find the mention of this officer in the military administration during the time of Harsha. During Rajputa period the chief military officer was known as *Senapati* and *Dandanayak* was his subordinate. Singhnayak the *dandnayak* of Vigrahpal IV Chahman supported *Senapati* Bhuvanaikmalla during the reign of Prithaviraj III. Generally *Mahabaladhyaksha* was known as *Mahadandanayak* during this age (Pandey 2012 : 126-27).

4. A terracotta seal-die is oval in shape **(Plate 25.3 d)**. It is parted in two compartments by two horizontal straight lines in center. The upper compartment has a net shaped design with two unidentified marks in its left and right. The lower compartment has four *Brahmi* alphabets (**Plate 25.3 e**). Letters are bold and sound which can be read as Cha (n) draverma च (˙)द्र वर्मा. It is obvious that this is the name of any official / person of that time but who was he? It is difficult to identify. We find the mention of the name of a king/feudal as Chandra verma in the 21st line of *Prayag Parasasti* of Samudragupta which runs as: रुद्रदेवमतिलनागदत्तचन्द्रवर्म्मगणपतिनाग नागसेनाच्युतनन्दिबलवर्म्माद्यनेकार्यावर्त्तराजप्रसभोद्धरणोद्धृतप्रभाव महतः The area around Sanchankot fell in the ancient boundary of *Aryavarta*. It may be after defeating this king Samudragupta got sovereignty over this area.

5. A bone dice, conical at both ends having a hole across to fasten it with thread (**Plate 25.4 a**) was found from trench T-4. It's measurement is: length 3.7 cm, width 2.7 cm. The seal die is well preserved and intact. A flake was removed from its lower side towards base during handling but it made no harm to the motif or legend engraved on its surface. The motif and legend is engraved in negative on its base (**Plate 25.4 b**). Its positive impression shows figure of a bird like duck floating on water surface with its upraised feathers. The surface is represented by a horizontal straight line. This scene represents the environment of Sanchankot located on the bank of river Sai. The legend contains four *Brahmi* alphabets with *visarga* mark in the last which can be deciphered as *Giridattah* (**Plate 25.4 c**). The letters are nail headed and seem to belong to Gupta period. The user of this seal die may be any officer residing at Sanchankot during that period. He may be looking after the business activities regulated through Sai River.

6. A terracotta seal die, circular in shape has a motif and legend in negative on its base measuring its diameter 4.0 cm. It is surrounded with a boundary of dots. In the upper left corner of the seal-die is a figure of frog floating in water. In the lower case legend runs in five *Brahmi* alphabets which can be deciphered as *Rudrachetasya* (रुद्रचेटस्य) (**Plate 25.4 d**). Here *Rudra* means Shiva and *Cheta* means servant of slave. It is the name of a person whose parent was Shaiva and named their son as Rudracheta faith full devotion to lord Shiva. It may belong to late Kushana period.

7. A terracotta seal – die, circular in shape, has only four *Brahmi* alphabets of Kushana / Gupta period. It can be read as *Granthilyasya* ग्र(˙)थिल्यस्य। It indicates towards a professional performing the job of binding of manuscripts.

8. There are some other seals and sealings in collection but they are not much clear. One of it (Plate 4.6) is circular. Its diameter is 2.5 cm. It is partly damaged and bears flower design on its base. Likewise another sealing was also found with floral designs (**Plate 25.4 e**).

Thus most of the seals and sealings are associated with religious activities which throw sufficient light on the fact that it was a great center of Shaivism. The near past of Sanchankot gives a glimpse of Buddhist influence in the area but during Shunga-Kushana period the scenario changed rapidly. Shiva worshipers occupied the place might be coming from Kalanjar. They made brick temples at different corners of habitation and promoted Shaivism in the area which became a responsible factor for the decline of Buddhism at the site. During the entire excavation we could not find terracotta or sculpture of Buddha. The popularity of Shiva worship in the region was maintained during Gupta period also. The remains of a Vaishnava temple excavated at Khambhamau indicates that the Vashnavite influence reached on the site during Rajputa period. No doubt Sanchankot flourished as a big city which is evident from massive and healthy brick structures as well as defense wall during Shunga-Kushana period. During the Gupta period Shanchankot became an important administrative centre and defense activities were controlled from this post. It may be possible that a *Mahadandanayak* of that time made his headquarter at Sanchankot.

References

1. The paper was presented by the author in the Joint Annual Conference of Indian Archaeological Society, Indian Society of Prehistoric and Quaternary Studies and Indian History and Culture Society, at Banaras Hindu University, 2013.
2. Beal S., Buddhist Records of the Western World, Page XLIII.
3. Fuhrer A., Archaeological Reports, Vol. I, p. 318; Archaeological Survey of India Reports, (New Series), Vol. II, 1891, p. 275.
4. Shukla K.S., Archaeology of Unnao District, 1986, p. 34.
5. Dutta N. and K. D. Bajpai, Uttar Pradesh Main Bauddha Dharma ka Vikas, 1956, Page 7.
6. Dighanikay, Part II, Page 16; Mahavastu Part I, P 348; Jatak , Part III, Page 270
7. Kiran Kumar Thaplyal and D.P.Tewari, Seal-Die of the Saiva Shrine Kalanjar from Sanchankot, Research Bulletin, Vishveshvaranand Vedic Research Institute, Vol. 4&5, December 2006, PP 451-456.
8. Arthasastra 2/33/3 तदेव सेनापतिः सर्वयुद्धप्रहरणविद्याविनीतो हस्त्यश्वरथचर्यासंघुष्टश्चतुरंगस्य बलस्यानुष्ठानं विद्यात्......... ।
9. Arthasastra, 10/1/1 वास्तुकप्रशस्ते वास्तुनि नायकवर्धकि मौहूर्तिकाः........... । and 10/6/6 अंगदशकस्यैकः पतिः पदिकः,पदिक दशकस्यैकः सेनापतिः, तद्दशकस्यैको नायक इति ।
10. Ghoshal, U.N., Indian Historiography and Other Essays, pp. 177-179.
11. Sharma, R.S., Prachin Bharat me Rajanitik Vichar Evam Sansthayen, 1990, pp. 288-289, and Foot note 31.
12. Journal of Royal Asiatic Society, 1924, p. 402, Line 5; Sharma R.S., Ibid, p. 289.
13. Bajpai K.D., Proceedings of Indian History Congress, 1958, p. 68, Line 2.
14. Altekar, A.S., Prachin Bhartiya Shasan Paddhati, Saka Samvat 2033, pp. 144-145; Archaeological Survey of India, Annual Reports, 1911-12, p. 152; Indian Antiquary, No. 12, p. 120.
15. Sircar, D.C., Select Inscriptions, 1965.
16. Archaeological Survey of India, Annual Reports, 1911-12, p. 54-55.
17. Ibid, p. 109.
18. Sharma R.S., Ibid, p. 317.
19. Pandy Krishna Murari. 2012. Prachin Bhartiya Rajnaya evam Prashasan, p. 126-127.

ASIAR – Archaeological Survey of India Annual Reports
CII – Corpus Inscriptions Indicarum

26

हिन्द–यवन शासकों की मुद्राओं पर अंकित 'गज' प्रतीक : एक विवेचन

विपुला दुबे

पश्चिमोत्तर भारत पर शासन करने वाले हिन्द–यवन, शक शासकों में यूक्रेटाइडीज[1], एण्टियालकिड्स[2], मावेस के कतिपय मुद्राओं के पृष्ठ भाग पर सिंहासनारूढ़ देवता के साथ गज के अग्रभाग का अंकन हुआ है। इन मुद्राओं पर प्रायः सिंहासन पर आसीन दवेता, जिसके दाहिने हाथ में माला, बायें में ताड़पत्र अथवा मशाल धारी हीकेट, मालाधारी नीके, बायें हाथ में राजदण्ड, के साथ दाहिनी ओर गज का शिरोभाग तथा पीछे बायीं ओर पर्वत सदृश कोई चिह्न **(Conical Object)** अंकित है तथा खरोष्ठी में क्रमशः लेख है 'कविषिये नगर देवता', 'महरजस जयधरस एन्टियालकिड्स' दोनों लेखों में प्रथम लेख, मुद्रा पर अंकित देवता को कपिशा का स्थानीय देवता घोषित करता है तो दूसरा लेख अपने राजा को विजयी। विजयोपरान्त माला धारण करना प्राचीन परम्परा रही है। सिंहासनारूढ़ देवता की पहचान रैप्सन एवं जे0एन0 बनर्जी ने यूनानी देवाधिदेव जीयस (Zeus) से की है जो समीचीन है। यद्यपि ह्वाइटहेड जैसे कतिपय मुद्रा शास्त्री इस पहचान से सहमत नही हैं[3], जिसका प्रमुख आधार मुद्रा पर गज का अंकन है। इसमें संदेह नहीं कि यूनानी दैवी अवधारणा में जीयस के प्रतीक चिह्नों में वज्र, राजदण्ड (Sceptre) सिंहासन, चील पक्षी, हीकेट (मशाल देवी), नीके प्रमुख हैं।[4] गज का प्रत्यक्ष सम्बन्ध जीयस से नहीं दिखायी देता फिर मुद्रा शिल्पी ने सिंहासन पर बैठे माला धारी देवता के साथ एक ऐसे पशु प्रतीक 'गज' को क्यों अंकित किया है जिसका सम्बन्ध उत्तरवैदिक काल से विशेष रूप में 'इन्द्र' से जुड़ता दिखायी देता है तथा जो देवता, यूनानी जीयस से समीकृत हैं। यह विचारणीय तथ्य है।

प्रस्तुत शोध–पत्र में जीयस के साथ मुद्राओं पर गज (इन्द्र वाहन ऐरावत) के अंकन की ऐतिहासिक पृष्ठभूमि क्या थी, तथा वज्रधारी दोनों देवता समाज में होने वाले किस परिवर्तन को समेटे हुए हैं, इस पर विचार किया गया है। इस शोध–पत्र में उस सांस्कृतिक परिवर्तन की पड़ताल की गयी है, जिसके परिप्रेक्ष्य में देवराज वज्रिण इन्द्र अश्व चालित रथ से उतर कर हाथी पर सवार हो जाते हैं[5] एवं पंचनद क्षेत्र में इस देवता का तादात्म्य 'गज' से जुड़ता है। ऐसा प्रतीत होता है कि इस पूरे परिवर्तन से मुद्राशिल्पी परिचित था तथा जीयस के ही समान धर्मा इन्द्र को मुद्रा पर अंकित किया जो कपिशा का नगर देवता था तथा जिसका वाहन ऐरावत था। ध्यातव्य है कि इन्द्र–वाहन ऐरावत को लगभग एक ही रूप में (गज का अग्रभाग) डिगेट्रियस यूक्रेटाइडीज, एण्टियालकिड्स एवं मावेस की मुद्रा पर अंकित किया गया (फलक 26.1 से 26.4 तक)।

गज एवं इन्द्र का सम्बन्ध पौराणिक काल से जुड़ता है, ऋग्वेद में[6] मात्र एक स्थल पर इन्द्र को युद्ध में 'हाथी' के समान भयंकर आक्रमण करने वाला कहा गया है। अन्यत्र इन्द्र अश्वचालित स्वर्ण रथ पर आरूढ़ ही विवृत हैं, लेकिन एक संदर्भ भी महत्व रखता है। वैदिक आर्यों के ओजपूर्ण अन्तरिक्ष देवता इन्द्र परवर्ती काल में किस प्रकार लोकपालों के

(Tutelary) रूप में परिगणित हुए तथा गज इन्द्र के वाहन ऐरावत के रूप में प्रतिष्ठित हुआ, इस तथ्य पर विचार के पूर्व हिन्द–यवन मुद्राओं पर सिंहासन पर आरूढ़ देवता जीयस एवं इन्द्र की प्रमुख चारित्रिक विशेषताओं, लक्षणों पर प्रकाश डालना आवश्यक है क्योंकि परवर्ती काल में नये प्रतीक पुराने प्रतीकों के निहितार्थ को समेटे हुए दिखायी देते हैं।

यूनानी देवमण्डल में जीयस (Zeus) का वही स्थान है जो वैदिक देवमण्डल में इन्द्र का। मैक्डानल ने संस्कृत के द्यौस–पितर (Dyausa-Pitar) एवं यूनानी जीयस–ज्यूसपेतर (Zeus-Pater) में साम्य बताया है। होमर के विवरण[7] एवं मुद्रासाक्ष्य[8] से विदित है कि यूनानी जीयस के प्रतीकों में वज्र, राजदण्ड, सिंहासन, माला, चील, हीकेट, मालाधारी, नीके आदि प्रमुख थे। यह देवता हिन्द–यवन, शक–पहलवों की मुद्राओं पर एक सुगठित, सशक्त शरीर से युक्त वृद्ध के रूप में अंकित है। इस सन्दर्भ में वैदिक वाङ्मय[9] में इन्द्र के लिए 'वज्रिण' विशेषण का पुष्कल प्रयोग तथा उनके शरीर को धातु निर्मित[10] कहा जाना दोनों देवताओं के साम्य का प्रमाण है।

इसी प्रकार जीयस द्वारा राजसत्ता के प्रतीक राजदण्ड को प्रायः धारण करना एवं इन्द्र का इन्द्रयष्टि, इन्द्रध्वज[11] से सम्बद्ध होने का संकेत ऋग्वेदीय युग से ही प्राप्त होता है, जिसकी भौतिक अभिव्यक्ति आहत मुद्राओं पर 'इन्द्र यष्टि' के रूप में हुई है। यह इन्द्र यष्टि उर्वरता, सम्पन्नता एवं राजसत्ता का प्रतीक था। इसकी पुष्टि पौराणिक आख्यानों से भी होती है यथा पौराणिक शासक वसु उपरिचर को इन्द्र द्वारा यष्टि प्रदान करना एवं यष्टि के व्याज से राजा को सार्वभौम शासक होने का आशीर्वाद देना है। इन लाक्षणिक विशेषताओं के अतिरिक्त 'सिंहासन' एवं विजय प्रतीक 'माला' (Wreath) का साहचर्य दोनों देवताओ से जुड़ा हुआ था। जिसकी अभिव्यक्ति मुद्राओं पर जीयस के साथ हुई है। इस सन्दर्भ में उल्लेखनीय तथ्य यह है कि इन्द्र के उत्तमोत्तम सिंहासन का उल्लेख उत्तर वैदिक साहित्य से मिलने लगता है।[12] सिंहासन के साथ ही कमल मालाओं से सुसज्जित सभा का उल्लेख भी महाभारत में हुआ है।[13] अथर्ववेद में इन्द्र के एक विशेषण के रूप में 'सुस्रजम्' आया है, जो इन्द्र के मालाधारी होने का प्रमाण है।[14] माला एक ऐसा प्रतीक था जो आरम्भ में राजा की विजय एवं शूरता को सूचित करता था। यूक्रेटाइडीज एवं एन्टियालकिड्स की मुद्रा पर[15] देवता को ताड़पत्र एवं माला लिए हुए दिखाया गया है, देवता के साथ गज का अग्र भाग है खरोष्ठी लिपि और प्राकृत भाषा में मुद्रा लेख है. . . . . विजयधरस, यहाँ विजय को धारण करने वाले राजा की विजय की अभिव्यक्ति प्रतीक एवं लेख दोनों के माध्यम से की गयी है। इन प्रतीकों के साथ गज के अग्र भाग के अंकन का अभिप्राय क्या था ? यह प्रमुख विचारणीय तथ्य है। इन्द्र की चारित्रिक विशेषताओं में कतिपय तत्त्व परवर्ती काल में जुड़े इनमें इन्द्र वाहन ऐरावत प्रमुख हैं।

पौराणिक आख्यानों से विदित है कि इन्द्र का हाथी ऐरावत पूर्व दिशा का दिग्गज, समुद्र मंथन से निकला श्वेतवर्ण, चतुर्दन्त था। इसे स्वर्ग के हाथी के रूप में उल्लिखित किया गया है। अमर कोश में दिग्गजों के वर्णन में ऐरावत का उल्लेख है।[16] इसे गजों में अग्रगण्य एवं नागमल्ल भी कहा गया है, नाग एवं हाथी एक दूसरे के पर्याय तथा जल से उद्भूत हैं। 'ऐरावत' इरावती का पुत्र कहा जाता है। 'इरा' का अर्थ जल होता है[17] तथा इरावती उस नदी का अभिधान है जो जल से परिपूर्ण है। पंजाब में प्रवाहित होने वाली 'रावी' का एक नाम इरावती भी मिलता है। इरा अर्थात् जल से उत्पन्न ऐरावत परवर्ती काल में उस क्षेत्र का वाची हो गया जो पाँच नदियों से सिंचित था। जीवन दायिनी जल तत्त्व इरा से ऐरावत का उद्भव प्रतीकात्मक महत्व रखता है क्योंकि इन्द्र धनुष को भी ऐरावत कहा गया है, जो वर्षा काल में दिखायी देता है तथा जिसने वज्र को स्थानापन्न किया। इस प्रकार ऐरावत जल, विद्युत दोनों का सम्मिलित रूप था। ध्यानार्ह है कि महाभारत के भीष्म पर्व के अष्टम अध्याय एवं जैन साहित्य में भारत के उत्तर भाग को 'उत्तर कुरू' के बदले ऐरावत कहा गया है।[18] यहाँ यह उल्लेखनीय है कि यास्क ने 'इरा' से ही इन्द्र को व्युत्पन्न माना है तथा इरा का अर्थ 'अन्न' बताया है। अन्न के बीज को वृष्टि के द्वारा जो अंकुरित करता है वह इन्द्र है। यह वृष्टि द्वारा इरा का स्वामी ऐरावत है।[19] इस प्रकार इन्द्र एवं ऐरावत एक दूसरे के पूरक, पर्याय थे। यूक्रेटाइडीज के मुद्रा के पृष्ठ भाग पर सिंहासनासीन देवता के साथ गज के अग्रभाग का अंकन, पर्वत सदृश चिह्न तथा 'कविषिये नगर देवता' लेख से स्पष्ट है कि कपिशा क्षेत्र में 'गज' का विशेष महत्व था। चीनी यात्री ह्वेनसांग का उल्लेख इस तथ्य की पुष्टि करता है कि कपिशा के दक्षिण–पश्चिम में स्थित पर्वत (Pi-lo-sho-lo) श्रेष्ठ हाथियों का आवास था। चीनी यात्री ने कपिशा के उपनगर को सि–पि–तो–फा–ला–त्जु (Si-Pi-to-fa-la-Tzu) कहा है जो 'श्वेतवातालय' का चीनी अनुवाद है। जे0एन0 बनर्जी ने अपनी पुस्तक 'द डवलपमेंट ऑफ हिन्दू आइकनोग्राफी' में इस पर विस्तार से चर्चा की है। ध्यातव्य है कि श्वेतवत्, इन्द्र एवं ऐरावत का एक उपनाम है एवं श्वेतवातालय इन्द्र का निवास स्थान अर्थात् इन्द्रपुर।[19] पश्चिमोत्तर प्रान्त में शासन करने वाले शासकों में पुरू की सेना में हाथियों की बहुलता, रावी का इरावती नाम एवं भारत के उत्तर क्षेत्र का ऐरावत अभिधान के साथ ही डिमेट्रियस के द्वारा गजमस्तक का शिरस्त्राण धारण करना, कैड्यूसस गज प्रकार की मुद्रा (द्र0 चित्र सं0–1 तथा 2) का प्रवर्तन एवं अन्य हिन्द–यवनों की मुद्राओं पर हाथी का अंकन अकस्मात् नहीं था बल्कि इस क्षेत्र के श्रेष्ठ हाथी तथा इनका देवराज इन्द्र से बनता नवीन समीकरण ही मुद्राओं पर अंकन के लिए प्रेरित किया।

इसमें सन्देह नहीं कि ऋग्वेद में मात्र दो बार (ऋग्वेद 1.64.7 एवं 7.16.14) हाथी का उल्लेख है। जिसमें एक मंत्र में यह कहा गया है कि हे इन्द्र देव ! आप शक्तिशाली हाथी के समान विकराल शत्रुओं की सेना को भस्मसात करते हैं,[20] लेकिन यह एक मंत्र ऋग्वेदीय युग से ही शत्रु सेना को ध्वस्त करने वाले एक विशाल पशु के रूप में 'गज' की पहचान की पुष्टि करता है। इन तथ्यों के साथ ही परवर्ती काल में इन्द्र का देवराज पद से च्युत होकर दिग्पालों में परिगणित होना,[21] अश्वचालित रथ से उतरकर हाथी पर सवार होना जाना एक ऐसे धार्मिक परिवर्तन का संकेतक है जिसकी आड़ में वैदिक जनों के प्रतिनिधि देव का वर्चस्व पुनः पंचनद क्षेत्र में स्थापित करने का प्रयास हुआ। इस परिवर्तन का पुरोधा बौद्ध धर्म था जिसके आभामण्डल से पश्चिमोत्तर भारत अछूता न था। यहाँ यह कहना अनुचित नहीं कि बौद्ध धर्म की प्रतिक्रिया में पौराणिक साहित्य में इन्द्र को एक ऐसे पशु (गज) का स्वामी बताया गया जो बौद्धधर्म में बुद्ध के अवतरण का प्रतीक था। इन्द्र की निम्न स्थिति का पुरातात्विक साक्ष्य इन्द्र का पंचशिख गन्धर्व के साथ बुद्ध के दर्शन हेतु गुहा में प्रवेश का दृश्य एवं उदक निःसृत ऐरावत नागराज द्वारा बोधि वृक्ष की पूजा है।[22] इससे ऐसा प्रतीत होता है कि इन्द्र एवं ऐरावत के समीकरण में बौद्ध धर्म एवं ब्राह्मण दोनों ही समान रूप से भागीदार थे। बौद्ध धर्म में बुद्ध का माया के गर्भ में प्रवेश श्वेत हाथी के रूप में हुआ बताया गया है तो ब्राह्मण परम्परा में इन्द्र को हाथी (ऐरावत) का स्वामी। दूसरी ओर बौद्ध गुफा, स्तूप चित्रों के साथ आभिलेखिक एवं मौद्रिक साक्ष्य से भी बुद्ध के समक्ष इन्द्र के नतमस्तक होने का उल्लेख मिलता है। यशोवर्मा के नालन्दा पाषाण अभिलेख में[23] इन्द्र द्वारा बुद्ध की स्तुति का उल्लेख है। मथुरा की कुछ वेदिकाओं पर सपक्ष हाथी के अंकन में बौद्ध धर्म के प्रभाव को देखा जा सकता है।[24] कौशाम्बी की पौर जनपदीय ताम्र मुद्राओं के एक भांत पर इन्द्रयष्टि के सम्मुख सोपान पर वामाभिमुख गज अंकित है, उसके पीछे चक्र, नीचे एक रेखा, उज्जयिनी चिह्न के साथ ब्राह्मी लिपि में 'कोशबि' लेख है,[25] जो लगभग द्वितीय शताब्दी ई0पू0 से इन्द्र के साथ गज के बनते नए सम्बन्ध का प्रबल साक्ष्य है। इस सम्बन्ध में महत्वपूर्ण भूमिका बौद्ध धर्म की कही जा सकती है क्योंकि इन्हीं मुद्राओं पर चक्र बना है जो बौद्ध धर्म का पवित्र चिह्न है।

इन तथ्यों के आलोक में ऐरावत देवराज इन्द्र के उस समग्र चरित्र का आख्यान प्रतीत होता है जो उसे वज्र, वृष्टि, जल, अन्न के देवता के रूप में प्रतिष्ठित करता है। दूसरी शताब्दी ईसा पूर्व तक आते–आते इन्द्र एवं उसके वाहन ऐरावत गज से इतना तादात्म्य स्थापित हो चुका था कि दोनों में कोई अन्तर नहीं था। यही कारण था मुद्राशिल्पी ने हिन्द–यवन एवं शक शासकों की मुद्राओं पर सिंहासनासीन देवता इन्द्र को जीयस के वेश में प्रस्तुत किया। लेकिन जीयस से उसके अन्तर को दर्शाने के लिए इन्द्र के नये वाहन गज के अग्रभाग का अंकन कर दिया। जो इस क्षेत्र में गज की बहुलता का भी संकेतक है। जल से उद्भूत एवं जल का स्वामी होने के कारण जीवनदायिनी शक्ति का प्रतीक ऐरावत (गज) था और यही कारण था कि यह मंगल, कल्याण देवता के रूप में बाद में प्रतिष्ठित हुआ।[26]

इन तथ्यों के आलोक में ऐसा प्रतीत होता है कि उत्तर वैदिक काल में 'ऐरावत' (श्वेत हाथी) का इन्द्र के साथ जो सम्बन्ध बना उसके दो पक्ष थे, प्रथम ऐरावत, जल, विद्युत, वीरता का सायुज्य था, जिसे इन्द्र के पुरातन चरित का संवाहक कहा जा सकता है तो इसका दूसरा पक्ष बौद्ध धर्म एवं ब्राह्मण धर्म की आपसी प्रतिस्पर्धा थी। बौद्ध धर्म में तुषित स्वर्ग से उतरते हुए 'श्वेत हाथी' को बुद्ध की माता महामाया की कुक्षि में प्रवेश का उल्लेख है[27] और इस प्रकार यह बौद्ध धर्म में बुद्ध के 'जन्म' (अवतरण) का प्रतीक बन गया। ध्यानार्ह है कि गया के शैल गुहा में बुद्ध के दर्शन हेतु जाते इन्द्र का चित्रांकन, बौद्ध ग्रंथ महामायूरी में इन्द्र का मात्र संरक्षक देवता (दिग्पाल) के रूप में उल्लेख अथवा परवर्ती काल में बुद्ध की वन्दना करते वर्णित 'इन्द' का सन्दर्भ इत्यादि इस तथ्य का परिचायक है कि बौद्ध धर्म ने वैदिक यज्ञवाद, कर्मकाण्ड, जातीय श्रेष्ठता का ही विरोध नहीं किया बल्कि वैदिक जनों के 'देवराज इन्द्र' को भी बुद्ध का शरणागत बना दिया। यहाँ यह कहना अत्युक्ति नहीं कि इसकी बौद्धिक प्रतिक्रिया हुई जिसका स्वर पौराणिक आख्यानों से सुना जा सकता है, जहाँ ऐरावत (स्वर्ग के हाथी, समुद्र मंथन से निकले श्वेत वर्णी गज ऐरावत, इरा का पुत्र) को इन्द्र के वाहन के रूप में प्रस्तुत कर उन्हें ऐरावत का स्वामी बताया गया। चूँकि पश्चिमोत्तर क्षेत्र में शासन करने वाले हिन्द–यवन, शक–पह्लव शासकों में वज्रधारी जीयस का अंकन मुद्राओं पर हो रहा था तथा इस देवता की चारित्रिक विशेषताएं 'इन्द्र' से अत्यन्त साम्य रखती थीं। यही कारण था कि कपिशा क्षेत्र के स्थानीय देवता 'इन्द्र' को मुद्राशिल्पी ने 'जीयस' के वेश में प्रस्तुत किया। इन्द्र के साथ उनके नये पशुवाहन (ऐरावत) गज के शिरोभाग का अंकन कर मुद्राशिल्पी ने यह दर्शाने का प्रयत्न किया कि यह यूनानी देवता जीयस नहीं बल्कि कपिशा क्षेत्र का देवता 'इन्द्र–ऐरावत' है। उल्लेखनीय है कि वराहमिहिर के बृहत्संहिता में वर्णित इन्द्र मूर्ति लक्षण एवं मुद्रा पर अंकित 'इन्द्र–ऐरावत' के अंकन में भी पर्याप्त साम्य है।[28]

सन्दर्भ

1. Percy Gardner, *The coins of the Greek and Scythic Kings of Bactria and India,* Sagar Pub. 72, Janpath New Delhi, 1971, p. 19, 25, Pl. VI & P.M.C. III, 131, Pl. VII, 10, 13, 14.
2. Banerji, J.N., *The Development of Hindu Iconography*, P. 148-149, Munshiram Manohar Lal Pvt. Ltd., 54 Rani Jhanshi Road, New Delhi; 1974 'Indra appears in the garb of Zeus on the coins of Eukratides, Antialkidas and on a few other Indo-Greek rulers and on those of, Maues.
3. तत्रैव, पृ0 148, White head doubted this indentification; he thinks that the enthroned deity is female and may stand for Demeter or Tyche; Numismatic Chronicyle, 1947, pp. 29-31.
4. तत्रैव
5. Donald, A. Mackenjee, *Indian Myth and Legend*, London, p. 3-4.
6. ऋग्वेद : 4.16.14 सूर उपाके तन्वंऽदधानो वि यत्ते चेत्यमृतस्यवर्पः
मृगो न हस्ती तविषीमुषाणः सिंहो न भीम
आयुधानि विभ्रत ।। 14।।
7. चट्टोपाध्याय, भास्कर, *द एज ऑफ दि कुषाणाज़,* पुंथी पुस्तक, कलकत्ता, 1967, पृ0 145.
8. Percy Gardner, *The coins of the Greek and Scythic Kings of Bactria and India*, p. 19, Pl. VI, 8, P.M.C. III, 131, p. 21, Pl. VII, 1 : Zeus holds winged thunderbolt and long Sceptre, Pl. IV, 1, p. 25.
9. ऋग्वेद : 10.96.6, 1.7.2.
10. तत्रैव : 10.96.8 हरिश्मशारूर्हरिकेश आयसस्तुरस्पेये यो हरिपा अवर्धत।। 8।।, अथर्ववेद : 20.69.4 त्वं सतस्यपीतये सद्यो वृद्धो अजायथाः। इन्द्र ज्यैष्ठाय सुक्रतो ।। 4।।
11. ऋग्वेद : 10.103.11.
12. महाभारत : भीष्म पर्व, अष्टम अध्याय
13. तत्रैव, एषा सभा मयराजन् दृष्टा पुष्करमालिनी ।। 30।।
14. अथर्ववेद : 20.129.15 स्वस्त्यश्च जैत्रायेन्द्रमा वह सुस्रजम् ।। 15।।
15. Percy Gardner, *The coins of the Greek and Scythic Kings of Bactria and India*, Delhi, 1971.
16. पाण्डेय, राजबली : हिन्दू धर्मकोश, 1988, लखनऊ, पृ0 146, अमरकोश : प्रथम काण्डे, 4, ऐरावतो पुण्डरीको वामनः कुमुदोऽञ्जनः।
पुष्पदन्तः सार्वभौमः सुप्रतीकश्च दिग्गजाः ।।4।
17. Heinrich Zimmer, *Myths and Symbols in Indian Art and Civilization*, p. 104.
18. निरूक्त : 10.1.8 इन्द्र इरां तृणातीति, इरां ददातीति वा, इरां दधातीति वा।
19. Banjerji, J.N. *The development of Hindu Iconography*, P. 148.
20. ऋग्वेद : 4.16.14.
21. वाजपेयी, कृष्णदत्त, ऐतिहासिक भारतीय अभिलेख जयपुर, 1992, पृ0 119, 145.
22. अग्रवाल, वासुदेवशरण, भारतीय कला, पृ0 147, 184.
23. गोयल, श्रीराम, मौखरि–पुष्यभूति–चालुक्य युगीन अभिलेख, मेरठ, 1987, पृ0 73.
24. अग्रवाल, वासुदेवशरण, भारतीय कला, वाराणसी, 1977, पृ0 228.
25. पाण्डेय, प्रभाशंकर, प्राचीन भारतीय कला में प्रतीक, नई दिल्ली, 2001, पृ0 159
26. Chattopadhyay, Bhaskar, *The Age of the Kushanas - A Numismatic Study*, Calcutta, 1967, p. 60.
27. अग्रवाल, वासुदेव शरण, भारतीय कला, पृ0 55.
28. बनर्जी, जे0एन0, द डवलपमेन्ट ऑफ हिन्दू आइकोनोग्राफी, पृ0 149.
शुक्लश्चतुरविषाणो द्विपो महेन्द्रस्य वज्रपाणित्वम्।
तिर्यग्ललाटसंस्थानं तृतीयमपि लोकनं चिह्नम्।।

27

STYLISTICS OF KALACHURI COINAGE IN CHHATTISGARH

Vishi Upadhyay

The setting

Dakśina Kosala, roughly corresponding to the boundaries of present Chhattisgarh, which was carved out of erstwhile Madhya Pradesh in 2000 has a long Numismatic history commencing from the Punch marked coins. After the Janapada type or punch marked variety, many coins of Mauryas, Sātavāhanas, Kuṣāṇas, Kṣtrapas and Guptas are yielded from this area. Posterior to Guptas, when there was a considerable decline in the trade and commerce leading to a sparse retrieval of coinage, many local dynasties of Chhattisgarh issued a rich typology of coins viz. Maghas of Malhār, Nala, Śarabhpuriyās, Kalaīchurīs of Ratanpur, Phaṇināgvamśīns and Nāgvamśīns of Chakrakota. The most significant contribution in this regards has been made by the Kalachuris (10th-13th CAD) who were the descendants of the Kalachurīs of Chedi or Dāhāla with their capital at Tripurī.

The coinage of Kalachurīs opens some new aspects of numismatic epoch of Chhattisgarh. Found from stratigraphic context as well as from stray hoards, there are numerous varieties of coins with plethora of motifs viz. deities (Lakśmī, Viṣṇu, Hanumāna), Fauna (Lion and elephant), mythical animals (Gajaśārdula) and few mint marks. These coins were minted on three metals-gold, silver and copper with higher and lower denominations. Devises on these coins present a riddle for Numismatists who present dubious decipherment and many a time wrong identification. The figure on the reverse of these coins is indeed crudely executed which has caused such a divergence of opinion among the scholars. The present paper entails an attempt to document the coinage of Kalachuris with a focus on the study of metallurgy, metrology, script, art having a bearing on the numismatic history of the region.

Previous work

Coins of Kalachuri rulers are reported from different hoards and excavations viz. Sarangarh[1] (Hoernle 1893: 92), Āraṅg[2], Sonsari[3] (Jain 1985: 33), Khudimudi[4] (IAR 1968-69 : 60), Balapur[5]

(IAR 1958-59 : 66), Kera[6] (IAR 1978-79) and from the excavations of Malhar 1974-76[7] (IAR 1974-75, 1975-76) and 2008-12[8] (Mitra: 2010: 214-221), Sirpur[9] (IAR 1955-56: 26) and Pachrahi[10] (Yadava 2007-08: 44) (See map). Few gold coins of Ratandeva and Pṛithvideva are found beyond the administrative division of Chhattisgarh i.e. at Puri distinct, Odisha (IAR 1954-55: 63)[11], which might have been transferred by the pilgrims. However, it shows a wide distribution of Kalachuri coins on a geographic expanse surpassing their political boundaries. Five kings of this dynasty issued these coins (see table) i.e. Pṛithvideva, Ratandeva, Jājalladeva, Pratāpamalladeva and Jagpāla (possibly a feudatory). The genealogical table of Kalachuris reveals that there were two rulers, with the same name of Ratandeva, two rulers with the name of Pṛithvideva and two rulers with the name of Jājalladeva. The coins do not bear any date, which makes their attribution to a particular king more difficult. Cunningham (1894: 73)[12], V.V. Mirashi (1941:26-39)[13], P.L. Gupta (1953: 82-83)[14], Vijay Lakṣmī Labh (1994:64-69)[15], Joe crib (2003-04: 71-81)[16], P.C. Roy etc. tried to analyse these similarity in names but did not arrive at any consensus. Possibly, these coins were meant to obliterate individually for an unhindered development of economy without being appellated to a particular ruler.

Metallurgy (Table 1)

Metals have been profusely used in the coinage of Kalachuri rulers viz. gold, silver and copper. Coins of Pṛithvideva (Pls. 27.1 - 27.3) and Ratandeva (Pls. 27.4 - 27.6) were issued in all three metals while the coins of Jājalladeva (Pls. 27.7 and 27.8) are found on gold and copper; coins of Jagpāla (Pl. 27.9) were issued only on silver. Copper was though the usual metal for the coins of Pratāpamalladeva (Pls. 27.10 and 27.11) but a solitary gold coin of Pratāpamalladeva has been retrieved from the excavation at Pacharahi; and another gold coin is noticed in the collection of a private individual at Nagpur, which is doubtful on its authenticity. The percentage of metals in these coins is as following:

Gold

It seems to be that the gold was the first metal which was used by Kalachuris of Ratanpur for their coins. Many coins have been investigated by me from the different collections and few gold coins also detected for knowing the gold percentage of coins. The gold percentage of these coins is as following; Ratandeva I 80.41%, Pṛithvīdeva I 79.96%, Jājalladeva I 60.78%, Ratandeva II 52.35%, 41.6%, 53.8% (Bar Chart 1), Jajalladeva II 61.84% and 56.4%. Here, it is noteworthy that coins of early rulers like Ratanadeva I. Pṛithvīdeva I. Jājalladeva I show the high percentage of gold while later coins show the debasement of gold (Bar Chart 2).

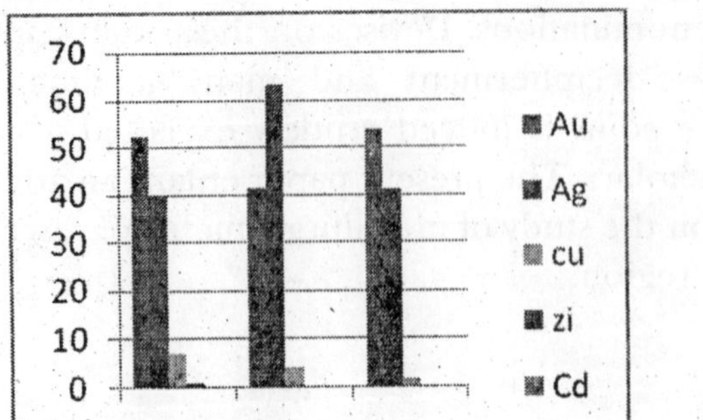

Chart 1 Metal percentage of gold coins of Ratandeva II (Alloy)

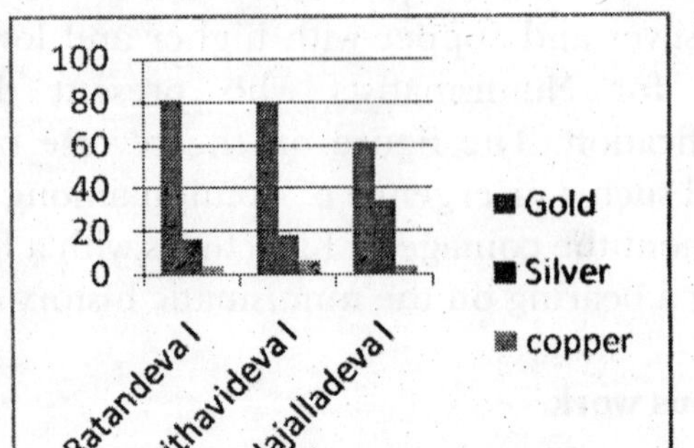

Chart 2 Percentage of metals in gold coins of Kalachuris

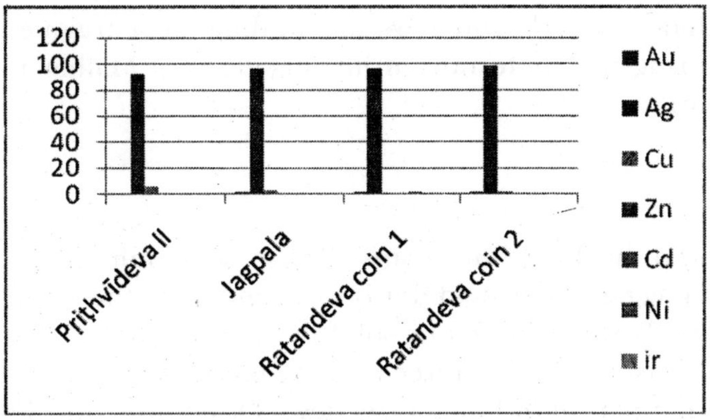

Chart 3 Percentage of metal in silver coins of Kalachuris of Ratanpur

Table 1 : Percentage of metals in coins of Dakśiṇa Kosala

King	Dynasty	Au (%)	Ag (%)	Cu (%)	Zn (%)	Ni (%)	Cd (%)	Ir (%)	Other base metal
Ratandeva I	Kalachuri	80. 41	16.12	3.04	-	-	-	-	-
Pṛiṭhvīdeva I	Kalachuri	79.96	17.93	1.63	-	-	-	-	-
Jājalladeva I	Kalachuri	60.78	33.26	5.75	-	-	-	-	-
Ratandeva II	Kalachuri	52. 35 , 41.6, 53.8	40.18,63.1, 41.2	7.25 , 4.48, 1.66	0.92		0.29	-	-
Pṛiṭhvīdeva II	Kalachuri	0.4	92.8	6.6		-	-	0.2	-
Jagpāla	Kalachuri	1.0	96.1	3.0	-	-	-	-	-
jājalladeva II	Kalachuri	56.4	37.4	3.98	1.65	0.31	0.26	-	-
Ratandeva III	Kalachuri	1.66, 1.48	96.6, 98.0	1.10, 2.46	0.30	-	2.46		-

Silver

Kalachuris issued their coin on this metal also. Few coins of Pṛiṭhvīdeva II, Ratanadeva III and Jagpāla (feudatory king of Kalachuris of Ratanpur) are represented to this metal. One coin of Pṛiṭhvīdeva II, one coin of Jagpāla and two coins of Ratandeva III have been detected by me for understanding the metal composition. The silver content of coins of Pṛiṭhvīdeva II is 92.8% in coin of Jagpāla, this percentage is 96.1% and in coins of Ratandeva III, this percentage is shown by 96.6% and 98.0%. These all silver coins were made by pure silver (Bar Chart 3).

The source of these metals is unknown till now because no ancient mine could be located anywhere in Chhattisgarh. Presumably, these metals might have been imported from outskirts of Chhattisgarh.

Bereft of the name of minting place, coins of Kalachuris are distributed over different localities of Chhattisgarh, making it difficult to decide that where the minting places were exactly situated in this period. Some additional letters on coins of Jājalladeva arrest the attention in this regard. The additional letter in proto Nāgari characters of tenth century recording '*Ma*' and '*Mā*' on the coins of Jājalladeva, according to some scholars, denotes the place of Malhār (Mallāla (Mirahi 1955: 161-65)[17] or Mallālapaṭṭana (Mirahi 1955:181-82)[18]). If this fact is true, the mint of

Kalachuris might be situated at Malhār, which was an important trade centre during the period under study. This evidence is supplanted by the finding of a fragment of mould from the stratigraphic context during the subterranean investigations at Malhār in 2011-12 (Mitra 2010: Personal communication)[19].

Mint Marks (Table 2)

Few marks are appeared in Kalachuri coins. These are only found in copper coins of Pratāpmalladeva e.g. 1) dagger and a solid dot is surrounded by the seven (*chakra*?) or eight tiny circlets. 2) Single dagger 3) single *chakra* or solid dot is surrounded by the seven or eight tiny circlets. It proves that at least there were three minting places though the exact locations of them are yet to be established in period of Pratāpmalladeva. Other gold and silver coins of Kalachuris do not show the mint marks but few letters viz. *ma, ta* are appeared , it probably shows the name of minting places e.g. Tumman, Malhar.

Table 2: Showing the mint marks on Kalachuri coins

Coin type	Name of ruler	Image of Coins	Coins	Mint marks	Letter
Elephant type	Pratāpmalladeva				
Lion type	Pratāpmalladeva				
Dagger type	Pratāpmalladeva				
Gajshar-dual type	Jajalladeva		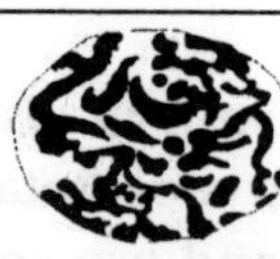		

Metrology (Table 3)

It would not be out of place to discuss here the names, the value of the Kalachuri coins and the weight-standard according to which they were struck. Coins of the early Kalachuri king Krishnaraja were called *rūpakas* and were struck to the standard of *hemidrachma*. The gold and silver coins of Gangeyadeva and the gold coins of Jajalladeva, Ratnadeva and Prithvideva were struck to the weight-standard of the *attic drachma* (67.5 grains), though they rarely reach that standard. Vincent Smith thought that all these coins were known as *drammas*. He drew attention to the great Siyadoni inscription in which the coins are so named. Accordingly he used the terms gold, silver and copper *drammas* in describing the coinage of the Kalachuris, the Chandellas and the Gāhadavālas (*Epigraphia Indica* 1895-96: 801)[20]. It is however doubtful whether the term *drammas* signified gold and copper coins as well. The Sīyaḍoṇī inscription mentions specifically the *Āivarāha* and *Vigrapālīya drammas,* referring evidently to the coins of the Gurjara-Pratihāra king Bhoja I and the Pāla king Vigrapāla I respectively. But these coins are almost all in silver. Besides, if the term *drama* qualified for coins of all the three metals, some words like *suvarṇa, rūpya* etc., would have been prefixed to *dramma* in order to indicate the intended class of coins(Howarth 1884: 301)[21]. *Dramma* seems therefore to have been the name of only the silver coin weighing about 65 grains. This conjecture receives support from the fact that in some inscriptions *drammas* are mentioned separately from *suvarṇas* which were undoubtedly gold coins. In the Cambay plates dated to āaka 852, for instance, the Rāshṭrakūta king Govinda IV is said to have donated, on the occasion of his *paṭṭabandha,* four lacs of *suvarṇa* and thirty-two lacs of *dramas* (Fleet 1903:40)[22]. The former were plainly gold coins and the latter silver ones. In later times *ṭaṇka* (Hiralal 1907-08: 168)[23] or *suvarṇa-taṇka* seems to have become current as the name of a gold coin. The Rewah inscription dated Kalachuri samvat 944 states that Malayasiṇha, the minister of the Kalachuri king Vijayasiṇha, incurred the expenditure of 1500 *taṇakakas* stamped with the effigy of the Bhagavat (Hiralal 1927-28: 299)[24] in constructing a tank near Rewah. The *Smriti-sthala,* a Marāṭhī Mahānubhāva work of about the 14th century A.D., mentioned *sona-ṭaṇka* (Sanskrit *suvarṇa-taṇka*) as the coin in circulation during that time.

As stated above, *dramma* was the name of a silver coin weighing about 65 grains. There were lower denominations prevalent i.e. one-quarter, two-quarter and three-quarter *drammas.* One-quarter *drammas* were called *pañchīyaka drammas,* as known from the Sīyaḍonī inscription which in line 37 lays down a cess of a quarter – *Ādivargha dramma* and then in the next line expresses the same cess in figures as *pamdra* 1, i.e., one *pañchīyaka drammas* (Kielhorn 1892: 175-77)[25]. In the same inscription a half *dramma* is called *drammārdha* and a three-quarter *dramma* as *dramma- tribhaga.*

The *drammas* are mentioned in the Besāni stone inscription dated Kalachuri samvat 958 from the Chedi country. But there is no record from Chhattisgarh which mentions about these coins. The Tahankāpar plates of Pamparāja, dated Kalachuri samvat 965, mention that 130 *Sarāhagaḍam āchhu* (Hiralal 1927-28: 299)[26] which may mean 130 silver coins minted in *Sarāhagaḍa* (modern Sarangarh). It is noteworthy in this connection that a similar Marāṭhī biography of Chakradhara, the founder of the Mahānubhāva sect, *āsu* appears to have been a silver coin current in Mahārāshṭra in the 13th CAD. It was equal in value to 24 *dāmas,* which were copper coins (Kielhorn 1892:262)[27]. The *Lilācharitra* speaks in one place of a *pāuna āsu* or three-quarter *āsu* which shows that lower denominations viz. one-quarter, one-half and three-quarter *āsu* were also in circulation.

The Siyaḍonī inscription mentions *vimśopakas* which were evidently copper coins. They were so called because they were equal in value to one-twentieth of a *dramma.* This appears quite clear from line 20 of this inscription which first mentions in words a monthly tax of half a *Vigrahatuṇgīya* (Hultzsch 1913: 84)[28] *dramma* and then states the same in figures as *vi* 10 (i.e. 10 *vimúopakas*); one *dramma* was therefore equal to twenty *vimúopakas.* The Bilhāri stone inscription mentions *shodaśika* (Cunningham: 72 and 74)[29] which, on the analogy of *vimśopaka,* might have signified a copper coin equal in value to one-sixteenth of *dramma. Paura* (Mirashi 1983: 329)[30], *kaparda* and *dyūa-kaparda* are other coins mentioned in the same inscription. The first was probably a silver coin and remainings are small copper coins.

It is not known to what weight-standard those copper coins were struck. The copper coins of Gāngeyadeva and Chandellas, described by Cunningham weighed from 41 to 61 grains, but it is not possible to assess the loss in weight due to rust, wear and tear. The average weight of fairly well preserved copper coins of the Kalachuris of Ratanapur is about 100 grains. Allowing for loss of weight due to wear and tear, they might have been struck to the ancient Indian standard of the

Kārshāpana which was 146 grains. These coins therefore represent the *vimśopakas* and *panas* which are mentioned in the records of medieval India. (Cunningham 1966:27)[31] The copper coins described by Cunningham were probably half-paḍas (Jain 2055:66)[32]. According to Vāchaspati cited by Mahendra, such half *paṇas* were called *bindukas.* Lower denominations of copper coins such as *vodrī* or *kakiṇī* and *gaṇḍa* mentioned by Sanskrit lexicographers and commentators; and some of them might represent the smaller Kalachuri copper coins which are often found in Chhattisgarh. But these coins are so much worn and so irregular in weight that it is often difficult to say what denominations they represent. *Kapardī* is the lowest copper coin denomination mentioned in the Kalachuri inscriptions.

Table 3 : Showing the metrology of the Kalachuri coins

King	Dynasty	Metal	Weight (gm.)	Denomination	Motif	Legend
Pṛithvideva II	Kalachuri	Gold, silver, Copper	3.00, 0.26, 2.00	Dramma, quarter dramma, Half dramma	Gajśārdula, Four handed deity by crushing the demon, Lakṣmī	Śrīmat Pṛithvideva
Jājalladeva I and II	Kalachuri	Gold, Copper	3.00, 0.21, 0.99	Dramma, quarter dramma, Half dramma	Gajśārdula, Hanumān by crushing the demon, Nagari letter Ma and Mā	Śrīmat Jājalladeva
Ratanadeva I, II and III	Kalachuri	Gold, silver, Copper	3.00, 0.23, 0.90	Dramma, quarter dramma, Half dramma	Gajśārdula, Lakśmī	Śrīmat Ratandeva
Pratāpmalladeva	Kalachuri	Gold, Copper	3.00, 0.21	Dramma, quarter dramma,	Gajśārdula, Lakśmī	Śrīmat Pratāpmallad eva
Jagpāla	Kalachuri (feudatory)	Silver	0.21.0.23, 0.25	quarter dramma,	Lakṣmī	Sijagpāla

Palaeography and orthography

All legends are commenced from the *Śrīmat* followed by the name of the king. The characters belong to the Nāgari alphabet of the northern class, commonly designated as the 'northern class of alphabets' and few letters denote to *Śāradā* script i.e *Ja, Ma, Ś* etc. All records and legends on coins are composed in Sanskrit which appears to have served as the official language. Local elements may be illustrated by numerous words viz. *Rāh* for *Rājā, Śrīmat* for *Śrīmān* etc.

As regards to orthographical peculiarities, consonants are used in numerous places and the cases of the employment of the vowel r are only limited to the coins of Pṛithvideva. Besides, the composite letters are used throughout the period on the coins of all Kalachuri rulers viz. for *Śrīmat,* letter *Śrī* is narrated separately and for '*mat*' letter '*Ta*' is joint with '*Ma*' on the top right corner in the shape of curved stroke. This form of *Śrīmat* is used on all Kalachuri coins except to silver coins of Jagpāla, Pṛithvideva II and Ratandeva III. There is *Śrī* in form of '*Si*' which shows the gradual changes on the script. Apart from it, few other joint letters are also noteworthy in this regard viz. on the coins of Pṛithvideva I and II, the letter *Ta* of *Śrīmat* is joint with the letter *Pṛi*, which is interesting that this kind of attempt is noticed only on coins of Pṛithvideva I and II, but on gold and copper coins of Pṛithvideva I, letter *Ma* is followed the coins of Gāngeyadeva. Another letter like *tha* is joint with *vi* on the coins of Pṛithvideva II. On the coin of Jājalladeva, letter *Ja* and *La* in double form and are overlapped to each-other. Legends of coins of Ratandeva are also interesting where a gradual change can be noticed on letter *Ma*. On previous coins, *Ma* shows with a parallel stroke on top right corner and Letter *Ta* is joint in the form of vertical stroke on top corner but on the coins of Ratandeva this vertical stroke is totally merged in letter *Ma* and represented on the bottom of letter *Ra* by a parallel stroke and half *Ta* is overlapped with letter *Na*.

As regards to the alignment of legends, it is found that all legends of coins were found straightly in two lines except the coins of Pratāpamalladeva, they are in three lines.

Onomastic studies reveal two aspects on the obverse of the coins namely the exalted title like *Śṛimat* and Name of the ruler like Pṛithvideva or Pratāpamalladeva etc. it reflects the dynastic appellation of regnal names throwing light on the political condition coeval to the Kalachuri period.

Technique

All coins were minted by double-die technique and circular in shape. This technique was influenced by the Greek coins prevalent in North West frontiers. Coin blanks in this process were prepared by clipping the sheet or were molded separately and hammered on top of the punch-die. Thus, the letters are usually in relief.

Art (Table 4)

The motifs on coins of Kalachuris are very interesting. There is a rampant lion attacking on elephant under a beaded border, few scholars called it Gajśārdula; This kind of device is found on the gold coins of Pṛithvideva II, Ratandeva II and Jājalladeva I and II and on the copper coins of Jājalladeva II. The figure of lion has drawn in linear form. The meaning of the representation of Gajśārdula is also cleared by the inscriptions and sculptures of Kalachuris. The Kalachuri kings styled themselves as powerful as lion and elephant representing the groups of enemies[33].

Along with it, many deities also adorned these coins i.e. Hanumān on copper coin of Jājalladeva while crushing the demon, four handed deity in standing position while crushing the demon and four armed Lakśmī found both in seating and dancing position.

Table 4 : showing different deities on Kalachuri coins

Name of King	Deity	Metal	Image of coins	Coins
Pṛithavideva I	Hanuman	AE		

Jājalladeva 1	Hanuman	AE		
Jājalladeva 1I	Hanuman	AE		
Ratanadeva	Lakshmi	AR		
Jagpal	Lakshmi	AR		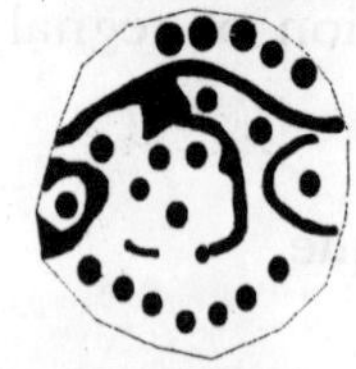
Pṛithavideva I	Lakshmi	AE		
Pṛithavideva I	Lakshmi	AE		
Pṛithavideva I	Lakshmi	AE		

Conclusion

After surveying the tradition of ancient coinage in Chhattisgarh, the fact clearly emerges that posterior to the punch marked coins, no local coinage could be flourished. Rulers of Nala and Śarabhapuriya, most probably issued the commemorative medals which are treated as coins by few scholars. Subsequently, after the lapse of many centuries, Kalachuris again commenced the local coinage of Chhattisgarh. Since the Kalachuri of south Kosala was a distinguished branch of Kalachuris of Tripuri, that's why the coins of this branch are much influenced by Tripuris in respect of devices and denominations. Tummān was the initial capital of Kalachuris in Chhattisgarh; after some eras they shifted their capital to Ratanpur and issued most of the coins from new capital. It might be possible that after transferring the capital to Ratanpur, they established a strong economy as known from the issuance of numerous coins from this place. Another point also supports to this fact that Tummān has not survived much cultural and architectural remains whereas Ratanpur was called the city of temples in this period. There are many temples, forts, around 120 water tanks and finding of coins are the strong evidences of cultural and economic development of this period. Apart from this the problem of attribution of coins of Kalachuris could not be resolved till now. There is a simple reason visible behind this problem that the Kalachuris were recommenced the local coinage of Chhattisgarh after a long gap, so for establishing the political stability and economic strength, they followed the same names of kings viz. Pṛitavideva I and II, Ratanadeva I, II and III, and Jajalladeva I and II. It might be helpful for continuity of circulation of currency through the eras.

Acknowledgement

I pay thanks from the core of my heart to my Ph.D. co- guide Late Dr. Subash Khamari (former Superintending Archaeologist, Archaeological Survey of India) for his proper guidance and editing in text of this article.

References and Notes

1. Hoernle, Report on Old Coins, *Journal of Asiatic Society of Bengal,* 1893,p. 92.
2. Ibid.
3. Jain B.C., *Numismatic Notes and Monographs,* No. 5, Varanasi, 1985, p. 33.
4. *Indian Archaeology – 1968-69, A Review,* ,P.60
5. Ibid,1958-59,p.66
6. Ibid, 1978-79, p. 90
7. Ibid, 1974-75 and 1975-76, p. 22 and p. 23.
8. Mitra, S.K. personal communication.
9. *Indian Archaeology-1955-56, A Review,* p. 26.
10. Yadav S.S., *Excavation at Pachrahi,* Directorate of Culture and Archaeology, Raipur , 2007-08, p. 44.
11. *Indian Archaeology –1954-55, A Review,* p. 63.
12. Cunningham A., *Medieval Coins of India,* Indological book house, Varanasi,1894, p. 73.
13. Mirashi V.V., The Coins of the Kalachuris, *Journal of Numismatic Society of India,* Vol III, 1941, pp.26-39.
14. Gupta P.L., A note on two coins of eastern Kalachuris, *Journal of Numismatic society of India,* Vol XIV, part1, 1953, pp. 86-87.
15. Labh, Vijay Lakshmi, Some observations on silver coinage during early medieval north India, *Journal of Numismatic society of India,* Vol LVI, 1994, pp. 64-69.
16. Cribb Joe, Silver coins of Jagapala, feudatory of the Kalachuri kings of Ratandeva, C.AD 1145. *Numismatic Digest,* Vol 27-28, 2003-04, pp.71-81.
17. Mirashi V.V., Malhar stone inscription of Prithavideva II, *Corpus Inscriptionum Indicarum* , Vol IV, 1955, pp. 161-65.
18. Mirashi V.V., Malhar Stone Inscription of Jajalladeva II, *Corpus Inscriptionum Indicarum* , Vol IV, 1955, pp. 181-82.
19. Mitra S.K., op.cit.
20. Allan has used the name *dingra* in referring to the gold coins of the Kalachuris of Mahgkoasala, but this name seems to have gone out of use in the age of these kings. The gold coin current in Konkan were called Gadiyg´as and Dhara´as, see Khgrapg´an plates of Ra´´argja, *Epigraphia Indica,* Vol. III, 1895-96, p. 801.
21. Howarth, H. Henry, Changej Khan and His Ancestors, *Indian Antiquary,* Vol XIII,1884, p. 301.
22. Fleet H.,Three Ganga Records in Mysore Government Museum of Banglore , *Epigraphia Indica,* Vol VII, 1903, p. 40.
23. Hiralal, Konkaer Copper Plates of Pamparajadeva,Ibid, Vol IX , 1907-08, p. 168.
24. Hiralal, The Rewah Inscription of Malayasimha,Ibid, Vol XIX, 1927-28, p. 299.
25. Kielhorn F., Siyadoni inscription, Ibid, Vol 1, 1892, pp. 175-77.

26. Hiralal, op.cit. p. 168.
27. Kielhorn F., op.cit., p. 175.
28. Kielhorn F., Bilhari stone Inscription of Rulers Chedi, Ibid, p. 262.
29. Hultzsch E., Critical Notes on Kalhanas eighth Taranga, *Indian Antiquary*, Vol XLII, 1913, p. 84.
30. Cunningham, A. op.cit, pp. 72 and 79.
31. Mirashi V.V., Kaman stone inscription, *Epigraphia Indica*, vol XXIV,1984, p. 329.
32. Cunningham, *Archaeological Survey of India Report*, Vol X Indological Book house, Varanasi,1966, p. 27.
33. Jain B.C., *Utkrina Lekha* (in Hindi), Directorate of culture and Archaeology, Raipur, 2005, p 66.

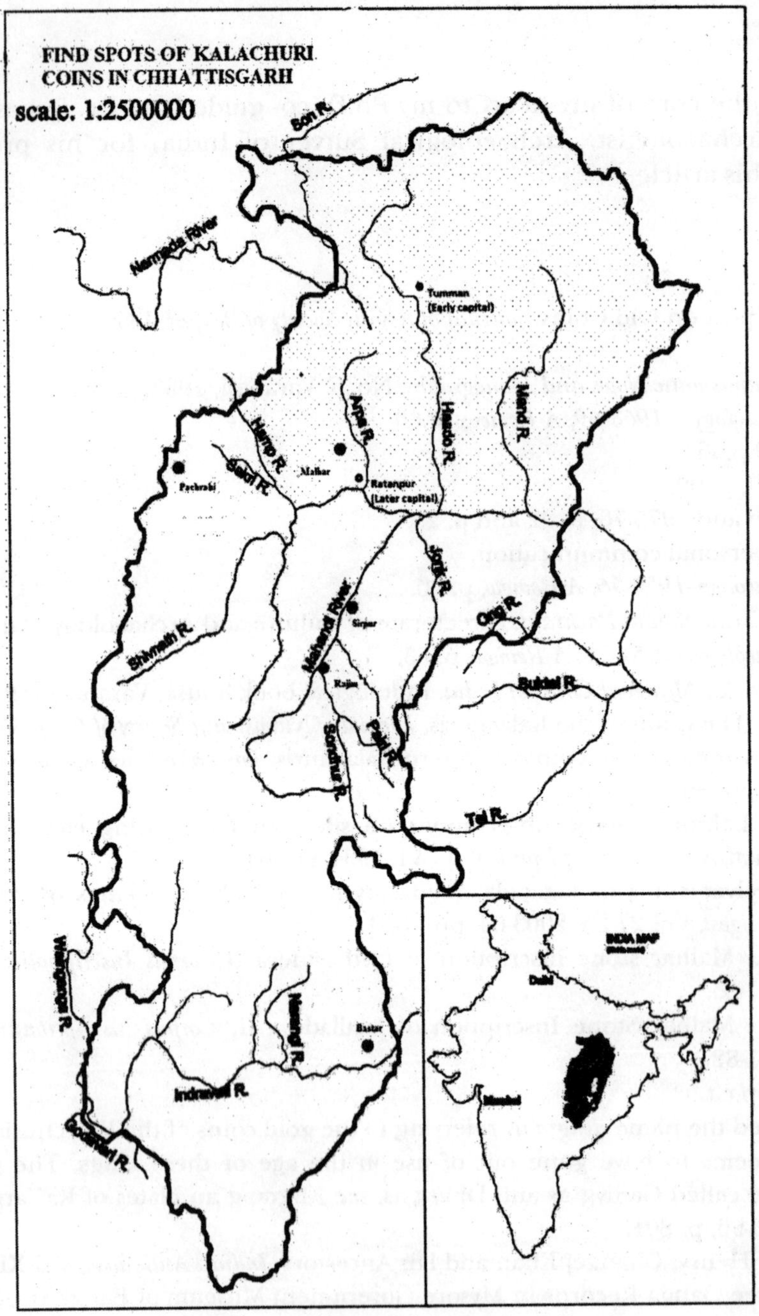

1 : Map of Chhattisgarh, India, Find spots of Kalachuri coins

Plate 3.1 : Main Section Belan Valley

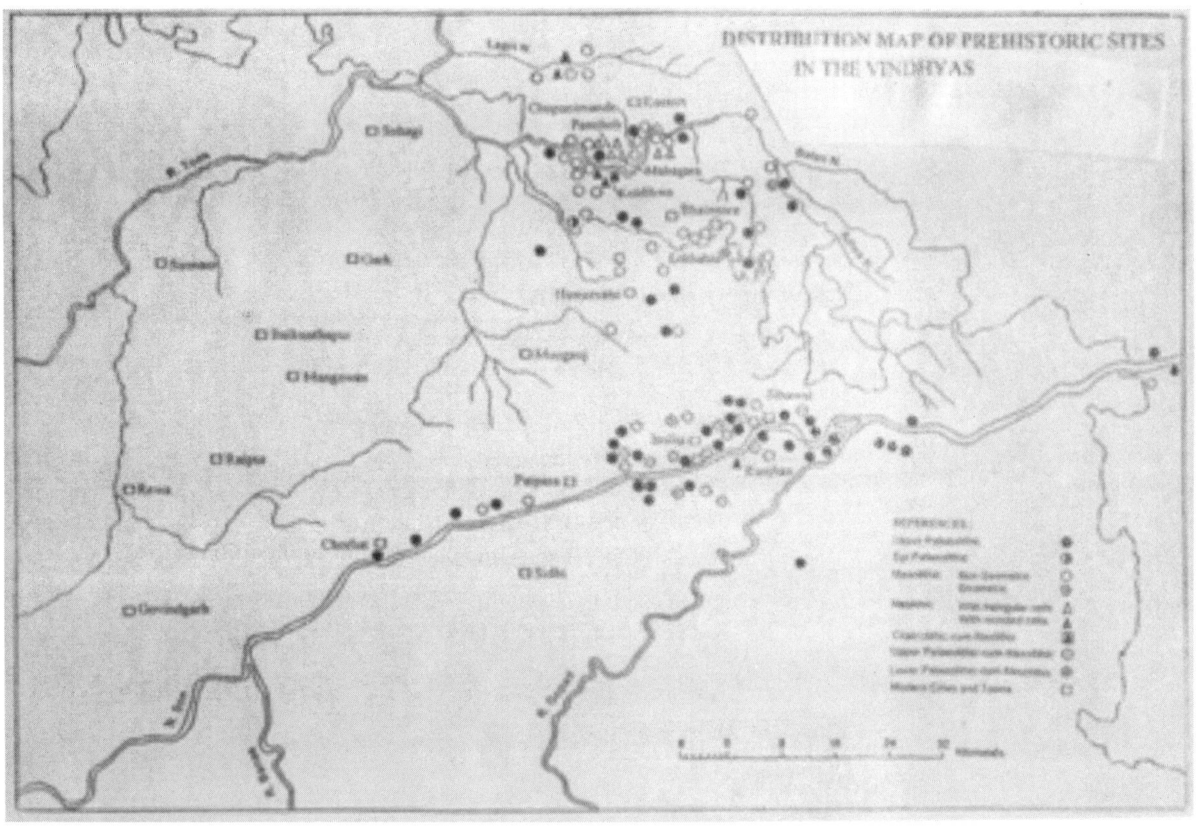

Plate 3.2 : Distribution of Sites in the Vindhyas

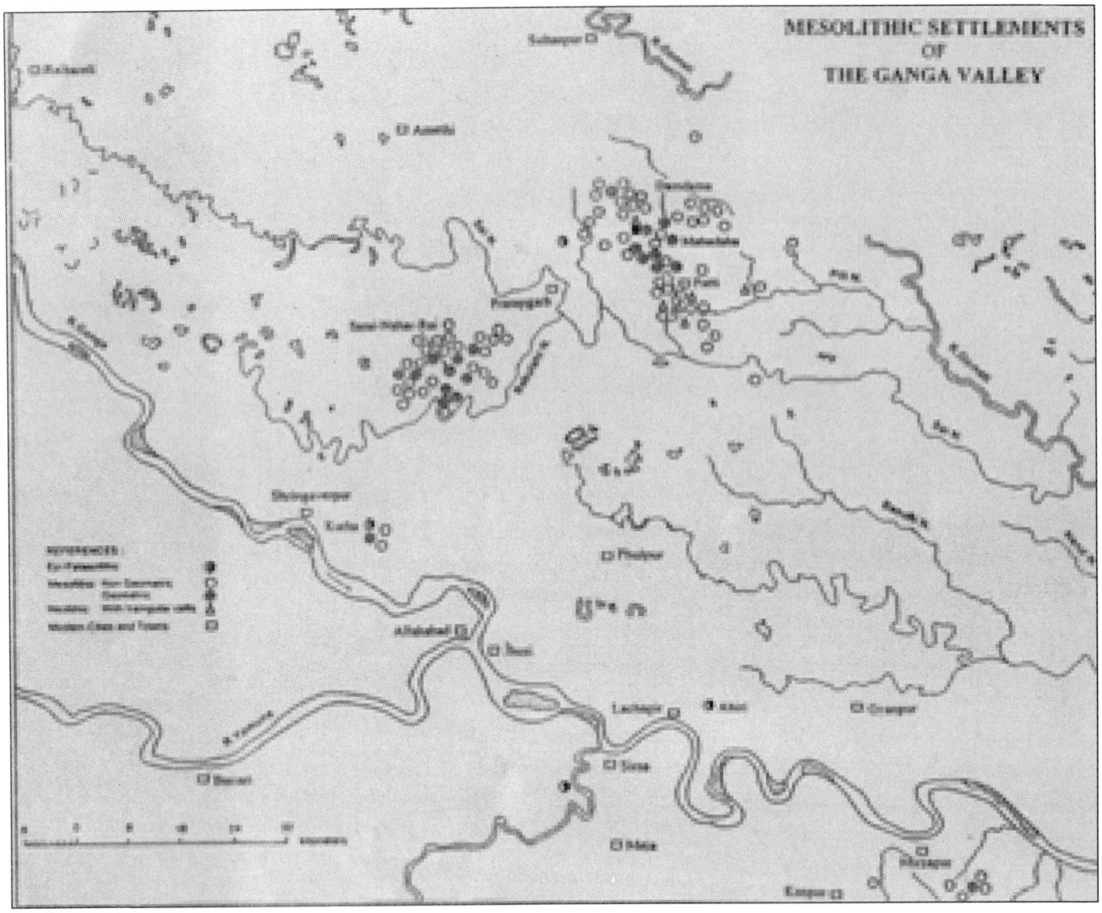

Plate 3.3 : Mesolithic Settlements of the Ganga Valley

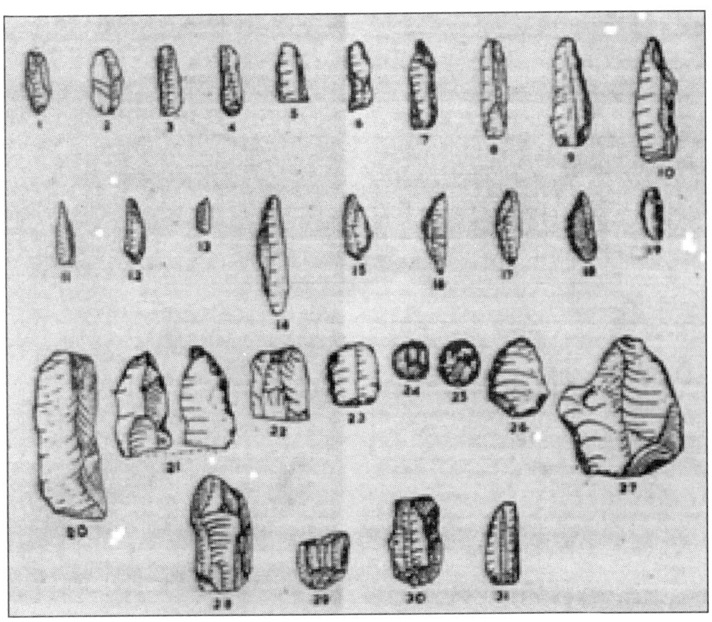

Plate 3.4 (a) Epi-palaeolithic Tools

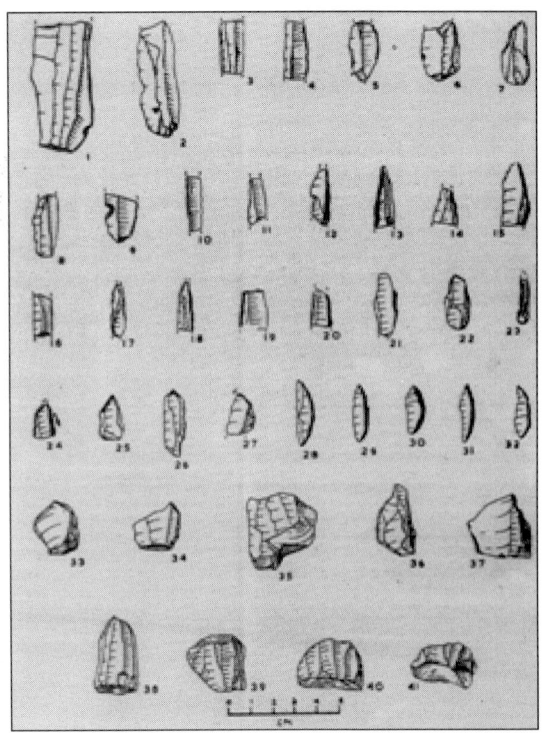

Plate 3.4 (b) : Tools Non Geometric Tools

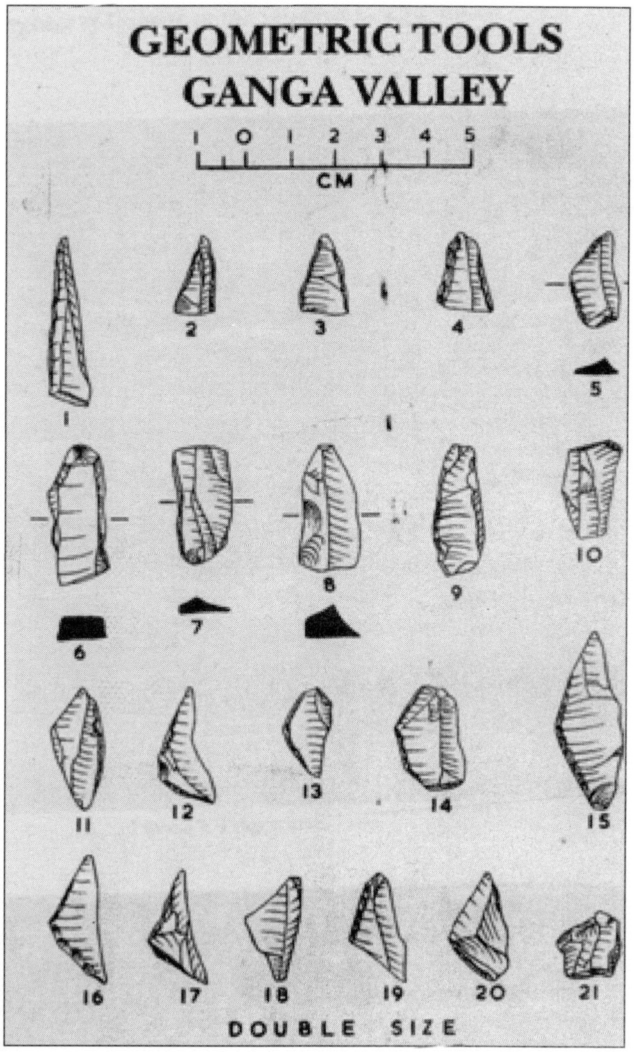

Plate 3.4 (c) : Tools Non Geometric Tools

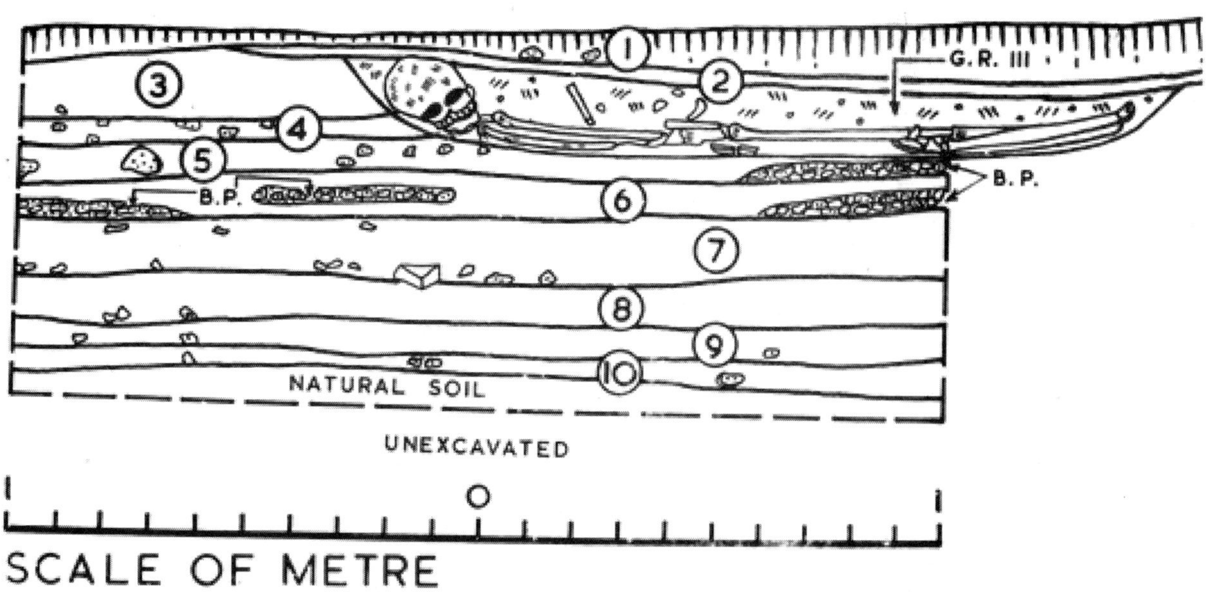

Plate 3.5 : Stratigraphy of Damdama

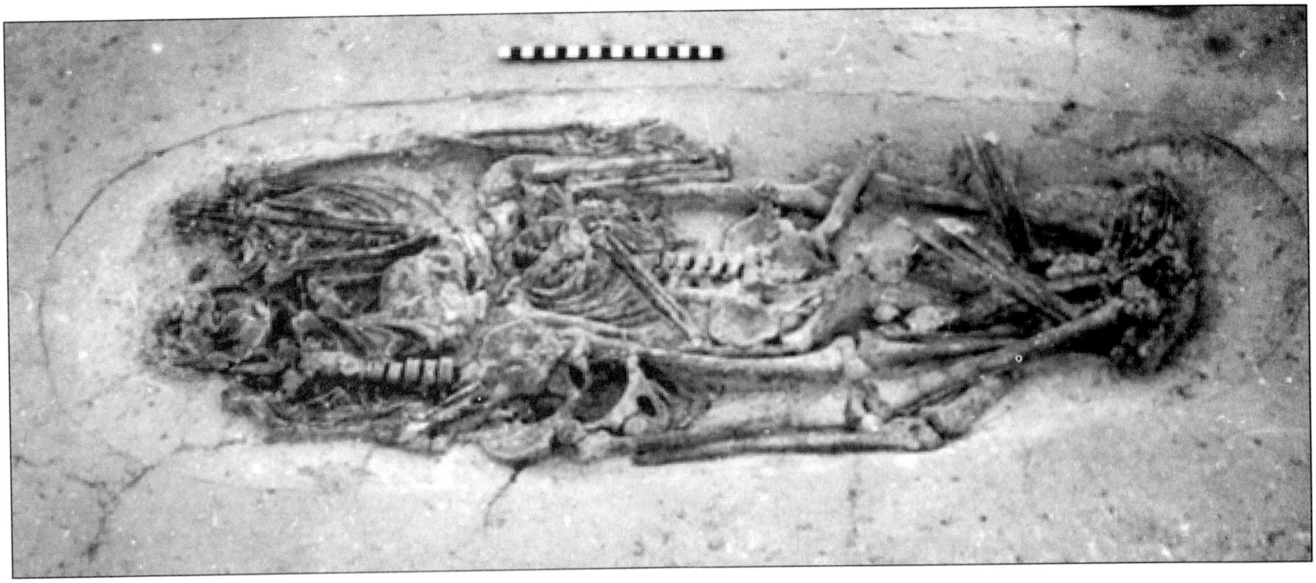

Plate 3.6 : Four Burials Sarai Nahar Rai-Couples

Plate 3.7 : Couple Burial Mahadaha

Plate 3.8 : Burils and Hearths of different periods

Plate 3.9 : Pit Hearth, Damdama

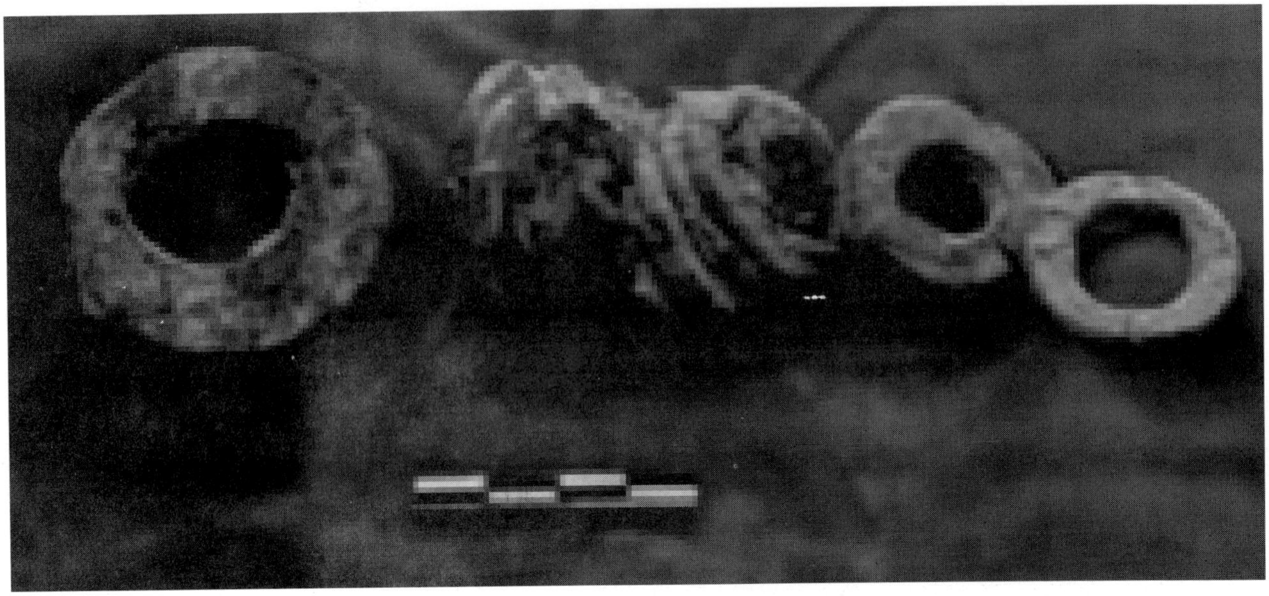

Plate 3.10 : Antler,Ornaments,Mahadaha

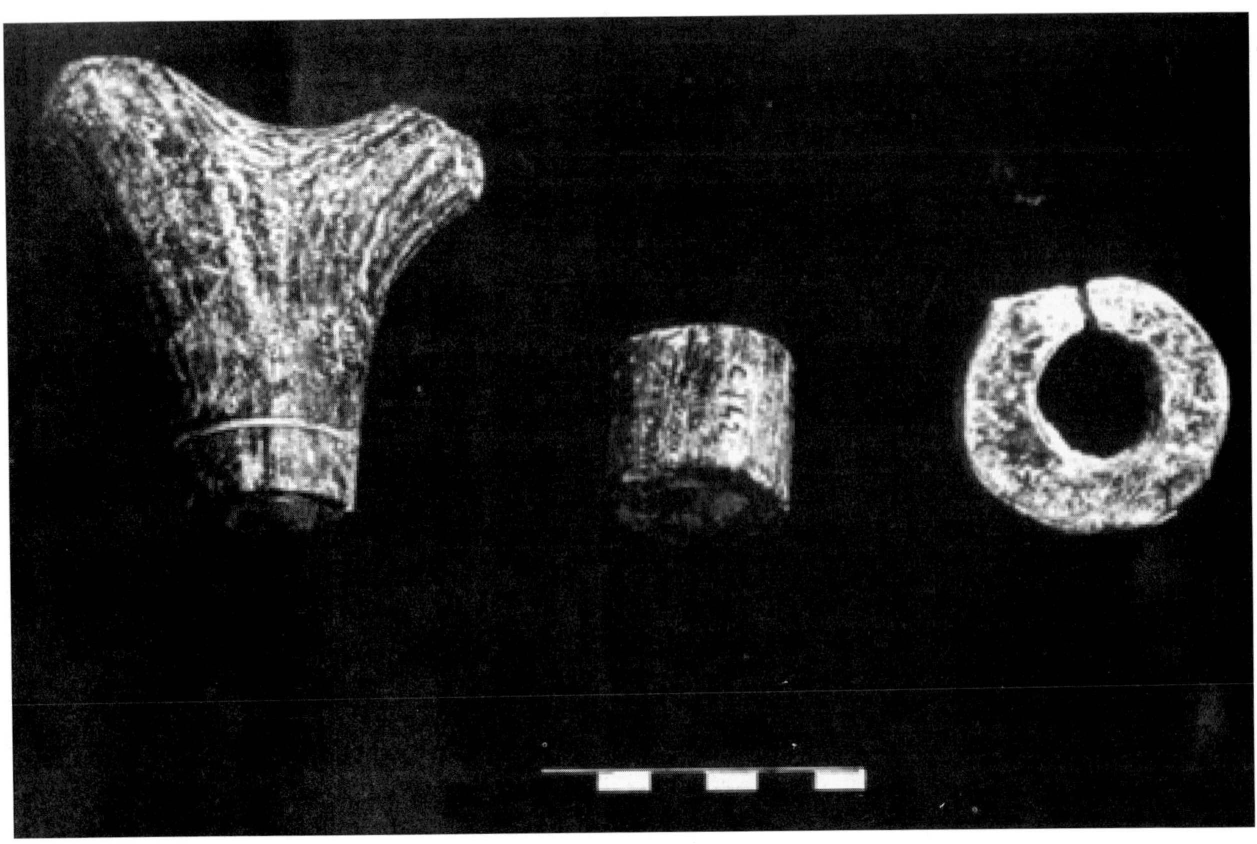

Plate 3.11 : Ornaments in the Manufacturing Stage

Plate 3.12 : Male Skeleton With ear rings

Plate 3.13 : Rock Painting; A group of Boars

Plate 3.14 (a) : General view of Ronp Shelter

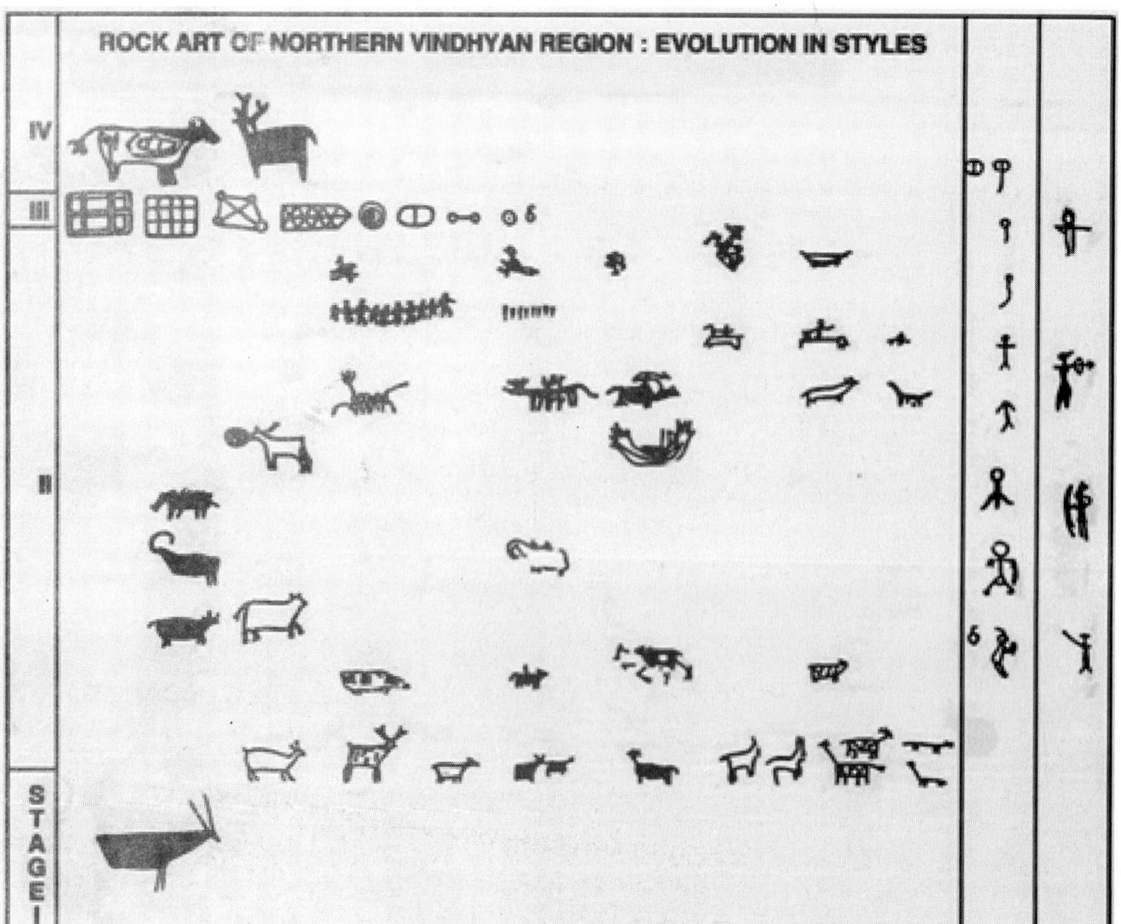

Plate 3.14(b) : Rock Art of Northern Vindhyan Region : Evolution in Styles

Plate 5.1 : King and queen in low relief, Manhai, Kausambi

Plate 5.2 : Nativity scene, Kausambi.

Plate 5.3 : Palm leaf capital, Manhai, Kausambi.

Plate 5.4 : Buddha in Bhumisparsha Mudra, Kausambi.

Plate 5.5 : Bodhisattva, Kausambi.

Plate 5.6 : Bodhisattva, Kausambi.

Plate 5.7 : Unfinished Sculpture, Kausambi.

Plate 5.8 : Gajalakshmi, Kausambi.

Plate 8.1 : Dwarka: Diving near Samudra Narayan temple (photo: UAW)

Plate 8.2 : Dwarka: A submerged structural remain after cleaning (photo: UAW)

Plate 8.3 : Dwarka: Excavations in Dwarkadheesh temple complex (photo: UAW)

Plate 8.4 : Dwarka: Partly broken circular structure in intertidal zone (photo: UAW)

Plate 15.1 : General View of the Mound, Waina, Ballia

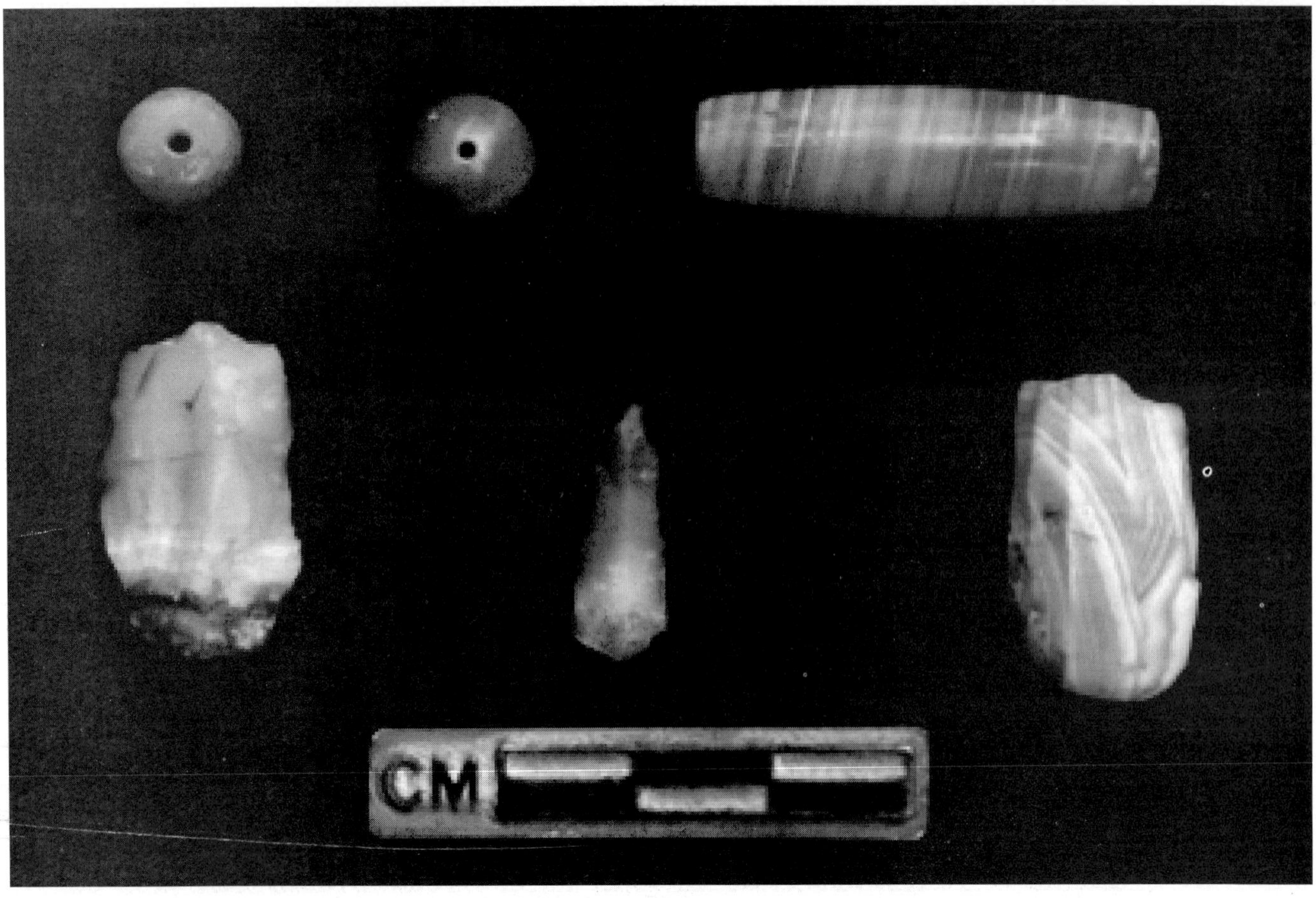

Plate 15.2 : Microliths of Waina, District Ballia (U.P.).

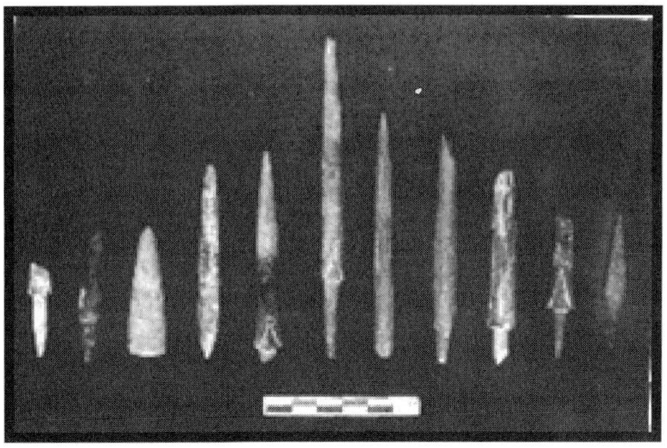

Plate 15.3 : Bone Points of Plate IB & II, Waina, Ballia.

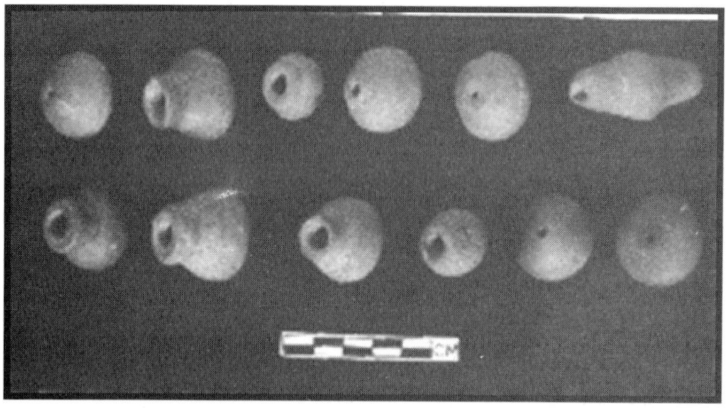

Plate 15.4 : Terracotta Beads of Plate IB, II & III, Waina, Ballia.

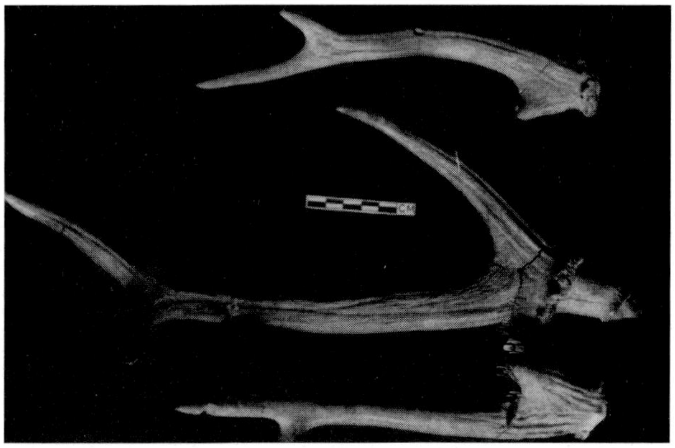

Plate 15.5 : Antlers of Plate II & III, Mound, Waina, Ballia.

Plate 15.6 : Occupation floor with Post-holes Plate III, Mound, Waina, Ballia.

Plate 18.1 : Lower Palaeolithic tools from Sohanpura

Plate 18.2 : Lower Palaeolithic tools from Sohanpura

Plate 18.3 : Lower Palaeolithic tools from Bheetaro

Plate 18.4 : Lower Palaeolithic tools from Bheetaro

Plate 18.5 : Lower Palaeolithic Handaxe from Reedh Ka Tila

Plate 18.6 : Lower Palaeolithic Handaxe from Reedh Ka Tila

Plate 18.7 : Lower Palaeolithic tools from Peer Baba Ki Bani

Plate 18.8 : Lower Palaeolithic tools from Peer Baba Ki Bani

Plate 18.9 : Lower Palaeolithic tools from Shobh

Plate 18.10 : Lower Palaeolithic tools from Shobh

Plate 18.11 : Middle Palaeolithic tools from Bageshwar

Plate 18.12 : Middle Palaeolithic tools from Bageshwar

Plate 18.13 : Middle Palaeolithic tools from Laloda

Plate 18.14 : Middle Palaeolithic tools from Laloda

Plate 18.15 : Upper Palaeolithic tools from Deoli Ki Dhani

Plate 18.16 : Upper Palaeolithic tools from Deoli Ki Dhani

Plate 20.1 : A cylindrical neck & collared mouth Chalcolithic Pot

Plate 20.2 : Fragmentary remains of Chalcolithic Earthen Pots

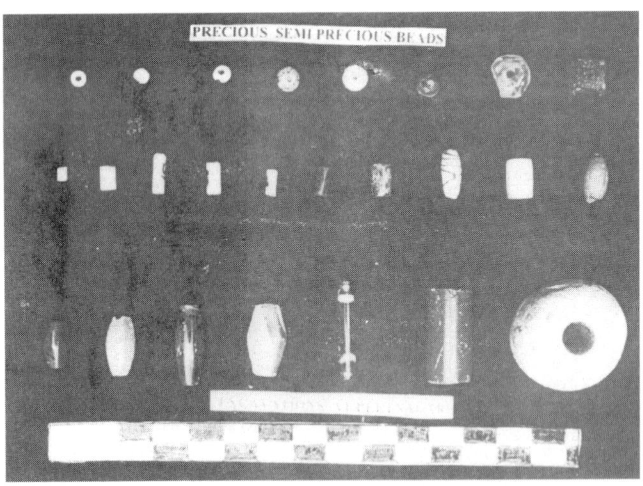

Plate 20.3 : Precious and Semi-precious stone bead excavated from Peetnagar

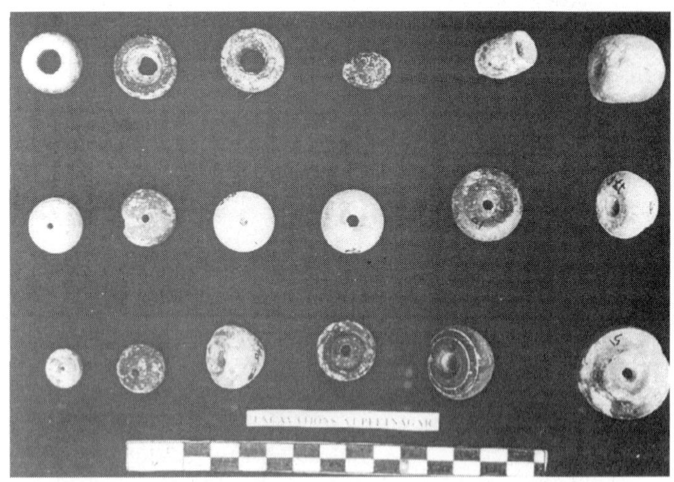

Plate 20.4 : Terracotta Beads

Plate 20.5 : Painted thin fragments of Lota & thick Globular Vessel

Plate 20.6 : Painted fragmentary pieces of Stand Bowls and Vessels

Plate 23.1 : Fragmentary Stone Inscription of Kachchhapaghāta Ratnapāla: V.S. 1165

Plate 23.2 : Close up of the upper left portion of the Stone Inscription of Ratnapāla

Plate 23.3 : Close up of the upper right portion of the Stone Inscription of Ratnapāla

Plate 23.4 : Close up of the lower right portion of the Stone Inscription of Ratnapāla

Plate 23.5 : Close up of the lower right portion of the Stone Inscription of Ratnapāla

Plate 25.1(A) : General view of the mound with its highest elevation

Plate 25.1 (B) : General view of mound on the bank of river Sai

a

b

c

d

e

f

Plate 25.2 : Terracotta Seals and Sealings

a

b

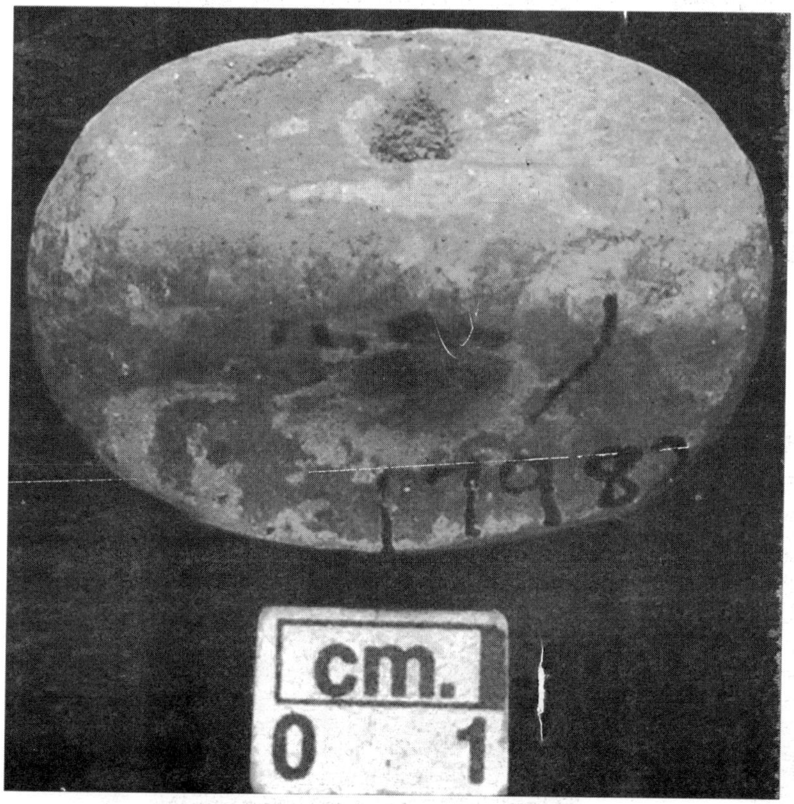

c

d

Plate 25.3 : Seals and Sealings from Sanchankot.

Plate 25.4 : Seals and Sealings from Sanchankot.

फलक 26.1 : गजमस्तक का शिरस्त्राण धारी डिमेट्रियस

फलक 20.2 : डिमेट्रियस की मुद्रा पर अंकित गज का शिरोभाग एवं अंकुश

फलक 26.3 : एण्टियालकिड्स की मुद्रा पर अंकित गज का शिरोभाग

फलक 26.4 : एण्टियालकिड्स की मुद्रा पर अंकित गज का शिरोभाग

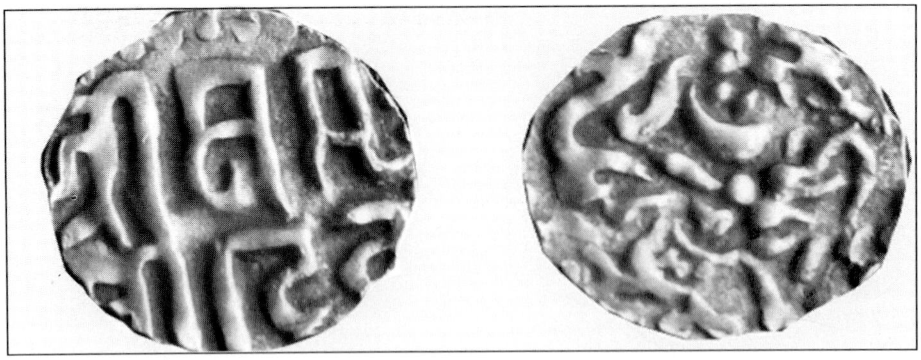

Plate 27.1 : Gold coin of Prithvideva obverse (in collection of Kamal Vaid) copy(1)

Plate 27.2 : Silver coin of Prithvideva Reverse (in collection of Prshant kulkarni) copy

Plate 27.3 : Copper coin of Prithavideva Reverse (in collection of L.P. Pandey) copy

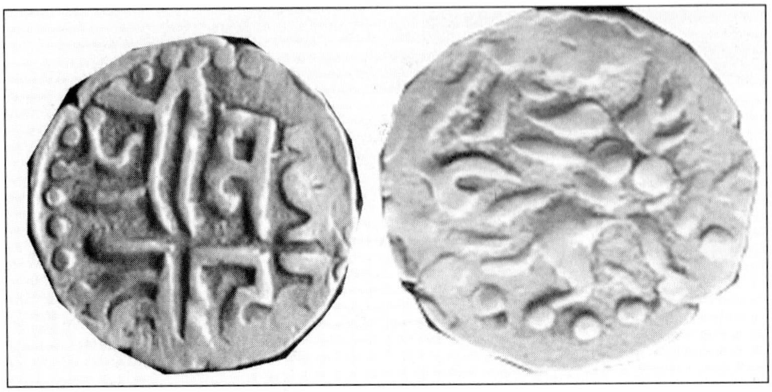

Plate 27.4 : Gold coin of Ratandeva obverse (in collection of Kamal Vaid) copy(1)

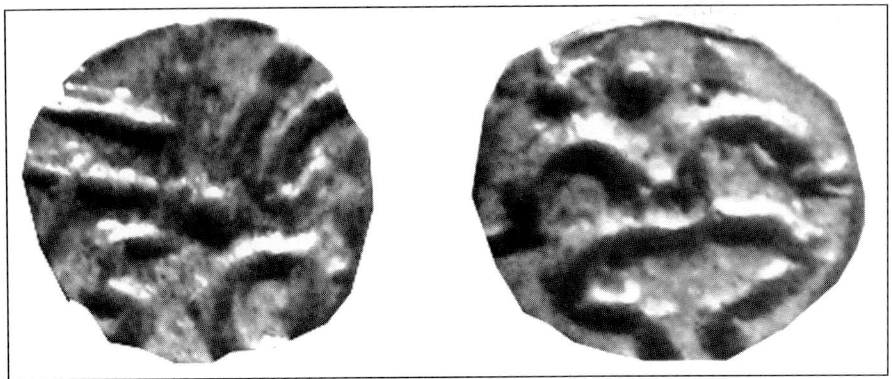

Plate 27.5 : Silver coin of Ratandeva, Reverse (in collection of Prashant kulkarni) copy

Plate 27.6 : Copper coin of Ratandeva obverse (in collection of Pushparaj Victor) copy(1)

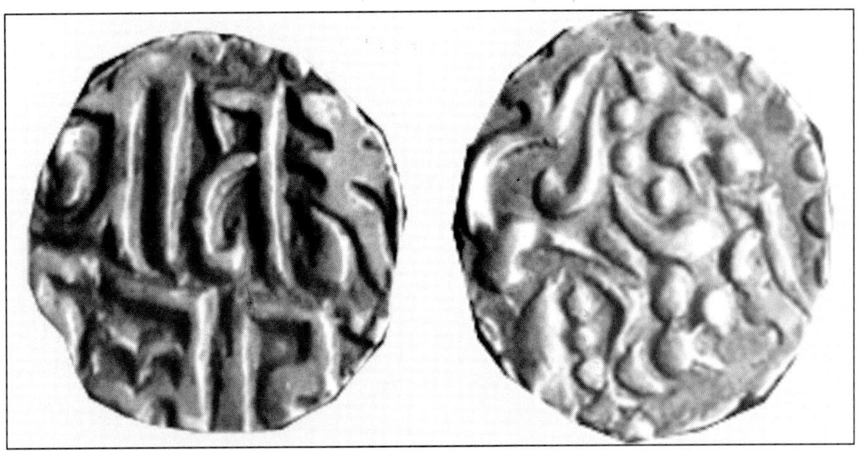

Plate 27.7 : Gold coin of Jajalladeva obverse (in collection of Kamal Vaid) copy

Plate 27.8 : Copper coin of Jajalladeva (in collection of Bhanupratap singh) copy

Plate 27.9 : Silver coin of Jagpaladeva obverse copy

Platc 27.10 : Copper coin of Pratapmalladeva copy

Plate 27.11 : Gold coin of Pratapmalladeva copy

Archaeology & Tradition

(Prof. D. N. Tripathi Felicitation volume)

Archaeology & Tradition

(Prof. D. N. Tripathi Felicitation volume)

Volume – II

Editors

B.R. Mani

I.D. Dwivedi

Vimal Tiwari

Agam Kala Prakashan

DELHI

First Published 2016

ISBN : 978-81-7320-169-1

Published by :
Dr. Agam Prasad, M.A., Ph.D., Diploma in Museology
for **Agam Kala Prakashan**
34, Central Market, Ashok Vihar, Delhi-110052
Ph. : 27212195, 65688806-7
Fax : 91-11-27212195
E-mail : agambooks@gmail.com, agambook@yahoo.com
Website : www.agamkala.com

Composed by :
Elegant Printographics
Delhi-110085

Printed by :
Chawla Offset
Ashok Vihar, Delhi-110 052

Printed in India.

Prof. D.N. Tripathi

Mrs. and Prof. Tripathi at their grand daughter's Marriage on 20 Nov. 2011

Contents

Editor's Note xi

Bibliographical Sketch xxvii

List of Contributors xxxix

List of Plates xlv

Tributes & Reminiscences

1	Colin Renfrew	Tribute to Professor Daya Nath Tripathi	l
2	अजय कुमार पाण्डेय	परम्परा के संवाहक परमाचार्य प्रोफेसर दयानाथ जी	li
3	कुवॅर बहादुर कौशिक	पुरातत्व के प्रमाता (प्रो0 दयानाथ त्रिपाठी)	liii
4	Devesh N Tripathi	An Untold Saga of My Papaji & Tribute (poem)	lv
5	देवेश नाथ त्रिपाठी	पिता–पुत्र	lxi
5	Sibesh Bhattacharya	My Friend Daya Nath, Indian Archeology --- Some Nostalgia, Some Rambling Thoughts	lxii
6	सुरेन्द्र दुबे	बहुस्तरीय संचरना का उत्कृष्ट व्यक्तित्व	lxv
7	ईश्वर शरण विश्वकर्मा	आचार्य–परम्परा के एक बहुआयामी व्यक्तित्व : मेरे गुरूवर्य	lxviii
8	राकेश तिवारी	सोहगौरा से सोहगौरा : प्रोफेसर दया नाथ त्रिपाठी	lxxi
9	Y Sudarshan Rao	Message	lxxiii
10	उमेश नाथ त्रिपाठी	आचार्य दयानाथ त्रिपाठी: मेरे पिता एवं प्रेरणा	lxxv
11	अंजुला शुक्ला	गर्व है पुत्री होने का	lxxvii
12	Irfan Habib	Professor D.N. Tripathi	lxxix

Volume - I

Section I : Archaeology

1 An Evolutionary Perspective on the Development of Human Culture — 1
– *Colin Renfrew*

2 Evolution of Society and Culture in Rajasthan — 6
– *V. N. Misra*

3 Over-view of the Mesolithic Culture of the Vindhya-Ganga Region — 15
– *Radhakant Verma*

4 The Iron Age Society of India: Pattern of Technology Adaptation and Culture Change 23
– Vibha Tripathi

5 Archaeology of Kausambi: Review of a City Site of the Lower Ganga-Yamuna Doab 45
– J N Pal

6 Early Agro-pastoral Cultures of India 56
– Vasant Shinde

7 Pakkākot: Transition from Rural to Urban Settlment: An Archaeological Study 64
– Sitaram Dubey & Santosh Kumar Singh

8 Dwarka: Traditions and Excavations 80
– Alok Tripathi

9 Climate, Environment and the Break-up of the Indus-Sarasvati Civilization 85
– Michel Danino

10 Jalore-Elana (Irina) and Swarnagiri: A Study 93
– K S Shukla

11 River Saraswati— The Cradle of Indian Civilization 96
– Rajesh Purohit

12 Archaeological Investigations along the Ancient Pilgrimage Route from Ayodhya to Sravasti 103
– Indudhar Dwivedi, Vimal Tiwari and *Abha Dwivedi*

13 सरस्वती नदी का प्रवाह तंत्र एवं तीर्थ (पुरातत्त्व के संदर्भ में) 119
– रत्नेश कुमार त्रिपाठी

14 विन्ध्य क्षेत्र की मध्यपाषाणिक संस्कृति में जीवन–निर्वाह के साक्ष्य 136
– रमाकांत सिंह

15 Archaeology of Bhrigu Kshetra (with special reference of Waina) 146
– Santosh Kumar Singh

16 Neolithic Culture of Saryupar Region 165
– Shitala Prasad Singh

17. Evolution of Early Farming Culture in Middle Ganga Plain 173
– Neelesh Kumar Pandey

18 Palaeolithic Tools from Shekhawati Region: A Preliminary Study 179
– Vineet Godhal

19. New Appearance of Beads in NBPW Culture in the Middle Ganga Plain 187
– Shanker Jaikishan

20. Excavations at Peetnagar 192
– D.K. Mathur

Section II : Epigraphy & Numismatics

21 A Study of Inscriptions: History and Administration 195
– T. P. Verma

22 The Allahabad Museum Copperplate grant of Raṇabhañjadeva-I 221
– G. C. Tripathi

23 Fragmentary Stone Inscription of the Kachchhapaghāta Ratnapāla: V.S. 1165 230
– Arvind K. Singh

24	The Tradition of Shaiva Ascetics and their Significance (with special reference of early Medieval Inscriptions) *– Rajesh Kumar Dhar Dubey*	235
25	Seals and Sealings from Sanchankot *– D P Tewari*	238
26	हिन्द–यवन शासकों की मुद्राओं पर अंकित 'गज' प्रतीक : एक विवेचन *– विपुला दुबे*	243
27	Stylistics of Kalachuri Coinage in Chhattisgarh *– Vishi Upadhyay*	247
	Plates	257

Volume – II

Section III : Art, Iconography & Architecture

28	Invocation of Sārasvatī Power in Jainism *– M N P Tiwari & S S Sinha*	289
29	Śaivism of *Tattvaprakāśa* and Parallels in the Śaiva images in *Samarāngaṇsūtradhāra* *– Susmita Pandey*	296
30	पूर्व मध्यकालीन जैन वास्तु में भेद अभेद के तत्व *– दिवाकर प्रसाद तिवारी*	301
31	A Note on the Newly Discovered Brick Temple and it's Site at Pipri, District Siddharthnagar, U.P. *– Praveen Kumar Mishra*	304
32	Yaksha Iconography: Thematic Variation and its Implications *– Namrata Singh*	309
33	Depiction of Brahma's Life through the Vaishnava Sculptures of Udayagiri Caves, Vidisa: A Proportionate Blend of Iconography and Philosophy *– Pooja Saxena & Apurva Sinha*	320
34	Sculptural Art of Trans-Ghaghara Region *– Neetu Tiwari*	323
35	Transformation of West Asian and Greco-Roman Elements in Indian Art *– Vinay Kumar*	329
36	खम्भात में अर्द्धकीमती पत्थर के मनके बनाने की पारम्परिक तकनीक *– राजेश कुमार मीणा*	333
37	Newly Discovered Painted Rock Shelters of Chandauli District, Uttar Pradesh *– Prabhakar Upadhyay & Om Prakash Kumar*	340
38	चम्पानेर–पावागढ के जैन बावनढेरी मंदिर के श्वेताम्बर मूर्तियों की पहचान एवं विवेचना *– बृजेश रावत एवं अनुपमा सिंह*	347
39	Earliest Human Bronze Image from Middle Ganga Plain and its Iconic Representation in the Rock Art of Kaimur region, India *– Sachin Kumar Tiwary*	353
40	Brahmanical Figures on the Terracotta-Art of Bihar *– Anantashutosh Dwivedi*	355

Section IV : Religion

41	The Human Stratum of the Rāma Story *– S R Goyal*	362

42 The Four *Varnas*: A Vedic Concept of Division of Society 376
– *Shashi Tiwari*

43 A Note on the Origin of the Āśrama Institution 381
– *Rajawant Rao*

44 The Nāynārs & Āḷvārs and their contribution to the Bhakti Movement in South India 385
– *Shankar Goyal*

45 The Living Saura Traditions of Gujarat 396
– *Atul Tripathi*

46 इक्ष्वाकु परम्परा एवं संस्कृति 405
– *ईश्वर शरण विश्वकर्मा*

47 राम चरित मानस का धर्मशास्त्रीय अध्ययन : परहित सरिस धरम नहिं भाई परपीड़ा सम नहिं अधमाई 412
– *संचिता घोष*

48 Athena Pallas : The Greek Goddess 417
– *Rekha Chaturvedi*

49. Deepaawali : Celebrations & A Message 423
– *R.C. Tripathi*

50 ऋग्वेद में मानव एवं मानवीय मूल्य 428
– *दिग्विजयनाथ*

51 The Concept of Mandal in Tantric Form of Mahayan Buddhism 433
– *Kamlesh Kumar Gautam*

52 पांचरात्र आगम में वैष्णवी दीक्षा 437
– *रामप्यारे मिश्र*

53 पांचरात्र संहिताओं में नृ–सिंह का स्वरूप 445
– *ध्यानेन्द्र नारायण दूबे*

Section V : Historiography

54 Purusha, Purana and Itihasa: History and Spiritual Understanding 450
– *Ramashray Roy*

55 The account of nearchos' voyage: an appraisal 466
– *U.P. Arora*

56 Lalitaditya Muktapida : The First Indian Antiquary 473
– *J. N. Pandey*

57 वेद–व्याख्या के नैरुक्त प्रस्थान में इतिहास की भूमिका 475
– *मुरली मनोहर पाठक*

58 यूनानी इतिहास–दर्शन : एक सर्वेक्षण 478
–*कुँवर बहादुर कौशिक*

59 भारतीय इतिहास की सनातन परम्परा 485
–*अजय कुमार पाण्डेय*

Section VI : General

60 Ancient Indian Ideals and Modern Realities 494
– *K. Paddayya*

61	The Indo-European Problem: A New Paradigm, A complete re-look – *Mohan Gupta*	503
62	A Cultural-Psychological Orientation to Self-Understanding – *Girishwar Misra*	518
63	A study of Human Evolution and Migration on the basis of Analysis of Deoxyribonucleic Acid (DNA) – *Ram Rudra Shukla*	526
64.	On Our History, Our Tradition and Astronomy – *Krisnanand Sinha*	530
65	Ganesh Shankar Vidyarthi and his Crusade Against Communalism (1915-1931) – *P.K. Shukla*	533
66	The Aesthetics of Sanskrit Theatre and the Structure of Sanskrit Drama – *Kamalesdatta Tripathi*	540
67	Shorapur: A Palace City of Late-Medieval Southern Deccan – *S. K. Aruni*	550
68	Water Resources and their Management in Ancient India – *Pragya Chaturvedi*	555
69	Lumbini: The Birthplace of Lord Buddha – *Gitu Giri*	560
70	प्रयाग और भरद्वाज – *राजेश मिश्र*	565
71	Power and Imagination : Representation of India in European Cartography – *Deepak Kumar* and *Ravindra Kumar*	569
72	"पूर्व वैदिक काल में स्त्रियों की स्थिति: एक ऐतिहासिक विमर्श" – *संगीता सिंह*	578
73	Banking in Ancient India – *Praveen Kumar Sharma*	582
	Plates	585

Editor's Note

It was the month of April 2014 when the idea of this felicitation volume came in the mind of pupils and well wishers of Professor D.N. Tripathi to felicitate him for his contribution to the subject. The theme of this volume titled 'Archaeology and Tradition' was chosen as this is the favourite subject of Professor Tripathi and most of his research was oriented to this topic.

Indology and archaeology represent faces of the same coin in an ideal combination. In most other countries with an ancient past like West Asia, China and Egypt, terms like Assyriologist, Sinologist or Egyptologist signify 'an expert in the study of human antiquities of the respective country, focusing on evidences drawn from archaeological excavations.' However, the term Indology has been defined as 'the study of literature and history of India.' The reason for this anomaly may be that an Indologist, in Indian parlance, has come to mean one who is not an archaeologist and is, therefore, not aware of the importance of the study of pottery and of modern dating methods. The situation is changing now. In post- independence India much of the writing of history is based upon the synthesis of archaeology and tradition. Archaeological cultural sequence for a given region is a paradigm with which the traditional culture-framework of the same region (as from Puranic data) will have to be compared. The resultant congruency will have to be taken as the best fitting restoration of the past. Traditional data in India does not necessarily lack authenticity of occurrence, but mainly lack chronological consistency or cohesion. Archaeological data provide this invaluable correction.

The answer of these problems could be found in its analysis on the basis of the data available to us both from Archaeology and Tradition. The history of ancient civilizations cannot be written correctly without the help of both. Schliemann was probably the first archaeologist who tried to identify the Greek traditions in its archaeological remains. With his complete faith in the historicity of Homer's Iliad, he started his search for the city of Troy and Mycenae. In 1872 he identified the "Palace of Priam" and "Priam's Treasure" which included two diadems, six bracelets, sixty ear-rings, 8,700 rings, buttons and ornaments of gold, an electrum vase and others of silver and bronze, and many bronze weapons. In spite of scholastic jeers of the contemporary academics, Schliemann continued his search, and in 1876, while excavating the Shaft Graves at Mycenae, he not only identified the 'Golden Mycenae' of Homer but also had a 'gaze upon the face of Agamemnon!' And then digging by Schliemann in Greece and Evans (1900) in Crete at Knossos, 'the Palace of Minos', and Sir Leonard Wooley (1926) at Ur—'Royal Tombs of Ur'— and many other excavations in Lebanon, Palestine and Syria with a view to locating the Bible cities or sites, have yielded good results.

In India, scholars turned to archaeology for the verification of the Epic stories quite late. B.P. Sinha may be correct in thinking that "this was partly because the earlier archaeologists from Cunningham onwards were very much concerned with Buddhist sites about which there were Chinese accounts and datable Buddhist and Jain literary texts". In the second decade of the last century, when archaeologists came to know of the Indus civilization accidentally, much of the energy and resources of the Archaeological Survey of India was invested in the study of this civilization. It was left to B.B. Lal to "embark on the adventure of testing Indian traditions in the crucible of archaeology", although Pargiter, a great proponent of the value of historical traditions, had asserted as early as 1922 that "the general trustworthiness of the tradition is the fact demonstrated, whenever it has been possible to test tradition by results of discoveries and excavations." In any case, the process once started by Lal in the field has been carried on by other historians and archaeologists in India and *Puratattva* No. 8 is largely devoted to the discussion of the theme 'Archaeology and Tradition'. The present position in India is that, whereas some scholars believe that the traditions contain some real truth, and that they refer to genuine historical traditions, scholars like D.C. Sircar think that the Indian traditions as stored in the Puranas and Epics and corroborative additional information gleaned from the vast Vedic literature are imaginary and provide no base for sober history. M.C. Joshi is of the opinion that the Indian tradition, Vedic or Puranic, is not "likely to help much in the interpretation of archaeological data" as they are "unhistoric and coloured". Tradition and archaeology should not be mixed together in any form at least as far as Indian protohistory is concerned. Romila Thapar also considers that "in the absence of contemporary written record or deciphered scripts, any attempt to correlate archaeological material with traditional accounts of the past becomes a venture into speculation." Despite these doubts, there are many historians and archaeologists in India who are trying to identify the tradition with archaeology. R.S. Sharma is of the view that the Painted Grey Ware phase of Indian archaeology is "comparable on many counts to the material culture of the later Vedic texts". Sankalia has been consistently arguing the case of identification of various Chalcolithic and Neolithic cultures of India with the Vedic and Puranic tribes. Malati J. Shendge may be right in saying that:

> It is possible to verify the literary tradition through archaeological findings and the literary tradition may also be used to throw light on the archaeological remains without which they may be best described as artefacts which do not seem to breathe life on their own ... if a coherent picture is to be drawn, both literary and archaeological evidence have to go hand in hand.

We all know that Lal, after having worked on the archaeology of Mahabharata, also worked on the national project of the 'Archaeology of Ramayana Sites'. Sānkalia and Gupta have also done work on the two great epics. Recognizing the importance of this subject, the Advisory Board of the Archaeological Survey of India, in its meeting held in November 1974, approved this project out of the list of twenty five problem-oriented national projects, which were required to be undertaken during the Fifth Five Year Plan (1974-79). Sinha may be right in admitting that the archaeology and literary traditions are the "twain that do not meet" today. Still we feel that in the near future we will strive and strive with success to make Archaeology and Tradition meet since all our traditions cannot be fully false. But in this effort the approach has to be "contextual rather than textual" and one will have to bear always in mind the caution given by Ghosh that ". . . It is indeed tempting to utilize archaeological evidence for substantiating tradition, but the pitfalls in the way should be guarded against, and the caution is necessary that fancy does not fly ahead of facts."

Traditional evidence yielded by literary texts and archaeological evidences can perhaps meet only at certain points. This perhaps may be possible by "undertaking a total structural study of society and the major trends of societal change in terms of both archaeology and literary tradition." Sankalia also holds the same opinion. He thinks "Our literary data are preserved in the Vedic and Puranic literature ... something about the political, social, religious and economic conditions, however, may be gathered to putting together the scraps of evidence from these sources."

Earlier attempts to correlate archaeology and the literary sources have, in the main, focused on the question of identifying the Aryans. Studies made on the basis of linguistic paleontology became acceptable to scholars only after the excavation of Boghazkeui by the German archaeologist, Hugo Winckler, in 1906-1908. About ten thousand inscriptions in cuneiform script were unearthed. When the Czech linguist, Freidrich Hrozny, read them in 1924, several issues concerning the Aryan problem seemed to have been solved. Ever since then the authority of the Vedic literature for interpreting the Aryan culture has been accepted by the scholars. Jean Deshayes in the beginning of the present century had identified the Aryan race on the basis of their copper and bronze tools found from Danube to the Ganga valley.

D.N. Tripathi became interested in the problem of tracing the material artifacts of the Aryan people who were surely the first users of copper and bronze artifacts on an industrial scale after his studies on the copper and bronze artifacts of the Mainland Greece (2600 B.C.-1450 B.C.). He has published several articles in his book *Archaeology and Tradition* which deals with this problem in detail.

New trends in Indian historiography since independence gained a new momentum and have been enriched by a variety of archaeological approaches. This has spurred scholars and students alike to have an archaeological look at the Aryan problem. The myth of a parent Indo-European language, the myth of an Aryan race speaking this language, the myth of a homeland for them in Central Asia or some region outside India, the myth of their invasion on India, and the myth of Arya-Dasa, Arya-Harappan or Aryan-Dravidian confrontation are completely exploded now. Prof. B.B. Lal (*Saraswati Flows on*, 2002) has first exploded the myth of Aryan invasion and only recently Michel Danino has quite convincingly discussed this problem in his book *The Lost River-on the trails of the Saraswati* (Penguin Books, 2010).

The origin of the Indus civilization is now dated in the fifth millennium BC (*Pre-Kot Dijian deposits at Harappa*: R.H. Meadow and Mark Kenoyer). Early Harappan phase now goes back to 3300 B.C.-3100 BC. A 4-meter deposit of the so-called early Harappans or Kot Dijian levels, Pre-Early Harappans or Pre-Kot-Dijian levels at Dholavira, and G.F. Dale's excavations at Bala Kot suggest that the early levels may go back to the 4th millennium BC. The Harappan civilization could easily now be placed along with Mesopotamian civilisation insofar as antiquities of both the civilisations are concerned. Vedic people were not the primitive nomadic pastoralists, as once Max Muller thought, but they were, in fact, fully aware of the craft specialisations of the urban culture. Since there is no other pre-600 B.C. urban culture in India except the Harappans, there is no way out but to accept the proposition that the Harappans and the Vedic were neither two different culture-complexes, nor the earlier proceeded the later. The Myth of Aryan invasion of the Harappan town was exploded long ago and the theory of non-presence of true domesticated horse at Harappan sites is no longer substantiated (cf. Mohenjodaro, Kalibangan, Ropar, Surkotda, etc.).

More than 30,000 miniature sculptures of clay, marble, bone, copper and gold from some 3000 sites of the Neolithic and Chalcolithic era in South Eastern Europe along with enormous models of temples and actual temples have been reported in recent years. Marija Gimbutas of California has identified various cosmogonical and cosmological images of moon, bull, snake, fish and primordial Egg in them. These archaeological images are well dated on the basis of the radio-carbon analysis and their calibration with dendochronology in circa 6500 to 3500 B.C.

The cosmogonical and cosmological images could be better explained and appreciated on the basis of the study of Vedic literature and Puranas which have a long tradition. Much has been written on the date of various works of the Vedic literature. While some scholars have attached a label of high antiquity to them, others have placed them not much farther from the historical period of written records. H. Jacobi and Shankar Balakrishna Dixit have fixed the date of the Satapath Brahmana in 3000 B.C. on the basis of the astrological calculation of a verse in it. Winternitz too 'agreed with them when he placed the beginning of the Brahman tradition in 2000 or 3000 B.C. On the basis of the date of the Brahmanas the date of Samhitas may be placed in the tenth to sixth millennium B.C.

We would like to draw the attention to the fact that the well dated proto-Indo-European images of southeastern Europe are really the material manifestations of the Vedic mythological concepts and legendary ideographs. None will doubt the fact that the Vedic literature is the first written record of the human race consisting the best thinking regarding the origin of universe, religion and philosophy carrying traditions of thousands of years.

The exact parallels of the Vedic legendary concepts are found in these archaeological records and, as such, it would not be incorrect to place the beginnings of the Vedic tradition in the sixth millennium BC rather than in the third millennium BC. The parallels drawn from the Proto-Indo-European art motifs, the Vedic ideograms and mythological concepts will certainly justify such an assumption.

The origin of this great civilisation lies in Indian soil. The birth of no civilisation lies in any single place or single factor because civilisation is a process and not an event. It took around 1000 years to integrate all the cultural elements of Pre-Harappan sites of Baluchistan through Harayana into an urban process the components of which were villages and townships interacting with each other and supporting the growth of Harappan civilisation. Effective long-distance trade with West Asia was the outcome of urbanization in India and not vice-versa.

On the basis of a detailed study of the representation of Primeval Water, Primordial Egg, Snake and Fish in the Proto-Indo-European and Indo-European art forms of circa 7000 BC to 4000 BC. Marija Gimbutas has rightly concluded that these representations are definitely associated with the cosmological myths of the Indo-European people. The parallels drawn from the Vedic literature and Avesta regarding the creation of the universe simply confirms the cosmogonical and cosmological associations of the above art motifs in the Indo-European contexts. A further study of the animals, plants and trees, both in the Indo-European art and Vedic literature, reconfirms the above parallelisms. It would, therefore, be not a mere fancy to conclude that the antiquity of the Vedas would go further in the past. Since no artistic representations similar to those found in the Old Europe of seventh and fifth millennium BC is available in India, the Vedic cosmogony and cosmology could not be archaeologically attested. But, in the light of the proto-Indo-European and Indo-European art representations discussed here it would not be unfair to rethink about the antiquity and geographical expanse of the Vedic literature. Stephen Knapp's book –*Proof of Vedic Culture's Global Existence* (Lexington, KY, USA, 2010) - clearly demonstrates the Vedic influence and proof of its existence found in such countries as Greece, China, Egypt, Middle East and Africa and its link with other ancient cultures, such as the Sumerians, Persians, Egyptians, Romans, Greeks, etc. He further asserts that "*the origins of world languages and literature are found in India and Sanskrit*".

Two areas for future research in the ancient history of India have been summarized in the above paragraphs, which involve matters of global interest and within each of which a number of interesting problems can be formulated which deserve further investigation on a fairly broad interdisciplinary basis. The prospects of such studies are fairly tremendous in India.

The present felicitation volume contain total 73 articles on different aspects of History, Culture, Archaeology, Epigraphy, Numismatics, Art & Iconography, Philosophy, Tradition, Historiography and other related subjects in the honour of Professor Tripathi. Out of 73 articles, 15 are in Hindi and 58 are in English language and divided into six sections i.e. Archaeology; Epigraphy & Numismatics; Art, Iconography & Architecture; Religion & Tradition; Historiography and General. Apart from article the volume also contains 12 tributes to Professor Tripathi. Section wise summary of the papers are as follows:

Section I – Archaeology

This section contains 20 articles. The first paper by Colin Renfrew titled 'An Evolutionary Perspective on the Development of Human Culture' recognizes the aspiration that the story of human cultural development over the past 100,000 years, and more especially over the past 10,000 years, be encompassed within the broad explanatory framework of Darwinian evolution.

V.N. Misra' paper titled 'Evolution of Society and Culture in Rajasthan' deals with the archaeological antiquity of the region and followed by the continuity of the components of different cultures in present days. Several parts of Rajasthan were inhabited during the Stone Age which has been divided in lower, middle and upper Palaeolithic and Mesolithic. After Stone Age, Protohistoric cultures i.e. Harappan, Chalcolithic, OCP and PGW and early historic cultures were developed in this region. The paper reviews main components of above mentioned cultures in the first part of the paper and in the second part it deals with the several features in the form of ceramics, structures, metal technology, agriculture products, decorations, ornaments, etc. which are still surviving in this region.

Paper of Radha Kant Verma titled 'Over-view of the Mesolithic Culture of the Vindhya-Ganga Region' is focused on the Mesolithic culture of this region. The term Mesolithic was used to denote a group of industries supposed to be transitional between the Palaeolithic and the Neolithic cultures. Three stages of Mesolithic culture have been noticed in this region i.e. Epi-Palaeolithic, early Mesolithic and advanced Mesolithic. This paper deals with the material culture of Mesolithic culture on the basis of the important excavated sites located in the Vindhyan region and Ganga valley.

Paper titled 'The Iron Age Society of India: Pattern of technology adaptation and culture change' by Vibha Tripathi is focused on the developmental stages of iron technology and its role in socio-economic changes that took place in ancient India especially in the Ganga plain. The copper was used for fashioning hunting and war weapons for several centuries after emergence of iron. Qualitative and quantitative improvement in iron objects was done during the middle Iron Age and the iron metallurgy attains greater heights during the late Iron Age i.e. opening centuries of Common Era. It took a long time to perfect the metallurgy of iron to produce good quality tools and implements superior to copper- bronze that was used prior to advent of iron. The metallurgy had to attain a status of efficiency to produce cheaper and affordable objects that too in sufficient quantity to be socially adaptable and effective.

J.N. Pal's paper titled 'Archaeology of Kausambi: Review of a City Site of the Lower Ganga-Yamuna Doab' is focused on the literary references of Kausambi in ancient literatures and archaeological investigations carried out at the site. The ancient site of Kausambi is located on the left bank of river Yamuna in district Kausambi of U.P. and was the capital of Vats Mahajanapada. This ancient city was one of the fortified cities of Northern India and has been frequently mentioned in various ancient literatures. The site was identified by A. Cunningham in the year 1861 and the Archaeological Survey of India under N.G. Majumdar excavated it in 1937-38 but the large scale excavations were only carried out by the University of Allahabad under G.R. Sharma between 1949 and 1965. The paper also deals with the several issues associated with the archaeology of the site.

Vasant Shinde presented a clear picture of Indian agro-pastoral cultures in his article on 'Early Agro-Pastoral Cultures of India'. Beginning of agriculture was an important phase of human history and before that the food economy of man was based on the wild plants and hunting. During last few decades several sites related with early farming have been explored and excavated. The paper reviews the evidences of early farming from the various sites of different regions of India i.e. Ganga valley, Western India, Deccan, South India, North-East India, etc. The paper also provides scope for future work for the study of origin and development of agro-pastoral societies.

Joint Paper of Sita Ram Dubey and Santosh Kumar Singh titled 'Pakkakot: Transition from Rural to Urban Settlement: An Archaeological Study' is basically a summary of the excavation carried out by the authors at the ancient site Pakkakot. The site is located in Ballia district on the ancient bed of Chhoti Saryu (*Tons*) river. The excavation had brought to light a six-fold cultural sequence ranging from Neolithic to Medieval periods without any break. The paper includes details of each period along with important findings.

The ancient city of Dwarka is mentioned in several ancient Indian texts and is of great religious significance for Hindus. Alok Tripathi's paper titled 'Dwarka: Traditions and Excavations' is based on the excavations conducted by him in the search of the city. The paper is divided in to two parts and the first part provides literary references of Dwaraka and previous attempts which were conducted by different institutions to locate the site. The second part of the paper demonstrates the preparation and process of underwater excavations carried out by him in collaboration with the Indian Navy.

Several studies have been carried out to solve the problem of downfall of Indus-Saraswati civilization. Michel Danino's paper titled 'Climate, Environment and the Break-up of the Indus-Sarasvati Civilization' is focused on climatic and environmental studies carried out by various scholars to solve this problem.

K.S. Shukla tried to identify the present town of Jalore, village Elana and Suvarnagiri hills with the literary evidences in his paper titled 'Jalore-Elana (Irina) and Swarnagiri: A Study'. Jalore is an important town and Elana is a small village and archaeological site in the district Jalore of Rajasthan. Suvarnagiri hill ranges are located in the same district and find mention in ancient literatures.

The river Saraswati and its tributaries gave birth to a mighty civilization presently termed as Indus-Saraswati civilization in the north-western part of Indian subcontinent around 3rd millennium B.C. Rajesh Purohit's paper on 'River Saraswati- The Cradle of Indian Civilization' is based on the human colonization in this region as exemplified by the archaeological sites and materials. The paper provides detail of literary references of river Saraswati available in various ancient works. The Rig-Veda mentions Saraswati as *Ambitame*, (the best among the mothers), *Naditame,* (the best among the rivers) and *Devitame*, (the best among the goddesses). A large number of habitational sites have been discovered along the palaeo-channels of river Saraswati in Haryana, Rajasthan and Gujarat. Discussion on the major sites of Harayana along these palaeo-channels has been made in this paper.

Paper of Indu Dhar Dwivedi and others titled 'Archaeological Investigations along the Ancient Pilgrimage route from Ayodhya to Sravasti' is based on the explorations carried out by the team of Lucknow Circle of ASI under the project titled 'Anctient Pilgrimage route from Kaushambi to Kapilvastu'. Ayodhya and Sravasti were politically as well as religiously very much important during different periods and were the capitals of ancient Kosala kingdom. The paper deals with the outcome of the exploration conducted between these two pilgrimage centers. Total 44 sites, 30 in Gonda district, 11 in Balrampur district and 3 in Sravasti district were located. These sites are associated with different cultural periods ranging from pre-NBP to late Medieval. Two routes are proposed from Ayodhya to Sravasti i.e. 1. via Nawabganj, Wazirganj, Gonda, Itiathok and Balrampur, 2. Nawabganj, Mankapur, Utraula and Balrampur. On the basis of the results of exploration, it is proposed that the first route was more popular during NBPW period. In later periods, both routes were used for travelling from Ayodhya to Sravasti.

Sarasvati was a gigantic river system that originated from Himalaya, entered the plains and flowed in southwesterly direction through present day Haryana, Punjab, Rajasthan and Gujarat before joining the Arabian sea. Ancient Civilization flourished along its banks and important cities flourished along this mighty river. It was a lifeline of northwestern and western India. Paper of Ratnesh Kumar Tripathi titled 'Saraswati Nadi ka Pravaah Tantra evam Teerth' deals with the river Saraswati and is divided in to two sections. The first section illustrates the water system of river Sraraswati from the Himalaya to the Gulf of Kachchh. The second section deals with the pilgrimage centers on the river Saraswati which were visited by lord Balrama, brother of lord Krishna.

The Vindhyan region of India is one of the oldest regions where remains of prehistoric settlements have been found. A large number of sites related with Mesolithic culture are reported from this region. These sites are located in either open areas or in the rock shelters. Excavation of some sites named Morahna Pahad, Bagahikhor, Lekhahia and Chopanimando have been carried out. Paper of Ramakant Singh titled 'Vindhya Kshetra kee Madhyapashanik Sanskriti me Jeevan Nirvaah ke Sakshya' is the review of subsistence pattern of Mesolithic culture of Vindhyan region on the basis of material evidence.

Paper of Santosh Kumar Singh titled 'Archaeology of Bhrigu Kshetra' is basically a report of excavation carried out at the ancient site Waina, located in Bhrighu ksetra (Ballia district of U.P.) on the confluence of rivers Ganga, *chhoti* Saryu and Magai. The site of Waina was excavated by Purushottam Singh of Banaras Hindu University in the nineties of last century. The first part of the paper comprises geographical scenario, water resources, historical background and archaeological scenario of the area. The second part of the paper comprises details of excavation carried out at the site. The site was first occupied for habitation during Neolithic period and was continued upto post Gupta period. The author has described important potteries and other antiquities in detail. He has also given details of structural, faunal, botanical and other important remains in his paper.

Saryupar region of middle Ganga plain is one of the most important regions where evidences of early farming have been found. Paper of Shitala Prasad Singh is based on the excavated remains of Neolithic culture of this region which titled 'Neolithic Culture of Saryupar Region'. He has provided details of all three excavated sites related to Neolithic named Sohgaura, Imlidih Khurd and Lahuradewa in his paper. Apart from Saryupar, he has also given a list of Neolithic sites in middle Ganga plain.

Paper of Neelesh K Pandey titled 'Evolution of early farming culture in middle Ganga plain' deals with the beginning of agriculture in middle Ganga plain. He has given details of crops identified during excavations at the sites of middle Ganga plain and their original habitats from where they probably transported to this region. He has divided the crops into three major groups on the basis of their origin i.e. Indian, Mediterranean and African.

Vineet Godhal's paper titled 'Palaeolithic Tools from Shekhawati Region: A Preliminary Study' is the study of explored sites and materials found by him during explorations in Shekhawati region of Rajasthan. He located 8 lower Palaeolithic [Sohanpura, Bheetaro, Reedh Ka Tila, Peer Baba Ki Bani (Badalwas), Udaipurwati (Kot), Salahadipura, Shobh (Chaneja Ki Dhani) and Gopalpura], 03 middle Palaeolithic [Bageshwar, Burja Ki Dhani, Laloda] and 01 upper Palaeolithic [Deoli Ki Dhani] sites in this region. He has also made the typological study of explored materials in his paper.

Paper of Shankar Jaikishan titled 'New Appearance of Beads in NBPW Culture in the Middle Ganga Plain' is based on the review of beads found during excavations from different NBPW sites of middle Ganga plain. He has given details of several sites of middle Ganga plain where excavations have been conducted and beads of different materials and shapes have been found. According to his paper some new materials like amethyst, basalt, coral, crystal, granite, lapis-lazuli, lime-stone, onyx, oyster, quartz, sardonyx, glass, ivory, paste, etc. were used for the first time for bead manufacturing during the NBPW period.

Last paper of this section titled 'Excavation at Peetnagar' by D K Mathur deals with the outcome of the excavation carried out at Peetnagar. The site is located on the left bank of the river Narmada in tehsil Badwaha of district Khargaon in Madhya Pradesh and the earliest level of the site is associated with the Ahar culture.

Section II - Epigraphy and Numismatics

It contains seven papers. T.P. Verma's paper titled 'A Study of Inscriptions: History and Administration' is a detailed work on the inscriptions. Inscriptions are considered as the most reliable source of Indian history. The earliest known inscriptions are found at the sites of Indus-Saraswati civilization but the script is still to be deciphered. Asoka's inscriptions are considered as the oldest inscriptions of India but some scholars claimed a pre-Asokan date for the inscriptions found at Sohgaura, Piprahwa and Mahasthan. Epigraphic records are classified into two groups: 1) those issued by the ruling authority, and 2) those issued by individuals or organizations. Being contemporary records these inscriptions provide welcome glimpses of social, religious, fiscal and administrative aspects which are otherwise unknown. The paper discussed important features of inscriptions like language, Prashastis, types of Raja-Shasana, process of writing on copperplate, etc. The paper also discussed the process of issuing land grants; offices and officers involved in this process; number of addressees in the copperplates, taxes, and many more related issues.

Rulers of Bhanja dynasty ruled over different parts of Orissa from the 5th-6th century onwards. Paper of G.C. Tripathi titled 'The Allahabad Museum Copperplate of Ranabhanjadeva-I' is based on the inscription of Ranabhanjadeva-I of the western Bhanja family who ruled in the second half of 10th century A.D. The paper is divided into two parts; the first is related with the history of Bhanjas while the second part is related with the copperplate grant. There are two copper plates and they contain total 23 lines; 12 on first and 11 on second. The inscription records the grant of a village by the king Ranabhanjadeva to a prominent Shivaite ascetic Shikhadeva for the purpose of establishing a monastery of his sect. The grant was issued in the 50th regnal year of the king and the inscription was written by Devachandra and was incised by Kulaputraka Divakara. According to the author this copper plate grant is a testimony to the fact that the Bhanja kings not only adopted Shaivaism as their personal and state religion but were also keen to propagate it throughout their empire by inviting learned Acharyas and scholars of Shaiva philosophy.

Paper of Arvind Kumar Singh titled 'Fragmentary Stone Inscription of the Kachchhapaghata Ratnapala: V.S. 1165' is a firsthand work on the inscription which was found at Gwalior fort and presently housed at Lucknow Museum, Lucknow. It consists of twenty-five lines and the language of the inscription is Sanskrit and the script is developed Nagari. The inscription is a eulogy and commences with the description of Krishna and Samkarshana followed by the description of the Kachchhapaghata rulers. The object of the present inscription is to record the construction of a temple of the Balarama on the top of the Gopa hill or Gwalior fort by Kulhana who was the 'lord of the entire army' and the 'chief minister' of the king. The last line of the inscription records that at the request of Ratnapala the *prashasti* was composed by Ananda who was the son of Manikantha. The date of the inscription is Samvat 1165 as given at the very end of the inscription. The paper also includes text of the inscription at the end.

Inscriptions are one of the very important sources of religious activities of the ancient India. Rajesh Kumar Dhar Dubey has tried to use the references of early medieval inscriptions for his paper titled 'The tradition of Shaiva Ascetics and their Significance'. References of Bilhari, Chirva, Abu, Achalesvara, Bheraghat and several other inscriptions are quoted by him in his paper which shows that the Shaiva sect was very popular in early medieval India and the Shaiva teachers and their pupils continued their tradition. They played very important role in society and politics of early medieval period. Some very learned teachers like Aghorshiva and Shrikumar composed many works related with Shaiva philosophy.

Seals and sealings are one of the most important antiquities recovered during excavations which provide information about the different aspects of the society/culture. The paper of D.P. Tewari titled 'Seals and Sealings from Sanchankot' is focused on the seals and sealings found during the excavations carried out by him in different field seasons at Sanchankot which is located on the Sai river in district Unnao of Uttar Pradesh. Most of the seals and sealings found from the site are associated with religious activities which throw sufficient light on the fact that Sanchankot was a great center of Shaivism.

The Greco-Bactrian king Demetrius I invaded India in the first quarter of second century BC and founded the Indo-Greek kingdom in northwestern part of Indian subcontinent. Near about 30 kings of this dynasty ruled and most of them are known only by their coins. The paper titled 'Hind-Yavana Shasakon kee Mudraon par ankit Gaja Prateek: Ek Vivechaṇ' by Vipula Dubey is the study of elephant symbols especially with Zeus on the coins of Indo-Greek rulers.

Paper of Vishi Upadhyay titled 'Stylistics of Kalachuri Coinage in Chhattisgarh' is the study of coins of Kalachuri dynasty who ruled between 10th and 13th century A.D. with their capital at Ratanpur in Chhattisgarh. These coins were minted on three metals- gold, silver and copper with higher and lower denominations with a large number of motifs i.e. deities (Lakṣmi, Viṣṇu, Hanumna), Fauna (Lion and elephant), mythical animals (Gajashardula) and few mint marks. She included study of metallurgy, metrology, script, artistic features, mint marks, etc. in her paper. She also used line drawings, tables, charts, etc. as supporting instruments.

Section III - Art, Iconography and Architecture

This section contains 13 papers. Paper of M.N.P. Tewari and Shanti Swaroop Sinha titled 'Invocation of Sarasvat Power in Jainism' is focused on the status of Saraswati in Jainism. Their study reveals that the worship and rendering of Sarasvati in Jaina tradition and art, popular from the Kushan period through the centuries, had the dynamics of rapid evolution from being the goddess of wisdom to the presiding goddess of music and fine-arts. She has been invoked mainly as benevolent goddess granting power of knowledge to the worshippers but in tantric invocation she has also been conceived in gruesome form with attributes like goad, noose and having such appellations as Kali, Kapalini, Kauli, Trilochana, etc. She was also given a status equal to the Jinas, as is evident from an image of Sarasvati from Deogarh depicting her with two Jinas on the same pedestal and in same composition and size.

Shaivism was the most popular sect between 9th and 12th century A.D. in the central India. Paramara king Bhoja was the great follower of Shiva. His two works named Samarangana Sutradhara and Tattva Prakash provides very useful information regarding philosophical as well as iconographical aspects of Shaivism. Shiva is called the upadana of all the elements. Paper of Sushmita Pande titled 'Śaivism of *Tattvaprakāśa* and Parallels in the Śaiva images in *Samarānganṇsūtradhāra*' is based on the study of these two important works of Bhoja.

The architectural remains of Jaina are found in the form of caves, stupas, viharas and temples. Diwakar P Tewari's paper titled 'Purva Madhyakaaleen Jaina Vastu me Bhed Abhed ke Tatva' is an analysis between the Jaina religion and the architecture related with the Jaina tradition.

Praveen Kumar Mishra's Paper Titled 'A Note on the Newly Discovered Brick Temple and It's Site at Pipri, District- Siddharthnagar, U.P.' provides a firsthand information of the exposed brick temple. The site of Pipri is a centrally protected site under the Archaeological Survey of India and yielded several small and large mounds. Scientific clearance work was initiated by the Lucknow Circle under the guidance of the author between December 2013 and February 2014 at one of the small mound. The exposed brick temple is a *pancha ratha* temple having three projections in each lateral side.

Yakshas have occupied an important place in Indian art and iconography through the ages. They were accepted within Buddhist, Jaina and Brahminical theology and assigned a subordinate status. The *Yaksha* sculptures are the earliest known anthropomorphic representation of any deity in stone in India and as such they have evoked considerable interest among scholars. Namrata Singh's paper on 'Yaksha Iconography' is the study of thematic variation in *Yaksha* iconography over space and time. She has grouped the *Yaksha* sculptures available from ancient India into four regional groups in accordance with the locations at which they have been found - Northern region, the Eastern region, the Western region and the Central region. She concluded in her paper that the most popular themes in *Yaksha* iconography have little correspondence with what the text tells us about the cult and it would be prudent if *Yaksha* iconography would be used as a source to study the *Yaksha* cult as well, instead of the sole reliance on textual sources and the *Yaksha* iconography also indicates that there were regional manifestations of the *Yaksha* cult at different places and time periods in ancient India.

Joint paper of Pooja Saxena and Apurva Sinha titled 'Depiction of Brahma's Life through the Vaishnava sculptures of Udayagiri caves, Vidisa: A Proportionate Blend of Iconography and Philosophy' is a deep study of iconography and literature. The Udaygiri caves at Vidisha are famous for the sculptures of Sheshshayee Vishnu and Varaha incarnation of Vishnu of Gupta period. The philosophical aspects of the iconography based on the puranic references have been explained by the authors in this paper.

Paper of Neetu Tiwari titled 'Sculptural Art of Trans-Ghaghara Region' is based on the primary and secondary sources. She has made explorations in district Deoria & Gorakhpur and taken references of sculptures found in this region. The region is located in the north-eastern part of the Uttar Pradesh covering 11 districts. After dealing the historical background and archaeological investigations carried out in this region, she discussed the concept and antiquity of image worship in India. She has incorporated several sculptures found in this region and related to the Maurya, Sunga, Kusana, Gupta, late Gupta and early Medieval periods.

Vinay Kumar's paper on 'Transmission of West Asian & Greco-Roman Elements in Indian Art' is the study of West Asian and Hellenistic elements which were adopted by the Indian Artisans with or without modifications during Mauryan, Sunga and Kusana periods. Beads are one of the important ornaments which are in use since ancient times.

The paper titled 'Khambhat me Ardhkeemti Patthar ke Manke banane kee Paramparik Takaneek' by Rajesh Kumar Meena is a documentation work of manufacturing technique of semiprecious stone beads presently under practice in Khambhat region of Gujarat.

Paper of Prabhakar Upadhyaya and Om Prakash Kumar titled 'Newly Discovered Painted Rock Shelters of Chandauli District, Uttar Pradesh' is focused on the painted rock shelters brought to light in course of explorations in southeastern parts of Chandauli district Uttar Pradesh and adjacent parts of Kaimur district, Bihar at Arjikalan, Nasopur, Kaurihar Khas, Ghurahupur, Tala, Tenui, in Chandauli district and at Diha, Basaha, Kharauli, Patesar and Ratanpurva in Kaimur district. The paintings executed in the rock shelters show superimpositions attempted by the artists right up to the historical period as clearly evinced by the subject matter of the paintings. The paintings depict day-to-day life-scenes of people. According to the authors, these paintings may be assignable to Upper Palaeolithc, Mesolithic, Chalcolithic and early historical periods.

Champaner and Pavagarh is located in the Godhara district of Gujarat and is a world heritage site. Antiquity of this place goes back to the prehistoric period. It was an important seat of Gujarat during the Medieval period and was came under the control of Kichchhi branch of Chahmaan Rajputs around 1300 AD. Later on, in 1484, it was conquered by the Mahmood Begda, the Sultan of Gujarat. Several Hindu, Jain and Muslim monuments are located at this place. Paper of Brajesh Chandra Rawat and Anupama Singh titled 'Champaner-Pavagarh ke Jaina Bavandheri Mandir ke Shwetambar Moortiyon kee Pahchan evam Vivechana' is focused on the documentation of Bavandheri temple which was constructed around 13th century AD. The paper illustrates nine sculptures which were identified by them.

Sachin Kumar Tiwary's paper titled 'Earliest Human Bronze images from Middle Ganga Plain and its Iconic Representation in the Rock art of Kaimur Region, India' is the study of similarities between the earliest bronze image of a male found from Chechar, Bihar during excavation and pictographs found in the Kaimur ranges.

Terracotta is considered as the most powerful and ancient mode for the artistic representation of human's emotion. Paper of Anantashutosh Dwivedi 'Brahmanical Figures on the Terracotta-Art of Bihar' is based on the terracotta having brahmanical figures over it found from the sites of Bihar. He has selected several specimens of terracotta in the form of seals, sealings and plaques found from the sites of Nalanda, Basarh, Bulandibagh and Chausa. He discussed the iconographic features of the brahmanical deities i.e. Brahma, Shiva, Ganesha, Ganeshini, Varaha, Narsimha, Duraga, Abhishek Lakshmi, Garuda, Chamunda, Harihara, Surya depicted on these terracotta remains along with Ramayana scenes. He has also included the inscriptional records engraved over these modes in his paper.

Section IV - Religion

Section IV contains 13 papers. S.R. Goyal's paper titled 'The Human Stratum of Rama Story' deals with the evolution of Ramayana. According to the author, the story of Ramayana acquired the shape of a Mahakavya in four stages. Its evolution began with the composition of stray gathas composed by unknown sutas who portray the character of Rama as a human hero and his story as a human story of a great king who has strength as well as weakness of a man. The final stage portrays Rama as an incarnation of Vishnu and a sole object of devotion. The paper also deals with several other aspects of Ramayana i.e. Dasaratha's promise of bride's price, two boons of Kaikeyi, nomination of the successor by Dasaratha, Rama's relation with his brothers. The outcome of the paper shows that Rama had no legitimate claim to the throne of Ayodhya and the atmosphere of the royal family of Ayodhya was full of factional intrigues, suspicion and hatred even before the question of Dasharatha's successor arose. Apparently Rama and Bharata both had a purely pragmatic approach to this problem.

Shashi Tiwari's paper on 'The Four Varnas: A Vedic concept of division of Society' throws light on the Vedic concept of four *Varna*. According to her the idea of classification of society into four groups is originally of Vedic Seers having intention to highlight inner quality based work- structure in the society. Nothing like caste was determined by birth. Duties of a person appear to have been based on activities rather than heredity. Undoubtedly it may be assumed that later developed caste system has its root in the *Varna* system of Vedic period.

The ancient Indian social life was divided into four stages termed as *Ashrama dharama* namely *Brahmacharya Ashrama, Grahastha Ashrama, Vanaprastha Ashrama* and *Sanyasa Ashrama*. The paper titled 'A Note on the origin of the Ashrama Institution' by Rajawant Rao shows that the scheme of the four Ashrama of life originated in eastern region during the post-Vedic period as a result of the conflict and comingle of the Shramana and Brahmana traditions. According to the author a clear reference to the of the Ashrama system is found in Jabalopanishad, which describes in sequence the four stages of an individuals' life, i.e., Brahmacharya, Grihastha, Vanaprastha and Sanyasa and the Jabalopanishad is definitely post-Buddhist.

The paper of Shankar Goyal titled 'The Nayanars and Aalvars and Their Contribution to the Bhakti Movement in South India' is based on the works of Nayanars and Aalvars for the revival and development of Vaisnava and Shaiva sect in South India. In South India till about the fifth century A.D. harmony and tolerance characterized the relations between the different religious sects. But thereafter a great change came about particularly in the Tamil region and people began to entertain fears of the whole land being converted to Jainism and Buddhism. Devotees of Vishnu and Shiva under the leadership of saints called the Alavars (Vaishnavas) and Nayanars (Shaivas) began to traverse the country through their ways. Sun worship has a very long tradition. The primitive men witnessed the miraculous power of Sun as the chief source of light, warmth and fertility. Its unique qualities aroused a deep sense of reverential emotions in the minds of primitive people.

The paper titled 'The Living Saura Tradition of Gujarat' by Atul Tripathi is the study of Sun worship in Gujarat. Gujarat lies closer to the area where the artistic activity of the *Saura* sect had first started and the region is still in possession of a sufficient number of sun temples roughly ranging from the 8th century to the 12th century CE presenting almost a continuous artistic, iconographic and architectural development for five centuries. Saurașhțra was an epicenter of the sun worshippers. In the Puranas and other religious texts Surya is shown attached to this region as his wife Sanjana Devi (locally known as Ravi Randal Devi or Ranna Devi) and father-in-law Vishwakarma were from the Prabhas Patan. The artisans and craftsmen of the region who consider themselves the descendants of Vishwakarma recognize her as their *phoi* (aunt). In any auspicious occasion they worship her and the folklore related to her marriage and married life having Vedic and Puranic backgrounds are parts of their cultural life. Many legends were also added and adopted by the society which later became part of the rituals and other ceremonies. The paper discusses in detail of those living Saura traditions which are part of the Ravi Randal worship and also of Saura festival Uttarayaṇa and focuses on the social persuasion and developments in this regard.

Paper of Ishwar Sharan Vishwakarma titled 'Ikshvaku Parampara evam Sanskriti' is focused especially on the tradition and culture of Iksvaku dynasty of Ayodhya. Although the other branches of this dynasty ruled over the Mithila and South Kosala. The genealogy of the Iksavakus of Ayodhya begins from Manu Vaivasvata. Iksavāku was the second, Mandhata was ninetieth, Purukutsa was twentieth and Dasaratha was sixtieth king of this race. The famous Iksavaku king Rama appears in the 61st generation while Vrihadabala of the same dynasty, who fought against the *Pandavas* in the Mahabharata war, was the 76th king. Sumitra was the last king of the Kosalan Empire.

Ramcharitmanas by Tulsidas is an epic dedicated to the life of lord Rama. It consists seven kands namely Bal, Ayodhya, Aranya, Kishkindha, Sundar, Lanka and Uttar Kand. Paper of Sanchita Sharma titled 'Ramcharitmanas ka Dharmashastriya Adhyayan' explains the role of Ramacharitamanasa in the society as a Dharma Shahstra.

Rekha Chaturvedi's paper titled 'Athena Pallas: The Greek Goddess' deals with the character of Athena who was the goddess of wisdom, war, polity and industrial art, etc. Athena Pallas is mostly shown on the coins Parthian king Andragoras, Apollodotus II, Menander, Dionysius, Zoilus, Apollophanes, Amyntas, Ranjabala, Azes, Azilises, Spalhores with Vinones, Spalagadames, Gondophares and Demitrious II. Author has given details of legends of Athena's origin, her attributes, epithets and her status among the goddesses. She also compared Athena with the Indian deity Saraswati in her paper.

Deepawali is an important festival which is celebrated on the Kartika amavasya every year. Paper of R.C. Tripathi 'Deepaawali: Celebrations & A Message' is focused on the celebration of Deepawali which is associated with the victorious return of Lord Rama and with the Nirvana of the Jaina thirankar, Sri Mahavira. Deepawali is a full five-day long festival, each day having specific worship and rituals. For this reason, it is also called "Pancha-raatra" mahotsava or celebrations and each of the five days has traditional / Puranic stories linked to its significance.

The Rigveda is the oldest in four Vedas and is a collection of 1017 hymns and about 10600 verses, organized in ten mandalas. Paper of Digvijayanath titled 'Rigveda me Manava aur Manviaya Moolya' is focused on the various aspects of human and human values in the Rigveda.

Paper titled 'The Concept of Mandal in Tantric Form of Mahayan Buddhism' by Kamlesh Kumar Gautam describes the origin and development of mandal in Buddhism which represents panch dhyani Buddhas named Vajrasattava in center, Vairocana in east, Ratnasambhava in south, Amitabh in west and Amoghsiddhi in north side. The intermediate directions are symbolized by four goddesses named Lochana, Mamaki, Pandaravasini and Tarini. Each goddesses represents one of the four elements – earth, water, fire, air respectively. Paanchraatra Aagam is one of the oldest sects of Vaishnavism.

Paper of R.P. Mishra titled 'Paanchratra Aagam me Vaishnavi Deeksha' is the focused on the different aspects of Deeksha or initiation mentioned in the various literatures of this sect.

Paper of Dhyanendra Narayan Dubey titled 'Panchratra Samhitaon me Nr-Singh ka Swaroop' is focused on the various types of worship of God Nr-Singh as mentioned in various Samhitas i.e. Sanatkumar, Jayakhya, Saatvat, Ishwar, etc. Lord Vishnu had taken his fourth incarnation as Nr-Singh to kill the demon Hiranyakshipu who was the father of Prahlad, a great devotee of him.

Section V - Historiography

Section V titled 'Historiography' contains 6 papers. 'Purush, Puran and Itihas: History and Spiritual Understanding' by Ramashray Roy is focused on historiography which can be broadly divided into two categories: secular and sacred. Sacred history belongs to the type of symbolic speculation that found its culmination not only in the Old Bible and writers such as Saint Augustine, Joachim of Fiora and others who used Christian symbolism in constructing the history of the world. It is also reflected in ancient historical writings, especially the *Puranas*. The purpose of the *Puranas* is not simply to describe in a neutral way what really happened in the mist of time but also to evoke in the people the need for adopting the most appropriate mode of living an exemplary life in conformity with the spirit of what had happened. History has three very distinct but important stages which can be symbolically identified as *Purusha, Purana and itihas.* These three symbols constitute the essence of history as the mode of describing man's participation in the flux of divine reality. Aim of the paper is to revive the link between *Purusha, Purana and Itihas* not only for apprehending reality better and presenting a realistic and holistic account of it but also for making man aware of his proper place in the cosmos so that he may not be affected by *pleonexisa* or *hybris*.

U.P. Arora's paper titled 'The Account of Nearchos' Voyage: An Appraisal' is a detailed exploration of references of Nearchos' expedition from the mouth of the Indus to the head of the Persian gulf available in different literary sources i.e. Arrian's *Indika*, and *Anabasis*, Strabo's *Geography* and Pliny's *Natural History*, etc. Nearchos was the admiral of Alexander's army who was selected by him for this expedition. Nearchos has given a long list of places on the coast lines, races, the number of stades sailed each day, the navigational facilities, climatic condition and some hints on the maritime trade. According to the literary records, he was deputed not to navigate the ocean, but to investigate the coast lying on the ocean, and the inhabitants of the coast, and its anchorages, and its water supplies, and the manners and customs of the inhabitants and what part of the coast was fertile, and what part was not.

Lalitaditya Muktapida was the ruler of Karkota dynasty of Kashmir who ruled between 724 and 760 A.D. Owing to his remarkable achievements, Lalitaditya became a halo of popular stories in the tradition of Kashmir. The paper of J N Pandey titled 'Lalitaditya Muktapida: The First Indian Antiquary' is focused on one of these stories mention by Kalhan in his work Rajatarangini regarding the king's initiative to expose two temples.

Murli Manohar Pathak's paper 'Veda-Vyakhya ke Nairukt Prasthan me Itihas kee Bhumika' deals with the knowledge of history to describe the verses of Vedas. To know the real meaning and pure pronunciation of Vedas, Vedangs were created. Shiksha, Kalpa, Vyakarana, Nirukta, Chhandas and Jyotisha are six Vedangas and out of these Nirukta is most important. To know the fundamental meaning of Vedas knowledge of Nirukta is necessary. It is also important to know the history and historical events to describe the verses of Vedas.

Kuar Bahadur Kaushik's paper 'Yunani Itihas Darshan: Ek Sarvekshan' and Ajay Kumar Pandey's paper 'Bhartiya Itihas ki Sanatan Parampara' deals with the Greek Historiography and Indian Historiography respectively.

Section VI - General

This section contains 14 papers on various aspects. India is a country of values and customs and these are continuing in the society since very ancient times. In other words, the past continues and lives into the present. The paper titled 'Ancient Indian Ideals and Modern Realities' by K.

Paddayya aim to explore certain dimensions of this connectedness or relationship between the past and the present.

The paper of Mohan Gupta titled 'The Indo-European Problem: A New Paradigm, A Complete Re-look' is a wonderful paper which is focused on the origin and mainland of the Aryans and traces the facts on the basis of four lanes viz. 1. Archaeology, 2. Archaeo-astronomy, 3. Cosmology and cosmogony, Linguistic paleontology, theology etc. and 4. the literary history, starting from Rigveda down to the Mahabharata. He concluded in his paper that the Vedic period extends from 9th millennium B.C. to 2000 B.C. and the Sapta Sindhu or the Brahmavarta is the homeland of Proto-Indo-European language and this language is none other than the Proto-Vedic Sanskrit. The Aryan migration or Aryan invasion theory is completely baseless. There is no indication in the entire vast Indian literature of any foreign origin or any reminiscence of a foreign land. The ancient Rigvedic Aryans in 7th, 4th and 2nd millennium B.C. were the carriers of Proto Vedic Sanskrit in the distant lands of Crete, Greece, Anatolia, Sumer, Egypt and Babylonia because they ruled these countries during various periods.

The paper titled 'A Cultural-Psychological Orientation to Self-Understanding' by Girishwar Misra is focused on the thoughts on the notion of selfhood. The notion of self may be characterized as a multifaceted, dynamic system that emerges in socio-cultural processes and subsequently regulates and mediates behavior at individual and group levels. It acts as an anchor and affords and constraints our behavior, perceptions, feelings, values and meanings held by the people.

DNA is the chemical basis of life for all living organisms, including humans. It is the blue-print of life, growth and differentiation as the information stored in its sequence is specific to every organism. Ram Rudra Shukla's paper titled 'A study of human evolution and migration on the basis of analysis of Deoxyribonucleic acid (DNA)' is based on the review of molecular biology methods used in predicting human evolution and migration.

Krishnanand Sinha's paper titled 'On Our History, Our Traditions and Astronomy' is focused on the astronomical facts recorded in ancient texts to establish our tradition. On the basis of astronomical references available in Valmiki Ramayana, dates related with the important events of lord Ram's life have been calculated by different scholars.

Ganesh Shankar Vidyarthi was born on 26 October 1890 and was assassinated on 25 March, 1931 in the wake of the Kanpur riot. He was a dedicated and prominent Congress leader, and one of the leading literary figures of India. Ganesh Shankar Vidyarthi was associated with the 'Pratap' newspaper. He wrote extensively against communal frenzy. The article of P K Shukla titled 'Ganesh Shankar Vidyarthi and His Crusade Against Communalism (1915-1931)' is based on Ganesh Shankar Vidyarthi's writings which discusses his crusade against the rising tide of communalism, and also focuses on his perception of India as nation, his concern for the distortions of India's past history in the writings of the imperialist historians.

Tradition of theatre is a very old practice in India. Bharata Muni is regarded as the preceptor of Drama and Theatre (Natya). His work Natyashastra is an encyclopaedic compendium of ancient Indian Theatre. Paper of Kamaleshdutta Tripathi titled 'The Aesthetics of Sanskrit Theatre and the Structure of Sanskrit Drama' deals with the practice of Sanskrit theatre in India.

Several capital cities and urban centers were established during the Medieval period in Karnataka. The paper of S.K. Aruni titled 'Shorapur: A Palace City of Late-Medieval Southern Deccan' is focused on the setup of the city of Shorapur located in the present day district of Yadgir in Karnataka. The city was founded by Raja Pid Nayaka-II around 1710 who divided the city into 14 quarters and assigned them to various classes of the society. The paper presents the details of the fort, palaces, temples, space arrangement of city, etc.

Water is one of the essential elements for the existence and no one can survive without it. Pragya Chaturvedi's paper on 'Water resources and their management in Ancient India' presents a variety of data for water and water resources in ancient India. She used literary references like Rigveda, Atharvaveda, Mahabhasya, Arthashastra, etc. and archaeological evidences from different sites and periods for water, water resources and water management for her paper and shown that these evidences reflect the ingenuity and wisdom of our ancestors who made water and its management an integral part of the native culture and community life. This water-wisdom at all levels of society ensured adequate availability of water for all, which in turn, formed the basis of all-round development and prosperity.

Lumbini is considered as one of the great centers of Buddhism as lord Buddha was born here. It is located in the Rupandei district of Nepal near the Indo-Nepal border. The paper of Gitu Giri titled 'Lumbini: The Birth Place of Lord Buddha' presents a wide range of information regarding Lumbini and its importance. The site was visited by King Asoka in his 20th year of kingship and an inscribed stone pillar was installed here. A large number of artifacts of the Mauryan, Sunga, Kushana and Gupta periods were recovered in course of various excavations. Due to its outstanding universal value it was inscribed in the World Heritage list in the year 1997.

Rajesh Mishra pointed out the importance of Allahabad (Prayaga) and its association with the sage Bharadwaja in his paper titled 'Prayaga and Bharadwaja'. Greatness of Prayaga is mentioned in various Indian texts i.e. Vedas, Brahmans, Epics, Puranas, etc. Bharadwaja was a great sage who lived on the bank of river Ganga at Prayaga. An archaeological site named Bharadwaj Ashrama is located in Allahabad city. Before the establishment of a city called Allāhabad by the Akbar in 1575 AD, Prayaga was known as a great religious center.

Maps are temporal frozen frame that are devoid of dynamic landscape processes but they do reveal themselves as a site of theater where ethnocentricity, racism and other biases play. The recent trends in the historiography of cartography are a step away from writing cartobibliography and viewing maps as simplistic representation of space. Paper of Deepak Kumar and Ravindra Kumar titled 'Power of Imagination: Representation of India in European Cartography' is an attempt to explore history of cartography in India to study maps and marginalia constructed by Europeans reflecting Imperial agendas, social stereotypes and other biases.

Paper of Sangeeta Singh titled 'Poorva Vedic Kaal me Mahilaon ki Sthiti: Ek Aitihasik Vimarsh' is focused on the role and condition of ladies during the early Vedic age as cited in the Vedic literatures i.e. Vedas, Upanishadas, Brahmanas, etc. During this period male and female have the same status and rights in the family and the society.

Praveen Kumar Sharma's paper titled 'Banking in Ancient India' describes the role of temples as banking centers in ancient India. The religious centers like temples were safe places for the protection of money and other valuable things. The temples in ancient India used to give loans to various customers from its own treasury with the stipulation that the fixed interest on the loan should be paid regularly into the treasury of the temple. The paper also discussed the terms and conditions of the loans which were disbursed by the temples.

Acknowledgement

We are thankful to all the contributors for their papers and tributes. We are also thankful to Dr. Agam Prasad of Agam Kala Prakashan, Delhi who has taken keen interest in the publication of this volume.

Bibliographical Sketch

Prof. Daya Nath Tripathi is one of those renowned academicians who don't need any introduction. His vast academic and research experience in the field of Archaeology and Ancient History shows his excellence, love and affection for the subject. He was born on 13th June 1938 as the eldest son of Smt. Krishna Devi and Pandit Ram Kishor Sharma of Jairam Purwa located in the Meja tehsil of district Allahabad (U.P.). He completed his primary education at Modern School, Allahabad and passed High School from Seva Samiti Vidya Mandir, Allahabad. After passing Intermediate from Government Inter College, Allahabad, he joined Allahabad University for Graduation. He has completed his Post Graduation from the department of Ancient History, Culture & Archaeology, Allahabad University, Allahabad in the year 1958. At the age of 19 year, he was married to Smt. Leela Tripathi. He joined Ancient History department of Gorakhpur University, Gorakhpur as Lecturer in 1958. He was promoted as Reader in the year 1979 and as Professor in the year 1989. Professor Tripathi has taken the charge of Head of the Department in the year 1994 and was retired from University in 1998. He received a lot of love and respect from teachers, students, administrative officers and employees during his about 40 years long teaching carrier. In addition, he possessed administrative responsibilities of Chief Proctor (1980-84) and Director of Rahul Peetha (1994-98) in the same University.

During his service at Gorakhpur University, he also served as the General Secretary of Gorakhpur University Teachers' Association between 1961 and 1964; Hon. Bn. Comdt. of U.P. Home Guards between 1963 and 1970; President of Gorakhpur University Teachers' Association between 1977 and 1979; Chief Proctor and Special Executive Magistrate of Gorakhpur University between 1980 and 1983; General Secretary of Federation of U.P. Residential Universities Teachers' Association, between 1985 and 1987 and President of Federation of U.P. Residential Universities Teachers' Association during 1987 and 1989. He was also deputed as the authorized Controller of Kishan Post Graduate College, Basti, U.P. in 1994 and continued till 1998.

Professor Tripathi has been awarded Greek Government Scholarship (1971-74), British Council Scholar (1974-76) and Studentship of British School of Archaeology at Athens, Rome, Ankara and Tehran (1971-76) and received Diploma in Greek language from Athens University in 1972 and awarded Ph.D. in 1976 by Southampton University (U.K.) under the guidance of Lord Colin Renfrew for his masterly work titled 'Bronze work of Greece'.

He has participated in the excavation at Kaushambi under the direction of Professor G.R. Sharma during his post graduation in 1957-58; at Sohgaura, an important Neolithic site, under the supervision of Prof. S.N. Chaturvedi between 1961 & 63; at Ahar, a well known Chalcolithic site of Rajasthan, under the supervision of late Prof. H.D. Sankalia in 1963-64. He was the co-director of excavation at Fazilnagar, district Kushinagar and was the director of excavation at Usmanpur Dih both in district Kushinagar. The first site was excavated in 1978-79 and the later was in 1997-98. Apart from the above, Prof. Tripathi was involved in finding new archaeological sites and between 1994 and 1998 more than 200 sites were explored by him in Gorakhpur division, located in Saryupar region. Apart from India, he has contributed in the excavations at Meneleon under the supervision of Dr. H.W. Catling, Director, British School at Athens in the year 1973-74 and at Pylos under supervision of Prof. G.S. Korres of Athens University in the year 1974-75. The above sites are located near Sparta in Greece.

Professor Tripathi received the chance to study the copper and bronze objects of the Aegean World kept in the museums of the Mainland Greece, The Cyclades, Dodecanese and Crete between 1971 and 1974. He also studied all the Pre and Protohistoric materials in the museums of Yugoslavia (Belgrade), France (Louvre), Germany (Munich, Bonn and Frankfurt), Italy (Rome), U.K. (Ashmolean, Cambridge, Southampton and London (British Museum), Egypt (Cairo), Turkey (Istambul and Ankara), and Iran (Tehran) between 1975 and 1977.

After his retirement from Gorakhpur University, he was the visiting Professor in Allahabad University in 1998-99, fellow of Indian Institute of Advance Study, Shimla between 1999 and 2002, visiting Professor at British Academy, London, U.K. in 2003. He was appointed a member of Indian Council of Historical Research (ICHR), New Delhi in 1998 and continued till 2004. In the year 2004 he was appointed as the Chairman of the same institution and completed his tenure in 2007. He was the member of cultural delegation of ICCR, Government of India to Indo-Greek festival in 1988; ICHR delegate to XXXVIth ICAANAS conference at Canada in 2000 and ICHR delegate to XIVth UISPP conference at Liege (Belgium) in 2001.

During his vast academic carrier Professor Tripathi completed several major research projects, attended and organized National and International conferences, chaired more than 50 academic sessions in National and International seminars held in India and abroad, delivered academic lectures in India and abroad and reviewed books. He has published several books and more than 50 research papers in prestigious National and International Journals and Felicitation volumes. 'Archaeology and Tradition' of University Grant Commission, New Delhi; 'Archaeolinguistics' of Indian Council of Historical Research, New Delhi; 'Hinduism & Hellenism' of Indian Institute of Advance Study, Shimla are the numerous projects which have been completed by him. More than half dozen students have received Doctorate and D.Litt. degree under his supervision.

Prof. Tripathi is a life member of Indian Society for Greeco-Roman Studies, Indian Archaeological Society, Indian History & Culture Society and Indian Society for Prehistoric & Quaternary studies. He is holding post of member of Madhya Pradesh Heritage Development Council, Bhopal and Allahabad Museum Society and its Governing Council, Allahabad at present.

Professor Tripathi has two daughters and two sons. The eldest daughter Smt. Aparna Shukla is a housewife and residing in Virginia, USA with her husband Dr. Ram Rudra Shukla. His second daughter Dr. Anjula Shukla is married to Shri Ashok Shuka and working as Associate Professor in B.Ed. Department of Buddha P. G. College, Kushinagar, U.P.. Dr. Umesh Nath Tripathi is the eldest son and working in the Department of Chemistry, DDU Gorakhpur University as Associate Professor and is married to Smt. Usha Tripathi. Dr. Devesh Nath Tripathi is working in the Defence Institute of Psychological Research, New Delhi as Scientist and is married to Smt. Jyoti Tripathi. Professor Daya Nath Tripathi is residing in Gorakhpur with his wife at present.

Books by Professor Tripathi

1. 2013. *India and Central Asia*- Indo-Russian Seminar Proceedings, ICHR & Aryan Books International, New Delhi.
2. 2012. *A Golden Chain of Civilizations: Indic, Iranic, Semitic and Hellenic from c. 600 BC to A.D. 600,* Vol. 1, Part 5 of the PHISPC, New Delhi.
3. 2007. *A Golden Chain of Civilizations: Indic, Iranic, Semitic and Hellenic up to c. 600 BC,* Vol. 1, Part 4 of the PHISPC, New Delhi.
4. 2005. *A Discourse on Indo European Languages and Culture*, ICHR, New Delhi.

5. 2004. *Hinduism and Hellenism,* Indian Institute of Advanced Study, Shimla.
6. 1996. *Cultural Interactions Between India and Greece,* K.P. Jayaswal Research Institute, Patna.
7. 1994. *Puratattva Paribhasha Kosha,* CSTT, Ministry of HRD, Govt. of India.
8. 1988. *Archaeology and Tradition,* Ramanand Prakashan, Delhi.
9. 1987. *Bronzework of Mainland Greece from 2600BC to 1450 BC*., Studies in Mediterranean Art Archaeology Series, Vol.69, Gottenburg University, Sweden.
10. *Rock Art of India and France*, Indo-French Seminar Proceedings, ICHR, New Delhi (In Press)

Published Articles of Professor Tripathi

1. 2015. "Art and Religion" in *Early India: Historical Probings*, S.R. Goyal Felicitation volume, Kusumanjali Prakashan, Jodhpur, pp. 1-7.
2. 2015. "Foreword" in *Mani-Sushma: Archaeology and Heritage*, Felicitation volume of Dr. B. R. Mani, B.R. Publishing Corporation, Delhi.
3. 2015. Tribute to Prof. V.S. Pathak in *Probings into Indian Culture: Prof. Pathak as a Historian*, Pratibha Prakashan, Delhi.
4. 2015. A Tribute to my friend Ramesh Chandra Tripathi in *Indian Culture and Art: Continuty and Change* (Shri R C Tripathi Felicitation Volume), pp. xvii-xx, Swati Publication, Delhi.
5. 2015. "Trading during the Prehistoric and Protohistoric periods: Perspectives from the Ancient Civilizations" in *Man and Environment Vol. XL(1)*, pp.94-104.
6. 2014. "Rewriting History: Archaeology and Tradition" in *Prachyabodha: Indian Archaeology and Tradition (Professor T.P. Verma Festschrift)*, B.R. Publishing Corporation, Delhi.
7. 2014. "Indian Archaeology and Tradition: A Historical Perspective" in *Itihas Darpana,* Vol.XIX (2), pp.209-217.
8. 2014. "Ethics & Civilization" in *Aitihya,* Journal of Ancient History, Culture & Archeology vol-5, pp.42-63 edited by A.K. Sinha, Anamika Publishers & Distributers Private Limited, Delhi.
9. 2014. "Art and Religion" in *Kala evam Purushartha*, Allahabad Museum, Allahabad.
10. 2013. "Preface" in *India, Central Asia and Russia: Three Millennia of Contacts*, ICHR and Aryan Books International, New Delhi.
11. 2013. "India and Western Asian Cultural Contacts" in *Itihas Darpana,* Vol. XVIII (2), pp.267-286.
12. 2013. "Dimensions of Indian Art, Heritage and Contributions of Buddhism" in History of Science, Philosophy and Culture in Indian Civilization, vol. VII, part 9 entitled *Buddhism*, Ed. by G.C. Pande, PHISPC, Centre of Studies in Civilization, New Delhi, pp. 791-818.
13. 2013. "Dimensions of Indian Art Heritage and Contributions of Jainism" in History of Science, Philosophy and Culture in Indian Civilization, Vol. VII, part 4 entitled *Jainism* edited by G.C. Pande, PHISPC, Centre of Studies in Civilization, New Delhi, pp. 503-36.
14. 2013. "Central Asia and Indo-Aryans" in *India, Central Asia and Russia: Three Millennia of Contacts*, ICHR and Aryan Books International, New Delhi.
15. 2013. "Archaeology and the date of Buddha" in History of Science, Philosophy and Culture in Indian Civilization, vol. VII, part 9 entitled *Buddhism*, Ed. by G.C. Pande, PHISPC, Centre of Studies in Civilization, New Delhi, pp. 3-40.
16. 2012. "Itihaas Lekhan me Greek-Roman Parampara" in *Itihaas Lekhan ki Vibhinn Drishtiyan*, ed. by P.K. Shukla, Granth Shilpi, Delhi, pp. 46-84.

17. 2012. "Brahman Samaj: Kal, Aaj aur Kal" in *Sarayu Chetana*, ed. by Harish Mishra, Noida, pp. 65-69.
18. 2011. "Philosophy of History and Indian Historiography" in *Bharti*, vol. 35, Bulletin of the Department of Ancient Indian History, Culture & Archaeology, B.H.U., Varanasi, pp. 1-16.
19. 2011. "Cultural Interaction between South India and South East Asia" in *Aitihya,* Journal of Ancient History, Culture& Archeology , Vol.2, pp.37-64 edited by A.K. Sinha, Anamika publishers &distributers private limited, Delhi.
20. 2010. Presidential Address entitled "Vedic Roots of Hinduism and Hellenism" published in the souvenir of the National Seminar on '*Vedic Foundations of Indian and Hellenic Cultures*' held at Maharshi Panini Sanskrit Vishwavidyalaya, Ujjain, on 16-18 August, 2010.
21. 2009. "Vedic Roots of Hinduism and Hellenism" in *Vikramshila Journal of Social Sciences*, vol. 6, no. 2, ed. by Panchanand Mishra, Vikramshila Research Institute, Bhagalpur, pp. 5-52.
22. 2009. "History and Historiography: Some issues" in *Approaches to History, Culture, Art Archeology: Essays in honour of Prof Om Prakash* edited by A K sinha, pp.61-78, Anamika Publishers & Distributer Private Limited, Delhi.
23. 2008. "Greeco-Roman Historiography and Writing of Ancient Indian History" in *Papers from the Aligarh Historian Society*, ed. by Irfan Habib.
24. 2007. "Trail of Proto-Indi-Europeans: Archaeological Evidence" in History of Science, Philosophy and Culture in Indian Civilization, Vol. I, part 4 entitled *A Golden Chain of Civilizations: Indic, Iranic, Semitic and Hellenic up to 600 B.C.* edited by G.C. Pande & D.N. Tripathi, PHISPC, Centre of Studies in Civilization, New Delhi, pp. 3-28.
25. 2007. "The Problem of the Aryan People and their Language" in History of Science, Philosophy and Culture in Indian Civilization, Vol. I, part 4 entitled *A Golden Chain of Civilizations: Indic, Iranic, Semitic and Hellenic up to 600 B.C.* edited by G.C. Pande & D.N. Tripathi, PHISPC, Centre of Studies in Civilization, New Delhi, pp. 29-65.
26. 2007. "Cosmogonic Myths of Indo-Europeans" in History of Science, Philosophy and Culture in Indian Civilization, Vol. I, part 4 entitled *A Golden Chain of Civilizations: Indic, Iranic, Semitic and Hellenic up to 600 B.C.* edited by G.C. Pande & D.N. Tripathi, PHISPC, Centre of Studies in Civilization, New Delhi, pp. 477-98.
27. 2007. "1857 ka Itihaas Vimarsh" in *Anbhai Sancha (Shaitya aur Sanskriti ki Traimasik Patrika)*, ed. by Dwarika Prasad Charumitra, Rohini, Delhi, pp. 49-57.
28. 2006. "Cellular Jail in Freedom Struggle" in Newsletter, vol.6, no.1 Indian Council of Historical Research, New Delhi, pp. 1-2.
29. 2005. "The Indo-European Homeland: An Indian Perspective" in *A Discourse on Indo-European Languages and Culture*, edited by D.N. Tripathi, ICHR & Manak Publications Pvt. Ltd., Delhi, pp. 21-41.
30. 2005. "Editorial" in *A Discourse on Indo-European Languages and Culture*, edited by D.N. Tripathi, ICHR & Manak Publications Pvt. Ltd., Delhi, pp. 1-20.
31. 2004. "The Concept of Man and Hinduism" in Tripathi, D.N. *Hellenism and Hinduism*, Indian Institute of Advance Study, Rashtrapati Nivas, Shimla, pp. 14-40.
32. 2004. "Origin and Evolution of Indo-European Languages" in Tripathi, D.N. *Hellenism and Hinduism*, Indian Institute of Advance Study, Rashtrapati Nivas, Shimla, pp. 14-40.
33. 2004. "Indian and Western sian Cultural Contacts" in *Studies in Humanities and Social Sciences*, vol. XI, no. 1, ed. by. R.N. Misra, IIAS, Shimla, pp. 1-28.
34. 2004. "Hellenism and Hinduism: An Archaeological and Historical Study" in Tripathi, D.N. *Hellenism and Hinduism*, Indian Institute of Advance Study, Rashtrapati Nivas, Shimla, pp. 1-13.

35. 2004. "Cosmogony and Cosmology" in Tripathi, D.N. *Hellenism and Hinduism*, Indian Institute of Advance Study, Rashtrapati Nivas, Shimla, pp. 41-81.
36. 2004. "Concept of Justice, Social Justice and Ethics" in Tripathi, D.N. *Hellenism and Hinduism*, Indian Institute of Advance Study, Rashtrapati Nivas, Shimla, pp. 82-110.
37. 2000. "New Archaeology and Vedic Cosmogony" in Man and Environment, vol. XXV (1), Journal of Indian Society for Prehistoric and Quaternary Studies, Pune, pp. 1-17.
38. 1998. "Saraswat Samskriti ki Puratatvika Anveshna" in *Facets of Indian Culture, Gustav Roth Felicitation Volume*, Bihar Puravid Parishad, Patna (India), pp.526-53.
39. 1994. "Pit-Dwellings: An Archaeological and Literary Study", Proceedings of the National Seminar on '*Rural Life and Folk Culture in Ancient India*', Department of Ancient History, Archaeology and Culture, Allahabad University, Allahabad, February, 1994.
40. 1994. "Emergence of Bhakti Cult and Indian Society" in the Proceedings of the National Seminar on '*The Bhakti-Cult and Indian Society through Ages*' at BHU, Varanasi, 7-9 April, 1994.
41. 1994. "Diffusion Vs. Evolution" in the Proceedings of the National Seminar on '*Models in Archaeology*', Allahabad Museum, Allahabad, 13 March, 1994.
42. 1994. "Chalcolithic Cultures and Indo-Aryan Problem", Proceedings of the National Seminar at Patna Museum, Patna, 14-15 May, 1994.
43. 1993. "Trade and Urban Centres", Proceedings of the National Seminar, BHU, Varanasi, 1 March, 1993.
44. 1993. "*Place names of Western Asia*" in the Felicitation Volume of Prof. V.S.Pathak, Gorakhpur University.
45. 1993. "*Metallurgy and the Emergence of Aegean Civilization*", Commemorative Volume of the Greek Pundit Galanos, Department of Ancient History, Culture and Archaeology, MJP Rhilkhand University, Bareilly.
46. 1993. "Indo-European Goddesses and Gods and the Indo-European Problem" in the National Seminar of Bharatiya Itihas Samskriti Sankalan Yojana on '*Dating in Archaeology*' at Mysore, 19-21 December,1993.
47. 1993. "Historical Geography of Madhyadesa", Proceedings of the National Seminar, Allahabad Museum, Allahabad, 22 March, 1993.
48. 1993. "Evolution of Symbols in Ancient Indian Art Tradition" Proceedings of the National Seminar , Allahabad Museum, Allahabad, 25-26 Feb. 1993.
49. 1992. Presidential Address on "History, Archaeology and Ecology", Proceedings of the National Seminar on the same subject held at HRPG College, Khalilabad, Sant Kabir Nagar (U.P.), 20 Nov. 1992.
50. 1992. "*Vedic Vajra*" in the Felicitation Volume of Prof. G.C. Pande, Allahabad University, Allahabad.
51. 1992. "*Archaeology and Tradition*" in the Felicitation Volume of Prof. Lallanlji Gopal, BHU, Varanasi.
52. 1991. "Swami Ramtirtha: His Socio-Cultural Contributions", Proceedings of the National Seminar on '*Indian Nationalism*' held at Hindi Sahitya Sammelan, Allahabad, August, 1991.
53. 1991. "Middle Helladic Bronzework", Proceedings of the International Seminar of Indian Society for Graeco-Roman Studies at MJP Rohilkhand University, Bareilly, 29-30 Nov. 1991.
54. 1991. "Ayas in Rigveda", Proceedings of the National Seminar on '*Archaeometallurgy*', BHU, Varanasi, 3-4 Oct.1991.
55. 1991. "Archaeology of Feudalism", Proceedings of the National Seminar on "*India in the Seventh Century A.D.*", Centre of the Advance Studies in Indology and Museology, Bhopal, 25-26 February, 1991.

56. 1991. "Archaeology and Indo-Iranian Language", Proceedings of the National Seminar on '*Aryan- A Myth or Reality?*' at APS University, Rewa, 6-8 Dec.,1991.
57. 1990. "Protohistory of Upper Ganga Valley", Proceedings of the National Seminar on "*Panchal through Ages*", MJP Rohilkhand University, Bareilly, 21-22 March,1990.
58. 1989. "*Archaeology and Language*" in the Felicitation Volume of Dr. Sampurnanand, Sanskrit University Varanasi.
59. 1988. "Vedic Vajra" in Tripathi, D.N. *Archaeology and Tradition* (The Heritage of India no. XV), Ramanand Vidya Bhavan, New Delhi, pp. 1-6.
60. 1988. "Tin in Ancient World: A Literary Study" in Tripathi, D.N. *Archaeology and Tradition* (The Heritage of India no. XV), Ramanand Vidya Bhavan, New Delhi, pp. 18-25.
61. 1988. "Prehistoric and Protohistoric Indi-Greek Cultural Interactions: An Archaeological Study" in Tripathi, D.N. *Archaeology and Tradition* (The Heritage of India no. XV), Ramanand Vidya Bhavan, New Delhi, pp. 46-55.
62. 1988. "Preface" in Tripathi, D.N. *Archaeology and Tradition* (The Heritage of India no. XV), Ramanand Vidya Bhavan, New Delhi, pp. vi-x.
63. 1988. "Pit-Dwelling: An Archaeological and Literary Study" in Tripathi, D.N. *Archaeology and Tradition* (The Heritage of India no. XV), Ramanand Vidya Bhavan, New Delhi, pp. 26-34.
64. 1988. "Original Indo-Iranian Sources of Vajra" in Tripathi, D.N. *Archaeology and Tradition* (The Heritage of India no. XV), Ramanand Vidya Bhavan, New Delhi, pp. 66-91.
65. 1988. "Metallurgy and Emergence of Aegean Civilization" in Tripathi, D.N. *Archaeology and Tradition* (The Heritage of India no. XV), Ramanand Vidya Bhavan, New Delhi, pp. 35-45.
66. 1988. "Indo-Aryan Sources on Ayas" in Tripathi, D.N. *Archaeology and Tradition* (The Heritage of India no. XV), Ramanand Vidya Bhavan, New Delhi, pp. 92-100.
67. 1988. "Copper in Ancient World: A Literary Study" in Tripathi, D.N. *Archaeology and Tradition* (The Heritage of India no. XV), Ramanand Vidya Bhavan, New Delhi, pp. 11-17.
68. 1988. "Ayas in the Rigveda" in Tripathi, D.N. *Archaeology and Tradition* (The Heritage of India no. XV), Ramanand Vidya Bhavan, New Delhi, pp. 7-10.
69. 1988. "A Study of Some Indo-Aryan Personal Names of Ancient Western Asia" in Tripathi, D.N. *Archaeology and Tradition* (The Heritage of India no. XV), Ramanand Vidya Bhavan, New Delhi, pp. 56-65.
70. 1987. "*A Parallel to OC-EO (Cambodia) Seal from Sunet*", Journal of the Numismatic Society of India, Vol. XLIX, Patrs I&2, pp. 68-69.
71. 1987 "*Copper Harpoons- their possible use*" K.D. Bajpayi Felicitation Volume, State Museum, Gauhati, Assam.
72. 1986. "A Study of the Indo-Aryan Personal Names of Ancient Western Asia", Proceedings of the National Seminar on '*The Cultural Contexts of Personal Names in India up to 12th century A.D*", University of Gorakhpur, 22-24 Feb.1986.
73. 1984. "A Study of the Social-ecology of the Professions in Ancient India", Proceedings of the National Seminar on the '*Sociology of Professions*', Department of Sociology, Jodhpur University, Jodhpur, 13-16 Oct. 1984.
74. 1983. "Copper and Tin in Ancient World", Proceedings of the International Seminar on '*Recent Advances in Indian Archaeology*', Deccan College, Pune, 13-14 December, 1983.

Addresses, Lectures, Radio Talks, Paper presentations, etc. by Professor D.N. Tripathi

1. 2015. Presidential Address at the National Seminar on *Indo-Greek Relations* held at Allahabad Museum, Allahabad on 13-14 February, 2015.

2. 2015. Key-note address entitled "Language and Archaeology", during the Centenary Year celebration of the BHU and National Seminar on *Recent Field Researches in Indian Archaeology and Literature* (24-26 April, 2015), Centre of Advanced Study, Department of A.I.H.C. & Archaeology, BHU, Varanasi.
3. 2014. Key-note address entitled "Sir Alexander Cunningham and the Indo-Greek Art" at the International Seminar on '*Sir Alexander Cunningham and the Art Heritage of India'*, Department of History of Art, Banaras Hindu University, Varanasi, February 20-22, 2014.
4. 2014. Inaugural Address in the National Seminar on *The Archaeology of Ancient Capital Cities in India* at Allahabad Museum, Allahabad on 5-6 February 2014.
5. 2014. Inaugural Address at the UGC sponsored National Seminar on "Technological Basis of Cultures of Vindhya-Ganga Region" held at the Centre of Advanced Study, Department of AIHC & Archaeology, BHU, Varanasi on 3-4 March, 2014.
6. 2014. Inaugural Address at the National Seminar on "Samskriti, Kala evam Darshana: Bhartiyata ke Pariprekshya me", Mahila Mahavidyalaya, Banaras Hindu University, Varanasi, March14-15, 2014.
7. 2014. Addressed the Inaugural function of the 10th Refresher Course on "New Dimensions in the Study of History, Culture & Archaeology" in the Department of Ancient History, Archaeology & Culture, DDU Gorakhpur University, Gorakhpur on 6th September 2014.
8. 2014. Acharya Vishambhar Sharan Pathak Memorial Lecture titled Indian Culture: New Perspective delivered in the Department of Ancient History, Archaeology & Culture, DDU Gorakhpur University on 19.12.2014.
9. 2014. "Concept of Humanism in Ancient Indian Tradition" lecture delivered at the UGC-Academic Staff College, DDU Gorakhpur University, Gorakhpur on 31 January 2014.
10. 2013. Valedictory Address in the National Seminar on *Rationality, Science and Theology*, organized by Department of Philosophy, DDU, Gorakhpur University, Gorakhpur on 22-24 December 2013.
11. 2013. Presidential address at the Refresher's Course on "The Concept of Bhakti and its Role in the Formation of Indian Culture", Department of Ancient History, Archaeology and Culture, DDU Gorakhpur University, Oct.4,2013.
12. 2013. Presidential Address at the Inaugural Session of the National Seminar on "*Kala aur Purushartha*", Allahabad Museum, Allahabad, March 16-17,2013.
13. 2013. Paper presented on the occasion of the 74th Indian History Congress at the Ravenshaw University Cuttack under the aegis of Aligarh Historian's Society's Panel on Merchant, Trade and Commerce, entitled "Commerce in Early Civilization" on 29th December, 2013.
14. 2013. Address at the UGC sponsored National Seminar on *Archaeology and Culture of Bundelkhand* organized by JRH University, Chitrakoot on 7-8 December 2013.
15. 2012. Inaugural Address of the National Seminar on Cultural Heritage of Buddhism , Buddha Study Centre, Buddha P.G.College, Kushinagar (U.P.), March 1-2,2012.
16. 2012. Addressed the Inaugural Session of the National Seminar on "Indian View of History: A Critical Investigation" as Chief Guest held on March 13-14,2012, at the HRPG College, Khalilabad, Sant Kabir Nagar, U.P.
17. 2011. Inaugural Address at the National Seminar on *R.Shamasastry: New Dimensions in Indian History*, Nov.8-10, 2011.
18. 2011. Chief Guest's Address in the National Conference on *Environment in Buddhist Literature* held on 23-24 February, 2011 at HRPG College, Khalilabad, Sant Kabir Nagar, U.P.

19. 2010. Presidential Address entitled *"Vedic Roots of Hinduism and Hellenism"* published in the souvenir of the National Seminar on 'Vedic Foundations of Indian and Hellenic Cultures' held at Maharshi Panini Sanskrit Vishwavidyalaya, Ujjain, on 16-18August, 2010.
20. 2009. Lecture on "Value Education: Humanism and Human Rights", Department of Education, DDU, Gorakhpur University, 27 March, 2009.
21. 2009. Lecture on "Indo-Greek Art", Allahabad National Museum, Allahabad, 15 February, 2009.
22. 2008. Presidential lecture at the ICPR's National Seminar on "Ethics and Epics: Reflections on Indian Ethos", held in the Department of Philosophy, DDU Gorakhpur University, 05 January, 2008.
23. 2008. Paper entitled "Cultural Interactions between South India and South East Asia" presented at the International Seminar held at the Allahabad National Museum, 11-13 January, 2008.
24. 2008. Lectures on "Dimension of Indian Art Heritage and Contributions of Jainism and Buddhism", Parshwanath Vidyapeeth, Varanasi, 17-19 October, 2008.
25. 2008. Inaugural Address at the National Seminar on *Bhartiya Samskriti ka Jeevan Mulya Ahimsa tatha Vartmaan Vaishvik Paridrishya me iski Prasangikta* held on 22-23 February 2008 at Chandrakanti Ramawati PG College, Gorakhpur.
26. 2008. A Lecture on "Graeco-Roman Historiographic Tradition", Indian Council of Historical Research, New Delhi, February, 2008.
27. 2007. Press interview titled 'Kam Nahi ho Sakti Itihaas ki Prasangikta' published in Hindustan Bhagalpur edition on 29.01.2007 at page 6.
28. 2007. Lecture as a Chief Guest on *"Meaning and Process of History: Socio-Economic Interpretations"* at the National Seminar in the Department of Ancient History, Archaeology and Culture, DDU Gorakhpur University, 18 January, 2007.
29. 2007. A Lecture on "History, Philosophy of History & Research Methodology" in Refreshers Course of the Department of Education, DDU Gorakhpur University, 01 October, 2007.
30. 2006. Professor R. Sathianathier Endowment Lecture titled *"South India and South-East Asia"* at the University of Madras, Department of History, Nov.10, 2006.
31. 2006. Press interview titled 'Arya Bahar se Nahi Aaye' published in Panchjanya on 16.07.2006 on page 5.
32. 2006. Presidential Address of the International Seminar on *"Reason and Tolerance in Indian History"* on the occasion of the 4th Centenary of Emperor Akbar's Death on 28th November 2006 at India International Centre (IIC) New Delhi.
33. 2006. Presented paper at the National Seminar on "Evolution of India's Composite Culture" on the occasion of the Indian History Congress at Vishwa Bharati Shanti Niketan. 28-30 January, 2006.
34. 2006. Lecture on '*Rewriting History, Archaeology and Tradition*' organized by the School of Historical Studies, Madurai Kamraj University on 13.11.2006.
35. 2006. Lecture on '*Philosophy of History*' at the National Institute of Advanced Study, JRD Tata Auditorium, Bangalore on 21.06.2006.
36. 2006. Lecture at the ICHR's National Seminar on the "Historiography of 1857: Debates in the Past and the present state of knowledge" at India International Centre, New Delhi, 9-10 December, 2006.
37. 2006. Lecture at the 3 Day International Seminar on "Identity, Emotion and Culture: Language of the Subcontinent, c.1900-1971" at Indian International Centre, New Delhi, 21-24 December, 2006.

38. 2006. Key-note Address at the Seminar organized by Kerleeyan Smarak Samiti, Malabar Institute for Research and Development on "*Nationalism, Peasantry and All India Kisan Sabha*" held at Calicut (Kerala) on 16-17, September, 2006.
39. 2006. Inaugural Address of the Seminar on '*Gender Equality*' at Kaktiya University, Warangal on 20.01.2006.
40. 2006. Inaugural Address of the ICHR Seminar entitled "*From Orality to Writing: Understanding Hundred Years of Change in Mizoram*", held at the Department of History, Mizoram University, Aizwal, on 2-4 May, 2006.
41. 2006. Inaugural Address of the 10th Annual Congress of the Rock Art Society of India (RASI) at Institute of Archaeology, ASI, Delhi on 11-12 February 2006.
42. 2006. Inaugural address at the ICHR National Seminar on "*The Tribe, Peasants and Modern Identity in Northeastern India (c,1800-2000 A.D.*", held at the Department of History, Tripura University on 5-7 April, 2006.
43. 2006. Golden Jubilee Year Lecture in the Department of Ancient History, Culture and Archaeology, Allahabad University On "Middle East and Indo-European Languages: Problems and Issues", 9 January, 2006.
44. 2006. General Presidential Address at the 43rd Annual Conference of the Institute of Historical Studies at Bhubaneshwar, 13-15 October, 2006.
45. 2006. Chief Guest's Lecture on "Recent Trends in the writing of Indian History" at the C.P.Ramaswamy Foundation, Madras, Nov.10, 2006.
46. 2006. Chief Guest's lecture on '*Jawaharlal Nehru and International Diplomacy*' delivered under the auspices of the Centre for Nehru Studies, Bharathidasan University, Tiruchirappalli on 14.11.2006.
47. 2006. Chairman's Address at the International Seminar on "*Reason and Tolerance in Indian History*" at India International Centre, New Delhi, on 28 October,2006.
48. 2006. Addressed one day symposium on "Gandhi: His Relevance in the Present Scenario" at Centre for Gandhian Studies (UGC Programme), Department of History, Chaudhary Charan Singh University, Meerut. 22 Dec. 2006.
49. 2006. Addressed as a Chief-Guest on the occasion of the releasing ceremony of the *Special Issue* on the "*1857 First War of Independence*" at N.A.S.P.G. College, Meerut, 14 September, 2006.
50. 2006. A Lecture on "Language and Archaeology" organized jointly by the U.P. State Archaeology Department and the Department of Ancient Indian History and Archaeology, Lucknow University at Lucknow on 17 April, 2006.
51. 2005. Lecture on "*Vraja Samskriti ki Vaidik Prishthabhumi*" in Dr. Ramdas Gupta Memorial Lecture at Vrindavan Shodh Samsthan, Vrindavan, 6 Dec. 2005.
52. 2005. Key-note Address of the Ancient Section of the Joint Indo-Turkish International Seminar (under the cultural exchange programme) on "Turkish and Indian Studies: An Appraisal" organized by the Indian Council of Historical Research, New Delhi. 9 February, 2005.
53. 2005. Inaugural Address of the Two-day Conference of the 6th Bihar History Conference at Langat Singh Postgraduate College, Muzaffarpur, Bihar, 29-30 July, 2005.
54. 2005. Inaugural Address of the National Seminar on "Literature, Art and Secular Thought in Medieval India", Aligarh Muslim University, Aligarh. April 5-7, 2005.
55. 2005. Inaugural Address at the Three-Day National Research Conference on "Rashtriya Chetana ke vikas tatha swadhinata aandolan me kaviyitri Srimati Subhadra Kumari Chauhan ka Yogadana" at Jabalpur University, Jabalpur (M.P.) on 28 Sept. 2005.

56. 2005. Inaugural Address at the Joint Conference of Indian Archaeological Society, Indian Society for Prehistoric and Quaternary Studies and Indian History and Culture Society at Bangalore, 15 Dec. 2005.
57. 2005. Chief Guest's Lecture at the 5th National Seminar on "The Jats: Their Role and Contribution to the Socio-Economic Life and Polity of North & North-West India", organized by Surajmal Memorial Education Society, New Delhi, April 30-May 1, 2005.
58. 2004. Special Guest's Lecture at the National Seminar on "Professor Vasudeva Sharan Agrawal and his contributions to Indian Art and Culture" organized by the Department of History of Art in Senate Hall of Swatantrata Bhavan, BHU, Varanasi, 28-30 November, 2004.
59. 2004. Paper presented at the National Seminar on "Indian Identity and Cultural continuity", organizes by the Indian Institute of Advance Study, Shimla at Delhi University Guest House, Delhi, 4-5 May, 2004.
60. 2004. Paper presented at the National Seminar on "India and Asia: Glimpses of the Aesthetic Discourse", Sponsored by India International Centre, Centre for the Study of Civilizations, Indian Council of Historical Research, New Delhi and Indian Institute of Advanced Study, Shimla, held at India International Centre , 26-27 April, 2004.
61. 2003. Paper presented at the International seminar on "Cultural Interface of India with South, Southeast and east Asia (Religion, art and architecture) at Indian Institute of Advanced Study, Shimla, 6-10 March, 2003.
62. 2002. Address at the National Seminar on "The Homeland of Indo-European Languages and Culture" Convened by the Indian Council of Historical Research, New Delhi at India International Centre, Conference Room No.II, IIC, New Delhi on 7-9 January, 2002. Paper presented at the National Seminar on "Historiography of Indian Culture: Language and Culture, at Indian Institute of Advanced Study, Shimla, 9-11 October, 2002.
63. 2001. Lecture on "Social Justice and Traditional Indian Thinking" at the Indian Institute of Advanced Studies, Shimla, 28 Sept., 2001.
64. 2000. Paper entitled "Indian Religious Traditions and Humanism" presented at the National Seminar on 'Indian Religious Traditions in their Interdisciplinary Profile' held at the Indian Institute of Advanced Study, on 7-9 May, 2000.
65. 2000. Paper entitled "Hellenism and Hinduism" presented at the International Seminar on 'Relevance of Ancient Classics in the New Millennium' held at the Department of Ancient History and Culture, M.J.P. Rohilkhand University, Bareilly on 5-8 February, 2000.
66. 1994. Video lectures of the U.G.C. "On the Original Homeland of Aryans and Vedic Language and Literature", New Delhi, 22-23 January, 1994.
67. 1994. Two lectures "On Second Urbanization of Mid-Ganga Valley" at the UGC Refresher's Course held at the Allahabad University, 26 February, 1994.
68. 1994. Two lectures "On Historical Geography of Mid-Ganga Valley" at the UGC Refresher's Course held at the Allahabad University, 26 February, 1994.
69. 1994. Presidential Address on "Identification of Kapilvastu", Kapilvastu Mahotsava, Siddharthnagar (U.P.), 30 March 1994.
70. 1994. Presidential Address in the Lecture Series of U.P. Government Buddhist Museum, Gorakhpur on "Decline of Buddhism" 28 Jan. 1994.
71. 1994. Four U.G.C.'s Extension Lectures on "The Aryan Problem and Research Methodology" at Kurukshetra University, Kurukshetra, Harayana on 12-13 Feb., 1994.
72. 1994. Delivered two lectures "On the evolution of political society in Ancient India" at the UGC Refresher's Course held at the Sampurnanad Sanskrit University, Varanasi, 27 February, 1994.
73. 1994. A Lecture on "Rahul and Buddhism" at the U.P. Government Buddha Museum, Gorakhpur, 31 May.1994.

74. 1993. Valedictory Lecture on "Facets of Indian Nationalism", M.J.P. Rohilkhand University, Bareilly, 15 Jan, 1993.
75. 1993. Two lectures on "New Archaeology" at the UGC'S Refreshers Course at DDU Gorakhpur University on 25 Nov. & 2 Dec. 1993.
76. 1993. A Lecture on "Prehistoric Art of Greece" at the U.P. Government Buddhist Museum, Gorakhpur on 29 Sept. 1993.
77. 1993. A Lecture on "Archaeology of Mid-Ganga Valley" at the Academic Staff College, Allahabad University, 3-4, Sept.1993.
78. 1993. "Archaeology and Indo-European Languages', in the Annual Conference of the IAS, IPQS,& IHCS, Bhopal, 16-19 Dec., 1991.
79. 1992. Two Lectures on "Historical Research Methodology" at the Academic Staff College of Allahabad University, 19 October, 1992.
80. 1992. A Lecture on "Minoan Religion and Art" at the Allahabad National Museum, Allahabad on 1 March, 1992.
81. 1992. A Lecture on "Archaeology and Tradition" at the Birla Museum, Bhopal , February, 1992.
82. 1991. Valedictory Lecture in the National Seminar on "India in the 7th century A.D." at Prachya Niketan, Barakatullah University, Bhopal, Feb. 1991.
83. 1991. Two Lectures on "Minoan-Mycenaean Art" at the National Human Resource Research Institute, Varanasi, 6 June, 1991.
84. 1991. Presidential Address in the National Seminar on "Archaeological Evidence of Religious Tolerance in Bundelkhand Region", Banda, 19-25 Nov.1991.
85. 1990. Presidential Lecture at the National Seminar on "Panchal through Ages" held at M.J.P. Rohilkhand University, Bareilly, 22 March, 1990.
86. 1990. "Archaeological Models for the Study of Rural Development", at the National Seminar on 'Rural Development: Problems and Prospects', Jodhpur University, Jodhpur, Rajasthan, 17-19 March, 1990.
87. 1984. Two U.G.C. Extension lectures on "Indo-Greek Relations through Ages" at the Jodhpur University, Jodhpur, 13-15 Oct. 1984.
88. 1984. A series of three lectures on "Theory and Methods in Archaeology" delivered at the U.G.C. Workshop in Higher Education, Gorakhpur University, Gorakhpur, on 20 Nov. & 9 Dec.1984.
89. 1984. "*Bharat ki Navapashanakalin Sanskritian*", A radio-talk, published in AIR Journal. Broadcast on 16 April, 1984 at 9.16 p.m.
90. 1983. A series of two lectures delivered On "Wonder that was Greece" at Saint Andrews Post-Graduate College, Gorakhpur under U.G.C. Scheme.

International Conferences attended by Professor Tripathi

1. 2015. 3rd International Dharma and Dhamma Conference, Indore (M.P.), Oct.24-26, 2015.
2. 2011. Indo-Turkish Seminar of ICHR at New Delhi.
3. 2008. 18th Vedanta Conference at Dartmouth, Massachusetts, USA, August 2008.
4. 2001. XIVth UISPP conference, Liege (Belgium), Sept. 2001
5. 2001. World Samskrit Conference, New Delhi, 4-8 April, 2001.
6. 2000. XXXVI ICAANAS Conference, Montreal (Canada), August 2000.
7. 1994. World Archaeological Congress, New Delhi, December, 1994.
8. 1991. IInd Congress International Di Micenologia, University of Rome and Naples, "Cultural Interactions between India and the Aegean World" 14-20 Oct. 1991.
9. 1990. International Seminar on "New Archaeology and India", New Delhi, January 1990.

10. 1989. World Archaeological Inter-Congress, South Dakota, U.S.A., “Sati Burial-A Myth or Reality” August 5-10, 1989.
11. 1987. International Colloqueum in Agean Prehistory, Athens, (through a paper). August 29-Sept. 7, 1987.
12. 1986. XXXIII, ICAANAS conference, Hamburg, Germany, “Vajra-An Archaological and Literary Study” August 25-30, 1986
13. 1986. World Archaeological Congress, Southampton-London, “The Origins of Middle Helladic Metallury” and “The Origins of the Early Hellladic Metallurgy'' Sept. 1-7, 1986.
14. 1986. International Seminar on Recent advances in Pre- and Protohistoric Studies in India, National Museum, New Delhi, January 3-6, 1986.
15. 1984. Indo-Greek Symposium, Delphi, Greece, “Prehistoric and Protohistoric Indo-Greek Cultural Interactions: An Archaeological Study” June 8-14, 1984.

Membership of Academic Bodies

1. Member, Board of Studies, Greek and Latin, Sampurnananda Sanskrit University, Varanasi (1979-82).
2. Academic Member of the Indian Delegation of the Ministry of External Affairs, Government of India at the Greek Festival in Athens and Delphi, Greece, June 1984.
3. Chancellor's Nominee in the Syndicate of Rajasthan University, Jaipur (1986-1989).
4. Chancellor's Nominee in the Executive Council of R. M. L. Awadh University, Faizabad (U.P.) (1992-1994).
5. Member of the Executive Committee of the Indian Archaeological Society, New Delhi, (1986-88), Indian History and Culture Society, New Delhi (1984-86), and Indian Society for Prehistoric and Quaternary Studies, Pune (1995-98).
6. Member Editorial Board of *Summerhill,* IIAS Review, Indian Institute of Advanced Study, Shimla. (1999-2002).
7. Member, Inquiry Committee, NCERT, New Delhi. (2003-2004).
8. Member CABA, Ministry of Culture, New Delhi (2004-2007).
9. Member, Governing Body, IIAS, Shimla. (2004-2007).
10. Member CBSE, Ministry of HRD, New Delhi. (2004-2007).
11. General Secretary, Indian Society for Graeco-Roman Studies, Bareilly.

List of Contributors

Abha Dwivedi
Depts of A.I.H. & Archaeology,
University of Lucknow,
Lucknow.
E-mail: jaydra.ad@gmail.com

Ajay Kumar Pandey
Principal
Hiralal Ramniwas P.G. College
Khalilabad,
Sant Kabir Nagar-272175(U.P.)

Alok Tripathi
Director
Centre for Archaeology and Museology
Department of History
Assam University, Silchar
Email: alok.asi@gmail.com

Anantashutosh Dwivedi
Bihar Heritage Development Society,
Patna, Bihar
E-mail:- adwivedi195@gmail.com

Anjula Shukla
Associate Professor
Buddha P.G. College, Kushinagar (U.P)

Anupama Singh
Asstt. Archaeologist
Archaeological Survey of India, Vadodara

Apoorva Sinha
98, Sindhu Nagar, P.O Manas Nagar,
Lucknow-226023
Email: apurvasinha3@gmail.com

Arvin K. Singh
Professor Depts. Of AIHC
and Archaeology, Jiwaji University,
Gwalior-474011 (M.P.)
E-mail: aks_archju@yahoo.co.in;

Atul Tripathi
Professor, Depts. of the History of Art,
Faculty of Arts,
BHU, Varanasi-221005

B.R. Mani
Former Additional Director General,
Archeological Survey of India
Janpath
New Delhi

Brijesh Rawat
Asstt. Professor Depts. Of History
Dr. Shakuntala Mishra Rehabilitation
University,
Lucknow (U.P.)

Colin Renfrew
Former Director
Mcdonald Institute of Archaeology
Cambridge University,
Cambridge (U.K.)

D.P. Tewari
Professor Depts of A.I.H. & Archaeology,
University of Lucknow,
Lucknow
E-mail : tewaridplu@gmail.com

Deepak Kumar
Research Scholar,
Depts of AIHC and Archaeology,
Gurukul Kangari University,
Haridwar
E-mail : deepakmeluha@gmail.com

D.K.Mathur
Former Director,
V.S.Wakanker Research Institute
State Museum Compounds
Shymla Hills,
Bhopal

Devesh N. Tripathi
Scientist
Defence Institute of Psychological Research,
New Delhi

Dhyanendra Narayan Dubey
Asstt. Professor Deptt. of AHA and Culture
DDU Gorakhpur University,
Gorakhpur

Digvijaynath
Associate Professor,
DDU Gorakhpur University, Gorakhpur

Diwakar Prasad Tiwari
Retd. Principal
D.N. Pandey State Girls College
Deoria, (U.P.)
5/444, Deoria Ramnath West,
C.C. Road, Deoria (U.P.)

Gaya Charan Tripathi
Director, B.L. Institute of Indology
Vijay Vallabh Jain Mandir,
G.T. Karnal Road, P.O. Alipur, Delhi-36
E-mail : gctripathi235@gmail.com,

Girishwar Mishra
Vice-chancellor
Mahatma Gandhi Antarrastriya
Hindi Vishwavidyalaya,
Wardha (Maharashtra)

Gitu Giri
Tribhuwan University,
Nepal

Indudhar Dwivedi
Superintending Archaeologist (Retd.)
Archaeological Survey of India,
Janpath, New Delhi
E-mail : indidhardwivedi@gmail.com

Irfan Habib
Prof. (Retd.)Depts. of History
Aligarh Muslim University,
Aligarh (U.P.)

Ishwar Sharan Vishwakarma
DDU Gorakhpur University,
Gorakhpur
E-mail: isvishwakarma@gmail.com

J.N. Pal
Department of AHC and Archaeology
University of Allahabad
Allahabad 211 002 (U.P.)
E-mail : Jnpal@hotmail.com

J.N. Pandey
Former Professor & Head
Depts of AHC and Archaeology
Central University of Allahabad,
Allahabad.

K.D. Tripathi
Advisor
IGNCA, Eastern Regional Centre
Ravindrapuri Extension
Varanasi-221005

K.K. Paddayya
Former Director and Emeritus Professor of
Archaeology
Deccan College (Deemed University)
Pune 411 006

K.S. Shukla
36, Shuklana
Bangarmau, Unnao (UP) 209868
E-mail : ksshukla50@rediffmail.com

Kamlesh Kumar Gautam
Dept. of Ancient History
DDU Gorakhpur University,
Gorakhpur

Kunwar Bahadur Kaushik
Vivekpuram,
Taramandal,
Gorakhpur, U.P.

Maruti Nandan Pd. Tiwari
Deptt. of History of Art
Banaras Hindu University,
Varanasi-221005
Email- mnptiwari@rediffmail.com

Michel Danino
Guest Professor
IIT Gandhinagar (Gujarat)
E-mail: micheldanino@gmail.com

Mohan Gupta
Former Vice Chancellor
Maharshi Panini Sanskrit evam
Vedic Vishwavidyalaya
Ujjain, M.P.

Murli Manohar Pathak
DDU Gorakhpur University
Gorakhpur-273009

Namrata Singh
Assistant Professor
University of Delhi, Delhi

Neelesh Kumar Pandey
C/o B.K. Pandey, A-206,
Indraprastha Villa,
Sector-61, Noida
Gautam Buddha Nagar, U.P.
E-mail : nileshpandey21@gmail.com

Neetu Tiwari
Independent Archaeologist
163/P, L.I.C. Colony
Patel Nagar, GONDA, U.P.
E-mail : neetudivedi@gmail.com

Om Prakash Kumar
Senior Research Fellow,
Department of AIHC & Archaeology,
Banaras Hindu University,
Varanasi-221005

P.K. Shukla
Former Member Secretary, ICHR and
Fellow, NMM & Library,
New Delhi

Pooja Saxena
HIG- 71, Shankaracharya Nagar,
Bagh Sewania, Bhopal (M.P.)
E-mail: poojabpl@yahoo.com

Prabhakar Upadhyay
Assistant Professor,
Depts. of AIHC & Archaeology,
Banaras Hindu University,
Varanasi-221005

Pragya Chaturvedi
Associate Professor
Depts. of AHA & Culture
D.D.U. Gorakhpur University
Gorakhpur

Praveen K. Sharma
Research Scholar
Depts. of History, Archaeology & Culture
DDU Gorakhpur University,
Gorakhpur

Praveen Kumar Mishra
Superintending Archaeologist
Archaeological Survey of India,
Patna Circle,
Patna (Bihar)
Email: pkmgkp@gmail.com

Radhakant Varma
Former Chairman
Allahabad Museum Society,
Allahabad (U.P.)

Rajawant Rao
Professor
Depts. of AHA and Culture
DDU Gorakhpur University,
Gorakhpur

Rajesh Kumar Dhar Dubey
Ex-Post Doctoral Fellow,
ICHR, 35, Firozshah Road,
New Delhi,

Rajesh Kumar Meena
Asstt. Archaeologist
Archaeological Survey of India
Jaipur Circle,
Jaipur

Rajesh Mishra,
Allahabad Museum,
Allahabad

Rajesh Purohit
Director,
Allahabad Museum,
Allahabad.

Rakesh Tewari
Director General
Archaeological Survey of India
New Delhi

Ram Rudra Shukla
46494 Cedarhurst Drive,
Sterling, VA 20165, USA
E-mail : shuklarr@yahoo.com

Ramakant Singh
Associate Professor and HOD
Department of History,
Nagric P. G. College Janghai,
Jaunpur U.P.

Ramashray Roy
Former Director and Emeritus Fellow
Centre for the Study of
Developing Societies (CSDS),
Delhi (India)

Rampyare Mishra
Asstt. Professor
Depts. of AHA and Culture
DDU Gorakhpur University,
Gorakhpur

R.C.Tripathi
Former Secratery General Rajaya Sabha,
A-1055,Girja Bhavan,
Lekhraj Marg, Indira Nagar,
Lucknow-226016

Ratnesh Kumar Tripathi
Asstt. Prof. (Guest), History Deptt.,
B.N.C. College, Delhi University,
Research Associate, Indian Old Study
Organisation
(Madhav Sanskriti Nyas), New Delhi

Ravindra Kumar
Associate Professor,
DIHRM, Qutub Institutional Area
18/A, Satsang Vihar,
New Delhi.
E-mail : ravindrakumar1101@gmail.com

Rekha Chaturvedi
Depts. of Anc. History and Culture
DDU Gorakhpur University
Gorakhpur

S R Goyal
Former Professor, Depts. of History,
JN Vyas University,
Jodhpur, Rajasthan

S.K. Aruni
Member Secretary
ICHR, 35, Firozshah Road, New Delhi
E-mail : skaruni@gmail.com

Sachin Kumar Tiwary
Assistant Archaeologist,
Archaeological Survey of India,
Sarnath Circle, Sarnath,
Varanasi-221007, UP.
E-mail : sachintiwary@rocketmail.com

Sanchita Ghosh
Associate Professor,
Deptt. of Ancient History
D.A.V. College,
Kanpur (U.P.)

Sangeeta Singh
11, Jai Nagar Colony,
Gilat Bazaar, Shivpur,
Varanasi-221002

Santosh Kumar Singh
Depts. of A.I.H.C. & Archaeology
Banaras Hindu University,
Varanasi-221005
E-mail: sksingh1169@gmail.com

Shankar Goyal
Department of History
Jai Narain Vyas University
Jodhpur (Rajasthan)

Shankar Jai Kishan,
Curatorial Associate
Bihar Museum, Patna
E-mail : jaikishan5183@gmail.com

Shanti Swaroop Sinha
Deptt. of History of Art
Banaras Hindu University,
Varanasi-221005
E-mail : sssbhu@gmail.com

Shashi Tiwari
Former Professor, Sanskrit,
University of Delhi & Secretary General,
WAVES, New Delhi
Resi : 54, Saakshara Apartments,
A-3, Paschim Vihar, New Delhi

Shitala Prasad Singh
Associate Professor
Depts. of AHA & Culture
D.D.U. Gorakhpur University,
Gorakhpur
Email : dr.shitalaprasadsingh@gmail.com

Sibesh Bhattacharya
Professor (Retd.)
Deptt. of Ancient History
University of Allahabad,
Allahabad

Sita Ram Dubey
Department of A.I.H.C. & Archaeology
Banaras Hindu University,
Varanasi-221005
Email: dr.sitaramdubey@yahoo.co.in

Surendra Dubey
Dean, Faculty of Arts
DDU Gorakhpur University,
Gorakhpur

Susmita Pande
Former Professor & Head
Depts. of AIHC& Archaeology
Vikram University,
Ujjain

T. P. Verma
397-A, Ganga Pradushan
C, Road, Bhagwanpur,
Varanasi-221 005

Umesh Nath Tripathi
Associate Professor
Department of Chemistry
DDU Gorakhpur University,
Gorakhpur

U.P. Arora
Former Emeritus Professor
of Greek Studies
Jawahar Lal Nehru University,
New Delhi

V.N. Misra
G-2, B Wing, Ganga Park,
Mundhawa Road,
Pune 411036
Email: vnmisra1935@gmail.com

Vasant Shinde
Vice Chancellor
Deccan College Post-Graduate and
Research Institute (Deemed University)
Pune, Maharashtra

Vibha Tripathi
Senior Academic Fellow
Indian Council of Historical Research
35, Firozshah Road,
New Delhi

Vimal Tiwari
Curator
Maharajadhiraj Lakshmishwar Singh
Museum
Darbhanga, Bihar
Email : vimal311@gmail.com

Vinay Kumar
Assistant Professor,
Department of AIHC & Archaeology,
Indira Gandhi National Tribal University,
Amarkantak, M.P.
E-mail : vinaykumar166@yahoo.com

Vineet Godhal
Agrasena Colony,
Near Power House, Kotputli,
District Jaipur (Rajasthan)
E-mail: vineetgodhal@gmail.com

Vipula Dubey
Professor, Depts. Of AIHC& Archaeology
DDU Gorakhpur University,
Gorakhpur

Vishi Upadhyay
Curatorial Associate, Bihar Museum,
Patna (Bihar).
E-mail : vishi.arch@gmail.com

Y. Sudarshan Rao
Chairperson
Indian Council of Historical Research
35, Firozshah Road,
New Delhi

List of Plates

Plate 3.1 : Main Section Belan Valley
Plate 3.2 : Distribution of Sites in the Vindhyas
Plate 3.3 : Mesolithic Settlements of the Ganga Valley
Plate 3.4 (a) : Epi-palaeolithic Tools
Plate 3.4 (b) : Tools - Non Geometric Tools
Plate 3.4 (c) : Tools - Non Geometric Tools
Plate 3.5 : Stratigraphy of Damdama
Plate 3.6 : Four Burials Sarai Nahar Rai-Couples
Plate 3.7 : Couple Burial Mahadaha
Plate 3.8 : Burils and Hearths of different periods
Plate 3.9 : Pit Hearth, Damdama
Plate 3.10 : Antler, Ornaments, Mahadaha
Plate 3.11 : Ornaments in the Manufacturing Stage
Plate 3.12 : Male Skeleton With ear rings
Plate 3.13 : Rock Painting; A group of Boars
Plate 3.14 (a) : General view of Ronp Shelter
Plate 3.14 (b) : Rock Art of Northern Vindhyan Region : Evolution in Styles
Plate 5.1 : King and queen in low relief, Manhai, Kausambi
Plate 5.2 : Nativity scene, Kausambi.
Plate 5.3 : Palm leaf capital, Manhai, Kausambi.
Plate 5.4 : Buddha in Bhumisparsha Mudra, Kausambi.
Plate 5.5 : Bodhisattva, Kausambi.
Plate 5.6 : Bodhisattva, Kausambi.
Plate 5.7 : Unfinished Sculpture, Kausambi.
Plate 5.8 : Gajalakshmi, Kausambi.
Plate 8.1 : Dwarka: Diving near Samudra Narayan temple (photo: UAW)
Plate 8.2 : Dwarka: A submerged structural remain after cleaning (photo: UAW)
Plate 8.3 : Dwarka: Excavations in Dwarkadheesh temple complex (photo: UAW)
Plate 8.4 : Dwarka: Partly broken circular structure in intertidal zone (photo: UAW)
Plate 15.1 : General View of the Mound, Waina, Ballia
Plate 15.2 : Microliths of Waina, District Ballia (U.P.).
Plate 15.3 : Bone Points of Plate IB & II, Waina, Ballia.
Plate 15.4 : Terracotta Beads of Plate IB, II & III, Waina, Ballia.
Plate 15.5 : Antlers of Plate II & III, Mound, Waina, Ballia.
Plate 15.6 : Occupation floor with Post-holes Plate III, Mound, Waina, Ballia.
Plate 18.1 : Lower Palaeolithic tools from Sohanpura
Plate 18.2 : Lower Palaeolithic tools from Sohanpura

Plate 18.3 : Lower Palaeolithic tools from Bheetaro
Plate 18.4 : Lower Palaeolithic tools from Bheetaro
Plate 18.5 : Lower Palaeolithic Handaxe from Reedh Ka Tila
Plate 18.6 : Lower Palaeolithic Handaxe from Reedh Ka Tila
Plate 18.7 : Lower Palaeolithic tools from Peer Baba Ki Bani
Plate 18.8 : Lower Palaeolithic tools from Peer Baba Ki Bani
Plate 18.9 : Lower Palaeolithic tools from Shobh
Plate 18.10 : Lower Palaeolithic tools from Shobh
Plate 18.11 : Middle Palaeolithic tools from Bageshwar
Plate 18.12 : Middle Palaeolithic tools from Bageshwar
Plate 18.13 : Middle Palaeolithic tools from Laloda
Plate 18.14 : Middle Palaeolithic tools from Laloda
Plate 18.15 : Upper Palaeolithic tools from Deoli Ki Dhani
Plate 18.16 : Upper Palaeolithic tools from Deoli Ki Dhani
Plate 20.1 : A cylindrical neck & collared mouth Chalcolithic Pot
Plate 20.2 : Fragmentary remains of Chalcolithic Earthen Pots
Plate 20.3 : Precious and Semi-precious stone bead excavated from Peetnagar
Plate 20.4 : Terracotta Beads
Plate 20.5 : Painted thin fragments of Lota & thick Globular Vessel
Plate 20.6 : Painted fragmentary pieces of Stand Bowls and Vessels
Plate 23.1 : Fragmentary Stone Inscription of Kachchhapaghāta Ratnapāla: V.S. 1165
Plate 23.2 : Close up of the upper left portion of the Stone Inscription of Ratnapāla
Plate 23.3 : Close up of the upper right portion of the Stone Inscription of Ratnapāla
Plate 23.4 : Close up of the lower right portion of the Stone Inscription of Ratnapāla
Plate 23.5 : Close up of the lower right portion of the Stone Inscription of Ratnapāla
Plate 25.1 (A) : General view of the mound with its highest elevation
Plate 25.1 (B) : General view of mound on the bank of river Sai
Plate 25.2 : Terracotta Seals and Sealings
Plate 25.3 : Seals and Sealings from Sanchankot.
Plate 25.4 : Seals and Sealings from Sanchankot.
फलक 26.1 : गजमस्तक का शिरस्त्राण धारी डिमेट्रियस
फलक 26.2 : डिमेट्रियस की मुद्रा पर अंकित गज का शिरोभाग एवं अंकुश
फलक 26.3 : एण्टियालकिड्स की मुद्रा पर अंकित गज का शिरोभाग
फलक 26.4 : एण्टियालकिड्स की मुद्रा पर अंकित गज का शिरोभाग
Plate 27.1 : Gold coin of Prithvideva obverse (in collection of Kamal Vaid)
Plate 27.2 : Silver coin of Prithvideva Reverse (in collection of Prshant kulkarni)
Plate 27.3 : Copper coin of Prithavideva Reverse (in collection of L.P. Pandey)
Plate 27.4 : Gold coin of Ratandeva obverse (in collection of Kamal Vaid) copy
Plate 27.5 : Silver coin of Ratandeva, Reverse (in collection of Prashant kulkarni)
Plate 27.6 : Copper coin of Ratandeva obverse (in collection of Pushparaj Victor)
Plate 27.7 : Gold coin of Jajalladeva obverse (in collection of Kamal Vaid)
Plate 27.8 : Copper coin of Jajalladeva (in collection of Bhanupratap singh)
Plate 27.9 : Silver coin of Jagpaladeva obverse
Plate 27.10 : Copper coin of Pratapmalladeva
Plate 27.11 : Gold coin of Pratapmalladeva

Plate 28.1 : Tritîrthî – showing Sarasvatî with two Jinas, Jaina Dharmashala Museum, Deogarh (Lalitpur, U.P.), 11th century CE.
Plate 28.2 : Six-armed Sarasvatî, southern adhiṣṭāna rathikā, Pārśvanātha temple, Khajurāho (Chhatarpur, M.P.), c. 950-70 CE.
Plate 28.3 : Sarasvatî, Pañcakūṭa Bastî, (Shimoga, Karnataka), 11th century CE.
Plate 28.4 : Sarasvatî joined by dancing divine figures, corridor ceilings, Vimala-Vasahî (Sirohi, Rajasthan), c. 1150 CE.
Plate 28.5 : Sarasvatî, Pallū (Bikaner, Rajasthan), now in National Museum, New Delhi, c.11th CE.
Plate 31.1 : View of Temple from North-eastern side
Plate 31.2 : View of Temple from Northern side
Plate 31.3 : View of the Temple from Southern side
Plate 32.1 : Patna - Yaksha - Mauryan Period
Plate 32.2 : Besnagar - Yakshi (2nd century BC)
Plate 32.3 : Parkham - Yaksha - Post Mauryan
Plate 32.4 : Atlantes - Yaksha - Sanchi
Plate 32.5 : Bowl Suporting Yaksha - Pitalkhora (2nd century BC)
Plate 32.6 : Moggarapani Yaksha - Satavahana period
Plate 32.7 : Kuber - Ahichhatra Kushan (2nd century AD)
Plate 32.8 : Yakshi - Sanchi (1st century BC)
Plate 33.1 : Udaygiri Hill, Vidisha
Plate 33.2 : Shehshayi Vishnu, Cave No. 13, Udaygiri Hills, Vidisha
Plate 33.3 : Mutilated figure of Brahma seated on lotus, Cave No. 13, Udaygiri Hills, Vidisha
Plate 33.4 : Nrivaraha, Cave No. 5, Udaygiri Hills , Vidisha
Plate 34.1 : Monolithic Pillar, Mauryan Period.
Plate 34.2 : Lion Capital, Mauryan Period.
Plate 34.3 : Yakshi, Sunga Period.
Plate 34.4 : Kuber, Kushan Period.
Plate 34.5 : Head of Bodhisattva, Kushan Period.
Plate 34.6 : Buddha, Kushan Period.
Plate 34.7 : Surya, Gupta Period.
Plate 34.8 : Rishabhnath, Gupta Period.
Plate 34.9 : Jaina Pillar with images of Teerthanakas, Gupta Period.
Plate 34.10 : Jaina Pillar with images of Teerthanakas, Gupta Period.
Plate 34.11 : Buddha in declining posture, Gupta Period.
Plate 34.12 : Image of Teerthankar, Gupta Period.
Plate 34.13 : Ekmukhlinga, Gupta Period.
Plate 34.14 : Navagrah Panel, Early Medieval Period.
Plate 34.15 : Uma-Maheshwar, Early Medieval Period.
Plate 34.16 : Mahishamardini, Early Medieval Period.
Plate 34.17 : Jeevant Swami, Early Medieval Period.
Plate 34.18 : Agni, Early Medieval Period.
Plate 34.19 : Neminath, Early Medieval Period.
Plate 34.20 : Vishnu, Pala Period.
Plate 34.21 : Agni, Early Medieval Period.
Plate 34.22 : Buddha, Early Medieval Period.

Plate 34.23 : Head of Bodhisattva, Early Medieval Period
Plate 35.1 : Horse on the abacus of Sarnath Lion Capital
Plate 35.2 : Lady of Auxerre in Daedalic style
Plate 35.3 : Tanagra Terracotta figures, about 250 B.C.
Plate 35.4 : Dancing girl, Patna Museum, Mauryan Period
Plate 35.5 : Open mouth of the lion in West Asian art
Plate 35.6 : Open mouth of the lion in Mauryan art
Plate 35.7 : So-called shrine of the Double headed Eagle at Sirkap.
फलक 36.1 : धूप में नमी को सुखाने के लिए रखा कच्चा माल
फलक 36.2 : प्रथम हीटिंग का दृश्य
फलक 36.3 : प्रथम चिपिंग के लिए प्रयोग किया जाने वाला लकड़ी का हथौड़ा
फलक 36.4 : प्रथम चिपिंग के लिए लोहे की पतली नोंक वाली छड़
फलक 36.5 : प्रथम एवं द्वितीय चिपिंग के लिए प्रयोग किये जाने वाले भैंस के सींग से बने हथौड़े
फलक 36.6 : मनकों की प्रथम चिपिंग
फलक 36.7 : मनकों में द्वितीय चिपिंग
फलक 36.8 : मनकों की घिसाई एवं पॉलिश के लिए प्रयुक्त एमरी व्हील्स
फलक 36.9 : मनकों की घिसाई
फलक 36.10 : मनकों की एमरी व्हील द्वारा पॉलिश
फलक 36.11 : छिद्र के लिए प्रयोग किये जाने वाले औजार
फलक 36.12 : मनकों में छिद्र प्रक्रिया
फलक 36.13 : मनकों को गर्म करने के लिए तैयार की गई भट्टी
फलक 36.14 : लकड़ी के बुरादे से भरी गई भट्टी
फलक 36.15 : भट्टी में आग का दृश्य
फलक 36.16 : अगले दिन सुबह भट्टी का दृश्य
फलक 36.17 : भट्टी में परिवर्तित हुए कार्नेलियन के मनकों का चित्र
Plate 37.1 : Map of the area under the discussion
Plate 37.2 : Rock Shalter Kaurihar Khas
Plate 37.3 : Hunter, Animale and Loade Carrier, Ghurahupur
Plate 37.4 : Humped Bull, Ghurahupur
Plate 37.5 : Depications of Budha, Stupa and female Dancer, Ghurahupur
Plate 37.6 : Painting Belongs to Deference Period, Tanui
Plate 37.7 : A bull shown with roap around in its neck Kharauli
Plate 37.8 : Mesolithic Rock Paintings, Ratanpurawa
फलक 38.1 : त्रिभंग शांतिदेवी, जैन बावनढेरी, चाम्पानेर–पावागढ़, गुजरात
फलक 38.2 : आसनस्थ सरस्वती, जैन बावन ढेरी, चाम्पानेर–पावागढ़, गुजरात
फलक 38.3 : त्रिभंग इन्द्राणी, जैन बावन ढेरी, चाम्पानेर – पावागढ़, गुजरात
Plate 39.1 : Earliest evidence of excavated bronze object from Chechar. (Photograph courtesy ASI, Patna Circle)
Plate 39.2 : Polychrome Pictographs of human executed on the wall of the shelter very much similar to the bronze image, Chand Block of Kaimur district, Bihar
Plate 39.3 : Pictographs of human holding hammer or stick like object on left hand and rope or symbolic form of an un-iconic form holding on right hand executed on the wall of the cave also very much similar to the bronze image, Chand Block of Kaimur district, Bihar

Plate 45.1 : Rāndala Mātā with Chāyā, a photograph commoly seen during worship in households in the Saurāṣṭra Region

Plate 45.2 : Mānat at Ravi Rāndala Mātā Temple, Daḷavā (Bhavṇagar) : For the ailments of the bodyparts devotees offer either small wooden replicas of the whole body or the part(s) which is/are affected; displayed on the left side here are the wooden replicas at a shop for sale. On the right side are the photographs of the new born children being put up after their mānat of childbirth is fulfilled.

Plate 45.3 : Diaspora of Ravi Rāndala Mātā : Rituals being performed by Non Resident Gujaraties outside a Hindu Temple at Leister in England.

Plate 45.4 : A scene of the celebrations during the inauguration of the International Kite Festival, Ahmedabad.

Plate 45.5 : A large number of domestic as well as foreign kite enthusiasts flying their kites at a vanue during the International Kite Festival at Ahmedabad.

TRIBUTE TO PROFESSOR DAYA NATH TRIPATHI

It is a pleasure and an honour to pay tribute to my friend (and former student) Daya Tripathi, for whom I had the privilege of acting in the formal capacity of supervisor during his years as a doctoral student at the University of Southampton, where I was at the time Head of the Department of Archaeology. In reality there was little "supervision", since Daya Tripathi, then as now, was a formidable scholar, and his time of research in Athens and then in Southampton had been well spent. His impressive doctoral dissertation was of course accepted and welcomed by the examiners, and was subsequently published (in Paul Åström's *Studies in Mediterranean Archaeology* series (SIMA)) with the title: *Bronzework of Mainland Greece from c. 2600 BC to c. 1450 BC*. It is a significant contribution to Aegean prehistory.

It is a great pleasure to contribute to this Felicitation Volume with a recent paper 'An evolutionary perspective on the development of human culture', which will fall within his wide range of interests. Among these is the still not fully resolved problem of the origin of the Indo-European languages, on which I would have wished to present a paper for the Felicitation Volume. But several chapters of the new *Cambridge World Prehistory*, written in collaboration with my colleague Paul Heggarty, have recently addressed this theme, so that I hope the 'evolutionary perspective' will be found acceptable.

It is my great please to offer warm felicitations and congratulations to Daya Tripathi, with every good wish for a long and happy retirement.

Colin Renfrew
(Lord Renfrew of Kaimsthorn)

परम्परा के संवाहक परमाचार्य प्रोफेसर दयानाथ जी

अजय कुमार पाण्डेय

प्रयाग के पवित्र भूमि के स्थित जयरामपुर पत्रालय दोहरिया के स्वर्गीय राम किशोर शर्मा तथा स्वर्गीय श्रीमती कृष्णा शर्मा का सम्पूर्ण परिवार भारत की सनातन हिन्दू परम्परा में संस्कारित था। इसी संस्कारित परिवार में गुरूवर प्रो0 दयानाथ त्रिपाठी उत्पन्न हुए, संस्कारित और दीक्षित हुए, जिसका प्रभाव उनके परम्परागत मानस में अद्यावधि विद्यमान है।

परम्परागत शिक्षा

ममतामयी माँ एवं पूजनीय पिता की छत्रछाया में गुरूवर त्रिपाठी को माता–पिता के संस्कार प्राप्त हुए। प्रो0 त्रिपाठी के पिताश्री स्वर्गीय पं0 राम किशोर शर्मा सर्वाय इण्टर कालेज, इलाहाबाद के प्रधानाचार्य थे और वे सनातन धर्मी थे। गुरूवर त्रिपाठी के पिताश्री और स्वर्गीय महिमामयी माँ दोनों हिन्दू धर्म के देवताओं की उपासना और पूजा करने के पश्चात ही प्रातः काल जलग्रहण करते थे। अल्पाहार के पश्चात रामायण, गीता और रामचरितमानस का पाठ करने के पश्चात ही विद्यालय प्रस्थान करते थे। प्रो0 त्रिपाठी माता–पिता के पूजा सामग्री, फल–फूल तथा हवन सामग्री आदि एकत्रित कर स्वयं माता–पिता के साथ कुछ समय पूजा करने बैठ जाते थे। पुत्र प्रो0 दयानाथ के इस पूजा रूचि को देखकर उनके प्रारम्भिक शिक्षा–दीक्षा को सनातन धर्म का संस्कार प्रदान किया। जो उनके जीवन का अंग बन गया।

अध्ययन–अध्यापन में परम्परा पालन– अपने प्रारम्भिक शिक्षाकार इलाहाबाद विश्वविद्यालय के प्राचीन इतिहास, संस्कृति और पुरातत्व विषय में प्रथम श्रेणी प्राप्त करने के अवधि में भी गुरूवर त्रिपाठी इलाहाबाद के हनुमान मंदिर का दर्शन करने जाते थे, लड्डू चढ़ाते थे, प्रसाद प्राप्त करते थे और अपने आवास पर लौट आते थे। अध्ययन अवधि में उनके अनेक सहपाठी उनका अनुकरण करते हुए हनुमान जी के मूर्ति के सम्मुख उपस्थित होकर हनुमत वंदना करते हुए प्रसाद प्राप्त कर अपने आवास पर लौट आते थे। विशेष ध्यातत्य तथ्य यह है कि प्रो0 त्रिपाठी के अध्ययन कक्ष में विभिन्न हिन्दू देवी–देवताओं के चित्रों के साथ हनुमान जी का सबसे बड़ा चित्र लगा रहता था और उस पर माला चढ़ाया गया होता था। क्रमशः हिन्दू परम्परा को मानते हुए हनुमान जी के प्रति उनके निष्ठा बढ़ती गई। गुरूवर का यह मानना था कि हनुमान जी की कृपा से ही उन्होंने एक अच्छे विद्यार्थी के रूप में अपनी पहचान बना ली।

इष्टदेव हनुमान

मैं दीनदयाल उपाध्याय गोरखपुर विश्वविद्यालय के प्राचीन इतिहास पुरातत्व एवं संस्कृति विभाग का विद्यार्थी था और गुरूवर प्रो0 त्रिपाठी की मुझपर पर्याप्त कृपा बनी रहती थी। प्रो0 त्रिपाठी जी प्रति मंगलवार को बेतियाहाता में स्थित हनुमान मंदिर पहुँचकर हनुमान जी का दर्शन करते और कुछ समय तक खड़े रहकर हनुमान जी की पूजा करते रहते थे। कभी–कभी मैं भी गुरूवर के साथ हनुमान मंदिर जाता था और उनके साथ पूजा भी करने लगा। राह चलते चर्चा में गुरूवर प्रो0 त्रिपाठी जी कहते थे कि मेरे इष्टदेव हनुमान जी हैं। मैं प्रतिदिन प्रातःकाल एक घण्टा हनुमान जी की पूजा करता हूँ और हनुमान जी की कृपा से ही मैं दीनदयाल उपाध्याय गोरखपुर विश्वविद्यालय के नियंता पद को स्वीकार कर विश्वविद्यालय में शांति व्यवस्था स्थापित करने में सफल हो पाया। उनका यह विश्वास रहा कि हनुमान जी कृपा से ही उन्हें निरन्तर उन्नति प्राप्त होती गई।

बहन से रक्षा बन्धन

गुरूवर दयानाथ त्रिपाठी भारतीय परम्परा से इतने अधिक आबद्ध हैं कि वे भारत के किसी भी भू–भाग में रहते हुए भी 'रक्षाबन्धन' के अवसर पर अपनी बहन (श्रीमती–शुक्ला) से अवश्य ही रक्षा बंधवाने के लिए उपस्थित हो जाते हैं। यदि गुरूवर विदेश में रहते हैं तो वही से अपनी बहन के रक्षा बन्धन हेतु द्रव्य प्रेषित करते हैं कि रक्षा बन्धन के एक दिन पूर्व बहन को निश्चित रूप से प्राप्त हो जाता है। परम्परा के प्रति इतनी अधिक घनिष्ठता और मान्यता प्रदान करने वाले व्यक्ति को मैं सदा प्रणाम करता हूँ। उनकी बहन भी रक्षा बन्धन के अवसर पर इस प्रत्याशा में निश्चित रहती है कि उनके भाई प्रो0 त्रिपाठी का कुशल क्षेम प्राप्त होगा और वह भाई के आरती के लिए दीपक और मिष्ठान की तैयारी पहले से ही कर लेती हैं।

पत्नी का परम्परा में सहयोग

आचार्य प्रवर प्रो0 दयानाथ त्रिपाठी का प्रिय शिष्य होने के कारण माता तुल्य श्रीमती (त्रिपाठी) का निरन्तर सहयोग गुरूवर को प्राप्त होता रहता है। गुरूमाता उनके पूजा, स्थल, पूजापीठ, पूजा सामाग्री के पात्र आदि की व्यवस्था पूजा प्रारम्भ के पूर्व ही कर देती हैं। गुरूमाता अस्वस्थता और स्वस्थता की स्थिति में भी गुरूवर के धर्माचरी के होने का पूर्ण दायित्व निभाती हैं। कभी–कभी पूजा सामग्री लाने का सौभाग्य मुझे भी प्राप्त हुआ है। यह मेरा परम सौभाग्य है कि गुरू, गुरूमाता तथा देव प्रतिमाओं के प्रति अपनी श्रद्धा समर्पित करने का अवसर सौभाग्य से प्राप्त होता रहा है।

मेरे शोध निर्देशक

मैं अत्यधिक भाग्यशाली हूँ कि ऐसे सनातन पुरूष और परम्परा के संवाहक मुझे एम0ए0 (प्राचीन इतिहास पुरातत्व एवं संस्कृति) विषय में शिक्षा प्रदान किया। मेरे पी–एच0डी0 के निर्देशक रहे तथा डी0लिट् के परामर्शी रूप में उनके वैश्विक पुरातत्व के अगाध ज्ञान का परिचय मुझे प्राप्त हुआ। मेरे डी0लिट् करने की अवधि में उत्पन्न बाधाओं का क्षणैक में समाधान प्रस्तुत करने वाले गुरूवरज्ञय के प्रति सदा नमित हूँ। मेरे अनुसंधान अवधि में अपनी सनातन परम्पराओं के परिपालन तथा विश्वविद्यालय के पूर्वायतन के आचार्य एवं अध्यक्ष के कार्य दायित्व का निर्वाह करते हुए भी मेरे अनुसंधान विषय पर लिखे जाने वाले प्रत्येक पृष्ठों का स्वयं अवलोकन करते हुए त्रुटियों का संशोधन एवं समाधान प्रस्तुत करने का समय निकाल लेते थे।

तीर्थयात्रा के तपस्वी

प्रो0 दयानाथ त्रिपाठी के जीवन चारिका की यह विशेषता यह रही है कि भारत के प्रमुख तीर्थो की यात्रा करते रहते हैं। यात्रा का प्रमुख उद्देश्य ऐतिहासिक संस्थानों, स्थानों, संग्रहालयों का निकट से अध्ययन एवं अवलोकन करना रहता था। परन्तु इस अध्ययन अनुसंधान यात्रा केन्द्रों के निकट स्थित राजगृह से लेकर जरासंध का अखाड़ा, नालन्दा विश्वविद्यालय के खण्डहरों, एवं विक्रमशिला विश्वविद्यालय के अवशेषों के साथ ही साथ बिहार के धर्म स्थलों का अध्ययन करते हुए काश्मीर से कन्याकुमारी तक धार्मिक स्थलों की यात्रा उनकी अत्यधिक अभिरूचि रही है। प्रत्येक मंदिरों में स्थापित देव मूर्तियों के तदानुकूल दर्शन एवं प्रसाद समर्पण का कार्य करते रहे। आज भी वे एक जीवन्त पुराविद् एवं परम्परा के संवाहक रूप में निरन्तर चारिका करते रहते हैं।

प्राचार्य
हीरालाल रामनिवास स्नातकोत्तर महाविद्यालय
खलीलाबाद, संत कबीर नगर, उ0प्र0

पुरातत्व के प्रमाता
(प्रो0 दयानाथ त्रिपाठी)

कुँवर बहादुर कौशिक

प्रयाग की प्रशस्त भूमि में प्रस्थित् इलाहाबाद विश्वविद्यालय के प्रख्यात पुरातत्ववेत्ता प्रो0 गोवर्धन राय शर्मा के सनिध्य में पुरातत्व की विभिन्न विधाओं का अध्ययन किया। कौशाम्बी उत्खनन में गुरूवर त्रिपाठी ने अपनी सक्रिय सहभागिता प्रस्तुत करते हुए पुरातत्व एवं परम्परा का प्रौढ़ ज्ञान प्राप्त किया। इलाहाबाद विश्वविद्यालय के प्राचीन इतिहास, संस्कृति एवं पुरातत्व विषय में स्नातकोत्तर उपाधि अर्जित करने के पश्चात ही दीनदयाल उपाध्याय, गोरखपुर विश्वविद्यालय के स्थापना उपरांत 1958 से ही 'प्राचीन इतिहास, पुरातत्व एवं संस्कृति' विभाग में प्रवक्ता, प्रवाचक एवं आचार्य–अध्यक्ष के रूप में 40 वर्षो तक निर्बाध पूर्वायतन की सेवा में संलग्न रहे। प्रवक्ता काल में ही आचार्य त्रिपाठी अपने कर्त्तव्यनिष्ठा के कारण विश्वविद्यालय के प्रमुख नियंता (1980–84) पद पर आसीन रहे तथा विभिन्न बाधाओं में सफलता–पूर्वक अपने कार्यकुशलता से विद्यार्थियों–अध्यापकों में अधिक लोकप्रियता प्राप्त की।

अनुसंधित्सु

पूर्वायतन् में इनके अध्यापन का मुख्य विषय पुरातत्व, प्राग इतिहास एवं पुरैतिहास रहा है। गुरुवर त्रिपाठी ने वर्ष 1971 से 1974 तक ग्रीक स्कालरशिप तथा 1974 से 1976 तक ब्रिटिश काउंसिल स्कॉलरशिप प्राप्त की तथा अपनी उपलब्धियों से यूरोपीय पुरातत्व के क्षेत्र में महत्वपूर्ण स्थान स्थापित किया। आचार्य त्रिपाठी को एथेंस विश्वविद्यालय से यूनानी भाषा की उपाधि 1972 में प्राप्त हुयी। विश्व प्रसिद्ध पुरातत्ववेत्ता लार्ड कोलिन रेनफ्रियू के निर्देशन में प्रो0 त्रिपाठी को 'साउथसेम्पटन विश्वविद्यालय, यूनाइटेड किंगडम' से पी–एच0डी0 की उपाधि 'ब्रान्ज वर्क ऑफ ग्रीस' नामक शोध प्रबन्ध पर प्रदान किया गया।

शोध–यात्रा

गुरूवर त्रिपाठी ने अपने यूनान के अध्ययन में ही ग्रीस, फ्रांस, जर्मनी, इटली, यूनाइटेड किंगडम, इजिप्ट तथा ईरान आदि देशों में प्रसिद्ध संग्रहालयों में संरक्षित पुरावशेषों का प्रत्यक्ष दर्शन करते हुए पुरातत्व विषय में अपनी पुरातत्व विषयक विधाओं का अध्ययन किया तथा भारत के संग्रहालयों में स्थित प्रमुख संग्रहालय– राष्ट्रीय संग्रहालय, नई दिल्ली, भारतीय संग्रहालय, कलकत्ता; इलाहाबाद संग्रहालय तथा मध्य प्रदेश, उत्तर प्रदेश, बिहार, राजस्थान के राज्य संग्रहालयों का पूर्ण अध्ययन एवं अवलोकन किया। अपने अध्ययन के आधार पर गुरूवर त्रिपाठी जी यूरोपीय देशों तथा भारतीय विश्वविद्यालयों में पुरातत्व विषयक शोध–पत्रों का वाचन और सम्बोधन करते हुए एक लब्ध प्रतिष्ठित पुराविद् के रूप में विख्यात हो गये।

यूरोपीय देशों में विशेषकर यूनान के पुरातत्व का गहरा अध्ययन करके आचार्य प्रवर – त्रिपाठी जी ने दीनदयाल उपाध्याय गोरखपुर विश्वविद्यालय में क्रमशः पूर्वायतन् के आचार्य एवं अध्यक्ष पद को सुशोभित करते हुए विभिन्न शैक्षिक संस्थानों इलाहाबाद विश्वविद्यालय, 1998–1999, इंडियन इंस्टीट्यूट ऑफ एडवांस स्टडीज शिमला के अनसंधित्सु (1999–2002) तथा ब्रिटिश एकाडमी, लंदन 2003 के विजिटिंग प्रोफेसर के रूप में प्रसिद्धि प्राप्त की।

अनुसंधान–परिषद के अध्यक्ष

आचार्य प्रवर प्रोफेसर दयानाथ त्रिपाठी पुरातत्व के साथ ही साथ परम्परा की सहचारिता के समर्थक विद्वान थे। वे भारतीय इतिहास अनुसंधान परिषद के सदस्य रूप में 1998–2004 तक महत्वपूर्ण स्थान भारतीय इतिहास एवं पुरातत्व के क्षेत्र में प्राप्त कर चुके थे। अखिल भारतीय स्तर पर प्रो0 त्रिपाठी की महत्ता का अनुभव प्रशासनिक क्षेत्रों में भी व्याप्त हुआ। इसी कारण प्रो0 त्रिपाठी को भारतीय इतिहास अनुसंधान परिषद, नई दिल्ली के अध्यक्ष पद पर वर्ष 2004 में नियुक्त किया गया जिसका सफलतापूर्वक निर्वहन उन्होंने अपनी कार्यावधि में किया। भारतीय इतिहास अनुसंधान परिषद के सदस्य के रूप में आचार्य प्रो0 त्रिपाठी की अध्यक्षता में एक अन्तर्राष्ट्रीय गोष्ठी का आयोजन

07–09 जनवरी, 2002 तक भारतीय अन्तर्राष्ट्रीय केन्द्र, नई दिल्ली में "A DISCOURSE ON INDOEUROPEAN LANGUAGES AND CULTURE" विषय पर कियागया जिसमें पुरातत्व, पुराभाषा, भाषिक पुरातत्व एवं संस्कृति विषय के अन्तर्राष्ट्रीय विद्वानों ने अपने शोध–पत्र प्रस्तुत किये। तीन दिनों तक इस विषय के विद्वानों ने प्रस्तावित विषय पर गम्भीर विचार – मंथन किया। परामाचार्य गुरूवरज्ञ प्रो0 त्रिपाठी की कृपा से मुझे भी इस अन्तर्राष्ट्रीय गोष्ठी अपना शोध पत्र हिन्दी भाषा में प्रस्तुत करने का सुअवसर प्राप्त हुआ।

पुरावशेषों के उत्खाता

गुरूवर त्रिपाठी जी ने सोहगौरा (बाँसगाँव–गोरखपुर) के त्रिपाठी परिवार से अपने सम्बन्ध को उद्घाटित करते हुए सोहगौरा के उत्खनन की एक योजना तत्कालीन आचार्य एवं अध्यक्ष प्रो0 विश्वम्भर शरण पाठक के सम्मुख प्रस्तुत किया। विभाग के वरीयता क्रम में गुरूवर त्रिपाठी का तीसरा स्थान था। इसीलिए द्वितीय स्थान के प्रवाचक प्रो0 शैलनाथ चतुर्वेदी को सोहगौरा के उत्खनन का दायित्व प्रदान किया गया। भारत के अहाड़ तथा यूनान के मेनीलियोन और पिलोस के उत्खनन का अनुभव होने के कारण सोहगौरा उत्खनन में अपना सक्रिय सहयोग प्रदान कर प्रो0 त्रिपाठी ने सोहगौरा के पुरावशेषों को भारतीय पुरातत्व के क्षितिज पर प्रतिष्ठापित किया। गोरखपुर परिक्षेत्र के फाजिलनगर और उस्मानपुर डीह (कुशीनगर) के उत्खनन का कार्य सम्पन्न किया। पुरातत्व के प्रमाता के रूप में लगभग 200 प्रमेय स्थलों को पुरातत्व का प्रमाण आधुनिक इतिहास के वस्तुनिष्ठता के लिए एक अनिवार्य तत्व के रूप में स्वीकार किया जाने लगा। इस दृष्टि से उन्होंने शताधिक राष्ट्रीय एवं अन्तर्राष्ट्रीय संगोष्ठियों में भाग लिया तथा उनके लगभग 50 शोध–पत्रों को प्रतिष्ठित राष्ट्रीय एवं अन्तर्राष्ट्रीय पत्रिकाओं में स्थान प्राप्त हुआ। गुरूवर त्रिपाठी ने विभिन्न राष्ट्रीय तथा अन्तर्राष्ट्रीय पुरातत्व, इतिहास एवं संस्कृति संगोष्ठियों की अध्यक्षता की तथा नई दिल्ली, शिमला एवं गोरखपुर में अनेक संगोष्ठियों का आयोजन करने का श्रेय उन्हें प्राप्त है।

शोध प्रकल्पों के प्रणिधि

आचार्य प्रो0 दयानाथ त्रिपाठी का व्यक्तित्व निरन्तर अध्ययन–अध्यवसाय में अद्यावधि व्यस्त रहता है। अपने व्यस्त क्षणों में भी विश्वविद्यालय अनुदान आयोग के वृहद प्रकल्प के रूप में 'आर्कियोलाजी इन ट्रेडीसन' विषय पर महत्वपूर्ण ग्रंथ प्रस्तुत किया और इस ग्रन्थ में उन्होंने पुरातत्व एवं परम्परा को सहचर रूप में प्रस्तुत करने का श्लाघनीय प्रयास किया है। प्रो0 त्रिपाठी ने भारतीय इतिहास शोध परिषद के पुरातत्वीय अनुसंधित्सु के रूप में 'हिन्दूइज्म एवं हेलनिज्म' शोध प्रकल्प में अपने इस शोध–पत्र के द्वारा अन्तर्राष्ट्रीय जगत में एक नवीन आयाम प्रस्तुत किया है। उनके निर्देशन में लगभग दसाधिक शोध छात्रों ने पी0एच–डी0 और डी0 लिट्0 की उपाधियाँ प्राप्त की। उनके शिष्य लोक सेवा आयोग, दिल्ली और उत्तर प्रदेश के अतिरिक्त विश्वविद्यालयों तथा उच्च शैक्षिक संस्थानों में कार्यरत हैं।

कृतित्व

पुरातत्व के व्याख्याता आचार्यवर त्रिपाठी ने 1987 में 'ब्रांज वर्क ऑफ मेन लैंड ग्रीस' (2600 ई0पू0–1450 ई0पू0) तक के यूनानी कांस्य सभ्यता पर अपना शोध ग्रन्थ लिखा है। 1988 ई0 में उन्होंने 'पुरातत्व एवं परम्परा' ग्रन्थ का प्रणयन किया, 'पुरातत्व–भाषा–कोष' का सम्पादन 1994 में किया, 1996 ई0 में 'कल्चरल इंटरएक्शन इंडियन ग्रीस' का प्रणयन किया, 2004 ई0 में 'हिन्दूइज्म एवं हेलेनिज्म' शोध निबन्ध प्रस्तुत किया, 2005 ई0 में 'ए डिस्कोर्स आन इंडो–यूरोपियन लंग्वेज एण्ड कल्चर' विषय पर आयोजित गोष्ठी में प्रस्तुत शोध पत्रों का सम्पादन किया, ए गोल्डेन चेन ऑफ सिविलाइजेशंस : इंडिक, ईरानिक, सेमेटिक एण्ड हेलेनिक', प्रथम भाग, 600 बी0सी0 तक विवरण इस ग्रंथ में प्रस्तुत है। 'ए गोल्डेन चेन फार सिविलाइजेशनः इंडिक, ईरानिक, सेमेटिक एण्ड हेलेनिक', 600बी0सी0 भाग दो का संपादन वर्ष 2012 में तथा वर्ष 2013 में इंडियन सेन्ट्रल एशिया – इंडो-रशियन सेमिनार की कार्यवाही में शोध प्रस्तुत किया।

व्यक्तित्व

पुरातत्व के प्रमाता गुरुश्रेष्ठ प्रो0 दयानाथ त्रिपाठी का विराट व्यक्तित्व पुरातत्व के प्रमेयों (पुरावशेषों) के अभिज्ञान तथा परम्परागत भारतीय लोक जीवन में प्रचलित शाब्दी परम्परा के सहचर की अन्वेषणा करने में सदा संलग्न रहा है। व्यक्तित्व की विराटता का अभिज्ञान उनके कृतित्व के साथ ही साथ समकालीन ऐतिहासिक, पुरातात्विक तथा सांस्कृतिक क्षेत्र की श्रेष्ठ संस्थाओं से अपनी सम्बद्धता सदा बनाये रखे है। प्रो0 त्रिपाठी ग्रीको–रोमन स्टडीज के भारतीय समिति के आजीवन सदस्य के रूप में, भारतीय पुरातत्व समिति, भारतीय इतिहास एवं संस्कृति समिति तथा प्री हिस्टोरिक एवं क्वाटर्नरी स्टडीज के आजीवन सदस्य रूप में अपना अमूल्य योगदान प्रदान करते रहते है। प्रो0 त्रिपाठी मध्य प्रदेश हेरीटेज डेवलपमेंट काउंसिल, भोपाल तथा इलाहाबाद संग्रहालय समिति के प्रशासकीय परिषद के पदाधिकारी रूप में पुरातत्व के क्षेत्र में अनवरत सहयोग, सम्मति परामर्श और निर्देशन के जीवंत साक्षी हैं। इस प्रकार पुरातत्व के प्रमाता के रूप में पुरावशेषों के प्रमेय एवं प्रमाण के सिद्ध पुरुष हैं। मैं उनका अन्तेवासी रहकर गुरूवर त्रिपाठी से अधिकाधिक प्राचीन भारतीय इतिहास, पुरातत्व एवं संस्कृति में ज्ञान प्राप्त करने का सौभाग्यशाली अध्येता हूँ।

AN UNTOLD SAGA OF MY PAPAJI

Devesh N Tripathi

Prologue

I am extremely happy to find the invitation to contribute something to Papaji's felicitation volume. "तेरा ज़िक्र हैया कि इत्र है, जब भी होता है महक जाता हूँ मैं : A M Turaz" (*It is your mention or perfume; whenever it happens I become fragrant*). I am addressing Professor D.N.Tripathi as 'Papaji' frequently in this paper because I am going to write something straight from my heart, as a proud son of this giant personality. Believe me, for past 20 years as a student and learner of psychology, I have a firm belief that no single test of personality in psychology can ever map Papaji's personality. At this juncture, few lines of Qateel Shifai sahib are worth mentioning, "आसमान जो शख्स है सबकी नज़र में उसको छू लेने की जुर्रत कर रहा हूँ मैं" (*I am daring to touch that individual who is a sky in everybody's eye*). He is far beyond the words as expressed in most of his vitae.

Though it's quite true that others can only perceive the overt personality however to build up this overt persona there are always many covert facets. When we refer about knowledge too, there is an explicit aspect that can be seen by everyone but the tacit aspect is always hidden and explicit knowledge is basically an offshoot of this tacit knowledge. Whatever is written in the vitae of any individual are basically his/her achievements in the worldly view. If we ever ask about it personally, we shall be enlightened that whatever world perceives to be as 'achievement' is basically nonentity in that person's view. Products take front stage; however, the process backstage also is equally important and interesting.

Life is not a destination rather it's a journey. When we start the journey, destinations are never seen but mere presence of them in our psyche drives ourselves towards them and we are so engrossed in thinking about these mirage destinations that at times, we forget to enjoy the pleasures of journey.

The Journey

To start this ever interesting journey of my father's untold, unknown, hidden aspect of personality, let me humbly accept this truth in few of these lines: "समंदर को समझना है तो उसकी तह में टहल कर, ये तो साहिल है यहाँ मछलियाँ कपड़े बदलती हैं।" (*To understand sea one has to go deep down at the base, this is the seashore only futile things happen here*). What Bashir Badr sahib has written in the aforesaid lines, I thought it was about my father and, I ponder whether Papaji ever met him? Also I am amazed because for few days I firmly believed that Badr Sahib had written these lines especially for my father. Later, in-depth evaluation of this ode made me realize that this was true for most of us in this dynamic and ever changing society.

Always I have felt that Papaji has been most talked and referred but least understood. He always presents tougher side of his persona to everyone he meets. Even if someone stubborn like me always clings to him then also he never reveals, especially his earlier struggles and sorrows. One has to understand him; he never divulges. He is alike sacred book which neither opens its pages to anybody nor asks others to read it, rather who so ever is interested can readily access him and if one is wise enough s/he will be able to understand that he is like a coconut. Who shall get the nectar of this coconut is basically dependent upon the desire, wish and striving of the person who wants to obtain it.

It is such a Herculean task to come up with a sketch of Papaji because of his multifaceted personality. Earlier life of Papaji reveals that as an individual he too has been a proud son of an honest and hence poor School Principal. In material sense Papaji was deprived yet an emperor. He didn't possess ever enough money but there were lot of values, ethics, culture, dedication, determination and confidence to prove his mettle. He always has been a go-getter type of person who never says die. Throughout his life he has been a true fighter to achieve whatever was justice. He is resolutely grounded yet elite minded. Most positive aspect of his personality has always been his non-compromising nature with life's struggle. No problems of life have ever deterred his ambitions to attain whatever is righteous. Like me, readers might be amazed to see the paradoxical nature of his personality.

It might be a revelation for many that Papaji is very emotional for everyone be it his parents, wife, Gurus, sons, daughters, students, down trodden persons or anyone whom he has known, yet he is very firm. In any context, emotionality seldom overshadows his decision making. Papaji is so successful because of his ability to take decisions, be it wrong at times, and is bold and firmly ever ready to face the consequences of the decisions so taken. In his whole life, his resilient nature has made him bounce back. The tougher the conditions life has offered him the stronger he emerges from that problem and has never complained about it to anyone. Even though suffering with various types of diseases he has been ever contended and satisfied with his life conditions. He always believes that, *"Whenever you feel depressed; keep this in mind, things are yet to happen, life is yet to go; this is just a bend not the end"*.

Any person evolves into such a multifarious personality because some habits become lifestyle of that individual. Lifestyle of Papaji is interwoven in few of these habits such as 'Paan', 'Puja', 'Paper', 'Paidal', 'Padhai' and 'Pehnawa'.

Anyone who has met him can never overlook his face especially his mouth filled with *paan*. Papaji without *paan* will be synonymous to sun without warmth. In the worldly affair, he knows and understands that it is not a good habit for health. Many a times he has attempted to quit this habit and often tells us too that never imitate this habit of mine but HABITS DIE HARD.

Another habit of Papaji is *puja*. Come what may, he never misses it. He is a firm believer of God especially Bajrang Bali. He believes, "मेरा मुहाफ़िज़ मेरा खुदा है, यही बहुत है; चिराग आंधी में जल रहा है यही बहुत है।" *(This is enough that lamp is lit in storm, his saviour is God).*He always has an unshakeable belief on his 'Karma' and 'Tail of Bajrang Bali'. Often he narrates that whatever has been portrayed as his achievements is basically blessings of Prabhu Hanumaan. He is resolute believer in the fact; "हानि लाभ जीवन मरण यश अपयश बिधि हाथ।" *(Loss, gain, birth, death, fame and ill repute are controlled by God).*In our memory, without fail, for past 40 years Papaji has been visiting to Hanuman Mandir preferably Betiahata Gorakhpur on every Tuesday. He incessantly prays to Almighty; "जेहिं बिधि होंहि नाथ हित मेरा करहुँ सो बेगि दास मैं तोरा।" *(O Lord! I am your servant, find a way out in what so ever manner my goodwill happens*).

For the past 50 years, he has a daily habit of reading at least three newspapers and penning down all his routine activities in his small diary: *'Geeta-Dainandini'*. Mornings start with green tea and newspaper. He considers newspapers are basically mirror of this society. After reading these papers often he is very disgusted to find perishing value system of this society. Alone retired professor attempts to reconnect himself with the happenings of the society. At times, he is so happy with any of the article/poetry published in any paper that immediately it is scribbled at any corner of paper, later to be sent to persons whom he feels they can appreciate the essence of it.

Another habit of Papaji is walking a few miles which I have listed as *paidal*. Despite of being diagnosed with osteoarthritis he is in a habit of walking daily in the evening. He makes it a point to collect his 'Paan' himself. Seeing my pumpkin shaped body he always passes on to me the famous quote of Mahakavi Kalidas, "शरीर माध्यम् खलु धर्म साधनम्।" *(The body is the means of fulfillment of Dharma).* In his age he is so disciplined about his body that he rarely misses yoga, exercises and walking, now with the help of a cane stick. When the sun sets and birds return to their nest no one can ever miss this lonely archaeologist walking silently, chanting Gayatri Mantra in the busy shrieking lanes of Bilandpur, Gorakhpur.

'Padhai' or reading has always enthralled Papaji. Few persons can ever beat him in reading. I believe reading habit is very close to his heart. He is not a bookworm but can hardly resist *padhai* for less than 3 to 10 hour/day. The library he possesses is worth watching. In addition to his favourite subjects– culture, linguistics, archaeology and tradition – it is stacked with archives of many historical accounts, literary and philosophical books along with dictionaries of many languages. He seems to be totally engrossed and happy, whenever he is dusting them. He is such a quick learner that with the technological revolution these days he is adept in reading e-books but still enjoys reading printed books.

Last of the habits of Papaji's *'Pehnawa'*. He is very cautious about the dress he wears. His wardrobe is always packed with different types of matching dresses and perfumes for various occasions. Also he never ever misses to take out sometime to get rid of budding hairs on his chin. I always felt that with such a magnetic personality whatever he wears will suit him but he never presents himself ill-dressed to anyone. This habit of him, I believe, is rooted in his British training. Moreover, he is of an era when being a university teacher he was supposed to be a role model to his students and other members of society.

Every individual seems to be composite of HABITS and various ROLES s/he plays during entire lifetime. How truly and effectively do we play our roles fundamentally indicates the significance of our being in this mortal world. In our complete chapters of life we are assigned various roles by The Supreme Playwright: The Almighty. We simply dance like a buffoon on the tunes of that rhythmic composer. Further, Papaji's untold saga encapsulates his dutiful personality for various roles to which he had been passionately committed.

As a son, Papaji, being the eldest child of his parents, assumed responsibilities in quite an early age. His parents lovingly called him *'Bachau'*. He joined Gorakhpur University in 1958 at the tender age of 21. He very efficiently delivered all his responsibilities as a son, and as an elder brother he even got his single sister married. Also he supported his younger brothers in the best way he could. He did his best of efforts to support his parents. He was quite fearful of my Grandfather and was very attached to his mother. His parents have been a whole world for him. Words of his parents behold Gospel for Papaji. I saw his eyes full of sea when my Grandfather, then Grandma and again when one of my uncle bid adieu to this world, in a very short span of time. As a souvenir Papaji has preserved letters written to him by my Grandfather. Even today anyone can find his parents' portrait in his *puja room,* next to God. As a son Papaji seems to be humming couplet of Manzar Bhopali sahib, "इसी से अज़मत की मंज़िलों का पतामिलेगा, ये जो बुज़ुर्गों की ख़ाक़–ए–पा है, यही बहुत है।" (*Services of one's parents is sufficient enough to understand the path of ultimate reality*).

As a loving husband, my father holds a lot of respect for my mother. He understands Mummy better than her. Always together they have shared their good and bad days. In his earlier struggling days, he had very less time for the household chores and children. The saying *'Behind every successful man there is a woman'* seems to be relevant in his life too. Till date, Papaji admires her dual responsibility both as father/mother. He often refers that it was she who took the pains of upbringing us. They share a very friendly and cordial relation. A lot of times it is amusing to find both of them affectionately teasing each other. They are made for each other and these days it seems to be a vacuum for them, if anyone of them is far. For these and many other reasons Papaji forever refers my mummy as *"Deviji"*.

I think words fall short when I have to elaborate the role of Papaji as a father. According to his basic personality he never expressed his true feelings of love, compassion and emotion to his children; but we as his progeny may probably express our feelings through these lines by Azm shakiri, "धूप में जल रहा था बदन, पाँव बांधे हुए थी थकन; तेरी बाँहों में आकर लगा ज़िंदगी ताज़ा दम हो गई।" (*My body was burning under sun, I was too tired, when I came into your lap I felt rejuvenated*). Papaji has ever been solution to the problems we face. The values, ethics, morality, character, straight forwardness, impartiality, fearlessness, discipline, punctuality, respect for elders, and courage to say *no,* are all his personality traits that has been imbibed by all of us. Due to our parents' effort we all are well settled and well placed at our respective places. If ever we had desired for anything in life, those have been silently fulfilled by them. At times in his role as father Papaji has been strict, but as a punishment for himself he missed his supper that day. Papaji has always been friends of his children and has always expected and did open communication on varied issues of life. Today we all have become parents and realize how much pain and sacrifice they did for us. I have heard this from my mother that due to our joint family he always put himself out of sight and steal a look to see my eldest sister playing and if ever he could be in the lone company of my sister he would shower all his love on her. Similarly, he has been attached to each one of us but never displays it before public. He has always respected others' individuality and never intervenes until it is very pertinent to do so. He has always taught us, "ज़िंदगी को हमेशा ज़रूरतों में रखो, ख़्वाहिशों की तरफ न ले जाओ; क्योंकि ज़रूरत फ़कीरों की भी पूरी हो जाती है और ख़्वाहिशें बादशाहों की भी अधूरी रह जाती हैं।" (*Keep yourself limited within necessities, don't ever desire too much because necessities of everyone is fulfilled; however desires of even emperors remain unfulfilled*).

About modern days Bashir Badr Sahib has stated very aptly: "कोई हाथ भी न मिलायेगा जो गले मिलोगो तपाक से, ये नये मिज़ाज़ का शहर है जरा फ़ासले से मिला करो।" (*In this materialistic world keep a distance while interacting, as no one will even shake hands if you are ever ready to embrace them*). These lines hold true when I think about Papaji as Friend. He is very cautious in selecting friends however he has always been a very devoted and loyal friend to those who are his real friends. He had many acquaintances but very few friends. These friends lovingly called him *'Panditji'*. In friendship he believes "शर्तें लगाई नहीं जाती दोस्ती के साथ, कीजिये मुझे कुबूल मेरी हर कमी के साथ।" (*one has to accept friends with all their negativities as you cannot lay a wager in friendship*). For his friends Papaji has been most dependable person on this earth and they would vouch for him in extreme conditions. Also this holds true about Papaji as he too would look forward towards them in his happiness and sorrow alike. As written by Goswami Tulsi Dassji, "धीरज धर्म मित्र अरु नारी, आपद् काल परिखिहहुं चारी।" (*Patience, Dharma, friends and wife are well tested during testing times*). He and his friends were time tested and even preferred to sacrifice their lives for each other.

At times seeing his immaculate tactical prowess and anger many of his acquaintances called him *Chanakya*– the strategist and others termed him *Durvasa*– the angry man, but for a friend who truly understands him Papaji is *Daya Nath*– Master of Kindness. I think across time and era no one can ever be equated with any other person in this universe. Each individual is unique and this forms the basis of psychology. One of the behavioural manifestations of kindness is forgiveness. Papaji has always believed "अपराध क्षमा गुर्वीणाम्" (*forgiveness has an edge over crime*) especially in the context of friendship. He has forgiven everyone even those foe and friend who at times have attempted to demean or even be-head him. Papaji seems to be articulating Munnavar Rana sahib's thought, "मुझे दुश्मनों से भी ख़ुद्दारी की उम्मीद रहती है, सिर किसी का भी हो कदमों में अच्छा नहीं लगता।" (*I expect self-respect even from my enemies as I am never delighted to see a surrendered self before other human being*). His philosophy of friendship and enmity may be summarized through this couplet of Bashir Badr sahib, "दुश्मनी जम कर करो, लेकिन ये गुंजाइश रहे, कि जब हम दोस्त बनें तो शर्मिंदा ना हों।" (*Even do enmity with lot of determination but always keep a chance that if ever again we be friends we are not ashamed*).

Above elucidated roles were performed by Papaji at personal level. At the professional level too, as a student Papaji is so attached with his teachers that in his office cum reading room photographs of both the *Gurus* Lord Colin Renfrew and Prof. G.C. Pande are easily traceable. It seems, he feels that till date whatever knowledge he acquires is bestowed upon him by these teachers. He has faced a lot of hardships to attain the position, he has. His relentless pursuit for knowledge and assiduous character as a student made him a success to overcome all the challenges life has ever posed before him. His multilingual ability, clarity of thought and clear goals in combination with the blessings of Almighty, his parents and *Gurus* made him a highly successful student who could further become a teacher, a role model for many students.

As a teacher, without fail Papaji made a point to complete the curriculum assigned to him. Despite of being busy in various activities he never missed his classes. He has always been a very methodical, well prepared, strict and punctual teacher. Papaji believes that life is a learning process and to be effective teacher one has to a continuous learner and student. Morality, character and ethics were the driving forces of this disciplined teacher and I think that who so ever possesses these qualities, people become fearful of him. I shall again refer to Manzar Bhopali Saheb, "मैं मुत्मइन हूँ कुफ़्र की आंधियों में मंज़र, चिराग–ए–ईमान जल रहा है, यही बहुत है।" (*I am contended even under the thunders of 'Kufra: Refuting the existence of Almighty'; this is enough for me that my character is intact hence attached to Almighty*).

As a teacher, Papaji never compromised with the values of this noble profession and had to face lot of anguish of his students but never subdued to anyone's unethical demands. As a teacher, he believed in himself and was very tenacious for what he believed as correct. For these reasons I can easily state about Papaji's role as a teacher through this poetry of Dr Kumar Vinod,

देखिये उस पेड़ को तन कर खड़ा है आज भी
आंधियों का काम चलना है, चलीं तो क्या हुआ?
कम से कम तुम तो करो खुद पर यकीं ऐ दोस्तों
गर ज़माने का नहीं तुम पर यकीं तो क्या हुआ?

(*Till date see that unwavering standing tree even if there were many storms, who cares? At least have the self-confidence, my friends! Who cares if the society does not believe you?*)

Papaji has always been a guide, mentor and motivator to many students. Even though he has always believed that one should not express his opinions regarding any problem unless sought but unobtrusively he never misses to indicate the correct path. "वो जब भी देते हैं मायूसी के लम्हों में जरा सा हौसला, हम कागज़ की कश्ती में ही समंदर में उतर जाते हैं।" (*Whenever I am depressed small motivation provided by him is enough for me to jump into the sea with a paper boat:* Anonymous). He has always been a true motivator, by his words and deeds. As a motivator and guide he exemplifies to think big, face challenges bravely without losing self-confidence. Many a times, by his speech and actions it seems he wants to reverberate the couplet of Rahat Indori sahib, "तूफ़ानों से आँख मिलाओ सैलाबों पर वार करो, मल्लाहों का चक्कर छोड़ो तैर के दरिया पार करो।" (*Face the adversaries, attack the enemy fleet, abstain from the expectation of any help, and just do self-efforts to swim across the sea*).

As an academician, Papaji's contributions are well known to the learned readers. I am reminded about the international conference organized single-handedly by him as Head of the Department, Ancient History and Archaeology, Gorakhpur University. All the scholars around the globe, in addition to the people of Gorakhpur marvelled at the organizing ability of Papaji at such a small place with meagre funds. It was his honest incessant effort and academic acumen that many well-known figures of the city, though poles apart in personal life came forward to contribute in this historical event. Also as an administrator and leader Papaji has been very successful. He held various positions with integrity throughout his career. As an administrator he believed to keep distance from the persons sitting at top, if there was no genuine reason of doing so. He had to face many obstacles, untoward incidences and opposition during enforcement of rules, regulations and discipline. I often thought, "ज़माना क्यूँ ख़िलाफ़त करता है हर बात में उसकी, हक़ीक़त में मुझे वो शख़्स तो खुद्दार लगता है।" (*Why he is always opposed by the society; in reality I feel that he is a person of integrity*). During his administrative regime whenever he and his Webley Scott .32 revolvers roared no other person even dared to perform any misconduct. Papaji has always been a fearless and risk taking individual for truth. When his bosom friends would advise him to refrain from such risky situations he seems to be saying in words of Shahid,

दुनिया उलझ रही है तो सुलझा रहा हूँ मैं
आँधी से कुछ तो सोच कर टकरा रहा हूँ मैं।
मुझ पर हंसो न तुम मेरी हिम्मत को दाद दो
ज़र्रा हूँ..... और पहाड़ से टकरा रहा हूँ मैं।
जारी रहेगी जंग हवाओं से सुबह तक
ये किसने कह दिया कि बुझा जा रहा हूँ मैं।

(*With certain faith I am opposing the thunders as I am attempting to solve the puzzles of this life. Don't laugh at me rather compliment my courage as being a miniscule I am fighting the mountain. Till the dawn, fight with adversaries shall keep on going, who says that I am lit off?*)
Papaji's tenure as Head of flying squad, President of FUPRUTA (Federation of Uttar Pradesh Residential Teachers Association) and as Chief Proctor, to name a few, can hardly be forgotten by people of that period. During these days too, he was so sagacious and sympathetic that he provided employment to many persons. As a leader, Papaji always gave importance to the tasks at hand but never overlooked his companions.

Epilogue

I am quite dissatisfied hence sad with myself that despite of my best efforts I was not able to convert my feelings and Papaji's accurate personality into words. Believe me, whatever has been experienced in this brief journey put in my words is just tip of an iceberg. May be, if you permit still I can say that Papaji possesses a magnetic personality. Papaji is versatile; utmost honest; man of character, integrity, ethics and values; astute; he hates lies; loves truth; straight forward; a true philosopher; methodical archaeologist; avid reader; prolific researcher; lover of semi classical music; precisely – a person who believes in no-nonsense; compassionate; magnanimous; impartial; uncompromising, etc. He is a true follower of simple living and high thinking. Papaji had never been part of minute rat races. He has always been a satisfied person with whatever has been provided to him by the Almighty. Manzar Bhopali sahib has truly stated, "मुझे फ़लक की बुलंदियों की हवस नहीं है, जो मेरे रब ने मुझे दिया है, यही बहुत है।" (*I don't have lust for top positions I am contended with whatever has been given to me by my Lord*).

Papaji is a person who enjoys discussing ideas not persons, for him work is worship and he understands that even if you give yourself to others, in this materialistic world once the chair is gone everyone will disown. Wrinkles of his face in a strong and echoic voice often communicate this verse to me, "टूट कर रोज़–रोज भी मुकम्मल खड़ा हूँ मैं, जिंदगी देख तुझसे कितना बड़ा हूँ मैं।" (*Though many hardships have been presented to me at various fronts still I am intact and bigger than life*).

पिता–पुत्र

देवेशनाथ त्रिपाठी

हमारा सम्बंध
पहले से स्थापित
नहीं हुआ कभी परिभाषित।
मैं देवदारु,
तुम हिमालय
मैं पत्थर
तुम शिवालय।
आधुनिकता ग्रसती जा रही है
सभी सम्बंधों को।
आज के पिता–पुत्र सम्बंधों को
देखिये अगर गौर से
तो मिलेगा
पिता अग्नि है
पुत्र धुंआ
पिता सागर है, तो
पुत्र कुंआ।
पिता स्वयं जलता है
और उसी से
पुत्र की उत्पत्ति होती है।
छोड़ देता है पिता
पुत्र को सहज ही
अपना आकाश टटोलने के लिए
और पुत्र भी बढ़ चलता है
असीमित ऊँचाइयाँ पाने के लिए
अपने पिता से दूर ....
यहाँ पिता जलता रहता है

और पुत्र
आकाश में जाकर
न जाने कहाँ
अपना अस्तित्व खो देता है
और पिता सिर्फ उसकी राह देखता
इंतज़ार करता रहता है
अपने पुत्र के लौट आने का।
हमारा सम्बंध तो
जस का तस है
मैं देवदारु
आपकी ही गोद में
अपनी जड़ें और मजबूत करता
बढ़ रहा हूँ
उन्हीं असीमित
ऊँचाइयों को पाने के लिए,
जो आधुनिक पुत्र
अपनी जड़ें खोकर पाते हैं।
मैं पत्थर ही सही मगर
खुश हूँ कि
मेरे पास शिवालय तो है।
मैं देवदारु सा
एकांतिक अकेला वृक्ष ही सही
बहुत खुश हूँ कि
मेरे पास हिमालय तो है।

My Friend Daya Nath, Indian Archeology --- Some Nostalgia, Some Rambling Thoughts

Sibesh Bhattacharya

Although we were batch mates in our postgraduate final class --- MA in Ancient History, Culture and Archaeology at Allahabad University, 1958 --- we were not very close then. My intimacy with Daya Nath developed later. There was no natural common platform for regular interaction during our earlier career. While Daya Nath joined Gorakhpur University as a teacher, I was fortunate to get an appointment in my alma mater itself. During postgraduate days our syllabus did not offer scope for choice or specialization; every student had to take same sets of papers. So area specialization could begin only at the research stage. I personally don't think it was such a disaster. Again speaking in purely personal vein, I don't think I had then the maturity and equipment to independently decide upon an area of specialization. In fact, my research topic was chosen more by my teachers, the research committee members of the department, than by me and for that I remain eternally grateful to them. It was in that manner that I was initiated into the area of socio-economic history of early India. I do not know the story of how Daya Nath came to the field of archaeology. I should assume that it must not have been very different from my own.

It was exciting time. The Freedom of the country still had freshness about it; the air of expectation had not yet taken flight. New ideas were arising or coming from outside. If there was clearly discernible enthusiasm for many of these ideas, there was an equal measure of unease and confusion about them. Meanwhile, important, even momentous, changes were taking place in the political, social and economic fabric of the country. Universal adult franchise had recently been introduced and two elections were already successfully conducted on that basis. Zamindari was abolished. States were being reorganized on linguistic basis and other local factors. Five Year Plans for channelized economic development had been launched. However, everything was not just positive; there was ample measure of negative things to worry about as well. The scar of partition had not fully healed and 'refugee' problem was not fully solved. The country was in the throe of food shortage and had to depend on foreign aids on that front. These led to considerable restrictions in trade and consumption, the 'ration' regime and 'license permit raj' breeding corruption. And then there was the shadow of the 'cold war' and the two contending ideologies. It was not that the everyday life of a young man in Allahabad or Gorakhpur was directly affected by all these, but the universities were sensitive places prone to reflect even distant issues. The intellectual discourse in the country naturally could not remain unaffected by the changes.

Among the various developments taking place --- all of them not always mutually harmonious or coherent --- two proved significant for moulding the thought world of the country. There was a growing sensitivity and appreciation of the problems of poverty. It was natural therefore that the deprived and the marginalized received considerable intellectual and academic attention besides that of the politicians and planners. Poverty and deprivation have of course remained a perennial milch cow for politicians of all hue and they perhaps account for a great deal of the depravity found in our public life. Our main interest here, however, is the thought-environment in which our generation grew and not so much the public life and politics directly. The growing sensitivity about poverty and deprivation and the urge for economic development led to a greater, deeper and a more critical interest in the roots of our civilizational history. Unfortunately, the 'critical interest' later in the hands of excessively ideologically oriented scholars became a synonym for the rejection of everything lock stock and barrel of early Indian heritage -- a clear case of pouring the baby out with the bath water. In the beginning, however, this sensitivity gave a fillip to the expansion and diversification of focus in the study of our early past. This was particularly true of archaeology. There was an upsurge of interest and a welcome expansion in archaeological studies of early India. The ground for that expansion to some extent was already laid by Wheeler when he invited universities to take up archaeological field works on equal footing with the Archaeological Survey. The University of Allahabad was among the first ones to respond to the call. Gorakhpur university too followed suit after it was opened. The career of Daya Nath very largely coincides with this happy phase of Indian archaeology.

The other development that I mentioned was the rising assertion of regional identities. This came to be described in the contemporary intellectual parley in various terms: regionalism, regional nationalism, sub-nationalism, multiculturalism, pluralism, and so on. It's most aggressive early expressions were in the North Eastern India and a slightly less aggressive one was the assertion of Dravidian identity. Our concern here, however, is not with the politics of the development, but with its impact on academic and intellectual field, particularly on the study of archaeology and early history of India. The expansion of archaeological work, with new areas coming under archaeologist's spade and exploration, universities contributing substantially towards it, was revealing distinct regional traits within a broad common pattern of development. These had two interesting characteristics: (a) emergence of certain common features that could be loosely described as 'Indian', and (b) within the rubric of the Indian, pluralistic trends. The cumulative effect of the new and expanding archaeological studies within the country was the emergence of a culture-profile that had three simultaneous strands interacting with each other. These three can be likened to three concentric circles: the local, the Indian, the global. While the general pattern more or less conformed to the universal sequence of human development, within it there was a distinctive Indian flavor and then even within that there were regional and local features.

Some ideas that held sway came to be challenged and some of the accepted neat divisions tended to become hazy or obliterated by the emerging new archaeological evidence; the pre-Aryan Aryan divide, for example. Inconsistency of the theory of the wanton total destruction of the pre-Vedic urban Drávidian high Harappan culture by the nomadic barbarian Aryan invading hordes became more and more evident; like its origin the end of Harappan culture too appeared to have been gradual. It never seemed to have died; it rather seemed to have merged into succeeding sequences providing the stimuli for the growth of a new phase of urban development in the Ganga valley and eastern India. The space for the purely nomadic/ pastoral Vedic culture, untouched by urbanism of any sort tended to dry up. All these necessitated re-looking at the overall development sequence during early India.

We may mention in passing another thing. The new archaeological methods and techniques appeared to make archaeology an autonomous subject. It seemed it was not necessary any longer (unlike the earlier phase when epigraphy, numismatics and study of monuments dominated archaeology, particularly in India) to correlate it to literary evidence. However, the narrowing gap between the waning of the Harappan and the subsequent urban development seem to be bringing back the issue of the relevance of the correlation of the archaeological and the literary evidence to the fore. Archaeology seemed in fact to be preparing a case and offering the ground for reexamining the relative chronology of the Harappan and Vedic, of the Samhita, Brahmana, Aranyakas and Upanishads, of the Vedic and the Puranas. The theory that the four classes of Vedic literature originated in four succeeding periods has been stoutly contested by Anirvana, for example. And, the general archaeological picture seems to point out that the profile of India right from the very beginning was predominantly pluralistic. It was pluralistic not only in regional cultural manifestations but equally strongly in patterns of living and economy as well; within the same region and within same period urban and rural, agricultural and pastoral, even hunting and gathering economy and way of life could and did coexist without too much frictions. While there could be a magnificent urban establishment at Kausambi, for example, not far from it, the

Vindhyan/ Mirzapur area continued to remain in hunting gathering state. This is also the general picture that we get from literature.

Daya Nath was well equipped to deal with the emerging challenges of Indian archaeology. He had close familiarity with the Bronze Age material of Greece and had done an important book on it. We have noted above that a good deal of the emerging problems of Indian archaeology actually related to the 'Bronze Age' phase and the knowledge of the Greek material surely was an advantage. His association with Renfrew gave him a vantage point in the interesting area of the archaeology of language. He had conducted significant archaeological explorations of the Rapti valley. He was also among the pioneers to attempt to relate Indian archaeology to tradition. In his later life, Daya Nath began moving from field work based archaeology towards comparative history, comparing Hinduism and Hellenism. Perhaps he was making a statement through this transition: value of archaeology ultimately lies in shedding light on the less illumined aspects of human past.

A few words on the human qualities of Daya Nath may not be out of place here. He is a friend par excellence. His loyalty as a friend has always touched me most. I would always remember those misty early dawns during winter months when I would get down from the train from Allahabad at Gorakhpur Station, the twilight had hardly broken, and Daya Nath would be there with his warm welcome smile to receive me. Those days I was a frequent visitor to Gorakhpur University and Daya Nath would be present every time without fail at the station to receive me. And then we would first go to the platform-teashop and have tea before proceeding towards the University Guest House. The sun was still hidden below the eastern horizon. Many a times Daya Nath would make me stay with him at his house. His hospitality has always been extremely warm and generous. I would also always remember the numerous meetings of various committees we attended together, the number of viva voce examinations we conducted together. I always found him ever conscientious and totally committed never sharking work or responsibility. On the occasions of viva voce examinations of PG classes, on the concluding days of the examinations, the filling of the mark sheet and the completion of the required formalities would take us almost into midnight! I don't remember Daya Nath ever betraying any sign of annoyance or impatience for this. Among the fondest memories of our long association of well over half a century are the days we spent together at Shimla at the Indian Institute of Advanced Study. I will treasure these memories for ever.

बहुस्तरीय संचरना का उत्कृष्ट व्यक्तित्व

सुरेन्द्र दुबे

आचार्य दयानाथ त्रिपाठी मेरे लिए गुरु कल्प आदरणीय सहयोगी और संरक्षक की भूमिका में रहे हैं। मेरे ऊपर सदैव उनका स्नेह और विश्वास रहा है। वे जहाँ एक ओर अपने विषय ख्यात आचार्य रहे हैं, वहीं दूसरी ओर उनकी प्रशासनिक क्षमता भी अद्वितीय रही हैं। विद्वान और प्रशासक के बीच उनकी तीसरी विशेषता है उनकी अद्भुत संगठन और नेतृत्व क्षमता। विद्वान, प्रशासक और नेता की यह त्रिवेणी ही उन्हें अपने समकालीन अन्यों से विरल बनाती है।

दीनदयाल उपाध्याय गोरखपुर विश्वविद्यालय, गोरखपुर के इतिहास का विलक्षण काल–खण्ड। परिसर–शिक्षण और आवासीय में अजीब दहशत का माहौल जारी था। जाड़े की रात–समय होगा कोई 7:30 से 8:00 बजे बीच का। एक वरिष्ठ आचार्य आवासीय परिसर की सड़कों पर टहल रहे थे कि अचानक किसी ओर से चोरों की तरह आकर कुछ गुण्डों ने उन पर आक्रमण कर दिया। एक निर्दोष व्यक्ति पर अकारण किया गया यह हमला सबको विचलित और हमप्रभ कर देने वाला था। खैर, उन्हें लेकर लोग सिविल अस्पताल गए। प्रारम्भिक जाँच और हल्की सुश्रुषा के बाद उन्हें छोड़ दिया गया। मैं उन दिनों शिक्षक संघ का महामंत्री था। अनेक शिक्षक साथियों के साथ अस्पताल से परिसर तक हमलोग चक्कर काटते रहे। उस दिन के बाद रात में पहरा देने का कार्यक्रम भी चला। दहशत इतनी कि लोग दिन ढलते ही अपने घरौदों में कैद हो जाते थे। इस कायरतापूर्ण हमले को अखबारों ने प्रमुखता से छापा। परिणाम वही हुआ जो होना था–हीरापुरी कॉलोनी के मुख्य द्वार पर पहला बंगला सुबह से ही आने जाने वालों से भर गया। लोग आते, हालचाल पूछते, अफसोस जाहिर करते और चले जाते। जाड़े का समय, चोटिल आचार्य धूप में अपने आंगन में लेटे थे। लोग चर्चा करते–हमले का कारण क्या है? क्या यह हमला एक कठोर अनुशासन लागू करने वाले आचार्य पर है? विश्वविद्यालय से लेकर प्रदेश स्तर तक शिक्षक राजनीति में अपने नेतृत्व कौशल और सक्रिय जीवन संघर्ष से एक स्थायी पहचान बनाने वाले शिक्षक नेता पर है? या ....अनेक तरह की खुसुर–फुसुर चलती रही। दोपहर ढल रही थी। शाम धीरे–धीरे आँगन में उतरने लगी। श्वेत वस्त्र और केश दाढ़ी वाले एक सज्जन चोटिल आचार्य जी के पास आते हैं। लोगों को लगता है कि आचार्य जी उनसे रात की घटना के विषय में कुछ महत्त्वपूर्ण सूचना देंगे या लेंगे। पर, यह क्या? ....इस दशा में भी आचार्य जी अपने किसी लेख के विषय में उनसे बात कर रहे हैं। ऐसे हैं आचार्य श्रेष्ठ प्रो. दयानाथ त्रिपाठी। यह देखकर वहाँ स्थित हम शिक्षकों को लगा कि इस व्यक्ति को अपने शरीर से ज्यादा अपने विषय से प्रेम है।

दीनदयाल उपाध्याय गोरखपुर विश्वविद्यालय के मजीठिया भवन का कमरा नं. 113। कुलपति श्री जी.सी. चतुर्वेदी का विदाई समारोह। इस समारोह के पहले तक हम लोगों को यह भरोसा था कि चतुर्वेदी जी को एक टर्म और मिल जाएगा। चतुर्वेदी जी ने विश्वविद्यालय के कीचड़ को स्वच्छ कर उसमें ज्ञान का कमल खिलाने का सार्थक प्रयत्न किया था। एक घनघोर अराजक माहौल से विश्वविद्यालय को मुक्ति दिलाई थी। संस्था को अराजक, अव्यवस्था और गुण्डई से मुक्त कर एक स्वस्थ वातावरण दिया था। विदाई समारोह में चतुर्वेदी जी की इन्हीं बातों की प्रशंसा हो रही थी। प्रशंसा जायज थी। शिक्षक के रूप में हमलोगों ने पहली बार पठन–पाठन का माहौल पाया

था। चतुर्वेदी जी ने जब अपनी बात कहने के लिए माइक सँभाला तो उन्होंने कहा–'मैंने जो किया, आप सबके सहयोग से किया। हाँ, मुझे एक जादू की छड़ी मिल गई थी। वह भी यहीं से। वह जादू की छड़ी थी–डॉ. दयानाथ त्रिपाठी। मैं इनके भरोसे बहुत कुछ कर सका। डॉ. त्रिपाठी उस समय मुख्य नियन्ता थे। यह थी उनकी अनुशासनिक और प्रशासनिक क्षमता। मुझे स्मरण है, उस समय विश्वविद्यालय में से अभी जौनपुर अलग नहीं हुआ था। जौनपुर और काशी विद्यापीठ का बहुत–सा हिस्सा गोरखपुर विश्वविद्यालय परिक्षेत्र में ही आता था। विश्वविद्यालय परिसर के साथ–साथ उसके परिक्षेत्र में आने वाले सभी महाविद्यालयों को नकल विहीन परीक्षा का वरदान देने वालों में डॉ. त्रिपाठी महत्त्वपूर्ण रहे हैं। डॉ. माहेश्वर मिश्र, डॉ. दयानाथ त्रिपाठी और डॉ. करुणाकर त्रिपाठी की इस तिकड़ी ने विश्वविद्यालय का जो कायाकल्प किया उसका मीठा फल, आज भी बिना किसी अतिरिक्त श्रम के हम खा रहे हैं। नब्बे के दशक के बाद की पीढ़ी के शिक्षकों को तो शायद यह बोध भी नहीं होगा नकल रोकने और विश्वविद्यालय में पठन–पाठन का अनुकूल वातावरण बनाने के लिए हमारे पुरखों ने किस तरह का जोखिम उठाया और आपने को दाँव पर लगाया था? इस संदर्भ में आज स्मरण में अनेक घटनाएं उमड़ घुमड़ रही हैं किन्तु आजमगढ़ की घटना तो अलग खड़ी आज भी स्मृति में जीवन्त है। ऐसी अनेक घटनाओं की कोख से निकला था डॉ. त्रिपाठी का कठोर अनुशासक व्यक्तित्व। इलाहाबाद विश्वविद्यालय के टॉपर और गोरखपुर विश्वविद्यालय के इस अत्यन्त तेजस्वी और लोकप्रिय शिक्षक ने शिक्षा के मंदिर को स्वच्छ करने के लिए अपने व्यक्तित्व को एक इतर रूप दिया था, जो विश्वविद्यालय के इतिहास में सदैव के लिए दर्ज रहेगा।

प्रो. त्रिपाठी ने अपनी उत्कृष्ट नेतृत्व और संगठन क्षमता का परिचय देते हुए विश्वविद्यालय शिक्षक संघ में सक्रिय भूमिका के निर्वहन के साथ ही आगे चलकर उ.प्र. आवासीय विश्वविद्यालय शिक्षक महा संघ के अध्यक्ष तक की लम्बी यात्रा तय की थी। महासंघ के गठन और उसके सुदृढ़ीकरण में जिन लोगों का उत्कृष्ट योगदान रहा है उसमें त्रिपाठी जी का महत्त्व उल्लेखनीय है। मुझे याद है 1983 का वह लम्बा आन्दोलन जिसने विश्वविद्यालय शिक्षकों को प्रोन्नति का अवसर सुलभ कराया। पहले विश्वविद्यालय के विभागों में रीडर और प्रोफेसर के बमुश्किल क्रमशः 3 से 4 और 1 से 2 पद हुआ करते थे। अनेक अपने विषय के ख्यातिलब्ध आचार्य प्रवक्ता पद से ही सेवानिवृत्त हो जाया करते थे। हताशा और कुण्ठा के उस दौर से शिक्षक समुदाय को उबारने में इस प्रोन्नति योजना ने बड़ी मदद की। इतना ही नहीं कैडर पद पर नियुक्ति के लालच में शिक्षकों का जिस तरह शोषण होता है वह अपने आपमें एक कटु अनुभव था। कभी–कभी बिना किसी प्रयत्न के मिली हुई सहज और सरल जीवनोपलब्धि हमें उसकी नींव के पत्थरों की याद ही नहीं दिलाती है। लगता है कि यह सब जो हमें मिल रहा है, वह मेरा पैतृक अधिकार है, जबकि ऐसा है नहीं। इस अधिकार को पाने के लिए और इसके रक्षण–पोषण के लिए कितने लोगों ने अपने को खपाया है जरा, उसे भी हमें स्मरण कर लेना चाहिए। प्रो. त्रिपाठी पर बात करते हुए मुझे वे दिन स्पष्ट आईने की तरह दिख रहे हैं, जब इन लोगों ने अपनी संघर्ष क्षमता से हमें यह सुखद अवसर उपलब्ध कराया। आज बिना किसी कठोर परिश्रम के मिली हुई यह उपलब्धि हमारे भीतर अकर्मण्यता और अक्षमता भी भर रही है। हम शोषण से मुक्त हो गए, प्रोन्नति के अवसर भी सुलभ हो गए, किन्तु हमारी अकादमिक उपलब्धियाँ आज कहाँ हैं? विषय और विभागों के प्रति दायित्वबोध एवं समर्पण कहाँ है? त्रिपाठी जी के बहाने अपने शिक्षक बंधुओं से प्रार्थना है कि जो सुअवसर हमें मिला है उसका हम सदुपयोग करें। अपने को माँज कर और अधिक तैयार करें। कहीं ऐसा न हो कि यह सुअवसर हमें जड़ बना दे। इस विषय पर मेरी प्रो. त्रिपाठी से कभी बात तो नहीं हुई है, किन्तु मुझे लगता है कि वे हमारी पीढ़ी की कर्तव्य–विमुखता को देखकर निश्चित ही पछताते होंगे। उन्हें लगता होगा कि किनके लिए हम लोगों ने संघर्ष किया? क्यों किया? उच्च शिक्षा की गुणवत्ता की अभिवृद्धि के लिए जिन लोगों ने अपना सब कुछ खपाया है ऐसे त्रिपाठी जी का स्नेह उन शिक्षकों के लिए निरन्तर मिलता रहता है जो अन्य प्रशासनिक या शिक्षक राजनीति में कुछ करते हुए भी अपने विषय में अपना सर्वोत्तम योगदान कर रहे हैं, क्योंकि उन्होंने स्वयं यही किया है।

प्रो. त्रिपाठी इलाहाबाद विश्वविद्यालय से स्नातकोत्तर उपाधि प्राप्त करने के बाद हमारे विश्वविद्यालय में प्रवक्ता पद पर नियुक्त हुए थे। उसी विभाग में प्रवक्ता, उपाचार्य और आचार्य पद पर कार्य करते हुए अध्यक्ष पद से

1998 में सेवानिवृत्त हुए। इस बीच ग्रीक सरकार की अध्येतावृत्ति (1971–74) लेकर ग्रीक भाषा में, डिप्लोमा तथा कालान्तर में ब्रिटिश काउंसिल की अध्येतावृत्ति के साथ पी–एच.डी. उपाधि प्राप्त की। सैकड़ों शोधपत्रों, संगोष्ठियों और कार्यशालाओं में अपने व्याख्यानों द्वारा पुरातत्त्व और प्राचीन इतिहास के क्षेत्र में अपना उल्लेखनीय योगदान किया। यह हमलोागें के लिए गौरव की बात है कि कौशाम्बी, सोहागौरा, फाजिलनगर, उस्मानपुर डीहा (कुशीनगर) की खुदाई आपकी देखरेख में ही सम्पन्न हुई। ये सब ऐसी बातें हैं, जिनकी चर्चा मात्र इसलिए कर रहा हूँ कि मेरी दृष्टि में ऐसे कई शिक्षक हैं, जो अच्छे प्रशासक रहे या अच्छे शिक्षक नेता रहे हैं, किन्तु यह सब रहते हुए भी अपने विषय में उत्कृष्ट योगदान करना निश्चित ही एक बहुमुखी प्रतिभा और बहुस्तरीय मनोसंरचना के व्यक्तित्व द्वारा ही संभव है। पुरातत्त्व और इतिहास को जीने वाले त्रिपाठी जी कालान्तर में भारतीय इतिहास अनुसंधान परिषद के अध्यक्ष बने। किसी भी इतिहासविद् के लिए यह सर्वोच्च उपलब्धि है।

आज प्रो. त्रिपाठी विश्वविद्यालय परिसर से जा चुके हैं। सेवानिवृत्ति के बाद किसी संगोष्ठी, पुनश्चर्या या किसी शैक्षणिक कार्यक्रमों में सादर आमंत्रित करने पर निश्चित ही आते हैं और अपनी ज्ञानराशि के अशेष पुंज को श्रोताओं पर लुटाना चाहते हैं, पर दुःख है कि हमारी और हमारे बाद की पीढ़ी के पात्र बहुत छोटे हैं। कुछ सुबुद्धजन दो–चार दिन उसकी चर्चा करके शान्त हो जाते हैं। काश, कुछ ऐसे जिज्ञासु और सुपात्र विद्यार्थी आते जो इस ज्ञानगंगा से कुछ बूँद चुरा लेते तो उनका जीवन भी धन्य हो जाता। हम बड़भागी हैं कि हमें त्रिपाठी जी की सन्निधि प्राप्त हुई थी, उनके व्यक्तित्व की सुगन्ध आज भी स्मृतियों में महक उठती है।

अधिष्ठाता कला संकाय
दीनदयाल उपाध्याय गोरखपुर विश्वविद्यालय
गोरखपुर

आचार्य–परम्परा के एक बहुआयामी व्यक्तित्व : मेरे गुरूवर्य

ईश्वर शरण विश्वकर्मा[1]

भारतीय मनीषा आचार्यतत्व से आलोकित हुई है। इसीलिए इसकी सुदीर्घ आचार्य–परम्परा विश्व संस्कृति में समादृत एवं आचरणीय रही है। यह श्लाघनीय परम्परा आचार्य (गुरू) के प्रति सदैव श्रद्धेय, सम्पूज्य एवं श्रेष्ठ भाव व्यक्त करती रही है क्योंकि यही परम्परा शिष्यों को 'आचार' या चारित्रय की शिक्षा प्रदान करता था। इसीलिए आचार्य यास्क ने निरूक्त में कहा है कि "आचार्यः कस्यात्।" आचार्य आचारं ग्राहयति" अर्थात् आचरण या विशुद्ध चारित्रय की शिक्षा ही आचार्य का उद्देश्य एवं जीवन है। महर्षि व्यास ने इसे और व्यापक तथा स्पष्ट किया है कि "आचार्य वह था जिसमें वेदों के प्रति उत्सर्ग की भावना हो, उत्तम परिवार का हो, श्रोत्रिय हो, शुचि हो, वैदिक भाषा का अध्ययन किया हो तथा जो आलसी न हो"

वेदैकनिष्ठं धर्मज्ञं कुलीनं श्रोत्रियं शुचीम्।
स्वाभाषाज्ञमनालस्य विप्रं कर्तारभीप्सतम्।।

महर्षि व्यास ने भारतीय आचार्यो के जिन गुणों का वर्णन किया है वही आचार्यत्व की आर्ष कसौटी है। मेरे गुरूवर्य प्रो. दयानाथ त्रिपाठी पर आचार्य यास्क और महर्षि व्यास की दोनों ही व्याख्याएँ ठीक बैठती है। उनके व्यक्तित्व के निरूपण तथा शिष्यों के प्रति भाव के लिए आचार्य परम्परा का निकष ही चरितार्थ होता है। एक पुरातत्त्ववेत्ता होने के साथ ही वैदिक परम्परा के प्रति उनकी आसक्ति सदैव बनी रही। 'आर्क्यालाजी एण्ड ट्रेडिशन–(1988) नामक प्रकाशित ग्रंथ तथा 'अयस् इन दि ऋग्वेद' शोध लेख उनकी इसी भावना को व्यक्त करते है। इसी प्रकार 'हिन्दुइज्म एण्ड हेलेनिज्म' (2004) नामक वृहत्प्रकल्प पर शोधकृति में इस भावना का वैश्विक विस्तार होता है। गुरूवर्य का सम्पूर्ण जीवन एक आचार्य की भाँति शुचितापूर्ण, सात्विकता से ओतप्रोत तथा सत्यपरक रहा है।

गुरूवर्य के बहुआयामी व्यक्तित्व में उनका उत्तम कुल में जन्म एवं श्रेष्ठ माता–पिता के वे संस्कार भी थे जिन्होंने उनमें आचरण, चरित्र, कर्मठता, अनुशासन तथा दया भावना का बीजारोपण कर उनको शिक्षा क्षेत्र में प्रस्तुत किया। मेरा यह सौभाग्य रहा है कि उनके पूज्य पिता स्वर्गीय पं. एम किशोर शर्मा तथा पूज्यामाता स्वर्गीया श्रीमती कृष्णाशर्मा का आर्शीवाद तथा सान्निध्य प्राप्त हुआ था। उनके पूज्यपिता एक आदर्श शिक्षक तथा स्वाधीनता आंदोलन के एक ऐसे सेनानी भी थे जिन्होने सेना की नौकरी छोड़कर इलाहाबाद के रामबाग मुहल्ले में स्थित सेवा समिति विद्या मंदिर इंटर कॉलेज में अध्यापक बने तथा बाद में सरयूपारीण इंटर कॉलेज, रामभवन, चौराहा, बहादुरगंज के प्रधानाचार्य पर से अपनी सेवापूर्ण की थी। इसी प्रकार उनकी पूज्यामाता जी परमसात्विक कुल से सम्बन्धित थी। वृन्दावन के स्वामी अखंडानन्द सरस्वती उनके संबन्धी थे तथा माधवानन्द सरस्वती उनके भतीजे थे। इस प्रकार गुरूवर्य के व्यक्तित्व के विकास में उच्च श्रोत्रिय कुल के संस्कार तथा उनकी कुल परम्परा के वंशानुगत लक्षणों का बड़ा योगदान रहा है।

यह एक उल्लेखनीय तथ्य है कि गुरूवर्य मूलतः गोरखपुर जनपद के कौड़ीराम के समीप स्थित प्रागैतिहासिक ग्राम सोहगौरा के निवासी रहे हैं। छः पीढ़ी पूर्ण पं. जयराम तिवारी ने सोहगौरा से जाकर इलाहाबाद मे बसना स्वीकार किया। मेजा तहसील में डोहरिया के पास का ग्राम अभी भी "जयरामपुरवा" कहा जाता है।

---

1 आचार्य, प्राचीन इतिहास, पुरातत्व एवं संस्कृति विभाग, दीनदयाल उपाध्याय गोरखपुर विश्वविद्यालय, गोरखपुर (उ.प्र.)–273009

इसीलिए गुरूवर्य के व्यक्तित्व में सनातनता पाण्डित्य तथा पूर्वजों के प्रति अनन्य श्रद्धाभक्ति का भाव मानों मोतियों की तरह सजे हैं।

यह गोरखपुर विश्वविद्यालय का सौभाग्य रहा है कि गुरूदेव प्रो. दयानाथ त्रिपाठी जैसा आचार्य व्यक्तित्व शिक्षक के रूप में मिला। 1958 में इलाहाबाद विश्वविद्यालय से एम.ए. करने के पश्चात् वे गोरखपुर विश्वविद्यालय के प्राचीन इतिहास विभाग में प्रवक्ता नियुक्त हुए। तब से लगातार चालीस वर्षो तक (1958 से 1998) इस विश्वविद्यालय की अविस्मरणीय सेवा अर्पित की। इस चारदशक की सेवा अवधि में उन्होंने विषम परिस्थितियों में अपनी उच्च शैक्षणिक अध्येतावृत्ति को बाधित नहीं होने दिया। अध्यापकीय जीवन में ही पीएच.डी. शोध हेतु उन्हें इन्डो–ग्रीक फेलो स्कॉलरशिप (1971–74), ब्रिटिश कौंसिल स्कॉलरशिप (1974–76), एथेंस में ब्रिटिश स्कूल ऑफ आर्क्यालाजी की अध्येतावृत्ति के साथ रोम, अंकारा, तेहरान में कार्य करते हुए यूनानी भाषा में डिप्लोमा (1972) तथा साउथस्पटन विश्वविद्यालय (यू.के.) से प्रख्यात पुराविद लार्ड कॉलिन रेनफ्र्यू के शोध निर्देशन में ब्रान्ज वर्क ऑफ मेनलैण्ड ग्रीस (2600 बी.सी.–1450 वी.सी.) विषय पर पीएच.डी. उपाधि प्राप्त कर विषय, विधा, विश्वविद्यालय तथा क्षेत्र को गौरवान्वित किया। गुरूवर्य सही अर्थों में प्राच्यविधा के महामनीषी हैं। भारतीय–यूनानी संस्कृतियों के समन्वय को उन्होंने अपने जीवन तथा अनुसंधान में व्यक्त किया है।

गुरूवर्य प्रो. त्रिपाठी के व्यक्तित्व में पुरातनता, पुरातत्व तथा पारम्परिकता का अद्भुत समन्वय है। पुरातत्व के प्रति उनके मन में अनुराग महज संयोग नहीं है। वे एक ऐसे ग्राम (सोहगौरा) के मूलनिवासी है जो भारत का प्राचीनतम ग्राम है और पिछले पांच हजार वर्षो से निरन्तर आवासित है। इसीलिए गोरखपुर विश्वविद्यालय के प्राचीन इतिहास विभाग ने प्रो. शैलनाथ चतुर्वेदी के निर्देशन तथा विभागीय सहयोगियों के कुशल नेतृत्व में 1962–65 में इसका पुरातात्विक उत्खनन कराया। इस नवपाषाणकालीन ग्राम ने राप्तीघाटी की संस्कृति को एक नई पहचान दी। इस प्रकार अपने प्राचीन ग्राम के इतिवृत्त तथा पुरातत्व के साथ गुरूवर्य सदैव जीवन्त रहते हैं तथा गर्वानुभूति का दृष्टान्त देते हैं। इसी पृष्ठभूमि ने आपको भारत तथा यूनान के अनेक पुरातात्विक स्थलों पर पुरातात्विक सर्वेक्षण तथा उत्खनन का सुअवसर प्रदान किया।

गुरूवर्य का ''शिक्षक–व्यक्तित्व'' सदैव प्रेरणास्पद, अनुकरणीय तथा आचारणीय रहा है। मुझे स्नातक एवं स्नाकोत्तर दोनों ही कक्षाओं में 1974 से 1978 तक (जब वे भारत में थे) शिष्य के रूप में उनका स्नेहिल सान्निध्य मिला है। वे विश्व की प्राचीन सभ्यताओं तथा विश्व प्रागितिहास के कुशल अध्येता, अध्यापक तथा आचार्य रहे हैं। यह विषय का ही प्रभाव था कि उनके व्यक्तित्व में विश्व की श्रेष्ठ सांस्कृतिक विरासत समन्वित होकर शिक्षण में सहयोगी रहती थी। यही कारण था कि उनके शिष्य के रूप में मुझे सदैव गर्व की अनुभूति होती है। महाकवि कालीदास ने गुरू–शिष्य के पारस्परिक सम्बन्ध को 'गुरूवो गुरूप्रियम्' कहा है। मेरे लिए उनकी गुरुता सदैव वन्दनीय तथा प्रंशसनीय रही है। वे सहज ही शिष्यों के विद्यानुराग से प्रभावित हो जाते थे तथा उन्हें 'शिष्य–पुत्र' बना लेते थे। यही घाती उनके व्यक्तित्व की विशालता का एक आधार है। एक श्रेष्ठ गुरू के रूप मे वे कुशल थे क्योंकि सदाचारी, प्रतिभावान और सुयोग्य शिष्य को चुनना गुरू की कुशलता कही गई है। वे ऐसे शिष्यों को सदैव अपने सानिध्य से योग्यतम बनाने के लिए सद्भाव रखते रहे हैं।

वर्ष 1998 में गोरखपुर विश्वविद्यालय से सेवानिवृत्त होने के पश्चात् वे निरन्तर अकादमिक सक्रियता के सद्गुण को संरक्षित किए है। सेवानिवृत्त होने के पश्चात् वे इलाहाबाद विश्वविद्यालय के प्राचीन इतिहास, संस्कृति एवं पुरातत्व विभाग में विजिटिंग फेलो (1998–99), भारतीय उच्च अध्ययन संस्थान, राष्ट्रपति निवास, शिमला के फेलो (1999–2002), विजिटिंग फेलो, ब्रिटिश एकेडमी, लन्दन (2003), भारतीय इतिहास अनुसंधान परिषद, भारत सरकार, नई दिल्ली के सदस्य (1998–2004), तथा परिषद के अध्यक्ष (2004–2007) के गौरवमय पदों को सुशोभित कर अघावधी अपनी अध्येतावृत्ति के साथ सक्रिय हैं। उन्होंने तीन वृहतशोध प्रकल्पों को पूर्ण कर अपनी शोधपरक पहचान बनायी है। इस दृष्टि से विश्वविद्यालय अनुदान आयोग इस स्वीकृत 'आर्क्योलॉजी एण्ड ट्रेडीशन' भारतीय इतिहास अनुसंधान परिषद द्वारा स्वीकृत ''आर्कियो लिंग्विस्टिक्स'' तथा भारतीय उच्च अध्ययन संस्थान शिमला द्वारा स्वीकृत ''हिन्दुइज्म एण्ड हेलेनिज्म'' विद्वत्वर्ग में समाहृत एवं प्रशंसित है।

गुरूवर्य के व्यक्तित्व का एक अनुकरणीय पक्ष उनका अनुशासन प्रिय होना रहा है। वे बचपन से (जैसा कि उनके पूज्य पिता एवं पूज्यामाता जी से सुना है) ही कठोर, अनुशासन प्रिय तथा विद्या के प्रति अनुसक्त रहे हैं। शैक्षणिक व्यवस्था तथा शिक्षा–परिसरों को अनुशासित बनाने में उनकी दृष्टि पारम्परिक रही है। वर्ष 1980–84 तक वे गोरखपुर विश्वविद्यालय के मुख्य नियंता एवं दंडाधिकारी रहे हैं जिसमें उनका परिसर की सुचिता, व्यवस्था आज भी स्मणीय है। इसी क्रम में गोरखपुर विश्वविद्यालय शिक्षकसंघ तथा उत्तरप्रदेश आवासीय विश्वविद्यालय शिक्षक महासंघ के अध्यक्ष रहे हैं जिसमें विश्वविद्यालयों के शिक्षकों के लिए अनेक उल्लेखनीय कार्य किया।

गुरूवर्य के व्यक्तित्व में स्पष्ट वादिता तथा सत्यनिष्ठता का अनुपम योग रहा है। वे निर्भीक, स्पष्टवादी तथा सत्यनिष्ठ रहे हैं। उनकी इस लाक्षणिकता से उनके शिष्य–मित्र परिचित हैं। उनकी इसी पहचान ने शिक्षा, राजनीति, प्रशासन, समाज आदि विविध क्षेत्रों में उनके प्रशंसकों की लम्बी पंक्ति खड़ी कर दी है। वे एक राजनीतिक सूझ–बूझ के धनी तथा समाज–कार्य में कुशल समाज–चितंक रहे है। उनकी शिष्य परम्परा में समाज के प्रत्येक क्षेत्र, वर्ग तथा श्रेणी के लोग सम्मिलित हैं। उनकी स्पष्टवादिता तथा सत्यपरकता ने शिष्यों तथा मित्रों को एक जीवन शैली दी है जिसका स्मरण कर उनके व्यक्तित्व को नमन् किया जाता है।

अपने गुरूजनों के प्रति असीम श्रद्धा तथा पूज्यभाव गुरूदेव के व्यक्तित्व का सबसे सुन्दर पक्ष है। अपने अध्ययन कक्ष, पुस्तकालय तथा कार्यालय आदि में वे भारती विद्या के महान आचार्य प्रो. गोविन्द चन्द पांडे तथा इंग्लैंड के गुरू लार्ड कॉलिन रेन्फ्यु को अपना प्रेरणास्त्रोत मानते है। यह भाव उनके जीवन में पाश्चात्य एवं पुरातत्व विद्या परम्परा के प्रति आदरभाव का प्रत्यक्ष दर्शन कराता हैं। यही कारण है कि गुरूवर्य के व्यक्तित्व में परम्परा एवं पुरातत्व का अनुपम योग है। भारतीय दर्शन, परम्परा, संस्कृति, कला तथा पाश्चात्य कला संस्कृति के समन्वय को वे अनुभव करते थे। ऐसा बहुआयामी व्यक्तित्व दुर्लभ होता है। ऐसे अभिनन्दनीय व्यक्तित्व को नमन्।।

आचार्यत्व के निकष पर निकषित व्यक्तित्व की एक बड़ी विशेषता उसका विद्यानुराग तथा विषयगत अध्ययन, अध्यापन एवं अनुसंधान है। गुरूवर्य एक विद्यानुरागी माँ शारदा के वरदपुत्र तथा गहन अध्येता एक पुरातत्व मनीषी आचार्य हैं। वे विश्व पुरातत्व के अध्येता रहे हैं। विश्व पुरातत्व परिषद (वर्ल्ड आर्क्योलाजिकल कांग्रेस), इण्डियन सोसाइटी फार ग्रीको – रोमन स्टडीज, इण्डियन आर्क्यालाजीकल सोसाइटी नई दिल्ली, इण्डियन हिस्ट्री एण्ड कल्चर सोसाइटी, नई दिल्ली, इण्डियन सोसाइटी फार प्री हिस्ट्री एण्ड क्वार्टर्नरी स्टडीज, पूना, मध्यप्रदेश धरोहर विकास परिषद, भोपाल तथा इलाहाबाद राष्ट्रीय संग्रहालय, इलाहाबाद के आजीवन सदस्य, पदाधिकारी तथा अध्येता रहे हैं।

एक पुरातत्वविद् के रूप में उन्होंने न केवल विषय को जिया अपितु क्षेत्रीय पुरातत्व को अपने पुरातात्विक सर्वेक्षणों, उत्खननों एवं विश्लेषणों से समृद्ध किया। गोरखपुर विश्वविद्यालय द्वारा उत्खनित पुरास्थल सोहगौरा, फाजिलनगर (उस्मान (डीह)) एवं वीरमाटीपुर के उत्खनन से प्रत्यक्ष सम्बद्ध रहे हैं। उन्होंने अपने विश्वविद्यालयी सेवा के अंतिम चरण में वीरभारी के उत्खनन का निर्देशन कर विभागीय पुरातत्व संग्रहालय को अमूल्य पुरावशेषों का धरोहर देकर उपकृत किया है। इतना ही नहीं उन्होंने यूनान प्रवास के समय मेनेलियॉन तथा पीलॉस जैसे पुरास्थलों के पुरातात्विक उत्खनन में महत्वपूर्ण योगदान दिया है। उनके द्वारा सर्वेक्षित पूर्वी उत्तरप्रदेश के लगभग 150 पुरास्थल भावी उत्खननों के दिशा प्रदर्शक हैं।

'चरैवेति चरैवेति' गुरूवर्य के जीवन का मंत्र रहा है। वे ऐसे पथ के पथिक हैं जहां चरणशीलता आचरण में है। अथक परिश्रमी, उद्यमी एवं पुरूषार्थी व्यक्तित्व के धनी हैं। प्रातः काल ब्राह्ममुहूर्त से प्रारम्भ दिनचर्चा मध्यरात्रि में विश्राम लेती रही है। चारिका, चंक्रमण एवं चर्चा की भांति वे अपनी गतिविधियों से विषय को समृद्ध करते रहते है। शांत, गंभीर, सौम्य, मितभाषी एवं मृदुभाषी जैसे सदगुणों से गुरूवर्य का व्यक्तित्व निरूपित हुआ है। पांडित्यपूर्ण जीवन की ये विधाएँ कठिन साधना तथा अध्यवसाय से प्राप्त होती हैं। गुरूवर्य को ये सौभाग्य मिला भी है, उपार्जित भी है। इसीलिए वे 'दयानाथ' है तथा उनके दो अनुज क्रमशः कृपानाथ (पं. कृपानाथ त्रिपाठी अधिवक्ता, इलाहाबाद) तथा स्व. शिवानाथ (स्व. शिवानाथ त्रिपाठी, पूर्व पुलिस उपाधीक्षक, मध्यप्रदेश विशेष सशस्त्र दल) सही अर्थों में नाम को चरितार्थ करने वाले हैं।

गुरूवर्य के बहुआयामी व्यक्तित्व की विनिर्मिति में अपना सम्पूर्ण जीवन अर्पित करने वाली उनकी धर्मपत्नी पूज्या अम्मा श्रीमति लीला त्रिपाठी का महत्वपूर्ण योगदान है। आज भी दोनों ऋषि परम्परा का जीवन व्यतीत करते हुए विद्या की साधना में लीन हैं। वे साक्षात देवी हैं। उनके चरणों में कोटिशः नमन है। वे प्रत्यक्ष अन्नपूर्णा हैं जिनका घर शिष्यों के लिए, विद्यार्थियों के लिए सदैव आश्रमवत खुला रहता है। मुझ जैसे शिष्य को उन्होने इसी परम्परा में शिक्षित कर विद्या के क्षेत्र में अग्रेसित किया।

ऐसे आचार्य मनीषी विद्वत्ता एवं वात्सल्य के पूर्ण मेरे गुरूदेव सदैव अभिनन्दनीय एवं श्रद्धा–स्पद भाव के साथ प्रणम्य हैं। उनका बहुआयामी व्यक्तित्व, छात्रों, अध्यापकों, अनुसंधित्सुओं सभी के लिए प्रेरणास्त्रोत तथा पाथेयपरक रहेगा। गोरखपुर के इन्द्रानगर मुहल्ले का उनका आवास'लीलानिलयम' सदैव एक आश्रम की भॉति प्रणम्य एवं गमनीय है। अंत में इस अभिनन्दन के अवसर पर अपने गुरूवर्य के श्री चरणों में प्रणाम निवेदित करते हुये उनके चिर यशस्वी वैदुष्यपूर्ण जीवन की कामना तथा ईश्वर से प्रार्थना करता हूँ कि वे "शतायुर्वे पुरुषाः" की परम्परा में अपने आचार्यत्व से विषय, समाज तथा राष्ट्र को समृद्ध करें। "तस्मै श्री गुरवे नम :"।।

सोहगौरा से सोहगौरा : प्रोफेसर दया नाथ त्रिपाठी

राकेश तिवारी

प्रोफेसर त्रिपाठी का नाम तो बड़े–बड़कवों से एक जमाने से सुनते रहे लेकिन पहली बार उनके दर्शन का संयोग बना 1997 में जब देश की आज़ादी की पचासवीं सालगिरह के मौके पर पिछले पाँच दशकों में हुई पुरातात्विक गतिविधियों से नफे–नुकसान का हिसाब बैठाने के इरादे से लखनऊ में पुराविद–संतों की जुटान में भागीदारी के लिए हमारा आमंत्रण स्वीकार कर पधारे।

मज़बूत कद काटी, प्रभावशाली गोल चेहरा, चौड़ा माथा, गहरी प्रभावशाली ऐसी आँखें कि जब चढ़ा कर बोले तो उनसे आँखें मिला कर बात करना सबके बस का ना रहे, मज़बूत कद काठी, एक बड़े विद्वान और मल्ल एक में मिला दिए जाएं तो उनका व्यक्तित्व बन जाए।

सेमीनार के दौरान जब सोहगौरा की चर्चा चली तो बेलौस बोले। राप्ती और आमी नदियों के संगम पर बसे इस गाँव का नाम 1962–63 में वहाँ लगाई गई छोटी सी खन्ती की गहराई से उभर कर पुराविदों के आकश में देदीप्यामान हुआ। इस खन्ती में उतर कर धरती की परतों में दबी पुरासम्पदा का महत्ता आंकने वालों में गोरखपुर विश्वविद्यालय में उस समय प्राचीन भारतीय इतिहास की कमान संभाल रहे प्रोफेसर गोविन्द चन्द्र पांडे की टोली में डॉक्टर शैल नाथ चतुर्वेदी के साथ वे भी शामिल रहे।

सोहगौरा के शोध से ऐसे साक्ष्य सामने आए जो आगे सरयूपार सहित पूरे पूर्वी उत्तर प्रदेश में मानव आवास के प्रारम्भ का काल दूसरी सहस्त्राब्दी ईसा पूर्व से भी पहले ले जाने के अनुमानों के आधार बने। प्राचीन आवासीय गतिविधियों की अटूट कड़ी ने सिद्ध कर दिया कि यह गाँव लगभग 4000 वर्ष से भी अधिक समय से उसी जगह आबाद रहा है। इस गाँव की चर्चा यहाँ से मिले एक ताम्र–पत्र पर अंकित लेख के लिए भी होती रही है जिसकी गिनती देश के सबसे पुराने लेखों में की जाती है।

सरवरिया ब्राह्मणों में सोहगौरा के तिवारियों या त्रिपाठियों का बड़ा मान रहा है, इतना ऊँचा कि किसी ज़माने में और काफी हद तक आज भी खेती–बारी, धन सम्पदा हो ना हो सोहगौरा का तिवारी होना ही अच्छे वर के चयन के लिए पर्याप्त रहा। कालान्तर में मालूम हुआ कि इलाहाबाद जिले में गंगा–पार के शुकुलपुरा गाँव के जिस पुरवे के वे मूल निवासी हैं उसका नाम 'सोहगौरन का पुरवा' पड़ने का कारण उनके पुरखों के किसी समय गोरखपुर के सोहगौरा गाँव से आ कर वहाँ बसने के कारण पड़ा। यह भी एक कारण रहा उनका सोहगौरा से विशेष लगाव रखने का।

उनका जन्म 1938 में इलाहाबाद में हुआ, वहीं पले–बढ़े पढ़ते हुए 1958 में इलाहाबाद विश्वविद्यालय से प्राचीन भारतीय इतिहास, संस्कृति एवं पुरातत्त्व विषय में स्नातकोत्तर की डिग्री हासिल करते ही अपनी मेधा के चलते उसी वर्ष गोरखपुर विश्वविद्यालय में लेक्चर के पद पर सुशोभित हो कर सोहगौरा की मूल धारा से जुड़ गए। उसके बाद 1971–74 के बीच ग्रीक सरकार की स्कालरशिप पा कर एथेंस यूनिवर्सिटी से ग्रीक भाषा में डिप्लोमा किया। 1974–76 में ब्रिटिश कौंसिल स्कॉलरशिप प्राप्त कर के 'ब्रॉन्ज़ वर्क ऑफ़ ग्रीस' विषय पर 'साउथेम्पटन यूनिवर्सिटी' (यू.के.) से प्रोफेसर कॉलिन रेनफ्रिउ के पर्यवेक्षण में, पी–एच. डी. की डिग्री पाने के सिलसिले में एथेंस, रोम, अंकारा और तेहरान की शोध–यात्राओं के अनुभव बटोरा। फिर, गोरखपुर विश्वविद्यालय में 1979 में रीडर और 1989–1998 तक प्रोफेसर के पदों को सुशोभित करते हुए सतत मुक्त हस्त विद्यादान में डूबे रहे। 1998–99 में अपनी मातृ–संस्था, इलाहाबाद यूनिवर्सिटी में विज़िटिंग प्रोफेसर रहे।

लगभग चार दशक पठन–पाठन में खपा कर भी विद्या–व्यसन से मुक्त नहीं हुए। विश्वविद्यालय से निकले तो 1999–2002 तक इंडियन इंस्टिट्यूट ऑफ एडवांस इंस्टिट्यूट, शिमला और 2003 में ब्रिटिश अकादमी, लन्दन के फेलो, और फिर, 2004–2007 तक इंडियन कौंसिल ऑफ हिस्टोरिकल रिसर्च के अध्यक्ष रहे। व्यक्तित्व के अनुरूप

1980–1984 तक गोरखपुर विश्वविद्यालय के चीफ प्रॉक्टर और 1997–1998 तक किसान पोस्ट ग्रेजुएट कॉलेज, बस्ती के अधिकृत नियंत्रक के प्रशासकीय पदों पर दायित्व सम्भाला। उनके विश्वविद्यालयों और शोध–संस्थाओं तथा उनकी विभिन्न कमेटियों के सदस्य एवं अन्य पदों को सुशोभित करते हुए महत्त्वपूर्ण योगदान किया।

भारतीय इतिहास, संस्कृति और पुरातत्व जगत में उनका नाम खूब जाना गया। शोध और अध्ययन के साथ साथ क्रमशः प्रोफेसर गोवर्धन राय शर्मा, प्रोफेसर शैल नाथ चतुर्वेदी तथा प्रोफेसर एच. डी. सांकलिया के पर्यवेक्षण में कौशाम्बी (1957–58), सोहगौरा (1961–63), और अहाड़ (1963–64) के अतिरिक्त क्रमशः डॉ. एच. डब्लू. कैटलिंग तथा प्रोफेसर जी.एस. कोर्रेस के पर्यवेक्षण में ग्रीस में स्पार्टा के निकट मेनेलिओन (1973–74) और पाइलोस (1974–75) के पुरातात्विकउत्खनन में भाग लेने का अनुभव प्राप्त किया। 1978–79 में फाजिलनगर (कुशीनगर) के उत्खनन का सह–निदेशन और 1997–98 में उस्मानपुर डीहा (कुशीनगर) के उत्खनन का निदेशन किया। इतना ही नहीं उनके दिशा–निर्देशन में 1994–1998 के बीच संपादित सर्वेक्षण से लगभग 200 पुरास्थल भी प्रकाश में आए।

अपने शोध सिलसिले में उन्होंने ग्रीस, युगोस्लाविया, फ्रांस, जर्मनी, इटली, यू.के., मिस्त्र, टर्की और ईरान तथा भारत के संग्रहालयों में संग्रहीत 'प्री एंड प्रोटो स्टिोरिक' पुरा सामग्री का अध्ययन किया। 'पुरातत्त्व और परंपरा' (1995–99) तथा 'हिंदुइज़म और हेलेनिज़म' (1999–2002) विषयों पर संपादित शोध आधारित प्रकाशन विशेष महत्त्वपूर्ण हैं। उनके निर्देशन में लगभग आधा दर्जन शोध प्रबंध प्रस्तुत हुए।

ताजिंदगी ज्ञान की पताका लहराते देश–विदेश के सौ से अधिक राष्ट्रीय–अंतर्राष्ट्रीय सेमिनारों में भारत और इंगलैण्ड, ग्रीस, इटली, जर्मनी, बेल्जियम, अमरीका और कनाडा के सभागृहों में डंका बजाते घूमते रहे और आज भी घूम रहे हैं। विशेषज्ञों को आमंत्रित कर उनके विचारों से लाभान्वित होने और विचार विमर्श के अवसर जुटाने के लिए उन्होंने समय–समय पर अनेक कॉन्फ्रेंस, सेमीनार, पाठ्यक्रम आयोजि कराए। 'ग्रीस–भारत सम्बन्ध', 'पुरातत्त्व और परम्परा', 'इंडो–यूरोपियन भाषा और संस्कृति', 'भारत और मध्य एशिया', 'पश्चिम एशिया से सांस्कृतिक सम्बन्ध' उनके प्रिय विषय रहे हैं जिन पर उनकी 9 किताबें और 50 से अधिक शोध–पत्र एवं समीक्षाएं प्रकाशित हैं। आज भी वे गहन अध्ययन–मनन में लगे रह कर इस कोष को भरते ही जा रहे हैं। प्राचीन अवशेषों से डी एन ए निकाल कर मॉलिक्यूलर पापुलेशन जेनेटिक तकनीक (आर्किओजेनेटिक्स) के माध्यमसे मानव, पशुओं और वनस्पतियों की विभिन्न प्रजातियों के इतिहास और उनकी आनुवंशिक परम्परा का अध्ययनउनका परम रुचिकर विषय बन गया है।

एक बार उनके पुरखों ने इलाहाबाद जा कर सोहगौरन का पुरवा बसाया था। लेकिन उन्होंने इलाहाबाद से गोरखपुर आ कर वापस लौटने से बेहतर अपनी सोर से जुड़ कर अपने मूल निवास प्राचीन 'सोहगौरा' ग्राम के निकटतम गोरखपुर में ही बसना पसंद किया। वे जहाँ रहते हैं वहाँ प्राचीन भारतीय इतिहास व उससे जुड़े विषयों के अध्येताओं का जमावड़ा लगा रहता है।

एक अवसर मिला था हमें खलीलाबाद (जिला संत कबीर नगर) के पोस्ट ग्रेजुएट कॉलेज में आयोजित समारोह में उनके एक और रूप से साक्षात्कार पाने का। वे वहाँ मुख्य अतिथि के रूप में आमंत्रित थे। खचाखच भरे सभागार में हम सब अपनी अपनी कुर्सियों पर बैठे उनके आने की प्रतीक्षा कर रहे थे। थोड़ी देर बाद मुख्यद्वार पर हलचल के साथ सभी लोग खड़े हो कर उधर ही देखने लगे। हमने देखा, सबसे आगे आगे अपनी विशिष्ट प्रभावशाली मुद्रा में एक सम्राट के समान माथा उठाए, 'रेड कार्पेट' पर धीरे–धीरे पग धरते बढ़ते प्रोफेसर दया नाथ त्रिपाठी, पीछे–पीछे उन पर फूल बरसाते जयकारा लगाते आयोजक। उनके अभिनन्दन में पढ़े गए व्यक्तव्य में परम वरेण्य जैसे अनेक संस्कृतनिष्ठ विशेषणों से परिपूर्ण माला ने गोरखपुर क्षेत्र की विशिष्ट शैली और त्रिपाठी जी के प्रति उद्गारों ने अभिभूत कर दिया। हम कामना करते हैं कि उनकी यह आन–बान–शान यूं ही बनी रहे और वे इससे भी ऊंची ऊंचाइयों पर आसनस्थ रहें।

महानिदेशक
भारतीय पुरातत्त्व सर्वेक्षण
जनपथ, नई दिल्ली

INDIAN COUNCIL OF HISTORICAL RESEARCH
(AN AUTONOMOUS ORGANTSATTON)
MINISTRY OF HUMAN RESOURCE DEVELOPMENT GOVT. OF INDIA
35. Ferozeshah Road, New Delhi-110 001

Y. Sudershan Rao
Chairperson

Phone : 23387 877, 23386033, 23382321, 23386973
23389021, 23388857, 23388747, 23384829
Fax : 23383421, 23387829
E-mail : ms_ichr@rediffmail.com,
support@ichrindia.org
Website : www.ichrindia.org

19 August 2014

It gives me great pleasure to hear that a Felicitation Volume is being brought out, titled 'Archaeology and Tradition', in honour of Prof. Daya Nath Tripathi. Prof. D. N. Tripathi is a renowned archaeologist and respected academician. His area of research was not just limited to a micro-area. The scope of his research covered India, Greece and England. He had also worked on linguistic parlances of early civilizations of the ancient world. Since I do not belong to this area of specialisation, I am not fortunate enough to give any critical assessment of his work but my recent interests fall in the ancient historical tradition of India's remote past, I have great appreciation for his contribution to our knowledge of the ancient world.

Unlike other countries, Indian culture is not based on material culture alone. Indian culture is basically evolved from Shastras formulated from the Vedic thought by the Rishis. Indian polity, social customs, traditions, faiths and material cultures are the developments out of meditation (single pointed attention), *Tapas* (wait for the result) and intellectual exercise (to make it comprehendable to others) of the ancient rishis. Archeology has helped us in tracing our ancient history from the past providing us material artefacts from about two centuries. The new trends in archeology are also stepping forward to consider the collective memory of generations as sources of history which are still available in form of tribal lore, folklore and Vedic-lore in form of Orature as sources for history. This would help us bridging-up the missing link between known and unknown worlds of the remote Indian past. Hope the historical researches in the coming years would address this problem to improve our understanding of ancient past.

I know Dr D N Tripathi for more than a decade as we were both members of ICHR in 2002. I developed a great regard for him for his positive outlook on Indian past. I wish him a long life and good health. May his scholarship and experience guide the succeeding generations of archaeologists to look at India's ancient past in a proper perspective and let our Indian historical tradition getneeded support from the 'new' archaeological explorations.

Warangal

Telangana State

Y.Sudershan Rao

आचार्य दयानाथ त्रिपाठीः मेरे पिता एवं प्रेरणा

उमेश नाथ त्रिपाठी

मैं अभिभूत हूँ और साथ ही साथ असमंजस में भी हूँ कि मुझे पापाजी के सम्मान में प्रकाशित होने वाले ग्रंथ में कुछ लिखना है। अभिभूत इसलिए हूँ कि मेरे पिता, जिन पर हमें लगता था कि उनका पुत्र होने के कारण, केवल हमारा अधिकार है, उनको चाहने और उनका सम्मान करने वाले दुनिया में और कितने लोग हैं? असमंजस में इसलिए कि जिन्होंने सब कुछ दिया उनके उपर क्या लिखूँ? मेरा नाम, मेरा पद, मेरी प्रतिष्ठा, मेरा परिवार, मेरा सब कुछ तो उन्हीं का दिया हुआ है। शायद अब यह बात समझ में आने लगी है कि क्यों संस्कृत के श्लोक में यह लिखा है –

त्वमेव माता च पिता त्वमेव, त्वमेव बन्धुश्च सखा त्वमेव।
त्वमेव विद्या द्रविणम् त्वमेव, त्वमेव सर्वम् मम देव देव।।

ईश्वर से सबका साक्षात्कार सम्भव नहीं है, इसीलिए ईश्वर माता – पिता के रुप में आकर अपनी संतानों का पालन पोषण करते हैं।

क्या लिखूँ, कहां तक लिखूँ, विज्ञान विधा का विद्यार्थी होने के कारण भाषा तथा अपने भावों की अभिव्यक्ति हमेशा से मेरे लिए कठिन कार्य रहा है। अनुसंधान मेरे लिए प्रयोगों से प्राप्त आंकड़े की विवेचना तक ही सीमित रहा है। वो व्यक्ति जिसका पूरा जीवन, अपने आदर्शों तथा दर्शन पर आधारित रहा है, उसकी विवेचना करना मेरे इस रसायनशास्त्रीय बुद्धि तथा विवेक से अतिरिक्त वस्तु है। परन्तु जो आपने (पापाजी ने) सिखाया आपको ही समर्पित करने की कोशिश कर रहा हूँ, मेरा इसमें लेशमात्र भी अपना कोई योगदान नहीं है।

हमेशा से सूरज पकड़ने की चाहत लिये मैं जब भी क्षितिज तक पहुँचता हूँ तब पता चलता है कि सूरज तो बहुत दूर है और मैं फिर बढ़ चलता हूँ, सूरज की किरण पकड़ते हुए।

मैं और मेरे पिता जी दोनों अपने पिता जी के सबसे बड़े लड़के हैं, पापाजी अध्यापक थे, मैं भी हूँ, ध्यातव्य है कि मेरे पितामह भी अध्यापक थे, पापाजी ने घर परिवार छोड़कर विदेश से शोधकार्य पूर्ण किया, उन्हीं के लिखने पर मैने भी महान रसायनज्ञ प्रो0 आर0सी0 महरोत्रा के साथ हास्टल में रहकर शोधकार्य किया। पापाजी गोरखपुर विश्वविद्यालय में थे, मैं भी अंततः यहाँ आ ही गया। अपने सेवा काल के दौरान विश्वविद्यालय की परीक्षाओं को सुधारने के लिए उन्होंने उड़ाका दल का नेतृत्व किया, कालंतर में मैंने भी वह दायित्व निभाया। पापाजी हीरापुरी कालोनी में रहे, मैं भी वहां रह रहा हूँ। पापाजी ने दयनीय स्थिति में पहुँच चुकी अनुशासन व्यवस्था को विश्वविद्यालय के मुख्य नियंता के रुप में ठीक किया, मैं भी नियंता मण्डल में अनेकों बार रहा। पापाजी ने विश्वविद्यालय तथा उत्तर प्रदेश विश्वविद्यालय शिक्षक संघ का नेतृत्व किया, मैं भी उनका अनुकरण करते हुए गोरखपुर विश्वविद्यालय शिक्षक संघ का अध्यक्ष बना।

हमेशा से पापाजी की परछाई पकड़ने की कोशिश करता रहा लेकिन जो कुछ उन्होंने किया, वो मैं क्या मुझे पूरा विश्वास है कि, कोई भी नहीं कर सकता है। कहावत है कि–

बाढ़ै पूत पिता के धर्मे, और खेती उपजै अपने कर्मे।

हम सभी उनके पुत्र तथा अनुयायी उनके ही पुण्य प्रताप का फल हैं। आज अनुभव हो रहा है कि जो कुछ भी हमने किया, जानते हुए या अंजाने में, प्रेरणा तो पापाजी ही रहे।

पापाजी ने अपने समय के जिन मूल्यों को जिया, तत्कालीन परिस्थितियों में भी उनका निवर्हन कठिन था। आज के समय में तो लगता है जैसे कि असम्भव है। आज की वर्तमान विश्वविद्यालयीय परिस्थितियों तथा पिता जी के समय के विश्वविद्यालयीय मूल्यों की विवेचना करना सवर्था उपयुक्त विषय है क्योंकि मूल्यों पर आधारित शिक्षा व्यवस्था पापाजी का सर्वाधिक प्रिय विषय रहा है।

मूल्यों की बात करना मेरे इस वैज्ञानिक बुद्धि के लिए अतिरेक तो होगा पर आचार्य प्रो0 दयानाथ त्रिपाठी (पापाजी) के जीवन को जितना देखा है, उसे ही आधार मानकर लिखने की कोशिश कर रहा हूँ।

बहुत बचपन का तो नहीं पर पांच या छः वर्ष की वय से पापाजी को देखने समझने का प्रयास कर रहा हूँ। मेरे अनुज डॉ0 देवेशनाथ त्रिपाठी के जन्म के सवा महीने पर होने वाली पूजा के पश्चात् पापाजी शोधकार्य करने हेतु यूनान चले गये और हम सब अपने पितामह के साथ रहने इलाहाबाद आ गये। हमारी ज्यादातर यादें तभी की हैं। हम सभी उस समय पापाजी के लिए हींग और मसाले पार्सल द्वारा यूनान भेजते थे जिसका पापाजी हमेशा विदेश में इंतजार करते थे। ऐसा उनके द्वारा लिखे पत्रों से ज्ञात होता था। उनके पत्र हमेशा ही अपने पिता जी के लिए और मेरी माता जी के लिए आते थे। उनके द्वारा अपने पिता जी को लिखे पत्रों से ज्ञात होता था कि उनका जीवन दर्शन अपने पिता जी द्वारा ही प्राप्त था। इस संदर्भ में एक बात का स्मरण आता है कि भारत में आपातकाल की घोषणा के बाद विदेश में रह रहे भारतीय छात्रों की छात्रवृत्ति भारत सरकार द्वारा बंद कर दी गई थी। पापाजी भी उस समय इंग्लैण्ड में अपने शोध निर्देशक के साथ ही थे। धनाभाव के कारण जीवन कितना कठिन हो जाता है, इसकी कल्पना अपने देश में ही रहने पर बहुत कठिन है, ऐसे में जो अपनों से दूर विदेश में हो उसकी कठिनाई का अनुमान लगाना भी आसान नहीं है। बहुत कठिनाई का सामना करते हुए जब समस्याएं बढ़ गई तो पापाजी को इंग्लैण्ड में रह रहे भारतीय समाज द्वारा धार्मिक उपदेश देने का कार्य दिया गया। उस समय शायद एक व्याख्यान का 25 पाउण्ड पारिश्रमिक तय किया गया। अपनी माता जी (मेरी पितामही स्वर्गीय कृष्णा शर्मा) द्वारा वर्णित धार्मिक कथाओं में पुरोहित कर्म को निंदनीय समझते हुए, उनका मन विचलित हो गया। इस संदर्भ में आपने अपने पिता जी से निर्देश मांगा। उनके द्वारा अनुमति मिलने पर ही आपने साप्ताहिक धार्मिक उपदेश द्वारा धन लेना स्वीकार किया। इसी तरह मैंने अपने बाल्यकाल से ही पापाजी को धनाभाव की चिन्ता न करते हुए अपने जीवन मूल्यों की रक्षा करते हुए पाया है। आज तो अध्यापक किसी कोचिंग संस्था में अपनी सेवायें धन के लिए आसानी से देने को तैयार हैं, और जरूरत पड़ने पर मूल्यांकन को भी प्रभावित करते हैं। कर्त्तव्य परायणता उनके जीवन मूल्यों में एक महत्वपूर्ण स्थान रखता है। इस संदर्भ में मुझे पापाजी के सेवाकाल से एक उदाहरण स्वरुप घटना आप सब सुधि पाठक के समक्ष रखने की इच्छा हो रही है। यह घटना उस समय की है जब गोरखपुर विश्वविद्यालय अराजकता की चरम पर था, सम्भवतः 1980–83 का समय था, प्रो0 जी0सी0 चतुर्वेदी जी कुलपति थे, एवं पापाजी मुख्य नियन्ता, विश्वविद्यालय परीक्षा को सुधारने हेतु उड़ाका दल का गठन पहली बार किया गया। उसमें तत्कालीन सभी संकायाध्यक्ष, प्रति कुलपति तथा मुख्य नियन्ता को सम्मिलित किया गया। रक्षा अध्ययन विभाग में परीक्षा चल रही थी, अराजकता के माहौल में कुलपति द्वारा निरीक्षण करने के बाद इसका निर्णय लिया गया कि उस दिन की परीक्षा को निरस्त कर दिया जाय। इस निर्णय के पश्चात आन्दोलन होना ही था। इस आंदोलन तथा विश्वविद्यालय की अन्य अराजकताओं में दोषी छात्र नेताओं को विश्वविद्यालय नियन्ता द्वारा काली सूची में डाला गया। उल्लेखनीय है इस सूची में हमारे कुछ रिश्तेदार तथा पापाजी के परम् मित्र श्री रविप्रताप सिंह जी (लल्लू चाचा) के रिश्तेदार भी सम्मिलित थे। समाज तथा मित्रों के दबाव के बावजूद इन लोगों का नाम उस काली सूची से निकाला नहीं गया। कुछ दिनों पश्चात पापाजी से मैंने पूछा तो उन्होंने कहा मुख्य नियन्ता का कार्य विश्वविद्यालय की अनुशासन व्यवस्था को सुधारना है न कि अपने रिश्तेदारों की मदद करना।

अपने कर्त्तव्य परायणता के लिए ही पापाजी एवं हमारे आवास पर तीन बार पूरी ताकत के साथ अराजक तत्वों ने हमला किया। इन घटनाओं में से पहली घटना के समय मैं नवीं कक्षा का छात्र था। बाहर लगभग हजार की संख्या में अराजक तत्वों ने हमारे आवास (20 हीरापुरी कालोनी) को घेर कर देशी तमंचों से गोली एवं देशी बम द्वारा प्रहार किया था। पापाजी ने भी लाइसेंसी रिवाल्वर द्वारा हवा में गोली चलाकर उन अराजक तत्वों को घर में प्रवेश करने से रोका तथा मुझे कहा कि कैन्ट थाने पर जाकर प्रथम सूचना रिपोर्ट पहुंचा दो। फिर मुझसे पूछा तुम्हें डर तो नहीं लग रहा है? यदि लग रहा है तो हनुमान जी का नाम लेते रहना। मेरे द्वारा प्रथम सूचना रिपोर्ट पर भी पुलिस प्रशासन द्वारा कार्यवाही नहीं होते देख, मैं पापाजी के उन्हीं मित्र श्री रविप्रताप सिंह जी के आवास पर गया, वो तुरन्त मेरे साथ ही उसी समय रिक्शे से हमारे घर आ गये। आज उस घटना के स्मरण मात्र से डर लगता है, परन्तु उस घटना से यह सबक मिलता है कि कर्त्तव्य परायणता के लिए पापाजी ने न केवल अपना, अपने सबसे प्रिय पुत्र तथा परिवार की भी चिन्ता नहीं की और शायद इसी कर्त्तव्य परायणता के कारण पूरा समाज उनका सम्मान करता है।

अन्ततः परिवर्तित होते हुए इस आधुनिक समाज में भी मूल्यों को संजोये और गुरू–शिष्य परम्परा का निर्वहन करते हुए सभी सम्पादकों को मैं साधुवाद देना चाहता हूँ, जिनके प्रयासों के फलस्वरुप पापाजी जैसे बहुमुखी प्रतिभा के व्यक्तित्व, जिसने अनेक कठिनाईयों के बाद भी कभी अपने आदर्शों एवं मूल्यों से समझौता नहीं किया, आज सुधिजनों के समक्ष आ सका।

डॉ0 उमेशनाथ त्रिपाठी
रसायनशास्त्र विभाग
दी0द0उ0 गोरखपुर विश्वविद्यालय, गोरखपुर

गर्व है पुत्री होने का

अंजुला शुक्ला

कक्षा में शिक्षण कार्य समाप्त कर जैसे ही विभाग में बैठी एक अन्जान नम्बर से मोबाइल की घंटी बजती है, मैडम आप डॉ0 अन्जुला शुक्ला बोल रही हैं। हाँ मैं बोल रही हूँ। मैडम मैं विमल तिवारी बोल रहा हूँ। मैं गुरूजी के ऊपर एक किताब प्रकाशित कर रहा हूँ, चाहता हूँ आप कुछ लिखें।

इतना सुनते ही मेरे मुख से निकला 'मुझे गर्व है उनकी पुत्री होने का'। शायद ही कोई इतना भाग्यशाली होगा जितना हम भाई–बहन हैं। प्राचीन इतिहास के विद्यार्थी ही नहीं अपितु भारतीय इतिहास, संस्कृति एवं पुरातत्व के सभी जानने वाले पापा पर गर्व करते हैं। बात उस समय की है जब सन् 1962 में चीन ने भारत पर आक्रमण किया था। दुर्भाग्यवश उसमें भारत को हार का मुंह देखना पड़ा था। ऐसे आपातकालीन समय में भारत सरकार ने देश के सभी नागरिकों से मदद की अपील की थी कि वे देश की सुरक्षा के लिए आगे आए। विश्वविद्यालयों में भी इसके लिए नाम मांगे गए और पापा ने देश सेवा के लिए सहर्ष अपना नाम आगे दिया था। इसी के निमित्त उन्हें जनवरी 1963 में केन्द्रीय आपात राहत प्रशिक्षण संस्थान, नागपुर में प्रशिक्षण के लिए भेजा गया। उसी समय मेरा जन्म 30 जनवरी 1963 को मेरे पैतृक आवास मुट्ठीगंज, इलाहाबाद मे हुआ। मेरे जन्म होने के साथ ही पूरे माहौल मे मायूसी सी छा गई क्योंकि मेरी एक बड़ी बहन पहले से ही थी। लोग कहने लगे, "लो फिर बेटी आ गई, यह तो मनतोरा अर्थात मन को तोड़ने वाली आ गई। पापा जब मार्च 1963 में अपना प्रशिक्षण पूरा करके लौटे और जब सुना कि लोग ऐसा कह रहे हैं, तो उन्होंने कहा यह मनतोरा नहीं मेरी मनबोधा अर्थात मन को भाने वाली है। तदुपरांत पापा ने मार्च 1963 से लेकर अपने शोध कार्य के लिए 30 नवम्बर 1971 में यूनान जाने के पूर्व तक गोरखपुर में होमगार्ड के डिप्टी कमांडेंट का अतिरिक्त पद भी संभाला और देश के लिए अपनी सेवाएं समर्पित की। यह घटना पापा के बेटियों के प्रति धनात्मक दृष्टिकोण और उनके बहुमुखी व्यक्तित्व की पहचान कराता है।

पापा उपर से जितने कठोर दिखते हैं, उतने ही अन्दर से मृदु हैं। हमारा जरा भी कष्ट उन्हें बर्दाश्त नहीं होता है। उन्होंने कभी भी लड़के और लड़की में भेद नहीं किया। हम जो विषय लेना चाहे, जैसा पढ़ना चाहे, उन्होंने पूरी स्वतन्त्रता दी। परन्तु अनुशासनहीनता उन्हें जरा भी नहीं पसन्द थी। हम सबको उन्होंने कठोर अनुशासन में पाला। जिसका स्पष्ट प्रमाण हम भाई–बहनों में दिखता है। उनके द्वारा दिया गया संस्कार आज इतनी विपरीत परिस्थितियों में भी हमें सही रास्ते पर चलना सिखाता है।

पापा जब विश्वविद्यालय में मुख्य नियन्ता पद पर थे, उन्होंने गोरखपुर विश्वविद्यालय में नकलमुक्त परीक्षा कराने में जितना साहस दिखाया वह सामान्यतः आज असम्भव है। उनके उपर गोली चली, आवास पर बम फेका गया परन्तु पापा ने साहस नहीं खोया और दृढ़ संकल्प के साथ अपने कार्य को सम्पादित किया। उनके इस पुनीत कार्य का प्रतिफल आज भी है कि, गोरखपुर विश्वविद्यालय नकलमुक्त परीक्षा करा रहा है। पापा से जुड़ी उनकी बहुत सी बातें प्रेरणादायक हैं। किन–किन का उल्लेख करूँ। घर और बाहर अपने विचारों को रखने की पूरी स्वतन्त्रता हमें दी और हमेशा शिक्षक का सम्मान करने की शिक्षा दी।

आज मैं जहाँ हूँ पापा एवं माँ के दिये संस्कारों के कारण सफलता पूर्वक अपने कर्तव्यों का निर्वहन कर रही हूँ। कक्षा में समय से जाना, अपने विषयवस्तु की तैयारी के साथ कक्षा में विद्यार्थियों के साथ सामन्जस्यपूर्ण व्यवहार करना, यह सब पापा के दिखाये मार्ग से ही सम्भव है।

विश्वविद्यालय शिक्षक नेता के रूप में भी पापा ने एक आदर्श शिक्षक अध्यक्ष के रूप में गोरखपुर विश्वविद्यालय एवं उत्तर प्रदेश आवासीय विश्वविद्यालय संघ में कार्य किया। गलत बातों को स्वीकार न करना, शिक्षकहितों के लिए संघर्ष करना यह सब उन्हीं से सीखा है। आज मुझसे लोग कहते हैं यह वह समय नहीं है परन्तु मैं कहती हूँ मुझसे गलत बात बर्दाश्त नहीं होगी क्योंकि मेरे अन्दर जिसका खून है वह व्यक्तित्व प्रो0 दयानाथ त्रिपाठी हैं। आज सामाजिक सम्बन्धों में एक संक्रमण सा हो गया है। व्यक्ति नितांत स्वार्थी होकर जी रहा है। परन्तु आज भी समाज में कुछ अच्छे लोग है जो 'बहुजन हिताय–बहुजन सुखाय' की भावना से प्रेरित होकर स्वयं के साथ दूसरों का भी जीवन सुखमय बना रहे हैं। मेरा मानना है कि यह समाज इन्हीं लोगों की वजह से चल रहा है। यद्यपि ऐसे लोग बहुत कम रह गये हैं परन्तु मैं गर्व से कह सकती हूं कि पापा उनमें से एक है। पापा की एक बात और प्रेरणादायक है कि वह उस व्यक्ति (शिक्षक) को अच्छा नहीं मानते हैं जो अपने विषय में कार्य न कर अन्य क्षेत्रों में कार्य करता है। उनका कहना है कि तुम जिस विषय के हो तुम्हारा प्रथम दायित्व है कि तुम अपने विषय को पढ़ो, समझो और उसमें कुछ नया करो। समकालीन समय में शिक्षक के रूप में उच्च शिक्षा के द्वारा एक तरफ जहाँ हमें अपने भविष्य निर्माताओं को तैयार करना है वहीं पर साथ ही साथ हमें इस बात का का ध्यान भी रखना है कि हमारा व्यक्तित्व गुण कर्म स्वभाव को परिष्कृत करने वाला हो। न केवल वैयक्तिक समृद्धि एवं सुख शान्ति के लिए वरन् सामाजिक सुव्यवस्था एवं प्रगति के लिए भी पापा जैसे ही परिष्कृत व्यक्ति की आवश्यकता है। ईश्वर से प्रार्थना है कि पापा स्वस्थ एवं दीर्घायु हों, जिससे हम लोगों को उचित मार्ग दर्शन मिलता रहे। उनके इतना तो आज करना मुश्किल लगता है परन्तु कुछ कर सकूँ यही ईश्वर से प्रार्थना है।

डॉ0 अंजुला शुक्ला
उपाचार्य, बी0एड0 विभाग
बुद्ध पी0जी0 कालेज, कुशीनगर

Professor D.N. Tripathi

Irfan Habib

Professor Daya Nath Tripathi (b. 1938) is a historian of eminence who has combined much work in archaeology with work in an area in which few Indian historians have ventured, viz. Hellenic studies. He has had the rare privilege of his Ph.D. work on Bronze work of Greece (Southampton University) supervised by anarchaeologist of the status of Lord Colin Renfrew. Besides this thesis which was published in the prestigious Mediterranean Archaeology series of the University of Gottenhurg, Sweden (1987), he has published widely on India's relations with Greece, notably *Cultural Interaction between India and Grece* (1996) and *Hinduism and Hellenism,* (2004). These and his other publications constitute substantive contributions to both History and Archaeology.

Professor D.N. Tripathi had an eventful term as Chairman, Indian Council of Historical Research (2004-07). He was able to bring together historians of all persuasions in fruitful collaboration and revived such important projects of archival importance as "Towards Freedom" (1937-47), "Epigraphical Dictionary" and "Economic History documentation". The volumes that were published or prepared during this term have won wide acclaim.

I cannot end this note without a reference to my personal experience. I always found him immensely considerate to friends and colleagues, always cheerfully dealing with the differences of opinion that are a natural part of the discipine of History. As he passes theage of seventy-six, I as a still older man, hasten to wish him a long life and further attainments.

28

INVOCATION OF SĀRASVAT POWER IN JAINISM

Maruti Nandan Pd. Tiwari, Shanti Swaroop Sinha

Sarasvatī (also called Śāradā, Bhāratī, Vāk, Vāṇī, Vāgīśvarī), the ancient most *Vaidik-Purāṇic* goddess of learning (*vidyā*) and music, also enjoyed unquestionable popularity among both the sects of the Jainas from at least Kushāṇa period. As Śrutadevatā she represents the personified knowledge (*Jñana-mūrti*) embodied in the sacred Jaina scriptures preached by the Jinas and the Kevalins (***Vyākhyā-Prajñapati****-11.11.430 and* ***Paümacariya****-3.59*). The ***Dvādasāṅga***- the twelve *aṅga*-texts are described as different limbs of Śrutadevatā, while the fourteen ***pūrva***-texts are said to be her ornaments. She virtually represents Sārasvat Power (*Jñana-Śakti*).

Sarasvatī, as the best power of knowledge and purity, has been endowed with symbols like swan (as mount), manuscript, rosary, *varada-mudrā* and water-vessel (in hands), which do represent her distinctive character. Subsequently by the end of ninth century, she also became the presiding goddess of music and hence provided with *Viṇā* (lute) in hands and peacock as mount. The popularity of worship of Sarasvatī in Jainism is established on the testimony of literary references in the ***Vyākhyā-prajñapti*** (c. 2nd -3rd cent. CE), the ***Pakṣika-sūtra*** of Śivaśarmā (c. 5th cent. CE), the ***Dvādaśāraṇyacakravṛtti*** of Siṁha sūri Kṣamāsramaṇa (c. CE 675), the ***Pañcāśaka*** of Haribhadra sūri (c. CE 775), the ***Saṁsāradāvānala stotra*** (also of Haribhadra sūri); the ***Mahāniśītha sūtra*** (c. 9th cent. CE) and the ***Śāradā-stotra*** of Bappabhaṭṭi sūri (c. 3rd quarter of the 8th cent. CE) and also by the archaeological evidence of the images of Sarasvatī from different Jaina sites ranging in date from 2nd to 14th cent. CE. A special festival held in the honour of Sarasvatī is called *jñāna-pañcamī* in the Śvetāmbara tradition and *Śruta-pañcamī* in the Digambara tradition[1]. Besides this festival, special penance like the Śrutadevatā – *tapas* and *Śruta-skandha* and *Śrutajñāna-vratas* are also observed by the Jainas[2].

The Jainas, particularly, the monks, friars and pontiffs such as Bappabhaṭṭi sūri, Hemacandra, Malliṣeṇa, Mallavādi sūri II, Naracandra sūri are reported in the medieval literature to have acquired Sārasvat power from Sarasvatī. The cause for such pursuit was not only to become a poet (*kavi*) of unequal merit and invincible dialectician (*vādī*)[3] but also to obtain certain supernatural powers. There are references which distinctly reveal that the Jaina *ācharyās* and poets sought to acquire the *Sārasvata-mantra,* a magic formula for obtaining mastery over speech. Hemacandra himself in his manual of poetics, the *Alaṅkāracuḍāmaṇi,* admits unreservedly of his faith in such means[4]. The Jaina works also make frequent references to the journey of Hemacandra and other Jaina *ācharyās* to Brāhmīdeśa i.e. Kashmir for wining the favour of goddess *Brāhmī* in order to overcome all their rivals in disputations (*vāda*)[5].

The ***Prabandha-kāvyas*** invariably refer to a story wherein Bappabhaṭṭi sūri is said to have invoked Sarasvatī for winning over a Buddhist dialectician Vardhanakuṅjara at the court of Āmarāja in Gopagiri[6]. Hemacandra (c. mid 12th cent. CE) was also blessed with Sārasvata power alongwith other magical powers[7]. Malliṣeṇa sūri (c. CE 1047), the author of ***Bhairava – Padmāvatī-kalpa*** and ***Bhāratī-kalpa*** (wrongly called ***Sarasvatī-mantra-kalpa***), was also blessed with Sārasvata power[8]. From the various titles mentioned for him in his works we gather that he was not only a great *māntric* but also a great poet of Sanskrit and Prākṛt, a grammarian, a dialectician and was favoured by Sarasvatī with a boon[9]. Another reference pertains to Bālacandra sūri, author of the ***Vasantavilāsa*** (c. early 13th cent. CE) who was well known as *Siddhasārasvata* i.e. one who had successfully practiced the *sādhanṇ* of Sarasvatī. He is described to have realized the form of *Śrī-Śāradg* in a yogic trance[10].

Sarasvatī is also invoked in Jaina texts of *tāntric* expression. The later *tāntric* Jaina works such as the ***Bhārati-kalpa*** by Malliṣeṇa and the enlarged version of the ***Sarasvatī-kalpa*** attributed, though wrongly, to Bappabhaṭṭi (c. 10th – 11th cent. CE), the ***Siddhasārasvata-stava*** (misread as of Sādhvī Śivāryā but in reality the composition of Hemachandra sūri) and ***Śāradāstavana*** by Jinaprabha sūri (c. 14th cent. CE) refer to her worship in all the *tāntric* rites such as the *śāntika, pauṣṭika, stambhana*[11], *māraṇa, ucāṭaṇa* etc. The various *tāntric* modes include her *sakalīkaraṇa, arcana, yantravidhi, pīṭhasthāpanā, saubhāgyarakṣā* and *vaśya-mantras* alongwith different rites to be performed. Apart from the propitiatory rites, the gruesome rites were also accepted and the terrific form of Sarasvatī was also visualized from about the 10th -11th cent. CE. The ***Bhāratī-kalpa*** of Malliṣeṇa, the ***Sarasvatī-kalpa*** of Arhaddāsa, ***Sārasvatayantra-pūjā*** of Śubhacandra (c. 10th cent. CE) and ***Jinasaṃhitā*** of Ekasaṁdhi enunciate the goddess in horrible form with three eyes and crescent in her *jaṭā* and also making terrifying sounds (*huṁkārangda*)[12]. These features bear testimony to her closeness with Śivā. Bappabhaṭṭi, in his ***Sarasvatī-kalpa*** invokes the goddess under the name Gaurī[13]. It may be noted in passing that the ***Sūtasaṁhitā*** of the ***Skanda-Purāṇa*** (c. 13th cent. CE) likewise describes Sarasvatī with three eyes and having *jaṭā-mukuṭa* with crescent[14]. A few Jaina works visualizing Sarasvatī with goad and noose in her hands further reveal her power aspect[15]. However, she is also addressed by various such names *as Kālī, Kapālinī, Kaulī, Trilocanā, Raudrī, Khaḍginī, Kāmarūpiṇī, Nityā, Tripurasundarī, Candraśekharī, Śūlinī, Cāmuṇḍā, Bhairavī* and so forth which attest to the amalgamation of *tāntric* features in her worship[16].

According to ***Vidyānuśāsana*** (c. 15th cent. CE) Vāgīśvarī should be worshipped in a form with sharp bare fangs and protruding tongue, three eyes and in terrific appearance. Her worship in this form with *khaḍga-mantra* results in removing all mishaps[17]. The ***Ācāradinakara*** of Vardhamāna sūri (c. A.D. 1412) includes Sarasvatī in the list of 64 *yoginīs* as well[18].

The ***Sarasvatī-kalpa***, the ***Bhāratī-kalpa*** and the ***Sārasvata-yantra-pūjā***, however, speak of different *yantra* or magical diagram for the *sādhana* of Sarasvatī[19]. The *Sārasvata-yantra* sometimes give interesting information on the *parivāra* of Sarasvatī as well. The *yantra-pūjā* envisaged in the *Sarasvatī-kalpa* of Bappabhaṭṭi sūri mentions *Mohā, Nandā, Bhadrā, Jayā, Vijayā, Aparājitā, Jambhā, Stambhā,* the sixteen Vidyādevis (*Rohiṇī, Prajṅapti* etc.), the eight Dikpālas, Aṣamātṛkas[20] and the Aṣṭa-Bhairavas to be worshipped in the *maṇḍala* or *yantra* of Sarasvatī[21].

Sarasvatī in Jainism, has distinct bearing of *Brāhmanic* Sarasvatī. This closeness can be established on account of their common attributes, like *pustaka, vīṇā, akṣamālā, kamaṇḍalu, sruk, aṅkuśa* and *pāśa* and also the mount. The ***Ācāradinkarā*** (1412 CE), however, envisages the same sets of symbol for *Śrutadevatā* and *Brahmāṇī*. The four-armed Sarasvatī here is visualized like *Brahmāṇī* as riding on *haṁsa* and holding *vīṇā, pustaka, padma* and *akṣamālā*[22]. The rendering of *sruk* in the hand of Sarasvatā, an invariate feature of Brahmā images, is also noticed in several examples, although it was never prescribed by any Jaina text[23].

Sarasvatī in Jaina texts is visualized in three varieties of forms, namely the two-armed, the four-armed and the multi-armed. In sculptures, as against the iconographic texts, sometimes she is also carved with six, eight and sixteen hands. The symbols invariably held by Sarasvatī are *pustaka* (manuscript), lotus, rosary and the *varada* or *abhaya-mudrā,* the former three being of more frequent occurrence. She rides a swan occasionally replaced by a peacock. She mostly appears as *sudarsanā* (beautiful) and seated on a lotus in *lalitāsana,* or standing in *tribhaṅga.* The *vāhana* of Sarasvatī in the Śvetāmbara tradition is swan while in Digambara tradition she rides a peacock.

The early Jaina works conceive Sarasvatī only with two hands and as holding either a book and a lotus or a water-vessel and a rosary, and riding a swan[24]. The ***Sarasvatī-yantra-pūjā*** of Śubhacandra, however, describes the two-armed *mayūravāhinī* with three eyes and holding a rosary and a book[25]. The four-armed Sarasvatī appears to have enjoyed the highest veneration among both the Śvetāmbara and the Digambara sects. The four-armed goddess in both the sects bear almost identical attributes, except for the *vāhana.* The āvetgmbara works invariably conceive her with the *varada-mudrā,* a lotus, a manuscript and a rosary[26]. The ***Sarasvatī-kalpa***, however, gives two sets of symbols for four-armed Sarasvatī; the first showing her with the *abhaya-mudrā,* the *varada-mudrā, pustaka* and a lotus while in other the *abhaya* and *varada-mudrā* have been replaced by a *vīṇā* and a rosary[27]. The ***Bhāratī-kalpa*** renders the *dhyāna* of the goddess showing *abhaya-mudrā, jṇāna-mudrā,* rosary and manuscript[28]. According to ***Nirvāṇakalikā*** of Pādalipta sři III (c. CE 900), Sarasvatī bears a book, a rosary, a lotus, the *varada-mudrā* and various other symbols in her hands[29].

The earliest representation of Sarasvatī is known from Mathura (CE 132). The image now preserved in State Museum, Lucknow (Acc. No. J.24), is inscribed and mentions the date and name of Sarasvatī on the pedestal. The two-armed goddess seated squatted on a rectangular pedestal, holds a manuscript in her left hand, while her mutilated right hand was in the *abhatākṣa.* The *haṁsa vāhana* is not carved in present instance. Deogarh (Lalitpur, UP), a prolific Digambara Jaina site, has yielded a number of independent figures of Sarasvatī, datable between c. ninth to 12th cent. CE. Sarasvatī in Deogarh, riding either a swan or a peacock, is represented either with two or four arms. The rendering of Sarasvatī twice in the group of 24 *yakṣis* on the facade of the temple no. 12 (A.D. 862) at Deogarh, is particularly interesting which represent her as the *yakṣis* respectively of Jina Abhinandana and Supārśvanātha with the labelling **"Bhagavatī Sarasvatī" and Mayūravāhinī (ni)**[31].

A non-pareil figure of Sarasvatī from Deogarh, carved on the exterior wall of temple no. 1 (now in the modern temple of Jaina Dharmashala, late 11th cent. CE), shows the goddess in the *tritirthi* image wherein Sarasvatī is depicted with two Jinas standing on the same pedestal (Plate 28.1). Sarasvatī occupying the left extremity of the *tritīrthī,* is shown equal in size to the Jina figures, which may, however, be interpreted that as Śrutadevatā, personifying *Jina-vāṇī,* she is given a status as honourable as that of the Jinas. The four-armed goddess, standing in *tribhaṅga* with peacock mount, shows the *varada-mudra,* a rosary, a lotus and a manuscript. She also finds representation on different door-lintels with (temple no. 12) *Cakreśvarī, Rohiṇī, Ambikā* and *Lakṣmī.*

The two-armed Sarasvatī in Deogarh usually bears the *abhaya-mudrā* and a manuscript (temple no. 16). The four-armed figures, either wearing a *dhammilla* or a *jaṭā-jūṭa,* show the *varada-mudrā,* the *vyākhyāna*-cum-rosary, a long-stalked lotus and a manuscript[32]. In one instance (temple no. 19) Sarasvatī is accompanied by fly-whisk bearers, tiny Jina figures and also the Jaina *ācāryas.* A few instances, carved mainly on the door-lintels, show her with *vīṇā*[33].

Khajurāho, a Digambara Jaina site (Chhatarpur, MP), has yielded eight figures of Sarasvatī wherein she, except for one instance[34], is always four-armed[35]. The figures datable between c. CE 950-1100, depict her in *lalita-mudrā* and as holding a manuscript, a *vīṇā* (either in one or two hands), a lotus (usually in two hands) and also the *varada-mudrā* (or a water-vessel or a rosary). However, the *vāhana*, swan is carved only in one instance of the northern *adhiṣṭhāna* of the Pārsvanātha temple (c. CE 950-70). The six-armed image of Sarasvatī, on the southern *adhiṣṭhāna* of the same temple, shows a lotus and a manuscript in upper pair of hands, while the middle pair of hands is engaged in playing on *vīṇā* (Plate 28.2). The remaining two hands, however, show the *varada-mudrā* and a water-vessel. The presence of female *cāmara*-bearers, adorers, hovering *mālādharas* and above all, small Jina figure overhead, signify that she was accorded a favoured position at the site.

Belonging as they do to Digambara tradition a few sculptures from different places in Karnataka have some indications as to the power aspect of Sarasvatī. Three such examples, datable to 11th-12th cent. CE, are known from the Pañcakūṭa-bastī, Humcā (Shimoga district, Plate 28.3), Shāntināthа-bastī, Jinanāthapura and ṛdināātha temple, Halebiḍ (Hassan) **[36]**. Sarasvatī, seated in *dhyāna-mudrā* without *vāhana,* in all the instances shows *abhayākṣa,* goad, noose and manuscript. The face, although much mutilated, has atleast some suggestion of power through large open eyes, open lips and even somewhat swollen nose.

The Śvetāmbara Jaina temples in western India have yielded sufficient figures of Sarasvatī coming as they do mainly from Osiāṅ, Kumbhāriyā, Mt. Ābū and Tāraṅgā. The figures on the Mahāvīra temple at Osiāṅ (Jodhpur, Rajasthan) (close of eight cent. CE) show the goddess both with two and four arms and riding either a peacock or a swan. The two-armed goddess holds a lotus and a manuscript, while the four-armed goddess (*mukhamaṇḍapa* on west) shows a *sruk,* a lotus, a lotus and a manuscript. The figures of five Jaina *devakulikās* at Osiāṅ (c. 10th-11th cent. CE) invariably show the four-armed goddess riding a swan and as holding a manuscript and a lotus in two hands, and the remaining two showing the *abhaya-mudrā* and a water-vessel or the *varadākṣa* and a book.

The figure from Vimala-Vasahī (latter half of 12th cent. CE) and the Lūṇa-Vasahī (13th cent. CE), Mt. Ābū, Rajasthan and the Ajitanātha temple at Tāraṅgā (Mahesana, Gujarat, 12th cent. CE) are particularly interesting since they exhibit the goddess with two, four, six and even 16 arms, thus distinctly suggesting her power aspect by way of increase in number of hands. Besides the usual four-armed figures of Sarasvatī with swan as mount and the *varada* (or the *abhaya-mudrā*), a lotus, a manuscript (sometimes *sruk* or *vīṇā* replacing lotus or manuscript) and a fruit (or a water-vessel) in hands, Vimala-Vasahī has two other such figures which deserve our attention. In one case, carved in the southern bay ceiling, Sarasvatī seated in *lalitāsana* on a *bhadrapīṭha* and holding *varadākṣa*, a spiral lotus, a manuscript and a water-vessel, is accompanied by two male figures, standing close to her with folded hands. These figures bear inscriptions, according to which the bearded figure to her right is *sūtradhāra* Loyaṇa while the figure to left with a measuring rod is *sūtradhāra* Kelā. The first seems to be the chief architect of the *raṅgamaṇḍapa* while the other was possibly the chief sculptor. The present figure apparently suggests that Sarasvatī here has been visualized as the goddess of fine-arts. The figure of 16-armed goddess carved in a *bhramikā*-ceiling, depicts her as sitting on a *bhadrāsana* in *lalita*-pose with swan and holding the *varada-mudrā,* a conch, small stick (possibly measuring rod in two hands), a chain (in uppermost pair of hands), an indistinct object, a goad, the *abhayākṣa,* a fruit, a manuscript and a water-vessel. The goddess is joined by six-armed dancing male figure on each side, thus suggesting her command over musical power (Plate 28.4).

The figures in Lūṇa-Vasahī show the goddess with four and six hands and riding a swan. An interesting point in this regard is the collective rendering of eight Sarasvatī figures on each of the four pillars of the *navacaukī* close to *raṅgamaṇḍapa.* The four-armed Sarasvatī in these instances shows the *varada-mudrā* (or *varadākṣa*), a long-stalked lotus (or manuscript), manuscript (or *vīṇā*) and water-vessel. There are two examples wherein Sarasvati possesses six hands. These figures are carved in the *bhramikā*-ceiling of *devakulikā* no. 11 and in the ceiling close to the *raṅgamaṇḍapa* on north. Accompanied by a swan, she in latter case bears the *abhayākṣa,* a double petalled lotus (in two hands), a water-vessel and the *jñāna-mudrā* (with the middle pair of hands). The other instance, again revealing her musical power, shows her as holding cymbals in middle pair of hands with a *vīṇā* in the upper left. The remaining three hands, as usual, show the *varadākṣa,* a spiral lotus and a manuscript.

The most exquisite of all the known figures of Sarasvatī are the two images from Pallū (Bikaner, Rajasthan). Of the two identical figures, one is in the National Museum, New Delhi (Acc. No. 1/6/278, Plate 28.5) while the other one is in the Gaṅgā Golden Jubilee Museum, Bikaner (Acc. No. 203). These figures, belonging to c. mid 11th cent. CE, show the four-armed goddess as standing in *tribhaṅga* on a lotus pedestal with a small figure of swan. The goddess, benign in appearance, is bedecked with beautifully carved ornaments and *karaṇḍa-mukuṭa.* The whole composition is endowed with divine grace and aesthetic qualities. She shows the *varadākṣa,* a full blown lotus, a manuscript and a water-vessel. The goddess is accompanied by two female figures playing on *vīṇā,* topped by another two figures playing on flute, thus revealing her musical power. What is particularly interesting about the image in the Ganga Golden Jubilee Museum, Bikaner is the beautiful *prabhā-toraāa,* containing the two-armed figures of 16 *Mahāvidyās* (goddesses with magical powers). Some of them may be identified with *Apraticakrā,* V*ajrāṅkuśā, Kālī, Rohiṇi* and *Prajñapti.* The figure on the *prabhā-toraṇa* possibly suggests that Sarasvatī here has been conceived as the superintending goddess of all the **Great-Powers** (*Mahāvidyās*).

Another beautiful image of Sarasvatī in marble is preserved in Modern Jaina Temple at Ladnun (Nagaur, Rajasthan). The image inscribed in V.S. 1219 (=CE 1162) gives the name of Sarasvatī and refers to its carving at the instance of *Śreṣṭhi's* wife Āshā Devā. Sarasvatī with a tiny seated Jina figure atop stands in *tribhaṅga* and wears tastefully chiselled *karaṇḍa-mukuta,* long *vanamālā* hanging down to the knees and other ornaments which make her *sarvābharaṇabhūṣitā.* Sarasvatī like Pallu images bears (clockwise) *varadākṣa,* spiral lotus, manuscript and water vessel in her four hands. The swan mount also is likewise shown in miniature form in the midst of beautifully delineated rolled lotuses on the pedestal exhibiting at its extremities male-female devotees (probably donors) with folded hands. Sarasvatī also being the presiding goddess of music is joined by the figures of two female musicians playing on flute and *vīṇā* alongwith two flywhisk bearing female attendants. The beautiful oval face with benign smile and supple body reveal ideal divine beauty and grace.

The present study thus reveals that the worship and rendering of Sarasvatī in Jaina tradition and art, popular from the Kushan period through the centuries, had the dynamics of rapid evolution from being the goddess of wisdom to the presiding goddess of music and fine-arts. She has been invoked mainly as benevolent goddess granting *Sārasvata*-power (power of knowledge) to the worshippers but in *tāntric* invocation she has also been conceived in gruesome form with attributes like goad, noose and having such appellations as *Kālī, Kapālinī, Kaulī, Trilochanā, Khaḍginī, Śūlinī.*

Owing to the fact that Sarasvatī in Jaina context was visualized as personification of the preachings of the Jinas (*Jina-Vāṇī*), she was provided not only with manuscript (symbol of Jinas preachings) but was also given a status equal to the Jinas, as is evident from an image of Sarasvatī from Deogarh depicting her with two Jinas on the same pedestal and in same composition and size.

References

1. The *jñāna-pañcamā* falls on the fifty day of the bright fornight of the month of Kāttika while the *śruta- pañcamā* is the fifth day of the bright half of Jyeṣṭha.
2. U.P. Shah, "Iconography of Jaina Goddess Sarasvatī", *Journal of University of Bombay,* Vol. X (New Series), pt. II, Sept. 1941, p. 196.
3. *Caturviṁśatikā* (of Bappabhaṭṭi sūri) Appendix A - *Śāradā Stotra*-11. As quoted in *Jaina-Stotra-Sandoha,* Vol.I, Ed. Amarvijaya Muni, Ahmedabad, 1932, p. 346.
4. *Alaṁkāracūāmaṇi* I, 4. (as quoted by G. Bḷhler in his '*The life of Hemacandrācārya* (tr. By Manilal Patel), Singhi Jaina Series-11, Santiniketan, 1936, p. 10).
5. G.Bḷhler, *op.cit.,* p. 10.
6. *Prabhāvakacarita* of Prabhacandrācārya, (Ed. Jinavijya Muni, Singhi Jaina granthamala-13, Ahmedabad-Calcutta, 1940), 11- *Bappabhaṭṭi sūri carita*; *Prabandhakośa* of Rājaśekhara sūri (Ed. Jinavijya Muni, 1st part, Singhi Jaina Series-6, Santiniketan, 1935) a - Bappabhaṭṭi sūri Prabandha.
7. G.Bḷhler, *op.cit.,* p. 54.
8. *Bhairava-Padmāvatī-Kalpa,* Appendix 11: *Sarasvatīmantra-Kalpa* (actually *Bhāratā-Kalpa*), verse 3. (Ed. K.V.Abhyankara, Gujrati trans., Sarabhai Manilal Nawab, Ahmedabad, 1937, p. 61).
9. Mohanlal Bhagwandas Jhaveri, *Comparative and Critical Study of Mantraśāstra,* Ahmedabad, 1944, p. 300.
10. Gaekwad Oriental Series, Vol.VII, p.5; also Kanailal Bhattacharyya, *Sarasvati* (A study on concept and Iconography), Calcutta, 1983, p.109.
11. Stambhana is defensive magical power for making the evil spirit motionless.
12. *Abhayajñānamudrākṣamālāpustakadhāriṇī/trinetra pātu mām vāṇī jaṭābālendumaṇḍitā//* Bhāratī-Kalpa, verse 2.
    *Candraprabhāṁ nīlagalaprayānaṁ, trinetramyāṁ svaguṇapratuṣṭām/*Sārasvatamantra-pūjā (as quoted by U.P.Shah in '*Iconography of Sarasvatī*', p. 201 & 211, in footnotes 29 & 71).
13. *Sarasvatī-Kalpa,* verse 6: as Appendix 12 of *Bhairava-Padmāvatī-Kalpa.*
14. T.A. Gopinath Rao, *Elements of Hindu Iconography,* Vol. I, pt. II, Delhi, 1971, p. 378.
15. The goad and noose, principal attributes respectively of Indra and Varuṇa (also of Yama), are suggestive of power since these are among the main attributes held by various *tāntric* deities in gruesome forms. Sarasvatī through these attributes perhaps control the evil spirits of ignorance.
16. *ārī Sarasvatīstotra,* Publ. in *Jaina-Stotra-Sandoha,* Vol. I, 107, pp. 345-46.
17. As quoted by U.P.Shah in his article on 'Supernatural Beings in the Jaina Tantras', *Āchārya Dhruva Commemoration Vol.,* pt. III, Ahmedabad, 1946, p.75.
18. *Ācāradinakara,* pt. II : *Pratiṣṭhāvidhi* (Bhagavatī maṇḍala), Bombay, 1923, p. 207.
19. U.P.Shah, "*Iconography of Sarasvatī*", pp. 211-12.
20. Brahmāṇī, Māheśvarī, Kaumārī, Vārāhī, Vaiṣṇavī, Cāmuṇḍā, Caṇḍikā and Mahālakṣmī —— *Sarasvatī-Kalpa,* p. 73.
21. *Sarasvatī-Kalpa* : Appendix 12 of *Bhairava-Padmāvatī-Kalpa,* pp. 69-76.
22. *Ācāradinakara* I, p.12, II, p.158, Bombay, 1923.
23. Such figures are in the Pārśvanātha temple (eastern façade) at Kumbhāriyā (c. 12th cent. A.D.), Ajitanātha temple at Tāraṅgā (c. 12th cent. A.D.), Vimala-Vasahī at Mt. Ābū (ceiling of cell no. 48, c. CE 1150) and Mahāvīra temple at Jalore (c. 12th cent. CE).
24. The *Caturviṁśatikā* (76.19) and the *Śāradā-Stotra* (verses 1-2,8) of Bappabhaṭṭi sūri respectively give two different sets of symbols for Sarasvatī who is visualized either holding *kamaṇḍalu* and rosary or *pustaka* and *padma.*
25. U.P.Shah, *op.cit.,* p.201, fn. 29.
26. *Nirvāṇakalikā* of Pādalipta sūri (c. A.D. 900), p.37 (Ed. Mohanlal Bhagwandas, Muni Shri Mohanlalji Jaina Granthamala 5, Bombay, 1926).
27. *Sarasvatī-Kalpa,* verse 6 and 11.
28. *Bhāratī-Kalpa,* verse 2.
29. U.P.Shah, *op.cit.,* p. 211, fn. 70.

30. K.D.Bajpai, "Jaina Image of Sarasvatī in the Lucknow Museum", *Jaina Antiquary*, Vol. XI, no. 2, Jan. 1946, pp. 1-4.
31. Klaus Bruhn, *The Jina Images of Deogarh*, Leiden, 1955, pp. 102 & 105: The four-armed mayūravāhanā *yakṣī*, with Supārśvanātha stands in *tribhaṅga* and shows the *vyākhyāna-mudrā*, a *cāmara-padma* (typical of Deogarh), a manuscript and a conch.
32. Of the three instances, two are in temple nos. 12 & 19 while the remaining one is near the entrance gate of the enclosure wall.
33. Door-lintels of temple nos. 5, 12, 13 and the pillar-figures of temple nos. 1, 4, 12, 24 and 25.
34. Figure on the southern adhiṣṭhāna of the Pārśvanātha temple.
35. Figures on the façade of the Pārśvanātha temple and the door-lintels of different temples.
36. Another image with the same symbol is preserved in the temple at Truparuttikuṭaram (Tamilnadu).

29

ŚAIVISM OF *TATTVAPRAKĀŚA* AND PARALLELS IN THE ŚAIVA IMAGES IN *SAMARĀNGAṆSŪTRADHĀRA*

Susmita Pande

Bhoja was the most famous of the Parmāra rulers who wrote the *Samarāngaṇsūtradhāra* sometime in the 11th Cen. CE. His special predilection for Śaivism is clear from his *Tattva Prakāśa* and invocatory verse of *Samaranganṇsūtradhāra*–

> *देव स पातु भुवनत्रयसूत्रधारः त्वां बालचंद्रकलिकांकित जूटकोटिः*
> *एतत् समग्रमपि कारणमन्तरेण कात्स्न्र्यादि असूत्रितमसूत्रयत येन विष्वम्*
> *1.1.ए*

This may be translated as "may the God protect you who is the sūtradhāra (architect) of the three worlds and whose matted hair is adorned by the new moon digit at the top as if by a bud (there is a pun on *kalikā* which is a bud and is also the diminutive of Kalā) and who composed the whole universe without another cause or joining thread.

Here we can see his view point as believing Śiva to be both the *Nimitta Kāraṇa* (efficient or intelligent cause) as well as *Upādāna Karaṇa* (material cause) of the universe although he is said to be a *Śaiva Siddhānti* by ancient scholars like Aghora Śiva.[1]

Śaiva Siddhānta was the most popular Śaiva sect between the 9th-12th Cen. CE which had many branches–*Amardaka, Mattamyura* and *Mādhumateya.*[2] It is well proven now that these branches had spread to Madhya Pradesh and were popular among rulers between 9th-12th Cen. CE. It has been suggested that the Mattamayura and Ranipadra monasteries extended their branches to Malwa also. One of the ascetics Lamba Karṇa of Ranipadra (of Kadwahas Branch) monastery was the spiritual Guru of Siyak. Hence they yielded influence over the Parmāra dynasty.[3] Lamba Karṇa is said to be regarded as a Bhairava at Avanti.

The names of several works composed by Hṛdaya Śiva of the Gorathika Maṭha at Dhārā are also known.[4]

Two ancient commentaries of Bhoja's *Tattva Prakāśa* are available. One is *Tātparyadīpikā* of Śri Kumara and the other is *Vṛtti* of Aghoraśivācārya (believed to be of 12th Cen.CE). Śri Kumara has interpreted *Tattva Prakāśa* monistically while Aghora Śivacarya has considered it under the dualistic philosophy of *Śaivasiddhānta*.

The truth is that the view point of Bhoj oscillates between two points of views *Śaivasiddhānta* philosophy with his original modification and glimpses of concrete monism. He does not clamp spiritual experience in strictly any one metaphysical system. The originality of Bhoja lies in relating the metaphysical diversity to the diversity of spiritual experience.

The main differences between Śankara's monism and Agamic systems is that Brahman in Śankara's thought is non active whereas in Agamika darshana the supreme truth Śiva is active and dynamic. The world in Śankara is a *vivarta* of Brahman and *pariṇāma* of *māyā*. Brahman alongwith the concept of *māyā* gives rise to the concept of Iśvara. The Śaiva Siddhāntis view God or Siva as the intelligent cause (निमित्त कारण) while *māyā* is the material cause (उपादान कारण) of the world. But in the *Tattva Prakāśa* of Bhoja Śiva is called the *upādāna* of all the elements and of the form of *jñāna* and *kriya* (Tattva Prakāsa 25). This is Śaiva Siddhānta with upaniṣadic leanings.

On the other hand in consonance with Southern Śaiva Siddhānta māyā is also called the *upādāna* cause of the universe in another verse. This māyā is one, eternal, all pervading, not samveta in Śiva.

शक्तयइहास्यकरणं मायोपादनमिष्यते सूक्ष्मा
एकनित्याव्यापिन्यनादिनिधना शिवासक्ता
T.P. 38

The doctrine of *Paśu*, *Pati* and *Pāśa* is common to all Agamic systems. The origin can be traced back to the *Śvetaśvatara Upaniṣad* where the doctrine of *Pati, Paśu*, and *Pāśa* has its genesis.[5] Pati is Śiva, Paśu is anu, and pāśā are the malas. Malas are obstructions to liberation.

Siva is devoid of all malas. He is पंचमन्त्रतनु.[6] He is ever free and is पंचकृत्यकारी which refer to his deeds like सृष्टि, स्थिति, संहार, तिरोधान and अनुग्रह.[7]

Paśu are of three types *vijñānākala* or *vijñānakevala, pralayākala pralayakevala* and *sakala vijñānākala* has only mala i.e. *āṇavamala* (beginningless mala), *pralayākala* has only *aṇava* and *karma mala* and *sakala* has all the malas.[8] The concepts of pāsas are also explained here in *Tattva Prakāśa*. *āṇavamala* is beginning less mala and is a veil over our enlightenment and power of action. *Karma Mala* is the bond forged by deeds. *Māyāmala* is the material cause of the world. It endows the world with means and objects of enjoyments.

The *Tattva Prakāśa* says that the *Vijñānākala* is of two types – those associated with impurities and those devoid of it – समाप्त कलुष and असमाप्त कलुष.[9] Those with *samāpta kaluṣa* get the grace of Śiva and are installed in *Vidyeśapada* located in Iśvara tattva, the others obtain *mantrarūpa* –in vidyātattva. They are seven crores (*saptakotayah)* in number.[10]

Among the *paralayākalas* those whose malas and karmas are over they get emancipated (मोक्ष) the rest are united with *puryaṣtaka* body (subtle body) and acquire various *yonis*. There are still some other *puryaṣtaka* who acquire *mantramaheśvara* status.[11]

Among the sakalas 118 get the *Mantreśa* status.[12] Among these the mandali or group of gahaneśa comprises of eight beings (1 Gahaneśa +7) eight beings of krodhas, (1 Krodhas and + 7 others), one Vireśa and one Śrikantha and hundred Rudras (8+8+1+1+100).

Here we can see another original point of view of Bhoja. Whereas in Southern Śaiva Siddhānta and *pratyabhijña* system even *Vijñānākalas* who have shed off their māyā mala and karma mala do not get liberated because aṇavamala is removed only by Śivas grace. But here we see that Śiva bestows his grace also on those some of the *pralayakalas* too. whose karma and āṇavamalas are over. (T.P.11)

Here the text says *pralayākala* but it refers to mala (aṇavamala and karma mala) whereas it should have said *Vijñānākala.*

The grace of Śiva is evident in other way also. The *mantreṣa* are those who do not have malas but by the help of Kala Para Śiva makes them "Sakala". the reason could be that Śiva creates such divine beings who are easily approachable by a person engaged in *dhyāna.*

Śiva is called the *upādāna* of all the elements. He is also the *upādāna* of all elements and of the form of Jñāna and Kriya.[13]

Śaiva Siddhānta accepts 36 tattvas. The first five are of the nature of pure consciousness (cidrupa) and belong to the realm of Śuddhadvā or pure creation. These five are Śiva, Śakti, Sadaśiva, Iśvara and Vidya.

In accordance with bestowing grace on *cit* and *acit* (paśu and paśa) he manifests himself as śakti tattva which is inseperable from him.[14] The third is *Sadāśiva* in which there is a balance of jñāna and karma in this according to *Tattva Prakāśa.*[15] This may be compared to the *pratyabhijña* system where *Sadāśiva* is the stage where ideal universe is experienced as an indistinct something in the depth of consciousness.[16] In this the experience is – I am this but (this) is a hazy experience.

The most interesting comparison between *Tattva Prakāśa* and *pratyabhijñā* system is in their concepts of *Iśvaratattva* and *sadvidyā tattva*. The definitions are just the opposite.

In *Tattva Prakāśa* this is a stage where *jñāna* is latent and *kriya śakti* blossoms.[17] In the *Pratyabhijñā* system, at this stage *jñāna* or knowledge is predominant although 'idam' or this side of experience becomes more defined.

Similarly the concept of *sadvidya tattva* differs. In the *Tattva Prakāśa* the *sadvidyā tattva* is explained as the stage when the *kriyaśakti* is latent and jñānaśakti blossoms being the form of jñāna it illumines the objects.

But in the *pratyabhijñā* system in this stage the *kriyāśakti* is predominant. The 'I' and 'this' in this stage are recognized with equal clarity.[18]

Bhoja in *Samarānganṣūtradhāra* treats of the representations of Śiva in two chapters–70 and 77. The first deals with Śiva in the form of Linga and the second with Śiva in anthropomorphic forms. But I would like to make it very clear that there is a difference between the cult images or *upāsya* bimbas and the illustration of mythical episodes in *lila murtis*. The former is the symbolization of some cosmological idea and the latter the playful artistic rendering of mythical episodes. Since we are concerned with expanding the Śaiva Siddhânti philosophy of Bhoja in this paper, I would like to point to the cult images in their philosophic background.

It is unfortunate that the text of 70th chapter is defective at numerous places but it deals with *Śivalingas* and chapter 77 with anthropomorphic forms of Śiva.

Chapter 70 enumerates different types of materials for making the Śivalinga. The use of पद्मराग (ruby) brings luck, crystals bring fame and a good progeny, *maṇi* leads to a good harvest etc. [19] Three sizes are mentioned short, middle and high (हस्तमध्यत्तिमाख्यानि)[20] The three parts of the linga are mentioned ब्रह्मभाग, विष्णुभाग and रूद्रभाग.[21] The first was the lowest and square in form, the second or middle was octagonal, the third or रूद्रभाग was the cylindrical top. This form was adopted in all the pillars of Paramāra art, especially in the Bhumija temples.

The Chapter says that the linga may have one, three or four faces–the chaturmukh linga is especially recommended.[22]

चतुर्मुखभवेल्लिङ्गमर्चितं सर्वकामदम्

The face has a pile of matted hair at the top and half moon as its ornament.

Although Bhoja does not explicitly mention the significance of the four faces of linga it can be inferred that they were symbolic representations of the metaphysical categories discussed by him in his *Tattva Prakāśa* which showed Āgamic influence. The interpretations may be gleaned from the *Viṣnudharmottarapurāṇa.*[23] Here five faces are mentioned as Sadyojāta, Vāmadeva, Aghora, Tatpuruṣa and Iśana. Sadyojāta is the eastern face and represents the elements of the earth. The southern face is Aghora or Bhairava or Rudra and represents fire. The western face is nandin or Tatpuruṣa and represents air. The northern face is of Uma or Vāmadeva and represents water Iśāna or Sadāśiva is the fifth or upper face. All have three eyes except Vāmadeva which has two Mahādeva or Sadyojata has rosary (akṣamala) and water pot (kamandala) in his hands. Iśana or Sadāśiva has bow and arrow. Bhairava or Aghora has staff (danda) and Citron (mātulinga). Nandi or Tatpuruṣa has shield and spear. Umā or Vāmadeva has mirror and blue lotus. The mirror stands for pure knowledge.

It may be stated here, that these different faces of Śiva were visualized to indicate how the same Lord was the source of different Agamic traditions. The Lord appears as Sadāśiva the supreme teacher and his five powers–Cit, Ānanda, Ichchā, Jñāna and Kriya are expressed as five faces from which proceed different Āgamas–dualistic, non-dualistic and mixed.

The five functions of the Lord also mentioned in *Tattva Prakāśa, Sriṣti, Sthiti, Samhara, Terodhana and Anugraha* may also be thought of here. *Tattva Prakāśa* accepts the metaphysical and other categories of based on the Śaivāgamas. Hence the above symbolic interpretations of the different faces of lingas could have been naturally acceptable to him.

In Chapter 77 of S.S. a basic distinction is made between benevolent and fierce aspects of Śiva.

चंद्रांकित जटः श्रीमान नीलकंठ सुसंयत
विचित्रमुकुटः शम्भुर्निशाकर –सम –प्रभ
दोर्भ्या द्वाभ्यां चतुर्मिर्वा मुक्तो व दोर्मिरष्टमिः
पट्टिश–व्यग्र–हस्तश्च पन्नगाजिन–संयुतः
सर्वलक्षणसपूर्णो नेत्रत्रितयभूषण
एवंविध –गुणैर्युक्तो यत्र लोकेश्वरो हरः
परा तत्र भवेद् वृद्धिर्देशस्य च नृपस्य च.

That country and its ruler will flourish where the lord of the world Hara is installed with matted hair marked by the moon (चंद्राकितजटः), beautiful dark throated, well trimmed (सुसंयत) with a marvelous crown (विचित्र मुकुट) with a spear or trident (पट्टिश) in his hand covered with snakes and skin (पन्नगाजिन संयुतः) complete with auspicious signs (लक्षण) and adorned by three eyes (नेत्र त्रितय भूषण).

It is noticeable that this iconography does not mention the consort of Śiva as an integral part of the image. Hence it is distinguished from the images of Soma Siddhānta which were known in Malwa at this time.

About the fierce aspect of Śiva it is stated that if his image is constructed in the forest (अरण्ये) or in cremation ground (श्मशान) his form should be as follows to be auspicious to the maker. He should have eighteen to twenty arms or sometimes one hundred or a thousand arms (अष्टादश भुजो दोष्णां विशत्या वा समन्वितः। शतबाहु कदाचिद्वा सहस्त्रभुज एव च।)

His fierce aspect is surrounded by his ganas, his upper covering being of the skin of a lion रौद्ररूपं गणवृतः सिंहचर्मोत्तरीयकः He should also have sharp jaws and teeth and garland of beads. तीक्ष्णद्रंष्टाग्रदशनः शिंरोमालाविभूषितः He should also be moon crested resplendent with a muscular chest, looking fierce चंद्रांकिंत शिरः श्रीमान पीनोरस्कोग्रदर्शनः-

In the capital Śiva should be made with two arms and in the port town (पत्तन) fourarms (द्विभुजो राजधान्यां तु पत्तने स्याद्चतुर्भुजः) in the forest or cremation ground however he should have twenty arms कर्त्तव्यों–विंशति भुजः, श्मशानारण्यमध्यगः।

Bhairava was already distinguished by large number of arms and skull ornaments.

Bhoja also touches a philosophical point when he says that although inherently auspicious the same Śiva has opposite aspects of benevolence and fierceness and this unique lord is diversely conceived for different places. ऐकोऽपिभद्रः भगवान् स्थानभेद विकल्पितः and also रौद्रसौम्यस्वभावश्च क्रियमाणो भवेद बुधैः

It is also interesting that while the inscriptions of Vakpatiraja have invocatory verses in praise of Śrikantha associated with Shankar and Śivas consort Girija, Bhoja in his several grants makes no reference to the consort of Śiva.

The fundamental basis of Śiva's iconography lay in the Agamic concept of five forms of Śiva. In the Vaiṣnava Panchratra Agamas the *vyūhas* of Vāsudeva are emanations showing the reality which proceeds from the subtle to the gross but in the Śaiva agamas and also in Tattva Prakāśa the different aspects of Śiva are not limited aspects but ideal states of manifestation.

The cult images are of various types अव्यक्त लिंग, व्यक्त लिंग (with faces) अनुग्रह मूर्ति वत सौम्य विग्रह as a yogi (with or without a consort), सौम्यविग्रह as creator (अर्धनारीश्वर or accompanied by spouse) Raudra or उग्र विग्रह वत संहार मूर्ति of Bhairava. Of these Bhoja omits the अर्धनारीश्वर विग्रह वत सौम्य विग्रह with consort.

This view can only signify the view of a particular Śaiva cult probably, *Śaivasiddhāntis* but with original points of Bhoja at many places.

In the Śuddhadhvā maya is not there but mahāmāyā is mentioned in *Tattva Prakāśa*. This might be the reason why we see the images of mahāmāyā in the Paramāra sculptures.

Hence we can conclude that Bhoja's *Tattva Prakāśa* has *Śaivasiddhanta* with significant original modifications. He does not clamp spiritual experience in strictly any one metaphysical system.

Parallels of his *Śaivasiddhānta* can be seen in his description of cult images in *Samarāngaṇsūtradhāra.*

The two texts contribute to Śaivism in a unique way.

References

1. *Tattva Prakāśa* by Bhoja, trans. Kameshwar Nath Mishra, Chowkhamba Orientation, Delhi 2010 also S.N. Dasgupta, *A history of Indian Philosophy*, Vol. V, p.160, Motilal Banarsidas, Delhi, 1975.
2. V.S. Pathak, *History of Śaiva Cults in Northern India from Inscriptions 700 AD-1200 AD*, p. 30, Abhinash Prakashan, Allahabad, 1980.
3. *Ibid*, p. 35.
4. The *Prāyascitta Samuccaya, Naimittika Kriyanusandhana and Pratiṣtha Darpana* were composed by Hṛdaya Śiva–*Iśāna Śivaguru Paddhati*
5. *Śvetaśvatara Upaniṣad Tattva Prakāśa* 4.16 and *Tattva Prakāśa*, 5
6. *Ibid*, 6.
7. *Ibid*, 7
8. *Ibid*, 8
9. *Ibid*, 9
10. *Ibid*, 10
11. *Ibid*, 12
12. *Ibid*, 13
13. *Ibid*, 25
14. *Ibid*, 27
15. *Ibid*, 28
16. Jaidev Singh, Śiva Sutras, commentary Vimarśini of Kṣemraja, translated into English, Introduction p.viii
17. *Tattva Prakāśa* 29
18. Jaidev Singh, op.cit. introduction, p.ix
19. *Samarāṇganasūtradhāra*, 70, 78-80
20. *Ibid*, 70.2
21. *Ibid*, 70-2
22. *Ibid*, 70 33-34
23. *Viṣṇdharmottara Purāṇa* 3.48.

30

पूर्व मध्यकालीन जैन वास्तु में भेद अभेद के तत्व

दिवाकर प्रसाद तिवारी

कलाकृति मूल्य या मूल्य संस्थान को प्रतीकों द्वारा रूपायित करने की एक माध्यम होती है जिसकी अभिव्यक्ति यद्यपि सामान्य होती है तो भी वह मूर्त होती है और उसे देखते हुए कलाकार मूल्या या मूल्य संस्थान को देखता है (मॉरिस)। भारतीय कला इसका अपवाद नहीं है। भारतीय कला में यह संकेतात्मकता अथवा प्रतीकात्मकता विभिन्न धार्मिक मतों एवं विश्वासों से प्रेरित तथा अनुप्रमाणित है और अवधारणा के स्तर पर इसमें ब्रह्माण्डीय व्यवस्था (Cosmic Order) के विभिन्न उपागम मूर्त हैं। प्रस्तुत शोध पत्र में जैन धर्म से अनुप्राणित वास्तुकला के अंग–उपांगों के मूल्य सापेक्ष विमर्श के साथ उसके भेद–अभेद (सादृश्य एवं वैषम्य) के तत्वों को एक सीमा तक निदर्शित करने का यत्न किया गया है। हिन्दू कला एवं बौद्ध कला के समान ही जैन कला को उसके कलात्मक प्रतिमानों के साथ वास्तुकला में मूर्त किया गया है। जैन वास्तकला के प्रमुख केन्द्र प्रकृति के सुरम्य एवं एकान्त वातावरण में प्रायः पर्वतों अथवा उनके अधित्यका में, स्तम्भ, गुफा, स्तूप, चैत्य, विहार और मंदिरों के रूप में स्थित हैं परन्तु जैन वास्तुकला का उत्कर्ष गुप्तोत्तर अथवा पूर्व मध्यकाल में जैन मंदिरों में ही देखने को मिलता है (जैन, 1962)।

विवेच्य युग में तंत्र ने सभी मतों को प्रभावित किया और जैन मत में भी इसे स्वीकार किया गया। हेमचन्द्र के योगशास्त्र में हठयोग का वर्णन है। नाथ पंथ के कुण्डनीय को भी जैनियों ने महत्त्वपूर्ण माना। मुम्बई के एक जैन मंदिर में गोरखनाथ की भी प्रतिमा विराजमान है। इस प्रकार युगीन प्रवृत्तियों के साथ समन्वय, सामंजस्य एवं साहचर्य के आग्रह ने जैन कला को एक वृहत्तर आयाम दिया।

वस्तुतः ब्राह्मण एवं श्रमण परम्पराओं से परिपुष्ट भारतीय वास्तुकला का स्वरूप 'एकं सद्विप्राः बहुधा वदन्ति' की दृष्टि का उद्घोषक है जिसमें एक तरफ समग्रता का आग्रह है तो दूसरी तरफ वैषम्यमूलक स्वतंत्र अधिरचना के तत्व प्रदर्शित हैं। इसका एक स्वरूप तो, विवेच्य काल में शासक राजवंशों (चालुक्य, चेदि, पाल, चन्देल आदि) द्वारा संरक्षण प्राप्त धर्मों–वैष्णव, शैव, शाक्त, बौद्ध आदि के लोकप्रिय देवी देवताओं को शिल्पियों द्वारा जैन मंदिरों पर मूर्त करने से प्रकट होता है। ये देवता–इन्द्र, रूद्र, शिव, अग्नि, ब्रह्म, विष्णु, कृष्ण–बलराम, राम–सीता, गणेश, स्कन्द, मुकुन्द, वासुदेव, नृसिंह, वैश्रवण (कुबेर), यक्ष, यक्षी, विद्यादेवियां, सरस्वती, लक्ष्मी, नैगमेषी, शलाका पुरुष, वामनदेव, कामदेव, सूर्य, नक्षत्र, श्री ह्रीं, धृति, कीर्ति, अज्जा (पार्वती या आर्या), महिषासुरवेधिका, विन्ध्यवासिनी, गंगा सिन्धु आदि हैं (अग्रवाल, 1966.............)। तत्कालीन राजाओं की धार्मिक सहिष्णुता की नीति ने कलात्मक स्वतंत्रता को पुष्ट किया। विभिन्न धर्मों–सम्प्रदायों में विभाजित तत्कालीन समाज के प्रत्यक्ष या परोक्ष दबाव तथा प्रभाव का यह एक परिणाम भी था। अतः शिल्पियों एवं निर्माण निर्देशक स्वामियों ने भी इस उदारता को कला संस्थानों में व्यक्त किया। तथापि जैन धर्मावलम्बियों ने अन्य धर्मों एवं विश्वासों को स्थान देने के बावजूद अपने मूल कथावस्तु को प्रमुखता से रूपायित किया।

विवेच्य काल में राजनीतिक–सामाजिक संघर्ष तथा आन्तरिक एवं बाह्य आक्रमणों से उत्पन्न स्थितियों का सामना करने के लिए आक्रामक एवं रक्षात्मक संश्लिष्ट देव रूपों की अवतारणा, ब्राह्मण, बौद्ध एवं जैन – लगभग सभी धर्मों में की गयी। स्वयं की रक्षा एवं शक्तिसंचय की दृष्टि से यह एक मनोवैज्ञानिक सम्बल था। अतः दो से अधिक भुजाओं वाले संहारक अस्त्रों से सज्जित देवी–देवताओं का अंकन प्रमुखता से हुआ। यहाँ भी जैन धर्म के समावेशी चरित्र का परिचय मिलता है। कला में तीर्थंकरों की श्रेष्ठता को बनाये रखते हुए ब्रह्मा, विष्णु, वैष्णवी, कार्तिकेय आदि को अंकित किया गया है। वस्तुतः 5वीं शताब्दी के बाद जैन देवमण्डल में जैन तीर्थंकरों के अतिरिक्त अन्य धर्मों के देवी–देवताओं को सम्मिलित कर उनकी विशेषतायें निरूपित की जा चुकी थीं जिसका विस्तृत उल्लेख जैन ग्रन्थों में मिलता है। ब्राह्मण धर्म का यह प्रभाव श्वेताम्बर एवं दिगम्बर दोनों सम्प्रदायों से सम्बन्धिक कलाकेन्द्रों में यक्ष, यक्षी, शिवा, कौमारी, सरस्वती, लक्ष्मी, बलराम, कृष्ण, अष्ट दिक्पाल, नवग्रह एवं क्षेत्रपाल आदि के मूर्तन में परिलक्षित है। ब्राह्मण देव कुल के इन्द्र, विष्णु, ब्रह्मा, शिव स्कन्दकार्तिकेय, काली, गौरी, सरस्वती, चामुण्डा और बौद्ध देवकुल की तारा, वज्र श्रृंखला, वज्रतारा एवं वज्रांकुशी के नाम व लक्षण जैन कला में ग्रहण कर लिये गये (तिवारी, 1983)। इस तथ्य की पुष्टि अनेक जैन कलाकेन्द्रों से होती है। देवगढ़ एवं मथुरा की नेमिनाथ की प्रतिमाओं के साथ हलधर बलराम एवं चक्रधर वासुदेव भी प्रदर्शित हैं। दिलवाड़ा के विमलवसही एवं लूणबसही के नेमिनाथ मंदिर में भी कृष्ण जन्म, कालिया–मर्दन, गोप–गोपियों के साथ होली का मनभावन अंकन कृष्ण भक्ति सम्प्रदाय के प्रति समादर का दृष्टान्त है। जयसिंह सूरि के कुमारपाल चरित (5.5) के एक संदर्भ के अनुसार जैन आचार्य हेमचन्द्र के परामर्श पर कुमारपाल ने हेमचन्द्र के साथ सोमनाथ जाकर शिव की आराधना की जिस पर शिव ने प्रकट होकर जैन धर्म की प्रशंसा की। कुमार पाल ने सोमनाथ मंदिर तथा चित्तौड़गढ़ के शैव मंदिर को ग्रामदान किया था। गुजरात के जैन नरेश सिद्धराज ने भी शिव के मंदिर की स्थापना करायी थी। गणधर सार्द्धशतक वृहद्वृत्ति में कहा गया है कि एक अच्छे जैन आचार्य के लिए आवश्यक है कि वह ब्राह्मण–दर्शनों का पूर्ण ज्ञान प्राप्त करे (शर्मा, बनर्जी, घोष, 1956, 1975)। निश्चित ही इस प्रकार की उदारता एवं कला में उसके प्रदर्शन से कलाकृति के दर्शन में अनुभव की जाने वाली एकरसता घटी होगी, वास्तु के विशाल–विस्तीर्ण आयामों को कलात्मक अभिप्रायों से भर दिया गया होगा और अन्य धर्मावलम्बियों को जैन धर्म के प्रति आकृष्ट करने में सहायता मिली होगी। खजुराहो का पार्श्वनाथ मंदिर (950 ई.) इसका उत्तम निदर्शक है जिसमें हिन्दू देवी–देवताओं का अंकन दोनों सम्प्रदायों में सद्भावनापूर्ण सम्बन्ध की स्थापना का प्रयास है किन्तु कुछ अंकन जैन परम्परा से अलग हटकर भी हैं यथा – इन मूर्तियों का उनकी शक्तियों के साथ, आलिंगन मुद्रा में तथा आयुधों के साथ अंकन (वर्मा, 1984)। यद्यपि खजुराहो के हिन्दू एवं जैन मंदिर सहअस्तित्व के द्योतक हैं तथापि इनके बीच की भौगोलिक दूरी संभवतः परस्पर टकराव की संभावना को टालने के लिए रखी गयी होगी। कामुक एवं अप्राकृतिक मैथुन के दृश्य भी इन जैन मंदिरों पर अत्यल्प ही उकेरे गये हैं। इसके विपरीत देखें तो खजुराहो में एक भी हिन्दू मंदिर ऐसा नही है जिस पर किसी जैन तीर्थंकर का अंकन हो जबकि जैन मंदिरों में ऐसा नहीं है। परन्तु मध्य प्रदेश के बजराज मठ के हिन्दू मंदिरों में तीर्थंकरों की प्रतिमायें भी प्रतिष्ठित हैं (तिवारी, 1981, 83)।

गुजरात और राजस्थान के जैन मंदिरों में भी समन्वय की यह प्रवृत्ति देखने को मिलती है। परन्तु अनेक स्थलों पर जैन शिल्पियों ने कुछ अधिक ही स्वच्छन्दता का परिचय दिया और जैन परंपरा के विरूद्ध विषयों को कला में स्थान दिया जिसकी पुष्टि देवगढ़ के मंदिर सं. 18 से होती है जिसमें एक जैन साधु को एक नग्न स्त्री के साथ प्रदर्शित किया गया है (तिवारी, 1983)। इसी प्रकार खजुराहो के पार्श्वनाथ मंदिर की भित्तियों पर उत्कीर्ण एक निचली पंक्ति में शक्ति के साथ आलिंगन मुद्रा में देवताओं को तथा अप्सराओं को अंकित किया गया है। इसके उत्तरी एवं दक्षिणी शिखर पर भी काम क्रिया में रत दृश्य उत्कीर्ण हैं (त्रिपाठी)। इसके विपरीत, यहां के हिन्दू मंदिरों पर भी जैन यतियों की मूर्तियों को रति मुद्राओं में प्रदर्शित किया गया है। यहाँ हरिवंश पुराण का वह उल्लेख ध्यातव्य हैं जिसमें कहा गया है कि जिन मंदिरों में, प्रजा के कौतक के लिए, कामदेव एवं रति की मूर्तियों को स्थान दिया जाए (हरिवंश पुराण, 29.1–4)। अतः यहां यह कहना अत्युक्ति नहीं होगी कि यद्यपि इस काल में जैन वास्तु का तीव्र गति से विकास तो हुआ किन्तु उस पर कामक्रिया सम्बन्धी ऐसे अंकनों से जैन धर्म की प्रगति अवश्य दुष्प्रभावित हुई होगी।

इस प्रकार विवेच्य काल में वास्तुकला के विकास के सम्पूर्ण परिदृश्य का विश्लेषण करते हुए उसकी समीक्षा करें तो कह सकते हैं कि –

1. जैन वास्तु में नृत्य–संगीत आदि के लिए सभा मण्डप का निर्माण जैन सिद्धान्तों के प्रतिकूल था क्योंकि इनके निर्माण का उद्‌देश्य तो योग एवं साधना को संवर्धित करना था।
2. जैन कला के समावेशी चरित्र, सहिष्णुता एवं उदारता, के प्रदर्शन के लिए जैन साधुओं सहित देवी–देवताओं की कामुक प्रतिमाओं का अंकन, जैन कला एवं धर्म के लिए शुभ लक्षण नहीं था। इसके समर्थन में यह तर्क बहुत स्वीकार्य नहीं हो सकता कि जैन धर्म में तंत्र का प्रभाव मंत्रवाद के रूप में प्रकट हुआ।

3. यह भी एक विचारणीय प्रश्न है कि जैन शिल्पियों द्वारा बौद्ध देवमण्डल के किसी प्रमुख देवमूर्ति का अंकन क्यों नहीं हुआ? इसी प्रकार अन्य धर्मावम्बियों को अपने मंदिरों में जिन प्रतिमाओं का प्रदर्शन अभिप्रेत क्यों नहीं था? क्या उससे द्योतित नहीं होता कि कला एवं धर्म में सहिष्णुता, समन्वय तथा सामंजस्य के प्रयासों के साथ–साथ आपसी वैमनस्य, असहिष्णुता, प्रतिस्पर्धा की अन्तर्धारा भी प्रवाहित थी?

संदर्भ

1. कुमार पाल चरित (जयसिंह सूरि कृत), निर्णय सागर प्रेस, बम्बई, 1926।
2. अग्रवाल, वासुदेव शरण, भारतीय कला, वाराणसी, 1966।
3. घोष, अमलानन्द (सं.) जैन कला एवं स्थापत्य (तीन खण्ड), भारतीय ज्ञानपीठ, नई दिल्ली, 1975।
4. जैन, हीरालाल, 'भारतीय संस्कृति में जैन धर्म का योगदान' भोपाल, 1962।
5. तिवारी, मा.न.प्र., 'जैन प्रतिमा विज्ञान, वाराणसी 1981' एलीमेन्ट्स ऑफ जैन आइकोनोग्राफी, वाराणसी, 1983।
6. त्रिपाठी, एल.के., द एरोटिक स्कल्पचर्स ऑफ खजुराहो एण्ड देयर प्राबेबुल एक्सप्लेनेशन, भारती–3 वाराणसी।
7. बनर्जी, जे.एन., 'दि डेवलपमेन्ट ऑफ हिन्दू आइकोनोग्राफी' कलकत्ता, 1956।
8. वर्मा, रत्नेश कुमार, 'खजुराहो के जैन मंदिरों की मूर्तिकला', वाराणसी, 1984।
9. शर्मा, बृजेन्द्र नाथ, 'सोशल एण्ड कल्चरल हिस्ट्री ऑफ नार्दर्न इण्डिया'।
10. यादव, अवधेश, 'पूर्वमध्य कालीन जैन कला', वाराणसी, 2007।
11. रे, हेमचन्द्र, 'डायनास्टिक हिस्ट्री ऑफ नार्दर्न इंडिया', भाग–2, दिल्ली, 1973।

31

A NOTE ON THE NEWLY DISCOVERED BRICK TEMPLE AND IT'S SITE AT PIPRI, DISTRICT- SIDDHARTHNAGAR, U.P.

Praveen Kumar Mishra

Pipri, a centrally protected site of Archaeological survey of India is located about a kilometer east from Madhubenia Bazar on the Naugarh- Birdpur road in District Siddharthnagar of U.P. The site comprises several mounds, some are having prominent shape and reaming are reduced in size. In the north of the mounds there is a pond extended in about an acre area. The traces of brick structural activities can be noticed from the surface which suggests the existence of Stupas or temples underneath, keeping the view that surrounding area has several sites with such structures like piprahwa and Ganwaria.

This motivated the author to conduct a scientific clearance, at least on one of the small mounds, to verify the nature of the structural activities at the site. In December 2013 the scientific clearance work was started and completed in the month of February 2014 produced an outstanding result in the form of a brick temple.

The temple unearthed is a north facing square shaped brick temple constructed on a plan of 6.35 m^2. The bricks have been used for construction are in the size of 30x20x5 cms. From the plinth, sixteen courses of the bricks in slant stepping (tapering) way have been so arranged to raise the walls as the thickness at the plinth became more widen than the top. The maximum thickness of the wall on the top at the central projection is 2.75 m. It seems that two parallel walls were constructed and the brick bats and rubbles were filled in between to make this much thick wall. The top portions of the walls are found sealed by brick bats masonry. The temple structure has been provided with an extensive pavement of the similar bricks used in the construction of the temple.

It is a *panch-ratha* temple having three projections in each lateral side. The central projection is 1.57 mtr wide and remaining two are 0.69 mtr each at either sides of the central one. There is an entrance (*Mukha Mandapa*) measuring 2.10 x1.21 mtr followed by a *Kapili* and a sanctum (2.66 x 2.62 mtr). The peculiarity is the arrangement of a *triratha peetha* for establishing the cult image. At the rear end of this *peetha,* a clear impression of a trapezium at the centre is still remaining on which the *vigrah* would have been established. Remains of *Pranali* (water outlet), running towards east, is also found.

The traces of fine lime plastering on the inner walls are also found. Though the plaster remains are not found applied on the outer side of the walls but while comparing with other contemporary brick temples of north and central India we find few of them are provided with plastering on both sides. The floor in the sanctum and mandapa is made by ramming and followed by a fine layer of lime mortar to give the floor a clean and smooth finishing.

Remains of another structure of similar brick also exists at the north-western corner of this temple, though partly exposed, indicates the possibility of *panchayatan* arrangements. Further clearance may add more information in this direction.

The pavement of the bricks is provided all around shows that temple has been fully constructed and completed in all respects. It is because that pavement work is normally done after completion of the main structure.

Keeping in view of the nature of debris found during the clearance work, especially from the sanctum and unavailability of a single antiquity including the cult image, it is assumed that after the falling of the super structure the stakeholders might have taken out the precious materials from the sanctum and abandoned the ruins. It is yet to find out the possible reasons of the collapse of the magnificent structure.

Since the clearance did not reveal any single antiquity it is difficult to establish the date of this temple, but on the basis of the plan of the remains of the temple and the bricks used in the construction may help in this regard. Such other square shaped temples in north and central India are datable to 8th-9th century A.D. Hence this temple remains can also be kept in this bracket until new evidences come out.

As mentioned in the starting the site comprises several mounds, hence it is obvious that this would have been a multi-structural complex, more particularly of brick temples. Upcoming research work will make the clear picture and add a new chapter in the study of brick temples in the Saryupar (Trans-Saryu) region.

The author is heartily thankful to Dr. Vimal Tiwari, the then Assistant Archaeologist of Lucknow circle of ASI for his dedication in conducting this clearance work. The courtesy is also dues to Shri U.N. Tiwari, I/C of conservation works and Shri Ravishankar Saxena, Draughtsman for their support at various levels. I am grateful to Prof. (Ret.) Amar Singh of Lucknow University for his kind guidance and encouragement.

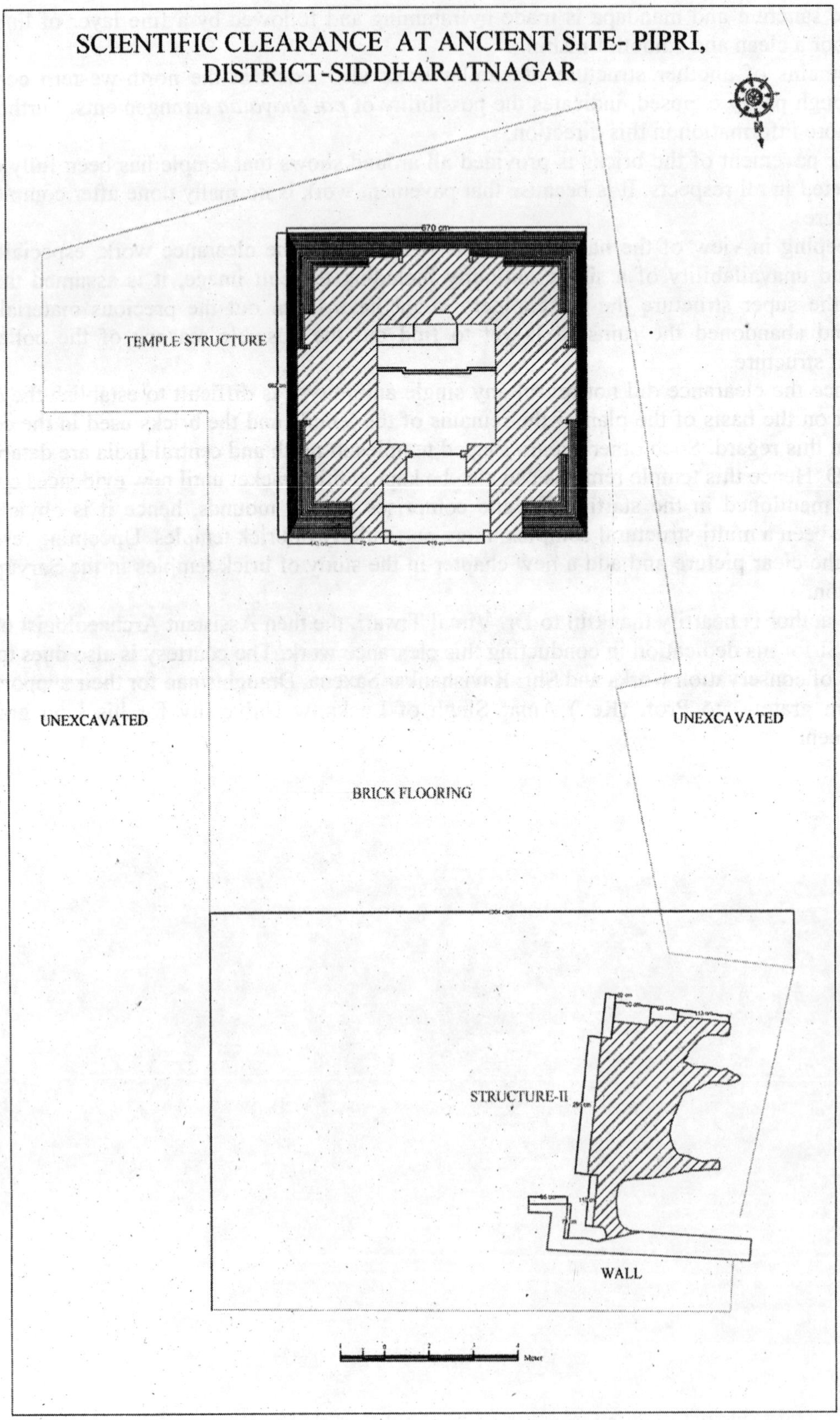

Fig. 1 : Scientific Clearance at Ancient Site – Pipri, District – Siddharathnagar

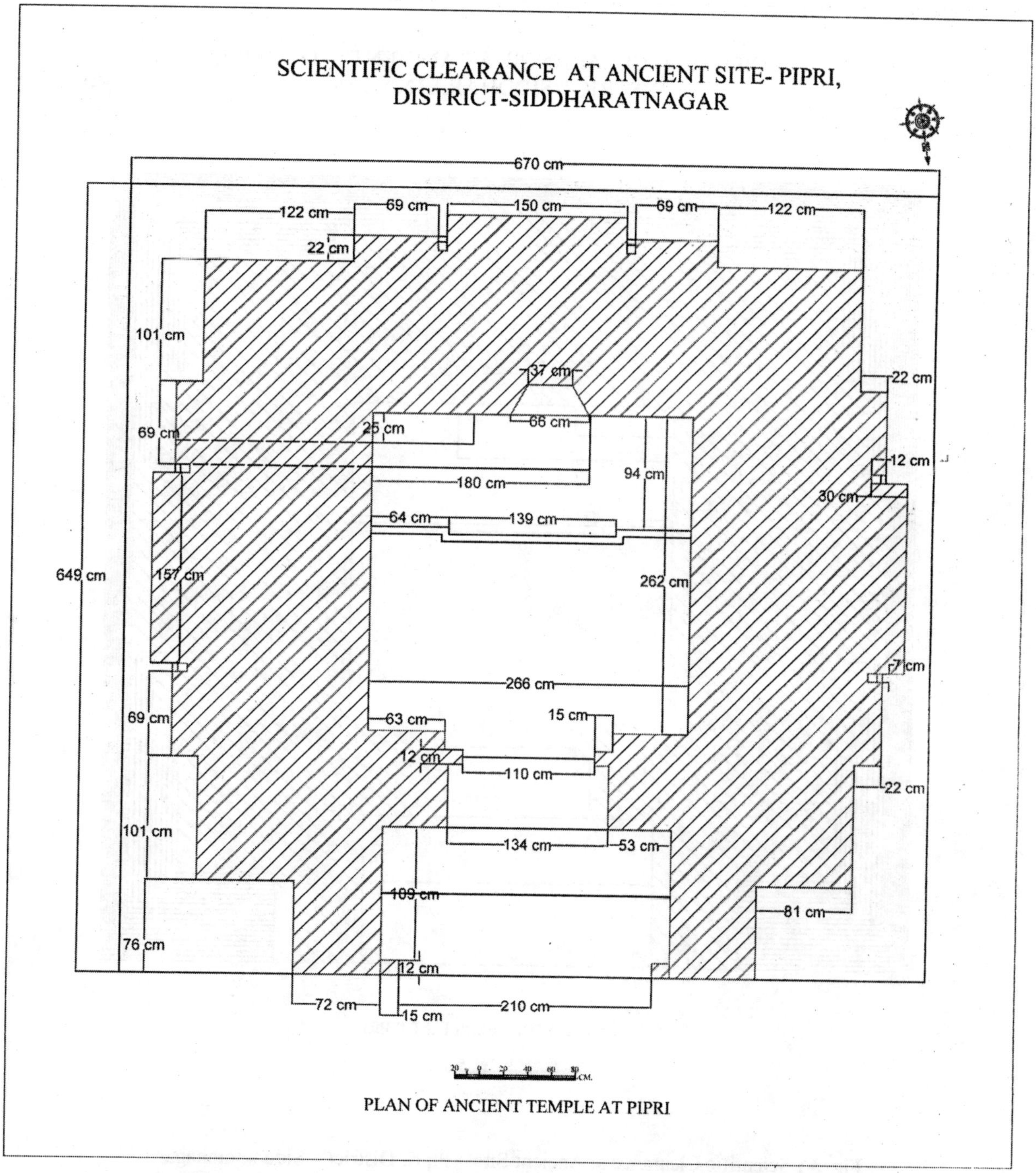

Fig. 2 : Scientific Clearance at Ancient Site – Pipri, District – Siddharathnagar

SCIENTIFIC CLEARANCE AT ANCIENT SITE- PIPRI,
DISTRICT-SIDDHARATNAGAR

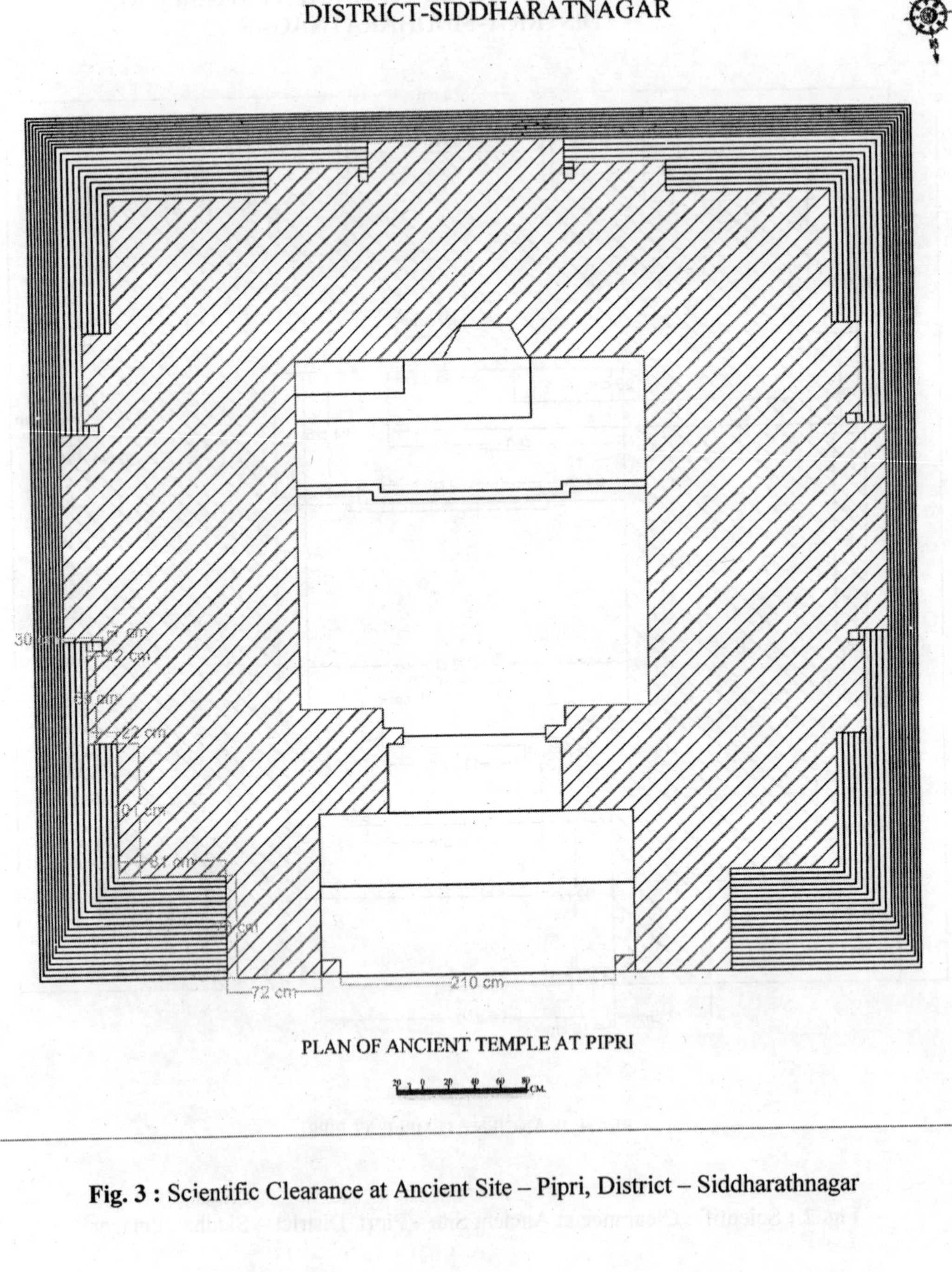

PLAN OF ANCIENT TEMPLE AT PIPRI

Fig. 3 : Scientific Clearance at Ancient Site – Pipri, District – Siddharathnagar

32

YAKSHA ICONOGRAPHY: THEMATIC VARIATION AND ITS IMPLICATIONS

Namrata Singh

Yakshas have occupied an important place in Indian art and iconography through the ages. *Yakshas* seem to have been indigenous non-Aryan deities, having beneficent powers of wealth and fertility in ancient times. They were later accepted within Buddhist, Jaina and Brahminical theology but assigned a subordinate status within their respective pantheons. The *Yaksha* concept has played an important part in the development of Indian mythology and the early *Yaksha* iconography has formed the foundation of later Hindu and Buddhist iconography. The *Yaksha* sculptures are the earliest known anthropomorphic representation of any deity in stone in India and as such they have evoked considerable interest among scholars.

The *Yaksha* cult and its development has received attention of various stalwarts like Coomaraswami, Motichandra, V.S. Agarwal and R.N. Misra and certain general features about the origin and development of this cult are accepted by all of them based on their reading of various Brahiminical, Buddhist and Jaina texts. It seems that the *Yaksha* cult was a primitive non-Aryan one associated with features of primitive religion like animism, ancestor worship and fertility. Owing to their immense popularity the *Yakshas* seem to have been later accommodated within Vedic religion with both benevolent and malevolent characteristics. Sometimes they were even associated with a higher spiritual plane and complex questions related to cosmology. The subsequent period was more significant for the evolution of the *Yaksha* cult. It is discernible that considerable efforts were made to eradicate belief in the *Yakshas* in the literature of the heterodox sects of Buddhism and Jainism and also the Brahmanical texts, yet, it seems their popular appeal among the masses ensured their enduring status as deities.

In the scholarly sphere, since the very beginning there has been a compartmentalization between the works dealing with the *Yaksha* cult on one hand and those related to *Yaksha* iconography on the other. The former rely mostly on literary sources, Brahmanical, Buddhist and Jaina, to discuss various themes related to the development of the cult , while those works which deal with *Yaksha* iconography mainly focus on the importance of the *Yaksha* sculpture as an object of art, its stylistic features and also on the role of *Yaksha* iconography in shaping the later Indian iconography. Hence, till date, the *Yaksha* cult and *Yaksha* iconography have been studied as two separate themes and the works dealing with the former use the latter merely for illustrative purposes. There has hardly been any attempt to explore what *Yaksha* iconography as a source of history reveals to us about the *Yaksha* cult as it existed in ancient India.

The over-emphasis on, one kind of source, that is, literary, in order to study the *Yaksha* cult has its obvious disadvantages. There might be certain aspects of this cult which the texts have kept us in the dark about, intentionally or unintentionally, which can be revealed by iconography. It is perhaps this attitude of over-emphasis on textual sources that led R.N. Misra to declare while talking about various anecdotes about *Yakshas* that got into scriptures that "they reveal uniformity in the *Yaksha* concept and image everywhere. This methodological consistency concerning the *Yakshas* reflects the universal dominance of the cult which percolated into different systems without any significant change in its core. In spite of several setbacks the kernel of belief in the *Yakshas* remained always the same and exists even today (Misra 1981)". This is an assumption which will be questioned in this paper.

The objective of this paper is to explore the thematic variation in *Yaksha* iconography in order to find out whether this popular cult has its regional manifestations which varied over space and time. Secondly, it will also be explored how far the popular themes in *Yaksha* iconography reveal a correspondence with the literary sources and what additional light can they shed about the *Yaksha* cult in ancient India.

The following methodology that has been followed : The various *Yaksha* sculptures available from ancient India have been arranged into four regional groups in accordance with the locations at which they have been found - Northern region, Eastern region, Western region and Central region. Two to three representative locations where the maximum number of *Yaksha* statues have been found have been assigned to each regional group. In Northern India, Mathura and its surrounding region has been considered as one locational category and the rest of Uttar Pradesh as another category. This is due to the fact that while there is no site other than Mathura and the area adjoining it where there is a concentration of *Yaksha* sculpture, one or two sculpture of different types have been found from many regions in Uttar Pradesh. In Eastern India, three sites have been taken up –Patna, Bodh Gaya and Dumdama in Orissa. In Western India -Sopara, Pitalkhora and Nasik and in Central India-Besnagar, Bharhut and Sanchi.

R.N Misra has done the commendable job of compiling information on most of the important *Yaksha* sculptures of ancient India at one place. Moreover, he has also arranged them chronologically, on the basis of their stylistic features and the opinions of the other scholars, into broad time frameworks-Mauryan, post-Mauryan, Satvahana-Kushan phase and post-Kushan phase (Misra 1981). The dating of various *Yaksha* sculptures is a controversial issue amongst the art historians and it is obvious that some scholars might differ on the dating of certain statues by Misra. However, for the purpose of this study, mostly Misra's chronological framework has been relied upon as his division into broad time periods rather than more exact dates is sufficient to give one a fair idea about the temporal frequency of various themes which is sufficient for the scope of this paper. *Yaksha* statues that have not been dealt with by Mishra have also been assigned under the above mentioned temporal divisions based on the opinions of scholars from whom information about them has been derived.

In this study sculptures belonging up to the Kushan period have been considered because after this period indigenous iconographic texts had started coming up which might have led to a certain standardization in *Yaksha* sculptures. Also, after this period, the *Yaksha* and *Yakshi* statues become rare because they had mostly ceased to have an independence status and appear mostly as decorative motifs.

In the ensuing paper, the first section consists of a discussion of the various themes in *Yaksha* iconography occurring in different regions over different time periods up to the Kushan phase. This is followed by an exploration of how far the popular themes bear a correspondence with the textual sources. Finally it is explored whether the thematic variations in *Yaksha* iconography indicate regional manifestations of the *Yaksha* cult at different times in ancient India. If so, this would question Misra's assertion that there was a uniformity of concepts in *Yaksha* cult everywhere and at all times in ancient India. In the description of the iconography the focus is on the themes rather that dress, style, ornamentation etc.

Northern Region

Mathura in the post-Mauryan Phase

Yaksha iconography in the Mathura region first appears in the post-Mauryan times. In this period, many detached colossal statues have been discovered around Mathura. They seem to have had an independent cult status and some of them were even under regular worship by the local population when first discovered.

A *Yaksha* from Parkham has a height of 2.3 meters and has an inscription incised in three lines below the feet on the surface of the pedestal. This has been finally read as, "the image was placed in the *puga* (guild) of *Manibhadra*" (V.S. Agarwal 1968: 117). The image has thus been identified as that of *Yaksha Manibhadra.* Both his arms and hands are broken off at the armpits but it has been concluded by most art historians that his right hand was raised in the *abhaya mudra* and the left had held a purse, the remnants of which are still visible on the statue. In fact the purse in the left hand has been declared as an identifying symbol of *Manibhadra* in the post-Mauryan phase as it is associated with two of his inscribed images at Parkham and Pawaya.

At Palwal, a colossal bust carved in red sandstone has been found holding a flower or a conch in the right hand which is raised up to the shoulder (V.S. Agarwal 1968:134, Misra 110). At Baroda village near Parkham, remains of a *Yaksha* statue have been found which when complete would be about twelve feet. It was being worshipped under the name of *Jakhia* when discovered (V.S. Agarwal 1968:119)

At Noh village in Bharatpur district adjoining Mathura, a *Yaksha* image has been found, eight feet in height. His legs and left hand are broken. His right hand is raised up to the shoulder in the *abhaya mudra* and he was still under worship when found (R.C. Agrawala 1967:64, Misra 1981:110)

Besides the *Yaksha* statue from Noh, the Bharatpur region is reported to have half a dozen *Yaksha/Yakshi* statues within a radius of nineteen miles (R.C. Agrawala 1969: 47). Remarkable among them and belonging to this period is a colossal image of a *Yaksha* from Biravai village. Its uniqueness lies in the depiction of a long sword hanging at the left back hip of the *Yaksha* tied to a belt worn across the right shoulder. In this form the *Yaksha* has been represented as *Vira* (repository of valour) and the existing name of the village as Biravai probably owes its derivation from *Vira* (R.C. Agrawala 1969: 48). The worship of the *Yakshas* as *Viras* is a cult that persists till modern times (V.S. Agarwal 1953: 68). In this period, two other statues from U.P. were sculpted in the *Vira* form. A figure of a seated *Yakshi* was discovered at Jhing-ka-Nagra, near Mathura, where she was worshipped as *Mansadevi.* The image carries an inscription which has been read as "*Yakshi* Layava has been caused to be established by ....together with his sons and made by Naka, pupil of Kunika (V.S Agarwal 1968:118)".

Yaksha sculpture from the various sites of U.P. in post-Mauryan phase

The Sarnath museum has the ram-horned head of a *Yaksha* figure. Another interesting piece shows a *bharwahaka* (load-bearing) *Yaksha,* headless, whose dwarfish stature illustrates a new mode in the *Yaksha* motif. (Misra 1981:111) It is not certain whether this *Yaksha* was supposed to be holding a building part or a bowl, two separate motifs which became much more common in the *Satavahana-Kushan* phase.

A headless torso from Partapgarh is deposited in the Allahabad museum. The arms are broken but the hands are partly preserved. The right hand seems to have been in the *abhaya mudra,* the left is kept on the waist. A *Yaksha* figure was discovered from Kosam in which the left hand is suspended low and is probably holding a purse. He has been identified as *Manibhadra.* In the right hand he holds a mace and thus has been depicted in the *Vira* form. The Sarnath museum has a sword bearing *Yaksha* figure, in which the sword is held horizontally over the head so probably it's a depiction of a *Yaksha* as *Vira* (Misra 1981:110-11)

The Allahabad municipal museum contains a seated image, in which a fierce-looking *Yaksha* is depicted squatting on a seat in the *pralambhapadasana-mudra.* He holds a cup in the right hand and with his left hand he shown holding a pig between his feet. (Misra 1981:112)

A huge sculpture recovered from Bhita in the Lucknow museum shows two well carved figures standing back-to-back while there are two more figures carved on the side in which only the heads are prominently shown, while the rest of the body is depicted in a hazy outline on the pillar, the lower portion of which is occupied by the figure of a lion of one side and a pig on the other. One figure holds a water bottle. According to R.N. Misra, the iconography of the images seems to indicate that they were supposed to be guarding the four quarter of the place where the images were consecrated (Misra 1981:112). This is because the figures are all different from one another and one of them holding the bottle might be *Kubera.* However, this cannot be said for certain as only two of them are shown prominently while of the rest only the heads are prominent. This iconography might have some other significance.

In the Bharat Kala Bhavan, Benaras there is a three sided block of stone which has a square pedestal below, each side is carved with a standing male figure in bold relief. The figures are rather dwarfish in stature, plump, and have their hands lifted up as in atlantis *Yaksha* figurines. Agrawal tentatively identified the image with *trimukha Yaksha,* although he concedes that literary sources offer no such *Yaksha*-name. According to Misra this image was for a tri-view (Misra 1981:113).

What is noteworthy is that although Benaras is often associated with *Yaksha* legends in the *Jataka* and *Puranas,* early images of *Yaksha* are rare in this region. This is something that has been pointed out by Misra also (Misra 1981:113).

In this period relief-art also assumed prominence and some *Yaksha* and *Yakshi* figure carved on railing pillars have been found at Moosanagar (forty two miles south-west of Kanpur), Kausambi and Amin. In Moosanagar there are three figures of *Yakshis* carved on railing pillars. They are standing without *vahanas* and holding flowers. Besides, in Moosanagar there is one *Yaksha* figure standing with folded hands while the other is holding some object at the chest with one hand. At Kaushambi two *Yakshis* have been represented standing cross legged, while one is holding a lotus in her right hand, the other *Yakshi* is headless and without attributes. Another *Yaksha* from there is holding a bunch of flowers in his left hand, while his right hand is held at his chest. Amin has provided two pillars, one containing a *Yaksha- dampatti* (*Yaksha* and *Yakshi*) clasping each other; which is one of the earliest representation of a pair in *Yaksha* iconography. The *Yaksha* holds a wine-cup in his left hand. The other pillar portrays a *padampani Yaksha* (*Yaksha* holding a lotus) (Misra 1981:120).

Mathura region in Satvahana – Kushan phase

In this phase a variety of new poses and attributes come up. *Yakshas*, by this time, had been reduced to the status of attendant deities and they rarely appear as genuine cult images excepting those of Kubera. The *Yaksha* statues are mainly of three types. The first category consists of grotesque dwarf *Yakshas*, most of them as carrier of bowls and at times building parts and female *Yakshis* shown on railing pillars. The second category consists of specific *Yakshas* who are mentioned predominantly in the Buddhist texts and the third category consists of many cult images of *Kubera*.

Some of the images of *Yakshas* in the first category are nude and are shown squatting and pot bellied with conspicuous genitals. A nude Kushan *Yaksha*, has been found from Palikhera (Mishra 1981:123). *Yaksha* supporting parts of building or capitals are also known. Early specimen of a series of load supporting *Yaksha* like the ones in Bharhut and Sanchi are rare in Mathura, whereas the motifs of *Yakshas* carved as single supporters frequently occurs (Mitterwallner 1989:375). A surprisingly large number of bowl-supporting *Yakshas* have been found at different sites in and around Mathura. A pot bellied dwarf *Yaksha* seated in *lalitasana* carrying a basket in upraised hands is also found (Misra 1981:123). One more *Yaksha* of this kind is preserved in the state museum of Ethnology in Munich (Mitterwallner 1989:375). Another example of this type of image is in Mathura museum which came from Maholi (Misra 1981:124). A similar *Yaksha* has been found from Govindnagar near Mathura which has been dated to the Ksatrapa period (Mitterwallner 1989:377).

A large number of railing pillars show female figures, some marked by their nudity, under trees, holding a branch or plucking flowers with a corpulent male dwarf under the feet. They have been called *salabhanjikas* or *puspapracayika* or *vrikshakhas* and they are generally put under the broad category of *Yakshis* (Misra 1981 :123).

Among *Yakshas* who occur prominently in the Buddhist texts are the images of *Moggarapani* and *Vajrapani*. The *Moggarapani* images are in the dwarf form. In one relief he is holding *musal* in the left hand with right hand in *abhaya mudra*. The figure is entirely nude. Elsewhere, he shown inside an arched *torana* with a mace in his right hand, his left hand is kept on his belly and his grotesque and corpulent figure has a grinning face. Coomaraswami identified an image (no. 24) in the Mathura museum as that of *Vajrapani Yaksha,* but Agrawal said that on account of the *Vajra* held in the right hand, the figure represents *Indra* (V.S. Agarwal 1949:11). However, a statue (no. 2501) from Mathura shows a corpulent figure of *Vajrapani* holding a double-headed *Vajra* (Misra 1981:124).

A large no of sculptures of *Kubera* belonging to the *Kushan* period (at least 30) in various poses have been found. They present *Kubera* alone or with his consort *Hariti* (who is shown holding a child in accordance with her role in the Buddhist texts); or with a number of devotees. The oft –presented objects in the hands are cup, goblet, purse, nectar (wine?), vessel, mongoose. He is sometimes shown holding his hands in *abhaya mudra*. An interesting image in this context is one belonging to the *Kushan* period (no. 1346) which shows a small figure of *Kubera* seated in *bhadrasana* on the pedestal of the main Buddhist image. This provides iconic proof of the cult rivalry between Buddhism and the cult of *Kubera* according to Misra (Misra 1981:69).

Yaksha sculpture from the various sites of U.P. in Satavahana – Kushan phase

In the Satvahana-Kushan phase, there are not many examples of *Yaksha* iconography from the rest of Uttar Pradesh. An interesting image from Ahichhatra is carved on a block of stone whose upper side must have served as a seat while the knees arms and legs of a pot-bellied *Yaksha* are shown supporting the seat. He has bulging eyes; teeth peeping through the mouth, moustache and large ears. He is shown stretching the two ends of his mouth with the index fingers of his hand (Misra 1981: 125). The head of a *Yaksha* with similar facial features has been found from Bhita, Allahabad District (Chandra 1970 :61). A statue from Kausambi shows a seated Yaksha with a squat, dwarfish figure on a stool with mouth open in a grimace, fang-like teeth, moustache, protruding eyes with right hand cupped and left hand holding a boar by the hind feet (Chandra 1970 :63)

Eastern India

Yaksha Iconography in the Mauryan period – Patna

The earliest example of *Yaksha* iconography in ancient India comes from Patna and is regarded as belonging to the Mauryan period. Among these, three are quite famous but the fourth one discovered by Cunningham in the outskirts of Patna is hardly ever mentioned perhaps because few people know about it. Three statues were discovered by Dr. Tyler outside the city of Patna of which only two were sent to Calcutta. A broken statue of a similar kind was still standing at the Agam Kuan just outside the city of Patna when Cunningham visited it. It was adorned with a new head and a pair of roughly marked breasts and was being worshipped as *Mata Mai.* The Agam Kuan is a very large and very old brick well outside the city of Patna and to the north of the Buddhist ruins of *Panch Pahari*. The broken statue is said to have been found in the well, Cunningham concluded that the first two statues must also have been found near the same place. The inscription of the third was also lost.(Cunnigham Reports, Volume 15 : 1). The first two statues are huge ones. They are inscribed as 1) *Bhagavan Akhayanivika* and 2) *sarvatanandi* (V.S. Agarwal 1968:60). No *Yaksha* in any text has been assigned these names. However, scholars are bent upon identifying these two *Yakshas* with *Nandi* and *Vardhana*, two *Yakshas* of a certain *Nandivardhana* town mentioned in the *Mahamayuri*. Although the arms of both the *Yakshas* have been lost the marks of a *chauri* or fly whisk is visible on the shoulders of one of them. This indicates that in Patna, in the Mauryan period itself the subordination of *Yaksha* cult has begun.

A *Yakshi* from Didarganj near Patna, also belonging to this period has been discovered. She holds a *chauri* which also shows her subdued status. The image is uninscribed. Art historians have tried to identify her with *Hariti* who is mentioned in the texts as a *Yakshi* of Rajgriha in the *Magadha janapada,* although the iconic attributes of *Hariti* associated with her later images are entirely absent in this image.

Yaksha Iconography in the post Mauryan phase-Bodh Gaya

In Eastern India in the post Mauryan phase *Yaksha* figures were carved on the railing pillars in Bodh Gaya although these are not too numerous. There is the figure of *salabhanjika* being helped to climb a tree by a man. There has also been found the figure of a standing *Yakshi* on a pillar shaft. Then there is the figure of a *Yaksha* standing on ram like quadruped and holding a bunch of plants with stalks who is sometimes identified as *Indra* posing as *Brahmin Santi* (Coomaraswamy 1928). Two other *Yakshi* figures are exhibited in the Bodh Gaya museum, both are in standing posture and one has a lion as her *vahana*. There are also reliefs of pot bellied, nude *Yaksha* with fruit and dwarf *Yakshas* attacking *makaras* (Misra 1981:120)

Yaksha Iconography in the Satvahana-Kushan phase-Odisha

In the Satvahana-Kushan phase the only examples of *Yaksha* iconography available from the Eastern India are the Dumduma *Yakshas* and one each from Badgad and Panchgan village all found near Bhubaneswar in Odisha by K.C. Panigrahi (Panigrahi 1961:207-8).

Two of the Dumduma statues have bulged out bellies, bent knees, are dwarfish in size and stylistically very similar to the Sanchi *Yaksha* figures on the western gateway. They have sockets on the head which evidently were inserted into some other structural part. They have been shown as bent under some structure. The third is also stylistically similar. The fourth has holes below the armpits which no other specimen has. Two other *Yakshas* of the same type are being worshipped in Badgad and Panchagan villages near Bhubaneswar. According to K.C. Panigrahi the *Yaksha* iconography of the above specimens indicates close cultural contacts between Bhubaneswar and Sanchi.

Western India

Yaksha Iconography in the post- Mauryan phase-Sopara, Pitalkhora, and Nasik

A sculpture from Sopara shows a colossal *Yaksha*, standing with two attendants flanking him. Of the main figure, only the lower part below the girdle is extant now. There was probably a *Vajra* near the left foot of the main figure. Of the attendants, the one toward the left is turned backwards and is being carried by a grotesque looking figure which has a huge head attached to a dwarfish body. The figure is similar to the grotesque *Yakshas* of *Maras's* army at Sanchi (Misra 1981:111)

At Pitalkhora a *Yaksha* sculpture has been found which is 3.5 feet high and represents a standing corpulent male *Yaksha* with its hands raised upwards to hold a shallow bowl. The expression of the face is full of joy resulting in a chuckle which exposes the teeth. The sculpture bears an inscription which is helpful in dating this sculpture. The inscription is written in clearly engraved letters of 2nd century B.C. and reads made by Kanhadasa, a goldsmith (Deshpande 1959 :82). Misra however assigns it to the Satavahana-*Kushan* phase (Misra 1981:121).

Besides Pitalkhora, in this phase, similar *Yaksha* figures carved in half–relief are shown at Nasik, on the plinth of cave 3 as atlantes supporting the *vihara* and at Kanheri on a lion pillar in front of a *chaitya* -cave. (Deshpande 1959:81)

At Pitalkhora, a *Yaksha* acting as a *dwarapala* was originally placed on the left side of the entrance to cave 3; in fact it was carved in one piece with the jamb of the doorway. Stylistically it has been dated to the Satavahana period. The right arm bent at the elbow, holds a heavy and long spear. A fragment of a sculptured plaster depicts a *Yaksha* and a female *chauri* bearer. The dwarf *Yaksha* has his hands raised upto support on the head the base of an oblong platform, the front of which is decorated with the *vedika*-pattern. The face has a jovial expression and bulging eyes. The *chauri*-bearer stands to the left of the *Yaksha* in a graceful pose and has dignified expression. A 3 feet high sculpture, carved on a plaster, portrays *Yakshi* with a *karanda* over her head. There is also a female door–keeper holding a spear in her right hand and a scabbard is held in position over her left hip.

Central India

Yaksha iconography in the post-Mauryan phase-Pawaya, Besnagar and Bharhut

A colossal *Yaksha* image was discovered by Garde at Pawaya, the site of ancient Padmavati. The headless image, corpulent and pot-bellied, is represented standing on a pedestal. The right hand is broken but from its upward rise it appears to have been held in *abhaya mudra*. In his left hand he holds a purse. An inscription of six lines is present on the pedestal which informs that the image informs that the image of *Manibhadra* was installed in a club (*goshthi*) by his devotees (V.S. Agarwal 1968:119).

A colossal statue of a *Yaksha* was discovered in 1952 in the river Betwa in Besnagar. It measures about 11 feet 3 inches excluding the pedestal. The right hand of the statue is placed near the chest. It probably held a cup of wine (R.C. Agrawala 1969:48). The left hand firmly clasps the upper portion of the tall purse or money bag. The statue has thus been identified as that of *Manibhadra* by Misra and *Kubera* by Agrawala. A *Yakshi* measuring about 6 feet 10 inches was also discovered in 1952. In her right hand she holds some indistinct object and carries a bunch of mango fruit in her outstretched left hand.

The Besnagar region has supplied two more *Yakshi* figures, one of which is now in the Indian Museum, Calcutta. Both of its hands are broken. It measures 6 feet 7 inches and when discovered by Cunningham, it was being worshipped as *Telin* (Misra 1981:110). A bust of a *Yakshi* with hands broken has also been found from this region.

Several *Yaksha* and *Yakshi* figures carved on railing pillars have been found at Bharhut. Some are accompanied with inscriptions identifying them as specific *Yakshas* or *Yakshis*, some other reliefs are not labeled, but from their general style they have been identified with certain *Yaksha* or *Yakshis* mentioned in literary sources. Sometimes they occur as a part of some scene (Barua 1934).

A relief of a *Yaksha* inscribed as *Ajapala* has been found at Bharhut. He is shown as standing on a monster with the body of a fish but human hands thrust into its mouth. He is holding a half blossomed lotus in the right hand. Among the *Yakshas* at Bharhut he alone doesn't hold his hands in the *namaskar mudra*. He is referred to as a terrific *Yaksha* in Buddhist sources. There is also a carving bearing the label *Cada Yakshi* - the *Yakshi Cada* (*Chandra*). She stands under a *Naga* tree, holding in the left hand a branch of the tree with flowers and the leaves and bending the branch by her right hand while her right foot is placed straight on the pedestal. The pedestal carries a *makara.* Any *Yakshi* from the literary work with this name has so far not been encountered.

Bharhut also has the first distinctive image of *Kubera* which is labeled as *Kupero Yakho*. Here he has been shown standing on a crouching, grotesque, male dwarf. This is the only ancient Indian sculpture which shows *Kubera* as a *nar-vahana* which is his description in the literary sources. He has been shown holding his hands in the *namaskar mudra*, a pose of supplication. He is positioned as a *Lokapala* guarding the north quadrant of the *stupa*. Besides, *Virudhaka Yaksha* is depicted on the south gate also standing in the *namaskar mudra* on a rock, while a sandalwood tree and lion have also been shown on the pedestal. The labels of *Dhritrashtra Yaksha* and *Virapaksha Yaksha* on the east and the west quadrant of the *stupa* have also been found although their figures are missing. The way these *Yakshas* have been depicted in the four cardinal directions indicates that the Bharhut *stupa* upheld the belief in *Yakshas* being the guardians of the four quarters.

The *Yaksha Gamgita* mounted on an elephant is also holding his hands in *namaskar mudra.* This *Yaksha* is not mentioned in any of the literary sources. The *Yaksha Sipavasa* (*Supravrisa*) similarly holding his hands in *namaskar mudra*, stands on a kneeling caparisoned elephant carrying a lotus flower in his extended trunk. The *Yaksha Shuciloma* (having needle-like hair) is also carved in the *namaskar mudra* with a hideous *Kapala* (skull) carved on the right side of his head, probably to indicate the terrifying nature of the figure. He is mentioned in texts as the serpent whom Buddha converted. The *Yakshi Sudasana* (*Sudarshana*) is shown standing on a fish-tailed *makar.*

Besides these *Yakshas* and *Yakshis*, some other inscribed and uninscribed demi-gods and goddesses generally identified as *Yakshas* and *Yakshis*, are also mentioned by B.M. Barua (Barua 1934). Certain female figures are carved as *Yakshis* but labeled as *Devatas*. These include *Sirima* (godess of lucky grace) and *Chulakoka* and *Mahakoka*, two hunter goddesses who are shown on the elephant and the ground respectively.

Besides these, at Bharhut there are also found reliefs of dwarf *Yakshas* as atlantes (carrying building parts) or sprouting lotus rhizomes. There is one reference to a bowl supporting *Yaksha* too (Mitterwalner 1989:382).

Yaksha Iconography in the Satvahana-Kushan phase-Sanchi

Sanchi has supplied several images of *Yakshas* and *Vrikshakas* (mostly as decorative motifs). Some of the *Yaksha* figures are dwarfish and grotesque which seems to have been the dominant trend in most regions in this phase. Some however are more dignified and graceful like those from Bharhut .

The Western Gate of Sanchi Stupa I has eight *bharvahaka Yaksha* figures, standing back-to-back, impressive in bulk and volume, but dwarfish in size. Some *Yakshas* are shown grinning while others have contorted features; all of them support the parts of the *torana* above. The second type of *Yaksha* figure is seen in the relief of the *Padmapani Yaksha* who stands under a tree holding a lotus (Misra 1981:122).

Two other *Padmapani Yaksha* are shown standing either side of the *Bodhi* tree elsewhere. Similarly, a *chauri*-bearing *Yaksha* has been shown standing on one side of a wheel. The *Yaksha* who must have stood on the other side is now missing. Another sculpture shows a *Yaksha* standing beside a tree holding a long spear in his hand. There is also a relief of many grotesque dwarfish *Yaksha* dancing in the *darbar* of *Mara* who is supposed to have tried to tempt the Buddha. (Coomaraswami 1928)

The theme which becomes popular as a decorative motif in this phase is that of *Yakshas* sprouting lotus rhizomes from their mouth or navel. The maximum numbers of such motifs are found in Amravati followed by Sanchi.

Correspondence of Some of the Popular Themes in Yaksha Iconography with Literature

Having dealt with the themes in *Yaksha* iconography in different regions the paper will now explore the correspondence of some of the common themes with what the texts reveal about the cult. Some of the popular themes up to the *Kushan* times in *Yaksha* iconography among those mentioned in detail in the previous section are –*Manibhadra*, *Yaksha* as *Viras*, *Yakshis* as *Salabhanjika* or *Vrikshashakhas*, *Yakshas* holding lotus or flowers (*Padmapani*), *Yakshas* with *vahanas*, Atlantes *Yakshas*, bowl –supporting *Yaksha*, *Yakshas* as guardians of the four quarters, *Dwarpala Yaksha*, *Kubera* and lotus sprouting *Yakshas*.

Manibhadra holds an enviable place in the *Yaksha* pantheon; however, in cult hierarchy he is second to *Kubera* in the literary sources. It is surprising however, that *Manibhadra* is more popular in *Yaksha* iconography than *Kubera* in the early phase while *Kubera* gains prominence only in the *Kushan* period. The iconography indicates that perhaps, in the earlier period *Manibhadra* enjoyed greater importance in popular perception than *Kubera*, unlike what is indicated in the literary sources. Later, *Kubera* seems to have acquired some of *Manibhadra's* iconic attributes like purse and crown tilted to left (*Parshvamauli*). *Manibhadra* is mentioned in the *Mahabharata* as the deity of traders and travelers which is confirmed by the inscriptions on his statues and also their location on the trade routes. However, while he is mainly associated with the eastern region in the literature, his images are found in north and central India while no image has been found in eastern or western India.

Yakshas as *Viras* (repositories of valour) are depicted only in north India-Bharatapur, Sarnatha and Kosambi. Interestingly, V.S. Agrawal has pointed out that in many villages of India *Yakshas* in modern times are worshipped as *Bira* or *Brahma*. In fact, there is a saying in Benaras which goes *Gaon – Gaon ko thakur, Gaon-Gaon ko Bir* -very village has its own Bir who is worshipped (Agarwal 1968 :90). It is quite possible that this practice of worshipping of *Birs* originated very early in north India where people worshipped *Yakshas* as *Viras* who gave them protection and this folk cult must have spread to the other parts of India through the ages.

Yakshis as *Salabhanjikas* or *Vrikshashakhas* is a popular theme in iconography. *Yakshas* and *Yakshis* seem to have been perceived as vegetative and fertility spirits and were often associated with trees in popular religion and this perception slowly crept into literature too. In the Epics, goddesses born in trees were to be worshipped by those desiring children. In iconography we find scantily clad *Yakshis* standing under trees, sometimes holding a branch, sometimes with one foot on the trunk. Coomaraswami points out that these figures seem to be singularity out of place if regarded with the eyes of Buddhist or Jaina monks. However these figures of fertility spirits were present there because of the people's expectations. Women, accustomed to invoke the blessing of a tree spirit, would approach the railing pillar images with similar expectations (Coomaraswami 1928 :33). Hence, this is a motif which survived through the ages.

Another popular theme is *Yakshas* holding lotus (*Padmapani*) or other flowers which was specially prevalent in north India during the post-Mauryan times. No text establishes a direct connection between the *Yaksha* cult and the lotuses, except the lotus being one of the *nidhis* or the sources of wealth of *Kubera*. According to Coomaraswami, the association of *Yaksha* with the lotus is mainly due to the fact that the lotus represents the waters or earth resting on the back of waters and *Yakshas* are also intimately associated with water (Coomaraswamy 1931). This may be true in case of lotus sprouting *Yaksha* iconography of Sanchi and Amrawati but in many cases lotus holding, or flower holding *Yakshas* have a terrestrial background. A simpler explanation would be that *Yakshas* holding flowers simply depict their role as vegetative deities or tree spirits (Misra 1981:114).

The *Yakshas* and *Yakshis* are often shown standing on many animal mounts (*vahana*) at Bharhut and at one or two other places like Gaya (*Yakshi* on a lion), Kausambi (*Yaksha* on *makar*). In literature the *Yakshas* are not associated with *vahanas* except *Kubera* who is called a *nar-vahana*. Ironically, there is only one representation of *Kubera* as *nar-vahana* from Bharhut. The association of specific *Yakshas* with their respective animal mounts like elephant, *makar* and lion must have existed in the popular aspect of the *Yaksha* cult and thus it is reflected in the iconography.

Yakshas are often depicted as Atlantes, supporters of buildings and super structures, early Indian art though mostly Satvahana-Kushan phase. These *Yakshas* are dwarfish in nature. The only reference to this theme is found in *Mahabharata* (2,10,3) where *Guhyas* (whose position was later taken by *Yakshas*) are said to support *Kubera's* flying palace and *Kubera* is *Guhyapati*. This theme is perhaps the most popular theme in terms of its acceptance in all regions - eastern India, western India, northern India and central India in Hindu, Buddhist and Jaina sites.

Bowl supporting *Yaksha* statues are a common theme in Mathura in the Satvahana-Kushan phase although the earliest one might be the one at the Pitalkhora, Sarnath or Bharhut. There has been much debate about the significance of this theme. The most acceptable explanation was however given by Vogel according to whom these bowls were kept on the heads of *Yakshas* to receive offerings of flowers or other kind of offering such as powdered perfume and fragrant incense at the entrance of the sacred precincts of a *stupa*. He came to this conclusion on the basis of two relief carvings, one in Amravati and one in Mathura where such a scenario is represented (Mitterwallner 1989 :375-76).

An interesting question however is why were *Yakshas* chosen to hold these bowls on their heads. We know through references of *Yaksha* worship in texts and also through the folk religion of the present times that flowers seem to have been the most popular offering to *Yakshas*. We also know that by the time the bowl supporting *Yaksha* iconography became common, they had already been reduced to the status of attendants, gatekeepers and decorative motifs. Perhaps, the motif of a bowl on the head of a *Yaksha* serving as a gatekeeper was introduced to accommodate the popular sentiments so that devotees could first offer their personal floral tributes to the gatekeeper *Yakshas*. It seems that a sort of compromise could have been made to fulfill both their roles as subsidiaries in Buddhism and their persisting popularity among the common folk. This would also explain why this theme is most popular in the Mathura region where the *Yaksha* iconography indicates that the cult had occupied a strong position since the very beginning.

Yakshas as *Lokapalas* or the guardians of the four quarters of the earth is a common theme in the literature but in iconography their only representation as such is in Bharhut. However, *Yakshas* are frequently represented in iconography as *Dwarapalas* or gatekeepers. Curt Maurey speaking on this theme states, "Few peculiarities of Indian iconography demonstrates the survival of the old religious deity and the perpetuation of his hold on the popular mind as implicitly as the *Yakshas* assignment as

Dwarapalas. In their apparently humble positions, they are essential sustainer of the divine world, indispensible to its preservation. The *Yakshas* role as *Dwarpala* proves that however their external dignity might have debased, his internal authority remained undiminished (Maurey 1969:28).

The most popular theme in the *Yaksha* iconography in Mathura in the Satvahana-*Kushan* phase is statues of *Kubera* in various poses. Considering that *Kubera* seems to have been the most important *Yaksha* in literature since the earliest times, his iconography begins quite late and is confined only to the Mathura region. However, the depiction of *Kubera* in this phase with the purse, wine goblet, nectar flask or his consort *Hariti* corresponds to his image in literature.

The lotus sprouting *Yaksha* iconography has come mainly from sites in central India that is Bharhut, Sanchi and mostly Amravati. The texts do not give us any idea about the significance of this theme. Coomaraswamy while elucidating the connection of *Yakshas* to water cosmology states that in this motif the *Yakshas* navel or mouth represents the procreative centre giving birth to life while the rest of the *Yakshas* represents water (Coomaraswamy 1931). Whether the artists and sculptors who created these reliefs were aware of the more abstract and cosmological aspects of the cult as pieced together by Coomaraswami is moot. The theme could have had some more intelligible and popular connotation which is lost to us.

Having discussed the correspondence of some of the most popular themes in *Yaksha* cult, it seems obvious that most of themes seems to have no parallel in literature and are thus based on the popular perception of the cult which might have existed over time. Most of the themes also seem to have been particularly conspicuous in specific regions at certain points of time while there might be one or two example of such a theme in other regions. Thus it is evident that there are a lot of aspects of the *Yaksha* cult which must have existed in the popular perception of the cult with regional peculiarities, about which the texts do not inform us.

It thus seems totally unnecessary why art historians over the years have tried to put a name tag on various *Yaksha* and *Yakshi* statues based on literary descriptions and a connection of their find places with the *Mahamayuri* list of *Yakshas* and *Yakshis*, although it is a text which comes up late vis-à-vis the *Yaksha* iconography. Instead, it would not be unjustified to consider that just as *Yaksha* iconography portrays certain aspects of the cult which the literature doesn't tell us about, similarly most of the *Yaksha* and *Yakshi* statues found must have been local deities about whom the local population shared knowledge in common, but these deities managed to stay away from the texts.

Thematic variation over space and time

Yaksha iconography had begun in Eastern region in the Mauryan period itself which indicates that initially the cult must have enjoyed popularity in this region. However, in this phase itself the beginning of subordination of the cult is evident because although the statues are massive cult figures, two of them were already carrying *chauris (*fly whisks), a symbol of subordination. In the post-Mauryan phase in eastern India there is a marked decline in *Yaksha* iconography as compared to other regions. There is no novelty in themes too, except perhaps the lion-mounted *Yakshis* of Gaya which indicates a similarity with the Bharhut tradition of associating *Yakshas* and *Yakshis* with *vahanas*. In the Satvahana-*Kushan* phase the cult seems to have lost its popularity altogether in the Eastern region and the only example we get from Orissa of dwarf Atlantes *Yaksha* indicates that *Yakshas* as cult figures were no longer being worshipped and they merely existed as decorative motifs in iconography. The quick and total subordination of the cult at least in terms of iconography may be due to the fact that Buddhism had been very strong in the Eastern region in those times.

In Northern India *Yaksha* iconography begins with the post-Mauryan phase and seems to have been particularly strong in the Mathura region. *Yakshas* were regarded as capable of great strength, providers of protection and objects of dignity. This is obvious from the fact that many of them were depicted in the *abhaya mudra* and most of them are independent cult statues. The worship of *Yaksha* in the form of *Vira* or the repositories of valour was particular to this region. Also the cult of *Manibhadra* seems to have been popular amongst the merchants and travelers. The iconography of flower holding *Yaksha* also indicates that in this phase, they were mainly regarded as tree spirits. In the Satvahana-

Kushan phase, from the dwarfish grotesque and nude *Yaksha* statues it is obvious that the cult had been subordinated to some extent. There is also a beginning of the practice of depicting Buddhist themes in iconography. However, the cult of *Kubera* seems to have become particularly popular in the Mathura region in this phase and the iconography also indicates that it gave some competition to Buddhism. The popularity of the bowl carrying *Yakshas* in Mathura in this phase shows that an attempt must have been made by Buddhism to reconcile itself somewhat to the popularity of *Yaksha* cult in the Mathura region.

In Western India we do not find many examples of *Yaksha* iconography. However, it is obvious from the iconography in Post- Mauryan phase that the *Yakshas* had been given a subordinate status. For the first time not only *Yakshas* but even *Yakshis* are portrayed as *dwarpalas.*

In Central India the earliest examples of *Yaksha* iconography come from the post-Mauryan phase. In places like Pawaya and Besnagar *Yaksha* were being worshipped as cult icons and the cult of *Yaksha Manibhadra* seems to have been popular. On the other hand, in Bharhut the iconography indicates that *Yakshas* had already been reduced to a servile status and except one all are shown in *namaskara mudra* as humble attendants of Buddha. This is in contrast to the *abhaya mudra* posture of the north Indian *Yakshas* of this phase. Also Buddhist themes in *Yaksha* iconography are more common here. In the Satvahana-Kushan phase, the tendency is to use dwarfish, grotesque *Yakshas* as attendants but also popular *Yakshas* like the *padmapani* form in direct attendance to the Buddha. The connection of the *Yakshas* with water cosmology is mostly shown in Central India where the *makara* is shown as their *vahana* and Sanchi and Amravati have various reliefs of lotus sprouting *Yakshas*. This is in contrast to their representation in north India mostly as tree spirits.

From the above analysis of various the themes in *Yaksha* iconography and their variations over space and time two observations might be made. Firstly, the most popular themes in *Yaksha* iconography have little correspondence with what the text tells us about the cult. Hence it would be prudent if *Yaksha* iconography (which has till date been studied mainly in terms of its contribution to Indian art) would be used as a source to study the *Yaksha* cult as well, instead of the sole reliance on textual sources.

Secondly, the *Yaksha* iconography also indicates that in ancient India there were regional manifestations of the *Yaksha* cult at different places and time periods. It challenges the impression given by the texts that the kernel of the belief in the *Yaksha* cult remained the same everywhere and at all times.

Bibliography

Agrawal V.S. "Catalogue of Mathura Museum". *JUPHS.* XXI, 1949.

Agrawal,V.S. "Bira-Baramha". *Janapadai.* Volume I, April 1953.

Agarwal,V.S. *Studies in Indian Art.* Varanasi: Vishwavidyalaya Prakashan, 1968.

Agrawala, R.C. "Yaksa Torso from Bharatpur Region". *Journal of the Oriental Institute.*Volume 17, 1967, 64-65.

Agrawal, R.C. "Unpublished Yaksha-Yaakshi Statues from Besnagar". *Lalit Kala.* No.14,1969

Barua, B.M. *Barhut :Stone as a Story Teller.* Volume 1.Calcutta:Indian Research Institute:1934

Coomaraswamy, Anand. K. *Yaksas.* Washington :Smithsonian Institute .1928, New Delhi : Munshiram Manoharlal. 1971.

Coomaraswamy, Anand. K. *Yakshas.* Part 2 Washington: Smithsomian Institute. 1931.

Coomaraswamy, Anand. K. *Yakshas : Essays in the Water Cosmology* ed. rev. and enl. Paul Schroeder. New Delhi : Indira Gandhi National Centre for the Arts, New York: Oxford University Press. 1993.

Chandra Moti. "Some aspects of the Yaksha Cult in Ancient India". *Bulletin of the Prince of Wales Museum of Western India.* No.3. 1954.

Chandra, Pramod. *Stone Sculptures in the Allahabad Museum: A Descriptive Catalogue* . Poona: American Institute of Indian Studies. 1970.

Cunningham, Alexander, *Cunningham's Reports published by Archaeological Survey of India,*Volume 15. Calcutta: Office of the Superintendent of Government Printing, Reprinted in 2000.

Deshpande M.N. "Rock-cut caves of Pitalkhora in the Deccan". *Ancient India, No. 19*, 1959,

Maurey,Curt. *Folk Origins of Indian art*, New York and London: Columbia University Press, 1969.

Misra, R. N. *Yaksha Cult and Iconography*, New Delhi: Munshiram Manoharlal , 1981.

Mitterwallner, Gritli V. "Yakshas of Ancient Mathura" in *Mathura the Cultural Heritage* ed. Doris M Srinivasan. 354-382, New Delhi: Manohar Publications, 1989.

Panigrahi K.C. *Archeological Remains at Bhubaneswar.* Bombay : Orient Longman. 1961.

33

DEPICTION OF BRAHMA'S LIFE THROUGH THE VAISHNAVA SCULPTURES OF UDAYAGIRI CAVES, VIDISA: A PROPORTIONATE BLEND OF ICONOGRAPHY AND PHILOSOPHY

Pooja Saxena, Apurva Sinha

Vaishnavism was at its peaks during the Gupta period which is observed by the display of Vaishnavism all over the Gupta Empire in central India. Gupta period is famous for its temples at Udayagiri, Eran, Nachna Kuthar, Bhumra, Deogarh, Bhittargaon that portray immense faith in Brahmanism that marks the revival of Brahmanical faith.[1] Apart from Udayagiri, all the other sites are either structural or partly structural. Udayagiri caves located Vidisa district of Madhya Pradesh[2] shows complete affinity towards the zealous Brahmanical faith. There are 20 rock-cut caves at Udayagiri of which 19 are Brahmanical and 1 is Jaina cave[3]. Maximum work of art is dedicated to lord Vishnu. The metaphysical forces of nature rest in the supreme Lord Vishnu. The copious depiction of Lord Vishnu leaves us with an impression as what was the mindset behind the greatest creation at Udayagiri. Going deep into the philosophy, the depiction at Udayagiri Caves is not merely a depiction dedicated to Lord Vishnu. The artist took care of the ancient scriptures such as Matsya, Vishnu, and Varaha Purana that led to the development of a vision or more of a multi-disciplinary approach as to how many ways the depiction at Udayagiri can be interpreted. As inspired by the Vishnu, Varaha and Matsya Purana, the iconography at Udayagiri seems to be much more philosophical than it appears to be.

For once witness the caves as a frame displaying the cosmic event of creation. The entire walk through of the rock-cut caves leaves us with an impression that the idea behind carving out the caves was not just to project zealous faith in Brahmanism but to focus on the genesis of the cosmos. There are two aspects of Vishnu that are exquisitely depicted at Udayagiri; they are Seshasayi Vishnu and his Varaha incarnation. The enormity of the sculptures gives a notion that the artist intended to publicise the creation of the cosmos. Keeping in consideration the panoramic view of the site a fresh interpretation of the Udayagiri caves has been derived to mark the creation of the Earth and the series of events that took place as mentioned in the Puranic literature.

The cave no.13 displaying Narayana is a rock-cut niche, facing north[4]. The rock-cut niche can be reached through a passage going adjacent to cave no.7. 'Nara' means water and 'ayana' means a resting place is the manifestation of Vishnu resting on water. The depiction of 'Narayana' in the cave numbered as 13 is an expression to show the end of the world (maha-pralaya) where only the Supreme lord survived who is shown resting on the waters on his serpent couch. Keeping a balance between iconography and philosophy, the entire panorama can be conceptually understood. The cave no.13 depicts Vishnu in slumber (sayana) and the figures depicted can be identified as Brahma seated on the lotus, issuing from Narayana's navel, Garuda in the bird form and Gada Devi and Chakra purusha who were created to slay the demons Madhu and Kaitab depicted on the extreme right. The Puranas testify that Vishnu created his attributes Gada and Chakra to kill Madhu and Kaitab. The Matsya purana gives a vivid description of the birth of Brahma[5], the creation of the Universe and how the Earth was brought up from the waters. In Kali era, the life of Brahma is hundred years. One day of Brahma is equivalent to a Kalpa[6]. There are 30 kalpa mentioned in the puranic literature. The life of Brahma is divided into two halves, '*Prathama Parardha*' and '*Uttara Parardha*[7]'. The *Prathama Parardha* began with the 'Brahma Kalpa' in which the present cosmos was born. Brahma was conceived in the golden egg and which is why he came to be known as *Hiranyagarbha*. At the end of the *Prathama Parardha* was '*Padma Kalpa*' when *loka Padma* or the louts of the *Lokas* appeared at the navel of Narayana. From the navel of Narayana, sprang Brahma seated on lotus. The origin of Brahma from the lotus marks the beginning of the process of creation. As stated in the Matsya Purana that, 'with the creation of Brahma the creation of the Vedas began. Brahma's task was to meditate'. It was while he was meditating, that the Vedas were revealed from his heart. The depiction of Narayana in this cave demarcates the origin of the process of creation, the conception of the Vedas in which was written the entire knowledge of the world. The depiction also expresses the protection of the knowledge (*jn ana*) of the world from the evils that were personified as Madhu and Kaitab.

Iconography is the study that deals with the depiction of the metaphysical and concrete forces of nature .The study helps in the identification of the figures. The cave no.13 at Udayagiri is dedicated to Narayana. Narayana is depicted as sleeping on waters on his serpent couch after the great deluge. There are total eight figures depicted above the figure of Narayana. Moving from right to left, the figures can be identified as a standing female attendant holding a lotus stalk. There is a lesser possibility of the figure being Goddess lakshmi as Goddess Lakshmi is always shown near the foot of Lord Vishnu. The lotus issuing from the navel of Narayana once had seated Brahma, now only the lotus is properly visible. Next to the depiction of Brahma is the depiction of Garuda in the form of a bird. Next to Garuda is the depiction of personified Gada and Chakra. Towards the extreme left there two standing figures depicted, they are identified as Madhu and Kaitab. The events of the creation of Brahma, revealing of the four Vedas from his heart and the procurement of Vedas from the demons Madhu and Kaitab was the significant event of the *Prathama Parardha* which is depicted in cave no.13.

The end of *Prathama parardha* or the *Padma Kalpa* is marked by the genesis of Brahma. The beginning of the *Uttara Parardha* which is depicted in cave no.5 is marked by the *Sveta Varaha Kalpa* where Vishnu appears in the form of a majestic boar (Varaha) to lift up the Earth from the waters. The niche facing east is shown depicting one of the significant incarnations of Lord Vishnu. The *Varaha Purana* acknowledges the quadruped signifying the four Vedas[8]. The colossal sculpture of Varaha is shown adorned with a garland made out of lotus flowers, exquisite jewellery and wears an Indian *dhoti*. He has his left foot placed on the Sheshanaga and the goddesses Earth is shown clinging on to his tusk. The depiction can be interpreted as the creation of the living beings on Earth as Vishnu rescues the Earth that is submerged in the water. The entire canvas portrays the rescuing of the Earth and then bringing life to the Earth. Vishnu Lifts the goddess personified as Earth. The heavenly triad i.e. creator, protector and destroyer are present in the panel. Vishnu, the protector in Varaha incarnation is shown as protecting the Earth, three faced Brahma seated on a lotus doing the act of creation along with Siva seated on a standing Nandi. Towards the right side is shown the emergence of rivers Ganga and Yamuna. The personified form of river goddesses Ganga and Yamuna is shown standing on their vehicles. The flowing of the river is felt by Marut that is shown just above the figures of Ganga and Yamuna. The Marut being the Wind God is identified because of his body posture as though flying. Below the depiction of Ganga and Yamuna is the depiction of God of sky and rain, Varuna who is shown standing in the waters holding a pot as though ready to regulate the flow of the rivers. The same depiction is shown on the left side of the niche too. The entire panel depicts numerous sages and musicians witnessing the event. Another noticeable factor of the panel is the depiction of the five basic elements of the creations that are known as *Panchamahabhoota.* They are the earth, the water, energy or fire, the wind and the sky. The earth is depicted as personified clinging on to the tusk of Varaha. The water is depicted through the wavy lines and is also marked by the presence of the God of waters, Varuna. The wind is depicted in the form of Marut that is shown in the flying posture above the personified river goddesses, Ganga and Yamuna. The flying posture of the wind God Marut is a characteristic feature of wind god and the God is identified because of this posture. The sky has no limits and is depicted as where the Gods, Brahma and Siva are depicted. The energy is depicted in the form of all the celestial forces depicted in the panel. In short, it can be said that Vishnu took the form of a wonderful boar to cleanse the Earth and make it dwell-able for life. This depiction at Udayagiri demarcates the *Sveta Varaha Kalpa* that is the beginning of life on the Earth or the awakening of the civilisation. The *Sveta Varaha Kalpa* also marks the 51st year of Brahma's life and as noted by some scholars, presently we are living in the 1st day of 51st year of Brahma[9]. The artist remarkably publicises the day, life on Earth came into existence.

The view of the Udayagiri caves can be interpreted by various means and mostly it is dependent on one's perception. This far reaching insight has been presented to mark the genesis of the Earth in a series of steps as mentioned in the Puranas. Brahma's life is divided into two *Parardha* i.e. two halves. By the end of *Prathama Parardha*, Brahma is born and he starts the work of creation in the beginning of *Uttara Parardha.* The cave no.13 shows the Brahma kalpa, of the *Prathama Parardha* where Lord Brahma is conceived and Brahma comes out seated on a lotus issuing out of Vishnu's navel in the *Padma kalpa*, the end of *Prathama Parardha*. The act of making Earth a dwell-able place and the creation of the living beings began in the *Sveta Varaha Kalpa* that is the first kalpa of *Uttara Parardha* which is portrayed in the cave no.5 in the form of a boar. To summarise, the rock-cut architecture of the Udayagiri caves remarkably is a complete blend of a philosophy and iconography where you are not just witnessing the enormity of the sculptures but also the very act of creation of the Earth and making it dwell-able for life.

References

1. Mookerji, R.K. 2007. *The Gupta Empire*. New Delhi: Motilal Banarsidass. Gazetteer of Vidisa district.
2. Khare, M D. 2009. *Vidisa*. Bhopal : Madhya Pradesa Hindi Grantha Akademi, India.
3. Patil, D. R.1948. *The monuments of the Udayagiri Hills*. Gwalior: Alijah Darbar Press, India.
4. Vyasadeva, Sri.1892. *Matsya Purana*. Lucknow : Published by Munshi Naval Kishore (C.I.E Printing Press), India.
5. A., Qeyamuddin (Ed.). 2008. *India by Al- Biruni*. New Delhi: National Book Trust, India.
6. Kalpa, a period at the beginning and end of which there is a conjunction of seven planets and their apsides and nodes in 0° of Aries.
   1 caturyuga= 12000 divya years
   72 caturyuga=1 manu
   14 manu= 1 kalpa
   Therefore,14 manus will have 72X14= 1008 caturyuga
   1008 caturyuga= 1 kalpa (1 day of Brahma)
   The first half of 504 caturyugas is called utsarpini (winter solstice) during which the sun is ascending, and the second half is called avasrapini (summer solstice), during which the sun is descending. The midst of the period is called sama.
7. Srinivasachariar, M.1974. *History of classical Sanskrit literature: Being an elaborate account of all*. New Delhi: Motilal Banarsidass, India.
8. Chaturvedi, B K. 2004. *Varaha Purana*. New Delhi: Adarsh Printers, India.
9. Srinivasachariar, M. 1974. Op.cit.

34

SCULPTURAL ART OF TRANS-GHAGHARA REGION

Neetu Tiwari

The Trans-Ghaghara region, popularly known as Saryupar, is the part of middle Ganga plain and it has the similar geographical features as the vast Ganga plain. It is a monotonous flat land sloping from the north-west (elevation 102 mt.) to south-east (elevation 70 mt.) and forms a distinct geographical and cultural entity.

The areas of Trans-Ghaghara covers north-eastern Uttar Pradesh comprising of modern districts of Deoria, Kushinagar, Gorakhpur, Maharajganj, Sant Kabirnagar, Basti, Siddharthnagar, Gonda, Bahraich, Balrampur and Sravasti; besides the adjoining terai area of Nepal which also come under it. It is bounded on the east by little Gandak, on the south and west by Ghaghara/Srayu river and on the north by the Nepal terai adjacent to Himalayan foot hills. The region has been broadly divided into three divisions viz (1) the *Terai* (2) the *Bhangar* or upland and (3) the *Kachhar* or the flood-prone lowland.

Historical Background

Rig-Veda mentioned Saryu River but its relevance is controversial. Zimmer, R.B. Sharma and other scholars recognized it as present Saryu (Majumdar 1965: 246). The Trans-Ghaghara region formed the eastern part of the ancient Kosala *Mahanjanpada*, which was ruled by the legendary kings of *Ikshavaku* lineage of the solar race.

On the basis of genealogical tables of the Puranas and other relevant ancient literatures, it is proposed that about one hundred and two kings of the aforesaid solar race ruled up to one or two generations later to the Buddha (Pushalkar 1951).

On the contrary the history of the Trans-Ghaghara region before Buddha is observed obscure or any body's guess. The legend of Videgha Mathava mentioned in *Satapatha Brahmana* (1.4; 1.14-20) indicates that the area west to Sadanira was occupied by the Aryans in early times. This area is well mentioned in the epics and Buddhist as well as Jain literatures too (Pathak 1963: 84-114).

In the pre-Buddhist period Kosala *mahajanpada* was expanded up to Kashi (for limited time). But during the Buddha period it is restricted only in region of Ghaghara (Saryu)-Rapti doab (Tewari 2004: 2). At the same time on this land some republic were established like Sakya, Kalam, Koliya, Moriya and Mallas. With zenith of Magadh and the period of Nanda-Maurya dynasty the geographical and political identity of this region attached with Magadha (Raichoudhary 1980: 143). In the Sunga period when the Greeks had marauded Panchala, Mathura and Madhymika with Saket; we came to know that this region corresponds to ancient Saket (Pargiter 1962: 53-4). This geographical region retained its political supremacy even during the Kushan-Gupta period. During the reign of Chandragupta-II Vikramaditya and Harshvardhan, Chainise trevellers Fa-Hian and Yuan-Chwang treveled respectively along with the region. They have given graphic picture of the cities and religious centers of this area also.

In the early medieval period this region known as 'Saryupar', Daddarandika and Daradgandika' (EI XXI: 169-71). Between this time period this region was ruled by several dynasties like Malayaketu, Kalchuri, Savarni, Gaharwal which is evidenced by the archaeological remains like- coins, inscriptions etc.

During the Mughal period and British period the region was under the Nawabs of Awadh. After their rule the area come under British empires during which some geopolitical changes took place.

Archaeological investigations were started in this region as early as in 19th century by Alexander Cunningham of Archaeological Survey of India. He and his team explored the region and excavated few sites to identify the Buddhist sites. After Independence the area was extensively explored by different institutions like Archaeological Survey of India, UP State Archaeology Deptt., Gorakhpur University, Banaras Hindu University and others and the sites like Sravasti, Sohgaura, Piprahwa-Ganwaria, Narhan, Imlidih, Dhuriapar, Siswania, Lahuradeva etc. were excavated. A large number of antiquities including sculptures have been came into light by these investigations.

Trans Ghaghara plain was the place of development of Vedic Brahman tradition and non-Vedic but Aryan-Shraman tradition. These traditions and the religious sects and thoughts originated from these traditions and influenced all the aspects of art of this region. So it was natural to receive the subject of sculptural art and architectural art from their tradition but the meaning of this is not that all the art traditions were influenced by these thoughts. There was a strong local tradition, other than the written religious literatures which affected the art tradition of the region.

Although the physical form of an icon is not exemplified in Vedic period still the Vedic literature presents various iconographic references. *Rigveda* (5.52.15) mentions at one instance a man saying "who will take my Indra in exchange of ten cows". But it does not, shows that the man is probably referring to an icon of Indra. But whether the man corresponding to an icon of Indra is not clear enough to conclude the image worship during that time. The Vedic literature refers to Indra, Surya, Agni, Chandra, etc. but these references do not confirm whether the icon of these Gods were made or not during the contemporary time.

Ṙigveda also refers to Sishna Devata and Bhura Deva. While describing them Sri Avinash C. Das & J.N. Banerjee have inferred that these words surely signify the practice of image worship (Misra 2002: 59). Probably there was a practice of phallus worship among the non-Aryan people. Bhurdeva probably refers to a god or power whose image was made of stone or many other static materials. In context to the origin and development of sculptural art if Aryans are credited for their contemplative references the non-Aryans are credited to give their intellectual thoughts an iconic form.

Literary evidences of sculptural art tradition of Mauryan period is available along with sculptures itself. *Patanjali* mentions that the images were carved for the betterment of economy "*Maurye Arthambhin Archcha Prakakalpita*". This reference is may be for those images whose sale increased the money in the royal treasury. There is a Sutra "*Jivikarthe Cha panye*" in the *Ek Sutra "Eva Pratikritau*" of *Panini*.

There is a tradition explained in this Sutra that if any image is carved for livelihood then "*ka*" suffix was not used for those. It is clear by these descriptions that there were two types of divine images during Panini's time, one for selling in the markets and the other for the establishments in the temples (Misra 2002: 59).

Sculptural art of Mauryas was very prominent. Chinese traveler Fa-hian and Yuan Chwang mentioned respectively six and fifteen pillars made by Asoka in their travel account.

Tibetian Lama Taranath who was very much influenced by the beauty of these pillars and he stated that Mauryans were helped by Gods and Yakshas in their different works which is resulted in the Pillars and buildings of that time (Hule: 102)

The extreme of art during Asoka time reflects in the high pillars with polished shaft and animal capitals. In the creation of these pillars there was not only the aptitude of craft but its imagination was also rudimentary and possibly given by the king himself.

There was a great respect for religion in the heart of the Asoka and he planned to erect the pillars with the teachings engraved over that. All erected pillars of Asoka are not surviving at present. Only a few pillars have been found in which they are mentioned by Fa-Hian and Yuan-Chwang.

Trans-Ghaghara plain is a witness of main events of Buddha's life. This region is not only the birthplace of Buddha but also the work place and the Mahaparinirvana place of Buddha.

The Lumbini monolith (Plate 34.1) of Asokan period is made of Chunar sandstone with tiny blackish specks and bears the characteristic of the Mauryan polish. The pillar has vertical Fissure down to the middle and its top broken off probably by lightening as noted by Hieuṇ-Tsang. A stone cap has been provided at the top to prevent the percolation of water. The height of extant part above the rough hammer dressed surface meant to be burried below ground is 7.391 mt. The lower portion of the pillar to a depth of 2.134 mt remains burried below the ground. The crowning elements except the bell shaped lotus member (in two halves), which was on the paved platform in front of the Rummindei temple; are now missing. The bearing of sun as capital of the column here has been interpreted to mean a horse, which symbolises the sun. It is also mentioned in the account of Hieun-Tsang. Fragments of Asokan pillars are also found from Nigliva and Gotihava, both sites in Nepalese Tarai area.

An Asokan lion capital (Plate 34.2) was found from Mahadeva in Tehsil Bansi of Siddhartha Nagar district (Mani 1998: 109). This pillar capital is in broken stage. Only inverted lotus, Kantha, broken abacus with floral motif and the feet of lion over abacus is available.

During the Mauryan period, where the pillar manufacturing was developing as the royal art on one hand, the manufacturing of image of local deities like Yaksha and Yakshi were developing as local art on other hand which developed as post-Mauryaṇ art in later times. Yakshas and Yakshis were established as lower class deities in the ancient society and local art or folk art.

The images were started to carve in the Mauryan period and received as a tradition in the field of sculptural art. The images of these Yakshis were found from Didarganj, Patna, Mathura, Bhita, Pratapgarh, Noh, Rajghat, Plaval, Besnagar, Vidisa, Pavaya, Sopara, Amaravati etc.

In this sequence an image of Yakshi with broken head of sand stone from Buddhi Khas (Mani 1998: 115; Plate 34.3) in district Siddharthnagar is mentionable. The image was found from a well by the villagers. In style, it resembles the famous Yakshi of Didarganj as it is also sculptured for having a view form all around. It is 86 cm. in height its palms, feet and head are broken. The upper portion of body iṣ naked. She is wearing a *Kanthahara* in neck and a decorated *kardhani* in waist, drapery is available at the lower portion of body, shoulder and on left hand. On the basis of dress, ornament and style of image it is assumed that this Yakshi image is related to Sunga period.

After Sunga period, new horizons of art were came into existence and new centers of art were established like Gandhara and Mathura school of art. The subject and tradition of Indian art extended in the region of west Asia with the expansion of state of Kushan rulers. The sculpture of Kushan period has been found in large numbers from Trans-Ghaghara region. These sculptures are made of red sand stone of Roopbas and Fatehpur Sikri.

1. Image of Kuber of red sand stone seated over an asana. Size of the image is 30 x 26 cm. Kuber has *usnisa* over head, *kundala* in ears. The image is two handed and holds purse in left hand and an unidentified object in right hand-probably wine cup. The other features are not very clear. On the basis of identified features this image belongs to Kushan period. This image is housed at Gorakhpur museum. (Plate 34.4)
2. Head of Bodhisattva of sand stone in Gandhara style. Size of this head is 27 x 19 cm. Image has curly hairs, ornamented headband, moustache, half closed eyes?, *urna* in the center of forehead. The image/head belongs to Kushan period. (Plate 34.5)

3. Image of Buddha within an arch. The material is red sand stone and the size is 31 x 29 cm. The arch has pillars at both sides. Buddha is seated in *Padmasana* and *abhayamudra*; he has *sanghati* over body and *usnisa* over head, ears are elongated and the face is in smiling form; eyes and half closed, *urna* is also present in the center of forehead. This image has *prbhamandala* behind head. The features show that the image belongs to Mathura school of Kushan period. (Plate 34.6)
4. Red sand stone image of Bodhisattva Padmapani. Its size is 95 x 38 cm. It is in *sthanakamudra*. It has crown over head, *kundala* in ears, necklace, and *uttariya* over body. He is holding *Padma* in right hand and the left hand holds *uttariya*. Other features are not clear. The above description shows that the image belongs to Mathura school of Kushan period.

Two schools of art were emerged and developed during Gupta Period in northern India including Trans-Ghaghararegion. These were Mathura and Sarnath schools of art. Many stone sculptures are noticed in Trans-Ghaghara region belonging to Gupta period.

1. Image of two handed Surya in standing posture found from Turpatti (Kushinagar) Sun temple. He is holding lotus in both hands and wearing crown, necklace, sacred thread, waist band, dhoti in lower part and shoes. *Prabhamandala* is available behind head and vidyadhars are shown on both sides. Usha and Pratyusha standing on the sides and Aruni in front of Surya. On the basis of the features this image belongs to Gupta period. Size of image is 115 x 49 cm and made of sand stone. (Plate 34.7)
2. Jaina Image in *Kayotsargamudra* found from Khukhundu in red sand stone. The size is 223 x 11 cm. *Triratna* is available on the chest. *Chauri* bearers are shown at lower part and flying *gandarva* on the upper part. *Simhasana* or pedestal has dharma chakra in center and bull (?) on both the sides of dharma chakra. On the basis of bull this image is identified with Rishabhanath. This image belongs to Gupta period. (Plate 34.8)
3. Jaina pillar from Kahaon in Deoria district. This pillar is squarish at the base and respectively octagonal, 16 sided and circular at the upper part. The upper part consists of a squarish abacus with floral motif, inverted lotus and a square block with Jaina images on four sides. The square base has also a Jaina image. This Jaina image is in *Kayotsargamudra*. Two devotees are present on the side. This image has *chhatra* of snake hood and the body of snake is visible at the back of the image. On the basis of the snake hood this image is identified with Parsvanath. This pillar belongs to Gupta period as it contains the inscription of Skandagupta. (Plate 34.9 & 34.10)
4. A monolithic Image of Buddha in declining posture made of red sand stone from Kushinagar. Size is about 6.10 mt. The pedestal is of bricks over which three stone plaques with sad devotees are available. The inscription at the pedestal refers that this image was established by Haribal in 5th century A.D. (Plate 34.11)
5. Sculpture of a Jain Teerthankara in red sand stone is housed in a modern temple at Kahaon, district Deoria. The image is in *kayotsargamudra* and it's legs are broken. The size of image is 145 x 45 cm. The sculpture has a *ushnisha* over head and *srivatsa* on the chest. On the basis of the features it is related to Gupta period. (Plate 34.12)
6. Ekamukhlinga in sand stone. Size of the image is 99 x 49 cm. It is housed at a modern temple at Mahen in Barhaj (Deoria distt.). In this Linga a beautiful face of Siva is shown with *jatajuta*, *trinetra* and half closed eyes, with a smiling face. Above the *jatajuta* portion a short portion of linga is shown. On the basis of the features it is related to Gupta period. Classical art of Gupta period is shown in this Image. (Plate 34.13)

The art of Gupta period was on the peak and the later tradition were highly surprised and over whelmed by Gupta art that they cannot be imagined.

Regionalism was developed in the place of unity. Even in different regions different scripts and languages developed. In the region of Ganga-Yamuna and Ghaghara-Rapti doab, Sarnath was the main center of art but staleness developed in the art and the old reflections were repeated continuously for which the tradition became conservative. Mathura also witnessed the same type of decline. In the images of Mathura where the imprint was survived but the typological ideals were lost. The change on the style of workmanship also affected the sculptural art of Trans-Ghaghara region. The image of this region was not only the imitative of Sarnath School; but the art tradition which was developing in the eastern India also influenced the art tradition of this region. The sculptures of eastern India have emotional manifestation than the spiritualism of Gupta period.

In the 8th century A.D. the images of this region have all aspects of beauty but all these are impulsive. It is compulsory to consider the images of Paharpur (Bengal) in the study of the images of Trans-Ghaghra region. These images, which were made during 7th century A.D., are slightly different from the images of other centers. The Pala tradition which flourished between 8th to 12th century A.D. did not witnessed any major changes. The Sarnath tradition was totally untouched from the Pala tradition. The images of this tradition were made of black smooth stone. All the aspects of images in different religions were developed till this time. Every god has its own specific attributes, which were showed in the images regularly. The ratio of body, its parts and forms were established and these were followed strongly; but the sculpturor got extreme in this work. Round and clear face, strong muscles, broad shoulders, handsome body are the main features of Pala images. The images of this period are highly ornate, polished and they look like metallic than stone finished.

Pala sculpturor were not adept for such imagination so they introduced jewellery as a medium of beautification. The Buddha image in this style is also ornated through jewellery. The parts of image got motion through the jewellery but the emotion became secondary.

Some noteworthy images of the Early Medieval period in the Trans-Ghaghara region are:

1. Navgraha panel in sand stone housed at Gorakhpur museum. The size is 40 x 28 cm. five grahas are broken and only 4 are available. From the right side first image is of Surya with Aruni then Soma, Mangala and Buddha. Soma, Mangala and Buddha are in *abhay mudra*. All are wearing crown and *prabhamandala* is available behind head. The panel belongs to Early Medieval period. (Plate 34.14)
2. Image of Uma-Maheshwara in black stone housed at Gorakhpur Museum. The size is 62 x 37 cm. Four handed Siva is seated in *Lalitasana* and Uma is seated over left lap of Siva. Siva is wearing *jatamukuta* and *hara*. He is holding trident in one hand and two lower hands are on the breast of Uma. Uma is holding *kamala* (lotus) in her left hand. Siva's right leg is over nandi and a lion is seated below Uma. Image belongs to the Early Medieval period. (Plate 34.15)
3. Image of eight-handed Mahisamardini in sand stone housed at Kushinagar Museum. The size is 78 x 45 cm. She is wearing *mukuta*, *kundala*, *hara* and holding shield, bow and arrow, *chakra*, sword and spear. Her right leg is on the Mahisa and she is (attacking) killing Mahisa by spear. Image belongs to the Early Medieval period. (Plate 34.16)
4. Image of Jeevanta Swami in black stone housed at Kushinagar museum. The size is 34 x 16.5 cm. The head, hand and legs below knee are broken. The image is highly decorated and it has *haras* in neck, *mekhla* in waist ad *dhoti* in lower part. *Srivatsa* is available on chest. The image belongs to Pala period. (Plate 34.17)
5. Image of four handed Agni in red sand stone housed at Gorakhpur museum. Agni is in *tribhanga mudra*. He is wearing *mukut*, *kundal*, *hara*, *yagyopavita* and *dhoti*. His left upper and right lower hand is broken. He is holding *shakti* in right upper hand and *kamandalu* in left lower hand. He is shown with beard and moustache. Ram is shown behind legs. The image belongs to early medieval period. (Plate 34.18)
6. Jaina Tirthanakara in sand stone found from Khukhundu, (Deoria district) and size of image is 28 x 17 cm. seated in *dhyana mudra*. Ears are elongated, face is smiling and the eyes are half closed. *Chhatra* is available over head, on the basis of the *shankha* symbol at pedestal this image is identified with the 22nd Teerthankara Neminath. On the basis of the features this image belongs to early medieval period. (Plate 34.19)
7. Image of Vishnu in standing position found from Hoi Park at Gorakhpur in black stone. The size is 168 x 99 cm. He is wearing *mukuta*, *hara*, *dhoti* till *Jangha* portion, which is ornated and a long *vanamala*, *srivstsa* is available in the center of chest. Vishnu is four handed, both front

hands are broken and holding a *Gada* (broken) on the upper right hand. Image of *Gadadevi* is on the right of Vishnu's leg and *Chakra Purusha* on the left, *Parikara* is decorated with devotees and attendants. On the basis of the features this image belongs to Pala period. (Plate 34.20)

8. Image of Agni in schist stone seated in *lalitasana* over a lotus throne. The size is 72 x 57 cm. and it was found from Rudrapur, Deoria. Agni is wearing *mukuta, kundala, hara,* sacred thread, bangle, *dhoti* and anklet. He is holding *kamandalu* in left hand and right hand is broken. Eyes are half closed and he has beard and moustache. Flames are shown in background. A goat (Ram) is seated in front of the *asana.* The image belongs to 11th century A.D. (Plate 34.21)

9. Image of Buddha in *bhumisparsh mudra,* from Kushinagar. It is made of Black basalt. The size is about 3 mtrs in height. Buddha seated on the *kamalasana,* which is placed over a *simhasana.* Elongated ears, smiling face and half closed eyes are the other features of this image. On the *parikara* figures of male and female devotees, *vidyadharas* and on the top Bodhi tree can be seen. On the basis of the inscription found on *simhasana* it can be dated to 10-11th century A.D. (Kalchuri period). (Plate 34.22)

10. Head of Bodhisattva, with half closed eyes of fairly neat workmanship. At the base of high *jata mukutra* is a short crown with an ornate triangular piece at each side and effigy of a *dhyani* Buddha (probably Ratna Sambhava). It is found from Lumbini. (Plate 34.23)

Above description and study show that starting from the early times many traditions of art developed in this region. The subject of the art was religious on hand and folk on the other. Terracotta and stone were the main medium for the expression of these subjects. Although a center like Sarnath was not develop in the region, but art spread between Sravasti and Kushinagar, was influenced by Sarnath School of art on the one hand and by the local tradition on the other. By the influence of regionalism in early medieval period a large number of sculptures were made in Post Gupta art tradition and Pala art tradition.

Acknowledgements

The author is grateful to B.R. Mani, Additional Director General, A.S.I.; A.K. Singh of Govt. Buddhist Museum, Gorakhpur; Officials of American Institute of Indian Studies, Gurgaon and D.P. Tiwari of D.N.P. Govt. Mahila P.G. College, Deoria for guidance and help in preparing this article.

References

EI- Epigrapica Indica.
Hule. Extracts from Taranath's history of Buddhism, *Indian Antiquity*, p.102.
Majumdar, R. C. 1965. *Vedic Age*, Bombay.
Mani. B. R. 1998. Two Seasons of Archaeological investigations in Trans Ghaghara Plains (Districts Basti & Siddharthnagar U.P.) 1995-97, *Pragdhara*, 8, Lucknow.
Misra. R. N. 2002. *Bhartiya Murti Kala ka Itihas*, Delhi.
Pargiter, F. E. 1962. *Purana text on the dynasties of the Kali Age*, Varanasi.
Pathak, Vishuddhanand. 1963. *History of Kosal*, Delhi.
Pusalakar. A. D. 1951. *Traditional History From The Earliest Time To The Accession Of Parikshit.*
Raichoudhary, H. C. 1980. *Political History.*
Tewari, Diwakar Prasad. 2004. *Gorakhpur Parikshetra ka Itihas*, Deoria.

35

TRANSFORMATION OF WEST ASIAN AND GRECO-ROMAN ELEMENTS IN INDIAN ART

Vinay Kumar

The first contact of India with West Asia and Greek world must have occurred during the 6th century BC when Cyrus the Great of Persia (558-535 BC) enlarged his kingdom to include the Greek cities of Asia Minor in the west and Afghanistan and the borderland of India in the east. His successor, Darius, extended the conquest even further eastwards by annexing eastern Punjab and Sindh in 578 BC. The Persian Empire served as a common meeting ground for the Indians and Greeks as subjects of the great Persian Emperor came in touch with one another through trade and commerce as well as the administrative and military services. This contact subsequently extended to interaction on the native soil of the two countries.

Among the first Greeks to arrive in India was Alexander who descended on the flat plains of the Punjab in 326 BC. He had come to assert his domination on the provinces which had formed part of the Achaemenid Empire. His victorious progress came to an abrupt end when his soldiers mutinied and his dream of developing the Indus region as a centre of Hellenistic culture departed with him. The brief expedition of Alexander led to some interesting consequences in every sphere. One of the spheres was the sphere of art and architecture. On Indian soil, Alexander's campaign resulted in numerous Greek settlements and the cities he founded served as urban centres amidst Indian villages. These cities, with their planned layout of streets and buildings, were modeled on Greek prototype. After Alexander the Great, the accord between the Seleucid and the Chandragupta Maurya had a beneficial effect on trade between the two kingdoms. The Royal Road that Chandragupta Maurya built, linking the frontier to the capital, facilitated the rapid transport of goods. The concept of Royal Road appears to have been derived from the road of the Persian kings, whom Chandragupta Maurya seems to have emulated in many aspects.

There are many art motifs, which are West Asian and Hellenistic in origin, but they underwent great formal changes on the soil of India and too from the very beginning as if it was deliberate, pre-planned and well thought of. These foreign motifs include the floral and faunal motifs, (honeysuckle, acanthus, laurel, vine, athemion flower nymphea papyrus bud, lion motifs, atlantes, tritons, dragon, griffin, winged animal motifs *etc.*) drapery and coiffeurs (toga, trousers, tunics, helmets *etc.*), geometric motifs such as bead and reel, ovolo, architectural motifs such as pillars, gable ends, pilasters, *etc.*

The Mauryan freely borrowed the architecture of the Persian Palace complex and adopted the kingly rituals of the Persian Courts. The artisans, craftsmen and technicians that streamed into India from Greece in the wake of Alexander's invasion were commissioned to build monumental palaces of stone which reflected the strength of the empire. The pillars and capitals that Ashoka, the Great king of

Mauryan dynasty, erected at various points in his empire were also of stone and their accomplished handling betokens the hand of a foreign craftsman. Since Achaemenid art borrowed few elements from Greece, Mauryan art too indebted to Greece. More direct parallels to Greek and Hellenistic art are evident in the motif of the horse on the abacus of Sarnath pillar capital **(Plate 35.1)** and many of the ornamental motifs such as honeysuckle and acanthus.

Besides that, perhaps more Greek in inspiration is the terracotta figurines found at Pataliputra and other sites. The Hellenistic influence reveals itself in the superb handling of the female figurines- the depiction of their drapery and physique- and recalls of Tanagra. The double mould technique employed in making the heads of these figurines again points towards Greek diffusion. Dedalic style of Greek art **(Plate 35.2)** can be seen in Pataliputra terracotta or even in the Mauryan and Sungan heads of mother goddesses. The late Hellenistic style of Tanagra style of art (*i.e.* East Mediterranean School) **(Plate 35.3)** is well reflected in Amaravati, Nagarjunkonda art. In this style the figures generally of women are elongated with very great charm in the face and delicate rendering in the pose. The drapery clings to the body upto the legs in looped folds. The terracotta of Pataliputra, Bulandibagh, Sonepur and Buxar had the source of inspiration from Greek art **(Plate 35.4)**.

When we analyze Mauryan art, we find that the vision of Asoka regarding Indian art appeared to be absolutely clear from the very beginning as can be seen from his art creations. In his inscriptions he proclaims, "We shall adopt from West Asia whatever suits our cultural ethos and in forms which will be modified according to our tastes and requirements." This process is generally called 'transformation'. It was not 'influence' or 'copying' anything but it was an incorporation through conscious efforts in the historical situation of close interaction of cultures of West Asian and Indian origins to adopt all that suited the nation's ethos. This was not the case in Mauryan art only, but in the art of subsequent periods too. The concept which was not gainfully adopted was rejected. All ideas and all models were transformed and were allowed to burst forth in thousands of new flowers. This is best reflected in the 'honeysuckle' or '*Nagapushpa*' motif. This motif has been exploited in a rich manner in Indian art as compared to West Asia and the Greek world. This motif has been the source of various forms of Indian art motifs, such as the *trisula* or Trident, *Triratna* and *Srivatsa*. It is not just the depiction of any particular flower that grows in nature but gradually it combined with *Padma* which later on completely replaced this honeysuckle motif in Indian art. Thus what was just a decorative element in Greek and Persian art, found on their architectural moulding, in effect became possibly the greatest source of inspiration for such a life pulsating motif in Indian art which even its innovators in West Asia would not have dreamt. This is transformation of a foreign motif. In this lies the perception of ideas, adaptability and genius of Indian artists. The process of transformation can be visualized in the various lion motifs of Ashokan pillars **(Plate 35.5** and **35.6)**.

While all lions in West Asian Art are looking ferocious and monstrous, none of the Mauryan lions look like that. In the decorative arts the lions were used by ancient Greeks and Romans as a form of supports for the gateways of palaces or parapet walls of the fortification, but in Mauryan India they crowned the pillars of piety, *dharmastambhas* and roared the triumph of *Dhamma i.e. 'Dhammaghosakas'* all over the Mauryan empire. This was the metamorphosis of a decorative element used by West Asian Kings in their court art and a rejection of the details which don't suit Indian taste by the Indian artists. The Mauryan lions are no carbon copy of any particular West Asian or Greek Model. It is a consciously adopted process by Kings and his artists. It was not 'influence' or 'copying' anything but it was an incorporation through conscious efforts in the historical situation of close interaction of cultures of west Asian and Indian origins to adopt all that suited the nation's ethos.

Many Hellenistic elements are well reflected in various art forms of subsequent Sunga period also. Dedalic style of Greek art was gradually indianized in Sunga heads of mothergoddesses. This process is well reflected in various other art motifs also, eg. There is a progressive change in palmette motif. In former examples it is like an unpraised leaf with lenticular outline while in the latter it is an extremely charming flower bud with petals either completely closed or partially opened. So many Greek gods and goddesses were indianised on the coins of this period. Various winged animals have been indianised during this period. In Sunga art we get *ihamrgas* in the form of winged lion, beaked lions, horned lions, winged bulls, stag with fish tail, sea-monsters etc. Such fabulous figures were either found in the Greek, Persian and Assyrian art from the seventh-sixth century BC and later on they were indianised.

After the disintegration of Mauryan Empire in 184 BC, Indo-Greek exercised control over all provinces west of Khyber Pass, Gandhara, *etc.* They penetrated eastwards as far as Pataliputra. In the area of art and craft they contributed significantly in the subsequent period. The art of ancient Greece had exercised an enormous influence on the art of not only India but also on the art of many countries from ancient times particularly in the areas of sculpture and architecture. In the West, the art of the Roman Empire was largely derived from Greek models and in the East, Alexander the Great's conquests initiated several centuries of exchange between Greek, Central Asian and Indian culture, resulting in the Gandhara art what is sometimes also called Greco-Buddhist art. In philosophy the Greeks showed great penetration into the causes and nature of things. This phenomenon was also conceived in Indian art. Representations of Greek gods and other mythological figures appeared on the reverse side of the coins of Indo-Greeks. Other objects manufactured from schist and other soft stones also portrayed scenes from Greek mythology. By the beginning of the Christian era, the Sakas subdued the Indo-Greek rulers of Hindukush Mountain. They occupied Greek territories and assumed Greek manners and methods of administration. They copied Greek coins and continued the existing tradition in the arts and crafts. They accepted the architectural forms of the Greeks as well as their town planning schemes. Conspicuous in this respect is the Saka temple at Sirkap with its Greek plan, Ionic pillars and classical mouldings. Remains of the temple at Sirkap and Taxila show transformed features such as huge base-mouldings and ionic capitals of the massive porch and vestibule columns. The double headed bird atop the *chaitya* arch is an emblem of a Scythian origin which later on emerged in South India as the *ganda – bherunda* **(Plate 35.7)**.

Over a period of time the Greek influence became diluted. After the death of Gondophores the Parthian authority in India began to weaken and they passed the way for the Kushan conquest. Diplomatic relations between India and the Rome during the time of Kushans helped to create the ambience for intellectual and religious activities. The artistic impulses expressed themselves into two district schools of sculpture- Mathura and Gandhara. In Gandhara and Mathura styles of art the foreign motifs were quickly indianised. Foreign elements were introduced in Mathura and Gandhara art but they were tried to indianise all these foreign elements according to the local taste by the artists of Gandhara and Mathura school. Various mythological scenes and subjects of Hellenistic world were also indianised gradually, such as Heracles and the Namean lion and Bacchanalian scenes etc. The process of transformation can also be seen in the contemporary jewellery, costumes and other items. Several types of caps, diadem, pointed head-gears were also the contributions of the scythians, especially the crown worn by Vishnu and Surya is considered to be of Iranian origin. In Gandhara School the alien traits were gradually rejected. It is first reflected in the Buddha garment which is now less stiff, released and light. Actually the thick wooly robe suited the requirement of the cold climate of the Gandhara region but it didn't suit Mathura which is quite hot. The outlavish cloth was adopted just for a change and the wave against the foreign elements prevailed, it made its frontal attack on the drappery and it was the beginning of the process of transformation.

The Gandhara School of sculpture effloresced in the north-western regions of the Indian sub continent with Taxila and Peshawar as its chief centres. Cultural currents from the Hellenistic world and Iran intermingled with the indigenous elements to produce a syncrete style which shaped figures in stone and stucco. In the art of Gandhara, Zeus became the inseparable companion of the Buddha by assuming the form of *Vajrapani*. He wears the characteristic dress of a Graeco-Parthian attendant, namely a short *Chiton*, "caught in round the waist and provided with a scalloped turn-over edge at the top." In this form, in an example the *Bodhisattva* as a standing and emaciated ascetic is seated in *padmasana*. On the left he is flanked by Indra and Brahma. On the left side is Sujata with food and at her back is *Vajrapani.* Sujata is dressed in a Greek *Chiton* reaching the feet and a *himation*. The artistic traditions of the region drew upon the Hellenistic heritage of Bactria and the philhellenic character of Parthian art to forge a suitable idiom. In its later articulations, it relied more heavily on Greco-Roman models. Even here, the Parthian mentality intervenes; it hardens the soft voluminous folds of the drapery seen in Roman examples into schematic ridges in Gandhara art. Classical antecedents are again encountered in motifs such as acanthus leaves and Corinthian capitals. Similarly the Greek art form of animation is well transformed in the frieze of

Gandhara art. Various architectural elements such as Corinthian pillar were transformed into pseudo-Corinthian pillars in Gandhara art.

Around the middle of fifth century AD the kingdom of Kushan was devastated by the horde of white Hunas. With the destruction of the Kushan Empire, the Greco-Roman element in Indian Civilization gradually lost its outward identity as it merged and dissolved into the variegated patterns of Indian culture.

Conclusion

Thus we can see that the list of West Asian and Hellenistic elements reflected in Indian art is very long and it does not end here. With the decline of the Kushan rule the process of transformation gained a further momentum and the art products of Mathura experienced it at every stage. During this period the foreign trends imported by the scythians and Kushans were either completely rejected or transformed. The Mathura-Gupta style was refined and perfected at Sarnath. The figure now became slim and slender and the expression suggested bliss and serenity. The youthful body is now full of energy and mobility. There is an overall improvement in carving which rejects grace, charm and delicacy. Thus Gupta sculpture affected all subsequent schools of art within and beyond India and also had a significant and lasting effect on Brahmnical art.

References

1. Agarwal, V.S. 1965. *Indian Art*. Varanasi: Prithvi Prakashan.
2. Asthana, Shashi Prabha & Jha, Bhogendra. 1999. *Gandhara Sculptures of Bharat Kala Bhavan* .Varanasi: Banaras Hindu University.
3. Asthana, Shashi Prabha. 2000. *Mathura Kala*. New Delhi: National Museum.
4. Basham, A.L. 2000. *The Wonder that was India.* New Delhi: Rupa & Co. Publication.
5. Charturvedi, Sarojini. 1985. *Foreign Influx and Interaction with Indian Culture*, Delhi: Agam Kala Prakashan.
6. Coomaraswamy, A.K. 1972. *History of Indian and Indonesian Art.* New Delhi: Munshiram Manoharlal Publishers
7. Gupta, S.P. & Asthana, Shashi Prabha. 2002. *Elements of Indian Art.* New Delhi: D.K. Printworld (P) Ltd.
8. Gupta, S.P. (ed). 1985. *Kushana Sculpture from Sanghol (1st-2nd century AD), A Recent Discovery*. New Delhi: National Museum.
9. Gupta, S.P. 1982. *The Roots of Indian Art*. New Delhi: B.R. Publishing Corporation.
10. Hallade, Madeleine. 1968. *The Gandhara style and the Evolution of Buddhist Art.* London: Thames and Hudson Publication.
11. Ray, Nihar Ranjan.1965. *Maurya and Sunga Art.* Calcutta: University of Kolkata.
12. Ray, Nihar Ranjan. 1975. *Maurya and Post Maurya Art*. New Delhi: ICHR.
13. Rowland, Benjamin. 1970. *Art and Architecture of India*. London: Pelican Books.
14. Sharma, R.C. 1994.*The Splendour of Mathura Art and Museum*. New Delhi: D.K. Printworld (P) Ltd.
15. Sivaramamurti, C .1974. *The Art of India*. New York: Abrams Publishes.
16. Taddei, Maurizio. 1978. *Monuments of Civilization (India),* New York: Grosset and Dunlop Publication.
17. Tomory, Edith. 2000. *A History of Fine Arts in Indian and the West*. Chennai: Orient Longman Publication.
18. Zimmer, H. 1960. *The Art of Indian Asia: Its Mythology and Transformation.* New York: Pantheon Publication.

36

खम्भात में अर्द्धकीमती पत्थर के मनके बनाने की पारम्परिक तकनीक

राजेश कुमार मीणा

प्रस्तावना

खम्भात के एक प्रमुख काश्तकार अनवर हुसैन के अनुसार उनका परिवार पिछले 200 वर्षों से मनके बना रहा है। ये लोग अर्द्धकीमती पत्थरों से विभिन्न आकार–प्रकार वाले मोती (मनके), कटोरे, मूर्तियां एवं सजावट की वस्तुएं बनाते रहे हैं। मैने खम्भात में मनके बनाने की तकनीक को समझने के लिए कानमेर पुरास्थल (गुजरात) के उत्खनन सत्र 2007–08 के दौरान खम्भात में मनकों की निर्माण तकनीक का अध्ययन किया।

मनकों के निर्माण एवं दूसरी अन्य वस्तुओं के उत्पादन के लिए अनवर एवं उसके पिता इनायत हुसैन को राष्ट्रीय पुरस्कार भी मिल चुका है। अनवर विभिन्न प्रकार के अर्द्धकीमती पत्थर यथा– ब्लड–स्टोन, रोज क्वार्ट्ज, फोसिल–स्टोन, मॉस अगेट, जैस्पर, चर्ट, हरा एवं सफेद स्ट्रेट अगेट, पीला अगेट, बैन्डेड अगेट, फेन्सी अगेट और अमेथिस्ट का प्रयोग मनकों के लिए करते हैं। अर्द्धकीमती पत्थरों का कच्चा माल औरंगाबाद, रतनपुर (मुख्यतः अगेट एवं कार्नेलियन) एवं मध्यप्रदेश से आयात किया जाता है। कच्चे माल की कीमत अर्द्धकीमती पत्थर पर निर्भर होती है।

कच्चे माल की कीमत (अनुमानित)

कार्नेलियनः 45 किलोग्राम 2500 रु, रतनपुर अगेटः 45 किलोग्राम 1500–2500 रु, दूसरे अन्य अगेट : 15 से 20 रु प्रति किलोग्राम, रोज क्वार्ट्जः 80–90 रु प्रति किलोग्राम, दूसरे अन्य अर्द्धकीमती पत्थरों की कीमत 4–6 रु प्रति किलोग्राम।

मनके बनाने के लिए विभिन्न चरण

अगेट व कार्नेलियन के मनकों के निर्माण के विभिन्न चरणों को रेखा चित्र संख्या 1 में दर्शाया गया है।

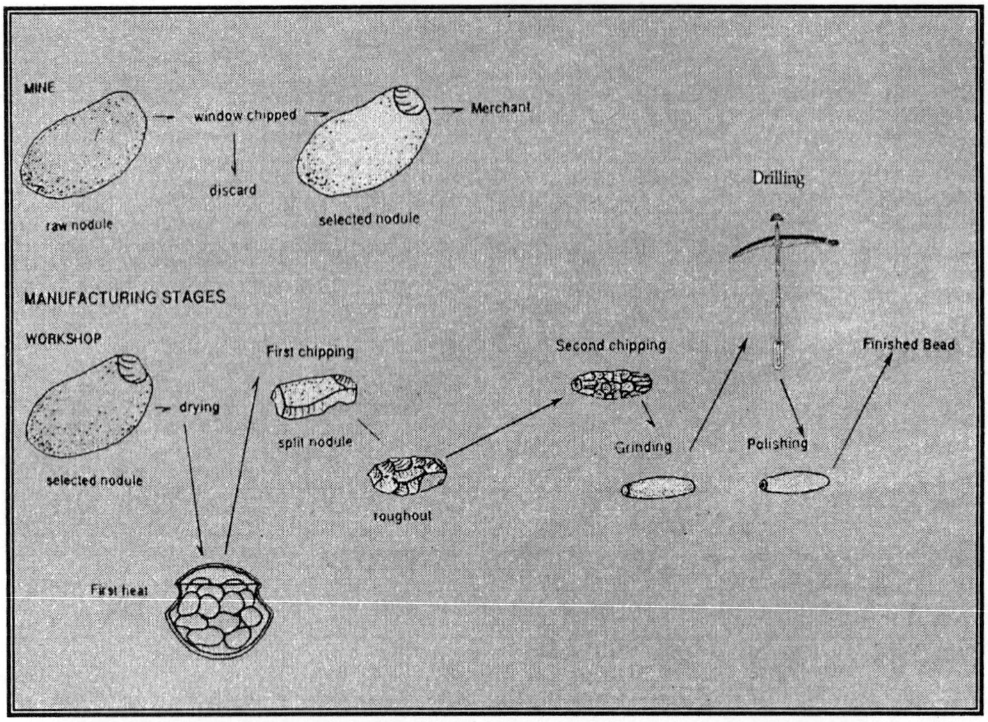

रेखाचित्र 1 : अगेट के मनके निर्माण के विभिन्न चरण (केनोयर के आधार पर)

प्रथम चरण – सुखाना

अर्द्धकीमती पत्थरों को खदान से निकाला जाता है उसके बाद उनको एक किनारे से तोड़कर गुणवत्ता की जांच की जाती है। अच्छी गुणवत्ता वाले पत्थरों की नमी को कम करने के लिए मार्च की शुरुआत में तीन महीनों तक लिए धूप में सुखाया जाता है। कुछ लोग इन्हें घरों की छतों पर व घर के बाहर सुखाते हैं (फलक 36.1)।

द्वितीय चरण – गर्म करना

अर्द्धकीमती पत्थरों के टुकडों को सूर्य की रोशनी में सुखाने के बाद इनको मिट्टी के छोटे घड़ों में भरकर साधारण गड़ढेनुमा भट्टी में गर्म करके इनकी कठोरता को कम किया जाता है, जिससे टुकड़ों को तोड़ने एवं छिलके निकालने में भी आसानी रहती है। गर्म करने के लिए चावल भूसी का प्रयोग किया जाता है। इससे करीब 100 से 200 डिग्री तक तापमान मिल जाता है। मनकों की बड़ी कार्यशाला में स्थायी रूप से भट्टी का ढाँचा बनाया जाता है जबकि छोटी कार्यशालाओं में प्राथमिक रूप से यह भट्टी ईंटों तथा अनगढ़ पत्थर के टुकड़ों से बनाई जाती है (फलक 36.2)।

तृतीय चरण– प्रथम चिपिंग

अगेट के टुकड़ों को गर्म करने के बाद तराशने के लिए तैयार किया जाता है। बड़े टुकड़ों को तोड़ने के लिए लकड़ी के हथौड़े का प्रयोग करते हैं (फ़लक 36.3)। यह हथौड़ा रायन (यह एक गुजराती पौधा है, इसकी लकड़ी बहुत ही कम भार की होती है) के पेड़ की लकड़ी से बना होता है, जिसका गुजराती नाम *अलुश्रिन* है।

प्रथम चिपिंग के लिए लोहे की पतली नोंक वाली करीब एक मीटर लम्बी छड़ को 45 डिग्री के कोण पर जमीन में गाड़ देते हैं (फलक 36.4)।

उसके उपरान्त हथौड़े का चुनाव (टुकड़ों के आकार तथा कच्चे माल के आधार पर) किया जाता है। हथौड़े की लम्बाई 3 से 5 सेमी. तथा इसकी मोटाई 2 से 2.50 सेमी. हौती है। इसे 1.05 सेमी. मोटी एवं 24 सेमी. लम्बी बाँस की छड़ी में जोड़ा जाता है (फलक 36.5) और छड़ी को पकड़ने में सीधे हाथ के अँगूठे तथा पहली दो अँगुलियों की महत्त्वपूर्ण भूमिका रहती है। यह हथौड़ा भैंसे के सींग से बना होता है। टुकड़ों को छड़ के नुकीले सिरे पर रखकर हथौड़े से प्रहार किया जाता है।

दक्षिणी एशिया में औजार बनाने के लिए इस पद्धति को अप्रत्यक्ष–आघात तकनीक कहा जाता है[1]। इस तकनीक का विकास प्रागैतिहासिक काल में मनुष्य ने पत्थर के औजार बनाने में किया था। हड़प्पा काल में जब मनुष्य लोहे से परिचित नहीं था, तब बारहसिंगा के सींग एवं बाद में तांबे का उपयोग किया था[2]। चिपिंग करने पर हथौड़े के प्रहार से आयताकार टुकड़े निकलते हैं (फलक 36.6)। पत्थर को हमेशा लम्बे आकार में तोड़ा जाता है। मनके का अच्छा कारीगर चिपिंग करते समय पत्थर के दोनों किनारों को नहीं तोड़ता है। इस आकार वाले लम्बे मनकों को चिपिंग करने में लगभग 30 मिनट का समय लगता है। चिपिंग का समय भिन्न–भिन्न आकार के मनके पर निर्भर करता है।

चतुर्थ चरण – द्वितीय चिपिंग

द्वितीय चिपिंग के लिए पहली छड़ के स्थान पर दूसरी अन्य छड़ें उपयोग में ली जाती हैं। यह छड़ पहले की अपेक्षा अधिक तीखी व नुकीली होती हैं तथा इस कार्य में छोटे हथौड़े का प्रयोग करते हैं। हथौड़े की लम्बाई 5 से 6 सेमी. एवं मोटाई लगभग 3 से 4 सेमी. होती है। इसे करीब 1 सेमी. मोटाई वाली एवं 24 सेमी. लम्बाई की बाँस की छड़ी से जोड़ा जाता है (रेखाचित्र 2)। द्वितीय चिपिंग में रफ ऑउट से छोटे–छोटे टुकड़े निकलने लगते हैं (फलक 36.7)। चिपिंग की पहली एवं द्वितीय तकनीक में एक हाथ से पत्थर को पकड़ते हैं तथा दूसरे हाथ से हथौड़े का प्रहार किया जाता है। साथ–साथ पत्थर को चारों ओर से घुमाते भी रहते हैं ताकि मनके का आकार समान रहे। द्वितीय चिपिंग में करीब 10 मिनट का समय लगता है, शेष बचे टुकड़ों को इकट्ठा कर लिया जाता है तथा इनसे छोटे आकार के मनके बनाये जाते हैं। छोटे मनके बनाने का कार्य घर की महिलाएं करती हैं। इनकी चिपिंग लोहे के करीब 1 से 1.50 सेमी. मोटाई एवं 2 से 3 सेमी. लम्बाई के हथौड़े द्वारा की जाती है।

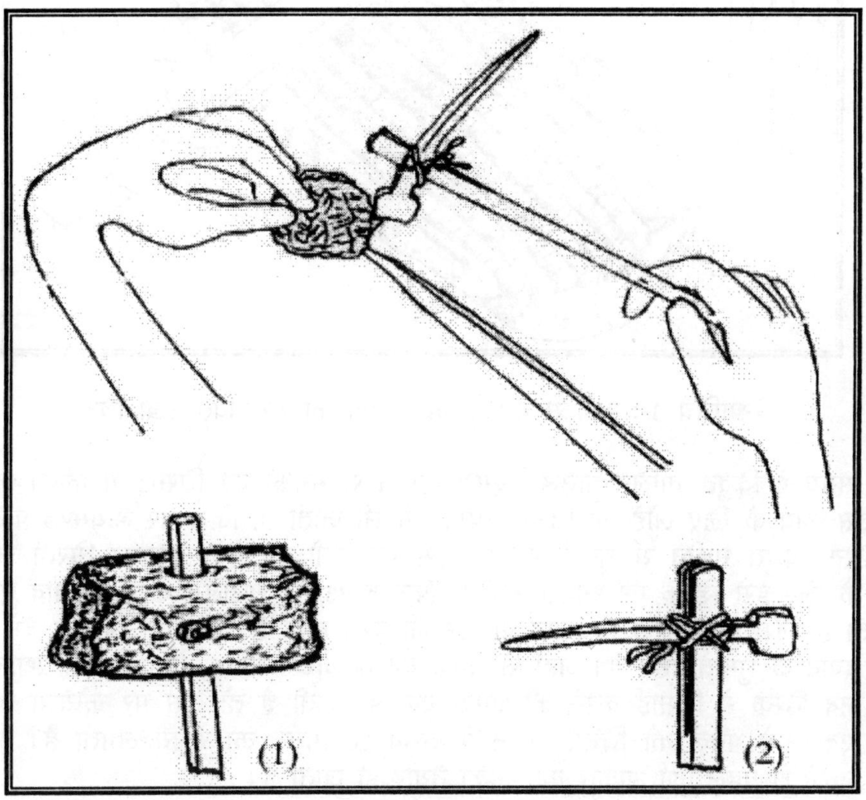

रेखाचित्र 2 : मनकों में चिपिंग का रेखा चित्र

पंचम चरण– घिसाई

विद्युत चालित पाउडर्ड एमरी व्हील्स से परिचित होने से पहले अनवर तराशे हुए मनकों की घिसाई एवं राउंडिंग कठोर बलुआ पत्थर और क्वार्टजाईट के बड़े पत्थरों से करता था। इस प्रक्रिया में बलुआपत्थर या क्वार्टजाईट के बड़े एवं चौकोर पत्थरों का प्रयोग किया जाता था। सर्वप्रथम अर्द्धतराशे मनकों से पत्थर में गहरी रेखाएं बनाने की

कोशिश की जाती थी, इसके लिए पानी की सहायता ली जाती थी। जब रेखाओं का आकार गहरा एवं चौड़ा हो जाता था तो इस पत्थर (ग्राइन्डर्स) पर एक या दो व्यक्ति आसानी से मनकों की घिसाई कर सकते थे। ग्राइन्डर्स का आकार मनकों के आकार पर निर्भर होता था। इस तरह के ग्राइन्डर्स में कई बार मनके टूट भी जाते हैं।

सम्भवतः प्राचीन समय में मुख्य रूप से ग्रूव बने हुए पत्थर छोटे गोल आकार के मनकों को घिसने के उपयोग में लिये जाते होंगे। मनके को लकड़ी के दो टुकड़ो में कसकर बाँधा जाता होगा एवं दोनों हाथों से लकड़ी को पकड़कर मनके की घिसाई की जाती होगी हालाँकि इस तकनीक से समय की खपत काफी होती होगी (रेखा चित्र 3)।

एक बड़े बाइकोनिकल आकार के मनके को ग्राइन्ड करने में लगभग तीन से चार घंटे का समय लगता होगा।

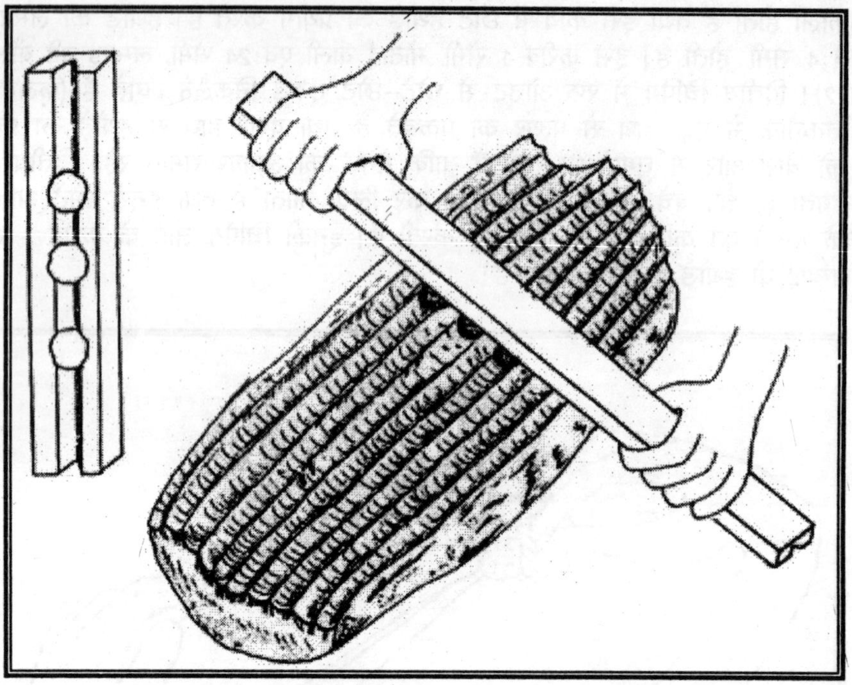

रेखाचित्र 3 : हाथ से मनकों की घिसाई का सम्भावित रेखा चित्र

वर्तमान समय में विद्युत चालित पाउडर्ड एमरी व्हील्स से मनकों की घिसाई में काफी कम समय लगता है (फलक 36.8)। इस कार्य के लिए लोहे की डिस्क उपयोग में ली जाती है, जिस पर डायमण्ड पाउडर की परत चढ़ी होती है। यह डिस्क विद्युत मशीन से घूमती है तथा इस पर पानी की बूँदे लगातार गिरती रहती हैं। मनके को गोलाकार बनाने के लिए इसे डिस्क पर रगड़ते रहते हैं (फलक 36.9)। राउंडिंग करने के बाद एक अन्य डिस्क का प्रयोग किया जाता है जिस पर अधिक डायमण्ड पाउड़र की परत होती है। अब पूर्ण आकार देने के लिए मनके को डिस्क पर बिना दबाव के घुमाते रहते हैं। जहाँ से मनके का आकार बदलना होता है उस स्थान पर अधिक दबाव दिया जाता है। जब डिस्क में घिसाई करने की क्षमता कम हो जाती है तो उस पर कोयला तथा ईंट का टुकड़ा घिसा जाता है। एक लम्बे मनके को घिसाई करने में करीब 20 मिनट का समय लगता है। इस प्रक्रिया के बाद छिद्र एवं पॉलिश करने से पहले पूर्ण आकार का मनका तैयार हो जाता है।

छठा चरण – पॉलिशिंग

अनवर के अनुसार पहले मानव द्वारा हाथ से चालित मशीन से पॉलिश की जाती थी। इसके लिए आम की लकड़ी की डिस्क का प्रयोग किया जाता था। इस तकनीक में एक हाथ से पहिये को घुमाया करते थे तथा दूसरे हाथ से मनके की पॉलिश की जाती थी (रेखाचित्र 4)। पूर्ण पॉलिश करने के लिए डिस्क पर फाइन चेल्सिडोनी पाउडर या *वारी* (पत्थर का पाउड़र) लगाते थे। इस तकनीक के माध्यम से एक लम्बे आकार के मनके को पॉलिश करने में लगभग तीन से चार घंटे का समय लगता था।

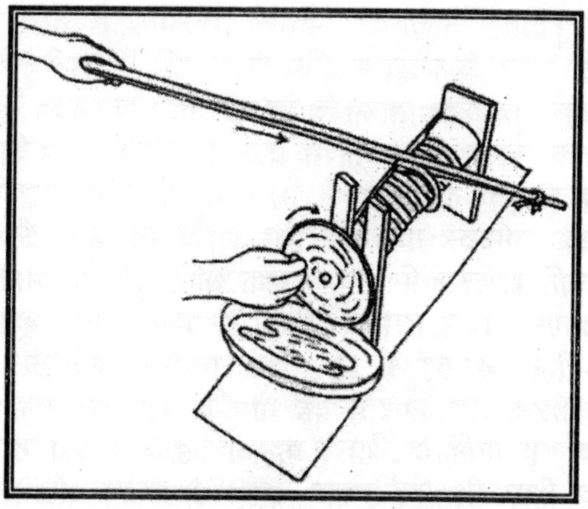

रेखाचित्र 4 : मनकों की हाथ से पॉलिश प्रक्रिया का सम्भावित रेखाचित्र

खम्भात में करीब पचास वर्ष पहले भी पॉलिश की अलग ही तकनीक थी। इस तकनीक में एक चमड़े के थैले के अंदर अब्रेसिव पाउडर एवं मनके भरकर जमीन पर रगड़ते थे। इससे एक साथ 100 मनकों की पॉलिश की जा सकती थी। इस पद्धति से पॉलिश करने में करीब पन्द्रह दिन का समय लगता था हालाँकि इस तकनीक से एक साथ सैकड़ों मनकों को पॉलिश किया जा सकता था किन्तु मनकों में चमक का अभाव नजर आता था।

इस तरह की तकनीक का प्रमाण खम्भात से 6 किमी. की दूरी पर नगर (तीसरी सदी ई.पू.) नामक पुरास्थल के उत्खनन से प्राप्त हुआ है[3]। अनवर वर्तमान में विद्युत चालित मशीन द्वारा पॉलिश की प्रक्रिया को अंजाम देता है। इस कार्य में बफ्फ की परत चढ़ी हुई डिस्क का उपयोग करते हैं तथा उसके समीप ही एक कटोरे में वारी पाउडर (सम्भवतया पत्थर का पेस्ट) भरा होता है। यह डिस्क तीव्र गति से घूमता है एवं उस पर पानी की बूँदे लगातार गिरती रहती हैं (फलक 36.10)। डिस्क पर वारी पाउडर लगाकर पॉलिश की जाती है। अधिक चमक के लिए हरे रंग का एवं कम चमक के लिए गुलाबी एवं सफेद वारी पाउडर का उपयोग किया जाता है। इस प्रक्रिया में लम्बे आकार (15 सेमी.) के मनके को पॉलिश करने में करीब 30 मिनट का समय लगता है।

वर्तमान में कई मनका बनाने वाले कारीगर लकड़ी की ढोलकनुमा वस्तु बनाकर उसे विद्युत मशीन से जोड़ देते हैं। इसमें मनकों के साथ एमरी पाउड़र तथा पानी डाल दिया जाता है। इस ढोलकनुमा वस्तु को 12 घंटे तक विद्युत मशीन के द्वारा घुमाया जाता है। इस तकनीक से करीब 1000 छोटे आकार के मनकों की पॉलिश की जा सकती है। घिसाई के बाद छिद्र एवं पॉलिश करने से पूर्व वांछित आकार का मनका तैयार हो जाता है। खम्भात में पहले मनकों में छिद्र किये जाते हैं उसके उपरान्त इनकी पॉलिश की जाती है। अनवर पहले मनकों में पॉलिश करता है बाद में मनकों में छिद्र किये जाते हैं।

सम्भवतया प्राचीन समय में घिसाई करने के लिए मनकों को चमड़े से बनी ढोलकनुमा वस्तु में डालकर इसे रस्सी के माध्यम से घुमाया जाता होगा (रेखाचित्र 5)।

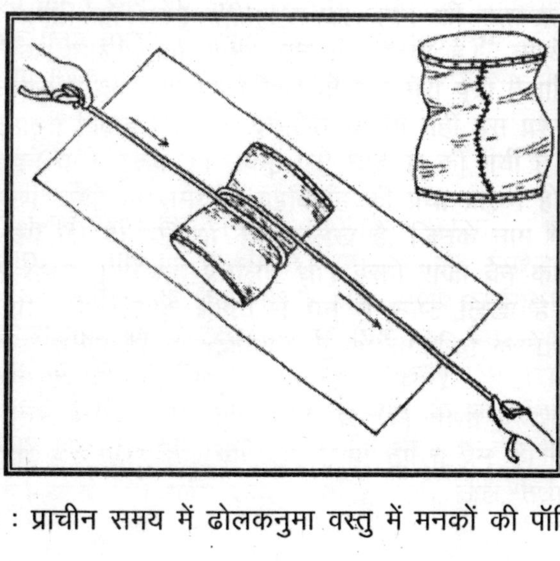

रेखाचित्र 5 : प्राचीन समय में ढोलकनुमा वस्तु में मनकों की पॉलिश प्रक्रिया

सातवां चरण– छिद्रण

मनकों में छिद्र करने वाले अधिकांश लोग खम्भात के नजदीक गाँवों में अपने खेतों के नजदीक रहते हैं। ये लोग मनकों में छिद्र करने के साथ–साथ कृषि कार्य भी करते हैं। अगले दिन हम अनवर के साथ खम्भात से 8 किमी. दूर नगर गाँव में गये। यहाँ के एक निवासी ने खेतों में अपना मकान बना रखा था। इसको स्थानीय लोग कोटेश्वर महादेव के नाम से जानते थे। मनकों में छिद्र करने वाले इस व्यक्ति का नाम प्रताप भाई था।

उसके अनुसार इस तकनीक में शुरुआत से अब तक कोई बदलाव नहीं आया है। प्रताप भाई सबसे पहले मनके को लकड़ी के शिकंजे में डालता है। इस शिकंजे का निचला सिरा बबूल तथा क्लैम्प्स का हिस्सा नीम की लकड़ी का बना होता है। छिद्र के लिए बॉ (धनुष) ड्रिल का उपयोग करते हैं, बॉ (धनुष) के लिए बाँस का प्रयोग होता है, जिस लकड़ी या हत्थे में छिद्रक लगे होते हैं वह नीम या सागवान का बना होता है। छोटे कपनुमा औजार से छिद्रक के हत्थे पर दबाव डालते हैं (रेखाचित्र 6) (फलक 36.11)। कप के लिए नारियल के कठोर खोल का उपयोग होता है। छिद्रक बनाने के लिए छाते में लगाने वाली लोहे की पतली छड़ को नुकीला बना कर उपयोग करते हैं। एक छिद्रक में दूसरे छिद्रक के नुकीले सिरे पर छोटा सा छिद्र करके उसमें बहुत छोटा डायमण्ड का टुकड़ा लगाया जाता है। छिद्र करने में दो प्रकार के डायमण्ड टिप्ड ड्रिल उपयोग में लिए जाते हैं। छोटे मनकों के लिए एक डायमण्ड वाले छिद्रक का उपयोग करते हैं जिसका आकार एक सेमी. होता है। इससे मनके में छिद्र करने में करीब 3 से 5 मिनट लगते हैं।

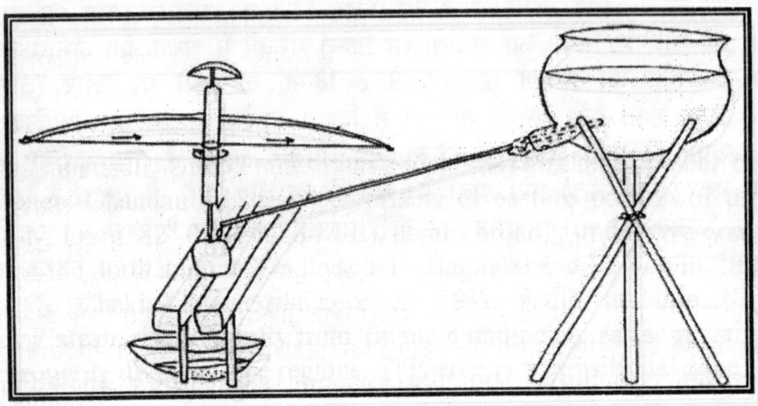

रेखाचित्र 6 : मनकों में छिद्रण प्रक्रिया का रेखा चित्र

लम्बे आकार के मनकों के लिए तीन विभिन्न प्रकार के छिद्रकों का उपयोग करते हैं जिनका व्यास प्रत्येक समय बढ़ता है और छिद्र करने में लगभग 45 मिनट से एक घंटा तक लग जाता है। छिद्रक को ठंडा रखने के लिए एक छोटा घड़ा लटकाया जाता है या इसे जमीन पर स्टैण्ड़ के ऊपर भी रखा जाता है एवं उस पर धागा लपेटा जाता है। यह पानी धागे से होकर तार के अंतिम सिरे तक पहुँचकर मनके पर बूँदों के रूप में गिरता है जहाँ पर यह छिद्रक घूमता है। लकड़ी के नीचे एक कटोरा रखा जाता है, उसमें पानी तथा अगेट पाउड़र (वारी) इकट्ठा हो जाता है (फलक 36.12)। प्रताप भाई द्वारा इस वारी पाउड़र को पॉलिश करने वाले को बेच दिया जाता है।

आठवां व अंतिम चरण – अंतिम तपाना

मनकों में पॉलिश तथा छिद्र करने के पश्चात् कार्नेलियन के मनके को (गहरे लाल एवं नारंगी) बनाने के लिए इनको गर्म किया जाता है। मनकों के कारीगर अधिकांशतया इस प्रक्रिया को शाम के समय शुरू करते हैं। अनवर ने सायं 5 बजे मनकों को गर्म करने की प्रक्रिया प्रारम्भ की। सबसे पहले उसने बिना गर्म किये अगेट के बैन्डेड एवं नॉन बैन्डेड मनकों को इकट्ठा किया। उसके बाद ईंटों से एक छोटे चौकोर आकार की भट्टी बनाई गई। इसके मध्य भाग में एक छोटे आकार का घड़ा रखा (फलक 36.13)। इस घड़े से भट्टी के अंदर के भाग की दूरी समान रहे, इसके लिए तिनके से बर्तन के चारों ओर की नाप ली गई। ताकि जब भट्टी में ईंधन डालें तो वह चारों तरफ समान मात्रा में तापमान दे सके। उसके पश्चात् बर्तन को आधा चावल की भूसी की राख से भर दिया। यह राख प्रथम हिटिंग में उपयोग किये गये ईंधन की थी।

इसके उपरान्त बर्तन में मनके रखकर ऊपर से राख द्वारा बर्तन को पूरा भर दिया (फलक 36.14)। बर्तन के अंदर भरी गई राख तापमान पर नियंत्रण रखती है। बर्तन को पूरा भरने के बाद भट्टी को ऊपर तक लकड़ी के बुरादे से भर दिया (लकड़ी का बुरादा विभिन्न लकड़ियों का होता है) (फलक 36.14)।

लकड़ी के बुरादे के ऊपर लकड़ी के टुकड़े, बाँस के टुकड़े एवं कण्डे आदि से आग जलाई जाती है। जब आग जलकर बुझ जाती है और उसमें धुंआ उठने लगता है तो इसे लोहे के पतले ढ़क्कन से ढ़क कर रात भर छोड़ दिया जाता है (फलक 36.15)।

अगले दिन सुबह छोटे घड़े को भट्टी से बाहर निकाला गया। अब तक लकड़ी का बुरादा पूर्ण रूप से राख में परिवर्तित हो चुका था। अभी भी भट्टी से धुंआ उठ रहा था। छोटे घड़े को भट्टी से बाहर निकाल कर करीब एक घंटे के लिए ठंड़ा होने को छोड़ दिया गया (फलक 36.16)।

छोटे घड़े को खाली करने के बाद देखा गया कि कुछ मनकों का रंग गहरा लाल हो गया है एवं कुछ मनकों के रंग में किसी प्रकार का अन्तर नहीं आया (फलक 36.17)। इनका अलग रंग भट्टी में पहुँचे तापमान पर निर्भर करता है। इनमें से कुछ मनके उचित तापमान के अभाव में टूट गये थे। इसलिए मनकों को गर्म करते समय तापमान पर अधिक ध्यान दिया जाता है।

निष्कर्ष

इस प्रक्रिया से कार्नेलियन के मनके बनाये जाते हैं। इनको बनाने में करीब 12 घंटे तक लगते हैं। पूर्ण आकार में बने मनके देश के विभिन्न शहरों एवं देश के बाहर भी भेजे जाते हैं।

एक लम्बे आकार के मनके को बनाने में खर्च :–

प्रथम चिपिंग	:	7 रु प्रति मनका
द्वितीय चिपिंग	:	7 रु प्रति मनका
घिसाई और राउन्डिंग	:	10 रु प्रति मनका
पॉलिशिंग	:	15 रु प्रति मनका
छिद्रण	:	15 रु. प्रति मनका (छोटे मनके), 30 रु प्रति (लम्बे मनके)

एक मनके को बनाने का कुल खर्च लगभग 59 रुपये से 74 रुपये तक होता है, लेकिन यह मनके के आकार एवं कच्चे माल पर निर्भर करता है। लम्बे आकार का मनका 135 से 140 रु प्रति नग तक बेचा जाता है।

संदर्भ

1. केनोयर, जे.एम., दी इण्डस बीड इण्डस्ट्रीः कोन्ट्रीब्यूशन टू बीड टेक्नालॉजी, *ऑरनामेंट* 10(1), 1986, पृष्ठ 18–23.
2. केनोयर, जे.एम., *शेल वर्किंग इण्डस्ट्रीज ऑफ दी इण्डस सिविलाईजेशनः एन आर्कियोलॉजिकल एण्ड इथनोग्राफिक परस्पेक्टिव,* पीएच.डी डिजरटेशन यूनिवर्सिटी ऑफ केलिफोर्निया एट बरकलै, 1983; क्लार्क, जे.ओ., वाई चेन्ज. एन एक्जाम्पल ऑफ दी टेक्नालॉजी फॉम इन्डिया एन्ड्यूरिंग पास्ट, *संस्कृत मेमारियल वोल्यूम, डेकन कॉलेज बुलेटिन 49,* 1990, पृष्ठ 83–98.
3. मेहता, आर.एन. ऐण्ड आर.डी. शाह, *एक्सकेवेशन एट नगर,* बडोदराः महाराजा सयाजीराव यूनिवर्सिटी, 1968.

37

NEWLY DISCOVERED PAINTED ROCK SHELTERS OF CHANDAULI DISTRICT, UTTAR PRADESH

Prabhakar Upadhyay, Om Prakash Kumar

Explorations in districts Chandauli, Uttar Pradesh have yielded a sizeable number of rock paintings of great historical significance. Chandauli district, comprising of eastern portion of old Varanasi district (Lat. 24^0 42'' - 23^0 32'' N; Long. 82^0 00^0 - 83^0 34'' E), comes broadly under two geographical regions – the Middle Ganga Plain in the north and the Vindhyachal – Baghelkhand Region in the south. The former, represented by part of the Chakia-Chunar plain, covers 70% of the total area. The second region, represented by Mirzapur Plateau, rises abruptly from the plain and occupies the remaining 30% area. The contour line of 91.44 m roughly divides these regions. This area is a transitional zone between the Ganga Plain and the peninsular upland.

The plateau area mainly consisting of quartzite and sandstones of different kinds rises abruptly from the plains and forms up to 60 m high escarpments. Numerous detached hillocks are seen in the foothill area. The plateau area with several rock shelters in hillocks has a northerly slope meeting with the escarpments forming zigzag line. A number of seasonal streams flowing down the escarpments to the plains have carved out the gorge like valleys and waterfalls in the plateau region.

The present paper is focused on the painted rock shelters brought to light in course of explorations conducted by us in southeastern parts of Chandauli district, Uttar Pradesh and adjacent parts of Kaimur district, Bihar. A good number of sites could be located by us in district Chandauli (U.P.) and adjacent parts of the hill ranges running into Bihar. There are important rock art sites located in villages like Arjikalan, Nasopur, Kaurihar Khas, Ghurahupur, Tala, Tenui, etc. in Chandauli district. The hills extending in the adjacent parts in Bihar reveal similar sites at Diha, Basaha, Kharauli, Patesar and Ratanpurva in Kaimur district, Bihar (See Plate 37.1). The paintings executed in the rock shelters show superimpositions attempted by the artists right up to the historical period as clearly evinced by the subject matter of the paintings. The important rock shelter sites and the painted scenes are briefly discussed below.

1. Arjikalan : The site of Arjikalan (25^0 00' 51" N; 83^0 18' 22" E) is located on Kapisha hill, nine km. east of Chakia town. A *nallah* known as Karatnala flows to the right of the site. During rainy season this nallah gets filled up and flows into River Karamnasa. Two rock shelters and a cave with prehistoric rock painting have been located there. In this rock shelter several paintings pertaining to different cultural periods have been executed. The rock painting- 1 appears to be of Mesolithic period depiction with of a buffalo comparable to one painted at Adamgarh (Wakankar and Brooks 1976: 96). Rock painting - 2 has a solitary human form painted in it. This type of depiction has been generally assigned to Neolithic-Chalcolithic period (Dubey 2007:1-21). The third rock painting at Arjikalan bears painting of couple of goats/sheep. Humped bull, wheeled cart etc. painted in ochre shows a stage of cattle and plant rearing as well as transportation of goods with the help of wheeled carts (Neumayer 1992: 215-241).

2. Kaurihar Khas : This place (25^0 00' 25" N; 83^0 15' 17" E) is located 5 km from Chakia bazaar and about 2 km in the east from Latif Shah where a dam is constructed on River Karamnasa. The height of rock shelter on Kapisha hills in Kaimur ranges is 110 ft. It is a pretty extensive rock shelter containing complex designs like intricate patterns and mythical animal figures (Plate 37.2). Five rock paintings have been noted at Kaurihar Khas.

In rock painting -1 animals like giraffe and elephant have been depicted. Such figures have been assigned to Mesolithic period on the basis of similar paintings found at Chiklod, district Raisen, Madhya Pradesh (Neumayer 1992: 215-241, fig 5 A).

In rock painting- 2 horned bull with prominent hump, cattle, deer etc. are depicted. On stylistic ground, similar paintings have been placed in Chalcolithic period by Wakankar (2005: 190-191).

The next Rock painting shows a herd of goats (?) being hunted by a human figure which is depicted quite prominently. This is superimposed by an anthropomorphic figure and a pack of dogs that is painted with ochre.

Another scene belongs to a solitary deer painted in solid colour. It is comparable with a similar depiction at Mandi in district Mandsaur in Madhya Pradesh which has been placed in Chalcolithic period by Wakankar (2005: 335-337).

Some mythical animals (?) and herds of deers decorated with wavy lines are painted nearby. Reptiles like lizard painted with criss-cross lines and herds of deer and monkeys are painted with ochre. Human- like figures with bow and arrow are also shown along with animals. An animal is shown with arrow struck in its body indicating hunting being pursued.

The scene on the extensive surface of the hill at Kaurihar Khas in district Chandauli is almost panoramic (Plate 37.2). If we pay attention to the scenes painted by the artist, we find reproduction of common activities in which people were engaged.

3. Ghurahupur : Ghurahupur village (25^0 00' 51" N; 83^0 19' 21"E) is a situated 11 km east of Chakia bazaar on border of Uttar Pradesh - Bihar in Kapisha hills of Kaimur hill range close to Karat Nala near Arjikalan. The rock shelter is located at about 155 ft height in village Ghurahupur in a rock shelter locally known as Baba ki Layan (Plate 37.3). It is of great archaeological importance because the rock shelter yields archaeological material like potsherds, a Buddha figure (?) along with paintings and inscriptions. One may identify a group of seven rock shelters there which are briefly described below:

Rock shelter-1 has the earliest depiction of a pregnant cow. It is typically a portrayal of agricultural society. Depiction of the pregnant animals in the rock shelter provides a glimpse into cattle rearing and its significance to early societies.

The next painting has been done in two stages. In the supposedly earlier stage, the depictions are done in silhouette style. On the contrary, the paintings done in the succeeding stage are linear in nature. Single lines are used to draw forms of animals. It contains long horned bulls, goats being herded by a human forms, masked figures, and monkeys. Depiction of boat here is interesting indeed.

We come across depictions both in silhouette as well as in outline with single lines. There are depictions of human beings carrying loads on their heads hunters as well as deer with arrow stuck in the body. It is comparable to Neolithic paintings in Bhutahia rock shelters in district Mirzapur assigned to the Neolithic period by Tewari (1992: 285-303).

Nearby, there is a painting showing banyan tree and an archer that appears to be a superimposition belonging to a relatively later period.

The stone appears earlier in time scale to shows two sets of depictions. In the first one there are intricate designs as generally assigned by scholars to Stone Age, especially to the Upper Palaeolithic and Mesolithic periods. Such depictions have been described as Pre-figurative or non-iconic symbolic motifs

(Sonawane 2008: 1-13). The second set of paintings is comparable to picture of rhinoceros, the like of which have been seen at Ghormangar in district Mirzapur,(U.P) which were discovered by J. Cockburn (Wakankar 2005: 45-46 and 282-293).

These Prehistoric scenes mention above have been superimposed by depictions of bulls, or cattle and other animals with ropes around their necks. A human figure seated on a lion appears to be much later. Another set of paintings belonging to Kohbar style is assignable to Chalcolithic period (Wakankar 2005: 309-310). There are depictions in it which are very conspicuous in style showing panthers, bulls, rabbits and even anthropomorphic figures. This has been superimposed by picture of an owl painted in two colours using white pigment and ochre. While the entire body has been painted with ochre; the eyes have been painted white. In view of Wakankar this style pertains to historical period (Wakankar 2005: 282-333). Noteworthy here are carvings of male and female forms. In this rock shelter certain tools of sandstone presumably Prehistoric in nature have been unearthed from a 10 cm deep deposit.

An interesting feature of this rock shelter is shallow steps cut into the rock near the front which is the approach to the Rock shelter 3. This shelter contains three sets of paintings. In the first set there are depictions of animals like cattle and sheep many appear to be pregnant. This suggests a stage of domestication of animals. Such depictions of domesticated animals and agricultural activities naturally belong to the Neolithic or Chalcolithic stage. This similar assumption is also has been made by Neumayer (1992: 215-247).

In the scene next to it there are two human forms painted in ochre colour. Stylistically, these depictions compare well with similar paintings found at Mirzapur and also with a few sites in M.P. like Singanpur, Mandi, Narsinghgarh and Kanwal respectively which are placed in Chalcolithic period by Wakankar (2005: 358-383).

The last set of paintings in rock shelter- 2 is done at two stages. The earlier ones depict birds, a reptile with thick tail, panther and a seat (throne?). The next series shows depiction of a seated Buddha having a halo. Noteworthy is the treatment of eyes that have been painted with white in these paintings.

Rock shelter- 3 at the approach of this rock shelter bears foot- prints engraved in the rock; locally it is revered as these are believed to be belonging to Lord Buddha who is painted in the rock shelter. There are also cupule marks along with these carvings of the footprints.

In Rock shelter 4 we find two sets of paintings in double outline. In the first one, there is a humped bull with prominent horns (Plate 37.4). It is painted with ochre in silhouette form. The next painting is that of Buddha in *Dharmachakrapravartan mudra* and also that of a dancing lady, nearby. The Buddha figure has a (*Chhatra*) three- tiered canopy above the head (Plate 37.5). There are inscriptions written with red ochre in Prakrit language above of the figure. There is a bench like structure in front of this painting. Interestingly, it has been polished that imparts it a shining smooth surface. This appears to be a place of worship used by monks who must have frequented the shelter. But obviously it belongs to a much later period. Potsherds have been collected from the floor of the rock shelter-5.

At the rock shelter at Ghurahupur, though no regular excavation has taken place but potsherds belonging to different periods have been collected from the upper layers of the rock shelter. This is a definite proof of the occupation of the shelter by a community which stayed and cooked meals there. On the stylistic ground these may be assigned to period ranging from the Chalcolithic to medieval period. A proper excavation, if conducted at the site may yield fruitful results.

4. Tala : The site is located (20^0 59' 29" N; 83^0 19' 03" E) in Jaja hill of Kaimur on the northern bank of River Karamnasa. There is a small rock shelter showing painting in black in single outlines. There are dancing figures. In view of Wakankar 'such single line drawings with ochre along with black pigment belong to much later period' assigned by him to circa 1700 BCE (Wakankar 2005:282-363).

5. Tenui : The survey of this site (24^0 59' 29" N; 83^0 19' 03" E) was undertaken with help of local people by the second author of this paper in the year 2008. It is located approximately 12 km. south-west of Chakia Bazaar in Kaimur range on Jaja hill. Two rocks shelters are located at a height of 90 ft. On the eastern side, there is a 4.16 m long shelter containing paintings in red ochrous colour (Plate 37.6). But due to age and perhaps due to encrustation and environmental impact a good number of depictions have almost faded and blurred beyond recognition. Some of the forms, however, may be identified. Mention may be made of an elephant, some human forms and a man with bow and arrow. The elephant figure is comparable in style with a similar one found at Adamgarh assignable to Middle Stone Age (Wakankar 2005: 288-289). The second stage paintings are in intricate design, a large sized Neelgai surrounded by hunters, masked human beings many of them dancing and playing instruments – all datable to Mesolithic period on comparative grounds (Sonawane 2008:1-13).

The paintings at third stage show bulls without hump, flock of deers, a prominent human form etc. Noteworthy is the depiction of a deer with arrow stuck in its body. Similar depiction is seen in a rock shelter at Mandi and Raisen (M.P.) depicting a bull and a deer, respectively. On a comparative ground these rock paintings may be placed in the Chalcolithic period (Wakankar 2005: 300-304). The fourth and final stage of paintings with animals decorated with diagonal latticed designs also belongs to Chalcolithic period.

Thus, at the rock shelters of Tenui, we came across a whole spectrum of activities from the Palaeolithic to the Chalcolithic period.

6. Nasopur : The rock shelters (25^0 01' 13" N; 83^0 17' 46" E) is situated about 8 km south-west of Chakia bazaar on Kapisha hills locally known a Raja Bhoj Ki Pahari. The rock shelter is located at a height of 230 ft. painted with ochre; it has depictions of herds of humped bulls, deer and geoconic human forms that appear to be riding on a cart in a standing position. The cart is a Chalcolithic depiction, according to Neumayer (1983:132-133). On closer investigation, the surface of this rock shelter yielded pieces of some broken potsherds and lumps of ochre. It indicates (1) occupation of this rock shelter at some point of time (2) use and preparation of ochre as raw material for pigment at the site itself.

In the nearby area of Bihar that is contagious to the series of rock shelters discussed above rock paintings have been located. Some of the important ones from the view point of the present theme are being discussed below.

7. Diha : The rock shelter (25^0 01' 47" N- 83^0 25' 51" E) is located about 25 km east of Chakia. There are petroglyphs as well as paintings in the Rock shelter there. Interesting is the depiction of cart which has somewhat blurred. This should be assigned to Chalcolithic period in view of scholars like Neumayer (1983: 132-33). Once farming became the dominant way of life transportation must have became a necessity.

8. Kharauli : The Rock shelters is located on the northern end of Kaimur in Mathia hill in Bihar (25^0 00' 57" N 83^0 20' 13" E) at a height of 100 ft.12 km from Chakia and barely one km away from the well known Ghurahupur rock shelter discussed above. A Sati stone has also been located here. A set of six paintings have been noted here that are being briefly discussed below:

The first painting shows a human form painted in solid colour that is placed by scholar in the Chalcolithic period on the stylistic grounds. The second one shows hunting and domestication scenes. Elephant, masked human figures and bull with a rope in the neck that is being led by a human form, an ass or donkey- like figure are noteworthy depictions in this painting (Plate 37.7). The elephant form has been decorated. Painting number-3 seems to have been executed at two stages. The first one is done in greenish colour showing intricate geometric design, the like of which are generally assigned to Upper Palaeolothic period by Neumayer (1993:43). In the next stage, a painting is superimposed on the earlier one that pertains to the stage of animal domestication. Goats and anthropomorphic figures are clearly visible in these depictions.

The fourth set of painting is done in solid form with herdsmen and stick like stylized human figures. Long-horned humped bulls, herds of goats along with a human form that seem to be leading the animals is seen in this depiction. Slightly away from this painting there appears a human form that is comparable to rock painting of Bhimbetka, Raisen, Mandi, etc. It has been placed in Neolithic–Chalcolithic period by scholars, (Wakanakar & Brooks 1976:97).

The next set of painting depicts an extra large sized animal decorated with intricate designs assignable to Mesolithic period (Tyagy1992: 303-317).

9. Ratanpurva : The Rock Shelter (25^0 00' 50" N 83^0 19' 45" E) is in Bhabhua (Kaimur) district of Bihar, located 11.5 km east of Chakia Bazar on eastern bank of River Karamnasa. There are a set of twenty paintings at the Rock shelter at Ratanpurva.

The first painting shows animals standing under a tree with herdsmen or a community of pastoralists. The depictions are done in single lines but filled up with paint. A lion in movement may also be seen in the painting. The scene is comparable with Chalcolithic paintings of auditorium rock shelter of Bhimbetka and some paintings at Mirzapur (Wakankar 2005. 282-309). The second one in rock shelter-1 that is 14 m. deep suggests use of metal to cut and shape the cave -like structure in which the paintings are executed. Traces of cow dung on the floor of the cave and presence of postholes suggest a stage of domestication of animals. There are also depictions of huts and cattle-pen which are indeed denominators of settled life with an agrarian base.

The painting No. 3 has been done in two stages. The earlier one depicts humped bull, wheeled cart and other animals. The cart wheel is comparable with Daimabad bison belonging to Chalcolithic period (Dhavalikar1997:166).

The painting of the second stage shows a tree, perhaps a banyan tree or a Bodhi tree as seen at the Sanchi stupa (Agrawala 2007: 234-244). The painting 4 has a humped bull, a human figure carrying something in his hand. Painting 5 depicts a 71 cm long bison painted with ochre in a silhouette. It is comparable to a similar depiction at Abchand in district Sagar, M.P. and placed in Mesolithic period (Wakankar 2005:102-103 and 281-289). The last painting has been done at apparently three consecutive cultural stages, *viz* the earliest one is a human form painted in black assignable to Chalcolithic period. At the second stage, we find paintings of deer, human forms with arrows, a cart-wheel and bull. In the third stage a huge anthropomorphic figure is drawn which may belong to a relatively later period.

The rock shelter-2 has two paintings. No.1 shows dancing human forms in ocher colour done in what is generally described as 'S' style. Similar ones are seen at several places other including at Bhimbetka in green colour and assignable to Upper Palaeolithic period (Wakankar1992: 319-336) or Mesolithic period in view of Tyagy (1992: 303-317). The next painting shows a large sized goat or an ibex comparable to the one seen at Latham rock shelter in Mirzapur and dated to Mesolithic period (Tewari1992: 285-303). At the second stage there are dancers, the likes of which are datable to Neolithic – Chalcolithic period. Similar figures found at Daura rock shelter in district Mirzapur have been placed in the Chalcolithic period (Tewari1992: 285-301). The third stage paintings portray cattle with herdsman carrying something in their hands.

Rock shelter-3 has 5 set of paintings. The first one belongs to historical period depictions of horse riders and warriors with evolved types of weapons of war. The second one has a rich repertory assignable to Mesolithic Period (Plate 37.8) (Tyagy 1992: 303-317). There are full range of painting from intricate designs to fully coloured animals like Neelgai and buffaloes with ochrous and black colour. The third painting depicts bulls which have similarity with bulls seen at Kupagal at Bellary in Karnataka that has Neolithic affiliation (Neumayer1992: 215-245).

The fourth set of rock painting is significantly shows domestication. There are cattle pen, dogs, goats and stylized human figures. It clearly shows a settled life with agricultural base. Interestingly, one may find this type of enclosures made with wood and straw in use even today in the modern villages in the surrounding region.

The next painting depicts wheeled cart and animals painted in black. As observed earlier, this type of depiction of toy cart has been found at Daimabad on Chalcolithic pottery (Dhavalikar 1997: 165-167). On the basis of this, the painting may be placed in the Chalcolithic period.

In the sixth painting, there are bisons and other animals that may be placed in Mesolithic period. It is superimposed both by linear and filled up depictions of humped cattle with prominent horns, stick-like human figures as well as herdsmen. In one such painting, there is semblance of a plough being carried by a man. There is a pot-like form dangling from the waist and the other hand of the man is engaged in feeding an animal. It is clearly a depiction of farming society. Neumayer (1991: 39-70) feels that such scenes belong to Neolithic period. The last scene belongs to the historical period.

The other painting has been executed in single linear method showing angular human forms and small horned humped cattle. This has been assigned to Chalcolithic period on stylistic grounds (Wakankar 1992: 319-336).

Rock Shelter-6 shows some vaguely painted figures. The forms that may be identified are that of humped cattle – some of them engaged in a fight with horns locked. There are more animals and angular human forms present in the scene. The bulls depicted in this painting compare well with Joara rock shelter placed on stylistic grounds in Chalcolithic period (Neumayer 1992: 215-247).

Discussion

This brief description of the rock shelters in the Vindhya-Kaimur region provides deep insights into the life and culture of humankind which occupied the region at different cultural stages. The paintings depict day-to-day life-scenes of people. There are hunting scenes by group of men - some kind of totem or ritual observed for successful adventure in the forest? There are depictions of animals which are difficult to identify. Is it a shortcoming of the painter or is it depiction of an animal that is now extinct? Giraffe-like animals are intriguing again. There are processions led by horse riders. There are scenes which are suggestive of man's march towards a settled life - domesticating cattle or sheep and goats, engaging in activities related to the early farming communities. The pastoralists who came to these parts seem to have taken to a more settled ways of life. These rock paintings are indeed witness to evolving ways of life from hunting-gathering to farming. Needless to underline, that the painted rock shelters bear the testimony of human activity spanning over the millennia. This fact is fully testified by the superimpositions of depictions in different colour schemes. The subject matter, the variety of colours in use, the style - all manifest use of specific rock surface over and over again by humankind over the millennia representing different cultural stages. The present description focuses on the activities of the early farming communities (Neolithic and Chalcolithic) as reflected in these rock shelters in Vindhya-Kaimur region.

We know now that in many regions including the Vindhya-Kaimur region, man started food production leaving behind food gathering and foraging during the later part of Mesolithic Age. The evolving life style finds its reflections in the artistic expression seen on the smoothened surface of rock shelters and caves. There are depictions of animals, many in x-ray style, stick-like human forms supposedly belonging to Mesolithic Period. While the hunting-gathering scenes still continued, there appeared depictions of animals being led by strings or ropes. These scenes show domestication of animals or being herded. The tools pertaining to earlier cultural stages painted in these rock shelters are by and large replaced by more evolved type and somewhat deferent In due course of time, with beginning of use of metal, there are sharper looking objects like arrowheads, spearheads, lances etc. that are depicted in these paintings. Carts with wheels are also shown along with cattle, especially bulls. Thus in a broad sense the rock paintings reflect the changing means and modes of life of their respective age. These are clear-cut depictions of economic priorities as well as ways and means of tool utilization a fact that can never be so clearly discernable in the archaeological excavations. Through these paintings one gets a direct peep into life as led by humankind during early stages of cultural development.

Acknowledgement

Authors are grateful to Vibha Tripathi, Department of AIHC and Archaeology, for her invaluable suggestions in preparation of the paper. Thanks are also due to ICHR, New Delhi and UGC, New Delhi for granting financial support for conducting fieldwork in Chandauli district, Uttar Pradesh.

References

1. Agrawala, Prithvi Kumar 2007. *Prachin Bharatiya Kala Evam Vastu.* Varanasi: Vishvavidhyalay Prakasan.

2. Carlleyle, A.C.L. 1883. Notes on Lately Discovered Sepulchral Mounds, Cairns, Caves, Cave-Paintings and Stone Implements. *Proceedings of the Asiatic Society of Bengal*, 49-55.
3. Cockburn J. 1883. On the Recent Existence of Rhinoceros Indicus in the Northeastern Provinces and a Painting from Mirzapur Reporting the Hunting of this Animal, *Journal of Asiatic society of Bengal*, 52(2): 56-64.
4. Dhavalikar, M.K.1997. *Indian Protohistory.* New Delhi: Books & Books.
5. Dubey, S.R. 2007. *Pragaitihasik Bharatiya Shailchitra Aur Unamen Pratibimbit Lok Sanskriti* (in Hindi), *Sanskriti Sandhan*, 20(1): 1-21.
6. Neumayer, Erwin 1983. *Prehistoric Indian Rock Paintings*. New Delhi: Oxford University Press.
7. Neumayer, Erwin 1991. Wheeled Vehicles and Mounted Animals in Prehistoric Indian Rock Art, *Man and Environment* 26(2): 39-70.
8. Neumayer, Erwin 1992. Rock Art in India. In *Rock Art in the Old World,* Michel Lorblanchet (Ed.), New Delhi: Indira Gandhi Nation Center for the Arts and Aryan Books International. Pp. 215-247.
9. Neumayer, Erwin 1993. *Lines on Stone, The Prehistoric Rock Art of India.* New Delhi: Manohar Publishers and Distributers.
10. Sonawane, V.H. 2008. Rock Art of India: A Historical Perspective, *Man and Environment*, 33(1):1-13.
11. Tewari, R. 1992. Rock Paintings of Mirzapur in Uttar Pradesh. In *Rock Art in the Old World,* Michel Lorblanchet (Ed.), New Delhi: Indira Gandhi Nation Center for the Arts and Aryan Books International. Pp. 285-301.
12. Tyagy, G.S.1992. Decorative Intricate Patterns in Indian Rock Art. In *Rock Art in the Old World,* Michel Lorblanchet (Ed.), New Delhi: Indira Gandhi Nation Center for the Arts and Aryan Books International. Pp. 303-317
13. Wakanker, V.S. & R.R. Brooks 1976. *Stone Age Painting in India.* Bomby: D.P. Taraporevala Sons & company Private Ltd.
14. Wakanker, V.S. 1992. Rock Painting in India. In *Rock Art in the Old World,* Michel Lorblanchet (Ed.), New Delhi: Indira Gandhi Nation Center for the Arts and Aryan Books International. Pp. 319-336.
15. Wakankar, V.S. 2005. *Painted Rock Shelters of India.* Bhopal: Director - Archaeology, Archives & Museums.

38

चम्पानेर–पावागढ के जैन बावनढेरी मंदिर के श्वेताम्बर मूर्तियों की पहचान एवं विवेचना

बृजेश रावत, अनुपमा सिंह

मध्य युगीन नगर चम्पानेर का भग्नावशेष जिसे 'समय का जमाव' कह सकते हैं, 450 वर्ष पूर्व अचानक परित्याग कर देने के कारण विद्यमान है। यहाँ पर बड़े पैमाने पर अनुत्खनित पुरातत्त्व, ऐतिहासिक एवं आवासीय सांस्कृतिक संपत्ति एवं प्राकृतिक भू–दृश्य प्रभावपूर्ण हैं। यहाँ के पर्वतीय दुर्ग हिन्दू प्रधान और अवशेष गुजरात सल्तनत को प्रकट करते हैं। इस पुरास्थल पर दुर्ग संरचनायें, महल, धार्मिक भवन, आवासीय स्थल, कृषक संरचनायें और जल संग्रह आदि विद्यमान हैं। यहाँ की निर्मित इमारतें एवं विविध रचनायें भग्नावशेष के साथ पूर्णतः भारतीय–इस्लामिक मिश्रित वास्तुकला को प्रस्तुत करते हैं।

चम्पानेर–पावागढ़ पूर्वी गुजरात के हालोल तालुका, जिला– गोधरा (पंचमहल) में, वड़ोदरा के उत्तर–पूर्व में 45 किलोमीटर की दूरी पर स्थित है। पावागढ़ पर्वत की ऊँचाई 830 मीटर है तथा यह पाँच स्तरों (उतरते क्रम) में विभक्त है, जो लम्बवत् खड़ी टीलों में विभाजित है। जिनके नाम हैं– कालिका माता, मौलिया, भद्रकाली, माची और अटक। यहाँ का सबसे ऊँचा पठार पश्चिम और दक्षिण भाग को आक्रमण से सुरक्षित रखता था। उत्तरी और पूर्वी दिशा में शांत पर्वतीय ढ़ाल है। इस पर्वत पर सुकली, जोरवन, विश्वामित्री झरने बहते हैं।

पावागढ़ के आग्नेय चट्टान पीत एवं रक्त आभा के प्रकाश प्रकट करते हैं। इन रंग द्रव्य चट्टानों और पत्थरों को चम्पक फूल के साथ तुलना कर सकते हैं अथवा अग्नि की लौ के सदृश्य रंग होने के कारण इसका नाम चम्पानेर नगर और पावागढ़ पर्वत पड़ा। यहाँ चम्पानेर शब्द से सम्बन्धित दो और बातें प्रचलित हैं – एक कि, चम्पारा अथवा चम्पराज गुजरात का चावड़ावंशीय शासक वनराज का मंत्री था, जबकि, दूसरी मान्यतानुसार भील के मुखिया को 'चम्पा' कहा जाता है। इस प्रकार चम्पानेर नाम पड़ा। सामाजिक, राजनैतिक एवं ऐतिहासिक दृष्टि से यहाँ की मान्यता परस्पर विरोधी है। इसलिए, भौगोलिक आधार पर ही यहाँ का नामकरण संतुष्टिपूर्ण है। प्राचीन पांडुलिपि के अनुसार पावागढ़ (वायुपर्वत), 12वीं शती के उत्तरार्ध में चन्दबरदाई ने पावागढ़ को "पृथ्वीराजरासो" में वर्णित किया है, कि पावागढ़ पर 'राम गौर तुवार' ने शासन किया था।

हिन्दू परम्परा के अनुसार पावागढ़ पर्वत देवी 'सती' के पाद के अंगूठे से बना है, संस्कृत तथा गुजराती साहित्य के एक नाटक 'गंगादास प्रतापविलास नाटकम्' और 'कलिका का गरबा' में काली माता के पूर्व अवतार का और नगर का वर्णन किया गया है। शख्तास के पीठ निर्णय के अनुसार पावागढ़ पर्वत तब स्थित हुआ, जब देवी कालिका का दाहिना अंगूठा यहाँ पर गिरा। ऐसा मानते हैं, कि यह पर्वत अंगूठे का रूप है। परसियन साहित्य सिकन्दर–बिन–मुहम्मद द्वारा रचित 'मिरात–ए–सिकन्दरी' अबुल फज़ल द्वारा रचित 'आइन–ए–अकबरी', एवं 'तबकात–ए–अकबरी' तथा मुहम्मद कासिम की 'तारीख–ए–फरिस्ता' में भी इस क्षेत्र का वर्णन मिलता है।

इस क्षेत्र का पुरातात्त्विक उत्खननन् करने से जोरवन नदी के किनारे से पाषाण काल के प्रस्तर से बने हथियार हस्तकुठार, गंड़ासा, इत्यादि प्राप्त होते हैं। मैत्रक शासकों के अधिकार क्षेत्र से कुछ मैत्रक सिक्के भी प्राप्त हुए हैं। सन् 1300 के लगभग पावागढ़ चौहान राजपूतों की किच्छी शाखा के नियंत्रण में आ गया, जिन्होंने 184 वर्षों तक राज्य किया। सन् 1418 और 1420 में अहमदशाह (सन् 1411–1441) ने चम्पानेर पर आक्रमण कर, वहाँ के दुर्ग को कब्जे में ले लिया। अहमदशाह ने सन् 1431 में चम्पानेर को विकसित करने का प्रयास किया, परन्तु कुछ कारणवश सफल नहीं हो सका।

सन् 1450 में मुहम्मद द्वितीय (सन् 1441–1452) ने आक्रमण किया और नीचे के कुछ दुर्गों पर जीत हासिल की। चम्पानेर का किच्छी शासक चौहान गंगादास मालवा के सुल्तान महमूद खिलजी का घनिष्ट मित्र था, मालवा के शासक और गंगादास के चम्पानेर आगमन पर, मुहम्मद द्वितीय ने गोधरा छोड़ दिया। पतई रावल अन्तिम राजपूत शासक था, जो महमूद बेगड़ा से पराजित हुआ। गुजरात के सुल्तान महमूद बेगड़ा के सैनिक घेराव के बाद 20 महीनों से भी अधिक समय में (अप्रैल 1483 से दिसम्बर 1489 में) विजय प्राप्त की। जीत हासिल करने के बाद महमूद बेगड़ा ने चम्पानेर को 'मुहम्मदाबाद' के नाम से अपनी दूसरी राजधानी बनाया। कहा जाता है, कि गिरनार और चम्पानेर के दो दुर्गों के नाम ऐतिहासिक आधार पर बेगड़ा (गुजराती–गढ़) के नाम से पड़ा।

महमूद बेगड़ा (सन् 1459–1511) के शासन काल में चम्पानेर अपने उत्कर्ष के सर्वोच्च शिखर पर था, किन्तु नगर का वैभव ज्यादा दिनों तक कायम नहीं रह सका, और सन् 1534 में मुगल बादशाह हुमायूँ ने सुल्तान बहादुर शाह के समय में आक्रमण कर, इसे जीत लिया। इसके बाद अहमदाबाद को पुनः गुजरात की राजधानी बनाया गया। मुगल सम्राट अकबर के शासन काल में महमूद तृतीय (सन् 1537–1554) ने चम्पानेर पर कब्जा कर लिया। बाद में, चम्पानेर शाह मिर्जा के अधिकार में आ गया, परन्तु उसके बाद चम्पानेर का तेजी से पतन हुआ। इस बात को 'मिरात–ए–सिकन्दरी' में दृढ़तापूर्वक कहा गया है, कि चम्पानेर एक खंडहरों का राज्य था, यहाँ के विकसित घर पतन की ओर थे एवं जहाँगीर के शासन काल (सन् 1605–1627) में स्थानीय लोगों ने इस क्षेत्र को छोड़ दिया। अधिकांश जनसंख्या राजसी बाड़े में एवं माची में आ गई; दूसरे स्थलों को भुला दिया गया और पहाड़ियों की ओर पलायन कर गये।

विगत समय में भारतीय पुरातत्त्व सर्वेक्षण द्वारा यहाँ के स्मारकों और पुरावशेषों का संरक्षण और परिरक्षण होता रहा है। किन्तु, फिर भी कतिपय स्मारक उपेक्षा के शिकार रहे। इन्हीं में से लकुलीश मंदिर (7वीं–8वीं) और जैन बावनढेरी मंदिर विशेष हैं। जैन बावनढेरी मंदिर का एक अन्य नाम पार्श्वनाथ मंदिर है, जिसके मात्र ध्वंशावशेष ही बुलंद इमारत की कथा–व्यथा कहते हैं। इन मंदिरों के बिखरे पड़े पुरावशेषों में वास्तुखंडों एवं मूर्तियों आदि का प्रलेखन कार्य अथवा अभिलेखीकरण (Documentetion Work) का दायित्व तत्कालिक अधीक्षण पुरात्त्ववविद् के० सी० नौरियाल, भारतीय पुरात्त्व सर्वेक्षण, वडोदरा मण्ड़ल, वडोदरा ने स्वयं पर लिया और अपने निर्देशन में इस कार्य को करने के लिए दो सहायक पुरातत्त्वविदों (लेखकों) को सौंपा।

बावनढेरी मंदिर का निर्माण लगभग 12वीं–13वीं शती ई० में हुआ था, किन्तु वर्तमान में यह पूर्णतः विध्वंसावस्था में हैं, इसकी मात्र संरचनाएं ही शेष हैं। बावनढेरी जैन मंदिरों में बावनढेरी मंदिर के निर्माण की एक विशेष परम्परा राजस्थान और गुजरात में रही है। मध्य में बड़ा मंदिर और इसके चारों ओर 51 छोटे–छोटे गर्भगृह का निर्माण होता था, जो एक चाहारदीवारी का भी कार्य करता था। मुख्य मंदिर का शिखर बड़ा, शेष छोटे–छोटे शिखरों से अच्छादित रहता था। इस प्रकार, एक ही स्थल पर बावन गर्भगृह होते थे, जिन्हें 'बावनढेरी' कहा जाता था। दरअसल, ढ़ेरी शब्द ढ़ेर से बना है, जिसका अर्थ 'इकट्ठा करना' होता है। चम्पानेर–पावागढ़ के इस मंदिर का मुख्य गर्भगृह पार्श्वनाथ का था। पुरास्थल पर पार्श्वनाथ मंदिर की संरचना स्पष्ट है। इसके सामने ही भारतीय पुरातत्त्व सर्वेक्षण ने कुछ छोटे गर्भगृहों को संरक्षित किया है। शेष मंदिर के पुरावशेष आस–पास पड़े हुए हैं, और अपने उद्धार हेतु पुराविदों की प्रतीक्षा में हैं। वर्तमान में उत्तर, दक्षिण और पश्चिम दिशा में नवीन जैन मंदिरों का निर्माण हो चुका है। वहीं से प्राप्त विलक्षण मूर्तियों का अध्ययन प्रस्तुत शोध–पत्र में किया जा रहा है। विवेच्य प्रतिमाएं गैरिक वर्णीय मोरंग प्रस्तर से निर्मित हैं। इन पाषाणों के कण छोटे न होकर मोरंग के समान काफी बड़े हैं। अस्तु, इन्हें गैरिक वर्णीय मोरंग प्रस्तर कहा जाना उचित होगा। वर्णित नौ विशिष्ट प्रतिमाओं में ईशान, शिव, इन्द्र लक्ष्मी, गणेश, शान्तिदेवी और सरस्वती हैं। प्रतिमाओं के व्याख्या के साथ ही जैन साहित्य में वर्णित उक्त देवी–देवताओं के वर्णन भी उल्लेखनीय हैं। प्रतिमाओं का विवेच्य क्रमांक जैन साहित्य में वर्णन के अनुसार है।

प्रतिमाओं का विस्तृत वर्णन

उक्त पुरास्थल से प्राप्त अनेकों मूर्तियों में से नौ विशिष्ट प्रतिमाओं का विस्तृत वर्णन प्रस्तुत है–

(1) त्रिभंग शिव – यह प्रतिमा खण्ड़ित स्तम्भ में उत्कीर्ण है। देवकोष्ठ के भीतर शिव त्रिभंग मुद्रा में अवस्थित हैं। देवकोष्ठ अत्यन्त अलंकृत है, इसका ऊपरी भाग आर्च के समान निर्मित है। प्रतिमा काफी क्षरित है, जिससे मुख एवं नासिका दर्शित नहीं होते किन्तु, सूक्ष्मता पूर्वक देखने से नेत्र के अवशेष प्रतीत होते हैं। कर्ण, ग्रीवा के वलय, देहयष्टि, कटि और जानु भाग सुरक्षित हैं। शिव चतुर्भुज हैं। वस्त्राभूषण में करंडमुकुट, कर्णकुण्ड़ल, वनमाला, ग्रीवा के हार, हाथों के कड़े, कटि के अधोवस्त्र एवं आभूषण भी सहजतापूर्वक दृष्टिगत होते हैं। इनके करों में त्रिशूल, शूल एवं अक्षमाला स्पष्ट हैं। चौथा आयुध अस्पष्ट है। नीचे शिव पुत्र गणेश निरूपित हैं। देवकोष्ठ के अर्धस्तम्भों में व्याल निर्मित हैं और उसके पार्श्वों में दो सहायिका वस्त्राभूषण से शोभित अवस्थित हैं। इस प्रकार यह प्रतिमा प्रतिमातिक लक्षणों के आधार पर कला के क्षेत्र में विशेष महत्व रखती है, जिसकी माप 41× 34× 43 सेमी0 है।

(2) त्रिभंग ईशान – दिक्पाल ईशान की मूर्ति भी द्वारशाखा में उकेरी गयी है। अत्यन्त अलंकृत देवकोष्ठ का ऊपरी भाग आर्चनुमा है। रथिका के मध्य में ईशान त्रिभंग मुद्रा में रूपायित हैं। मूर्ति काफी क्षारितावस्था में है, जिससे उसके शारीरिक अंग स्पष्टतः परिलक्षित नहीं होते हैं। ईशान के मुखमण्ड़ल, कर्ण, ग्रीवा, चार भुजाएं, देहयष्टि, नाभि, कटि और पादों को सरलता से देखा जा सकता है। वस्त्राभूषणों में करंडमुकुट, वनमाला, कर्णकुण्डल, गले के हार, कटिबन्ध, अधोवस्त्र, पादों के कड़े आदि स्पष्ट हैं। इनके आयुधों में शूल, त्रिशूल और अक्षमाला निरूपित हैं। चौथा कर व आयुध अनुपस्थित है।

ईशान का वाहन वृषभ भी उत्कीर्ण है, किन्तु इसमें भ्रम हो सकता है। वाहन को सूक्ष्मता से देखने पर उसके खुर स्पष्ट हैं, जिससे भ्रम की स्थिति दूर हो जाती है। देवकोष्ठ के बाहरी अर्धस्तम्भों पर दोनों पार्श्वों में व्याल निर्मित हैं तत्पश्चात् दो सहायिकाएं कलश लिए दोनों ओर वस्त्राभूषण से शोभित त्रिभंग मुद्रा में खड़ी हैं। कलागत वैशिष्ट्य के आधार पर इस प्रतिमा का कलाक्षेत्र में विशेष स्थान है। इसकी माप 41× 35× 22 सेमी0 है।

(3) त्रिभंग शिव – प्रस्तुत शिव प्रतिमा भी स्तम्भ में उत्खचित है। देवकोष्ठ पूर्व की भांति है। शिव त्रिभंग मुद्रा में हैं। देवकोष्ठ अत्यन्त अलंकृत है। इसका भी ऊपरी भाग आर्चनुमा है। इसके अर्धस्तम्भों में व्याल भी निर्मित हैं। देवकोष्ठ के मध्य शिव अपने पुत्र गणेश के साथ रूपांकित हैं। इनके मुखमण्ड़ल का आधे से अधिक भाग टूट चुका है। तीसरा और चौथा हाथ भी भंगितावस्था में है। मूर्ति में कर्ण, ग्रीवा, चौड़े स्कन्ध, विशाल वक्ष, नाभि, कटि और पाद स्पष्ट हैं। देहयष्टि सुगठित व सुड़ौल है। इनके वस्त्राभूषण में कर्णकुण्ड़ल, वनमाला, ग्रीवा के हार, कंकण, कटिबन्ध और अधोवस्त्र आदि रूपायित हैं। शिव के आयुधों में शूल, त्रिशूल और एक कर में अक्षमाला दृष्टिगत है, जबकि एक अन्य कर व उसके आयुध भंगितावस्था में हैं। मूल प्रतिमा के बायें पाद के समीप गणेश स्थानक मुद्रा में रूपायित हैं। रथिका के पार्श्वों में सहायिकाएं त्रिभंग मुद्रा में वस्त्राभूषण से सुसज्जित खड़ी हैं। बायीं ओर की देवी क्षतिग्रस्त हैं। इस मूर्ति का प्रतिमातिक लक्षणों के आधार पर कला जगत में विशेष योग है। इसकी माप 41× 34× 43 सेमी0 है।

(4) नृत्य गणेश – गणेश की यह विशिष्ट प्रतिमा रथिका के भीतर उत्कीर्ण की गयी है, जो नृत्य मुद्रा में है। इसका देवकोष्ठ पूर्व की मूर्तियों के देवकोष्ठ से पृथक निर्मित है। पूर्व के देवकोष्ठ के अर्धस्तम्भ गोलाकार थे और उनमें बाहर की ओर व्याल निर्मित थे, जबकि इसमें अर्धस्तम्भ चौकोण हैं और व्याल नहीं है, और न ही, आर्चनुमा अलंकरण निर्मित है। गणेश की शारीरिक संरचना मांसल और आकर्षक है।

गणेश का सिर, मस्तक, बड़े कर्ण (सूर्पकर्ण), सूंड़, ग्रीवा, चार भुजाएं, वक्ष, बड़ा उदर, नाभि और मांसल जंघा आकर्षक निर्मित हैं। इनके वस्त्राभूषणों में करंड़मुकुट, ग्रीवा के हार, बाजुबन्द, धोती, पादों के कड़े को सूक्ष्मता से देखा जा सकता है। आयुधों में त्रिशूल और अंकुश है। मोदक का भी अंकन है। एक हाथ भग्न है। सूंड़ का भी कुछ भाग टूटा है। गणेश के दाहिने पाद के समीप इनका वाहन मूषक भी निरूपित है, किन्तु स्पष्टता का अभाव है। रथिका के दोनों पार्श्वों में नृत्यरत, सहायिकाएं वस्त्राभूषण से शोभित उत्कीर्ण हैं। दायीं ओर की सहायिका के किनारे पानगोष्ठी का दृश्य है। इस भांति यह प्रतिमा अपने कला जनित विशिष्टताओं के कारण जैन कला क्षेत्र में विशेष महत्व रखती है। इसकी माप 41× 46× 28 सेमी0 है।

(5) त्रिभंग शांतिदेवी – यह विशिष्ट प्रतिमा शांतिदेवी की है, जो एक वास्तुखण्ड़ में निरूपित हैं। शांतिदेवी खड़ी हैं। ये चतुर्भुजधारिणी हैं। मूर्ति काफी क्षारितावस्था में है। जिससे मुखमण्ड़ल के अवयव दृष्टिगत नहीं होते हैं। इनका मुखमण्ड़ल, कर्ण, ग्रीवा और उसके वलय, स्कन्ध, भग्न वक्ष स्थल, उदर, नाभि, कटि और पादों को आकर्षक निर्मित किया गया है। देवी के वस्त्राभूषणों में मुकुट, संवरे केश, कर्णकुण्ड़ल, वनमाला, ग्रीवा के हार, हाथों के कड़े और चूड़ियां, भुजबन्द, कटिबन्ध, धोती और पादों के कड़े विशेष उल्लेखनीय हैं। इनके दो आयुध पद्म ऊपर के दो हाथों में स्पष्ट है तथा दो भंगित अवस्था में हैं। एक पद्म बायें पैर के समीप भी निरूपित है। वास्तुखण्ड़ का ऊपरी भाग

पत्रवल्लरियों से युक्त है। शांतिदेवी के दोनों पार्श्वों में वस्त्राभूषण से युक्त त्रिभंग मुद्रा में कलशधारणियां निरूपित हैं। ऐसी शांतिदेवी की मूर्तियां बहुत दुर्लभ हैं। कला वैशिष्ट्य एवं प्रतिमातिक लक्षणों के आधार पर यह प्रतिमा कला जगत में अति महत्वपूर्ण स्थान रखती है। इसकी माप 70× 49× 24 सेमी0 है (फलक–38.1)।

(6) इन्द्र – इन्द्र की यह प्रतिमा भी वास्तुखण्ड़ में निरूपित देवकोष्ठ के भीतर उत्कीण है। इसमें इन्द्र अपने वाहन ऐरावत पर ललितासन अवस्था में आरूढ़ हैं। यह देवकोष्ठ भी औरों से भिन्न है। इस देवकोष्ठ में वर्गाकार दो–दो अर्धस्तम्भ निर्मित हैं। और, चारों अर्धस्तम्भों में घटपल्लव उकेरित हैं। इन्द्र चतुर्भुज हैं, किन्तु इनके तीन हाथ टूटे हैं। ऐरावत का भी मुखभाग भग्न है। बायें पाद के घुटने में भी एक फलक (Chip) निकली हुई है। इनका भी मुखमण्ड़ल क्षरितावस्था में है। जिस कारण अन्य अवयव दर्शित नहीं होते हैं। सिर, मस्तक, कर्ण, ग्रीवा, और उसके वलय, चौड़े स्कन्ध, विशाल वक्षस्थल, उदर, कटि और पाद स्पष्ट हैं। देहयष्टि सुडौल और आकर्षक है। इनके वस्त्राभूषण में मुकुट, कर्णकुण्ड़ल, ग्रीवा के हार, बाजूबन्द, कड़े, कटिबन्ध एवं अधोवस्त्र विशेष दर्शित हैं। आयुधों में मात्र अंकुश ही परिलक्षित है। इनका वाहन ऐरावत भी आभूषण से युक्त है। यह प्रतिमा कलागत विशेषताओं के आधार पर कला क्षेत्र में विशेष योग रखती है।

(7) त्रिभंग सरस्वती – यह स्वतन्त्र प्रतिमा श्रुत देवी सरस्वती की है, जो त्रिभंग मुद्रा में रूपायित है। इसका भी देवकोष्ठ अत्यन्त अलंकृत है। देवकोष्ठ में ज्यामितीय अलंकरण बने हैं और इसमें कोई सहायक मूर्तियां निरूपित नहीं है। देवकोष्ठ के भीतर चतुर्भुजधारिणी सरस्वती का सिर, मस्तक, दो कर और बायां पाद टूटा हुआ है। इनके नेत्र, कर्ण, नासिका, ओष्ठ, कर्ण, ग्रीवा और उसके वलय, स्कन्ध उन्नत किन्तु भग्न, वक्षस्थल, उदर, नाभि, पतली कटि और पाद स्पष्ट दृष्टिगत हैं। वस्त्राभूषणों में मुकुट, कर्णकुण्ड़ल, वनमाला, ग्रीवा के हार, बाजूबन्द, कंकड़, कटिबन्ध, धोती आदि भी दर्शित हैं। बायीं ओर के नीचे का कर वरदमुद्रा में है। दायीं ओर के ऊपरी हाथ में वीणा है। दायीं ओर ही नीचे हंस निर्मित है, जिससे पता चलता है, कि यह मूर्ति सरस्वती की है। प्रतिमा क्षरित होने के बावजूद भी आकर्षक है। कलाजनित विशिष्टताओं के कारण इस मूर्ति का कलाक्षेत्र में विशेष महत्व है। इसकी माप 50× 24× 23 सेमी0 है (फलक–38.2)।

(8) त्रिभंग इन्द्राणी – यह प्रतिमा भी वास्तुखण्ड़ में निरूपित देवकोष्ठ के भीतर उत्कीर्ण है। देवकोष्ठ के अर्धस्तम्भ वर्गाकार हैं, जिनके भाग में घटपल्लव निर्मित हैं। इसके पार्श्वों में वस्त्राभूषण से सज्जित त्रिभंग मुद्रा में दो कलशधारिणी सहायिकाओं के रूप में खड़ी हैं। इनके पश्चात् पानगोष्ठी का दृश्यांकन भी है।

मूल प्रतिमा भी वास्तुखण्ड़ में निरूपित देवकोष्ठ के भीतर त्रिभंग मुद्रा में इन्द्राणी खड़ी हैं। ये चतुर्भुजधारिणी हैं। मूर्ति काफी क्षरित हो गयी है, जिससे मुखमण्ड़ल के अन्य अंग स्पष्टतः दिखलाई नहीं पड़ते। किन्तु, सूक्ष्मता से देखने पर सिर, मस्तक, भौंहें, नेत्र, नासिका, ग्रीवा, स्पष्ट हैं। मुखमण्ड़ल गोलाकार हैं। साथ ही स्कन्ध, उन्नत वक्षस्थल, उदर भाग, नाभि पतली कटि और पादों का सुन्दर निरूपण है। इनके वस्त्राभूषणों में करंडमुकुट, बाजूबंद, ग्रैवेयक, एकावली, करधनी, धोती आदि दृष्टिगत होती हैं। इन्द्राणी के आयुधों में अंकुश, पाश और वरदमुद्रा स्पष्ट हैं। जबकि, एक अन्य हाथ के आयुध का ज्ञान नहीं हो पाता। इनके वाहन गज का बैठी हुई अवस्था में निरूपण है। प्रतिमा जनित लक्षण के आधार पर इसका कला के क्षेत्र में विशेष महत्व है और इसकी माप 41× 56× 28 सेमी0 है (फलक–38.3)।

(9) आसनस्थ इन्द्राणी – प्रस्तुत मूर्ति स्तम्भ में उत्कीर्ण है। प्रतिमा अलंकृत रथिका के भीतर अवस्थित है। यह इन्द्राणी की ललितासन मुद्रा की मूर्ति है। देवी के केश, मस्तक, भौहें, नेत्र, नासिका, ओष्ठ क्षरित होने के पश्चात् भी सूक्ष्मता से देखने पर स्पष्ट होती हैं। ग्रीवा दृष्टव्य नहीं है। स्कन्ध, चार हाथ, उन्नत वक्ष, उदर, गहरी नाभि, पतली कटि और पाद दिखलाई पड़ते हैं। मुखमण्ड़ल लगभग वृत्ताकार है। इनके वस्त्राभूषणों में मुकुट, बड़े वृत्ताकार कुण्ड़ल, कण्ठहार, ग्रैवेयक, बाजूबन्द, कंकड़, कमरबन्द, अधोवस्त्र और पादों के कड़े भी सूक्ष्मता से गढ़े गये हैं। इन्द्राणी के बायें पाद के नीचे अत्यन्त क्षरित अवस्था में गज निरूपित हैं। इनके आयुधों में अंकुश, पाश तथा मातुलिंग है। और एक हस्त वरदमुद्रा में रूपायित है। कलागत विशिष्टाओं के आधार पर मूर्ति का कला क्षेत्र में विशेष महत्व है। साथ ही इसकी माप 30× 44× 31 सेमी0 है।

जैन साहित्य में उल्लेख

मध्यकाल आते–आते जैन धर्म में हिन्दू धर्म की लोकप्रिय देवी–देवता जैसे शिव, सरस्वती, लक्ष्मी, इन्द्र, गणेश इत्यादि को सम्मिलित कर लिया गया, जिन्हें कुछ संशोधनों के साथ तीर्थंकरों के सहयोगी के रूप में जैन शिल्प में स्थान मिला। इन्हीं में से कुछ देव–देवियों का उल्लेख किया जा रहा है।

शिव – परवर्ती काल में दिशाओं के स्वामी दिक्पाल या लोकपालों का पूजन वास्तु देवताओं के रूप में भी लोकप्रिय था।[1] लगभग 8वीं–9वीं शती ई0 में जैन देवकुल में दिक्पालों की धारणा विकसित हुई। दिक्पालों के प्रतिमा निरूपण से सम्बन्धित शुरूआती वर्णन निर्वाणकलिका एवं प्रतिष्ठासारसंग्रह में मिलता है। किन्तु जैन मंदिरों में इनका रूपांकन लगभग 9वीं शती ई0 में ही प्रारम्भ हो गया था, जो ओसियां (गुजरात) के महावीर मंदिर पर हैं। जैन कला में अष्ट दिक्पालों का उत्कीर्णन ही लोकप्रिय था।[2] परन्तु जैन ग्रन्थ में दस दिक्पालों के उल्लेख मिलते हैं। ये दस दिक्पाल–इन्द्र (पूर्व), अग्नि (दक्षिण–पूर्व), यम (दक्षिण), निऋत (दक्षिण–पश्चिम), वरूण (पश्चिम), वायु (पश्चिम–उत्तर), कुबेर (उत्तर), ईशान (उत्तर–पूर्व), ब्रह्मा (आकाश) एवं नागदेव या धरणेन्द्र (पाताल) हैं। जैन दिक्पालों की लाक्षणिक विशेषतायें हिन्दू दिक्पालों से प्रभावित हैं।

जैन ग्रन्थों में ऐसे देवों का भी उल्लेख है, जिनकी पूजा लोक परम्परा में प्रचलित थी और हिन्दू एवं बौद्ध धर्मों में भी लोकप्रिय थे।[3] जैसे– रूद्र, शिव, स्कन्द वासुदेव, नाग, भूत, पिशाच, यम, वरूण देवियों में श्री, ह्री, धृति, कीर्ति, अज्जा आदि।[4]

सरस्वती – सरस्वती का उल्लेख प्रारम्भिक जैनग्रन्थों में 'मेधा' एवं 'बुद्धि' के देवता या श्रुति देवता के रूप में मिलता है। इसे 'श्री; ह्री', 'धृति', 'कीर्ति' तथा 'लक्ष्मी' के साथ सम्बद्ध किया गया है।[5] अंगविज्जा में भी 'मेधा' एवं 'देवता' के रूप में सरस्वती का उल्लेख है।[6] कला में जैन सरस्वती का अंकन सर्वप्रथम कुषाणकाल में ही हो गया था।

शान्तिदेवी – जैन धर्म एवं संघ की उन्नतकारिणी शांति देवी की धारणा 10वीं–11वीं शती ई0 में विकसित हुई। देवी के प्रतिमा निरूपण से सम्बन्धित प्रारम्भिक उल्लेख शेभनसूरिकृत स्तुतचतुर्विंशतिका एवं निर्वाणकलिका[7] में है। जैन कला में शांतिदेवी श्वेताम्बर स्थलों पर ही लोकप्रिय थीं। खजुराहो की भी कुछ जिन मूर्तियों में सिंहासन के मध्य में शान्तिदेवी निरूपित हैं। गुजरात तथा राजस्थान के श्वेताम्बर स्थलों पर स्वतन्त्र प्रतिमाओं में तथा जिन् प्रतिमाओं के सिंहासन के मध्य में शान्तिदेवी आमूर्तित हैं। देवी की दोनों करों में या तो पद्म हैं या फिर, एक में पद्म तथा दूसरे में पुस्तक है।

गणेश – हिन्दू देवकुल के लोकप्रिय देवता गणेश को लगभग 11वीं–12वीं ई0 में जैन देवकुल में सम्मिलित किया गया।[8] यद्यपि अभिधानचिंतामणि में गणेश का उल्लेख है[9] परन्तु लाक्षणिक विशेषताएं सर्वप्रथम आचारदिनकर[10] में विवेचित हैं। जैन गणेश की लाक्षणिक विशेषताएं स्पष्टतः हिन्दू गणेश के समान हैं।

इन्द्र – जैन साहित्य में इन्द्र[11] का उल्लेख है। जिन्हें तीर्थंकरों का प्रधान सेवक कहा गया है। स्थानांगसूत्र[12] में इनके कई नाम मिलते हैं। जैसे– नामेन्द्र, स्थापनेन्द्र, द्रव्येन्द्र, ज्ञानेन्द्र, दार्शनेन्द्र, चरित्रनेन्द्र, देवेन्द्र, असुरेन्द्र तथा मनुष्येन्द्र। सम्भवतः यह इनके नामों के पर्यायवाची हैं। यह भी वर्णन है, कि तीर्थंकरों के जन्म, दीक्षा एवं कैवल्य प्राप्ति के अवसरों पर देवेन्द्र का शीघ्रता से पृथ्वी पर आना होता है। इसी ग्रन्थ में वज्रधारक और ऐरावत पर आरूढ़ शुक्र का देवताओं के राजा के रूप में उल्लेख है।[13] जैन साहित्य में इन्द्र द्वारा तीर्थंकरों के जीवनवृत्तों– जन्म, दीक्षा एवं कैवल्य प्राप्ति से सम्बन्धित अंकनों में ग्यारहवीं–बारहवीं शती ई0 में इन्द्र को अमूर्तित किया गया।[14]

विवेचना

विवेच्य प्रतिमाओं में तीन शिव की मूर्तियां हैं, जिनमें से दो स्पष्टतः शिव हैं। क्योंकि, दोनों में ही शिवपुत्र गणेश का रूपांकन है, जबकि जैन साहित्य में गणेश को शिव के साथ रूपायित करने का वर्णन प्राप्त नहीं होता। यह प्रतिमा विज्ञान की दृष्टि से पृथक है। एक अन्य प्रतिमा शिव की ही है, जो उत्तर–पूर्व दिशा के स्वामी दिक्पाल ईशान हैं, समीप ही इनका वाहन वृषभ भी उत्कीर्ण है। यहाँ एक विशेष तथ्य यह है, कि ईशान चतुर्भुज हैं, जबकि, जैन साहित्य के अनुसार ईशान के मात्र दो भुजा ही होनी चाहिए। अस्तु, यह भी प्रतिमा विधान से साम्यता नहीं रखता। गणेश की नृत्यरत प्रतिमा उल्लेखनीय है। पांचवीं प्रतिमा शान्तिदेवी की है, जो श्वेताम्बार स्थलों से प्राप्त होती हैं। यह लक्ष्मी का भी रूपांकन हो सकता है ? स्पष्टतः कुछ भी नहीं कहा जा सकता, क्योंकि दोनों के प्रतिमा लक्षण समान हैं, किन्तु खड़े होने की मुद्रा लक्ष्मी की नहीं है, इसलिए निश्चित–सा होता है, कि मूर्ति शांतिदेवी की है।

अगली प्रतिमा निश्चित ही श्रुतदेवी सरस्वती की है। ऐरावत पर आसीन इन्द्र चतुर्भुजधारिणी हैं, किन्तु जैन साहित्य में इनका भी उल्लेख द्विभुज के रूप में ही है। शेष दो मूर्तियां इन्द्राणी की हैं। एक त्रिभंग मुद्रा में और दूसरी ललितासन मुद्रा में निरूपित है। इनका वाहन गज भी रूपायित है। जैन साहित्य में उल्लिखित प्रतिमा लक्षण

के अनुसार उक्त दोनों मूर्तियां पूर्णतः विधि सम्मत नहीं हैं। हिन्दू प्रतिमा विधान के अनुसार गज, पाश और अंकुश इन्द्र की पत्नी इन्द्राणी के विशिष्ट आयुद्ध हैं। किन्तु, जैन साहित्य में इन्द्राणी को स्थान प्राप्त नहीं है। फिर भी, यह इन्द्राणी की प्रतिमा है, तो जैन स्थल पर विधि सम्मत नहीं है। इसलिए इनकी निश्चित पहिचान प्रस्तावित है। यह भी कहा जा सकता है, कि शिल्पकार मूर्ति विधि–बन्धनों का खण्ड़न करते हुए, स्वतन्त्रता का परिचय दिया है। गणेश और शान्तिदेवी की उपस्थिति से निश्चित होता है, कि यह मंदिर श्वेताम्बर सम्प्रदाय का था। बावनढ़ेरी अथवा पार्श्वनाथ मंदिर अभिनव प्रयोगों की विविधताओं से परिपूर्ण था।

सन्दर्भ

1. बी.सी. भट्टाचार्य, 'दि जैना आइक्नोग्रॉफी', लाहौर, 1939, पृ0 148
2. एम. एन. तिवारी, 'जैन प्रतिमा विज्ञान', वाराणसी, पृ0 42
3. यू. पी. शाह, 'बिगिनिंग्स ऑव जैना आइक्नोग्रॉफी', संग्रहालय पुरातत्त्व पत्रिका, लखनऊ, अंक–9, पृ0 10
4. भगवतीसूत्र, 3.1.134
5. भगवतीसूत्र, 11.11.430
6. अंगविज्जा, 58.82.223
   'एकाणंसा सिरी बुद्धि मेघ कित्ती सरसती एवमादीयाओं उवलद्व्वाओ भवन्ति।'
7. शोभनसूरिकृति, 'स्तुतिचतुर्विशतिका', 12.4.137
8. एम. एन. तिवारी, 'सम अनपब्लिश्ड जैन स्कल्पचर्स ऑव गणेश फ्रॉम वेस्टर्न इण्ड़िया', जैन जर्नल, 9, अंक–3, पृ0 90–92
9. अभिधानचिंतामणि, 2.129
10. आचारदिनकर, भाग–2, गणपति–प्रतिष्ठा, 1–2, पृ0 210
11. एम. एन. तिवारी, 'जैन प्रतिमा विज्ञान', वाराणसी, पृ0 33
12. स्थानांगसूत्र
13. तथैव, 13
14. कल्पसूत्र, 14

39

EARLIEST HUMAN BRONZE IMAGE FROM MIDDLE GANGA PLAIN AND ITS ICONIC REPRESENTATION IN THE ROCK ART OF KAIMUR REGION, INDIA

Sachin Kumar Tiwary

Introduction

Present small paper is based on the remarkable object of bronze human image in Indian context after Indus Civilization. The time frame of the present search has been chosen from sixth century BCE to the beginning of current era, which includes a wide time frame of Northern Black Polished ware, the Mauryan period and prior to the Kushana period. The main objective of this paper is to find out archaeologically (from the excavated remain of metal object recovered) whether metal was truly one of the major factor for the rise of power in the said region.

Brief about Geo-coordinate and early history of the Bihar state

The said object is recovered from the Bihar state of India. Bihar comprising Chhotanagpur plateau is situated in the North-eastern part of the country between 24°20'10"N -27°31'15"N latitude to 82°19'50" E - 88°17'40" E longitude with Nepal in the North, Jharkhand in the South, Uttar Pradesh in the West and West Bengal in East. The plain is divided into two unequal halves (North Bihar and South Bihar) by the river Ganges which flows through the middle from west to east. Continuous evidence of Human settlement was noted in this plain since prehistoric time special noted from the sites of Paisra, Rajgir, Lota Pahar, Senuwar, Chirand etc., but with the emergence of state which took place with Sixteen *Mahajanapadas* from 600 BCE, evidence of proper urban settlement was noted in the plain. By 5th century BCE Magadh emerged as a powerful state with Rajagriha as its capital under the kingship of Ajatashatru. It was during his time Pataliputra emerged as an important port town in this region which later became the capital of Magadha during Mauryan period.

About the finding Site

The site Chechar-Kutubpur is located on the northern bank of river Ganga in the district of Vaishali, Bihar. It was discovered in 1967 by the team of archaeologist from Patna Circle of Archaeological Survey of India, Patna[1]. *Padma Shree* R. S. Bisht of the Patna Circle then Mid-eastern Circle of the Survey conducted small-scale excavation at the site, with a view to ascertaining the cultural sequence of the site.

The excavation yielded a three-fold cultural sequence. The occupation strata of Period I is represented by compact deep yellow alluvium overlying the natural soil. Although no metals were recovered from this period, the general evidence speaks of a developed rural economy in which agriculture as well as hunting, including angling played an important role. Fire places dug into the flooring were encountered at the centre of the houses. Polished stone tools are also noticed. However, the divergences that exist within this Period are strong enough to justify the division into three phases A, B and C. Period II is marked by the appearance of the Northern Black Polished Ware with its associated wares. A huge pit, more than 2 m deep and 5 m wide, belonging to this phase was encountered. It yielded baked bricks and iron pieces. In case of Middle Ganga Plain the earliest evidence of bronze figurine has been discovered from the Period II, Mauryan period from the excavated site at Chechar. Period III is represented by a large brick structure represented essentially by the ghost walls and four successive floor-levels. On the basis of pottery, this structure seems to have been constructed in the Kushana period and continued into the following Gupta period[2].

Iconography and similarity in rock art study with the bronze image

The recovered caste bronze image of a male is standing (fig.14.1) on square flat base. Head of the image is shown conical in shape, having beautiful decorated hair style. Both the ears prominently shown pressed, which left one is partially damage. He is holding either arrow or flower buns or corn- cropia in his left hand and either a stick (*lathi*) or bow is holding by his right hand. It is quite interesting that the bronze image is very much similar to the pictographs discovered in the Kaimur range of Kaimur district, Bihar[3]. In my opinion they were very aware with such kind of artistic work on the cave or shelter walls as well as they were developed in metal art too. Similar image in the form of pictographs are recorded from the cave, in which the human figure standing in position holded same kind of object, it may be weapon or simple daily life use equipments in his both hand (fig. 14.2 and fig. 14.3). Bothe the pictographs are in dynamic pose. It is difficult to ascertain the time frame of the pictographs, whereas with the study of other associate material culture those recovered from the shelter and cave it may be framed in Chalcolithic to Early historic period.

References

1. Indian Archaeology 1976-77—A Review, Archaeological Survey of India, New Delhi, p. 14.
2. Indian Archaeology 1977-78-A Review, Archaeological Survey of India, New Delhi, pp. 17-18.
3. Author's unpublished thesis on Rock Art of Kaimur Region-Bihar, submitted in the Social Science Faculty of Patna University, 2013.

40

BRAHMANICAL FIGURES ON THE TERRACOTTA-ART OF BIHAR

Anantashutosh Dwivedi

The clay master in Ancient India had achieved a great height in shaping the clay images of the deities. They have well versed with the iconographic features of the deities. The terracotta of Bihar played a vital role in reconstructing the Art history of India. Here an analysis would indicate how artistically they described the features of Hindu Gods and Goddesses.

Brahma

Brahma, also known as *Prajapati*, is the creator of the Universe and the foremost of the Brahminical deities. In the Brahminical texts, he has been described as the creator of the universe. But in spite of this, his position in the pantheon is somewhat of lesser importance as compared to *Vishnu, Shiva, Ganapati, Surya, Durga* and the likes. But in spite of this he has got a prominent place in Indian plastic art from the earliest time in stone, bronze as well as miniature paintings etc. The terracotta artists did not overlook *Brahma* altogether, though his presence is rarely found in the available evidences.

A circular seal elongated on the top from Nalanda[1], has the image of *Brahma* with three faces seated on a lotus with heavy ear-rings. He holds a rosary in the right hand and a long necked vase (*kamandalu*) in the raised left hand. He has a pot belly. The legend in two lines reads:

I. Prakasha(?) – kalapaka
II. Trividya – Brahamana

A baked oval clay seal found from Nalanda[2] has a large hole passing through both its ends and depicts three faces of *Brahma*, seated over a lotus seat. He has a pot belly and two arms. The right one holds a rosary and the left a small vase. The heads are enriched with halo. In the lower field the legend with two lines reads as follows:

I. Shriman Navaka[rmmathanam(?)]
II. Traividyasya

A similar circular seal from Nalanda[3] with a three headed corpulent *Brahma* figure is shown seated over a lotus above two horizontal lines. The legend reads as follows: *Vasantagra-vataka-agrahara*

Traividya (sya), i.e., "The Traividya of agrahara of Vasantagravataka". The back has an impression of inserting something. These *agrahara* seal seems to be Brahmanical in nature.

Another circular seal from the same site[4] is divided into equal spaces by two lines, the inner space is dotted. Above two horizontal lines, the *Brahma* figure (Fig. 1) with a pot belly, seated over a lotus seat, has a heavy ear ring, crescent to the right and Sun to the left. He is holding a rosary in his right hand and a narrow necked vase in his left hand. It has the following legend:

I. *Bhallatvataka-agrahare(sa)*
II. *Srimat- Traividyasya*

"Of the illustrious Traividya, the chief of agrahara of Bhallatvataka". The seal is partially damaged and a hole pierces through both the ends. The presence of the *Brahma* in these seals is quite conspicuous which possibly belong to Gupta period.

1

2

Shiva

Shiva happens to be the mightiest of the gods of Hindu trinity. He has been dominating the Indian religious scene from the remote past. Though his antiquity could be traced to the Vedic literatures, but in Rigveda, he had been popular more as a *Rudra* than *Shiva*. Besides the literature, *Shiva* was represented in the Indian plastic art as well. *Shiva* is represented in two forms in the terracotta art of Bihar i.e. *linga* and human form.

The right side of the seal of the Catur monks of Nalanda[5] bears a *Shiva* figure seated on a *chauki* with a tree on his right side and a *trishula* on his left. It has two horizontal lines, an obscure legend of one line read *Mallirasala - gramasya*. It seems *Mallagrami(?)na- gramasya*.

A seal from Basarh[6] depicts a *linga* (Fig. 2) on a yoni flanked by two tridents. The legend of the seal is *Amratakeshvara* i.e. the lord of *Amrataka. Amrtakeshvara* is mentioned in the *Matsya Purana* as one of the eight *Guhyalingas*, situated in the *Avimukta* region in Varanasi. A seal of the district office at Nalanda has a device of a crescent tapped *linga* flanked by two female attendants, one on either side. The device could represent *Shiva* as *Shashanka-Shekhara*, in his an iconic form. This has been interpreted by Banrejea[7] as *Shiva* in theriomorphic form with a crescent over the head. Nalanda[8] seal depicts a *linga* in the upper half. The *linga* is flanked by female worshippers. A crescent is at the top. The lower half has a legend in two lines:-

I. *Shon-antarala-visaye*
II. *Adhikarnasya*

"of the court of justice in the district (*visaya*) of the Son-*doab*". The river Son is known to be a large tributary of the Ganga. The seal shows that there was a district named after it by the 8th century A.D. and that *Shiva* was a deity worshipped by the holder of the seal.

An oblong yellowish seal of Nalanda[9] bears in its upper part, a corpulent male seated cross-legged under the canopy of the serpent hoods with a *linga* and a tree on its left. On the *linga*, there is a symbol which either represents a trident or an umbrella. The legend reads:-

I. *Sri Purik agrahare*
II. *Srimat- Traividyasya*

Ganesha

Shiva has a large number of *ganas* and *Ganesha* has been described to be the foremost among them. His adoration has been of comparatively later period, as compared to *Brahma, Vishnu, Shiva* and other deities. But his depiction in Indian plastic art has been made in various ways. A number of *Ganesha* figures have been made in terracotta art in Bihar. The seal of Nalanda is fine example. The right side of the seal of Catur monks of Nalanda[10] bears an oval impression showing seated *Ganesha* with four arms, holding a *parasu* in the upper right, a rosary in the lower right hand, a dish of sweets in the upper left hand and an *ankusha* (?) in the lower left hand. Below two horizontal lines a legend reads as *Udumbaraka-gramasya*, i.e. "Of the village Udumbaraka". This village also must have its own establishment at Nalanda.

Ganeshani

The Catur monastic seal of Nalanda[11] on left, an oval sealing shows a seated goddess *Ganeshani* (Fig. 3) with a child to the left and having a tree to her right. The lower field separated by two lines has legend:

I. *Ankathasatta (?)grama*
II. *Sya*

3

4

Garuda

The *Brahma Purana* (3.95) describes *Garuda* and *Aruna* as the two sons born to *Vinata*. Eighth verse in the fourth chapter of this text testifies to the crowning of *Garuda* as the king of birds *Garudanchaiva Pakshinam*. The *Garuda* is described as the vehicle of *Vishnu*. A number of seals from Nalanda exhibit the depiction of *Garuda*. Some of them are intact and some are broken.

A seal from Nalanda depicts *Garuda* as a vehicle of *Vishnu* with wings spreading on both sides. The upper field separated by a thick straight line, shows apparently *Vishnu* riding on *Garuda* (Fig. 4), as can be surmised from the plumage and the claws of the bird and the *gada* or mace symbol of the deity in the right upper hand – the symbol in the right lower hand is indistinct but might be a conch or lotus. The legend begins like that on the *Maukhari* seals and would lead us to think that the seal is a *Maukhari*[12] token. The clay seal from Nalanda belonging to Kumargupta III[13], has device of *Garuda* (Fig. 5) in hybrid form. He has a body of a bird but the face of a human. The head is decorated with *jata*, falling on either side of the head. The forehead has a pointed Vaishnavite mark. The Sun to the right and the crescent to the left could be identified on the aforesaid-seal. The Sun and the moon are two witnesses of our actions or *karmas* and to represent them on such documents is very appropriate. A snake is coiled around the neck and the talons rest on two parallel lines. The legend of eight lines appears below the parallel lines. An elliptical seal of Buddhagupta[14] with a raised border shows *Garuda* in composite form showing full human face and the left side is that of a plumage and the right side of which is damaged. The main bird is lodged over the two parallel lines below which comes a legend. A fragmentary seal of Narsimhagupta[15] shows the deep groove at the back. The effigy of *Garuda* on the upper side is mostly gone and only ends of the left wing and the claws are preserved. The legend consists of eight lines.

Narsimha

This is the forth incarnation of Vishnu and has been described in the various *Puranas*. The incarnation of *Narsimha* is represented in Indian plastic art in his individual capacity as well as in *Dashavatara* panels in stone, bronze, wood work as well as the miniatures. But his representation in terracotta art is few and far between. The Spooner's list of Basarh[16] seal of Gupta period projects the figure of *Narsimha*, facing front but intended to be turned slightly to the left, seated in the *lalitasana* on a pedestal. His right hand is raised while the left rests on the hip. The legend occurs in very small letters below this device.

5

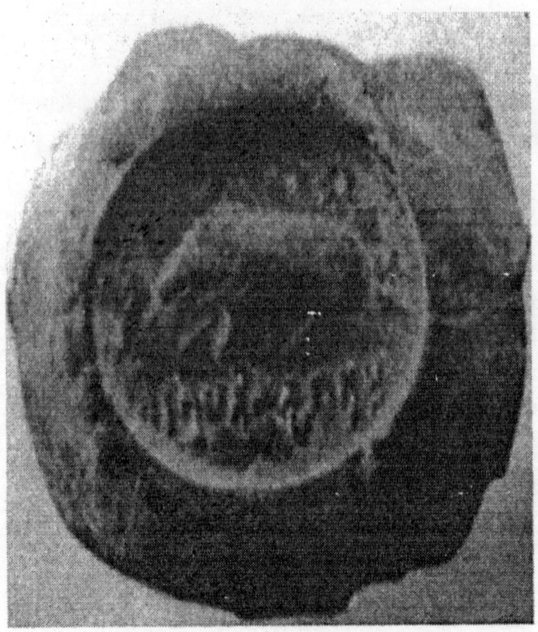

6

Varaha

The original concept of *Varaha*, the third incarnation of *Vishnu*[17] lies in the *Vedic* literature followed by the *Brahmanas* and other subsequent literature. But the representation of boar incarnation of *Vishnu* though evolved evidently during Shunga- Kushana period became popular in the sculptural art of Gupta period, wherein both the theriomorphic and therioanthromorphic types occur frequently. The *Parambhagvata* Gupta kings favoured this incarnation for saving the country from the depredations of the foreign invaders like Shaka and Hunas.

The boar figure is found to occur on the Basarh sealing. It occurs on no. 18 of the Bloch's list[18] (Fig. 6) and no. 54 in the list of Spooner in Basarh seals. No.54 from Basarh is unique example and a very handsome one with a legend of one line. The crescent and the Sun are also carved on the upper field above the boar. It is a finely executed figure of a boar recumbent to left as its device. The seal is unusual in the artistic excellence.

Harihar (?)

The Catur monastic seal from Nalanda[19] has an oval impression showing a seated four-armed deity i.e. *Harihar*(?), holding a *Cakra*(?) in right upper hand and *trishula* in left upper hand. It is a very peculiar seal due to the change of position of *Vishnu* and *Shiva* .The symbols of the lower hands are not clear. The legend below two lines reads: *Nandana-gramasya*, i.e., of the village of *Nandana*.

Surya

The seal of the Spooner's[20] collection represents the very fine temple seal No.607 at Basarh. It contains the perfect example of fire-alter with probably with the solar disc placed above it. The legend in the Gupta characters is *Bhagavata Adityasya*, i.e., "seal of the temple" of the blessed Sun. This particular seal must be the seal of the some temple, presumably in eastern India, to the divinity to the blessed Sun as worshipped in the cults of the Persians domiciled in India , we are to understand the eastern Iranians who migrated to India in large numbers with their cults in the early post-Christian period. Bloch illustrated a seal found by him from Basarh[21] with the significant legend: *Ravidasa(h)*, 'the slave of the Sun'. It is one of the best depiction of fire-alter (Fig. 7) not only in Bihar but also in India in the terracotta art. A black terracotta plaque of Mauryan-Shunga period discovered from Bulandibagh, Patna[22], depicts Surya standing over a chariot drawn by four horses. He wears a coat of mail and quiver and shoots an arrow from his bow. The charioteer on his right holds with his left hand the reins of the four horses and in the right hand with a long staff. A bird is perched behind the chariot. Bell-shaped tassels hangs with the chariot and with the harness of the horse. A hole to the left of Surya's head-dress can also be seen. The back part of the plaque is impressed with two concentric rings, the outer with crescent shape and inner with the deeply holed dots set in a zig-zag manner. It has a circle in the middle with an indistinct floral pattern.

Ramayana' Scene

The scene from the *Ramayana* on the moulded brick from Chausa[23] in Bihar, which is damaged considerably, portrays a scene from the *Ramayana*. There are six figure in the panel of which there are three monkeys and three humans. The person sitting the left cross-legged is possibly engaged in the conversation with the other which is invisible. The anxiety is writ large on the faces of all the group of humans and the monkeys. Their hand gestures are superb. The panel is unique in displaying of the expression of feelings. This belongs to the 4th-5th century A.D.

Durga

Nalanda is also important for the presence of the seal of *Durga*. It is an elongated oval piece with oval running from bottom to top for a string. The upper field is occupied by eight armed *Durga*[24] seated on a lion above two lines, below which a legend reads:

I. *Ghananjana-grama-ja-[ja]-*
II. *Napadasya*

It refers the present name of the village Ghenjana which is in Jehanabad district, where some Buddhist remains are still preserved as protected monuments.

Chamunda

A unique seal from Nalanda depicts the figure of *Chamunda* on the upper field of two lines. Seal is an oblong, brown piece, groove and a palm leaf mark on the back. It is enclosed in oblong line. Four armed *Chamunda*[25] is facing right, skull in right lower hand, dagger in left upper, trident in left lower and goad in right upper hand. Her mouth is open and tongue is protruding. Below two horizontal lines the legend reads:

I. *Alikapṛistha-grama-*
II. *Janapadasya.*

7

8

Abhishek Lakshmi

The seal of Nalanda[26] depicts *Abhishek Lakshmi* which is standing in the centre with an elephant and a *mangala-kalash* on each side. Halo is also shown behind the head of *Abhishek Lakshmi*. The lower field which is divided by one straight line has a legend in two lines which reads:

I. *Nagara-bhuktau kumaramatya-adhi-*
II. *Karanasya*

Another seal from Nalanda[27] depicts *Abhishek Lakshmi,* seated at two horizontal lines and flanked by a male figure. Each side of her hand stands an elephant, apparently in the act of offering lotus. The lower field has a legend in one line: *kumaramatya-adhikaranasya*. Another seal from Nalanda[28] gives the depiction of *Abhishek Lakshmi*. The concentric circles with dots in the intervening space enclose both the fields. The upper field exhibits the *Abhishek Lakshmi* figure standing on the lotus and flanked by a seated male figure above whom stands an elephant with his trunk raised and possibly holding a lotus to offer to the goddess. The lower field has a legend:

I. *Magadha-bhuktau kumaramatya-*

II. Adhikarnasya.

Basarh[29] is also important for the seal of *Abhishek Lakshmi. Abhishek Lakshmi* is standing and she is flanked by seated male figure. Many bag in the front, from which he throws down small round objects (coins?). Above the seated male figure, elephant is standing with his raised trunk and holding a lotus to offer to the goddess. Two horizontal lines below:

I. Shri-Yuvraja-bhattaraka-padiya-
II. Kumaramatya-adhikarnasya.

"(Seal) of his highness, the illustrious *Yuvraja* (and) *Bhattaraka*, the chief of prince's ministers". Basarh is also known for the beautiful depiction of *Abhishek Lakshmi* on the seals of Bloch's[30] (Fig. 8) and Spooner's[31] lists. It is more or less in the same manner like the seals of Nalanda.

On the basis of systematic study of the representation of Brahmanical images and their mount in the terracotta art of Bihar exhibits the mastered of the artistic development both, human and animal figurines. The aforesaid examples stands testimony to the fact that the figures in the early terracotta art of the deities were not so well executed and their outward finish also left much to be desired, but with the passage of time right from pre-Mauryan to Shunga times, the quality and execution was improved while during the Gupta period and the subsequent time their execution reached the zenith possibly with the royal patronage as well as the continuous development of the iconographical features of the deity.

References

1. *Memoirs of the Archaeological Survey of India* (MASI), No.66, 1942, reprint 1999, Delhi, pp. 54-55, S.I No.801, Pl. VI, h.
2. Ibid., p. 55, S.I, No.691, Pl. VII, a.
3. Ibid., p. 56, S.I, No.782, Pl. VII, b.
4. Ibid., p. 56, S.I, No.350, Pl. VII, c.
5. Ibid., p. 41, S.I, No.645 & 811, Pl. III, h.
6. *Archaeological Survey of India : Annual Reports* (ASIAR), 1903-04, Delhi, P.110, No. 30, Pl. XL, 2.
7. Banerjea, J.N., *Development of Hindu Iconography*,1956, Kolkata, p. 179.
8. MASI, op.cit., p.51, S.I , No.790, Pl. V, j.
9. Ibid., p. 56, S.I , No.791, Pl. IV, f.
10. Ibid., p. 41, S.I, No. 789, Pl. III, g.
11. Ibid., p. 42, S.I, No.836 & 807, Pl. III, i.
12. Ibid., p. 70, S.I , No.347, Pl. IX, c.
13. Ibid., p. 65, S.I , No.849, 843, Pl. VIII , d-e.
14. Ibid., p. 64, S.I, No.660, Pl. VIII , a.
15. Ibid., p. 65, S.I , No.650, Pl. VIII, b.
16. ASIAR, 1913-14, Delhi, p.133, No.191, Pl. XLVI.
17. Banerjea, J.N., op.cit., p.194.
18. ASIAR, 1903-04, Delhi, p.109, N0.18, Pl. XLI, 15.
19. MASI, op.cit., p. 42, S.I, No.831, Pl. III k.
20. ASIAR, 1913-14, Delhi, p. 141, No. 607, Pl. XLIX.
21. ASIAR, 1903-04, Delhi, Pl. XL ,9.
22. Akhtar, Naseem, *Patna Museum Catalogue: Terracottas and Metal images*, 2001, Patna, No.8570, p. 56.
23. Nagar, S.L., *Deities in Terracotta Art*, p. 32, Pl. 24.
24. MASI, op.cit., p. 46, S. 9, R.19, Pl. IV, j
25. Ibid., p. 48, S. 9, R.IA, Pl. V ,d.
26. Ibid., p. 52, S.I, 797, Pl. VI ,b.
27. Ibid., p. 52, S.I, 787 Pl. V ,l.
28. Ibid., p. 51, S.I, 813,817,808,691, Pl. V , k.
29. ASIAR, 1903-04, Delhi, p. 107, No.6, Pl. XL ,11.
30. Ibid., Pl. XL 8,10,13.
31. ASIAR, 1913-14, Delhi, No. 200, Pl. XLVII.

41

THE HUMAN STRATUM OF THE RĀMA STORY

S.R. Goyal

Stages in the Evolution of the Rāma Story

It was the *Vālmīkīya Rāmāyaṇa* that established the essentials of the story of Rāma for the entire subsequent Hindu tradition. The later ancient Indian works, except Buddhist and Jaina, give only a modified version of the story or interpret it in different ways. Even the *Adhyātma Rāmāyaṇa* and the *Rāmacharitamānasa* of Tulsidas take the basic framework of the story of Rāma as given by Vālmīki.

As has been stated in the *Rāmāyaṇa* itself the story of Rāma originated and developed among the kings of the Ikshvāku dynasty (*Rāmā.*, I.5.3); it acquired the shape and form of a *Mahākāvya* only gradually. Like the *Mahābhārata* its evolution began with the composition of stray *gāthās* composed by now unknown *sūtas.* When the *sūtas* composed the original *gāthās,* which must have been unconnected with each other, they tended to portray the character of Rāma as a human hero and his story as a human story of a great king who had strength as well as weaknesses of a man. That is proved, as is seen in the sequel, by the internal evidence of the *Rāmāyaṇa* itself. The composition of these stray *gāthās* was the *first stage* in the evolution of the Rāma story. Now, we do not know anything about the contents of that stage of the Rāma saga except what one can conjecture and deduce on the basis of the second stage which we will discuss presently. Later on when these *gāthās* were collected and given the form of a *kāvya* or *Mahākāvya* by some poet—probably Vālmīki—Rāma became an ideal human hero who, by definition of an Epic hero, could not have been depicted as doing anything which was less than just and true. In the beginning of the *Vālmīkīya Rāmāyaṇa* Nārada is asked by Vālmīki: "Who is there in this world today who is great and heroic, who knows dharma and duty, speaks the truth and is firm in his vows ? And who is endowed with good conduct, is helpful to all creatures, and who is learned, able, handsome, self-controlled, slow to anger, wise, free from jealousy, and—when stimulated to wrath—can terrify the gods in battle ?" (*Rāmā.*, I, 1.2-4). This provides right at the beginning an idea of what an ideal hero of an epic should be and the contours of the human personality and character of Rāma, which was of course noble and blameless but nevertheless human, not divine. It was what Vālmīki originally wished to portray. That was the *second stage* of the evolution of the Rāma story.

As is generally believed the first and the last *Kāṇḍas* of the *Rāmāyaṇa* are later than the *Kāṇḍas* II to VI (which also contain numerous interpolated passages), though some portions of the first or Bāla Kāṇḍa may belong to the original story. Therefore, the original poem of Vālmīki must have been much smaller in volume than it is today. However, there is no reason to doubt that Vālmīki composed at least part of the *Rāmāyaṇa.* Its *phalaśruti* says that the work was written by Vālmīki—*Rāmāyaṇam Vālmīkinā kṛtam* (VI. 128. 107, 112, 114). He is mentioned more than once in the first and the last Kāṇḍas. The *Mahābhārata* and other later sources agree on the point that Vālmīki was its author; there is no need to doubt this as a basic fact.

The life of Vālmīki is shrouded in mist. According to Bulcke[1] he lived in Kosala about the turn of the fourth century B.C. and was a lover of Kosala, a lover of nature, and well-travelled in North India but not in Central or Southern India. By the first century B.C. (the approximate time of the Bāla Kāṇḍa according to Bulcke) he was considered to have been a famous *muni* of Rāma's time with an *āśrama* near the Gaṅgā. Two centuries later, when the Uttara Kāṇḍa was taking shape, he was thought to be a friend of Daśaratha of Ayodhyā, and also a scion of the clan of the Bhārgavas. The association of the word *valmīka* meaning anthill with his name gave rise to the legend that he practiced asceticism for so long that an anthill grew up around him. Insofar as he is said to have taught Rāma's sons Kuśa and Lava he himself may well have been an itinerant singer—*kuśīlava*—a word which in view of the present writer might have been the original from which names Kuśa-Lava were derived. According of later traditions he was a robber and of low caste.

Much interpolations were made in the text of Vālmīki at a later date. It is generally believed, and rightly, that much of the Bāla Kāṇḍa, almost the whole of the Uttara Kāṇḍa and several passages in the other kāṇḍas were added in the text much later. And it is also a fact that these additions were mostly made when the figure of Rāma had become transformed from human to divine—from a royal prince to an *avatāra* of Vishṇu. That may be regarded as the *third stage* in the evolulion of the Rāma Kathā.

The Bāla Kaṇḍa tells us that Vālmīki composed the *Rāmāyaṇa* "with the Uttara", that is with the Uttara Kāṇḍa. But the seventh or Uttara Kāṇḍa appears to be a later addition. The opening part of this Kāṇḍa begins with the stories told by certain sages to Rāma when he was back in Ayodhyā. They include tales about Vishṇu and Rāvaṇa which were intended to portray Rāma as an *avatāra* of Vishṇu. The *Rāmāyaṇa* itself sees the Uttara Kāṇḍa as something of a postscript. As with the Bāla Kaṇḍa it also differs from the main story in language and style. The two tables of contents in I.1 and I.3 also indicate that the Uttara Kāṇḍa is a later addition. In it Rāma is portrayed as an avatāra of Vishṇu. Some scholars feel that some parts of the Uttara Kāṇḍa are authentic.

But B. M. Barua[2] takes the Uttara Kāṇḍa as a whole to be an interpolation except certain cantos or their portions which relate to the episode of Sītā's banishment and its sequel. However, C.V. Vaidya[3] argues that Sītā's disappearance and the description of Rāvaṇa's greatness are part of the main story.

The view that like the Uttara Kaṇḍa, much of the Bāla Kāṇḍa is also a later addition has been popular since the days Jacobi.[4] The main arguments in favour of this view have been that the Bāla Kāṇḍa portrays Rāma as an *avatāra* of Vishṇu, the main story does not. Then it gives two introductions for the *Rāmāyaṇa.* In the first (I. 1) the events of the Bāla Kāṇḍa are not mentioned; in the second (I.3) they are. The language and style of the Bāla Kāṇḍa are quite drab and different from the poetic style of the main story (II-VI). Much of the material of the Bāla Kāṇḍa has little or no connection with the main story and there are internal contradictions between some of its later material and other material in the main story.

The main figure of Rāma that emerges from *Rāmāyaṇa* is of a man and king who is the upholder of dharma, who is an example for others, who is a hero and who is (mainly in the first and last or the seventh Kāṇḍa) an incarnation of Vishṇu. But in the *Rāmāyaṇa* the divinity of Rāma does not go further. It is the *Rāmacharitamānas* of Tulsī and the *Adhyātma Rāmāyaṇa* that give us a seemingly very different image of Rāma. In them the divine aspect of Rāma becomes prominent and stress is laid upon his *bhakti* not merely as an *avatāra* but as the sole object of devotion. The *Adhyātma Rāmāyaṇa* sees Rāma not only as a personal God but also as *nirguṇa Brahman,* and propagates that salvation may be found only by union (*sāyujya*) with him. That may be regarded as the *fourth stage* in the evolution of the divinity of Rāma.

Kernel of the Rāma Kathā

The story of Rāma as given in the *Rāmāyaṇa* of Vālmīki is regarded by many as a composite story of Rāma's life in Ayodhyā, the tale of the Vānaras given in the Sundara Kāṇḍa and the story of Rāma's struggle against the demon-king Rāvaṇa. How far this view of the Rāma Kathā is correct we will discuss it elsewhere. Here, we propose mainly to analyse the Ayodhyā Kāṇḍa story with a new and, in our opinion, correct approach.

The central theme of the Ayodhyā Kāṇḍa is undoubtedly the succession of Rāma to the throne of Ayodhyā. As the seventh Kāṇḍa of the *Rāmāyaṇa* is admittedly a later accretion, the accession of Rāma must have been the *phalāgama* of the original *Rāmāyaṇa.* However, even in its present form this work presents quite a compact and well-knit story in which the character of Rāma is portrayed on so noble a design that even after divesting it of divine elements it retains its idealism and almost superhuman qualities. But from the historical point of view, in the actual story the attitude of Rāma, and also of Bharata, towards their respective prospects of acquiring the throne obviously must have been more human.

As is well-known and has been stated in the *Rāmāyaṇa* itself, the story of Rāma originated and developed among the kings of the Ikshvāku dynasty.[5] It was natural, therefore, for the *sūtas*, who composed the original *gāthās*, to present the story of Rāma in such a manner as to make him, despite his human weaknesses, an embodiment of all the kshatriya virtues. Later on, when these *gāthās* were collected, collated and given the form of a *mahākāvya* by some poet—probably Vālmīki—the character of Rāma was portrayed in most glorious colours, because as the hero of an epic he could not have been depicted as doing anything which was less than just and true. And subsequently, after he acquired the status of an *avatāra* (a fact which led to many alterations and additions in the *Rāmāyaṇa*), nobody could think of casting even an aspersion on his conduct and character.

The portrayal of Rāma in the *Rāmāyaṇa* was influenced by another factor also. As V.S. Pathak has pointed out for the writers of the *kāvyas* and historical dramas notionally the end (*phala*) of the story used to be the starting point. In this reverse process, Pathak argued, his (poet-historian's) endeavour used to be not much to develop gradually the consequences of a given initial situation, as to arrange antecedent events in such a way that they necessarily culminated into the known outcome. "Further, since a man can hardly grasp and describe life in all its mutifarious aspects, the historian selects only that series of events through which he can explain the end in question."[6] Moreover, "the concern of the historian is not so much to bring out the consequences which would inevitably follow if a person with certain given qualities were placed in the initial situation, as to divine in his character those qualities which make the known outcome appear rational and inevitable. Therefore, besides conditioning the treatment of antecedent events, the end (*phalāgama*) also influences the characterization."[7] However, in his attempt to weave a coherent story such a poet-historian usually inadvertently left several loose ends which ultimately give a lie to the central tale exposing the motive of the author. The author or rather authors of the *Rāmāyaṇa* also certainly tried to remove such contradictions and make their story compact and homogenous. Nevertheless they inadvertently left many a loose ends in it—anomalous fragments that are neither integrated with the core of the story nor are required by it. They are more or less refractory snippets of the main story which apparently defied the attempts of the author of the Epic to harmonise them with the rest or were left inadvertently. But by striking discordant notes they help us in removing the various layers of transmutations and interpolations by which the author of the Epic had sought to conceal the worldly atmosphere of jealousy, greed and ambition which dominated the royal family of Ayodhyā. As we will see, even though woven carefully, these anomalous fragments present an intelligible, even if somewhat disjointed and incomplete, pattern which sometimes cuts the central tale at its vital points.

Popular Version of the Ayodhyā Kāṇḍa

Let us begin with the story of Rāma in the form in which it has influenced the popular mind. According to it, king Daśaratha had four sons : Rāmachandra, the eldest, was the son of the chief-queen Kausalyā; Bharata, the next one was the begotten on Kaikeyī; and Lakshmaṇa and Śatrughna were the sons of the second queen Sumitrā. Daśaratha in his old age decided to coronate Rāma as the next king (or declare him as heir-apparent only, the point is not clear). But Kaikeyī, on the advice of her maid Mantharā (who had come with kaikeyī at the time of her marriage from her mother's country), embarrassed him by asking him to honour the two boons he had promised her earlier. By the first boon she secured the kingdom for her son Bharata (who had, at that time, along with Śatrughna, gone on a visit to the kingdom of his maternal grand-father) and by the second demanded the exile of Rāma for fourteen years. Rāma did not protest and along with his wife Sītā and step brother Lakshmaṇa (son of Sumitrā) went to Chitrakūṭa. After his departure the old king died. Bharata and Śatrughna were hastily summoned from the Kekaya kingdom but on his arrival contrary to the wish and expectation of Kaikeyī, Bharata refused to ascend the throne. Instead, he went to Chitrakūṭa and pleaded with Rāma to accept the burden of sovereignty, Rāma did not agree to it and argued that he must fulfil the vow of his father and should, therefore, remain in exile. But when he was pressed by Bharata, he agreed to ascend the throne of Ayodhyā after the expiry of the fourteen year period. On his part, Bharata agreed to carry on the burden of administration in the meanwhile after installing the *pādukās* of Rāma on the throne. Both of them lived upto their respective promises. Shorn of the refractory snippets this is the popular version of the story of *Vālmīkīya Rāmāyaṇa.*

It is obvious that in the popular version of the Rāma story the right of Rāma to his ancestral throne emanated from the fact of his being the eldest son of his father. It is explicitly mentioned in the *Rāmāyaṇa* at several places. "Among all the Ikshvākus", Vasishṭha told Rāma, "the eldest son undoubtedly becomes the ruler; while an elder son is present a younger son is never consecrated as king. The eldest alone is so consecrated. Being one of the Rāghavas, you as such ought not violate the time-honoured usage of your house. Like your father, highly illustrious as you are, rule the earth abounding in precious stones and consisting of numerous dominions."[8] Lakshmaṇa, the most outspoken supporter of Rāma, pointedly refers to this custom on several occasions.[9] Bharata also made the same statement when he exhorted Rāma to return to Ayodhyā.[10] This argument was also accepted unquestioningly by the Indian people and all the subsequent authors of the Rāma story. Most modern historians have supported it even though without analysing it critically. For example N.N. Law writes : "In Rāma's case the normal rule had almost been carried into effect when Daśaratha proposed to have Rāma formally declared as his successor in the presence of priests, nobles and the people, who cheerfully assented to the proposal. The installation of Bharata as crown-prince to the exclusion of Rāma, the eldest brother, at Kaikeyī's instance is an exception to the normal rule. This deviation was only possible for the reason that Rāma himself, the subject of the exclusion, instead of making any protest like Lakshmaṇa, voluntarily gave up his right."[11] Further, he states, "for crown-princeship Rāma alone was pre-eminently eligible by both nature and custom; and unless the legal incumbent by his own accord, gives up his right the way is barred for anybody else. What led Rāma to this voluntary self-sacrifice is another matter—a self-sacrifice which was not forced upon him by the mandate of an autocratic sovereign, but was the spontaneous outcome of Rāma's unfettered, individual decision."[12] Ramashraya Sharma agrees with N.N. Law fully when he opines that "Rāma alone, under the rule of primogeniture, was competent to create a vacancy for Bharata."[13]

Outer Layers of the Popular Version of the Two Boon Story

But the popular notion that the throne of Ayodhyā unquestionably belonged to Rāma overlooks the fact that as the ruling sovereign Daśaratha could and did override the right of Rāma and give his kingdom to his younger son Bharata.[14] From the story it is clear that the two boons asked by Kaikeyī were complimentary to each other and the exile of Rāma was demanded not only to emphasize his exclusion from sovereignty but also to make the accession of Bharata secure from any possible threat from Rāma.[15] Thus both the bones had some direct or indirect implications for Rāma. Now, in the *Rāmāyaṇa*, it has been repeatedly emphasized that Rāma, as a devoted son of his father, was very anxious to see that the words of his Sire were fully honoured.[16] And yet we find that at Chitrakūṭa he succumbed to the persuasion of Bharata and agreed to ascend the throne after the expiry of the period of exile which was something excluded by the combined import of the two boons given to Kaikeyī.

The reason of this *volte-face* on the part of Rāma is not far to seek. To us it appears that even after his exile and clear-cut exclusion from sovereignty, Rāma had not given up the desire of obtaining the ancestral throne. While discussing with Lakshmaṇa the impending arrival of Bharata in their *āśrama* at Chitrakūṭa, he explicitly stated that he was still desirous (*ichchhāmi*) of obtaining the kingdom.[17] Not only this he expressed the fond hope that Bharata had come to offer (*dātum*) the kingdom to him.[18] This desire of Rāma for sovereignty is the key for understanding the subtle but definite change which took place in his attitude towards the two boons awarded by Daśaratha to Kaikeyī, though apparently he continued to insist on honouring the words of his father.

Rāma's conversation with Bharata at Chitrakūṭa opens with this statement of Bharata : "Father pacified my mother by giving her the two boons; mother gave the kingdom to me and now I am offering it to you. You please enjoy it without impediment."[19] In reply to this Rāma initially takes the natural and very correct stand that whatever was given to anybody by his father in his life time, no one, including he and Bharata both, could alter.[20] But after at few verses he himself quite unnecessarily adds that when he will return after the expiry of the period of exile, he will rule the kingdom along with Bharata.[21] Here he definitely puts a new interpretation to the boons given to Kaikeyī and separates his exile from the award of kingdom to Bharata.

After adopting this position it was only a small step for him to agree to ascend the throne after the period of exile as the sole king and also to create the myth of his continued sovereignty by permitting Bharata to put his (Rāma's) *pādukās* on the throne. But this stipulation was not in accordance with the obvious implications of the two boons and constituted a *volte-face* from the position that 'the decision of Daśaratha could not be revoked by anybody, including Rāma and Bharata both'.

Further, even if Bharata was not willing to accept the burden of sovereignty, Rāma should not have accepted its offer from his younger brother. He should have politely but firmly rejected the offer of Bharata. Further, it is also a moot point whether Bharata was legally competent to offer the crown to Rāma. He could have offered it to Rāma if he had first accepted it in accordance with the first boon awarded to Kaikeyī. But he did not do so and therefore he had no *locus standi* in the matter. In such a situation the crown should have gone to Lakshmaṇa, Śatrughna and other male members of the Ikshvāku royal family successively according to their failure to accept it. But instead of asking Bharata and others to follow this proper procedure Rāma permitted himself to be persuaded by the entreaties of his younger brother.

Bride Śulka Story

However, there is another aspect of this episode which Vālmīki very successfully tries to relegate into the background without actually concealing it. According to it, Daśaratha had granted not only two boons to Kaikeyī discussed above, but at the time of their marriage had also promised the bride's price in the form of his throne for her would-be son. This important and highly significant fact is revealed by Vālmīki at a very unexpected place. When Bharata rebukes Kaikeyī at Chitrakūṭa, Rāma defends her and informs Bharata : "In the past, while marrying Kaikeyī, O brother, our celebrated father promised to your maternal grandfather the kingdom (of Ayodhyā in favour of her issue) as the best price (for the marriage)."[22] As is well-known, the payment of bridge's price by husband to the bride or her family was a widely prevalent practice in ancient India. It is mentioned in the *Mahābhārata* also as a custom then prevalent in the Vedic Kshatrīya dynasties. Therefore, such a promise of Daśaratha at the time of his marriage with Kaikeyī changes the entire complexion of the *Rāmāyaṇa* story. It proves that the throne of Ayodhyā had been promised by Daśaratha to Bharata even before the birth of the latter. This promise could not have been a secret. As it was made by a king to his would be queen and her family including her father, himself a king, on a matter which concerned the fate of the entire kingdom of Ayodhyā it must have been a talk of the town. Bhāsa, an author of pre-Kalidāsa period, refers to this story in his Pratimā Nāṭaka repeatedly. In the Act I of this drama Rāma pointedly asks the chamberlain who accuses Kaikeyī of being greedy when she demanded the throne of Ayodhyā for her son Bharata : "If for the sake of her son she begs the kingdom stipulated for in her bride-price, is the greed hers, not of us who take away our brother's kingdom ?"[23] later on also Rāma concedes that the kingdom of Ayodhyā was legally the property of Kaikeyī (sva dhanam, I. 22). In the Act III the Devakulika asks Bharata, whom he had not recognised : "Why don't you ask about this image of Daśaratha who gave up his life and kingdom for the sake of a bride's price?"[24]

That Bharata was aware of this fact was also known to Bhāsa according to whom Bharata himself reconstructed the possible course of events in his absence thus: "Recalling that wretched bride's price, she (Kaikeyī) said, 'let my son be king' and on its strength she boldly said to my elder brother, 'son, go to the forest', and on seeing him clad in the tree bark, the king did indeed meet with an unbefitting death. And all the fitting words of censure flowing therefrom are thrown indeed on me by the subjects."[25]

In the same Act, Kaikeyī also defends herself with the words : "Is it a question to be put to one who claims her bride's price ?" (*śulka lubdhā nanu prashṭavyā*). Significantly Rāma himself knew this fact from the very beginning (he did not have any occasion to learn it from his father after the latter's visit to the *kopabhavana* of Kaikeyī). Actually a fact of this magnitude could not have remained a secret; it must have been known to everbody (as the Pratimā Nāṭaka of Bhāsa brings out).

Nomination of the Successor : A Privilege of the Ruling Sovereign

Here it may be argued, as N.N. Law and R. Sharma have done, that Daśaratha had no right to offer his throne to his younger son Bharata.[26] But whether these scholars accept it as legally justifiable or not, according to the *Rāmāyaṇa* Daśaratha did exercise this right. Initially he declared the nomination of Rāma as his successor in the presence of the various *prakṛtis* but afterwards he gave away the entire kingdom to Bharata as a boon to Kailkeyī without consulting his friends, ministers, elders or anybody else on this point.[27] It is apparent not only from the course of events but also from what he himself stated : "No deliberation was made," he said, "by me with the elders clever in giving counsel, dictated as I was by Kaikeyī of sinful birth and intention. Without taking counsel with my well-wishers and ministers including those well-versed in the Vedas, was this step precipitately taken by me through excessive infatuation in order to please my wife."[28]

Thus, evidently Daśaratha had the right of giving away his kingdom to a younger son in supersession of the claim of the eldest without any offence on the part of the later. Secondly, we must also remember that in his turn Rāma also distributed his empire among his own sons and nephews. The argument that Rāma did not distribute his paternal kingdom among his nephews, what was given to them was the later accretions made to the ancestral kingdom during the reign of Rāma himself,[29] does not cut much ice. For Rāma divided his ancestral kingdom itself into two parts and gave one each to his two sons. Thirdly, here it may be recalled that the talk of the legal incompetency of Daśaratha is totally irrelevant because, our legal authorities have not mentioned such a situation regarding royal succession anywhere. How then can one raise the question of the constitutional validity of Daśaratha's action?[30] Fourthly, it should not be forgotten that the selection of a younger son by a king in preference to the eldest was a well-known practice in ancient India. According to the Paurāṇika tradition king Yayāti of the Lunar race installed Puru, his youngest son, as his heir in his ancestral kingdom in supersession of the claim of his other sons including that of Yadu, the eldest.[31] Several generations later in the same royal family king Pratīpa was succeeded by his younger son Śāntanu who has been explicitly accused of being a *parivetta* (one who violated the rights of his elder brother by accepting the ancestral throne) in the *Bhāgavata Purāṇa.*[32] The case of Devavrata (who is better known by his later name Bhīshma), the son of Śāntanu, also offers, mutatis mutandis, a close parallel to the bride's price story of the *Rāmāyaṇa.* According to the account of the *Mahābhārata* Devavrata was the son of Śāntanu's queen Gaṅgā. Later on, when Devavrata was already a youngman, Śāntanu desired to marry Satyavatī, the daughter of a fisherman. But she was not willing to marry Śāntanu unless the king promised to give his kingdom to her son that might be born of their marriage. Thereupon Devavrata renounced his title to the throne in favour of the would-be son of Satyavatī and, in order to assure her further, vowed to remain celibate throughout his life. He did not ascend the throne even when the sons of Satyavatī died without leaving any issue.[33] Another case in which the title of the eldest son to the throne was set aside by the ruling king, though because of a different reason, is offered by the Solar royal family in which we are told the king Sagara, one of the ancestors of Rāma, discarded his eldest son Asamañjas on the ground that the latter was cruel to the citizens.[34]

Thus we find that in the Vedic age the will of the reigning king was usually, though not always, the most important factor in the selection of the heir-apparent. Therefore, Daśaratha may be regarded as well within his rights when, at the time of his marriage with Kaikeyī, he promised that the son born of her would succeed to his throme.[35]

Role of the People and Prakṛtis

In order to prove the legitimacy of Rāma's succession Ramashraya Sharma has argued that at that time the "state primarily belonged to the people, the king being there not for his personal benefit but for the prosperity and welfare of the people."[36] Therefore "succession in the royal families........ necessarily required the approval of the officers of the state and the representatives of the people. Moreover, the succession of the eldest son of the ruler was not binding upon the people in each and every case."[37] But the argument, if valid, which it is not, would cut the very root of the theory of the legitimacy of Rāma's succession because the claim of Rāma to the throne of Ayodhyā emanated solely from his being the eldest son of his father, not because the people selected him as their king. But we do not feel that this reasoning is correct. For-in ancient India the voice of the people did not have any effective role to play in the selection of the successor to a king. It was only in exceptional circumstances that the people's voice made any difference in this matter. So far as the *Rāmāyaṇa* is concerned, the *rājakartāraḥ* or the *prakṛtis* seem to have been quite indifferent to the question of selection of the successor of Daśaratha. They welcomed the decision of Daśaratha to install Rāma on the throne. Incidentally, Daśaratha merely informed them of his decision[38] after he had already made arrangements for the coronation of Rāma;[39] he did not ask them to nominate his successor. And later on, when he took a different decision and without consulting anybody[40] gave his kingdom to Bharata, they accepted the new verdict without any protest. Still later when Daśaratha died and no son of his was available (Rāma and Lakshmaṇa had gone into exile and Bharata and Śatrughna were with the maternal uncle of the former) they even thought of installing some other Ikshvāku prince on the vacant throne.[41] However, when Bharata was recalled from the Kekaya country they showed no hesitation in requesting him to accept the burden of sovereignty. After the last rites of Daśaratha had been performed the *rājakartāraḥ*, it is said, assembled and approached Bharata and requested him to ascend the throne.[42] Thus it is obvious that so far as the *Rāmāyaṇa* is concerned the people and *prakṛtis* of Ayodhyā had neither any voice in the matter of selection of the successor of Daśaratha and nor any particular preference for Rāma or Bharata. They were interested in having a ruler only.

As regards the common folk, though the author/authors of the *Rāmāyaṇa* have repeatedly referred to their lamentations on the exile of Rāma,[43] there are certain passages which indicate that they also did not have any special preference for him. For example, at one place Lakshmaṇa exhorts Rāma to capture the kingdom by force and significantly adds that "if the people of Ayodhyā shall oppose your accession I shall kill all of them."[44] Later on, he tries to convince Rāma that if he will capture the throne by force, the likelihood of a popular revolt against him is very slight. And if a revolt shall take place he would defend his kingdom with all his might.[45] It was probably in order to avoid the possibility of the popular revolt against Rāma that Lakshmaṇa asked the former to capture the throne before the story of the selection of Bharata leaked out.[46] Obviously the supporters of Bharata and those who could oppose the accession Rāma were not an insignificant factor.

Other Outer Layers of the Succession Story

From the above discussion it is obvious that Rāma did not have any special claim to the throne of Ayodhyā as his father had promised it to the would-be son of Kaikeyī as a bride's price to her. Daśaratha was perfectly within his right to do so even if his people in general or his officers in particular were opposed to his decision, for which there is absolutely no evidence. But if the story of bride's price is correct, one can hardly escape the conclusion that the story of the two boons given by Daśaratha to Kaikeyī after the nomination of Rāma was a concoction of later writers when the figure of Rāma had acquired the status of a popular idol. Other ancient authors of the authors of the *Rāmakathā* are either unaware of the two-boon story or radically differ on the number and nature of boons and the occasion when they were granted.[47] The facts that the two boons are said to have been given to Kaikeyī at the conclusion of a mythical war between gods and demons in which Kaikeyī, a female, also participated against the custom and tradition of those days, and that it is put into the mouth of Mantharā who 'reminded' Keikeyī of this episode, make it highly suspicious. Significantly Lakshmaṇa expressed his grave doubts in the genuineness of the two-boon story. He told Rāma : "It is a matter of surprise how there is no suspicion in your mind about that wicked couple (Daśaratha and Kaikeyī).... Nay, if (the story of) the boon granted by the one and received by the other had been real, it would have been granted even before (the preparations for the installation were taken in hand).... Since this interruption (in your installation), though brought about through machination (in the shape of connecting the story of a boon granted by the emperor), is not being recognized (by you) as such agony is caused to me on that account."[48]

As regards the question why was the story of the two boons invented when Kaikeyī had a perfect case in the form of Daśaratha's bride's price promise the answer is be quite simple : It was invented to put the character of Rāma, the 'hero' of the Epic, on a high plane untouched by the selfishness associated with the petty court-intrigues. The story of the bride's price to Kaikeyī implied that Rāma even before his selection as heir-apparent, knew that the throne had been promised long before by his father to the would-be son of Kaikeyī and yet he, the 'ideal hero', agreed for his own coronation. That was unbecoming of the hero of an epic and therefore totally impossible. Hence the story of the two boons in which he agreed to ascend the throne earlier while the demand of Kaikeyī for the fulfillment of the two boons was put forward later, when Daśaratha met her in the *kopabhavana*.

But if the two-boon story was a later fabrication and Bharata's title to the throne emanated from the bride's price promised by Daśaratha to Kaikeyī, the exile of Rāma must have been caused by circumstances other than the award of the two-boons to Kaikeyī. And consequently, it must also be admitted that the story of Bharata's visit to Chritrakūṭa (which was supposedly prompted by the'unjust' and'sinful' conduct of his mother!) and his return with the *pādukās* of Rāma was also a later fabrication. In that case the possibility emerges that after his return from the Kekaya country Bharata accepted the throne and ruled as a fullfledged king and not merely as the 'regent' of Rāma. It gets some confirmation from a tradition preserved in the *Rāmāyaṇa* itself. In the Kishkindhā Kāṇḍa, when Rāma kills Vālin fraudulently and the latter accuses the former of un-Kshatriyalike conduct, Rāma defends himself by claiming that the Ikshvākus have a right to kill those who transgress the path of dharma. In that connection he declares that at that time Bharata, whose mind was set on virtue, ruled over the whole earth,[49] and that "so long as the said Bharata, a tiger among rulers of men, who is fond of virtue, rules over the entire globe, who can do something repugnant to righteousness ?"[50] In several verses he very explicitly states that he himself was subject to the authroity of Bharata. "Keeping before us the command of Bharata (भरताज्ञां पुरस्कृत्य)" he declares, "we who are devoted to our paramount duty, duly punish him who has strayed away from the path (of virtue)."[51] "In fact Bharata is the ruler of the earth while our duty is to carry out his behests."[52] "Taking the behests of Bharata as our authority, O Lord of the monkeys, we are bent upon punishing people like you who have transgressed the bounds of morality."[53]

From this speech put into the mouth of Rāma himself, the indubitable fact emerges that Bharata ruled over Ayodhyā not only as a regent, but as a king in his own right. At least this statement cannot be regarded as consonant with the story of Bharata's visit to Chitrakūṭa and his return from there with the *pādukās* of Rāma which was apparently a device by which in later ages the myth of Rāma's continued sovereignty even during the period of his exile was created. But if the story of the bride's price is correct and the evidence of Rāma's speech quoted above has any validity, the course of events (viz. Bharata's Chitrakūṭa visit and his return with the *pādukās* of Rāma) which follows as a sequel to the spurious two-boon story could not have taken place. That is simple logic; one cannot escape from it.

Internal Discrepancies

Now let us try to remove the inner layers or rather discrepancies of the *Rāmāyaṇa* story by which its authors sought to transform the personalities of the main characters in order to portray an ideal picture of their mutual relations. According to the overall impression given by the *Rāmāyaṇa* the mutual relations of the various members of the royal family of Ayodhyā were simply ideal till Kaikeyī was misled by Mantharā. Earlier Kaikeyī herself was very much pleased when she was told of the nomination of Rāma as the next king.[54] Similarly, Bharata had nothing except deep respect for Rāma and could not even think of acquiring the ancestral throne for himself by disputing the 'rightful' and 'just' claim of his elder brother. Even afterwards the mutual relations of all the four brothers (with the occasional fury of Lakshmaṇa against Bharata which is explained as due to his misunderstanding the motives of Bharata) and their attitude towards other members of their family were full of love and respect. But if Daśaratha had promised his kingdom as bride's price to the would-be son of Kaikeyī, viz. Bharata, such a picture of the mutual relations of the various members of the royal family is difficult to be imagined. Daśaratha's promise meant that Bharata had a just and rightful claim on the throne of Ayodhyā; but as Rāma was the eldest son of the chief-queen of Daśaratha, in normal circumstances it was he who should had ascended the throne. In such a situation one would expect that the royal family would had become divided into at least two mutually hostile camps respectively favouring the candidature of Rāma and Bharata. That is what appears to have actually happened though the authors of the Rāmāyaṇa tried to show otherwise.

Factionalism in the Royal Family

Let us begin with an analysis of the relations of Rāma with his brothers. In her speech to Kaikeyī, Mantharā contrasted the attitude of Rāma towards Bharata and Lakshmaṇa thus : "Having attained sovereignty shorn of enemies, Rāma on his part will surely send Bharata into exile or even to the other world (लोकान्तरम्). Indeed Lakshmaṇa will protect Rāma and Rāma too will protect Lakshmaṇa; their brotherly love, which is akin to the love of Aśvins, is widely known in the world. Therefore, Rāma will not do any wrong to Lakshmaṇa. Against Bharata, however, he must perpetrate a wrong; there is no doubt about it."[55] That

Rāma was very much attached to Lakshmaṇa was quite well-known. When he was assured by Daśaratha that his coronation shall take place the next day, he broke the good tiding to Lakshmaṇa in this fashion: "Rule you beneficently over this earth with me O Lakshmaṇa ! You are my second self. This royal glory has come to you. O son of Sumitrā ! enjoy the pleasures coveted by you as well the rewards of sovereignty. I desire to live and rule only for your sake".[56] According to Rāma, a brother like Lakshmaṇa could not be found anywhere in this world[57] and without him victory in war, company of Sītā and his own life had no meaning.[58] The devotion of Lakshmaṇa to Rāma was also well-known. When Lakshmaṇa heard that Rāma's claim to the throne had been set aside by Daśaratha, he became very angry and told Kausalyā that in his old age Daśaratha had become perverse[59] and suggested that he (i.e. Daśaratha) should either be imprisoned or killed.[60] Later on he explicitly stated that he will not tolerate the accession of anybody except that of Rāma.[61] He placed himself entirely at the disposal of Rāma and sought permission of the latter to conquer the whole world on his behalf.[62] And when Rāma decided to go to the forest, Lakshmaṇa gave him company, though his exile was not included in the boons granted to Kaikeyī. These facts clearly bring out the close relationship between Rāma and Lakshmaṇa. On the other hand, Rāma's attitude to Bharata, in some passage at least, betrays a singular lack of confidence. For example, when Rāma went to meet Sītā to inform her of the situation created by the award of the two boons to Kaikeyī and ask her to stay in Ayodhyā in his absence, he advised her not to praise him in the presence of Bharata lest the latter should become angry with her.[63] Sītā also refers to Bharata as her enemy.[64] Rāma was also certain in his mind that after obtaining the kingdom Bharata will not look after Kausalyā and Sumitrā properly, devoted as he will be to Kaikeyī.[65] Later on, when he returned from Laṅkā, Rāma sent Hanumāna to Nandīgrāma not only to inform Bharata of the developments which had taken place in Laṅkā, but also to assess the reaction of Bharata at the news of Rāma's return to Ayodhyā and find out whether Bharata wanted to keep the kingdom to himself or was willing to give it back to Rāma.[66]

That Bharata was looked upon with suspicion by the supporters of Rāma can hardly be doubted. Guha, the king of Nishādas, for example, asked Bharata when the latter was going to meet Rāma at Chitrakūṭa whether he (i.e. Bharata) was going to the *āśrama* of Rāma with some evil intention.[67] The same doubt was expressed by Bharadvāja when Bharata visited his *āśrama* on his way to Chitrakūṭa.[68] The attitude of Lakshmaṇa to Bharata was of plain and unconcealed hostility. When Bharata was due to arrive at Chitrakūṭa, Lakshmaṇa speculated that after acquiring the whole kingdom Bharata was coming with the intention of killing them. He referred to Bharata as 'our enemy' and sought the permission of Rāma to kill Bharata and Kaikeyī both.[69]

That the hostility of the two factions of the royal court was quite deep-rooted and long-lasting is also proved by a very interesting fact recorded towards the end of the Yuddha Kāṇḍa. According to it, after his return to Ayodhyā Rāma offered crown-princeship to Lakshmaṇa and not to Bharata who was elder of the two. It was only after Lakshmaṇa had declined the offer that Bharata was installed as heir-apparent[70] (though later on it were the sons of Rāma who inherited the ancestral kingdom).[71] This partiality of Rāma towards Lakshmaṇa at the cost of Bharata can hardly be reconciled with the general drift of the *Rāmāyaṇa* story in which Rāma had nothing except heart-felt affection for Bharata.

Here we may add a few words about the attitude of Rāma and his supporters to Kaikeyī and that of Bharata and his supporters towards Kausalyā. At one place Rāma explicitly accuses Kaikeyī of playing a fraud on the king Daśaratha (कैकेय्या वंचितो राजा) by asking the two boons in the way she did.[72] He very conveniently forgets the bride's price story at that place which he himself relates to Bharata at Chitrakūṭa and lays the entire blame on the shoulders of Kaikeyī. At another place he suspects that in his absence Kaikeyī might kill Daśaratha[73] and give poison to Kausalyā and Sumitrā.[74] His mother Kausalyā also did not have any affection for Kaikeyī. She exhorted Rāma to take her with him to the forest because, she could not live peacefully with her co-wives (आसां राम सपत्नीनां वस्तुं मध्ये न मे क्षमम्).[75] That Sītā and Lakshmaṇa also did not have any respect for Kaikeyī is also apparent from numerous passages. In the opposite camp also Bharata and his mother did not seem to have any genuine respect for Kausalyā. Rather they were always a source of great botheration for her. When Rāma broke the news of his exile to Kausalyā and sought her permission to go to the forest, she lamented: "No good fortune or happiness was enjoyed by me in the past through the efforts of my husband. Hope was, however, entertained by me, O Rāma, that with my son in power I might see both in abundance. Senior-most queen though I am, I shall in my present plight hear many unpalatable words from my junior co-wives, who will rend my heart thereby. Even with you by my side I have been despised; how much more shall I be despised when you are away, O dear child ?........ Not esteemed by my husband I have always been greatly snubbed. I have been treated on a par with or even on a lower footing than Kaikeyī's servants. Whosoever serves me or speaks kindly to me would no longer speak to me on perceiving Bharata. Reduced to a bad plight, my son, how shall I possibly be able to cast my eyes on those lips of Kaikeyī uttering harsh words due to her becoming constantly angry?''[76] This statement of Kausalyā which, one should remember, describes her plight before the nomination of Rāma was announced, is corroborated by another passage in which Mantharā tells Kaikeyī : ''It is improbable that your co-wife Kausalyā, who has been slighted by you in the past out of pride born of your being loved by your husband will not reply her grudge to you (when Rāma shall become the king).''[77] These facts clearly prove that the atmosphere in the royal family even before Rāma was formally selected as the successor of Daśaratha was far from peaceful and cordial.

Attitude of Daśaratha

That in his last years Daśaratha was in favour of Rāma can hardly be doubted. But at the same time he was very much infatuated with Kaikeyī. He also knew that the claim of Bharata was just as the kingdom had been promised to him even before his birth at the time of her mother's marriage. Put in such a situation what he did was a fraud on Kaikeyī and Bharata : he sent Bharata to the capital of Kaikeyī's brother and tried to enthrone Rāma in his absence. In the *Rāmāyaṇa* it is said that he called all the high officials of the various cities and *janapadas* of his realm and other great kings of the whole earth[78] to attend the *durbār* in which Rāma's nomination was announced, but he is said to have done it so secretly and hurriedly that Kaikeyī became informed of it only after the festivities had already begun in the palace and the capital.[79] His invitation to all the great 'kings of the earth' to this *durbār* may also be contrasted with the non-invitation to the king of the Kekaya country as well as to Bharata who was at the time, along with Śatrughna, staying with the Kekaya king. The author or authors of the Rāmāyaṇa explain that they could not be informed because the durbār was called in haste and they could hear the 'good news' later (त्वरया चानयामास पश्चात् तौ श्रोष्यतः प्रियम्).[80] But in that case how could the other great kings of 'the whole earth' reach in time to participate in the *durbār*? According to the *Rāmāyaṇa* itself when, after the death of Daśaratha, Bharata was suddenly called from the Kekaya country he completed the journey from that kingdom to Ayodhyā in only seven nights arriving in time for the last rites of his father.[81] Therefore, he and the king of the Kekaya country could easily be invited for the *durbār* in which the decision regarding Daśaratha's successor, to which Bharata was a natural party, was taken. With regard to the Kekaya king it is possible to argue that Daśaratha was under no compulsion to send an invitation to him (though this argument will not be valid since Daśaratha, at the time of his marriage with Kaikeyī, had assured the Kekaya king that the son of Kaikeyī would be the next king of Ayodhyā) but the attempt of the authors of the *Rāmāyaṇa* to give an explanation, though a flimsy one, for the omission of invitation to the Kekaya king betrays the real motive behind it. Evidently, Daśaratha, who was planning to nominate Rāma as his successor in contravention to his earlier promise given to that king, thought it prudent to avoid his presence along with that of Bharata on that occasion. It is also quite possible that Bharata was intentionally sent to the Kekaya kingdom so that the accession of Rāma could take place smoothly. That may also explain as to why the nomination of Rāma was kept a secret from Kaikeyī. Therefore, Mantharā was not very much wide of mark when she accused Daśaratha of sending Bharata to the capital of the brother of Kaikeyī and anointing Rāma fraudulently in his absence.[82] But despite all these precautions taken by him, Daśaratha could not free himself from apprehension of some trouble. That is why, soon after the aforesaid *durbār* in which Rāma's crown-princeship was declared, he called Rāma to his private chambers and advised him to get himself anointed as soon as possible before Bharata returned from the kingdom of his maternal uncle. He further explained that though Bharata was the follower of the path shown by the great ones, it was quite possible that his mind would be swayed by greed and jealousy.[83]

The group politics of the royal family of Ayodhyā was obviously of ordinary human level. There was a lot of loose talk of violence. On several occasions Lakshmaṇa threatened to kill all the supporters of Bharata along with Kaikeyī.[84] He suggested that Daśaratha should either be killed or imprisoned.[85] Later, at Chitrakūṭa, he threatened to kill Bharata and destroy his army.[86] His proposal of murdering or imprisoning Daśaratha was not opposed even by Kausalyā. She merely commented to Rāma : ''Son! you have heard what

Lakshmaṇa has said. Do what you think is proper."[87] When Bharata and Śatrughna returned from Kekaya country, Śatrughna angrily asked why did Rāma not imprison Daśaratha[88] while Bharata talked of the justification of murdering Kaikeyī.[89] He repeated his statement even in the presence of Rāma.[90] Satrughna is on record of having beaten Manthrā.[91] Even Rāma himself is said to have expressed the fear that in his absence Kaikeyī would kill Daśaratha[92] and poison her co-wives. From all this (which is based entirely on the evidence of the *Rāmāyaṇa* itself) it is evident that in the original *gāthās* on which the story of *Rāmāyaṇa* was woven the figure of Rāma was purely of a human prince who had all the failings and weaknesses as well as strong points which may be found in any ordinary mortal.

Story of the Anomalous Fragments

From what has been discussed above, it is obvious that towards the close of the reign of Daśaratha the royal family of Ayodhyā had become divided into two rival camps.[93] The first wanted to enthrone Rāma as the next king. His title to the throne emanated from the fact of his being the eldest son of Daśaratha. His case was supported by Kausalyā, Sumitrā and Lakshmaṇa.[94] The second camp wanted Bharata to be declared the heir-apparent. Like Rāma, Bharata was also a very able prince.[95] His claim to the throne emanated from the bride's price which Daśaratha had promised at the time of his marriage with Kaikeyī in the form of his kingdom to her son. His candidature was mainly supported by his mother.[96] The group of Kaikeyī was smaller but her case was legally stronger and she had the advantage of being the most favourite queen of Daśaratha—he is said to have spent most of his time in her palace.[97] Daśaratha himself favoured the candidature of Rāma, but he was rather fickle-minded[98] and fully under the spell of Kaikeyī's beauty. His position was also weakened by his promise given to Kaikeyī at the time of their marriage. Therefore, instead of taking a bold stand on the question, he played a fraud on Kaikeyī by sending Bharata to the Kekaya country and declaring Rāma as his successor in an open durbār[99] without consulting or even informing Kaikeyī about it.[100] But Kaikeyī turned the table at the eleventh hour with the result that Rāma had to go into exile and Bharata obtained the ancestral throne instead. As the story of the two boons is almost certainly a later fabrication, all the events that follow as its sequel, viz. Bharata's visit to Chitrakūṭa and his resolve to carry on the administration of Ayodhyā on behalf of Rāma should also be regarded as later accretions. The real cause of Rāma's exile is not known. Other ancient works on the story of Rāma materially differ on this point.[101] It is, however, quite likely that Rāma left Ayodhyā because he was afraid of the conspiracy of his step-mother, as some Buddhist works have asserted. It is also not beyond the bounds of possibility that Rāma, a practical politician and realist as he was,[102] voluntarily decided to leave Ayodhyā temporarily in order to collect an army of the forest-folk. Kauṭilya in his *Arthaśātra* suggests this course of action for a prince who is put by circumstances in such a position.[103] After all, it is not without significance that he returned to Ayodhyā, not alone but with a large number of powerful Vānaras and Rākshasas, who had very recently crushed the mighty king of Laṅkā. Their arrival at Ayodhyā from far-off Laṅkā and Kishkindhā (wherever they were located) could not have been merely due to their desire to have a glimpse of that city. At any rate, it is obvious that in face of this show of strength,[104] Bharata could have no option except agreeing to the accession of Rāma and making professions of his fraternal loyalty. From the above discussion it is apparent that the story which emerges from the anomalous fragments of the central story of Bāla Kāṇḍa of the *Rāmāyaṇa* runs in the opposite direction cutting across the central story at its vital points. In the central story Rāma has a just claim to the ancestral kingdom and there is a noble struggle between the two brothers, Rāma and Bharata, each of whom persuades the other to ascend the throne. Further, it assumes that all the members of the royal family had nothing but deep-rooted love for each other until Kaikeyī was misled by Mantharā. But the tale of the anomalous fragments suggests the reverse of it. It indicates that Rāma had no legitimate claim to the throne of Ayodhyā and the the atmosphere of the royal family of Ayodhyā was full of factional intrigues, suspicion and hatred even before the question of Daśaratha's successor arose. Apparently Rāma and Bharata both had a purely pragmatic approach to this problem, at least in the story as revealed by the anomalous fragments.

References

1. *JOI*, VIII, Dec. 1958, No. 2, pp. 121-31.

2. In *Sir Asutosh Mookerjee Silver Jubilee Vol.*, III, Orientalia - Part I, Calcutta, 1922, p.397.
3. The Riddle of the *Rāmāyaṇa*, pp. 47-48.
4. Jacobi, Das *Rāmāyaṇa*, pp. 50-59.
5. *Rāmāyaṇa*, 1.5.3. Here we have used the Gita Press (Gorakhpur) edition of the *Rāmāyaṇa* because it is easily available. However, the Ayodhyā Kāṇḍa of the other editions of this work, with which we are mainly concerned, is not much different.
6. Pathak, V.S., *Ancient Historians of India*, p. 45.
7. *Ibid.*, p. 47 ff.
8. *Rāmāyaṇa*, 2.110.36-37.
9. Cf. for example, 2.96.23.
10. *Ibid.*, 2.101.10; 2.102.2. Before she was misled by Mantharā, Kaikayī is also said to have accepted the claim of Rāma.
11. Law, N.N., *Aspects of Ancient Indian Polity*, p. 53.
12. *Ibid.*, p. 58.
13. Sharma, R., *A Socio-Political Study of the Vālmīkīya Rāmāyaṇa*, 1971, p. 299.
14. The contention of R. Sharma (*op. cit.*, p. 298) that Daśaratha did not expressly say yes to the boons of Kaikeyī, is not correct. Cf. *Rāmāyaṇa*, 2.34.31-38.
15. *Rāmāyaṇa*, 2.9.21, 31.
16. Cf. *Rāmāyaṇa*, 2.18.28-30; 2.19.5; 2.19.8; 2.21.30; 2.21.60; 2.34.48; 2.101.27; 2.105.4; 2.107.8.
17. *Rāmāyaṇa*, 2.97.5.
18. *Rāmāyaṇa*, 2.97.12.
19. *Rāmāyaṇa*, 2.105.4.21.
20. *Rāmāyaṇa*, 2.105.4.
21. *Rāmāyaṇa*, 2.111.31-32.
22. *Rāmāyaṇa*, 2.107.3.
23. *Pratimā Nāṭaka*, III.15
24. *Pratimā Nāṭaka*, III.8
25. *Pratimā Nāṭaka*, III.11
26. Law, N.N., *op. cit.*, p. 59; Sharma, R., *op. cit.*, pp. 299 ff.
27. Incidentally this fact shows that the general notion that in the choice of his successor a king was guided by the wishes of his prakṛtis is not correct.
28. *Rāmāyaṇa*, 2.59.18-19.
29. Sharma, R., *op. cit.*, p. 29.
30. The non-inclusion by our judicial authorities such as Mishra (cf. Law, N.N., *op. cit.*, p. 56) of the gift of the kingdom by its ruler in the lists of the invalid gifts by a king may be regarded as an indication of their tacit approval of this custom.
31. *The Vedic Age*, ed. by Majumdar, R.C. and Pusalker, A.D., p. 278; cf. Law, op. cit., pp. 52-63.
32. *Bhāgavata Purāṇa*, 9.22.15 (Gita Press ed., Vol.II).
33. *The Vedic Age*, p. 299.
34. *Ibid.*, p. 291.
35. In the historical period also the cases of the selection of a favourite son as heir-apparent by the reigning king are quite numerous. For example, we know that in the Gupta dynasty Samudragupta was selected as successor by his father Chandragupta I, even though his selection was not taken kindly by other princes. Later on Samudragupta himself selected Chandragupta II, his younger son, as the next king, superseding the claim of his eldest son Rāmagupta. In the Western Gaṅga dynasty on the advice of his guru Vijayakīrti, a king set aside the claim of his son Durvinīta to the throne and nominated his another son by a different wife. According to Bāṇa the king Prabhākaravardhana of the Pushyabhūti dynasty asked his younger son Harsha to ascend the throne after him, by-passing the claim of Rājyavardhana who was elder to Harsha. According to Sulaiman, the Muslim traveller, the kings of the Rāshṭrakūṭa period named their own successors. In doing so they sometimes violated the law of primogeniture. The emperor Dhruva, for example, nominated his third son Govinda for succession overriding the claim of the elder son Stambha. Not only this, he probably abdicated in favour of Govinda in order to make the position of the latter secure in his own life-time. In the *Vikramāṅkābhyudaya* of Someśvara III it is claimed that Someśvara I, the Chālukya emperor of Kalyāṇī, favoured the succession of his second son Vikramāditya VI in preference to that of the eldest son Someśvara II. In Mewar Rana Lakshasimha or Lakha (c. 1405-20 A.D.) of the Sisodia family promised a bride's price in the form of his throne to the would-be son of Haṁsabai, the Marwar princess, whom he wanted to marry and thus superseded the rights of all of his living sons, including the eldest son Chunda. It reminds one of the favour shown by Daśaratha to Kaikeyī and Bharata. The Rathore ruler of Marwar, who married his young daughter Haṁsabai to Rana Lakha of Mewar, was Rao Chunda. Now this Chunda also had numerous sons of whom Ranamalla was the eldest. But Chunda desired that

Kanha, the issue of his favourite wife, should succeed him. Accordingly he asked Ranamalla to renounce his right in favour of Kanha. Ranamalla followed the will of his father, left Marwar and settled down in Mewar.

36. Sharma, R., *op. cit.*, p. 300.
37. *Ibid.* Some instances are generally quoted to prove that in ancient India people and Prakṛtis or the high officials elected a king's successor. But they are all of dubious nature. For example, the Junagadh inscription of Rudradāman I (Sircar, D.C., *Select Inscriptions*, pp. 176 ff.) states that he was approached by all the *varṇas* to become their king. But the same inscription also mentions that he had acquired *rājalakshmī* when he was in his mother's womb and also that he earned the kingdom by his own valour. Similarly, in the Khalimpur grant of Devapāla (Maity, S.K. and Mukherjee, R.R., *Corpus of Bengal Inscriptions*, p. 96) it is said that in order to put an end to 'the rule of fishes' (*mātsya nyāya*), that is anarchy, the *prakṛtis* elected Gopāla as king. But this record also informs us that Gopāla was born in a royal family and that his father, their 'vanquisher of enemies', had decorated the earth extending upto the sea with his fame. Apparently Gopāla had inherited the throne of his father. The fact that there was no system of election of the successor of a king in the Pāla dynasty is also proved by the absence of any reference to the election of Dharmapāla and Devapāla in this record. It is quite possible that both Rudradāman I and Gopāla had acquired their respective ancestral thrones with the help of some nobles or officers. A reference to their election is merely a literary motif to describe such an event.
38. *Rāmāyaṇa*, 2.6.45.
39. *Ibid.*, 2.2.214.
40. *Ibid.*, 2.59.18-19. See fn. 100.
41. *Ibid.*,2.67.6-8.
42. *Ibid.*, 2.67.1-5.
43. *Ibid.*, 2.85.5-8.
44. *Ibid.*, 2.21.10.
45. *Ibid.*, 2.23.27-28.
46. *Ibid.*, 2.23.27-28.
47. *Ibid.*, 2.21.8.
48. For a detailed summary of the various traditions concerning the boons granted by Daśaratha to Kaikeyī vide, Bulcke, *Rāmākathā*, (in Hindi), pp. 399-401.
49. *Rāmāyaṇa*, 4.18.7.
50. *Ibid.*, 4.18.10.
51. *Ibid.*, 4.18.11.
52. *Ibid.*, 4.18.23.
53. *Ibid.*, 4.18.25.
54. *Ibid.*, 2.7.32-36.
55. *Ibid.*, 2.8.27, 30-31.
56. *Ibid.*, 2.4.43-44.
57. *Ibid.*, 6.101.15.
58. *Ibid.*, 6.101.50.
59. *Ibid.*, 2.21.3. His sentiment can be put in Hindi thus : बुढ़ापे में राजा सठिया गये हैं।
60. *Ibid.*, 2.21.12.
61. *Ibid.*, 2.23.10.
62. *Ibid.*, 2.23.35-40.
63. *Ibid.*, 2.26.24-25.
64. *Rāmāyāṇa*, 2.30.19.
65. *Ibid.*, 2.31.44.
66. *Ibid.*, 6.125.14-18.
67. *Rāmāyaṇa*, 2.84.3-4.
68. *Ibid.*, 2.90.10-13.
69. *Ibid.*, 2.96.17. Cf. also 2.75.11-16 where Kausalyā speaks tauntingly to Bharata.
70. *Ibid.*, 6.128.92
71. In the *Adhtyātma Rāmāyaṇa* (6.16.26) and *Ānanda Rāmāyaṇa* (1.12.169) Lakshmaṇa actually became the heir-apparent of Rāma. In the Uttara Purāṇa (68.663) of Guṇa Bhadra, Rāma and Lakshmaṇa both ascend the throne (cf., Bulcke, K., *op. cit.*, pp. 596-97).
72. *Rāmāyaṇa*, 2.24.11.
73. *Rāmāyaṇa*, 2.53.7.
74. *Rāmāyaṇa*, 2.53.18.
75. *Ibid.*, 2.24.19.
76. *Ibid.*, 2.20.38-39, 41-44.
77. *Ibid.*, 2.8.37.
78. *Ibid.*, 2.1.45.

79. *Ibid.*, 2.7.
80. *Ibid.*, 2.1.48.
81. *Ibid.*, 2.72.8.
82. *Rāmāyaṇa*, 2.7.26.
83. *Rāmāyaṇa*, 2.4.25-27.
84. *Ibid.*, 2.96.17-31.
85. *Ibid.*, 2.21.12.
86. In the *Bhāvārtha Rāmāyaṇa* (2.15) an actual war takes place between Bharata and Lakshmaṇa (Bulke, *Rāmākathā*, p. 392).
87. *Rāmāyaṇa*, 2.21.21.
88. *Ibid.*, 2.78.3.
89. *Rāmāyaṇa*, 2.78.22.
90. *Rāmāyaṇa*, 2.106.9.
91. *Ibid.*, 2.78. In the *Ānanda Rāmāyaṇa* (1.6.96) it is Bharata who beats Mantharā.
92. *Rāmāyaṇa*, 2.53.7.
93. *Ibid.*, 2.53.18.
94. It is interesting to note that when the selection of Rāma was announced, Kausalyā celebrated it along with Rāma, Sītā, and Lakshmaṇa (2.4.31). Kaikeyī was either not called or did not come to the palace of Kausalyā.
95. According to the *Rāmāyaṇa* during his regency the treasury of Ayodhyā increased ten-fold.
96. It is also quite possible that the royal family of the Kekaya country also played some role in this family feud. According to the *Anāmakam Jātakam* Rāma retired to forest when he heard that Bharata's maternal uncle was coming with an army (Bulcke, *op. cit.*, p. 400). Mantharā, the maid of Kaikeyī belonged to Kekaya deśa, (2.7.1). Later on, the sons of Bharata namely Pushkala and Taksha, alongwith their father, went to the Kekaya country and carved out independent kingdoms in the adjoining region of Gandhāra.
97. *Rāmāyaṇa*, 2.72.13. At several places Lakshmaṇa, Rāma and Śatrughna, etc. very pointedly mention the weakness of Daśaratha to the charms of Kaikeyī. Cf. e.g. *Rāmāyaṇa*, 2.21.3., Cf. also 2.10.23-24. 2.11.1; 2.11.17; 2.23.12; and 2.31.12.
98. Cf. his changing attitude towards the question of his successor from the time of his marriage with Kaikeyī onwards. At several places Lakshmaṇa, Śatrughna and others accuse him of being fickle-minded (e.g. 2.21.19). Daśaratha himself was aware of his own weakness. E.g. in 2.4.20 he asks Rāma to get himself coronated before he (i.e. Daśaratha) changed his mind.
99. It is also quite likely that Daśaratha followed the maxim that a prince who may prove himself troublesome should be sent to the kingdom of his maternal uncle (the view of Āchārya Koṇapadanta quoted by Kauṭilya); cf. *Arthaśāstra*, ed. by V. Gairola, p. 65.
100. The *durbār* was held as a mere formality because Daśaratha had already asked his ministers to make preparations for Rāma's coronation (2.1.45) even before he sent invitations to his officers and subordinate kings to attend the *durbār.*
101. For the various causes of Rāma's exile as given in the different *Rāmakathās*, see Bulcke, K., *op. cit.*, pp. 399-401.
102. From several episodes connected with the life of Rāma his sagacity and realism become quite clear. For example, he did not hesitate to kill Vālin fraudulently. He justified his un-Kashatriyalike conduct on the plea that Vālin had committed the crime of violating Rumā, the wife of Sugrīva (*Rāmāyaṇa*, 4.18.18-20). But the hollowness of this plea becomes apparent when we find that he did not punish Sugrīva when the later violated Tārā, the wife of Vālin. Instead, as Tārā herself stated, it was with the help of Rāma that Sugrīva had acquired her along with the kingdom of Vālin (*ibid.*, 4.35.5). After the death of Vālin, Hanumāna raised the question of the coronation of Aṅgada, the son of Vālin (*ibid.*, 4.21.11) which was quite justified from the legal and moral points of view. But instead of Aṅgada, Rāma placed this own friend Sugrīva on the throne of Kishkindhā. In Laṅkā when Vibhīshaṇa sought refuge with Rāma, the latter at once recognised that the former had come with the hope of getting the kingdom of Rāvaṇa (ibid., 6.18.13).
103. *Arthaśātra*, Gairola's ed., pp. 71-2. In this passage Kauṭilya says that if a prince finds that his father, being under the influence of other princes or women and is not pleased with him, he should reitre to the forest. There he should enter into an alliance with a powerful, reliable and truthful king, increase his power and wealth and enlist the support of the forest people. In the subsequent passages Kauṭilya describes how that prince should regain his ancestral kingdom. That is what precisely Rāma appears to have done. Cf. also the case of Chandraguptga Maurya who captured Magadha by adopting the same course of action, though it was not his paternal kingdom.
104. Cf. the message which Hanumāna was asked by Rāma to convey to Bharata : "Tell him that Rāma, after getting victory over his enemies as well as great fame is coming back with his highly powerful friends such as Vibhīshaṇa, the king of the Rākshasas and Sugrīva the king of Vānaras, and others." (*Rāmāyaṇa*, 6.125.12-13). If put bluntly, it could give the impression of being almost a threat.

42

THE FOUR *VARNAS*: A VEDIC CONCEPT OF DIVISION OF SOCIETY

Shashi Tiwari

Nothing dominates the life of a Hindu more than religious institution; and no institution is more tyrannical in its influence than the caste-system. Its ugly inconsistencies and bitter tyranny have gone far to make the Hindu community what it is generally looked upon today. The impact of this single institution has been immense on the structural growth of Hindu society. This is not a place to refute or justify this system, but we are only concerned with the question where there is anything like the present caste-system evidenced by the hymns of the *Rigveda,* the oldest text of *Sruti* literature, regarded as the final evidence *(param pramana)*. Do the other Vedic texts mention the caste- system? Do we find out the origin of present caste system in the Vedic Scriptures? What was its original form in India? In reference to these questions here an effort is made for the analytical study of the *Shruti* literature to know the Vedic concept of division of society which later developed as the basis of *Jati*-system.

Generally we consider Vedas as the treasure-house of all knowledge and foundation of all Indian ideologies pertaining to society, religion and philosophy. But nothing like the present divisions and sub-divisions found in contemporary Hindu society has any place anywhere in ancient Vedic literature. It has often been observed that no trace of caste system can be recognized in the *Rigveda.* For example the Creator (Vishvakarma, Tvashta) is what would now be called a *Shudra.*[1] In the *Rigveda* two words – *Chashani* 'wanderer' and *Krishti* 'Ploughman' are generally used for 'folk' or 'people' indicating them typically agricultural. In many passages *Pancha Charshanayah* or *krishtayah* replaces the more usual *pancha janah.*[2] Although the four characteristic functions of priest, ruler, farmer, and craftsman are distinguished, one and all of these are 'ploughmen'. What this implies is a state of affairs in which the individual of a given type is still in full possession of all the possibilities of being in the mode of that type. A caste system on the other hand reflects a posterior condition in which the individual realizes in himself only a part of the potentialities that are proper to the type generically; priest, king, etc., are now specific determinations, the names alluding to the one and only function which the individual can properly fulfill, and which is his 'vocation.'[3]

In the Vedas we find *Brahma* and *Chatram*[4] two words simultaneously used for denoting intellect and strength, thus indicating two types of persons having intellectual and physical excellence. These two living palladiums can also be seen in the Roman concept of state[5]. In addition to, *Brahmana, Kshatriya, Vanik,* and equivalent terms are used disjointedly in the *Rigveda* and *Atharvaveda* to refer specific individuals with certain qualities.

Brahmana are called followers of certain tenets and regulations (*vrata*)[6]; they drink Soma and recite *Mantras*[7]; as *Vipra* they are magnificent[8] and have good conduct[9]. Besides this *Vipra, Dvija* and

Brahmanaspati terms are also explained by ancient commentators for the meaning of *Brahmana* in the *Rigveda*. The word *Brahmana* is used frequently in the *Atharvaveda*[10]. Another term '*Chatriya*' is seldom used independently in the *Rigveda*[11] and *Atharvaveda*[12] denoting the person of discipline, strength and vigor; while the word *Chatra* also represents these qualities. The third category of persons is indicated by the terms *Vanika, Visha*[13] who have money, and never-ending treasures and also by *Vaishya*[14].

Earliest reference of four classes of society is found in the *Rigveda*[15]. This authoritative passage referring four-fold division is in the hymn known as *Purusha- Sukta*. The term *Varna* is not used here. It only refers to the division of society, comparing it to the different organs of the human being. This *Sukta* describes Creator as verily 'all this' visible world and 'lord of immortality'[16]. Here creation is described through a metaphor of sacrifice i.e.'*Yajya*' where different parts and things of universe are created by gods performing the sacrifice with *Purusha* as offering. This imaginary sacrifice shows that this all universe is nothing but the Creator himself. *Purusha* is the spiritual cause and effect of material creation, it is from him, not from the ideal or real sacrifice, that all things originate. *Rrik, Saman, Yajus, Chandas, Ashva, Go* etc. were produced from him. The eleventh *Mantra* put a question, 'When they (gods) immolated *Purusha,* into how many portions did they divide him? What was his mouth called, what his arms, what his thighs, what were his feet called?'

The twelfth *Mantra* answers, 'His mouth became the *Brahmana*, his arms became the *Rajanya*, his thighs became *Vaishya,* the *Shudra* was born from his feet.'

Brahmano asya mukhamasit bahu rajanyah kritah/
Uru tadasya yadvaishyah pabhyam shudro ajayata//

The *Mantra* has allegorical significance behind it. The verse says that 'The mouth of the *Purusha* became *Brahmana*'. It means the *Brahmana* has not come from the mouth of this primary being, *Purusha*, but his mouth became the *Brahmanical* division, that is to say, was transformed into it. Mouth is the seat of speech. The allegory thus points out that the *Brahmanas* are teachers and instructors of mankind. If the two arms of the *Purusha* are said to have been made a *Rajanya (Kshatiya)*, that means then, that he has to carry arms to defend the empire and to protect the people. The arms represent the symbol of strength and valor. The thighs of the *Purusha* were transformed into the *Vaishya* means that, as the lower parts of the body are the principal repository of food taken; the *Vaishya* class is destined to provide food to the people. The creation of the *Shudra* from the feet of the *Purusha* indicates that he is destined to be a servant to the others, just as the feet serves the other parts of the body as a firm support. It is this verse which is generally put forth as foremost evidence from *Rigveda* for the determination of four-fold division of society, which is later known as four *Varnas*.

Here the whole social organization is conceived symbolically as one human being with its organs representing the different social classes. In fact, the *Purusha* refers to mankind as a whole. It is important to note that body of *Purusha* is here a metaphor for the human- society. This shows the principle of integration and co-ordination that will have to be maintained for the smooth functioning of the society and the body too. As each part has to perform its duty in order to maintain the strength of the body, so the different classes have to live in harmony for a healthy society. As all limbs of a body are important for a human being so are all the classes of the society. All limbs according to their functioning power and capacity used to work for the benefit of the whole body so these classes must do, this is indicative. If one part of the body quarrels with another part of the body, the whole body has to suffer including those parts. All are interlinked and therefore, the question of superiority or inferiority of *Varna* does not arise.

It establishes the principle that these four types of people performing their duties and responsibilities can build a prosperous and harmonious society. In Vedic view there is no discrimination among these classes, rather according to qualities their activities are assigned.

II

The *Purusha Sukta* is regarded by many scholars as being late production on account of several indications on its modern character. Thus it is argued by them that even the conception of the four divisions of men is foreign to the *Rigveda*.

Other scholars, however, hold that the hymn may not be necessarily regarded as modern in character, because such speculative notions are met with in about every part of the *Rigveda* and here allegory is most significant and enlightening. The hidden allegorical sense must be explained. According to the *Rigvedic* verse, the primal man, *Purusha* created human society from himself. This *mantra* is regarded as an evidence for the determination of caste by birth. *Mantra* says: 'The different classes (i.e. *Varnas)* were created from different parts of his body. The *Brahmanas* were created from his head; the *Kshatriyas* from his hands; the *Vaishyas* from his thighs and the *Shudras* from his feet'. The supremacy of these classes can be determined by the descending order of the different organs from which these were created. The *Brahamans* are instructors of mankind. The *Kshatriyas* have to carry arms to defend the empire. The *Vaishyas* have to provide food for others. The *Shudras* are servants to the others. On the basis of this some religious theory claims that the *Varnas* were created from the body organs of Brahma, who is the creator of the world. Even the passage from *Gita* which affirms that the fourfold division of caste depends upon qualities and actions as opposed to birth,[17] is interpreted by some scholars differently laying stress on the word '*Srishtam*' to prove that castes are by birth. The Vedic *mantras*, having mysterious connotations, may be explained variously due to their deep meanings '*Annatah hi Vedarthah'*.

III

The *Brihadaranyaka Upanishad*[18] states that in the very beginning *Brahman* was all alone and so he was not able to perform magnificent actions, so he created *Kshatriyas* and *Kshatriya* deities as Indra, Rudra, Parjanya, Yama. *Brahmanas* were there to perform *Rajasuya Yajya* for them. Soma is *Brahmana* deity. He was not able to perform without people of trading, so he created *Visha* and their deities as Vasus, Marut, Adityas and Rudras. These deities are in group because generally a group of people is able to do business. Even being with them, Brahman was not able to perform as he need service class, therefore he created *Sudras*. Pusha deity represents *Sudra* because he serves the whole earth. Finally, He created *Dharma* to control them all. Here we see that all the four classes are told essential for the proper performance of any deed, even by *Brahman*, and deities are classified in the same way on the basis of their actions and attributes. This passage shows that the ordering of society has been constant endeavor of Vedic Seers.

IV

It is important to note that according to Vedic point of view, *Varnas* were not a barrier to gain knowledge, as knowledge can be imparted to anyone who is desirous from a person who is knowledgeabie . All have a right to get knowledge. No one can claim to be knowledgeable due to his position or family. Similarly due to the mode of livelihood no one can be condemned. In the *Upanishads,* there are so many instances where we see that people of any *Varna* would go to a knowledgeable person of any *Varna* for instructions in the field of higher intellectual pursuit. Father of Svetaketu, Uddalaka Aruni went to kind Pravahana to gain the knowledge of *Brahman.* With the same intention King Janasruti approached to charioteer Raikva in the *Chandogya Upanishad.* Another story in the *Chandogya Upanishad* says that Rishi Uddalaka Aruni inspired five *Brahmanas* to go to King Asvapati for the higher pursuit of Self-knowledge. Hence, stories of *Upanishads* highlight the importance of scholarship above *Varna.*

Social mobility was not hindered at all for any reason of any *Varna* in ancient times. The Sun God advised Samba, son of Shri Krishna, to go to Sakadvipa, and bring the Maga priests well versed in the ritual of sun-worship who alone could cure his leprosy. A whole *Purana, Samba Purana,* narrates that 18 Maga families traveled to India, settled down at Mitravana and established their cult of the Sun in Sambas temple.

V

The Vedic classification of society into four classes later known as *Varnas* was aimed at the distribution of duties and responsibilities in order to build a healthy and prosperous society. The four

Varnas have been referred to the four classes of the society and these have been determined by the natural tendencies, qualities and actions of the persons. In the *Varna* system, natural tendencies and profession are correlated. In later times *Varna* came to be loosely interpreted as caste. The word *Varna* is derived from the Sanskrit root *vri* which means 'to choose' or 'the select'.

An individual is capable of choosing his path of life which will be in conformity with his innate tendencies or temperaments. Four categories of innate tendencies are said to be found in man which are bases on three qualities (*Gunas*). The biological theory claims that all existing things, animated and in-animated, inherent three qualities in different apportionment. *Sattva* qualities include wisdom, intelligence, honesty, goodness and other positive qualities. *Rajas* include qualities like passion, pride, valor and other passionate qualities. *Tamas* qualities include dullness, stupidity, lack of creativity and other negative qualities. People with different doses of these inherent qualities adopted different types of occupation. According to this theory who inherent *Sattva* qualities are the *Brahmans*. Who inherent *Rajas* qualities are *Kshatriyas* and *Vaishyas*. And who inherent *Tamasa* qualities are the *Sudras*. This principle to classify *Varnas* point out that *Varna* are not fixed by birth or any other way, rather they can be changed after word. Rishi Vishvamitra is its example.

Strictly speaking caste it is not *Varna*, it is *Jati* .The word *Jati* is derived from the Sanskrit root *jan* which means 'to take birth'. The seed of caste system was sown in the community on the basis of *Varna* system when qualities of a man became indecisive of his personality and nature. In the new setup, a group of *Brahmana,* named priests, became powerful and made the kings subordinate to themselves. The new elite were more concerned with the enjoyment of power, status and wealth, for which purpose they engaged themselves in the task of elaborating the concept of *Brahmanas* at the cost of neglect of previous spiritualism and scholarship[19].

VI

Every practice has its positive side too. The *Varna* system enlarged as *Jati* system in India kept away the invaders socially, as they could not penetrate families by marrying them. The womenfolk sanctified by the *Varna* structure led to the preservation of our culture. The four *Varnas,* though reproduced into thousand of *jatis*, yet they kept the foreign hordes at bay from all sorts of relationship for thousand years. *Varna* and *Jati* with all their prohibited elements became the defender of our cultural continuity and social integration. Caste system played a useful role in the cultural history of India. The occupation of a caste was passed on from one generation to another. This system helped sufficiently in the preservation of several arts and crafts in ancient Indian society. Every phenomenon has a negative aspect, and negative *Varna-jati* fence stopped social growth variously as we see today artificial distinction between different sections of the society which led to restriction of education for women, inequality, untouch-ability, discrimination at sacred places, restriction in matrimonial alliances etc. This now dominates political spectrum also. With modernity, we continue to treasure our social norms whose core and primary unit is *Varna* and *Jati.*

The four pillars sustaining our society were power of intellect, law and order by governance, economic development, and dynamic activity of labour. They were crystallized in Hindu society as follows the *Brahamana* as keeper of intellection and sanctity, the *Kshatriya* as defender of social order, the *Vaishya* as the productive management of economy, and finally the *Sudra* as the work force. All the four were interactive ingredients of a healthy and strong order. The two greatest poets of India, who authored the epics of Ramayana and Mahabharata were born in low *Varna* according to popular sayings. They are the most venerated sages, and have been the most powerful formative authority in our ethos who influenced the whole literary traditions of all the Indian languages. It indicates that *Rishis* can be born in any *Varna.*

According to Vedic teaching, the ultimate aim of each and every human being is realization of the Divine and Self-fulfillment. Therefore, the pursuits of our entire life should be directed towards this end. The *Varna* System was invented to help man to move collectively towards this end, for man is not merely the body, but he is much more than the body; he is the body as well as spirit. The main noteworthy point that emerges from this study is that the idea of classification of society into four groups is originally of

Vedic Seers having intention to highlight inner quality based work- structure in the society. Nothing like caste was determined by birth. Duties of a person appear to have been based on activities rather than heredity. Undoubtedly it may be assumed that later developed caste system has its root in the *Varna* system of Vedic period.

References

1. Vidyanivas Mishra (Ed.), *Perception of the Vedas,* Ananda K. Coomaraswamy, Indira Gandh For National Centre for Arts, New Delhi, 2000, p.110
2. *Rigveda* (RV) 5.86.2,7.15.2,9.101.9
3. Vidyanivas Mishra (Ed.), *Perception of the Vedas,* Ananda K. Coomaraswamy, Indira Gandh For National Centre for Arts, New Delhi, 2000, p.110-11
4. *Brahma ca Chatram ca.Yajuveda32.16 ;Kathopanishad 1.2.25*
5. Lokesh Chandra, *Varna-Jati System,* in *Sanskrit Vimarsh,* Vol. 5, Journal of Rashtriya Sanskrit Sansthan, New Delhi 2011, p. 191.
6. RV 7.103.1
7. RV 7.103.8
8. RV 1.82.2
9. RV1.8.6
10. *Atharvaveda* (AV) 5.17.1;12.5.4;5.18.1,4;519.6;12.5.11
11. RV 4.12.3,8.67.1, 8.25.8
12. AV 4.22.1;7.103.1
13. RV 1.112.11, 5.45.6
14. AV 5.17.9
15. RV 10.90.12
16. *Purusha evedam sarvam... Utamritatvasyeshano.* RV 10.90.2
17. *Chaturvarnyam maya srishtam gunakarmavibhagashah. Gita 4.13*
18. *Brihadaranyaka Upanishad* 1.4.11-15
19. M. Sundarraj, *Rgvedic Studies,* International Society for Investigation of Ancient Civilization, Madras, 1994, p. 457.

43

A NOTE ON THE ORIGIN OF THE ĀŚRAMA INSTITUTION

Rajawant Rao

The scheme of the four stages of an individual's life, known as Āśrama Dharma, is regarded as an important feature of the ancient Indian social life. Literally the word means a hermitage or a 'resting place', but technically it means a stage in the life of a Hindu. The origin of the Āśrama Institution is shrouded in obscurity. We do not find any direct clear reference to this system in the pre-Buddhistic Vedic Literature. According to the authors of the Vedic Index the word Āśrama does not occur in any Upnishad which can be regarded as Pre-Buddhistic.[1] The earliest use of the word Āśrama is found in the expression 'atyaśramibhyah' which occurs in Śvetaśvatara Upnishad.[2] But according to G.C. Pandey this expression seems to imply that mendicancy was as yet beyond the ken of the Āśramas.[3] A clear reference to the Āśrama system is found in Jābālopanishad[4], which describes in sequence the four stages of an individuals' life, e.i., Brahmacharya, Grihastha, Vānaprastha and Sanyāsa, but the evidence provided by Jābālopnishad is definitely not pre-Buddhist. The Dharmasutras of Āpastamba, Gautama, Baudhāyana and Vaśishtha, mention the four stages of life, but the difference in the nomenclature and in the sequence adopted by them proves that the system was not fully recognized as yet: Thus, Āpastamba speaks of Grihastha, Ācharyakula, Mauna, and Vānaprastha.[5] Gautama mentions Brahmachāri, Grihastha, Bhikshu and Vaikhānasa[6], while Vasistha[7] and Baudhāyana[8] speak of Brahmachāri, Grihastha, Vānaprastha and Parivrājaka. Thus, we find that during the age of Dharmasutras the fourth Āśrama was known to be associated with the bhikshus and parivrājakas. It appears that these terms were interchangeable during the age of the Dharmasutras, as the munis, Bhikshus and parivrājakas belonged to one and the same milieu which was characterized by austerity and negation of mundane life.

This is to be noted that the Vedic tradition, which put special emphasis on sacrificial religion, disapproved the ascetic way of life. Though Gautama and Baudhāyan mention four stages of life in their works, they mince no words in stating that only Grihastha Āśrama is worth following[9]. Baudhāyan further informs that the theory of the four Āśrama was initiated by a Asura named Kapila, who was son of Prahlāda and therefore the wise men should not follow it[10]. This is pertinent to note that Kapila, according to Baudhayan, was a Asura and was opposed to Devas. The passage suggests that the fourfold division of life was not in accordance with the rules promulgated by the Gods and it was the creation of a demon. Baudhāyana clearly attacks the ascetic way of life and takes it as an anti-vedic tradition.

Interestingly enough, both Kapila and Prahlāda have been mentioned in the Bhagvadgita, the first as a muni[11] and the second as a demon (daitya).[12] Thus, it appears that the ascetic way of life which was associated with the munis parivrajakas and bhikshus was essentially non-vedic in nature. In the introduction of his commentary on Gita, Sankaracharya has observed that the Vedic religion is two-fold Pravrtti-Dharma and Nivrtti-Dharma. Scholars such as S.K. Chatterji and R.P. Chanda opine that the two tendencies may be attributed to different ethenic traditions- Aryan and non-Aryan, the ascetic tradition being the contribution of the letter. G.C. Pande also admits that the Vedic religion was, in the beginning essentially Pravritti Dharma but later on partly through inner evolution and more, through the influence of the muni-śramanas it developed Nivritti Dharma as a tendency within its fold.[13]

Now our attention is drawn towards the muni-śramana tradition which was opposed to the ritualistic brahmanical tradition. This is to be noted that the Buddhist and Jain literatures very often use the term Śramana to denote all the non-Brahmanical systems collectively. The Dighanikaya, the Indica of Megasthanese and the inscriptions of Aśoka indicate that heterodox sects represented by the Śramanas claimed equality of status with the Brahmanas belonged to rival groups[14]. The muni śramana tradition ran parallel to vedic tradition. The earliest literary reference to munis comes from the Rigveda. The term muni occurs once in a hymn to the Maruts[15], where it appears to mean a person in esctacy. At another place Indra has been said to have been the friend of the munis[16]. The most striking description of the muni is found in the Keśi Sukta[17] which delineates him as long-haired (Keśi), Clad in dirty tawny coloured garments (Pisanga vasate malā), living by air (Vatarasanāh), delirious with the state of being a muni (unmadita mauneyena) and inspired. He enjoyed the friendship of Vāyu and drank poison with Rudra.[18] On the basis of the above description G.C. Pande opines that the munis were alien to Rigvedic culture. The vedic Aryans were filled with a certain sense of wonder and awe at the sight of miracle performing munis.[19]

According to Goyal they were the marginal men of the Rigvedic period.[20] But gradually the impact of muni-śramana culture was felt in the vedic society, when some Aryans were attracted towards the nivritti ideal of the munis. Tapa, an essential feature of Śramanism was given due recognition in the later vedic age.[21] The later vedic literature is not only more acquainted with the munis but has sometimes respectful attitude towards them. For example, Atharvaveda refers to a Devamuni who acquired mysterious powers by the dint of asceticism.[22] Similarly we find references to munis in Aitareya Brāhmana and Panchavimsa Brāhmana.[23] The Taittariya Aranyaka speaks of the Vatarasanā Śramanas, who led a celibate life and could disappear at will and teach to the Brāhmanas the way beyond sin. It also makes obeisance to the munis of Gangā and Yamunā.[24] As suggested by some passage in the later vedic literature, the gradual development of the concept of the four stages of life was a result of the conflict and conflux of the Brahmanical and Śramanic ideals of life. In the Brāhmanical tradition the importance of the life of house-holder was supreme while the śramana philosophy denounced it and preached a life of austerity and renunciation. An echo of the conflict of two ideas is found in the well known passage of Aitareya Brāhmana[25] which states "What use is there of dirt (mala), what use of skindress (ajina) and what use of austerity (tapas)? O Brahmana, desire a son; he is a worth to be highly praised." According to Kane this is perhaps the earliest reference of the four aśramas in the vedic literature.[26] He interprets 'mala' in the sense of sexual intercourse and takes it as representing the life of a grihastha. According to him the 'ajina' denotes brahmacharya, shmashru, denotes vānaprastha and 'tapa' is indicative of sanyasa āśrama.[27] But to find here a reference to four āśramas appears to be too speculative. Actually the passage in question speaks of the two contradistinctive ideals of nivritti and pravritti and rejects the first one. Commending procreation of a son, it loudly speaks of the importance of the worldly life. In the passage under review 'mala', 'ajina', 'shmashru' and 'tapa' collectively point towards the life of an ascetic. Here, "mala' stands for dust or ash used by the escetics even in later times. As it is evident through a number of passages in Dharmasutras[28] and Mahābharata[29], ajina, shmashru and tapa were closely associated with Vānaprasthas or Vaikhānasas. Thus, the passage clearly presents a contrast between the life of a householder and the life of an ascetic. An attempt to harmonize the two contradictory ideals of the pravritti and nivritti is found for the first time in chhandogya upnisad[30], which mentions three sections of Dharma the first comprising sacrifice, sacred study and liberality, the second being austerity and the third being studentship. The passage in question presents a nebulous description of the first three stages of life. On the basis of the data available it may safely be presumed that only three āśramas were known during the age of the Upnisads and three was as yet no clear distinction between the third and the fourth āśrama.[31] However, the passage clearly suggests that the asceticism was gradually accommodated in the vedic scheme of life, which originally recognized only the first two āśramas. It was the growing impact of the muni-śramana tradition under which Brahmanical values changed partially and some sections within the vedic society tended the accept the ascetic way of life. The need to synthesize the two value systems gave birth to the concept of the āśramas. Nevertheless the distinction between the third and fourth āśrama and a clear concept of the system of four āśramas crystallized gradually during the age of Dharmasutras and smritis. There is reason to believe that the concept of the four stages of life evolved in the eastern part of India, under the influences of the muni-śramana culture. The later Vedic literature bears it out that the Vedic Aryans were influenced by the ascetic tradition in their eastward movement. A passage in Satapatha Brāhmana suggests that the sacrificial religion could not find favour from the people living on the eastern bank of Sadanira.[32] On the other hand Aitareya Aranyaka expresses a sense of respect to the munis living in Gangā-Yamunā region. Asceticism had become very popular in eastern region during the post-vedic age. We have frequently about the ascetics living in āśramas located in different parts of eastern U.P. and Bihar. Verses of Mahābharat refer to the ascetics living in Naimisaranya. The Ramayan also refers to number of āśramas such as of Valmiki, Bhāradwaja and others in the Gangetic valley. The Buddhist texts furnish evidence for the presence of a number of ascetics in eastern India. Thus, we know from Vinayapitaka that at the time of Gautama Buddha, a large number of Jatilas lived in Gayā region.[33] There can scarcely be any about that these Jatilas were Vānaprasthas.[34] The same text further informs us that more than two hundred parivrājakas were living near Rājagriha under the leadership of Sanjaya Velathiputra.[35] There are, besides, frequent reference to Nirgranthas and Ajivikas in early Buddhist literature. These evidences leave no doubt that long before Buddha's time a large number of ascetics used to live in the mid gangetic valley and further east. It is not a mere coincidence that Risabhanātha and Parśvanātha, the two jain tirthankaras belonging to pre-Buddhist period and preaching the ascetic way of life are said to have belonged to Kośala and Kāśi respectively. Even Gautama Buddha and Mahāvira the two great preceptors of ascetic ideals were the products of eastern U.P. and Bihar. This is interesting to note that Kapila the son of Prahalāda, who has been held responsible for the introduction of the system of the four āśramas in Baudhāyana Dharma-sūtra, is also associated with this region. Buddhist literature informs us that the ascetic Kapila had his hermitage at the place where the township of Kapilvastu developed later.[36]

In short, it may be submitted that the scheme of the four āśramas of life originated in eastern region during the post-vedic period as a result of the conflict and commingly of the śramana and Brahman traditions.

Notes and References

1. Vedic Index, Vol. 1, p.68.
2. Śvetaśvatara Up. VI. 21.
3. Pande, G.C., Origins of Buddhism, p. 322.
4. Jābālopanisad, 4.
5. Āpastamba, 2.1.21.
6. Gautama, 3.2.3.
7. Vasistha, 7.1.2.
8. Baudhāyana, 2.11-14.
9. Gautama, 3.3-5, Baudhāyana 2.6
10. Baudhāyana, 2.6 एकाश्रम्यं त्वाचार्या अप्रजनत्वादिरेषाम् तत्रोदाहरन्ति–प्रह्लादिर्ह वै कपिलो नाम असुर यांस, स एतान्मेदांश्चकार दैवेस्सह. सिद्धानां कपिलो
11. Gita, 10.26 सिद्धानां कपिलो
12. Gita, 10-30.
13. Pande, G.C., Studies in the Origins of Buddhism, p. 261.
14. Agrawal, V.S., India as known to Panini, p. 383 F
15. RV VII, 56.8
16. RV. VIII 3.5.
17. RV. X. 136.
18. Griffith interprets Visha as water, while V.S. Pathak takes it in the sense of intoxicant.
19. Pande, Op.Cit. , P. 258

20. Goyal, S.R., A Religious History of Ancient India, P.92.
21. Brh.Up. IV. 3.22: Chh.Up. II, 23.1.
22. AV. VII. 74.1.
23. Ait. Br. VI 33; Panch,Br.X. 14.47.
24. Ait, Aranyaka 2.20.1
25. Ait Br. 33.1. किं नु मलं किमजिनं कि श्मश्रूणि किं तपः।
    पुत्रं ब्राह्मण इच्छध्वं स वै लोके बदावदः।।
26. Kane, P.V., History of Dharmasastra Vol. II. P. 419-20
27. Ibid.
28. Gautam, 1.3, 25-26
    वैखानसो वने मूलफलाशीं जटिलश्चीराजिन वासाः
    भूमिशय्याजटाश्मश्रुर्चर्मवल्कलधारणम्।
29. MB, Anusasana Parva 141, p.5922
30. Chh.Up. 11.23.1.
31. Hist. of Dharmashastra, Vol. II, p.420-21.
32. Sat.Br. 1.4.1.14
33. S.B.E. XIII. 118
34. Majumdar, Corporate life, p.272
35. S.B.E. XIII. 144-48
36. Saundarananda I, 5.57.

44

THE NĀYANĀRS AND ĀḶVĀRS AND THEIR CONTRIBUTION TO THE BHAKTI MOVEMENT IN SOUTH INDIA

Shankar Goyal

I

In South India till about the fifth century A.D. harmony and tolerance characterized the relations between the different religious sects. But thereafter a great change came about particularly in the Tamil region and people began to entertain fears of the whole land being converted to Jainism and Buddhism. Consequently, missionary parties of the devotees of Vishṇu and Śiva under the leadership of gifted saints called the Āḷvārs (Vaishṇavas) and Nāyanārs (Śaivas) began to traverse the country singing, dancing and debating all through their way. This great wave of religious enthusiasm attained its peak in the middle of the seventh century A.D. and had not fully spent itself by the middle of the ninth. The Chinese pilgrim Yüan Chwang, who visited South India in 642 A.D. when the Hindu devotional revivalism was just gathering momentum, failed to notice the new movement. He indeed regrets that Buddhism was on the decline, but remarks repeatedly that it had yielded to Digambara Jainism.[1] It seems that the triumph of the Hindu revivalism was largely achieved in the two centuries that followed him. Public disputations usually led rulers to transfer their allegiance from one creed to another, but more significant was the impact of the soul-stirring compositions of the Śaiva Nāyanārs and the Vaishṇava Āḷvārs and the fact that these were set to simple popular tunes. The Nāyanārs and Āḷvārs, especially the earlier ones, were simple-hearted bhaktas rather than philosophical or theological scholars. They were god-intoxicated people who transmitted their divine infatuation to millions of their contemporaries. But some of them were talented singers also and have left behind them an imperishable legacy of devotional poetry which has rarely been equalled anywhere else in quantity and quality.[2]

We owe the collection and preservation of the devotional songs of the Śaiva and Vaishṇava saints to the labours of two religious leaders, Nambi-Āṇḍār-Nambi and Nāthamuni. The former arranged the available Śaiva hymns into eleven *Tirumuṛais.* The first seven of these (collectively called *Tevāram* or *Devāram*), bring together the hymns of Sambandar, Appar and Sundarar. The eighth (called *Tiruvāchakam*) is the work of Māṇikkavāchakar, the ninth is a miscellaneous collection, the tenth brings together the mystic outpourings of a sixth century Śaiva yogī, Tirumūlar, and the eleventh and the last *Tirumuṛai* is another miscellany of poems from Nakkīrar to Nambi-Āṇḍār-Nambi. Similarly, Nāthamuni, the Vaishṇava counterpart of Nambi-Āṇḍār-Nambi, arranged the extant Vaishṇava hymns into a colossal collection, called *Nāḷāyira Divya Prabandham*, which is a veritable treasure-house of devotional poetry. The four thousand hymns included in this collection are the work of twelve Āḷvārs including a woman mystic, Āṇḍāl.

II

Śaiva bhakti became widespread throughout the Tamil land because of the zeal of the Nāyanārs, the Śaiva mystics and bhaktas. Their movement reached its peak in the seventh century A.D. and had not spent itself entirely by the middle of the ninth century.[3] Their hymns are full of and noble sentiments of devotion, but their main emphasis is on the majesty and greatness of God and the feeling of submission, self-abnegation and surrender to God. Later tradition counted sixty-three Nāyanārs, individual and collective, as the most prominent leaders of this revival. The individuals included a woman Kāraikāl Ammaiyār (the woman of Kāraikāl) and a pariah, Nandan from Āḍanūr, besides a general of the Pallava forces, Śiruttoṇḍar. Their main contribution lay in the creation of a firm foundation of Tamil mysticism and bhakti philosophy. They made no distiction of caste, creed or sex in the cause of devotion.

The relationship of the Nāyanārs to the Śaiva Āgamas is somewhat similar to that of the Āḷvārs to the Pāñcharātra Āgamas. Tirumūlar, the author of the tenth *Tirumuṛai*, whom a myth makes a permanent door-keeper (*dvārapāla*) of Śiva, refers to the Āgamas being as divine as the Vedas. He enunciates in his work called *Tirumantiram* the Śaiva Siddhānta doctrine of three *padārthas* — Pati, Paśu and Pāśam. *Pati* or Śiva is the creator of the universe and the saviour of the soul. *Paśu* or soul is distinct from *Pati* but is eternal, individuated consciousness having the powers of cognition and activity. *Pāśam* is ultimately rooted in *mala* which binds the soul to ignorance, passions and sufferings. Since *mala* is a substance it cannot totally disappear without the action of God's grace. Tirumūlar believed that the spirit no less than the matter must be accepted as real, for it is impossible to conceive of one quite independently of the other.

About a century after Tirumūlar, Māṇikkavāchakar and the other three great Śaiva Samayāchāryas — Appar, Sambandar and Sundarar — flourished in the Tamil land. It is now generally agreed that Appar and Sambandar were contemporaries, and that Sundarar lived two or three decades after Appar's death in 681A.D.[4] But whether Māṇikkavāchakar preceded or came after the three *Tevāram* singers is not certain.

Tirunavukkaraśu or Appar is generally believed to have been a contemporary of the Pallava ruler Mahendravarman I. Though born in an orthodox Śaiva family he was attracted to Jainism in his early years, and joined the Jaina monastery at Pāṭaliputra (Cuddalore) as a monk with the adopted name of Dharmasena. His elder sister, a devout Śaiva, who had watched his change of faith with extreme anguish and dismay, implored Śiva's help. As if in answer to her prayer, Dharmasena became afflicted with an incurable abdominal disorder. When all his fellow Jainas failed him, he was compelled to go and seek his sister's help. She succeeded in securing his cure by the grace of Śiva. But because of his defection, the Jainas poisoned the mind of the Pallava ruler of the country against him. According to the tradition, he was subjected to many trials and tortures which, however, by the grace of Śiva he easily surmounted. Finally, the king himself was convinced of the superiority of Saivism, and embraced it. A verse in a Trichinopoly inscription of Mahendravarman's time does indeed suggest that the king turned to Śaivism from some other creed.[5] The rest of Appar's life was spent in pilgrimages during which he met many contemporary Nāyanārs, of whom Sambandar was the most notable, indeed the greatest of them all.

Appar's contribution to *Tevāram* consists of 313 hymns. He conceives a personal relationship with God — who is mother, father, and a relative for him. Every perfection in man and nature is a sign of God's love for man. Appar also had a profound sense of sin and hence his bhakti is marked by humility, penitence and repentance.[6] But in spite of all this he is optimistic about salvation through the Divine Grace.

Jñānasambandar or Sambandar was a Brāhmaṇa of the Kauṇḍinya *gotra* from Shiyali in the Tanjore district. According to a legend, as a child of three he got the milk of the divine knowledge from Pārvatī herself and narrated this incident to his father in a song. At that time the Pāṇḍya country was almost completely overrun by Jainism. Sambandar betook himself to Madurā, foiled the conspiracies of the Jainas against him, vanquished them in debate and converted the king and his subjects to Śaivism. It is said that on this occasion 8,000 Jainas were put to death by impalement. This, however, according to K.A. Nilakanta Sastri, is a little more than an unpleasant legend and cannot be treated as sober history.[7]

Sambandar is said to have been absorbed into the god-head at the age of 16 only. Probably it only means that he died in the prime of his life. He is reputed to have composed 10,000 hymns, though only 384 of these are now extant.

Some decades later than Sambandar came Sundarar, or Sundaramūrti Nāyanār. He was the last of the four great Śaiva Samayāchāryas. He was born of poor Brāhmaṇa parents. His beauty as a child was such that he attracted the attention of a local chieftain who, with the consent of the parents, brought him up. When his marriage with a girl of his own caste was about to take place it was stopped, it is said, by the mysterious intervention of Śiva who claimed him as his slave. A little later Sundarar fell in love with two women, one a dancing-girl and the other a Śūdrā. Their jealousies were resolved by Śiva himself. Like the other Nāyanārs, Sundarar is also credited with many miracles, and the contemporary Chera ruler, Cheramān Perumāl, is said to have been his friend. Sundarar's devotion to Śiva was that of an intimate friend (*sakhyabhakti*) so that he was given the title *Tambirān-Toḷan* ('Friend of God'). During his incredibly short life of only eighteen years, he crowded a career of astounding service in the cause of the Divine. Of the tens of thousands of songs said to have been composed by him hardly one hundred have survived which are included in the seventh book of the *Tirumuṛai*. In these God is conceived as madly in love with his devotees. Sundarar's hymns are on every devout Tamil bhakta's lips to this day, and are sung by the musicians in temples and maṭhas.

About a century after Sundarar came the illustrious Māṇikkavāchakar who was also born of Brāhmaṇa parents. Legend makes him the minister of a Pāṇḍyan king; and on his account Śiva, the presiding deity of Madurā, is said to have performed many miracles. He is said to have debated with the Buddhists who came from Ceylon at Chidambaram and to have utterly vanquished them. The collection of fifty-one hymns known as *Tiruvāchakam* is, as if, Māṇikkavāchakar's spiritual autobiography. Mystical writings reached their climax, it is said, in the writings of Māṇikkavāchakar. They melt the heart and purify all sins. He who remains unmoved by them is called a veritable stone. *Tiruvāchakam* seems to bring out the quintessence of Tamil Śaivism — especially by its doctrine of self-surrender to the Supreme God — even more completely than *Tevāram*.[8]

III

The Āḷvārs[9] (meaning 'divers into the qualities of God' or 'those who delved deep in wisdom') represented the Vaishṇava wing of the Bhakti movement. They were looked upon as 'wise seers who exercised spiritual sovereignty over the hearts of men'.[10] Their bhakti was certainly more intense than the bhakti advocated in the *Gītā*. Hooper calls them the morning stars of the medieval bhakti movement.[11] They had before them a tradition of the Upanishads and the *Gītā* which helped them form their own basic philosophy concerning God. Their theology was completed by accepting the ideas of the Pāñcharātra Āgamas and the Purāṇas. They may not have succeeded in making much positive contribution to philosophical thought, but their revelation of a depth of fervour produced by the idea of Deity as incarnating Himself out of love for His creatures, and desiring in return their whole-hearted devotion, is worth noting.

The Āḷvārs hailed from different parts of the Tamil land. The Pallava country contributed the first four Āḷvārs, namely, Poygai, Bhūtattār, Pey, and Tirumaliśai; Chola Deśa was the home of Toṇḍaraḍippoḍi, Tiruppān, and Tirumaṅgai; the Chera country produced Kulaśekhara; while to the Pāṇḍya Nāḍu belonged the rest, notably, Nammāḷvār, and also Āṇḍāl, one of the supreme women mystics. It is also worthy to note that the twelve Āḷvārs, like the sixty-three Nāyanārs, were a cosmopolitan group, and came from all castes and various strata of the society. Nammāḷvār, like Appar, was a Veḷḷāḷa by caste, Tirumaṅgai came from a robber's family, Kulaśekhara was a princely ascetic while Periāḷvār was a Brāhmaṇa.

There are three main sources for the study of Āḷvārs — (1) legendary lives of the saints narrated in the Guruparamparās, (2) contemporary inscriptions on stone or metal, and (3) collections of their hymns called *Nāḷāyira Divya Prabandham,* compiled by Nāthamuni. Of these Guruparamparās are not of much historical importance. They mix facts and fiction so liberally that they are of little value to the historian. However, they provide religious and mythological colour to the lives of the saints. Contemporary inscriptions furnish authenticity to the meagre data available to us while the *Nāḷāyira Divya Prabandham* acquaints us with the essence and soul of the Āḷvārs' teachings. There cannot be two opinions about its poetical and spiritual fervour.

Tradition found in the Guruparamparās arranges the Āḷvārs into three groups and gives them precise but impossible chronology:[12]

(1) *Ancient* group of Poygai, Bhūtattār, Pey and Tirumaliśai Āḷvārs which is placed in 4203 B.C.

(2) *Middle* group of Nammāḷvār, Madhurakavi, Kulaśekhara, Periāḷvār and Āṇḍāl. It is placed between 3102 and 3005 B.C.

(3) *Last* group consisting of Toṇḍaraḍippoḍi, Tiruppān and Tirumaṅgai Āḷvārs (2814-2706 B.C.).

These seemingly precise dates are, however, of no use whatsoever as historical data. According to the traditional accounts, the earliest of the Āḷvārs, Poygai, Pey and Bhūtattār and also their contemporary Tirumaliśai were born in the Dvāpara yuga in Toṇḍaimaṇḍalam and lived at the time of the Pallava domination over that region. But it is impossible to believe that the Āḷvārs flourished in the Dvāpara age because of the following reasons :

(1) Now we know that the Pallavas first came to Kāñchī not earlier than the second century A.D.[13] Therefore, the early Āḷvārs who lived at the time of the Pallava domination cannot be placed there earlier than that.

(2) Tirumaliśai Āḷvār mentions the Śramaṇas (obviously the Jainas), the Bauddhas and the Śivabhaṭṭārakas. But Buddhism and Jainism had not come into being in the Dvāpara yuga. Therefore, the Āḷvārs who refer to these religions cannot have lived earlier than the Buddha who belonged to the sixth century B.C.

(3) A verse of Tirumaliśai seems to be an adaptation from the famous *Tirukkuṛal,* a work which belonged to the Saṅgam period, variously dated from the 2nd to the 6th century A.D.

(4) Bhūtattār Āḷvār refers to Māmallai as his own birth place which is the same as the modern Mahābalipuram. This town did not probably exist before the time of Narasiṁhavarman I, for it was this king who is said to have founded or at least enlarged it and gave it the name of Māmallapuram after his own name Māmalla. Therefore, Bhūtaṭṭār and his contemporaries cannot be assigned to a period earlier than the middle of the seventh century of the Christian era, the date of this king, before whom this city, even if existed, could not be known as Māmallai.

(5) Some facts contained in an Anaimalai inscription first brought to notice by T.A. Gopinatha Rao[14] records many things which are in striking consonance with those found in the Guruparamparās regarding Nammāḷvār. For example, it mentions a disciple of Nammāḷvār who was known as Madhurakavi.

(6) In one of his verses Nammāḷvār also shows his acquaintance with the famous *Tirukkuṛal,* a work composed in the Saṅgam age.

(7) Kulaśekhara Āḷvār was, according to the tradition, next to Nammāḷvār in point of time. In his work there is a reference to a historical incident which alludes to the defeat and death of a Pallava king at the hands of Kulaśekhara Āḷvār. After discussing the history of the Pallavas of that period, Gopinatha Rao has suggested that the Pallava contemporary of Kulaśekhara was someone later than Nandivarman Pallavamalla and that Kulaśekhara probably joined the Pāṇḍya king in assailing and probably also killing the Pallava king Dantivarman sometime about 825 A.D. It is perhaps this event that is alluded to in the *Perumāl Tirumoḷi.*[15]

(8) Apart from the *Tirukkuṛal,* the Āḷvārs were familiar with several other Tamil classics. In the *Tirumālai* of Toṇḍaraḍippoḍi, for instance, there occur two feet of a verse which is identical with two feet of a verse belonging to the work of the Śaiva saint Appar. Since we know that Appar lived about the middle of the seventh century A.D., we must hold that Toṇḍaraḍippoḍi could not belong to the twenty-ninth century B.C.

For reasons such as these, modern scholars do not believe in the tradition that the Āḷvārs flourished in 4203-2706 B.C. According to S. Krishnaswamy Aiyangar, the earliest of the Āḷvārs must have flourished in the second century A.D., but most of the other scholars place the earliest Āḷvārs about the sixth or seventh century A.D. In any case, the Āḷvārs cannot be placed earlier than the Gupta age. Nilakanta Sastri also argues from the non-sectarian simplicity of their hymns, style and metre that the earlier Āḷvārs could not have been later than the fifth or sixth century A.D. On the other hand, all the Āḷvārs almost certainly flourished before Vaishṇava Āchārya Nāthamuni (10th or 11th century A.D.). In the present state of our knowledge one cannot be surer and more exact than this.

IV

The twelve Āḷvārs came from diverse social groups and backgrounds. Though some of them were Brāhmaṇas, one was a Chāṇḍāla (Tiruppān); though most were men, one was a woman (Āṇḍāl); though one was a king (Kulaśekhara of Travancore), one was a thief and a brigand (Tirumaṅgai). But despite such differences in their social and cultural background, they were accepted by the tradition as saints.

The first three Āḷvārs — Poygai, Bhūtattār and Pey are known to have had miraculous origin as they are believed to have been born out of flowers.[16] Poygai, according to a tradition, was born in Kāñchī from a golden lotus; Bhūtattār in Mahābalipuram, just outside Chennai, again from a lotus; and Pey, in the suburb of the present-day Chennai known as Mylapore, again from a lotus, though in a well. All of them are said to have been incarnations of important Vishṇu symbols — Poygai of Vishṇu's conch named Pāñchajanya, Bhūtattār of Vishṇu's mace, and Pey of Vishṇu's sword Nandaka.[17]

The three early Āḷvārs did not know one another until Vishṇu simultaneously induced in each of them a desire to visit his shrine at Tirukkovalur (Koval).

Poygai, Bhūtattār and Pey were early voices in the evolution of a personal poetry of devotion in Tamil. By that time the age of classicism in Tamil literature was coming to a close, therefore the classical influence is not pervasive in their poems. Nevertheless, many of their verses display or extend classical motifs and techniques.[18]

The first three Āḷvārs contributed one hundred verses each in praise of the Lord. Their poems are embroidered with references of Vishṇu's sports in His various *avatāras* ; but their key-note is a mystical longing for Him. Their bhakti was gentle simple dovotion, altogether free from a sectarian outlook. This fact, and their employment of the *veṇbā* metre in their songs, are regarded as pointers to an early date for them.

Poygai Āḷvār was fascinated by various myths, such as, the myth of ocean-churning, and the Vāmana myth, and speaks of the measureless qualities of the Lord revealed in those myths.

Bhūtattār was also greatly impressed by the various *avatāras* of Vishṇu. He enumerates the exploits of Vāmana, Trivikrama, Varāha and Nṛsiṁha *avatāras.* The various episodes from the life of Kṛshṇa held particular interest for him, e.g. the Pūtanā incident and the episode of Kṛshṇa getting down from the chariot to kill Bhīshma in spite of his vow not to take a weapon in his hands in the Bhārata War. This incident, Bhūtattār believed, shows the utmost love of God for His devotees. Bhūtattār claimed a constant vision of the Divine in sleep as well as in the waking state and emphasized the importance of constant remembrance. This is reminiscent of the *Dhruvā Smṛti* of Rāmānuja.

The greatness of Pey lay in his knowledge and vision of the Divine from a deeper perception of God's eternal divinity as the Divine Two, comprising Nārāyaṇa and his consort Śrī.[19] He mentions numerous exploits of the Lord especially the incidents of Dantavaktra, Pūtanā, Hiraṇyakaśipu and Gajendramoksha. The Trivikrama exploit is the one which he most frequently refers to.

After the early Āḷvārs came Tirumaliśai or Bhaktisāra born in Chingleput district. He became famous after the name of the village where he was born. He is said to have been an incarnation of the Sudarśana Chakra of Vishṇu. Most probably he was an elder contemporary of the Pallava ruler Mahendravarman I. It is said that at birth he was a shapeless mass of flesh abandoned by his parents and was brought up by a Śūdra. He is said to have practised Jainism, Buddhism and Śaivism in turn before he became a Vaishṇava yogī. His poems show a more controversial tone than those of the first three Āḷvārs, and this was quite natural for his age. He gives a more personal description of God and describes His *vibhavas* and *vyūhas.* According to him, God runs after His devotees and grants them grace if they adopt the path of *śaraṇāgati.*[20]

Tirumaliśai appears to have been ideologically a militant Vaishṇava extremely hostile to the Buddhists, Jainas and Śaivas. He was also uncompromising in his monotheism, and his learning was prodigious. The single-minded devotion, that is *ekāntika* bhakti, of Tirumaliśai finds expression in assertions like this : "Be it today or tomorrow or some future day, Your grace is surely mine; I shall take refuge in none other than you, Neither will you ever abandon me, O Nārāyaṇa."[21]

Tirumaṅgai, who may be placed after Tirumaliśai, is variously described as 'a petty chieftain', 'leader of a big gang of robbers', and 'a military chief who was weaned away from his worldly career by the redemptive grace of God'. His life seems to have been highly colourful. He was skilful versifier, though as a mystic poet he is usually rated below Nammāḷvār. There is a story that Tirumaṅgai was a contemporary of the Śaiva saint Tirujñāna- sambandar or Sambandar who was himself a contemporary of the Pallava king Narasiṁhavarman I (630-68 A.D.) of Kāñchī. But K. A. Nilakanta Sastri says that Tirumaṅgai mentions the siege of Kāñchīpuram by Vairamegha, who is usually identified with the first Rāshṭrakūṭa ruler Dantidurga (mid. 8th century A.D.). However, there are many resemblances in literary form and religious sentiments between Sambandar and Tirumaṅgai. According to the legends, he became a highwayman in order to carry off and marry the daughter of a higher caste Vaishṇava for whom he also changed his religion. He is said to have stolen a solid golden image of the Buddha from a monastery in order to pay for renovation of the temple of Śrīraṅgam.

Tirumaṅgai's hymns are full of good poetry and attack Jainism and Buddhism. To Śaivism he shows a friendlier attitude. His hymnal collection comprises the *Periya Tirumoḷi* and constitutes almost one-third of the *Nāḷāyira Divya Prabandham.* He sings passionately of his seeking for the Lord and of His grace which gives refuge to all, however lowly.[22]

A little later than Tirumaṅgai, about the close of the eighth and the beginning of the ninth century, came a number of Āḷvārs. Periyāḷvār, also known as Vishṇuchitta, was a Brāhmaṇa by caste. He is said to have won a religious disputation in the court of the Pāṇḍya king Śrīmāra Śrīvallabha (815-62 A.D.). In his verses he assumes the role of Kṛshṇa's parents or associates showing *vātsalya* and *sakhya bhāva.* Renunciation for him meant renunciation of everything except the service of God. He contributed about five hundred hymns to the 'Four Thousand'. He also composed the *Tirumoḷi,* a splendid imaginative recreation of Lord Kṛshṇa's life.

Āṇḍāl or Kodai (Skt. Godā) was the real or adopted daughter of Periyāḷvār. She is deemed to have been a form of Vishṇu's consort Lakshmī. According to the tradition, Periyāḷvār found a child Āṇḍāl at the foot of a tree and brought her up with more than a fatherly affection.

From the outset Āṇḍāl or Godā thirsted for the Divine, and poured forth her divine love into some of the finest poetry she wrote. She regarded herself as one of Kṛshṇa's gopīs, sought Him with singular fervour and determination, and is believed to have achieved union with Him at last at Śrīraṅgam. In her intense devotion to Vishṇu she dreamt of her marriage with him, and described her experience in her hymns. This mystical union was the only one she knew.

The devotion of Āṇḍāl shows *mādhurya bhakti* in the most intense form like that of the gopīs of the *Bhāgavata* and of Mīrā of Rajasthan. Her two works *Tiruppāvāi* and *Nāchchiyār Tirumoḷi* are full of hymns showing this aspect of bhakti. Śrī or the Divine mother is sought by her as the supreme teacher, companion and guide who also acts as a mediator between the soul and the Divine. Her *Tiruppāvāi* is a lyrical essay on the dynamics of true devotion. In her *Nāchchiyār Tirumoḷi* she constantly dreams of her beloved and prays sleeplessly for the fulfilment of her desire. She seems to be lost in dreaming about her dalliance with God. Vedāntadeśika in his *Godāstuti* declares that all the other Āḷvārs have transmuted their bhakti into *śṛṅgāra* taking their cue from Godā. Her hymn '*varaman ayiram*', etc. speaking of her dream-marriage with Vishṇu is still sung at all Vaishṇava, Brāhmaṇa marriages.

Tiruppān was responsible for only ten verses. He belonged to the Chāṇḍāla caste, and was not permitted to enter the temple of Lord Raṅganātha at Śrīraṅgam and was thus a Vaishṇava counter-part of Nandan. But so great was his devotion to Raṅganātha that the Lord is said to have asked the Brāhmaṇa priest of the temple to bring Tiruppān on his shoulders to His presence. He is said to have been fond of his *vīṇā* to abstraction. It is said that he often fell into deep *samādhi* whilst playing it. Being a Chāṇḍāla he could not enter any temple, so he would pray and sing on the banks of the Kāverī.[23] In his verses God is described as taintless, origin of all, resplendent, immaculate and holy and upholder of the right. He refers to the Trivikrama and Rāma *avatāras* of the Lord.[24]

Toṇḍaraḍippoḍi ('the dust of the feet of the devotees') was a Brāhmaṇa from Tanjore district whose real name was Vipranārāyaṇa. His intolerance of Buddhism and Jainism was as great as that of Tirumaṅgai. He sang of the nature of God, His beauty and His grace. Fifty verses of his are extant. He lived for a time with a courtesan and got into trouble, but was ultimately saved by Raṅganātha. According to Toṇḍaraḍippoḍi, God is the First Being and has three functions of creation, preservation and destruction of the world. His beauty is beyond description. Even if a sinful person utters His name, he attains the highest state. 'There is no other God than He to save'. He slew Rāvaṇa in order to save the world from *adharma.* He revealed Himself in the temple at Śrīraṅgam. This is the *archā* form of the Lord in which he has descended for the sake of his devotees.

Toṇḍaraḍippoḍi says that he does not even want Indraloka, but wants to address the Lord forever on this earth. He says that his purpose of being born will not be fulfilled if he will not spent all his time offering flowers at the feet of the Lord, and will not speak faultless words describing His qualities. He remembers that even monkeys and squirrels helped the Lord when he was crossing the sea to reach Laṅkā and therefore he feels the necessity of doing his bit too.[25] He prays to the Lord to take away the food of those who do not take His name and give it to dogs.

Kulaśekhara was a king of Travancore. He was proficient in Sanskrit and Tamil both. His hunger for the Divine made him more and more unworldly till at last he renounced the throne and devoted himself whole-heartedly to the service of the Divine.

The works of Kulaśekhara are known as *Perumāḷ Tirumoḷi* and *Mukundamālā*. The latter is often compared with the *Gīta-govinda* of Jayadeva. His *Tirumoḷi* consists of 105 hymns and is divided into ten sections. He fancies all sorts of relationships with the Lord — mother-child, child-mother, beloved-lover, father-child, etc. and prays for His grace.

Nammāḷvār was born in a Veḷḷāḷa family. He was one of the greatest god-intoxicated men. His personal name was Māṛan and he seems to have gained the name Śaṭhakopa as well on the occasion of his initiation. He renounced the world in his thirty-fifth year to practise yoga. His hymns, the largest in number after those of Tirumaṅgai, are rightly regarded as embodying the deepest religious experience and philosophic thought of one of the greatest seers of the world as is evident from his following declaration : "My tongue sings to me divine songs. My body dances as if it is possessed by a Deity, worships the Lord and turns back to Him. ... He does not take a few deserving only. He does not leave off the undeserving. He is not vexed with wrong-doers nor does He love the good only. He is unseconded nectar to those who join and love him."[26]

Nammāḷvār is venerated as the super mystic of Vaishṇavism, and as the founder of the *prapatti* school. The *prapanna* bhaktas are those who advocate utter surrender to Vishṇu as the only or at least the most ideal way to *moksha.* He is held in high esteem by the Vaishṇavas so much so that he has become a symbol of the Divine experience. Later, his icon was placed in every temple.

Nammāḷvār was considered so devout that tradition holds that he sat in deep *samādhi* under a tamarind tree for sixteen years right from his birth. His four major works — the *Tiruviruttam, Tiruvāśiriyam, Tiruvāymoḷi,* and *Periyatiruvantādi* — are often spoken of as Śrī Vaishṇavas' four Vedas. His *Tiruvāymoḷi* has been called *Dramiḍopanishad* by Vedāntadeśika. In this work love poetry, mythology, philosophy and heroic poetry alternate with one another and blend together in new ways. It consists of 1102 stanzas. It has been described as the 'universal compendium' (*saṁhitā sārvabhaumī*) of the essence of the Vedic and Paurāṇika lore.

Madhurakavi was a Brāhmaṇa by caste. He was a disciple of Nammāḷvār. He was highly devoted to his *guru* and adored him as God incarnate. His short hymn in praise of Nammāḷvār is sung even now by the Vaishṇavas. He claims that he understood the inner meaning of the Vedas from his *guru* and had become a realized soul by having sought refuge with his *guru.* It has to be remembered that although the importance of the teacher is an ancient tradition it came to be one of the most striking features of the medieval Indian mysticism.

From the tradition of these saints emerged the teachers or Āchāryas including Nāthamuni (born in Tanjore district, 824 A.D.) who is credited with compiling the Āḷvār canon.

V

The bhakti of the Nāyanārs and Āḷvārs was socially an all-embracing movement in the sense that it knew no barriers of caste. Therefore, there has been a general assumption among historians and sociologists that the concept of bhakti, as expressed in the Āḷvār and Nāyanār hymns, initiated a movement of protest and reform particularly aiming at caste hierarchy and Brāhmaṇa exclusiveness in Tamil society. But, as R. Champakalakshmi points out, 'this view represents an inadequate understanding of their hymns'.[27] According to her, the bhakti hymns are dominated by three major themes. First, the idea of devotion to a personal god; second, a protest against orthodox Vedic Brāhmaṇism and the exclusiveness of the Brāhmaṇas in their access to divine grace and salvation, that is, against an elitism in the religious sphere; and, third, a vehement denunciation of the Jainas and Buddhists as non-believers and heretics. In other words, the theistic and pietistic religion of the Śaiva and Vaishṇava saints was also at least partly a reaction against the impersonal and atheistic tendencies of the two ascetic religions.[28]

The hymns of the Āḷvārs and the Nāyanārs reveal that the general nature of their bhakti was similar, i.e., of dispassion in relation to the world and intense longing for personal union with God, the sense of despair and ecstasy and a claim for a personal relationship between the bhakta and the Lord. "The general metaphysical assumption of an individual soul as lying midway between the world and God seeking to move from the world to God, and of a God who as the Supreme Soul creates and governs the universe determining the destiny of souls in accordance with their deeds and yet conferring grace on them by its own miraculous and mysterious power — these are common assumptions of the Āḻvārs and Nāyanārs and also of the Pāñcharātra and the dualistic Śaiva Āgamas."[29] One marked difference, however, is in relation to the concept of incarnation. For the Vaishṇava saints God is more recognizably human and historical, and there is a better scenario for the *līlā* of the Lord and the possibility of a greater synthesis with matters and events of ordinary life.[30]

There is a great similarity between the Upanishadic teachings and hymns of the Āḻvārs. We can glean in the hymns of Poygai Āḻvār, for example, the teachings of *Īśopanishad.* He says that he will not hanker after anyone's wealth, and that everything belongs to Him, which reminds one of *Īśāvāsyamidaṁ sarvaṁ yatkiñcha jagatyāṁ jagat,* etc. of the Upanishads. Poygai says that those who meditate on the name of God do not tread the path of pain. The *Īśopanishad* also states, "For him who has seen himself in God and God in himself where is the delusion, where is fear." When Pey Āḻvār says, 'To such a God who has completely occupied me both within and without, have I become a slave', he also echoes the Upanishadic saying that 'the Divine is in all, pervading both inside and outside'.[31] In the *Bhagavadgītā* the supreme spirit is humanized in the concept of the incarnation. This places the relationship between man and God in the centre of worship. In the *Gītā,* however, it is simultaneously realized that God's approach to man as an incarnation also facilitates man's approach to him.[32]

Almost all human relationships which are based on love are conceived of by the Āḻvārs — mother-child, slave-master, and lover-beloved. This makes their love very intense and a personal one. The Āḻvārs accepted the five-fold manifestations of God described in the Pāñcharātra Āgamas, especial importance being given by them to the *archā* form. For them the icon is not a mere symbol of God, but God himself.

The grace of God is an important aspect of the Pāñcharātra Āgamas. The Āḻvārs also accepted this. We attain Him through His grace and not by our works, efforts, intellect or charity. Service to the Lord is, therefore, more important than liberation. This is suggested by numerous verses especially those of Vishṇuchitta. In such a view the ultimate aim for a devotee is a perfect union with God and not a complete merging in Him. Here again, the Āḻvārs seem to have been impressed by the Pāñcharātra philosophy. However, as Hooper says, the goal of the Āḻvārs is seen to vacillate between two alternatives as is the case with mystics of every country and every period. Firstly, there is a normal human longing for a relation of conscious love and trust between man and God, and secondly, there is the goal of complete absorption as suggested in the stories of Āṇḍāl and Tiruppān.

It is the second theme, namely, protest against orthodox Vedic Brāhmaṇism, that needs to be specially examined from the point of view of the social significance of the Nāyanārs and Āḻvārs. Their hymns made bhakti a well-established ideal for all and sundry and thus carried an earnest message of personal religion to all the people. But that created a situation in which some conflict between the saints and the established social order became inevitable. Champakalakshmi finds hints of this struggle between the privileged Brāhmaṇas on the one hand and the saints on the other in the bhakti literature. And indeed there was an element of protest or dissent in the Āḻvār and Nāyanār poetry, representing an attempt to provide avenues of social acceptance and even mobility to less privileged castes and economic groups. A certain reformatory zeal characterizes some of the bhakta saints or religious teachers like Rāmānuja.[33] Madhurakavi says that the Chaturvedins (those who recite the four Vedas) regarded him as vile and that he accepted only Nammāḻvār (a Śūdra) as his teacher. This is an expression of the solidarity of the bhakta community with the down-trodden against the orthodox Vedic Brāhmaṇas. Hence, their opposition seems to be against orthodox religious attitudes. "It stemmed primarily from the need to defend the bhakti tradition not by denying the superiority claimed by orthodox *brāhmaṇas* but by hailing the devotee's status as higher than even that of the *brāhmaṇa.* In other words, to be a *bhakta* was more important than being a *brāhmaṇa*."[34] Toṇḍaraḍippoḍi asserts that even those who recite the Vedas and know the six *aṅgas*, if they speak ill of the devotees of Vishṇu, are equal to the *pulaiyar* (outcastes).[35] He further holds that even the Chaturvedins become slaves if they are not devotees of Vishṇu, whereas even those actually born among the *kuṭis*, who work on the lands of others, are better than the Brāhmaṇas (if they are His devotees). The *Bhāgavata Purāṇa* also reiterats this position when it says that even a chāṇḍāla or a śvapāka (dog-eater), who is a true devotee, is better than a 'virtuous' Brāhmaṇa who has turned away from Vishṇu's feet. The story of Tiruppān, who was of low caste, and who was carried to the temple by a Brāhmaṇa on his shoulders, implies such a struggle between the authors of these hymns and the Brāhmaṇical priests. "The relation between the *bhaktas* and the *varṇa* system is represented here as one of tension. ... If anything like a direct rejection of caste can be recognized in the Śaiva hymns, it is only in the hymns of Appar, as in the following verse: 'O rogues who quote the Law Books: Of what use are your *gotra* and *kula* (clan). Just bow to Māṟperu's lord as your sole refuge'." Appar says that he would worship even the 'leper with rotting limbs, the outcaste, even the foul *pulaiyan* who skins and eats cows, even these men, if they are servants of Him (that is, Śiva) who shelters the Ganges in his long hair'.[36]

References

1. Cf. S.R. Goyal, *Fundamentals of Paurāṇika Hinduism*, Jodhpur, 2009, p. 115.
2. K.R. Srinivasa Iyengar, in *The Classical Age*, eds. R. C. Majumdar and A.D. Pusalker, Bombay, 1954, p. 327.
3. K. A. N. Sastri, *Development of Religion in South India*, Madras, 1963, pp. 40-41.
4. C.V. Narayana Ayyar, *Origin and Early History of Śaivism in South India*, Madras, 1936, p. 642.
5. K. A. N. Sastri, *A History of South India*, Madras, 1966, p. 424.
6. Susmita Pande, *Birth of Bhakti in Indian Religions and Art*, New Delhi, 1982, p. 132.
7. Sastri, *op. cit.*
8. *The Classical Age*, p. 331.
9. Cf. D.C. Sircar, 'Early History of Vaiṣṇavism', in *The Cultural Heritage of India*, Vol. IV, ed. Haridas Bhattacharyya, Calcutta,1969, pp. 143 ff.; H.V. Sreenivasa Murthy, 'Revival of Bhakti Movement in the Tamil Country by the Āḷvārs', in *The Bhakti Cult and Ancient Indian Geography*, ed. D. C. Sircar, Calcutta, 1970, pp. 82-87; R.N. Saksena, *Indian Social Thought*, Meerut, Year not given, pp. 92-93; K. Rajayyan, *Tamil Nadu : A Real History*, Madurai, 2005, pp. 75-86; Sastri, *op. cit.*, pp. 422-36; Pande, *op. cit.*, pp. 111-29; Goyal, *op. cit.*, pp. 115-20. It is an interesting and significant fact that the Nāyanārs and Āḷvārs have been studied intensively by some Hindi scholars also. Cf., for example, Yaduvamshi, *Saiva Mata*, Patna, 1955, pp. 139-64; Hazari Prasad Dvivedi, *Madhyakalina Dharma-sadhna*, Allahabad, 1956, pp. 38-48; Parashuram Chaturvedi; *Madhyakalina Prem-sadhna*, Allahabad, 1957, pp. 53-74; idem, *Bhakti Sahitya men Madhuropasana*, Allahabad, 1962, pp. 35-42; Munshi Ram Sharma, *Bhakti ka Vikasa*, Varanasi, 1958, pp. 352-60.
10. Pande, *op. cit.*, p. 114.
11. J. S. M. Hooper, *The Hymns of the Āḷvārs*, Oxford, 1929, p. 6.
12. Vide Iyengar, in *The Classical Age*, pp. 332-33.
13. Sircar, in *The Classical Age*, pp. 275 ff.
14. Cf. T.A. Gopinatha Rao, *Sir Subrahmanya Ayyar Lectures on the History of Śrī Vaiṣṇavas*, Madras, 1923, pp. 18 ff.
15. *Ibid.*, p. 22.
16. *Ibid.*, pp. 2-3.
17. *Ibid.*
18. A. K. Ramanujan and Norman Cutler, 'From Classicism to Bhakti', in *Essays on Gupta Culture*, ed. Bardwell L. Smith, Delhi, 1983, p. 194.
19. Pande, *op.cit.*, p. 119.
20. Cf. *The Classical Age*, p. 332.
21. *Ibid.*, p. 335.
22. Pande, *op. cit.*, p. 121.

23. I. Kesarcodi-Watson, in *Bhakti Studies*, eds. G.M. Bailey and I. Kesarcodi-Watson, New Delhi, 1992, p. 115.
24. Pande, *op. cit.*, p. 123.
25. *Ibid.*, p. 125.
26. Quoted in Saksena, *op. cit.*, p. 93.
27. R. Champakalakshmi, 'From Devotion and Dissent to Dominance : The Bhakti of the Tamil Āḷvārs and Nāyanārs', in *Religious Movements in South Asia 600-1800* , ed. David N. Lorenzen, New Delhi, 2006, p. 54.
28. M.G.S. Narayanan and Veluthat Kesavan have also written on the bhakti movements in South India, especially in the Tamil region. According to them, these represent a new wave of Aryan or Hindu influence which was basically a religious phenomenon albeit with a social content that reflects the elements of dissent, protest and reform. Beginning with a framework of definitions and concepts, they have analyzed the apparent religious movement against its socio and political and economic background, also within the larger perspectives of Indian civilization (M.G. S. Narayanan and Veluthat Kesavan, 'Bhakti Movement in South India', in *Indian Movements : Some Aspects of Dissent, Protest and Reform*, ed., S.C. Malik, Simla, 1978, pp. 33-66).
29. Pande, *op. cit.*, p. 134.
30. *Ibid.*
31. *Ibid.*, p. 116.
32. *Ibid.*, p. 112.
33. Champakalakshmi, *op. cit.*, p. 55.
34. *Ibid.*, p. 56.
35. *Ibid.*
36. *Ibid.*, p. 57.

45

THE LIVING SAURA TRADITIONS OF GUJARAT

Atul Tripathi

Abstract

Sun-worship in one form or the other was very widespread since prehistoric times. The primitive men witnessed the miraculous power of Sun as the chief source of light, warmth and fertility. Its unique qualities aroused a deep sense of reverential emotions in the minds of primitive people. The prehistoric men of Gujarat like those of other cultures of the world must have realized the importance of Sun as the immediate creator and ordainer of existence. Wide popularity of the Sun during the proto-historic period is established from the available symbolic representations from different archaeological Harappan sites in Gujarat. The admiration of the anthropomorphic representation of the Sun and the Purāṇic description regarding his marriage and married life made the affinity more strong. As a result, we find more and more importance given not only to the deity but also to other family members. Many legends were also added and adopted by the society which later became part of the rituals and other ceremonies. Moreover, the admiration of the deity is ascertained from the available architectural remains and sculptures which were in worship till twelfth century CE. Later on, we find the Sun goddess Rāndala Dēvī (Purāṇic Sañjñā Dēvī) more attached to the public sentiments of the people and many legends got associated with her and became part of their customs. The paper discusses in detail of those living Saura traditions which are part of the Ravi Rāndal worship and also of Saura festival Uttarāyaṇa and focuses on the social persuasion and developments in this regard.

The customs and traditions of India have been reformed and moulded by the long and dynamic history of Indian society. Through its distinct geography and social adaptation to new cultures, traditions, and ideas, and national heritages, India stands as a monumental example of cultural and social diversity. India's great accomplishment as a culture and nation is its diverse and ample collection of cultural practices, languages, customs, and traditions that have developed and shaped the nation of India for the past five millennia. Very few countries in the world has a social and religious structure which withstood invasions and persecution and yet kept its identity by being resilient enough to absorb, ignore or reject all attempts to radically change or destroy them. Indian culture is unique because of its diversity and variety in physical, religious, racial, linguistic and artistic fields.

In India religion is a way of life, being an integral part of Indian tradition. Many dances, theatrics and folklore are religious and based on Indian mythology and folk legends. India is a pluralistic and multi-cultural society where many faiths and belief systems regulate the life of individuals. Many religious traditions, both indigenous and foreign, have been established over the years here and Gujarat is one of them. The state is having long coastal area and unique geographical set up and lies closer to the area where the artistic activity of the Saura sect had first started. The region is still in the possession of a sufficient number of sun temples roughly ranging from eighth century to the 12th century CE and presenting almost a continuous artistic, iconographic and architectural development for five centuries. Saurāṣṭra, located on the Arabian Sea coast of the state, was an epicentre of Sun worshippers.

In the *Purāna*-s and other religious texts *Sūrya* is being shown associated with this region; his wife *Sajñā Dēvī* (locally known as *Ravi Rāndal Dēvī* or *Rannā Dēvī*) and father-in-law *Viśvakarmā* are believed to be native of Prabhas Pātana. The artisans and craftsmen of the region who consider themselves the descendant of *Viśvakarmā* recognize her as their *phoi* (aunt). In any auspicious occasion they worship her and the folklore related to her marriage and married life having Vedic and *paurānic* background are part of their cultural life. The present paper discusses in detail of those living Saura traditions which are part of the *Ravi Rāndala* worship and *Uttarāyana* festival and also focuses on the social persuasion and developments in this regard.

Ravi Rāndala Mātā Worship

The worship of *Sūrya* and his consort *Rajñi Dēvī*, also known as *Rannā Dēvī* or *Ravi Rāndala Mātā*[1] is still met within the folk life of Gujarat, particularly in the Saurāṣṭra region. The deity is considered as the daughter of the great architect *Viśvakarmā* and therefore the artisans and craftsmen of the region consider themselves as their descendents and recognize her as their *Phoi* (aunt). In any auspicious occasion, be it *yajñōpavīta, sīmanta*, or the wedding of son, the installation and consecration ceremony known as '*jāga*' is held for at least eight days at their home. She is invoked like *Ganapati* before the starting of any auspicious work.[2]

Motherhood is a significant part of a woman's life, the deity is worshipped in the region as the goddess of fertility and the devotees ask for her to be blessed with sons. Among many families she is also worshipped as their *kuladēvī* (patron goddess). As the deity is associated with fertility, pregnancy and birth, her worship is performed in several ways by the devotees to fulfill their desires. On *Navarātri* and *Gaurī vrata* she is worshipped as *Ganapati*. Barley is sown after her worship and if it grows quicker the devotees believe that it is because of her blessings. Like this she is worshipped for the growth and prosperity. A special function is also held either within five years of the first child or during his marriage. Vase and coconut are installed at home during this ceremony[3].

Regarding origin of the name '*Rāndala*'[4] there is a mythical story prevalent in the region which tells that *Sūrya* asked *Rāndala Mātājī* to go to '*mrityu lōka*' (earth) to rescue the lives of people from the antisocial elements and show them the right path of religion and truth. It was hard for her to go on earth in her original form. So, she had to find some other alternative. *Mātājī* took the form of a child; sat under a tree like a dumb without making any sort of noise. Since it was famine in the region[4]; the shepherds of *Māladhārī* [5](a tribe) were roaming here and there for fodder to feed their cattle. One of the shepherds saw that child under the tree. He went directly to that child and asked about her identity and cause of her loneliness in the jungle? *Mātājī* didn't speak anything but through expressions conveyed that she is dumb and alone. *Māladhārī* felt pity on her and took her with them and named her *'Rāndala'*, as she was found in the desert.

It is said that the wife of *Māladhārī* cared enough of the child like her own; soon they observed a miracle as the famine got over and rain were aplenty. Also many family members who were disabled, blind, and leprous were cured by her and renewed their health. *Māladhārī* people were unable to identify her. Once *Māladhārī* camped near the river Vasavadi, on the bank of which was a city named Dhutarpur (later renamed as Vasavad). Servants of the King were taking milk, curd etc. from *Māladhārī*-s. *Rāndala Mātājī* showed herself as a beautiful young girl to them. Her beauty amazed the servants. So they praised her beauty before the king. On hearing this, the king got crazy about her and went to the camp and asked them to see her. But *Māladhārī*-s were surprised to hear it as *Rāndala Mātā* was with them in the form of a child. The King thought that *Māladhārī-s* didn't want to give the girl and hence he ordered his soldiers to kill everyone in the group. The soldiers started killing the people very cruelly. At that time *Rāndala Mātājī* couldn't control herself and became angry. She put her hand on a cow and converted it into a lion. She sat on its back and started killing the soldiers. The King and other people immediately realized their mistake and got that she is none other than goddess *Jagdamba!* They bowed down before her and asked for her pardon as they did not know the real truth. *Mātājī* calmed down and gave life to the dead soldiers. Though *Rāndala Mātājī* blessed the *Māladhārī*-s, she however warned them and extorted a promise from king that he will not repeat the mistake again. It is believed that the place where the fight took place got to be known as '*Dalavā*'[6].

Presently there are three *Dalavā*-s (*Rāndalanā*) associated with *Ravi Rāndala Mātā* at Amreli (Amreli tālukā), Bhavnagar (Umrala tālukā) and Junagadh (Manavadar tālukā) districts respectively in Saurāṣṭra. The devotees from all over Gujarat, other parts of India as well as those expatriated, come here in large numbers irrespective of their caste, creed and religion.

There are many local beliefs regarding the deity's marriage and married life. The social beliefs and customs related with her are very popular in Saurāṣṭra. The mythological story regarding *Sūrya's* marriage with *Rāndala* informs us that when *Rāndala* was young, *Sūrya* got attracted by her charm and beauty; as he couldn't stop himself, he went directly to her father *Viśvakarmā* with the marriage proposal which was strongly rejected. Regarding their marriage the most pervasive belief still prevalent in many parts of Saurāṣṭra tells us that once *Rāndala Mātā*'s mother went to *Sūrya's* house to borrow a baking plate made of clay. *Sūrya*'s mother gave it on a condition that it should not break otherwise she will ask her daughter's hand for marriage with *Sūrya*. *Sūrya* thought it to be the right occasion to use a trick to compel *Rannā Dēvī's* mother to fulfill her promise. He made two bulls fight on her way while she was carrying the plate. Somehow the plate fell down and got broken. Now she was bound to fulfill her promise and thus she married her daughter to *Sūrya*[7].

Rāndala had with *Sūrya* a son (*Yamarāja*) and a daughter (*Yamunā*). But *Rāndala* found it difficult to bear the resplendence and heat of *Sūrya*. Because of the extreme light and shine of *Sūrya*, she wasn't able to look at him and this created a misunderstanding between them. *Sūrya* doubted that *Rāndala Mātā* is proud of her beauty and because of this she is ignoring and not looking at him. Hence, he cursed that both of her children (*Yamarāja* and *Yamunā*) will suffer by roaming in jungle.[8]

We find similar stories in the *Purāna*-s. It is said in the *Matsya Purāna* that on the request of sages, *Rōmaharaa* explained the brief history of the solar line as '*Aditi* and the sage *Kaśyapa* gave birth to the sun-god *Vīvasvāna* or *Sūrya*, as a son. *Sūrya* had three wives, *Sanjñā*, *Rājñi* and *Prabhā*. *Rājñi* had a son named *Revata* while *Prabhā* had a son named *Prabhāta*. *Sūrya* with *Sanjñā* had two sons and a daughter, the eldest was *Vaivasvata Manu* and the remaining two descendants were twins - *Yama* and *Yamunā*.'[9] The Sun's radiance was however too much for *Sanjñā* to bear. After a while, she could not bear it any longer. She therefore created a woman out of her own body that looked exactly like *Sanjñā* and it was named *Chāyā* (shadow).[10] There was no way of telling the two apart. *Sanjñā* said to her 'stay here and pretend to be me. Look after my husband and my children. No one will know the truth unless you tell them. As for me, I am going away.'

Sūrya did not realize that *Sanjñā* had left. He took *Chāyā* to be his wife and had with her two sons and two daughters. The sons were *Savarni Manu* and *Śani* (Saturn) and the daughters were *Tapati* and *Vishti*.[11] *Chāyā* was clearly fonder of her own children and neglected *Sanjñā's* and this favouritism made *Yama* to resent. In a fit of petulance, he raised his foot to kick *Chāyā*. *Chāyā* cursed *Yama* by saying 'I curse you that your foot may be devoured by worms. May it be infected with pus and blood.'[12] This alarmed *Yama* and he rushed to his father and told 'My mother has cursed me. I am only a child. Even if I did commit a sin, should a mother ever curse her children? I have serious suspicion whether she is our mother.' When *Sūrya* presented *Chāyā* with this, she came out with the truth and *Sūrya* learnt that *Sanjñā* had already left him. *Sūrya* went to his father-in-law *Viśvakarmā* to find out if he knew anything of *Sanjñā*'s whereabouts. "Indeed, I do, replied *Viśvakarmā*. When *Sanjñā* left your house, she came to me in the form of a mare. But I refused to let her live in my house, since she had left her husband's house without seeking his permission. She is living at the moment in the desert. But what *Sanjñā* did is because of the fact that she could not bear to stand your energy and radiance. If you permit, I shall shave off some of the excess energy, so that people can look at you". And *Viśvakarmā* shaved off some of the Sun's energy.

It is said in the *Matsya Purāna* that with the excess energy were constructed many of the weapons of the gods such as *Visnu*'s *cakra*, *Siva*'s *triśūla* and *Indra*'s *vajra*. This made the Sun's appearance much more pleasant and bearable. The only parts of *Sūrya*'s body that were not thus modified were his feet.[13] *Sūrya* now went to look for *Sanjñā* (*Rāndala*) and found her in the form of a mare. He too adopted the form of a horse and at the union of both; horse-faced *Aśvin*-s were born who later became the physicians of the gods. *Sūrya* and *Sanjñā* later returned to their usual forms.

Rāndala Mātā no Lōtō

Another story popular in the region, particularly in Saurāṣṭra is that when *Sūrya* brought back *Rāndala Mātājī* to his house, at that time *Chāyā*, who was left with *Sūrya* as her surrogate asked Mātājī to do something for her. *Rāndala Mātājī* promised her that whoever will perform the '*Lōṭās*' (a rituals done by the people of the region after the fulfillment of their desires known as '*Rāndala Mātā no Lōṭō*') ceremony, should always be in pairs i.e. one for the *Rāndala Mātājī* and the other for her shadow-image i.e. *Chāyā*. *Sūrya* also promised her that he will remain present in the form of a horse during this ritual to make it successful. This ceremony is known among the devotees as '*Ghodo Khunda*'.

'*Rāndala Mātā no Lōṭō*' is a famous ceremony performed by the devotees of the region and expatriates **(Plate 45.3)**. During my visit to the temples at *Daḷavā*-s I observed many Non Resident Gujarātīes (NRG) especially from European or East African countries coming to these temples for *Rāndala Mātā* worship and performing rituals like the '*Lōṭās*' ceremony. These ceremonies are usually performed at home on any auspicious day, most preferably on Saturday, Sunday or Monday. First, the priest is consulted for the most favourable day to perform this auspicious ceremony. He makes a list of items required for the purpose. The success of the ceremony depends on the number of *Gōynī*'s invited for the ritual. Woman of any caste or faith can be a *Gōynī* but she must be fit to eat well and should not be pregnant. It is believed that on this particular day the *Gōynī* represents the form of *Rāndala Mātājī*. The number of *Gōynīes* is determined by the number of *Lōṭā* used in the ceremony. *Lōṭās* are always counted in pairs with 14 *Gōynī's* for each pair of *Lōṭās*.

Rāndala Mātājī's Mudh

The '*Rāndala Mātājī's Mudh*' is a ceremony in which the *mudh* is made by the priest who comes on Saturday evening and sets up it in the *pūjā* room. On Sunday i.e. the next day, the priest arrives early in the morning and performs the *pūjā*. First of all *Gaṇēśa* is invoked before the auspicious beginning of the ceremony to remove the obstacles, if any. Later on, other important gods and goddesses, ancestors, planets, holy rivers and above all *Rāndala Mātājī* are worshipped and prayed. During this *pūjā* two *ghee* lamps remain lighted as it is believed that a ghee lamp has more capacity to attract the *sātvika* vibrations present in the surrounding atmosphere. Once lit, the lamps must remain alight until the ritual on Monday. The lamps are witnesses to the ceremony. They signify the continuity throughout the following days of ritual. Milk is offered to *Mātājī* after which the priest is allowed to leave. Two spiritual foods, the *kheer* and *paar* are prepared on this particular occasion. After the *pūjā*, householders go to *Rāndala Mātājī's mudh* to invite a *Bhuy Mā* or a *Bhuvor* in the form of *Rāndala Mātājī* as a part of the tradition of the ceremony to extend a formal invitation. It is advised that the householders should carry *kumkum*, rice, fruits and a coconut with them, as offerings. The *Bhuya Mā* or *Bhuvor* explains the rituals at this time. The householders pray that *Rāndala Mātājī* comes back to their home and give them her blessings.

It is still early morning by this time and the special foods for the ceremony are prepared. The *kheer* and *paar* should remain in the house at all times. *Rāndala Mātājī* is offered *kheer* and *paar* on a *thal*. Special *garabā* songs made for the occasion are sung during this. The *Gōynīs* arrive with their families and they are treated with great respect. It is believed that *Rāndala Mātājī* is physically present as *Gōynīs*. The first mark of respect for her is washing their toes. Few grains of rice are attached to the *chāndalo* (forehead); the big toe of the *Gōynīs* foot is now washed. Again the toe of each *Gōynīs* feet is washed with warm water followed by milk and again by warm water. After the toe is washed, they apply another *chāndalo* with rice to the *Gōynīs* washed toe. This is done to show love and devotion towards *Rāndala Mātājī*. It is advised that this act should be performed by a household woman. At last the *Gōynīs* are offered a present which includes a *chāndalo* and *supārī* (betel nut) and after that they are invited to take the food in the household and in this *kheer* and *paar* are served first. *Mātājī*'s *garabā* is performed for maintaining the spiritual atmosphere.

On the Sunday afternoon at around 4.00 pm everyone assemble around the *pūjā* room for the singing of *garabā* songs. In the meantime someone goes to the *mudh* to invite the *bhuy mā* or the *bhuva* over to the house where the ceremony is taking place. The *bhuya mā* or *bhuva* will become the channel through which *Rāndala Mātājī* speaks to the devotees. While the household continues to sing *garabā*, the *bhuya mā* or the *bhuva* will enter the shrine and perform his or her own personal ritual at the *mudh* to prepare oneself for what is to come. This part of the ceremony is called the *ghoro kundwo*. As singing progresses the *bhuy mā* experiences surge of energy that transforms her into the mouthpiece of *Mātājī*. It is said that the stronger presence of the deity during the *ghoro kundwo* is based on the performance of the *garabā*. The householders will now ask *Mātājī* through the *bhuya mā* whether the ceremony has been successful. They should ask for forgiveness for any mistakes. There is no particular form of words for this conversation. But it should be loving and respectful. *Mātājī's* reply comes to the householders only through the *bhuya mā* or *bhuva*. *Garabā* songs during this period should be sung in full swing as *prasāda* and milk is offered to *Rāndala Mātājī*. Special *garabā* invites *Mātājī* to come to eat. If necessary the *bhuya mā* will guide the householders on the procedures to be followed. After the *thāl*, the devotees perform *āratī* and then the householders' fast is over.

Once again the householders must fast till the Monday morning rituals are over. *Daatan* (a special toothbrush stick) and milk is offered to *Rāndala Mātājī*. The priest returns early on the Monday morning to perform another *pūjā* to give thanks to *Rāndala Mātājī*. In this *pūjā*, *khuller* and coconut are offered for every two *Lōṭās* placed in the *mudh*. This *prasāda* is the divine goddess's breakfast. It is offered in a specific order: *dātan*, milk, *khuller*, and coconut. This ceremony must be completed by 12.00 noon and after that the *mudha* is dismantled.

According to the *Maher*[14] family tradition, the ceremony is to be performed after the marriage, when the daughter-in-law is welcomed into a new home. It is supposed that the ceremony will bring happiness and blessings to the new couple. The ceremony is also associated with the first pregnancy, done on the seventh month of the pregnancy, to call for blessings upon the baby conceived by the 'would be mother.' Some parents perform the ceremony for an infant boy after his head is shaved at his *bālmuvara* ceremony. *Rāndala Mātājī*'s blessings are taken for the healthy and fruitful life of the child. At the time of *yajñōpavīta* also, the ceremony is performed and it is believed that by doing so *Rāndala Mātājī* will give blessings to the boy and make him safe and successful in his studies.

Thus, the living *Saura* traditions can be seen in Gujarat through the worship of *Ravi Rāndala Mātā* in Gujarat, particularly in Saurāṣṭra. Various rituals and ceremonies related to the deity represent the *Purānic* mythological stories adopted by the devotees from time to time. Worship of *Chāyā* parallel to *Rāndala* (*Sañjñā Dēvī*) is unique here and reminds us of the *Purānic* story in which a commitment is made by *Sañjñā* (*Rāndala*) *Dēvī* to her that she will not be ignored and will remain worshipped parallel to her **(Plate 45.1)**. By the time of the *Harivamśa* (c. 8th century CE) *Saranyū* (*Saranyu*) is called *Sañjñā* and her double is reduced to her shadow or reflection *Chāyā* whom she places in her place, which was created by illusion to take care of her children and later the promise given to her regarding her worship in pairs along with *Sañjñā*. It is noteworthy here that like *Harivamśa* most accounts consider *Chāyā* to be the reflection or shadow of *Saranyu (Sañjñā) - Sūrya*'s first wife; *Bhāgavata Purāṇa* tells that *Chāyā* was a sister of *Sañjñā* and the daughter of the divine architect *Viśvakarmā*.

Since *Sūrya*'s wife *Rāndala* (*Sañjñā Dēvī* in the *Purānas*) and his father-in-law *Viśvakarmā* are believed to be from Prabhāsa Pāṭaṇ (Saurāṣṭra), the artisans and local people consider them as their ancestors and thus they are part of their traditions. In due course of time we find the *Purāṇic* stories and beliefs adopted in the society in a more practical manner. The deity is also worshipped to overcome many social and physical problems including ailments of the hands and legs. For this the sufferer or his/her relatives usually come to the temple at *Daḷavā*-s to offer the small wooden replica of the ailed parts to the temple **(Plate 45.2)**. It is remarkable here that we find a story in the *Purāna*-s that *Sūrya* reduced the curse cast by *Chāyā* to *Yama* in which his leg got affected. In the *Mārkandeya Purāna*[15] also, we find *Sūrya* grants *Yama*, a cock to eat the worms from his leg. In the *Rāndala* temples at *Daḷavā*-s we also find wooden cocks in the shops for the offering to get rid of the disease.

The role of the deity as a fertility goddess is more popular in the region as in many folk songs she is worshipped in that capacity. It may be possible that the physical features, geographical set up and climatic condition forced her worship as 'the goddess of fertility'. The popularity of the deity can be seen in every stage of life whether its baby shower (*śrīmanta*), *choul samskāra* (*balmovara*), *janoi* (*yajñōpavīta*), or wedding ceremony, including welcoming of a new daughter-in-law into the new home. In short, we can say that the deity with its mythological background is very popular in the region and associated to every phase of life.

Uttarāyana-A Saura Festival with an International Exposure

Festivals have rich tradition throughout Indian culture which originated either out of a shared agrarian heritage, as a celebration of a successful harvest or as an opportunity for families to reunite and offer prayers for future health and prosperity. *Uttarāyana* or *Makara Sankrānti* is a festival of the Hindus usually celebrated on 14th January every year. *Uttarāya□a* (derives from the Sanskrit words *uttara* and *āyana* meaning movement towards north), is the six-month period between Winter solstice (around December 22) and Summer solstice (around June 21), when the sun apparently travels towards the north on the celestial sphere. It marks the end of a long winter with the return of the sun to the northern hemisphere. According to the Hindu astronomy the sun enters the zodiac of *makara* (capricorn). Hence it is called *Uttarāyana* or *Makar Sankrānti*. The period involves pilgrimages and festivals and collides with the *pausa māgha* month. It is believed that on this day *Gangā* reached the earth from heaven. Hence, *māgha* bath is also considered to be important. Auspicious activities like *yajñas*, austerities, marriages, *mundanas* etc. are considered to be auspicious during this period. According to the *Purāna*, *Bhīsma Pitāmaha* chose this particular day to leave for his heavenly abode.

The festival represents selfless giving. Kites are flown in thanksgiving to the Sun, which gives life to the world without seeking any reward. Because of its selflessness, the Sun symbolizes the attributes of *karma yoga*. Spring is celebrated as a season of enlightenment and spiritual growth. It represents the triumph of light over darkness and positive qualities over the negative.

There are three legends which add to the significance of this day in the Brahmanical tradition: (i). The Sun, reputedly did not like his son *Śani*; but during the period of *Uttarāyana*, the Sun stays in the house of his son for a month, symbolizing the importance of the relationship between father and son. (ii). It is also said that it was on the first day of spring that lord *Visnu* banished the evil committed by the *asuras* who were unruly and destructive. *Uttarāyana* represents the end of mischief and disorder and the beginning of peace and righteousness. (iii). We find different versions of this story- According to a legend, an ancient wise man named *Kapila* was abused by the sons of the King. The sage turned the princes into dust. They could only be revived by the water of the Ganges. On *Uttarāyana*, a king named *Bhagīratha* performed the rituals and prayed until the curse was lifted and the Ganges came down on earth.

Spirituality of Kite Flying

The kite was said to be the invention of the famous 5th century BCE Chinese philosophers Mozi and Lu Ban.[16] It was recorded in the year 549 CE that paper kites were being flown and were being used as a message for a rescue mission. Ancient and medieval Chinese sources list other uses of kites such as for measuring distances, testing the wind, lifting men, signalling, and transmitting communications for military operations. Kites were decorated with mythological motifs and legendary figures; some were fitted with strings and whistles to make musical sounds while flying.

Kites were known throughout Polynesia, as far as New Zealand, with the assumption being that the knowledge diffused from China along with the people. Anthropomorphic kites made from cloth and wood were used in religious ceremonies to send prayers to the gods. Polynesian kite traditions are used by the anthropologists to get an idea of the early "primitive" Asian traditions, which are believed to have at one time existed in Asia.

Kites were late to arrive in Europe, although windsock-like banners were known and used by the Romans. Stories of kites were first brought to Europe by Marco Polo towards the end of the 13th century, and kites were brought back by sailors from Japan and Malaysia in the 16th and 17th centuries. Although they were initially regarded as mere curiosities, by the 18th and 19th centuries kites were being used as vehicles for scientific research. Kites have been used for scientific purposes, such as Benjamin Franklin's famous experiment proving that lightning is electricity. Kites were the precursors to the traditional aircraft, and were instrumental in the development of early flying craft. Alexander Graham Bell experimented with very large man-lifting kites, as did the Wright brothers and Lawrence Hargrave. Kites had a historical role in lifting scientific instruments to measure atmospheric conditions for weather forecasting. In fact, the period from 1860 to about 1910 became the "golden age of kiting". Kites started to be used for scientific purposes, especially in meteorology, aeronautics, wireless communications and photography; many different designs of man-lifting kite were developed as well as power kites.

Kites or '*patangas*' are believed to have first arrived in India either through Muslim traders coming eastward through Persia or Buddhist pilgrims coming from China in search of sacred texts. Either way, they have a long history in this part of the world with numerous classic miniature paintings of typical scenes depicting people flying kites. Since Gujarat is at the westernmost edge of India, it is one of the regions where Muslim and Hindu cultures have blended to a great degree in many aspects. Hence, kites probably introduced by the Muslims, end up as the symbol for celebrating *Uttarāyana.* Still, no one knows exactly when this tradition began but the kite festival can be seen as the best example for national integrity and secularism of India.

Kite festivals are a popular form of entertainment throughout the world which includes large local events, traditional festivals which have been held for hundreds of years and have become major international festivals. Kites are very popular in Gujarat, notably for the kite fighting festivals. Kites of all shapes and sizes are flown, and the main competition is to engage in a battle with the nearby kite-flyers by snapping to cut their strings and bringing down their kites. Many cities in Gujarat organize kite competitions between their citizens where all the people compete with each other. Days before the festival, the market is filled with participants buying their supplies. For this, people find their favoured kite-makers who prepare strong resilient kite bodies with springy bamboo frames and kite-paper stretched to exactly the right tension. Lastly, the kites are attached to a spool (or *firkin*) of *manjhā*[17], special kite-string coated with a mixture of glue and glass powder to be as sharp as possible for cutting the strings of the rival kite fliers. Production of kites and kite supplies can be seen on the streets of Ahmedabad beginning in November, to get ready for *Uttarāyana*. During the festival week the markets are flooded with kite buyers and sellers. In the heart of Ahmedabad, there is a famous Kite market- *Patanga Bazaar*, which during the festive week remains open 24 hours a day with buyers and sellers negotiating and buying in bulk. Moreover, many families in Ahmadabad start making kites in home and setup small shops in their home itself.

The people of Gujarat celebrate *Uttarāyana* with a lot of enthusiasm and it is such a huge celebration that it has become a public holiday for two days in Gujarat. The festival is a uniquely Gujarātī phenomenon, when the skies over most cities of the state fill with kites from before dawn until well after dark. Kite flying begins at dawn and continues without a pause throughout the day. People of all ages including men, women, boys, girls and grandparents gather on terraces or rooftops and engage in kite flying. There is music in the air and traditional delicacies are especially prepared for this day. Friends, neighbours and total strangers battle with one another for supremacy and cries of triumph rend the air when someone cuts the line of a rival. A tremendous variety of kites are seen and the connoisseur can choose precisely what he wants. Highly manoeuvrable single-string paper and bamboo kites are flown from the rooftops while using line friction in an attempt to cut each other's kite lines, either by letting the cutting line loose at high speed or by pulling the line in a fast and repeated manner. The atmosphere is wonderfully festive, as whole families gather on the rooftop, special foods like *laddoos*, *udhīyu* (a mixed vegetable including yam and beans) or *surati jamun*, sesame seed brittle and *jalebis* are prepared for eating over the course of the day, and friends and neighbours visit each other for group kite-flying fun. Often people look out for which of their friends has the optimum terrace for kite flying and many will congregate there. At night, kite fighters send up bright white kites to be seen in the darkness, and skilled flyers will send aloft their illuminated kites known as *tukkals* (illuminated box kites) into the sky to compete with the stars. The *tukkals* with strings of brightly lit lanterns in a long line leading back down to the rooftop compete with the stars. Thus, *Uttarāya□a* provides lots of fun and beautiful sights to remember for a long time from early morning to late at night.

Since 1989, the city of Ahmedabad is hosting the 'International Kite Festival' as part of the official celebration of *Uttarāyana*, bringing master kite makers and flyers from all over the world to demonstrate their unique creations and surprise the crowds with highly unusual kites **(Plate 45.4 & 45.5)**. Almost every known variety of kite can be seen in the skies over Sardar Patel Stadium or the Ahmedabad Police Stadium, where people lay down to see the sky filled with thousands of kites, from box kites to high-speed sport kites, from windsocs and spinsocs to hand-painted artistic kites. This festival attracts international kite flyers and local champions as well who demonstrate their skills in flying exotic kites. This Kite festival has become an important tourist attraction and is one of the flagship attractions of Gujarat tourism. Visitors come from all over India for the celebration; many Gujarātīs who live outside the state choose this time to make their trip home. International visitors also make their appearance during this time. Usually the prominent countries include Japan, Italy, the UK, Canada, Brazil, Indonesia, Australia, the USA, Malaysia, Singapore, France, China, and many more. In 2012, the Tourism Corporation of Gujarat mentioned that the International Kite Festival in Gujarat was attempting to enter the Guinness World Records book due to the participation of 42 countries in it. There is also a Kite Museum, located at Samskāra Kendra in the Paldi area of Ahmedabad. It was established in 1985, which has a wide range of collection of unique kites.

Concluding Remarks

Gujarat lies closer to the area where the artistic activity of the *Saura* sect had first started and the region is still in possession of a sufficient number of sun temples roughly ranging from the eighth century to the 12th century CE presenting almost a continuous artistic, iconographic and architectural development for five centuries. Saurāṣtra was an epicenter of the sun worshippers. In the *Purāna*-s and other religious texts *Sūrya* is shown attached to this region as his wife *Sanjñā Dēvī* (locally known as *Ravi Rāndal Dēvī* or *Rannā Dēvī*) and father-in-law *Viśvakarmā* were from the Prabhās Pātan. The artisans and craftsmen of the region who consider themselves the descendants of *Viśvakarmā* recognize her as their *phoi* (aunt). In any auspicious occasion they worship her and the folklore related to her marriage and married life having Vedic and *Purānic* backgrounds are parts of their cultural life. The kite festival is a uniquely Gujarati phenomenon in Gujarat, when the skies over most cities are filled with kites from early dawn until late in the evening. As the kite flying festival has no religious connotation, it is celebrated by the Hindus, Jains, Muslims, Christians, Parsees, Jews, Sikhs and Buddhists in the state as it provides fun-filled get-togethers for family and friends on rooftops. The *'pols'* or old quarters of Ahmedabad are the major centers of kite flying. The Gujarat State Tourism is hosting the 'International Kite Festival' as a part of the official celebration of *Uttarāyana* since 1989 to promote tourism in Gujarat in order to popularize the festival. The festival often features contests and competitions, exhibitions, workshops, aero-sports demonstrations, and sightseeing tours.

References and Notes

1. The *Sañjñā Dēvī* of the *Purāṇa*-s is the present '*Rāndala Mātā*' or '*Rannā De*' of the region.
2. Atul Tripathi, "Sun Worship in India with Particular Reference to Saurāṣṭra", Masatoshi Konishi, ed., *Indo-Koku-Kenkya* (Rikkyo University, Tokyo, 2006), pp. 64-65.
3. *Ibid.*
4. The information collected through interacting the priests, devotees, and villagers at *Daḷavā* and nearby region.
5. The *Māladhārīs* (meaning "owner of animal stock i.e. cattle") are tribal herdsmen living in Gujarat. They are notable as the traditional dairymen of the region who once supplied milk and cheese to the palaces of *rājās*. The *Māladhārī* have been living in the Banni grasslands for nearly 700 years. In different regions, they belong to different castes. The *Māladhārīs* living in Gir Forest National Park are mainly *Chāraṇ*, and their villages are known as *ness*.
6. The local literature available in the shops at *Daḷavā (Rāndalnā)* as well as the folklore popular among the people provides this mythical story.
7. As known from the priests, devotees and available local published material at *Daḷavā (Randalnā)*.
8. The folklore is presently popular in the region with its origin in ancient religious texts.
9. V.S.Agrawala, *Matsya Purāṇa-A Study*, Varanasi, 1963, pp.86-87.
10. *Chāyā* is described as the shadow-image or reflection of *Saranyu (Sañjñā)*, the first wife of *Sūrya*. She is usually described as the mother of *Śani, Tāptī* and *Savarni Manu*, destined to be the next and eighth *Manu* (progenitor of mankind) - the ruler of the next *Manvantara* period. Unlike the later *Purāṇas* where *Chāyā* is a mere shadow of *Saranyu*, in the *Ṛgvēda*, *Savarṇa* is of the same-kind as *Saranyu*, but mortal (Light corresponds to the immortal creation of *Puruṣa* and shadow to the mortal creation of *Prakṛti*). *Savarṇa* has no children from *Sūrya*. A later (500 BCE) addition to the original *Ṛgvēda* by *Yāska* in his *Nirukta* says that *Manu* (the progenitor of mankind, called *Savarṇi Manu* in later *Purāṇic* text) was born to *Savarṇa*. While the original text says "they" (interpreted as the gods) substituted *Savarṇa* for *Saranyu, Yaksa*'s *Nikuta* tells that *Saranyu* created *Savarṇa* and substituted her. *Bṛhad devatā* calls the prototype of *Chāyā* as *Sadrisha* ("look-alike"), a woman who looked like *Saranyu. Sadrśa* begot *Manu* by *Sūrya*, who became a royal sage. (Doniger, Wendy, "Saranyu/Samjna" in John Stratton Hawley, Donna Marie Wulff. *Devī: goddesses of India*. Motilal Banarsidas, New Delhi1988, pp.154–7).
11. The second daughter named *Viśti* does not usually occur in the other *Purāṇa*-s.
12. We find it another way which tells that *Yama* had been cursed by *Chāyā* that his feet would rot and be infected with worms. To mitigate the effects of the curse, *Sūrya* gave *Yama* a bird which ate up all the worms. Thereafter, *Yama* went to a *Gōkarṇa tīrtha* and started to pray to *Śiva*. For thousands of years he prayed and eventually managed to please *Śiva. Śiva* granted *Yama* the boon that he would be the god of death. He would mete out punishments to sinners in accordance with the sins (*pāpa*) that they had committed. He would also keep account of the store of merit (*puṇya*) that righteous people accumulated.
13. No one can bear to look at *Sūrya*'s feet and it is forbidden to visualize the Sun's feet when one is praying to him. It is said that a person who does not follow this injunction is a sinner and is made to suffer from leprosy.
14. The *Maher* or *Mers* community is having a rich and diverse history involving many battles, valour and sacrifice to uphold their honour & values. They are divided into 14 exogamous lineages. They worship Hindu gods and goddesses and observe all the major Hindu festivals. They have their own temple for the community members. Each clan has its own clan Goddess worshipped by the head of the household on various occasions. The clan's deity separates one clan from the other. They make special offerings to her during the *Navarātrī* festival in the month of *Aśvin*.
15. The *Mārkaṇḍēya Purāṇa* tells the tale of *Sañjñā-Chāyā* twice; the tale is similar to that in the *Harivanśa*, but Sañjñā leaves *Sūrya* as she is unable to bear his splendour and heat. The curse to *Yama* is a little different. *Yama* abuses *Chāyā* and picks his leg up to kick her. *Chāyā* curses *Yama* to have his leg affected with worms and sores. *Sūrya* grants *Yama*, a cock to eat the worms from his leg. (Doniger, Wendy, Ibid., p. 163)
16. As in China the materials ideal for kite building were readily available: silk fabric for sail material; fine, high-tensile-strength silk for flying line; and resilient bamboo for a strong, lightweight framework.
17. The line used for flying the Indian Fighter is called a '*māñjhā*'. This is typically a cotton thread coated with a mixture of finely crushed glass, glue and various abrasives. Long before the festival, we can see *māñjhā* makers applying the abrasive materials and reeling the line onto spools called '*phirkis*'.

46

इक्ष्वाकु परम्परा एवं संस्कृति

ईश्वर शरण विश्वकर्मा

इक्ष्वाकुओं का इतिहास विश्व इतिहास का एक गौरममय इतिहास है। भारतीय परम्परा में आख्यात सृष्टि के आरम्भकर्त्ता मनु की संतानों में ज्येष्ठपुत्र इक्ष्वाकु एवं पुत्री इला के इतिहास एवं संस्कृति तथा वैश्विक प्रसार से 'वसुधैव कुटुम्बकम्' का आदर्श चरितार्थ होता है। क्योंकि इक्ष्वाकु तथा इला की संततियों ने विश्व के विभिन्न भूभागों पर सुशासन द्वारा श्रेष्ठ राज्यादर्श स्थापित कर जीवन के मूल्य निर्धारित किए (वर्मा 2010 : 25–61)। किन्तु वास्तविक परम्परा इक्ष्वाकु इक्सठवीं पीढ़ी में दाशरथि राम के आख्यान से ही ज्ञात है। राम के पूर्व का इतिहास अभी इतिहास एवं पुरातत्व की एक जटिल समस्या बनी हुई है। इसलिए इक्ष्वाकु परम्परा एवं संस्कृति अनुसंधान का नवीन क्षेत्र प्रदान करता है।

यह सर्वस्वीकृत तथ्य है कि रामाख्यान के विविध प्रसंगों की ऐतिहासिक सत्यता एवं सांस्कृतिक मूल्यवत्ता चिंतन की सभी विधाओं में मान्य एवं तत्त्वतः सिद्ध है। इसीलिए विचार, वाणी और क्रिया की त्रयी इस आख्यान का आरम्भिक बिन्दु बन कर लोक की चिरकालिक साधना में संचरणशील है। रामाख्यान के इस तात्त्विक चिंतन में एक महत्वपूर्ण पक्ष राम के कुल (वंश) की पहचान है। आदि कवि वाल्मीकि ने रामायण के बालकाण्ड के प्रथम सर्ग में इस प्रसंग को उठाया है वह है, देवर्षि नारद द्वारा महर्षि वाल्मीकि को संक्षेप में श्रीरामचरित सुनाना। वाल्मीकि और नारद के इस संवाद से रामायण की रचना प्रारम्भ होती है। महर्षि वाल्मीकि ने इस संसार में गुणवान्, वीर्यवान्, धर्मज्ञ, कृतज्ञ, सत्यवादी, दृढ़वादी, सदाचारी, समस्त प्राणियों का हित साधक, विद्वान्, सामर्थ्यशाली, एकमात्र प्रियदर्शन, आत्मवान, जितक्रोधी, कांतिमान, अनुसूयक, संग्राम में कुपित होने पर देवताओं को भी भयभीत करने वाले ऐसे एक पुरूष को जानने की उत्सुकता व्यक्त की।[2]

"एतदिच्छाम्यहं श्रोतुं परं कोतूहलं हि में।
महर्षे त्वं समर्थोऽसि ज्ञातुमेवंविधं नरम्।।" (रामायण, बालकाण्ड 1/5)

महर्षि वाल्मीकि के कौतूहलपूर्ण वचनों को सुनकर त्रैलोकज्ञ नारद ने सम्पूर्ण दुर्लभ गुणों से युक्त जिस पुरूष का वर्णन किया है, वे इक्ष्वाकुवंश में उत्पन्न है तथा लोक में 'राम' के नाम से विख्यात हैं। आगे के बारह श्लोकों (5 से 19 तक) में राम के गुणों का अद्भूत वर्णन है, किन्तु आश्चर्य तब होता है कि जब नारद एकमेव श्रेष्ठ परमसुख राम का विचार करते समय उनके इक्ष्वाकुवंश में उत्पन्न होने को महत्वांकित करते हैः

"इक्ष्वाकुवंश प्रभवो रामो नाम जनैः श्रुतः।
नियतात्मा महावीर्यो द्युतिमान् धृतिमान् वशी।।"[3] (रामायण, बालकाण्ड 1/8)

इस प्रकार नारद की दृष्टि में राम का इक्ष्वाकुवंश में उत्पन्न होना एक अत्यन्त महत्वपूर्ण गुण है। इसके विपरीत रामाख्यान के परवर्ती कवियों ने राम की पहचान 'रघुपति', 'रघुवर', 'रघुनन्दन', 'रघुकुल तिलक' आदि रूपों में की है। गोस्वामी तुलसीदास ने वाल्मीकी–नारद संवाद को नवीन रूप में युगधर्म के परिपेक्ष्य में प्रस्तुत किया है।

बालकाण्ड में उद्धृत करते हैं कि "हे प्रभो! मैं आपको पूछता हूँ कि वे राम कौन हैं? हे कृपानिधान! मुझे समझाकर कहिए।"

"रामु कवन प्रभु पूछउँ तोही। कहिअ बुझाइ कृपानिधि मोही।।"

(रामचरितमानस, बालकाण्ड 45/3)

इस पर मुनि का उत्तर है कि–

"एक राम अवधेश कुमारा। तिन्ह कर चरित विदित संसारा।।"[5]

(रामचरितमानस, बालकाण्ड 45/4)

इस प्रकार वाल्मीकि एवं तुलसीदास दोनों की रामाख्यान परम्परा के राम की पहचान या प्रथम विशेषण के प्रयोग के समीक्षण से यह तो स्पष्ट है कि **प्रथमतः राम इक्ष्वाकुवंशी** है। यह बात अलग है कि सोलहवीं शताब्दी तक आते–आते कोशल, अयोध्या और राम के एकत्व में इक्ष्वाकुवंश के प्रतापी सम्राट तथा राम के प्रपितामह महाराज रघु के दिग्विजयी प्रजावत्सल एवं लोकल्याणकारी राज्य के संस्थापक की छवि लोक में मान्य हुई और तुलसीदास तथा अन्य कवियों ने भी 'कोसलपुर राजा', 'अवधेस कुमारा' तथा रघुपति (रामचरितमानस, बालकाण्ड 16/3 , 'रघुपति कीरति विमल पताका', 17/2 रघुपति चरन उपासक जेते', 36/1 "रघुपति महिमा अगुन अवाधा', 18/1 'वंदउँ नाम राम रघुवर को' आदि) विशेषण को भी उभारा। इससे यह विश्लेषित है कि राम की श्रेष्ठता, परमपुरूषत्व तथा सभी गुण इक्ष्वाकुवंश के प्रतापी राजाओं की परम्परा से संचित होकर अभिव्यक्त हुए हैं। इसलिए इक्ष्वाकुवंश का इतिहास तथा उसकी राजनीतिक, सांस्कृतिक एवं मूल्यपरक अन्य परम्पराएँ रामाख्यान की पृष्ठभूमि में विचारणीय हैं।

इक्ष्वाकुः इतिहास एवं वंश परम्परा

राम से सम्बद्ध इक्ष्वाकुवंश अत्यन्त प्राचीन एवं पारम्परिक है। भारत ही नहीं अपितु, सम्पूर्ण विश्व के इतिहास निर्माण में इस वंश की राजत्व, प्रजापालकत्व एवं प्रतापी परम्परा का महत्वपूर्ण योगदान रहा है। मूलतः 'इक्ष्वाकु' एक जन थे। इनकी प्राचीनता प्राग्वैदिक है। **ऋग्वेद** (10.60.4), **अथर्ववेद** (19.39.9) तथा **पंचविंश ब्राह्मण** में एक–एक स्थान पर प्रसंगतः 'इक्ष्वाकु' का उल्लेख है। इन सीमित उल्लेखों के आधार पर यह तो स्पष्ट है कि यह एक वैदिक जन था जिनकी गणना वैदिक भरतों एवं पंचजनों (अनु, द्रह्यु, यदु, तुर्वसु एवं पुरू) के अतिरिक्त की गई है। पुरूओं की एक शाखा भरतों की थी जो अपनी यज्ञ–परम्परा, प्रताप तथा इतिहास बोध के कारण वैदिक काल में ख्यातिप्राप्त थे, जिनकी परम्पराओं ने 'भारत' को यह अभिधान प्रदान किया। इसीलिए साहित्य एवं इतिहास के मनीषी विद्वान् डॉ. राम बिलास शर्मा (1996a : 58–59; 1996b : 13–16) यह स्वीकार करते हैं कि वैदिक काल में इक्ष्वाकु जन एवं उनका वंश एक प्रतापी वंश रहा होगा । यहाँ वे ऋग्वेद की उस ऋचा का अनुवाद प्रस्तुत करते हैं कि "जिस राष्ट्र में धनवान शत्रुओं के संहारक इक्ष्वाकु राजा शासक के कार्य में वृद्धि को प्राप्त करता है, उस राज्य में पाँचों वर्णों के लोग स्वर्ग के समान संकल्पसिद्ध होकर सुख प्राप्त करते हैं।" यहॉ पंचकृष्टयः से तात्पर्य पंचजनों से है जो कृषि कर्म के कारण स्थायी निवास की ओर अग्रसर हो गये थे। यह प्रक्रिया बतलाती है कि इक्ष्वाकु जन एक क्षेत्र विशेष में राज्य करते थे।

अथर्ववेद में कुष्ठ के प्रसंग में प्राचीन काल के इक्ष्वाकु का उल्लेख है। पुरूकुत्स ऋग्वेद में एक राजा का नाम है जो **शतपथ ब्राम्हण** के अनुसार इक्ष्वाकुवंशी है। इसी प्रकार एक राजा त्र्यरूण त्रसदस्यु है जो **पंचविंश ब्राह्मण**के अनुसार इक्ष्वाकुवंशी माना गया है। इस ग्रंथ के त्र्यरूण त्रैधात्व इक्ष्वाकु को वृहद्देवता का त्र्यरूण त्रैवृष्ण और ऋग्वेद के त्र्यरूण त्रसदस्यु को एक माना गया है। इन उल्लेखों के पारस्परिक सम्बंधों के आधार पर इक्ष्वाकुओं और पुरूओं में एकत्व स्थापित किया जाता है। इस एकत्त्व के आधार पर ही इक्ष्वाकुओं के वैदिक स्वरूप तथा उनकी ऐतिहासिक परम्परा को उद्घाटित किया जाता रहा है। इतना ही नहीं इक्ष्वाकुओं के इतिवृत्त तथा उनके अभिजन को निरूपित करने में ऋग्वेद में उल्लिखित सरयु (5.53.9), गोमती (10.75.5–6; 5.61.19 आदि), राम (10. 93.14), वशिष्ठ (7.33.32;7.23.6 आदि), विश्वामित्र (3.53.13;3.1.21;3.18.4) तथा अथर्ववेद की अयोध्या (10.2.31–33) आदि के साथ इक्ष्वाकुओं की स्थिति को स्पष्ट किया जा सकता है।

वैदिक उल्लेखों तथा सम्बद्ध परम्पराओं के आधार पर इक्ष्वाकु जन की आरम्भिक स्थिति, अभिजन एवं मूल अधिवास क्षेत्र का निश्चयन इतिहास की एक जटिल समस्या बनी हुई है। वैदिक एवं पौराणिक साहित्य के मर्मज्ञ अमेरिकी विद्वान डेविड फ्राउली (2001 : 65–66) (वामदेव शास्त्री) ने अपनी पुस्तक **'दि ऋग्वेद एण्ड दि हिस्ट्री ऑफ इण्डिया'** में इक्ष्वाकुओं के इतिहास पर प्रकाश डाला है। उनके अनुसार इक्ष्वाकु मूलतः सरस्वती घाटी के निवासी थे। भरत एवं कुशिक वंशों की तरह इक्ष्वाकुवंश भी मूल पुरूवंश की एक शाखा था। फ्राउली के अनुसार, "सरस्वती घाटी से विस्तार क्रम में इक्ष्वाकु सरयू के किनारे अयोध्या पहुँचे। बाद में उनकी एक दूसरी शाखा सरस्वती से सदानीरा (गंडकी) के पास पहुँची और विदेह कहलायी।" किन्तु, राम विलास शर्मा (1996a : 53–54)

ने भाषाई–भूगोल का सूक्ष्म विश्लेषण करते हुए यह निष्कर्ष निकाला है कि इक्ष्वाकुओं का मूलक्षेत्र अयोध्या (कोसल) थी, क्योंकि वैदिक क्रिया पदों के मूल रूप कोसल के हैं। इस प्रकार इक्ष्वाकुओं के मूल अधिवास क्षेत्र कोसल तथा राजधानी अयोध्या के पक्ष में सर्वाधिक प्रमाण उपलब्ध होते हैं।

इक्ष्वाकुओं की मूलभूमि कोसल का क्षेत्र था। जैन, बौद्ध एवं पौराणिक परम्पराओं से यह तथ्यतः प्रमाणित है। जैन ग्रंथों में प्रथम जैन तीर्थकर ऋषभनाथ को 'इक्खाग भूमि'(=इक्ष्वाकु भूमि) से संबद्ध माना गया है। **आवश्यक निर्युक्ति** (382) में इक्ष्वाकु भूमि को अयोध्या (अयोज्झा) का ही एक नाम बताया गया है और इसे प्रथम तीर्थकर उसभ (ऋषभ) की राजधानी बताया गया है। इसकी पुष्टि **रामायण** के उत्तरकाण्ड के उस विवरण से होती है जहाँ कहा गया है कि, राम के जाने के बाद अयोध्या बहुत दिनों तक सूनी पड़ी रहेगी, फिर राजा ऋषभ के समय यह पुनः आबाद होगीः

"अयोध्यापुरी रम्या शून्या वर्षगणान् बहून्।
ऋषभं प्राप्य राजानं निवासमुपयास्यति।।"

यह भी सर्वविदित है कि इक्ष्वाकु भूमि के शासक ऋषभनाथ के पुत्र भरत के प्रतापी एवं दिग्विजयी शासन में भरत देश भारत की विशेष ख्याति बढ़ी थी। इसीलिए जैन परम्परा यह मानती है कि देश का नाम 'भरत' पड़ने का एक कारण भरत का कर्त्तव्य था। इतना ही नहीं इक्ष्वाकु भूमि अयोध्या जैन धर्म की सृजन भूमि रही है। जैन धर्म के पाँच तीर्थंकरों –ऋषभनाथ, अजितनाथ, अभिनन्दननाथ, सुमतिनाथ, अनन्तनाथ की जन्मभूमि अयोध्या तथा पुष्पदन्त की जन्म स्थली काकण्डी (खुखुन्दू, देवरिया जिला, उत्तर प्रदेश) इक्ष्वाकु क्षेत्र ही रहा है।

इसी प्रकार कोसल से सम्बद्ध इक्ष्वाकुओं की बौद्ध परम्परा भी है। बौद्ध पालि साहित्य में ओक्काक (मालालसेकर 1937 : 461–62 (इक्ष्वाकु) की चर्चा है। छठीं शताब्दी ईसापूर्व के सभी गणतंत्रों–शाक्य, कोलिय, मल्ज, मोरिय आदि इक्ष्वाकु से संबंधित थे। **दीघनिकाय** के अम्बट्ठसूत्र (1.3) में शाक्यों की उत्पत्ति में प्रसंग में स्पष्टतः उल्लिखित है कि शाक्य राजा इक्ष्वाकु को पितामह मानते हैं। 'ओक्काक' (इक्ष्वाकु) उनका पूर्वज था। इसी प्रकार **महावंश** में 'ओक्काक' के वंशजों की चर्चा है। बौद्ध ग्रंथ **महावस्तु** मे। इक्ष्वाकु, कोसल और अयोध्या को महत्व के साथ उल्लिखित किया गया है। यहाँ यह विशेष रूप से उल्लेखनीय है कि **बुद्धचरित** में अश्वघोष ने शाक्यों के पूर्वजों को 'इक्ष्वाकवो' सिद्धार्थ के पिता शुद्धोधन को 'इक्ष्वाकुवंश प्रभवस्व राज्ञः' तथा बुद्ध को 'इक्ष्वाकुकुल प्रदीप' और 'इक्क्षाकुकुल चन्द्रमा' कहा है। **थेरगाथा** में तो कपिलवस्तु के शाक्यों को 'भगीरथ' कहा ही गया है। इस प्रकार यह स्पष्ट है कि इक्ष्वाकुवंश कोसल से सम्बद्ध रहा है। यह इक्ष्वाकुवंश भारतीय राजवंशों तथा श्रेष्ठ राजत्व की तापस (प्रताप) एवं चक्रवर्तिन् दोनों ही परम्पराओं का मूल अधिष्ठान रहा है। इसीलिए वाल्मीकि–नारद संवाद के इस वंश में उत्पन्न संसार के श्रेष्ठतम पुरूष 'राम' को इसमें उद्भूत बतलाकर उनमें सभी श्रेष्ठ गुणों का एकमेव अधिष्ठान बताया गया है।

ऐतिहासिक तथ्यों से यह भी स्पष्ट है कि वैदिक इक्ष्वाकु जनों ने आगे चलकर एक आदर्श राजवंश की परम्परा का स्वरूप विकसित किया। भारत की प्राचीनतम राजवंश परम्परा में परिभाषित और पारम्परिक वंश के रूप में प्रतिष्ठित होने के कारण इक्ष्वाकुवंश का सभी ऐतिहासिक राजवंशों में श्रेष्ठतम स्थान है। सर्वाधिक समृद्ध वंश परम्परा इक्ष्वाकुओं की ही रही है। पुराणों में इसका विस्तारपूर्वक विवरण मिलता है।

भारत का इतिहास विश्व इतिहास की 'नाभि' है, क्योंकि यहाँ का इतिहास सृष्टि से आरम्भ होता है। सृष्टि के सर्जन–विसर्जन तथा उस पर दीर्घकाल तक शासित वंशों एवं राजवंशों का दीर्घ इतिवृत्त है। चौदह मनुओं का इतिहास इसकी आधारशिला है। सूर्य से उत्पन्न इस इक्ष्वाकुंश के इतिहास में सातवें मनु वैवस्वत से ही वंशों का इतिहास आरम्भ होता है। पौराणिक परम्परा बतलाती है कि मनु के नौ पुत्र (इक्ष्वाकु, नृग, धृष्ट, शर्याति, नरिष्यन्त, प्रान्सु, नभाक, करूप और पृषघ) तथा एक पुत्री 'इला' थी। मनु का वंश 'मान्ववंश' ही 'इक्ष्वाकुवंश' कहलाया, क्योंकि मनु के पुत्रों में इक्ष्वाकु ज्येष्ठ एवं श्रेष्ठ थे। **इक्क्षाकु** को अयोध्या का राज्य मिला, नृग का राज्य कहीं मध्यप्रदेश में, धृष्ट से धार्ष्टिक क्षत्रियों की उत्पत्ति हुई जो पंजाब के वाहीक क्षेत्र में शासन करते थे, **शर्याति** से शर्याति क्षत्रिय हुए जो गुजरात के आनर्त्त क्षेत्र में राज्य कर रहे थे, **नरिष्यन्त** सम्भवतः 'शक' कहलाये, नाभाक उत्तरी बिहार में स्थापित थे जिनके वंशजों में राजा विशाल ने वैशाली नगर की स्थापना की, करूष का राज्य क्षेत्र आधुनिक रीवा में सोन नदी की घाटी में करूष जनपद था तथा **पृषघ्र** को कोई राज्य नहीं मिला, क्योंकि उसने गुरू की गाय का वध किया था। (वर्मा एवं गुप्त 2001 : 127) इक्ष्वाकुवंश की पौराणिक वंशावली अत्यन्त समृद्ध है। मनु के ज्येष्ठ पुत्र इक्ष्वाकु ने ही वंश की नीवं डाली इसीलिए सूर्य एवं मनु का सम्पूर्ण वंश 'इक्ष्वाकुवंश' कहलाया। कुछ पुराणों में इक्ष्वाकु के 100 पुत्र बतलाये गये हैं, जिनमें छः का ही नाम मिलता है– विकुक्षि, निमि, शकुन, विराट्, दण्डक एवं दशास्व। इसमें शकुनि आदि 50 पुत्रों को उत्तरापथ का राज्य मिला। विराट् आदि 40 दक्षिणापथ के शासक थे। इनमें सर्वाधिक महत्त्वपूर्ण विकुक्षि, निमि और दण्डक थे। विकुक्षि अयोध्या का उत्तराधिकारी बना और निमि ने विदेह (मिथिला) में राज्य स्थापित की तथा दण्डक ने दक्षिण कोसल में राज्य स्थापित किया जिसे दण्डकारण्य कहा गया। इस प्रकार

इक्ष्वाकु के पुत्रों ने ही भारत के सभी क्षेत्रों में राजवंश परम्परा की नींव डाली। इक्ष्वाकु के पुत्रों द्वारा स्थापित राजवंश भी इवाकुवंश ही है।

इनमें सबसे समृद्ध और प्रतापी राजाओं की परम्परा अयोध्या के इक्ष्वाकुवंश ही है। यह प्रतापी वंश था। राजाओं ने अग्नि–अर्चा (यज्ञ–यागादि) से जो ताप–प्रताप प्राप्त किया उससे वंश की ख्याति बढ़ी और विश्व के प्रतापी वंशों में इनकी गणना हुई। इसीलिए इस वंश में काकुस्थ्य, युवनाश्व, पृथु (त्रसदस्यु), पुरूकुत्स, मुचुकुन्द, त्रय्यारूण, सत्यव्रत, त्रिशंकु, हरिश्चन्द्र, सगर, भगीरथ, अम्बरीष, ययाति, मान्धाता, सुदास, कल्माषपाद, दिलीप, रघु, दशरथ, राम, लव, कुश आदि महाप्रतापी सर्वगुण सम्पन्न आदर्श राजाओं ने राज्य किया। महाभारत युद्ध के समय इक्ष्वाकुवंश परम्परा में बृहद्वल शासन कर रहा था जो अभिमन्यु के हाथों मारा गया था।

यह तथ्य स्पष्ट है कि इतिहास–पुराणों में सर्वाधिक पूर्ण वंशावली केवल अयोध्या के इसी इक्ष्वाकु शाखा की मिलती है, जिसके महाभारत युद्ध पर्यन्त 91 राजा और भारतयुद्ध से कल्पान्त तक 24 राजाओं के नाम मिलते हैं, जिसमें अंतिम राजा सुमित्र था। इक्ष्वाकु से सुमित्र तक 115 राजाओं के नाम कथित हैं, फिर भी इक्ष्वाकुवंशावली अपूर्ण मानी जाती है। एफ.ई. पार्जिटर (1972), कुँवर लाल जैन 'व्यासशिष्य' (पुराणों में वंशानुक्रमिक कालक्रम), विशुद्धानन्द पाठक (1983), ठाकुर प्रसाद वर्मा आदि ने इक्ष्वाकुवंश की वंशावली पर महत्वपूर्ण कार्य किया है। इन विद्वानों का मानना है कि इक्ष्वाकु (लगभग 12,500 वि.पू.) से सुमित्र (लगभग 1800 वि.पू.) तक इस वंश के लगभग 150 राजाओं ने लगातार दस हजार वर्षों से अधिक काल तक राज्य किया। विश्व का इतिहास साक्षी है कि इतने दीर्घकाल तक पृथ्वी पर राज्य, सुराज्य स्थापित करने वाला कोई वंश नहीं है। पृथु, सगर, भगीरथ, सुदास, रघु एवं राम के दिग्विजयी सुशासन से विश्व इतिहास परिचित है। रघु का दिग्विजय, मान्धाता की उत्तरकुरू विजय तो साहित्य एवं शिल्प की कथावस्तु बनी। इसीलिए वाल्मीकि रामायण में राम का प्रथम परिचय इक्ष्वाकुवंशी राम के रूप में कराकर देवर्षि नारद ने सांकेतिक रूप से इक्ष्वाकुओं के राजत्व का राम पर आरोपण कर दिया। इसीलिए 'राम' एवं 'इक्ष्वाकुवंशी' पर्यायी है।

वाल्मीकि एवं तुलसीदास के मध्य सहस्त्राब्दियों का अन्तराल है। वाल्मीकि तक इक्ष्वाकुवंश की लोकप्रतिष्ठा पराकाष्ठा पर थी। इक्ष्वाकु राजाओं द्वारा स्थापित राजनीतिक, सांस्कृतिक, धार्मिक एवं आर्थिक जीवन की श्रेष्ठ मौलिक परम्पराएँ लोक में सम्पूजित तथा लोक नियमन का आधार थी। इसके विपरीत गोस्वामी तुलसीदास का युग संक्रमण का युग था। इक्ष्वाकुओं द्वारा स्थापित मूल्यों पर मध्येशियाई अमर्यादित संस्कृति का दबाव था। इसीलिए तुलसीदास ने दिग्विजयी रघु और धर्नुधारी राम का आदर्श लोक में गाया जो कालान्तर में भारतीय संस्कृति के संरक्षण का आधार बना। यही कारण था कि तुलसीदास ने 'रघुपति', 'रघुवर', 'अवधेस कुमारा' जैसे विशेषणों का प्रयोग कर राम की पावनी गाथा को लोकमंगल के लिए रचित किया। (वर्मा एवं गुप्त 2001)

इक्वाकु संस्कृति : वैशिष्ट्य एवं अवदान

'राम' से सम्बद्ध इक्ष्वाकुवंश वस्तुतः राजनीतिक एवं सांस्कृतिक इतिहास का मूल उत्स है। कोशल (अयोध्या), मिथिला (विदेह), आनर्त्त, दण्डकारण्य, माहिष्मती, आन्ध्र आदि क्षेत्रों में जिस वंश परम्परा ने दीर्घकालिक राज्य स्थापित किया वह आज भी किसी न किसी रूप में जीवित है। इस वंश ने मिथिला में जो राज्य स्थापित किया वहाॅ जनक उपाधिकारी राजाओं की विश्वविख्यात तेजस्वी मेधासम्पन्न परम्परा शुरू हुई। सीता के पिता सीरध्वज जनक परम्परा के एक शासक थे। जनक का प्रथम परिचय कृष्णयजुर्वेदीय **तैत्तिरीय ब्राह्मण** (30/10/09) में प्राप्त होता है। वहाँ जनक वैदेह देवताओं से मिलते हैं। भारतीय इतिहास में जनक इतने विद्वान तत्त्वज्ञ के रूप में सामने आते हैं किवे याज्ञवल्क्य को भी शिक्षा देते हैं और स्वयं ब्राह्मण बन जाते हैं। इसीलिए यदि इक्ष्वाकुओं के वैशिष्ट्य का चिंतन होता है तो इक्ष्वाकुओं से संबंधित सभी परम्पराओं का समन्वित रूप आवश्यक है।

इक्वाकुवंश श्रेष्ठ राज्य व्यवस्था का प्रतिपादक एवं पालक वंश रहा है। कोसल से सम्बद्ध इक्ष्वाकुवंश की परम्परा में ही परवर्ती ऐतिहासिक राजवंशों की परम्परा मिलती है। छठीं शताब्दी ईसापूर्व से लेकर वर्तमान लोकतंत्रीय राज्य व्यवस्था का राज्यादर्श 'राम राज्य' ही है। भारत एवं दक्षिण पूर्व एशिया के साहित्य एवं अभिलेखों में राजाओं के जो विरूद एवं उपाधियाँ मिलती हैं, उनमें 'इक्ष्वाकुकुल प्रदीप', 'इक्ष्वाकुकुल चन्द्रमा', 'रघुकुलतिलक' और 'रघुकुल ग्रामणी' तथा उपमाओं में 'पृथुराघवाद्याः इव' जैसी उक्तियाँ सहज ही प्राप्त हैं। महाभारत के भीष्मपर्व (915–7) में 'भारतप्रशस्ति' की जो काव्यमय प्रस्तुति मिलती है, वह इक्ष्वाकु परम्परा के यशस्वी राजाओं की है, जिसकी पृष्ठभूमि ऐतिहासिक है। राजाओं का इतिहास एवं कर्त्तव्य बतलाया है कि मनु से उत्पन्न वंश इक्ष्वाकु ने मानव जाति को सुशासन, सुराज्य, सुसंस्कृति, सभ्यता, सत्य, तप एवं धर्म पर आधारित बनाने में विलक्षण एवं चिरकालिक योगदान दिया है। वाल्मीकि रामायण में वशिष्ठ ने राम के पिता राजा दशरथ के लिए जो संबोधन दिया है, वह इक्ष्वाकु परम्परा के वैशिष्ट्य का एक उदाहरण हैः

"इक्ष्वाकूणां कुले जातः साक्षाद् धर्मइवापरः।
धृतिमान सुव्रतः श्रीमान् न धर्महातुमर्हसि।।
त्रिषुलोकेषु विख्यातो धर्मात्मा इति राघवः।
स्वधर्म प्रतिपद्यस्व नाधर्म वोढुमर्हसि।।" (बालकाण्ड 21/6–7)

राजनय, प्रजा वत्सलता, प्रजा पालकत्व, दौत्य प्रविधि, कराधान, अर्थव्यवस्था, धर्माचरण आदि सभी पक्षों को दृष्टि में रखकर इक्ष्वाकुओं ने लोकपाल का ही कार्य किया। राजाओं में चक्रवर्तित्व की अवधारणा पर जीवन का क्रम संयोजित करने वाले मार्ग का आलोक इसी परम्परा की देन है। प्रत्येक कार्य में इक्ष्वाकुओं के आदर्श 'सूर्य' रहे हैं, क्योंकि यह सूर्य से उद्भूत वंश था। जिस प्रकार सूर्य अपनी ऊर्जा से जगत् को आलोकित और चैतन्य रखता है, उसी प्रकार सूर्यवंशी इक्ष्वाकुओं ने राज्य, शासन, बलि (कर) आदि का आदर्श सूर्य रखा। कालिदास ने रघुवंश में स्पष्ट लिखा है किः

"प्रजानामेव भूत्यर्थ स ताभ्यो बलिंग्रहीत।
सहस्त्रगुणं उत्स्त्रष्टुं आदत्तं हि रसं रविः।।"

अर्थात् जिस प्रकार सूर्य पृथ्वी से जल ग्रहण कर पुनः वर्षा के रूप में प्रदान करता है, उसी प्रकार रघुवंश के राजा बलि अर्थात् कर को प्रजाहित में ही ग्रहण करते हैं। यह किसी भी राज्य के शासन का चरमोत्कर्ष है। इसीलिए 'षष्ठांशवृत्ति' अर्थात् उपज का छठाँ भाग एक आदर्श कर व्यवस्था के रूप में लोक में मान्य हुआ।

लोक में सत्य एवं धर्म की व्यवस्था की स्थापना में इक्ष्वाकु सबसे अग्रणी रहे हैं। हरिश्चन्द्र, सगर, भगीरथ आदि का उदाहरण प्रत्यक्ष है।

इक्ष्वाकु परम्परा का वैशिष्ट्य 'आर्यत्व' की प्रतिष्ठा में दिखाई देता है। इक्ष्वाकुओं ने आर्य धर्म को जीवन का श्रेष्ठ मार्ग निरूपित किया। यह मार्ग ब्राह्मण एवं श्रमण दोनों ही संस्कृतियों में महत्वांकित है। वस्तुतः 'आर्य' जीवन दृष्टि इक्ष्वाकुओं की देन है। रामायण, महाभारत एवं संस्कृत वाङ्मय में इक्ष्वाकुओं का प्रिय सम्बोधन 'आर्य' मिलता है। संस्कृत कवि भास ने **प्रतिमानाटकम्** (पृ. 83) में भरत–देवकुलिक संवाद के प्रसंग में देवकुलिक के मुँह से कहलवाया है कि "आर्येति इक्ष्वाकुकुलालापः खल्वयम्" अर्थात् निश्चित रूप से इक्ष्वाकु कुलक्रम 'आर्य' हैं। इस आर्यत्व में सत्य, धर्म, दिव्य, पवित्र, पूर्णतेज, यशस्विता आदि वे सभी गुण आते हैं जो धर्म के लक्षणों में परिगणित हैं। सत्य, दृढ़प्रतिज्ञ, वचन का पालन (प्राण जाय पर वचन न जाई), धैर्य, बुद्धि, जीवलोक की रक्षा, प्रजावत्सलता, नैष्ठिकता आदि विशिष्ट गुणों के लिए इक्ष्वाकु प्रसिद्ध रहे हैं। यही जीवन दृष्टि भारत की आत्मा है जो प्रत्येक समाज तथा प्रत्येक काल में प्रासंगिक है। इसीलिए मौर्यवंशीय इक्ष्वाकु शासक अशोक ने अपने सिंहशीर्ष स्तम्भों की जो प्रतीकात्मक शिल्प कृति निर्मित की उसे हम आज 'सत्यमेव जयते' के रूप में स्वाधीनता के पश्चात् स्वीकार किये हैं। जैनों और बौद्धों ने भी क्रमशः 'आयाग पट्ट' तथा 'चत्वारि आर्य सत्यानि' के रूप में इसे लोक में प्रतिष्ठापित किया । आर्यत्व ही ईश्वरत्व है, इसीलिए इक्ष्वाकुवंशी राम ईश्वर हैं, आर्य है, आर्य–पुत्र हैं। यही आर्यत्व हम भारतीयों की सांस्कृतिक पहचान है। आर्यत्व के गुण ही हिन्दुत्व के लक्षण है।

इक्ष्वाकुवंश वर्णाश्रम व्यवस्था का प्रतिष्ठापक एवं पालक था। समाज की व्यवस्था का आरम्भिक सूत्र इक्ष्वाकुवंश के राजाओं तथा प्रजा जीवन में दिखाई देता है। कर्म के सिद्धान्त पर वर्णों का नामकरण एवं उसके विहित कर्त्तव्यों की पृष्ठभूमि इक्ष्वाकुवंशीय थी। ब्राह्मण, क्षत्रिय, वैश्य एवं शूद्र सभी को महत्व प्राप्त था। मान्धाता संततियों के प्रसंग में ज्ञात होता है कि आरम्भ में वर्ण व्यवस्था सुदृढ़ नहीं थी। श्रेष्ठ कर्मों के कारण वर्णों के धर्म परिवर्तित होते थे। युवनाश्व तृतीय ने पुत्र हरित आंगीरस गोत्र के ब्राह्मण बन गये। दिलीप एवं राम का जीवन जंगली जातियों के बीच व्यतीत हुआ। जातियों में एकत्व की स्थापना इसी वंश परम्परा में दिखाई देती है। विवाह का श्रेष्ठतम् आदर्श भी इक्ष्वाकुओं ने रखा। मिथिला में सीता स्वयंवर में पहुँचे राम के साथ ही जनक की शेष तीनों पुत्रियों का दशरथ के पुत्रों से विवाह आज भी विलक्षण स्मृति है। पारस्परिक सौहार्द्र तथा समाज में श्रेष्ठ परम्पराओं की स्थापना इक्ष्वाकु कुल की क्रमागत परम्परा रही है। पारिवारिक संगठन, माता–पिता, भाई–बहन आदि के बीच उच्च मर्यादित आदर्श केवल इक्ष्वाकुओं ने ही स्थापित किये। इसीलिए राम के जीवन में उनका मर्यादित पुरूषोत्तमत्व सामने लक्षित होता है।

कृषि एवं अर्थव्यवस्था के क्षेत्र में इक्ष्वाकुओं का श्रेष्ठ अवदान सर्वस्वीकृत है। मिथिला के इक्ष्वाकुवंश में जनक सीरध्वज द्वारा सोने के हल से खेत जोतना और उसकी हराई से 'सीता' की उत्पत्ति केवल काल्पनिक विवरण नहीं है। वास्तव में सीता और जनक अन्न के प्रतीकात्मक रूप हैं। इसीलिए सीता का एक रूप पृथ्वी है। इसके पूर्व इक्ष्वाकुवंशी राजा पृथु का उदाहरण है। वे पहले राजा हैं जिन्होने पृथ्वी को कृषि योग्य बनाया और विभिन्न प्रकार के उत्पादों का सृजन किया। कृषि, पशुपालन, व्यापार आदि इक्ष्वाकुओं की आर्थिक समृद्धि के मूलाधार थे। दिलीप की गो–सेवा प्रतीकात्मक है। राम का वनवास सायास है। इन सभी कारणों से इक्ष्वाकु कुल सदैव प्रेरणा तथा प्रोत्साहन का केन्द्र रहा है। राम स्वयं गोपालक थे। एक रोचक प्रसंग में उनके गोदान का एक अद्भुत वर्णन हैः

"गवां सहस्रमप्येकं न च विश्राणितं मया।
परिक्षिपसि दण्डेन यावत्तावदवाप्यसे।।
स तीर्त्वा सरयूपारं दण्डस्तस्य कराच्चयुतः।
गोव्रजे बहुसाहस्रे पपातोक्षणसंनिधौ।।"

(रामायण, अयोध्याकाण्ड 32/36–38)

इस प्रकार आर्थिक वैशिष्ट्य के अनेक प्रसंग वाल्मीकि रामायण तथा अन्य रामाख्यानों में सुरक्षित हैं जो सार्वकालिक महत्त्वपूर्ण एवं प्रासंगिक है। इक्ष्वाकुओं ने संरक्षित ग्राम, नगर, अरण्य आदि सभी क्षेत्रों को पुरस्कृत किया। यही चिन्तन किसी भी देश की समृद्ध अर्थव्यवस्था का आधार है।

भारत की धार्मिक परम्परा का सुदृढ़ीकरण भी इक्ष्वाकुओं की देन है। इक्ष्वाकु राजा धर्मनिष्ठ तथा आश्रम–परम्परा के पालक थे। राम ने स्वयं 'शिव' की पूजा कर धर्मों के अन्तर्सम्बन्धों को प्रमाणित किया। इक्ष्वाकु प्रजापालक थे इसीलिए विष्णु के रूप में मान्य हुए। धार्मिक प्रक्रिया में लोकविहित कर्मों को करते हुए किस प्रकार लोकाराधन किया जाय यह इक्ष्वाकु परम्परा में भरा पड़ा है। वैष्णव परम्परा लोक कल्याणक है। शक्ति की प्रतिष्ठा तथा अन्य अनेक शक्तियों की लोक प्रसिद्धि में इक्ष्वाकुओं का बड़ा योगदान था। इसी प्रकार कला एवं संस्कृति के क्षेत्र में इक्ष्वाकुवंशीय राजाओं के स्थापित आदर्श आज भी मान्य एवं अनुकरणीय है।

वाल्मीकि ने रामायण के सुन्दरकाण्ड के 58वें सर्ग में एक रोचक प्रसंग दिया है। जब जाम्बवान् के पूछने पर हनुमान अपनी लोक यात्रा का वृतान्त सुनाते हैं तब एक प्रसंग है कि सीता जी की दारूण दशा देखकर उनसे वार्तालाप का जो उपाय सोचते हैं वह इक्ष्वाकुवंश की प्रशंसा है:

"इक्ष्वाकुकुल वंशस्तु स्तुतो मम पुरस्कृतः।
श्रुत्वा तु गदितां वाचं राजर्षिगणभूषिताम्।।"

हनुमान कहते हैं कि राजर्षियों से विभूषित मेरी वाणी सुनकर देवी सीता के नेत्रों में आँसू भर आया, फिर वे बोलीः

"कस्त्वं केन कथं चेह प्राप्तो वानरपुडगव।।95।।
का च रामेण ते प्रीतिस्तन्मे शंसितुमर्हसि।95 1/2।"

(रामायण, सुंदरकाण्ड 58/95)

इस प्रकार इक्ष्वाकुवंश का वैशिष्ट्य और उसकी सांस्कृतिक थाती से साहित्य एवं परम्परा समृद्ध है। विश्व का ऐसा कोई भी देश नहीं है जहाँ यह परम्परा न गई हो। आज वैश्विक स्थिरता में यदि कोई परम्परा प्रासंगिक है तो वह है– इक्ष्वाकुवंशीय परम्परा। इक्ष्वाकुओं ने पृथ्वी के प्रति सदैव अपना रागात्मक सम्बन्ध व्यक्त किया। मनु से लेकर राम, लव, कुश, चन्द्रकेतु आदि की परम्परा में यह मूल तत्त्व है। सीता का पृथ्वी, जगजननी जानकी एवं राम का 'जननी जन्मभूमिश्च स्वर्गादपि गरियसी' की उक्ति इक्ष्वाकुवंश में उत्पन्न होना है। राम नर से नरोत्तम बनने का सूत्र देते हैं। इसीलिए वाल्मीकि कहते है–

"नास्ति रामस्य सदृशे विक्रमे भुवि कश्चन्।"

(रामायण, युद्धकाण्ड, 30/29)

इस प्रकार नारद मुनि द्वारा वाल्मीकि को संसार में श्रेष्ठ सर्वगुण सम्पन्न पुरूष का जो वर्णन है, वह एक सुदीर्घ, समृद्ध एवं भारत की राजवंश परम्परा में इक्ष्वाकुवंश का सांकेतिक निरूपण है। रामाख्यान के प्रत्येक चरण इक्ष्वाकु परम्परा के श्रेष्ठ आदर्शों एवं मूल्यों से आप्लावित हैं। इस पृथ्वी पर प्रथित, पुरातन एवं पारम्परिक केवल एक ही वंश है, वह है– 'इक्ष्वाकुवंश'। इक्ष्वाकु कुल में राम 61वीं पीढ़ी के बाद के शासक हैं। राम में प्रत्येक पीढ़ी के श्रेष्ठ गुणों का संचित रूप विद्यमान था। इसीलिए रामचरित मानस के उत्तर काण्ड में तुलसीदास को कहना पड़ता है कि,

"राम कृपा नासहिं सब रोगा। जौं एहि भाँति बनै संजोगा।।"

(12/13)

यहाँ यह तथ्य उदाहरणीय है कि इक्ष्वाकुओं का इतिहास एवं संस्कृति साहित्य एवं परम्परा से पूर्णतः प्रमाणित है किन्तु पुरातत्व की दृष्टि से राम के पूर्व का इतिहास अभी भी अन्वेषणीय तथा स्थलों के पहचान की अपेक्षा करता है। पुरातत्त्ववेताओं ने राम से सम्बद्ध पुरास्थलों की तो पहचान तथा उत्खनन किया है। किन्तु पूर्ववर्ती इतिहास की कड़ी भारत एवं विश्व इतिहास के कालानुक्रम के लिए आवश्यक है।

संदर्भ

1. वर्मा ठाकुर प्रसाद "मानव इतिहास की आदिभूमि एशिया में ऐक्ष्वाकु तथा ऐलवंश", *कोशल का इतिहास एवं संस्कृति,* (लोक भारती प्रकाशन, इलाहाबाद, 2010), पृष्ठ 25–61
2. शर्मा, राम विलास, *भारतीय साहित्य की भूमिका,* (राजकमल, दिल्ली, 1996),

3. शर्मा,राम विलास, *इतिहास दर्शन*, (वाणी प्रकाशन, नई दिल्ली, 1996)
4. फ्राउली डेविड, *ऋग्वेद एण्ड दि हिस्ट्री ऑफ इण्डिया*, (नई दिल्ली, 2001) पृष्ठ 65–66।
5. मलालसेकर, जी.पी., *डिक्शनरी ऑफ पालि प्रापर नेम्स*, वाल्यूम1, (लन्दन, 1937)
6. वर्मा ठाकुर प्रसाद एवं गुप्त स्वराज प्रकाश, *अयोध्या का इतिहास एवं पुरातत्त्व*, पृष्ठ 12 (नई दिल्ली, 2001)।
7. पार्जिटर, एफ. ई., *एंशिएण्ट इण्डियन हिस्टॉरिकल ट्रेडिशन्स* (1972, पुनर्मुद्रण)
8. पाठक, विशुद्धानन्द, *हिस्ट्री ऑफ कोशल अप टू दि राइज ऑफ मौयोज* (गोतीलाल बनारसीदास, नई दिल्ली, 1983)

47

राम चरित मानस का धर्मशास्त्रीय अध्ययन

परहित सरिस धरम नहिं भाई
परपीड़ा सम नहिं अधमाई

संचिता घोष

वस्तुतः रामचरितमानस एक धर्म शास्त्र है। उसमें धर्म शास्त्र के समस्त तत्व, विशेषताएँ, लक्षण एवं स्थापनाएँ घटित होती हैं। सामान्य जनता उसे धर्मग्रन्थ के रूप मे ही मानती है। उसकी अत्यधिक लोकप्रियता तथा प्रतिष्ठा का मूल हेतु भी उसका धर्म शास्त्र होना है। यह एक अभिनव धर्मशास्त्र है। इसे कान्ता सम्मति कह सकते हैं, क्योंकि इसमें धर्मशास्त्र की नीरसता तथा रूक्षता का अभाव है। यह धर्मशास्त्र है और आचार शास्त्र भी। उसमें सिद्धान्त तथा व्यवहार दोनों का स्वर्णिम समन्वय है। इस धर्मशास्त्र के जनगीता बनने का श्रेय इस तथ्य में निहित है कि इसमें सिर्फ उपदेश तथा निर्देश ही नहीं मिलते अपितु उनको जीवन में सफलतापूर्वक चरितार्थ करने के लिए भगवान राम का जीवन चरित्र भी उपस्थित किया गया है। इसलिए 'मानस' का प्रभाव अन्य भारतीय धर्मशास्त्रों की अपेक्षा सर्वाधिक तथा सर्वोत्कृष्ट रूप में दिखाई देता है।

तुलसी के लिए काव्य एक माध्यम तथा निमित्त मात्र है। धर्म और मर्यादा उनके लिए लक्ष्य है। वह मुक्ति को धर्म पर्याय के रूप में ग्रहण करते हैं। 'मानस' में सभी हिन्दू धर्मशास्त्रों का निचोड़ विद्यमान है। विगत चार सौ वर्षों से हिन्दू मानस इस जीवित धर्मशास्त्र को अपना प्रकाश स्तम्भ एवं प्रेरणा स्त्रोत मानकर कार्य करता चला आ रहा है। न 'मानस' के समान कोई धर्मग्रन्थ जनप्रिय बना और न उसने जनता जनार्दन को इतने अधिक रूप में प्रभावित ही किया। वेद, उपनिषद, महाभारत, मनुस्मृति, पुराण, श्रीमद्‌भगवत गीता आदि अनेक धर्मशास्त्रों का वह प्रभाव नहीं पड़ा जो अकेले 'मानस' का।

तुलसी ने लिखा है–

नाना पुराण निगमागम सम्मतम यद
 रामायणे निगदितं क्वचिदन्यतोऽपि
स्वान्तः सुखाय तुलसी रघुनाथ गाथा
 भाषा निबन्ध मतिमंजुलमातनोति[1]

कवि मैथिलीशरण गुप्त ने लिखा है कि कहने को तो हम लोग वेद शाखाओं का नाम लेते ही हैं परन्तु सच्ची बात यह है कि आज रामचरितमानस ही हमारा धर्म ग्रन्थ है। मैं यह समझता हूँ कि उसे यह पद देकर कुछ भी नहीं खोया, उल्टा सब कुछ एक साथ पा लिया है।[2] तुलसीदास जी ने लोक और वेद से जो कुछ भिक्षाटन कर के पाया, सब अपने प्रभू को सर्मपण कर दिया। उस योग का प्रसाद जिसने पाया उसका भी लोक परलोक बन गया।

शास्त्र कतिपय नियमों, सिद्धान्तों तथा परिपाटियों से बनता है, 'मानस' भी अनेक धार्मिक तथा दार्शनिक सिद्धान्तों से परिपूर्ण है जो तुलसी का धर्म तथा दर्शनशास्त्र का मौलिक प्रदेश्य है। 'धर्मशास्त्र' में मौलिक भेद है जो पूजा जाता है उसे हम धर्मग्रन्थ कहते हैं परन्तु जिसमें धर्म सम्बन्धी मानवाचरण, शास्त्रीयता तथा नियमगत प्रतिपादन निहित रहते हैं, वह धर्मशास्त्र के रूप में अभिहित होता है। 'मानस' धर्मग्रन्थ, धर्मशास्त्र तथा महाकाव्य–तीनों का उत्कृष्ट निर्देशन है। तुलसी का 'मानस' हिन्दू धर्म की विराटता, विशालता, व्यापकता तथा उर्वर पाचन शक्ति का प्रतिनिधि, प्रमुख एवं महत्वपूर्ण ग्रन्थ है।

रामरत्न भटनागर ने 'तुलसी' नवः मूल्यांकन में लिखा है कि तुलसीदास का 'रामचरितमानस' मध्यदेशी हिन्दू धर्म परम्परा का अन्तिम ग्रन्थ कहा जा सकता है जिसका आरम्भ ऋग्वेद से होता है। तीन हजार वर्षों के अन्तर से हमें ये ग्रन्थ मिलते हैं परन्तु इनकी समानताओं और विभिन्नताओं के आधार पर हम भारतीय चेतना के विकास की परिकल्पना भली–भांति कर सकते हैं। वास्तव में दोनों ग्रन्थ दो सांस्कृतिक उन्मेषों के चरम बिन्दु हैं।[3] 'रामचरितमानस' से हमें आर्य सांस्कृतिक का एक दूसरा रूप मिलता है जो 600 ईसवी में लगभग हिन्दी के पश्चिमी प्रदेश में पांचरात्र भक्ति दर्शन और वासुदेवोपासना से आरम्भ होकर विष्णुवाद और अन्त में वैष्णव धर्म और अवतारवाद के भीतर से वाल्मीकि के राम को केन्द्र बनाकर इसी प्रकार एक चरम बिन्दु की सृष्टि करता है जिस प्रकार ऋग्वेद में इन्द्र सम्बन्धी ऋचाओं में वैदिक शौर्य, साहस और दीप्ति का एक सर्वोपरि ज्योति–बिन्दु कल्पित हुआ था।

तुलसी के एकेश्वरवाद अर्थात् राम ने तैंतीस करोड़ देवताओं को एक फूंक में उड़ा दिया और एक प्रकार का शास्त्र और एक ईश्वर की मध्ययुगीन धारणा एवं सांस्कृतिक माँग को सार्थक परिपूर्ति की। तुलसी का 'मानस' उपदेशों, आचार–विचार, नैतिकमता, आचरण तथा सदवृत्तियों से परिपूर्ण है जो एक सटीक धर्मग्रन्थ के लिए परमावश्यक है। 'मानस' आचार को आचरण से जोड़ने वाला धर्मशास्त्र है। उसमें शास्त्रीयता को व्याख्यात्मक कामनीय कलेवर प्राप्त हुआ है वह विचार को व्यक्तित्व प्रदान करता है वह सिद्धान्त को सांसारिकता की मायावी दुनिया में परखता है।

विद्यानिवास मिश्र ने 'साहित्य की चेतना' नामक ग्रन्थ में लिखा है कि रामचरितमानस पर संस्कृत के काव्यों में सबसे अधिक श्रीमद् भागवत का प्रभाव पड़ा है, श्रीमद् भागवत यदि परमहंसों की संहिता है तो मानस जन परमहंसों की लीला भूमि है।[4]

तुलसी ने धर्मशास्त्र का निर्माण अल्मारियों की शोभा बढ़ाने अथवा पण्डितों के शास्त्रार्थ हेतु नहीं किया था अपितु वह एक ओर अपने युग की धार्मिक अनावारिता तथा विश्रृंखलता का प्रतिबिम्ब है तो दूसरी ओर वह एक आदर्श परिवार एवं नैतिक समाज के अभ्युत्थानों हेतु सक्रिय योगदान देता है। तुलसी का समाज धर्मनिष्ठ है वह भारत की पारम्परिक धर्मशास्त्रीय मान्यताओं के सर्वथा अनुकूल है। इसीलिए आचार्य रामचन्द्र शुक्ल ने लिखा है कि गोस्वामी जी का समाज का आदर्श वही है जिसका निरूपण वेद, पुराण, स्मृति आदि में है अर्थात् वर्णाश्रम की पूर्ण प्रतिष्ठा।

सर्वप्रथम हम तुलसी की धर्मदृष्टि को लेते हैं। उनकी धर्मदृष्टि श्रद्धालु और धर्मप्राण व्यक्तियों के लिए है–

यह न कहश्र सठहो हठसोलहि।
जो मन लाइ न सुन हरि लोलहिं।।

उनको धर्मदृष्टि का उद्देश्य समय जीवन है। उसकी चरम परिणति के दो केन्द्र बिन्दु है

–प्रथम मानवता–

परहित सरिस धरम नहिं भाई
परपीड़ा राम नहिं अधमाई

और द्वितीय अद्वैत दृष्टि–

सियाराममय सब जग जानी।
करेउ प्रणाम जोरि पानी।।

हिन्दू धर्मशास्त्रों तथा बौद्ध धर्मग्रन्थों के समान उन्होंने साहित्यिक शैली का प्रयोग किया है। वह देववाणी संस्कृत को छोड़कर प्राकृतवाणी 'भाषा' में, जो लोकभाषा है अपना महान् ग्रन्थ लिखते हैं। उन्हें विद्वानों का धर्मशास्त्र नहीं लिखना था। इसलिए लोग 'मानस' को ही धर्मशास्त्र का पर्याय तथा प्रतिनिधि मानने लगे।

तुलसी के प्रसंग में जब हम धर्म की बात करते है तो स्वाभाविक रूपेण अधर्म का भी प्रसंग उत्पन्न होता है। वह राम विमुखता को अधर्म मानते हैं। उनके चरित्र चित्रण कला का आधार ही यह है कि रामभक्ति से विपरीत पात्र उनकी दृष्टि में तमोगुणी व निकृष्ट है यथा रावण, शूर्पणखा, मन्थरा आदि। तुलसी का समूचा साहित्य भक्तिवाद का पूर्ण उन्मेष हैं वे भक्ति को ही जीवन का वास्तविक धर्म मानते हैं। भक्ति ही उनका सबसे बड़ा धर्मशास्त्र है। नारद भक्ति सूत्र से शक्ति के एकादश भेद निरूपित किये गए हैं– गुणमाहात्म्या, रूपाशक्ति, पूजाशक्ति, स्मरणशक्ति, दास्यशक्ति, संख्याशक्ति, कांताशक्ति, वात्सल्याशक्ति, आत्मनिवेदनाशक्ति, तन्मयाशक्ति तथा परमाविरहाशक्ति के अतिरिक्त सबको मान्यता दी है। उनके साहित्य में पूजा शक्ति एवं स्मरणशक्ति अत्यल्प है। अरण्यकाण्ड में राम ने शबरी से नैवेद्य भक्ति का वर्णन अधोलिखित रूप में किया है–

प्रथम भगति सन्तन्ह कर संगा।
दूसरी रति मन कथा प्रसंगा
गुरूपद पंकज सेबा, तीसरि भगति अमान।
चौथि भगति में गुणगन, करई कपट तजि जान।।
मंत्र जाप मम दृढ़ विश्वासा
पंचम भजन सो वेद प्रकासा।।
छठ दम शील विराति।।
निरत निरन्तर सज्जन धरमा।।
सातवां सम मोहि मय जग देखा।
अष्टम मोहे अधिक संत कर लेषा।
सपनेहुं नहि देखई पर दोषा।।
नवम सरल सब ही छल हीना।
मम भरीस हिय हरष न दीना।।
नवमहुं एकउ जिन्हके होई।
नारि पुरूष सचराचर कोई।
सोई अतिशयप्रिय भामिनी मोरे।
सकल प्रकार भगति दृढ़ तारें[5]

तुलसी उत्तरकाण्ड के पुरगीता के संदर्भ में भक्ति के निम्न लक्षणों का प्रतिपादन करते हैं–

बैर न विग्रह आस न त्रासा।
सुखमय ताहि सदा सब आशा।।
अनारम्भ अनिकेत अमानी।
अनव अरीष दच्छ विज्ञानी।।
प्रीत सदा सज्ज संसर्गा।
तृन सम विषय स्वगौ उपवर्गा।
भगति पच्छ दृढ़ नहिं सठताई ।
दुष्ट तर्क सब पूति बहई।।
मन गुन ग्राम नम रत, गत ममता मदमीह।
ताकर सुख सोई जानई, परानन्द सन्दोह।[6]

तुलसी ने अपने धर्मशास्त्र को तीन ग्रन्थों का स्वरूप प्रदान किया है–

(क) रामचरित मानस (ख) विनय पत्रिका (ग) वैराग्य–संदीपिनी। दर्शन में रामानुजाचार्य और धर्म के क्षेत्र ने तुलसी प्रायः समान हैं। 'मानस' विभिन्न धार्मिक मत–मतान्तरों को एक केन्द्र पर संस्थित कर दिया गया है।

'मानस' मूलतः भक्ति महाकाव्य है। उनके प्रायः सभी पात्र बाहर या अन्दर से राम भक्तिमय है। बालकाण्ड में सतरूपा मं तपश्चर्या के पश्चात प्रभू के समक्ष इच्छा व्यक्त की है–

सोइ सुख सोइ गति भगति, सोइ
निज चरन सनेहु,
सोइ विबेक सोइ रहनि प्रभु
हमहि कृपा कर देहु

तुलसी स्वयं श्रीराम तथा अन्य देवताओं से भक्ति की याचना करते हैं। 'मानस' में ऋषि मुनि, देवता, धर्मग्रन्थ और पात्र राम से भक्ति का ही वरदान मांगते हैं। उत्तर काण्ड में वेद की यह स्थिति है–

करूणायतन प्रभु सद्‌गुनाकार
देव यह वर मांगहीं
मन वचन कर्म विकार तजि।
तब चरन अनुरागहिं।।[7]
'मानस' का फलागण भी राम भक्ति ही है। मंदोदरी भी कहती हैं–
नाथ भजहु रघुनाथहिं अचल होइ अहिवास।।[8]
तुलसी की दास भक्ति है–
सेवक सेव्य भाव बिनु
भव न तरिअ उरगारि।
भजहु राम पद सकज।
उस सिद्धांर विचारि।।
तुलसी को शान का मार्ग का स्वीकार नहीं–
शानपथ कृपान कै धरा।
परत खगेश होइ नहि बारा।
जो निविघ्न प्य विर्वहई।
सी कैवल्य परम पद लहई।
अति दुर्लभ कक्वल्य परम पद
संत पुरान निगम आगम वदे।
अनइच्छित आवे बरिआई।

तुलसी का धर्मशास्त्र समन्वयवादी है उन्होंने शैव, शाक्त, पुष्टिमार्गी, रामभक्त, बिन्दु माधव आदि को समन्वित करने का ऐतिहासिक प्रयास किया। समूचे 'मानस' में शिव को प्रमुखता मिली है। रामकथा के प्रथम उद्‌गाता भी स्वयं शिव हैं। तुलसी ने 'पार्वती मंगल' भी लिखा।
तुलसी–मानस में शक्ति की प्रार्थना के लिए प्रावधान करते हैं–
नहि तब आदि मध्य अवसाना।
अमित प्रभाव वेद नहिं जाना।
भवमय विभव पराभव कारिनि।
विस्व विमाहिनि स्वबस विहारिनि।

तुलसी ने पुष्टि मार्ग के समन्वय प्रसंग में 'कृष्णा गीतावली' की रचना की। बाल–इष्टदेव–उपासना का प्रसंग भी उल्लेखनीय है–
जब जब राम मनुज तन धरहीं।
भगत हेतु लीला बहु करहीं।
तब तब अवधपुरी मैं जाऊं।
बालचरित विलोकि हरषाऊ।
जन्म महोत्सव देखउ जाई।
इष्टदेव मम बालक रामा।
सोभा बपुष कोरि सतकामा।
तुलसी निर्गुण ब्रह्म, सगुण ब्रह्म तथा दशरथ पुत्र राम में एकात्मकता स्थापित करते हैं–
(क) तन बिनु परस नयन बिनु देखा।
ग्रहइ घ्रान बिनु बास असेसा।।
असि सब भांति अलौकिक करनी।
महिमा जासु जाय नहीं बरनी।।
जेहि इमि मावहिं बुध,
जाहिं धरहिं मुनि व्यान।
जाहिं दशरथ सुत भगत हित,
कोसलपति भगवान।।

(क) अगुन अरूप अलाव अज जोई।
भगत प्रेम बह सगुन सो होई।
जो गुन रहित सगुन सोइ कैसे।
ज्लु हिम–उपल विलग नहिं जैसे।

कतिपय विद्वानों का अभिमत है कि तुलसी ने विविध दर्शन धाराओं का भी सामंजस्य किया है श्री रामदास गौड़ (रामचरितमानस की भूमिका)[9] और पण्डित रामनरेश त्रिपाठी (रामायण–टीका की भूमिका) का कथन है कि तुलसी ने दायर्शनिक भावों की अवधारणा के लिए ही रामचरितमानस के चार घाट की कल्पना की है। प्रत्येक घाट पर वक्ताओं द्वारा एक विशेष दर्शन सन्प्रदाय के मत का प्रतिपादन किया गया है।[10]

श्री रामानुजाचार्य, शंकर के अद्वैतवाद का विरोध करके अपने विशिष्टाद्वैतावाद का सूत्रपात करते है। मध्वाचार्य ने द्वैतवाद का प्रचार किया और निम्बार्काचार्य ने द्वैताद्वेतवाद का प्रचलन किया था।

तुलसी अपने धर्मशास्त्र में अद्वैतवाद तथा विशिष्टाद्वैत का समन्वय करते है। रामानुजाचार्य के अनुसार जीव को ईश्वर का अंश मान कर मिथ्या बताते है।

ईश्वर अंस जीव अविनासी।
चेतन अगल सहज सुख रासी।
सो माया बस भएउ गोसाई।
बध्यो की मर्कट की नाई।

वे शंकराचार्य की भांति जीव को बह्मस्वरूप तथा जगत् को ईश्वर बताते हैं–

सोइ जानइ जेहिं देहु जनाई।
जानत तुम्हहि तुम्हहि होई जाई।
जनमु मरनु जह लगि जगलालू।
धरनि धासु धानू पुर परिवारू।
सरगु नरकु जहं लगि व्यवहारू।
देखिय सुनिअ गुनिअ मनमाहीं।
मोहमूल परमारथ नाहीं।

तुलसी का धर्मशास्त्र सरलता, सुगमता तथा संर्वगम्तया के तत्वों का संग्रही हैं। उन्होने श्री राम को पहले प्रतिष्ठित किया और बाद में धर्मशास्त्र को बनाया। उनके मतासुनार नियम, सिद्धांत तथा शास्त्र व्यक्ति या मानव के लिए होते है। मानव उनके लिए नहीं होता। वह अभिनव तथा लोककल्याणकारी धर्मशास्त्र रचयिता थे। उनका प्रदेय अप्रतिम है।

पाद–टिप्पणी

1. रामचरितमानस–पृष्ठ 111
2. हिन्दी भाषा सम्मेलन अध्यक्षीय भाषण
3. तुलसी नवः मूल्यांकन–डा0 रामरत्न भटनागर पृष्ठ 69–77
4. साहित्य चेतना – डा0 विद्यानिवास मिश्रा पृष्ठ 87–89
5. कही– अरण्य काण्ड पृष्ठ 98–99
6. कहीं–उत्तर काण्ड पृष्ठ 100–102
7. कही–बालकाण्ड पृष्ठ 60–61
8. कही– लंका काण्ड पृष्ठ 330
9. रामचरितमानस की भूमिका – श्री रामदास गौड़ पृष्ठ 113/114
10. रामायण टीका भूमिका– पंडित रामनरेश त्रिपाठी पृष्ठ 100–102

सन्दर्भ ग्रन्थ सूची

1. राम चरित मानस, गीता प्रेस गोरखपुर
2. साहित्य की चेतना, डा0 विद्यानिवास मिश्र
3. तुलसीः नवः मूल्यांकन, डा0 रामरत्न भटनागर
4. हिन्दी भाषा सम्मेलन, कवि मैथिलीशरण गुप्त प्रयाग (1950) (अध्यक्षीय भाषण)
5. रामचरितमानस की भूमिका, श्री रामदास गौड़
6. रामायण टीका की भूमिका, पंडित रामनरेश त्रिपाठी

48

ATHENA PALLAS: THE GREEK GODDESS

Rekha Chaturvedi

Athena is the name of an important goddess of the Greeks, whose character is without a Flaw. Originally as it would seem is a conscious impersonation of the divine wisdom and therefore fable to have sprung, fully grown from the head of Zeus. She became a distinct and sustentative deity at a very early date and was recognized as the goddess of wisdom, war, polity and industrial art.[1]

Homer places her together with zeus and Apollo on a higher platform of divinity than the other deities,[2] and makes her even oppose Zeus. When he is wrong, thwart him and vindicate right and truth in his character.[3] It has been said for her that she is without feminine weaknesses, the type of composed, majestic and unrelenting force.[4] This is so far true that she has certainly little softness, absolutely no weakness, and not many distinctly faminine characterstics.[5] But at times she was also recognized like her Egyptian counterpart Neith, as the goddess of Good housewifery, patronising handicraft and expert at weaving with the loom and Spindle,[6] no less than as the wise directress of wisemen and warriors.

Athena's Connection with Great Mother Cult

Zeus, the father of Athena had dual character. On one hand he is the male god of vegetation and fertility, subordinate to Mother Goddess in the Minoan Mycenian Cult, on the other hand in his purely Hellenised form he was the sky father and the head of the patriarrchal pantheon. The legends of his union with the Earth and corn goddess like Hera, Dione, Demeter and Semele, etc. are Indicative of his pre- Hellenic Characterstics. It seems as Hera is originally concerned mainly- with birth, marriage, menstural cycle and maternity. The secret rites connected with her cult reveal her origin in hoary antiquity.[7] In the Mycenean age the Minoan civilization was dominant in Greece at that time the cult of the Goddess was firmly established in many parts of the land. The Great mother goddes took the form of Rhea, the mother of Zeus. Poseidon and other deities. She became Hera the goddess of Argos, Athena in Attica, Artemis in Arcadia and at Corinth under formative Influence she became Aphrodite.[8]

The goddess Athena was also of a Certain origin, the survivor of the Minoan- Mycenean household goddess bearing a shield, the protectress of Cities. Eventually she acquired a military character but she never abandoned her earliest female attributes and functions.[9]

J.J. Bachofen[10] advocated that Athena was originally a maternal figure stable in her security and poise but was caught up and perverted by a patriarchal society, that especially dwelt in Athens. The goddess was adapted but could very easily be seen as a God.

Legends of her origin

Athena is said to be the offspring of Zeus alone. Though we find the story of her birth in several versions. One most commonly cited is that Zeus had a lust towards Metis the titaness who turned into many forms untill she was caught at last. Zeus lay with Metis, the goddess of crafty thought and wisdom and she got pregnant with a child. An Oracle of Mother Earth then declared that this would be a girl child and if Metis conceived again, she would bear a son who was fated to depose Zeus. Just as Zeus had deposed Kronos and Kronos had deposed Ouranos.[11] But immediately zeus feared the consequences. It had been prophesied that Metis would bear children more powerful than the Sire, even Zeus himself.[12] In order to forestall these dire consequences having coaxed Metis to a couch with honey quoted words, put her away inside his own belly, he swallowed her down all of a sudden[13], that was the end of Metis. Though Zeus claimed that she gave him counsel from inside his belly, but zeus was too late as Metiz had already conceived. By swallowing the oceanid and her unborn child Zeus became pregnant with Athena. Zeus was not built to deliver a baby, though he seems to have gastated the baby in his head.

There was still one more problem to contend with, lack of an opening that would serve for birth Canal. In due process of time he was seized by a raging headache as he walked by the shores of lake Triton, his skull seemed about to burst and he howled for rage untill the whole fermament echoed. The new goddess needed to be born. She was pressing from the inside of his head outwardly with increasingly excruciating insistence. Prometheus, Hephaestus Hermes and Ares or Palaemon cleaved Zeus's head with the double headed Minoan axe. Hermes sent Hephoustus to fetch his wedge and beetle and they make a breach in Zeus's skull from which Athena sprang fully armed with a mighty shout.[14] She was full grown, in with a full set of armour.[15] Due to the manner of her birth she has dominion over all things of intellect. She pealed to the broad sky her clarion cry of war.[16] Thus Athena was the daughter of Zeus not from inter course but when the god had in mind the making of a world (logos) his first thought was Athena.[17] Here we are reminded of Vedic goddess 'Vak' (logos) as she is called in the Brahman books, later merged in the persona of Sarasvati. In Cratylus (40B) Plato gave the etymology of Athena's name as signifying the mind of god.

Thus Pallas Athena, the glorious goddess, bright eyed, inventive, unbending of heart, pure virgin, saviour of cities, courageous, tritogeneid, from his awful head, wise zeus himself bear her arrayed in warlike arms of flashing gold, awe seized, all the Gods as they gazed at her, but Athena sprang quickly from the immortal head and stood before Zeus who hold the aegis shaking the sharp 'spear', great Olympus began to reel horribly at the might of bright eyed goddess and earth round about cried fearfully, and the sea was moved and tossed with dalk waves, while foam burst forth suddenly. The bright son of Hyperion stopped his swift footed horses a long while, untill the maiden Pallas Athene had stripped the heavenly armour, from her immortal shoulders and wise Zeus was glad.[18]

Athena was the favourite daughter of Zeus[19] though he had a number of other offsprings namely- Artemis, Aphrodite, The Muses, The Graces, Ares, Apollo, Dionysus, Hebe, Hermes, Heracles, Helen of Troy, Hephoestus, Minos, Perseus and Porus.

Attributes

Athena is very popular in Greek mythology as she is called Athena, Athene, Athenaia, Athenaic and Pallas, the goddess of wisdom, courage, inspiration, civilization, law and justice, just warfare, divine Intelligence, skilled in arts and crafts, mathematics, metal work, strength strategy. She possessed the disciplined strategic side of war, in contras to her brother Ares, the patron of violence, blood, lust and slaughter.[20] Athena disliked the fighting without purpose and preferred to use wisdom to settle predicaments.[21] Athena's wisdom includes the cunning intelligence of Metis.[22] As the patron goddess of Athens[23], her Roman counterpart was Minerva[24]. Some Greek scholars have derived natural symbols from the etymological roots of Athena's names to be acther, air, earth and moon.[25]

Epithets : Athena's epithets include- Atrytone (the unwearing), Parthenos (Virgin), Promachus (the first fighter or one who fights in the front) Glaukopis (bright eyed or gleaming eyes).[26] Glaukos has the root glaux (owl) presumably because of the birds own distinctive eyes. The owl sees well in the night, is closely associated with the goddess of wisdom. Now the owl is known as Athenian mascot and like olive tree a sacred symbol. Aethyia also signifies for here as diver and relates her with art of ship building and navigation but I think word diver her means one who helps in crossing the worldly river Tritogenia (Triton born) as well as Tritonia meaning tripple born from Metis, Metis and Zeus and only from Zeus, Hippea (horse) or the inventor of chariot.

Athena exercised an elevating experience on the nobler spirits of both sexes, as combining the three attributes of purity, strength and wisdom in the highest possible degree, and so furnishing at once a model for imitation and support and stay for feeble souls.

Guardian of Artists

In Greek mythology she is depicted as the guardian of artists and craftsmen, specially of weaving and she taught and defeated Archne in this craft. She was the patron of metal work also and as Athena Ergane she was honoured at festivals such as chalceia and also as the personification of wisdom. Her title Pallas is indicative of sexual rites connected with the primitive form of worship. Her association with craftsmanship was derived from the domestic Minoan prototype as a goddess of household. Indian goddes Vak or Sarasvati is also associated inseparaply with learning untill she actually became the goddess of learning in the Puranic age. Bharati is her another name a patronyme of Bharat (India), like Athena of Athens Though a virgin she is venerated as mother goddess. Besides learning she is the patron of fine arts such as music, poetry, dance, drama etc. She herself plays Veena and holds the manyscript and sings the 'Samageet', the songs of Sammaveda. She sists on the lotus which is a symbol of immortality, purity freshness and non- attachment to worldly gains.

The War Goddess

Athena was a tutelary goddess who subsequently raised to the dignity of the republican state, the important Attic city being named after her, so her more warlike characteristics became dominant Being patroness of the city taking the place of the king she involved in its wars and acquired a military character untill eventually she was a mighty and furious war goddess fighting all and sundry[27]. She led battles (Athena Promochos) or warrior maiden as Athena Parthenos.[28] Her symbols are a thunderbolt, shield, spear, helmet, gorgoneion, aromors, owls, olive trees, snakes, aegis etc.

According to one legend the semen of the god Hephaustus fell on a foot of the goddess Athena in his attempt to rape her. She wiped of the Semen with a handful of wool, which she threw away and it fell on the ground and mother earth impregnated by it, resulting the birth of Eriehthonius who became the king of Athens and Athena as a foster mother brought him up and counselled him time to time.[29] In Indian mythology it is mentioned in the Devi Bhagvata Purana that a Asur named Rakta Beeja whose each drop of blood fell on earth impragnated her and she produced number of Asuras[30]. Similarly in Greek legends Athena's fore father Kronos who mutilated his father Ouranos, the blood dropped from heaven impnagnated earth who in due time delivered giants.[31]

Athena is the shrewd companion of heroes and is goddess of heroic endeavour. She is the helper of many heroes including Odysseus, Jason and Heraclese. She is dubbed as the goddess of nearness due to her mentoring and motherly probing.[32]

The Virgin Goddess

It is said for Athena that she never consorts with a lover, nor does she ever marry. This is known as Athena Parthenos which stands for virgin Athena. It is not merely the observation of virginity but a recognition of her role as enforcer of rules of sexual modesty and ritual mystery even beyond recognition. The Athenians allotted the goddess a value based pureness of virginity as it would upheld a rudiment of female behaviour in the patriarchal society. Athena accredits her verginal toponyme to be a result of the relationship to her father zeus and a vital cohesive piece of her character throughout the ages.[33]

Here we can compare Athena with Indian goddes Sarasvati. Sarasvati is also called the manas-kanya (born of thought) of Brahma, as Athena was born of Zeu's head. In Indian mythology Brahma committed incest with his-daughter Sarasvati and in Greek mythology Hephaustus attempted a rape on Athena which failed, but in both the mythologies they are mostly conceived of as a virgin. Sarasvati is an external projection of prima dia. In mythological language Sarasvati is the daughter of Durga and is the Kumari (virgin) aspect of Durga herself.[34] The Virgin goddess has many parallels. Athena was worshipped at the temple of 'Parthenon' and the word emphasises her virginity. The virgin goddesses mother while in many myths remained virgin. As in India Durga is called Kumari or Kanya Kumari (Virgin damsel) and worshipped on the ninth day of 'Navaratra' Called 'Kumari Puja'. She is invoked as Brahmachariani (Observing Celibacy)[35]. One more thing is also common in both the goddesses that Athena's father lived on Olympus while Durga's husband lived on Kailash, the Himalayan mountant. The fact contributes their association with mountains. The sacred mountains are the centre of the earth and the source of its life giving energies as Sarasvati has association with water the prima-element.

Potniya or the Mistress of Athens

Once Athena Competed with Poseidon to be the patron deity of the City which was yet unnamed. They agreed that each would give the citizens one gift and they would choose the gift they preferred. Poseidon struck the ground with his trident and a salt water spring sprang up. This could give them a means of trade and water but the water was salty and useless for drinking.[36] Athena offered them the first domesticated olive tree. The king Cerocrops and the citizens accepted the olive tree and the patronage of Athena. The olive tree brought wood, oil and food. Robert Graves believes that the myth reflects the conflict between matriarchal and patriarchal religions.[37]

Potniya is a cognate of Vedic term Patni or Avestan Pathini with its Indo-European cognates means the female ruler, owner in her own right or a property holder, ruler of men or the queen of the community, the patron and protector, be it male or female, all are under her domain. In Greek language Potnia is near to Posnia- means (पालयित्री), one who brings up, cares, feeds and protects. Potniya is a king or rular, to cite a few example despotnia (queen).

Apion writes in his book Grammatius that 'Potnia' is Thepon- the queen of beasts in the company of Artemis, etc. contras with Alxos, i.e. wife, literally means a bed fellow. Alxos does not inherit property because her position is only of a bed sharer while as Potnia, she is the rightful owner of his household property,[38] just as Indian Patni or Jaya, the biggeter of children.

The epithet simply signifies woman's position of ownership and dominance. Anthropologists view that there was matriarchy and mat-riliny in the early society but which gradually subverted to patriarchy and patriliny.

We also find her epithet, Athena diwya or diwia means 'divya' or divine as well as A-ta-nu-dju-wa-ja or Myceanian di-u-ja or di-wi-ja. According to Vertis and Chadwick it stands for her dual forms (i) Weaver and deity of craft and (ii) Athena's mind (nous) and intelligence (dianoba) but I think it stands for 'dwij' or 'twice born' one birth from Metis and the other from Zeus.

City Protectress

The Athenians founded the Parthenon on the Acropolis of her names sake city Athens in her honour. Athena's Veneration as the patron of Athens seems to have existed from the earliest times and was so persistent that archaic mythic about her were recast to adapt to cultural changes. As a protector of city (Polis) the people through out the Greek world worshipped Athena as Athena Polias. The city of Athens and goddess Athena essentially bear the same name.[39] She is considered as protectress of other cities like Argos, Sparta, Cortyn, Lindos and Larisa. Sparta where the cult of Athena Alea had its sanctuaries in Mantineia and Tegea which was an important religious center of ancient Greece containg the temple of Athena Alea. Athena Khalkioikos (of Brazen House) often latinized on the Spartan acropolis, bronze roofed where the most solemn religious activities in Sparta took place.

The ancient Greeks believed that Athena had visited many mythological places such as Libya's Triton River in North Africa and Phlegraen Plains[40]. Scholars like Martin Bernal Created the Controversial Black Athena theory[41] to explain that the conception of Neith was brought to Greece from Egypt along with an enormous number of features of civilization and culture in the third and second millennia.[42]

The Parthenon at Athens marked the zenith of Greek Doric architecture. The frieze of the temple was covered with figures designed by the Greek sculptor, Phidias containing one pediment showed the birth of Athena from the brow of Zeus in the other portryaed the strife between Athena and Poseidon for the control of Attica. Originally a statue of Athena, 42 feet high occupied the interior which contributes the rare beauty of Parthenon.[43]

Athena Pallas is shown mostly on the coins of the Greek and Sythic kings of Bactria and India.[44] On the reverse of the coins Pallas is shown standing, holding spear or a shield in her hands. On the shield the face of the Gorgan is found. She is the goddess of light, warmth and dew and a goddess of vegetation and fertility.

She is shown on the coins of Parthian king Andragoras, Apollodotus II, Menander, Dionysius, Zoilus, Apollophanes, Amyntas, Ranjabala, Azes, Azilises, Spalhores with Vinones, Spalagadames, Gondophares and Demitrious II.

On some coins Pallas is shown standing, Clad in Chiton and peplos with a shield adorned with Gorgon's head behind her spear or in the left hand holding aegis and in the right hurling thunderbolt or standing Pallas with right hand advanced holding spear and shield in the left hand or her granuel flying her right hand extended before her altar, or crowning herself, or wearing helmet and holding wreath in the right hand and in the left hand holding spear and shield bound with fillet sword slung round waist or fighting holding thunderbolt and shield.

It is a firm belief of the Greeks that Athena was the true mentor acted as a strong reinforcement to the power of conscience which the young Greek felt might be the voice of Athena speaking within him, advising him for path of honour and duty. Athena's special connection with Athens and Attica added much to her importance in the Greek religious system, since it brought the best minds and most generous natures of Hellas peculiarly under the Influence of a thoroughly high and noble religious conception.[45]

Reference

1. Homer and the Homeric Age, Vol. II, p. 47.
2. Homer, 'Iliad', II, 1.371; IV, 288,VII,132, etc. 'Odyss', IV.341; XVII, 132 etc.
3. 'Iliad' VIII, 132 etc.
4. Grote, History of Greece, Vol. 1, p. 47.
5. Rowlinson, G., The Religions of the Ancient World, Award Publishing House, New Delhi, 1980. p. 221.
6. History of Greece, Vol. 1, p. 47.
7. Farnell, L.R., Cults of the Greek States, Edinburgh, 1909, I. p. 179.
8. Farnell, Greek Religion, II, 9-11 See, Hastings, J. Encyclopaedia of Religions and Ethics, VII, 396, High Aspects of Greek Religion, New York, 1912, p. 8FF. Nilsson, History of Greek Religion, Oxferd, 1925, Chapter 1, III, IV.
9. Nilsson, M.P. Minoan- Mycenean Religion, Oxford, 1950, p. 487.
10. J.J. Bachofen, "Mother Right : An investigation of religious and juridicial character of matriarchy in the ancient world", Myth, Religion and Mother Right. London : Routledge and Kegan Paul, 1967.
11. Arora Udai Prakash, Motifs in Indian Mythology : Their Greek and other Parallels, Indira Publishing House, New Delhi, 1981, p. 78.
12. Compare the prophecy concerning Thetis.
13. Hesiod, Theogony 890ff and 924ff.
14. Apollodorus : III, 4.3; Hesiod. Theogory, 866-900. Pindar : Olumpion Odes, VII.34; Jane Ellen Harrison's famous characterisation of this myth element as, "a desperate theological expedient to rid an earth-born Kore of her matriarchal conditions" has never been refuted (Harrison 1922 : 302).
15. Apollodorus, L,III.6, Hesiod. Theogony, 886-900.
16. Pindar, Seventh Olympion, Ode.

17. Justin, Apology 64.5 quoted in Robert McQueen. Grant, Gods and the One God, vol. 1 : 155, who observes that it is Porphyry "who similarly identifies Athena with "forethought".
18. Homeric Hymn to Pallas Athena by Evelyn White, is in, Public domain, XXIII, to Athena (18 Lines) 'About. Com Ancient/ Classical History.
19. According to Hesiod's Theogony, Metis was Athena's mother, but, according to Homer's Iliad, after Zeus swallowed Metis because she was pregnant with Athene (to prevent the birth), Athene sprang forth from the head of Zeus nonetheless and later it was declared that she "had no mother".
20. Darmon. "Athena and Ares". Chicago and London : University of Chicago Press, 1978.
21. Loewen, Nancy. Athena. ISBN 9-7368-0048-4.
22. Goldhill, S. Reading Greek Tragedy (Aesch. Eum. 737). Cambridge : Cambridge University Press, 1986.
23. "Athena". Myths Encyclopedia. Archived from the original on 4 January, 2010. Retrieved 2009-11-24.
24. Johrens, Athenahymnus, 438-453.
25. George Liddell, Henny, Robert Scott, 1940, A Greek-English Lexicon, ISBN 0-19-864226-1, online version at the Perseus Project.
26. Rowlinson, G., op.cit.; p. 222.
27. O'Malley, Bengal District, Gazetteer, Khulna, Calcutta, 1903, p. 61. See, Bhattacharyya, N.N., The Indian Mother Goddess, Delhi, 1977, p. 57-58.
28. Herrington, C.J., Athena parthenos and Athena Polias. Manchester : Manchester University Press, 1955.
29. Apollodorus III, 14.6; See, Arora, U.P. Op.cit. p. 56.
30. Devi Bhagvata Purana, 63.
31. Hesiod. Theogony, 183.
32. Otto, W.E., Die Gotter Griechenlands (55-77). Bonn : F. Cohen, 1929.
33. Kerenyi, K., Die Jungfrau und Mutter der griechischen Religion. Eine Studie uber Pallas Athene. Zurich. Rhein Verlag, 1952.
34. Bhattacharji, Sukumari, The Indian Theogony : A Comparative Study of Indian Mythology from the Vedas to the Puranas, Cambridge University Press, 1970, p. 164.
35. Mahabharata, IV,6;VI.23,3-16 and Markandey Purana- Durga Sapta Shati.
36. Graves, 1960:16.3 p. 62.
37. This sanctuary had been respected from early days by all the Peloponnesians, and afforded peculiar safety to its suppliants" (Pausanias, Description of Greece, iii.5.6).
38. Chaturvedi, Rekha, Reading in Indian History, Delhi, 2003, "Panchali a classical Myth', p. 45-46.
39. Burkert, 1985, 139.
40. Aeschylus Eumenides, 292-293. Cf. the tradition that she was the daughter of Neilos : see, e.g. Clement of Alexandria Protr. 2.28.2; Cicero, De Natura Deorum. 3.59.
41. Mary R. Lefkowitz, Black Athena Revisited, The University of Noth Carolina Press, 1996, on Google books; Jacques Berlinerblau, Heresy in the University : The Black Athena Controversy and the Responsibilities of American Intellectuals, Rutgers University Press, 1999, on Google Books; M. Bernal, Black Athena : The Afroasiatic Roots of Classical Civilization (New Brunswick : Rutgers University Press, 1987), 21, 51-53.
42. Walter Burkert, Greek Religion, 1985 : VII "Philosophical Religion" treats these transformations.
43. Swain, James Edgar, A History of World Civilization, New Delhi, 1984, p. 135-136.
44. Gardener, Percy; The Coins of the Greek and Sythic king of Bactria and India, Sagar Publications, New Delhi, 1971.
45. Rowlinson, G., Op.cit. p. 222.

49

DEEPAAWALI : CELEBRATIONS AND A MESSAGE

R.C. Tripathi

India has a host of festivals all along the year. These relate deeply to Indian life and culture and underline Indian vision of celestial and terrestrial unity in diversity. The Indian calendar, in fact, is based on the movement of the heavenly bodies, the Sun, the moon and the earth's rotation and revolution, including the ecliptic and the zodiac, and thereby correcting the lunar synodic year of around 354 days by providing an intercalary month, called the adhik or purushottam or mal-maas, an extra- month, once in thirty-two solar months of the Indian calendar, during the month having no solar ingress or transit from one zodiac sign to the next one. We are also aware that Sun transits almost one zodiac sign of thirty degrees every month and the transit day or the tithi, is known as Sankranti. Every sankranti is an occasion for prayers, worship and celebrations. The mesha (or vaishakhi) and the makar (lohari) sankratis are quite well-known. The Pongal and Onam are also sun-relared and sankranti-based. There is a month-long congregation every year on makar sakranti during the Magha mela (January-February) at Allahabad. For the Kumbha or the Ardha-Kumbha mela, Jupiter's motion is also taken into consideration in addition to those of the sun and the moon. The Onam and the Pongal are also the sun-based sankranti festivals.

All the twelve sankrantis are related to the sun's transit from one zodiac sign to the next zodiac sign. However, most of the Indian festivals are based on tithis or the lunar movement. Every twelve-degree separation or distance from the sun of the moon counts in the Indian calendar as a 'tithi', beginning with the bright- phase of the moon, the shukla paksha-the purnima falling at 180 degrees, opposite to the sun and making a conjunction with the sun on the amavasya, the fifteenth day of the dark-phase, the krishna Paksha, completing its orbit of 360 degrees around the earth.

A day in the traditional Indain calender is counted from sunrise-to-the-next-sunrise, unlike the western calculations where the day begins at the mid-night meridian. The tithi at the sunrise holds good for the whole day. That is why tithis sometimes end before the sun-rise leading to its kshaya (loss) or extend beyond the next sunrise leading to gain (vridhhi) of a tithi. This phenomenon very often causes confusion in the mind of a common man since the moon-based festivals follow the tithi concerned and commonly worship takes place in the evenings or night, signifying lunar presence. Some important moon-based festivals are the Chaitra (spring) Navaratri and the Shardiya (autumn) Navaratri , the Ramnavami, the Krishnajanmashtmi, the Rakshabandhan, the Dashehra, the Deepaawali , the Ganesha Chaturthi, Vasant Panchmi, Mahashivaratri , the Holi, only to name a few of them.

We concern here ourselves with the Deepawali festival, an Indian festival, popularly known as 'Diwali', the 'Festival of Lights'. Literally, Deepaawali is combination of two words: deepa (meaning lamp/light) + awali (meaning a row or string) and, thus, the word Deepaawali-(Row of lights) gets formed. The festival is associated mainly with the worship of Lord Ganesh, the god of wisdom and goddess Lakshmi, the goddess of wealth and prosperity. In eastern India, the Festival is called "Kali Puja", worship of the Goddess Kali, as distinct from the Navaratra 'Durga-Puja' preceding the Vijaya Dashami/Dushehra).

Deepawali is associated with the victorious return of Lord Rama after defeating the demon King Ravana of Lanka to Ayodhya, the capital of his kingdom, Koshala, and, therefore, a joyous occasion of celebrations and merry-making by the people of the capital city and entire Kingdom. The festival is also associated with the Nirvana of the Jaina thirankar, Sri Mahavira, commemorating his nirvana or emancipation and, thus, an auspicious occasion to remember the Great Liberator, his message of ahimsa (non-violence) and celebrate the great event by elaborate ceremonies, rituals and illumination.

The Deepawali follows the autumn Navarartra- Durga- puja and Dashehera by about three weeks. The period coincides with the end of the monsoon season and is associated with maturing of the kharif, the monsoon crops and reaping their harvest. There are also beginnings of the change of weather. With the harvesting of the kharif (monsoon) crops, preparations for the rabi, the winter crops get into full swing to the keep pace of sowing etc. of crops with the changing weather. These activities are essential for any society and more so in agrarian societies like ours in India for sustenance, trade and commerce.

India is a tropical country and the monsoons in a tropical country are accompanied with growth of wild vegetation, insects and mosquitoes. Since time immemorial, festivals in India have been associated with drives of cleansing and white-washing of houses, cattle-sheds and work places to rid off dirt and filth from places of use and living. There is a strong belief that goddess Lakshmi would not make a filthy place or house her abode; and so if houses are unclean and untidy, there would be dim chance of Lakshmi, the goddess of wealth and prosperity favoring it as making that her abode. There are many myths and apocryphal stories forming part of the Deepawali worship and narrations during the Deepawali-puja, eulogizing how the poor and the wise became rich by keeping their house neat and tidy and well illuminated on the pitch-dark night of the Deepawali, so as to attract attention of the goddess Lakshmi to their modest but tidy and well- lighted dwelling. How deeply and sincerely we desire that such drives become normal and routine, every-day conduct of our country-men and not confined merely to festive occasions like that of Deepawali, serving useful preventive health care measures to fight disease and ill-health!

Deepawali is not a one or two-day festival. It is a full five-day long festival, each day having specific worship and rituals. For this reason, it is also called "Pancha-raatra" mahotsava or celebrations. Deepawali Festival commences from the thirteenth day of the Dark-Moon of the Kaartik month (October-November) of the Indian Lunar calendar, the Vikram Samvat and lasts up to the second-day of the Bright Moon fortnight of the Kaartik month. The main day of Deepaawali falls on the amavasya, the fifteenth darkest moon night, with complete conjunction of sun and the moon. Thus, celebrations are spread over five days and each of the five days has traditional / Puranic stories linked to its significance. The religious celebrations traditionally are spread throughout the five days. Friends and relations visit each other freely all these days, exchanging sweets, gifts and presents and youngsters pay respect to elders/relations. However, the practice, particularly in urban areas, is now getting restricted to less number of days.
The five days of this festival are known as the following:

1) The Dhanvantari Trayodashi or dhanteras;
2) The Naraka chaturdashi or Chhoti Diwali;
3) The Deepaawali;
4) The Annakuta, and
5) The Bhrartri Dwitiya.

Every thirteenth tithi, both in the krishna and shukla paksha, of Indian calendar is known as 'Pradosha' (the thirteenth of the krishna-paksha being called also the 'maas-shivaratri) and is dedicated to Lord Shiva. The thirteenth of the Phalguna-krishna paksha is the Sri-Mahashivaratri. Incidentally, Indian tradition does not treat number (13) thirteen as inauspicious. It is a Christian tradition, where one the thirteenth present at the Last Supper, exposed Jesus, the Christ, to the Romans leading to the crucifixion of Jesus. Unlike the Christians, the 'thirteenth' is associated with Lord Shiva, the great Benefactor. There are various synonyms of Lord Shiva; one of them is Vaidynatha, the Lord of Knowledge and Medicine. The Dhanvantari-trayodashi, popularly called Dhanateras, happens to fall on the thirteenth tithi of Kartika krishna-paksha. It is associated with Dhanavantari, the Physician of Gods. The story of 'Samudra-manthan' (Churning of Oceans) by the gods and demons for 'amrita' (nectar of life) is too well- known to be recounted here. The Puranic depictions convey that 'fourteen' jewels emerged out from the samudra-manthan. The 'kalkuta' (the most deadly poison), Goddess Lakshmi and Dhanvantari with the 'amrita-kalasha'(Pitcher of Nectar) are amongst the fourteen jewels. Dhanvantari trayodashi is, thus, associated with amrita (nectar of life), cleanliness- next only to godliness, health and healing. Houses are decorated by this day and in the evening Ganesh and Yama (and Kuber at some places) are worshipped for health, well-being and solvency and deep-dana is offered for pleasing Yama, the god of death/ justice (yamayaprityartham). In practice, the day has come to mean purchase of new utensils, clothes, expensive items of luxury and often vulgar display of wealth. The concepts underlining sound health, solvency and living with satisfaction appear to have been marginalized, almost forgotten. Its association with Shiva and Dhanvantari, and sound health as the basis for all growth, activity and prosperity can be ignored only at one's own peril. This is the first day of the Deepawali.

The second day is known as the Naraka Chaturdashi, also known as Chhoti or small Diwaali. Naraka means 'Hell' in Sankrit and Chaturdashi is the fourteenth-day of dark-moon night, symbolizing dark, evil and the hideous. This day is associated with the killing of the demon king, Narakasura or Bhaumasura (born of earth) of Pragjyotisha, who had seized and collected more than 16000 damsels in his harem, daughters of gods, gandharvas and men. Narakasura is attributed with carrying away the ear-rings of the goddess Aditi and also with having outraged modesty of Visvakarman's daughter. Lord Krishna eliminated Narakasura on this day leading to redemption of the captive damsels and the world of the evil devil king. According to the Vayu-Purana, this day is associated with the birth of Lord Hanumana, the monkey-God. Hanumana is symbol of strength, velour and eliminator of evil and dispenser of well-being to the devout and faithful. In north India, this day is widely celebrated as the birth-day of Hanumana. On this day, deep-dana is made and the earthen lamps are placed at important points in the house and outside, more particularly on the drains going out of the premises. Special offerings and prayers are made in the evening to Hanumana for propitiation commemorating his birthday.

Deepaawali, the amavasya, the darkest-night of the Kartika krishna-paksha, is the third and the main day of this festival. People decorate their houses elaborately with floral and auspicious designs and motifs. Visiting friends, family members and relatives, exchange of gifts, sweets and suitable presents and paying respect to elders is a chief customary practice of this festival. Various delicacies are prepared in each house-hold. Fire-crackers of different varieties are brought home in substantial quantities so that children could play with them after the Deepawali- puja. The most auspicious hours of the worship are notified. From dusk-hours to deep mid-night, every house-hold and business community select most suitable hour for themselves for worship. In the Tantrika tradition, Deepawali night is most opportune time for the successful completion of tantrika and occult practices and worship; their hours for worship are mid-night hours.

Lord Ganesh, the god of wisdom and Laksmi, the goddess of wealth and prosperity are the main deities for this worship. Some also worship the Yaksha-lord, Kuber, the lord of riches, for propitiation and conferment of plentiful riches. Kuber is the half-brother of the demon king, Ravan of Lanka, who had ousted Kuber from Lanka. Ravan was defeated and killed by lord Rama. The puja is generally confined to family members; intimate friends may be invited occasionally. People have elaborate puja; the family members seek blessings and favor of Ganesh and Lakshmi for wisdom and prosperity for the family and every member. 'Prasad', consisting of roasted paddy seeds and sweets is given to everyone. The entire house is decorated, at all floors and around, with lighting of rows of earthen-lamps with mustard oil with cotton-wicks; now being replaced rapidly by electrical strings to decorate and illuminate houses, shops, work places. There are lot of fire-crackers and such fireworks that are played by children and all after the puja. A sumptuous family feast is accompanied with a lot of merry-making. In some families, there is also the practice of playing card-games with the belief that winnings and loses would harbinger the kind of year to be countenanced with. Not infrequently, cases of heavy drinking could be seen as fashionable part of the celebrations, sometimes leading to disasters. All this needs to be corrected and modified.

At the cost of a minor digression, it may not be out of place to mention that there follows a festival known as the Dev-Deepawli,(the Gods 'Festival of Lights), which falls around fifteen days later, on the Kartika Purnima, the full-moon night. There is a belief that on this day, Lord Visvanath, Lord of the Universe and the Guardian deity of Varanasi, destroyed the demon king, Tripurasura, who had become menace to the gods and the world, earning thereby the epithet of Tripurari. Gods celebrate this festival in Heavens and the humans on the earth. There is deepdaana in Varanasi along the Ganga on all the ghats and all water bodies. The practice is followed at other places on river banks but these have little to compare with Varanasi.

To revert to our Deepawali festival, the fourth day is known as the 'Anna-Kuta' or 'Govardhana' Pujaa. Anna-kuta means a mountain of cereals and govardhana literally means giving fillip worship of cattle-animal wealth. This is the Kartika shukla-pratipada, the first day of the bright-moon fortnight. The festival is also associated with Lord Krishna who very ingeniously saved the lives, property and cattle wealth of the people of the Gokul and the Braja mandal from the wrath of rain- god Indra. In the city of Varanasi, there is a temple dedcated to the Goddess, Annapurna, the goddess of plenty & an epithet of Parvati, the consort of Lord Shiva. Due the merciful dispensation of this Goddess, it is the popular belief that no soul goes to sleep hungry in that city. It is appropriate to mention here that the Annapurna temple in Varanasi has an annual feature of the Goddess giving away Annakuta offerings to the devotees beginning with the DhanvantarTrayodashi to the day of Annakuta , for four days. Lord Shiva is also believed to stand in the line. Every devotee is given 'annakuta' and a coin. There are around hundred-thousand devotees every day. After all, this day is the 'annakuta, a peak of mountain; 'go' means cows or cattle (*also the 'senses'*)and 'vardhana' meaning to increase and improve; thus, indicating plenty of cereals and material wealth and also improving one's perception of life and things. On this day, traditionally an anthropomorphic figure of Govardhana is made of cow-dung. All the cattle are taken and washed in the nearest river or tank and cattle are decorated with colorful designs giving a very festive atmosphere. The Govardhana is worshipped with 'annakuta' prepared of all the vegetables of the season and food items are prepared from the newly arrived cereals. A large range of Indian dishes are cooked from milk, curd, rice, millets and other cereals. This is the day to enjoy and celebrate the plenty. Lights are put up in the evening to illumine the houses. This day is also associated with the commencement of the New Year in the western India, with traders and business men balancing their books of account.

Bhratri or bhratritva (brother) or Yama duja/ dwiteeyaa is the fifth-day of Deepawali, theKartika Shukla-paksha dwitiya, the second day of the bright-moon fortnight. 'Yama' literally means control and self-restraint as also the 'twin'. Dwiteeyaa or Duja means 'second day' of any lunar fortnight. This day is believed to have been once a brotherhood- celebration, for giving and sharing, now confined and limited to brothers and sisters largely. There is a story that Lord Yama, the God of Death, is supposed to have granted boon to his 'twin' sister, Yamuna the river, for the long life of happiness to brothers and sisters who bathe in the river that day or meet with on this day exchanging respect and gifts. Sisters put vermillion 'tilaka' on the forehead of brothers and offer sweets and delicacies to them, praying for each other's welfare and long life.

Festivities are, thus, spread over the five days in varying ways from house to house, village to village and region to region. Since the Festival coincides with the end of the rainy season (the monsoon) and the arrival-home of monsoon crops, there is emphasis on cleanliness and enjoyment. However, the worship of various gods and goddesses sometimes is questioned by persons as superstitious and meaningless. Lord Ganesha, the elephant God symbolizing wisdom and discrimination, and Goddess Lakshmi, the Goddess of wealth and prosperity, are worshipped during Deepawali. Indian iconography has figurative and allegorical meanings. Allegorically, Lakshmi is the Goddess of wealth and prosperity, another synonym being 'shri', is daughter of the Ocean-God and emerged out from the Ocean (ratnaakara=the abode of jewels/wealth) as a product of the Churning of Ocean (Samudra-manthana'-churning of life) by all, gods and demons all put together. Wealth and prosperity require sound physical and mental health and persistent sincere efforts as pre-conditions to success and achievement. Therefore, Dhanavantari, the Physician of Gods, has to precede the Goddess of Wealth to demonstrate that the Nectar of Life can come only after the 'samudra-manthana' (churning of Ocean of life) by a good deal of efforts by each and every person. This is applicable to societies as also to individual lives. It is only by eliminating the demonic or evil or bad habits that one celebrates Deepaawali for the blessings of Lakshmi and therefore, the Narakachaturdashi. To eliminate evil or bad habits, one has to have the qualities similar to Hanumaana or the' Vajraanga Bali', (the strong man of steely frame). With these assets, one would be able to enjoy wealth and prosperity, with the wisdom and discretion of Lord Ganesha and possess plentiful of assets like cereals, cattle, means of production, sharing, distribution and generating wealth and happiness for the 'annakuta'. 'Bhai duja or the Bhratri duja' is now largely for brothers & sisters, but has spirit of common brotherhood. In fact, universal brotherhood (vishva-bandhutva) of humankind, as concomitant of self-restraint and brotherhood. Incidentally, the fifth day is also a day of 'Yama', the God of Death, forewarning control and self-restraint, to make festivities and life memorable and lasting.

Let there be a word about 'dyuta' (gambling) and also 'UlooKa'(Owl), the vehicle of Goddess Lakshmi. Lord Shiva and his spouse, Paarvati are sculpted in the famous Ellora Kailaasha temple (rock-cut in the hill from top-down), playing dice and in the next adjoining frame, Paarvati is leaving the game a bit anguished. Why? It is any bodies guess! The game is dicey, deceptive and wealth is fickle. Each and every one should remember that fact. Or else, the fortunes change quickly and one may come to bickering, dispute and grief.

Goddess Lakshmi demands effort, industry and labor and comes only after hard-work to industrious, sharp and intelligent persons. One, who strives even in hardships, would be rewarded by Lakshmi. One is reminded of the Bridaranyaka Upanishad (1.3.28) prayer of "leading from untruth to truth; from darkness or ignorance to light or knowledge; and from death to immortality."

One need not lose heart even in the darkest and hardest of times. Nothing can be darker than the darkest midnight of the dark-moon fortnight. Tough times do not last; tough people do. It is the 'Owl', which has the vision, skill and capacity to find its prey, a way to survive and flourish despite difficult circumstances. Therefore, Lakshmi has harnessed 'ulooka' as the vehicle. Deepaawali has celebrations, festivities, realities of life, all built together.

So, Always a very Happy Deepawali to celebrate & enjoy.

50

ऋग्वेद में मानव एवं मानवीय मूल्य

दिग्विजयनाथ

इतिहास मानवीय मूल्यों एवं मानवीय क्रिया कलापों का अध्ययन है। साहित्यिक परम्परा एवं वैज्ञानिक अनुसंधानों में मनुष्य को ही सर्वश्रेष्ठ प्राणी माना गया है। साथ ही मनुष्य, संसार के सर्वाधिक रहस्यमय प्राणियों में से भी एक है। इसके उत्पत्ति और विकास, संचेतना और आत्मा, भौतिक और रासायनिक संरचना सभी, अन्वेषणा के विषय बने हुए हैं। भारत में इसे एक ओर विकासवादी सिद्धान्त के अनुसार स्वयं क्रियता (Self Automation) के द्वारा लम्बे समय के विकास की प्रक्रिया का परिणाम माना जाता है तो दूसरी ओर ईश्वर (ब्रह्म) के निर्देशन में इसी रूप में उत्पन्न एवं गतिमान प्राणी माना जाता है।

ज्ञानी मानव के सम्बन्ध में प्राचीनतम एवं व्यवस्थित साहित्यिक साक्ष्य ऋग्वेद है, जिसमें मनुष्य को, उसकी संचेतना, विवेक, मनन क्षमता एवं हस्त कौशल के आधार पर सर्वश्रेष्ठ कहा गया है और इसकी विभिन्न विशेषताओं के आधार पर ऋग्वेद में इसके अनेक पर्यायवाची शब्द प्राप्त हैं। ऋग्वेद में मनुष्य (Individual) के लिए मनुष्य, मर्त्य, मर्त, मर्य, धव, हरि, जन, जन्तु, नर, पुरूष, नहुष आदि शब्द प्राप्त हैं। यहाँ उल्लेख्य है कि ऋग्वेद में मनुष्य के पर्याय प्रायः पुरूष वर्ग (Male) के सन्दर्भ हैं, स्त्रीवर्ग के सन्दर्भ में नहीं हैं साथ ही यहाँ पुरूष विमर्श ने स्त्री विमर्श की तुलना में अधिक स्थान प्राप्त किया है।

भारोपीय काल में व्यक्ति से सम्बद्ध कतिपय मौलिक धारणायें थीं जिनके प्रमाण प्रायः शब्दों के तुलनात्मक अध्ययन से उपलब्ध होते हैं और उनमें दो सर्वाधिक प्रमुख हैं– प्रथमतः व्यक्ति का पर्याय वह मानव है जो अपने हस्त प्रयोग से वस्तुओं का निर्माण करने में सक्षम है। द्वितीयतः चिंतन का सामर्थ्य है।

हस्तकौशल और चिंतन सामर्थ्य व्यक्तित्व का केन्द्रीय बिन्दु है, क्योंकि व्यक्तित्व निर्माण की सतत प्रक्रिया में इनकी भूमिका प्रति क्षण दिखायी पड़ती है। 'मन्' धातु से व्युत्पन्न मन, मनुष और मानुष मनुष्य की मननशीलता को दर्शाते हैं। मन से ही सम्बद्ध जर्मन गाथिक शब्द परम्परा का मूल 'मन्न', टेसीटस के 'मान्व' में भी सुरक्षित है। स्लाव भाषा का 'माजी' शब्द भी इसी 'मन' का समानार्थी है। मन– मनुष–माजी–मूज–मोगस आदि एक तरफ चिंतनशीलता से सम्बद्ध है तो दूसरी ओर हस्तकौशल से। लैटिन में मनुष्य मूलतः हैण्ड (हस्त) से सम्बद्ध है और व्यक्त करता है कि व्यक्ति वह है जो हस्त से कार्य करता है।[1] ऋग्वेद में मनुष्य शब्द का प्रयोग अधिकांशतः चिंतनशील एवं हस्त कौशल के अर्थ में किया गया है।[2] यास्क के अनुसार वे मनुष्य इसलिए कहलाते हैं, क्योंकि वे अपने कार्यों को चिन्तन के पश्चात् करते हैं।[3] पुनः 'मनस्यति' क्रिया मनस्वी होने के अर्थ में प्रयुक्त होती है।

व्यक्ति से सम्बद्ध द्वितीय मौलिक धारणा 'मरणशीलता' है। संस्कृत मर्त्य, मर्त एवं मर्य, अवेस्ता का मस्य, प्राचीन फारसी मर्तिया, आमीनियन मर्द यूनानी, व्रोतोस (ब्रिटिस) और लैटिन 'मार्तस्' आदि सभी के पीछे मरणशील और नश्वर प्रकृति ही है। ऋग्वेदन में व्यक्ति के लिए मर्त्य के अतिरिक्त मर्त और मर्य शब्द का भी प्रयोग मिलता है। मर्य का अर्थ है वह जो मरणशील है।[4] सायण ने इसका तात्पर्य मनुष्य से लगाया है। ऋग्वेद के प्रथम मण्डल की एक ऋचा में आये 'मर्त्य' शब्द में मनुष्य का अर्थ समाहित है। वहाँ कहा गया है– ''हे अग्नि तुम्हारा जो महान कर्म है उससे बड़ा न तो देवता का है, न मनुष्य का।''[5] अन्यत्र एक ऋचा में आये 'मर्त' शब्द का अभिप्राय भी मनुष्य

है– वहाँ कहा गया है– ''परिश्रमपूर्ण कर्मों का उत्साह से सम्पादन करके यज्ञ प्रवर्तकों ने मर्त होते हुए भी अमरता प्राप्त की।'' एक स्थल पर कहा गया है कि 'हे मित्र, ऐसा हो कि वह मर्त्य अन्न एवं दुग्ध में समृद्ध हो।''[6] यह धारणा यहाँ मानव के साथ सम्बद्ध है।

ऋग्वेद में मनुष्य के लिए एक शब्द 'धव' व्यवहृत है। धव शब्द 'धु' कम्पने धातु से व्युत्पन्न है।[7] जिनके अंग कम्पायमान हैं अर्थात् जो शरीर को कार्य में प्रवृत्त करते समय इस स्थिति में होते हैं अथवा जो मृत्यु से कांपते रहते हैं अथवा युद्ध करते हैं। ऋग्वेद में मनुष्य के लिए हरि शब्द भी प्रयुक्त है यह 'हृ' धातु से उत्पन्न है।[8] यहाँ पदार्थों का हरण करने अथवा मृत्यु के द्वारा बलपूर्वक हरण किये जाने के कारण वह 'हरि' है। उल्लेख्य है कि यह शब्द हरणशीलता अथवा मरणशीलता के अर्थ में अभिव्यक्त हुआ है।

मनुष्य के सम्बन्ध में एक अन्य विशिष्ट अवधारणा जनन से सम्बद्ध है। वैदिक सजन, जन्तु, अवेस्ता के जन्तु और यूनानी गेनोस समानार्थक शब्द समूह हैं। प्रजनन की प्रक्रिया रक्त सम्बन्ध के माध्यम से मानवों में, समूह विशेष बनाने में सक्षम रही है। ऋग्वेद में जन शब्द का उल्लेख अनेक स्थलों पर किया गया है और इन प्रसंगों में इसका अभिप्राय प्रजनन से ग्रहण किया जाना उचित है।[9] जन्तु शब्द जनी प्रादुर्भावे से व्युत्पन्न है।[10] चूँकि वह उत्पन्न होता है, इसलिए जन्तु है।[11] इसके साथ ही विभिन्न जन्मों को धारण करने के कारण भी मनुष्य 'जन्तु' नाम से अभिहित है। सायण ने ऋग्वेद के प्रथम मण्डल में प्रयुक्त जन्तु का अर्थ 'मुनष्य' किया है,[12] जो बाद तक इसी अर्थ में बना रहा।[13]

व्यक्ति के लिए अन्य महत्वपूर्ण पर्याय है 'नर'। 'नृ' धातु से उत्पन्न नर का अभिप्राय नेता है। संसार चक्र को आगे बढ़ाने के कारण व्यक्ति का नर अभिधान है, अथवा पदार्थ होने के कारण एक स्थान से दूसरे स्थान तक वह ले जाया जाता है इसलिए नर है।[14] पुनः पुनः कर्मों में गति करने के कारण भी व्यक्ति नर है। ऋग्वेद में अनेक ऋचाओं में 'नर' शब्द नेता अर्थ में प्रयुक्त हुआ है।[15]

व्यक्ति की अत्यन्त महत्वपूर्ण धारणा 'पुरुष' शब्द में समाहित है। पुरूष अभिधान का सर्वप्रथम विवरण ऋग्वेद के 'पुरूषसूक्त' में उपलब्ध होता है।[16] सायण उसे प्राणि समूह की समष्टि के रूप में स्थित ब्रह्माण्ड शरीरी विराट् आख्या वाला बताते हैं। निरूक्तकार के अनुसार पुरूष का अभिप्राय है पुर अर्थात् शरीर में निवास करने वाला। यह पूर्णार्थक धातु से व्युत्पन्न है।[17] परमात्मा सर्वत्र पूर्ण है जिसका साक्ष्य श्वेताश्वर उपनिषद् में उपलब्ध है।[18] शतपथ ब्राह्मण में 'पुरिशेते' व्युत्पत्ति मिलता है।[19] कठोपनिषद् में एकादशीय द्वार पुर है।[20] वृहदारण्यकोपनिषद् में वर्णित है, 'सृष्टि में सर्वोपरि होने तथा सभी पापों को दग्ध करने की क्षमता रखने के कारण वह पुरूष नाम से अभिहित है।[21] इन प्रसंगों से प्रतिपादित होता है कि पुरूष में विशिष्ट ज्ञानेन्द्रिय संरचना से युक्त भाव का समावेश है। इससे आभ्यन्तरिक सत्ता का बोध होता है। यहाँ पुरूष में उस भाव का समावेश है, जो शक्ति, ऊर्जा, स्फूर्ति प्रत्युत्पन्न मति और तेज का उत्पादक है। पुरूष का एक प्रयोग अनन्त, अखण्ड, सर्वत्र व्याप्त एवं ब्रह्म के रूप में भी ऋग्वेद में दिखायी पड़ता है। सभी विषय पुरूष के सम्बन्ध में ही अर्थ का रूप धारण करते हैं। वैदिक पुरू और अवेस्ता का 'पोउस', पूर्ण, विशाल और सब अर्थ में प्रयुक्त होता रहा है, अख्मेनियन 'परू' का अर्थ भी पूर्ण है। ऋग्वेद में मनुष्य के लिए एक शब्द 'नहुष' उल्लिखित है।[22] नहुष का अर्थ है बाँधने वाला।[23] मानव को संसार का माचाचक्र आबद्ध करता है, लीन करता है, जोड़ता है और अपने अनुसार चलने को बाध्य करता है।

उपरोक्त सन्दर्भों में ऋग्वैदिक काल में मनुष्य के उन गुणों तथा तत्सम्बन्धी शब्द पर्यायों का उल्लेख है जो सर्वमान्य एवं सार्वभौमिक हैं। वस्तुतः व्यक्ति में पर्यावरण से संघर्ष करने की क्षमता पूर्व काल से ही रही है जो उसे ज्ञानेन्द्रियों एवं कर्म इन्द्रियों से उपलब्ध होती है। इस क्षमता का विकास निरन्तर होता रहा है, इन पर्यायों से भी यही आभास मिलता है। ऐसा प्रतीत होता है कि ऋग्वैदिक काल के मनुष्य को भी एक ओर अपने प्राकृतिक अस्तित्व का बोध है तो दूसरी ओर अलौकिक शक्ति का आभास भी, जो जगत् को संचालित करता है। इसका प्रबल प्रमाण ऋग्वेद के प्रत्येक ऋचा का देवता से सम्बद्ध होना है। ऐतिहासिक विकास क्रम में हम एक तरफ उसे औजार की खोज में देखते हैं तो दूसरी ओर मृतक संस्कार एवं अदृष्ट शक्तियों (प्रकृति प्रमुखों) की उपासना में संलग्न पाते हैं। मानव इतिहास में सर्वत्र लौकिक एवं आध्यात्मिक बोध का द्विविध रूप प्रस्तुत किया गया जो व्यक्तित्व का स्थायी आधार सा है। ज्ञातव्य है कि भौतिक कार्य–कारण का ज्ञान जागतिक व्यवहार में फलदायी है, किन्तु आंतरिक तृप्ति का यह हेतु नहीं है।

व्यवहारिक जीवन में ज्ञान के एक स्तर पर अलौकिक आदर्श की प्रेरणा व्यक्ति को अपने लौकिक चेतना का आकलन करने के लिए प्रेरित करती है।

सारांशतः 'मनुष्य' में चिन्तनशीलता एवं हस्तकौशल, 'मर्य' एवं 'मर्त' में मरणशीलता, 'धव' में गतिशीलता–क्रियाशीलता, 'हरि' में हरणशीलता, 'जन' में जननशीलता, 'जन्तु' में उत्पन्नशीलता, 'नर' में नेता, 'नहुष' में बंधन और 'पुरूष' में पूर्णता का भाव समाहित है।

इतिहास दर्शन में व्यक्ति पर अधिक विमर्श किया गया है। एक मान्यता के अनुसार व्यक्ति एक पंख रहित द्विपाद है, कुछ लोगों की दृष्टि में मनुष्य एक आत्मा है, कुछ मानते हैं कि मनुष्य एक हंसने वाला जानवर है जो यंत्रों का उपयोग करता है, पर सभी में उसके आभ्यन्तर पक्ष को छोड़ दिया गया है। वस्तुतः मनुष्य एक विवेकशील प्राणी है उसमें चिंतन सामर्थ्य और हस्तकौशल है जो उसे पशु से अलग करती है। मनुष्य में वनस्पति एवं पशुओं के तत्व होते हुए भी ज्ञान इसे इन दोनों से अलग कर देता है।

वस्तुतः मनुष्य मात्र की प्रतिष्ठा, उसके मूल अर्थात् मूल्य के साथ युक्त रहने के कारण बनी रहती है। 'मूल्य' शब्द, स्वतंत्र रूप से तथा जीवन मानव आदि पदों के साथ उत्तर पद के रूप में प्रयुक्त होकर वर्तमान में एक विशिष्ट अर्थ में परिभाषित है। यह शब्द प्रतिष्ठा अर्थ की वाचक मूल धातु के साथ यत् प्रत्यय जुड़ने से बना है। तद्नुसार मूल्य शब्द का शाब्दिक अर्थ हुआ 'प्रतिष्ठा के योग्य'। अमरकोश के टीकाकार कृष्ण मित्र ने 'मूल्य' शब्द का अर्थ किया 'मूलेनानाभ्यम्' अर्थात् मूल से न झुकने योग्य। वृक्ष की प्रतिष्ठा तब तक है जब तक उसका मूल स्थिर है। वृक्ष का आरम्भ मूल से है। मनुष्य की मनुष्यता एवं प्रतिष्ठा का कारण भी मूल या मूल्य है। समाज का प्रमुख व्यक्ति 'मूल–पुरुष' कहलाता है। नवीन सकारात्मक चिन्तन या विचार 'मूल–विचार' कहलाता है। इस प्रकार किसी भी वस्तु का अपने मूल से हर समय जुड़े रहना उसमें प्रतिष्ठित रहना तथा कभी भी उससे अलग न होना मूल्य है। मूल से जुड़े रहना मूल्य की अनिवार्य शर्त है। जो वस्तु जिस कार्य के लिए है उसका उसी में उपयोग मूल्य है तथा उससे अलग उपयोग अवमूल्यन है। ऋग्वेद में मूल्य का पर्यायी शब्द 'वस्न' व्यवहृत है। वरन शब्द वस् धातु से न प्रत्यय के योग से बना है जिसका अर्थ है जो उसमें निवास करता है। मूल्य सदा मूल में निवास करता है।

मनुष्य अपने ज्ञान, विवेक एवं चेतना के विकास के साथ सुसंस्कृत एवं श्रेष्ठतम मनुष्य के सृजन के लिए निरन्तर प्रयत्नशील रहा। इस प्रयत्न में उसने मूल्यों एवं मूल्य तथा संस्कारपरक संस्थाओं का सृजन किया और मूल्यों तथा संस्थाओं के विकास एवं ह्रास का उत्तरदायी भी स्वयं रहा। ये मूल्य एवं संस्थाएं अलग–अलग समाजों (संघों) में अपनी ही बेहतरी को ध्यान में रखकर निर्मित किये गये जो समकालीन भौतिक एवं सांस्कृतिक परिस्थितियों एवं परम्पराओं के सापेक्ष थे। दूसरे शब्दों में – किसी देश–काल व परिस्थिति में जन सामान्य की उदात्त मान्यताएं ही मानव मूल्य की संज्ञा से अभिहित हुयी। जहाँ तक ऋग्वेद में मानव मूल्यों के संदर्भ का प्रश्न है वहाँ आश्चर्यजनक रूप से श्रेष्ठ मानवीय मूल्यों का विवरण प्राप्त है। इनमें ऋतु, सत्य, अहिंसा, मैत्री, अभय, विवेक, बुद्धि, दानशीलता, पवित्रता, कर्म (परिश्रम), समात, सुभावना, नैतिकता और माधुर्य मुख्य हैं। यद्यपि भाष्यकारों ने इनकी अलग–अलग व्याख्या प्रस्तुत की है तथापि सभी में आन्तरिक एकता देखी जा सकती है।

'ऋत्' को ऋग्वेद में प्रतिपादित चरित्रगुणों में सर्वोच्च स्थान प्रदान किया गया है। ऋग्वेद में यह शब्द तीन प्रमुख विचारों का सूचक है– ब्रह्माण्ड नियम, यज्ञ के धर्म की नियमितता और नैतिक नियम।[24] ऋत् सदाचार का मानदण्ड है। जहाँ यह कार्य करता है वहाँ अव्यवस्था या दुराचार नहीं रहता। देवताओं को ऋत् से उत्पन्न, ऋत् के पालक, ऋत् के प्रेमी और ऋत् से सम्पन्न कहा गया है। ऋत् की शक्तियाँ बहुत है और उसकी बुद्धि पापों को नष्ट करती है।[25] ऋत् के मार्ग से जाने वाले ही सुगम और कण्टक रहित मार्ग पाते हैं।[26] वरुण ऋत् के अधिष्ठाता और सर्वोच्च नियामक देव हैं। वरुण के ऋत् में ही हमें सर्वप्रथम मानवों के लिए निर्धारित नैतिक कार्यक्रम के दर्शन होते हैं। ऋत् से प्रेरणा प्राप्त करके ही प्राचीन भारतीयों ने नैतिकता के नियमों को जन्म दिया।

'सत्य' ऋत् का सहोदर है ऋग्वेद के अनुसार महान दीप्तिमान तप से ऋत और सत्य पैदा हुए हैं।[27] संसार को यदि ऋत चलाता है तो मानव जीवन को सत्य चलाता है। ऋत ही मानव जीवन में सत्य कहलाता है। कष्ट सहकर भी मनुष्य को सत्य के मार्ग पर दृढ़ रहना चाहिए।[28] सातवलेकर के अनुसार– 'ये दोनों ही मानव के व्यवहार में आने चाहिए। ऋत् और सत्य का मूल यौगिक भाव है– 'प्रगति और अस्तित्व।'[29] वचन और कर्म दोनों से ही सत्य के पालन की प्रतिज्ञा की जानी चाहिए।[30] स्पष्ट है कि ऋत और सत्य दोनों ऋग्वैदिक काल में मानवीय मूल्य हैं।

'अहिंसा' वैदिक आचारों में प्रमुख है। आर्यों ने अपने देवताओं को हिंसा रहित, अहिंसक आदि गुणों से विभूषित किया है।[31] देवों से हिंसा रहित धन प्रार्थनीय है।[32] इसी प्रकार अहिंसक बुद्धि की याचना की गयी है।[33] इन्द्र हिंसकों तथा दुष्ट, हन्ता शत्रुओं के विनाशक देवता हैं। मंत्रों में हिंसकों के विनाश और अहिंसकों की सुरक्षा की कामनाएं वैदिक आर्यों की अहिंसा में दृढ़ आस्था व्यक्त करती हैं। स्पष्ट है ऋग्वेद में अहिंसा भावना को मानव मूल्य के रूप में मान्यता दी गयी है।

'मैत्री' भाव वेदों में सर्वत्र द्रष्टव्य है। वहाँ सब प्राणियों को मित्रवत् देखने की कामना की गयी, देवों से मित्रता चाही गयी जिससे वे समय पर सहायक हों। ऋग्वैदिक ऋषि का यह प्रतिपादन मैत्री भावना की प्रशस्ति है कि– 'जो विद्वान, मित्र को छोड़ देता है उसकी वाणी में कोई फल नहीं रहता, वह जो कुछ सुनता है व्यर्थ ही सुनता है वह सत्कर्म का मार्ग नहीं जानता है।[34] मित्र के हित की सदा आकांक्षा करना मित्रता का सबसे बड़ा गुण

माना गया है। इन्द्र को हितकारी मित्र कहा गया है।[35] इस प्रकार ऋग्वैदिक काल में, सबके प्रति सहानुभूति, सहयोग, प्रेम और उपकार का भाव मानसिक संकीर्णता त्याग कर व्यापक दृष्टि ग्रहण करने का परिचायक है।

'अभय' जैसे उत्कृष्ट मानव मूल्य की स्थापना, 'मा भैषीः' जैसी ऋग्वैदिक प्रार्थनाएं करती हैं, समानता, स्वतंत्रता और स्वावलम्बन निर्भयता से ही प्रश्रय प्राप्त करते हैं। ऋचाओं में स्वाभाविक रूप से एक दूसरे के प्रति अभय की भावना व्यक्त की गयी है। हे अग्ने ! तुम हमें दृष्ट और अदृष्ट भयों से बचाओ।[36] हे द्यावापृथिवी! यहाँ अभय होवे, सूर्य–चन्द्र हमारे लिए निर्भयता सिद्ध करें[37], इत्यादि प्रार्थनाओं से प्रगट होता है कि निर्भयता ऋग्वैदिक आर्यों का अभिसिप्त गुण था।

'मेधा', धी या विवेकबुद्धि मनुष्य को सांसारिक प्राणियों में श्रेष्ठ बनाती है। इसलिए ऋग्वेद में सद्बुद्धि प्रार्थनीय है। सविता ! देव प्रज्ञा को प्रेरित करें,[38] इन्द्र बहुविध बुद्धि प्रदान करें[39] अग्नि बुद्धि को ले आये[40] इत्यादि प्रार्थनाओं में बुद्धि की कामना की जा रही है तो दूसरी ओर दुर्बुद्धि निवारण के लिए भी प्रार्थना है।[41] यहाँ श्रेष्ठ एवं सफल जीवन जीने के लिए ही बुद्धि की अभिलाषा की गयी है। जो श्रेष्ठ मानव जीवन के रूप में यहाँ वर्णित है।

'दान' मानव का गुण है। ऋग्वैदिक मंत्रों में इसकी प्रशंसा एवं प्रतिष्ठा देखी जा सकती है। वैदिक ऋषि का कथन है– दाता सदा अदाता के ऊपर रहता है[42] दाताओं की मृत्यु नहीं होती है[43] अग्निदेवता से प्रार्थना है कि हमें दानशीलता (दिति) दें और कंजूसी (अदिति) से हमारी रक्षा करें,[44] प्रतिस्पर्धा की तुलना में दानशीलता श्रेयष्कर है।

'पवित्रता' बाह्य एवं अभ्यंतर दोनों स्तर पर आवश्यक है। ऋग्वैदिक काल में वैराग एवं निराशावादी जीवन दर्शन नहीं था। फिर भी वे तपोमय एवं रागरहित जीवन पद्धति से परिचित थे तथा व्रतों, नियमों एवं मंत्रों से दैवीय सिद्धियां प्राप्त करने में उनका विश्वास था।[45] सविता देवता से ऋग्वेद के एक मंत्र में प्रार्थना की गयी है कि वे स्तोता को दर्शनार्थ पवित्र करें।[46] अन्यत्र कहा गया है कि विद्या मनुष्य को पवित्र करती है।[47] पवित्रता विषयक प्रार्थनाएं यजुर्वेद में भी बहुलता से प्राप्त होती हैं।

'कर्म' के बिना मनुष्य श्रेष्ठ नहीं होता। ऋग्वेद के अनुसार मनुष्य अपने श्रेष्ठ और महान् कार्यों से प्रसिद्ध होता है– ''कर्मभिर्महदियः सुश्रुतोभूत्''[48] अन्यत्र कहा गया बिना परिश्रम के देवताओं से मित्रता नहीं मिलती।[49] तात्पर्य यह है कि देवता भी उसी की सहायता करते हैं जो कर्म (परिश्रम) करता है। कर्म प्रशंसनीय है जहाँ कर्म है वहीं पर सुख है।[50] जिस प्रकार इन्द्र आदि देवता उत्तम कर्मों के कारण श्रेष्ठ हुए उसी प्रकार उत्तम कर्म मनुष्य की लक्ष्य प्राप्ति के लिए आवश्यक है यही ऋक्संहिता का संदेश है। अक्षसूक्त उद्यम का ही उपदेश देता है।

'सद्भावना' भी वैदिक आर्यों का मूल्य था। वे सभी को सुखी व सम्पन्न देखना चाहते थे– इसलिए अधिकांश प्रार्थनाएं बहुवचन में हैं। मनुष्यमात्र को सद्भावना और सौहार्द का उपदेश देने वाली ऋग्वैदिक ऋचाएं साहित्य की अनमोल निधियाँ हैं। संज्ञानम सूक्त[51] समष्टि भावना का प्रचारक सूक्त है। इसमें भी मनुष्यों को सामंजस्य की प्रेरणा दी गयी है।

'माधुर्य' गुण (वाणी का) मानव जीवन की श्रेष्ठता के लिए श्रेयष्कर है। वाणी की मधुरता से एकता और सद्भावना अधिक बलवती होती है। सविता देव 'अद्रोहवाक्' है। इसीलिए वह सुख स्वरूप (सुवेशम्) है। अहिंसक वाक्यों से युक्त वाणी का प्रयोग मनुष्य को सुख और शुभ की ओर ले जाता है।

इन्हीं उपरोक्त अवधारणाओं से ही क्रमशः भारतीय चिंतन में मानव मूल्यों का विकास हुआ। यद्यपि वर्तमान भारतीय समाज और संस्कृति में जिन मानवीय मूल्यों को मनुष्य की श्रेष्ठता अथवा मानवता का आधार माना जाता है, जिन सद्गुणों एवं नैतिक आचारों को अनुकरणीय बताया जाता है जिन दुर्गुणों और दुराचारों को व्यक्ति एवं समाज की उन्नति में बाधक माना जाता है प्रायः इन सभी विचारों की स्थापना ऋग्वेद में दिखायी पड़ती हैं, तथापि इनके विकास में परवर्ती चिंतन धाराओं का भी पर्याप्त योगदान था।

सन्दर्भ

1. सी0टी0 ओनियन्स, दि आक्सफोर्ड डिक्शनरी ऑफ इंग्लिश एटियोमोलॉजी, पृ0 550.
2. ऋग्वेद– 1.77.3; 115.2; 163.18; 173.2; 303107; 4.20.5; 9.93.2 आदि।
3. निरुक्त– 3.7; मत्वा कर्माणि सीव्यन्ति। मनस्यमानेन सृष्टाः।
4. ऋग्वेद– 1.5.10; 30.20; 64.13; 72.4; 147.5; 163.7; 2.23.7; 3.59.2; 4.41.2; 5.50.1; 6.1.9; 2.4; 13.4; 8.19.5; 9.101.13 आदि।
   मर्य के लिए– 1.6.3; 64.2; 77.3; 115.2; 3.31.7; 4.20.5; 5.59.3; 8.43.25; आदि
   द्रष्टव्य निरूक्त– 2.27; 3.15; 4.2;
5. ऋग्वेद– 1.19.2 नहि देवो न मर्त्यो महस्तव क्रतुं परः। पर सायण भाष्य पृ0 107 मर्त्यमनपुष्यश्च।
6. ऋग्वेद– 3.59.2 प्र स मित्र मर्त्रो अस्तु पयस्वान्यस्त आदित्य शिक्षति व्रतेन।
7. ऋग्वेद– 3.59.2
8. ऋग्वेद– 1.16.1; 101.10; 164.47; 3.43.6; 50.2; 53.4; 4.16.1; 6.30.1; 2.44.3;
   निघण्टु 2.10 'हृञ हरणे भूषादिः' हृ प्रसस्य करणे जुहोत्पादिः।

इन सर्वधातुभ्यः
(उ0 4.117) इतीन् प्रत्ययः हरन्तिपदार्थान प्रसह्यीक्रियन्ते वा
मृत्युनेति वा। तथा च मृत्युवाक्यम्'
द्र0 निरूक्त– 4.19; 5.12; 6.21; 7.6; 9.36 आदि

9. डॉ0 वी0के0 सिंह– 'व्यक्तित्व की भारतीय अवधारणा', पृ0 3.
10. निघण्टु 2.4 पर दुर्गाचार्य का भाष्य 2.4; 'जनी प्रादुर्भावे'
11. तत्रैव, 'जायन्ते जन्तवः'
12. ऋग्वेद पर सायण भाष्य, पृ0 319; 'जन्तवः प्रजासूत्पन्ना'
13. द्रष्टव्य– ब्राह्मण साहित्य, उपनिषद–साहित्य एवं भगवद्गीता आदि।
14. निरूक्त 3.7 पर स्कन्द स्वामी भाष्य– णीं प्रापणे (भू0उ0) नयर्तीऽच्च (उ0 2.93) इति ऋन्प्रत्ययतः। नयन्ति संसार चक्रम पदार्थत्वात् देशान्तर नीयन्ते वा स्थानोत्तर कालेन।
द्रष्टव्य– वामनशिवराम आप्टे– संस्कृत हिन्दी कोश पृ0 511 एवं मैनफ्रेड मेरहॉफर, ए कनसाइज एटीमालाजिकल संस्कृत – इंग्लिश डिक्शनरी, भाग– 2, पृ0 138.
15. ऋग्वेद– 1,121,2; 184.2; 186.6; 2.14.8; 7.1.1;
16. ऋग्वेद– 10.90.1
17. ऋग्वेद– 10.90.1 पर सायण भाष्य, पृ0 288 सर्व प्राण समष्टि रूपो ब्रह्माण्ड देहो बिराडाख्यो यः पुरूष सोऽयं सहस्रशीर्षा।
18. श्वेताश्वर उपनिषद– 5.3.9.
19. शतपथ ब्राह्मण 13.6.2.1
20. कठोपनिषद 2.3.1 पुरमेकादशद्वारीयमजस्यावकृन्वेतसः। अनुष्ठायन सोचनि विमुक्तश्य विमुच्यते।
21. बृहदारण्यकोपनिषद् 1.4.1
22. ऋग्वेद– 1.31.11; 133.8; 5.12.6; 6.26.7; 7.6.5; 8.8.3; 9.88.2; 80.6; 99.7; आदि।
23. निरूक्त 2.9 जहबन्धने (दि0उ0) जनेरूसि (उ0 2.18)
24. घाटे द्वारा ऋग्वेद पर व्याख्यान (अनुदित) दिल्ली, पृ0 121.
25. ऋग्वेद– 4.23.8.
26. ऋग्वेद– 1.41.4
27. ऋग्वेद– 10.190.1
28. डॉ0 भीखन लाल आत्रेय, भारतीय नीतिशास्त्र का इतिहास, पृ0 39.
29. सातवलेकर,,ऋग्वेद का सुबोध भाष्य, सप्तम मण्डल, पृ0 226.
30. ऋग्वेद– 1.113.4
31. ऋग्वेद– 1.31.13; 1.33.1
32. ऋग्वेद– 1.185.3; 6.22.10
33. ऋग्वेद– 7.67.5.
34. ऋग्वेद– 10.71.21.
35. ऋग्वेद– 3.55.21
36. ऋग्वेद– 10.7.7
37. ऋग्वेद– 10/63/7
38. ऋग्वेद– 3.62.10
39. ऋग्वेद– 1.5.3
40. ऋग्वेद– 1.22.10
41. ऋग्वेद– 8.67.15; 10.76.4
42. ऋग्वेद– 10.117.7
43. ऋग्वेद– 10.107.7
44. ऋग्वेद– 4.2.11
45. विश्वेश्वरनाथ रेड, ऋग्वेद पर एक ऐतिहासिक दृष्टि, 1967, पृ0 89.
46. ऋग्वेद– 9.67.25
47. ऋग्वेद– 1.3.10
48. ऋग्वेद– 3.36.1
49. ऋग्वेद– ''न ऋते श्रान्तस्य देवाः'' 4.33.12
50. ऋग्वेद– 3.3.3

51

THE CONCEPT OF MANDAL IN TANTRIC FORM OF MAHAYANA BUDDHISM

Kamlesh Kumar Gautam

The devotees of Tathagata trace the roots of his teaching in the profound super normal realization of their great prophet. It is only natural for the followers of their religion to credit their founder of their faith with power of insight and penetion into the nature of truth and reality. Buddhism developed into great religion, for the people at large and gained support and was firmly conceded in eastern part of India. With the passing centuries Buddhism spilt into two parts namely : Hinyana & Mahayana. The development of Hinyana & Mahayana Tantrayan, Vajrayan were caused by complex factors.

The development of Mahayana Tantricism in Tibet was caused by different factors. Some Indologists suggest that it must have been the result of not only the natural development of some latent tendencies in the original Buddhism but also of the influence of contention of other Indian religious sects like the Bhagavatas and the Saivas, Iranian religion and culture, Christianty and of the pursuance of propaganda among the new semi-barbarous tribal communities.

Buddhism was broadly be divided into three Yanas – Hinayana, Mahayana and Tantrayan. The term Hinayana was usually adopted for early Buddhism which commenced with the Pariniravana of the Tathagat. The Mahayana grew out of the Hinyana, though it traces its final authority to the Buddha himself. Other terms used respectively for these two branches of Buddhism are (i) Buddhayana or Tathagatayana or Budhisattvayana and (ii) Sravakayana or Pratyka-Buddhayana. However the terms Mahayana and Hinayana are the most popular ones. The causes usually given for prefixing *maha* (superior) and *hina* (inferior) to *yana* (vehicle) in that the former carries to followers to the highest aim of Buddhahood as well as perceived by Siddharatha Gautama, while the latter carries a person only to the stage of an Arhat, which is, in many respects, inferior to that of the compassional Buddha. Further, as argued by Asanga in his *Sutralankara,* the Mahayanaists never seek their own salvation before others have attained it. They take the vow that they will attain *bodhi* only after they have done all that is necessary for making all others beings attain the truth or reality. On the other hand, the Sravakyanists or Pratyeka-Buddayanists seek their own salvation first which Asanga calls selfish and justifies thereby the use of the prefix *hina* for their path, and *maha* for his own creed.

In order to impart authenticity to their religion, the followers of Mahayana proposed the doctrine of two fold truth in the teachings of the Buddha : the outer exoteric truth meant for ordinary people and esoteric truth meant for the highly evolved ones. The Hinayana is concerned with the exoteric truth while the Mahayana is concerned with the esoteric truth.

Since Buddhism develop with Hinduism, hence the philosophy of history is similar a cyclic view. The Buddhist text describe the high power developed by Buddhist monks who had arrived at higher stage. The later development of Buddhist Mahayanism, Tantric Buddhism had the perception of spiritual world and materialistic world accordingly. The description of Mandal in Tantric form of Buddhism has been impressively significant in the study of Mahayana Buddhism and Tantric Buddhism.

The word Mandal suggest the magical circle. Bhikshu Shantrakshit the great exponent of Buddhism thinks of Mandal not as a magic circle but as symbol of profound significance and visual representation of diagram form of Mahayana Buddhist philosophy of total Universe having a function of reintegration of devotee with cosmic reality.

The mandal has important role in Tantric form of Buddhism in Tibet. It is also found elsewhere in Mahayana Buddhism. It is indisputedly admitted that Yoga practice was very ancient much as before Indus Valley civilization. The Tantric Yoga practices of Buddhism in Tibet as well as those of Hinduism are misconstrued by western thinkers. The most attractive of these is the biography of great Tibetian Yogi Milarepa. Milarepa attended highest goal of spirituality. The Mandal is the graphic representation of Tantric Yoga followed by Milarepa.

The Buddhist Chakra is similar in function not as similar to Hindu Mandal called Yantra. A book Myths and reality in Indian Art & Architecture symbols gives us the design and meaning of the symbol Shaivtt Tantric Yantra which is also called Sri Yantra. The Sri Yantra is different as compared to the Mandals. Mandal is perceived as square in shape with four gateways. Inside the square there are four concentric circular lines and in this there is ring of sixteen lotus petals. There are five cone shaped triangles pointing upwards and five pointing down wards of all same shape and size. The scholars explained the triangles with the meaning. The triangle pointing down symbolizes female creative energy. The five male and five female triangle intersect each other symbolizes the creation of dynamic world. The four gateways makes the frame of Swastik. The Swastik, a sun symbol signifies the Sansar. The four gateways are stair ways to upper spiritual planes of cosmos.

The central point of diagram represent the world of spiritual form and gross bodily forms. The Tantric devotee who uses Yantra for intense concentration is able to realize his identity with centre, the absolute reality or transcendental Shiva, whose Maya is the Samsar of world of physical and spiritual and finite existence. Therefore the devotee who is microsm relates himself with marcosm, who is both absolute and relative world.

The Tibetian Buddhist Mandal is also understood in Cosmic Diagram. In the Tantricism of Tibet the interpretation of material and spiritual world Sansar and Nirvan. These are the symbolize in Buddhist Tantra as Compassion and Wisdom and not like Shiva and Shakti of Hindu Tantric view. The philosophical basis of representation is of material and spiritual world is found in these sources :-

> The teaching of Yogachara School says that all things are manifestation of absolute mind. The Madhyamic School says that absolute mind is transcendental form of Sunyata. The Central Idea of Avatansake School Sutra is the idea of interpretation of transcendental void and Sansar world. The Tantric emphasizes the realization of the truth with faculty of Vigour; (one of five Buddhist Spiritual faculty) The four other are faith concentration, mind fullness and wisdom.

The Tantric disciples aims to experiences directly transcendental unity and interpretation of things. The perception of Mandal are as follows in Mahayana Buddhism of Tibet :

The first example of Mandal is simplest which is called five fold manifestation, like all Mandals it is circle in symbolic forms. The core of the Mandal represents Adi Buddha Vajrasattava. He represents the absolute and symbolizes the unity of Pragya and Upaya form where the Sansar world exist. The aim of desciples is realization of state of Vajrasattava.

Around Vajrasattava in the circle there are northern, sourther, eastern and western are four Buddha called Tathagat. The Buddha of eastern quarter in this Mandal is Vairocana. His skandha is "form", his quality is delusion, his wisdom is the mirror-like knowledge, his colour is white.

The Buddha of sourthen quarter is Ratnasambhava. His skandha is "feeling" and his quality is malignity, his wisdom is knowledge of Sameness, his quarter of annual cycle is spring.

Amitabh is the Buddha of western quarter. He is red in colour, his skandha is "perception", his evil quality passion, his wisdom is perceptual knowledge.

The Buddha of northern quarter is Amoghasiddhi. His colour is dark green and he is shown with crossed vajra as his spiritual symbol, his skandha is "impulses" and his evil quality envy, his wisdom is knowledge of needful activity.

The intermediate direction of space are symbolized by four goddesses : Locana, Mamaki, Pandaravasini and Tarini. Each goddesses represents one of the four elements – earth, water, fire, air respectively. Each has the evil of Sansar world-delusion, wrath, passion and envy respectively.

A cosmic diagram of this kind is considered a true picture of reality than that perceived in ordinary everyday human experience. This is because the diagram shows two nature of spiritual and material world. In this contraction upon a such a Mandal, the yogi is enabled to see reality as a whole, as a cyclic on emanation and return of the Absolute the Dharmadhatu. The world of plurality after this experience seen in a new light as the reflection of Absolute. Ego-consciousness is extinguished. These are the basic concepts of Mandal in Tantric form of Buddhism.

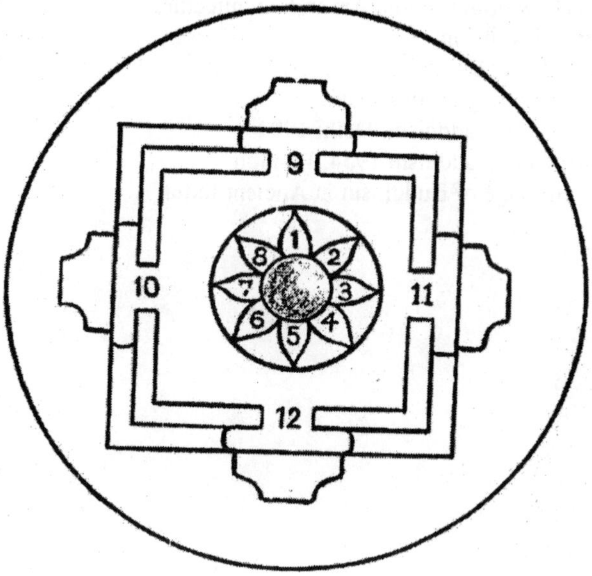

Cosmic Diagram of Mandal

1. Vairochana : Form, East
2. Locana : Earth
3. Ratnasambhava : Feelings, South
4. Mamaki : water
5. Amitabha : Perception, west
6. Pandaravasini : Fire
7. Amoghasiddhi : Impulses, North
8. Tarini : Air
9. 10, 11, 12 : The four quarter of Earth

   Centre : Vajrasattva

References

1. Winternitz M, History of Indian Literature, Calcutta, 1933.
2. Pandey G.C., Itihas Swaroop, Siddhant, Jaipur, 1973.
3. Dubey, Sita Ram, Sam Samuik Itihas lekhan.
4. Prasad H.S. Essay on Time in Buddhism, Delhi, 1991.
5. Pathak V.S., Essay on Time in Buddhism, 1966.
6. Warder A.K., In Introduction to Indian historiography, Bombay, 1972.
7. Wardner, A.K. Indian Buddhism, Delhi 1970.
8. Kern H, Manual of Indian Buddhism Stiausberg, 1986.
9. Mishra G.S.P., age of Vinay, Delhi,1972.
10. Phillips, C.H. Ed Historians of Indian, Pakistan and aylon oxford, 1961.
11. Dutta, N. Bajpai, K.D. Uttar Pradesh nein Baudh dhram Ka Vikas LKO, 1956.
12. Yazdani, G. Early history of deacon, Hyderabad,1960.
13. Ryyas Davids, T.W., History of Indian Buddhism, 1897.
14. Charles, Eliot, Hinduism and Buddhism London, 1954.
15. Suzuki, B.L., Outlines of Mahayan Buddhism, London,1907.
16. Hazara, K.L. Royal Patronage in of Buddhism in Ancient India, 1984.
17. Pandey GC, Studies in origin of Buddhism, Allahabad, 1957.
18. Coomarswamy A.K. Buddha and Gospel of Buddhism, New York,1928.
19. Upadhyaya, K.N. Early Buddhism & Bhagwatgita, Delhi, 1971.
20. Anagrik Govind – Principle of Tantric Buddhism
21. Bapat P.V. – 2500 years of Buddhism, Delh 1959
22. Henric Zimer – Myth and symbol in India Art and Architecture.
23. Kern – Manual of Indian Buddhism
24. N. Dutta – Aspect of Mahayan Buddhism.
25. Suzuki B.L. – Outlines of Mahayan Buddhism.
26. Prasad H.S, Essay on Time in Buddhism, Delhi 1991
27. Charles Eliot – Hinduism and Buddhism 1954, London
28. Hazara K.L. – Royal Patronage of Buddhism in Ancient India.

52

पांचरात्र आगम में वैष्णवी दीक्षा

रामप्यारे मिश्र

पांचरात्र आगम वैष्णव धर्म के सर्व प्राचीन मतों में से एक है। पांचरात्र आगम का वाङमय अत्यन्त विपुल है। यह चार भागों में विभक्त है– ज्ञान, योग, क्रिया एवं चर्या। इस शास्त्र में मन्त्रशास्त्र, यन्त्रशास्त्र, तन्त्रशास्त्र, योग, मायायोग, मन्दिर निर्माण प्रतिमा–निर्माण, प्रतिमा–प्रतिष्ठा, प्राण–प्रतिष्ठा, दीक्षा–विधान, आदि अन्याय विषयों का व्यापक उल्लेख हुआ है। वैष्णवी दीक्षा, दीक्षा शब्द की उत्पत्ति, अर्थवत्ता, प्रकार एवं परिभाषा का सुन्दर विवेचन इन आगमों, संहिताओं एवं तन्त्रों में उल्लिखित है।[1] प्रपंचसार[2], कुलार्णव तंत्र[3], शारदा तिलक[4], नित्योत्सव[5], ज्ञानार्णव 24वाँ पटल,[6] विष्णुसंहिता[7], महानिर्वाणतंत्र[8] एवं लिंग पुराण[9] में दीक्षा का विस्तृत उल्लेख हुआ है। दीक्षा के लिए उपदेश, गुरु, पंचसंस्कार, पुत्रक, प्रार्थना, शिष्य, समयिक, साधक, वर्ण एवं तत्व दीक्षा भी पांचरात्र संहिताओं द्रष्टव्य है। दीक्षा एक कार्य विशेष न होकर अनेक विशिष्ट क्रियाकलापों का समूह है।[10] दीक्षा प्रथमतः दिव्यज्ञान देती है तदनन्तर पापक्षय करती है। इस कारण समस्त तन्त्र **ग्रन्थों** की सम्मति से यह दीक्षा कही गयी है[11] – (विश्वसार तन्त्र, पटल 2)। दीक्षा से बढ़कर न कोई ज्ञान है, न तप है और न समय है, इसी कारण दीक्षा सर्वश्रेष्ठ है (पुरश्चरण सोल्लास–प्रथम पटल)। ब्रह्मा ने पूर्वकाल में दीक्षा को चतुर्विध बतलाया है यथा– क्रियावती, कलावती, वर्णमयी एवं बोधमयी। सभी दीक्षाएं सम्पदा देने वाली तथा शुभप्रद हैं (विश्वसार तन्त्र–उत्तर खण्ड)।

दीक्षा शब्द यौगिक है अर्थात् दो शब्दों के योग से बना है यथा – 'दी' एवं 'क्षी'।

दीक्षा के लिए विष्णु संहिता में बड़ी ही सुन्दर विवेचना की गयी है जो इस प्रकार है–

दीयन्ते सिद्धयः सर्वाः क्षीयन्ते ग्रन्थयोऽप्यतः।
दीक्षात्वमेवं दीक्षायाः धर्माधर्महृदात्मनः।।

अर्थात धर्मगुरुओं द्वारा प्रतिपादित दीक्षा एक धार्मिक संकल्प है जो कर्मकाण्डीय रीति करने के लिए योग्य बना देती है। यह शब्द तन्त्रवेत्ताओं द्वारा अपने कार्य हेतु विविध रूप से निःसृत है। दीक्षा शब्द की उत्पत्ति के संबन्ध में विष्णु संहिता के पटल (102) द्रष्टव्य है।

दीयते यदनया शिवभावो दीक्षया हि पशवोऽत्र ददातेः।
क्षीयतेऽस्य पाशपशुत्वं भिक्षयार्थपरिनिष्ठित धातोः।।

ईशान शिव गुरुदेव पद्धति (क्रियापाद, पटल 10.2) में दीक्षा शब्द की उत्पत्ति उल्लिखित है।

ददाति यस्मादिह दिव्यभावं
मायामले कर्म च सक्षिणोति।
फलं चतुर्वर्गमयंचयस्या–

स्तम्मात् तु दीक्षेत्यभिधानमस्याः।।

चूँकि यह शब्द दो अक्षरों से निर्मित है इसलिए यह अत्यन्तम महत्वपूर्ण है। प्रथम अक्षर 'दा' है जिसका अर्थ है देना, स्वीकृति देना, प्रतिपादित करना, प्रदान करना आदि। इसमें दूसरा अक्षर 'क्षी' का अर्थ नाश करना, समाप्त करना या अन्त करना आदि है। अतः दीक्षा शब्द का अर्थ होता है शिव एवं शिवभाव जो सांसारिक मोह को नष्ट कर देता है।

दीक्षा शब्द की दूसरी व्याख्या निम्नलिखित शब्दों में की गयी है जो इस प्रकार है (पटल 11.2)।

संसारार्णवमग्नानां पशूनां पाशुमुक्तये।
त्वमेव शरणं देव! सदा त्वं भक्तवत्सल।।
देवदेवानुजानीहि प्राकृतै पाशबन्धनैः।।
पाशितान् मोक्षयिष्यामि त्वत्प्रसादात् पशूनिमान्।।

लेखक के द्वारा पशु–पाश की अवधारणा विष्णु संहिता, पटल 10.39–40 में निम्न प्रकार से उद्धृत है। यहाँ यह ध्यान देने योग्य है कि पशु जीव को कहा गया। पाश बन्धन को कहते हैं। पशु (जीव) सांसारिक पाशों (बन्धनों) यथा–कलह, फूट, ईर्ष्या, द्वेष, राग, मोह एवं क्लेश की अन्तिम अवस्था अभिनिवेश में फंसा है। दीक्षा से ज्ञान की प्राप्ति होती है और पाशविक वासनाओं का क्षपण अर्थात् नाश होता है। इसीलिए तत्व चिन्तकों ने इसे दीक्षा कहा है। योगिनी तंत्र में दीक्षा शब्द की व्याख्या निम्न प्रकार से दी गयी है–

दीयते ज्ञानमत्यर्थं क्षीयते पाशबन्धनम्।
अतो दीक्षेति देवेशि कथिता तत्वचिन्तकैः।।

ध्यातव्य है कि मन्त्र दीक्षा का भी विशद विवेचन वैष्णव आगमों में भी हुआ है।[12]

दीक्षा किसी भी व्यक्ति को पूजा करने योग्य बना देती है इसमें पंच संस्कार की क्रिया भी सम्मिलित है (द्र0 रंगाचारी, वैष्णव, ब्राह्मणाज, पृष्ठ 100)।

कुलार्णव तंत्र में वर्णित है कि 'सज्जन लोग इसे दीक्षा कहते हैं क्योंकि यह दिव्यज्ञान प्रदान करती है, सभी पापों का क्षय करती है और इस प्रकार संसार के बन्धन से मुक्ति देती हैं।[13] शारदातिलक में उल्लिखित है कि –'क्योंकि यह दिव्य ज्ञान प्रदान करती है और पापों का नाश करती है अतः तान्त्रिक गुरुओं द्वारा यह दीक्षा कहलाती है।[14] अग्निपुराण में दीक्षा के सन्दर्भ में तान्त्रिक मन्त्रों एवं क्रियाओं का उल्लेख हुआ है[15]। ज्ञानार्णव तंत्र में विवेचित है कि दीक्षा के समय गुरु को अपने शिष्य को छः चक्रों मूलाधार, स्वाधिष्ठान, मणिपूर, अनाहत, विशुद्ध एवं आज्ञा) के साथ प्रत्येक के दलों की संख्या, रंग तथा प्रत्येक के अक्षरों का ज्ञान करा देना चाहिए[16]।

उत्तरवर्ती धर्मशास्त्र–ग्रन्थों ने मन्त्र–दीक्षा के लिए तन्त्र ग्रन्थों का सहारा लिया है। दीक्षा एवं उपदेश में अन्तर है, क्योंकि उपदेश में मन्त्र–ज्ञान सूर्य–चन्द्र–ग्रहण में, तीर्थस्थान में सिद्धक्षेत्र या शिवालय में प्रदान किया जाता है[17]। महानिर्वाणतन्त्र में यह भी कहा गया है कि जब शिष्य शैव, वैष्णव, शाक्त, सौर या गाणपत्य हो तो गुरु को उसी सम्प्रदाय का होना चाहिए, किन्तु कौल सभी के लिए अच्छा गुरु है।

ज्ञातव्य है कि दीक्षा के चार प्रकार बतलाये गये है। यथा–क्रियावती, वर्णमयी, कलावती तथा वेधमयी। श्रीप्रश्न संहिता में तीन प्रकार की दीक्षा का उल्लेख है– 'दीक्षा सा त्रिविधा प्रोक्ता स्थूला, सूक्ष्मा परा तथा' – श्री प्रश्न संहिता – 16.23। पुनः दीक्षाभेद से त्रिधा भी और चतुर्विधा भी कही गयी है– 'पुनर्दीक्षा विभेदन त्रिधा सापि चतुर्विधा। श्रीप्रश्न संहिता– (16.24)

पांचरात्र मतावलम्बियों के अनुसार दीक्षा गुरु को अन्य सभी गुणों के साथ योगस्वाध्याय तत्पर, तन्त्रान्तर विचक्षण, तन्त्र अन्तरज्ञ, मन्त्रज्ञ एवं यन्त्रविचक्षण भी कहा गया है। स्पष्ट है कि पांचरात्र–गुरु कोरा भक्त नहीं, अपितु वह योगी तथा मन्त्र–यन्त्र विशेषज्ञ भी होता है[18]। गुरु की योग्यताओं और शिष्य के गुणों का सुन्दर विश्लेषण तन्त्रसार में उल्लिखित है।[19]

अहिर्बुध्न्य संहिता के बीसवें अध्याय का प्रतिपाद्य विषय दीक्षा विधान के रूप में उल्लिखित है। दीक्षा परम्परा की उत्पत्ति वैदिक है[20]। तांत्रिक साधना में दीक्षा एक रहस्यमय क्रिया होती है। इसी संहिता में एक आदर्श आचार्य[21] या गुरु की सुन्दर परिभाषा दी गयी है[22]। आचार्य का लक्षण बतलाते हुए कहा गया है कि आदर्श आचार्य वह है जो अन्य बातों के अलावा दूसरों के सुख, दुःख दोनों में समान रूप से भागी हो तथा अन्य बुद्धि वाले पुरुषों के प्रति भी दयालु हो–

अमत्सरी परोत्कर्षें पर दुःखे घृणापरा। अहिर्बुध्न्य संहिता, 20.2 उत्तरार्द्ध।
दयावान सर्वभूतेषुदृष्टः परसुखोदये।। तत्रैव, 20

यही नहीं वह वेद एवं वेदान्त का ज्ञाता हो तथा पांचरात्र तथा अन्य ग्रंथों का भी ज्ञान रखता हो। वह अध्यात्म में कुशल हो, तथा कर्मकाण्डीय ज्ञान में निपुण हो एवं जितेन्द्रिय हो[23]।

अहिर्बुध्न्य संहिता में[24] शिष्य का लक्षण बतलाते हुए कहा गया है कि चाहे वह विवाहित हो या अविवाहित लेकिन उसे द्विजाति का होना चाहिए। विनम्र, सुसंस्कृत तथा पवित्र होना चाहिए। गुरु की आज्ञा से क्या करना चाहिए एवं क्या नहीं करना चाहिए का निर्णय लेना चाहिए। उसे ब्रह्मचारी तथा स्वदारा में अनुरक्त होना चाहिए। उसे गुरु से नीचे आसन पर बैठना चाहिए[25]।

अहिर्बुध्न्य संहिता के अनुसार शिष्य का द्विजाति होना आवश्यक है। उसे ब्रह्मचर्य, व्रतधारी, जगत के अंगारों के मध्य अपने कर्मों के दाह से दुःखी शिष्य 'मैं तुम्हारी शरण में आया हूँ', ऐसी वृत्ति रखने वाला शिष्य ही पांचरात्र मत का अधिकारी है[26]। ध्यातव्य है कि यहाँ शरणागति के सिद्धान्त पर बल दिया गया है। स्वयं में पूर्ण आस्था रखने वाले शिष्य को आचार्य कुछ दिनों तक परवीक्षा पर रखने के पश्चात् निश्चित कर लेने पर कि वह लोभ से रहित तथा गोपनीय परम्परा[27] (रहस्यांनाम–गोपिन) की रक्षा करने में समर्थ है, उसे दीक्षा देता है[28]। तान्त्रिक परम्परा में दीक्षा का अत्यन्त ही महत्वपूर्ण स्थान रहा है 'दीक्षा बिना न मोक्षः तथा 'आचार्य बिना न दीक्षा' के विधि–विधान का उल्लेख बड़ा ही वैज्ञानिक है।[29] इस दिशा में प्रथमतः साधारण न्यास का विधान वर्णित है, तदनन्तर सुदर्शन मन्त्र की दीक्षा प्रदान की जाती है। इस मन्त्र में तीन ऋषियों को सम्बोधित किया जाता है– परमात्मा (परमशक्ति), संकषर्ण (सूक्ष्म) एवं अनिरूद्ध (स्थूल) इसके अलावा शरीर को भी सम्बोधित करने का विधान है। इस अवसर पर स्थूल, सूक्ष्म तथा अणुमय शरीर को सम्बोधित किया जाता है। सूक्ष्मशरीर को 'पुर्यष्टक' कहा गया है[30]।

अहिर्बुध्न्य संहिता में शिष्य के कर्तव्यों के सम्बन्ध में विस्तृत वर्णन है[31]। शिष्य के आत्मसंयम पर बल दिया गया है। मन्त्र के प्रयोग के सन्दर्भ में प्रकाश डाला गया है[32]। मन्त्र का प्रयोग विनाश एवं तुच्छ वस्तु की सम्प्राप्ति के लिए वर्जित है। इसीलिए मन्त्रों की गोपनीयता तथा कल्याणकारी कार्यों के लिए प्रयोग का विधान बतलाया गया है। मन्त्र शब्दमात्र नहीं है। यह परमात्मा का स्वरूप है। मन्त्र एवं गुरु में कोई भेद नहीं है। मनन एवं त्राण मन्त्र के दो धर्म है। पूर्णहन्ता अथवा परावागत्मक अनुभूति ही मन्त्र हैं। मन्त्र नित्य होते हैं किन्तु इनकी नित्यता त्रिकालाबाधित नहीं है। देवता के सूक्ष्म शरीर ही मन्त्र हैं।

मन्त्र दीक्षा के समय इस बात पर बल दिया गया है कि मन्त्र का प्रयोग क्षुद्र कार्यों के लिए न किया जाय। मन्त्र का प्रयोग लोकरक्षा, राज्य रक्षा आदि परोपकारी कार्यों के लिए किया जा सकता है, दूसरे के उच्छेद (नाश) के लिए नहीं[33]। पर्वत, नदी–तीर, विष्णु–मंदिर, आश्रम, सिद्धालय या ग्राम–मंदिर साधना के स्थान हैं एवं लाखबार या अधिक बार जप करने से 'मंत्रनाथ' प्रसन्न होते हैं[34]।

गरुड़ पुराण के अंगन्यास को पूजा, जप एवं होम का अंग माना है[35]। नारदीय पुराण[36] भागवत पुराण[37] या ब्रह्मपुराण[38] ने मन्त्रों के न्यास के लिए 'ऊँ नमो नारायणाय' एवं ऊँ नमो विष्णवे नमः' का उल्लेख किया है। ब्रह्म पुराण में 'ऊँ नमो नारायणाय' नामक मन्त्र के न्यास का उल्लेख है जो अंजलियों एवं शरीर के अन्य अंगों पर अवस्थित किया जाता है उसमें करन्यास एवं अंगन्यास (28.26) का वर्णन हुआ है[39]। पद्मपुराण में शरीर में शिर से लेकर पैर तक के अगों पर विष्णु के नामों के न्यास का वर्णन हुआ है[40]। इसी पुराण में 'ऊँ नमो भगवते वासुदेवाय' के मन्त्र के साथ अंगन्यास एवं करन्यारा का वर्णन है[41]।

न्यास के सन्दर्भ तन्त्र–ग्रन्थों से पुराणों द्वारा योगियाज्ञवल्क्य, अपरार्क एवं स्मृतिचन्द्रिका के कई शताब्दियों पूर्व ग्रहण की गयी थी[42]। गौतमीय तन्त्र के अनुसार दीक्षा सर्वासिद्धि प्रवर्तिका है, दीक्षा के बिना शत वर्ष में भी मन्त्रों की सिद्धि नहीं की जा सकती। यह दिव्यता प्रदान करती है। पाप–संतति का क्षय करती है, अतएव तन्त्रपारग मुनियों के द्वारा इसे दीक्षा कहा गया है[43]। पांचरात्र आगम की नारदीय संहिता का मत है कि 'दीक्षया दिक्क्षयं यान्ति' कहते हुए दीक्षा के दिक्क्षय अर्थात् सांसारिकता के क्षय का निर्देश किया है[44]। श्री प्रश्न संहिता में उल्लिखित है कि जिस कर्म से विष्णु का परम पद दिखलायी पड़ता है और अखिल संसार खण्डित होता है उसे दीक्षा कहते हैं[45]। दीक्षा एक व्रताचरण है तथा उसका प्रयोजन शारीरिक तथा आत्मिक शोधन है[46]।

शिष्य को यह प्रतिज्ञा लेनी पड़ती है कि वह पांचरात्र शास्त्र के रहस्य को गुप्त रखेगा[47]। अन्य तांत्रिकों की तरह प्रथमतः अंगन्यास को किया जाता है[48]। न्यास एक तांत्रिक पूजा – कृत्य है जिसका तात्पर्य है कि शरीर के कुछ अगों पर अवस्थित होने के लिए किसी देवता या देवताओं, मन्त्रों का मानसिक जप से आहवान करना जिससे शरीर पवित्र हो जाय तथा पूजा एवं ध्यान के योग्य हो जाय तथ शरीर में देवता का निवास हो 'देवो भूत्वा देवं वजेत्'। न्यास के अनेक भेद हैं–यथा–मन्त्रन्यास, हंस–न्यास, प्रणव–न्यास, मातृका–न्यास, करन्यास, अंगन्यास, पीठन्यास[49]। 'मातृका' एवं मन्त्रोचारण द्वारा शिष्य के विभिन्न अंगों पर स्वर व्यंजनों तथा देवताओं की प्रतिष्ठा की जाती है[50]। तदनन्तर सुदर्शन मन्त्र दिया जाता है। इस मन्त्र के तीन ऋषि हैं। मन्त्र के परारूप के ऋषि हैं परमात्मा, सूक्ष्म रूप के संकर्षण एवं मन्त्र के स्थूल रूप के ऋषि हैं अहिर्बुध्न्य अर्थात् तांत्रिकों की तरह पांचरात्र आभ्यांतरिक अर्थ पर सर्वत्र बल देता है। शरीर के भी मन्त्र की तरह तीन रूप बताये गये हैं। प्रत्यक्ष, पुर्यष्टक (Grossbody) या सूक्ष्म तथा आणव (Atomic)[51]।

श्रौतसूत्र आदि ग्रन्थों में सोमयाग से पूर्व यजमान द्वारा सम्पाद्यमान विविध कर्म समुच्चय को दीक्षा कहते हैं। अनेक भारतीय विद्वानों ने दीक्षा शब्द की इसी परिभाषा को माना है। इन विद्वानों के अतिरिक्त पाश्चात्य विद्वानों में ओल्डेनवर्ग, कीथ आदि के नाम उल्लेखनीय है[52]। श्रौत प्रक्रिया में दीक्षा को अत्यन्त महत्वपूर्ण कृत्य माना गया है। इसी कारण अनेक वैदिक संहिताओं, श्रौतसूत्रों एवं ब्राह्मण ग्रंथों ने इस विषय का सम्यक विवेचन किया है[53]।

पांचरात्र आगम के अनुसार दीक्षा गुह्यात् हितकारक कहा गया है। विष्णुमण्डल में दीक्षा प्राप्ति के उपरान्त महापातकी तथा उपपातकी भी शीघ्र ही मुक्त हो जाते हैं। कर्मदुष्ट, बीजदुष्ट, आहारदुष्ट तथा संकरकारक भी एक बार अध्वर में दीक्षा प्राप्ति के बाद मुक्त हो जाते हैं।

दीक्षा निर्वाणदा होती है। पशुपति के लिए दीक्षा का न्यास कर चंचल चित्त का शोधन भी किया जाता है। इस प्रकार बन्धन से मुक्त होने का उपाय दीक्षा है[54]। अदीक्षित जनों का विष्णु की आराधना में अधिकार नहीं होता अर्थात् दीक्षा के पश्चात् ही वैष्णव भक्त भगवत् पूजा की अर्हता प्राप्त करते हैं[55]। दीक्षा प्राप्त कर मनुष्य मरणोपरान्त अभिमत पद को प्राप्त करता है। एक दीक्षा कैवल्य फलदा, दूसरी भोग तथा कैवल्यदा तथा तीसरी केवल भोगदा कही गयी है। वे सभी दीक्षायें आचार्यानुमत एवं फललाभ के अनुष्ठेय हैं[56]।

दीक्षा–प्रदान–क्रम में गुरु भगवान् के प्रति विज्ञापन करता है। उस विज्ञापन से दीक्षा के उद्देश्य तथा दीक्षा की विशेषता पर भी कुछ प्रकाश पड़ता है। आचार्य अथवा गुरु हाथ में देव को ग्रहण कर कहता हैः 'हे देव! संसार–पाशबद्ध पशुओं के पाशमोक्ष में मात्र तुम्हीं शरण हो, दूसरी कोई गति नहीं है। तुम्हारी आराधना ही इसमें हेतु है। अतः जन्मपाश में आबद्ध पशुजन्म वाले इस शिष्य को पाशमुक्त करने के लिए हे आदिदेव! अनुज्ञा प्रदान करो[57]।

अस्तु उपर्युक्त विवेचन से स्पष्ट है कि संसार–बन्धन से मुक्ति की प्राप्ति के लिए दीक्षा आवश्यक है। यह भी स्पष्ट है कि दीक्षा के बिना मनुष्य पशु रहता है। अर्थात् दीक्षा–द्वारा पशुत्व का निवारण कर शिष्य को उच्चता प्राप्त करायी जाती है। दीक्षा के तत्त्वहोमादि के द्वारा शुद्धदेह शिष्य निर्वाणाख्य पद को प्राप्त करता है जिस प्रकार जले हुए बीज से अंकुर उत्पन्न नहीं होता उसी प्रकार वैष्णवी दीक्षा–प्राप्त शिष्य पुनः पशुता को नहीं प्राप्त कर सकता, फिर पाशबन्ध होने का प्रश्न ही कहाँ उठता है[58]।

नारदीय संहिता में गौतम ने स्पष्ट कहा है कि बिना वैष्णवी दीक्षा प्राप्त किये इस पांचरात्र शास्त्र में या विष्णु की आराधना में किसी को अधिकार नहीं होता। इसी कारण गौतम सर्वप्रथम वैष्णवी दीक्षा प्राप्त करते हैं तदनन्तर नारद वैष्णव शास्त्र का उपदेश देते हैं। अर्थात् दीक्षा के बिना पांचरात्र शास्त्र में अधिकार नहीं होता। अतः पांचरात्र–ज्ञान–प्राप्ति की योग्यता के लिए दीक्षा–ग्रहण आवश्यक है[59]। यह विषय अन्यत्र संहिताओं में भी प्रायः इसी तरह देखा जा सकता है[60]।

नारदीय संहिता ने विष्णुहस्त–प्रदत्त शिष्य को जीवन्मुक्त होना कहा है– 'जीवन्मुक्तः स विज्ञेयः विष्णुहस्ते समर्पिते'[61]। विष्णुहस्त समर्पण दीक्षा का ही एक अंगभूत कर्म है। स्पष्ट है कि दीक्षा की पूर्णता के बाद दीक्षार्थी जीवन्मुक्त हो जाता है।

जयाख्य संहिता जो पांचरात्र आगम की अतिप्राचीन संहिताओं में से एक है सामान्य रूप से दो प्रकार की दीक्षा का निर्देश दिया है– 1. सामान्या दीक्षा, 2. विशेषाख्या दीक्षा। सामान्या दीक्षा के तीन भेद बतलाये गये हैं। संक्षिप्ता, मध्यमा तथा अतिविस्तृता। इसी संहिता में दीक्षा के प्रकारों तथा प्राप्त फलों का उल्लेख है[62]। ईश्वर संहिता ने भी तीन प्रकार के दीक्षाओं का निर्देश दिया है और तीनों दीक्षाओं के अन्त में गुरु शिष्य को शक्ति, भूषण तथा वाहन आदि प्रदान करता है[63]। ईश्वर संहिता में भूमि पर मण्डप तथा पीठ एवं उपपीठादि – कल्पन विधि का विस्तृत उल्लेख किया गया है[64]। नारदीय संहिता ने भी पर्वत–पृष्ठ, नदियों के मनोरम संगम–स्थल या महानदी का मनोरम किनारा दीक्षा–विधि सम्पादन के लिए उपयुक्त माना है। इन स्थलों में से किसी जगह भू–परीक्षण कर मण्डपादि–कल्पनापूर्वक दीक्षा–सम्पादन का विधान बतलाया है। ज्ञातव्य है कि नारदीय संहिता ने यहाँ इस प्रसंग में भू–परीक्षण के प्रायः उन्हीं विधियों का निर्देश किया है, जो वास्तु कल्पन प्रसंग में वर्णित है। यथा–भू–खनन पुनः उसका पूरण आदि क्रम[65]। पादम संहिता में सामान्य रूप से प्रतिष्ठा–विधि की तरह पवित्र देश में दीक्षा–मण्डपादि–कल्पन का निर्देश किया है[66]। कुछ अन्य संहिताओं ने पाद्म संहिता का अनुकरण किया है। दीक्षा क्रम में कुण्ड संस्कार उल्लेख पांचरात्र संहिताओं में विस्तार के साथ उल्लिखित है[67]। श्रीप्रश्न संहिता में 14 प्रकार के अग्निकुण्डों का उल्लेख है साथ ही विनियोग का विस्तृत विवेचन वर्णित है। नारदीय संहिता में उक्त कुण्डों में होम के विधान को बतलाया गया है[68]। जयाख्य संहिता में नित्य तथा नैमित्तिक होम के लिए वृत्त या चतुरस्र होम–कुण्ड का विवेचन है[69]। श्री प्रश्न संहिता ने दीक्षा प्रसंग में कहा है–

चतुरस्रं ब्राह्मणानां वृत्तं कुण्डं तु भूपतेः।
वैश्यस्य चापकुण्डं स्याच्छूद्रजातेस्त्रिकोणकम्।।

अर्थात् ब्राह्मणों की दीक्षा के समय चतुरस्र अग्निकुण्ड में, क्षत्रियों की दीक्षा के अवसर पर वृत्ताकार अग्निकुण्ड में, वैश्यों की दीक्षा के समय चापकुण्ड में तथा शूद्रों की दीक्षा के समय त्रिकोण अग्निकुण्ड में होम विहित है[70]। पाँच

अग्नि जिह्वाओं के विनियोग का क्रम नारदीय संहिता में वर्णित है। यहीं यह भी कहा गया है कि पूर्वास्य जिह्वा में शान्तिहोम, पश्चिम जिह्वा में प्रायश्चित्त होम, उतरास्य जिह्वा में सर्वकामार्थ होम, दक्षिणास्य जिह्वा में आभिचारिक होम, मध्यमास्य जिह्वा में सिद्धिलाभदायक होम किये जाते हैं[71]। अग्नि संस्कार पूर्वक अग्नि में होम करने का विधान बतलाया गया है। अग्नि–कार्य के पश्चात् दीक्षा के अंगभूत कार्य मण्डल आराधन का अवसर आता है। यद्यपि जयाख्य संहिता ने आढ्य शिष्य के लिए महामण्डलार्चन पूर्वक दीक्षा विधान का उल्लेख किया है तथापि सभी पांचरात्र आगम ग्रन्थों ने सामान्य रूप से दीक्षा विधि के वर्णनक्रम में सभी के लिए दीक्षांगभूत मण्डल के अर्चन का उल्लेख आवश्यक रूप से किया है। पांचरात्रिक वैष्णवों के लिए अनेक अवसरों पर, कुम्भ, मण्डल, अग्नि तथा बेरार्चन, चतुस्थानार्चन का विधान किया गया है। पांचरात्र प्रक्रिया में मण्डलों का सर्वाधिक महत्व रहा है। मण्डलार्चन का विशद वर्णन पौष्कर संहिता में उल्लिखित है जिसमें 25 मण्डलों का विवेचन है[72] तथा स्थूल रूप से कीर्तन भी किया गया है। नारदीय संहिता में सामान्यतः दो मण्डल स्वरूप का वर्णन है – भद्रमण्डल तथा चक्राब्ज मण्डल। सामान्य रूप से भद्रक मण्डल के एकादश अंग या विभाग देखे जा सकते हैं। अब्जयुक्त मण्डल सामान्यतः ये विभाग सभी जगह दिखलाई पड़ते हैं। अर्थात् कमल स्वरूप की तरह कल्पित इस मण्डल में कमल के सभी अंग–प्रत्यंग, विभाग एवं उपविभाग दिखलायी पड़ते हैं। नारदीय संहिता के दीक्षार्थ मण्डल के लिए मण्डप तथा पीठ कल्पन का वर्णन सातवें अध्याय के अन्त में है[73]। मार्कण्डेय संहिता में भी मण्डल के सन्दर्भ में वर्णन हुआ है[74]। मण्डल के स्वरूप आदि के वर्णन के उपरान्त विविध वर्ण विन्यास का अवसर आता है जिसका विस्तृत उल्लेख पाद्म संहिता एवं नारदीय संहिता में है[75]। मण्डल कल्पना एवं वर्णापादन के उपरान्त मण्डल के अंगों में उनके देवताओं की आराधना का विधान किया गया है। देवाराधन का विधान नारदीय संहिता में वर्णित है। इन देवताओं के अर्चनाक्रम में नमः शब्दान्त तत्तत् अध्व के सामाराधन का विधान विहित है[76]।

प्रसंगात् ध्यानार्ह है कि दीक्षाक्रम में शिष्य की शुद्धता के आपादान के लिए षडध्व हवन का विधान किया गया है। पाद्म संहिता के षडध्वों का उल्लेख करते हुए निम्नलिखित अध्वों का निर्देश किया है[77]। विश्वामित्र संहिता ने भी शिष्य में अध्वशोधन का निधान करते हुए षडध्वों का निर्देश किया है। ये षडध्व संख्या में छः है[78]। ईश्वर संहिता में भी षडध्वों का निर्देश अन्य पांचरात्र संहिताओं की तरह उल्लिखित है[79]।

शब्दब्रह्म के रूप में लक्ष्मी के प्रथम उन्मेषका नाम वर्णाध्व है[80]। अतः स्पष्ट है कि दीक्षा विधान में वर्णाध्व, तत्वाध्व, मन्त्राध्व, पदाध्व, एवं भुवनाध्व का महत्व उल्लेख्य है। माया से लेकर पृथ्वीपर्यान्त भुवन पद्धति को भुवनाध्व कहते हैं[81]। भुवनाध्व को अशुद्ध तथा मल पङ्किल कहा गया है[82]। त्याज्य के त्याग तथा प्राप्तव्य की प्राप्ति के लिए मुमुक्षु को षडध्व शोधन करना चाहिए। षडध्व से मुक्त होकर पर–ब्रह्म को प्राप्त करता है। शब्दब्रह्म ही षडध्व के रूप में परिणामित होता है। अतः मुमुक्षु शब्द ब्रह्म से अतीत को अर्थात् पर–ब्रह्म को प्राप्त करता है।[83]

विष्वक्सेन संहिता में दीक्षा के विषय में केवल एक ही अध्याय में विचार किया गया है जो दीक्षा से सम्बद्ध शकुन–विचार है[84]।

दीक्षा के समापन पर गुरु शिष्य को विष्णुहस्त प्रदान करता है। इससे पुरुष वासुदेव के समान हो जाता है[85]। इसमें करन्यास करके देहन्यास किया जाता है। यह न्यास सृष्टि, स्थिति एवं संहार रूप से तीन प्रकार का होता है। गुरु शिष्य के दोनों हाथों के मध्य सोम तथा सूर्यकला का न्यास भी करता है। कलाओं के न्यास के उपरान्त दक्षिणहस्त की अंगुलियों के पर्वों में ये कलायें न्यस्त होती हैं। सोलहवीं कला निर्वाणाख्या कला कही गयी है। इसी क्रम में गुरु पहले दक्षिण हस्त शिष्य के मस्तक पर रखते हैं। उसके द्वारा पातकों के वह्निकला का ध्यान कर पाशजाल का दहन किया जाता है[86]।

इन सभी क्रियाओं के सम्पादन के उपरान्त दीक्षा–निर्वतन करते हैं। अग्नि में ब्रह्म का ध्यान कर होम के सम्पादन पूर्वक कला–व्याख्यान योग से यह निर्वर्त्तन होता है। इस प्रकार विष्णुहस्त प्रदत्त शिष्य जीवन्मुक्त कहा गया है[87]।

उपर्युक्त तथ्यों के आलोडन, अवलोकन एवं विश्लेषणोपरान्त स्पष्ट है कि पांचरात्र संहिताओं, तंत्रों, आगमों में 'दीक्षा' शब्द की उत्पत्ति एवं अर्थवत्ता पर प्रकाश डालते हुए यह विवेचित है कि भक्त वैष्णव दीक्षा के उपरान्त ही विष्णु–पूजा के अर्ह होता है। दीक्षा के लिए आचार्य के लक्षणों को बतलाते हुए कहा गया है कि गुरु अन्य गुणों के साथ योग स्वाध्याय तत्पर, तन्त्रान्तर विचक्षण, मन्त्र एवं तन्त्रज्ञ होना चाहिए। इसीलिए श्री प्रश्नसंहिता में कहा गया है– 'आचार्यो मन्त्र सम्पूर्णः क्रिया पुर्णास्तु शिल्पिनः', (49–468.9)।

दीयते दिव्य सद्ज्ञानं क्षीयते पशुवासना।
दान क्षपण संयुक्ता दीक्षा तेनेह कीर्तिता।।

अर्थात् जिससे दिव्य ज्ञान की प्राप्ति होती है। पाशविक वासनाओं का क्षपण यानी नाश होता है, ऐसे दान और क्षपण युक्त क्रिया को दीक्षा कहते हैं। पांचरात्रिक दीक्षा प्राप्त दीक्षित भक्त वैष्णव जीवनमुक्त हो जाता है क्योंकि दीक्षा निर्वाणदा होती है, कैवल्यदा होती है तथा मुक्तिदा होती है। साथ ही 'आचार्य विना न दीक्षा, दीक्षा विना न मोक्षः' के

वैशिष्टय पर विशेष बल दिया गया है। इसी कारण तन्त्रपारग मुनियों, मन्त्रद्रष्टा ऋषियों, तपस्वियों, साधकों, चिन्तकों, यतियों, योगियों, सभी सम्प्रदाय के आचार्यों के मतों एवं सिद्धान्तों में इसे महिमान्वित किया गया है जो सामाजिक, सांस्कृतिक एवं धार्मिक अध्ययन की दृष्टि से अत्यन्त उपादेय है।

संदर्भ

1. अगस्त्य संहिता[2], अध्याय 8, (रामन्मन्त्र), अ0 17 (राम गायत्री); अनिरुद्ध संहिता, 4–4,(परिभाषा), 187–215 (ब्राह्मणों के लिए शास्त्र, सभी के लिए मन्त्र), अहिर्बुध्न्य संहिता, अ0 15,.37 अ (यज्ञ–दीक्षा–मनुष्य का तृतीय जन्म); ईश्वर संहिता[1], अ0 21. 1–558, 1–510 : पाँच प्रकार, 54–74, : दीक्षा के लिए द्रव्य, 23–25 ; जयाख्य संहिता पटल 16.1–369, 54–61अ (शिष्य के लिए दीक्षा), 61–89 (कर्म), अ0 17.1–62, अ0 18.1–93 अ, अ0 19.1–37 अ, ज्ञानामृत सार संहिता I–9 (यत्र–तत्र), III–7, अ0 9, (यत्र–तत्र) : 5. I : 4 ; नारदीय संहिता, अ0 .7.1–110 अ, अ0 8.1–91 अ, अ0प्र0 91–347 अ ; परम संहिता, 7.1–70, अ0 8.1–82, अ0 17.1–21 (राजा एवं मंत्री के लिए) ; पराशर संहिता, अ0 3.129–136, अ0 4.143, अ0 6.1–66 (मन्त्र दीक्षा), पादम संहिता, चर्यापाद, अ.2.1–86 (दशमी), पुरुषोत्तम संहिता, अ 22..1–80 (परिभाषा), 13 परिभाषा ; पौष्कर संहिता, 1, 1–32, अ0 38.47–71; बृहद् ब्रह्म, 1.5 6–42, 6.1–108 (मन्त्र), 7.1–110 (मन्त्र), 3.3; मार्कण्डेय संहिता, 7.14 ब–36 अ; लक्ष्मीतन्त्र, 41.1–66; विश्वामित्र संहिता, 9.0 1–94 अ (चक्रमण्डलदीक्षा); विष्णु संहिता, 10.1–94 अ(सबसे अच्छा मास 31 अप्रैल–जुलाई, दूसरा चयन नवम्बर–फरवरी 11.1–82 अ), 29.1–52, विष्णुतिलक संहिता, 4.187–215; विष्वक्सेन संहिता, 15 ब – 112 (शकुन विचार); शाण्डिल्य संहिता, 1.8.1–46, 10.1–32, 19 (यत्र–तत्र गोपाल, गायित्री); श्री प्रश्न संहिता, 16.19 अ (परिभाषा)16.19 अ (परिभाषा), 21–33 (पाँच प्रकार के स्तर), 34–56 द्रव्य, सनत्कुमार संहिता, इन्द्ररात्र, 4.1–55 (चक्रमण्डल, 9 प्रकार), 9.84ब – 92 (चारभाग), ऋषिरात्र, 5.1–44; सात्वत संहिता, अ. 16 – 17 अ0–18 –19 अ (तीन प्रकार की दीक्षा)।
2. प्रपंचसार, 5 एवं 6
3. कुलार्णव तंत्र, 14.39
4. शारदा तिलक, चतुर्थपटल
5. नित्सयोत्सव, पृ0.4–10
6. ज्ञानार्णव, 24वाँ पटल
7. विष्णु संहिता, पटल.10
8. महानिर्वाणतंत्र, 10.112–119
9. लिंगपुराण, 2.21
10. पांचरात्रागम, राघव प्रसाद चौधरी, बिहार राष्ट्रभाषा परिषद् पटना, 1987, पृ0 266
11. विष्णुसंहिता, ऐन इन्ट्रोडक्शन बाइ एन0पी0 मुनी, पृ0 102, नाग पब्लिशर्स, जवाहर नगर, दिल्ली, 1991
12. अनिरुद्ध संहिता, 4.4–5; अहिर्बुध्न्य संहिता, 1–58, जयाख्य संहिता, 16.1–369; ज्ञानामृतसार संहिता, 1.2. यत्र–तत्र, 3.7, 8,9 यत्र–तत्र वर्णित है, 5.1–14; नारदीय संहिता, 9.213–246 (यत्र–तत्र); पराशर संहिता, 6.1–66; लक्ष्मीतन्त्र, 41.9–34; शेष संहिता, 14.26; ब–74अ; श्रीप्रश्न संहिता, 51.1–103, 52.1–202 अ; सनत्कुमार संहिता, ऋषिरात्र, 6.16–182 अ; सात्वत संहिता, 17.1–454, 18.1–232, 19.1–182,
13. कुलार्णवतंत्र, 17.51
14. शारदातिलक, 4.2
15. अग्निपुराण, 27.81–89 एवं 304
16. ज्ञानार्णव तंत्र, 24.45–53
17. धर्मसिन्धु पृ0 32; रघुनन्दन दीक्षा तत्व, भाग 2, पृ0 645–659
18. अहिर्बुध्न्य संहिता, भाग एक, पृ0 184–185
19. तन्त्रसार; 1, गन्धर्व तन्त्र 2; शारदा तिलक, 2.142–144, 'सर्वा ममाना सारज्ञः सर्वशास्त्रर्थ तत्त्ववित। अमोघ वचनः शान्ती वेदवेदार्थ पारगः।
20. तैत्तिरीय संहिता, 6.1.1.3, 7.4.8; ऐतरेय ब्राह्मण, 1.3; शतपथ ब्राह्मण, 3.2.1.19 एवं 22, अथर्ववेद, 7.1.1, किन्तु तांत्रिक परम्परा ने इसका स्वरूप प्रदान किया है– द्र0 प्रपंचसार, 5 एवं 6; कुलार्णव तंत्र, 14, 39; शारदातिलक पटल, 4; नित्योत्सव, 4–10; ज्ञानार्णव, पटल 24; विष्णु संहिता, 10; महानिर्वाण तंत्र, 10.112–219; लिंग पुराण 2.21; रघुनन्दन दीक्षा तत्व 2.645–659
21. गुरु की योग्यताओं और शिष्य के गुणों का सुन्दर विश्लेषण तन्त्रसार 1 में वर्णित है, गन्धर्व तन्त्र–2 शारदातिलक, 2. 142–144–'सर्वा ममाना सारज्ञः सर्वशास्त्रार्थ तत्ववित'। अमोघ वचनः शान्ति वेदवेदार्थ पारगः। योग मार्गानुसन्ध्यायी देवता हदयंगमः।' तुलनीय, कुलार्णव तन्त्र, उल्लास 12 एवं 13, शारदा तिलक, 1.145–53; ज्ञानसिद्धि, 139–12 तथा प्रज्ञोप्राय विनिश्चय सिद्धि 3.9–16
22. अहिर्बुध्न्य संहिता, 20.1–7
23. संसारङ्गार मध्यस्थः पच्मानः स्वकर्मभिः। भवन्तः शरणं प्राप्त उपसन्नोऽस्म्यधीहि भो। अहिर्बुध्न्य संहिता, भाग–1, पृ0 185
24. तपः संतोष शौचाढ्यो योग स्वाध्याय तत्परः। पांचरात्र विधानज्ञस्तन्त्रान्तर विचक्षणः।। तन्त्राणामन्तरज्ञश्च मन्त्राणां कृत्य तत्ववित्। पदवाक्य प्रमाणज्ञो हेतुवाद विचक्षणः।।

अहिर्बुध्न्य संहिता, 20.4–5

25. अहिर्बुध्न्य संहिता, 20.8–10,शिष्य को शुद्धात्मा एवं पुरुषार्थ के प्रति अनुरक्त होना चाहिए। द्र0 मत्स्य सूक्त तन्त्र, 13, प्राण तोषिणी, 108
26. भवन्तं शरणं प्राप्त उपसन्नोस्म्यधीहि भो, अहिर्बुध्न्य संहिता, 20.10 उत्तरार्द्ध विस्तृत विवरण के लिए द्र0 अहिर्बुध्न्य संहिता : संक्षिप्तरूपरेखा, डॉ0 किरण कुमारी श्रीवास्तव, एक्सेलेंस पब्लिशर्स, इलाहाबाद, 1993, पृ0 68–69
27. 'रहस्यामायगोपिने'– तत्रैव, 20–12 का उत्तरार्द्ध
28. तांत्रिक परम्परा के मतानुसार गुरु एवं देवता में कोई भेद नहीं होता दोनों एक हैं। द्र0 योगिनी तंत्र–1, सर ज्ञान वुडराफ, इन्ट्रोडक्शन टू तंत्रशास्त्र पृ0 66, लिंग पुराण–1.85 'यो गुरुः स शिवः प्रोक्तोयः शिव स गुरुस्मृतः, प्रपंचसार, 6.12; शारदातिलक, 5.113–114, ब्रह्माड पुराण 43.68–70; देवीभागवत में कहा गया है कि मानसिक उपचारों से विधिपूर्वक गुरुदेव की प्रार्थना करे– 'गुरु ही विष्णु है, गुरु ही देवता है, गुरु ही महेश्वर है अतः उस श्रीगुरुदेव के लिए मेरा नमस्कार है– 'गुरुर्ब्रह्मा गुरुर्विष्णुर्गुरुर्देवो महेश्वरः। गुरुखेव परमब्रह्म तस्मै श्री गुरुवे नमः।। देवीभागवत, 11.1.49.
29. बिना दीक्षां न मोक्षः स्यातदुक्तं शिवशासने। सा च न स्यादिलाचार्यमित्याचार्य परम्परा।
कुलार्णव तंत्र, उल्लास, 14.3
30. 'पुर्यष्टकं तु सूक्ष्माख्य' – अहिर्बुध्न्य संहिता 20.32 । 'पुर्यष्टकं' शब्द का अर्थ है अष्टभुजा से युक्त नगर अर्थात् शरीर। द्र0 डॉ0 किरणकुमारी श्रीवास्तव, पूर्वोद्धृत पृ0 69
31. अहिर्बुध्न्य संहिता, 20.43–48
32. तत्रैव, 20.48–51
33. तत्रैव, पृ0 188
34. 'मन्मनाथः प्रसीदति', तत्रैव, पृ0 192
35. गरुणपुराण, 1.126, 31, 32
36. नारदीयपुराण, 2.57. 13–14
37. भागवत महापुराण, 6.8, 40वां श्लोक द्र0
38. ब्रह्मपुराण, 60.35–40
39. तत्रैव, 60–35–39
40. पद्मपुराण, 6.79.17–30
41. तत्रैव, 85–26 साथ ही द्रष्टव्य, मत्स्य पुराण, 226.29; देवी भागवत, 11.16–76–91, देवीभागवत, 11.7–26–38; कालिका पुराण, 53.36; बृहद्योगियाज्ञवल्क्य (स्मृति चन्द्रिका 1. पृ0 198 – 'अंगुष्ठे चैव गोविन्दं तर्जन्यां तु महीधरम् । मध्यमायां ऋषीकेशमनामिक्यां त्रिविक्रमम्। कनिष्ठक्यां न्यसेद्विष्णुं हस्तमध्ये च माधवम् (स्मृति चन्द्रिका (1. पृ0 198) ने इसे योगियाज्ञवल्क्य का स्वीकार किया है। साथ ही राघव भट्ट (शारदा तिलक 5.4) तथा महानिर्वाण तन्त्र(5.176–178) में भी द्रष्टव्य है।
42. विस्तृत विवरण के लिए द्र0 काणे, धर्मशास्त्र का इतिहास, पंचमभाग, अध्याय 26, पृ0 64–65
43. अथ दीक्षां प्रवक्ष्यामि सर्वासिद्धि प्रवर्त्तिकाम् । यां विना नैव सिद्धिं स्यात्मन्त्रः वर्षशतैरपि। ददाति दिव्य भावं च क्षिणुयात् पापसन्ततिम्। तेन दीक्षेत् विख्याता मुनिभिस्तन्त्र पारगैः। गौतमीयतन्त्रम्, 7.1–3 चौखम्भा संस्करण 1977
44. भ्रमन्ति योनिमार्गेषु प्रविष्टाः पाशपंजरैः। दीक्षया दिवक्षयं यान्ति दीक्षा निर्वाणदा भवेत्।।
नारदीय संहिता, 7.7
45. ईक्षते कर्मणा येन तद्विष्णोः परमंपदं। द्यति सांसारमाखिलं तेन दीक्षेतिभण्यते।
श्रीप्रश्न संहिता, 16.18–19 अ।
46. द्र0 पांचरात्रागम, राघव प्रसाद चौधरी, बिहार राष्ट्रभाषा परिषद, पटना, 1987, पृ0 268
47. अहिर्बुध्न्य संहिता भाग 1, पृ0 185
48. देवप्रतिष्ठा तत्व, पृ0 505
49. जयाख्य संहिता, पटल–11, प्रपंचसार, 6; कुलार्णवतन्त्र, 4.18; शारदातिलक, 4.29–41; महानिर्वाणतन्त्र, 3.41–43, 5.11–118
50. अहिर्बुध्न्यसंहिता, पृ0 185
51. तत्रैव, पृ0 188
52. सिग्निफिकेन्स ऑफ दीक्षा अनाल्स ऑफ द भण्डारकर ओरियण्टल इन्स्टीट्यूट, पूना वाल्यूम 11, भाग–1–4, 1970
53. शतपथ ब्राह्मण, 3.2.1; कात्यायन श्रौत सूत्र, 7.2.4
54. नारदीय संहिता, 7.3–9
55. ईश्वर संहिता, 21.1
56. ईश्वर संहिता, 21.247–249
57. पाद्म संहिता, चर्यापाद, 2.29–31
58. नारदीय संहिता, 9.27–28
59. नारदीय संहिता, 1.18–20
60. ईश्वर संहिता, 21–419–20; नारदीय संहिता, 9.321
61. नारदीय संहिता, 9.344
62. जयाख्य संहिता, 16.54–61
63. ईश्वर संहिता, 21.448–460
64. ईश्वर संहिता, 21.44
65. नारदीय संहिता, 7.10–14

66. पाद्म संहिता, चर्यापाद, 2.3, विश्वामित्र, 9.3–4
67. नारदीय संहिता, 7.22.28, जयाख्य संहिता, पटल 16.95–104, ईश्वर संहिता, 21.98 एवं आगे, पाद्म संहिता चर्यापाद, 2.9–14, विश्वामित्र संहिता, 9.12–19
68. नारदीय संहिता, 7.41–46
69. जयाख्य संहिता, पटल–15–31
70. श्रीप्रश्न संहिता, 16.40
71. नारदीय संहिता, 7.55–76
72. पौष्कर संहिता, 5.1–18
73. नारदीय संहिता, 7.102–106
74. मार्कण्डेय संहिता, 12.1–21
75. पाद्म संहिता, चर्यापाद, 7.1–46; नारदीय संहिता, 8.59–61
76. नारदीय संहिता, 8.61–74
77. कलाध्वा च पदाध्वा च भुवनाध्वा तथैव च। मनत्रध्वा मन्त्रवर्णाध्वा षडध्वानः प्रकीर्त्तिता।।
    पाद्म संहिता, चर्यापाद, 2.51
78. विश्वामित्र संहिता, 9.57–58
79. ईश्वर संहिता, 21.13–216
80. 'उन्मेषः मस्तस्य वर्णाध्वापरिकीर्तितः'। लक्ष्मीतंत्र, 22.12
81. तत्रैव, 22.27–28
82. तत्रैव, 22.28
83. लक्ष्मीतंत्र, 22.31, 51.32 – विस्तृत विवरण के लिए द्र0 अशोक कुमार कालिया, लक्ष्मी तन्त्र : धर्म और दर्शन, अखिल भारतीय संस्कृत परिषद, लखनऊ, 1977, पृ0 111
84. विष्वक्सेन संहिता, 37.16–91
85. जयाख्य संहिता, 16.334
86. पांचरात्र आगम, राघव प्रसाद चौधरी, विहार राष्ट्र भाषा परिषद् पटना 1987, पृ0 307–308
87. नारदीय संहिता, 9.321–345

53

पांचरात्र संहिताओं में नृ–सिंह का स्वरूप

ध्यानेन्द्र नारायण दूबे

नारसिंहाविर्भाव

सनत्कुमार संहिता पांचरात्र परम्परा की प्राचीन संहिताओं में एक है।[1] इस संहिता में नारसिंहाविर्भाव का ''पुराण'' वर्णित है। इसके इन्द्र–रात्र नामक तृतीय खण्ड (रात्र) के पुराणाध्याय के अन्तर्गत वराह, नारसिंह, मत्स्य, कूर्म, तार्क्ष्य (गरूड़), वामन से लेकर राम और सात्वत (कृष्ण) तक के आविर्भावों के ''पुराण'' का वर्णन करते हुए कहा गया है कि लोकहित की कामना से जो सात्वत उनके शिष्य और भक्त का ध्यान करते हैं, वे सभी सात्वत कहलाते हैं और उन्हें ही कोई सात्वत, कोई भागवत, कोई वैष्णव तो कोई पांचरात्रिक कहता है।[2]

नारसिंह आविर्भाव के उत्तम पुराण का संक्षिप्त वर्णन करते हुए यहाँ कहा गया है कि हिरण्यकशिपु नामक एक दुर्जेय महासुर हुआ जिसने अपने बल व तेज के द्वारा सभी देवताओं को पीड़ित कर दिया। अस्तु दुरात्मा दानवों से पीड़ित सभी देवता संत्रस्त और आकुल चित्त के साथ रूद्र की शरण में पहुँचे। रूद्र सभी देवताओं के साथ ब्रह्मा समस्त देवगण को साथ लेकर महादेव अनिरूद्ध की शरणगति में आ पहुँचे। देव–मण्डल को अपने सम्मुख देखकर पुरूषोत्तम अनिरूद्ध नागशय्या से उठे तो देवताओं ने उनके चतुर्मख रूप की आसन–पानादि से पूजा अर्चना की और उन्हें प्रसन्नचित देखकर उनकी करबद्ध प्रार्थना की।[3] सर्व व्यापक परब्रह्म परमेश्वर के चित्त में देवताओं की प्रार्थना से तत्क्षण नारसिंह नामक पर रूप अभिनिविष्ट हुआ। फलतः उनका विलक्षण ''सिंह वक्त्र नराकार'' रूप प्रकट हुआ। उस महादेव के नेत्रयुगल अंगार सदृश्य प्रदीप्त थे, चन्द्ररश्मि प्रतीकाश भयनाशक भैरव नारसिंह का रूप अद्भुत था। शंख, चक्र और गदा धारण किये हुए नृसिंह देव तत्काल हिरण्यकशिपु–वध के निमित्त चल पड़े।[4] संध्याकाल में प्रकट होकर अपने दोनों जंघों पर दैत्यराज के हृदय को विदीर्ण कर डाला देवताओं की हित कामना से हिरण्यकशिपु–वध करके सुरेश्वर नारसिंह दक्षिण दिशा में चले गये।[5]

नृसिंह स्वरूप–विवेचन

पांचरात्र आगम की संहिताओं में विभव नृसिंह स्वरूप का बहुविध वर्णन उपलब्ध है। उनके ध्यान–मंत्र, वक्त्र–मंत्र और अंग–मंत्रादि के वहाँ वर्णन हुए हैं। इस तरह के वर्णन त्रिरत्न संहिताओं से लेकर पश्चात्वर्ती संहिताओं में मिलते हैं जिसमें नृसिंह देव के स्वरूप का परिचय मिल जाता है।[6] इसके अतिरिक्त नृसिंह मूर्ति विषयक वर्णन भी संहिताओं का प्रतिपाद्य रहा है, जो प्रतिमा–शास्त्रीय आगमिक परम्परा के अध्ययन के लिए उपयोगी है।

नृसिंह–मंत्र–विधान आदि में अभिव्यक्त रूप

जयाख्य संहिता के वक्त्र–मंत्र–साधन नामक उन्तीसवें पटल में नृसिंह–वक्त्र–मंत्र, नृसिंह के मूर्ति–मंत्र, नृसिंहानुचर मूर्तियों के ध्यान प्रकार, नृसिंह के शक्ति–मंत्र, नृसिंह शक्तियों के ध्यान प्रकार और नृसिंह–मंत्र–सिद्धि से उत्पन्न सामर्थ्य को उपवर्णित किया गया है।[7] यहाँ नृसिंह के वदन को "कल्पान्तार्कायुतप्रभ" कहा गया है[8] और मूर्ति–चतुष्टय का ध्यान किया गया है। ये चतुर्मूर्तियाँ क्रमशः सूर्य लोकप्रद, अग्नि प्रभाकर अत्युग्रदर्पषमन और विश्वशूकर कहलाती है। ये सभी नृसिंह मूर्तियाँ चर्तुभुजी रूप में ध्येय कही गयी हैं।[9] उन्हें सकल विप्लव विनाशक, नखों से प्रहार करने के कारण विष्ययारब्य रूप में विशिष्ट मुद्रा में स्मरणीय बताया गया है।[10] नृसिंह के शक्ति मंत्रों के निर्देश में और उनके ध्यान प्रकार के वर्णन में नृकेसरी के भीषण रूप का निदर्शन हुआ है।[11]

सात्वत संहिता में श्री नृसिंह के मूर्त साकार परब्रह्म स्वरूप का ध्यान किया गया है। उनके लिए बृहन्मूर्ति और सुभीषण जैसे विशेषण प्रयुक्त किये गये हैं। यहाँ निष्टप्तकनकाय देव को नृकेसरी कहा गया है, जिसके शरीर से प्रज्वलित अग्नि स्फुलिंगों के द्वारा एक विलक्षण आभा–मण्डल अभिव्यक्त होता है। यह वृहन्मूर्ति सात्त्वत संहिता के भाष्यकार अलषिंग भट्ट द्वारा प्रस्तुत पाठान्तर में "ब्रह्म मूर्ति है, जिसका अभिप्राय है – बृहत्काय। सत्व एवं रज श्रेणी दीप्त जिसके दोनों कर अभय मुद्राओं में शुद्ध सत्व मय नख–पंक्ति विराजित जिसके युगल कर वरद–मुद्रा की अभिव्यक्ति करते हैं।[12] पौश्कर संहिता में केवल नृसिंहावतार स्थान विन्ध्यारण्य में निर्दिष्ट है। तथा इस देवता को समस्त जीवों का पापहन्ता मृगेन्द्रात्मा कहा गया है। ईश्वर संहिता नाम की दो कृतियाँ उपलब्ध है। पहली पच्चीस अध्यायों में उपलब्ध और तेलगू तथा देवनागरी से प्रकाशित भी है।[13] दूसरी कृति नृसिंह–कल्प के नाम से विख्यात है तथा इसकी मातृका पत्रकार (ग्रन्थ) लिपि में प्राच्य–विद्या–संस्थान बड़ौदा (सं0 7967) में सुरक्षित है। जैसा कि इसके विख्यात नाम से स्पष्ट है, इसमें नृसिंह–मंत्र आदि की महिमा अभिव्यक्त है। नृसिंह–मंत्र को यहाँ अतिशय सामर्थ्य से युक्त तथा सभी वर्गों के लिए उपयुक्त बताया गया है। इसके चतर्थ अध्याय में नृसिंह–मंत्र के 77 प्रकार बताये गये हैं। इनमें दो विशिष्ट प्रकारों के नाम हैं – मुद्राबन्धन और अग्नि–पाकार। विभिन्न ध्यान पद्धतियों के जो उदाहरण यहाँ मिलते हैं वे अनुष्टुभ मंत्र के अन्तर्गत है। इनमें से एक पद्धति को पुच्छ–सिंह कहा गया है तो दूसरे को एकवीर। इस मंत्र का प्रयोग निश्चय ही दूसरों को प्रभावित और पराभूत करने की दृष्टि से किया जा सकता है। जब कोई 'पंचमुखी नरसिंह' का स्मरण करता है तो उस देवता का प्रत्येक भाग भयानक दिखायी देता है फिर तो इस मंत्र का प्रयोग न केवल विभिन्न रोगों का निदान करता है अपितु भयंकर व्याधियों का शमन, यहाँ तक कि विशापह्रण भी कर देता है।[14]

इस संहिता में नृसिंह–यंत्र और उसके महत्व का वर्णन इसके पाँचवें अध्याय में हुआ है, जहाँ नृसिंह मंत्र सहित यह यंत्र शत्रु दलन, ऐश्वर्य–प्राप्ति, रोग–मुक्ति आदि के लिए वरेण्य माना गया है। यह यंत्र किसी कपड़े के टुकड़े पर, पत्ते पर अथवा ताबीज के रूप में धारण किया जा सकता है।[15] इस संहिता के अगले अध्यायों में नृसिंह–मंत्र के साथ मुद्राओं तथा अन्य अनेक विध क्रियाओं का वर्णन है।[16] इसके ग्यारहवें अध्याय में नरसिंह के भयानक स्वरूप का ध्यान किया गया है। उनका वर्णन करते हुए कहा गया है कि वे आठ भुजाओं से युक्त है, उनके केश रक्तवर्णीय है, आँखें लाल हैं और पवित्र लक्षणों से युक्त उनके साथ लक्ष्मी विराजमान है। उनके इस रूप के स्मरण के साथ ऐसा निर्देश है कि सिंह मंत्र का जाप निरन्तर करना चाहिए। इसे अतिशय फलदायी कहा गया है। इसके अतिरिक्त हवन कर्म तो और भी फलदायक माना गया है। बताया गया है कि इस नृसिंह महामंत्र को विष्णु ने ब्रह्मा को और ब्रह्मा ने अगस्त को प्रदान किया था। ब्रह्मा ने इसे सनक तथा अन्य ऋषियों को भी दिया था।[17]

ईश्वर संहिता नाम से प्रसिद्ध जो ग्रन्थ प्रकाशित है उसका चौबीसवां अध्याय मुद्रा–लक्षण भगवद् ध्यानादि प्रकार कहलाता है। इसमें विभव रूपों का वर्णन करते हुए अन्ततः नरसिंह स्वरूप का भी वर्णन किया गया है।[18] यहाँ इस वर्णन का प्रतिपाद्य नृसिंह–विभव का ध्यान है।

तेलगू लिपि में उपलब्ध पराशर संहिता के पन्द्रहवें अध्याय (हंस मत्स्यादि मंत्र विधि) में नरसिंह मंत्र[19] एवं ध्यान मंत्र[20] भी देखा जा सकता है। इसी अध्याय में नरसिंह गायत्री उल्लिखित है।[21] पुनः नरसिंह मंत्र के जाप के लिए उपयुक्त पावन स्थलों का निर्देश किया गया है।[22] पराशर संहिता के अगले अध्याय में सुदर्शननारसिंह–मंत्र का विवेचन उपलब्ध है, यहाँ वस्तुतः सुदर्शन मंत्र के व्याख्या के उपरान्त नरसिंहानुष्टुभ चक्र और सुदर्शन नरसिंह मंत्र पर विमर्श किया गया है।[23] पराशर संहिता के ही अन्तिम अध्याय में नृसिंह मंत्र के चौसठ प्रकारों का विवेचन करते हुए उस पर सम्यक् विमर्श किया गया है।[24] वे सर्वाभरण भूषित हैं, दाहिने हाथ में चक्र तथा बायें हाथ में शंख धारण करते हैं। सभी अवयवों से पूर्ण सर्वसिद्धि कर शुभ श्वेत पर्वत के समान सबके दुःख का विनाश करते हैं। रक्त–चन्दन से दिग्ध है जिनके अंग, शरच्चन्द्र–कला के समान दाँत वाले, क्रुद्ध रूप, दुष्टों के संहारकर्ता, नृसिंह के रूप का यहाँ वर्णन किया गया है।[25]

शेष संहिता में नृसिंह मंत्र का निर्देश है।[26] इसी संहिता के अगले अध्याय में सुदर्शन नरसिंह के बीज–मंत्रों का वर्णन हुआ है।[27] अन्यत्र लक्ष्मी–नरसिंह के बीज–मंत्र वर्णित है[28] पुनः वराह–नरसिंह–बीजमंत्र[29] एवं हयग्रीव नरसिंह–बीजमंत्र[30] निर्दिष्ट है। इसी संहिता का एक अध्याय नरसिंह राजांग मंत्र के रूप में वर्णित है।[31] एक अन्य अध्याय में मंत्र–रत्न इसके मंत्र के साथ विवेचित है[32] जो इस संहिता के एक पूर्ववर्ती अध्याय सुदर्शन–नरसिंह की याद दिलाता है, जहाँ इस विषय पर सम्यक् प्रकाश डाला गया है।[33]

हयशीर्ष संहिता के वनयागपटल में नरसिंह–पूजा का संकेत है, वहाँ वाह्य क्षेत्र अरण्य में इस पूजन का विधान वर्णित है। नरसिंह की स्तुति करने और दुरात्माओं के भाग जाने के आह्वान के बाद एक रात्रि पर्यन्त उपवास एवं शयन के पश्चात् आचार्य शिल्पियों के साथ प्रस्तर तक्षण यंत्र (छेनी) के साथ पूर्व निश्चित प्रस्तर निर्मित चौकी तक जाता है। शिल्पी अथवा पूर्वाभिमुख तक्षण कार्य आरम्भ करता है। प्रस्तर के समान ही काष्ठ शिल्प के लिए भी यही विधान यहाँ वर्णित है।[34] अन्यत्र प्रतिमा–लक्षण के सन्दर्भ में नृसिंह पूजन के सन्दर्भ ध्यातव्य हैं।[35] श्री–प्रश्न संहिता के मंत्रोद्धार विधि प्रसंग में नृसिंह का ध्यान करते हुए उन्हें समस्त व्याधियों का शमन करने वाला, पिशाचों का निवर्तन करने वाला कहा गया है और उनके मंत्र जाप का निर्देश किया गया है।[36] परम संहिता के काम्य शीर्षक **26**वें अध्याय में भी नरसिंह–मंत्र एवं नरसिंह वक्त्र–मंत्र का विधान है।[37] यहाँ कहा गया है कि योगासन पूर्वक इसके प्रयोग से व्यक्ति अपने आकांक्षाओं की पूर्ति कर सकता है।

उपर्युक्त विवेचन नारसिंह–मंत्र, वक्तत्र–मंत्र एवं अंग–मंत्रादि आगमिक परम्परा की ओर ध्यान आकृष्ट करते हैं। इनके महत्व अर्थात् इनके फल का प्रतिपादन भी यत्र–तत्र किया गया है। नारदीय संहिता में कहा गया है कि नृसिंह के जिन–जिन पूजनों का विधान किया गया है, उनसे सभी कामनाओं की पूर्ति हो जाती है।[38]

नृसिंह–यंत्र

नृसिंह का स्वरूप अपने आप में ''तांत्रिक–यंत्र'' की अभिव्यक्ति करता है और वैष्णव संहिताओं में इसके इस रूप की प्रतिष्ठा भी रही है। पूर्व निर्दिष्ट नृसिंहकल्प (ईश्वर संहिता–2) के एक अध्याय में नृसिंह–मंत्र के साथ, शत्रु–दमन, ऐश्वर्य–प्राप्ति और रोग मुक्त, आदि के लिए वरेण्य माना गया है। वहाँ कहा गया है कि यह मंत्र कपड़े के टुकड़े पर पत्ते पर अथवा ठीकरे पर अंकित करके ताबीज रूप में धारण किया जा सकता है।[39] परमेश्वर संहिता में संयोगात् इस संदर्भ में दो विशिष्ट अध्याय मिलते हैं। इसका तेइसवाँ अध्याय (सुदर्शन नृसिंह महायंत्र स्वरूप कथन) कहलाता है और चौबीसवाँ अध्याय ''मंत्रराज मंत्रोद्धार विधान'' कहलाता है। इस संहिता के अंतिम दो अध्याय अर्थात् पच्चीस एवं छब्बीस भी इसी विषय से सम्बद्ध है, जिनका सम्बन्ध इसके कर्मकाण्डीय पक्ष से अधिक है। इस संहिता के वर्णन के अनुसार ज्ञात होता है कि यह ज्ञान शिव से प्राप्त हुआ है। शिव को इसका ज्ञान साक्षात् नारायण से प्राप्त हुआ था, उद्देश्य था इसकी सिद्धि से ब्रह्मा के पाँच शीर्षों में से एक को काटकर अलग कर देना।[40] इस यंत्र का रहस्य शिव से इन्द्र को, इन्द्र से लोकपालों को, लोकपालों से अखिल जगत को प्राप्त हुआ। ऐसा कहा गया है कि जो जगत का कल्याण चाहते हैं, उन्हें मन्दिर में इसकी बिम्ब प्रतिमा सहित मंत्र–विधि का पालन करना चाहिए। किन्तु यह स्वरूप जब एक मंदिर में प्रतिष्ठित कर दिया जाय तो उसकी उपेक्षा नहीं करनी चाहिए। उसकी सतत् उपासना अनिवार्य है। इस अध्याय के कुछ भाग सुदर्शन और नृसिंह यंत्र की रूप रचना सम्बन्धी लक्षणों के विवरण देते हैं, इतना ही नहीं इस महायंत्र के ऊपर उनकी प्रतिमाओं की प्रतिष्ठा का वर्णन भी किया गया है। यहीं कहा गया है कि व्यक्तिगत उपयोग की दृष्टि से यह यंत्र एक ताबीज अथवा गुह्य तत्व के रूप में भी निर्मित हो सकता है।[41]

पारमेश्वर संहिता के चौबीसवें अध्याय का मूल विषय ''यंत्रराज सुदर्शन'' के मंत्रोद्धार विधान से सम्बद्ध है तद्नुसार सनकश्शाण्डिल्य से पूछते हैं कि यंत्र में निहित शक्ति किस प्रकार उपासक में प्रतिस्थापित होती है। महर्षि शाण्डिल्य कहते हैं यंत्र रचना का ज्ञान संकर्षण के द्वारा शंकर को और उनके माध्यम से मुझे (शाण्डिल्य को) प्राप्त हुआ। उन्होंने यंत्र में निहित विभिन्न अक्षरों का विश्लेषण किया। इस प्रकार नरसिंह यंत्र अष्टाक्षर नरसिंह मंत्र सहित यहाँ वर्णित है और उसके सामर्थ्य को इंगित किया गया है। शाण्डिल्य ने अन्ततः इस महत् कार्य के लिए आराध्य के प्रति भक्त के मन में प्रपत्ति का (शरणागति) भाव आवश्यक बताया है।[42]

परमेश्वर संहिता के पच्चीसवें अध्याय में नरसिंह–यंत्र की उपासना पद्धति पर प्रकाश डाला गया है कि इस प्रकार आचार्य अपने आप को इस कार्य के लिए तैयार करता है मन्दिर जाता है एवं उसके द्वार खोलता है और अर्चा (जिसके भीतर यंत्र अंकित है) के सम्मुख आसन ग्रहण करता है। ये क्रियाएँ तथा मौन उपासना की अन्य क्रियाएँ ''मानस योग'' के अन्तर्गत वर्णित है। इस क्रिया के सम्पादन के बाद दूसरी निरन्तर उपासना ''वाह्ययाग'' के रूप में उपवर्णित है और यह वर्णन होम विधान तक सम्पूर्ण होता है।[43]

उक्त वर्णित सुदर्शन महामंत्र की अर्चना में अग्नि कार्य विधि का वर्णन पारमेश्वर संहिता के अंतिम अध्याय में किया गया है। यहाँ यज्ञशाला का वर्णन है, जिसके बीचों–बीच ''चक्राब्ज मण्डल'' बना होता है ताकि उसके

चतुर्दिक समस्त कृत्य संपादित किये जा सकें। पूर्णाहुति के पश्चात् आचार्य यज्ञशाला से गमन करता है और पितरों को बलि प्रदान करता है। इस संहिता में आगे कहा गया है कि 'सुदर्शन नरसिंह'' की उपासना के दैनिक कर्म–काण्ड से जुड़े होने के कारण आचार्य विशिष्ट गुणवत्ता अर्जित करता है। इसके माध्यम से वह दूसरों को उनके रोग, दोष, भय आदि के निमित्त प्रेरित कर पाता है।[44] इसी अध्याय के अंत में कहा गया है कि पारमेश्वर संहिता मात्र योग्य व्यक्ति को ही प्रदान की जानी चाहिए। ऐसे योग्य जनों को जो दिव्य या देवीय सत्य के उद्‌घाटन की आकांक्षा रखते हों, क्योंकि इस संहिता के वचन वेद के समान है।[45] इस अभिव्यक्ति में वस्तुतः उक्त मंत्र विधान की महिमा एवं गरिमा का संकेत मिल जाता है।

शेष संहिता का भी एक अध्याय सुदर्शन नृसिंह यंत्र[46] और नृसिंह यंत्र[47] का विवेचन करता है।

संदर्भ

1. दसवीं शताब्दी के मनीषी ओर आगम–प्रामाण्य के प्रणेता यामुनाचार्य ने इस संहिता का उद्धारण दिया है तथा पाद्यम्, पारमेश्वर और बाद की अनेक संहिताओं में इसके उल्लेख मिलते हैं। देखित–डेनियल स्मिथ, एच0, डिस्क्रिप्टिव बिब्लियोग्राफी, भाग–2, पृ0 504–506 ।
2. सनत्कुमार संहिता, इन्द्ररात्र, तृतीय अध्याय, 1–83 ।
3. सनत्कुमार संहिता, इन्द्ररात्र,, 3.10ब–20 ।
4. तत्रैव, 21.22.23 ।
5. तत्रैव
6. द्र0 ईश्वर संहिता, सात्वत संहिता, पारमेश्वर संहिता आदि।
7. जयाख्य संहिता, 29.1–58 ।
8. यत्तनृसिंवदनं कल्पान्तार्कायुतप्रभम्
तथ्याङ्ऽगश्ङ्गङकसंयुक्तं श्रृणु मूर्तिचतुष्टयम् ।।2।। जयाख्य संहिता, 29.2 ।
9. सूर्यलोप्रदष्वतुर्थो द्वितीयोग्निप्रभाकरः ।।8।।
अत्युग्रदर्पषमनष्वतुर्थो विश्वसूकरः।
नृसिंहभूतयः (मूर्तयः?) सर्वे ध्येयास्सर्वे चतुर्भुजाः ।।9।।10 जयाख्य संहिता, 29.87–9 ।
10. नखप्रहारणाश्चैव विश्वोपप्लवहानिदाः।
विस्मयाख्यां स्मरेन्मूद्रां सर्वेशां च करद्वये।।10।।
करेण तु करं ध्यायेन्मर्दयन्तमीव हि।
अतष्वोद्रिक्त रुपाणां ध्येया मुद्रा परा मुने।।11।।
11. तत्रैव, 29.12–26 ।
12. द्र0 सात्वत संहिता, 12.73–अ–75 पर अलषिंग भट्ट का भाष्य
13. मत्स्यात्मा भगवानप्सु अथ्वात्मा बवामुखे।
रसातले तु कूर्मात्मा विन्ध्यारण्ये तु पौष्कर।।
विज्ञातव्यो मृगेन्द्रात्मा पापहा सर्व देहिनाम्।
सौकरीयेन रूपेण क्षेत्रे तत्संज्ञके तु वै।।
14. डैनियल स्मिथ, तत्रैव, भाग–दो, पृ0–66 एवं आगे।
15. तत्रैव, पृ0 87–89 ।
16. ईश्वर संहिता, (नृसिंह कल्प) पंचम अध्याय।
17. तत्रैव, अध्याय 6–10 ।
18. तत्रैव अध्याय 11 ।
19. ईश्वर संहिता, (कांजीवरम्, सुदर्शन प्रेस, 1923) 11.265–270 ।
20. पराशर संहिता, 15.152–159 ।
21. तत्रैव, 15.160–164 ।
22. तत्रैव, 15.166–170 ।
23. तत्रैव, 15.171–180 ।
24. नरसिंहानुष्टुभ् चक्र के लिए द्र0 पराशर संहिता 16.19.24 और सुदर्शन नारसिंह मंत्र के लिए 16.25–39 ।
25. तत्रैव, 31.1–14 ।
26. विश्वक्सेन संहिता, 11.57 अ–64–ब ।
27. शेष संहिता, 23.11–44अ ।
28. तत्रैव, अध्याय 24 ।
29. तत्रैव, 27.1–7 ।
30. तत्रैव, 28.15 ब–20अ ।
31. तत्रैव, 29.15 45–अ ।
32. तत्रैव, अध्याय–45 ।
33. तत्रैव, अध्याय–52 ।

34. तत्रैव, अध्याय–31 ।
35. हयशीर्ष संहिता, आदि खण्ड, 16.2 ब–10 ।
36. तत्रैव, 8.15–23 ।
37. नारायणं तपयेद्यः स याति परमं पदम्।
नृसिंहादीनि मुर्तानि तन्मंत्रैर्य उपसते ।।161।।
नृसिंहमौषधं कालं गृहीयान्मन्त्रवित्तमः।।
जपेल्लक्षं शत्रुनाशो व्याधिनाशो भवेद रमें167।।
सर्वव्याधिप्रशमनं पिशाचादेर्निवर्तनम्।
जपेत् प्रत्यक्षरं लक्षं देवासांनिध्यमाप्नुयात्।।170।।
सनारसिंहननुं देवि सर्वव्याधिनिवारणम्।
सर्वशत्रुक्षयकरं ब्रह्मराक्षसनाशनम्।।171।।
38. परम संहिता, 26.1–3 तथा 26.7ब–10
39. यद्यदुपं नृसिंहस्य तदन्तेनैव पूजयत्।
सर्वान् कामानवाप्नोति मन्त्री तन्मयतां गतः।।35।।
40. नृसिंह कल्प, ईश्वर संहिता 2 का पंचम अध्याय।
41. पारमेश्वर संहिता, 23.1–12 ।
42. पारमेश्वर संहिता, अध्याय 23 ।
43. पारमेश्वर संहिता, अध्याय – 25 ।
44. द्र0 पारमेश्वर संहिता का सुदर्शन महामंत्र बाह्ययाभ्यन्तर याग निर्णय, 97.1–2 ।
45. द्र0 पारमेश्वर संहिता का सुदर्शन महायंत्रार्चने अग्निकार्य विधि शीर्षक अध्याय, 26 ।
46. तत्रैव, 26.49–51अ ।
47. शेष संहिता, 31.1–127 ।

54

PURUSHA, PURANA AND ITIHASA: HISTORY AND SPIRITUAL UNDERSTANDING

Ramashray Roy

> The historical imagination has never flown so far, even in a dream,; for now the history of man is merely the continuation of that of animals and plants; the universal historian finds himself even in the utter depth of the sea, in the living slime. He stands astounded in the face of the enormous way that man has run, and his gaze quivers before the mightier wonder, the modern man who can see all the way! He stands proudly on the pyramid of the world process; and while he lays the final stone of his knowledge, he seems to cry aloud to listening Nature: "We are the completion of nature.
>
> —Nietzsche, *The Use and Abuse of History*, p. 55.

I

Historiography can be broadly divided into two categories, secular and sacred. The former concerns itself primarily, even exclusively, with the pragmatic existence of man. In writing secular history, the historian opts for a unity of meaning and uses it to arrange his facts around it rather elegantly. The selection of the unity of meaning depends on the historian's background, training and ideological inclinations. But irrespective of the background, training and ideological preferences of historians, they are impelled in writing history by the objective of making a sense out of the confusing heap of multitudinous facts relating to a particular area of the pragmatic existence of man. For this, they impose on the chaotic mass of facts some semblance of order that can be rationally justifiable. Without it, history turns out to be simply a retailing of facts. The stress here is on rational explanation for satisfying the need to build historical knowledge by organizing facts around a rationalistic ideal of history.[1] The emphasis on rationalistic explanation brushes aside all histories that make use of what Hobbes calls "rhetoric."

In contradistinction to this, there is another, quite different genre of history which is known as sacred history. History of this kind belongs to the type of symbolic speculation that found its culmination not only in the Old Bible and writers such as Saint Augustine, Joachim of Fiora and others who used Christian symbolism in constructing the history of the world. It is also reflected in ancient historical writings, especially the *Puranas*. The method of symbolization is *spiritalis intelligentia,* spiritual understanding of world content by placing it under the scrutiny of sacred principles. History written from this perspective differs radically from profane or secular history in the method it uses. The result of the use of myths and symbols in writing sacred history cannot obviously be, as Voegelin points out, "a rational scientific picture of the world and the picture cannot be changed by progressive criticism. The movement of symbolic thought has to originate in the realm of sentiments determining the purpose to which the he symbolic method is to be put."[2]

The fundamental divide between the two broad type of historiography raises certain important but bothersome questions. They must, however, be answered if we are to apprehend what the term "history" substantively signifies and what kind of relationship does it have with man's existence in the world of here and now. To begin with, can the meaning of history be confined to rationalistic ideal of history without distorting or perverting the idea of man's existence? If the rationalistic ideal of history alone is the desideratum of historiography, what relevance do we attach to what we call sacred history?

Are we to follow Descartes when he says in his *Discourse on Method* that we should regard all that is probable as nearly completely false? Should we, then, not treat sacred history as exemplified by the Puranic literature as not only irrelevant but also completely false? If so, what sense must we make of the traditional conception of symbolic mode of participation in the world-transcendent being that constitutes the source of true order in personal and social existence? And if we do recognize the importance of sacred history, how do we reconcile the claim that intra-mundane factors, that impinge on human existence and give it a particular shape and direction, must be the only focus of proper history?

To do full justice to the questions raised above, it is necessary to examine the nature of profane history first. This involves, on the one, hand, a discussion of those factors that make it a dominant even exclusive, mode of history-writing in the modern times and, on the other, a reference to major philosophical/logical milestones in the history of ideas that account for the dominance of profane history today. A general overview of these two dimensions related with the rise of secular history as the dominant type of historiography will help us assess its merits and demerits. It will also help us ascertain the nature and evaluate the worth of sacred history, in this case, *Puranas* as a particular instance of *spiritalis intellegentia.*

II

The point of departure for this exploration is, of course, Hobbes who insisted on recognizing as proper historiography that is organized around a rationalistic ideal of history. For him, historiography reaches its pinnacle in Thucydides' *Peloponnesian War.* He praised Thucydides for his research into the objective conditions under which human actions take place and for his attempt to apply a kind of 'medical' rationalism to history. This meant the reconstruction of historical man as natural object. Thus, for Hobbes, Thucydides was unique because as a historian, he was committed to rigorous and objective reconstruction of the conditions that constitute not only a context but also a conditioning, limiting factor for human action. Such a history requires that one should steer clear of a set of prioristic, ethical principles for a better understanding of historical process as it unfolds in time.

Following Thucydides, Hobbes sets up three fundamental characteristic as defining criteria of the object and method of historiography. These are: (a) truth as central object of history; (b) the search for truth as the methodological problem concerning the historian's impartiality and the critical shifting of evidences; and (c) the use of correct methodologies of inquiry in order to understand the dynamism of history. Obviously, these characteristics are in tune with the scientific spirit of the age in which Hobbes lived and worked. This age was marked, on the one hand, by the quest for a universal language capable attaining the transparency and precision of numbers and, on the other, by the aspiration of creating a unified science fostering the idea of universally applicable mode of historical analysis.[3]

Such a universal language requires the formulation of clear and unambiguous definitions that can serve as axioms.[4] It will make the construction, with the help of accurate deductive reasoning, of a purified language of science to escape the spell of and the confusion created by ambiguous words.[5] The creation of unified science would, it was hoped, yield two benefits. It would facilitate the apprehension of the final truth which is only one from one single point of view.[6] It would also check the proliferation of perspectives or points of view that create the babble of tongue in perceiving the world and generate differences, tension and conflict. Needless to say that this scientific aspiration symbolizes the odyssey of human reason representing a tale of mind's progressive deliverance from fraudulent modes of perceiving the world and discarding of "all forms of discourse that could neither assume the form nor provide the clarity of mathematics."[7]

Inspired by the scientific spirit, Hobbes relied upon ideas of motion and substance to build the methodological presuppositions for the apprehension of reality. Accordingly, he sought to create, following the example of Aristotle, a rigorous, deductive and universal science just by using a limited number of proper definitions, postulates and axioms. This, Hobbes believed, would rid the writing of history of ideology and extrinsic principles that have been a bane of what Hobbes called, "rhetorical historiography." It would, he also believed, promote the writing of history that would present a viable alternative to rhetoric and clear the path for making the sole quest of truth the objective of writing history. By truth Hobbes meant nothing else than the belief that authentic knowledge could be built upon a proper use of language if definitions of meanings of words and their order within speech were correct. What is important for Hobbes, then, is not reality as it is but reality as it is apprehended through he medium of language, that is, definitions of meanings of words and their relationship. This is undoubtedly a notable example of reducing truth in reality to truth in language or truth as seen through the mediating screen of language.

Identifying truth as the artefact of language, Hobbes aimed at eliminating the babble of tongue by reducing the number of contentious principles and points of views from which one can perceive reality. However, it has, in fact, contributed to the proliferation of such principles and perspectives. The reason for this is not far to seek. The pragmatic aspect of human existence constitutes a world that is characterized by diversity; this gives rise to a diversity of points of views from which one can perceive the world. Consequently, there arises a plurality of meaning centres from which one proceed to approach the writing of history. It is needless to say that these meaning centres represent different aspects of a single, undivided reality. As such, it cannot be expected that they would either be mutually compatible or would, when aggregated, present a total and complete picture of the world.

This is so because reconstruction of the whole by the aggregation of all partial perspectives represents only a mechanical act, whereas the relationship between whole and parts is organic. For, it is with reference to a single higher principle that the different elemental poles of reality are unified in a field that is defined by separate but complementary elements. However, two factors have conspired to reject outright the idea of whole.

First, due to a radical shift In the world-view brought about by Renaissance and Reformation in Europe, the idea of whole was jettisoned. Second, rationality does not recognize any authority, whether sacred or secular, outside itself as the governing principle for the operation of reasoning process. With the rejection of the idea of whole as the unifying principle, man's existence came to be transformed into a diversified field of competing, often incompatible and conflicting, forces giving rise to a plurality of meaning centres. Each of these meaning centres competes with others for articulation, ascendance and control with a view to providing unchallenged specific meaning to history.

Compelled to deal with such a diversified field of forces, historians seek to tease out some meaning of history that can organize the chaotic diversity into an ordered and rationally explicated perspective. But such an effort often signifies only a monomaniacal desire to force the diversified field of human existence into a unified perspective of speculative history. Or lacking the imagination to speculate, historians take the line of least resistance and remain content with recounting the ways men act in different historical situations and/or focus on events that take place in different times and places. In most cases, what passes as history is nothing more than a multitude of speculations about what might have happened or will happen in the unfolding of history or, alternatively, a plethora of facts without any effort to relate to any meaningful unity of meaning that may impose on facts a semblance of order. The result is that one speculative theory about the meaning of history follows another in quick succession.

These theories range from attaching a *telos* to the flow of time to conceptions of history as moving towards some eschatological end. When, however, new facts and materials become available or the fashion of opinion changes, new constructions of the movement of time in history are offered as final truth. Even if historical materials do not exist at all for a fresh construction, ideology or speculation takes over to weave fanciful theories. This goes on undeterred despite the obsolescence of earlier constructions; the fancy for speculative theory or collection of new facts gains momentum. As a result, "if you are not happy with the progress of history from the unenlightened priests of Egypt to the enlightened intellectuals of the eighteenth century, or with its progress from primitive to final communism, take your choice and have your history advancing from stellar to earthly astronauts."[8]

III

The effort to create a unitary perspective on history in a situation marked by a plurality of meaning centres, thrown up by the diversity of intra-mundane forces, yields only a multiplicity of points of views. It is this fragmented perspective that historians endeavour to explore, evaluate and pass judgment on a particular facet of experience in man's existence in history or the entire course of history, if possible. This throws up three questions about the writing of history. First, in what ways does this multiplicity of perspectives on history make its appearance in historical writings? Second, what are the philosophical/theoretical factors that have led to the emergence of a multitude of perspectives on history? Third, when different perspectives identify different subjects of history—empires, civilizations, mankind, etc.—who or what really is the subject of history? Satisfactory answers to these questions alone can help us apprehend the status of *Puranas* as sacred history.

To begin with, in a world that has become more or less indifferent to or unmindful of *spiritalis intelligentia*, the central problem for historians has been and it still continues to be the quest for a universal that can impose some order on the multitude of particulars in a sensible way whether symbolic or rational. As long as Platonic mode of construction of knowledge, whether in history or in other fields, remained influential, the *apeiron* (the absolute) constituted the universal since it was considered to be the origin of all things and in which all things perished. Elaborating on the Anaximandrian insight into the structure of reality, Plato observes:

> There is a gift from gods to men, so at least it appears to me. From their abode, they let it be brought down by someone like Prometheus together with fire exceeding bright. The men of old, who were better than we are and dwelt nearer to the gods, passed on this gift in the saying: That all things are ever said to exist have their being from One and Many, and conjoin in themselves Limited (*peras*) and Unlimited (*apeiron*).[9]

When the One changes into Many and the *apeiron* transforms into *peras*, there arise between the two poles of reality number and form of things. This area of form and thing is the In-Between (*metaxy)* of the *apeiron.*[10] which constitutes the domain of human knowledge. It is this One that is the cause (*aitia)* and is present in all things. From the differentiation of the One and the Unlimited there emerges the new symbolism of an In-Between reality, *metaxy,* that receives its specific meaning from its continuation through the divine ground, i.e. the *Nous.* It is the In-Between reality, that is, between God and man, between knowledge of divine ground and its ignorance, that becomes the realm of spiritual experience which initiates a dialogue between God and man. The spiritual powers Interpret and convey things human to the gods and things divine to men; carrying prayers and sacrifices from below, the answers and commandments from above; being themselves midway between the two, they bring them together and weld them into one great whole....For God with man does not mingle; only through the mediation of the spiritual powers can man, whether walking or sleeping, have converse with gods.[11]

The dialogue that Plato refers to takes place when the soul "dialectically" investigates its own suspension between knowledge and ignorance. When this investigation yields an insight, it does not take the form of information about reality but that of an event in which the process of reality becomes luminous to itself, as an insight into the structure of reality. The subject-object divide, that plays such an important role in the writing of history in the modern times, does not apply to the event of an "experience-articulating-itself." Though this dialogue occurs in one man's soul, it is not, as Voegelin points out, one man's idea about reality" but an event in the *metaxy* where man has converse with the divine ground of the process that is common to all men."[12] It is the continuance of this dialogue in myths and rituals that brings man under the suzerainty of the world-transcendent entity, i. e., the *apeiron*. It is this dialogue that provides the basis of *koinonia* (community) between man and God and society and the world. It is the idea of *koinonia* that provides, in the Platonic perspective, the universal for historians for organizing disparate data about the pragmatic affairs of man in a meaningful pattern.

With the loss of this universal, we are back to a particular centre of meaning, which must be used to illuminate the meaning of pragmatic affairs of man on a moving time scale. This is fully reflected in, to take just three examples: Herodotus, Thucydides and Voltaire. Herodotus, for example, refers to "a wheel (*kyklos)* of human affairs, which, turning, does not suffer the same men to prosper always."[13] With this pronouncement, Herodotus treats history as something that has its *arche* in divine entity or something that is guided by providence, as Bossuet was to argue much later; its movement is now governed by the ebb and flow in the fortunes of the brave and the powerful.

In this ebb and flow, what counts as the most important thing in life is success measured in terms of the acquisition and retention of power and pelf or the inability to hold on to them is supposed to be by the intervention into the human affairs of divine superpowers. They are led to intervene because of their *phthosos* (envy).[14] Needless to say that Herodotus faithfully reflects the Homeric conception of the relationship between men and gods. Homeric gods intervene in human affairs whenever they get envious of the increasing power of men or when they feel that individual persons have been bitten by the bug of *hubris.* Be that as it may, what is crystal clear is the fact that "the mystery of *apeiron* and Time has been eclipsed by the imagery of a power tension between mortals and immortals.... The reality of the process is not denied, but the "thing" called man does not participate in it with the whole of his existence.[15]

Histories of Herodotus is a definite deviation from Plato's conception of history in which *apeiron* is not only the *arche of history* but also its sub-stratum. The central ordering conception for Herodotus is not man's participation in any transcendental entity but the power game between mortals and immortals. However, his historical accounts reflect his consciousness of the fact that too much emphasis on success brings into play the wrath of immortals who do not forbear man's *hybris* because it represents turning one's back to a reality that is impregnated with divine presence. This exodus makes concupiscence the impelling force behind the movement of history. Despite this, however, Herodotus shows his awareness of higher powers even though they are no more a living, dynamic element in man's existence. But Thucydides makes power game the central theme of history. In this game, the powerful seeks to hold on to power while other seek to loosen their grip on the reins of power. Thucydides does not refer to any other principle than the libidinous indulgence of the power-self. This is evident from the Milesian Dialogue in his *Peloponnesian War:*

> Of the gods we believe, and of the men we know, that by a necessity of nature they rule whenever they can. We neither made this law nor were we the first to act on it; we found it to exist before us and shall leave it to exist forever after us, we only make use of it, knowing that you and everyone else, if you were as strong as we are, would act as we do.[16]

Thucydides' stark realism is symptomatic of his interpretation of reality not in terms of its being influenced by divine powers but in terms of inexorable and inevitable law of nature and its manifestation in power-game. Also he does not justify his realism with reference to some higher moral law or political preference or ideological predilections. His conception of reality is self-justifying without moralistically appealing to the dogma of any ultimate truth. Note, for example, that Athenian ambassadors dispense with all pretences of justice and honourable conduct, which, they say, nobody believes. They allude to the fact that they do not derive any right of empire from their victory over the Persians, nor do they accuse the Melians of having done any wrong. Empire is just an empire, the ultimate reality.[17] It is this reality of empires following one another in quick succession that peoples history in its onward march.

When we come to the modern age, the intra-mundane basis of the forward march of history gains complete ascendance but it does so with a tinge of moralistic/ideological overtones. Voltaire, who is perhaps the first historian to give this trend a big boost, offers the best example. He wrote at a time when the three symbols—*sacrum imperium* (the Holy Roman Empire), *corpus mysticum* and *corpus Christi*— of the unified world-view of Christianity had lost their relevance for guiding the life of man in medieval Europe. Out of the ashes of this world-view was emerging a new world-view standing on two important props, science and history. The emergence of science and history as two of the central organizing principles became possible only when God was forced to retreat from his own creation leaving behind the problem of making a sense of the world as well as of making it a better place to live. The first problem was sought to be solved by adopting a mode of knowledge construction that is primarily factual rather than rational (in the sense of *sophia*) and/or theoretical. Similarly, the world seemed unfinished since it lacked resources for making man's life a better one.

Thus, the world came to be viewed both from the perspective of science and of history. "Viewed historically, it appears to be something in the making, something which can at best be only tentatively understood since it is not yet finished. Viewed scientifically, it appears as something to be manipulated and mastered, something to adjust ourselves to with the least possible stress."[18] This way of looking at the world has three important consequences insofar as the question of understanding the world is concerned. First, it leads, on the one hand, to the quest for a universal language characterized by transparency and precision of numbers and, on the other, to the aspiration of developing a universally applicable model of unified science.

Second, if the world is not yet finished, it needs to be made a better one over time through the transformation/manipulation of nature with the help of science and technology. If the world can be made perfect in history, then, it follows that everybody's desires could also be satisfied. And, lastly, the belief that this world can be made into a better one, gives birth to the idea of progress. This, in turn, leads to the belief that civilization contains a *telos* which propels it on the path of uninterrupted progress towards the destination of establishing a terrestrial paradise on this troubled planet. Kant's idea of universal history is just one example of this hope.

The complex of these ideas gives a new direction to the writing of history. If the marriage between science and history is not to prove barren, then, the writing of world history must reflect transparency and precision of scientific language; it should also aim at completeness by incorporating as many facts as can be available about the variety of peoples, their culture and civilization. Thus the central problem of history is to weave the diversity into a meaningful unity that can make the plethora of facts easily comprehensible. This has led to the search of a unity of meaning capable not only of weaving diverse facts into a whole in addition to endowing them with meaning and relevance since facts by themselves have no meaning. To employ a unity is to project a conceptual framework on the world of facts.

The need for a conceptual projection on the world of facts implies the rejection of any a priori design in the universe. As such, there is no need to apprehend the purpose of a designer God. The apprehension of reality now restricted to appearance alone means a complete representation of the phenomenal world. This transforms the world, as Heidegger puts it, into a picture. The world as picture does not simply mean a set of propositions arrived at by "scientific" investigation. It also means, in a normative sense, that the world itself consists of nothing else than the picture drawn by "scientific" investigation relying on particular conceptual projections.

Three important consequences flow from this for the way we view what history is and how we must go about writing historical accounts. First, it becomes necessary to go beyond the Christian world, the focus of history till the disintegration of the Christian world-view, and to seek completeness by including all known civilizations or centres of power. Second, this means gathering as many facts as possible in order to make a proper sense of the world whose history we write. And, lastly, since the world of facts is so variegated and vast, it is not at all possible to gather and use all facts for a comprehensive history. It is, therefore, necessary to organize facts in some fashion so that the task of writing history becomes manageable.

All these elements of history writing are present in Voltaire who, reacting to Bossuet's *Discours sur l'histoire universelle* (1681) wrote his own account of history.[19] He rebutted Bossuet's thesis that history was guided by providence so that humans ought neither unduly to fear terrestrial misery nor unduly to admire terrestrial grandeur. Bossuet had argued that the sacred and the profane are distinguishable. However, they intermingle to give direction to the course of history. In opposition to this Voltaire argued that there was but a singular history, an inner worldly chain of events, an immanent stream of genesis that nevertheless contained or expressed a universal meaningful order of human history. Anything else, he declared, was a pack of tricks we play on the dead. Voltaire sought to remove the gravest default of Bossuet's historical accounts, that is, his equation of the history of the world with the birth and spread of Christianity. This left several important parts of the world untouched. Voltaire, therefore, defined completeness as one of the criteria of proper history.

This insistence makes it necessary to gather all facts. But since facts, he argued, distort, historians must rely on one central theme as organizing principle which can illumine the process of the selection of facts germane to the task at hand. For Voltaire, this central theme is *l'histoire de l'esprit humaine*, the history of human spirit as it moves on the scale of time. This central theme helped Voltaire to "trace the steps by which we have advanced from the barbarian rusticity of (feudal times) to the *politesse* (politeness) of our own" Voltaire believed that the story he was telling was indeed of "the extinction, rebirth, and the progress of the human spirit."

Voltaire's historical enterprise is questionable on three important counts. First, the insistence on completeness is unavailing since the discovery of new facts would automatically lead to the revision of the unity of meaning or, at least, the conclusions the historians arrive at. Second, even if the goal of completeness becomes attainable, it would not itself yield a unity of meaning. The selection of a unity of meaning may help in providing a comprehensive and accurate account, but two deficiencies detract from its usefulness. In the first place, the unity of meaning imposed on the world of facts, unavoidably implies a selection process which includes some facts and excludes others. However, no plausible reason is offered justifying a particular selection process. In the second place, the selection of the unity of meaning is justified and considered relevant not on any theoretical or rational ground; its relevance becomes a matter of initial conceptual definition.

Here, again, it is never revealed why a particular set of concepts have been employed and how relevant they are to the topic under discussion. And, lastly, the unity of meaning Voltaire employs in historical account is the movement of *l'esprit humaine*. This movement represents the march of history towards a more perfect state and after reaching that state, history will perhaps come to an end. suggests It does not need to be pointed out that the idea of progress and the conception of the perfect state may vary from one historian to the next as is exemplified by the writings of Kant, Hegel, Marx, etc. As such, the selection of the unity of meaning or any interpretative framework, for that matter, proves more to be a matter of doctrines than a theoretically well justified principle. And these doctrines are derived from zeitgeist, political preference, or personal idiosyncrasies. The selected framework is, then, used to describe the object as it occurs in history and to penetrate from the obvious occurrence to the elements that may have entered the composition of the complex result.

IV

To impose a unity of meaning on the world of facts represents an attempt to view the world from an absolute perspective with the implied claim that no other unity of meaning is valid or relevant than the one employed. But, as already noted, the selection of a particular unity of meaning does not depend on any theoretically justified principle; it depends on the doctrine that the historian embraces or prefers. What also needs to be pointed out is that while the writing of history offers accurate account of certain historical happenings, the underlying meaning of these accounts tends to vary from one historian to the next due to differential value commitment of historians. It is not at all surprising that an event or happening may be analyzed to yield meanings at variance with each other.

Two consequences of this state of affairs must be noted here. First, since every historical account is considered to be scientific, different accounts relying on different perspectival projections on the world of facts create only confusion insofar as it becomes difficult to decide which account is scientific and, therefore, credible. Second, the numerous projections on the same world of facts but using different unities of meaning express a particular value commitment entailing a specific metaphysical understanding of and a pre-determined notion about the nature of reality. Driven by this notion, it is claimed that only a particular historical account is correct, no other account is. It is also claimed that reality is nothing else but as depicted in a particular account. As such, the supposition that different historical accounts of the same segment of reality are true turns out to be dubious.

The submission of the theory of history to the structure of intra-mundane forces, particularly in the modern times, has been the cumulative result of many factors that have not only influenced our sensibilities but also the course of history as well as its writing. As already indicated, the modern sensibilities, insofar as the writing of history is concerned, have been the direct result of the fragmentation of the universe of discourse. This fragmentation impinges not only on the way we look at the world and make a sense of it, but also on how we view history. Three distinct stages in the transformation of our outlook towards the world and, with it, towards history can, for the sake of convenience, be identified here.

The first stage is defined by a perspective that posits an entity beyond the world which, when in the process of transformation, becomes this world. As Voegelin notes:

Though the divine reality is one, its presence is experienced in two modes of Being and the Beginning. The Beyond is present in the immediate experience of movements in the psyche; while the presence of the divine beginning is mediated through the experience of the existence and the intelligible structure of things in the cosmos.[21]

The term "Beginning" signifies that the world is not an accidental concourse of cause-and-effect, not simply a material body without any significance of its own. On the contrary, it is a medium through which the Beyond or the *Apeiron* manifests itself and installs order on whatever it creates. The cosmic order is, therefore, the symbol of the presence of the Beyond in the phenomenal world and constitutes, at one and the same time, the paradigm for man to emulate for becoming a better man than his nature makes him to be.

This underlines an intimate relationship between the Beyond and the ordered succession of things in the phenomenal world; this relationship is consequent upon the very act of the Beginning. It is because of this that human existence is considered to be an act of participation in the world-transcendent entity, the Beyond. On this view, history is nothing else but an account of the manifestation of the Beyond on the moving scale of time. Needless to say that the awareness of the Beyond takes a definite shape in someone's—e.g. sage's, mystic's or philosopher's—consciousness, whether noetically or experientially awakened, which constitutes the basis of the organization and regulation of personal and collective lives and relations.

What then begins "as an insight into the mystery and the structure of the process leads on to the experience that has become articulate in the insight and further to its recognition as an act of consciousness by which man participates in the process of reality."[22] History, in this perspective, is an account of man's participation in the process of the unfolding of reality. What makes it distinctive is that if it is the Beyond whose apprehension, whether noetically or experientially, provides the basis for organizing and regulating pragmatic affairs of life. It is the consciousness of the presence of the Beyond that provides impetus to the movement of individual psyche and of history as the combined result of the actions of individual beings. However, the relationship between the Beyond and the world depends on the particular apprehension flowing out of one's experience. It is true that there might at any moment exist different ways in which the experience of the Beyond is articulated and the practical shape this experience assumes in organizing and regulating the pragmatic affairs of man. However, as long as the succession of events in any society reflects the conscious presence of the Beyond, the structures of power, too, would be subordinated to the structure of spiritual experience.

Second, the intimate relationship between the world of here and now with the experienced presence of the Beyond could not continue for long. The earthly powers organized in different territorial units rose to assert their autonomy from the restraints imposed upon them by their subordination to spiritual power. With the search for autonomy by the earthly powers "the attempts at ordering society by the truth of existence, be it the revealed word of God or the philosopher's love for wisdom, appeared to have come to their end."[23] Different societies came to be formed, they were cast not in accordance with the truth of the prophets or philosophers but in the shape of empires. It was very clear to the thinkers that the pragmatic order of history did not go the way of spiritual order. As a result, the course of order in history came to be divided on pragmatic and spiritual lines. The fact that the disorderly course of pragmatic history did not keep in tune with the spiritual order evoked different responses in different thinkers. The examples of two such thinkers—Paul and Augustine-- should suffice here.

To take the first example, Paul does recognize that the establishment of the Roman Empire is a fact that cannot be gainsaid. It is also true that in its initial stage, the earthly empire did not give allegiance to the spiritual empire of Christ. But beyond this earthly empire there does exist a spiritual empire represented by the Catholic Church. These two empires need not, however, go their different ways and prove antagonistic to each other. As a matter of fact, both can be reconciled in a way that the earthly empire becomes the vehicle of establishing and consolidating the rule of the spiritual empire. This is possible if the *telos* of the spiritual empire is superimposed on and embraced by the earthly empire while remaining true to its own objectives.

The subordination of the earthly empire to the spiritual empire in such a way that the former becomes the vehicle of spreading the word of Christ would help a universal community of human beings bound together in the love of God to emerge. As Paul declares: "This gospel of the kingdom (of God) shall be preached over the whole ecumene, as a testimony to all the nations. And then the end (*telos*) shall come."[24] Thus, even if different nations are organized differently and remain committed to pursuing their power game, they could still be united in a universal community of humanity if they become the vehicle of spreading the Christian word.

Augustine's point of departure is his recognition of the existence of two different realms, *civitas Dei* (kingdom of God) and *civitas terrena* (kingdom of earth), the former symbolizing the spiritual power and the latter indicating the organization of power in the phenomenal world. These two kingdoms have their separate locations in the soul of man. Augustine identifies these locations as love of self and love of God. There always exists a tension between these two centres in man's soul; he always tends to move away from the love of God and fall into the love of self. But man always remains conscious of the fact that he should orient himself to the love of God. Augustine did consider it necessary that both the terrestrial and the spiritual powers should intermingle and ultimately the spiritual must triumph over the earthly power. But the ultimate triumph of the spiritual power means, for Augustine, "the existential exodus from the pragmatic world of power."[25]

However, since this exodus is not possible for all because of the pull of the love of self, Augustine had to end up with the acceptance of both these separate realms with none of these interfering in the affairs of the other. He, however, postponed the victory of the spirit till the end of history when the eschatological event in the shape of the Resurrection could liberate mankind from the bondage to the love of the self.. Till then the two realms represented by the Holy Roman Empire and the Catholic Church would continue to run on their separate tracks.

It is true that the tension between the earthly empire and the heavenly empire provide stimulation to the thinking of various thinkers and statesmen who proposed various schemes of the relationship that should exist between these realms. These proposals and reconstructions kept the hope alive that the realm of spirit would govern and regulate the course of pragmatic history. It is true that each of these conceptions and reconstructions thought of this relationship in different ways. However, the important thing is the singularity of ethos that kept the universality of discourse intact. The real significance of the medieval period in this regard is its valiant struggle for safeguarding the universality of Christian ethos.

This struggle involved the reconstitution and preservation of the universality of the Christian world-view as a fruitful vantage point from which to look at the world and its history. The three pillars of the Christian world-view represented three important symbols—*regnum Christi, corpus mysticum, and sacrum imperium*—expressed in their interaction the European civilizational voices of the antiquity in the medieval western civilization. It was the earthly imperial body of *sacrum* imperium that was supposed to be the vehicle of supporting and spreading the word of Christ all over the world. This was the hope Paul had expressed; he was confident that the *sacrum imperium* would bring the entire humanity within the fold of a universal community in the presence of Christian God.

The increasing tension between the two jurisdiction of *sacerdotium* and *regnum* spurred intellectual efforts to justify and legitimize the medieval world-view. Such efforts produced not only a diversity of perspectives but also prompted attacks on the medieval world-view. As such, the struggle was defined as the effort to realize a single order of temporal and spiritual order and to adjust to the movements and forces that rendered this aspiration finally impossible to realize. Different thinkers favoured the singularity of order under God based on the belief that these two orders could still be brought within one all-embracing public order. It was this aspiration that defined the medieval world-view.

Most of the thinkers favouring the continuance of the singular public order believed that there is only one order that has its source in God and that this order can hold together both the orders, that is.

sacerdotium and royal powers and harmonize them since they were inferior orders. As David Walsh notes:

The papal and imperial authorities occupy their position not because of their achievement in organizing the whole, but primarily because there is a whole that must be given expression through the recognition of their cooperative authority. It is the wholeness of ethos, rather than of power, that accounts for the peculiar tolerance of resistance and diversity within the medieval commonwealth.[27]

The medieval period in Western Europe thus represented a constant struggle to rearticulate the universality of the Christian world-view against the forceful stirrings of intra-mundane forces. But this struggle failed to protect and preserve this universality. Efforts in this direction were ultimately given up when the realization gradually dawned that the universality of Christian world-view was lost perhaps for ever. The break-down of this universality was signalled emphatically by the emergence of several competing Christian churches and movements. Along with this, there emerged a new community substance that functioned as a substitute Christian universality. It was the rise of nationalism as a new political force signifying both a faith in the nation as a chosen people and the claim that parochial national civilization represented civilization writ large that spelt the doom of Christian universality.

Both these developments were instrumental in creating a plurality of centres of meaning from which one could view the world and its history. Thus the diversity of parochial institutions expressed the diversified field of intra-mundane social forces that finally led to the banishment of God from his own creation. As a result, secularism came to the fore. With this, dualism of sacred and profane history disappeared. The two merged at the level of secularized history. Secularization, in this connection, signifies the attitude whereby history, including religious phenomena, is conceived as an intra-mundane chain of human events while the belief in the universal meaningful order of human history is retained at the same time.

Lastly, then, as a result of the de-divinization of the world, the idea of history came to be subordinated to the structure of intra-mundane forces. This meant a radical transformation in the perception of what is history and what is the proper manner of writing it. First, the diversified field of intra-mundane forces did create a plurality of meaning centres from which to view the world. This prevented the emergence of a philosophical point of view that could have been accepted as a unifying, integrating perspective on man and his world. This encouraged an open field of theoretical expressions and speculations, each of which illumines only a fragment of meaning and, therefore, fails to yield a complete understanding of man and his world. In the lack of a holistic philosophical/theoretical foundation, these theoretical expressions and speculations are forced to derive their inspiration from zeitgeist, ideological preferences or personal idiosyncrasies.

One result that flowed from this was the sharpening of the distinction between history internal to a society's existence and history in which societies come into being and go out of existence.[28] However, parochialism inherent in the history of the first kind is sought to be overcome by focusing on the history of a civilization of which a particular society may form only a miniscule part. But, then, the question how to view a civilization presses for a satisfactory answer. Civilization may be taken to signify a mechanical concatenation of institutional phases, divisible into periods of genesis, growth and decay, succeeding one another till the civilization itself passes away. Or, alternatively, it can be understood as a mode of participation in the world historical process of attunement to the truth of being with a view to establishing the order of existence within this world. The de-divinization of the world has, however, made untenable the view that the moving spirit behind the movement of history is some world-transcendent entity. But to treat civilization simply as a concatenation of institutional phases divisible into periods of genesis, growth and decay leaves the question of what it is that undergoes the process of genesis, growth and decay unanswered.

It is needless to say that an entity, whether a society or a civilization, which is subject to change, cannot be the subject of history. And yet we are forced to suffer the suspense "between the assumption that history must be the history of something—empires, city-states, nation-states, civilizations or mankind—and the uneasy suspicion that the process of history cannot be predicated on societies which appear and disappear in its course."[29] This suspense remains unresolved as long as some intra-mundane entity is selected as the subject of history. Even if one seeks to understand the movement of history in terms of certain intra-mundane universal factors, such as progress or human spirit, it does not help in removing this suspicion since they prove to be , as Jacob Burckhardt puts it, "impertinent anticipations" because "eternal wisdom has not informed us about its purpose."[30]

Burkhart's critical and scathing remark rests on his understanding that the attempt to identify a *telos* in history is, in fact, superimposition on a field, marked by ups and downs, a perspective that sees in the movement of history linearity where there is none. The ups and downs in human existence are the hallmarks of irregular development. But these irregularities do not cancel each other out in the long haul of time to produce linearity in the movement of history. Thus we cannot say that history moves towards a predestined goal and proceeds straight to realize this goal. Thus the scaffold of ideas on which historians hang diverse and often incompatible facts go their own way without offering any clear understanding of why one should accept the propriety of the scaffold or the reconstruction of the inner meaning of the movement of history.

V

Who, then, is the subject of history if not any society, nation-state, civilization or the mankind? If they are so variable and prone to change, at times very drastic change, how can they become the subject of history? If one focuses on just one society or a nation-state or, for that matter, one civilization, for historical reconstruction, then, one must be able to make a distinction between two varieties of history, one dealing exclusively with history external to a particular society and the other focusing on history in which societies come into being and go out of existence. But this distinction can be justified only if the factors that shape the movement of history in particular societies are unique to that society.

Moreover, it has been also to be shown that none of these factors is the part of the larger civilizational forces. If this can be the case, the claim that history is something that records the movement of a universal propelling force on the moving scale of time must be given up. If, on the other hand, the forces shaping history internal to a particular society are but the reflection of a particular unity of meaning imposed on history, the perception of a plurality of societies different in certain ways from each other is, then, meaningless. Whatever may be the case, no matter how we look at history, the fact remains that a plurality of societies, just as a plurality of civilizations, is an undeniable fact. It, then, follows that human beings organized in different societies also differ in certain essential attributes from those in other, different societies.

It must be emphasized that differentiation of human beings in distinct groupings is neither haphazard nor an accident. Every differentiated civilization or society subsists on its own self-constitution. It is this self-constitution that accounts for not only differences between one society and the next but also for the uniqueness of each society. Whether it is a civilizational unit or a social order, its distinctive character is formed by the substantive idea of who man is. Without such an idea we do not have any frame of reference for designating human phenomenon as relevant or irrelevant. But how this idea of man is constructed, on the one hand, and how it is sustained over time, on the other? These two questions clamour for answer. In answering these questions, it is necessary to remember that man is engage in the creation of social order physically, biologically, psychologically, intellectually and spiritually only some of these engagements admit of general laws.

This means that the proper understanding of man will remain elusive if we focus only on those factors that are easily perceptible leaving out those not so perceptible but are influential in shaping the self-understanding of man. This calls for identifying the factor that shapes man's identity. This factor pertains to who man is substantively conceived to be. As Heschel notes, "the truth of a theory about man is either creative or irrelevant, but never merely descriptive. The image of man affects the nature of man."[31] It is clear, then, that who man is cannot be apprehended either by behavioural clues, historical generality, or, for that matter, mathematical or quasi-mathematical laws pregnant with predictability.

Since not all engagements of man can be reduced to general laws, it must be admitted that man is a resident of two orders of existence. One of these orders is defined by the external relationships that develop in the course of the management of his pragmatic affairs. The other is internal that is related with his consciousness that moulds and supports his identity and infuses his linkage with the larger world with meaning and value. What is important is the internal, imperceptible and implicit aspect of man's existence that forms the substratum of the external, perceptible and explicit aspect of man's existence. Externally, social life and relations assume a particular form because of the concatenation of the effects of action men engage into for realizing their ordinary life needs and purposes. But these needs and purposes draw their inspiration from, receive their particular modes of expression, and ormer derive their legitimacy from ideals and principles that are beyond the dominion of the eye.

The external aspect of man's existence is shaped, governed and regulated by the internal world of meaning and values. It is because of this that the civilizational form of a society is endowed with a distinctive character and significance. If the internal aspect of meaning, value and understanding can be called culture, the external aspect of the social order must be called civilization. It is the external aspect that gets imprinted with a distinctive form by the transmutation of the former into action congealing into relations and artefacts; it is this transmutation that gives birth to civilization. If culture is the soul, civilization is the body.

When looked at from this perspective, culture is prior to and, therefore bound to have its roots in something other than civilization itself. This something other is, as Voegelin puts it, "the idea that there is humanity, that there is a mankind, and that one can generate about man appears only when certain revolutionary insights occur. These are spiritual outbursts."[32] The recipients of such revelatory insights are sages, mystics or philosophers who, rebelling against the existing order of things, become the founder of a new order based on their insight into the structure of order. Every such insight begins a revolution of considerable dimensions in the sense that it defines the meaning of essential humanity, forms man, and provides clues to the creation of institutions, and shapes thought-ways and work-ways. And since there are several such outbursts, there are different types of culture inspired by and based on these outbursts. Each culture posits the idea of who man is.

It is needless to say that these spiritual outbursts are widely scattered in time and space over concrete human beings in concrete human societies. Even though these outbursts are based on the insight of one person, they are claimed to be true for all men in all ages. What one person experiences something beyond the phenomenal world forms the consciousness of many persons and leads to three different situations. First, there comes the consciousness that the phenomenal world, the *idam sarvam,* is not the only world that counts. Over and above the phenomenal world is a world beyond. Moreover, it is the world beyond that is not only the source and substratum of the phenomenal world but also the ground of its significance for man. Also, the awareness dawns that while the world beyond and its ground are unbounded and timeless, the phenomenal world is perishable; it appears, stays for some time and then disappears in that from where it has sprung.

Second, the experience of the Beyond yields the realization that there now exist two varieties of existence, one attuned to the spiritual world and the other pertained to human existence and its concerns in the phenomenal world. The realization that there is a world beyond does not in way make the world of here and now the any less real. What is distinctive is the awareness that reality must now be interpreted as having two poles, one defined by the presence of the Timeless and the other by the dynamic presence of Timeless in the flow of time. The existence of these two inter-related poles, however, poses a problem.

The transformation of the Timeless into flowing time is, it is true, real but not in a way that can be apprehended by sense perception or discursively recounted. This transformation expresses itself through what Voegelin calls "the sound of gentle stillness" in the inner core of a person's being and must be made articulate and comprehensible through a cosmogonic tale of what Plato calls "the likely story of creation." The cosmogonic tale is, of course, a myth, but myth happens to be the only symbolism through which man can express his experience of divine reality.

The awareness of the Timeless does not signify two different realities. The divine reality along with its manifestation is one, although its presence is experienced in two modes of the Timeless and the flowing time that has a definite beginning in the transformation of the Timeless. The experience of the Timeless occurs in the soul which is the sensorium of divine; its presence in the flow of time is "mediated through the experience of the existence and intelligible structure of things in the cosmos."[34] But since the structure of things in the cosmos and the cosmos itself are impregnated by the Timeless, these two modes of experiences are but two dimensions of man's consciousness. As such, the two modes interpenetrate each other and shape the character of man's existence in the world of here and now.

On this view, history touching upon man's existence must be concerned not only with the existence of man in the phenomenal world alone but also with man's existence as it is touched or remains untouched by the experience of the Timeless. It is in this sense that history is more than "a stream of human beings and their actions in time, (it is) the process of man's participation in a flux of divine presence."[35] It has as its end an ideal state of human existence. Thus the process of history is preceded by a spiritual outburst, which has its *arche* in the Timeless. It is the experience of the Timeless that assumes the form of a spiritual outburst, which is not a phenomenon "in a history of mankind, but is the source of meaning in history and of such knowledge as man has of it."[36]

Thus understood, history has an *arche* in the form of the Absolute; the Absolute is, of course, timeless but enters the stream of time. By virtue of this, the finite is linked to the Absolute; this linkage is made articulate and comprehensible with the help of myths and symbols. The awareness of this linkage enters human consciousness and shapes human existence in history. History becomes an account of human experience over time of a reality shaped by the tension between its two poles identified earlier. History is, then, the account that begins with the descent into matter of the Absolute who constitutes the *arche of* history by entering the stream of time and joins the present with its beginning in the mist of time. Thus, history, as the mode of accounting the experience of man's participation in the flux of divine reality has three very distinct but important stages which can be symbolically identified as *Purusha, Purana and itihas.* These three symbols constitute the essence of history as the mode of describing man's participation in the flux of divine reality.

VI

As is evident from the Purusha Sukta *(Rigveda* X, 90), Purusha as the absolute represents all; he is all this (the visible world), all that, and all that is to be; he is immortal and the lord of the mortals. But before he transforms himself into *vishwa* (the cosmos), he subsists on his own intrinsic strength as pure consciousness (*Rigveda* X, 129). But then he is affected by the desire to create; it is this desire that becomes the first seed of mind and acts as a link between the existent and the non-existent (*Rigveda* X.129.4). This decision to create moves the Purusha to sacrifice himself totally by performing what is called the *sarvahuta yajna*. Three parts of him ascend to the world beyond the phenomenal world with the fourth undergoing diversification into various animate and inanimate forms (*Rigveda* X.90.4). The transformation of the Absolute into the cosmos is expressed through three important symbols: *Brahma, Yajna* and *Vishwa. Brahma* constitutes the *arche* that transmutes itself through the process of *yajna* into the cosmos, the *vishwa*. This, in short, is the essence of the Vedic cosmogonic tale.[37]

The significance of the *Purushamedha Yajna* lies in the fact that the *sarva,* that is, the cosmos and all that it contains in itself becomes the *medha* (food) of the *Purusha.* To put it differently, the *idam sarvam* itself becomes the *avas* (residence) of *Isha;* what it also implies is that the *idam sarvam* must be made a proper residence by offering itself as the *medhya* of *Purusha.*[38] The *sarvahuta yajna* performed by *Purusha* is the process through which the One transforms into many. It is in this process that the constitutive elements of the cosmos, its operative principles and the patterns of interaction among different constituents of the cosmos are generated, encoded and made integral to these components. All these components are governed by the laws of *Rita* which not even the gods can violate. Thus, "in the Vedic vision, the universe manifests in accordance to an inherent law which is the very basis of its structure; it unfolds not in a haphazard manner, but in strict order, a progression, all other laws being but the development of and, therefore, subordinate to this one fundamental law."[39] All beings are bound by *ritasya panthah*.

To follow *ritasya panthah* is necessary for upholding the inner logic of the cosmos and to safeguard its metabolism. But this is threatened when man ignores the dictates of his soul and becomes what Plato calls "the slave of many mad masters." This signifies the life of passion or what Aristotle calls *"apaulistic* life"; such a life leads to alienated existence in rebellion against the ways of God. The life of passion buries the soul deep down under the frenzy of the body from where it becomes difficult to excavate it. When the rule of the soul is overthrown, the sense of what Heraclitus calls *"xynon"* (shareable commonality) lying deep in man's being is also deadened.

While *xynon* remains active or is actively acknowledged, man remains awake, as Heraclitus puts it, to his essential relatedness with his maker and to his fellow-beings. "Only one cosmos... exists for the 'waking' alone, while the 'sleepers' each have their own private world, a world of dreams."[40] When the world of dreams takes possession of men, consensus as the basis of society is destroyed. Value subjectivity produces a situation of eristics in which people stick to their own guns. This is symptomatic not only of disease of the soul but also of the breaking down of the bridge of common humanity, as Voegelin puts it.[41] This bridge can be built only if man becomes what *Chhandogya Upanishad* calls *swarat*, that is, if he submits himself to the *Purusha* within him and obeys his command.

Submission to the *Purusha* within cures the soul of its disease that afflicts it when it becomes the slave of many mad masters. It is then capable of laying the foundation of building the bridge of common humanity. It also becomes the source and support of a culture that helps man to rise to a far greater and higher power. This is possible only when the deliberate effort of knowledge and will is aimed at attaining an end that derives its significance from an ideal vision of life. It is culture in this sense that shapes the society's internal substance and external form. With it, society begins its journey in the phenomenal world towards the desired goal. Its *arche, that is, the Purusha,* constitutes the point which must provide the framework for any historical account of that society.

It is true that the cosmogonical tale yields the knowledge of the Timeless and of the way it descends into the flow of time and influences the way people must live, think, and act. But this is not enough. With the passage of time, active relationship with this tale grows dim and the danger of complete forgetfulness raises its head. That is why it is necessary to make the memory of man's primordial connection with the Absolute ever alive. That is what *Puranas* do. They constitute a process of *upabrimhan,* or augmenting, that is, keeping the text up-to-date by revising its contents as often as necessary.[42] *Upabrimhan,* as Agrawal notes, performs three different purposes: (a) *phalastuti,* that is, grafting of new composition on the old; (b) emboxing of new portions in the lap of other existing portions in such a way that later text forms a coherent part of the theme in which it is placed; and (c) repetition of old but already disposed of legends, but now with a different purpose and different motif.[43]

Irrespective of the purpose different *Puranas* serve, all of them have to talk about the Vedic *bhavavritta* even when the recounting of the process of creation may differ from one *Purana* to the next. In this sense, then, *Puranas* trace the origin of the world as it is conceived in the Vedic likely story of creation and make this story up-to-date. But *Puranas* do not stop here. Almost all of them engage in the exercise of what Voegelin calls "historiogenesis": it means the use of symbolism to underline the fact of absolute point of origin for a particular society, as a part of the cosmic order itself. From this point of origin, the history of that society descends to the present, that is, the period when a particular author of *Purana* was engaged in writing. But as Voegelin notes:

The story of the events between the origin and the present is not the homogeneous tale it pretends to be; rather, it proves to consist of two parts of widely different character. For only the latter part of the story, the part that issues into the author's present, can claim to relate *res gestai* in the pragmatic sense; the earlier part, covering an immense time-span of thousand and sometime hundred thousands of years, is filled with legendary and mythical event.[44]

It is not at all surprising that all *Puranas* contain genealogical charts of legendary and real kings.[45] The purpose of the authors of the P*uranas* in combining the mythical with the real is not only to include historical materials but also to link these materials, through the device of mythopoesis, with the emergence of order in the cosmos, so that events would have meaning that make them worthy of transmission to posterity.[46] This combination allows them to speculate on the origin of the specific realm of being. This speculation does not differ in principle from the Vedic *bhavavritta* that identifies the *arche* *a*nd its movement in time in the stream of life. This exemplifies the character of the linkage between the finite and the infinite; it thus joins together the Timeless and life under the presence of the Timeless in the flow of time.

And, finally, P*uranas* constitute *itihas* in the real sense of the term. If history for the authors of the *Puranas* signify something that happened (iti+ha+as) in the dim past , it means that whatever had happened whose account is contained in the Vedic *bhavavritta* and made up-to-date in the *Puranas* is still the paradigm for human beings since it is the myth that makes man and society rather than the other way around. The account of the *arche and* its movement in the flow of time are necessary for making man conform to the cosmic *Rita.* In this the *Puranas* make their own contribution in two ways. They keep the flame of spiritual awakening alight; they also describe the way this flame can illumine the lives and relations of the people so that their journey in the phenomenal world proves less troubled. *Purans,* therefore, contain accounts not only of what the gods did but also of how the sages lived and what kind of disciplined life people should lead by performing certain rites, rituals and *vratas.* Thus the purpose of the *Puranas* is not simply to describe in a neutral way what really happened in the mist of time but also to evoke in the people the need for adopting the most appropriate mode of living an exemplary life in conformity with the spirit of what had happened.

VII

Thus *Puranas* exemplify a particular type of historiography that is completely out of tune with modern sensibilities. As Voegelin points out, the moderns take the ancients to task for not writing history in a manner approved by positivist historians.[47] What they resent most is the mixing of facts with myths and symbols. But in condemning this act of mixing modern historians commit certain errors which are not righted either by seeking to account for all facts or by embracing a particular unity of meaning in selecting facts that support a particular point of view of a historian or justifying a particular ideological perspective on historiography. The first error they thus commit is to deny that myth is a part of life whether in ancient or modern times.

The second error they commit is that, lacking any well considered theoretic perspective, they suffuse whatever facts they marshal in support of their position with values which may not be acceptable to others—an endeavour they themselves condemn but always engage into. And, lastly, we have historians who look at what must have happened according to the Vedic likely story from the point of view of their own prejudice or ideological persuasion. As a result, historiography is reduced to an open field for historians to define what history must mean. As such, they turn the purely intellectual and spiritual endeavour to power game. One ideological position challenges another and the ensuing contention hurts truth, inflicts wound on it and, finally, truth goes into comma.

It is against this background that it becomes necessary to resurrect and revive the link between *Purusha, Purana and Itihas* not only for apprehending reality better and presenting a realistic and holistic account of it but also for making man aware of his proper place in the cosmos so that he may not be affected by *pleonexisa or hybris.*

Footnotes and References

1. This is what Thomas Hobbes insists on in his, *Eight Books of Peloponnesian War by Thucydides* (London: The author, 1629); also in the *English Works of Thomas Hobbes of Malmsbury,* ed. William Molesworth and publishe in London 1839-45 as volume VIII.
2. Eric Voegelin, *History of Political Ideas: The Middle Ages to Aquinas,* ed. and intro. By Peter von Sivers (Columbia: University of Missouri Press, 1997), II, p. 126.
3. On this point, see Thomas H. Spragen, Jr., *The Irony of Liberal Reason* (Chicago: the University of Chicago Press, 1981), p. 30.
4. Hobbes, *Leviathan* (New York: Dutton, 1950), p. 26.
5. Cf. Descartes:

   If someone were to explain correctly what are the simple ideas in human imagination out of which all human thoughts are compounded, and if his explanations were generally received, I would dare to hope for a universal language very easy to learn. The greatest advantage of such a language could be the assistance it would give to men's judgment, representing matters so clearly that it would be almost impossible to go wrong. *Philosophical Letters,* trans. & ed. by Anthony Kenny (Oxford: Clarendon Press, 1970), p. 6.
6. John D. Alembert, *Preliminary Discourse to the Encyclopedia of Diderot,* trans. Richard N. Schwab (Indianapolis: Bobbs-Merill, 1963), p. 83.
7. Spragen, op. cit. P. 39.
8. Voegelin, *Order and History: The Ecumenic Age* (Baton Rouge: Louisiana State University Press, 1974), IV, p. 4.
9. *Philebus* 16c-17a.

10. *Ibid, 16d-e.*
11. *Plato, Symposium* 202e-203a.
12. *Voegelin,* op. cit, p. 186.
13. *Histories*, i, 207.
14. *Ibid, 1.32; III.40; Vii.10.*
15. Voegelin, op. cit, p. 180.
16. Thucydides, *Peloponnesian War,* V.105.
17. Ibid, V.89.
18. Carl L. Becker, *The Heavenly City of the Eighteenth Century Philosophers (*New Haven: Yale University Press, 1952), pp. 27-28.
19. It is contained in the *Complete Works of Voltaire,* ed. Robert L. Walters, B. D. And W. H. Barker (Oxford: Voltaire Foundation, 1992).
20. The terms "Beyond" and "Beginning" refer to a particular mode of writing history and have been used by Voegelin in his *Ecumenic Age,* op. cit.
21. Ibid, p.17.
22. Ibid, p. 177.
23. Ibid, p. 115.
24. Mathew 24.14.
25. On this, see Voegelin, *The Ecumenic Age,* p. 172.
26. Voegelin, *History of Political Ideas*, III, Introduction, p. 6.
27. Ibid, p. 7.
28. On this point, see Voegelin, *The Ecumenic Age,* p. 173.
29. For a detailed discussion of the reasons why either civilizations or nations or humanity cannot be treated as the subject of history, see Voegelin, "Configurations in Hisory," in Paul Kuntz, ed. *The Concept of Order* (Seattle: The University of Washington Press, 1968), pp. 23-42.
30. Quoted in Voegelin, *The Ecumenic Age*, p. 195.
31. Abraham J. Heschel, *Who is Man?* (Stanford: Stanford University Press, 1965), p.8.
32. Voegelin, "Configurations....", p. 38.
33. Ibid.
34. Voegelin, *The Ecumenic Age*, p. 17.
35. Mircea Eliade, *The Myth of Eternal Return,* tr. Willard Trask (New York: Pantheon Books, 1954).
36. Ibid.
37. For details, see Ramashray Roy, *Beyond Ego's Domain: Being and Order in the Veda* (Delhi: Shipra Publications, 1999).
38. *Shatapatha Brahman, 13.6.2.1.*
39. Jeanine Miller, *The Vision of the Cosmic Order in the Vedas* (London: Rutledge and Kegan Paul, 1985), p.38.
40. Heraclitus, quoted in Werner Jaeger, *Paideia* (New York: the Oxford University Press, 1965), I, p.180.
41. Voegelin, *Order and History: Plato and Aristotle* (Baton Rouge: Louisiana State University Press, 1957), III, p.29.
42. Vasudev S. Agrawal, *Matsya Purana :A Study* (Varanasi: All India Kashiraj Trust, 1963), Preface.
43. Ibid
44. Voegelin, *The Ecumenic Age,* p. 59.
45. Voegelin argues that no historiography can be found in India. As he observes:"There is the spiritual outburst of the late *Upanishads* and also the *Mahabharat* and of the Buddhists scriptures, and there are empires...and yet no Indian has ever written history." Op. cit, pp. 28-29

    This invites at least two comments. First, Voegelin is completely off the track when he identifies spiritual outburst in India not with the Vedas but with Upanishads. Second, that *Puranas* do deal with historiography is amply evidenced by the writings of Pargiter, Warder and others. See, Shibesh C. Bhattacharya, "The Historical Universe of Puranas," Typescript.
46. Voegelin, *The Ecumenic Age,* p. 59.
47. Ibid, p. 63.

55

THE ACCOUNT OF NEARCHOS' VOYAGE: AN APPRAISAL

U.P. Arora

The voyage of Alexander's admiral Nearchos from Patala at the mouth of the Indus, to the head of the Persian gulf is the first voyage of discovery of which we have any detailed narrative. Known to us mainly through the text of Arrian's *Indika*, it was reproduced there in a summarised form. Some passages also occur in Arrian's *Anabasis*, Strabo's *Geography* and Pliny's *Natural History*. The work falls in the category of those *Periploi* Greek texts which contain reports of navigators by pioneers along unexplored coasts. It furnishes an account of the places and the races encountered, the number of stades sailed each day, the navigational facilities, climatic condition and some hints on the maritime trade[1].

The motivating force behind this adventure was Alexander himself, whose notion of India at the beginning of his campaigns was based on his teacher Aristotle, who had the confusion of accepting river Indus as the source of Nile and nearness of Eastern Ocean from the Northern mountains (Tarn, *CAH*, VI, pp.402-3). It is said that this Eastern Ocean was also a curiosity which had motivated Alexander to invade India. But once the mistake (F.20=Strabo, XV, 1, 26) realised and ambition of reaching the Eastern Ocean failed, the emperor appears to have given little further thought to Punjab and concentrated instead on a second best plan, i.e., the colonisation of the Persian gulf. Nearchos writes that Alexander had a vehment desire (*Pothos*) to sail the sea which stretches from India to Persia, but he disliked the lenghth of the voyage and feared that they would find a land uninhabited, either without harbours or with an impossible climate and so the fleet would be lost.

Nearchos says that Alexander discussed with him that whom he should select as an admiral of the fleet. After much discussion and thought Alexander became ready to appoint Nearchos for fulfilling Alexander's *Pothos* of finding a way to the mouth of the Euphrates (F.1=Arr.*Ind*, XX, 1-8). There is also another passage which speaks about the purpose of the voyage. It occurs in Nearchos' description of the conversation with his lieutenant Onesikritos, at Cape Maceta on the Arabian coast, during their voyage. In rejecting the proposal of Onesikritos that they should sail across to the Arabian side instead of following the coast line on the right, Nearchos stated that Onesikritos was a fool if he was ignorant of "Alexander's prupose in dispatching the expedition. It was not because Alexander was unable to bring all of his army safely through on foot that he had sent out the ships; but because he wished to reconnaitre the coasts that lay on the line of the voyage, the roadsteads, the islets, to explore thoroughly every bay which appeared, cities which lay on the sea-coast, and to find out which land was capable of bearing crops and which was desert land (F.1= Arr. *Ind.*, XXXII, 9, 12).

This speech of Nearchos was reported by Arrian in his other work *Anabasis* (F.1e=Arr. *Anab.* VII, 20,10)) also. There he says that he was deputed not to navigate the ocean, but to reconnaitre the coast lying on the ocean, and the inhabitants of the coast, and its anchorages, and its water supplies, and the manners and customs of the inhabitants and what part of the coast was fertile, and what part was not. It may be noted here that besides the works mentioned in the *Indika*, one more work, i.e., "the investigation of the manners and customs of the inhabitants" was also added in *Anabasis*. It appears from such statement that Alexander was not so much interested in discovering the fastest and most direct sea route from India to Persia, but he wanted a thorough reconaissance of the coast line made and a report on the conditions of life there, presumably as a preliminary to opening up the route between India and Mesopotamia, as Darius had done before. The great improtance was attached to the success to this voyage by Alexander, for in order to support the fleet he chose the closeby land via Gedrosia, so that he may support the fleet from the land, by digging wells and leaving supplies along the shore wherever possible, even though it meant exposing the army to great hardships of a march through the Gedrosian desert (F. 3a= *Anab.*, VI, 24).

The route followed by Nearchos might not have been known to Alexander's companions before their voyage, it was undoubtedly very old. India's contacts with its Western neighbours have been known from ancient times. The Indus seals have been found at various Mesopotamian sites[2]. The results of the excavations done at Lothal in India and ancient Telman (Barein) bear testimony to the fact of the existence of the coastal route between the two[3]. The *Atharvaveda Samhita* mentions at one place to a well known Babylonian myth (5, 13). The Asuras of the Brahmana literature have been connected with the Assyrians or the Iranians[4]. The *Jatakas* mention Babylon as Baveru[5].The references to ocean pilots throughout the route in Nearchos' account are proof of the fact that the route was already in use. It was an Indian pilot through whom the knowledge of so called first stage of the monsoon discovery was conveyed to the Greeks. He had warned the admiral Nearchos that the movements of south west monsoon was unfavourable for his retreat journey, therefore he waited for a change in the movement of the seasonal winds (*Anab.* ,VI, 17).

Whether Nearchos had any idea of the coastal route before his departure remains uncertain. It is also difficult to ascertain that he had any knowledge of the voyage made by Skylax. In view of the probability that Nearchos knew the work of Herodotos[6] and the fact that Aristotle had cited Skylax in an Indian context[7], it seems probable that the voyage of the latter was known.

Nearchos' own account seems to have some of the features of a *Periplus* or *Periegetes*, for which the work of Skylax may well have been the model and some scholars (Kiessling and Lehmann-Haupt) even believe that Nearchos had the work of Skylax before him during the voyage. But this is all mere conjecture. Not much is known about Skylax' work and it is not even certain that he enterned or described the Persian gulf (Schiwek, H.P. 14) and there is no indication that even existence of Persian gulf was known to Herodotos (Bunbury, Vol. I, p. 220). From the narrative it appears that Alexander and almost every body else regarded the expedition by sea as a desperate venture (Nearch. F.1=Arr. *Ind.* XX, 1-9), but if Nearchos believed that Skylax had accomplished his task, he might well think himself able to do what Alexander wanted which was not to repeat the votage of Skylax but to do something different and easier, i.e., not to sail from India to Egypt, but from India to the Persian-gulf.

In Nearchos' account of the voyage there is a long list of place names given on the coast lines named as the country of Arabies, Oreitai, Ichthyophagoi (Fish-eaters), Karmania, Susiana and Persis. As the place names have not yet been identified, a thorough investigation of this coastal route by a traveller is necessary for this purpose. The country of Arabies which was reported by Nearchos as a part of India, was probably extended upto somewhere near modern Cape Monze of Pakistan. The Arabies living on the river Arabis (mod. Porali in Baluchistan) were mentioned as the last Indian in the westward direction (*Ind.* XXII, 10). They were bordered by the country of Oreitai (the hinterland of the modern Sonmiyani Bay, in the former Las Bela state of Pakistani Baluchistan) whose last station was mentioned Malana (Ibid, XXV, 1-2) which may be identified with Ras Malan of Pakistan. The coastal people Ichthyophagoi lived below the Gedrosians (Ibid, XXVI, 1-2) i.e., Makran, the coastal region of Pakistani and Persian

Baluchistan as far west as the straits of Hormuz, whose country Alexander and his army had much pains in traversing. The Ichthyophagoi had their sway till the place called Dagasira (Ibid XXIX, 6-7) which has been identified with the island known as Jask, a small Iranian port in Hormozgan province on the Makran Coast (www.cais). The coast of Karmania corresponded with modern Laristan, while those of Persis and Susis with Fars and Khuzistan respectively[8]. Regarding Oreitai it was said that they were not much different from the Indians. Nearchos says that Oreitai who lived inland away from the sea, dressed as the Indians and equipped themselves similarly for warfare but their dialect and customs differed (F.I.=Arr.*Ind.*, XXV, 2). Differing with Nearchos the modern scholars like Cunningham (pp. 259-62) and Bevan (*CHI*, vol. I, p. 382) included Oreitai among the Indians, but on the other hand, in agreement with Nearchos, Tarn made a difference between the two. He is of the view that whereas Arabioi were the last Indians, the Oreitai were Iranians (Tarn, 1950, II, 250). In order to make his account interesting, the seafaring Nearchos also adopted the style and even material from *Odyssey*, which may be seen particularly in Nearchos' description of the race Ichthyophagoi (Nearch., F.I=Arr.*Ind.* XXV, 3).

We are also given the number of stades sailed each day, with only a few omissions and thus the length of the coast line of the Arabies, the Oreitae, and the Fish eaters, of Karmania, Susiana and Persis are known to us. But the distances have been overstated. For example from the mouth of the river Indus to the mouth of the river Arabis, i.e, the modern Poralia, the distance of 1000 stadia is far from reality. The length of the coast of Oreitae was stated 1000 stadia in Arrian's *Indika*, while its real length is only 100 miles. Nearchos' figures were no more than rough estimates, which appear to have made by him, after he had learnt the official figure for the overland route through Gedrosia and Karmania. Infact, it was not required in a literary work like this to write distances in stades for every stage of the itinerary. In the Greek tradition of *Periploi*, it was time, not mileage, which mattered to a sailor. In the voyage of Persian gulf Nearchos' predecessor Skylax too had given his distances in terms of daily voyages and not in stades (No. 709, F.6). It would have been more helpful indeed if, instead of giving these estimated distances, he had been more precise in his count of days and made it clear how long they sailed each day. Nearchos often noted early starts "when it was still night'' or "just before dawn", but hardly ever mentioned how early or late they reached anchorage. The trouble to furnish figures in stades appears to be on the insistence of Alexander, who wanted figures in stades in all reports of journey, whether measured by bematists or not.

However, the number of sailing days of Nearchos' journey can be counted with moderate certainty. A careful computation of Dr. William Wincent (p. 495) leads us to believe that the voyage had occupied approximately five months from the time the fleet left India. This period looks too short in view of the time of thirty months taken by Skylax. Moreover, Nearchos had experienced great difficulty in making his shorter vogage even with the help of the land forces. The explanation of this difference between the two can be made keeping in mind the fact that the voyage of Skylax incorporated the difficult circumnavigation of Arabia also in addition to the distance travelled by Nearchos and that he too could have been delayed for a long period by unfavourable winds such as those that impeded Alexander's admiral.

Although there is little evidence of Nearchos having met traders during the voyage, the commercial curiosity must have played significant role in making the voyage real. Nearchos probably failed to understand the seaworthiness of the native craft, which he did see on the coast of Ichthyophagoi. It should also be kept in mind that the delta was left by Nearchos before the beginning of the regular sailing season. Moreover the coastal trade may also have been disrupted by Alexander's campaigns in this region. In the western world there was an interest in knowing the sources and habitats of the various luxury commodities, such as spices, aromatics, and dyestuffs, which were already reaching the Eastern Mediterranean region from the semi-legendary lands along the Indian Ocean shores. We have for example references to Ophir in the *Old Testament*, the true form of which in Indian appears to be Sauvira in the gulf of Cambay which from time immemorial has been the chief seat of Indian trade with the west (Arora, 1996, pp.1, 11, 34, 62, 75-76).

Taking first the country of Arabies in connection with the informations of economic or commercial significance in course of the voyage, mention may first of all be made of pearl oysters

(F.1=Arr.*Ind.* XXI, 13), which the soldiers of Nearchos had hunted along with mussels and *solenes*, during their stay at Alexander's harbour, somewhere near the mouth of the Indus.

Nearchos' report of mentioning them as of unusual size and much larger than those of the Greeks appears to be in the ancient Greek tradition of describing everything of immense size in the remote east (see esp. Herod. III, 106). Nearchos had fortified his position at Alexander's harbour (F.1=Arr.*Ind.*, XXI, 12) which may indicate the presence of natives in the vicinity for the sake of things mentioned above.

The large haul of the plunder which was yielded by the country of Oreitai[9], indicates the prosperity of that country. Its importance may also be realised by the fact that a gold crown was awarded to the General Leonnatos for his victory over them[10]. Their prosperity appears to have been based primarily on the export of the spices, which grew in abundance in the western part of their territory[11]. It was probably to protect this commercial interest that the Oreitai were prompted to oppose Macedonians.

The evidence for the existence of local shipping (F.1=Arr.*Ind.*XXVI, 9-10) and the presence of pilots on the coast of Ichthyophagoi suggest that sea traffic and trade along this coastline must have been plentififul (Schiwek., 55, cf.p.39, note 77). Among the pilots mention may especially be made of an experienced Gedrosian pilot Hydrakes, who was able to guide the fleet completely from Mosarna (Ras Shanal Bandak) to Karmania[12].

It is difficult to explain his presence at Mosarna unless it is assumed that he had often travelled this route and that there was a regular demand for his services. Nearchos tells us that navigation from Mosarna westwards was easier (F.1=*Ind.*, XXVII, 1). Mosarna may have been the intermediate point where goods were handed over to Arabian or Persian merchants[13], although the proposed Sanskrit derivation of the name Dendrobosa may indicate the penetration of Indian traders further west[14] as in earlier days.

It was mentioned by Nearchos that at Cape Maceta in Arabia, the soldiers were informed by the guides that from there the Assyrians were importing Cinnamon and other spices (F.1=Arr. *Ind.*, XXXII, 7). The Maka of Oman and perhaps also the inhabitants of Bahrein (Makai in *RE*, XIV, 614 f. Also Schiwek, p.61) may be said as the main carriers of these spices which must be from India. From the ideal position of the country of Makai in particular it may also be postulated that they may already had been sailing more directly from the Arabian Coast to India via the open sea. Nearchos' reference to spices in Cape Maceta is an interesting notice for the light it throws on Arabian trading activities by sea in Indian spices particulary cinnamon which was considered even in the times of Eratosthenes as an Arabian product and long continued to be attributed to South Arabia and East Africa due to deliberate silence about its true place of origin by the Arabians who carried it to the western world[15]. From the above reference of Nearchos it is not clear to what extent Nearchos was aware of the connectors of Makai with India and the Indian goods. Probably he thought that the reports of the guides confirmed the view of Herodotos (III, 107) that all the incenses and spices originated in South Arabia. Aristoboulos had reported that cinnamon grew in south India (Quoted by Strabo XV, 22) which may mean that he had seen South Indian or Ceylonese cinnamon that had been imported in Sind, but even if he also had seen cinnamon in India, Nearchos would probably have concluded that this report confirmed Herodotos' statement that it was also an Arabian product. The middleman role of Arabs was probably not understood by him.

Towards the end of 325 B.C. Nearchos reached Harmozeia. He left his fleet and went into the interior to meet Alexander. There is no doubt that on account of the inhospitable nature of the Gedrosian Coast, Nearchos had faced hardship and losses during the voyage but the losses compared with those of the army in Godrosia on land route were very slight. If the right time of the year was chosen for the voyage, there were safe anchorages between the mouth of the Indus and Harmozeia. The water was available over most of the coasts and experiencd and friendly tribals could be found to guide the fleet the whole way from Pattala to Karmania. Nearchos must have also told Alexander the fact, that the passage on this route would be easier for smaller fleets carrying fewer soldiers. His report must have convinced Alexander that it would be possible to open up communication by sea between India and Mesopotamia.

Nearchos' journey of the Northern shore of the Persian gulf was made more easily, particularly on account of the guidance of experienced pilots. (F.I=*Ind.*, XXXVII, 5ff; XXXVIII, 8; XXXIX, 8 ff etc). The sea traffic between Harmozeia and the head of the gulf was frequent and well organized. The pearl fishing was seen by Nearchos on the island of Ilas (Jazineh-ye Hendorapai) (*Ind.*, XXXVIII, 3) perhaps most important of all was the trade in Arabian spices of Diridotis-Teredon (Kuwait), the emporium at the mouth of the Euphrates[16]. Near Susa in early 324 B.C, when the fleet and army were reunited[17], Alexander must have been greatly encouraged with report of the Northern shore of the gulf, form Nearchos.

Despite lackness of accuracy, overstatement of distances, no distinct account of the point of departure, etc. in the account of the voyage, its significance cannot be undervalued. The more arduous voyage of Skylax in the same seas was either forgotten or disbelieved, and it seems certain that no full or authentic record of it had been preserved. But the voyage of Nearchos has attracted an increased and in some degree a disproportionate amount of attention in modern times, from its having been preserved to us in a form so much more complete and authentic than any other record that we possess of similar character. As a commander of naval force on the great voyage of exploration, Nearchos offered an authentic narrative which no one of antiquity could match (Bunbury, E.H. Vol. I, 526-41). Arrian treated his account with respect[18] and took the truthfulness of Nearchos' account for granted. No one except Strabo (II, 1, 9) ever accused him for distorting the facts.

Abbreviations

CAH *Cambidge Ancient History.*
CHI Rapson, E.J. 1922, repr. 1962, *Cambridge History of India* Vol. I. Combridge, New Delhi repr.
F. 'F' refers to 'fragment' in F. Jacoby. *Fragmente Griechischer Historiker* (I-II D Berlin 1923-30; III a- III c, Leiden, 1954-58).
GGM 1855-61, *Geographica Graeci Minores*, C. Muller, Paris
N. N. refers to author "number" in F. Jaacoby. *Fragmente Grie chischer Historiker* (I-II D Berlin 1923-30' III a-III c. Leiden, 1954-58).
RE Pauly, G. Wissowa, *Realencyclopadie d. Klassichen Altertums wissen schaft*, 1983, Stuttgart.
T. 'T' refers to 'testimonia' in F. Jaacoby. *Fragmente Grie chischer Historiker* (I-II D Berlin 1923-30' III a-III c. Leiden, 1954-58).

Notes and References

1. For the whole text of Nearchos voyage, see, No. 133, F,1 (Arr. *Ind.* XVII-XLII); F1 a (Strabo, XV, 2, 5); F1 b (Strabo, XV, 2, 11-13); Ic (Strabo, XV, 2, 13); F Id (Strabo, XV, 2, 14); F. Ie (Arr. *Anab.* VII, 20, 9-10); F 1 f (Strabo, XV, 2, 14); F. 1 g (Strabo, XI, 13, 6); F 1 h (Pliny, *Natural Histrory*, VI, 124)
2. Star, pp.85-87; Wheeler, 1960, pp.84-89; Mackey, pp. 146-50; Piggott, pp. 110, 117-118; Dixit, 1967, p.57.
3. Rao, S.R., 1956-57, p.84; 1963 p.96, *Antiquity*; Glob, 1958, pp. 54-55; Wheeler, 1959, pp. 110-11.
4. Banerjee, A.P; Misra, Dwarka Prasad.
5. Chattopadhyaya, K.C., 1978; Meyer, Eduard; *Jataka* (Fausboll), No. 339, Vol. III, p.126.
6. For Herodotos influence on Nearchos see, Person, L. 1960, ch.V, especially 124 ff.; Murray, O.
7. No. 709, F.5 (Aristotle, *Politics*, VII, 13, 1).
8. The elucidation of many of the topographical problems here was undertaken by Wilhelm Tomaschek, 1890, 71, no. 8, 1-88. Also see Potts, D.T., 1999, p.21.
9. See Curtius, II, 10,7; Diod. Sic., XVII, 104, 7.
10. F.1 (Arr. *Ind.*, XXIII, 6); Arr. *Anab.* VII, 5, 4-5.
11. See Arr. *Anab.* VI, 22, 4-5 (from Aristoboulors); Cf. *Periplus*, 37 and Schoff's *Periplus*, 163 ff. Also Tarn, 1950, Vol. II, p. 252.
12. Nearchos, F-1 (Arr. *Ind.*, XXVII, 1). The presence of other pilots is indicated at Kyiza (Arr. *Ind.*, XXX, 3- modern Jiwari) at Mosala (*Ind.*, XXXI, 3- modern Astolah island) and when Cape Maketa was sighted (*Ind.*, XXXII, 7). The importance of Hydrakes is clear from the fact that he is one of only five persons mentioned in the *Indika*, the other four being Nearchos himself, Onesikritos, Archias of Pella and Mosenes, who had acted as a pilot in the Persian Gulf.
13. See Schiwek, p.60. In Markianos I, 28 ff. (Muller, *GGM* I, 532 ff). Mosarna appears as the boundary between Gedrosia and Karmania and the city from which the coastal distances were reckoned.
14. Tomaschek, W., 30, art. See also 'Dendrobosa' in *RE*, vol. V, 1, 215f.
15. Erat. In Berger's Fragments, III B, 48, p. 291 (Strabo, XV, 4,4).
Tarn, (1952, p. 244) says " The Alexandrian traders had no direct knowledge of India before the voyage of Eudoxus and the trade was carried out through the Arab middlemen. They were guarding their monopoly so

zealously that no Indian was allowed inside Bal-el-Mandeb and Eratosthenes knew nothing east of the Hadrament which Alexander's expedition had already heard".

16. *Ind.* XLI, 6ff; Schiewk, 62; 'Euphrates' in *RE*, VI, 1, 1206.
17. F.1 (Arr. *Ind.* XLII, 7ff). For the Chronology see Niese, *Geschichte*, 157 (note4).
18. *Indika*, XVII, 5-7. The Scholars like Susemihl (I, p. 653), O. Murray, Pearson (p.112) all believe in the authenticity of Nearchos' account.

Bibliography

Aristotle, *Politics*, Loeb Classical Library

Arora, U.P. 1981, *Motifs in Indian Mythology-Their Greek and other Parallels*, New Delhi, Munshiram Manohar Lal.

__________ 1982, "India Vis-a-Vis Egypt Ethiopia in Classical Accounts" *Graeco-Arabica* Vol. I, Athens, pp. 131-140.

__________ 1983, "Greek Attitude towards the Indians" *JGKSV:" Baldev Upadhyaya Felicitation Volume*, XXVII, Pt, 1-4, Allahabad pp. 97-109.

__________ 1989, "Folk literature in Ancient India and Greece" in Trivedi S.D. (ed.*) Essays on Indology Polity and Administration in honor of R.K. Trivedi* Vol. 2, New Delhi, Agam Prakashan, pp. 341-49.

__________ 1991, "Classical Accounts on India. Some Observations" in *G1* (ed.) New-Delhi, Ramanand Vidya Bhawan, pp. 86-108.

__________ 1991, Roman Age Authors on Ancient India" *Yavanika* I, Bareilly, ISGARS, pp. 21-46.

__________ 1991-92"The *Indica* of Megasthenes: An Appraisal", *ABORI Amrta Mahotsava volume*, LXXII & LXXIII, pp. 307-329.

__________ 1992, "Understanding Greek Nomenclatures in Classical Accounts of India" *Yavanika* No. 2. Bareilly ISGARS, pp. 85-96.

__________ 1994, "Graeco-Roman Accounts on Indian Animal World" *Yavanika*, No. 4 Bareilly ISGARS, pp. 31-76.

__________ 1994-95, "Early Greek Accounts on the Urbanization of North Western India," in *JGKSV* vol. L-L 1, Allahabad, pp. 155-176.

__________ 1996, *Greeks on India: From Skylax to Aristoteles*, Bareilly ISGARS.

__________ 2001, "Ancient India and Ancient Greece" in *Life Thought and Culture in India (From C. 600 B.C. to C.A.D. 300), edited by* Pande, G.C. and Chattopadhyaya, D.C. (General Editor) in the series *History of Science, Philosophy and Culture in Indian Civilization* Vol. I Part-2 New Delhi, Chap. 13, pp. 1045-1070.

__________ 2003, "Ancient India and the Greeks", *PIHC*, Kolkata, pp. 29-85.

__________ 2006, "The Roman Age Writings and the Political History of India" in Sinha, C.P. (ed.). *Art, Archaeology and Cultural History of India (U.N. Roy FelicitationVolume)* Pt II, Delhi: B.R. Publishing Corporation, pp. 287-292.

Arrian, 2000 (Reprint), *Anabasis of Alexander and Indica*, Text with Eng. Trans by P.A. Brunt, 2 Vols., Camb. Massac London, Loeb Classical Library.

Atharvaveda Samhita, 1966 (repr. of 1924), Hrsg. Von R. Roth & W.D. Whitney, Dritte Auflage, Bonn & Stuttgart.

__________ 1905, Ed. C.R. Lamman, Trans. W.D. Whitney, Harvard Oriental Series Vols. VII & VIII, Cambridge, Mass.

__________ 1895-96 With Sayana's Commentary, Pt. Panduranga (ed.), 1895-96, 4 vols., Bombay.

Banerji, A.P., 1926, *Asura India,* Patna.

Bunbury, E.H., 1879, 1959 (New edition) *History of Ancient Geography*, 2 vols, London, New York.

Chattopadhyaya, K.C., 1978, *Studies in the Vedic and Indo-Iranian Religion and Literature*, Benaras, Amar Printing Press.

Demosthenes, J.H., 1962-84, *Demosthenes Speeches* I-VII trs. and eds.

Diodorus Siculus, 1983, Diodours of Sicily *Bibliotheca* VIII, *Books XVI, 66-95* and XVII, C.B. Welles, ed. & trans., Camb. Mass, and London, Loeb

Dixit, K.N., 1967, *Prehistoric civilization of the Indus valley* 2nd edition, Madras, University of Madras Press.
Vince, C.A. Vince, A.T. Murray, N.W. Dewitt N.J.De
Witt, Camb. Mass. London, Loeb Classical Library.

Eratosthenes, 1880, *De Geographischen Fragmenta Des Eratosthnes,* H.Berger (ed.), Leipzig.

Glob, P.V., 1958, Jan. 11. "Excavation at Bahrein Citadel of 5000 years ago and sea links with Ur and Mohanjodaro" illustrated London News.

Herodotus,, 1960, 4 vols., text and trans. by A.D. Godley, Loeb Classical library.

Jataka Texts 1877-97, V. Fausboll (Ed.), 7 vols., London.

Hindi Trans by Bhadanta Ananda Kausalyayan. Eng. Trans, 1895-1913, (ed.) by various hands under the editorship of E.B. Cowell in 7 vols.

Mackey, E.J.H., 1948, *Early Indus Civilization*, London, Clay and sons Ltd., 2nd enlarged and revised edition by D.Mackay, London, Luzac.

Meyer Eduard., *Encyclopaedia Britannica* XXI, pp. 204 b.

Misra, Dwarika Prasad.1973, *Bharat Ka Adya Itihasa.*

Murray, O., 1972, "Herodotus and Hellenistic Culture" *CQ* in Vol. XXII, 206 ff.

Niese, B., 1893, *Geschichte der griechischen* und Makedonischen *Staaten seit der Schlacht bei Chaeronea (Geschichte)* 3 vols. Gotha.

Pearson, L., 1960, The Lost *Histories of Alexander the Great*, London. New York. *Periplus Maris Erythraei (Periplus of the Erythraean Sea).*

1989, text with Eng. trans and commentary by L., Casson, Princeton. Princeton university Press Publication.

Piggott, Stuart, 1950, *Prehistoric India*, Baltimore, Penguin.

Pliny, 1947, *Natural History,* Eng. Trans. H. Rackham, 10 Vols. Camb. Mass-London, Loeb Class. Lib.

Potts, D.T., 1999, *The Archaeology of Elam, Formation and Transformation of an Acient Iranian State,* Cambridge world Archaeology, Cambridge Unviersity Press.

Quintus Curtius, Curtius Rufus, 1971, 1976, Quintus Curtius. *History of Alexandr I-II*, trans notes text, J.C. Rolfe, Camb. Mass. London. Loeb Cl. Lib.

Rao, S.R., 1956-57, "Excavations at Lothal", *Lalit Kala*, Nos. 3-4.

__________ 1963, "A Persian Gulf Seal from Lothal", *Antiquity*, Vol. XXXVII, No. 146.

Schiwek, Heinrish, 1962, "*Das Persische Golf als schiffahrts-und seehandels route in Achamenidischen Zeit und in der Zeit Alexanders des Grossen," Bonner Jahrpucher des Rheinischen Landesmuseums in Bonn und des vereins Von Altertumsfreunden in Rheinlande.*

Star, R.F.S., 1941, *Indus Valley Painted Pottery: A Comparative study of the Design on the Painted Wares of the Harappa culture*, Princeton.

Strabo, 1917-32 (reprint), *The Geography of Strabo,* with Eng. Trans. by Jones, H.L., 8 Vols. Mass Camb. London, Loeb Classical Library.

Susemihl Fraz., 1891, *Geschichte der griechischen Literature in der Alexander inerzeit*, Vol. I Leipzig.

Tarn, W.W., 1923, "Alexander and the Ganges" *JHS* Vol. XLIII, pp. 93-101.

__________ 1950, *Alexander the Great*-II *Sources and Studies*, Cambridge

__________ 1952, *Hellenistic Civilization*, London, 3rd Edn.

Tomaschek, Wilhelm, 1890, "Topo graphische Erlauterungen der Kustenfahrt Nearchs vom Indus biszum Euphrat." *Sitzungsberichte der roster reichischen Akademie der Wissenschaften in Wien, Philosophisch-historische Klasse.*

Wheeler M., "Iran and India in Pre-Islamic Times" in *Ancient India*, No. 4, pp 85-101.

__________ 1955, *Rome Beyond the Imperial Frontiers*, London.

__________ 1959, *Early India and Pakistan*, London.

__________ 1960, *Indus Civilization*, 2nd edition, Cambridge.

56

LALITADITYA MUKTAPIDA : THE FIRST INDIAN ANTIQUARY

J.N. Pandey

The *Rajatarangini*[1] (the Chronicle of the Kings of Kashmir) by Kalhana, composed in 1148-49 C.E. is not confined in its scope to political history of Kashmir, but is a work of varied contexts. *Rajatarangini* is divided into eight *tarangas* or books of very unequal size, each dealing with a single dynasty or a pair of them. The first three books (I-III) which deals with the earlier periods, do not furnish us with a critically reliable account. From Book IV onwards we possess in it a truly historical record which grows more and more as we approach the time of the author. From the advent of Karkota dynasty in Book IV, we approach historical reality. There are indeed digressions even in Book IV, but modest in kind, and it is in one of them that we find the story about antiquarian interest of king Lalitaditya Mutkapida (724-760 C.E). Of the reign of Lalitaditya, the youngest son of Pratapaditya of *Karkota* dynasty, the chronicle gives a very detailed account. Kalhana represents Lalitaditya as a mighty monarch, who, "being eager for conquest", passed most of his time in expeditions abroad," (moving round the earth like the sun)" (Stein 1961 : 131). Owing to his remarkable achievements, Lalitaditya became surrounded in Kashmirian tradition by a halo of popular stories. Kalhana reproduces several of these stories in Book IV of *Rajatarangini*, and antiquarian story is one of them.

The story as narrated in Book IV of *Rajatarangini* runs as follows (Stein 1961 : 147-48) "Once Lalitaditya Muktapida, who was proficient in the knowledge of horses, took out himself and alone an untrained horse into a wasteland, to break it in. There far away from men, he (king) saw two beautiful maidens, one singing and the other dancing. After a short time, while the king was exercising the horse, he noticed that after completing their song and dance, the two girls bowed slightly and went away." "Mounting that horse, king Lalitaditya, came day by day to that place, and seeing two charming girls exactly in the same fashion, one day the king came up and questioned them in his surprise." The girls told the king, "We are dancing-girls belonging to a temple. Here in the village of *Suravardhamana*[2] is our home. By the direction of our mothers, who got their living here, we perform at this spot the dancing which our descent makes incumbent. This custom, handed down by tradition, has become fixed in our family. Its reason we cannot know, nor any one else." "When king Lalitaditya heard from them this information, he was astonished, and the next day had the whole ground, in accordance with their indications, dug by skilled workmen." "The when, the workmen had made a deep excavation, he (king) saw two dilapidated and worn out temples with closed doors."

"On opening the closed doors, he (king) saw there two images which as the inscriptions engraved on the bases (pitha) showed, were those of Rama and Lakshamana. The illustrious king Lalitaditya after erecting a separate stone temple by the side of the temple of Vishnu *Parihasakesava*[3], had the image of Ramasvamin consecrated there. The image of god *Lakshamana* was put up by the queen *Chakramardika* by the side of Siva *Chakresvara*[4] after she had obtained it by request from the king."

According to another closely related story occurring in Book IV of *Rajatarangini*, "the silver statue of Ramasvamin was broken into pieces by the soldiers of a *Gauda king*[5], who was treacherously murdered by assassins of Lalitaditya (Stein 1961: 152-153). Kalhana informs us that "to this day the temple of Ramasvamin is seen empty" (Stein 1961:153).

References

Stein, M.A. 1961 : *Kalhana's Rajatarangini* (Reprint) Delhi.

Notes

1. Kalhana's *Rajatarangini* was translated with an introduction Commentary and Appendices by M.A. Stein, Vol. I (Introduction, Book I-VII) and Vol. II (Book VIII, Notes, Geographical Memoirs, Index, maps) West-Minster, 1900. The critical edition of this work was published by the same scholar in 1892. Motilal Banarasi Das, Delhi has reprinted in 1961.
2. The Suravardhamana village has not been identified so far.
3. The temple of *Parihasakesava* was situated at the temple-town named Parihasapura. The name of *Parihasapura* is preserved in that of the Pargana Parspor. The identity of the names Parihasapura and Parspor is evident on phonetic grounds. M.A. Stein visited Parspor in September, 1892, in order to study the question on the spot. He was able to trace the actual remains of the buildings described by Kalhana in *Rajatarangini*; Book IV : 195-204, and thereby to fix with certainty the site of Parihaspura (Stein 1961 : 301). The five great buildings erected by Lalitaditya at Parihasapura are named in the Chronicle (Stein 1961 : 303), *Parihasakesava, Muktakesava, Mahavaraha, Govardhanadharsvamin* and *Rajavihara*. The first four were temples dedicated to the worship of Vishnu. The last, as its name suggests, was a Buddhist convent. According to Stein (1961), "The character of the ruins at Parspor agrees exactly with that of the shrines mentioned in Kalhana's account. These ruins were the only ancient remains of any significance in the neighbourhood not otherwise identified." The temple of *Ramasvamin* was built by Lalitaditya, "by the side of the temple of *Parihasakesava.*"
4. The position of *Linga,* called *Chakresvara* cannot be ascertained. According to Stein (1961 : 148) "*Siva* was worshipped under that name in not less than four distinct localities : the bank of *Madhumati,* the neighbourhood of *Vijayesvara,* the spring called *Chakratirtha,* close to *Isesvara* near Srinagar and in a cave near the *Harsesvara.*
5. It appears from the subsequent account that under the pretext of visiting the Shrine of the goodess Sharda, the *Gauda* soldiers came to Kashmir after the murder of their king with the object of revenging death of their king by the destruction of the favorite object of Lalitadiya's devotion, the image of *Parihasakesava.*

57

वेद–व्याख्या के नैरुक्त प्रस्थान में इतिहास की भूमिका

मुरली मनोहर पाठक

वेद के शुद्ध उच्चारण तथा वास्तविक अर्थावगति–हेतु ही वेदाङ्गों का प्रादुर्भाव हुआ। इसके छह अङ्गों –शिक्षा, कल्प, व्याकरण, निरुक्त, छन्दस् और ज्यौतिष में निरुक्त को श्रोत्रस्थानीय माना गया है– 'निरुक्तं श्रोत्रमुच्यते'। अतः इसके अध्ययन के बिना मनुष्य कानों के होते हुए भी वेदार्थ के विषय में बधिर ही है। सामान्य जन को यह ज्ञात नहीं हो सकता कि वेद में आधिदैविक और आध्यात्मिक अर्थों को भी उपन्यस्त किया गया है। वह तो इसमें केवल आधिभौतिक अर्थों का ही अनुसन्धान कर सकता है। सम्पूर्ण वैदिक विज्ञान दैवतवाद पर आधारित है। देवों की संख्या कितनी है? उनका स्वरूप क्या है? उनकी चेतनता तथा अचेनतनता का विचार, उनके कर्त्तव्य इत्यादि का ज्ञान वेदार्थावबोध में अपेक्षित है। ये सभी विषय निरुक्त में सम्यक्तया विवेचित हैं। इसलिए वेद के मौलिक अर्थज्ञान–हेतु निरुक्त का अध्ययन अपरिहार्य है।[1]

आचार्य यास्क ने अपने निरुक्त में यत्र–तत्र वेदों की व्याख्या के लिए आवश्यक नियमों का निर्देश किया है। इन्हें अधोलिखित रूपों में समझा जा सकता है–

(i) मन्त्रों की व्याख्या प्रकरण के अनुसार ही करनी चाहिए, पृथक् से नहीं। .. वे कहते है।– 'न तु पृथक्त्वेन मन्त्रा निर्वक्तव्याः। प्रकरणवश एव तु ते निर्वक्तव्याः।[2] प्रकरण चार हैं– याज्ञ, दैवत, अध्यात्म और इतिहास।

(ii) मन्त्रों की व्याख्या परम्परागत पद्धति से ज्ञानपूर्वक की जानी चाहिए। उसमें तर्क एवं यौक्तिकता का सन्निवेश भी होना चाहिए।[3]

(iii) वेदों में कुछ विशिष्ट अर्थ अत्यन्त निगूढतया सन्निहित हैं, उनके अवबोध–हेतु आर्षदृष्टि तथा तपश्चर्या अपेक्षित हैं।[4]

(iv) मन्त्रों का प्रतिपाद्य मुख्यतः एक ही परमात्मा है। विभिन्न गुणादि के आधार पर उसके ही विभिन्न नाम दृष्टिगत होते हैं। वस्तुतः वे सभी उस एक के ही प्रत्यङ्ग हैं।[5]

(v) आचार्य–परम्परा से शास्त्र का श्रवण करने वाले विद्वानों में अधिक विद्यावान् श्रेष्ठ माना जाता है। ऐसा विद्वान् अस्पष्टार्थक मन्त्रों का भी सरलता से अर्थ कर सकता है।[6]

उक्त नियमों के अतिरिक्त यास्क ने वैदिक शब्दों के निर्वचन–हेतु कुछ सिद्धान्तों का भी प्रतिपादन किया है। इन सिद्धान्तों के आधार पर शब्दों के मूलार्थ तक पहुँचा जा सकता है। इसके अतिरिक्त यास्क की व्याख्या–पद्धति में एक और वैशिष्ट्य यह दृष्टिगत होता है कि वे शब्दों का निर्वचन करते समय अपने पूर्व में प्रचलित मतों का भी सादर उल्लेख करते हैं। इनमें अधिदैवतवादी, आध्यात्मिक, ऐतिहासिक, नैदान, नैरुक्त, परिव्राजक, पूर्वयाज्ञिक, याज्ञिक इत्यादि का उल्लेख किया जा सकता है।

वेद में हमें ऐसे अनेक मन्त्र उपलब्ध होते हैं, जिनका सम्बन्ध ऐतिहासिक आख्यानों से है और जिन्हें जाने बिना वेदार्थ नहीं किया जा सकता। यास्क का यह वैशिष्ट्य है कि वे इन आख्यानों को स्पष्ट करने के बाद ही ऐसे

मन्त्रों की व्याख्या करते हैं। जैसे– 'नूनम्' इस निपात को समझाने के लिए व्याख्येय मन्त्र की व्याख्या करने के पूर्व वे उसका प्रसङ्ग स्पष्ट करते हुए कहते हैं–

'अगस्त्य इन्द्राय हविर्निरूप्य मरुद्भ्यः सम्प्रदित्साञ्चकार। स इन्द्र एत्य परिदेवयाञ्चक्रे।'[7] अर्थात् अगस्त्य ने इन्द्र को प्रदान करने के लिए 'हवि' तैयार करके उसे मरुद्गण को दे दिया। इस पर वह इन्द्र आकर मन्युपूर्वक विलाप करने लगा। उस विलाप में ही वह मन्त्र है, जिसमें 'सन्देह' के अर्थ में 'नूनम्' का प्रयोग किया गया है। मन्त्र इस प्रकार है–

'न नूनमस्ति नो श्वः कस्तद्वेद यदद्भुतम्।
अन्यस्य चित्तमभिसञ्चरेण्यमुताधीतं विनश्यति।।'[8]

अर्थात् आज तो मुझे यह 'हवि' मिली नहीं। जो वस्तु आज नहीं मिली, वह कल भी नहीं मिलेगी– कल के लिए उसकी क्या आशा की जा सकती है? जो अभी हुआ नहीं है, उसे कौन जानता है? अन्य दूसरे का चित्त (अस्थिर बुद्धि वाले का चित्त) चञ्चल होता है और आज जब मेरी अभीप्सित हवि नहीं मिली, तो वह कल भी नष्ट हो सकती है। प्रस्तुत मन्त्र की व्याख्या, उक्त ऐतिहासिक आख्यान के बिना नहीं की जा सकती है।

यास्क ने इस प्रकार के स्थलों की व्याख्या करते समय इतिहास का कण्ठतः उल्लेख किया है। अन्तरिक्ष के सोलह नामों में पठित 'समुद्र' शब्द की व्याख्या करते समय यास्क ने 'सागर' और 'अन्तरिक्षवाचक' 'समुद्र' की प्रकरणानुसार व्याख्या करने का निर्देश दिया है। इन दोनों अर्थों को प्रदर्शित करने के लिए उदाह्रियमाण मन्त्र के पूर्व वे इतिहास बताते हैं– 'तत्रेतिहासमाचक्षते। देवापिश्चार्ष्टिषेणः शन्तनुश्च कौरव्यौ भ्रातरौ बभूवतुः। स शन्तनुः कनीयानभिषेचयाञ्चक्रे। देवापिः तपः प्रतिपेदे। ततः शन्तनो राज्ये द्वादशवर्षाणि देवो न ववर्ष। तमूचुर्ब्राह्मणाः– अधर्म स्त्वयाऽऽचरितो ज्येष्ठं भ्रातरमन्तरित्याभिषेचितम्। तस्मात्ते देवो न वर्षतीति। स शन्तनुर्देवापिं शिशिक्ष राज्येन। तमुवाच देवापिः– पुरोहितस्तेऽसानि याजयानि च त्वेति। तस्यैतद् वर्षकामसूक्तम्। तस्यैषा भवति।'[9] अर्थात् ऋष्टिषेण के पुत्र–देवापि और शन्तनु, दो कुरुवंशीय भाई हुए। उनमें जो छोटा भाई शन्तनु था, उसने अपना राजतिलक करा लिया। इसके बाद देवापि ने तप करना प्रारम्भ कर दिया। तब शन्तनु के राज्य में बारह वर्षों तक पानी नहीं बरसा। ब्राह्मणों ने उससे कहा– तुमने अधर्म का आचरण किया है। अपने बड़े भाई का अतिक्रमण करके तुमने अपना अभिषेक करा लिया है। इसी कारण से तेरे यहाँ देव नहीं बरस रहे हैं। इसके बाद उस शन्तनु ने देवापि से राज्य लेने की प्रार्थना की। देवापि ने उससे कहा– मैं तुम्हारा पुरोहित बनूँ और तुझसे यज्ञ कराऊँ। उसी के विषय में यह वर्षकामसूक्त है। उसकी पाँचवी ऋचा इस प्रकार है–

'आर्ष्टिषेणो होत्रमृषिर्निषीदन् देवापिर्देवसुमतिं चिकित्वान्।
स उत्तरस्मादधरं समुद्रमपो दिव्या असृजद्वर्ष्या अभि।।'[10]

अर्थात् ऋष्टिषेण का पुत्र, देवापि नामक ऋषि देवताओं की कल्याणकारिणी बुद्धि को जानता हुआ यज्ञार्थ बैठ गया। उसने ऊपर के समुद्र–अन्तरिक्ष से निचले समुद्र–सागर को लक्ष्य करके उत्तम सस्य–सम्पत्कारी वर्षा के जलों को छोड़ दिया– वृष्टि करा दी। उपर्युक्त ऐतिहासिक कथा जाने बिना इस मन्त्र का अर्थ करना सम्भव नहीं था।

यास्क न केवल मन्त्रार्थ करते समय उससे सम्बद्ध आख्यान का ही उल्लेख करते हैं, अपि तु वे विभिन्न शब्दों के अर्थ के विषय में भी इतिहासविदों के मत को सादर उपन्यस्त करते हैं। ऋग्वेद के एक मन्त्र (I.32.10) में आए 'वृत्र' शब्द की व्याख्या करते हुए वे कहते हैं–

'तत्को वृत्रः ? मेघ इति नैरुक्ताः। त्वाष्ट्रोऽसुर इत्यैतिहासिकाः।'[11] अर्थात् वृत्र कौन है ? वह 'मेघ' है, ऐसा नैरुक्तों का सिद्धान्त है। ऐतिहासिकों का मानना है कि वह 'वृत्र', 'त्वष्टा का अपत्य असुर' है।

इसी प्रकार द्युस्थानीय देवताओं की व्याख्या के क्रम में प्रथमतः परिगणित अश्विनामक देवताओं पर विचार करते हुए यास्क कहते हैं–

'तत्कावश्विनौ द्यावापृथिव्यावित्येके। अहोरात्रावित्येके सूर्याचन्द्रमसावित्येके। राजानौ पुण्यकृतावित्यैतिहासिकाः।'[12]

अर्थात् ये अश्विनामक दो देव कौन हैं ? कुछ आचार्य ऐसा मानते है कि 'ये द्युलोक और पृथिवीलोक' ही हैं। अनेक नैरुक्तों का मानना है कि 'ये दिन और रात' ही हैं। कुछ लोग इन्हें 'सूर्य और चन्द्रमा' के रूप में मानते हैं। ऐतिहासिकों की मान्यता है कि 'ये अश्विन् पुण्यकर्मा दो राजा हैं', जो अश्ववान् हैं। यहाँ यह ध्यातव्य है कि यास्क ने विभिन्न मतों का उल्लेख करते हुए उनके प्रतिपादकों का नाम नहीं लिखा है, जबकि ऐतिहासिकों का मत–उल्लेख करते समय वे उन्हें नामसहित सम्मानित करते हैं।

द्युस्थानीय देवताओं के व्याख्या–क्रम में ही 'सरण्यू' के प्रसङ्ग में यास्क एक मन्त्र उद्धृत करते हैं–

'अपागूहन्नमृतां मर्त्येभ्यः कृत्वी सवर्णामददुर्विवस्वते।
उताश्विनावभरद् यत्तदासीदजहादु द्वा मिथुना सरण्यूः।।'[13]

मन्त्र के अन्तिम चरण में आये– 'द्वौ मिथुनौ' की व्याख्या करते हुए वे कहते है।– "द्वौ मिथुनौ सरण्यूर्मध्यमं च माध्यमिकां च वाचमिति नैरुक्ताः। यमं च यमीं चेत्यैतिहासिकाः।"[14] अर्थात् नैरुक्तों के अनुसार 'उस सरण्यू ने दो मिथुनों– मध्यम तमोभाग तथा उसके अन्तर्गत माध्यमिक वाक् को छोड़ दिया।' इतिहासविदों के अनुसार 'उसने विवस्वान्' के पास से दो बच्चों– यम और यमी को जन्म दिया तथा इसके बाद वह चली गई।' ऐतिहासिकों के इस अर्थ की पुष्टि के लिए यास्क एक उपाख्यान प्रस्तुत करते हैं– 'तत्रेतिहासमाचक्षते ....।'[15] आख्यान का स्वरूप यह है कि त्वष्टा की पुत्री सरण्यू ने विवस्वान् आदित्य से यम और यमी के जोड़े को उत्पन्न किया। वह सरण्यू दूसरी समान रूप वाली को अपना प्रतिनिधि बनाकर अश्व जैसा रूप धारण कर के भाग गई। वह विवस्वान् आदित्य भी अश्व का रूप धारण कर के उसका अनुसरण कर के उसी के साथ रहने लगा। उन दोनों से युग्म अश्विन् उत्पन्न हुए। समानरूप वाली से वैवस्वत मनु उत्पन्न हुए। उसके बाद सरण्यू नष्ट हो गई। इस प्रकार यह स्पष्टतः परिलक्षित होता है कि ऐतिहासिकों द्वारा उक्त मन्त्र की कृत व्याख्या कितनी समीचीन है। साथ ही आख्यान भी मन्त्रार्थ को स्पष्ट करने में महत्त्वपूर्ण भूमिका का निर्वहन करता है।

युद्धोपकरणों की व्याख्या के क्रम में आए 'द्रुघण' का अर्थ, यास्क ने 'द्रुममयो घनः'[16] अर्थात् लकड़ी का बना हुआ 'घन' या गदा किया है। इसे समझाने के लिए वे एक ऋचा उद्धृत करते हैं–

'इमं तं पश्य वृषभस्य युन्जङ्काष्ठाय मध्ये द्रुघणं शयानम्।
येन जिगाय शतवत्सहस्रं गवां मुद्गलः पृतनाज्येषु।।'[17]

अर्थात् किसी ने मुद्गल से पूछा– हे मुद्गल! तुमने एकमात्र वृषभ की सहायता से उस राजा को कैसे हरा दिया ? मुद्गल उत्तर देता है– सङ्ग्राम–भूमि के मध्य में वृषभ के सहयोगी उस पड़े हुए द्रुघण–गदा को देखो, जिसकी सहायता से मुझ मुद्गल ने एक हजार एक सौ गौवों को युद्ध में जीत लिया।

उक्त मन्त्र का अर्थ जानने के पूर्व इसका प्रसङ्ग जानना अपेक्षित है। इस हेतु यास्क इतिहास बताते हैं– 'तत्रेतिहासमाचक्षते–मुद्गलो भार्म्यश्व ऋषिर्वृषभं च द्रुघणं च युक्त्वा संग्रामे व्यवहृत्याजिं जिगाय।'[18] अर्थात् भृम्यश्व के पुत्र मुद्गल ऋषि ने वृषभ और गदा को जोड़कर युद्ध में इनका उपयोग कर आजि–लड़ाई जीती थी। इस ऐतिहासिक आख्यान को जान लेने पर ही मन्त्रार्थ स्पष्ट हो सकता है।

अन्ततः निष्कर्ष के रूप में यह कहा जा सकता है कि यास्क ने मन्त्रों की व्याख्या करते समय ऐतिहासिक आख्यानों एवं इतिहासविदों द्वारा मान्य अर्थो का अपेक्षित उपयोग किया है। इस प्रकार वेद–व्याख्या के नैरुक्त प्रस्थान में इतिहास की महती भूमिका निर्भ्रान्त रूप से हमारे सम्मुख उपस्थित होती है।

संदर्भ

1. पाणिनीय शिक्षा–41
2. प्रकरणानि पुनः याज्ञं दैवतमध्यात्ममितिहासश्चेति चत्वारि।
   – निरुक्त – 13.12, दुर्गवृत्ति
3. अयं मन्त्रार्थचिन्ताऽभ्यूहोऽभ्यूढोऽपि श्रुतितोऽपि तर्कतः। – निरुक्त – 13.12
   (मन्त्राणामर्था मन्त्रार्थास्तेषां चिन्ता तस्या अभ्यूहः – वितर्कणा भवति)
4. न ह्येषु प्रत्यक्षमस्ति, अनृषेरतपसो वा। वही, 13.12
5. माहाभाग्याद्देवताया एक आत्मा बहुधा स्तूयते। एकस्यात्मनोऽन्ये देवाः प्रत्यङ्गानि भवन्ति। वही, 7.4
6. पारोवर्यवित्सु तु खलु वेदितृषु भूयोविद्यः प्रशस्यो भवति। वही, 1.16
7. वही, 1.5
8. ऋग्वेद – I.170.1, निरुक्त–1.6 में उद्धृत।
9. निरुक्त–2.10
10. ऋग्वेद – X. 98.5, निरुक्त– 2.11 में उद्धृत।
11. निरुक्त – 2.16
12. वही, 12.1
13. ऋग्वेद, X. 17.2, निरुक्त– 12.5 में उद्धृत।
14. निरुक्त– 12.5
15. वही
16. वही, 9.18
17. ऋग्वेद– X. 102.9, निरुक्त–9.18 में उद्धृत।
18. निरुक्त– 9.18

58

यूनानी इतिहास–दर्शन : एक सर्वेक्षण

कुँवर बहादुर कौशिक

इतिहास दर्शन में यह विशेष ध्यातव्य है कि ऐतिहासिक घटनाओं के पीछे मानव–मस्तिष्क की भूमिका निर्णायक होती है। अतीत की घटनाओं के अन्तःस्थल में प्रवेश कर जब इतिहासकार क्रियाकलापों के परिवेश में मानवीय मस्तिष्क की प्रक्रिया को समझने का प्रयास करता है, तो इतिहास दर्शन का स्वरूप ग्रहण कर लेता है।[1] विज्ञान वाह्य–जगत तथा दर्शन–आतरिक जगत का अध्ययन है।[2] वाल्श ने इतिहास दर्शन के अन्वेषण का श्रेय इटालियन दार्शनिक विको (1680–1740) को दिया है। हर्डर (1784) ने अपनी रचना (Idea for Philosophy of History of Man Kind) द्वारा इतिहास–दर्शन को प्रकाश में लाया तथा हीगल ने अपने कृति (Lectures on Philoshophy of History) के माध्यम से इतिहास को एक गूढ़ विषय के रूप में समाज के सम्मुख प्रस्तुत किया।[3] प्रख्यात इतिहासविद् प्रो0 गोविन्दचन्द पाण्डेय का विचार है कि– इतिहास नेयार्थ है। नेयार्थ का अर्थ है कि ऐसी अभ्यर्थना जो अपनी मूल्यावत्ता के कारण नेय, वहनीय अथवा धरणीय होती है। अभ्यर्थना से हमारा तात्पर्य अन्वेष्यार्थ से है। अन्वेष्य स्वभावतः मूल्यवान होता है, परिणामतः नेय भी। नेयता अतीत और वर्तमान का भविष्य के लिए धारण करना है और अन्वेष्यता भविष्य का वर्तमान में धारण है। ये दोनों परस्पर सापेक्ष हैं और यह सापेक्षतया काल के ऐतिहासिक होने के लिए अनिवार्य है। अतीत, भविष्य के लिए और भविष्य के अतीत में धारण किये हुए बिना काल केवल प्रतिविम्वित वर्तमान होता है। प्रतिविम्बित वर्तमान के अर्थ में कालिकता जीवधर्म है, जो उसे अजीव से पृथक् करता है, किन्तु अर्थानुपुष्टि कालिकता मनुष्य की विशेषता है।[4]

डॉ0 कुँवर बहादुर कौशिक ने भारतीय इतिहास दर्शन की व्याख्या में मूल शब्द 'इति' को स्वीकार किया है। इति का अर्थ गति है और विश्व की सभी गतियाँ शक्ति पर निर्भर करती है। इसलिए गति ही शक्ति है और शक्ति ही गति है। वाह्य शक्ति और आंतरिक शक्ति को प्रथम स्थान प्रदान करता है। इसी आंतरिक शक्ति को पंडित दीनदयाल उपाध्याय ने 'राष्ट्रीय–चिति' कहा है।[5] इस चिति–चेतना में उस राष्ट्र की गतियाँ–इतियाँ, शक्तियाँ निहित हैं; जिसे उस दिक्–काल का इतिहास कहा जाता है। ''इसी इतिह'' पर ''आसीन'' (आस) होने की विद्या का नाम इतिहास है।[6] इतिहास–दर्शन की अनेक विधि अवधारणाओं के परिप्रेक्ष्य में यूनानी इतिहास दर्शन का एक संक्षिप्त सर्वेक्षण अनुवर्ती पंक्तियों में ध्यातव्य है।

यूनानी इतिहास दर्शन

यूनानी भाषा में यूनानी स्वयं को 'हेलीनेस' (एलीनेस) तथा अपनी भाषा को हैलीनिकी (ऐलीनिकी) कहते है। सम्भवतः ऐतिहासिक युग के उदय के साथ ही यूनानियों ने ऐसा कहना प्रारम्भ किया होगा।[7] यह हेलीनेस जाति ही आगे चलकर 'ग्रीक' जाति के नाम से प्रसिद्ध हुई। प्राचीन गाथानुसार उनके आदि पुरूष का नाम 'हेलेन' था। हेलास यूनानियों के देश का नाम था, परन्तु रोमनों द्वारा हेलास का उपनिवेशीकरण करने के पश्चात ग्रीस (GREECE) नाम दिया, जो रोमन भाषा के 'ग्रेइ' (GRAI) शब्द से उत्पन्न हुई, जिसका अर्थ है औपनिवेशिक। ग्रीक का नाम

'यूनान' पड़ने का कारण एशियामाइनर के 'आयोनियन' जाति के कारण यूनान शब्द की उत्पत्ति हुई जिसे अरब और पारसिक लोगों ने प्रयोग करना प्रारम्भ कर दिया। यूनान कभी राष्ट्र नहीं था। बुखारेस्ट की संधि (1913) के परिणामस्वरूप मकदुनिया और थ्रेस आदि यूनान में सम्मिलित कर लिए गये और यूनान को एक राष्ट्र की मान्यता प्राप्त हुई।[8] यूनान अपनी भौगोलिक परिस्थितियों के कारण कभी एक राष्ट्र के रूप में इसलिए विकसित नहीं हो पाया कि विभिन्न पर्वत श्रेणियों, नदियों, समुद्र और मैदान के कारण राजनीतिक रूप से यूनानी नगरों (City State) को ही राज्य मानकर उनके अपने पृथक विधान और नियम थे, जैसे– स्पार्टा, एथेंस, मकदुनिया आदि परस्पर विभाजित थे। इसलिए यूनानी दर्शन में यूनान के विभिन्न ऐतिहासिक गतिविधियों को संग्रह करके एक यूनानी दर्शन का स्वरूप निर्धारित किया गया जिसके प्रमुख बिन्दु अग्रिम पंक्तियों में अवधेय है– यूनानी इतिहास चेतना के सर्वेक्षण से यह ज्ञात होता है कि यूनानी चेतना ''हेल्लास'' से विकसित हुयी। इसका मुख्य लक्षण मूर्तता, सकारता और स्थायित्व का अन्वेषण था। फिशर ने लिखा है कि ''यूरोपीय' हेल्लास की संतान है। यूनानी चितंन पद्धति स्थायी, मूर्त और साकार तत्वों के आधार पर अग्रसर हुयी। यूनानियों के अनुसार मानव मस्तिष्क उसी तत्व को ग्रहण कर सकता है, जिसका निश्चित स्वरूप और आकार हो। इसलिए यूनानियों ने मूर्त, साकार और स्थायी चिन्तन को आधार बनाकर इतिहास को प्रथमतः उद्‌भूत किया। हर्बट बटरफील्ड[9] ने पश्चिम में पूर्व शास्त्रीय काल में मुख्यतः तीन तरह की रचनाओं को चिन्हित किया है, जिसमें किसी की ऐतिहासिक ज्ञान है। लोक–आख्यान, काव्य और महाकाव्य, शासकों की स्मृति में रचे गए वृतांत और हिब्रू धर्मग्रंथ आदि हैं।

मनुष्य अपने अतीत के अनुभव याद करता है और उन्हें स्मृति में सुरक्षित रखता है। लेकिन व्यक्ति के विपरीत समाज की कोई जैविक स्मृति नहीं होती, अपने अनुभव की अपने सदस्यों द्वारा सुनाई गई कथाओं से ही किसी आदिम समाज को अपने अतीत का ज्ञान होता था। बार–बार सुनाई जाकर ये कथाएँ अपने कबीले की परंपरा बन जाती थी और स्थानीय 'लोक–अख्यान' काव्य में परिवर्तित हो जाते है। दीर्घावधि में मौखिक संप्रेषण के कारण इन 'लोक–कथा–काव्य' की सामग्री किंवदंतियों के जुड़ने से परिवर्तित हो जाती थी। कुछ लोक आख्यानों को काव्यों के रूप संगठित किया गया, जैसे प्राचीन बेबीलोन वासियों का गिल्गमेश या यूनानियो का इलियड। पेशेवर कथावाचको द्वारा संप्रेषित लोक आख्यान काव्य या महाकाव्य हालांकि इतिहास नहीं थे जैसे हम आज परिभाषित करते हैं, लेकिन वे अतीत में रच जाते थे और आख्यान की एक तकनीक मुहैया कराते थे।[10]

मिस्री, हित्ती और असीरियाई जैसे महान साम्राज्यों के शासकों के लिए तैयार किए गए वृतांत पूर्व शास्त्रीय काल में एक अन्य तरह की ऐतिहसिक रचना हैं। महलों और मंदिरों की दीवारों पर उत्कीर्ण ये वृत्तांत शासकों की विभिन्न गतिविधियों के बारे में बताते हैं, खासकर उनकी सैनिक सफलताओं के बारे में। वृत्तांत, संस्मरणात्मक इतिहास का प्रतिनिधित्व करते है। हित्ती वृत्तांत शायद इनमें से सबसे विशिष्ट हैं। प्राचीन सुमेरी और मिस्री राजवंशावलियां एक तरह से ज्यादा विश्वसनीय इतिहास है। जहाँ संस्मरणात्मक अभिलेखों में अतिशयोक्ति की गुंजाइश रहती है, राजवंशावलियों में ऐसी विकृति की संभावना कम होती है। पहले बेबीलोनी साम्राज्य की सूची में वर्षों का नाम घटनाओं पर दिया जाता था, हर वर्ष के लिए एक घटना ऐसी तिथि सूचियों को कालाध्यानों का पूर्ववती गाना जा सकता है। साथ ही प्राचीन असीरियाइयों के खूबसूरत और प्रभावशाली उत्कीर्ण चित्र चित्रात्मक इतिहास के बेहतरीन उदाहरण है।[11]

सभी आदिम जनजातियों की तरह प्राचीन यहूदी भी सदियों से अपने बच्चों को कथाएं सुनाते, गाना गाते और लोकप्रिय किन्वदंतियों को बताते आये थे। इस तरह कम से कम डेविड के समय (1000 ई0पू0) से एक अनवरत मौखिक परंपरा रही जिसमें किंवदंती और इतिहास के बीच स्पष्ट विभाजन किया जा सकता था। यह विभाजन प्राचीन यहूदियों के धर्म ग्रंथ ओल्डटेस्टामेंट की किताबों का आधार है। इनमें प्रचुर ऐतिहासिक जानकारी है। हालंकि उनकी रचना ऐतिहासिक उद्‌देश्यों के लिए नहीं हुई। हिब्रू धर्मग्रंथ की 39 किताबों में 17 स्पष्ट तथा ऐतिहासिक हैं और पांच प्रमुख एवं बारह गौण पैंगबर भी लगभग ऐतिहासिक हैं।

(क) होमर का काव्यात्मक इतिहास

होमर की दो कृतियों 'इलियड' और 'ओडिसी' महाकाव्य को यूनानी इतिहास में वही स्थान प्राप्त है, जो भारतीय इतिहास में वेदव्यास और उनके द्वारा सम्पादित ग्रंथो को है। होमर ने इन महाकाव्यों की रचना की थी अथवा नहीं, यह प्रश्न विगत शताब्दी वर्षों से यूरोपीय विद्वानों को आकुल करता रहता। परन्तु अद्यावधि अन्तिम निर्णय नहीं हो पाया। परन्तु ऐतिहासिक तथ्य यह है कि इन दोनों महाकाव्यों में यूनान के प्राचीन वीर पुरूषों की उपलब्धियों एवं कृतियों का उल्लेख है। 'इलियड' में 'ट्राजन' युद्ध का वर्णन है। यह युद्ध 10 वर्ष तक चलता रहा और हेक्टर को दफनाने के पश्चात कथा समाप्त हो जाती है। 'इलियड' में 'एकियन' राजाओं के शासन काल में हुयी घटनाओं का वर्णन है, जिसमें उस युग की सभ्यता की धुंधली सी झांकी उपलब्ध होती है।[12]

छठी शताब्दी ई0पू0 ग्रीस में बौद्धिक संक्रमण का काल था। एक महत्वपूर्ण परिघटना थी कविता के साथ–साथ गद्य का विकास, जिसमें ग्रीक मस्तिष्क कल्पनाशील से ज्यादा मननशील होने लगा तथा यह नया बौद्धिक रवैया काव्यात्मक चिंता की कल्पनाशीलता पर अंकुश का काम करने लगा। भूगोल कालगणना आकार लेने लगी तथा पहले दर्शन और विज्ञान का उदय हुआ।[13]

इस बौद्धिक संक्रमण में आयोनिया ने शेष यूनान का नेतृत्व किया। 'इलियड' आयोनिया में ही लिखा गया, जो ग्रीक गद्य, दर्शन और विज्ञान का धन बन गया। विकसित वैज्ञानिकता ने वहां खुद को इतिहास में भी लगाया।

(ख) लोगोग्राफी का उदय

यूनानीयों का ईरान के साथ सम्पर्क होने से राजाओं की वंशावलियों, संधि, विग्रह के लेखों आदि के संरक्षण की ओर ध्यान गया। आयोनिया के लेखकों से सरल गद्य में नगरों, निगमों, जातियों, राजवंशों और मंदिरों की परम्पराओं तथा किंवदन्तियों को लिपिबद्ध करने लगे। सामूहिक रूप से इन्हें 'लोगोग्राफी' कहते हैं। इन लेखकों में अकूसिलौस–कादमस, हिलेनिकस, डाथोनिसस, चारोन और हिकेरियस प्रमुख थे। हेराडोटस के पूर्व इन्हीं को गद्य, लेख, इतिहास का काम देते थे।[14]

पड़ोसी लोगों के बारे में जानने की कोशिश में यूनानियों ने प्रत्यक्ष अनुसंधान का महत्व पहचाना जो इतिहास के अर्थ का मूल है। इस शैली में लिखने वाले लोग लोगोग्राफर कहलाए, जो सरल गद्य में नगरों, लोगों, राजकुमारों, मंदिरों आदि के उद्भव से सम्बन्धित मौखिक परम्पराओं और जनश्रुतियों को प्रस्तुत करते थे। हिकारियस, हिलेनिकस, शारोन और डायोनिसियस ज्यादा महत्वपूर्ण लोगोग्राफी मिथक से इतिहास में संक्रमण के बिन्दु पर स्थित है। स्थानीय इतिहास उनका विषय है, स्थानीय मिथक उनका स्रोत। पर नितांत अविश्वसनीय चीजें उन्होंने इन मिथकों से निकाल बाहर की। हिकारियस ने अपनी वंशावलियों से वे बातें निकाल दी जिन्हें वह हास्यास्पद समझता था। उत्सवों पर लोगोग्राफी की कलात्मक रचनाओं का सार्वजनिक किन्तु आंशिक वाचन होता था। इनकी शैली कलात्मक होती थी।[15] इतिहास की सबसे प्राचीन प्रजाति कथात्मक इतिहास है। लंबे समय तक अस्तित्व जिसकी नियति है। क्योंकि आख्यान ऐतिहासिक घटनाओं की स्मृति अक्षुण्ण रखने की स्थायी आवश्यकता पूरी करता है। पाँचवी सदी ई0पू0 में हेरोडोटस और थ्सीडाइडिस के कामों में लोगोग्राफी पूर्ण इतिहास के रूप में विकसित हो गई दिखती है। होमर के पश्चात उसकी विसंगतियों को दूर तक तैथिक क्रम में वीरगाथा कालीन वीर पुरूषों को प्रस्तुत करने का प्रयास किया गया। कालान्तर के कवियों ने यूनानी वीर पुरूषों के वंश को यूनानी देवताओं के साथ क्रमिक रूप से सम्बद्ध करने का प्रयास किया।[16] हेसिओड (Hesiod) नामक कवि ने सर्वप्रथम इतिहास की अवधारणा में युग–चक्र सिद्धांत को प्रस्तुत किया। इसने चक्र कल्पना की और इनका नामकरण चार धातुओं युगो के नाम पर रखा।

सातवीं शताब्दी के कवि हेसिओड (Hesiod) ने ऋतु चक्रों के आधार पर जो विचार दिया उसका विनियोग इतिहास में किया गया।

क– स्वर्ण युगः– इस युग में क्रोनोस का स्वर्ग में शासन था। मनुष्य स्वयं देवताओं के साथ कार्य करता था तथा देवता उसके कार्यों में सहयोग करते थे। वह भी उनके साथ ही काम–काज करता था और पृथ्वी स्वतः उन्हें सभी श्रेयस्कर वस्तुएँ देती थी।

ख– रजत युगः– युग चक्र का यह द्वितीय चरण अपनी पूर्ववर्ती (स्वर्ण) युग का अपेक्षा हीनता अवस्था में पहुँचा गया था। इस युग में मनुष्य की श्रेष्ठता में कमी आई। मनुष्य धीरे–धीरे निराशा की ओर अग्रसर होता जा रहा है। पारस्परिक संघर्ष में व्यस्त रहने के कारण देवताओं की आराधना के प्रति उदासीन होने लगा। उसकी प्रवृत्तियाँ कुछ हीन हुईं तथा देवताओं का पहले जैसा सन्निध्य और सहयोग रूक गया।

ग– काँस्य युगः– इस युग में मानवीय गुणो का उत्तरोतर ह्रास होता गया। शक्तिशाली मनुष्य दयाभाव से सर्वथा शून्य हो गया। इस युग के भवन कांस्य निर्मित होते थे। अब मनुष्य पतनोत्मुख होने लगा था। मनुष्य के गुणों में और कभी आना इस युग का विशेषता थी। पारस्परिक मारकाट, कलह तथा संघर्ष इस युग में मुख से विद्यमान था।

घ– लौह युगः– यह युग चक्र का अंतिम चरण था। इस युग के वीर पुरूष अपने पूर्वजों की तुलना में अधिक वीर तथा न्यायप्रिय थे। इस युग में 'द्राय तथा 'धेबीज' के युद्धों में वीर पुरूषों ने भाग लिया। वर्तमान कालीन लौह युग में श्रम तथा दुख से मानव समाज मुक्त नहीं है। अर्थात इस युग का मनुष्य कार्य अधिक करने को विवश होता है तथा दुखों का भी उसे अधिक सामना करना होता है।

युगों के चक्रात्मक विकास का यह सिद्धांत, इस मान्यता पर आधारित है कि जैसे रात–दिन, चन्द्रमा की वृद्धि और क्षय, मास, पक्ष अथवा एक ऋतु के पश्चात दूसरे का अनुगमन होता रहता है, इसी प्रकार सम्पूर्ण ब्रह्माण्ड में भी परिवर्तन की चक्रात्मक प्रक्रिया चलती रहती है। परन्तु यह एक आधुनिक विवेकशीलता की कल्पना मात्र है,

क्योंकि किसी भी लम्बे युग चक्र को रात–दिन; पक्ष या ऋतु चक्र में समाहित नहीं किया जा सकता। इसकी पृष्ठभूमि ऐतिहासिक होनी चाहिए और मनुष्य की पीढ़ी दर पीढ़ी से चलती हुई स्मृतियों के साथ ही वहाँ आये थे, लेकिन जिस युग चक्र की मान्यता प्रचलित थी, उस संस्कृति से उन लोगों का सम्बन्ध कब रहा था। इसका कोई काल–निर्धारण नहीं किया जा सकता। युग चक्र सिद्धान्त अपने मौलिक रूप में भारतीय सिद्धांत है, जो अनन्त काल से भारत में मान्य ही नहीं रहा है बल्कि भारत में युगों की अवधि भी निर्धारित है तथा उसकी पूरी व्याख्या भी है, जो युगचक्र को मन्वन्तर काल का एक भाग मानती है।[17]

हेरोडोटस

हेरोडोटस और थूसीडाइडिस की इतिहास मेधा ने दो अपराजेय लगने वाली कठिनाइयों पर विजय पाई, यथा–अभिलेखों का अभाव और इतिहास विरोधी दर्शन, जो इतिहास को एक निराशाजनक उद्यम मानता था।

हेरोडोटस का जन्म एक उच्च कुल में 484 ई0पू0 में हुआ था। अपने चाचा के दुस्साहसिक कारनामों के कारण उसे 32 वर्ष की उम्र में निर्वासन भोगना पड़ा। दूर–दराज की यात्राओं के रूप में इस भावी इतिहासकार ने अपने निष्कासन का लाभ उठाया। ये यात्राएं उसे कीनिशिया; मिस्त्र, सीरीन, सूषा और अंततः काले सागर के यूनानी नगर राज्यों तक ले गई। बिल ड्यूरां लिखते है 'जहां भी वह गया, उसने वैज्ञानिक की नजर और बच्चे की जिज्ञासा से निरीक्षण और अनुसंधान किया, और जब वह एथेंस में 447 ई0पू0 में बसा तो वह भू–मध्यसागरीय राज्यों के भूगोल, इतिहास और शिष्टाचार सम्बन्धी नोट्स के समृद्ध संग्रह से लैस था। इन नोट्स और हेकाटियस तथा अन्य पूर्ववर्तियों के काम से टीपे गए कुछ अंशों के आधार पर उसने अपना सबसे प्रसिद्ध इतिहास रचा जिसमें उसके अपने मिथकीय उद्भव से लेकर पर्शियन युद्ध के अंत तक का मिस्त्र निकट पूर्व और ग्रीस का इतिहास दर्ज था।[18]

इतिहास का जनक माना जाने वाला व्यक्ति अपनी भूमिका में घोषित करता है कि उसके इतिहासों का उद्देश्य यूनानियों और बर्बर (पर्शियनों) के महान कार्यों को भावी पीढ़ियों के लिए बचाकर रखना और उनके युद्ध के कारणों को उद्घाटित करना है। नौ भागों की इस रचना, जिसका हर भाग कलाओं की नौ देवियों में से किसी एक को समर्पित है का मुख्य कथ्य यूनानी–पर्सियन संघर्ष है। जिसका महान अंत 480 ई0पू0 में सलामिस में हुआ।

लेकिन हेरोडोटस अपने आख्यान में 24 विभिन्न पूर्वी भू–मध्यसागरीय लोगों के रीति, रिवाज, परिधानों, शिष्टाचार, नैतिकता, और मान्यताओं के दिलचस्प विवरण भी शामिल करता है। पुस्तक का विशाल फ्रेमवर्क एक सीमित अर्थ में उसे एक सार्वभौमिक इतिहास बनाता है।

दूसरे–तीसरे व्यक्ति से सुनी गई दूरदराज की घटनाओं के बारे में लिखना हेरोडोटस की पद्धति थी। जिज्ञासा निरीक्षण की तेज ताकत के बल पर वह जानने की कोशिश करता कि चीजें कैसे हुई थी। वह तार्किक व्याख्यानों की तलाश करता, जो जलवायु और भौगोलिक कारकों का प्रभाव बताती। लेकिन उसमें महत्वपूर्ण घटनाओं के छोटे मोटे महत्वहीन कारण बताने की प्रवृत्ति थी जैसे औरतों का प्रभाव या एकदम निजी बातें। अति प्राकृतिक चीजों में विश्वास के कारण वह अपने आख्यान में अपनी भविष्यवाणियों, दिव्यदृष्टि और आगामी दुर्घटनाओं के बारे में दैवी चेतावनियां शामिल करता था। उसकी बाल सुलभ जिज्ञासा अक्सर उसे बाल सुलभ भोले विश्वासों की ओर ले जाती। स्ट्रावो ने तो लिखा भी कि 'हेरोडोटस की रचनाओं में बहुत ऊटपटांग भरा पड़ा है। वह सोचता था कि इथियोपिया के लोगों का वीर्य काला होता है, मिस्र की बिल्लियां आग में कूद जाती हैं, डैन्यूब किनारे के लोग गंध से ही नशे में आ जाते हैं, पेडागस में एथीना की पुजारिन के भारी दाढ़ी थी, ने बूचइनेजार औरत था, और आल्प्स नदी थी। लेकिन उसने अपने बचाव में लिखा, जो कहा जाता है उसे बताना मेरा दायित्व है। परन्तु उसे मानने को मैं बाध्य नहीं हूँ, और इस इतिहास में हर आख्यान के बारे में वह सही मानिए।[19]

जो भी हो देश काल के परिप्रेक्ष्य में मनुष्य को देखने वाला हेरोडोटस पहला व्यक्ति था। सिसेरो ने उसे 'इतिहास का जनक' कहा और अधिकतर प्राचीनों की तरह लू सियन ने उसे थूसीडाइडिस से ऊपर दर्जा दिया, शारवेल ने उसे पर्सियन युद्धों का होमर कहा है, एच0ई0 बार्न्स के अनुसार वह पहला लेखक हुआ, जी मानता था कि इतिहासकार का काम मनुष्य के पूरे पिछले जीवन को पुननिर्मित करना है। वह संपूर्ण इतिहास लेखन के क्रम में सबसे दिलचस्प कथावाचकों में एक था।

कालिंगवुड हेरोडोटस को वैज्ञानिक इतिहास के सृजन का श्रेय देता है। वह हेरोडोटस को आधुनिक इतिहासलेखन की सभी चार परीक्षाओं से गुजारता है और तार्किक साक्ष्य एवं व्याख्या पर अपना आख्यान आधारित नहीं करने की सिर्फ कमी पाता है जो सिर्फ प्रश्न पूछने के हुनर से उसने पिछली मानवीय गतिविधियों की जानकारी पाना सम्भव बनाया जिसे पहले असम्भव माना जाता था। इस (इतिहास) शब्द के प्रयोग और उसके निहितार्थ हेरोडोटस वो इतिहास का जनक जानते हैं। जनुश्रुति लेखन को इतिहास के विज्ञान में बदलना पाँचवी सदी का अविष्कार था और हेरोडोटस वह आदमी था जिसने यह आविष्कार किया।[20]

थूसीडाइडिस

एथेंसी पिता और थ्रेसी माता की संतान थूसीडाइडिस को एथेंस में जितनी शिक्षा प्राप्त हो सकती थी उतनी उसने प्राप्त की। वह 430 ई0पू0 में प्लेग का शिकार हुआ, लेकिन मौत ने उसे इतिहास के हित में छोड़ दिया। पोलोपोनेशियार्ड युद्ध के आरम्भ से ही उसने उसका रोजानामचा दर्ज करना शुरू किया। थ्रेस के खिलाफ एक नौसैनिक अभियान के लिए उसे 424 ई0पू0 में दो में से एक सेनापति चुना गया। लेकिन सैनिक विफलता के कारण उसे एथेंस से निर्वासित कर दिया गया। यह दुर्भाग्य, इतिहास के लिए सौभाग्य सिद्ध हुआ।

क्योंकि थूसीडाइडिस ने अपने अगले 20 साल यात्राओं में गुजारे, खासकर पेलोपोनस में। 404 ई0पू0 की कुलीनतांत्रिक क्रांति ने उसका निर्वासन समाप्त किया और वह एथेंस लौटा। उसकी मृत्यु, कुछ लोग कहते है कि हत्या थी, 396 ई0पू0 में हुई जिसके कारण उसका ''पेलोपोनेशियार्ड युद्ध का इतिहास'' अधूरा छूट गया।[21]

युवावास्था में थूसीडाइडिस ने एथेंस में हेरोडोटस के 'पर्सियन युद्धों का इतिहास' का सार्वजनिक वाचन सुना था। हेरोडोटस जिसका दायरा युग से युग और स्थान से स्थान तक फैला था के विपरीत थूसीडाइडिस ने अपना दायरा पेलोपोनेशियार्ड युद्ध तक सीमित रखा और अपनी कथा को कठोर काल क्रमानुगत ढांचे में ''ग्रीष्म और शीत'' के क्रम में नियंत्रित रखा। पेलोपोनेशियार्ड युद्ध का इतिहास में आठ पुस्तकें हैं और आठवी पुस्तक 441 ई0पू0 के एक अभियान के बीच में अचानक खत्म हो जाती है। थूसीडाइडिस ने मानों इतिहासकारों को जानकारी देने और मानों राजनेताओं को दिशा निर्देश देने के इरादे से ही लिखा। उसके लिखने के लक्ष्य थे ''वे अनुसंधानकर्ता जो अतीत का ठीक–ठीक ज्ञान इसलिए चाहते हैं कि भविष्य की व्याख्या में मदद मिले, जो मानवीय कार्यकलापों के क्रम में अतीत जैसा ही होगा। ईमानदार और गंभीर थूसीडाइडिस चाहता था कि उसका काम 'क्षणिक वाहवाही प्राप्त करने वाले निबंध की तरह न होकर सार्वकालिक महत्व का हो'। चूंकि उसकी नजर में एक जैसी स्थितियां और समस्याएं दोहराई जाती रहती हैं। इसी कारण से एक युग के पाठ दूसरे में भी उपयोगी होंगे।

सही और भरोसेमंद ब्यौरा देने के लिए एक कड़ी पद्धति जरूरी थी। भोले विश्वासी हेरोडोटस के विपरीत थूसीडाइडिस अपने स्रोतों पर कड़ी वैज्ञानिक पद्धति लागू करता था और स्पष्टतम आकड़ों के आधार पर ही आगे बढ़ता था। वह मानता था कि ऐतिहासिक प्रक्रिया अतिप्राकृतिक और अति मानवीय ताकतों से अप्रभावित एवं तार्किक प्रक्रिया है। इसलिए उसे भविष्य वक्ताओं पर विश्वास न था और वह मिथको, किंवदंतियों, आश्चर्यों एवं चमत्कारों के पीछे हाथ धोकर पड़ता था। हेरोडोटस इतिहास के जनक भले ही हों, पर थूसीडाइडिस की सोची–समझी तथ्यपरकता और सच्चाई उसे इतिहास की वैज्ञानिक पद्धति का जनक बनाती है, और इतिहास में असाधारण व्यक्तियों की भूमिका मानते हुए भी थूसीडाइडिस का सुझाव निर्वैयक्तिक अभिलेखन तथा कारण विकास एवं नतीजो पर विचार की ओर था। पर उसने भी चरित्र के मुंह में अक्सर शानदार भाषण तलकर सच्चाई और तथ्यपरकता से कई बार समझौता किया।[22]

थूसीडाइडिस के इतिहास चिंतन के कठोर तार्किक आधार आधुनिक इतिहास चिंतन के लिए महत्वपूर्ण निष्कर्ष हैं। एथेंस का यह प्राचीन इतिहासकार विश्लेषण की जो गहराई इतिहास लेखन के लिए लेकर आया उसका स्थायी प्रभाव पड़ा। वह इतिहास प्रक्रिया का सिर्फ क्या नहीं बल्कि कैसे और क्यों भी जानना चाहता था। जबकि हेरोडोटस ज्यादातर पहले सवाल तक ही सीमित रहा। थूसीडाइडिस ज्यादा गहरी जांच करना चाहता था और मानवीय क्रियाओं के पीछे के इरादे और प्रक्रियाओं को तलाशना चाहता था। अपने समय के विज्ञान से प्रभावित उसने हिप्पोक्रेटिक चिकित्साशास्त्र के सिद्धांतों और पद्धतियों को राजनीति पर लागू करने की कोशिश की ताकि सभी कुछ की तार्किक व्याख्या की जा सके। विश्लेषण क्षमता ने उसकी गहरे कारणों को किसी धरना की तात्कालिकता से अलग पहचानने और आम निष्कर्षों तक पहुंचने के मदद की उसने जब धन और सत्ता के सम्बन्धों या एथेंसी साम्राज्यवाद के पीछे के अभावुक तर्को का विशलेषणं किया। थूसीडाइडिस के लिए इतिहास एक जैविक प्रक्रिया है, वह एक दूसरे से तार्किक व्यवस्थित और स्थायी क्रम से जुड़ी घटनाओं का अध्ययन है। बीसवीं शताब्दी में जो इतिहासवादी कहलाया, यह विश्वास हमें उसकी याद दिलाता है साथ ही आधुनिक इतिहास पद्धति जो रचनात्मक तर्क करती है, उसका सबसे पहले उपयोग करने वाला थूसीडाइडिस ही था। जब जानकारी के सकरात्मक स्रोत विपल हो जाते थे थूसीडाइडिस अनेम्सागोरा की उल्टी तार्किकता अपनाता था यानी वह पीछे से बस करता था, जाने हुए से अनजाने की तरह ताकि किसी घटना के कारण व कारणों का पता लगाया जा सके।

''यूनानी इतिहास पद्धति और उसकी सीमाएं हेरोडोटस और थूसीडाइडिस के लिए ऐतिहासिक स्रोतों का मतलब था प्रत्यक्षदर्शियों द्वारा तथ्यों का बयान और इतिहास पद्धति का मतलब था इन आख्यानों को प्राप्त करना। तथ्यों की पुष्टि के लिए दोनों इतिहासकारों ने अदालत की तरह गवाहों से कड़ी जिरह की होगी। कालिंगवुड का मानना है कि हेरोडोटस और थूसीडाइडिस के ठोस एवं सुसंगत आख्यानों के पीछे चश्मदीदो की गवाहियों के

इस्तेमाल की यह पद्धति है। लेकिन वह ध्यान दिलाता है कि उस समय एक मात्र उपलब्ध इस पद्धति की तीन सीमाएं हैं। एक यह उपयोगकर्ताओं पर परिप्रेक्ष्य की एक संक्षिप्ता थोपती है। प्रत्यक्षदर्शियों के ब्यौरे जीवित स्मृति के परे नहीं जा सकते थे। यह पद्धति उपयोगकर्ताओं को ऐसी ओर बांधती है जिसकी लंबाई जीवित स्मृति की लंबाई है। यही कारण है कि हेरोडोटस और थूसीडाइडिस जीवित स्मृति के पीछे की जो बातें बताते हैं (मसलन छठी शताब्दी ई0पू0 की) उन पर भरोसा नहीं किया जा सकता। क्योंकि उनकी पद्धति और स्रोत अतीत के दूरस्य कालखंडो तक नहीं पहुंच सकते, लेकिन यह विफलता नहीं थी यदि दूरस्थ नहीं तो हाल के अतीत को वैज्ञानिक इतिहास के दायरे में लाना पांचवी सदी के यूनानी इतिहास लेख की महत्वपूर्ण उपलब्धि हो चुकी थी। जो घटनाएं इसकी जीवित स्मृति में हुई थी वह सिर्फ उन्ही के बारे में लिख सकता था। इसकी हास्यजनक विडंबना कालिंगवुड के इन शब्दों में व्यक्त होती है। इतिहासकार द्वारा विषय के चुनाव के बदले विषय इतिहासकार को चुनता है। इतिहासकार सही मायनों में इतिहासकार न होकर महज अपनी पीढ़ी का आत्यकधवार था। तीसरे प्राचीन ग्रीक इतिहास में सुधार था, इसका पुनर्लेखन किया जा सके। यदि कोई इतिहास अपनी पीढ़ी की आत्मकथा है तो वह जिस साक्ष्य पर आधारित है उसे नष्ट हो जाना है। ऐसे कार्य को एक बड़ी संपूर्णता में समाहित करना भी असंभव है, 'क्योंकि वह एक कलाकृति है, एक मूर्ति के व्यक्तित्व या अद्वितोयता के साथ। इतिहास जैसी किसी बड़ी संपूर्णता का अंग नहीं बनाया जा सकता था।[23]

हेलेनिस्टिक काल में इतिहास लेख

सिकन्दर की विजयों से लेकर मिस्र पर रोमन विजय तक के 200 साल इतिहास के हेलेनिस्टिक युग में आते है। कालिंगबुड के अनुसार इस काल में यूनानी इतिहास लेखन ने अपनी तीन सीमाओं पर विजय पाई।

पहली तो यह कि ग्रीक लोगों ने धीरे–धीरे अपना सांस्कृतिक विशेषवाद त्याग दिया यानी वह संकीर्ण नजरिया जो यूनानियो और कथित बर्बरों के बीच के भाषाई और सांस्कृतिक अंतरों से निर्मित था। सिकन्दर के हथियारों द्वारा जीते गए साम्राज्य में यूनानी संस्कृति फैल चुकी थी और सिकंदरिया, पेर्गामम, ऐटियॉक तथा रोड्स जैसे कई शहर ग्रीक सभ्यता के महान केन्द्र बन चुके थे। इस दौरान यह भी पता चला था कि यूनानी भाषा तहजीब और रीति रिवाज सीखकर बर्बर भी ग्रीक बन सकते थे। सिकंदर और उसके दस हजार सैनिकों की एशियाई पत्नियाँ थीं; तीस हजार ईरानी लड़कों को यूनानी भाषा और मकदूनियाई फौजी तकनीक सिखाई गई। ग्रीक लोगों ने भी कुछ एशियाई तौर–तरीके सीखे, शंहशाह ने खुद पूर्वी परिधान, रीति–रिवाज और शिष्टाचार अपना कर उदाहरण प्रस्तुत किया। हेलेनिस्टिक काल में यूनानियों और गैर यूनानियों के बीच संपर्क के परिणाम से एक साझा संस्कृति बनी। दूसरी यह कि सिकंदर की विजयों के फलस्वरूप यूनानियों ने अपने नगर राज्य विशेषतावाद से निजात पाई, सिकन्दर की टुकड़ियों के साथ–साथ ग्रीक चिंतन भी दुनिया को जीतने निकला था। 'दुनिया' एक भौगोलिक अभिव्यक्ति से कही ज्यादा एक 'ऐतिहासिक अभिव्यक्ति' भी हो गई। ऐड्रियाटिक से सिंधु और डैन्यूब से सहारा तक सिकन्दर के साम्राज्य के सभी प्रदेश एक इतिहास का हिस्सा बन गए। ग्रीक दुनिया के इतिहास का हिस्सा। एक ऐतिहासिक इकाई के रूप में पूरे विश्व की अवधारणा एक विशिष्ट स्टोइक अवधारणा है। और स्टाइसिज्म, हेलेनिस्टिक काल का विशिष्ट उत्पाद है। यूनानी इतिहास–बोध में उपुर्यक्त परिवर्तन प्रतिबिबित हुए।

इतिहास की पुरानी अवधारणा जिसमें उसे एक खास कालखंड के एक खास सामाजिक इकाई या नगर का इतिहास माना जाता था, बदल गई। वह विकसित होकर एक विश्व दृष्टि हो गई और इसके अनुरूप उसका कालखंड भी विस्तृत हो गया। कालिंगबुड की स्पष्ट राय है कि हेलेनिज्म ने सार्वभौमिक इतिहास की धारणा सृजित की। पद्धति के मामलों में यूनानी इतिहास लेख ने अपनी तीसरी विजय पाई। मानवीय स्मृति को सीमाओं से बंधी प्रत्यक्षदर्शियों की गवाही के बल पर विश्व इतिहास की रचना नहीं की जा सकती थी। एक नई पद्धति खोजी गई यानी संग्रह, जिसके लिए सामग्री 'अधिकारी' विद्वानों' से प्राप्त होती थी। यानी उन पूर्ववर्ती इतिहासकारों से जो खास कालखंडों में खास समाजों का इतिहास लिख चुके थे। कालिंगवुड इसे 'कैंची और गोंद' इतिहास पद्धति कहते हैं। जो प्रत्यक्षदर्शियों की सूचना पर आधारित पांचवी सदीं की सुकराती पद्धति से निश्चित ही कमजोर थी। सामग्री संचयन और प्राप्त सूचनाओं को एक इतिहास में डालने में सक्षम इतिहासकार के लिए अब किसी भी आकार में एक नए तरह का इतिहास लिखना संभव हो गया। पोलिवियस में हमे नए तरह का इतिहास पूर्णतः दिखता है।[24]

सन्दर्भ

1. एन0 बी0 बनर्जी : कॉन्सेप्ट ऑफ फिलॉसाफी 1967, पृष्ठ –51

2. तत्रैव
3. वाल्श, पृष्ठ 12
4. गोविन्द चंद्र पाण्डेय, – इतिहास स्वरूप तथा सिद्धान्त पृष्ठ– 183–201. प्रकाशक – राजस्थान हिन्दी ग्रंथ अकादमी, जयपुर, 1971
5. कुँवर बहादुर कौशिक, इतिहास दर्शन एवं प्राचीन भारतीय इतिहास लेखन, विद्यार्थी पुस्तक भण्डार, षष्टम – 2008 पृष्ठ – 7।
6. तत्रैव
7. उदय प्रकाश अरोरा, प्राचीन यूनान : इतिहास एवं संस्कृति पृष्ठ – 258, अनामिका पब्लिशर्स एण्ड डिस्ट्रीब्यूटर्स, दरियागंज, नई दिल्ली।
8. तत्रैव, पृष्ठ – 20
9. बटरफील्ड, हिस्टोरियोग्राफी इन डिक्सनरी ऑफ हिस्ट्री ऑफ आयडियाज, वाल्यूम–2, पृष्ठ– 464–66।
10. कालिंगवुड, आइडिया ऑफ हिस्ट्री, पृ0– 9–10
11. तत्रैव
12. जेम्स टी0 शाटवेल, दि हिस्ट्री ऑफ हिस्ट्री, वाल्यूम एक पृष्ठ– 163
13. ई0 श्रीधरन, इतिहास–लेख, ओरिएंट ब्लैकस्वान प्राइवेट लिमिटेड, 1/24 आसफ अली रोड, नई दिल्ली, 2011 पृष्ठ 7–9
14. तत्रैव, पृष्ठ– 167
15. ई0 श्रीधर, तत्रैव पृ0 5–6
16. तत्रैव
17. कौशिक, तत्रैव, पृ0 56–57
18. बिल डूरेण्ट, हिस्टोरी ऑफ सिविलाइजेशन भाग–दो : दि लाइफ ग्रीस, पृ0 430
19. उदय प्रकाश अरोरा, तत्रैव, हेरोडोटस।
20. कालिंगवुड, आइडिया ऑफ हिस्ट्री, पृ0 19
21. यू0पी0 अरोरा, तत्रैव, थयूसीडाइसिस
22. एच0ई0 बर्नेस, ए हिस्ट्री ऑफ हिस्टोरिकल राइटिंग, पृ0 31
23. कालिंगवुड, आइडिया ऑफ हिस्ट्री
24. ई0 श्रीधरन, तत्रैव, पृ0 16–17

59

भारतीय इतिहास की सनातन परम्परा

अजय कुमार पाण्डेय

दिक् एवं काल के आयामों में आबद्ध इतियों–प्रमुख घटनाओं का वैशिष्ट्य मापक कार्य–सम्मत स्वरूप ही ऐतिह्य है। सृष्टि के सर्जन–विसर्जन, जातियों के उत्थान–पतन, चुनौती–प्रत्युत्तर, व्यष्टि–समष्टि के वैभव–पराभव का कारणात्मक तथा परिणामात्मक विश्लेषण ज्ञान के विभिन्न विधाओं के माध्यम से किया जाता है। परन्तु काल के नाभिक–बिंदु विविध व्यासों से निर्मित वृत्तों की इतियों (गति–विधियों–प्रघटनाओं) का अर्थ–अवधारणा–परिभाषा में सत्ता प्रज्ञापक ही इतिहास है।[1]

भारतीय इतिहास का अध्ययन करने वालों के लिए यह विशेष ध्यातव्य है कि आयातित ''हिस्ट्री'' शब्द की अपेक्षा भारतीय वाड्.मय में प्रयुक्त ''इतिहास'' शब्द के धात्वर्थ–मूलार्थ का अभिज्ञान सर्वप्रथम प्राप्त किया जाय। क्योंकि अंग्रेजी भाषा के शब्दों की व्युत्पत्ति नहीं है। संस्कृत–व्याकरण–दर्शन की ऐतिह्य–परम्परा, शाब्दी (नाम) पदार्थी (रूप) को भी व्याकृत करने में समर्थ है।

भारतीय इतिहास की सनातन परम्परा वैदिक काल से प्रारम्भ होकर अद्यावधि प्रचलित है, जिसका संक्षिप्त परिचय अनुवर्ती पंक्तियों में प्रस्तुत है–

पुराण शरीर है और इतिहास उसकी 'आत्मा' है। इस पुराण–शरीर के बिना इतिहास का क्रम स्मरण नहीं रह सकता। पुराण, इतिहास की सूची है। अतः इतिहास की भारतीय परिभाषा में युगपत रीति से दोनों (इतिहास–पुराण) का भाव सम्मिश्रित है।[2]

अथर्वा ऋषि की संघीय–दृष्टि – वैदिक ऋषियों के तीन परिवारों अथर्वों, अंगिरसों तथा भृगुओं के सम्मिलित स्वरूप का विवरण ऋग्वेद में ही प्राप्त होता है। तीनों परिवार का संघीय–एकीकरण का विकास अथर्ववेद के 'व्रात' में विकसित हुआ। इतिहास की प्रथम तथा प्राचीनतम परिभाषा 'व्रात–संघ' ने प्रस्तुत की। ऋग्वेद में उल्लिखित 'शर्ध शर्ध ता एषां व्रातं गणगणं सुशास्तिभिः अनुक्रामेय धीतिभिः''।[3] सातवलेकर जी ने 'व्रात' का अर्थ संघ तथा 'गण, का अर्थ सैन्य–दल किया है।[4] यहाँ तीनों शब्दों (शर्ध, व्रात–गण) का प्रयोग शक्ति सम्पन्न संघ संगठन के अर्थ में किया गया है। ऋग्वेद में – ''सेनानीर्महतो गणस्य राजा व्रातस्य प्रथमो बभूव'' का उल्लेख किया गया है।[5] इस ऋचा पर सायण का भाष्य है कि– ''हे अक्षाः वः युष्माकं महतो गणस्य संघस्य यः अक्षः सेनानी नेता वभूव भवति व्रातस्य च''। गण व्रातयोः अल्प भेदः। सायण 'गण' और 'व्रात' में अल्प भेद स्वीकारते हैं। इस ऋचा से ऐसा प्रतीत होता है कि संघ एक वृहत्तर संगठन था और गण उसका एक प्रकार का सैनिक संगठन था, जिसके प्रमुख को सेनानी अथवा सेनापति कहा जाता था। सातवलेकर जी का भाष्य है कि ''हे अक्षो। वः महतः गणस्य यः सेनानी'' तुम्हारे वृहद–संघ का जो प्रमुख नायक है और (व्रातस्य–प्रथमः राजा वभूव) जो सर्वश्रेष्ठ राजा है, (तस्मै अहुं दशा प्राचीः कृणोभिः) मैं उसको अपनी दोनों अँगुलियाँ जोड़कर नमस्कार करता हूँ।[6]

ऋग्वेद की एक ऋचा में तिरपन व्रातों के विहार की चर्चा की गयी है– ''एषां त्रिपंचाशः व्रातः'' इन तिरपन का संघ ''सत्य–धर्मा सविता देव=इव=सत्य धर्मा सविता (सूर्य) के समान क्रीडति=विहार करता है।[7] सायण ने इस

ऋचा में प्रयुक्त 'व्रात' शब्द का अर्थ संघ किया है।[8] इन व्रातों के विहार की तुलना सत्य स्वरूप सविता (सूर्य) के जगत में विचरण से की गयी है। इसमें आगे यह भी कहा गया है कि व्रात–संघ उग्र से उग्र व्यक्तियों के सम्मुख भी नतमस्तक नहीं होता अर्थात उनके वश में नहीं आता। राजा तक इस संघ को नमस्कार करते है।[9] ऋग्वेद में 'कौशिक–व्रात' और 'गण' का उल्लेख किया गया है।[10] ध्यातव्य है कि ऋग्वेद में अंगिरस–व्रात का– ''पुनर्नः पतिरौमनो ददातु दैत्यों जनः'' जीवं व्रातं सचेमहि'' का उल्लेख किया गया है।[11] इस ऋचा पर सायण का भाण्य है कि

''न अस्माकं पितरः पितृभया अंगिरसः जनः तेषां संघ इत्यर्थः।

सच जीवं प्राणादिन्द्रिय संघातं पुनः ददातु। तथा दैत्योजनः। जन शब्द संघ वचनः देवाना संघोऽपि जीवं व्रातं च ददातु वयं च तदुभयं सचेमहि प्राप्नुयाव''।

ऋग्वेद की ऋचाओं और उनके भाष्य में 'व्रातं, का क्रमशः 'कौशिक' तथा 'आंगिरस' से सम्बद्ध होना, संभवतः इसका पराक्रमी लोगों का एक संघ होना प्रमाणित करता है। क्योंकि कौशिक तथा आंगिरस व्रात–गण सैन्य कार्यो से सम्बद्ध है। ऋग्वेद में 'सबन्धवः पंच व्राता' का उल्लेख बन्धु–भाव से रहने वाले 'पंच व्रात=पचं जन (संघ) का द्योतक है।[13] अतः यह निष्कर्षित है कि व्रात=संघ ने विश्व के सम्मुख इतिहास की प्रथम परिभाषा प्रस्तुत किया कि–

1. अथर्ववेद

''स वृहती–दिशमनु त्यऽचलत। तम इतिहासश्च पुराणं च गाशांश्च नाराशंसीश्च अनुल्यऽचलन।।

इतिहासस्य च वै स पुराणस्य च गाथानां च नाराशंसीना च–प्रियं धाम भवति, य एवं वेद''।[14]

अर्थात् व्रातों का संघ (स) संगठित होकर महान् (वृहती) लक्ष्य (दिशा) की ओर चला, उस व्रती संघ (तम) के अनुकूल इतिहास, पुराण, गाथा, और नाराशंसी चले, जो यह जानता है, (य एवं वेद), वह इतिहास, पुराण गाथा, और नाराशंसी में प्रतिष्ठित स्थान प्राप्त कर लेता है। (प्रिय धाम भवति)।

व्याख्याः– अथर्वा–आंगिरस ऋषि की यह दृष्टि है कि जिस समाज–राष्ट्र के व्रती, संघ रूप में किसी महान् लक्ष्य प्राप्ति हेतु अग्रसर होते हैं उनके कृतित्व–कीर्ति का कीर्तन इतिहास, पुराण, गांथा नाराशंसी करते है और, जो अपने राष्ट्रीय इतिहास को जानता है वह संघीय–समाज में प्रतिष्ठित होता है।

2. शतपथ ब्राह्मण के प्रणेता याज्ञवल्क्य का मत है कि विभिन्न विधाओं में 'इतिहास' एक विधा है, जिसका अध्ययन–अध्यापन किया जाता था–

(क) ''पदनुशासनानि विधावा को वाक्यम्
इतिहास पुराणं गाथा नाराशंस्यः–
य एवं विद्वान् अनुशासनानि विधवो का
वाक्यम् इतिहास पुराणं गाथा नाराशंसीरित्यहरहः स्वाध्याय–धीते''[15]

(ख) ''य एवं विद्वान् वाको वाक्यम इतिहास–पुराण इति अहरहः स्वाध्यायम धीते''।[16]

जो विद्वान ऐसा जानता है, वह नित्य (अह्वारह) इतिहास आदि विधा का स्वाध्यायम अधीते–अध्ययन करता है। यहाँ यह तथ्य विशेष ध्यातत्य है कि विभिन्न विधाओं में इतिहास एक विधा है, जिसका अध्ययन प्राचीन काल में किया जाता था। इस प्रकार की परिभाषा किसी भी पाश्चात्य विद्वान ने नहीं दिया है कि इतिहास आदि सभी विधाएँ मधु=मधुर–आहुतियों के रूप में देवताओं, पितरों तथा विद्वानों को समर्पित की जाती थी। शतपथ ब्राह्मण का कथन है कि ''विद्वांसो हि देवाः।[17]

शब्द का अर्थ उद्यमी–अध्यवसायी विद्वत्जन का पूर्ण सत्कार करना अर्थात् इतिहास एक विशिष्ट विद्या है, जो विद्वानों को मधुर आहुतियों से तृप्त करता है।

3. इतिहास ज्ञान (वेद) की एक शाखा है

पंच वेदान निरभिमीत .... इतिहास वेद पुराण वेदं''[18]

इतिहास वेद (ज्ञान) के विषय में कहा गया है कि–

'उदीच्या इतिहास वेद'[19] अर्थात उत्तर दिशा से इतिहास वेद का निर्माण हुआ इतिहास से 'महत' (ज्ञान) की उत्पत्ति हुई।

''(महदितीतिहास वेदांत)''

ध्यातत्य है कि इस देश में ज्ञान का इतना मान रहा है कि यहाँ की प्रथम पुस्तक का नाम ही 'वेद' अर्थात् ज्ञान रख दिया गया। यह ज्ञान–वेद ही भारतीयों का चरम–उपास्य है।

''एवम इमें सर्वे वेदा निर्मिताः सकल्प सरहस्याः सब्राह्मणाः सउपनिषत्का स इतिहासाः सान्वारूयाः सपुराणा'':[20]

अर्थात् इतिहास ज्ञान (वेद) की वह शाखा है जिसके निर्माण की प्रक्रिया कल्प, ब्राह्मण, उपनिषद, अनुख्यान तथा पुराण के रहस्य से समन्वित–समिश्रित है।

4. चरक ब्राह्मण – सायण ने अपने ऋग्वेद भाष्य 18 में लिखा है कि–

''ऐतिहासिक पक्षे चरक ब्राह्मणो इतिहास आम्नायते''[21]

अर्थात् ऐतिहासिक दृष्टि से चरक ब्राह्मण, इतिहास को परम्परा प्राप्त राष्ट्रीय प्रचलन कहते हैं। यह परम्परा सागोपांग वेद, ब्राह्मण, उपनिषद तथा आरण्यक द्वारा समर्थित राष्ट्रीय में है। निघण्टु के टीकाकार देवराज यज्वा चरक ब्राह्मण का एक प्रमाण उद्धृत करते है–''
तथा च चरकाध्वचूणां ब्राह्मणो इतिहासः श्रूयते''[22]

अर्थात इतिहास वैदिक ऋत्विजों द्वारा कथित श्रुति–परम्परा है, जिसका वर्णन ब्राह्मण ग्रंथों में किया गया है। यह प्रमाण काण्व संहिता (36/7) में भी प्राप्त होता है। दुर्ग अपनी निरूक्त टीका में ''चरकाध्वर्यवः .... गृहणान्ति। तथा ''चारके पुनराध्वर्यवे श्रुति''[23] लिखकर मैत्रायणी संहिता[24] तथा[25] को क्रमशः उद्धृत करते हैं। स्कन्द स्वामी भी अपने भाष्य में इस तथ्य को स्वीकारते हैं कि चरक–ब्राह्मण नामक एक यजुर्वेदीय ब्राह्मण ग्रन्थ में इतिहास की आम्चाय परम्परा समर्थक परिमाण प्राप्त हैं।[26]

5. शाट्यायन–ब्राह्मण – यद्यपि यह ब्राह्मण ग्रन्थ अनुपलब्ध है, तथापि इसके उद्धरण विभिन्न ग्रन्थों में प्राप्त होते हैं। प्रसिद्ध विद्वान 'अर्तल' ने इस ब्राह्मण ग्रन्थ के सम्बन्ध में एक महत्वपूर्ण लेख लिखा है। सायण एक शाटायायन ब्राह्मण के पाठ का उद्धरण देते हैं – ''अत्र शाट्यायनि इतिहासम् आचक्षेत[27] .... अर्थात् शाटायायन की दृष्टि ऐतिहासिक है। उन्होंने ऋग्वैदिक घटनाओं को मानवी–क्रिया कलापों को दैवी घटना न मानकर ऐतिहासिक घटना माना है। अर्थात् सम्पूर्ण वैशिष्ट ज्ञापक मानवी–घटनाएँ इतिहास है तथा पुराण के रहस्य से समन्वित=समिश्रित हैं।

6. तित्तिरमुनि – तित्तिर मुनि का कथन है– ''यद् ब्राह्मणानि इतिहासान् पुराणानि कल्पना गाथा– नाराशंसर्मेदाहुतयो देवानामभवन्''[28] तैत्तिरीय आरण्यक के प्रणेता तित्तिरमुनि का कथन है कि इतिहास, वेद के समान ही देवताओं के प्रिय आहूति सम है।

7. बृहदारण्यक उपनिषद का कथन है कि – इतिहास, स्रष्टा (परमेश्वर) का श्वास है।
''अरेऽस्य महतोभूतस्य निःश्वासितमेद् यद्रग्वेदो यजुर्वेदः सामवेदोऽथर्वागिरस' इतिहास पुराणम्''[29]
अर्थात् महाभूतात्मक स्रष्टा के श्वास से इतिहास–पुराण–वेदों की सत्ता है।

इस परिभाषा में इतिहास को सजीव भौतिक सत्ता रूपके में उद्घाटित किया गया है।

8. छान्दोग्य उपनिषद में उल्लेख है कि – ''इतिहास वेदानां वेदं हैः–

विद्–धातु से व्युत्पन्न– 'विद्यन्ते ज्ञायन्ते लभ्यन्ते वा एभिः धमीदि पुरूषार्था इति वेदाः''[30] अर्थात् जिससे धर्मादि पुरूषार्थो की सत्ता का परिचय मिलता है उनकी उपलब्धि होती है, ज्ञान प्राप्त होता है, उसे वेद कहते है।

सायणाचार्य ने ऋगादिभाष्यों में लिखा है–

''प्रत्यक्षानुमान आगमेषु प्रमाणेषु अन्तिमों वेदः'' अर्थात् प्रत्यक्ष अनुमान और आगम प्रमाणों में वेद अन्तिम प्रमाण है। मनु का वचन है– ''सर्वज्ञानमयोहिसः'' अर्थात् वेद सभी प्रकार के ज्ञान से परिपूर्ण है।[31]
''इतिहास पुराणा पंचम वेदानां वेद्म''

छान्दोग्य उपनिषद[32] अर्थात् पांचवा वेद इतिहास ज्ञान का भण्डार है। ऐतिहासिक घटना यह है कि एक बार नारदमुनि पढ़ने के लिए सनत्कुमार के पास गए। सनत्कुमार ने पूछा कि अब तक तुमने क्या–क्या पढ़ा है। नारद ने कहा

(क) ''ऋग्वेदं भगवो अध्येभि यजुर्वेदं
समवेदं आथर्वणं चतुर्थम–

इतिहास पुराणं पंचम वेदानां वेदम'' अर्थात चारों वेदों के वेद इतिहास– पुराण का अध्ययन मैंने किया है, जो ज्ञान का ज्ञान है। इसी प्रकार का उल्लेख छान्दोग्यों उपनिषद में अन्यत्र भी किया गया है।[33]

(ख) ''वाग्या ऋग्वेदं विज्ञायति यजुर्वेद–
सामवेदम आथर्वणं चतुर्थम
इतिहास पुराणं पंचम वेदानां वेदम्।

(ग) ''इतिहास पुराणं पुष्प''=

इतिहास पुराण समाज में मधुरता के उत्पादक है। अथर्वा आंगिरसा ऋषियों ने पुष्प रूपी इतिहास से मधु का संकलन कर समाज–राष्ट्र के लिए किया।''

अथर्वागिरस एवं मधु कृतः इतिहासपुराणं पुष्प .... ते वा एते
अथर्वागिरस एतद्–इतिहास
पुराणामश्यतपन,''।[34]

9. आश्वलायन गृहय सूत्र के अनुसार – इतिहास स्वाध्याय का विषय है

क– ''अथ स्वाध्यायमधीयीत .... इतिहास
पुराणानीति[35]

ख– ''इतिहास पयस–धृत–मधु की अमृत
मयी आहुतियाँ है''

यद्चोडधीते पय

आहुतिभिख ....

धृताहुतिभिर्यत्सामानिमध्वाहुतिर्यदथर्वागिरसः सोम आहुतिभिः यद् ब्राह्मणामि कल्पानगाथा नाराशीं इतिहास पुराणनि इति अमृत आहुतिभिः''।[36]

ग– इतिहास देव, पितरों के लिए दूध–घृत मधु आदि की नहरें हैं।

''यद्चो अधीते पयसः कुल्ता–धृतस्य कुल्या मध्वः कुल्याः सोमस्य कुल्या यद् ब्राह्मणनि .... इतिहास पुराणानि इति अमृतस्य कुल्याः''

घ– इतिहास मंगल दीप हैः–

''तं दीपयमाना आसत आ शान्त रात्रात आयुष्मतां कथा कीर्तयन्तो मांगल्यानि इतिहास पुराणानि इति आख्यायप्यमानाः'' आर्थात् आयुष्मान मनुष्यों के कृतियों का मंगलदीप्यमान कीर्तन इतिहास है।

10. वाल्मीकि–इतिहास पुरावृत्त है –

''श्रूयतां यत पुरावृत्त पुराणेषु मया श्रुतम'' (बाल काण्ड)[37]

पुरावृत्त का पर्यायी शब्द इतिहासः पुरावृत्त कथा (बा0का0)[38] व्यास (महाभारत अनुशासनपर्व[39] शौनक (वृहद्देवता)[40] शुक्राचार्य (शुक्रं नीति–शास्त्र,)[41] अमरकोश[42] तथा विष्णु पुराण की श्रीधर स्वामी कृत टीका[43] आदि में इतिहास तथा पुरावृत्त को समान पद माना गया है– अर्थात् प्राचीन इतिहास की पुरावृत्त है, जिसमें प्राचीन ऋषियों–राजाओं के उत्तम उपलब्धियों का वर्णन किया गया है।

11. वेद–व्यास– ''भारतस्य इतिहासस्य
पुण्या ग्रन्थार्थ संचुताम''[44]

भारत का इतिहास पुण्प से युक्त ग्रन्थ रूप में है।

'जय ही इतिहास है।

क– विश्व गुरू व्यास ने इतिहास को परिभाषित करते हुए लिखा है–

'' जय नाम इतिहासो अयं श्रोतत्यों विजिगीषुणां''[45] अर्थात हे विजयाकांशी लोगों इस जय नामक इतिहास (महाभारत) को सुनो, इसके श्रवण–अध्ययन से ''मही विजयते राजा शत्रुंश्चापि पराजयते''[46]

ख– जय का मूल जि/जी+अच=

'अभिभवे 18 का ही रूपान्तर प्राकृत भाषा में जिण = जिन में हुआ है।'' हम अनुदिन 'जयन्ती का आयोजन करते हैं, जयकार, जय घोष में भारत माता की जय, गाँधी जी की जय, गंगा मइया की जय, जय श्री राम, जय राम, जय माता दी आदि तथा लोक अभिधान में व्यक्ति नाम जय, विजय, अजय आदि तथा जयपुर विजय नगर आदि के साथ ही राम जी, माता जी, पिता जी, दुर्गा जी, गणेश जी आदि का विविध प्रयोग भारतीय इतिहास–संस्कृति के प्रभामण्डित ललाट का विम्ब जी/जय है। भारत गण राज्य का प्रतीक शब्द ही 'सत्यमेव जयते' में प्रद्योतित है।'

ग–

इतिहास की निरूतरता है

वेद–व्यास ने लिखा है कि–

'आचरत्युः कवयः केचित सम्प्रत्याचयक्षते
परे आख्यास्यन्ति तक्षैव अन्ये इतिहास इयं भुवि''[47]
''इतिहास पुराणानाम उन्मेष निर्मितं च यत।
भूत भव्यं भभिष्यं च त्रिविधं काल संज्ञितम।।''[48]

अर्थात इतिहास पुराण का उन्मेषक काल सनातन है। इतिहास की सत्ता सनातन–त्रिकालिक है।

घ– इतिहास लोक प्रतिष्ठित महाज्ञान है–

''इदं तु त्रिषु लोकेषु महत् ज्ञानं प्रतिष्ठितं।
विस्तरेः च सामासैः च धार्यते यद् द्विजातिभिः।[49]

अर्थात महत ज्ञान देने वाला यह (इतिहास) त्रिलोक में प्रशंसित (प्रतिष्ठाप्राप्तं)।– विद्वान (द्विजः) लोग इसकी व्याख्या विस्तृत तथा संक्षिप्त रूप में करते है।

ङ– महाभारत सर्व–विषय समाहित लक्षणों से युक्त इतिहास ग्रन्थ है–

''इतिहासः सर्वेयाढ़या विविधाः श्रुतोऽपि च''।
इह सर्वम् अनुक्रान्तं युक्त ग्रन्यस्य लक्षणम्।।[50]

इतिहास ग्रन्थ के लक्षणों से युक्त, इसमें सभी अनुषांगिक विषय समाहित है।

जयात्मक इतिहास मोक्ष प्रदाता हैः–

''जय नाम इतिहासो अयं श्रोतत्यो मोक्षभिच्छता''[51]

12. आचार्य शौनक – ऋषियों द्वारा कीर्तित पुरावृत इतिहास भारत युद्ध के पश्चात शौनक ने इतिहास की महत्वपूर्ण परिभाषा अति संक्षिप्त रूप में लिखा है–

''इतिहास : पुरावृत्तं ऋषिभि : परिकीर्त्यते''[52]

अर्थात ऋषियों द्वारा किसी कृति 'कृतित्व का कीर्तन यशगान : प्रसिद्धि वर्णन प्रामाणिक है। क्योंकि ऋषि प्रत्यक्ष 'द्रष्टार : तथा प्रवक्तार : है। आज भी प्रवक्ता प्राचीन पुरावृत्त का विद्यालयों में कीर्तन करता है।

13. निरूक्ताचार्य यास्क – इतिहासम् आचक्षेत'

वेदों के अर्धज्ञान के लिए निरूक्त की प्राचीन
ऐतिहासिक परम्परा केवल भारत में प्रचलित रही।
इसीलिए निरूक्त को वेदांग कहा गया है।
'छनद : पार्दो तु वेदस्य हस्तौ कल्पोऽय पठ्यते
ज्योतिषामयनं चक्षुः निरूकतं श्रोत्रमुच्यते।।
शिक्षा घ्राणंतु वेदस्य मुखं व्याकरणं स्मृतम्।
तस्यान संगमधीत्यैव ब्राह्मलोके महीयते।।''[53]

अर्थात छन्दशास्त्र वेदो के पैरों के समान है निरूक्त कान के समान है, ज्योतिष वेदो की आखें है। व्याकरण मुख के समान है, शिक्षा–शास्त्र वेद की नासिका है और कल्प शास्त्र वेद के हाथ है। इन सभी अंगो सहित वेदो को पढ़ने वाले वेदज्ञों की ब्रह्मलोक में प्रतिष्ठा प्राप्त होती है। वैदिक मंत्रों के अर्थ निर्वचन में नैदानाः वैयाकरणाः याजिकाः की तरह ऐतिहासिका : परम्परा प्रचलित थी–

''तत्को वृत्र इतिह नैरूकताः, त्वाष्ट्रोऽसुर इति ऐतिहासकि[54]

अर्थात वृत्र कौन है, मेघ है ऐसा नैरूक्तो का मत है। त्वाष्ट्र असुर है ऐसा ऐतिहासिको का मन्तव्य है इसी प्रकार यास्क में अन्यत्र भी लिखा है।

''अनहाद द्वा भिधुना सरष्यू महयमं च महायमिकां च वाचम्–इतिमेरूकता :, यमं च यमी च इति ऐतिहासिका[55]

अर्थात 'अजहाद द्वा भिधुना'' में मध्यम देव और माध्यमिका वाक् है, ऐसा नैरूक्तो का मत है। यम और यमी है ऐसा ऐतिहासिको का मत है। यास्क के अनुसार वैदिक मंत्रों का अर्थ करने वाले ऐतिहासिक सम्प्रदाय का अस्तित्व वैदिक काल में ही उत्पन्न हो गया था, जिसका विकास आधि दैविक आध्यात्मिक, आधिभौतिक रूप में हुआ। आधुनिक काल में वैज्ञानिक अर्थ भी प्रस्तुत किया जा रहा है। यास्क ने इतिहास की अपनी परिभाषा में लिखा है –

''इतिहासम् आचक्षेत, इति आख्यानम्।''

अर्थात दृष्ट घटना का कथन ही इतिहास है, जिसे वेदो में आख्यान कहा गया है। क्योकि यास्क ने आख्यान–विदो को 'ऐतिहासिक' कहा है।[56] इतिहास का पर्यायी पद आख्यान को विद्वानों ने माना है।

14. पाणिनि – विश्व के व्याकरणचायों में पाणिनि अप्रतिम एवं अद्वितीय विद्वान थे उनके अष्ठाध्यायी नामक व्याकरण दर्शन का ऐतिहासिक–सांस्कृतिक अध्ययन प्रो0 वासुदेव शरण अग्रवाल ने सूत्रों को आधार बनाकर किया है। भागवत ने लिखा है कि भारतीय वांङमय में इतिहास शब्द से मिलता जुलता दूसरा शब्द ऐतिह्य है। उन्होंने इतिह शब्द से मानकर त्यज प्रत्यय से ऐतिह्य शब्द की सिद्धि किया है– ''पराभ्पर्योपदेश : स्याद ऐतिह्यम् इति अत्थयम्। अर्थात् परम्परा : उपदेश, शिक्षा–निर्देश ही इतिहास है परम्परा का अर्थ है उत्तरवर्ती का उत्तरवर्ती; आगे के आगे या श्रेष्ठ से श्रेष्ठ।

इसलिए परम्परा में पूर्ववर्ती का समावेश तो है, पर उससे आगे जाने की बाते भी है, पूर्ववर्ती का सातत्य है, आधिपत्य नही। परम्परा में अंशत: स्वीकार और अंशतः परिहार संस्कार दोनों है। परम्परागत उपदेश एक ऐतिहासिक आदेश है।

15. आचार्य कौटिल्य – भारतीय इतिहास के विराट–विक्रान्त महाआचार्य विष्णुगुप्त चाणक्य ने इतिहास की परिभाषा का विस्तार किया है–

''पुराणं इतिवृत्तम् आख्यायिका उदाहरणं।
धर्मशास्त्रम् अर्थशास्त्रम् च इति इतिहासः।''

अर्थात् पुराण : इतिवृत्त आख्यायिका उदाहरण, धर्मशास्त्र तथा अर्थशास्त्र आदि विद्याए इतिहास में समाविष्ट है। कौटिल्य के इस परिभाषा में विशेष ध्यातव्य शब्द 'उदाहरण है। महाभारत शांतिपर्व में बहुधा लिखा गया है कि ''अत्रापि उदाहरन्ति इमम् इतिहासं पुरातनम्'' अर्थात कौटिल्य के पूर्व वेदव्यास ने भी पुरातन इतिहास को प्रमाणित रूप से प्रस्तुत करने के लिए प्राचीन उदाहरणों को इतिहास का एक महत्वपूर्ण अवयव माना है। इतिहास में अथवा लोक जीवन में प्रघटित प्रचलित घटनाओं, कथन लेखन को प्रमाणित करती है। प्रत्यक्ष घटित घटनाओं का आकलन अनुमान प्रमाण पर वर्तमान में किया जाता है। न्याय शास्त्र के प्रमाणीकरण में अनुमान के पंचावयवी प्रतिज्ञा हेतु उदाहरण उपनय तथा निगमन की परम्परा प्रचलित है। रूप और शब्द के ज्ञान में– हेतु में साध्य की और साध्याभाव में हेत्वाभाव की व्याप्ति का उदाहरण (दृष्टान्त) द्वारा बोध कराने वाला वाक्य उदाहरण कहा जाता है। जैसेः– यह पर्वत धूमवान होने से वहिमान है। इस प्रकार प्रतिज्ञा और हेतु के प्रयोग के बाद जो–जो धूम युक्त है वह अग्रियुक्त है जैसे महानस (भोजन पकाने वाला घर) गौतम मुनि ने उदाहरण के लक्षणों में दृष्टांत का समावेश और पृथक–पृथक निर्देश भी किया है। वात्स्यायन ने इस वैषम्य का समाधान करते हुए कहा है कि दृष्टान्त ही न्याय वाक्य में प्रयुक्त होने पर उदाहरण कहा जाता है।

''उदाह्यते अनेन धर्मयो : साहय साधनभाव इति उदाहरणाम् अवयवेषु च उदाहरणाय कल्पत इति

भासर्वज्ञ के अनुसार भी दृष्टान्त का सम्यक अभिधान उदाहरण है। गंगेश ने अनुभिति के कारणी भूतलिंग (परम्परागत प्रतीक) परामर्श से उत्पन्न होने वाले तत्यात्मक; शब्द बोधात्मक ज्ञान के जनक व्याप्यत्व रूप से स्वीकृत धूम आदि से निष्ठ नियतत्व अभिमत सम्बन्ध (व्याप्ति सम्बन्ध) के बोध के जनक वाक्य रूप की उदाहरण कहा है।

''तंत्र अनुमति हेतु लिंग परामर्श वाक्य जज्य ज्ञज्ञन जनक व्याप्तात्व अभियतवत निष्ट नियतत्व अभिमत सम्बन्ध बोध जनक शुद्धत्वम उदाहरणत्वम् यथार्थ में व्यतीत तथ्यों के अभिमान तथा उद्घाटन का तथ्य परक ज्ञानार्थ अनुमान प्रत्यक्ष के आधार पर प्रचलित परम्परागत प्रतीकों की व्याख्या उदाहरण रूप में प्रस्तुत कर प्रघटना को प्रमाणित किया जाता है। आधुनिक काल का कोई भी वक्ता, प्रवक्ता लेखक बिना उदाहरण के अपने लेखन कथन को प्रमाणिक नहीं कर सकता है। अतः उदाहरण स्वयं एक ऐतिहासिक सत्य है। क्योंकि उसकी व्याप्ति सर्व स्वीकृति होती है।

16. मनुस्मृति इतिहास स्वाध्याय 'श्रवण का विषय है:– ग्रन्थ 'मनुस्मृति में कहा गया है–

'स्वाध्यायं श्रावयेत् पित्रेय धर्मशास्त्राणि चैव हि।
आख्यातानि इतिहासंश्च पुराणानि जिलानि च।।

अर्थात पूर्व पुरूषों के श्राद्ध में धर्मशास्त्र, आख्यान इतिहास पुराण तथा वैदिक खिल का स्वाध्याय श्रवण किया जाता है।

17. याज्ञवल्क्य स्मृति– आध्यात्मिक ज्ञान की विद्या इतिहास है।

वैदिक ऋषि याज्ञवल्क्य की स्मृति में लिखा गया इस स्मृति का कथन है कि–

वेद अधर्व पुराणानि सइतिहासानि शक्तितः।
जययज्ञ सिद्धयर्ध' विद्या च अध्यात्यिकी जयेतं।''[57]

अर्थात वेद, अधर्व, पुराण इतिहास द्वारा जय यज्ञ की सिद्धि के लिए तथा अध्यात्म विद्या के लिए यथा शक्ति जाप करे।

18. पातंजल, इतिहास शाब्दी प्रयोग का प्रमुख विषय है। शाब्दी परम्परा के भाष्यकार पातंजलि अपने युग के महान पुरोहित ने लिखा है कि–

''याको वाक्यम् इतिहास : पुराणं वैद्यकम् इति एतावत् शवस्य प्रयोग विषय :।

अर्थात वाकोवाक्य, इतिहास, पुराण और वैद्यक आदि प्रयोगाभ्यास विषय है। इन विषयों का शाब्दी प्रयोग से हस्तान्तरण प्राचीन काल से होता चला आ रहा है।

19. आचार्य शुक्रः– राजकृत्यो का पुरावृत्त ही इतिहास है। भारतीय लोक जीवन को प्रभावित करने वाली राजनीतिज्ञ शक्तियों के कृत्यों को आधुनिक काल में राजनीतिक इतिहास कहा जाता है। शुक्राचार्य ने अपनी परिभाषा में लिखा है–

''प्राग्वृत्त कथनं चैक राजकृत्यभिवादितः।

यास्मिन् स इतिहासः स्यात् पुरावृत्त। स एवं हिः।

20. आचार्य चरकः– इतिहास आप्तोदेश है।

चरक संहिता के विमान स्थान में लिखा है कि–

''ऐतिह्यम नाम आप्तोदेशो वेदादि''[58]

अर्थात चरक मुनि के अनुसार ऐतिह्य इतिहास एक हेतु है और उसके द्वारा वेदादि शास्त्र का ज्ञान लिखा जा सकता है। आचार्य चरक के इस परिभाषा में 'आप्त' तथा आप्तादेश' विशेष अवधेय शब्द है। 'आप्त का अर्थ व्याप्त है जो शब्द, वचन, कथन अधिक लोगो द्वारा स्वीकृत मान्य होता है वह आप्त वचन होता है। अतः शब्द प्रमाण की दृष्टि से 'आप्त शब्द' इतिहास में प्रमाणिक वचनोपदेश है। आप्त का विकृत रूप अंग्रेजी उच्चारण में आप्टे हो गया। त का अंग्रेजी भेट होता है। अथार्थ उपदेश करने वाले व्यक्ति (आप्त/के द्वारा प्रयुक्त होने पर ऐसे ही शब्द वाक्य (उपदेश) इतिहास में प्रमाण कहे जाते है।

''आप्तवाक्यंशब्द : आप्त : तु यथाभूत : अर्थस्य उपदेष्टा पुरूष :''

भगवान बुद्ध के उपदेश को प्रमाणिक माना जाता है क्योंकि वे आप्त पुरूष थे। जैन आचार्य सिद्धसेन दिवाकर, मणिक्यनन्दी, देवसूरि, प्रभाचन्द्र यशोविजय आदि ने शब्द प्रमाण के लक्षणों मे 'आप्त' शब्द को भी समाविष्ट किया है।

क– 'आप्त' वचनात जातम् अर्थज्ञानं आगमः

ख– आप्त वचनादि निबन्धनम् आगमः''

ग– आप्त वचनात आविर्भूत – अर्धज्ञान आगम :[59]

जैन आचार्य के अनुसार मोह, राग द्वेष आदि शंकाओं से रहित व्यक्ति ही 'आप्त' होता है।

क– ''यथा स्थित अर्थ परिज्ञान पूर्वक हितोपदेश प्रवण आप्तः''

ख– ''आप्त शंक रहित : शंकाहि सकल मोहराग द्वेषादउय :''

ग– ''आप्त प्रत्यत प्रयित संकल अर्धत्व सतिपरम हित उपदेशक :''

इसी प्रकार ईश्वर कृष्ण ने विश्वसनीय वचन को आप्तणक्य कहा है–

''आप्तश्रुति : आप्त वचनं तु।''

(साांध्यकारिका 5)

अर्थात जो व्यक्ति वस्तुनिष्ट (प्रघटनाओं) का साक्षात ग्रहण करके यथार्थ ज्ञान कराता है यह उस विषय में आप्त कहा जाता माना जाता है। ऋषियों, मुनियों, महापुरूषो के वचन आप्ता देश है।

इतिहास कथन लेखन ये उनके शब्द वाक्य अधिकृत विद्वानों द्वारा प्रयुक्त है। योग दर्शन के व्यासभाष्य में उल्लेख है कि अपने वोध का सम्प्रेषण करने के लिए तत्वज्ञानी अर्थात यथार्थ द्रष्टा 'आप्त पुरूषो' द्वारा शब्द के माध्यम से जो उपरदेश किया जाता है वह आगम प्रमाण है। गौतम के न्यायसूत्र पर भाष्य करने वाले वात्स्यायन का कथन है कि जो वस्तु जैसी है उसको वैसा ही बताने वाले पुरूष के उपदेश को आप्तोपदेश' कहा जाता है। वस्तुओं को साक्षात् ज्ञान है 'आप्ति और आप्ति (व्याप्ति) पद के अभाव में शब्द प्रमाण की परिभाषा ऐतिहय् पर भी अतिव्याप्ति हो जाती; क्योंकि उपदेश का तत्व तो ऐतिह्य ये भी है ही। वात्स्यायन द्वारा प्रयुक्त 'उपदेष्टो और चिरव्यापयिषा' शब्द साभिप्राय है। इससे यह ध्यातित होता है कि आप्त व्यक्ति का वीतराग (सम्बद्ध तथ्य के कथन में उसका कोई स्वार्थ न हो तथा उपदेश कुशल आवश्यक है। जयन्त के विचार में आप्तता की सम्बन्ध कुल की उच्चता से नहीं हैः–

ऋषि, आर्य, मलेच्छ सामान्य वक्तव्यं च आप्त लक्षणम'' केशव मिश्र तथा अन्नभट्ट जैसे उत्तरवर्ती नैयायिको ने 'आप्तवाक्य' को शाब्दी प्रमाण माना है–

''आप्त वाक्यं शब्द :''

(तर्क संग्रह पृ0 182)

आप्त वाक्यं शब्द :, आप्त तु यथाभूतस्य अर्थस्य उपदेष्टा

(तर्क भाषा, पृ0 122)

अतः इतिहास की परिभाषा में आप्तोदेश की मान्यता आज के युग में अधिक है। विवेकानन्द, गांधी, मार्क्स आदि आप्त पुरूषों के वचन, उसी प्रकार मान्य है, जैसे बाल्मीकि, व्यास, महावीर, बुद्ध आदि ऐतिहासिक पुरूषों के उपदेश को ऐतिहासिक प्रमाण माना जाता है।

21. आचार्य दुर्गः – निश्चित घटित–प्रघटना का कथन इतिहास है'

व्याकरण शास्त्र के विख्यात विद्वान दुर्गाचार्य अपने निरूक्तभाष्य वृत्ति में इतिहास शब्द पर लिखा है–

''इति हि एवय् आसीद् इति यः कथ्यते स इतिहास

अर्थात यह (प्रघटना) निश्चित : इस प्रकार प्रघटित हुआ था यह जो कहा जाता है वह इतिहास है। आचार्य दुर्ग की यह निरपेक्ष परिभाषा पूर्णतः आग्रहयुक्त है।

22. आचार्य अमरः – स्वर्णयुग के निर्माता गुप्त सम्राटों के काल में परम्परा से प्रचलित 'इतिहास पुरावृत्त है' का संकलन अमर सिंह ने नामलिंगानुशासन में लिखा है कि :–

क– ''इतिहास : पुरावृत्तम्''

इस परिभाषा का उपवृंहण 'ऐतिहयम्

पद से करते हुए अमर ने लिखा है–

ख– ''पारम्पर्योपदेश : स्याद ऐतिहयम् इति अत्ययम्''

अर्थात इतिह अत्यय है और ऐतिध्य (इतिहास) के साथ सम्पृक्त होने से परम्परागत महान पुरूषों के उपदेशों को इतिहास तथा पुरावृत्त कहा गया।

23. बाणभट्टः – इतिहास में अख्यान आख्यायिका समाहित है।

कादम्बरी में लिखा है

''कदाविद अख्यान – आख्यायिका – इतिहास – पुराण – आकर्णनेन ....।

इतिहास के सनातन परम्परा वाणभट्ट के पश्चात वात्सयायन के न्यायदर्शन, भट्टभाष्कर, हेमचंद, सागर नन्दी आदि के साथ ही भागवत पुराण, पदमपुराण तथा वायुपुराण के पश्चात भी यह परम्परा प्रचलित रही।

सन्दर्भ ग्रन्थ सूची

1. डॉ0 कुँवर बहादुर कौशिक, प्राचीन भारतीय इतिहास दर्शन पृष्ठ–1, विद्यार्थी पुस्तक भण्डार, गोरखपुर, 1972।
2. ऋग्वेद, स्कन्द स्वामी भाष्य, विश्वबंधु विश्वेश्वरानन्द वैदिक शोध संस्थान, होशियारपुर, 1965
3. ऋग्वेद, तत्रैव
4. ऋग्वेद, दामोदर पाद सातवलेकर, स्वाध्याय मंडल, 1958
5. ऋग्वेद, 10/34/12
6. ऋग्वेद, सातवलेकर, तत्रैव
7. ऋग्वेद, 10/34/8
8. ऋग्वेद, सायण भाष्य, शंकर पाडुरंग पंडित बम्बई 1995–98.
9. तत्रैव
10. ऋग्वेद, 3/26/6
11. ऋग्वेद, 10/57/5
12. ऋग्वेद, 10/26/6
13. ऋग्वेद, 9/14/2
14. अथर्ववेद, दामोदरपाद सातवलेकर, स्वाध्याय मण्डल, 1958
15. याज्ञवल्क्य– अपरार्क टीका, आनन्दाश्रम, पूना, 1903
16. शतपथ ब्राह्मण, 11/5/6/8 ए वेवर लिपजिंग, 1965,
17. शतपथ ब्राह्मण, 3/7/3/10
18. गोपथ ब्राह्मण, पूर्वभाग 1/10, राजेन्द्र चंद्र मिश्र तथा हरचंद विद्याभूषण, कलकत्ता, 1872
19. तत्रैव

20. तत्रैव
21. ऋग्वेद, 8/77/10, सायण भाष्य, वैदिक संसोधन मण्डल, पूना, 1941
22. चरक ब्राह्मण, यादव जी विक्रम जी आचार्य, निर्णय सागर, मुम्बई, 1935
23. निरूक्त टीका, राजाराम लाहौर भगवतदत्त, अमृतसर 2021
24. मैत्रेयणी संहिता– 1/3/11, F.O. श्रेडर, लिपजिम, 1923
25. मैत्रेयणी संहिता– 4/6/3, दामोदर सातवलेकर, स्वाध्याय मण्डल, पारडी, सूरत
26. तत्रैण
27. शाकट्टायन ब्राह्मण, शम्भुनाथ तिवारी, भारतीय॰ज्ञान पीठ प्रकाशन, 1971
28. तित्तरमुनी, तैतरीय आरण्यक, कृष्ण यजुर्वेदीय बाबा शास्त्री फडके, आनन्दाश्रम, पूना, 1872
29. वृहदारण्य उपनिषद– 2/4/11, लिमये तथा वाडेकर वैदिक शोध मण्डल, पूना 1958
30. छान्दोग्य उपनिषद– तत्रैव
31. मनु 2/7, मेघातिथि भाष्य, गंगानाथ झा कलकत्ता
32. छान्दोग्य उपनिषद, 7/1/2 तत्रैव, चन्द्रकान्त तकलिद्वार, कलकत्ता, 1909।
33. छान्दोग्य उपनिषद, 7/2/1
34. छान्दोग्य उपनिषद, 3/41/12
35. आश्वालायन गृहसूत्र, 3/3/1, वासुदेव शर्मा पड़शिकर निर्णय सागर बम्बई 1894
36. आश्वालायन गृहसूत्र, 3/3/2
37. वाल्मीकि रामायण, बालकाण्ड, 9/1 बड़ोदा संस्करण 1960, लाहौर संस्करण 1928–47 मैसूर संस्करण 1960।
38. बालकाण्ड 39/12
39. महाभारत, अनुशासन पर्व, 67/3 भण्डारकर ओरियण्टल रिसर्च इन्स्टीटीयूट, पूना, नीलकण्ठ भाष्य, पंचानन तर्करत्न भट्टाचार्य कलकत्ता 1904।
40. वृहद्देवता, 4/6 ए0.ए. मैकडानल, 1940 राजेन्द्र लाल मित्र, कलकत्ता।
41. शुक्रनीति, 4/31
42. अमर कोष, 1/6/4 हरदन्त शर्मा तथा सारदेसाई, पूना, 1941, आर0 राय शास्त्री, मैसूर, 1920
43. विष्णु पुराण 1/14, श्रीधर स्वामी टीका, प्रिय बाला शाह बड़ौदा, 1958
44. महाभारत, आदि. पर्व, 1/17/21
45. महाभारत, उद्योग पर्व, 136/18
46. महाभारत, 62/20
47. महाभारत आदि पर्व, 1/26
48. महाभारत, 1/63
49. महाभारत आदि पर्व, 1/27
50. महाभारत आदि पर्व, 1/50
51. महाभारत, 5/5
52. वृहद्देवता, 4/46
53. पाणिनी शिक्षा 41, 42 दयानन्द सरस्वती कृत धड़ीधर कृत, गोपाल शास्त्री नेने तथा सुदामा शर्मा मिश्र च0सं0सी0
54. निरूक्त, 26/16 कौशत्बय प्रणित दुर्गवृत्त, बी0के0 राजवाणे, पूना
55. निरूक्त, 2/10
56. यास्क, तत्रैव
57. याज्ञवल्क्य स्मृति, 1/101, तत्रैव
58. चरक संहिता, विमानस्थान, 8/4 तत्रैव
59. यशोविजय, 2 जैन तर्क भाषा पृ0–18, सिन्धी जैनगंध माला, 1938

60

ANCIENT INDIAN IDEALS AND MODERN REALITIES

K. Paddayya

Introduction

India is one among the four or five ancient regions of the Old World. In the areas covered by the Mesopotamian and Egyptian civilizations, there appears to be a disjunction between the past and the present in the sense that the present-day societies do not draw upon images from the past in conducting their day-to-day life. We further understand that the events and characters from Homer's classics the *Iliad* and the *Odyssey* are no longer freely invoked into the social space of modern Greek life.

But China and India present a different picture; here the past continues and lives into the present. This paper aims to explore certain dimensions of this connectedness or relationship between the past and the present with reference to India. Here the use of the past ranges from donning personal names after gods and goddesses taken from ancient texts and mythology to coming to grips with life-situations by invoking concepts from the past. V.S. Sukthankar (1957), for instance, pointed out long ago that the soul of India would be lost if one excluded the epic *Mahabharata* from the Indian way of life.

The Indian Mind

This unique relationship between the past and the present in India has been captured in a beautiful way by the celebrated art historian of South Asia, Ananda Coomaraswamy. In a remarkable essay entitled "What has India contributed to Human Welfare?", first published in *Athenaeum* (London) in 1915, he drew attention to the distinction between the value which people in the West attach to philosophy and the way an ordinary Indian employs it. In the West philosophy is essentially an academic/mental exercise, while philosophizing is an integral aspect of the Indian way of life. In Coomaraswamy's own words: "In Europe and America the study of philosophy is regarded as an end in itself, and as such it seems of but little importance to the ordinary man. In India, on the contrary, philosophy is not regarded primarily as a mental gymnastic, but rather, and with deep religious conviction, as our salvation (*moksha*) from the ignorance (*avidya*) which forever hides from our eyes the vision of reality. Philosophy is the key to the map of life, by which are set forth the meaning of life and the means of attaining its goal. It is no wonder, then, that the Indians have pursued the study of philosophy with enthusiasm, for these are matters that concern all" (Coomaraswamy 1985: 2-3). He further stated that all other elements of the Indian mind follow from this major attribute. In another illuminating paper entitled "On the Pertinence of Philosophy",

(Coomaraswamy 1989) defined philosophy as the love of wisdom rather than the love of knowledge and further remarked that wisdom is the criterion of value which governs decision-making in particular or general cases.

One of the common manifestations of this philosophizing attitude adopted by the ordinary man in India is the employment, in day-to-day situations, of an assortment of ideals or values embodying the essence of the past. These values or ideals are put in the form of various concepts, aphorisms, proverbs, similies and metaphors, and many do's and don'ts. These form the mortar of all kinds of transactions in life – social, economic, political, religious, etc. These concepts pervade the life transactions of the literate as well as the vast non-literate segments of the Indian population.

Elsewhere I cited some actual instances to illustrate the pervasive use of these ideals or concepts in ordinary man's life; the sources from which these are derived; and the methods adopted for this purpose (Paddayya 2011: 8-10). These are briefly repeated below:

1. "Protect *Dharma* and you will be protected by *Dharma*!" – *Bhagavadgita*'s exhortation inscribed in Telugu on a truck forming part of the public transport system.
2. *Laxmanrekha* – subtitle of a commercial product called Crazy Lines for keeping cockroaches away from cooked food items.
3. Observance of *Laxmanrekha* is as important in international affairs as in interpersonal life. – Former Prime Minister P.V. Narasimha Rao in his Address to the joint session of the U.S. Congress.
4. 'You are truly personification of Sita' – An elderly gentleman's statement at a wedding reception in Delhi after he unexpectly prostrated himself before Deepika Chikalia who had played the role of Sita in the T.V. serial *Ramayana*.
5. 'Modern women ought to remember the tribulations suffered by Sita by voluntarily proceeding to forest along with her consort Ram.' Statement forming part of a Judgement given by Bombay High Court (May 2012) while disposing of a divorce case filed by a government employee against his wife who had refused to join him at the place he was transferred to.
6. 'Please don't play the role of Narada *muni*!' – Congress Party spokesman Dr. Abhishek Singhvi's request to T.V. anchor Arnab Goswami who was trying to pit him against the B.J.P. spokesman on the show.
7. 'Mahabharat in the Ambani family!' Newspaper headlines when the business feud between Mukhesh Ambani and his brother Anil Ambani was at its zenith and taken to the Supreme Court.
8. 'Ram, Ram … Ram, Ram' – Mode of greeting each other common among the peasant folk of the Deccan.

One can easily multiply such instances; these are commonplace in various parts of the country. Where do the people derive these precepts from? The sources are many and varied:

a) The Vedic texts including the Upanishads.
b) The stories or anecdotes from the epics *Mahabharata* and *Ramayana*, which cover both original Sanskrit texts as well as the various regional versions which localize the events and places, thereby bringing the themes and ancient personalities closer to the hearts of people.
c) Do's and Don'ts laid down in the *Bhagavadgita*.
d) The Puranas and other religious as well as secular writings of the historical period.
e) The Buddhist and Jaina writings.
f) The devotional (Bhakti and Sufi) writings of the early and late medieval periods.
g) Episodes depicting the heroic deeds of famous personalities of the medieval period, e.g. Chhatrapati Shivaji, Maharana Pratap, Palnadu heroes of Andhra Pradesh, etc.

As concerns the methods adopted for securing information, people belonging to the literate segments have access to the written sources (primary or secondary) and have in some cases come up with their own excellent commentaries. More importantly, the messages drawn from these various religious and secular sources are reached even to the non-literate sections of population by a variety of folk techniques and methods of communication. The principal ones are noted below:

a) Tales and myths about the past and great personalities narrated at home to children by parents and elders; comics like *Amarchitra Katha* published by the late Anant Pai.
b) Late evening performances (dramas, *Yakshaganas*, plays, dance-dramas, *Harikeertans,* shadow-plays, *burra-kathas, powadas,* etc.) which enthral village audiences. To a great extent these folk media have now been supplanted by the T.V. and cinema.
c) Recitations from ancient texts on various religious and secular occasions like marriages, house-warming and festival-time temple ceremonies, including almanac-reading by the village priest on the New Year eve.
d) Long or short-distance pilgrimages to religious centres which, as pointed out by Radha Kumud Mukherjee (1954) and other scholars, reinforce the geographical and cultural unity of India.

Commenting on the impact that these oral and visual presentations of themes adopted from the past have on the minds of the people, Max Müller wrote long ago: "… We are told that the ancient epic poems of the Mahabharata and Ramayana are still recited in the temples for the benefit of visitors, and that in the villages large crowds assemble around *Kathaka*, the reader of these ancient Sanskrit poems, often interrupting his recitations with tears and sighs, when the hero of the poem is sent into banishment, while when he returns to his kingdom, the houses of the village are adorned with lamps and garlands …" (1883: 81). We might recall that Pandit Nehru (1960: 45) went to the extent of calling his recognition of this attribute of the folk mind (he designated it as Old Indian Tradition) a real discovery and lamented that he missed it in "our middle classes."

The values or ideals that lie embedded in the deep sense of the past have moulded the Indian character across ages. It is this component which has given strength and solidarity to the Indian society even in times of political and religious unrest. This is precisely the reason why stories from the epics and Puranas as well as the writings of medieval saints continue to exercise undiminished influence on the minds of Indian people.

Questions are often raised about the mythological or fictitious nature of many of the characters and episodes depicted in the ancient texts. These are valid queries and need to be attended to. But it is important to remember here that many writers from Kant to Nietzsche have commented on the fact that human societies exist not only on objective facts about the nature but also draw upon various kinds of "necessary postulates" (Kant) or "necessary illusions" (Nietzsche) or belief goods – or, in short, myths (for details, see Brezinka 1994: 33-80). Belief goods play a preeminent role in the Indian society.

Then sometimes doubts are raised about the extent to which the average Indian mind can capture the true meanings of the higher order concepts or values. We need to remind ourselves here that the Indian mind, even that of the non-literate person, has the innate ability to sift fact from fantasy. As one enters the threshold of adulthood and begins to experience the human deeds and happenings in nature in a direct way, even those who lack 'read and write' literacy start realizing that behind all the divinities they worship every day and the whole lot of rituals and rites they perform there are some underlying principles and concepts. I would like to illustrate this statement with reference to an insightful observation made by Max Müller more than a century ago. He remarks that the discovery of the *Brahman* or *Paramatman* no doubt requires observance of moral and intellectual disciplines but quickly reminds that even "… Those who had not yet discovered it, were allowed to worship lower gods, and to employ more poetical names to satisfy their human wants. Those who know the other gods to be but names or persons – personae or masks, in the true sense of the word – *pratikas,* as they call them in Sanskrit – knew also that those who worshipped these names or persons, worshipped in truth the Highest Self, though ignorantly …" (Max Müller 1883:251-2).

One can put the same matter in different words and say that an ordinary Indian is a Vedantin to a smaller or greater extent. From this background follow certain important and positive attributes of the Indian mind. As early as 1888 Seymour Keay, a British Member of Parliament, paid a rich compliment to the Indians when he said that "…Perhaps there are no other people in the world who show so much in their characters the *advantageous effects of their own civilization* (emphasis added). They are shrewd in their business, acute in reasoning, thrifty, religious, sober, charitable, obedient to parents, reverential to old age, amiable, law-abiding, compassionate towards the helpless and patient under suffering" (as quoted in M.K. Gandhi 2006: 92).

So far we have considered three important aspects of the Indian psyche: a) that it is imbued with a deep sense of the past, with much of it taking the form of myths and fables; b) that this consciousness of the past has endowed the people with an assortment of values and ideals as embodied in various precepts and concepts; and c) that these ideals have been a positive factor in the lives of people and have imparted cohesion and stability to social life across millennia. So far so good. The crucial issue that crops up now is: To what extent these ideals continue to guide various transactions of life in modern India? Is there a serious erosion of these time-hallowed ideals such that social life is confronted with a large degree of disorder and chaos? Here it seems useful to make a distinction between a) the level of observance of these values or ideals among the various sections of ordinary people including the large sector comprising rural folk who lack 'read and write' literarcy and b) the level of observance among the literate sections largely living in urban areas.

The Malaise

Let us first take the case of ordinary people. This is a vast category encompassing both non-literate and semi-literate groups mostly occupying the rural landscape. There are also some groups which are located in the urban or semi-urban areas with an average level of literacy. This is for sure the major component of the Indian population ranging from the landless workers and small farmers of the rural areas to people in urban and semi-urban areas engaged in small businesses comprising such diverse groups as fruit- or vegetable-vendors, owners of small groceries, cycle- or motor-mechanics, street corner tea-stall owners, rag-pickers like aged but industrious Manohar Waghmare and many others. Without meaning to glorify or romanticize these groups, I wish to say that in general they go about their work/business with sincerity and dedication, marked by a fair degree of transparency and honesty. They normally put up hard work of 10 to 12 hours a day, braving rain, heat and cold, to earn a limited income. These transactions are also characterized by an element of service to the people. It is far from true that these people are devoid of initiative and drive and that they do not wish to raise their status in the society. On the contrary, many of them do well in their respective areas of activity, but without taking recourse to wrongful paths.

I can illustrate this argument with some instances. Take the case of our aged friend Ishaq Khan, a road-side peanut-vendor in an urban setting. He probably has a small job during the day as an office assistant. In the evening he is on the road-side with his small push-cart laden with peanuts and a coal-using oven for sand frying these. Asked why he is still charging the same old five rupees for 100 grams of peanuts despite the fact that prices of all fruits, vegetables and much else had been raised three or four times, he would pause for a moment, point to the sky and reply: "The supreme force above is giving me two square meals a day. Why should I go out of the way to make money?!." All of us have had many such learning experiences with ordinary people. Even at the risk of being branded as naïve, my inference is that the ordinary man's life in India is still guided by the basic values like dignity of labour, contentment, service to others, and promotion of one's interests by socially acceptable methods of business, not by aggressive salesmanship. These attributes derive their sustenance from age-old concepts such as belief in a higher force, conception of all in one and one in all, service to others, and *karma* as the principle of causation. This is the true character of the Indian way of life, which disallows breakdowns of social life irrespective of the convulsions in the larger politico-economic-religious spheres.

What is the situation like in the case of upper classes of the Indian population? Going by the news one sees in the print and electronic media, it appears that there is a large degree of disparity between age-old norms and practice. The scams that have hit the headlines in recent times, such as the ones about Satyam Computers or Commonwealth Games or the 2G Spectrum, are among the biggest examples of mismanagement of public money. These instances present a sharp contrast to the Indian ideals of *aparigraha* or non-possessive attitude. One is reminded here of the speeches which Gandhiji gave in 1936 in the Malabar region after the famous Padmanabha temple decided to keep open its doors to all sections. In these speeches Gandhiji made a pointed reference to the first verse of the *Ishopanishad* (Gandhi 2010: 650-55). He was so fascinated by the thought contained in this verse that he felt that Hinduism would still survive if it so happened that all its other texts were reduced to ashes. He was particularly attracted by the precepts of all pervasiveness of God in the universe, pleasure in giving away things to others, and need to abstain from the desire of coveting things belonging to others.

The undercurrents of the present society seem to be running in an opposite direction. As Tagore (2007) deplored, wealth acquisition has become "a matter of science and not of social ethics." And we seem to be finding joy in amassing wealth even at the cost of others rather than in giving way some of it. Theoretically, there is nothing wrong in acquiring riches. But the matter is one of our attitude towards it. This applies equally to the big public positions which people hold in all domains, which provide scope for display of nepotism, bias and misuse of power in various ways, including financial irregularities. The difference in attitude is one between the ideal of being a master or owner and that of a trustee or keeper. We do come across on one hand elected representatives who wear in public kilos of gold on their bodies and also industry magnets who live in multi-storied mansions with superlative facilities and annexes but surrounded by shanty-dwellers. In sharp contrast to this we had persons like J.R.D. Tata who sold his old house to create a charitable trust for disadvantaged women and children and chose to live in a rented apartment with the drawing room also serving as the bed room. We have others like Azim Premji who donated a vast sum of money for promoting school education but travels by economy class and wears only Indian made clothes.

Let us take another important concept from our past – the ideal of tolerance towards other points of view and in fact appreciating them in a positive way. Confronted as he was with the pluralistic nature of the society from religious and other points of view, the emperor Ashoka more than 2000 years ago was already persuading the various segments of his empire's population to live together amicably by respecting each other's faith. This and other exhortations of Ashoka form part of his *Dhamma* policy, which was already anticipating what Pandit Nehru later designated as the scientific temper of mind (Paddayya 2012). In some of his edicts, Ashoka calls upon people: "Respect or honour the other man's faith just as you would like your own faith to be honoured." This is a cardinal principle applicable to any society characterized by diversity. And India is one country where this pluralism encompasses practically every domain of life—religion, language, and ethnic and cultural spheres. All our nationalist leaders were keenly aware of the importance of the spirit of positive appreciation for putting up with this diversity. The critical issue is the extent to which this great precept is actually followed. While the norm still governs day-to-day interactions at person-to-person level in a large way, the same cannot be freely said about group or community level interactions. At these levels serious disruptions do occur, leading to national level chaos and even violence, e.g. the Ayodhya-Babri Masjid dispute. There are many such instances at regional and local levels, covering ethnic, religious, social and linguistic matters.

One can extend this analysis to other ideals or values like *satya*, *ahimsa*, *dharma* and *Lakshmanrekha* forming part of the moral fabric of the nation. One notices here too widespread violations and misuse. How does one account for these aberrations? It is important to remind ourselves here that money mismanagement is only one form of corruption. Corruption assumes a myriad other forms and requires a more comprehensive definition. It is the straying away of the human mind from accepted norms of behaviour. This debasement of mind finds expression in things like unlawful accumulation of wealth, neglect of one's duties, nepotism and many other lower and higher level misdeeds of life.

I am tempted to cite two well-known confessional cases illustrating how a disjunction between accepted values and actual behavior led to disastrous consequences. The famous golfer Tiger Woods finally accepted that he landed in dark recesses of extramarital relations eventually leading to divorce from his wife because he had strayed away from his Buddhist family values. Then there is the case of Ramalinga Raju, the founder of Satyam Computers, who realized the significance of Buddha's teachings only after having been put behind bars for various fraudulent actions.

Remedial Measures

In social theory one often comes across the famous statement of Karl Marx: 'Philosophers have for long interpreted the world, and the task now is one of changing it.' There are two ways of changing unsavoury situations like the ones mentioned above. One consists of short-term curative steps to correct a wrong situation. Another way is to invest time and efforts on a long-term basis in order to prevent mishaps themselves as much as possible. As the old saying goes, prevention of the ailment is after all better than its cure. The first approach is what I call the headache-and- saridon method – trying to get relief from a bout of headache by swallowing an analgesic tablet. This is what we notice when a bureaucrat or a minister, after having been found guilty of mishandling a financial matter, is made to quit or sent to jail. Then the whole episode is forgotten till a similar happening takes place after some time. In other words, we are only curing the symptoms of the malady, not coming to grips with its very nature and source. Theoretically speaking, the widely publicized movement against corruption being spearheaded by Anna Hazare and now the Aam Admi party of Arvind Kejariwal belong to this category of remedies.

A true Gandhian or Gandhiji himself would have considered the whole issue as a malady of the human mind and thought of nipping it in the bud by devising an appropriate scheme for educating the mind itself. What I mean to say is that there is a need to devise an elaborate scheme of liberal education for brightening up the minds of people. This is an extension to and elaboration of traditional and informal methods of value education we used to receive from elders and folk media. Elsewhere I have argued at length that the values enshrined in ancient Indian thought should be an integral component of courses in liberal education, both at school and college levels (Paddayya 2002). I would like to repeat some of these suggestions about the possible contents of such courses in liberal education.

In his book *Religion and Ritual in the Making of Humanity* Roy A. Rappaport (1999) states, as the title itself suggests, that ritualistic and sacralizing attitudes played, alongside the materialistically oriented adaptive methods, an important role in the development of humankind as a special biological species. In a way, he was already anticipating Robert Fuller's (2001) concept of SBNR-spiritual but not religious. He cites the conception of cosmos being an organized whole as an important concept in the social life of man. In fact, this and several other cognate concepts constitute the essence of Upanishadic thought. Some additional comments are warranted here. The *Nasadiya Sukta* or Rigvedic Hymn of Creation, dedicated to the unknown God, represents the beginnings of an intense quest to investigate and understand other worldly matters. This hymn talks of the ineffable force that existed before creation. A.L. Basham, in his widely read book *The Wonder that was India,* designated it as "one of the oldest surviving records of philosophic doubt in the history of the world… (and it) marks the development of a high stage of abstract thinking" (Basham 1963: 247).

The methods adopted by the Upanishads are not the same as the experimental approach of modern science but still display a highly developed rational outlook. R.D. Ranade identified as many as ten methods (called the enigmatic, aphoristic, etymological, mythical, analogical, dialectic, synthetic, monologic, *ad hoc* and regressive) that were adopted by the Upanishadic teachers for conducting their deliberations (1968; see also 1970). The whole endeavour or quest was seen not as a closed process but as one that was open to debate and discussion.

A major principle of the Upanishadic thought is the unity of existence which encompasses the diverse and manifold aspects of the universe. This all-embracing approach to the phenomenal world leads, in Nehru's (1960: 80) words, to metaphysical democracy: "He who sees the one spirit in all, and all in the one spirit, henceforth can look with contempt on no creature". Speculation about the nature of Ultimate Reality or Creation is another noteworthy feature of the Upanishadic writings. This quest about Ultimate Reality is considered as man's saving knowledge. Creation has variously been viewed as arising from cosmic sex, from water, from fire, from wind and, then at other places, it is attributed to self-consciousness of the primeval person (*Purusha*). *Purusha* is the creator and all-pervasive force and *Prakriti* is his agent and plays an instrumental role in organizing the world. Thus creation is seen as movement of time, without beginning and without end. Here we are reminded of the steady state theory of the universe advocated by Fred Hoyle and the more recent theory of cycles of time put forward by Roger Penrose (2011).

Brahman is one aspect of Creation or Ultimate Reality expounded by the Upanishads that has made the widest appeal to both ancient and modern minds (eastern and western). Sankaracharya's *Vivekachudamani* is entirely devoted to an exploration of this theme. Knowledge of the *Brahman* is valued as the highest achievement and viewed as the true liberating force. In the Taittiriya Upanishad Varuna is asked by his son Bhrigu about the fit topic of inquiry. Varuna replies: "That spirit, from which these created beings proceed; through which having proceeded from it, they live; toward which they tend and in which they are ultimately absorbed, that spirit to know; that is *Brahman*". The centrality of knowledge of the *Brahman* is brought out by the injunction given in the *Brahmasutras*: "Athato Brahma-jignasa—Now therefore the desire to know the Brahman".

In Europe the spread of knowledge about the Indian thought gave rise to what Raymond Schwab (1984) called Oriental Renaissance, which brought an "antiquity more profound, more philosophical and more poetical than that of Greece and Rome." The great German philosopher and thinker Arthur Schopenhauer paid tribute to the depth of the Upanishadic thought in these words: "From every sentence of the Upanishads deep, original and sublime thoughts arise, and the whole is pervaded by high and holy and earnest spirit ... In the whole world there is no study ... so beneficial and so elevating as that of the Upanishads ... They are the products of the highest wisdom..." Further he remarked that "The study of the Upanishads has been the solace of my life. It will be the solace of my death" (as quoted in Max Müller 1879: lxi).

The view is often expressed whether the common man in India does not find Vedantic thought as too esoteric and abstract in nature and rather unconnected with the happenings of his day-to-day life. This fear, I believe, is unfounded. It is not uncommon to come across even non-literate people in both urban and rural parts of the country who do attach far more importance to spiritual matters rather than material conditions of existence. Commenting on how pervasive is the spirit of Vedantism in the Indian way of life, Max Müller (1883: 250) wrote: "... and so long as India is India, nothing will extinguish that ancient spirit of Vedantism which is breathed by every Hindu from his earliest youth, and pervades in various forms the prayers even of the idolater, the speculations of the philosopher and the proverbs of the beggar." While recommending the study of Vedanta to one and all, he further remarked that "...It will bring before them a view of life, different from all other views of life which are placed before us in the History of Philosophy. You saw how behind all the *Devas* or gods, the authors of the Upanishads discovered *Atman* or Self. Of that Self they predicated three things only, that it is, that it perceives, and that it enjoys eternal bliss..."(Max Müller 1883: 251, see also 1911). Continuing his exhortation to the Europeans, Max Müller (1883: 6) further stated that ancient literature of India offers that "corrective which is most wanted in order to make our inner life more perfect, more comprehensive, more universal, in fact more truly human..."

This is at once a gentle reminder to all those who worship many gods at home or else in temples but still miss the God and an open invitation to those who are in quest of a pool of ideas which can restore one's mental poise. In fact I have a strong feeling that the themes broached by Max Muller in his famous orientation lectures before Cambridge University in 1882 for young British recruits to Civil Services in India – published the very next year as a book under the title *India: What can it teach us?* — are actually so relevant in the context of modern India itself that this book should be retitled as *India: What can it teach Indians?* and translated into various Indian languages.

Apart from these and other principles enshrined in the Vedanta, the proposed liberal education could also incorporate many concepts and propositions drawn from other indigenous sources. These could encompass socio-political, philosophical and religious thought, scientific achievements, arts and literature. Take, for instance, the concept of *Dharma.* The various episodes given in the two epics emphasize the importance of observing one's Dharma in life. The essence of Kurukshetra battle is the tussle between the forces of *Dharma* and those of *Adharma* (see Das 2010). Rama's self-exile for 14 years and later his sending away Sita to a forest hermitage are acts done by a ruler in deference to sentiments of people for upholding the path of *Dharma.* The emperor Ashoka's edicts planted at various places in the sub-continent, espousing the *Dhamma* policy, are the earliest known instance in recorded history of the implementation of the concept of welfare state. Look at his famous proclamation espousing a paternalistic attitude in matters of governance: 'All people are my children and it is my desire to promote their welfare'. The measures he took towards this end are well known and need no mention here. The Buddhist principle of *Patichcha samuppada,* advocating multifactorial causality, is useful both in personal and public life. Then there are the concepts of *Din-Ilahi* or Divine Monotheism and *sulh-i kul* or Absolute Peace advocated by Mughal emperor Akbar. One could cite a host of other ancient and medieval Indian concepts which can bring many salutary effects on the modern way of life.

The limited instances cited above will suffice to emphasize the importance of ancient Indian thought as a rich source of ideas for developing a system of liberal education. It is hoped that this value-impregnated liberal education, once it is made an integral part of the curriculum right from the school level, will keep at bay basal instincts of the human mind that are the root cause of all corrupt actions and elevate the human mind to a level where it is at peace with itself, particularly in the context of many kinds of allurements being offered by modernized and globalized setting of life and at a time when the very meaning of happiness has changed from a contented mental state to an objectified quality of life (Nandy 2012).

Conclusion

I should admit that the topic dealt with in this paper has been commented upon by many workers for the last two hundred years and more. For example, in a famous oration delivered in the University of Oxford in 1773, Sir William Jones emphasized that "...speculation is only commendable, as far as it may supply us with Wisdom and Valour in active life, and that all arts, literature, science, cease to be laudable, as soon as they cease to be beneficial" (Jones 1807: 13). In his book *Moral Education* published in 1925, the French Sociologist Emile Durkheim called attention to the need for promoting what he called secular morality in order to create "new (human) beings" (Durkheim 1961). On the other side of the Atlantic this theme was developed by John Dewey and other educationists. In a memorable statement Dewey points out: "...Discipline, natural development, culture, social efficiency, are moral traits – marks of a person who is a worthy member of that society which it is the business of education to further. There is an old saying to the effect that it is not enough for a man to be good; he must be good for something. The something for which a man must be good is capacity to live as a social member so that what he gets from living with others balances with what he contributes. What he gets and gives as a human being, a being with desires, emotions, and ideas, is not external possessions, but a widening and deepening of conscious life – a more intense, disciplined, and expanding realization of meanings..." (Dewey 1976: 359). Writers on corruption in governance have already called for individual responsibility and obligation, sacrifice, compassion, justice, striving for the highest good, and acting morally (Caiden and Dwivedi 2002; see also Tripathi 2009).

In our own country the importance of ancient Indian ideals of education has been commented upon by more than one worker. In a lecture on 'The Aims and Ends of College Education' delivered at the Deccan College in Pune in 1868, Sir Ramakrishna Gopal Bhandarkar invoked the Indian concepts of *Vinaya* and *Samskara* and said that "the acquisition of clear ideas, and of the power of observation, comparison and criticism, the freeing of the mind from narrowness consequent on prepossion or prejudice, and a positive knowledge of certain subjects constitute, I believe, the aim of mental education." And he went on to emphasize that "the faculty of moral judgement is the most important of the ends to be attained by education. A man has no right to be called an educated man if he has not acquired the habit of controlling himself, and shaping his action in accordance with truth and justice or the dictates of an enlightened or cultured conscience" (Bhandarkar 1933: 463-4).

References

Basham, A.L. 1963. *The Wonder that was India.* Bombay: Orient Longmans Ltd.

Bhandarkar, R.G. 1933. The Ends and Aims of College Education. In *Collected Works of R.G. Bhandarkar* (N.B. Utgikar and V.S. Paranjpe Eds.), Volume I, pp. 461-75. Pune: Bhandarkar Oriental Research Institute. Based on a lecture delivered in 1868.

Brezinka, Wolfgang 1994. *Belief, Morals, and Education – Collected Essays on the Philosophy of Education.* Translated from German by James Stuart Brice. Aldershot: Avebury.

Caiden, Gerald E. and O.P. Dwivedi 2002. Official Ethics and Corruption. In *Where Corruption Lives* (G.E. Caiden, O.P. Dwivedi and J. Jabbra Eds.), pp. 244-55. Bloomfield: Kumarian Press.

Coomaraswamy, A.K. 1985. What has India contributed to Human Welfare? In *The Dance of Siva – Essays on Indian Art and Culture* (A.K. Coomaraswamy), pp. 1-13. New York: Dover Publications. Originally published in 1915.

Das, Gurcharan 2010. *The Difficulty of Being Good: On the Subtle Art of Dharma.* New Delhi: Oxford University Press.

Coomaraswamy, A.K. 1989. On the Pertinence of Philosophy. In *What is Civilization and other Essays* (A.K. Coomaraswamy), pp. 13-32. Delhi: Indira Gandhi Centre for Arts and Oxford University Press.

Dewey, John 1976. *Democracy and Education: An Introduction to the Philosophy of Education.* New Delhi: Light and Life Publishers. Originally published by Macmillan Publishing Co. in 1916.

Durkheim, Emile 1961. *Moral Education: A Study in the Theory and Application of the Sociology of Education.* Original French Edition published in 1925. Translated by E.K. Widson and H. Schnurer. New York: The Free Press of Glencoe, Inc.

Fuller, Robert C. 2001. *Spiritual but not Religious.* New York: Oxford University Press

Gandhi, M.K. 2010. *Great Works of Mahatma Gandhi.* Delhi: Jaico Publishers.

Jones, Sir William 1807. *The Collected Works of Sir William Jones,* Volume 1 (edited by Lord Teignmouth). London: John Stockdale and John Walker.

Keay, J. Seymour 1883. Comments on India made in 1883. As quoted in M.K. Gandhi *Hind Swaraj or Indian Home Rule, 2006,* pp. 92. Ahmedabad: Navjivan Publishing House. Eighteenth Reprint. Originally published in 1907.

Max Mueller, F. 1879. *The Upanishads,* Part I. Oxford: Clarendon Press.

Max Mueller, F. 2000. *India: What can it teach us?* (A Course of Lectures delivered before the University of Cambridge in 1882). London: Longmans, Green, and Co.

Max Mueller, F. 1911. *Three Lectures on the Vedanta Philosophy* (Delivered at the Royal Institution in March 1894). London: Longmans, Green, and Co. Originally published in 1894.

Mookerji, Radha Kumud 1954. *The Fundamental Unity of India.* Bombay: Bharatiya Vidya Bhavan.

Nandy, Ashis 2012. The Idea of Happiness. *Economic and Political Weekly* 47(2), January 14, 2012: 45-48.

Nehru, Jawaharlal 1960. *The Discovery of India.* London: Meridian Books.

Paddayya, K. 2002. Ancient Indian Thought: A Component of Liberal Education. *University News* 39 (53) (31 December 2001 – 6 January 2002): 3-9.

Paddayya, K. 2011. The Place of the Past in the Indian Mind. *Journal of the Asiatic Society* 53(1): 1-18.

Paddayya, K. 2012. On Nehru's Concept of Scientific Temper of Mind and its Place in Modern India. *Propagatio* 3(1): 23-26

Penrose, R. 2011. *Cycles of Time: An Extraordinary New View of the Universe.* London: Vintage Books.

Ranade, R.D. 1968. *A Constructive Survey of Upanishadic Philosophy: Being An Introduction to the Thought of the Upanishads.* Bombay: Bharatiya Vidya Bhavan. First published in 1926.

Ranade, R.D. 1970. *Vedanta: The Culmination of Indian Thought.* Bombay: Bharatiya Vidya Bhavan.

Rappaport, Roy A. 1999. *Religion and Ritual in the Making of Humanity.* Cambridge: Cambridge University Press.

Schwab, R. 1984. *The Oriental Renaissance: Europe's Rediscovery of India and the East, 1680-1880.* New York: Columbia University Presss.

Sukthankar, V.S. 1957. *On the Meaning of the Mahabharata.* Bombay.

Tagore, Rabindranath 2007. City and Village. *In English Writings of Rabindranath Tagore* (Lectures and Addresses), Volume 7, pp. 689-701. New Delhi: Atlantic Publishers. Originally published in 1924.

Tripathi, A.N. 2009. *Human Values.* New Delhi: New Age International Publishers. Third Edition. First published in 2004.

61

THE INDO-EUROPEAN PROBLEM : A NEW PARADIGM, A COMPLETE RE-LOOK

Mohan Gupta

Prof. Daya Nath Tripathi is a well known name among the eminent scholars of this country and the world, particularly in relation to in the field of archaeology and ancient history. His scholarship combines a deep and detailed study of ancient Indian literature on one hand and the vast field experience extending from India to Greece, France, Germany, Italy, United Kingdom, Egypt, Iran etc. This field experience is not just the visits or casual observations of the archaeological material placed in the musea of these countries but down to earth first hand experience of over 200 excavations and explorations. His approach to ancient history and archaeology for arriving at a conclusion is absolutely scientific as he has not relied upon archaeology alone but has drawn from the wealth of conclusions of archaeo-linguistics, archaeo astronomy and allied sciences. The first collateral methodology probably is perhaps due to the vary eminent British archaeologist and historian Lord Colin Renfrew, who was guide to the Ph.D. thesis of Prof. Tripathi for his masterly work entitled 'Bronze work of Greece'. My good fortune for the first acquaintance of such an eminent scholar came in Shimla when he was a fellow of Indian Institute of Advanced Studies between 1999-2002 and in relation to the second methodology which he adopted, viz. the Archaeo-astronomy. The credit for putting archaeo-astronomy as a reliable tool to come to the pointed conclusions regarding ancient history goes to Prof. G.C. Pande and Prof. Daya Nath Tripathi. To me he has proved like a beckon light in the unknown labyrinths of the vast terrain of ancient history. In fact, he took me seriously into the field of ancient history literally holding my finger so that I am not awed or discouraged by the vast and unknown horizons of this field. Its really a great pleasure that a felicitation volume is being published in his honour, which he richly deserves and I feel happy and fortunate in registering my presence, may be in a very small way in it, I express my gratitude and venerations to this great scholar and pray Lord Mahakala to give him a long illustrious and happy life.

So far as the subject of this article i.e. 'The Indo-European Problem : A New Paradigm, A Complete Re-look' is concerned, whatever I present here is like श्त्वदीयं वस्तु गोविन्द तुभ्यमेव समर्प्यते (O Govind! It is your graceful gift which is being offered to you). Because when Prof. Tripathi was Chairman of the Indian Council of Historical Research, I was given a project on Vedic Chronology. I worked on this subject for several years and drew my conclusions using as it where four lanes to come to a conclusion as near the truth as possible. These four lanes are 1. Archaeology 2. Archaeo-astronomy 3. Cosmology and cosmogony, Linguistic paleontology, theology etc. and 4. the literary history, starting from *Rgveda* down to the *Mahabharata*.

I know the limitations of such felicitation volumes and give in brief three stages of my article : 1. What do I mean by Paradigm shift 2. Broad arguments in support of my conclusions and 3. The conclusions themselves.

Stage : 1

Vedic Sanskrit is the oldest Indo-European language present in its entire majesty with a very rich and divergent literature, complete grammar, a treatise on phonetics and a huge vocabulary. Besides, the Rgveda is the oldest work of any Indo-European language. Naturally, Vedic Sanskrit and Rgveda are closest to any conceived proto Indo-European language which is non-existent at present. Therefore, in dealing with the question of Indo-European problem both historically and linguistically, Rgveda and Vedic Sanskrit and thereby the entire Vedic literature acquire great importance. That is why it is quite imperative first to look into the issues related to the Indo-European problem attempt to find its home-land and in the process attempt at the chronology of the Vedic literature historically.

2. Colin Renfrew in his famous work "Archaeology and Language" (1987) has dealt with in details the Puzzle of Indo-European Origins. He has very honestly without falling into the trap of racial superiority or imperialistic hang over tackled the issue stage-by-stage and has come to a plausible conclusion, tracing the stages of Indo-European languages and archeological findings and making a very intelligent synthesis of them.

But like earlier scholars such as Gustav Kossinna, V. Gordon Childe, Marija Gimbutas and such other scholars he has also taken the route to find out the 'unknown' from the 'unknown'. What I mean is that all these scholars have attempted to find out the homeland, the so called *Urheimat* of the Indo-European languages by first conjuring-up the non-existent conceptual proto Indo-European language through the process of taking up some common words in these languages - generally termed as proto lexicon - and then with the help of these few words imagining the culture of the people who might have spoken that language and then finding out the location of those people. One can understand how much farfetched and unscientific this process is ? Thus, earlier scholars by finding out some common words relating to professions, trees and vegetations and animals came to the conclusion that the people who spoke proto Indo-European were pastoral kind of people. Hence, they concluded that their habitat or the homeland of this language could be northern Europe or the steppes of Russia etc. No doubt, Renfrew has decried this process and has termed the construction of a language in such a way as not legitimate but with regard to archaeological processes combined with the linguistic processes, he has almost followed the same route. While dealing with the problem he complained there is very little in the early histories or literature of the languages concerned to explain the links between them. Here, then, is one of the most notable and enduring problems in the prehistory of the Old World. [1] In the next breath, he realizes that there is one exception to the lack of historical information and mentions the hymns of the Rgveda as remarkable source in India. But because of a very unclear or rather confused picture of the date of Rgveda till then putting it as late as 1200 B.C. he did not opt to examine the Vedic Sanskrit as the oldest language of the Indo-European family or to examine the culture of the Rgvedic people to tackle the puzzle of Indo-European origins. The latest researches by various scholars both indigenous and foreign have placed the date of Rgveda (which will be dealt with in great details later in this article) before 3000 B.C. or even earlier, by examining the state of mighty Saraswati river mentioned several times in Rgveda, the urban nature of the people of Rgveda and discarding the very unfounded dichotomy between the Vedic civilization and indus-valley civilization. Therefore, with the new horizons opened due to new researches on the culture of Rgveda and the status of Indus-Valley civilizations vis-à-vis Vedic civilization, it calls for a paradigm shift to consider the Indo-European problem afresh in a rather hitherto untreaded way inasmuch as to try to know the unknown from the known basis i.e. from known very ancient Indo-European Language called Vedic Sanskrit instead of attempting to create the non-existent Proto Indo-European language by collecting some common vocabulary of the ancient Indo-European languages which is certainly an unknown factor and not quite legitimate. Renfrew himself questions this process. 'One important question is the extent to which it is legitimate to reconstruct a Proto Indo-European language, drawing upon the cognate forms of the words in the various Indo-European languages that are known. Certainly it is questionable whether the nouns (for linguistic paleontologists make little use of verbs or adjectives) can legitimately be used in the way advocated by Pictet and by Schrader to create an inventory, as it were, of the *Urheimat*, the original homeland of these Proto Indo-Europeans.[2] This was therefore an unknown and invalid factor to embark upon a research. Instead, I propose to examine an existing fully developed ancient Indo-European language i.e. Vedic Sanskrit and its vast literature to understand the type of culture and civilization which the people of Rgvedic times followed to embark upon the question of the homeland of the Indo-European languages and their dispersal as it were in the world.

Stage : 2 - The Arguments

A glimpse of the four lane royal road to the homeland of Indo-European languages :-

These four lanes as mentioned earlier have been discussed in detail in my long thesis on the subject consisting of more than of 200 pages. Herein I give a glimpse of these four lanes i.e. archaeology, archaeo Astronomy, Cosmology, theology and linguistic paleontology and the literary history. My main plank for the chronology of early history of India has been archaeo astronomy. Therefore, I give here two very clear and unambiguous examples regarding the dating of Vedas.

Archaeo-astronomy

A very explicit time reference we come across in Maitrayani Upanisad : सूर्यो योनिः कालस्य। तस्यैतद्रूपं यन्निमेषादि कालात्संभूतं द्वादषात्मकं वत्सरम्। एतस्याग्नेय मर्द्धमर्द्ध वारूणं मघाद्यं श्रतिष्ठार्धमाग्नेयं क्रमेण – उत्क्रमेण सार्पाद्यं श्रविष्ठार्धान्तं सौम्यम्' (Mait. Up. 6.14).

'The sun is the cause of time. This is its form – the twelve-fold year, constituted of bits of time such as nimesa (16/75th of a second – a winking time) etc. Half of it is fiery and half cool; beginning with Magha and ending with half sravistha is the fiery half in order, conversely beginning with Aslesa and ending with half-sravistha is the cool half'.

The Magha-period

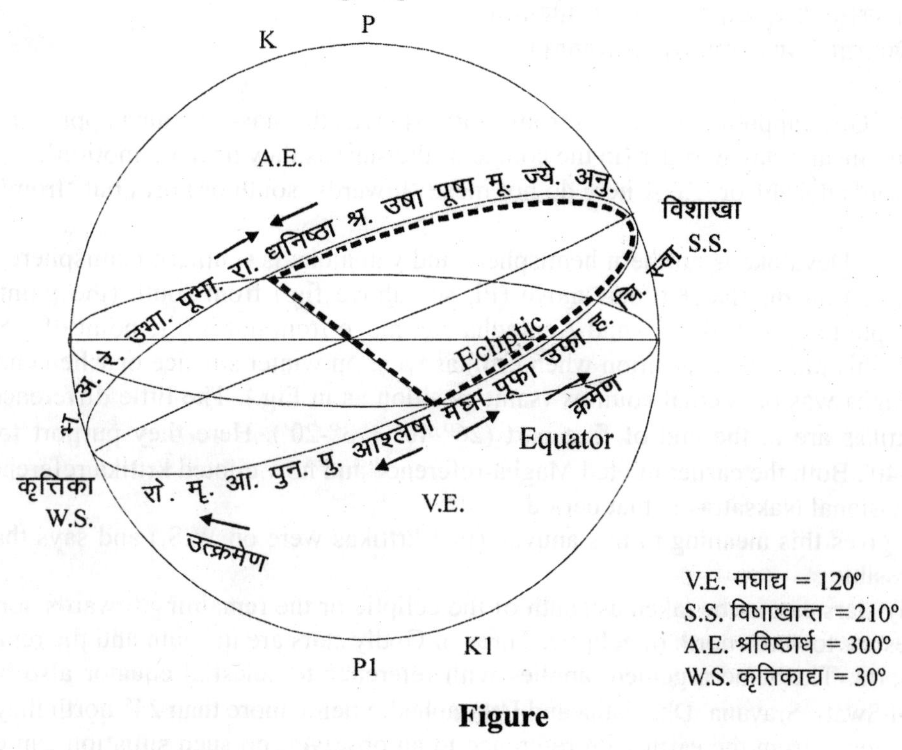

Figure

With the above figure, the meaning of this anuvak of Maitrayani Upanisad becomes clear. There are two halves of the year, one is fiery (आग्नेय) another is cool (वारूणम्). The fiery one is from Magha to half of Dhanistha – obviously when there is heat in the northern hemisphere i.e. the portion enclosed by dots in the figure. The cool half is the when the sun is in the southern hemisphere when the northern hemisphere is cold. In the figure, the lower half is the cool-one. From Aslesha to half of Dhanistha in reverse order (shown by arrows as continuous line) (वारूणम् or सौम्यम् = सोमस्य अयं सौम्यम्) Obviously this description does not fit well with the present meaning of Uttarayana and Daksinayana (vertical halves) because in that case neither half will be fully fiery or cool as both will have cold season for half period and hot season for another half. This confirms my interpretation given earlier that during Vedic times Udagayana or Uttarayana meant sun's north-hemisphere course above the celestial equator and Daksinayana meant its journey below the celestial equator in the southern hemisphere. Hence only the Uttarayana was called the day of the Gods (Sun V.E. to AE) and Daksinayana as the day of Asuras or Pitrs (Sun A.E. to V.E.) in Geeta, Smrtis and religious treatises which tripped even scholars like Varaha Mihira. So, Magha in this reference is neither at winter solstice as some scholars put it nor at summer solstice as some people think comparing with Vedanga Jyotisa, it is clealy and unmistakably at the Vernal equinox. Also, for the first time here, there is reference to divisional naksatras.

Computation of Time 120°/0-0-49″ = 8816-285
= 8531 B.C. or 8500 B.C.

There is another supporting statement for this reference of Maitrayani Upanisad and it is in Taittiriya Brahmana which corroborates the above conclusion without any doubt :

देवग्रहा वै नक्षमाणि। .... कृतिकाः प्रथमम्। विषाखे उत्तमम्। तानि देव नक्षत्राणि। अनुराधाः प्रथमम्। अपभरणी रूत्तमम्। तानि यम नक्षत्राणि। यानि देव नक्षत्राणि तानि दक्षिणेन परियन्ति। यानि यम नक्षत्राणि तान्युत्तरेण।

'Krttikas first; Visakhas ultimate; they are the stars of the Gods. Anuradha first, Apabharani ultimate; they are the stars of Yama (the God of manes). Those which are stars of Gods travel from south (दक्षिणेन) and those of Yama from north' (उतरेण). For the meaning of the words 'दक्षिणेन' and 'उतरेण' here, the commentary of Bhatta Bhaskar Misra helps :

'देव नक्षत्राणि देवलोकं दक्षिणेन परियन्ति
यम नक्षत्राणि तु यमलोक मुत्तरतः परियन्ति
परिपाट्या क्रमेणावतिष्ठन्ते गत्यभावात्।'

'The stars of Gods approach Devaloka from south whereas the stars of Yama approach Yamaloka from north; Pariyanti means stay in order (in the course of the sun) as they have no motion'.

Thus the words दक्षिणेन or उतरेण here do not mean 'towards' south or north but 'from' south and north.

We know that Devaloka is northern hemisphere and yamaloka is southern hemisphere. Therefore the anuvak (statement) means that Krttikas move (Pl. see above fig.) from south (the point of winter solstice) to north (upto the point of S.S.) and Anuradha etc. move from north (the point of S.S.) to (upto the point of W.S.). This indicates a position when krttikas were on winter solstice or when end of Aslesa or beginning of Magha was on Vernal equinox (same position as in Fig.). The little difference is that in the above fig. Krttikas are at the end of first part (26°-40′ + 3°-20′). Here they purport to be in the beginning i.e. 26°-40′. Both the earlier quoted Magha-reference and now quoted krttika reference indicate the existence of divisional Naksatras in that period.

S.B. Dixit gives this meaning to this anuvak (that krttikas were on W.S.) and says that no other meaning of it is possible :

'The Godly stars cannot be taken as south of the ecliptic or the remaining towards north because Krttikas themselves are towards north of ecliptic. Three of Godly stars are in south and the remaining two are again in the north. The same argument applies with reference to celestial equator also because the northern latitude of Swati, Sravana, Dhanistha and Uttarabhadra being more than 24° north they can never come south of equator… from the earth with reference to an observer, no such situation can ever obtain when 13 stars are towards his one side and the remaining 13 on the other. Therefore, the meaning of this anuvak is they are in the path of sun as it travels from south to north and vice versa. This means the Uttarayana (in the present sense) or winter solstice was in the beginning of Krttikas. He calculated this period as 8750 B.C. We can also verify it :

If W.S. is the beginning of Krttika i.e. 26°-40′
The V.E. would be (26°-40′) + 90° = 116°-40′
@ 48″ per year this amounts to

$$\frac{116° - 40'}{0 - 0 - 48''} = 8750\,\text{B.C.}$$

But to be precise, the average is to be taken as 49″ and not 48″ and zero Ayanamsa year being 285 AD, this is to be deducted from the result. So that a more precise value would be

$$\frac{116° - 40'}{0 - 0 - 49''} = 8571 - 285 = 8286\,\text{or}\,8300\,\text{B.C.}$$

Magha period is 8500 B.C. thus this anuvak confirms this same period.[3]

Archaeology

B.B. Lal in his article "Identifying the Rgvedic people : An Archaeological Approach" reports : In north-eastern Afghanistan there lies the site of Aq Kupruk. Over there we have a good sequence of habitation from the epi-Paleolithic times, dating back to ca.15th millennium BCE (Dupree 1972; Shaffer 1978). This was followed by a Neolithic stage which produced evidence of domestication of animals, but there was no pottery yet. On the basis of two radiocarbon dates, viz. 8565±240 and 6960±105 BCE (uncorrected; half-life 5730), these levels clearly go back to 8th-7th millennia BCE. In the succeeding period there turned up the pottery and for these pottery-bearing levels there are four Carbon-14 dates, viz. 5806 BCE, 5638 BCE, 5292/5286/5241 BCE. It would thus be seen that a Neolithic economy, with domestication of animals and production of pottery, had come into being in north-eastern Afghanistan by the beginning of the sixth millennium BCE.

Besides, there are on record the finds of Mehargarhf, Kile Gul Mohammad etc. Recently, there have been excavations at Lohradewa Dist. Sant Kabir Nagar in U.P. and the findings of these excavations presented by five eminent archaeologists in the Journal of U.P. Archaeology Department indicates the availability of the cultivation of rice at a period 6-5th millennium B.C. The archaeologists observe - "the appearance of cultivated type of rice is the culmination of the effects of manipulations of wild rices by hunter-gatherers for thousands of years and the conscious human selection, prior to the emergence of early farming communities. There is a strong possibility that people have been living in Ganga Plain since late Paleolithic and interacted with the communities living in Vindhyas, Himalayas and other areas."[4] This observation suggests that a rice cultivation is available in 6th millennium BC. The crude practices of agriculture must have started some 2000 years back i.e. in this middle Vedic period. We observe from Vedic studies that there is mention of Gangetic plain in Rgveda itself and other northern and eastern territories of India up to Magadha and Utkal in Yajurveda. Thus developed farming must have started in India in 6th-7th millennium B.C. itself.

Excavations at Nevali Cori and Gobekle tepe

About the excavations at both these places in Turkey, B.G. Siddharth vide an article "The Astronomy, Chronology and Geography of the Vedas" has observed "The excavations at Nevali Cori and Gobekle tepe (both within a few kilometers of each other) near Urfa (in Turkey) have turned the history books upside down. Here, most amazingly is revealed amongst many other sculpted artefacts, the head of a Vedic priest, complete with the shikha or pigtail. There are also several pillars and structures with all the astronomical motifs that could be found in the Rgveda and indicative of a high degree of artistry. ..... Another striking motif on the Gobekli tepe pillars is that of a bird with a circular disc - they represent Garuda the bird which carries Vishnu, the Sun and the Sun itself. So also images of the bird Garuda carrying a snake as described in the Puranas." Though, we do not agree with the dating of these excavations by B.G. Siddharth on the basis of Star, Aja Eka Padh rising in the east which he places at 10000 B.C. because the correct period of the rising of Aja Ek Pada in the east is 7200 B.C. We also do not agree with his other finding that Anatolia was the homeland of Rgvedic Aryans. The findings simply suggest the presence of Indo-Aryans in Anatolia in 7-8th millennium B.C. which means they were there during their westward journey to Anatolia and Greece.

Cosmogony, mythology and Philosophy of Indo-Europeans

Dayanath Tripathi a noted scholar of archaeology and Ancient History has done an excellent study of cosmogonic myths of Indo-Europeans. This period was the age when the cosmogonic myths of India took some concrete shape. These have been described in details by Mr. Tripathi comparing them with the cosmogonical myths of the other European countries. He observes - "Ancient Indian cosmogonies may be divided into three categories : those beginning with the material principles like water, earth, fire, ether, etc.; those beginning with the abstract principles like chaos, time, night, desire, non-being, etc.; and those beginning with the divine principles like Prajapati, Brahman, Visvakarman, etc. This holds good in the cosmogonical speculations of other countries also. Of these three categories, the first is probably the most primitive. It appears that the conception of a divine principle as the creator of the universe marks the latest stage in the development of cosmogonic ideas, though not in all cases.

It seems perfectly reasonable to the primitive peoples who saw land growing from the accumulations of river-borne silt and desert wastes rendered cultivable by irrigation, to conclude, for instance, that water was the primary element and the source of all that existed. In the famous creation hymn of the Rgveda (X.129) the question is raised whether the fathomless waters existed before the formation of the world and the answer is given in the affirmative. The conception of the cosmic ocean recurs in other mythologies as well, notably in some Greek cosmogonies and in the Egyptian and Babylonian legends of creation. Among the Greeks a number of cosmogonies were devised, the prime component of the universe being ocean according to Homer; water and earth, according to Athenagoras; and water, according to Thales. The ancient Egyptians believed that at the beginning of the world was a waste of water called Nu or Nun, and it was the abode of the great father."[5]

Mr. Tripathi has quoted Marija Gimbutas and Mallory profusely to explain his point. "Gimbutas has described in detail various conventionalized and abstract ideograms, recurring on figurines, stamp seals, dishes, cult vessels, and as part of the pictorial decoration of vases and house walls, which explain the cosmogony and cosmology of the people of that period as well the functions of the deities it sustained. She has divided the symbols into two basic categories: those related to water or rain, the snake and the bird; and those associated with the moon, the vegeta life-cycle, the rotation of seasons, the birth and growth essential to the perpetuation of life. The first category, according to her, consists of meanders, and spirals. The second group includes the cross, the encircled cross and more complex derivations of the basic motif, which symbolically connects the four corners of the world, the crescent, horn, caterpillar, egg and fish.

The cosmogonic myths of the Indo-European speaking peoples may be varied, but there are also a sufficient number of common elements to suggest the existence of an underlying Proto-Indo-European myth or myths whose general structure can be at least partially recovered. Mallory has divided creation myths of the Indo-Europeans into two broad types : a cosmogonic myth that explains the origin of both the physical and social worlds, and a 'foundation' myth that is more directly associated with the origins of mankind (anthropogonic) or the establishment of specific people.

Mr. Tripathi observes that "more than 30,000 miniature sculptures of clay, marble, bone, copper and gold from some 3000 sites of the Neolithic and Chalcolithic era in South Eastern Europe along with enormous models of temples and actual temples have been reported in recent years. Marija Gimbutas of California has identified various cosmogonical and cosmological images of moon, bull, snake, fish and primordial Egg in them.

I would like to draw the attention of scholars to the fact that the well-dated proto-Indo-European images of southeast Europe are really the material manifestations of the Vedic mythological concepts and legendary ideographs. None will doubt the fact that the Vedic literature is the first written record of the human race consisting the best thinking regarding the origin of universe, religion and philosophy carrying traditions of thousands of years.

The exact parallels of the Vedic legendary concepts are found in these archaeological records and, as such, it would not be incorrect to place the beginnings of the Vedic tradition in the sixth millennium BC rather than in the third millennium BC. The following parallels drawn from the Proto-Indo-Europeans art motifs, the Vedic ideograms and mythological concepts will certainly justify such an assumption.

The most important cosmogonic myth of the Indo-Europeans is centered on the dismemberment of a divine being - either anthropomorphic or bovine - and the creation of the universe out of its various elements. Such myths are there in the Old Norse, Old Irish, Old Russian, Celtic and Germanic sources, Greco-Roman traditions offer us Ovid's account of Atlas in the *Metamorphoses* (4.655-662), which relates how giant's beard and hair become forests, his bones become stone, his hand the ridges of mountains, etc. Some such myths are to be seen in the Middle Persian *Sken Gumanig Wizar* (16.8-20) of the ninth century AD. But the earliest comes from the *Purusasukta* of the Rgveda (X.90), which describes how Purusa, the (primeval)' man', was divided so that his eyes became the sun, his mouth the fire, his breath became the wind, his feet the earth, etc."[6]

In this period the philosophical concepts of the Vedic rishis must have formulated into concrete conceptions. The very first curiosity of any civilized people is about the secrete of creation called *Sristi Vidya*. Rgveda has a very rich conceptual framework for this *Sristi Vidya*. "The Vedic Srstividya offers a very rich fare of cosmological thinking as compared to cosmogonical stories prevalent in other cultures. Needless to say that the process of the One becoming the Many is the process of creation. In this connection, certain questions need to be satisfactorily answered. For instance, What does the term 'creation' signify? What are the elements that go into the making of the cosmos? In speaking about cosmos, one must take into account the elements that do, in fact, or promise to, maintain order. One must therefore ask: What are these elements? Are they engendered in the process of creation itself that help maintain order at the macro-cosmic plane and keep alive the possibility of gaining or regaining order in the human world?

The source or the maker of this Universe is universally acclaimed to be an entity that is all-pervasive but avyaya (inexhaustible), anirukta (inexplicable or undeclared), aparimit (immesurable, aperon in Greek), etc. The process of creation begins when aperon, as Plato puts it, is boundred by peras (limits). The process of the One turning into the Many raises four inter-related questions. First, what is the nature of this Boundless? Second, what is the process through which the One turns into the Many? Third, does the One exhausts itself fully by turning into the Many? And, lastly, if the whole process of creation is invisible even though occurring every moment before or beyond our eyes, what could be the most likely account of creation that can be rendered?

The Boundless, the avyaya, Idea (Eidos) (tatva) to use the Platonic term, assumes many names (nama) and forms (rupa) and becomes embodied idea (enhylon eidos). This can happen in two alternate ways. First, the Boundless is a creator who makes use of materials that are already available but only in an incompletely fashioned form for creating this universe himself standing outside it; he is a Demiurge or a deus ex machina. Alternatively, the creator is not outside this creation; the Boundless is the one substance which transforms himself into many modes of being. These many modes constituting the universe are considered to be either a parinama (transformation) or a vivarta (transfiguration) of the One. In either case, the universe is pervaded by the One."[7]

Linguistics Paleontology and Glottochronology

In this connection, I would like to begin with the observation of Dr. Govind Chandra Pande[8] in his recent work 'Vedic Sanskriti' :

In fact, the vary identity of the Aryas is their language. Without language by merely physical culture they can not be identified, otherwise their indicators are found from Neolithic period to the iron age. The original Aryan race their original home land, the original Aryan culture and pre history of Aryas can be discovered with the help of linguistic evidence only. Without linguistic evidence, this discovery is like horns on the head of a hare (which means it is impossible because a hare has no horns).

Based on certain morphological and phonological similarities between various Indo-European languages, it has been conceived that there must have been an original language from which all these languages such as Sanskrit, Greek, Latin, Avestan, etc. and their modern derivatives have emerged. Their original vowel and consonant sounds have been worked out and an Indo-European comparative grammar has been attempted.

A comparison of the verb 'to bear' or 'to carry' in five different Indo-European languages would indicate that they are kins not only in terms of phonetics but also morphology.

English	***Sanskrit***	***Greek (Doric)***	***Latin***	***Old High German***	***Old Slavonic***
I bear	bharami	phero	fero	biru	bera
(thou bearest)	bharasi	phereis	fers	biris	berasi
he bears	bharati	pherei	fert	birit	beretu
we bear	bharamas	pheromes	ferimus	berames	beremu
you bear	bharata	pherete	fertis	beret	berete
they bear	bharanti	pheronti	ferunt	berant	beratu

Thus not only there are striking resemblances between words for six basic relations of a family i.e. father, mother, brother, sister, daughter and son or the numerals or the names of the trees and animals but in verb forms also there are striking similarities and the above examples indicate the three persons - first person, second person and third person, the singular and plural numbers of the verbs in all these five languages. They seem to be following the phonetic rules of Panini because in third person plural number, the '*anti*' sound is there in Greek, Latin and Old High German. Only in old Slavic this sound is not there as of course in Sanskrit also, there are some plural verb forms without *anti* sound. Observing such similarities, the English Judge Sir William Jones in 1786 gave his famous utterance which was the foundation stone of modern linguistics. In 1813, the English scholar Thomas Young coined the term Indo-European for this widely spread group of related languages and Indo Germanic is occasionally used in the same sense. As per Collin Renfrew following are the languages of Indo-European family :

Indo-European language family

Anatolian Italic Slavonic Armenian Tocharian

Hellenic Illyrian Germanic Baltic Celtic Indo-Iranian

Glottochronology

One other recent development in the field of historical linguistics is of great potential relevance to the historical understanding of particular languages and language groups. This is the approach known as glottochronology. The basic idea is a very simple one. It begins with the general observation that the greater the time-depth which separates the members of a language family from the point of separation from their common ancestor, the greater the degree of differentiation between them.

It was concluded that the average retention rate was 81 per cent per millennium. When the original word list was shortened to the hundred words listed above, the rate was adjusted to 86 per cent per millennium.

Based on this procedure, the glotto-chronologists Escalante and Swadesh have prepared the following diagram indicating the time of separation between various languages in centuries before 13th century BC.

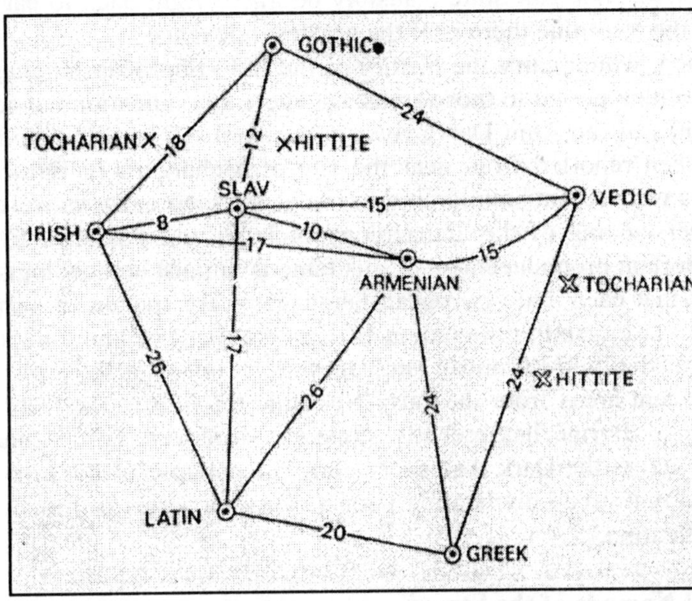

Figure : Relationships between different Indo-European languages based on glotto-chronological correlations. The numbers indicate the notional time in centuries prior to the 13th century BC when divergence between the pairs of languages took place

From the above diagram it would be seen that Gothic and Greek have separated from the Vedic Sanskrit some 2400 years before 13th Century which means Vedic is 2400 years older than the Greek and Gothic.

Renfrew has equated the first farmers of Europe with the Indo-European speaking people and as first points of settlements of these farmers and thus of Indo-European speakers, he takes as the Greece and Anatolia. He is convinced that "the equation between mixed cereal and livestock farming and the Indo-European languages is striking one."[9] He holds that the Indo-European languages of Europe can be traceable back to the first farmers of Greece who themselves have spoken an early form of Indo-European and the language of these first farmers in Greece around 6500 BC would be carried across the whole Europe.

The process of bringing a farming economy to Europe began somewhere shortly before 6000 BC in Crete and Greece. We should say that farming reached Greece sometime before 6500 BC. It had reached the Orkney Islands, at the northern tip of Scotland, and the rest of Europe also by about 3500 BC.

The Two Hypotheses of Renfrew

After a detailed discussion, Renfrew arrives at two hypotheses regarding the question of the origin of farming communities of Anatolia. His basic premise is "however the logic of the model identifies east Anatolia as part, although not necessarily all, of the early 'homeland' of people speaking a very early form of Indo-European, around 7000 BC.

Hypothesis A : Neolithic Aryas

Referring to the Mehargarh findings, he argues "In this way it might be argued that, from the very earliest farming times, as represented by Mehargarh and by other sites later, an early Indo-European language was spoken in the Indus Valley and in areas to the north and west..... there is no inherent reason why the people of the Indus Valley civilization should not already have been speaking an Indo-European language, the ancestor of the Rigveda. The arguments of Raymond and Bridget Allchin in favour of Indo-Aryan features back in the Harappan period could certainly be taken in support of Hypothesis A. Since the development of the civilization can quite plausibly be traced right back to early roots in the finds at Mehargarh, the origin of the Neolithic there is of the greatest relevance.

Hypothesis A, then, would carry the history of the Indo-European languages in north India and Iran back to the early Neolithic period in those areas. .... There are indications of settlements of the Indus Valley culture on the banks of the Amu Darya river in northern Afghanistan, and graves of bronze age Turkmenian type have been reported from near the site of Mehargarh in Baluchistan... Certainly the assumption that the Aryas were recent 'immigrants' to India, and their enemies were 'aborigines', has done much to distort our understanding of the archaeology of India and Pakistan. Finally, after a detailed discussion comes the important pronouncement of this famous linguist archaeologist Renfrew -

"This hypothesis that early Indo-European languages were spoken in north India with Pakistan and on the Iranian plateau at the sixth millennium BC has the merit of harmonizing symmetrically with the theory for the origin of the Indo-European languages of Europe. It also emphasizes the continuity in the Indus valley and adjacent areas from the early Neolithic through to the floruit of the Indus Valley civilization - a point which Jarrige has recently stressed. Moreover the continuity is seen to follow unbroken from that time across the Dark Age succeeding the collapse of the urban centres of the Indus Valley so that features of that urban civilization persist, across a series of transformations, to form the basis for later Indian civilization."[10]

Hypothesis B : Mounted Nomads of the Steppe

After discussing the stages of Central Asian Nomad Pastoralism and the primary pastoral economy, Renfrew concludes that - "One of the main ideas constituting Hypothesis B is that, with the development of chariotry and then of military horse riding, a new possibility for elite dominance emerged."

The Choice of Hypotheses : A Versus B

"At present it is not easy to see how one should choose between these two hypotheses. Both accept the major premise of this book that central and eastern Anatolia was the key area where an early form of Indo-European language was spoken before 6500 BC., From there the distribution of the language and its successors into Europe was associated with the spread of farming.

Hypothesis A suggests that the zone of early farmers speaking Proto-Indo-European extended east to northern Iran and even to Turkmenia at the outset. The spread of Indo-European speech to the south, to the Iranian plateau and to north India and Pakistan, can then be seen as part of an analogous dispersal, related to the demographic changes associated with the adoption of farming.

Hypothesis B does not take this view. It suggests instead that the crucial development for the eastern area was the development in the Eurasian steppes of nomad pastoralism, and that this took place first at the western end of the steppes. In this way, it was argued, the nomad pastoralists of the steppes spoke an Indo-European language at the outset. Their later dominance in Iran and in the Indus is then ascribed to their military effectiveness, based largely upon the use of the horse.

It is of course possible to blend these two hypotheses. Even if we accept Hypothesis A, it is still likely that the first steppe nomads did indeed speak Indo-European languages, and that their adaptation to the steppes first took place in the Ukraine."[11]

While the evidence advanced by Renfrew himself weighs in favour of hypothesis A i.e. Neolithic Aryas being the farming community present in Anatolia in 7th millennium BC, it can further we confirmed by the fact that there is ample evidence in Rgveda and Atharvaveda regarding the farming practices, the cultivation of rice, barley and wheat as we have discussed in connection with the Indus Valley civilization. There is also evidence of voyages and navigation by the Aryas to match perfectly with the requirement of the farming community that Renfrew is speaking about. Besides, neither the pastoral nomads of steppe nor the people of Anatolia can be conceived to speak Indo-European language at the outset. It is surprising why Renfrew has not taken into account the fact that no where in the world the Indo-European language can be spoken at the outset without first taking Indian element in it. Therefore, with the linkages so well established between the Neolithic Aryas of India and the farming community of Anatolia, the clear picture that emerges is that the Indo European language originated in Sapta Sindhu area of Rgveda and the first archaeological signs of this culture are seen in Mehargarh findings. From there the civilizational wave dispersed further west to Mesopotamia and then to Egypt, Anatolia and the Greece. The conjecture of Renfrew taking Anatolia as the centre and conceiving the dispersal of Indo-European speaking people first to the west Europe from Anatolia and then to the east upto India via Mesopotamia and Iran is not sustainable, for the simple reason that the Indo-European language can not originate in Anatolia and that the qualities that Renfrew prescribes to the farming community of Anatolia are all available in the same antiquity in the Rgvedic Aryans.

Besides, there can be blend of two hypothesis also as suggested by Renfrew himself. Inasmuch as there was an element of elite dominance, not of the pastoral nomads of steppe, but of warning Aryan princes who moved to the west with their knowledge of chariotry and horse riding. The evidence of a number of kings from Indian origin in Babylonia, Sumer and Egypt as also the names like Minos and Menes as the first kings of Crete and Egypt suggests that the princes from the Sapta Sindhu from India, moved to the west in different streams from time to time and carried with them the proto Vedic Sanskrit which is equivalent to the proto Indo-European. As we shall see, our literary history supports this premise. With them went the elite people in charge of administration and religious practices. Because the proto Vedic Sanskrit was the language of the ruling class and the elite, it established its roots in their western lands and gave birth to what is today called the Indo-European language.

Literary History

This was a period when the Krta Yuga was coming to a close. The pious, straight-forward and righteous man functioning perfectly within the obits of *rta* (dharma or righteousness) which was the hallmark of the entire Krta Yuga and because of which there was neither violence nor aggressiveness nor infringement upon the rights or property of others and hence there were no quarrels. This state of society has been very aptly described in Mahabharata in the Shanti Parva.

न वै राज्यं न राजाऽऽसीन्न च दण्डो न दाण्डिकः।
धर्मेणैव प्रजाः सर्वा रक्षन्ति स्म परस्परम्।। (महाभारत, शांतिपर्व, 59/14)

'There was neither the state nor a king; neither there was punishment or an authority imparting such punishment. The whole society was protecting each other on the basis of dharma i.e. righteousness.'

Like when the stars and the planets move in the respective orbits, there is no collision among them, similarly when people act according to their rights and duties perfectly under their orbit of dharma, there is no quarrel or animosity among them.

But with the laps of time this situation of extreme piousness started changing and the transition from the piousness to crookedness, from straightforwardness to deceit from satisfaction from ones own possession to the greed was being witnessed, necessitating the need of a ruler. This mental metamorphosis resulting in the changed behaviour of the human beings has also been aptly described in this Shanti Parva of Mahabharata.

Constantly functioning under the rigors of *rta* people started feeling uneasy and as is the nature of human beings they wanted to have more than the others which caused a veil of ignorance in their minds. Due to this ignorance they started the feeling of greed as also the covetousness. Due to these vices they did not no what is worthy of their action and what is not. With the result, the violence and the offences started.

तांस्तु कामवशं प्राप्तान् रागो नाम समस्पृशत्।
रक्ताश्च नाभ्यजानन्त कार्याकार्ये युधिष्ठिर।। (महाभारत, शांतिपर्व, 59/19)

Thus possessed of covetousness, the greed came in them and because of this greed they did not know what is worthy of doing and what is not.

The first result of this brewing uneasiness and growing adharma was the battle between the progeny of Druhyu, Angarsetu and Mandhata, the Iksavaku king - a battle which lasted for fourteen months and thus must have devastated many people. Harivansha Purana gives a glimpse of it :

द्रुह्योश्च तनयो राजन् बभ्रुः सेतुश्च पार्थिवः।
अंगारसेतुस्तत्पुत्रो मरुतां पतिरुच्यते।। 86।।
यौवनाश्वेन समरे कृच्छ्रेण निहतो बली।
युद्धं सुमहदस्यासीन्मासान्परि चतुर्दश।।87।।
अंगारस्य तु दायादो गान्धारो नाम भारत।
ख्यायते तस्य नाम्ना वैगान्धारविषयो महान्।।88।।[12]

O King! the son of Druhyu was Babhru and his son was Setu. The son of Setu was Angarsetu. He is called Marutpati also. This Angarsetu was killed in a fierce fight with Mandhata, the son of Yuvnasva of Iksavaku dynasty. This battle lasted for fourteen months and king Angarsetu fell along with his army. His son Gandhar ran away to the northern territories where he established a country by his own name i.e. Gandhar (modern Afghanistan).

This is the first movement from the main land Sapta Sindhu to outer territories.

Because of the feeling of possessiveness among the people of the society of this time, ethnic groups were formed and according to their capacity and power, they occupied various areas of Sapta Sindhu. Shivaji Singh has recognized these various ethnic groups of Rgvedic times very aptly "The 'Five Peoples' called Pancha-janah (RV, 1.89.10; 3.37.9; 59.8' etc.) are the most frequently mentioned group of ethnic units in the Rgveda. They are designated also as Pancha-jata (RV, 6.61.12), Pancha-manushah (RV, 8.9.2), Pancha-charshanyah (RV, 5.86.2; 7.15.2; 9.101.9), Pancha-krishtayah (RV, 2.2.10; 3.53.16; 4.38.10; etc.) and Pancha-kshitayah (RV, 1.7.9; 176.3; 5.35.2; etc). Some of these nomenclatures seem to refer to the developing stages of their social formation. Thus, while Charshanyah, from root char (to move), may point to their predominantly nomadic pastroal condition, krishtayah, from root krish (to cultivate), may indicate their settled agricultural situation. Similarly, kshitayah, from root kshi (to possess, to have power over), may express their still more developed status when these peoples had acquired territorial consciousness about the areas they occupied (Nandi 1986-87 : 156-57). The names of the ethnic units constituting this group of five peoples is not explictly stated in the Rgveda resulting in certain wild speculations by some ancient and medieval authorities (Cf. Aitareya Brahmana, 3.31; Yaska, Nirukta, 3.8; Sayana on RV, 1.7.9; etc.). However, on circumstantial evidence, modern scholars in general agree that the Anus, Druhyus, Purus, Yadus and Turvasas are the Rgvedic 'Five Peoples'. They are clearly mentioned together in one verse (RV, 1.108.8) and, substituing Yakshu for Yadu, in another hymn too (RV, 7.18). It is also clear that initially all these five peoples lived on the banks of the Saraswati (RV, 6.61.12) though later on in the Rgvedic period itself several of them moved to other areas.

The Bharatas have received maximum notice in the Rgveda though they are not included in the group of the 'Five Peoples' mentioned above. Though pitted against these 'Five Peoples', they were themselves a branch of the most important among them, the Purus. Their relationship with the Tritsus is not very certain. However, the data at hand suggests that the Tritsus were the royal family of the Bharatas. The Kusikas constituted another family of the Bharatas to which belonged Visvamitra, the former priest of the Bharata chief Sudas later replaced by Vasistha. The Bharatas are depicted as performing sacrifices on the banks of Saraswati, Apaya and Drishadvati (RV, 3.23.4) showing that they were living in the region between the rivers Saraswati and Yamuna, that is, in the Kurukshetra area."[13]

As far as archaeology of this period is concerned, S.P. Gupta observes that the Indus Saraswati civilization was preceded by a series of cultures from almost about 8000 BC. Broadly, these cultures are Pre-ceramic Neolithic cultures (8000-6000 BC) and Ceramic Neolithic cultures (6000-5000 BC)[14], where the settlements were found (site : Mehargarh) nuclear agricultural villages as well as extended villages with intensive agricultural pursuits, and long distance exchanges of commodities. According to S.P. Gupta, the earliest period of Mehargarh find[15] dates back to 8215-7215 BC.

Stage : 3 - The Conclusions

On the basis of detailed discussions in the forgoing paragraphs after examination of archaeological, archaeo-astronomical, religio-philosophical, linguistic and literary evidence, the following conclusions emerge regarding the Vedic chronology, the original homeland of the Indo-European language and the dispersal of Indo-Aryans from the Sapta Sindhu or *Brahmarshi Desha* to the West Asia, Egypt, Anatolia, Southern, Western and North-Western Europe : -

1. The Vedic period extends from 9th millennium B.C., the end of the last glacial period to 2000 B.C., the period of the drying up of Saraswati river and the Mahabharata War, coinciding with the declining phase of Vedic Harappan civilization with intermediatary stages, very clearly defined. There are reminiscences of earlier cycles, extending up to 27000 B.C. from 12800 B.C., the date from which the present cycle of Vedic civilization starts with the advent of Krta Yuga and first kings of Indian dynasties like Iksavaku, Pururva etc.

2. Sapta Sindhu or the Brahmavarta is the homeland, the u*rheimat* of Proto-Indo-European language and this language is none other than the Proto-Vedic Sanskrit which can be termed as *Urusprache*, the *Uruwolk* being the earliest Rgvedic people, inhabiting the area between Vedic river Saraswati and Drishadvati - the land known as Sapta Sindhu or Brahamarshi Desha. Proto-Vedic Sanskrit being the earliest existing Indo-European language with literature endorsing clear memories of the dispersal of the Rgvedic people towards the north and the west in the distant places, no other area in the world fits in the requirement of the homeland of the Proto-Indo-European.

3. The estimated period of the first dispersal of these Rgvedic people towards the west is about 7500 B.C., sometime after the battle of 10 kings mentioned in the Rgveda. From there Rgvedic people migrated to the various areas in the north and the west in three streams -

(i) the first stream as indicated above, was around 7500 B.C. after the Dasrajna battle (the battle of 10 kings) towards Anatolia, Crete and Greece. A little after this, Iranians must have separated from Vedic Indians. The Dasrajna battle suggests that successors of Anu dynasty went towards Iran, successors of Druhyu dynasty went towards West Asia and Turkey and successors of Turvasu, probably occupied the Syria and the Mesopotamia. This hypothesis fits well with hypothesis A of Renfrew who testifies presence of Indo-European speaking neolithic aryan farming community in Anatolia in 7000 B.C.

(ii) the second stream of dispersal took place around 4000 B.C. after the decline of Iksavaku dynasty. Agnivarna's grandson named Manu appears to have established the Egyptian first dynasty, its first ruler being Menes. Waddell identifies Menes of Egypt and Menos of Crete with Indian king Manasyu. But the proper identification taking the collateral circumstances and the time frame in account is with Manu, the grandson of Agnivarna - a fallen king of Iksavaku dynasty.

(iii) the third stream and probably bigger than the earlier two, took place around 2000 B.C. after the drying up of the Saraswati river and the Mahabharata War. The princess who were defeated in the Mahabharata War, the people who were annoyed because of the stoppage of Indra worship by Shri Krishna and the people who were affected by the drying up of Saraswati river and thus creating ecological imbalance must have fled to the west. They are the ones who established Mesopotamian, Sumer and Babylonian dynasties with the relations in Egypt.

4. The Aryan migration or Aryan invasion theory is completely baseless. Conjecture and motivated fraud perpetrated upon unwitting Indians who were a subject race to the English people. There is no indication what so ever in the entire vast Indian literature of any foreign origin or any reminiscence of a foreign land. The theatre of all happenings of Rgvedic civilization is squarely the Sapta Sindhu area of North West India and Aryan civilization a continuous civilization from the earliest Rgvedic days down to the present day - the Indus-Saraswati civilization included.

5. The ancient Rgvedic Aryans in 7th, 4th and 2nd millennium B.C. were the carriers of Proto Vedic Sanskrit in the distant lands of Crete, Greece, Anatolia, Sumer, Egypt and Babylonia because they ruled these countries during various periods. A foreign language easily establishes its roots in a country if the rulers of their country are the speakers of that language. By trade contacts alone, a language cannot spread. The class example of modern days is English which spread throughout the globe, because English people ruled the world for two centuries. Thus the root cause for the spread of Indo-European to the major

part of the world is because the Rgvedic Aryans ruled those areas in various periods of history and their language became the language of the ruling class. With the rulers went the aristocracy and the priestly class also which helped in the spread of their language. A branch of the Proto-Vedic Sanskrit went towards East also which accounts for Indo-European languages like Slavonic and Tocharian.

Shrikant Talageri has analyzed these language dispersals to the various parts of the globe connecting them with the dispersal of the people of Druhyu, Anu and Turvasu dynasties after the battle of 10 kings, so prominently mentioned in the Rgveda.

"The Indo-European languages, in the Original Homeland itself, had split into Satem and Kentum dialects which later developed into the present-day Satem and Kentum branches.

The Puranas, however, classify the Indo-European peoples to the north and west of the Vedic Aryans (the Purus) into only two categories : Anus and Druhyus. The facts therefore, suggest the following logical hypothesis : the Anus were probably the speakers of Satem dialects (and not just the Iranians), and the Druhyus were probably the speakers of Kentum dialects.

The present-day Indo-European languages are divided into nine branches of which four are Kentum : Germanic (or Teutonic), Italic, Celtic and Hellenic; and five are Satem : Indo-Iranian, Baltic, Slavonic, Thraco-Phrygian and Illyrian. But, as we have seen, the classification suggested by the puranas is slightly different : while we may roughly identify the early speakers of Kentum dialects with the Druhyus, and the early speakers of Satem dialects with the Anus, the Indo-Iranians do not fall into the Anu category in toto. While the Iranians were Anus, the Vedic Aryans were Purus, and the speakers of the ancestral forms of the Inner-Indo-European dialects were variously Yadus, Turvasus, Iksavakus, Pramsus, etc. Keeping this in mind, we must count only Iranian and not Indo-Iranian, as a branch of the Satem category.

All this confirms the validity of our interpretation of the Puranic and Vedic evidence.

This story of the dispersal of the different branches of Indo-European languages from India is, in fact, the only theory which accounts for every single factor.[16]

This conviction is borne out by sound scientific logic and not merely the conjecture born out of the indigenousness of a few Indian scholars. Collin Renfrew has a given a key to tackle this problem. We have applied that key to find out the solution of the problem with the little difference that we moved this key a little more eastward to come to the final conclusion. Renfrew applied the key only partially and his view is that the homeland was Anatolia. But the question is during that antiquity of 7000 B.C. was there any culture in Anatolia so rich that it could have created the language which is the mother to all Indo-European languages. Till now there is no evidence whatsoever for such a culture nor there is any literature from Anatolia which may suggests such a culture. On the other hand in Sapta Sindhu there is both the oldest, the most perfect, the most archaic Indo-European language of the world and the oldest and the richest literature of the world by way of Rgveda. Renfrew's key is "It seems likely then that the first Indo-European languages came to Europe from Anatolia around 6000 B.C., together with the first domesticated plants and animals, and that they were in fact spoken by the first farmers of Europe. That, I suggest, is the key to the solution of the Indo-European problem." Domesticated plants and animals as also quite improved farming is attested in the Rgvedic period and later the period of Yajurveda and Atharvaveda. Hence, the key of Renfrew applies squarely in the case of Sapta Sindhu i.e. North-West India. From out of the many derivations that Renfrew has made in his famous book "Archaeology and Language" he himself suggests the original homeland of Indo-European languages East of Anatolia either contiguous with it or otherwise ..... This hypothesis that early Indo-European languages were spoken in north India with Pakistan and on the Iranian plateau at the sixth millennium BC has the merit of harmonizing symmetrically with the theory for the origin of the Indo-European languages of Europe. It also emphasizes the continuity in the Indus valley and adjacent areas from the early Neolithic through to the floruit of the Indus Valley civilization - a point which Jarrige has recently stressed. Moreover the continuity is seen to follow unbroken from that time across the Dark Age succeeding the collapse of the urban centres of the Indus Valley so that features of that urban civilization persist, across a series of transformations, to form the basis for later Indian civilization."[17]

Renfrew himself admits that first farmers of Anatolia did not develop farming there, but there was some advance beginning further in the East beyond Turkey. Here he has all but indicated the possibility of the development of Indo-European farming community in India when we compare this opinion of his with the findings that he has made in relation to Indus-Valley civilization and Mehargarh findings. He says, " It is likely that the first farmers of west Anatolia did not develop farming there, on the spot, from wild prototype species, and we should imagine the wave of advance beginning rather further to the east, perhaps in the Konya Plain, where the site of Catal Hyyuk is located, or further east still."[18]

From the whole bulk of evidence, archaeological, archaeo-astronomical, linguistic, mythological, theological etc. inescapable conclusions that emerge is that Sapta-Sindhu of the North West India is the *Urheimat* of the Indo-European languages and early Rgvedic people are the *Urvolk* who spoke proto-Vedic Sanskrit which is their *Ursprache*.

References

1. Colin Renfrew, *Archaeology and Language*, Penguin Books, 1987, Page 12
2. Ibid, page 18
3. Dr. Mohan Gupta, Astronomical Observations in Later Samhitas, Brahamanas and Sutra Literature; in *A Golden Chain of Civilizations : Indic, Iranic, Semitic and Hellenic upto c. 600 B.C.*, pp. 779-782
4. *Pragdhara* : Journal of the U.P. State Archaeology Department, 2002-2003 No. 13, p.37.
5. Dayanath Tripathi : Cosmogonic myths of Indo-Europeans, in *A Golden Chain of Civilizations : Indic, Iranic, Semitic and Hellenic upto c. 600 B.C.*, p. 477.
6. Ibid, pp.479-480.
7. Ibid, pp. 482-483.
8. Govind Chandra Pande (2001) : *Veic Sanskriti* (Allahabad : Loka Bharti), p. 39
9. Colin Renfrew, *Archaeology and Language*, Penguin Books , p.152
10. Ibid, p. 196
11. Ibid, p. 205
12. *Harivansa Purana*, Gita Press Gorakhpur, Samvat 2044, p. 116
13. Shivaji Singh, quoted above, p. 160.
14. S.P. Gupta, *The Indus Saraswati Civilization*, p. 8.
15. Ibid, p. 22.
16. Shrikant Talgiri, *The Aryan Invasion Theory : A Reappraisal*, 2003, p. 331-332
17. Renfrew Colin, *Archaeology and Language*, quoted above, p. 170-171.
18. Renfrew Colin, *Archaeology and Language*, quoted above, p. 170-171.

62

A CULTURAL-PSYCHOLOGICAL ORIENTATION TO SELF-UNDERSTANDING

Girishwar Misra *

When we have passed beyond individualising, then we shall be real persons.

- Sri Aurobindo

Preoccupation with various aspects of self is a common feature of everyday life. Wes spend a great deal of waking time in engagement with self. But people's ways of experiencing, presenting and expressing self are quite diverse and so are the ways of differentiating between the notions of self and other, me and they. The notion of "I" (a subject or agent, in a physical, social and or spiritual world!) becomes critical to our existence. In the limited sense of ego the sense of self confines people to his or her body, one's possessions and things that enhance this kind selfhood. There are very few people who strive to go beyond this limited notion of self and venture to relate to society and address the broader concerns. Professor Daya Nath Tripathi is one of them. During his academic career spanning over half a century Professor Tripathi, a reputed scholar from Allahabad school of cultural and historical studies, has endeavored not only to enrich the disciplinary discourse but has been a great source of inspiration to numerous students, colleagues and friends. He has shaped their lives and substantially contributed towards building many academic institutions. His efforts toward promotion of the spirit of autonomy and practice of dialogue in the world of academia are remarkable. I have been privileged to be associated with Professor Tripathi for a long time as a younger colleague. I have observed him with great admiration in the course of Professor Tripathi's leadership in academic, social and administrative spheres. As a token of appreciation and gratitude to him I take this opportunity to offer some thoughts on the notion of selfhood which constitutes a key facet of life at individual and group levels.

Facets of Selfhood

The study of self constitutes a major part of intellectual analysis of self at global level. It is present in almost all the philosophical traditions. Scholars have opted for diverse positions while thinking about selfhood. These positions range from self as an illusion (e.g. Buddhism's *Anatta*) to the post modernist

---

* This paper draws from an earlier work of the author entitled "Construction of self: A cross-cultural perspective" published in Kiran Rao (Ed.) (2007). *Mindscapes: Global Perspectives on Psychology and Mental Health* (pp.32-42). Bangalore: National Institute of Mental Health and Neurosciences.

view of multiple selves. In between there are positions of monism and dualism. The self-views in Indian thought traditions constitute a major part of various texts of various schools such as Vedanta, Mimansa, Samkhya, Yoga, Sufism, Buddhism, Jainism, Charvak, and Sikhism. They document a multifaceted and complex view of self which is beyond the scope of present deliberation. Most of the accounts of self, however, appear to draw a distinction between the 'bodily self' and a higher self like *'Atman'*. This implies that self is not only a body centered and personal phenomenon but has transpersonal, collective and spiritual aspects too. It is also noted that the prevailing self-related discourses often endorse a more inclusive but non-physical/spiritual notion of self as true/real self and an ideal state of being which is positive. The idea of self or conceptual self often forms the basis of self as an experiential phenomenon. The ideas of self are often rooted in the texts, artifacts, customs and other practices prevalent in the cultural region.

Interestingly enough diverse cultures promote different views of self and help articulating ways of partitioning the world of experience between self and non self. Congruent with the culturally preferred ways of selfhood cultures organize the life world. This brief analysis tries to share current understanding of self in the context of cultural diversity It argues that the structure and processes of self are cultural products. The cultural practices are not only sources of personal and social identity but also operate as strategies for managing self, designing its relationship with the rest of the world and projecting the same. As we will notice in the following discussion the psychological essence of self is an outcome of a reflective dialogical relationship between the subject (I) and object (Me).

Within the modern discipline of psychology the first serious analysis of self was attempted by William James (1890). Viewing it a "puzzling puzzle" William James noted that *"self is the center of the psychological universe and is the lens through which other aspects of the world are perceived"*. Subsequently the notion of self was marginalized under the impact of mechanistic, objective and quantitative framework of behaviorism. Being philosophical 'self' was held less appropriate for objective and empirical investigations privileged in the course of behaviorist analysis. While sociological theorists like Cooley, Mead, Blumer, Goffman and the Neo Freudians like Adler, Horney, and Sullivan did develop various perspectives on self, it was only during the last quarter of twentieth century that self could resurface as a central theme in the mainstream psychology.

The Current Foci in Psychological Research on Self

The revival of interest in the study of self owes to many factors including interest in the role of self-esteem, cognitive revolution, and development of several quantitative measures of various self-dispositions. The current interest of psychologists in the study of self is following two lines of research emphasizing cognitive and motivational-emotional processes, respectively (Leary & Tangney, 2007). In particular the culturally engaged psychological studies have provided key impetus for going beyond Euro-American perspectives on self (see Bruner, 1990; Gergen, Gulerce, Lock & Misra, 1996; Misra & Gergen, 1993).

While going through current psychological literature one is impressed by the abundance of self-related constructs (e.g. self-awareness, self-consciousness, self-construal, self-categorization, self-disclosure, self-determination, self-esteem, self-enhancement, self-efficacy, self-monitoring, self-presentation, self-reference, self-schema and self-worth). The psychologists are examining the various facets of self including its contents and processes as well as their role in regulating various psychological processes. Underlying these constructs is a causally active and somewhat unitary self-structure. It is often treated as free, autonomous, conscious, morally responsible, author of action, and agency enjoying certain rights. To some self is nothing but continuity of one's memory of mental events while others hold it as a prewired feature of human brain. Some scholars identify and acknowledge the notions of private, public and collective selves. The notion of possible self, interpersonal self and remembered self have also generated interest among the researchers.

In contrast to the above analysis with a focus on individualized notion of self the cultural approach looks at self as a product of the membership in some local cultural community and through a history of symbolically mediated unique and shared experiences of that group. It assumes that the nature and experience of self depends to a large degree on person's early socialization, peer interaction and subsequent experiences. Our perception and experiences of self, therefore, are colored by culture(s) that we belong to. The prevalent cultural dialogues, myths, narratives and other social discourses inform the way self is described, responded to and evaluated. Thus cultural experiences programme the ways of representing and experiencing selfhood. It may however be noted that while culture does supply the scripts how to be and how to participate in the personal and social worlds people too are active agents and constituents of culture in their own right (Oyserman & Markus, 1993).

The Emerging Perspective

As indicated in the preceding discussion the notion of self may be characterized as a multifaceted, dynamic system that emerges in socio-cultural processes and subsequently regulates and mediates behavior at individual and group levels. It acts as an anchor and affords and constraints our behavior, perceptions, feelings, values and meanings held by the people. However, in the course of increasing use of the term self has acquired several meanings and functions. The term 'self' is also used independently or interchangeably with other constructs such as 'total person', 'personality', 'experiencing subject', 'beliefs about oneself', and 'executive agent' (see Leary & Tangney, 2003) and has been assigned different roles in conceptualizing psychological processes. Indeed its genesis in the social context and functions as knower (*Jnata)*, actor or doer (*Karta)* and experiencer (*Bhokta)* have led to much theorization and research (Paranjpe, 1998). It is not only an object of knowledge but also as the subject of experience. It is "*a mental capacity that allows an animal to take itself as the object of its own attention and to think consciously about itself*" (Leary & Tangney, 2003, p. 08). This view takes into account the basic quality of self- the human ability to take oneself as the object of one's attention and thought. The experience of self primarily involves the relationship between the subject and the object or the 'I' and 'me'.

The sense of self awareness (I) and its mental representations (Me), therefore, provide the building blocks for the construct of self. The core of self appears to be the process for self reflection which makes 'self' as object of attention and deliberates consciously about the same. Its domain has fuzzy boundaries where diverse concerns originating in different disciplines and schools of thought meet and interact. The issue of continuity and flux in self-experience is now made more complex in the post modern view of multiple selves.

It may be noted that becoming aware of oneself and engaging with self- reflection is central to the lay understanding of human behavior. Such a reflexive consciousness is treated as core of being human. The nature of human nature implies and issues of morality, ethics and responsibility need our acknowledgement of selfhood. This self reflexive capacity, however, is not independent of the cultural meanings and practices within which people grow and develop. Human life is substantially organized by the set of cultural understanding and our cultural participation that are embedded in culturally particular meanings and practices. It is therefore, not surprising to find that the ontologies and ideologies of self vary across cultures. The way of being a person is not a natural category but depends on cultural models of personhood and person's role in personal and social life (Shweder & Bourne, 1984).

Capturing the experiences of selfhood (e g. Process, structure and contents) in its varied symbolic constructions across cultures is a huge task. It is more so because psychology has not been much responsive to the historical and cultural boundedness of self and other psychological processes. However, gradually realization of the relevance of culture is taking place due to increasing globalization of economy, acceptance of multiculturalism, and increasing assertion of cultural identity. The evidence is emerging which indicates that self processes may differ across cultures and shape psychological processes in diverse ways. In the following section an overview of the learning from culturally engaged psychological analyses is presented.

Culturally Grounded Self Views: Independent Vs. Interdependent

It is now accepted that culture and self are inextricably intertwined and they mutually constitute each other. The cultural perspective is open to alternative assumptions about agency and basis of coherence and units of personality. From a cultural perspective the idea of an individualized, separate, and distinct self is a Euro-American construction. In this tradition individuals are treated as separate, autonomous and self contained entities with well defined boundaries. Such a view does not help to understand non-Western construal of self. The collectivist cultures tend to emphasize group orientation, are sensitive to the goals and needs of others, and show readiness to cooperate and maintain permeable boundaries (Markus & Kitatyama, 1991). In rent years the individualistic / independent and relational / interdependent models of self construal have received increasing attention. While former maintains separateness and indivisibility of self the latter holds that the two are inseparable from the surrounding context and people. They are held as continuous. As a result the individual experiences 'self-in-relation-to-other'. People find themselves as meaningful in terms of their capacity to relate to others or the relationships of which they are parts. While Western view emphasizes on personal choice and freedom the non Western view emphasizes on duties, roles and obligations. Research in the Western cultural settings has often shown that the individual is a separate, unconnected indivisible entity. This notion has its genesis in the Cartesian dualism, individual reason, free will and capitalism. It projects the unified, integrated, autonomous, and objective view of self. The same guides the child rearing practices, and modes of relating to environment and community.

In contrast, the interdependent mode of self-construal questions the decontextualized individualistic view of self and locates it in an encompassing framework that stresses on the social and spiritual/divine aspects of human existence. Such a model is prevalent in many Asian countries including Japan, Korea, China and India (Chao, 1995; Cousins, 1989; Kapur & Misra, 2005; Mascolo, & Bhatia, 2002; Misra, 2001; Roland, 1988; Singelis, & Sharkey, 1995). It is held that self is inseparable from the surrounding context and people. Accordingly the goal of self development is not individuation but of dissolving the self/other boundary and expanding the boundary of selfhood. Such models assume that an individual is an open system which communicates with other selves. To realize selfhood one is not to express the internal attributes but to connect, identify and become part of group, community and divinity. Such a non-egoistic perspective demands developing strategies of self-control and self-discipline. In this sense Patanjali's Yoga Sutras pronounce that the goal of Yoga is controlling and regulating the mental functioning (*Yogaschittavritti nirodhah).*

It may be noted that the independent and interdependent modes of self construal closely correspond to individualism / collectivism syndrome of values. People in the individualist cultures often give priority to their personal goals even if they conflict with the goals of an important in-group. Individualism is very high in the United States and generally high in English speaking countries (Hofstede, 1980). In collectivist cultures, the self is defined in terms of membership in in-groups which influences a wide range of social behaviors. Collectivists are usually organized hierarchically and tend to be concerned with the results of their actions on members of their in-group. They share resources with in-group member, and feel interdependent and involved in their lives. A relationship orientation is very strong in them. They tend to follow social norms and maintain normative or obligatory relationships (Sinha, 1990; Sinha & Verma, 1987; Sinha & Kanungo, 1997).

In collectivist cultures the self is often viewed as connected with others. People tend to pursue the goal of interdependence. They recognize that one's behavior is a joint achievement, and organized by what the actor perceives to be the thoughts, feelings, and actions of others in the relationship and seeing oneself as part of a network of encompassing social relations. Individuals, therefore, must be receptive and responsive to the needs, expectations, hopes and desires of relevant others. Thus in an interdependent mode self/other boundary has to be dissolved because the goal of selfhood is to fit in with others / context and become part of interpersonal relationship. The notion of control therefore is a distributed notion and involves self-discipline and tolerance, instead of ability to influence others.

Some Empirical Studies of Indian Self

The Indian notion of self appears to be continuous with others and shares their space and is in immediate relation with them. The individual develops through participation in the unity of all things. This demands emphasis on diverse and contrasting goals including engagement as well as dissociation and detachment. The inter-personal behavior mainly depends on the role occupied by the person, place of interaction and relationship with the people. Kakar (1978) has observed that the basis of relationships is mutual caring, involvement and emotional affinity. The empirical investigations often point to greater prevalence of social identity (see Dhawan, et al. 1995; Srivastava & Misra, 1997) and contextuality (Lalljee & Angelova, 1995) in self-descriptions. Misra and Giri (1995) observed that interdependent as well as independent both kinds of self-construal co-exist among Indians.

A number of researchers have noticed that there is considerable degree of tolerance for dissonance and coexistence of disparate elements in the Indian world view and the experience of self (Boss, 1964; Marriott, 1976; Ramanujan, 1990; Sinha & Tripathi, 1994; Sinha, et. al. 2001; Sinha & Pandey, 2007; Varma, 2004). Mascolo, Misra and Rapisardi (2004) found that individual and relational concepts of self were present in Indian as well as American samples. The cultural differences arose in specific ways the two notions are constructed. We, therefore, need to look within as well as between cultural differences in self construal.

The preceding overview of studies indicates that the Indian view on self is not based on a firm boundary between self and non self (object). Its continuity with other things occupying the universe broadens the deliberations about selfhood. In contrast to the Western psychological view in which every thing is defined with reference to self, the Indian view appears to be 'indexical'. The Indian notion of "self is not an entity existing independently from the relationships and contexts in which it is presented. It is constituted by social interactions, contexts, and relationships" (Landrine, 1997). The indigenous Indian perspective on self, however, goes beyond the dichotomies and offers an alternative model.

The Indigenous Indian View

The complexity of self and the process of self understanding in the Indian context may be illustrated by examining the way the Atman or inner self is held as the real self. It transcends the empirical self that is socially embedded, context sensitive and subject to continuous change. Spiritual interiority and social duty both occupy an important place. The individual (Jivatman) is construed in terms of structure with five sheaths (Panch Koshas). They include the body, the senses, the mind, thinking organ (manas), or ego (ahamkara), intellect or reflection (buddhi) and finally the Atman. The self consists of Atman which is a spiritual in nature. The Atman is the realization of one's true or essential self. Also, it is indistinguishable from absolute reality called Brahman, which is not only ubiquitous but also free of both form and matter.

Owing to ignorance (Avidya) Atman is fused with the material elements and we misidentify ourselves with acquired identities (Upadhis) and develop attachment with them. The realization of Atman (moksha or freedom/bliss) demands lifelong and effortful process. The Atman is a non-material or metaphysical self, as opposed to the material, and empirical self, which is placed hierarchically lower than the metaphysical self (Bharati, 1985). The empirical self or ego (Ahamkara) is a source of bondage and therefore needs to be transcended.

The goal is to expand the empirical self and identify with the higher and more inclusive spiritual self. This is treated as the chief pathway towards self realization. The Indian world view organizes the stages of life (Ashramas) accordingly. But concern for transcendent spiritual reality is combined with the web of social life. Thus Dharma (righteous action) Artha (wealth), Kama (pleasure) and Moksha (spiritual emancipation) are considered equally important goals of life. The primary aspect of dharma is performing the duties that pertain to one's stage in life. The social responsibilities toward the other are mandatory rather than optional. Through devotional practice Bhakti, involving yoga, meditation and righteous action, one may cultivate the awareness that one's true self is indistinguishable from the transcendental Brahman. This discourse necessitates going beyond the dichotomy of independent and interdependent selves and move towards relational and encompassing models of self conceptions.

Roland (1988) argues that the notion of detachment from immediate emotional connection, a theme central to Hindu spirituality, in some sense marks out the spiritual self as a realm of autonomy within the larger Hindu experience of unity. Renunciation during adulthood stage in the service of spiritual discipline seems to be a step in the loosening of the personal attachments and obligations and a reaching toward personal autonomy in the spiritual sphere (Collins,1991; Roland, 1996).

In the Indian tradition considerable emphasis has been given on self discovery and self realization. In the modern period Sri Aurobindo has made a serious attempt in this direction. A brief account of his perspective based on Dalal (2001) is presented in the following section.

Self Discovery: An Outline of the Integral Vision of Sri Aurobindo

Sri Aurobindo states that the way we know about ourselves presents very limited picture, something like "*a bubble on the ocean of our existence*". It is through spiritual discipline of yoga that we become aware of the complex nature of self or being which has many parts. He identifies two systems: one is concentric and the other is vertical. The concentric system comprises of outer being, inner being and innermost being. The first two have three parts i.e. mental, vital and physical. The vertical system has several levels of consciousness below and above ordinary consciousness. They are: *The Inconcient, The Subconscient, The Physical, The Vital, Mind, Higher Mind, Illumined Mind, Intuition, Overmind, Supermind, and Sachchidanand.* The movement along these levels of being involves evolution. Sri Aurobindo says 'life is the first step of this release of consciousness; mind is the second; but the evolution does not finish with mind, it awaits a release into something greater, a consciousness which is spiritual and supra mental. 'In the ordinary condition the Self is bound and governed by its instrumental nature–body, life and mind and fail to realize the awareness of Purusha, witness or Sakshi'. Sri Aurobindo further states that ' *the highest truth , the integral self knowledge is not to be gained by this self-blinded leap into the Absolute but by a patient transit beyond the mind into the Truth-Consciousness where the infinite can be known, felt, seen, experienced in all the fullness of its unending riches.*' It is by detaching himself from all identifications with mind, life and body one can get back from his ego to the consciousness of the true Individual, the Jivatman, who is the real possessor of mind, life and body. Looking back from this Individual to that of which it is the representative and conscious figure, he can get back to the transcendent consciousness of pure Self, absolute Non-Being, three poises of the same eternal Reality. Sri Aurobindo states that 'the true spiritual individual appears in its complete truth when we get rid of the ego and our false separative sense of individuality, realize our oneness with the transcendent and Cosmic Divine and with all beings'. While self realization of the *Atman* (real self) may not be a common practice for every Indian it does inform the mind set that works against ego (*Ahamkara*) and creates space for others through self discipline.

Concluding Comments

The present analysis suggests that while Indians are collectivistic and indicate more interdependence they also evince strands of individualistic tendencies and spiritual orientation. The indigenous notions of self available in texts, narratives and in-depth case studies indicate the need for a more comprehensive and complex treatment of selfhood. The relationship of self and culture is becoming more and more complex as the coexistence of alternate cultural demands is becoming a hard reality. A complete and thorough understanding demands a vision which recognizes the whole range of our being covering all the layers of existence including the outer being, inner being and the innermost being is necessary. So far the attention has been confined to the outer and egoistic dimensions. This over concern has led to increasing degree of conflict, violence, stress and anxiety. Envisioning self as a process of overcoming such tendencies and opting for an expanded or encompassing view appears to be more viable option. To this end the Indian insights deserve greater attention.

References

Bharati, A. (1985). The self in Hindu thought and action. In G. Marsella, A.J. DeVos, & F.L.K Hsu (Eds.), *Culture and self.* New York: Tavistock.

Brunner, J.B. (1990). *The acts of meaning*. Cambridge Mass: Harvard University Press.

Chao, R. K. (1995). Chinese and European American cultural models of the self reflected in mother's childrearing beliefs. *Ethos, 23,* 328-354.

Collins, A. (1991). From Brahma to a blade of grass: Towards an Indian Self-psychology. *Journal of Indian Philosophy, 19*, 143-189.

Cousins, S.D. (1989). Culture and selfhood in Japan and the U.S. *Journal of Personality and Social Psychology, 56,* 124-131.

Dalal, A.S. (2001). *A greater psychology*. Pondicherry: Sri Aurobindo Ashram.

Desai, P., & Collins, A. (1986). Selfhood in context: Some Indian solutions. In M.I. White & S. Pollak (Eds.). *The culture transition* (pp. 261-290). London: Routledge & Kegan paul.

Dhawan, N., Roseman, I.J., Naidu, R.K., Thapa, K. & Rettek, S.I. (1995). Self-concepts across two cultures: India and the United States. *Journal of Cross Cultural Psychology, 26,* 606-621.

Gergen, K. J., Gulerce, A., Lock, A. & Misra, G.(1996). Psychological science in cultural context. *American Psychologist, 51,* 496-503.

Hermans, H.J.M. (2001). The dialogical self: Toward a theory of personal and cultural positioning. *Culture and Psychology, 7,* 243-281.

Hofstede, G. (1980). *Cultures' consequences*. Beverly Hills, CA: Sage.

James, W.C. (1980). *The principles of psychology.* Cambridge, M.A.: Harvard University Press (Reprinted 1983).

Kakar, S. (1978). *The inner world: A psycho-analytic study of childhood and society in India.* New Delhi: Oxford University Press.

Kapur, Preeti & Misra, G. (2003). Image of self in the Sikh community: Continuity of the core and global presence. *Psychology and Developing Societies, 15,1,*103-116

Lalljee, M., & Angelova, R. (1995). Person descriptions in India, Britain, and Bulgaria, *Journal of Cross Cultural Psychology, 26,* 645-657.

Landrine, H. (1992). Clinical implications of cultural differences: The referential versus the indexical self. *Clinical Psychology Review, 12,* 401-415.

Leary, M.R. (2007). Motivational and emotional aspects of self. *Annual Review of Psychology, 58,* 317-344.

Leary, M.R., & Tangney, J.P. (2003). The self as an organizing construct in behavioral and social sciences. In M.R. Leary & J.P.Tangney (Eds), *Handbook of self and identity* (pp.3-14) . New York: Guilford.

Markus, H.R., & Kitayama, S. (1991) Cultural and the self: Implications for cognition, emotion and motivation. *Psychological Review, 98,* 224-253.

Marriott, K. (Ed.) (1990), *India through Hindu Categories,* New Delhi: Sage.

Marsella, A., De Vos, G., & Gsu, F.L.K. (1985). Culture and self. In M.H. Bond (Ed.) *The Cross-cultural challenge to social psychology* (pp.266-281). Beverly Hills, CA: Sage.

Mascolo,M.F. , & Bhatia, S.(2002). The dynamic construction of Culture, Self, and social relations. *Culture and Developing Societies,14,* 55-92.

Mascolo, M.F.,Misra, G. & Rapisardi, C.(2004) Individual and Relational Conceptions of Self in India and the United States. *Culture and Developing Selves: Beyond Dichotomization, 104,* 9-26.

Misra, G. (2001). Culture and self: Implications for psychological inquiry. *Journal of Indian Psychology, 19(1&2), 1-20*

Misra, G., & Gergen, K.J. (1993). *On the place of culture in Psychological Science, International Journal of Psychology, 28,* 225-243.

Misra, G., & Giri, R. (1995). Is Indian Self predominantly interdependent? *Journal of Indian Psychology, 11,* 15-19.

Oyserman, D., & Markus, H.R. (1993). The sociocultural self. In J. Suls (Ed.), *Psychological perspectives on the self* (Vol. 4, pp. 187-220). Hillsdale, NJ: Erlbaum.

Paranjpe, A.C. (1998). *Self and identity in modern psychology and Indian thought.* New York: Plenum.

Ramanujan, A.K. (1990). Is there an Indian way of thinking? An informal essay. In M. Marriott (Ed.) *India through Hindu categories, New Delhi: Sage.*

Roland, A. (1988). *In Search of self in India and Japan: Towards a cross cultural psychology.* Princeton, NJ: Princeton University Press.

Roland, A. (1996). Cultural pluralism and psychoanalysis: The Asian and North American experience. *New York: Routledge.*

Roland, A. (2001). Another voice and position: Psychoanalysis across civilizations. Culture & Psychology, *7(3), 311-321.*

Shweder, R.A. (1991). Thinking through culture. *Cambridge Mass: Harvard University Press.*

Shweder, R.A., & Bourne, F. (1984). Does the concept of the person vary cross-culturally? In R.A. Shweder & R.A. Levine (Eds.), *Culture theory: Essays on mind self and emotion,* (pp. 158-199). New York: Cambridge University Press.

Singelis, T.M. & Sharkey, W.F. (1995). *Culture, self construal, and embarrrasability. Journal of Cross-cultural Psychology, 26,* 622-644.

Sinha, D., & Tripathi, R.C. (1994). Individualism in a collectivist culture: A case of co-existence of opposites. In U.Kim, H.C. Triandis, C. Kagitcibasi S. Choi & G. Yoon (Eds.). *Individualism and collectivism: Theory, method and applications* (pp. 123-136). Thousand Oaks: Sage Publication.

Sinha, D., & Naidu, R. K. (1994).Multilayerd hierarchical structure of self and not self: The Indian perspective. In A.M. Bouvy, F.J.R. van de vijver, P. Voski, & P. Schmitz (Eds.) *Journey in to cross-cultural psychology* (pp.41-49). Lisse: Swets & Zeitlinger.

Sinha, J.B.P. (1990). The salient Indian values and their socio-ecological roots. *Indian Journal of Social Sciences, 3,* 477-488.

Sinha, J.B.P., & Kanungo, R.N. (1997). Context sensitivity and balancing in organizational behavior. *International Journal of Psychology, 32,* 93-105.

Sinha, J.B.P.; Sinha, T.N., Verma, J., & sinha, R.B.N. (2001). Collectivism coexisting with individualsism : An Indian Scenario. *Asian Journal of Social Psychology, 4,* 133-145.

Sinha, J.B.P., & Verma, J. (1987). Structure of collectivism. In C. Kagitcibasi (Ed.), *Growth and progress in cross-cultural psychology* (pp. 123-129). Lisse: Swets & Zeitlinger.

Sinha , J.B.P., & Pandey, A. (2007). Indian's Mindsets and the conditions that evoke them. *Psychological Studies, 52,* 1-11.

Srivastava, R. & Misra, G. (1997). Self construal, control and eastern orientation. Unpublished manuscript, Department of Psychology, University of Delhi.

Tangney, J.P., Baumeister, R.F., & Boone, A.L. (2004). High Self-Control Predicts Good Adjustment, Less Pathology, Better Grades, and Interpersonal Success. *Journal of Personality, 72,* 271-324.

Taylor, Charles (1989). *Sources of the self: The making of the modern identity.* Cambridge: Cambridge University Press

Triandis, H.C. (1989). The self and social behavior in differing cultural contexts. *Psychological Review, 96,* 506-520.

Triandis, H.C. (1995). *Individualism and collectivism.* Boulder, CO: Westview Press.

Tripathi, R. C. (1988). Aligning development to values in India. In D. Sinha & H. S. R. Kao (Eds.), *Social values and development: Asian perspectives* (pp. 315-332). New Delhi: Sage.

63

A STUDY OF HUMAN EVOLUTION AND MIGRATION ON THE BASIS OF ANALYSIS OF DEOXYRIBONUCLEIC ACID (DNA)

Ram Rudra Shukla

I am honored to contribute to this commemorative collection of articles alongside noted historians and archaeologists of India. While I am a biochemist by profession, I have an interest in history, particularly in interpreting and analyzing the relationship between Science and Hindu religion and history.

I got married to Aparna, Prof. Tripathi's eldest daughter in 1980 just after completing my M. Sc. in Biochemistry. A few years after, I left India to pursue my post-doctoral research in the USA and later decided to settle there as well. During these years, my interactions with my father-in-law occurred when I visited Gorakhpur or when he visited the USA. However, in the last decade with the advent of technology, particularly videophone calls, the frequency of our interactions has increased. This has also allowed us to have frequent discussions on varying academic interests.

I have been most impressed by my father-in-law's quest for learning, particularly regarding new technology. Among his other strong attributes are his discipline to follow a strict schedule and his determination. In my opinion these qualities have empowered him to achieve success in both professional and personal endeavors. When I was invited to write for this volume I was faced with a dilemma as I am neither a historian nor an archaeologist. However, I recounted one of the discussions we had recently regarding his participation in a conference at the Banaras Hindu University on archeology and evolution. As a non-historian I thought I could review molecular biology methods used in predicting human evolution and migration in simple language. I hope the following discussion will help historians and archeologists understand molecular basis of evolution.

How did the first human civilization begin in India? Are modern Indians indigenous to India or did they migrate from other continent(s)? Another question that is repeatedly asked is whether the caste system was a part of Indian civilization from its beginning or was it introduced at a later point by societies migrating to India? Archaeologists and anthropologists have tried to answer these questions by using traditional tools such as the excavation of ancient sites, artifact analysis, fossil study and human behavioral studies. Additionally, with the discovery of De-oxy ribonucleic acid (DNA) in the 1950s, the chemical basis of life, and the sequencing of the human genome in the last decade, the sequences of human DNA has been used to answer these same questions. The goal of this article is to provide a review of DNA based methods that are used to answer some of the questions. As I am not a historian or archaeologist, I will limit my discussion to the scientific techniques and leave anthropological and historical considerations to the experts in these fields. At the end of the article I will provide a list of recent reviews that would provide more in depth analysis of these methods.

DNA is the chemical basis of life for all living organisms, including humans. It is the blue-print of life, growth and differentiation as the information stored in its sequence is specific to every organism. The DNA of almost all organisms is made up of four building blocks- A (adenine), T (thiamine), G (guanine), and C (cytosine). These building blocks are linked to one another like beads of a pearl string andthe order of these building blocks in DNA is specific to an organism. Furthermore, two strings of these building blocks are entwined with each other to form a specific structure called the double helix. An organism's DNA could have 100,000 to several billion building blocks. To stabilize such a large string and pack them efficiently into a cell, the string of building blocks is bound to other biological molecules such as proteins and carbohydrates and form structures called chromosomes. Specific regions of a chromosome act as templates for copying the genetic information contained in these regions to produce a message that is then translated into proteins which perform all the metabolic functions of a cell and in turn of an organism. These regions are called genes. The number of chromosomes in a cell isfixed and when the cell divides its chromosomes are duplicated so that same number of chromosomes is constant in thenew cells. As the complexity of an organism's structure increases, the number of genes and corresponding proteins increases too.

In last seven decades since DNA was discovered as the genetic material, the chemical and physical properties of DNA, its stability and characteristics have been extensively studied. DNA has been isolated from organisms that grow under extreme conditions such as in boiling water or in subzero temperatures. DNA has also been isolated from human tissue samples such as from bones and tissues of human remains frozen or from archaeological artifacts that are centuries old such as from mummified humans. These studies have demonstrated that DNA is stable even under extreme conditions.A human cell has about 3 billion building blocks and may have about 20,000-25,000 genes.

Although they do not produce proteins, the regions of DNA that do not form genes do carry out other functions and may add to the complexity and specificity of cell structure and function. When a cell divides to produce progeny cells, the DNA of the cell is copied to make an exact copy by a duplication method, called replication. Replication has a built in correction mechanism for any errors created during duplication. Still there are situations where a few errors may remain that are then carried to the progeny cells. These errors are called mutations and when such errors occur in genes that make proteins, they may lead to diseases. Alternatively, these errors could occur in the non-coding parts of DNA and not affect the organisms. During DNA replication parts of the chromosome exchange sequences in a process called recombination. The process of DNA duplication and its error correction mechanisms are very precise and the rate of possible errors in DNA duplication can be predicted. However, certain errors skip correction and the exchange of sequence during recombination result in adding variation to the DNA in the new cells. Additionally, mutations can occur in DNA for a number of other reasons. Based on various studies, the rate of mutation in genomic or other DNA can be predicted. This has allowed scientists to calculate and predict the number of possible changes in the DNA of an organism over a period of time and also to calculate when a change could have occurred. Mutations introduced in the structure of DNA produce variations in the structure of DNA that could be mapped using various methods. The level and type of variation in the DNA of a population (genetic diversity) can be used to correlate origin and migration routes of a population.

An analytical method that has helped in mapping variation and mutations in human DNA is Restriction Length Fragment Polymorphism (RFLP) analysis. In RFLP analysis, DNA is treated with enzymes (restriction enzymes) that recognize specific sequences in the DNA and create precision cuts. When a DNA molecule is treated with a defined collection of restriction enzymes and the fragments produced are analyzed, they create a map that is unique to that molecule of DNA. If a mutation had occurred at a site(s) where a restriction enzyme makes a cut, the restriction enzyme would be unable to cut the mutated DNA and a fragment of different length will be produced. RFLP analysis can distinguish between the DNA of different organisms or between people from distinct populations.

One of the most important techniques used in DNA analysis is Polymerase Chain Reaction (PCR) that amplifies micro amounts of a DNA sample by synthesizing multiple copies of the sample allowing for the production ofthe DNA in sufficient amounts to analyze and determine its sequence. Additionally, high speed computing and software that can process large amounts of data and carry out complex statistical analysis have facilitated analysis and application of DNA.

When the DNA sequences of a part of human genome from several individuals are aligned and compared, any change or variation at a particular nucleotide position is called aSingle Nucleotide Polymorphism (SNP). When the DNA of several individuals is compared, if the comparison contains some SNPs at specific points but has largely the same code, these individuals share common ancestral DNA. SNPs are estimated to occur about once every 1000 nucleotides, although the density of SNPs can vary by as much as 100 fold across the human genome. While SNPs occur over the entire length of human genome, most SNPs occur in a region of DNA that is non-coding or does not produce protein(s). Determining the location of SNPs over the entire sequence of human DNA has helped in creating a map of human genomic DNA that can then be compared across populations and within populations to determine ancestry.

A combination of the techniques described has created a template of human DNA that can be compared across members of a population to determine relatedness, common ancestry and population member profiles. A group of individuals which share the same RFLP pattern, mutations and SNPs in a defined part of DNA make a haplogroup. Arranging haplogroups based on their relatedness as indicated by mutations, RFLP map and SNPs creates a template that can map the migration of humans from one part of the world to another.

The genomic DNA of organisms ranging from single cell organisms to humans have been isolated and their sequences determined. Comparing these DNA sequences of various organisms provides strong support to the theory of evolution of life beginning with simple organisms and resulting in more complex organisms, including humans. This has also helped in determining when the first humans evolved from the Chimpanzee, the human's closest mammal relative, and when humans migrated to various parts of the world. The complete sequence of the entire human genomic DNA, which is over 3 billion nucleotides long has been determined.

Comparing the sequence of DNA isolated from diverse organisms has indicated that there is a lot of sequence similarity across organisms. There is a very small difference in the DNA sequence of two humans (about 0.1%) and the difference between a humans and our nearest related animal species (chimpanzee) is about 4%. While the difference between the DNA sequences of two human cells is only about 0.1%, this small difference is responsible for the stark diversity observed among humans. While large difference in the genomic DNA of various animal species and organisms are evident, the analysis also reveals that DNA shares similarities and a clear difference when two different animal species diverged.

Mitochondrial DNA

Most of the DNA in a cell is present in its nucleus and is called genomic DNA. However, DNA is also present in mitochondria, the part of a cell responsible for its energy production. A cell typically has between 100-1000 mitochondria, with its own unique copy of mitochondrial DNA. These 100-1000 copies of mitochondrial DNA are far greater than genomic or nuclear DNA that only has one copy. This allows for the characterization of DNA from fossil samples. Contrary to nuclear DNA, the mitochondrial DNA of a cell does not undergo recombination. Furthermore mitochondria lack DNA repair mechanisms and as result experience a higher rate of mutation when compared to genomic DNA. Additionally, the mitochondrial DNA of an individual is derived only from the maternal sex cell (ova) or mother. This allows researchers the opportunity to trace related lineages back through time without the interference of paternal DNA. In mitochondrial DNA there are haplotypes that share the same RFLP or SNP map. A haplotype is represented by an alphabet and is defined by the presence of specific molecular markers. Within each of these haplogroups, there can be multiple haplogroups based on further characterization of the mutations and molecular markers in the mitochondrial DNA.

Y chromosome

Human cells carry a total of 46 chromosomes, of which there are 22 pairs of autosomes, each pair with exact copies and two sex chromosomes. The sex chromosomes could be two X chromosome (female) or one X chromosome and one Y chromosome (male). In a female, one of the two X chromosomes is of maternal origin and the other is of paternal origin. In a male, the X chromosome comes from the mother and the Y chromosome comes from the father. Since the Y chromosome is derived from the paternal side, characterizing its sequence and creating maps has also been used for tracing human lineage. Additionally, like mitochondrial DNA, the Y chromosome does not undergo recombination. The Y chromosome sequence has been determined and mapped using molecular markers such as SNPs, RFLPs and nucleotide markers. As mitochondrial DNA is used as a tool to trace female human migration and ancestry, the Y chromosome has been used in determining male human migration and ancestry.

Based on mitochondrial DNA and Y chromosome characterizations, four gene pools have been identified (i) a sequence signature that is related to the first humans in Africa; (ii) a sequence that is characteristic of the Ancient North Indian (ANI) population (iii) a sequence that is characteristic of an Ancient South Indian (ASI) population; and (iv) a sequence that contains both ANI and ASI markers (an admixture of the ANI and ASI sequences). Based on these gene pools it has been suggested that there was a migration of humans from Africa to India about 30-70 thousand years ago to the Andaman and Nicobar area and that there were distinct North Indian (ANI) and South Indian (ASI) human populations. The ANI human population contains signature sequences that are attributable to the Eurasian population that migrated to India about 4000 years ago. There is evidence of admixing of the ANI and ASI gene pools in the modern day population of India. While there are suggestions of a relationship between the caste system in India to these various gene pools, a larger sample size of various populations and amongst populations as well newer molecular markers would provide better insight of these relationships.

Selected Articles

1. Single nucleotide polymorphisms: From the evolutionary past. . .Mark Stoneking. *Nature* 2001; 409, 821-822.
2. A review on SNP and other types of molecular markers and their use in animal genetics. Alain Vignal et al. *Genetics Selection Evolution*. 2002; 34, 275-305.
3. Mitochondrial DNA analysis reveals diverse histories of tribal population from India. Richard Cordaux et al. *European Journal of Human Genetics*. 2003;11:253-264.
4. The human Y chromosome: an evolutionary marker comes of age.
5. Mark A. Jobling and Chris Tyler-Smith. *Nature Reviews Genetics*. 2003; 4, 598-612.
6. The application of molecular genetic approaches to the study of human evolution. L. Luca Cavalli-Sforzaandand Marcus W. Feldman. *Nature Genetics*. 2003; 33, 266 – 275.
7. Mitochondrial DNA and human evolution.Brigitte Pakendorf and Mark Stoneking. *Annual Review of Genomics and Human Genetics*. 2005; 6:165–83
8. Reconstructing Indian population history. David Reich et al. *Nature* 2009; 461:489-494.
9. The Indian origin of paternal haplogroup R1a1 substantiates the autochthonous origin of Brahmins and the caste system. Swarkar Sharma et al. *Journal of Human Genetics*. 2009;54:47-55.
10. A Revised timescale for human evolution based on ancient mitochondrial genomes. Qiaomei Fu et al. *Current Biology* 23, 553–559, April 8, 2013
11. A calibrated human Y-chromosomal phylogeny based on resequencing. Wei Wei et al. *Genome Research* 2013; 23: 388-395
12. Sequencing Y chromosomes resolves discrepancy in time to common ancestor of males versus females. G. David Poznik et al. *Science*. 2013; 341: 562–565.
13. Genetic evidence for recent population mixture in India. Priya Moorjani et al. *American Journal of Human Genetics*. 2013;93:422-438.
14. Genetic and archeological perspectives on the initial modern human colonization of southern Asia. Paul Mellars et al. *Proceedings of the National Academy of Sciences USA*. 2013;110:10699-10704.
15. Timing the first human migration into eastern Asia. Roscoe Stanyon. *Journal of Biology*. 2013; 8:18.

64

ON OUR HISTORY, OUR TRADITION AND ASTRONOMY

Krisnanand Sinha

The British were in a habit of recording events in chronological order and this could be in the form of writing diaries or making notes. It additionally resulted in recording the events of the state. So, once they arrived in India, finding no such records, it was easy for them to surmise that the country had no history and it lived in myths and superstitions. But again, thanks to the British who formed the Asiatic Society for Researches and some very highly motivated individuals including the high and mighty who worked untiringly and relentlessly to unravel the wonder and the grandeur of an ancient civilization that was India.

As Indians, we do precious little to preserve our monuments, be it in the form of manuscripts, structures or something similar. The remnants of old fallen structures were consumed in the construction of new buildings and the precious old coins of gold and silver were melted to convert them into valuable jewellery. It needed an order by Alexander Cunningham forbidding Dewan Jagat Singh of Sarnath to stop excavating and using the bricks of *Dhamek Stupa* to construct a house! Such activities by Cunningham resulted in the beginning of the process of preservation of the heritage.

We had probably been in the habit of glorifying and emulating the feat of great people who served the humanity. This should have been the theme and form of folklores and rituals we perform at different times during the year. Most interestingly here lies, in the opinion of the author, the sinews of recording history in our own way. But which is the calendar to associate our history with?

To digress but to record here an important point we state that a calendar is nothing else but a record of celestial events and their association with things happening on the Earth such as the SEASONS! Here, it is amply clear and must be borne in mind that whereas Astronomy deals essentially with the science of celestial events and bodies, Astrology deals with the art of interpreting the impact or influence of some such events on human life !! No wonder that the development of calendar also depended upon the development of our own understanding of the objects in the sky.

The Sun and Moon because of their huge apparent size in the sky immediately attract our attention. If the Sun freed the living beings from the uncertainties of the deathly dark night, the Moon served as a clear crusader in the background of point like asterisms shining as diamonds, serving as markers and pointing towards the approaching dawn. Continuous, yet rigorous observations showed the repetitive path of the Moon. It was realized that the Moon takes some 29 ½ days to go round the Earth and 12 such rounds were enough to mark a year which was almost the same time when the Sun rose in the beginning of the year. But later on it became clear that the arrival of seasons that were so important for agriculture had to be associated with the heliacal rising of stars. This finally lead to a 365 ¼ day solar year instead of the previous 354 day lunar year. Any mention and discussion of the other and finer improvements in the calendar make the article lengthy and hence treated as avoidable.

It may be remarked here that the planetary movements serve as sufficiently accurate clock! We know that Jupiter takes about 12 years to go round the Sun and Saturn does the same in 30 Years. Therefore, any relative position of these two cannot be repeated before the passage of a good 60 years. This is akin to saying that the hour and minute hands of a clock do not repeat their relative positions before the passage of an hour! Now add to the planetary movements, the motion of, say Mars (1.88 years period) and Venus (0.615 years period). Instead of making the picture complicated, here we make it fascinating and serve with a system which is precise, self sustaining and valid for years to come. The moment we add the motion of the Vernal Equinox to this system, we get a calendar for roughly 26,000 years with the planetary movement serving as the many hands of a conceptual clock (Bhatnagar, 2004)!

Now, let us see how the above can be utilized to put our history in chronological order. We do not precisely know when the practice of preparing horoscope began in the country. We note in particular that Buddhists never believed in Astrology and when Buddhism became weak, probably the Greek influence took over and the occult had its way (Kay, 1924).

In Valmiki Ramayan, the position of the planets at the time of birth of Sri Ram is given as follows :

1. Sun (*Surya*) in Aries (*Mesha*),
2. Saturn (*Shani*) in Libra (*Tula*),
3. Jupiter (*Brihaspati*) in Cancer (*Karka*),
4. Venus (*Shukra*) in Pisces (*Meen*),
5. Mars (*Mangal*) in Capricorn (*Makar*),
6. Lunar month of *Chaitra*,
7. Ninth day after no moon (*Shukla Paksh, Navami Tithi*),
8. Moon near Pollux in Gemini (*Punarvasu in Mithun*),
9. Cancer as *Lagna* or Cancer rising in the East and
10. Jupiter above the horizon.

Using the above and with the help of the software Planetarium Gold, Bhatnagar (2004) found the date of the birth of Sri Ram as 10 January, 5114 BC. Yet another fact is also clearly brought out by him that owing to the precession of the equinoxes, during those ancient days, *Chaitra* used to fall between 15 December and 15 January instead of the present 15 March to 15 April. Use of a different software does not affect the result (Bhatnagar, 2012). However, Vartak (1989) in his calculations without a software and using a different but astronomical approach obtained the date as 04 December, 7323 BC. The difference provides further scope for research. Arguably, different results are mentioned or believed in literature as the dates for *Ramnavami* but the differences including those due to methods other than astronomical considerations need a rigorous and close scrutiny.

The above also leads us to an interesting aspect. Sri Ram was exiled for 14 years on his 21st birthday. Obviously, his return to *Ayodhya* should be on or about the same day! Then why do we celebrate *Deepawali* in the month of October-November and the birth in March-April? The answer is not too far to seek. If we assume that during the *Vedic* period lunar calendar was in vogue then a short fall of 11 days every year would make it 154 days or 5 months and about 6 lunar days in 14 years. This precisely fills the gap between the time period of October-November and March-April! A controversy related to the *Vanvaas* of the *Pandavas* arose during *Mahabharat,* if they had completed the 12 year period. The controversy was similarly resolved by Bhishm (Mishr, 1930) in the favor of the Pandavas !! We thus clearly see how a horoscope and a precise mention of the celestial objects can be utilized to obtain important dates in history !!

Another interesting aspect is *Maha Shivratri*. When did we begin observing the same? It is well known that every new moon day (*Amavasya*) is a *Shivratri.* Obviously, the day when the night or the *Amavasya* is the longest! But such a night occurs on 22/23 December whereas we celebrate the festival in February or March. Abhyankar (2007) has explained this apparent discrepancy. Accounting for 1 day every 71 years he goes on to illustrate that the practice of observing began some 3000 years BC! Similarly, the present author believes that the practice of *Makar Sankranti* might have begun since the time of Aryabhat (I) !! Also, on the basis of visibility of the star Canopus (Agastya), Abhyankar fixes the period 5000-4000 BC for the sage Agastya to cross over the Vindhya.

Rao et al (2011) point towards stone alignments constructed between 1400 and 1000 BC at Murardoddi in Mahbubnagar district of Andhra Predesh. Observations show that the rows of the stones are aligned to the directions of sunrise and sunset on calendrically important events like equinoxes and solstices. Sunrise and sunset observations and the patterns of the shadows of stones were used to measure time, days and fractions of the day. Archaeological study to accurately date the monument is required.

The above, illustrates very clearly how the astronomical facts recorded in our epics, in folklore and/or even in traditions can go on to establish our golden heritage and a place in history. In this context efforts to know when a certain tradition or ritual was begun and who started it can be initiated by unearthing facts from some known/unknown texts.

References

1. Abhyankar, K. D. 2007, *Pre-Siddhantic Indian Astronomy* (A Reappraisal), Institute of Scientific Research on Vedas, Hyderabad, p. 52.
2. Bhatnagar, A. K. 2012. in (ed.) Bala, S. and Mishra, K., *Historicity of Vedic and Ramayan Eras*, Institute of Scientific Research on Vedas, Delhi Chapter, p. 55.
3. Bhatnagar, Pushkar. 2004. *Dating the Era of Lord Ram*, Rupa & Company, p. 06.
4. Kay, G. R. 1924. *Memoirs of the Archaeological Survey of india, No. 18 Hindu Astronomy*, Government of India Central Publications Branch, 8. Hastings Street, Calcutta, p. 97.
5. Kejriwal, O. P. 1998. *Bharat ke Ateet ki Khoj* (1784-1838), Manish Prakashan, p. 9.
6. Mishr, Sriradhakrishnaji. 1930. (in) *Kalyan Ramayananak*, Gitapress, p. 306.
7. Rao, N. K., Thakur, P. and Mallinathpur, Y. 2011. Journal of Astronomical History and Heritage, 14(3), p. 211.
8. Vartak, P. V. 1999. *The Scientific dating of the Ramayana & the Vedas*, Veda Vidyana Mandala, Pune.

65

GANESH SHANKAR VIDYARTHI AND HIS CRUSADE AGAINST COMMUNALISM (1915-1931)

P.K. Shukla

Ganesh Shankar Vidyarthi[1] (born 26 October 1890 and was assassinated on 25 March, 1931 in the wake of the Kanpur riot) was a dedicated and prominent Congress leader, and one of the leading literary figures of India. He was a disciple of Gandhiji, though he often differed with him on the question of non-violence. He accepted his leadership to further the cause of liberation of India from British rule, but he never allowed himself to be guided by his creed of non-violence. He argued that non-violence was a matter of policy and not the *dharma* (code). In his presidential speech delivered at the Fatehpur district committee in 1922-23, he made it clear that violence was inherent in the nature of a common man[2]. For having justified the relevance of violence, he was imprisoned for a year and a fine Rs. 100 was imposed on him. This article based on his writings discusses his crusade against the rising tide of communalism, and also focuses on his perception of India as nation, his concern for the distortions of India's past history in the writings of the imperialist historians.

Vidyarthiji's commitment to the cause of the nation is reflected in his writings and the affection he expressed towards Ram Prasad Bismil, Ashfaqullah Khan and Roshan Singh who were involved in the Kakori case. He extended material and moral support to these revolutionaries and criticized the unsympathetic attitude of the Congress leadership towards them.[3] While supporting the action of Shaheed Bhagat Singh and Batukeshwar Dutt in the Lahore Conspiracy case (1929), he argued that there should be no discussion on the relevance of violence and non-violence when animalism and atrocities reigned supreme in the country. He pleaded that the people could not remain non-violent forever if the oppression committed by the colonial rule had continued for centuries.

Vidyarthiji was influenced by the writings of John Stuart Mill and Thoreau. Soon after his M.A. from Allahabad University he came to Kanpur in search of a job. Here he came in contact with Pandit Sunderlal and his weekly the *Karmajogi* (Hindi) and the *Swarajya* (Urdu). Later, he came in contact with Mahavir Prasad Dwivedi and his weekly, the *Saraswati* through which he developed his highly literary talents. His political views were moulded by the columns of the *Abhyudaaya*, edited by Madan Mohan Malaviya. It was during the same period that he read Shakespeare, Victor Hugo, Austen, Sinclair, Tolstoy, Bernard Shaw, Tulsidas, Surdas, Kabir, Bharatendu and Rabindranath Tagore. The writings of these great men left a deep impact in shaping his social, political and cultural views on the country and its welfare. In his writings, one can find a synthesis of religious and rational ideas.

It is necessary to mention his life long association with the newspaper, the *Pratap*. Initially, the Pratap was weekly magazine and he became its editor in 1913. Later it was converted into a daily newspaper. Vidyarthiji attached much importance to the development of humankind and in order to achieve this goal, he emphasized the development of India as a nation. India, according to him, was suffering on account of the neglect of agriculture, trade, education and art. He thus began to lay emphasis on India's national integration and its overall development. Through his comments and editorials published in the *Pratap*, he began to educate the people about their rights. He argued that the country belonged to the people irrespective of various castes and communities.

In its phase, the *Pratap* published numerous articles for 17-18 years and underscored the problems of the country. His along with his colleagues and friends like Shiv Narayan Mishra, Narayan Prasad Arora began to dispatch the paper while sitting on the floor of the building. Initially it contained 16 pages and but by 1930 it consisted of 40 pages. Its office was raided many times by the colonial government. In 1915 the paper was fined Rs. 1000 for publishing anti-British articles like *Saudawatan*. It remained closed for a year or so and reappeared again on 8 July 1918 in which the oppressive nature of the government was brought to the notice of the public.

The *Prabha* weekly was edited by Makhanlal Chaturvedi from Khandva and Jabalpur. It was later brought out as an associated paper by Vidyarthiji between 1920 and 1925. Such newspapers and magazines imparted training to young journalists committed to the nationalist cause. In addition, he established a publishing house known as *Prakash Pustakalaya*. Among its important publications included a book on the biographical sketch of Lenin known as *'Bolshevik Jadugar'* written by Rama Shankar Awasthi.

Vidyarthiji went to jail on five occasions, out of which three times due to objectionable pieces published in the *Pratap* and twice for his anti-British speeches. He led the Kisan Andolan in Rai Bareilly (1921) in which many kisans lost their lives. Pandit Motilal Nehru, Pandit Jawaharlal Nehru and 50 others were witnesses in the case, but the order of the Session court was against the *Pratap* and its printer. He wrote not only against British imperialism, but also against the exploitation of the peasants by the feudal landlords; the stooges of British imperialism and the apparatus of the *Raj*, the bureaucracy.

Though he was largely committed to the ideology of the Congress, he sympathized and helped revolutionaries like Ram Prasad Bismil, Ashfaqullah Khan, Roshan Singh, Surendra Bhattacharya, Raj Kumar Sinha, Ram Dulare Trivedi, Bhagat Singh, Chandrashekhar Azad, Vinay Kumar Sinha, Batukeshwar Dutt. They were family friends. It may be noted that he gave them shelter, extended political advice and helped them monetarily. He worked with them as their friend, philosopher and guide. He kept Bhagat Singh with him. Bismil's autobiography was published by the *Pratap*. He performed the ritual of a father, when Roshan Singh's daughter was married. A day before Ashfaqullah Khan was to be hanged, he informed Vidyarthiji by telegram that he should come to Lucknow station at 2.30 p.m. to have a final meeting with him. Vidyarthiji along with eight others went to the railway station and saluted him there. He took his photograph, which is still available. Through his own effort he constructed a *mazar* over his place of burial[4]. Such a contributions in the first phase of his career shows that he was not a patriot but a crusader in arousing the political consciousness of the literature middle class against the alien rule.

As early as in 1915 when he was just 25 years old he wrote a few pieces entitled *'nationalism'*[5] and hope for the nation[6] in which he not only drew the attention of the youth to fight the cause of nation against British imperialism, but also made a sharp distinction between nationalism and religious identities. He said that nationalism should not be based on communal identity and its origin depended on the nature of the state. He said that natural boundaries and diversity kept the nation aloof from the world and the growth of national feeling was a step towards the development of human mankind. It was spontaneous, based on certain ideals and nurtured true patriotism. He felt that religion was always an obstacle to the human progress. National feeling was a wave that had swept the world in the nineteenth century. Those who believed in *Hindu Rashtra*, according to him, were befooling the people because they could not understand the meaning of nation. Though he was not a soothsayer, he predicted that so long India was ruled by an alien power there could not be a *Hindu Rashtra*. He admonished followers of Islam not to consider Turkey or Kabul, Mecca or Jeddah as their birth place for when they die' their graveyards would be dug in India alone.

In order to lay the solid foundation of Indian nationalism he appealed to the youth by reminding them of the glory of the Panchayati system flourishing during the Muslim rule. During this period people lived peacefully with no animosity between the two communities.[7] His remark is endorsed by the fact that during the Mughal rule there were only four cases of communal commotion recorded in the contemporary works covering the entire span of one hundred years. Yet, the term 'riot' in our contemporary sense cannot be applied to any such occurrences as none of them generated widespread frenzy, led to bloodshed and destruction of property. The Hindus and the Muslims enjoyed complete freedom to equip themselves for self-defense, but did not turn against each other even when few mischievous individuals stirred up tension. The strife was primarily caused by conflicting economic interests and competitive politics rather than by communal feelings.[8]

Vidyarthiji was a victim of communal frenzy which had erupted in Kanpur in 1931, but he continued to oppose those forces engaged in communal bitterness from 1917 onwards. In order to pacify communal strife he drew the attention of both the communities to refrain from religious acrimony. People from both the communities faced similar problems under the colonial rule, as misery and unhappiness were common to both. He cited examples on the differences prevailing between the communities throughout the world as well in India, yet such a situation ought not be created at the cost of the nation, especially when both the communities were fighting against the alien rule. He appealed to both the communities, the Hindus and the Muslims to create an atmosphere of mutual trust, and jointly fight for achieving Swarajya as a common goal. He asked both the communities to refrain from antagonizing each other and to avoid the beating of drums in front of the mosque and temple on the occasion of Dusshera and Muharram. He felt that festivities could be celebrated without creating communal tension[9].

People thought that the ideals of Swarajya had united both the communities against the alien rule but unfortunately on the eve of Bakrid, a communal riot occurred in Arrah (Bihar) in 1917 in which most of the victims were Muslims. Inspired by the alien authorities, the riot provoked Muslim mobilization on communal lines. They held a number of meetings in Arrah, Kashi (Varanasi), Lucknow, Aligarh and Jehangirabad. Most of these meetings were organized by the *Mullahs* and the *Maulvies* who were encouraged by the Raja of Jehangirabad. The Hindu-Muslim pact was criticized and the Swarajists were accused of being anti-Islam. The meeting organized at the initiative of Raja of Jehangirabad adopted many resolutions including the one which considered cow slaughter as essential for Islam. Similar sentiments here spread by most of the Muslim newspapers, which provoked the Muslim youth.[10]

Ganesh Shankar Vidyarthi wrote extensively against communal frenzy. He did not wish to appease the Hindus or to criticize the Muslims. He considered the attitude during the time of communal riots as jingoistic. He also maintained that both the communities here are victims of such passions. Yet the entire community should not be held responsible or victimized and butchered for the wrong committed by a handful of anti-social elements. He wondered why the poor, helpless Muslims born in this country should become victims of the atrocities committed by only a handful. He appealed to the common people to unite against the British imperialism. He wrote that "we are neither Hindus nor Muslims and the welfare of the motherland is our duty". He regarded the Hindus and the Muslims as twin brothers of the motherland. Vidyarthi adopted two methods to introduce meaning of the *Dharma* to both the communities[11]. Even though he failed in his attempt he never refrained from attacking the fundamentalists who were determined to take revenge upon one another. He considered such an attitude to be a sign of foolishness and asked for the broadening of the mental horizon so as to respect the religious sentiment of each other. He warned that if they did not do so reactionary and dark forces would be detrimental to the existence of both the communities and the cause for the nationhood would suffer. Should such a situation arise it would invite the alien power to interfere in the day-to-day administration of Hindustan. He did not adopt a negative attitude towards the Hindu Sabha, especially when it had been consolidating its position against the Muslims. He drew its attention towards the deteriorating condition of the Hindu social structure which was dominated by the *thikedars* of the temples. He blamed the *Baba Bairagi* for the backwardness of the Hindu society. He demanded reformation in social, economic and moral structures of the Hindu society. He hinted at the immoral use of the religious places, comparing them with the places of prostitution. He desired that women's honour should be protected from the *Pandas* and the *Goondas*[12]. He asked the Hindu Mahasabhaites not to encourage religious fanaticism and rituals prevalent at religious places. He wanted that all religious places like Haridwar, Ayodhya, Prayaga and Avantika should be converted into a trust and the wealth accumulated by them should be used for the uplift of the poor Hindus. He wanted that all religious preachers should work without any selfish motives.

In four other articles, all published in the *Pratap*,[13] during 1923-1926, Vidyarthiji discussed how common people were mobilized along communal lines leading to the emergence of communal riots. In 1924' there were 14 communal riots in U.P. then followed by 27 in 1927. It was during this period that the Non-cooperation movement was fading away. In 1924, communal tension was at its height when processions playing music before the mosques became a common occurrence. This was the main bone of contention between the two communities. Though inspired by vested interests, common people like Ramua Pasi and Budhoo Mian were ready to sacrifice their lives in the name of religion. The conspirators strove to manipulate common people in order to maintain their hegemony over their respective communities. Vidyarthiji wrote at length on how the ignorant and poor people of both the communities were misled and misguided by the *thikedars* spreading communal frenzy. He believed that in the name of religion poor people were often mislead for ulterior designs. He admitted the Mahatma Gandhi was a deeply religious person but his religion was different from the kind of religious frenzy propagated by undesirable elements. Vidyarthi was against the misuse of religion and remarked that if that was so then God would favour those non-believers who had high moral character and who took care of the plight of the human beings[14].

An outstanding journalist and publicist, Vidyarthiji wrote passionately against the mixing of religion with politics:

> We pray to God that our readers may lean to rely not on the weak crutches of religious organizations and diffident, moderate, political tactics but on the true strength of the country, which is found in her millions or ordinary people... The days of religion and religious organizations are numbered, the trend of world history and the future of India are against them. Whosoever wishes to be a 'Hindu' or 'Musalman' was welcome to be a 'Hindu' or a 'Musalman' inside the home[15].

He conceived of Indians as an agglomeration of communities. In fact in its early phase the national movement had conceived India as a collection of communities: Hindu + Muslim + Christian + Parsi + Sikh and so on. Drawing on this concept Vidyarthiji wrote extensively in the *Pratap* and other vernacular newspapers.

Vidyarthiji not only took a serious note of the deteriorating communal situation in the Punjab in 1925. He criticized the Mohammad Ali Jinnah, Lala Lajpat Rai and Veer Savarkar who were negotiating the question of representation of different communities in the Municipal Boards on the basis of proportional representation in jobs. He was critical of their ideas. He demanded a scientific study of religion and rejection of obscurantism. He made a appeal to the youth to follow the teachings of Nanak, Kabir, Guru Gobind Singh and Ramanuj in order to maintain communal harmony.

In one of the commentaries[16] he blamed the divide and rule policy of the government. Vidarthiji cited numerous examples of how people and leaders of one community were encouraged to provoke the other in religious matters. The government structures played off one community against the other, as exemplified in the encouragement given to Abdul Rahim in Calcutta and Fazli Hussain in Punjab. He highlighted the government's insensitivity in taking effective measures to control the anti-social elements indulging in religious violence in Calcutta, Punjab, Aligarh, Gowhati, and Rawalpindi.

Vidyarthiji lamented how the two misguided sons of the motherland were quarreling with each other over petty issues at the cost of the unity of the nation. In order to pacify the mounting tension, he cited an example from the life of the Prophet for giving shelter to the non-Muslims of Yemen. He also evoked and appreciated the Medieval Indian practice of celebrating Ramlilas in front of Mosques and how people would gather around the Mosques to garland the main actor of the Ramlila[17]. While criticizing social evils in Indian society from Vedic times to British raj, he commented positively on the famous saints and reformers like Guru Nanak, Kabir, Guru Gobind Singh, Ramanuj, Ballabhacharya, Dayanand Saraswati and Rammohun Roy who introduced social reforms in Indian society. It was not through the performance of rituals that the grace of God was bestowed upon them. He quoted extensively from Kabir and Nank, emphasizing that religion was omniprent[18].

For Vidyarthiji the true meaning of religion should be pursued. Religion should be perceived in its vastness. The god is neither confined to the mosque nor to a temple. He argued that no true Hindu would sanction the demolition of a mosque as his religious commitment and no true Muslim would consider cow slaughter as part of his religious practice. Commenting on Hindu Sabha's negative attitude towards the *Dalit's* temple entry at the instance of some *Marwaris* of Kolkata[19], he did not spare its president Lajpat Rai. Critising the caste affiliation to religion he lamented that the poor *dalits*, Christians and Muslims, unfortunately born in this country, were not allowed to take water from the same wells and to enter the god's places of worship[20].

He criticized the huge amount donated by a Brahmin, Darbhanga Maharaj for maintaining the *Varnashram Dharma*. Vidyarthiji sarcastically observed that without wealth *Dharma* could not be protected. Vidyarthiji did not find anywhere Dharma or the four-fold caste-system. What he found was the supremacy of *Karma*. He justified the conversion of the *Dalits* on account of their continual oppression by upper castes.

Vidyarthiji did not spare the Muslim foundamentalists and their view on Hindu Maha Sabha[21]. Though some of the papers were highly critical of Lala Lajpat Rai, Madan Mohan Malavia, Swami Shradhanand and Bhai Parmanand for their pro-Hindu views, Dr Kithcew's paper *The Tanzim* was sympathetic to the cause of the Dalits and it appealed to the Hindu Maha Sabha to initiate social reforms among the Hindus. But Vidyarthi thought that the Muslim paper was instigating the Hindu Maha Sabha. He asked the Muslim brothers not to encourage the Dalits to convert themselves into Islam and Christianity, thought he himself was not against conversion perse. Vidyarthiji's views of conversions in the past is justified on the ground that it did not lead to any serious social conflicts. After all, the change in religious a affiliation has not been sudden and total transformation but has been so gradual to be nearly imperceptible, mostly, involving an entire group, family of kinship network, or a local community[22].

Along with his numerous writings on language and literature, he wrote some excellent pieces how the history of India was distorted by foreign scholars. Such distorted picture of India's past was far from the objective and scientific history. Such writings on Indian history were detrimental to the emergence of healthy nationalism. History books taught in Indian schools demonstrated this trend quite clearly, he wrote[23]. Realizing the absence of objective and factual narration of the India's past by Indian scholars, he criticized the historical writings of foreign scholars as distortion of facts. He considered such histories as biased, racial and full of stereotypes[22].

The foreign writers were hostile to the Muslim rule. They considered Indians as uncivilized, barbarous and illiterate, and depicted the Hindu-Muslim relationships as mutually antagonistic. They disregarded the ways in which the Hindus and Muslims found common ground commonalities in art, literature and culture. They aimed at suppressing facts which were against Indian heroes. They found only evils in India's past history. Hindus and the Muslim were always at conflict with each other, and India therefore described an autocratic rule. Brahmins were symbols of 'cruelty' the Maratha was a caste, Shivaji was a 'hilly cat', a conspirator, a plunderer and a dacoit. There was only chaos and confusion on the eve of conquest of India. Such historical writings were taught in the school text books which denigraded India's past.

The distortion of historical facts about India's past in imperialist writing, as depicted by Vidyarthiji in his numerous writings was supported by the Cawnpore Riots Enquiry Committee[23] with Bhagavan Das as its Chairman. Other members of the Committee were Pandit Sunderlal, Purushottam Das Tandon, Zafarul Mulk, Abdul Latif Bijnori and Manzai Ali Sokhata. The Committee held that the histories available to the public perpetuated a false view. The imperialist school of history offered a blinkered perspective on India's historical past so as to justify the British rule and to perpetuate enmity among Indians. Though the report of the Committee was brought to the notice of the public after 1933, Vidyarthiji had discussed misrepresentation of historical facts as early as and thereafter. The death of Ganesh Shankar Vidyarthi was envied and admired by Gandhiji himself. He said that his blood was the cement that would bind the two communities. But the poison of communal passion had gone so deep that the blood of Vidyarthiji was not enough to bring about peace and tranquility. While paying his tribute to

Vidyarthiji, Gandhiji made a prophetic remark by saying that "let this noble example stimulate us all to similar effort should the occasion arise again"[25]. In fact, Gandhiji himself became a victim of such communal passion after 17 years, in 1948.

Besides Gandhiji, Pandit Nehru, Premchand, Acharya Mahavir Prasad Dwivedi Pandi Sunderlal, Maithalisharan Gupta, Vrindabanlal Verma and a host writers paid rich tribute to Vidayarthiji. While condoning his brutal assassination, Pandit Nehru said that his death taught a lesion to the people of India for the cause of Hindu-Muslim unity. He also wished like Gandhiji that the people of India should imbibe the same spirit and boldness for preserving the communal peace and harmony. He quoted a few sentences from the writings of Bernard Shaw to express his grief:

"This is the true joy in life, the being used for a purpose recognized by yourself as a mighty one, the being thoroughly worn out before you are thrown on the scrap heaps, the being a source of nature, instead of a feverish, selfish little clod of ailments and grievances complaining that the world will not devote itself to the making you happy"[28].

Prenchand and in his two-page tribute remembered Vidyarthiji and said that he was fully devoted to the cause of Hindu-Muslim unity and he never allowed communalism to be the political arms for the patriotic leaders.[29] It is high time that such patriot should be remembered and made availabie as an inspiration and an example for the unity and integrity of the country.

Note and References

1. Suresh Salil, ed. "Ganesh Shankar Vidyarthi Rachanawali, IV Vols." Anamika Publishers and Distributors, New Delhi, 2004. Most of his writings on various aspects of national movement have been compiled and edited covering 1899 pages.
2. *Ibid.*, Vol. I, p. 19.
3. *Ibid.*, op.cit., p. 19.
4. *Ibid.*, op.cit., p. 33.
5. *Rashtriyata* in the weekly, the *Pratap*, 21 June 1915, Reproduced in op.cit., Vol. I, pp. 69-71.
6. *Rashtra ki Asha*, op.cit., pp. 110-119.
7. *Rashtra ki Neeb*, 26 June 1915 in the op.cit., p. 121.
8. Z.U. Malik, "The Core and the Periphery: A Contribution to the Debate on the Eighteenth Century" in the *Proceedings of the Indian History Congress*, 1990 p. 189.
9. *Pariksha ka Samaya* (Trying Tims), op.cit., 15 October 1917.
10. *Katheen Samasya*, 12 November 1917, op.cit., pp. 297-300.
11. *Hindu Mahasabha Se*, 5 May 1924, op.cit., pp. 301-304.
12. *Ibid.*, p. 303.
13. *Dharma ki Aar*, 27 October, 1924, op.cit., pp. 305-307; Desh ki Un Atamaon se, op.cit., pp. 308-311; Josh Mein Na Ainye, op.cit., pp. 312-314.
14. *Dharma ki Aar*, op.cit., p. 307.
15. Sidhartha Varadarajan 'The Ink Link', in K.N. Panikkar ed., *The Concerned India's Guide to Communalism,* Penguin Books India, 1999, p. 178.
16. *Hindu-Muslim Vidwesh Aur Bharat Sarkar*, 25 July 1926, op.cit., pp. 319-322.
17. *Jehad ki Jarurat,* 30 May 1926, in the *Pratap*, op.cit., p. 31.
18. *Ekata ke Liya Udyoga*, 29 September 1924, Vol. III, op.cit., p. 263.
19. *Hinduon ki Kupmandukta*, 20 April 1925, op.cit., pp. 324-328.
20. *Samundra Mathan*, 8 August 1926, op.cit., p. 326.
21. *Hindu Mahasabha ke Musalman Alochak*, 4 May 1925, op.cit., pp. 333-335.
22. (Sumti Sarkar, 'Hindutva and the Question of conversion' in *The Concerned: India's Guide to Communalism,* ed. by K.N. Panikkar, Penguin Books, India, 1999, p. 78.
23. *Bharatiya Schooluon Mein Itihas ki Pusatakenya*, Vol. 1, op.cit., pp. 186-191.
24. *Ibid.*, p. 187.
25. Cawanpore (Kanpur) Riot Enquiry Committee (1931) was constituted by the Congress with Bhagavan Das as its Chairman "to discover the causes of the tension and to take such measures as may be necessary to heal the breach and to prevent the poison from spreading to the adjoining areas and district". It was appointed after the Kanpur riot of 1931 in which Ganesh Shankar Vidyarthi was killed on 25 March, while he was trying to save the lives of the people. Since the report of the Enquiry Committee charged the British government with anticipating the riot and then doing nothing to contain it, the report was banned by the

government. In this riot about 400 people died and over 1200 received injuries. See for details N. Geneal Barrier ed., *The Roots of Communal Politics*, Arnold-Heine Mann, 1976, New Delhi, pp. 6-27. The findings of the report of the Congress and Vidyarthiji's observations on historical writing by the imperialist historians are largely supported by J.S. Grewal, *Muslim Rule in India: The Assessment of British Historians*, OUP, 1970, pp. 165-194.

26. N.G. Barrier, op.cit., p. 14.
27. The *Young India*, ed. M.K. Gandhi, Vol. XIII, Ahmedbad, 9 April, 1931 p. 1.
28. See for details an excellent book (in Hindi) entitled *Gaṅeshshankar Vidyarthi Aur Unaka yug* ed. by Suresh Salil, New Delhi, 2014, pp. 19-20.
29. *Ibid*., p. 24; his tribute was published in the *Hans*, 1931, part III.

66

THE AESTHETICS OF SANSKRIT THEATRE AND THE STRUCTURE OF SANSKRIT DRAMA

Kamaleśadatta Tripathi

Background and Introduction

Sanskrit theatre has emerged to occupy the central place in contemporary theatre movement in recent decades. Growing interest of the scholars in the performance of Sanskrit plays is clearly discernible. The search for the identity of Indian theatre which started in the 6th decade of this century culminated in a serious inquiry into traditional folklore of India as well as classical Sanskrit Theatre.

The introduction of Kālidāsa's *Śākuntalam* to the western world at the close of 18th century generated keen interest in Indian thought in general and in Indian literature and arts in particular. Likewise, the discovery that Bhāsa's plays were being preserved and performed in the living tradition of the Sanskrit theatre in Kerala directed the attention of scholars towards the performative aspects of Sanskrit plays.

Publication of the fourth volume of Bharata's *Nāṭyaśāstra* complete with 'Abhinavabhārati' from Baroda in 1964 coincides with a fresh interest of theatremen and artists not only in *Nāṭyaśāstra* itself, but also in Sanskrit plays, Kudiyāṭṭam and numerous forms of traditional folk theatre scattered throughout India.

The *Nāṭyaśāstra* (hereafter NŚ) is an encyclopaedic compendium of ancient Indian theatre. It covers a wide range of artistic subjects such as music, dance, aesthetics, architecture and draws upon disciplines as diverse as philosophy, psychology, myth, ritual, grammar, phonetics, geography. Bharata has been regarded as the preceptor (ācārya) of Nāṭya (Drama and Theatre) as well as of Kāvyaśāstra (Poetics). He inherited the traditions of Brahmā and Sadāśiva and perhaps, that of Viṣṇu, which are direct antecedents of Bharata's *Nāṭyaśāstra.*[1]

The Tradition

Historically, there were attempts to systematize the tradition of theatre even before Bharata. Pāṇini, the grammarian of 5th of 6th century B.C., speaks of the Manual for Actors (*Naṭa-sūtra*) by Śilālin and Kṛśāśva (4.4.3.110,111). Besides, we are aware of the continuity of a dance and theatrical tradition in India from the earliest period for which we have records.

The danseuse figurine from Indus valley civilization, and the term for danseuse (nṛtu) in the early Ṛgvedic hymns, as well as the term for actor (*Śailūṣa*) in *Śukla Yajurveda* (30.6) and *Taittirīya Brāhmaṇa* (3.4.2.1) testifies to a tradition of performance from the 4th millennium B.C. It shows at this early era the existence of a spontaneous theatrical tradition, which, perhaps, had yet to be codified. The word '*Naṭa*' used in this context links the art of acting to the art of dancing. Both words '*Naṭa*' and '*Śailūṣa*' appear in the *Rāmāyaṇa* (2.30.8), which speaks of a *Śailūṣa*'s wife, an actress, who played various roles. The *Mahābhāṣya* of Patañjali (2nd century B.C.) refers to an actress (*Naṭa-bhāryā*) as well as theatrical performance.

Buddhist sources also refer to a flourishing theatrical tradition. There is mention of a village of actors and their chief, the '*naṭagrāmaṇī*'. In the '*Gāmaṇī Saṃyutta*' (Discourse to headmen) (*Samyutta Nikāya*, 4.2), a chief of the actors submits to Lord Buddha the common belief stated by Bharata at the end of NŚ that actors attain merit that help them reach heaven. V. Raghavan maintains that this chief is certainly the '*Sūtradhāra*' or, the director of the performance whose name, Talapuṭa, underlines dance as forming part of drama. This passage refers also to the stage (*raṅga*) and the assembly (*Samāja*), where and for whom, the performance takes place ('*raṅga-majjhe*', '*samajja-majjhe*').[2]

In Pali, a significant term occurs that describes the nature of stage reality as 'true false' (*sajjālīka* = skt. *styālīka*). A deeper ontological inquiry into the nature of theatre emerges in the NŚ and its commentary. The *Brahmajāla-suttanata* of the *Dīgha Nikāya* first refers to the practice of discourse on various arts, crafts, games, pastimes and schools of philosophical thoughts current among the Brāhmaṇas. The word used here for the plays is '*pekkhā*' or '*prekṣā*', in later Sanskrit writings. A pastime known as '*Sobhanāgāraka*' identified by Patañjali as '*Śobhanaka*', a form of theatrical art, has also been mentioned there.[3]

Such is the background of the NŚ. This unique tradition of Nāṭya and an excellent school of Nāṭyaśāstric exposition has been preserved in the *Abhinavabhāratī*, *Bhāva-prakāśana*, *Saṅgītaratnākara* and the commentaries of Kallinātha as well as Siṁhabhūpāla thereon. According to Indian Śāstric tradition, every Śāstra (discipline) was first composed in Sūtra, the most concise presentation of the disciplines in an aphoristic style, and was later developed by the 'Vārtika', 'Vṛtti' and 'Bhāṣya' (different forms of commentary). For instance, there is the tradition of Pāṇinian grammar where Pāṇini is the author of Sūtras, Kātyāyana is the author of Vārtikas and Patañjali composed the Bhāṣya, whereas *Kāśika* is the well-known Vṛtti on Pāṇini.

Similarly, the '*Sūtras*' (aphorism in prose form) and 'Kārikās' (versified aphorisms) of Bharata found an author of 'Vārtika' in Harṣa and an author of 'Vivṛti' or a commentary in Abhinavaguptapādācārya. The words of Udbhaṭa, Kīrtidhara, Bhaṭṭa Yantra, Bhaṭṭa Lollaṭa, Śrī Saṅkuka and Bhaṭṭa Nāyaka, Bhaṭṭa Tota, to name a few, were also in the form of commentaries. They are all now lost. Whatever little has been preserved in the form of prima facie views and references to earlier works, in the *Abhinavabhāratī*, *Bhāva-prakāśana* and *Saṅgītaratnākara* is of immense help in understanding the tradition of the NŚ and its diverse interpretations. Sometimes large passages and even a full chapter has been reproduced from the earlier works. For instance, Hemacandra reproduces numerous passages from *Abhinavabhārati* and Kallinātha, copiously quotes from Kohala on '*Vartanā*' and '*Cārī*'. Thus an uninterrupted school of Nāṭyaśāstric tradition has been preserved from circa 2nd century B.C. to 18th century. A number of texts written in different regions of the Country carry forward the tradition and diffuse it in multiple streams of Indian classical as well as folk theatre, and dance forms. From Abhinavagupta to the most recent Śāstric texts, a living and creatively diversified tradition of '*prayoga*' (performance) has been preserved and expanded by registering the views of different '*ācāryas*' and incorporating innumerable '*sampradāyas*' (schools). It is not simply an exercise of preserving a fossilised tradition; but rather it is a magnificent effort of carrying forward the tradition which pulsates with life and to which everyone has to make his or her own contribution.

Nature of '*Nāṭya*'

Such a long and rich tradition of '*prayoga*' (performance) as well as '*Śāstra*' (Discipline of Theatre) envisages not only a systematic and complete codification of the 'body language', but some deeper thinking on the nature of theatre and aesthetic experience.

The myth of the origin of *Nāṭya* and the story of the first dramatic performance occurring in the first chapter of the NŚ are important from this angle. In particular, the failure of the First Performance whose theme was the defeat of *Daityas* (Demons) is significant.

Angry as they were, *Asuras* and *Dānavas* (Demons) created troubles during the first dramatic performance. The objection against the performance raised by *Virūpākṣa*, together with the host of the *Daityas* and *Vighnas* (obstacles) has got deep implications. The *Daityas* said to Brahmā, "This knowledge of theatre which your lordship has created at the behest of gods, has humiliated us. Oh *Pitāmaha* of the entire world, this ought not to have been done by you in this way."

The first performance was of the nature of '*anukṛti*' (Imitation) and it is apparent that the Daityas took the '*anukṛti*' too literally. Brahmā tried to remove the demons' misgivings about the nature of *Nāṭya* by describing it "as the glorious retelling of the Bhāvas, or the emotive states, of the entire triple universe."

Although Bharata defines drama as "*anukaraṇa*" elsewhere, Abhinavagupta emphasizes that *Nāṭya* is essentially "*anukīrtana*" (Re-telling) of the '*Bhāvas*' (Emotive states) and not '*anukaraṇa*', i.e. 'imitation'. Abhinavagupta raises deeper ontological and aesthetic questions when he asks whether there is a comprehension of *Nāṭya* as reality (*tattva*) or as similarly to it (*sādṛśya*), as in the case of a twin or as an error (*bhrānti*) as in the case of silver mistakingly recognized as such in a piece of mother of pearl. Or theatrical reality is the superimposition (*āropa*) as in the case of viewing the face of the beloved as moon, or as identification (*adhyavasāya*) as when one says, "This man from the land of Vāhika is a bull." Or can we say that reality in theatre is a metaphoric supposition (*utprekṣyamāṇatva*) as when moon is fancied as the face of night or it is a replica (*pratikṛti*) as in the case of painting or a model, or as imitation or reproduction (*anukaraṇa*) as in the case of the intense desire of the pupil to recite the words of the Vedas as they are taught by his teacher. Or can we explain it as a sudden creation (*tātkālika-nirmāṇa*) as in the case of magic, or as an appearance of something (*tadābhāsa*) reproduced by tricks as in the case of the illusion created by a sleight-of-hand?[4] Abhinavagupta offers a number of options mentioned above to explain ontologically the nature of '*Nāṭya*' and denies all such hypotheses.

He singles out the concept of '*anukaraṇa*' in his brilliant analysis and argues that imitation (*anukaraṇa*) amounts to be a farcial and comic copy of the 'real'. Therefore, it is essentially a distortion (*vikaraṇa*). It makes the indifferent one simply laugh and may cause indignation in those who belong to the side of the imitated one.

The concept of '*anukīrtana*' is deeply rooted in the Vedic and Āgamic idea of '*Yajña*' and '*Vāk*'.

Kapila Vatsyayan has underlined the Vedic background of the *Nāṭyaśāstra* in her article on 'Dance or movement techniques of Sanskrit theatre' and in her own celebrated book *The Square and the Circle of the Indian Art* as well as in the paper entitled "The Indian Arts: Their Ideational Background and the Principles of Form" appearing in the work entitled "*Rūpa Pratirūpa*."[5] Earlier F.B.J. Kuiper, a well-known Dutch scholar and M.C. Byrski, the well-known Polish scholar did remarkable work in this direction. Kapila Vatsyayan maintains, "In enunciating his theory and in evolving a grammar of Artistic expression, Bharata undoubtedly accepted the organic world view inherent in the earlier speculative thought and the ritual. He brings together into one fold the essentials of this speculative thought, particularly the complex system of establishing correspondences between the limbs and the organs of human body, the senses and aspects of cosmos as also the methodology (the *Vidhi*) of the Brāhmaṇas, where earth, space, time are consecrated to suggest a cosmic order and the repetitive rhythm of cosmic time. He enunciates another path of experiencing the Brahman or Formless through the world of manifold names and form (*Nāma* and *Rūpa*)."[6] She further elaborates the idea and states that "the imagery of *Upaniṣads* which contain metaphysical ideas is translated into an actual technique of using limbs and organs of the human body and the senses with the objective of establishing correspondences between them and impersonalised states of being. Bharata thus develops a system wherein the very language of name and form (*Nāma* and *Rūpa*) evokes that beyond form or without form (*Pararūpa* and *Arūpa*), however momentarily."[7]

Āgamas also share the Vedic view of universe and man and emphasize the '*śakti*' or '*kriyā*' (creative) aspect of consciousness in order to explain the riddle more satisfactorily. For example, the primal creative act has been explained in the following words in Non-dualistic Kashmir Śaivism:

> "*Śiva* intent on creativity in the form of expansion by the means of energy of the great '*mantra*' of supreme primal word, viz. the perfect 'I' in union with '*Śakti*' in whom the urge of expansion is explicit and in whom abounds the bloom of compactness of their energy, becomes engaged in the act of creative expansion."[8]

The Āgamas try to explain the process of mundane as well as aesthetic and spiritual experience in terms of '*Śakti*' or potentiality and energy or the activity arising from our 'Freedom'. Thus creation and activity, being an activity, may be explained in terms of Vedic '*yajña*' as well as Āgamic '*kriyā*'.

Indian aesthetic tradition views art as the 'manifestation' of the 'unmanifest', which is an act involving the entire cosmos. Thus Pannikar maintains that "It is neither a merely divine affair, nor a purely human endeavour, nor a blind cosmic process, it is human, divine and cosmic–all in one. This reveals the inter-relation and the unity of the cosmos."[9]

The *Nāṭya* as '*Kriyā*' is creative '*anukīrtana*' of the 'Bhāva'. Bharata, at the same time views, '*Nāṭya*' as the '*anukaraṇa*' of the 'threefold universe' and 'the seven continents' (*Sapta-dvīpa*). This Indian concept of '*Anukaraṇa*' may be distinguished from the Greek concept of 'mimesis' in terms of its capacity to create a new world, whereas mimesis represents the world. In the Indian concept of '*anukaraṇa*', "the model is forgotten as soon as the creation is complete."[10] Abhinava upholds the view of his celebrated teacher, Bhaṭṭa Tauta that no recreation of the original historical 'Rāma' is possible. An actor only re-tells the historical or the present reality in traditional Indian theatre in a glorious way. Moreover, '*Nāṭya*' is the celebration of reality.

Thus, Nāṭya may be viewed experientially as '*Rasa*'. While '*anukīrtana* of the '*Bhāvas*' is a creative act in the sense of '*kriyā*', '*Rasa*' is an experience (*Anubhava*) of the 'Self' as 'Vimarśana' ('I'-consciousness), the subtlest, the most intrinsic, indivisble, fundamental, fullest and purest aspect of the '*Kriyā*' (activity) as '*Śakti*' or Potentiality lying dormant in our consciousness.

It is an '*anuvyavasāya*' (re-cognition), '*Prakāśa*' (luminosity), and *Ānanda* (bliss) as the "I-consciousness" characterised by such '*bhāvas*' as love (*rati*), sorrow (*śoka*), etc. Hence, it is wonderful. It is known by such synonyms as relishing (*rasa, rasana, āsvādana*), mastication (*carvaṇā*), flash of wonder (*camatkāra*), immersion (*niveśa*) and enjoyment (*bhoga*).

Ancient Indian culture experienced an integral viw of creativity and aesthetic experience in this concept of theatre, that has its basis in the holistic view of the universe and in the circular concept of time.

Bharata declares: "Nothing proceeds on the stage without reference to '*Rasa*'. He and his commentators emphasize that when all the components of the drama beginning with *Vibhāva* (the cause of the 'emotive states' and the environment in which they take place), *Anubhāva* (the 'consequents' expressive of those 'emotive states') etc. are presented, the realisation of *Rasa* manifests itself in the spectator. Similarly, when any element required for the manifestation of 'Rasa' is missing, the *Rasa*-realisation is rendered difficult, indirect, or incomplete.

Since cosmic multiplicity was created through the primordial act of sacrifice, therefore, unity may be regained through the same sacrificial act, freeing the self from its spatial and temporal limitations. The same creative act takes place in the sphere of aesthetic experience. The *Sahṛdaya* (aesthete) of traditional Indian art, literature and theatre attains repose in his deeper 'Self' (*ātmaviśrānti*) for a moment and experiences '*Rasa*' after having transcended the duality of relationship seen in temporal and spatial differentiations. It is an experience in which we move beyond ordinary temporality and spatiality, an experience which begins with the awareness of the 'relationship', but ultimately transcends it. However, the experience of westerns art-forms is confined to the awareness of either affirmation or negation of a specific relationship, and is therefore entirely different from its Indian counterpart.

Art forms in which one has to transcend the temporal and spatial differentiations manifested in the world of relationship offer a very different aesthetic experiences. Although in such art-forms, one begins with the delineation of the '*vibhāvas*' (the causes), *anubhāvas* (the consequents) and the '*sañcāri-bhāvas*' (relatively fleeting emotions), and the '*sthāyi-bhāvas*' (lasting or permanent emotions), the point of culmination is '*sādhāraṇīkaraṇa*' (de-personalization, universalization) in which these '*vibhāvas*' etc. neither appear belonging or not belonging to the aesthete nor belonging or not belonging to inner self or to others (either an enemy or a friend or some one quite different), for there is neither affirmation nor negation of the specific relationship at the stage of universalization.

In our ordinary mundane life, emotions or feelings (*bhāvas*) are evoked by some one who is their *āśraya* or substratum and by some specific environment working as stimulus. Emotions, feelings and dispositions can be permanent or lasting, such as love and anger etc., or fleeting, such as bashfulness or envy etc. It is sometimes difficult to determine which emotions is permanent and which is fleeting. Therefore, Bharata's opinion is final in such matters. Permanent emotions are called '*sthāyi-bhāvas*' and fleeting emotions are named '*sañcāri-bhāvas*'. The '*sthāyi-bhāvas*' are only eight or nine, while '*sañcāri-bhāvas*' are thirty-three in number. The *bhāvas* are made known or visible to others through the '*anubhāvas*' such as gestures, language and facial expressions.

When depicted, for instance, in a play, the 'cause' is known as '*vibhāva*'. The one on whom emotion rests is called '*ālambana vibhāva*' and the stimulating surroundings, as '*uddīpana-vibhāva*'. In our ordinary life a dominant emotion is often mingled with various fleeting emotions. A pervasive portrayal of life can never have only one sentiment. One dominant emotion will always be interwoven with various fleeting emotions. In an accurate portrayal of real life, the depiction of '*vibhāvas*', '*anubhāvas*', '*sthāyi-bhāva*' and '*sañcāri-bhāvas*' are present, but it must always culminate with the unity of *bhāvas*, known as '*Rasa*'. The means by which art attains this unity is '*sādhāraṇīkaraṇa*' or 'universalization', which leads to the transcendence of the specificity of relationship, or the individuation. In this way, it paves the way for transcending time and space, and thereby for attaining the repose into one's own deeper self (*ātmaviśrānti*) which is indivisible and pure consciousness (*cit*) and bliss (*ānanda*). This is *Rasa*.

The term '*nāṭya*' has been employed primarily to denote '*Rasa*' and secondarily, through Lakṣaṇā, 'abhinaya' endowed with its four genres–*Vācika, Āṅgika, Sāttvika* and *Āhārya*. '*Abhinaya*' is the means for expressing the '*bhāva*' and for evoking '*Rasa*'. This '*abhinaya*' stays in the actor or '*naṭa*' and reveals the '*vibhāvas*' etc. imbued in the dramatic texts. It means that the '*vibhāvas*' described in the dramatic text are elaborately delineated by the actor who concretizes them into corporeal images, his '*āṅgika*' or corporeal '*abhinaya*'. This corporeal '*abhinaya*' is usually accompanied with '*vācika*' or 'speech', '*sāttvika*' or emotional acting and '*āhārya*' or make up, costume and (required) properties. Very often other elements are also necessary such as '*dharmī*', the highly conventional or less conventional and more natural modes of representation, '*vṛtti*', modes of verbal, corporeal, and emotional activity, '*svaras*' the melodies, '*gāna*' the songs, '*ātodya*', the percussions and other instruments, and '*raṅga*' or stage and the auditorium. Traditional Indian Theatre integrates all these elements and thus, may be termed as an 'Integral Theatre'. The aesthetic experience emerging from such a theatre is 'holistic'. It is truly an integrated, holistic theatre.

The Structure of Drama

Bharata and Abhinava distinguish '*nṛtta*' from '*nāṭya*'. They relate '*nāṭya*' to '*rasa*' and '*bhāva*' as '*kāvyārtha*', the ultimate poetic meaning. '*Nṛtta*' is completely bereft of such poetic meaning. As such, it is related to life and termed as '*pāramārthikā*' (Real) by Abhinava. However, later texts distinguish '*nṛtta*' from '*nṛtya*' and relate '*nāṭya*' to '*rasābhinaya*' and '*nṛtya*' to '*bhāvābhinaya*' which express the meanings of poetic text. Whereas, *nṛtta* has been defined in terms of pure dance ("*Nṛttam tālālayaśritam*"). In earlier texts there is no distinction between '*nāṭya*' and '*nṛtya*', but in later texts it is found. However, all the texts agree that '*nāṭya*' and '*nṛtya*' both are related to '*kāvyārtha*' and thereby '*rasābhinaya*', whereas '*nṛtta*' is independent of '*kavya*'. Thus, '*nāṭya*' is '*rasa*', which is the very soul of the dramatic text (*pāṭhya*), i.e. the text entirely composed by the playwright or handed down orally by tradition in order to be performed.

Sanskrit theatre has a long history of prewritten text. According to the myth of origin of '*nāṭya*' occurring in NŚ, Brahmā created '*Nāṭya-veda*' by deriving '*pāṭhya*' from the '*Ṛgveda*', '*gīta*' from the '*Sāmaveda*', '*abhinaya*' from the '*Yajurveda*' and '*Rasa*' from the '*Atharvaveda*'. He created '*Itihāsa*' which remains a source for the '*pāṭhya*' or the text recited, i.e. the dramatic text. The *Ṛgveda* has the triple '*svaras*' (musical accent). This is the reason that '*pāṭhya*' endowed with the '*saptasvaras*' (seven melodies), is derived from the *Ṛgveda*. The '*svaras*' remind us immediately of the melodic '*svaras*' reaching its full development with *gīta, ātodya* in *Sāmaveda*. Hence, '*gīta*' including '*ātodya*' is also derived from the '*Sāmaveda*' in order to add pleasure (*rañjana*) to '*Nāṭya*'. '*Nāṭya*' is essentially a '*kriyā*' or activity in time and space. The *Yajurveda* is related to sacrifice, which is again, action. Therefore, the '*kriyā*' that is the '*abhinaya*' was derived from the *Yajurveda*. The accounts of the origin of *Nāṭya* help effect the realisation of the unity of the art and the transcending of multiplicity through '*avadhāna*' (concentration, aesthetic contemplation) and ultimately through the rise of '*sattva*' (the state of being in one's own 'Being'). '*Avadhāna*' is needed in performing the '*śānti*' and '*puṣṭi*'-*karmans*, i.e. the religious and magical acts prescribed for 'pacification' (*śānti*) of the troubles and attainment of nourishing growth (*puṣṭi*) taught in the *Atharvaveda*. Hence '*rasa*' is derived from the '*Atharvaveda*', which cannot be experienced without emergence of '*sattva*'. '*Sattva*' is aroused through concentration and aesthetic contemplation.

This myth of origin of drama makes it clear that the theatre consists in four major elements already present in Vedic tradition and '*nāṭya*' emerged spontaneously from this tradition. To summarize, these basic parts of the theatre are '*pāṭhya*' or the dramatic text together with recitation and verbal acting, '*gīta*' or the songs and percussive as well as other form of theatre music, '*abhinaya*' or the acting and '*Rasa*' or the ultimate aesthetic experience.

The '*pāṭhya*' is the verbal body of '*nāṭya*'. The structural frame of the dramatic text is built through the '*Itivṛtta*' or plot. This plot may be derived either from the sources like '*Itihāsa*' and '*Purāṇas*' or from popular tradition or even from the poet's own imagination.

Everyone embarks upon an activity with a specific objective ('*kārya*'). Therefore, action constitutes the basis of a plot and it is divided into five phases (*avasthā*)–beginning of the effort, a hope of attainment of the fruit, the frustration and then the certainty of attaining at fruit, and finally its attainment.

Including the description of the phase scheme of dramatic action, the NŚ underlines that it is a universal concept applicable to each and every action. The phase scheme treats action in its temporal aspect. There is yet another concept '*arthaprakṛti*' or subject matter, which describes its texture of thickness. Elaborating the concepts of '*avasthā*' and '*arthaprakṛti*', M.C. Byrski maintains that the phase scheme underlines a purely linear aspect of action which it requires when seen in the perspective of time and space as the sequence of five stages. On the other hand, the concept of '*arthaprakṛti*' takes into account that the time factor, important as it is, should not falsify the true character of each and every action, "for it would be naive to conceive an action which lasts, for instance five hours, the first hour would be dominated by desire, the second by an effort, the third by hope, etc. It is obvious that all these actions function simultaneously. Only at different stages different ones come to the forefront. It is precisely the nature of the subject matter that expresses their idea."[11] The '*arthaprakṛtis*' are five in number, namely '*Bīja*', '*Bindu*', '*Patāka*', 'Prakarī' and 'Kārya'. Strictly speaking only three of the five, the germ (*Bīja*), the drop (*Bindu*) and the action (*Kārya*) describe the nature of main sphere of action.

These are the co-relative notions to the five phases. The Botanical image of the '*Bīja*' in the subject-matter scheme suggests development factor until its fruition. The image of '*Bindu*' refers to continuity of action or its uninterrupted flow. The next two categories are known as '*Patāka*', or the subsidiary plot, and '*Prakarī*' or the chain of episodes in which the hero receives assistance from others bringing on first the stage of hope and then certainty of success. The course of development joins with the unfolding of the dramatic action, identified as the five junctures (*Sandhi*): the opening, the progression, the development, the pause and the conclusion. This is the logic of the plot structure in Sanskrit drama.

The types of heroes namely '*Dhirodātta*', '*Dhīralalita*', '*Dhīroddhata*' and '*Dhīraśānta*' together with the types of heroines and accompanying characters, are also important in determining the structure of tenfold Sanskrit plays, i.e. 'Rūpakās'.

F.B.J. Kuiper, among others, has revealed some interesting aspects of the structure of Sanskrit theatre. In his work entitled 'Varuṇa and Vidūṣaka', he draws attention to the cosmogonic battle between the 'Devas' and 'Asuras' during which they not only employed normal weapons, but also verbal combat. He refers to the use of 'Vivāc' (lit. speaking variously in dispute with one another).[12] He posits a connection between this cosmogonic fight and the preliminaries (*Pūrvaraṅga*) of Sanskrit drama.

Byrski and Kuiper both view Sanskrit drama as the re-enactment of the cosmic creation and trace the structure of Sanskrit theatre to the re-enactment of that cosmic event. As already mentioned, there is a constant reference to 'trailokya' or 'triple universe', in defining the nature of '*nāṭya*'.

The whole concept of auditorium in the NŚ and the construction of the theatre space is related to cosmogony. A host of Gods and Goddesses as well as Asuras, Rākṣasas, Yakṣas, Gandharvas, Kinnaras, Apsaras and Nāgas are worshipped and given place in the auditorium in order to protect it and the performance in it. No wonder that Sanskrit theatre had an elaborate scheme of preliminaries entitled '*Pūrvaraṅga*' consisting of the elements which are '*Pāramārthika*', the acts of real life, such as the *Nāndi* or the prayer and the other elements with the definite theatrical purpose. As Brahmā occupies the central place of the stage, so does the *Sūtradhāra* in the preliminaries. *Sūtradhāra* is accompanied by '*pāripārśvikas*' or assistants in the *Pūrvaraṅga.* According to Kuiper, *Sūtradhāra* represents the creator, the two '*pāripārśvikas*' represent Indra and Varuṇa. Again the hero in the drama proper represents Indra, the *Vidūṣaka,* Varuṇa and the heroine, 'Sarasvati'.[13] One may quibble over details but it cannot be denied that the *Sūtradhāra,* the *Vidūṣaka* and the hero form the basic structure of Sanskrit drama and Sanskrit theatre. The evolution of two characters, *Sūtradhāra* and *Vidūṣaka* determine the development of traditional Indian theatre itself.

It is interesting to observe that, in later traditional 'folk' theatre forms, we see the survival of the *Sūtradhāra* in a predominant way, whereas elsewhere, it is the *Vidūṣaka,* who predominates. Mostly in 'temple theatre forms', the *Sūtradhāra* survives, and in the forms enacted outside the temple, the *Vidūṣaka* occupies the dominant place, especially when it comes to deal with changing social reality. As wit and humour have been employed in classical Sanskrit theatre in order to highlight the social contradictions so also they are used in traditional folk-theatre-forms for the same purpose.

The linguistic structure of Sanskrit drama is also very significant. The multi-language structure from the very beginning has provided a unique theatricality in Sanskrit drama. The simultaneous presence of Sanskrit, Prākṛta and even Apabhraṁśa infuses a unique theatrical strength to Sanskrit theatre, so much so that recently even modern Indian language have found place in the structure of theatrical texts, for example, in a Kuḍiyāṭṭam performance *Vidūṣaka* elaborates his Prākṛta dialogue into Malayalam.

Vṛttis (modes of activities of speech, mind and body), namely *Bhārati, Sattvati, Ārabhaṭi* and *Kaiśiki* also play important roles in determining the structure of Sanskrit drama. For instance, *Nāṭaka* and *Prakaraṇa* have all the *vṛttis,* while the rest are devoid of the delicate vṛtti. The '*Ḍima*' should have only two *vṛttis* whereas '*Utsṛṣṭikāṅka*' should be devoid of all with the exception of *Bhārati.*

The number of acts is the next common distinction. The NŚ gives the exact number of acts for eight Rūpakas. *Vyāyoga, Īhāmṛga, Bhāṇa, Vithi, Utsṛṣṭikāṅka* are single act play. Samavakāra is a three-act play and *Ḍima* a four-act play. *Nāṭaka* as well as *Prakaraṇa* are composed with five to ten acts. NŚ does not specify the acts in '*Prahasana*', but Abhinava maintains that *Śuddha* (Pure) *Prahasana* is a one-act play, whereas '*Saṃkirṇa*' (mixed) *Prahasana* consists of many acts.

We have already noticed that music was an integral part of Sanskrit theatre from the very beginning–music was added in order to provide 'pleasure' (*rañjana*) to '*pāthya*'. Sanskrit drama utilises music according to the needs of theatre. NŚ speaks of the employment of '*Dhruvā*'. Kālidāsa and some of the later dramatists refer to the employment of *Dhruvā,* but give no clues to its use in the play. The dialogues that of prose and verse continue to be integral to the dramatic structure throughout the history of Sanskrit theatre. But the integration of the music lies in the introduction of '*gāna*' and '*ātodya*'. It served not only to determine the pace and rhythm of the movement, gait, *cārī,* exit and entry, etc., but also to integrate '*lāsyāṅgas*' (theatrical forms integrating pure dance and songs in them) into the body of the text. The progress of the Sanskrit theatre from '*Rūpakas*' to '*Uparūpakas*' is marked by the increasing use of music. The tendency was already present even in the time of Kālidāsa and *Harivaṅśa-purāṇa,* and it gathers momentum with the passage of time. Music becomes more and more essential and '*Uparūpakas*' often came to be called '*Saṅgītakas*'. It is important to note that music and dance acquire more dominant a place in the dramatic text and theatrical structure during this entire period. Although as previously plays were written with maximal dramatic scripts, the theatre practice began to rely increasingly on musical forms. This conclusion is based on references found in the *Abhinavabhāratī* and the *Bhāva-prakāśana* and such other texts.

A deeper study of the link between the '*Uparūpakas*' and the surviving 'folk' dance and 'Folk-theatre-form' may throw light on the later development of Sanskrit theatre and other traditional theatrical forms. Indeed, the tendency of connecting 'folk' forms and Sanskrit play performance is very old. The directions in the name of playwright himself to '*Vikramorvaśīya*' , a unique play from the point of view, reveals the immense emploment of musical and dance forms in the play-performance. Many terms occurring in '*Vikramorvaśīya*' are not traceable either to NŚ or to later Nāṭyaśāstric texts. They appear to be taken from the popular theatre tradition of the early mediaeval period which remained in perfect harmony with NŚ Directions given in '*Vikramorvaśīya*' prove that Kālidāsa's plays have an unbroken tradition of performance upto the early mediaeval period. This detailed account and appreciation, presented in highly śāstric language employing the terminology of NŚ proves the undiluted continuity of the NŚ tradition as late as 10th century A.D. It helps to explain Abhinavagupta's intimate and deep understanding of the practical aspect of the NŚ in the following centuries. References to the performance of IV Act of *Ratnāvalī* in *Kuṭṭanimatam* also proves the continuity of Nāṭyaśāstric tradition in premediaeval India.

Kallinātha's elaborate choreographical account of the *Nāndī* of '*Vikramorvaśīya*' also makes it clear that not only Sanskrit plays in general, but '*Vikramorvaśīya*' performances in particular continued upto his time (mediaeval period) and that the style adopted was highly '*nṛtya*'-oriented.[14]

Thus, the theatre which comes into existence at the initiative of gods headed by Indra is a theatre of '*Anukīrtana*', of *Bhāvas* and of the aesthetic experience of *Rasa*. It is a 'holistic theatre' consisting of a highly evolved text, pre-written as well as orally floating among the community of artists. It assimilated '*gīta*', '*ātodya*' fourfold *abhinaya, Nṛtta, Bhāva* and *Rasa* as its integral elements. Although the tradition of pre-written text continued, the tradition of floating oral text easily grasped by an audience fully familiar with the content of the text and the story gradually strengthened and became popular over time. This 'floating oral text' became the main vehicle for the performance by the traditional artists in the medieval period.

The theatre which has been essentially a theatre of free creative activity of '*Anukīrtana* of *Bhāva*' and the experience of '*Rasa*', has also been an object of life's diversion, namely the play which is both visual and audible. Sometimes it has been viewed as a ply (*krīḍā*) in terms of '*Māya*', when the entire expanse of the phenomenal world is viewed as an illusion according to the 'Advaita Vedānta'. It has also been seen as '*krīḍā*' (free activity) when this grand expansion of the plurality is the manifestation of '*Śakti*' (Power, Potentiality), and *Svātantrya* (Freedom). The latter approach towards the artistic creation and theatre occurs from an early period. The notion of Theatre as 'Līlā' is seminally present in the NŚ. Somewhat later developments occur with theatre as 'Freedom' (*Svātantrya*) and theatre as 'repose in the self' ('*svatmaviśrānti*') found in Kashmir Śaivite tradition. The concept of '*Bhāvānukīrtana*' and '*Rasa*' occurring to NŚ seems to be fully captured in the concept of theatre as 'Play' or 'Free creative activity'.

The tradition continues uninterruptedly even in our own times. 'Imitation' and 'Conflict' and so on is not the only view of theatre. There is a powerful alternative view of theatre in Indian tradition in consonance with an equally powerful view of the universe.

References

1. Abhinavabhāratī on NŚ I.1, p. 2, Nāṭyaśāstra, Vol. I, Baroda, 1956.
2. 'Sanskrit Drama in Performance,' pp. p-13, Ed Baumer and Brandon, The University Press of Hawaii, Honolulu, 1981.
3. *Ibid.*, p. 11.

4. Abhinavabhāratī, NŚ, Vol. I, p. 35.
5. Rūpa Pratirūpa, pp. 11-26, Ed. B. Baumer, Biblia Impex Pvt. Ltd., New Delhi, 1982.
6. *The Square and the Circle of the Indian Arts*, Kapila Vatsyayan, p. 9, New Delhi, 1983.
7. *Ibid.*, p. 39.
8. Parātriśikā-Vivaraṇa, Trans. Dr. Jaideva Singh, p. 42, Motilal Banarsidass, Delhi, 1988.
9. *Vedic Experience*, R. Panikar, p. 73, Motilal Banarsidass, Delhi, 1983.
10. Dramatic Concepts: Greek and Indian, Bharat Gupt, p. 98, New Delhi, 1994.
11. Prof. M.C. Byrski, *Methodology of the Analysis of Sanskrit Drama*, Warszawa, 1979.
12. *Varuṇa and Vidūṣaka*, Prof. F.B.J. Kuiper, p. 193, Amsterdam, 1979.
13. *Ibid.*, p. 118-240.
14. Kallinātha, pp. 186-189, Saṅgītaratnākara, Vol. IV, Adyar Library, 1953.

67

SHORAPUR: A PALACE CITY OF LATE-MEDIEVAL SOUTHERN DECCAN

S.K. Aruni

The medieval Karnataka witnessed foundations of a large number of capitals cities or urban centres and these capital cities or urban centres are till today continued to be headquarters of the districts or talukas. These medieval capitals with high walls and other important structures of defence architecture were primarily meant to protect the towns and society of the region for examples Halebid, Talakad, Gulbarga, Vijayanagara, Bijapur, Keladi, etc. With the adoption of certain urban features like palaces, gardens and other courtly structures these fortified towns later became symbols of expression of power. One of such capital city of the late medieval period is Shorapur (also known as Surapura), the taluka headquarter of the same name in Gulbarga district. The citadel complex, several living quarters for selected groups of the society, temples within the enclosed walls and location of a number of suburbs on the outskirts of the Shorapur city are noteworthy and good example of *sastric* model city of the region.

Shorapur was capital seat of the Surapura Samsthana (Samsthana means a small semi-independent kingdom). Surapura Samsthana was one of the important Samsthana of the post-Vijayanagara period in North Karnataka. This small kingdom came to power with the grant of Jagir from the Adil Shahis of Bijapur in the middle of 17th century A.D. The earlier capital was Wagingera lies 9 km to the southwest of Shorapur town. The importance of the principality's history lies in their battle against Mughals in 1705. Soon after the capture of Bijapur, Aurangazeb demanded Pid Nayaka II (1687-1726) to surrender his kingdom, but he refused to do so and also he revolted against Mughal powers in the Deccan. This led to begin Mughal campaigns against the Pid Nayak at Wagingera. Finally the Mughal emperor, Aurangazeb, had to personally lead the campaigns against Pid Nayaka-II. After the capture of the fort Aurangazeb camped at Devapur where he fell ill. He was eighty-seven years old and he died at Ahmadnagar in 1707. Thus the battle of Wagingera is an important event in the history of Deccan as it was the last military expedition undertaken by Aurangazeb. Another highlight of the Samsthana's history is the participation of last king, Raja Venkatappa Nayaka IV in the 'Sepoy Mutiny' in 1858. He rebelled against the British East India Company and involved in the Mutiny. Thus this led to capture the capital and the Samsthana came to an end in A.D.1858.

History of the city

Shorapur is the headquarter of the taluka of same name in the district of Yadgir. The city Shorapur lies 10 km to the north of the river Krishna on the Gulbarga-Bangalore highway. It is located in a shallow valley formed by the granitic hills which rise 560 m to 580 m above the Mean Sea Level. The city was founded soon after the death of Aurangazeb (1710) by Raja Pid Nayaka-II is also known as Pitambar Bahari Pid Nayaka). He built a fort at Shorapur and he divided the city into many sectors for different sections of the people. He laid foundation for a royal temple known as Venugopalaswamy temple. The city became the capital seat of the his Samsthana. His successors like Raja Venkatappa Nayaka-I (1747-1752), Raja Pama Nayaka III (1752-1774) and Raja Venkatappa Nayaka IV (1842-1858) built several temples and renovated the palaces, fort and gateways during their respective reigns. The city continued not only the political seat of the Samsthana but also the cultural destiny of the North Karnataka throughout the Samsthana period. After the brief occupation of British army in 1858 after the 'Sepoy Mutiny', the Shorapur became district headquarter under the Hyderabad Nizams State.

The Fort

The city is protected by the a massive fort wall, this runs on top of the hills and across the valley to form an oval shape. The total length of the fort wall is approximately 6400 m and covers approximately an area of 2 km X 1.5 km. and has a total of 34 circular and semi-circular bastions at strategic locations. There are six gateways built in different directions. *Devapur-agasi* (Southern Gate), *Mull-agasi* (Eastern Gate), *Kappalabenchi-agasi* (Western Gate), *Rangampeth-agasi* (Northeastern Gate), *Siddapur-agasi* (Northwestern Gate) and *Venkatapur-agasi* (Southeastern Gate). Among these gates the Devapur-agasi is intact and is an impressive one. The gate is strengthened with two circular bastions on either side. To protect the enemy's direct attack on the gate they built a rectangular barbican-court in front of the entrance. The gate walls have a group of musicians sculptural reliefs which indicate the traditional welcome to the city. *The Siddapur, Mull-agasi* and *Kappalabenchi-agasi* gates are in collapsed due to recent roads.

The City

Importance of the city lies on its physiography. The city is located in a shallow valley 80 m above the surrounding place and the hills and hillocks provide natural defence to the city. The central part of the city is occupied by the citadel complex. To the west of the citadel complex is a temple called Venugopalaswamy-*gudi* which houses the deity of royal family. The city is divided into Vaishnavaite, Saivaite, Bedars, craftsmen (Visvakarmas) and Muslim quarters. The capital city accommodated the ruling royal class, administrative class, elite class, scholars or *pandits* class and servants. According to chronicles, the founder of the Shorapur capital Raja Pid Nayaka-II (1687-26) divided the city into 14 quarters and assigned them to various classes of the society.

1. *Nadugeri*
2. *Mayeri*
3. *Hande-vajirgeri*
4. *Donnigeri*
5. *Jaggadakeri*
6. *Hulkadikeri*
7. *Boyigeri*
8. *Rampurgeri*
9. *Kurabargeri*
10. *Gurikarkeri*
11. *Sarsbadgeri*
12. *Gonalkeri*

13. *Palledkeri and*
14. *Gantinayakanageri*

Palace Complex

The citadel complex (*Bala-Hisar*) forms an important aspect of the medieval strongholds. These citadels strictly served to accommodate the rulers and built away from the city's population. The Hindu type for laying of the capitals in Medieval South India was accommodating the citadel (as recommended in the ancient texts or *Sastras*) in the central part (*mandala*) of the city. Bijapur and Warangal (A.P.) contain the citadels in the central part of the city and are good examples in the Deccan. At Shorapur the citadel complex is in the central part of the city. The complex is enclosed with high walls with a gate on the east. The walls are now in bad condition. The eastern wall is modified into a row of shops. In the middle of these shops is a large size entrance known as *Darbar-agasi.* This leads to the complex. The complex contains two distinctive palaces known as Hale Darbar (old palace) on the north and *Naya Darbar* (New palace) on the south of the complex.

Palaces

Hale *Darbar* or Old palace was built by Raja Venkatappa Nayaka I (A.D.1747-1752). This palace is now being used as primary school. Once it was audience hall and other activities complex of the Samsthana. This palace has several structures including a tower-like four-storeyed structure at southwestern corner, two vaulted rectangular halls, a rectangular hall with five arched openings and several large rectangular court-yards and few water fountains. The tower like four-storeyed structure dominates the *darbar*. To the south of this structure is a large hall which is now used as girl's high school.

The *Naya Darbar* or New palace is still under occupation of the royal family of the Samsthana. The palace is on the south of old palace and is standing as a prominent structure of the old capital city. Interesting part of the building is that this structure is laid on the east-west axis to the royal temple--Venugopalaswamy. One can see the main deity of the Venugopalaswamy temple from the balcony of the palace. It is said that the queens or royal persons were used to see the deity from the palace itself. Originally this palace had two large pillared halls, a large royal residence, harem, and a long stable for royal horses. Now only the royal residence is remained and bases of pillared halls are still can be seen on the east of the royal residence. The royal residence is three storyed. This consists number of rooms and open courts. The prominent feature of the palace is the wood carvings. The two storyes have well carved wooden pillars and beams and reminds us the western Indian Maratha palaces.

Venugopalswamy- The Royal Temple

To the west of the palace complex is the royal temple, Venugopalaswamy, it is located on a small hillock faces the east (palace). The Samsthana's state religion was the Vaisnava. the founder of the city, Raja Pid Nayaka-II laid the foundation of this temple built in the same axis to the palace. It is tradition that the royal temples should be face the royal residences (palace) and palaces should be below the temple's *sikhara.* This tradition is evident in the Shorapur. Since it is the royal temple, it has an elaborate plan which consists of all components of the temple such as *garbhagriha*, *antarala*, *ardhamandapa*, *sabhamandapa*, pillared *mukhamandapa*, rectangular pillared veranda, a *vahanamandapa* and *dvajastamba*. The temple is enclosed by high *prakara* walls. A broad flight of steps on the east leads to the temple from the ground. The carvings of pillars found in the *mukhamandapa* are noteworthy. These receive our attraction for their delicate carvings. These pillars and sculptures exhibit both the Deccani and Vijayanagara art features. The *sikhara* of the temple is of *Dravida* order and is built with brick and stucco. The parapet of the temple has many stucco sculptures. A blend of the Deccani and Vijayanagara styles can be seen in this temple and can be taken as representative temple of the post-Vijayanagara temple architecture in Karnataka.

Space Arrangement of the City

The city is broadly divided into Vaisnava, Saiva, Muslim sectors. The Vaisnva sector is located on the northern and northeastern part of the city or on the left side of the citadel complex locally known as Brahamanara-Oni, the Saiva sector occupies the south and southeastern part of the city and the Muslim sector is on the southeastern edge of the city. These sectors are indicated by the temples dedicated to respective deities and the mosques to the Muslims. The Vaishnvaite sector has many temples dedicated to the Vaishnava cult namely Narasimha, Panduranga, Vithala, Ramadeva and Prasanna Venkatesha temples. Similarly the Saiva sector has the Saiva temples and monasteries namely Kashi-Vishvanatha, Sugureswara, Isvara temples and Kadalappa monastery. The Muslim quarter shares a small area has few Muslim families and a mosque in the centre. The understanding of the town-plan of Shorapur appears to be followed the Mandala system as recommended in the ancient texts of the county. However, the lay-out of the Shorapur city may be partly ascribed to the ancient sastric model, with the royal residence in the central mandala and the others occupied by different classes of the society - the Saivites, Vaishnvites, Muslims and other classes.

Other Temples

A large number of temple are found in the city which were built by the rulers of the Samsthana. To the west of the palace are Vaisnava temples namely Narasimha, Panduranga, Venkateshvara, Prasanna Venkata and Ragavendraswamy temples while on the north of the palace are Isvara, Sugureswara, Kasi-Vishvanatha temples and a Kadalappa Matha. Both Saiva and Vaisnava temples are follow the royal temple – Venugopalaswamy - plan and other components. The Narasimha temple has octagonal sikhara which a sole example Maratha temple architecture influence on the Samsthana temple architecture. The Venkatesvara and Panduranga temples have very beautiful sikharas.

Muslim Quarter

The rulers of the Surapura Samsthana also provided a separate sector for the Muslims and built mosques. The Muslim quarter is in the southeastern sector of the town and contains two mosques: *Hire Majid* and *Naya Masjid*. The *Hire Masjid* occupies the eastern part of the Muslim quarter and consists of a small prayer room, a rectangular hall, a large open court, a conical *minar* and an arched gate. The interesting feature of the mosque is the conical *minar*. The *minar* stands on a raised square platform. The minar is adorned with a large number of projected slabs and it has miniature balcony-like on top. This conical *minar* resembles the *Dipamala* of the Maratha temples.

Taylor Manzil

Col. Meadow Taylor, who was great administrator and archaeologist of 19th century. He was serving in the Hyderabad Nizam State. Due to unsettled disputes between the Nizam and the Samsthana, the British East Company sent Taylor to the Samsthana to deal the disputes. Taylor came to Shorapur as 'Political Agent' in 1842 and served for 8 years. In his autobiography (Story of My Life) five chapters are dealt with Samsthan's history and his relation with the Samsthana. During his stay at Shorapur Taylor built a mansion for himself and this is known as Taylor *Manzil*. The Taylor *Manzil* is located on a high hillock called Kudaregudda. The plan and design of the complex was prepared by Col. Taylor himself and this building was completed in 1844. This complex follows the European style in layout and it consists of a house and a large rectangular office (*Darbar*). Both the house (*Manzil*) and *Darbar* face east. The house has a rectangular drawing hall flanked by large bed-rooms and a dining hall. Two porches are on the eastern and western ends; these have circular columns in the facade. Taylor lived in this house for ten years.

Water Supply

Although the city is located in the middle of the hills, the city never had any water shortage throughout the history. The selection of the site by the rulers is admirable. Due to geological setting like two major dykes, provided water sources. There are two geological dykes found on either sides of the city and are locally known as *Sitha-ka-Seragu*. These two dykes maintain a favorable ground-water level in the city. The city has a number of wells and large tanks. To trap the rain water the rulers have built number of tanks in the city. These wells and tanks provide water to the large habitants of the city.

Suburbs

Founding new settlements around the capitals was tradition in the medieval period for example Vijayanagara rulers found new settlements around the capital namely Kamalapuram, Nagalapuram, etc. Similarly the rulers of the Samsthana founded number of villages around the capitals. These are;

1. Kumarpet
2. Narasingampeth
3. Sibarbandi
4. Venkatapur
5. Satyampeth
6. Rukmapur
7. Lakshmipur
8. Timmapur
9. Rangampeth
10. Hasnanapur and
11. Siddapur

These new village were named after the queens or mothers names. These settlements not only provided shelter to the ever growing population, but also functioned as a second chain of defence to the capital. The capital cities are usually populated by the nobility or elite class and the surrounding settlements were inhabited by other classes. Venkatapur has a large temple known as *Basavanna-gudi.* The temple is also good example of Surapura Samsthana temple architecture. The nandi-mandapa has a large size *nandi* (Basava). Rangampeth has a large monastery known as *Rudraswamy-matha.* The walls of the *matha* have decorated a paintings which are very good example of Surapura style paintings. A large stepped well is found at Sataympeth known as Khanbhavi.

Paintings

Shorapur was one of the main centre of the fine arts. The paintings which set a new trend in the region is unique for its features and known as Shorapur school of painting. A blend of two different styles namely Vijayanagara or South Indian and the Deccani, are found in the Shorapur school of paintings. This school was flourished from the middle of 18th century to end of the Samsthana rule. A large number of paintings of this school are missing and few are preserved in various museums. The South Indian iconic features and elegance of the Deccani paintings are found in these paintings. Till today the old paintings are available in royal residences and old houses. Even these days the features of the Shorapur style are common among new artists of the region.

68

WATER RESOURCES AND THEIR MANAGEMENT IN ANCIENT INDIA

Pragya Chaturvedi

Like air, water is critical for living beings including humans. Therefore, since time immemorial man looked to the water bodies which could be a perennial source of water for him. It is because of this natural necessity that the primitive man used to occupy those parts of lands which could be a good source of water supply, and it was surely because of it that human settlements - villages, towns and cities - emerged either on the banks of rivers or some reliable source of water, a phenomenon which is observed even today.

Water being essential for existence was considered critical since the emergence of early societies. In fact, it was attached with the sense of religiousity in the ancient Indian tradition. The Rigveda, the oldest Indian text refers to *'Apah'* in four hymns.[1] They are also invoked in many detached verses along with other deities. The personification is only incipient, hardly extending beyond the notion of their being mother, young wives and goddesses who bestow boons and come to the sacrifice.[2]

The water is mentioned several times as bestowing remedies and longlife, immortality and healing are contained in them. They watch over man's health in house. They dispose of boons and wealth and bestow excellent strength and immortality.[3]

Sarasvati which was taken to be most sacred has been referred as best among the Goddesses (*Devitame*) and best among the mothers (*Ambatame*).[4] Obviously, being the perennial source of water the rivers nourished the mankind like mothers. The Harappans too considered the water sacred as is evident from the example of the 'Great Bath of Mohenjodaro'. In the Puranas digging of waterbodies such as well, ponds and tanks was considered to be the most pious acts which earned *'punya'* for those who indulged in their creation. It is significant aspect of the *'purta dharma'* depicted in the Puranas.

In the beginning when the people were not aware of the groundwater or about its procurement they had to depend on the celestial or rainwater. However, it is not available all the times and even rivers and other water bodies containing it were prone to dry, in case of no rain or severe droughts. Presumably, it was in these kinds of situations that people would have indulged into water storage in the man-made water bodies and would have searched the devices to outsource the ground water. Reliable evidence regarding these types of efforts occurs in proto-historic cultures including Harappan.

Development of reliable sources of water like storage tanks, wells, reservoirs, ponds, lakes, irrigation canals, anicuts etc. came to be regarded as an essential part of good governance. Our ancient religious texts and epics give a good insight into the water storage and conservation system prevailing in those days. Emperors not only built various water bodies but also encouraged the village communities and individuals to build these on their own. Several laws were made for maintenance and preservation of water and its proper distribution and use. Water came to be regarded as precious and its conservation and preservation was sanctified by religion.

The Mohenjodaro and Harappan ruins have thrown light on the fact that people of even that early period had given importance to proper water supply for domestic purposes, irrigation and public baths. There are archaeological evidence of water supply systems from a large number of wells with brick-lining. Dholavira, an important site of Indus valley had several reservoirs to collect rain water.[5] The city of Dholavira in Kachchh was built during Harappan civilization in a semi-arid region averaging 260 mm. rainfall annually. The city had an impressive and unique water harvesting and management system. These were no perennial water sources so they built storage tanks and wells. Similar evidences have been found at Mohenjodaro and Harappa. In Lothal (Gujarat) and Inamgaon (Maharashtra) and other places in north and western India small bunds were built by the local people to store rain water for irrigation.

Rigveda contains references to the water of wells being used for watering the fields and we have several words for well like *'Avata'*, 'Well', *'Kupa'* etc.[6] The water seems to have been raised by means of a wheel (Chakra) to which buckets of wood were fastened. The another passage of Rigveda shows that sometimes this water was poured into channels and sent to different parts of the field.[7] In Atharvaveda, we find a description of canal-digging[8]. In this reference the newly-cut canal is described in figurative language as a calf to the river which is as the cow. From these evidences it is clear that where there was scarcity of water people had to depend on the water of well, canals etc. Moreover, river or canal water which contains a good deal of silt, organic debris and salts which when carried would undoubtedly favourably influence the soil as also the crop irrigated.[9]

The Arthasastra of Kautilya gives an extensive account of dams and bunds that were built for irrigation during Mauryan period.[10] The water supply systems were well managed within the framework of strict rules and regulations. Different types of taxes were collected from the cultivators depending upon the nature of irrigation. The tax rate was 25% of the produce in respect of water drawn from natural sources like rivers, tanks, springs etc. From water drawn from storages built by the king the tax rate varied according to the method of drawing water. Water bodies like reservoirs, bunds, tanks were also privately owned and the owner was free to sell them. The owner could also sell water to others in return for a share of the produce. In the absence of the owner, the water bodies were to maintained by the people of the village. A set of punishments were prescribed for various violations of water laws like causing damage to another's plough or sown field, by letting water overflow from tank, causing damage to bunds, failure to maintain the water bodies, death penality was also prescribed for breaking a reservoir of tank full of water etc. [11]

Different methods were adopted to raise the irrigation water to permeate the fields. According to Kautilya these included carrying water by manual labour (*hastapravartimam*), water on shoulders, (*skandha-pravartimam*) conveyance of water by channels, (*srotoyantrapravartimam*) and by means of wind power (*vatapravartimam*) etc. Kautilya says that tanks and wells should be built in barren and less fertile parts of the country.[12] The Rock and Pillar edicts of Asoka refers to the digging of wells on highway at an interval of every half a *kosa* from each other.

Strabo refers to the embanked canals from which the water was distributed into the channels so that all could be benefited.[13] The excavations at Besnagar by D.R. Bhandarkar yielded a canal (300 B.C.) having a length of 185 feet towards the river with the masonary brick walls serving as embankments. The water of this canal, was probably brought up by suitable appliances to irrigate the fields in the vicinity.[14] Another canal of the Mauryan dynasty has been discovered at Kumrahar (Patna) appears to have been originally linked with the river Son and then with the river Ganga. It was utilised for internal transport and for irrigational purposes.[15]

Likewise, Mora brick inscription of the time of Bahasatimita reveals the construction of a well in the region of Kausambi.

In the post-Mauryan period Patanjali refers to *kulyah* for irrigation purposes.[16] The Hathigumpha inscription of Kharvela records that in his fifth year of reign a canal originally opened out by King Nanda 300 years earlier, to be brought to his capital from Tanasuli.[17] In the South, the Chola king Karikala built embankments along the Kaveri river to control its water and distribute them to irrigate the barren regions.[18] According to Dio-Chrysostom (Ist C.A.D.) there were many channels - large and small to convey water from the rivers in the country.[19] The Nasik Buddhist cave inscription of Ushavadata records that he made arrangements for distribution of water of rivers such as Iba, Parada, Damana, Tapi, Karabana and Dahanuka.[20] The Nasik Buddhist cave refers to the term *'Odayantrikas'* which is rendered by Senart as workers faricating hydraulic engines, water clocks or others. It seems that the engines had some connection with raising water from different sources for irrigation.[21] The widespread excavations at Nagarjunikonda have revealed a huge construction of ancient canal belonging to the time of Ikshvaku dynasty.[22] It has been observed that the paucity of either the religious or secular edifices in this area this canal was primarily built for irrigation purposes. The Satvahanas introduced the brick and ringwells.

These references indicates that from early times in the flat plains, the land was cut by canals running from the great rivers and dotted with artificial reservoirs, which were made by damming smaller streams or enlarging lakes by stopping their outlets. From these water supplies, whether natural and artificial, water was raised by counterpoised "sweeps' and fed into smaller channels, which watered the fields.[23] The Mathura stone slab inscription of the reign of Mahakshatrapa Sodasa records construction of a tank (*pushkarini*), the western tanks and a reservoir (*udapana*) by his treasurer.[24] From the Junagarh rock inscription of Rudradama we learn that the lake was built during the reign of first Mauryan emperor. It had strong embankments and was suitably provided with conduits and drains for proper distribution of water to the cultivated fields as also they served to safeguard against dirty water passing into the lake.

In the time of Rudradaman, a heavy flood caused a serious breach of a length of 420 cubits in the lake. But the state carried out the work of its repair and ensured prosperity to the people of Saurashtra whose fields were largely dependent on this source. Among the minor works of irrigtion tanks, well and artificial reservoirs etc. seem to have received more attention in ancient India.

A verse in the Bodhayana Dharmasastra shows that some of the villages entirely depend on wells for their water source.[25] In the newly formed villages, the king was expected to construct reservoirs (setu) with perennial water supply or with water drawn from some other source. The Pali and Sanskrit Buddhist text frequently refers to the construction of tanks, wells and reservoirs etc. both by the rulers and the ruled in many parts of North-eastern India.[26] At the Buddhist site of Sanchi there are three ancient tanks to store rain water from the hill slopes.

Epigraph on the colosal seated image of Kanishka mentions the construction of a temple, tank and a well.[27] Likewise the Gupta inscription of Chandragupta II and Skandagupta threw light on the large scale development of tank, well, canal for public welfare. In addition; the archaeological excavations have brought to light great terracotta ringwells, tanks and reservoirs. Most of them belong to the Mauryan and Post-Mauryan age and some might have served the purpose of irrigation. Such discoveries have been made at Hastinapur,[28] New Delhi[29], Mathura[30], Ujjain[31], Nasik[32], Rupar etc. Numerous votive tanks and ringwells belonging to the Pre-Kushana and Kushana periods have been unearthed at Thanesar, Ahar, (Udaipur), Ahicchatra[33], Sahet, etc.

In comparison to other works of irrigation, ponds and pools generally supplied water to the limited area of land. The Pathyar (Kangra valley) rock inscription records the pond (pukarini). Thus, it is evident that the cultivators of Pathyar region also depended on ponds for watering their fields.[34] From the Mahavastu, we came to know that ponds and pools full of cool water on both sides of the roadway in Banaras were quite prominent.[35] Thus, ponds and pools which impounded the rainwater fed the gardens and fields close to them.

The Rajput dynasty promoted irrigation works in northern India. The 647 Sq. km. Bhopal lake was built under the guidance of king Bhoja. In eastern India Pal and Sena kings built a number of large tanks and lakes in their kingdoms. Rajatarangini of Kalhana gives a detailed account of tanks, wells, lakes, reservoirs etc. developed in Kashmir.

In the south, the Pallavas expanded the irrigation system. The famous Cauvery anicut was built during this period. Large scale construction of tanks (*Tataka*) for tapping rainwater was also built in Tamil Nadu. The Chola period also witnessed the introduction of quite, advanced irrigation systems, which brought about prosperity in the Deccan region. This included not only anicuts across rivers and streams but also chain tanks i.e. a number of tanks with connecting channels.[36] This new system was more reliable in terms of water availability and provided better flexibility in water distribution. Some Chola kings are credited with initating tank and canal construction. For instance, Rajendra I is supposed to have begun the construction of the Cholaganga tank and canal network. However, when it came to the construction members of the village community played a central role. There are epigraphic references to tank maintenance committees (*erivariya*). James Heitzman had analysed references in Chola inscriptions from five taluks in Central Tamil Nadu - Kumbakonam, Tiruchirappalli, Tirukkoyilur, Tiritturapundi, and Pudukkottai and identified the distribution and changes in irrigation technology during the Chola period. The references to irrigation works - tanks, wells, canals, sluices - often occur in the descriptions of the boundaries of gifted land. Kumbakonam and Tiruchirapalli taluks constituted as much as 85 percent and 84 percent of the irrigation works. Kumbakonam taluk is the lower Kaveri valley and Tiruchirapalli taluk is further upstream. In Tirutturaippundi taluk, canals constituted 79 percent of the mentioned irrigation works and tanks 15 percent. If the data is put together the picture that we get is as follows : In the Kumbakonam taluk, the development of the irrigation network began before the Chola period, and its basic nature remained unchanged through the period of Chola rule. In Tirrukkojillur taluk, tanks were initially the most important source of irrigation but in course of time, river-led canals became increasingly important. In Pudukottai taluk, canal development may have peaked in the 11th century after which it plateaued. In Tiruchirappalli taluk, investment in canals was relatively low in the 11th century, but ment up in the 12th century.[37]

Most of the old temples in South India built centuries ago have large tanks in their premises. These tanks are either fed by harvested rain water or by tapping underground springs. In Tamilnadu alone there are 39 temples tanks with areas varying from 0.25 to 3 hectares. These are all fed by rain water and were used mainly for bathing and religious purposes.

These evidences reflect the ingenuity and wisdom of our forefathers who made water and its management an integral part of the native culture and community life. This water-wisdom at all levels of society ensured adequate availability of water for all, which in turn, formed the basis of all-round development and prosperity.

References

1. Rigveda. 7, 47.49; 10, 9.30.
2. Macdonnel, A.A.; Vedic Mythology,. p. 85.
3. Rigveda 10, 9^5, 30^{12}.
4. Rigveda 2, 41, 42.
5. Sankalia, H.D., Journal of International association of Sanskrit Studies, Vol. XXI - XXII (1996-97) pp. 263-269.
6. Rigveda - 85 . 10; 1.6, 9.IV, 7.6; VIII.49.6; x.5.4.
7. Vedic Index. 139.
8. Athravaveda, III p. 13.
9. Kher, N.N., Agrarian and fiscal economy, p. 167.
10. Artharastra, 13.2.
11. Sankalia, H.D., Journal of International association of Sanskrit Studies, Vol. XXI - XXII (1996-97) pp. 263-269.
12. Arthasastra, II.24, III.9.
13. Strabo XV.1.50.
14. A.S.I.R. 1914-15, pp. 9-71.
15. Indian Archaeology 1`954 - 55, p. 19, Altaker, A.S. and Mishra V., Kumrahar excavation (1959), p. 30, fig. 5.
16. Mahabhasya 1.1.24. 'Satyartham kulyah praniyanti.
17. Barua, Old Brahmi Inscriptions in the Udayagiri and Khandgiri Caves, p. 43. Pandey, R.B. Historical and Literary Inscriptions, p. 46.
18. Indian Archaeology, p. 233.
19. Mc Crindle, Ancient India as described in classical literature, p. 175.
20. Epigraphica India, VIII, p. 78. LL. No. 113.
21. Epigraphica India, VIII, p. 89.
22. Subrahmanyam, R. Indian Archaeology, 1958-59, A Review, p. 8, Pl XII.A.
23. Basham, A.L., The wonder that was India, p. 192.
24. Select Inscriptions, p. 119, Epigraphica Indica, p. 247.

25. Bodhayana Dharmasastra, 11, 6, 11, 25.
26. Mahavastu, 1.220, Buddhacharita 11.12, Lalitavistara XVII, p. 249.
27. Banerjee, C.P., Hellinism in Ancient India, p. 91-92.
28. McGindle, J.W., Ancient India, p. 16.
29. Indian Archaeology, 1954-55, p. 14.
30. Ibid, p. 16.
31. Ibid, p. 17.
32. Indian Archaeology, p. 14.
33. McGindle, J.W., Ancient India, No. 4, p. 125.
34. Gazetter of the Kangra district, Vol. I, 1883-84, p. 88.
35. Mahavastu, p. 308.
36. Technical document on water harvesting and artificial recharge, Department of drinking water supply, Government of India (2004), p. 3-11.
37. Singh, Upindra, A History of Ancient and Early Medieval India (from the stone age of the 12th century), p. 595.

69

LUMBINI: THE BIRTHPLACE OF LORD BUDDHA

Gitu Giri[*]

Abstract

Lumbini, the birthplace of Lord Buddha, is located at Rupandehi district, Lumbini zone in the western terai region of Nepal. Asoka had visited Lumbini with his spiritual teacher Upagupta in the third century BC. He had erected a monolithic pillar with inscription in Brahmi script. He has mentioned that Lumbini village is the birthplace of Shakyamuni and stone pillar indicates the exact point of birth. Asoka pillar is even standing at the site. It is the real evidence to identify the exact point of Buddha's birth spot. The Buddhist texts *Lalitavistara, Jataka Nidana katha, Divyavadana* and *Mahavamsa* have stated Lumbini as the birth place of Lord Buddha. Chinese pilgrims Shui-Ching-Chu, Fa-Hien, Hiuen-Tsang and Wu-Kung have given a more accurate and authentic description of Lumbini in the fourth, fifth, seventh and eighth centuries respectively. The monumental and habitation structures; stone sculptures, terracotta human and animal figurines, fragments of pottery belonging to the Mauryan, Sunga, Kushana, Gupta, Vardhan and Sena-Pāla periods, found here prove that Lumbini was well-populated till the early-medieval period and was frequently visited by the monks, nuns and other devotees from time to time. Structural remains of Mayadevi temple, Asoka monolithic pillar, Brahmi inscription, ancient stupas, vihars, marker-stone (conglomerate stone), and nativity sculpture of Buddha, Puskarini tank and fragments of pottery are the archaeological findings, which are real evidences to identify Lumbini as the birthplace of Buddha. Due to the establishment of outstanding universal value of the sacred site, it has listed as the world property list in 1997. Eminent scholars of India and Nepal have identified the birthplace of Buddha with Lumbini, which is situated in Rupandehi district, Lumbini zone, and the western terai region of Nepal.

Key Words

Lumbini, Buddhist literature, Chinese pilgrims, Versions of eminent scholars, structural remains, artifacts, identification

* Prof. Giri had completed Ph.D degree under the supervision of Prof. Dr. D.N. Tripathi in 2001.

Introduction

Lumbini, the birth place of Lord Buddha, is situated about 22 km from Bhairahawa (Siddharthanagar), the foot hills of the Himalayas, on the western bank of Telar river in Rupandehi district of Lumbini zone in Nepal. It is about 34 km. from Naugarh Railway Station on the North Eastern Railway of India. Buddha, known as the Lord of Asia, was born in Lumbini during the full moon day in the month of *Vaiśakha* in 563 BC. He was born under a *sal (Shorea robusta)* tree when Mayadevi was going to her maternal town on the occasion of delivery (Rockhill, 1972:15-17). *Suttanipata* has mentioned the earliest description of the birth of Buddha in Lumbini. After the birth of Buddha he took seven steps towards north and looking in all directions, he declared that "I am the foremost of all creatures to cross the riddle of the ocean of the existence, this is my last birth and here after, I will not be born again". The site is spelt as Rummin dei or Rupandei (beautiful lady), the perverted form of Rupadevi, the queen Anjana of the king of Devadaha which was situated to the east of Kapilvastu in ancient time (Warren 1986:45). The site is called Lun- min and La-Fa-Ni by the Chinese pilgrims Fa- Hien and Hiuen- Tsiang respectively. In course of exploration of the ancient Buddhist sites General Cunningham has mentioned La-Fa-Ni is Sanskrit Lavani, a beautiful lady. In Buddhist literature it is known as *Pradimokha vana* blessed with various trees and flowers, which is compared to the *Chittalata* grove of Indra's paradise in heaven. The earliest Pali text *Suttanipata* has mentioned that, "The wisdom- child, that Jewel so precious that can not be matched, has been born at Lumbini, in the Shakya land for well being and joy in the world of men". A Muslim historian of India named Abul Fazal has called Mokta (Cunningham 1990:351). It is also known as Paderiya (Parariya) where the Asoka pillar is located in the Nepalese Terai (Smith 1905:1-4). The name of the site is spelt *Lumminigame* and Lumbini *Vana* in the Asoka pillar Edict still standing at the same place. Mukherji has also mentioned the name Rummin-dei in his report. In the Magadhi language, being used in the north-eastern pillar edicts in India and Nepal, 'la' is invariable subsisted for 'ra'. The location of Lumbini is pointed out in the Buddhist literature, as well as, in the records of the Chinese pilgrims who visited India in the fourth, fifth, seventh and eighth centuries AD. As mentioned in *Jataka* story this *sal* garden was in joint possession of the Shakayas and Koliyas during the life time of Buddha. The *Mahavamsa*, a Ceylones chronicle, and *Nidana katha* have also located it between Kapilvastu and Devadaha. The sa*l* garden was the place of recreation during the reign of the Shakyas and Koliyas. *Buddha charita* of Asvaghosa describes Lumbini as "gay like the garden of *caitra ratha* with trees of every kind. According to Fa- Hien it is located about 50 *li* east of Kapilvastu (Giles 1981:38). Hiuen- Tsiang had also pointed out that it was about 80 or 90 *li*. (21.729 or 24.445 km.) north-east of arrow-well (Beals 1994:24). It was linked through popular *'Uttara path'* to Kapilvastu, Ramagrama and other important cities during the Buddhist period. The present location of Lumbini, the exact birth place of Lord Buddha, is absolutely clear (Rijal 1996:7).

Pilgrimage and Identification

The Buddhist texts *Lalitavistara, Jataka Nidana katha, Divyavadana* and *Mahavamsa* have stated Lumbini as the birth place of Lord Buddha. When Buddha was lying down on the death bed at the age of eighty in Kusinagar his disciples, monks and nuns surrounded him. On that occasion, he advised with feeling of holy reverence and awe, viz. the place where the *Tathagata* was born (Lumbini grove), the place where he had reached perfect enlighten (Bodha-Gaya), the place where for the first time he had proclaimed the law (Deer park near Varanasi), and the place of his final extinction (Kusinagar). Thus, Lumbini was declared as the sacred spot to the pilgrims and was visited by the scholars, nobles, Royalties and devotees from all over the world. According to *Kundala Vadana* of *Divyavadana* having led King Asoka into the Lumbini jungle, venerable Upagupta indicated with his right hand and said "*Asmin Maharaja pradase bhagavan jatah*", meaning 'Oh great King! here the blessed one was born!" King Aśoka made an offer of one hundred thousand gold coins and established the first *cetiya* or pagoda. In the next chapter *Asoka vadana of Divyavadan* we find the description of the site. In the Asoka pillar of Lumbini it is inscribed that "Here *Bhagwan Sakyamuni* was at the Lumbini village". It is translated by Fuhrer as to mean King *Piyadasi* beloved of the Gods (or dear to the Gods), having been anointed 20 years came himself and worshipped saying: " Here Buddha Shakyamuni was born", and he got a stone (capital) representing a horse, and the stone pillar erected. Because here the worshipped one was born, the village of Lumbini has been made free of taxes and a recipient of wealth (Fuhrer 1972:33). According to Hultzsch it mean, 'when king, beloved of gods, had been anointed twenty years he came himself and worshipped (this spot).' Hiuen-Tsiang's remark that the capital of the pillar contained a horse figure confirms to this interpretation. "As quoted by Rhys Davids, Buhler also says that "a stone horse was made and put on a stone pillar". King Aśoka installed the stone column with a clear legend inscribed on it that it is the spot of Lumbini where the blessed one was born. In Lumbini a brick railing was erected at a distance of 48.76 cm. from the base of the pillar and it had dentils also. After the visit of Emperor, many monks and nuns had started visiting the place. A large number of monasteries and vihars must have been built for their stay in this sacred complex. A large number of artifacts of the Mauryan, Sunga, Kushana and Gupta periods were recovered in course of various excavations. It is thus clear that it continued to be a place of pilgrimage since the third century BC till to date (Giri 2003:177-322).

Chinese pilgrims have given a more accurate and authentic description of Lumbini. Shui-Ching-Chu describes that at Lumbini the Aśokan tree which was gripped by Mayadeví at the time of Siddhartha's birth was still in a living condition and an image of Mayadeví was placed there where devotees used to offer *puja* articles. The spot where Siddhartha's feet touched the earth first, Aśoka got the Siddhartha's foot prints shielded with stones. His description has been ratified by the noticeable findings discovered during the joint excavation of the Department of Archaeology, Lumbini Development Trust and Japanese Buddhist Federation from 1993 to 1997. It is clearly seen that Aśoka had shielded the Siddhartha's footprints with stones in order to secure it. This significant news of the findings of the excavation was publicly declared by then Honorable Prime Minister Sher Bahadur Deuba on February 4, 1996. According to Fa-Hien in Lumbini the queen (Mayadevī) having entered the pool to bathe, came out on the north side , and after walking twenty paces, raised her hands and grasped the branch of a tree. She brought forth the Heir Apparent facing to the east. On reaching the ground, the Heir Apparent walked seven steps, and two dragon- kings washed his body. At the time of washing the tank was used. In this context Hiuen-Tsang had stated that there was the bathing tank of the Shakyas, the water of which was clear as a mirror and the surface of which was covered with a mixture of flowers. 24 or 25 paces to the north of this there was fallen Aśoka flower tree on the birth place of Bodhisattva. To the east from this place there was a stupa built by Aśoka-*raja* on the spot where the two dragons bathed the body of the prince. Bodhisattva walked without assistance in the direction of the four quarters, seven spaces in each direction, and said, "I am the only Lord in heaven and earth; from this time forth my births are finished". To the east of this stupa were two fountains of pure water, by the side of which two stupas were built. To the south of this was a stupa, where Sakra, the Lord of Devas, received Bodhisattva in his arms. Close to the site there were four stupas to denote the place where the four heavenly kings received Bodhisattva in their arms. When Bodhisattva was born they wrapped him in a golden coloured cotton vestment, and brought him to his mother, and placed him on a golden slab (*bench*). They said," The queen may rejoice indeed at having given birth to such a fortunate child!" If the Devas rejoiced at the event how much more could the men. By the side of these stupas there is a great stone pillar, on the top of which was the figure of a horse built by Aśoka. It was broken off in the middle and fell to the ground due to the contrivance (thunder stroke) of a wicked dragon. By the side of it is a little oil river flowing to the south-east, where Mayadevi had brought forth her child to wash and to purify herself (Beal 1994:25). After Hiuen-Tsang many other pilgrims had visited this place from time to time. One of them was Wu-Kung who came in 764 AD. Due to the absence of records very little is known about the condition of the area. The monumental and habitation structures, stone sculptures, terracotta human and animal figurines, fragments of pottery belonging to the Mauryan, Sunga, Kushana, Gupta, Vardhan and Sena-Pāla periods, found here prove that Lumbini was well-populated till the early-medieval period and was frequently visited by the monks, nuns and other devotees from time to time. The names of Jitari Malla (1287-89 AD) and Ripu Malla (1312 AD) were engraved on the stone columns (pillars) at Nigalihawa and Lumbini garden (Fuhrer 1972:33-34). It consists of the words, "*Om mani padme hum, shree Ripumallaschiran jayatu, 1234*". The former portion is a Mahayani Buddhist prayer and the later portion means "prince Ripu Malla, be victorious for long 1234". The year 1234 in the Saka era, corresponding to 1312 AD. Bhuwan Lal Pradhan has claimed that Sikandar Lodi (1489-1517 AD) and Aurangzeb (1668-1707AD) were mainly responsible for the destruction of cultural heritage and property of the Lumbini- Kapilvastu region. During the reign of Mukunda Sen I (1540-1575 AD), Mukunda Sena II (1750-82 AD) and Mahadatta Sena (1782- 93 AD) in Palpa the previous religious condition in the region could not be retained. The site was lost in the dense forest until the discovery of General Rana, Governor of Palpa.

Discovery

From the last decade of the eighteenth century British scholars in India got interested in the rich cultural potentiality of the region. Sir William Jones and others formed the 'Asiatic Society' in 1784. Under the aegis of this organization scholars like James Prinsep, A. Cunningham and others put a great effort to expose the ancient cultural and archaeological potentiality on the region. Archaeological Survey of India started the search of the possible location of Lumbini. First of all Lassen had suggested that a part of Gorakhapur in India might be ancient Kapilvastu. Cunningham purposed Nagar khas with ancient Kapilvastu and Carllyle identified it with Bhuiladih (Cunningham 1990:350). He had proposed Lumbini between Shepour and Burhapara in Uttar Pradesh. During this period when Ranas were ruling in Nepal foreign research scholars were not allowed to explore the cultural and archaeological sites in the Nepalese Terai. In March 1895, Fuhrer was sent to take photos of the inscription on an Aśoka pillar supposed to have been found at Bairat near Nepalguńj (Fuhrer 1972: preface). At that time he did not find the Aśoka pillar, but only two broken pieces of an inscribed Aśoka pillar were found on the bank of Nigali sagar at Taulihawa. On the information of the local people, the Nepalese team had already started digging under the aegis of General Khadga Shamsher. Several meters of earth around the pillar were dug, and there remained only 91.43 cm. from the base to be dug out. This Asoka pillar must have been seen by many of the Nepalese inhabitants of the Terai before Major Singh saw it in 1893, and before Khadga Shamsher was encouraged to do excavation by Fuhrer on December 1, 1896. At the end of November 1896, Fuhrer had gone to Niglihawa to supervise the contemplated excavations there. By a lucky chance he had gone to meet Rana at Bhagavanpur, near the village of Paderiya, in General's camp. Close to the camp, near the debris of four stupas, stood a slightly mutilated pillar rising about 3.04 m. above the ground (Fuhrer1972:27). The pillar inscription pointed out the birth place of Lord Buddha and Lumbini garden as described in the Buddhist literature and Chinese accounts. Surmounted horse capital, as described by Hiuen Tsang, may undoubtedly be buried under the surrounding ruins according his version (Ibid, 28). When Fuhrer saw the pillar on the first December, 1896, only a small portion, about 3.64 m. high, was above the ground and was covered with pilgrim's records. The importance of the reminded pillar inscription for understanding the history of Ancient India in general and the sacred history of the Buddhism in particular were published on 23rd December 1896. Dr. Buhler, A. Barth and Khadga Samsher had also written articles about the exposed site of the Lumbini and its importance in the Buddhist religion and culture. Waddell has said that "...Dr. Fuhrer did not initiate, he took a copy of the inscription. This work was done by the Nepalese officials".

Present Position

All the programs are running under the aegis of the Lumbini Development Trust in the sacred complex of Lumbini. The area is 770 hectares of land as mentioned in the master plan. The area is divided into New Lumbini village, International Monastery Area and Sacred Garden. New Lumbini Village is developing as a community center providing facilities of comfortable lodges, restaurants and other facilities. International Monastery Zone is developing as a sacred complex to the pilgrims and devotees. In this complex forty-two plots of lands are set a side (Tange, 1978). Different nations, Institutions and organizations can erect shrines in various sectors and in different styles under the permission of the project. In the complex the monasteries of Japan, South Korea, Myanmar, France, Viettnam, Nepal and India are under construction. In this process, International Research Institute, Museum and Auditorium have been operating and providing facilities for meeting, seminar and study. The circular sacred garden contains the Aśoka pillar, Mayadevi temple, sacred pond, ruined structures of stupas and vihars and other objects within barbed area. In the complex ornamental flower and hedge plantation has been done by

Japanese Overseas Co-operation Volunteers (JOCV) to create a reverent atmosphere conducive to remembering and exercising Lord Buddha's Universal message of peace and harmony.

Conclusion

Lumbini, the birthplace of Lord Buddha, is a sacred complex for the peace loving people all over the world. Buddha had advised to his disciples that all of you had visited four sites, belonged to the life of Buddha, including Lumbini. In course of pilgrimage the Buddhist sites; Aśoka had visited Lumbini with his spiritual teacher Upagupta in the third century BC. He had erected a monolithic pillar with engraving inscription in Brahmi script. He has mentioned that Lumbini village is the birthplace of Shakyamuni and stone pillar indicates the exact point of birth. Asoka pillar is even standing at the south corner of Mayadevi temple. It is the real evidence to identify the exact point of Buddha's birth spot. The Buddhist texts *Lalitavistara, Jataka Nidana katha, Divyavadana* and *Mahavamsa* have stated Lumbini as the birth place of Lord Buddha.

The structural remains and antiquities found here prove that Lumbini was well populated between Mauryan and early medieval periods and was frequently visited by the monks, nuns and other devotees from time to time. Due to its outstanding universal value, it has been listed in the world heritage property list in 1997. With the support of UNO, UNDP and other international agencies, Lumbini Development Master Plan has implimented by the interest of the concerned countries as well as agencies. Myanmar, Sri Lanka, Thailand, Cambodia, India, Korea, China, Viettnam, France, Germany, Japan, Austria and various Nepalese groups have been involved to complete their proposed plans as mentioned in contract letter. Undoubtedly Lumbini has established as the birthplace of Buddha. It is the sacred place all of the peace loving human beings.

References

1. Beal, Samuel (Trans), 1994, *Si- Yu -Ki Buddhist Records of the Western World;* Part II, Delhi: Motilal Banarashidas Publications.
2. Cunningham, A., 1990, *The Ancient Geography of India;* Reprinted, Delhi: Low Price Publishers.
3. Fuhrer, A., 1972, Antiquities *of the Buddha's Birth Place in the Nepalese Terai;* Reprinted, Delhi: Indological Book House.
4. Giles, H. A (Trans.), 1981, *The Travels of Fa- hsien (399-414 A.D.) or the Records of the Buddhists Kingdoms;* Reprinted, America: Green Wood Press, Publisher West Point C.
5. Giri, Gitu, 2003, *Art Remains in the Western Terai Region of Nepal*; New Delhi: Adroit Publishers.
6. _______, 2008, *Sacred Complex of Lumbini;* New Delhi: Adroit Publishers.
   _______, 2013, *Lumbini and Kapilvastu Museums*; Lumbini: Lumbini International Research Institute.
7. Petech, L. , 1950, *Northern India According to the Shui-Ching-Chu;* Vol. II, Rome: Series Orientale Rome II, IsMEO.
8. Rijal, B.K., 1996, *100 years of Archaeological Research in Lumbinī, Kapilvastu and Devadaha;* Kathmandu: S.K. International Publishing House.
9. Rock hill, W.W., 1972, Life *of Buddha;* Reprinted, Varanasi: Orientale Indica.
10. Smith, A. Vincent, 1905, "Rummindei Inscription, Hitherto Known As the Padariya Inscription of Asoka" *The Indian Antiquary*; Vol. XXXIV.
11. Tange, Kenzo and Urtec, 1978, Master *Plan for the Development of Lumbini Phase I Final Report;* Kathmandu: Lumbini Development Committee.
12. Warren, Henry C., 1986, The *Life of the Buddha;* Reprinted, Delhi: Eastern Book Linkers.

70

प्रयाग और भरद्वाज

राजेश मिश्र

प्रयाग अर्थात् वर्तमान इलाहाबाद[1] की महिमा का बखान ऋग्वेद के खिलसूक्त (22.1) ब्राह्मण ग्रन्थों, महाकाव्यों, पौराणिक आख्यानों तथा क्लासिकी संस्कृत साहित्य के ग्रंथों से लेकर अकबर इलाहाबादी और उसके बाद तक अव्याहत रूप से लगभग किया गया है, बाद में भी सभी की आस्था व आकर्षण के केन्द्र संगम को गंगा–जमुनी संस्कृति का प्रतीक बताया गया, यही नहीं द्वादश माधव, नागतीर्थों, अक्षयवंट, मध्य व आधुनिक काल की इमारतों, यहाँ तक की इलाहाबादी अमरूद[2] पर बहुत कुछ लिखा–कहा गया है,

प्रतिवर्ष के माघ मेले और हर छठें बारहवें वर्ष पर लगने वाले अर्द्धकुंभ और कुंभ पर तीर्थराज प्रयाग की महिमा का अनुगायन भी सदियों से होता आ रहा है, यह भी स्वीकार किया जाता है कि यह एक अन्तर्वेदी थी। राजशेखर यहाँ पूरी परम्परा का मत रखते हैं। जिस पर ब्रह्मा ने यज्ञ किया था और प्रकृष्ट याग के कारण यह यज्ञभूमि प्रयाग कहलायी।[4] वेद और यज्ञ प्रयाग में मूर्तिमान हैं।[5]

किन्तु प्रयाग के महिम–मण्डन तथा संवादभूमि के रूप में प्रतिष्ठित करने की पृष्ठभूमि बैठे ऋषि के विषय में आज कथाक्रम में कहने के अतिरिक्त ऐतिहासिक दृष्टि से कुछ भी नहीं कहा जाता।

जबकि प्रयाग में उनका आश्रम परम्परा और पुरातत्व दोनों के द्वारा चिन्हित व प्रमाणित है। इलाहाबाद के वर्तमान भू–आकृति में भी यदि अकबर द्वारा निर्मित बाँध हटाकर देखा जाए तो गंगा की धारा आज भी वर्तमान में चिन्हित भरद्वाज आश्रम के निकट से ही बहेगी।

ऋक्संहिता के मण्डल द्रष्टा ऋषियों में गृत्समद, विश्वामित्र, गौतम, अत्रि, भरद्वाज, वसिष्ठ और कण्व के नाम मिलते हैं। इसमें गृत्समद् को छोड़कर लगभग सभी ऋषि नाम रामायण व उसके बाद तक आते हैं। भागवत कथा के समय सभी ऋषि शुकताल में उपस्थित हैं। इनमें भरद्वाज संभवतः पहले ऋषि हैं, जिनका निवास स्थान और जिनकी परम्परा प्रयाग में थी। यह निश्चित है। बाल्मीकि के समय में यह क्षेत्र विशाल वन था, जिसमें एक वटवृक्ष की छाया में ब्राह्मण श्रेष्ठ रहते थे।[6] ये महामुनि, महातेजा–महातपा हैं। कालिदास केवल संगम का वर्णन करते हैं।[7] रामचरित टीका में कोटाटवी तथा दशकुमारचरित में विन्ध्याटवी का उल्लेख है। आभिलेखिक स्रोतों में आलवक (गाजीपुर) से डभाल (जबलपुर), पर्यन्त राज्य आटविक था। समुद्रगुप्तकालीन आटविकराज्य विन्ध्याटवी में स्थित थे। यहाँ से एक पथ दक्षिण की ओर जाता था, पाणिनि और कात्यायन इसे कान्तार पथ कहते हैं।[8] यह भी उल्लेखनीय है कि गुप्तकाल में अन्तर्वेदी (गंगा–जमुना दोआब एवं ऐरकिण प्रदेश में शर्वनाग नामक विषयपति गुप्त सम्राट् के प्रतिनिधि के रूप में शासन कर रहा था।[9] महाराज हर्ष और उनकी प्रयाग–परिषद् और प्रयाग प्रेम सुविदित और प्रमाण पुष्ट है। हवेनसांग ने भी यहाँ देवालय और पवित्र स्थल देखे थे। प्रयाग महोत्सव पांच वर्ष पर होता था हवेनसांग छठें में शामिल हुआ था, ऐसा उल्लेख है।[10]

यदि विश्वास करें तो तुलसीदास को भी संवत् 1628 विक्रमी में प्रयाग माघ मेले के अवसर पर भरद्वाज और याज्ञवल्क्य के दर्शन हुए थे।[11] इसके अतिरिक्त त्रिस्थली सेतु (16वीं सदी), तीर्थप्रकाश (17वीं सदी) तथा प्रयागमाहात्म्य शताध्यायी (18वीं सदी) तक तीर्थराज के रूप में प्रयाग–महिमा और यहाँ होने वाले धार्मिक अनुष्ठानादि का विवरण प्राप्त होता है। 1575 ई0 में जब बादशाह अकबर ने राजनीतिक केन्द्र के रूप में इसे विकसित किया तब इसका नाम "इल्हाबास" अर्थात् 'प्रकृति का जाहिर होना' रखा, जिससे इतना तो स्पष्ट है कि वह प्राकृतिक सौन्दर्य मध्यकाल तक बना रहा जिसके आकर्षण ने बादशाह को शहर बसाने पर मजबूर कर दिया, पृष्ठभूमि में गंगा–जमुनी तहजीब के विकास का सियासती मकसद का बीज वपन भी रहा होगा, यह एक अलग संवाद की दृष्टि हो सकती है। अबुल फजल लिखता है– 'बादशाह ने एक शहर बसाया और उसका नाम इल्हाबास रखा। इससे पहले यह प्रयाग नाम का तीरथ था।'[12] 14 नवम्बर 1583 को इलाहाबाद में अकबर ने किले का निर्माण शुरू कराया।[13]

इन सारे साक्ष्यों के आलोक दो बातें स्पष्ट हैं– 1. शहर के रूप में इलाहाबाद 1575 ई0 से अस्तित्व सम्मत हुआ। 2. इसके पहले यह तीरथपति प्रयाग के रूप में प्रतिष्ठित यज्ञभूमि, संवादभूमि, महोत्सव अथवा आध्यात्मिक आस्था की भूमि थी साथ ही प्राकृतिक सौन्दर्य के कारण सबके सम्मोहन की भी केन्द्र थी। तुलसीदास के रामचरितमानस में राम–कथा का प्रतीकात्मक प्रारम्भ तत्कालीन त्रिवेणी और तीरथराज के रूप में प्रयाग के परिवेश वर्णन से ही होता है। यही नहीं प्रसंगानुसार तुलसी तीन बार प्रयाग का वर्णन मानस में करते हैं। जिससे यह तो स्पष्ट हो जाता है कि संवत् 1631 विक्रमी तक प्रयाग का स्वरूप क्या था। यहाँ तुलसीदास केवल वैष्णव संत नहीं अपितु अपने समय तक के भारतीय के इतिहास, संस्कृति व परम्परा को सम्पूर्णता में प्रस्तुत करने वाले लेखक हैं। इस प्रकार वह द्वितीय स्त्रोत होकर भी प्रथम स्त्रोत हो जाते हैं[14] तुलसी के इस पूरे प्रयाग वर्णन के केन्द्र में ऋषि भरद्वाज हैं, जिनके यहाँ संत समागम होता है और जहाँ–

ब्रह्म निरूपण धरमविधि, पावहिं सब मनकाम।
कहाहिं भगति भगवंत कै, संजुत ग्यान–बिराग।।

–रामरचितमानस– बालकाण्ड, 44।।

जैसाकि पहले कहा जा चुका है कि भरद्वाज एकमात्र ऐसे वैदिक ऋषि हैं जो प्रयाग में थे, यह प्रमाण पुष्ट है। चरक चिकित्सा में इनके जन्म की कथा प्राप्त होती है, उसके अनुसार– ब्रह्मा के अयोनिज पुत्र अंगिरा के उतथ्य और बृहस्पति दो पुत्र हुए। उतथ्य की पत्नी ममता और बृहस्पति के संयोग से भरद्वाज कृतयुग के अन्त और त्रेता के आदि में हुए जिसका वर्णन, मत्स्य, अग्नि, ब्रह्म, हरिवंश और भागवत में भी है। इसी कारण वे पृषत् हुए।[15] वह सबसे दीर्घायु हुए।[16] महाभारत में इनका उल्लेख द्रोणाचार्य के पिता और पांचालराज पृषत् के मित्ररूप में हुआ है, जो द्रुपद के राजा बनने के बाद पृषत की मृत्यु के पश्चात् दिवंगत हुए।[17] तैत्तिरीय संहिता के एकादश अनुवाक् में प्राप्त विवरण के अनुसार भरद्वाज ने आयु के तीन भाग में ब्रह्मचर्यवास किया। बुढ़ापे में पड़े ऋषि के पास इन्द्र ने आकर कहा– भरद्वाज मैं तुझे चौथी आयु दूँ तो तुम क्या करोगे। उसने कहा ब्रह्मचर्यवास करूँगा। इन्द्र ने उसे पहाड़ों जैसे तीन ढेर दिखाये और उनसे एक–एक मुट्ठी निकालकर कहा– भरद्वाज, वे वेद हैं, अनन्त हैं, तुमने जितना वेद–अध्ययन किया है, वे ये तीन मुट्ठियाँ हैं। शेष तुमने देखा ही नहीं, आओ इसे समझो, यही सारी विद्या है तत्पश्चात् भरद्वाज को सावित्र अग्नि का उपदेश किया, उसे जान वे अमृतत्व को प्राप्त हुए।[18]

भरद्वाज को धरती पर आयुर्वेद का संस्थापक भी स्वीकार किया जाता है–

ब्राह्मण हि यथा प्रोक्तमायुर्वेदं प्रजापतिः

x x x

ऋषि प्रोक्तोभरद्वाजस्तस्माच्छक्रमुपागत...।

x x x

तेमनायुरभितं लेभे भरद्वाजं सुखान्वितम्...।

x x x

ऋषयश्च भरद्वाजाज्गृहुस्तं प्रजाहितम्।
दीर्घमायुश्चि वीर्षतो वेदवधर्नमायुषः।।

–चरकसंहिता– 11.27

चरकसंहिता मूलतः अग्निवेशतंत्र का प्रतिसंस्कृत स्वरूप है। भरद्वाज ऋषि से यह ज्ञान आत्रेय तक पहुँचा और उनसे अग्निवेश, भेल, जतुकर्णि, पराशर, हारीत और क्षारपाणि तक काल की दृष्टि से वर्तमान चरकसंहिता के तीन स्तर हैं– (1) अग्निवेशतंत्र का काल या उत्तर वैदिककाल (2) मौर्य–शुड्गकाल (3) परवर्ती शास्त्रीय युग की

त्रिधातु दोष पर आधारित चिकित्सा पद्धति।[19] इसके पूर्व रुद्र और अश्विन् वैदिक वैद्य या दिव्यभिषक् कहे गये हैं। रूद्र के साथ शीतल औषधियां हैं, रुद्र सिन्धुघाटी की मुहर पर भी हैं, अतएव भैषज्य की परम्परा सिन्धुघाटी तक जाती है। औषधिसूक्त में क्रमशः रोगों के नाम व पहचान को खोजा जा सकता हैं, यथा– प्रमेहण, वाजीकरण, गर्भ–प्रसवण, विषहरण तथा कासहरण के रसायन आदि जैसी अनेक चिकित्सा विधियों का वर्णन है।[20] यहाँ यह भी उल्लेखनीय है कि शल्यक्रिया का उपदेश सुश्रुत को धनवन्तरि या काशिराज दिवोदास से मिला।

इसी प्रकार पाणिनी का समय छठीं से चौथी सदी ई.पू. के मध्य[21] चाहे जो स्वीकार करें किन्तु इतना स्पष्ट है कि व्याकरणशास्त्र भी पाणिनि पूर्व का है, क्योंकि वेदों में अनेक व्याकरणशास्त्रीय संज्ञायें मिलती हैं, स्वयं पाणिनि ने अपने पूर्ववर्ती दस आचार्य–आपिशलि, काश्यप, गार्ग्य, गालव, चाक्रवर्मन, शाकटायन, शाकल्य, सेलक तथा स्फोटायन के क्रम में भरद्वाज का भी उल्लेख किया है। परम्परा के अनुसार ब्रह्मा से बृहस्पति, बृहस्पति से इन्द्र और इन्द्र से भरद्वाज तथा भरद्वाज से अन्य ऋषियों और उनसे ब्राह्मणों ने प्राप्त किया, जो प्रारम्भ में अक्षर समाम्नाय के रूप में था।[22]

प्रयाग और भरद्वाज के इन सन्दर्भों से दोनों की अन्योन्याश्रिता तो संपुष्ट है साथ ही आयुर्वेद और व्याकरणशास्त्र जैसी संजीवनी तथा संवादविद्या के प्रदाता के रूप में भरद्वाज और उनकी परम्परा का योगदान अक्षुण है। यद्यपि इन आख्यानात्मक विवरणों को पुरातात्विकों और पाश्चात्यों का समर्थन चाहिए क्योंकि सम्प्रति वस्तुनिष्ठ और वैज्ञानिक इतिहास लेखन के लिए मिट्टी से खोदा गया सत्य और उस पर पाश्चात्य लेखकों की सकारात्मक व्याख्या का आधार होना ही चाहिए अन्यथा सब अन्धविश्वास है। प्रश्न है कि क्या इतनी सहजता से भारतीय परम्परा का निरास सम्भव है। अपनी पारम्परिकता ऐतिहासिकता के पुरातात्त्विक संदर्भों को अभी तक अन्वेषित न कर पाने अथवा ढूंढ़े गए साक्ष्यों को परम्परा से न जोड़ पाने जैसी स्वयं की अक्षमता को अंधविश्वास कह देना कहाँ तक उचित है।

भारतीय इतिहास की सनातनता अनादिसिद्ध है। इसके अंतर्गत ऋषिचरित, वीरचित और देवचरित तीनों ही आदिकालीन आख्यानात्मक इतिहास के अंतर्गत मिलते हैं। इन आख्यानों में इतिवृत्त रूपक और रहस्य जुड़े हैं और इन्हें अलग–अलग करना एक दुष्कर कार्य है फिर भी यह स्पष्ट है कि मूल ऋषि देवकल्प और चमत्कारी माने जाते थे। वे देवताओं के कृपापात्र थे और यज्ञ–संस्था के प्रवर्तक भी। इनका ऐतिहासिक चरित कल्पना प्रचुर आख्यानों में लुप्त हो चुका है। प्रायः यही हालत उस युग के राजाओं की है। इस आख्यानात्मक इतिहास के बीज वेद में मिलते हैं, जो पुराणों में पल्लवित होता है, वंश और वंशानुचरित के रूप में यह पौराणिक इतिहास नामों और वंशावलियों के अद्भुत अवदानों से संसृष्ट रूप में स्मरण दिलाता है। पौराणिक आख्यान के इस परिवेश जहाँ मनुष्यों और देवताओं का साहचर्य द्योतित है वहीं एक ओर ऋषियों और राजाओं में देवत्व और दूसरी ओर देवताओं में मनुष्यत्व आरोपित मिलता है। प्रतीति और कल्पना का मिश्रण दोनों ही तरफ है। साक्षात्कार और कल्पना के द्वार से मनुष्य और देवता दोनों निकट आते हैं और इसी स्थिति में उनके धर्मों का पारस्परिक आरोप सिद्ध होता है। साधनासिद्ध ऋषियों एवं वीरों में इसी कारण देवत्व की प्रतीति होती है, यथा– *महती देवता ह्येषानररूपेण तिष्ठति* आदि। इसी प्रकार नाना देवताओ के वर्णन में बहुत सी बातें समान मिलती हैं। अचिन्त्यशक्ति से सम्पन्न देवताओं के आयुध, वाहन और अलंकार उन्हें प्राकृतिक और मानवीय व्यापारों से सम्पृक्त करती है, यज्ञ में वे सभी उपास्य हैं, द्रष्टा ऋषियों के भाव के अनरूप उनके नाम–रूप कृतभेद सिद्ध होते हैं, जिनके जन्म–कर्म–चरित आदि का वृत्तान्त आख्यानों द्वारा ऋषियों के सूक्तों में मिलता है। इनमें अभिव्यक्त काव्यात्मक और प्रतीकात्मक अनुभूतियों एवं रहस्यों को वस्तु वृत्तान्त मानकर परम्पर व्याहत और मिथ्याकल्पना की उड़ान मानना उनको न समझना है और सम्पूर्ण वैदिक परम्परा को असंस्कृत बुद्धि के लोगों की रचना मानना है जबकि स्थिति ठीक उलट है। देवताओं तक मनुष्यों की चेतना को पहुँचाने का कार्य ऋषियों का है। ऋषि मानव होते हुए भी असामान्य मानव हैं उनकी ज्ञान और शक्ति अलौकिक है। भृगु वरुण के दत्तक पुत्र हैं वे अग्नि को मनुष्य तक लाए। अथर्वा ने यज्ञव्यवस्था स्थापित की उनके पुत्र दध्यंच् बाद में दधीचि कहलाए। ऐसे ही अंगिरा नवम् मंडल, अत्रि पंचम् मण्डल, कण्व, अष्टम् मंडल के द्रष्टा हैं। कुत्स इन्द्र के मित्र हैं। काव्य उशना, गौतम, विश्वामित्र वामदेव और वशिष्ठ की भांति भरद्वाज भी मंत्रद्रष्टाओं में हैं, जिनके देवताओं से संबंध थे।[23] सुदास से लेकर महाकाव्यकालीन वीर और राजा तक ऋषियों और देवताओं से जुड़े दीखते है। अतएव प्रयाग में निवास कर रहे ऋषि भरद्वाज द्वारा प्रयाग में यज्ञ, ज्ञान व संवाद की निरन्तरता को कायम रख इसे संवादभूमि के रूप में प्रतिष्ठित व प्रयाग को महिमामण्डित किया गया। इसे निर्विवाद रूप से स्वीकार किया जाना चाहिए, जिसे इनकी शिष्य परम्परा ने भी किया।

मुण्डक, प्रश्न तथा वृहदारण्यक आदि उपनिषदों में सत्यवह भरद्वाज, सुकेशा भरद्वाज आदि नाम मिलते हैं, जो अंगिरा, पिप्पलादि तथा याज्ञवल्क्य जैसे ऋषियों से संवाद करते हैं। गोत्र के रूप में भी भरद्वाज बहुतायत में मिलता है। धर्मशास्त्र के इतिहास में तो यहाँ तक निर्देश है कि जिनका गोत्र भूल गया हो वे भरद्वाज और कश्यप

अंगीकार कर सकते हैं। जिससे यह प्रतीत होता है कि भरद्वाज की शिष्य परम्परा पूरे भारत में फैली थी जो इस ऋषि की महत्ता एवं स्वीकार्यता को स्थापित करती है।

सन्दर्भ

1. आइने अकबरी
2. कुछ इलाहाबाद में सामां नहीं बहदूद के।
यों धरा रखा है क्या अकबर के और अमरूद के।।–अकबर इलाहाबादी का शायरी संग्रह, संपादक शमीम–हनफी
3. विनशन प्रयागयोर्गगायमुनयोश्चान्तरमन्तर्वेदी। तदपेक्षया दिशो विभजते इति आचार्या।– राजशेखर, काव्यमीमांसा, पृ0 230
4. एषा यजनभूमिर्हिदेवानामभिसंस्कृता। – महाभारत, वनपर्व, 85.82
5. तत्रवेदाश्च यज्ञाश्च मूर्तिमन्तः प्रयाग के। –महाभारत, वनपर्व 85.19
6. ददर्श रम्योटजवृक्षषण्डं महद्वनम् विप्रवरस्य रम्यम्। – बाल्मीकि रामायण, 89.23
यत्र भागीरथी गंगा यमुनाभिप्रवर्तते।
जग्मुस्तं देशमुद्दिश्य विगाहय सुमदद्वनम्।।– वही, 54.2
7. रघुवंशम्, 8.10.55–56
8. 1.उदयनारायण राय, *गुप्तराजवंश और उसका युग*, पृ0 33 प्रयाग प्रशस्ति– *परिचारिकीकृत सर्व आटविक राजस्य।*
2.साष्टादशाटवी राज्यभ्यन्तरं डभाला राजमन्वयागतम्– संक्षोभ का खोह ताम्रलेख (गुप्त संवत् 209–529 ई0)।– *कार्पस इन्सिक्रिप्सन्स इंडिकेरम्– 3.114*
9. उदयनारायण राय, *गुप्तराजवंश और उसका युग*, पृ0 ।33 एवं प्रयाग प्रशस्ति, पंक्ति 24
10. ह्वेनसांग का यात्रा विववरण
11. तुलसीदास की जीवनी, रामचरितमानस, गीता प्रेस, गोरखपुर
12. *अकबरनामा*, उद्धृत सैय्यद मुहम्मद अकील रिजवी, *इलाहाबाद की संस्कृति और शायरी*, प्रकाशित, इलाहाबाद संग्रहालय
13. वही, पूर्वोद्धृत
14. रामचरितमानस, बालकाण्ड दोहा क्रमांक–2, अयोध्याकाण्ड, 104 से 109 एवं 203– 215 तक
15. चरक चिकित्सा भाग–1 सूत्र–1, सम्पादक– गिरिधर शर्मा चतुर्वेद
16. भरद्वाजो ह वा ऋषीणामनूचानतमो दीर्घ जीवितमस्त परिस्वतमआस...। ऐतरेय आरण्यक
17. भरद्वाजोऽपि भगवानारूरोह दिनं तदा। महाभारत, आदिपर्व– अध्याय–13।
18. तैत्तिरीय ब्राह्मण, 3.10.11.13
19. प्रियव्रत शर्मा आयुर्वेद का वैज्ञानिक इतिहास, पृ088
20. ऋग्वेद, 10.97 तथा अथर्ववेद, 8.7; 11.6।
21. गोल्डस्टूकर, पाणिनि एण्ड हिज एज इन संस्कृत लिट्रेचर
22. यथाचार्याः ऊचुः ब्रह्मा बृहस्पतये प्रोवाच, बृहस्पतिरिन्द्रायेन्द्रो भरद्वाजाय, भरद्वाजोऽपि ऋषिभ्यः, ऋषयो ब्राह्मणेभ्यस्तं खल्विममक्षर समान्नायम्।– युधिष्ठिर मीमांसक, व्याकरणशास्त्र का इतिहास, जिल्द 1, पृ0 79 से आगे
23. गोविन्द चन्द्र पाण्डे, वैदिक संस्कृति, पृ. 88–89.

71

POWER AND IMAGINATION: REPRESENTATION OF INDIA IN EUROPEAN CARTOGRAPHY

Deepak Kumar, Ravindra Kumar

Abstract

Maps are temporal frozen frame that are devoid of dynamic landscape processes but they do reveal themselves as a site of theater where ethnocentricity, racism and other biases play. The recent trends in the historiography of cartography are a step away from writing cartobibliography and viewing maps as simplistic representation of space. The present research is on the same track attempting to explore history of cartography in India to study maps and marginalia constructed by Europeans reflecting Imperial agendas, social stereotypes and other biases.

Introduction

Ideas and cultural practices of renaissance period influenced mapmaking and its functions in an unprecedented manner. Although the earlier functions of maps continued albeit with less emphasis. However, new functions of maps emerged that made them an instrument for territorial expansions and trade control. In the beginning, European nations viewed India as a commercial region to make profits from, which later became a cause of struggle between them that finally resulted into the complete conquering of India, in which maps played an important role. Trautmann observes that "the beginning of Britain's empire in India coincided with a new knowledge formation directed toward the purposes and intellectual consequences of rulership" (Trautmann 2009: 155). The maps constructed during this time have been subjected to rigorous readings by historians of cartography as well as that of the post-colonial studies for embedded expressions of imperialism (Edney 1997; Barrow 2003).

The arrival of Vasco da Gama in Calicut in CE 1499 was a historic event whose ramifications were far reaching, shifting subsequent trajectory of the world history, altogether. In the next century after the discovery of India by Portuguese, India became a locus for convergence, where Europeans, with their notions of enlightenment encountered Indians, with their tradition and culture. This period of discoveries of new lands, territorial expansions, and rising trading activities also witnessed the simultaneous development of sciences which transformed geography and cartography completely. The development of modern cartography was in conjunction with European colonization of the Asia, Americas, and Africa.

The religiosity or the erroneous nature of the medieval cartography now paved way for the new cartography that was strengthened by the development of new knowledge.

There are several references in ancient literature of India that indicate towards the existence of indigenous maps in India. However, there is not even a single indigenous map to corroborate this. Whatever the Indian cartographic material exist today does maintain a traditional Indian character and provides the idea of the maps produced in the past (Gole 1989; Schwartzberg 1992). Some maps drawn by Indians were even employed by James Rennell in 1782, for his *map of Hindoostan*. The Europeans considered the indigenous maps of India as unworldly and of religious nature, therefore out of the ambit of the definitions of maps. While looking deep into this attitude of Europeans on indigenous maps of India one finds that the European and Indian concept of Time was at clash. The indigenous maps of India were based on the *Kairos* time which is usually unchanging and spiritual in nature, in contrast to the European cartography basedon the *Chronos* time, which according to the wertern writers is dynamic and secular in nature (Dickason 2011: 14-26). Another dimension of conflict between them was of chronologies—Europeans, having shorter chronology opposed to Indians with long chronology spanning over million years, failed to interpret and translate indigenous maps in conjunction with Indian concepts and perception of time and space (Trautmann 2009: 25-52).

The mapping of India, indigenous as well as foreign has been studied by various scholars from multiple points of view. A substantial amount of research over the last few decades has provided a detailed account of the progress of cartography in India from prehistoric times to the present. Although most of these studies are carto-bibliographic in nature, however, the focus of the work that has emerged in the last decade has shifted towards the critical perspective on the axis of structure and agency. We will discuss briefly some of the important studies here.

Leo Bagrow's *History of Cartography,* written in 1939, while focusing only on early modern European maps has literally nothing for India, which he believes had no cartography of its own (Bagrow 1964). In the multi-volume *History of Cartography* series by J. B. Harley and David Woodward (Harley and Woodward 1987-2021), India is covered in the first book of the 2nd Volume from late prehistory onward, mostly by Catherine Delano Smith (Smith 1994: 1-22) and Joseph E Schwartzberg. Smith has shown that India is rich in representations of space, objects and events, as rock art, pottery and other artefacts from prehistoric sites and Indus Valley Civilization demonstrate. The work of Schwartzberg focuses largely on the cosmographical maps from India. On similar lines Susan Gole's work on indigenous maps of India in her *Indian Maps and Plans* covers comprehensively around 200 indigenous maps but excludes those which are cosmographical and astronomical in character. Another significant work is Gole's *India within the Ganges* (Gole 1983), a corpus of European cartography of India with an interesting narrative.

In the late 90's of the last century, beginning with Matthew Edney's, *Mapping an Empire: The Geographic Construction of British India1765–1843,* and P.L. Madan's (Madan 1997), *Indian Cartography: A Historical Perspective,* we see a development in the writing history of Cartography of India focusing on the colonial regime to demonstrate how map production is socially and politically constituted. In the current century, the work of Kapil Raj is significant who has given more importance to the role of native workers for the cartographic construction of India (Raj 2001: 119-134; Raj 2007). Ian Barrow in his work *Making History, Drawing Territory: British Mapping in India, c. 1756–1905* has shown how British mapping of India is linked with history writing.

Other noteworthy work in this track is by Kalpagam, who has linked the cartographic representation of India with the colonial projects (Kalpagam 1995: 87-98). Michael Mann in *Mapping the Country: European Geography and the Cartographical Construction of India, 1760-90* has demonstrated how cartographical construction of India paved way for the British expansion into India (Mann 2003: 25-46).

In the present research on European cartography of India emphasis will be laid to use Edward Said's study of orientalism as a framework to focus on the orientalist discourse inherent in cartography of India in order to analyze the way in which these maps echoed imperialist projects and imagined India. Although there are number of maps that have embedded imperialist connotations, however, because of limited space and time we have chosen only few of them in the present study. We will examine cartographs of India constructed by Europeans, to understand how these acted as an instrument to meet the requirements of imperial projects in India for economic and political advantages. We will also discern these cartographs and marginalia as a representation of the other to identify the imperial attitudes towards India.

Orientalism and Cartography

In the study of representation of India, orientalism as a framework makes the relationship between political hegemony and knowledge conceivable. It makes us review the Western discourse about India on a power/knowledge axis. Edward Said, in his magnum opus, *Orientalism* (Said 1978) elaborated the concept of orientalism as a discourse through which Orient (culture, literature, people, languages, history of the East), was methodically discovered, created, and represented. It is 'a kind of Western projection onto and will to govern over the Orient'. The Western biases and misrepresentation of East as inferior and primitive are at the core of orientalism. Orientalism also enables us to see how West defined 'self' by creating the Orient, 'other'.

Thomas Trautmann makes distinction in Orientalism, while the old Orientalism acquired knowledge of Hebrew, Aramaic, Syriac, Arabic, Persian and Turkish, the New Orientalism explored India to reveal its buried past. The old Orientalism paved way for the new Orientalism as it was through Persian that Europeans attempted to know India and its culture. For Trautmann "every intellectual project derives its meaning in relation to larger, collective projects that long preceded and will long outlive the individual and that the text written by an individual contains within it many voices of a continuing conversation" (Trautmann 2006: 3). In his work (Trautmann 2009: 155-188) of constructing an intellectual history in the *Longue Durèe,* looking for patterns of change over a long period, he identifies Ptolemaic space for mapping of the earth's surface as one of the locational projects that was generated by Claudius Ptolemy in 1st Century Roman Egypt. He argues that modern mapping of India was not framed in Colonialism on the contrary it was an extension of the Ptolemaic space project of the deep past.

It is in this background that we have examined the European maps to reveal how ideas about India that were seeded during the time of the Greeks and Roman continued, reinforced and transformed in the colonial times concurring with new information. These maps embedded with orientalist biases prove that by 'othering' Indians as a historical, incompetent and uncivilized. European endeavors of cartography in India specifically that of the Britain were maintained and defended.

India in European Cartography

India as a mysterious land of unusual customs and enormous wealth has always been a subject of imagination for Europeans. Since earliest times there were many Indias as the term was applied to various known and unknown places by the Europeans, 'India within Ganges' meant India proper and 'India beyond the Ganges' denoted the regions beyond. There were other terms like 'India orientalis' representing Japan and beyond and 'India superior' or 'Upper India' covering up to Northern China. Marco Polo in his book '*The Travels*' has described other terms, 'Grater India' and 'Lesser India' as well (Yule and Burnell 2013: 269; Trautmann 2009: 159 ; Gole 1983).

Before Europe's colonial encounter with India, westerners knew India only through the Greeks writers, e.g., Herodotus, Skylax, Magesthenes, Strabo and Eudoxos. Some of them actually visited India and have provided vital information about India. After the Alexander's expedition to India there was an increase in the Greeks knowledge about India. These writers remained primary source information on India for the subsequent generation of writers to come.

The early Greek writing about India had taken the literal form on maps. The earliest representation of India can be seen in maps of Claudius Ptolemy (CE 150) from his book *Geographia* which survived through centuries, translated into Arabic, Greek and then Latin was first published in CE 1475. On its tenth table there is a list of places with their coordinates of longitude and latitude accompanied by a map of unbounded India. The shape of India given in this map is hard to identify as the peninsula of India is flattened due to the inaccuracy in the measurements by Ptolemy still this shape of India was carried by European cartographers until the 16th Century.

The quality declined dramatically in medieval cartography represented by *Mappa Mundi* of the middle ages which was mostly church-sponsored. The woodcut map made by Heinrich Bunting representing the world in the form of a Pegasus shows the area of 'India within the Ganges' and 'India beyond the Ganges' on the thigh portion of the Pegasus. The oriental portion of the Catalan World Atlas of 1375 illustrated Indian cities and is one of the earliest map showing the peninsula of India albeit inaccurate. Later the proper shape was given by Ruysch in 1508.

The discovery of. America and the parallel exploration of Africa and Asia, along with the progress in measuring techniques, invention of the printing press and new explorations, fundamentally transformed cartography. As the new information started pouring in, the cartographers began redrawing Ptolemy's maps or adding entirely new outlines to the maps of Asia and newly discovered Americas. The discovery of India by Portuguese reproduced in manuscript maps containing necessary information were treated as top secret as it offered access to the overseas trade in the Indian Ocean. The top secret, however, soon disclosed and cartographers came forward with new maps that depicted peninsula of India and newly added information sought from the travellers. The maps from this period were mostly based on the cartographic assumptions of the Ptolemy, Marco Polo and other travelers.

During seventeenth century, South Asia became accessible to European travelers, whose accounts became important source for the cartographers and with this we see the beginning of imperial cartography linked to colonial project of expansion, although in nascent form. The travel literature such as that of Jan van Linschoten' *sitenarario, voyage ofteschipvaert* and Theodor De Bry's *Les Petit Voyages* or *India Orientalis* series provided textual and visual records of India. Georg Braun in his *Civitates orbisterrarum* has provided bird's eye view of the world cities including Indian cities of Diu, Cananor, Goa and Calicut. Other traveler's work also flooded the markets, portraying geography and the social and cultural aspects (Gole 1983: 50). The attention of map-making soon started shifting from the coastal areas to the interior parts of India. These books through maps and images, contained in them, offered readers' visual information of 'distant', 'unknown' and 'strange' territories.

In the eighteenth century India, developments in cartography and surveying coincided with the conflict of French and British in Asia and Europe in which British eventually overpowered French. The East India Company under the governorship of Robert Clive (1758-62) gave great importance to the cartographical recording of India. The scientific mapping started after Clive's acquisition of Bengal. The first task that was required by British to further their expansion into India was to collect information about India and its people and the first step towards this began with the Select Committee at Calcutta in August 1769 and Joint Commission from Bengal and Bombay in 1792 (Mann 2003:28-29). The British initiated three surveys in India—topographical, the trigonometrical and the revenue survey, resulting into the complete and detailed mapping of India.

Representation, Milieu, and Function

The corpus of cartography of India from the earliest times to the recent in independent India is a graphic history that needs to be studied cautiously. The study of these cartographs and the elements it is composed of will provide a better understanding of the mapping of India (the process), cartographers and their artistic sense and the political and cultural environment in which these cartographs were made.

The presence of artistic motifs in cartography has been there since very early times to represent geographical space, towns, people and their culture, etc. The marginalia refer to the images at the margins of maps and one such image from the *frontispiece* of *Theatrum Orbis Terrarum* (Fig-1) by Abraham Ortelius, first published in Antwerp in 1570, shows an architectural structure that houses female allegories of the four continents. Europe is shown on top head covered with the imperial crown and seated under a palisade of vine leaves and clusters of grapes, seems to be dominating the world. Asia is shown on left side of the title elaborately adorned with jewels while Africa on the right side and America on the bottom are shown stereotypically. What is striking in this image is the superior position of Europe in relation to other continents.

Another example comes from Sebastian Munster, whose maps are enriched with artistic images often relegated to the margins. In his *Typus Cosmographicus Universalis* (Fig-2) included in Johann Huttich and Simon Grynaeus's *Novus Orbis Regionum ac Insularum Veteribus Incognitarum*, first printed in Basel in 1532, there is a representation of the four continents in each corner. India on the upper right corner is represented by the Indian spice plants clove, musk, pepper and bow and arrow carrying natives dressed with feathers. The misrepresentation of the feathers and bow & arrow which is American Indian stereotype with the natives of India resulted from the mistake that there are two Indies. Another marginalia (Fig-3) in map of Asia from his edition of Ptolemy's *Geography*, first published by Henricum Petrum in Basel in 1540, depicts monsters from India, a man using his big feet as an umbrella, dwarfs fighting with the cranes, two men with face on the chest, and a dog-headed man. These monster races from India also reappear in his *Cosmographia* first published in Basel in 1544.

These images were produced at the time when new territories were being explored, new discoveries were in the making and new knowledge was forming. This was the first time when west encountered India in an ever before seen scale and intensity. The past images from the accounts of Magesthenes, Marco polo and other travelers reappeared and reverberated in the maps and marginalia of this period. These marginalia according to G.N.G Clarke are a representation of "ownership and control, as well as of information and accurate (often inaccurate) knowledge about the continent", therefore they have to be understood in the manner they represent spatial and cultural information (Clarke 1988: 455-475).

The demand for the military maps increased with the expansion of British dominence in India. Support for military use of maps was seen in the writings of Robert Orme and also in James Rennell words and it was not a coincidence that Surveyor General and his staff were later assimilated into the Military Department (Mann 2003: 31, 38-39). Maps were now being made from military point of view.

The Bengal Atlas and Map of Hindoostan by James Rennell (1742-1830), the first Surveyor-General of India and founder of the British Survey of India, were efforts that provided the foundations for the imminent control of India. His Bengal Atlas subtitled *maps of the theatre of war & commerce* carried inscriptions and notes of thanks to Robert Clive, Warren Hastings, Hector Munro, and Verelst (Kalpagam 1995: 87). This is an example that shows shared visualization of colonized space as revenue generating one and which can be achieved only if they work together (Virmani 2012: 107-122). Rennell's *Map of Hindoostan* (Fig-4) has an allegorical cartouche that shows Brahmins delivering the *shaster* (Sanskrit Literature) into the shelter of Britannia, which is supported by a pedestal on which military victories are engraved. The place names visible are Trichinopoly, Plassey and Wandiwash and the Sepoy has been shown pointing the recent military gains of Sholingur and Porto Novo to his Comrade (Edney 1997: 13). In the distant background there are plowman and loading gang serving the European ships behind them. In this depiction, Trautmann observes "Rennell makes the connection of the new orientalism with empire completely transparent; indeed, he draws attention to it and celebrates it", (Trautmann 2009: 168).

Arundhati Virmani observes that maps were essential to administrative goals and key instruments of colonial control and domination, symbols of power and propaganda, manipulation and subjection. In British maps color played a crucial role conveying different meanings. For example, the figure 5, a nineteenth century map, shows British territories in three shades of pink to indicate territories acquired in three phases. The native territories are shown in yellow while the French, Portuguese and Danish territories are shown in Blue, Green and Yellow respectively.

Conclusion

The entire colonial discourse of mapping India can be seen as continuation of the project that began with the Ptolemy's *Geography*, in Alexandria. The colonial method of ordering of space saw emergence of science and technology that helped in maneuvering and achieving European objectives in India effectively. It is in this scientific representation that the imperial biases were for long time went unnoticed, revealing the true power of maps. The cartographic representation of India reveals not only the Imperial agendas of Conquest and control of India but also the mindset of 'othering' India as inferior and uncivilized that needed to be ruled. The above discussion shows that the very idea of Empire is visible in the orientalist writings and in the maps and marginalia. There are numerous evidences only few of which have been examined here. Thus, what essentially required is to reread the history of cartography of India, particularly of the colonial period to expose the hidden meanings and messages they convey.

Figure 1 : Frontispiece of Abraham Ortelius's *Theatrum Orbis Terrarum* (CE 1570), with allegories of the four continents (Courtesy: Sandra Sáenz-López Pérez *Marginalia in Cartography, Marginalia in Cartography: Exhibition at the Chazen Museum of Art, Madison,* Madison, February 28-May 18, 2014).

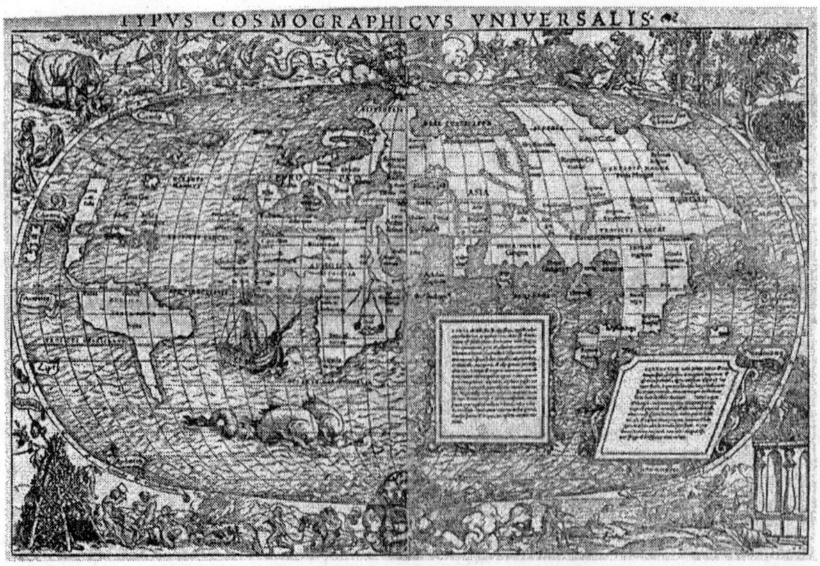

Figure 2 : Sebastian Münster's *Typus Cosmographicus Universalis* showing Asia in the upper right corner represented by plants and natives from India (Courtesy: Sandra Sáenz-López Pérez *Marginalia in Cartography: Exhibition at the Chazen Museum of Art, Madison,* Madison, February 28-May 18, 2014).

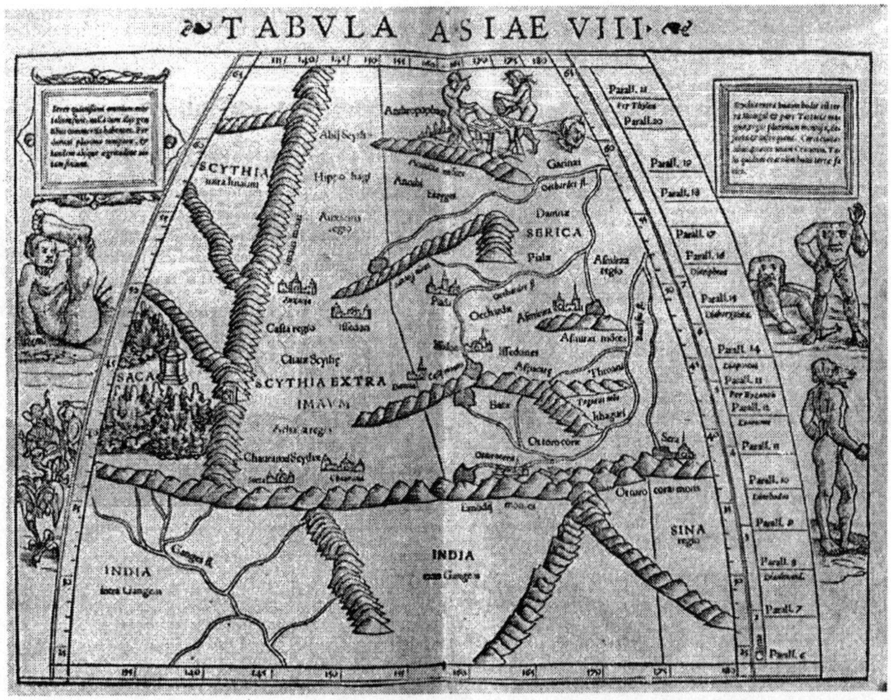

Figure 3 : The eighth map of Asia in Sebastian Münster's edition of Ptolemy's Geography 1542, shows monstrous races in India (Courtesy: Sandra Sáenz-López Pérez, *Marginalia in Cartography: Exhibition at the Chazen Museum of Art, Madison,* Madison, February 28-May 18, 2014).

Figure 4 : Title Cartouche from James Rennell's *Map of Hindoostan* (Courtesy: Trautmann, Thomas R, The Clash of Chronologies: Ancient India in the Modern World. Yoda Press: New Delhi, 2009.

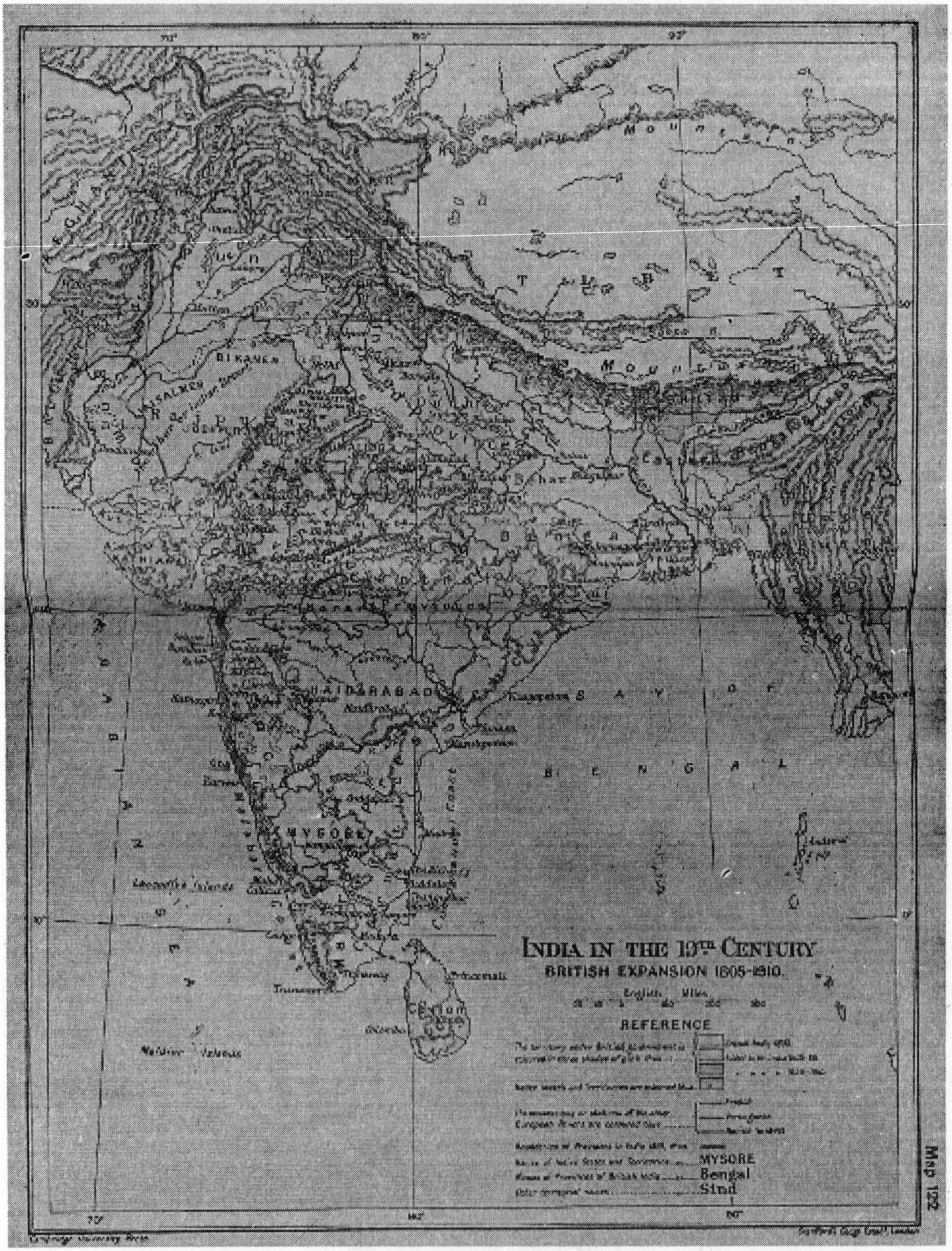

Figure 5 : Historical Map of India in the 19th Century: British Expansion 1805-1910, From the Cambridge Modern History Atlas, 1912).

***Note :** The paper was originally presented at the 2nd South Asian History Congress, 2014, Patiala by the first author. This is revised and updated version.

Bibliography

Bagrow, Leo. 1964. *History of Cartography*. Translated by D. L. Paisley. Rev. and enl. R. A. Skelton. London: C. A. Watts.

Barrow, Ian J. 2003. *Making History, Drawing Territory: British Mapping in India, 1756–1905*. New Delhi: Oxford University Press.

Clarke, G.N.G. 1988. 'Taking Possession: The Cartouche as Cultural Text in Eighteenth Century American Maps', *Word and Image*. 4:2.

Delano Smith, Catherine.1994.'Prehistoric Cartography in Asia', Cartography in the Traditional East and Southeast Asian Societies, vol. 1. *The History of Cartography*, edited by J. B. Harley and David Wood-ward. Chicago: University of Chicago Press.

Dickason, David G. 2011. 'The Future of Historical Cartography', *The Indian Cartographer,* vol. 31.

Edney, Matthew H.1997. *Mapping an Empire: The Geographic Construction of British India, 1765–1843.* Chicago: University of Chicago Press.

Gole, Susan. 1983. *India within the Ganges*. New Delhi: Jayaprints.

Gole, Susan. 1989. *Indian Maps and Plans*. Delhi: Manohar Publishers.

Harley, J. B., and David Woodward. 1987 -2012.eds. *The History of Cartography*,(in six vols.) Chicago: University of Chicago Press.

Kalpagam, U. 1995. 'Cartography in Colonial India', *Economic and Political Weekly*, vol. 30, No 30.

Kapil Raj. 2007. *Relocating Modern Science: Circulation and the Construction of Knowledge in South Asia and Europe, 1650 – 1900*. New York: Palgrave-Macmillan.

Madan, P.L. 1997. *Indian Cartography: A Historical Perspective.* New Delhi: Manohar Publishers.

Mann, Michael. 2003. 'Mapping the Country: European Geography and the Cartographical Construction of India, 1760-90, *'Science Technology & Society*, vol. 8, no. 1, March.

Raj, Kapil. 2001. 'Colonial Encounters and the Forging of New Knowledge and National Identities: Great Britain and India, 1760–1850', *Osiris* 2.

Said, E. 1978. *Orientalism.* New York: Vintage Books.

Schwartzberg, Joseph E. 1992. 'Introduction to South Asian Cartography', (ed) J. B. Harley and David Woodward, *History of Cartography.* Book 1,vol. 2.Chicago: University of Chicago Press.

Trautmann, Thomas R. 2006. *Languages and Nations: the Dravidian proof in Colonial Madras*. London: University of California Press.

Trautmann, Thomas R. 2009. *The Clash of Chronologies: Ancient India in the Modern World.* New Delhi: Yoda Press.

Virmani, Arundhati. 2012. 'Mapping Indian History: A New Historical Challenge,' *India International Center Quarterly*, vol. 40, no. 1, New Delhi.

Yule, Henry and A.C. Burnell. 2013. *Hobson-Jobson the Definitive Glossary of British India,*(ed) Kate Teltscher. Oxford: Oxford University Press.

72

पूर्व वैदिक काल में स्त्रियों की स्थितिः एक ऐतिहासिक विमर्श

संगीता सिंह

स्त्रियों की सामाजिक, आर्थिक तथा राजनैतिक स्थिति में सुधार तथा उसके सशक्तिकरण के विषय में सम्पूर्ण विश्व में चिन्तन, मनन तथा जागरूकता अभियान चलाया जा रहा है क्योंकि अपनी आधी आबादी को निर्जीव और पंगु रखकर कोई भी देश व समाज विकसित होने का दावा नहीं कर सकता। शिक्षित, सुसंस्कृत एवं उन्नत स्त्रियों का समाज उन्नत होगा और अशिक्षित एंव अनुन्नत स्त्रियों का समाज अनुन्नत होगा। भारतीय धर्मशास्त्र में नारी सर्व–शक्ति सम्पन्ना मानी गई है तथा विद्या, शील, ममता, यश और सम्पत्ति की प्रतीक समझी गई है। पूर्व वैदिक काल में स्त्रियों की स्थिति सम्मान जनक थी।

पूर्व वैदिक साहित्य के अध्ययन से ज्ञात होता है कि भारतीय सामाजिक व्यवस्था में स्त्रियों का स्थान प्राचीन समय से ही आदर्शात्मक और मर्यादायुक्त था। उनके प्रति समाज की स्वाभाविक निष्ठा और श्रद्धा थी। कन्या पत्नी तथा माता के रूप में परिवार तथा समाज में उनका आदर था और उनके योगदान का सर्वदा महत्व और गौरव रहा है। ऋक् संहिता[1] में 'स्त्री' शब्द का पुमांस (मनुष्य) और एक बार ''वृषन'' (पुरूष) के विपरीत प्रयोग हुआ है। 'स्त्री' शब्द की व्युत्पत्ति करते हुए ''स्त्यायाति गर्भो यस्यमिति'' ऐसा कहा गया है, सत्यै– स्त्यायते से डट् प्रत्यय ङीव होने से 'स्त्री' रूप बनता है[2]। क्षीर स्वामी ने भी कहा है कि नारी को स्त्री कहा जाता है, क्योकि गर्भ की स्थिति उसके भीतर स्थित रहती है। पूर्व वैदिक काल में पुत्र की भाँति पुत्रियों को भी आदर व स्नेह प्राप्त था। ऋग्वेद में प्रभूत संख्या में वाणों को धारण करने वाले इषुधि की प्रशंसा 'अनेक' पुत्रियों का पिता कहकर की गई है[3]। श्रीमद् भागवत के अनुसार सन्तान के अभिलाषी वैवस्वत मनु महाराज व उनकी पत्नी ने पुत्रेष्टि यज्ञ के अवसर पर 'होता' से कन्या के लिए याचना की थी–

'तत्र श्रद्धा मनोः पत्नी होतारं समयाचत,
दुहित्रर्थमुपागम्य प्रणिपत्य पयोव्रता[4]।

पूर्व वैदिक कालीन स्त्री शिक्षा उच्चतम शिखर पर थी। पुत्रों की शिक्षा पर जितना ध्यान दिया जाता था उतना ही ध्यान पुत्रियों की शिक्षा पर भी दिया जाता था। शिक्षा का आरम्भ उपनयन संस्कार से होता था। उपनयन संस्कार के बाद ही बालक या बालिका को वैदिक संहिताओं के अध्ययन का अधिकारी माना जाता था, आचार्यों के आश्रम में रहकर बालकों की भाँति ही कन्याएँ भी ब्रह्मचर्य का पालन करती हुई यज्ञोपवीत, मौंजी, मेखला और वल्कल धारण करती थीं। ऋकः यजुः अथर्व संहिताओं में ब्रह्मचारिणियों का उल्लेख है। अथर्वसंहिता में उल्लिखित है कि ''ब्रह्मचर्य व्रत का पालन कर शिक्षा समाप्त करने वाली कन्याएं योग्य पतियों को प्राप्त करती हैं।[5] वैदिक कालीन कन्या शिक्षा प्राप्त करने के दौरान गणित, वैद्यक, संगीत नृत्य और शिल्प आदि का भी अध्ययन करती थी।[6] अनेक पूर्व वैदिक कालीन विदुषी स्त्रियाँ थीं, जिन्होंने अनेक वैदिक मंत्रो का प्रणयन किया। लोपामुद्रा, विश्ववारा सिक्ता, घोषा, अपाला, गार्गी, मैत्रेयी आदि ऐसी ही विख्यात दार्शनिक थी।[7] जो दर्शन जैसे गूढ़ और गम्भीर विषय में

भी पारगंत थी। बृहदारण्यक उपनिषद् में उपलब्ध ''गार्गी–याज्ञवल्क्य संवाद' गार्गी की तीक्ष्ण एवं विवादशीला प्रज्ञा का परिचायक है।[8] ऋग्वेद में उल्लिखित है कि अपने पति अगस्त्य के साथ 'लोपामुद्रा' ने ऋग्वेद के प्रथम मण्डल के 179वें सूक्त का दर्शन किया।[9] 'अपाला' एवं रोमशा के साथ सूर्यपुत्री 'सूर्या' ने भी मन्त्रों की रचना की थी।[10] इन्द्रदेव की पत्नी इन्द्राणी ने ऋग्वेद के दशम मण्डल के सूक्त की रचना की थी।[11] पूर्व वैदिक कालीन स्त्रियों ने अध्यापन का भी पवित्र कार्य अपनाया और वे गुरूकुलों में अध्यापक के पद पर आसीन होकर अध्यापन का कार्य किया करती थीं। महर्षि पाणिनि ने अध्यापन की सहधर्मिणी तथा स्वयमेव अध्यापिका होने वाली स्त्रियों के लिए विभिन्न नामों की सृष्टि की है। साथ ही स्त्री शिक्षणशाला का भी उल्लेख किया है।[12] धीरे–धीरे समाज में स्त्री का महत्व इतना अधिक बढ़ कि उसके बिना पुरूष को अपूर्ण समझा गया। 'यावत् जायां न विन्दते, असर्वो हि तावद भवति।[13] आर्य पुरूष स्त्रियों का अत्यधिक सम्मान करते थे। वे गृह को नहीं अपितु नारी को ही गृह मानते थे– 'जायेदस्त'[14] और गृहस्थ धर्म के पालन में नारी की ही प्रधानता स्वीकार करते थे।[15] उनके विवाह करने का प्रयोजन था– नारी के साथ रहकर धर्मानुष्ठान और यज्ञ सम्पादन। नारी के बिना गृह का अस्तित्व कहाँ और गृह के बिना गृहस्थ धर्म का सम्पादन ही कैसे हो सकता है? स्त्री सहधर्मिणी थी उसी के साथ धार्मिक कृत्यों का अनुष्ठान सम्पन्न होता था इसलिए अपत्नीक व्यक्ति यज्ञ के अधिकार से वंचित था।[16] विवाहोपरान्त पतिगृह में वधू को सम्मानपूर्ण स्थान प्राप्त था। पत्नी अपने पति की चिरसंगिनी होती थी ऋषि प्रार्थना करते हैं कि उन्हें ऐसी पत्नी प्राप्त हो जो उनके आन्नद के क्षणों में साथ रहे।[17] नारी की शक्ति और महत्व स्त्रोत उसके प्रेम में होता था तथा वही पति भाग्यवान समझा जाता था जो प्रेममयी पत्नी को प्राप्त कर सके।[18] पति और पत्नी का सम्बन्ध अभेद्य एवं अविच्छिन्न होता था एक के बिना दूसरे का जीवन अधूरा समझा जाता था। पति और पत्नी का सामूहिक नाम ही दम्पति है, इसका अर्थ है– घर का स्वामी और स्वामिनी अर्थात दोनों मिलकर ही घर के स्वामी होते थे।[19] परिवार में पति एवं पत्नी की स्थिति एक समान मानी जाती थी। यह अथर्ववेद के इस मन्त्र से सूचित होता है– ''मै ज्ञानी हूँ, तू भी वैसी ही ज्ञानी है, मै साम हूँ तो तू, .ऋक हैं, मै द्यौः हूँ तो तू पृथ्वी है। ऐसे में हम दोनों यहाँ साथ मिलकर रहे और सन्तान उत्पन्न करें।[20] ऋग्वेद में पत्नी को पति का 'नेम'–भाग या अंग कहा गया है तैत्तिरीय संहिता का भी यही मंतव्य है।[21] शतपथ ब्राह्मण में इसकी व्याख्या करते हुए पति–पत्नी को एक दाने के दो दालों की भाँति कहा गया है जो दो होते हुए भी एक है।[22] आर्य जन विवाह के समय एक स्त्री से दस वीर पुत्रों की उत्पत्ति के लिए प्रार्थना करते थे।[23] ऋग्वेदीय विवाह पद्धति से स्पष्ट से स्पष्ट है कि उस समय युवास्था में ही विवाह होते थे, बाल विवाह के संकेत नहीं मिलते है।[24] विवाहोपरान्त पत्नी–पति के साथ धार्मिक कृत्यों में भाग लेना ही अपना आदर्श नहीं मानती थी अपितु वह स्वंय स्वतन्त्ररूप से धार्मिक कृत्यों कों भी सम्पन्न करती थी। स्त्रियाँ कभी–कभी अपनी रूग्णावस्था दूर करने के लिए, कभी पुत्र–प्राप्ति के लिए, कभी पति एवं परिवार पर अपने शासन के लिए तपस्या, यज्ञ तथा देवस्तुतियाँ किया करती थीं। उदाहरणस्वरूप 'घोषा' ने अपने रोग की निवृत्ति के लिए[25] 'वध्रिमति' ने पुत्र प्राप्ति के लिए[26] शचि–पैलोमी[27] ने पति को वश में करने के लिए यज्ञानुष्ठान सम्पन्न किये थे। स्त्री को भी अधिकार था कि वह प्रतिदिन घृत और सामग्री लेकर प्रातः सायं यज्ञ करे।[28] शतपथ– ब्राह्मण से स्पष्ट होता है कि 'उद्गाता' का कार्य भी पत्नियाँ करती थीं।[29]

गृहस्थाश्रम के नियमों का पालन करने वाले गृहस्थ की सुख सुविधाओं का वर्णन ऋग्वेद के अनेक मन्त्रो में उल्लिखित है जैसे–पति की आज्ञाओं का पालन करने वाली पत्नी[30] संतति का प्रेमपूर्वक पोषण करने वाली गृहिणी[31] पति के साथ आहुतियाँ देने वाली सहधर्मिणी[32] का विस्तृत वर्णन उपलबध है। ऋग्वेद से ज्ञात होता है कि उस समय विवाह योग्य किसी भी युवती को अपने मनोनुकुल वर चुनने की स्वतन्त्रता थी।[33] वैदिक कालीन समाज में युवक एवं युवतियों में पारस्परिक प्रेमालाप की अनेक घटनाएँ दृष्टव्य है।[34] ऋग्वेद के एक मंत्र में पत्नी द्वारा यह प्रार्थना की गई है कि मेरे पुत्र शत्रुओं का नाश करने वाले हों और मेरी पुत्री तेजास्विनी हो।[35]

पूर्व वैदिक युग में बहुपत्नी विवाह की प्रथा प्रचलित थी या नहीं इस प्रश्न पर विद्वानों में मतभेद है। ऋग्वेद के एक मन्त्र में दो पत्नियाँ रखने वाले पुरूष की उपमा ऐसे घोड़े से की गयी है कि जो रथ की दोनों धुरों के बीच में दबा हुआ चलता है।[36] ब्राह्मण ग्रन्थों के समय में बहुविवाह की प्रथा प्रारम्भ हो चुकी थी, इसमें कोई सन्देह नहीं है। शतपथ ब्राह्मण में याज्ञवल्क्य की दो पत्नियों का उल्लेख है, जिनके नाम मैत्रेयी एवं कात्यायनी थे।[37] ऋग्वेद संहिता[38] में स्पष्ट है कि उस समय पुनर्विवाह प्रचलित था। इसमें राजा वेन का उल्लेख है, जिसे 'पृथी' या 'पृतु' कहा गया है, यह वही वेन राजा है, जिसके विषय में मनु ने स्पष्ट लिखा है कि उसने विधवाओं का बलपूर्वक पुनर्विवाह करवाया था।[39] ऋग्वेद संहिता में एक विधवा स्त्री को सम्बोधित करते हुए कहा गया है कि तुम मृत पति को छोड़कर भावी पति को प्राप्त करो।[40]

गृहिणी पद के अतिरिक्त वैदिक काल मातृत्व पद का भी गौरव प्रस्तुत करता है। माता शब्द पारिवारिक जीवन के लिए अमृत का भण्डार है। वह परिवार के लिए त्याग तप व प्रेम की त्रिवेणी है। माता का पद पिता और गुरू से भी श्रेष्ठ माना गया है। ऋग्वेद में माता शब्द अन्तरिक्ष, नदी, जल, तथा पृथ्वी के अर्थ में भी व्यवहृत है।

व्याकरण 'मातृ' शब्द को मान्+तृच से बनाते हैं। मान का अर्थ है आदर, अतः मातृ शब्द का अर्थ 'आदरणीय' है। यास्क के मत में मातृ का भाव निर्माण करने वाली जननी भी है, परन्तु आदि युग से लेकर आज तक मानव जिसे असीम श्रद्धा भेंट करता रहा और जिससे अजस्र अक्षय स्नेह प्राप्त करता रहा केवल जन्मदात्री नहीं है। वह इससे बहुत बड़ी है। उसका स्थान स्वर्ग से भी ऊचाँ और गुरू से भी अधिक पूज्य है।[41] पुत्रों को जन्म देने के कारण वैदिक काल में माता का स्थान श्रेष्ठ था और राजगृहों में पुत्रों को जन्म देने वाली रानी को 'महिषी' के पद पर सुशोभित किया जाता था।[42] अथर्ववेद संहिता में कहा गया है कि उस समय पुत्र सदा माता की इच्छाओं के अनुकुल आचरण करता था, क्योंकि संहिता सन्देश उन्हें सुनाया जाता था। माता अपने अमृत तुल्य दूध से सन्तान का पोषण करती थी।[43] ऋग्वेदानुसार माता सर्वाधिक घनिष्ठ और प्रिय सम्बन्धी है, भक्त परमात्मा को पिता की अपेक्षा माता कहकर अधिक संतुष्ट होता है, माता–पिता के समास में माता को प्रथम स्थान दिया गया है।[44] एक स्थल पर दिव्य माता–पिता धावापृथ्वी से प्रार्थना की गई है कि 'मधुर वचन वाले, शोभन हाथों वाले यशस्वी माता–पिता प्रत्येक युद्ध में हमारी रक्षा करें।'[45] मृत व्यक्ति को दफनाते हुए भूमि से प्रार्थना की जाती थी कि हे भूमि! इसे ऐसे आच्छादित कर लो जैसे माता पुत्र को आंचल से ढ़क लेती है।[46] फलतः वेद में कहा गया है 'मातृदेवों भव'।[47] ऋग्वेद में उल्लिखित है कि कि 'तान्व' (औरस) पुत्र के होने पर उसकी बहन 'रिक्ख' (पैतृक सम्पत्ति) की कोई भाग प्राप्त नहीं करती।[43] यदि माता–पिता की सन्तान केवल कन्याएँ हों तो पैतृक सम्पत्ति की अधिकारिणी मानी जाती थी, विवाह हो जाने पर भी कन्या धन प्राप्त करने के लिए पितृकुल में आया करती थी।[49] पूर्व वैदिक युग में पत्नी व्यक्तिगत सम्पत्ति की भी स्वामिनी होती थी। पत्नी की यह सम्पत्ति उसके वस्त्र, आभूषण एवं धन राशि के रूप में होती थी, पत्नी विवाह के अवसर पर दहेज एवं भेंट में यह सम्पत्ति प्राप्त करती थी। इस सम्पत्ति पर पत्नी का पूर्ण अधिकार होता था।[50]

निष्कर्ष

पूर्व वैदिक काल में स्त्रियों की स्थिति उत्तम थी। उन्हें शैक्षिक, राजनैतिक एवं आर्थिक अधिकार प्राप्त थे। किसी भी स्थिति में एक पुरूष के समान ही स्त्री के भी अधिकार सुरक्षित थे। स्त्री पुरुष दोनों में समान रूप से समाज के लिए महत्वपूर्ण थे। वर्तमान समाज में स्त्री जिन अधिकारों के लिए संघर्ष कर रही है वह सभी अधिकार पूर्व वैदिक काल में स्त्रियों को स्वेच्छा से प्राप्त थे। पूर्व वैदिक काल की भाँति नारी का सम्मानजनक स्थान समाज में निर्मित हो सके इसके लिए प्रत्येक क्षेत्र में पूर्वाग्रह से मुक्त होकर उसे समान अधिकर प्रदान करना होगा। घर परिवार से लेकर समाज, देश, राष्ट्र एवं सम्पूर्ण पृथ्वी पर नारी के लिए भयमुक्त कार्य क्षेत्र का निर्माण हो। व्यक्तिगत सोच में स्त्री के लिए सम्माननीय सोच विकसित हो। आज की नारी पूर्व वैदिककालीन नारी से किसी भी प्रकार से कम नहीं है आवश्यकता है तो केवल प्रोत्साहन एवं सहयोग की। ईश्वर के पश्चात हम सर्वाधिक ऋणी स्त्री के है– प्रथम तो जीवन प्रदान के लिए फिर उसको जीने योग्य बनाने के लिए। और अन्त में जयशंकर प्रसाद के शब्दों में ''नारी की करूणा अन्तरंजगत का उच्चतम विकास है, जिसके बल पर समस्त सदाचार ठहरे हुए हैं।''

सन्दर्भ

1. ऋक् संहिता, 1.164.16, 5.61.6, सायण भाष्य सहित वैदिक संशोधन मण्डल, पूना–2
2. मैत्रायणी संहिता, 4.6.4
3. बृहदारण्यक उपनिषद, 1/4/3
4. श्रीमद भागवत पुराण, सं. वी. एल. पन्निकर, बम्बई, 1920
5. अथर्ववेद, 11.9.16, सं. श्रीपाद दामोदर सातवलेकर, स्वाध्याय मण्डल, परड़ी, बम्बई
6. ऋग्वेद, 1.9.2–4, सं. श्रीपाद दामोदर सातवलेकर, स्वाध्याय मण्डल, परड़ी, बम्बई
7. बृहदारण्यक उपनिषद, 2/4, 4/5
8. पूर्वोक्त, 3/6/1
9. ऋग्वेद, 1.17
10. ऋग्वेद, 10.9, 10.85
11. ऋग्वेद, 10.145
12. पणिनी अष्टाध्यायी, 6/2/47, सं. गंगदत्त शास्त्री, गुंरूकुलकांगड़ी वि.वि., सं0 2007
13. शतपथ ब्राह्मण, 5/2/1/16, सं. वेबर, लिपजिंग,1924
14. ऋक् संहिता, 3/6/1
15. अथर्ववेद, 14/2/75
16. तैत्तिरीय ब्राह्मण, 2/1/2/6
17. अथर्ववेद, 14.2.71

18. ऋग्वेद, 10.85.37
19. ऋग्वेद, 5.37.3
20. ऋग्वेद, 5.3.2, 8.31.5
21. तैत्तिरीय संहिता, 6.1.8.5
22. शतपथ ब्राह्मण, 14.4.2.4.5
23. ऋग्वेद, 10.85.27
24. ऋग्वेद, 10.85.9
25. ऋग्वेद, 1.117.7
26. ऋग्वेद, 1.116.13
27. ऋग्वेद, 58.159.1
28. ऋक संहिता, 7/1/6
29. शतपथ ब्राह्मण, 14/3/1/33
30. ऋग्वेद, 1.112.2
31. ऋग्वेद, 7.81.4
32. ऋग्वेद, 8.43.15
33. ऋग्वेद, 10.27.12
34. ऋग्वेद संहिता, 7.62.9; 9.56.3 ; 10.30.6
35. ऋग्वेद, 10.159.3
36. ऋग्वेद, 10.101.11
37. शतपथ ब्राह्मण, 11.5.18
38. ऋग्वेद संहिता, 10.85.41
39. ऋग्वेद संहिता, 10.93.14; 1.112.15
40. ऋग्वेद संहिता, 10.18.8
41. कल्याण नारी अंक पृ0, 140
42. अथर्ववेद संहिता ; 3.23.3
43. अथर्ववेद संहिता, 18.3.3.50
44. ऋग्वेद; 4.6.7
45. ऋग्वेद संहिता, 6/50/7
46. ऋग्वेद संहिता, 10/18/11
47. तैत्तिरीय संहिता, 1.11.2
48. ऋग्वेद, 3.31.2
49. ऋग्वेद, 1.124.7
50. तैत्तिरीय संहिता, 6.2.1.1

73

BANKING IN ANCIENT INDIA

Pravin Kumar Sharma

Banking is, now, a very significant part of our life. Our all activities, education, social, agricultural, trade, travel and other activities, are related to this immanent system. No doubt, Money acts a dominant role in today's life. Forms of money have evolved from coin to paper currency notes to credit cards. Commercial transactions have increased in content and quantity from simple banker to speculative international trading. Hence the need arose for a third party who will assist smooth banding of transaction, mediate between the seller and buyer, hold custody of money and goods, remit funds and also to collect proceeds.

The religious places were considered safe place for money and other valuables materials. In those days, people had not big and huge home for the view of security, therefore, most wealthy people held accounts at their temples. All the relevant person of temple complexes like priests or temple workers were both devout and honest always occupied the temples, adding a sense of security. There are records from Greece, Rome, Egypt and Ancient Babylon that suggest temples loaned money out, in addition to keeping it safe. The fact that most temples were also the financial centers of their cities and this is the major reason that they were ransacked during wars. Usually giving loan by the temple was one of the significant social services.

The Rig Veda refers only gold, silver, copper and bronze and the later Vedic texts also mention tin, lead, iron and silver. Recently iron coins were found in very early levels at Attranji Kheri (U.P.). From the days of Buddha, there was money economic system existed. In ancient India during the Maurya dynasty, an instrument called 'adesha' was in use, which was an order on a banker desiring him to pay the money of the note to a third person, which corresponds to the definition of a bill of exchange as we understand it today. During the Buddhist period, there was considerable use of these instruments.

Trade guilds acted as bankers, both receiving deposits and issuing loans. The larger temples served as bankers and in the south the village communities economically advanced loans to peasants. There were many professional bankers and money lenders like the sethi, the word literally means "chief". It has survived in the north India as seth. Small purchases were regularly paid for in cowry shells (varataka), which remained the chief currency of the poor in many parts of India. Indigenous banking grew up in the form of rural money lending with certain individuals using their private funds for this purpose. The scriptures singled out the vaishyas as the principal bankers. Exports and import were regulated by barter system Kautilya's Arthasastra mentions about a currency known as panas and even fines paid to courts were made by panas.

In ancient India, temples were consisted as a people's bank. But the temple did not discharge all the functions of a modern bank. One of the main functions of a bank is to give interest to the depositors but the temple never gave any such interest. The fixed deposits invested in the temple were mostly donatives in nature and were made for certain purpose. These fixed deposits were not repayable to the depositor, but at the same time the temple had no power to use them for other objects or to spend them in disregard of the terms laid down in its grants, so temples of early period served not as a modern bank but as prototype of it.[1] Sometimes the people used to give loans even to the merchant guilds and village assemblies.

Generally, village assemblies, singly[2] or jointly, farmers[3], Brahmanas[4], priests or managers[5] were the customer of the temple bank. The loans included both cash and kind. The temple used to work as bank in two ways - direct and indirect. By the first way the temple used to give loans to various customers from its own treasury with the stipulation that the fixed interest on the loan should be paid regularly into the treasury of the temple.[6] On the other hand, indirect loans were those transactions in which the donors, instead of giving grants directly to the temple would entrust them to some individuals or corporate bodies[7]on the condition that the yearly interest amount accrued from the grants should be utilized for providing some service to the temple.[8]Apparently in such transactions the temple was nowhere concerned with this sort of indirect loans. But when one looks at it deeply it becomes evident that these loans were available to people only because of the temple. Thus, the temple was indirectly responsible for these transactions taking place. Sometimes, the persons attached to temples in the capacity of Pujaris[9]or managers[10]or ascetics[11] residing in the temples would be entrusted with the grants and asked to arrange certain services to the god out of the interest from those grants. Thus the temple had an indirect hand in the disbursement of this loans.[12]

The temple played a prominent role mobilizing developmental funds within a region by giving loans to the village assemblies for developmental purposes. Most of the loans were given for productive activities such as cultivation, cattle-breeding and trade.[13] The temple also early received loans from individuals[14]and other bodies pledging its property.

The village assemblies such as 'Sabha', 'Ur' and 'Nagaram' stood first among the customers of the temple-bank. Moreover, donations made over to the temple was either entrusted or lent out to the village assemblies. The corporate bodies, in turn, distributed this donated amount to people on the condition that they should give the interest perpetually to the temple in order to fulfil the purpose of the donation. In A.D. 910, a record from Kilaiyur states that the donated gold for supply of ghee to god on new moon days was deposited in the temple treasury and these in charge of Srikariyam were asked by the Sabha of the village to look after the stipulated offerings.[15]

In the case of security, either the property of the debtor or the property of somebody on his behalf was pledged[16]or some individual or institution had to give assurance or to stand surety for the debtor.[17]Joint security was also obtained while giving the loans to the individuals.[18]

Generally, the authority of temples was very strict in the matter of getting interest. The interest was paid either in cash or kind. The interest to be paid in kind was mainly in terms of ghee, paddy, rice and other necessary requirements of temple. If the interest was to be paid in kind, mostly paddy, the temple used to impose so many conditions to be sure that it would get qualitatively and quantitatively good paddy and within time limit.[19] The paddy should have to be brought to the temple courtyard, got cleaned and freed from stones, chaff, sprouting and diseased grains and measured out fully with the same measure with which the debtor had received paddy from the temple.[20]

'If by any chance the debtor failed to pay the interest within the specified time, the temple used to sent two or three of its representatives or officers to his house to collect the interest. They would stay with him till he paid the interest. And as long as they stayed he would have to feed each of them with two full meals a day. If the debtor happened to be the village assembly or any corporate body, these officers could even forbid the entry of five and water in to the village, cut off communication with our villages and could detain cattle for collection purposes. In case one tried to obstruct them (officers) the obstructer would be held responsible for any injury that might be caused by such obstruction. Even after all these efforts, if the debtor failed to pay the interest, the elite of the region under whose protection the charity was, would levy a fine besides compelling the debtor to supply the paddy forever.'[21]

Kautilya's Arthasastra, the Dharmasastra and the Smritis give the normal rate of interest as fifteen percent or 1/8 part of the actual capital per month. But the rate of interest changed according to time and place. It ranged between nine to twenty five percents per annum.[22] The interest of the loans let out by the temple was usually fixed on a permanent basis. The interest in the case of cash was calculated annually[23]or once in every crop[24]or six month once[25]or monthly.[26]

Generally, the interest in the kind like ghee, rice, etc., was usually paid daily in order to meet out the day-to-day requirement of the temple.[27] But in some cases, the interest in kind was also paid at the time of certain special occasions.[28]

There were many agencies involved in the act of fixing and receiving fines from the defaulters. The Mahesvaras[29]and the Sraddhamantas[30]are often referred to have been involved in imposing fines on the defaulters. The former in addition to his were also empowered to receive the fine on behalf of the temple.[31]

The interest regularly paid by the borrowers, helped very much the temple in the perpetual maintenance of various services. But at the same time the borrowers were also benefited in many activities. So that temple, in ancient India, played an eminent role in economic life of society.

Banks were started from religious places of the ancient world but their basic economic ideals have not changed. Banks issue credit to people who need it, but demand interest on top of the repayment of the loan. Although history has altered the fine points of the business model, a bank's purpose is to make loans and protect depositors' money. Temple was acted important role in this specific area and provided a base for its. Modern bank is a developed form of ancient banking system specially related to temples.

Notes and References

1. B.K. Pandeya argues that the medieval South Indian temples functioned as money-lenders, but not as a bank- "Temple Economy Under the Cholas" (Thesis), pp.177-211
2. Epigraphia Carnatica, IX, Cp.129; Hyderabad Archaeological Series, no.18, Ins. no.1
3. Epigraphia Carnatica, V, BI.83
4. Annual Report of Mysore Archaeological Department, 1942, Ins.no.23; Epigraphia Carnatica, V, Arsikere, 174; Epigraphia Carnatica, XIV, Tn.225.
5. Annual Report of Mysore Archaeological Department, 1937, no.30
6. Epigraphia Carnatica, IX, Cp. 129.
7. Hyderabad Archaeological Series, no.18, Ins. no.1.
8. Epigraphia Carnatica, VII, Sk.164 and 165.
9. Annual Report of Mysore Archaeological Department, 1937, no.30; Epigraphia Carnatica, VII, Sk, 87.
10. Epigraphia Carnatica, XIV, In.270
11. Epigraphia Carnatica, VII, Sk. 164 and 165; Epigraphia Carnatica, XIV, Tn.225
12. K. Ismail, Karnataka Temple, Their Role in Socio- Economic Life, pp 103-104
13. South Indian Inscription, II, 94, 95
14. South Indian Inscription, XIX, 163
15. South Indian Inscription, XIX, 67
16. South Indian Inscription, VIII, 331; South Indian Inscription, XII, 103
17. South Indian Inscription, XII, 42; South Indian Inscription, XIV, 10
18. South Indian Inscription, XIV, 18, 46, 60
19. K. Ismail, op.cit. p.105
20. Epigraphia Carnatica, IX, Cp.129
21. K. Ismail, op. cit. pp. 105-106
22. Pran Nath, A Study in the Economic Conditions of Ancient India, Banaras, pp.93
23. South Indian Inscription, XII, 99
24. South Indian Inscription, III, 94
25. South Indian Inscription, XII, 87, 88, 90, 91, 100, 103; South Indian Inscription, III, 96, III, VII, 525.
26. South Indian Inscription, XIX, 161.
27. Annual Report on Indian Epigraphy, 14/1930-31; 162/1937-38; South Indian Inscription, VIII, 308; South Indian Inscription, VII, 503; South Indian Inscription, XIV, 12a, 12b, 20.
28. D. Dayalan, op. cit. p.152.
29. Epigraphia Carnatica, XX, 3a, 3b, South Indian Inscription, III, 48, 44.
30. South Indian Inscription, VII, 421.
31. South Indian Inscription, V, 624, South Indian Inscription, XII, 61.

Plate 28.1 : Tritîrthî – showing Sarasvatî with two Jinas, Jaina Dharmashala Museum, Deogarh (Lalitpur, U.P.), 11th century CE.

Plate 28.2 : Six-armed Sarasvatî, southern adhiṣṭāna rathikā, Pārśvanātha temple, Khajurāho (Chhatarpur, M.P.), c. 950-70 CE.

Plate 28.3 : Sarasvatî, Pañcakūṭa Bastî, (Shimoga, Karnataka), 11th century CE.

Plate 28.4 : Sarasvatî joined by dancing divine figures, corridor ceilings, Vimala-Vasahî (Sirohi, Rajasthan), c. 1150 CE.

Plate 28.5 : Sarasvatî, Pallū (Bikaner, Rajasthan), now in National Museum, New Delhi, c. 11th century CE.

Plate 31.1 : View of Temple from North-eastern side

Plate 31.2 : View of Temple from Northern side

Plate 31.3 : View of the Temple from Southern side

Plate : 32.1 : Patna - Yaksha - Mauryan Period

Plate : 32.2 : Besnagar - Yakshi (2nd century BC)

Plate : 32.3 : Parkham - Yaksha - Post Mauryan

Plate : 32.4 : Atlantes - Yaksha - Sanchi

Plate : 32.5 : Bowl Suporting Yaksha - Pitalkhora (2nd century BC)

Plate : 32.6 : Moggarapani Yaksha - Satavahana period

Plate : 32.7 : Kuber - Ahichhatra Kushan (2nd century AD)

Plate : 32.8 : Yakshi - Sanchi (1st century BC)

Plate 33.1 : Udaygiri Hill, Vidisha

Plate 33.2 : Shehshayi Vishnu, Cave No. 13, Udaygiri Hills, Vidisha

Plate 33.3 : Mutilated figure of Brahma seated on lotus,
Cave No. 13, Udaygiri Hills, Vidisha

Plate 33.4 : Nrivaraha, Cave No. 5, Udaygiri Hills , Vidisha

Plate 34.1 : Monolithic Pillar, Mauryan Period.

Plate 34.2 : Lion Capital, Mauryan Period.

Plae 34.3 : Yakshi, Sunga Period.

Plate 34.4 : Kuber, Kushan Period.

Plate 34.5 : Head of Bodhisattva, Kushan Period.

Plate 34.6 : Buddha, Kushan Period.

Plae 34.7 : Surya, Gupta Period.

Plate 34.8 : Rishabhnath, Gupta Period.

Plate 34.9 : Jaina Pillar with images of Teerthanakas, Gupta Period.

Plate 34.10 : Jaina Pillar with images of Teerthanakas, Gupta Period.

Plae 34.11 : Buddha in declining posture, Gupta Period.

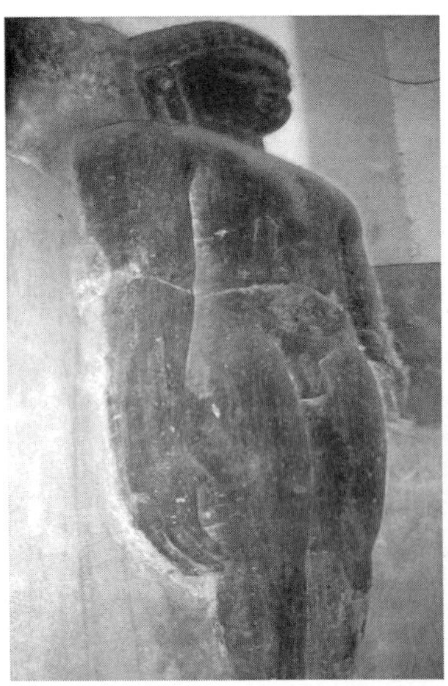

Plate 34.12 : Image of Teerthankar,

Plate 34.13 : Ekmukhlinga,

Plate 34.14 : Navagrah Panel, Early Medieval Period.

Plate 34.15 : Uma-Maheshwar, Early Medieval Period.

Plate 34.16 “ Mahishamardini, Early Medieval Period.

Plae 34.17 : Jeevant Swami, Early Medieval Period.

Plate 34.18 : Agni, Early Medieval Period.

Plate 34.19 : Neminath, Early Medieval Period.

Plate 34.20 : Vishnu, Pala Period.

Plate 34.21 : Agni, Early Medieval Period.

Plate 34.22 : Buddha, Early Medieval Period.

Plate 34.23 : Head of Bodhisattva, Early Medieval Period

Plate 35.1: Horse on the abacus of Sarnath Lion Capital

Plate 35.2 : Lady of Auxerre in Daedalic style

Plate 35.3 : Tanagra Terracotta figures, about 250 B.C.

Plate 35.4 : Dancing girl, Patna Museum, Mauryan Period

Plate 35.5: Open mouth of the lion in West Asian art

Plate 35.6: Open mouth of the lion in Mauryan art

Plate 35.7: So-called shrine of the Double headed Eagle at Sirkap.

फलक 36.1 : धूप में नमी को सुखाने के लिए रखा कच्चा माल

फलक 36.2 : प्रथम हीटिंग का दृश्य

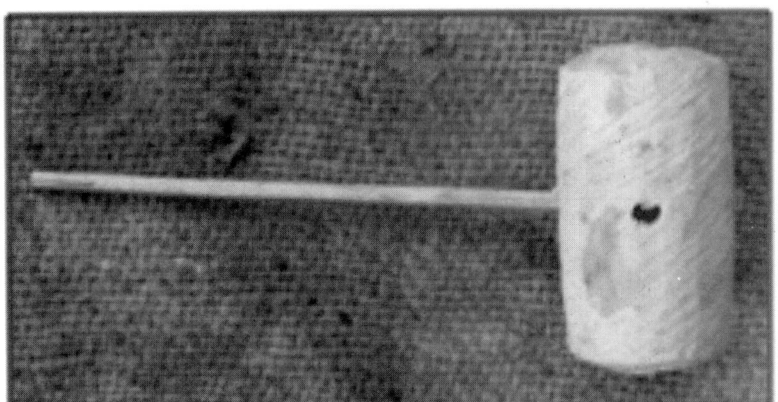

फलक 36.3 : प्रथम चिपिंग के लिए प्रयोग किया जाने वाला लकड़ी का हथौड़ा

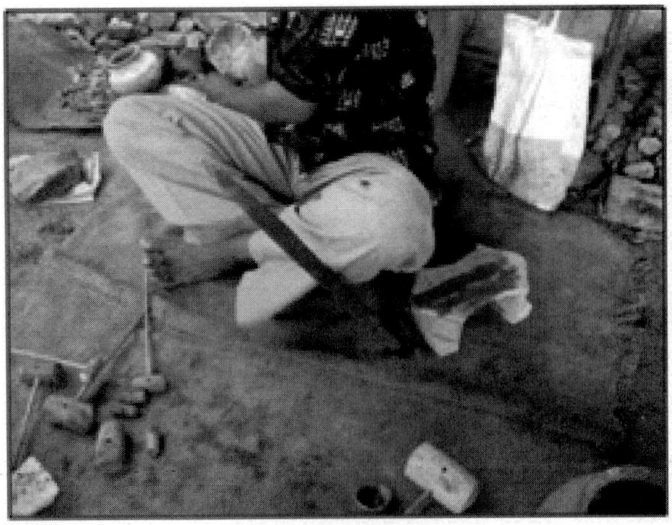

फलक 36.4 : प्रथम चिपिंग के लिए लोहे की पतली नोंक वाली छड़

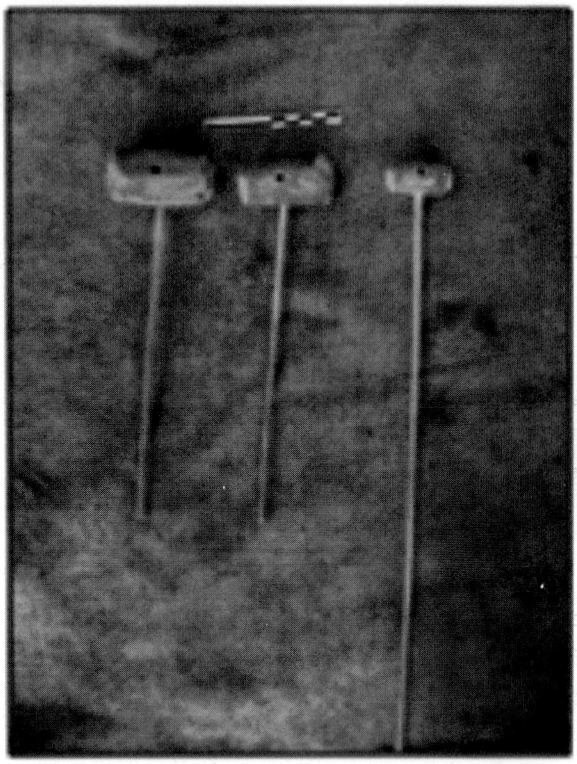

फलक 36.5 : प्रथम एवं द्वितीय चिपिंग के लिए प्रयोग किये जाने वाले भैंस के सींग से बने हथौड़े

फलक 36.6 : मनकों की प्रथम चिपिंग

फलक 36.7 : मनकों में द्वितीय चिपिंग

फलक 36.8 : मनकों की घिसाई एवं पॉलिश के लिए प्रयुक्त एमरी व्हील्स

फलक 36.9 : मनकों की घिसाई

फलक 36.10 : मनकों की एमरी व्हील द्वारा पॉलिश

फलक 36.11 : छिद्र के लिए प्रयोग किये जाने वाले औजार

फलक 36.12 : मनकों में छिद्र प्रक्रिया

फलक 36.13 : मनकों को गर्म करने के लिए तैयार की गई भट्टी

फलक 36.14 : लकड़ी के बुरादे से भरी गई भट्टी

फलक 36.15 : भट्टी में आग का दृश्य

फलक 36.16 : अगले दिन सुबह भट्टी का दृश्य

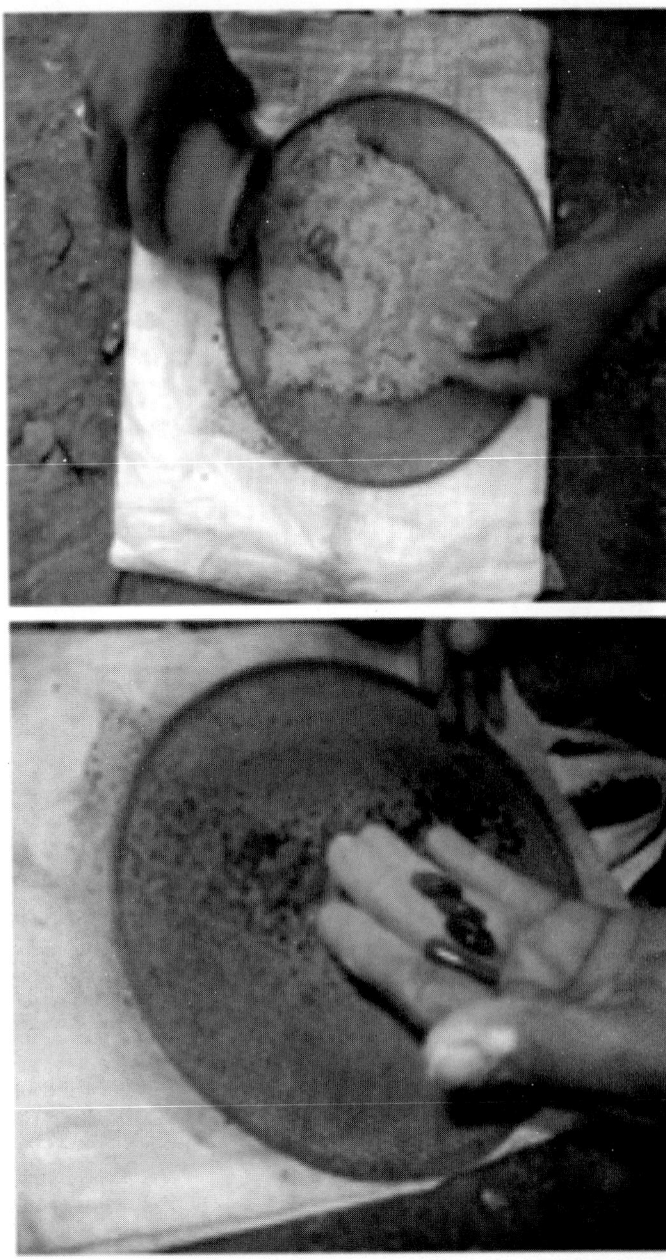

फलक 36.17 : भट्टी में परिवर्तित हुए कार्नेलियन के मनकों का चित्र

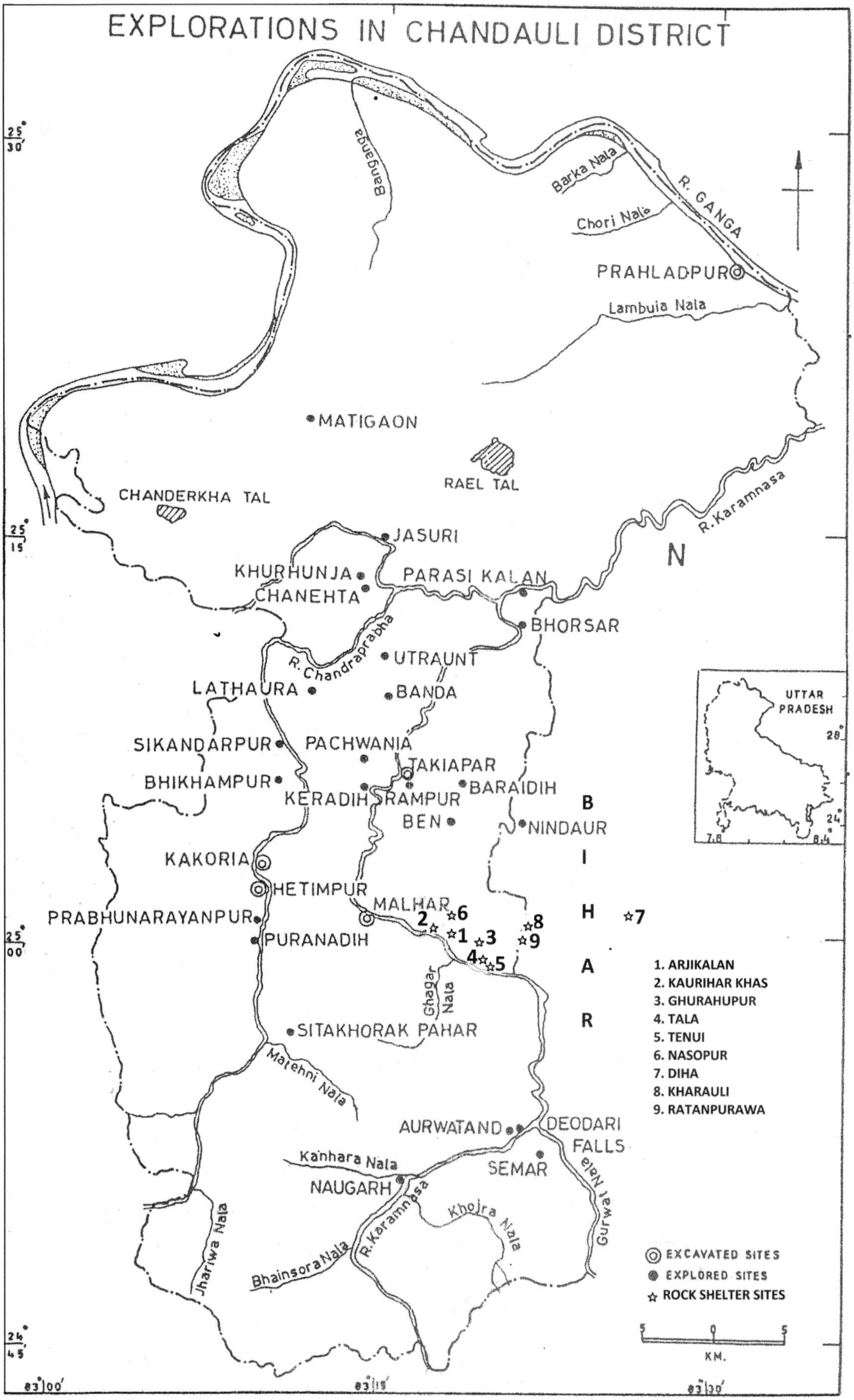

Plate 37.1 : Map of the area under the discussion

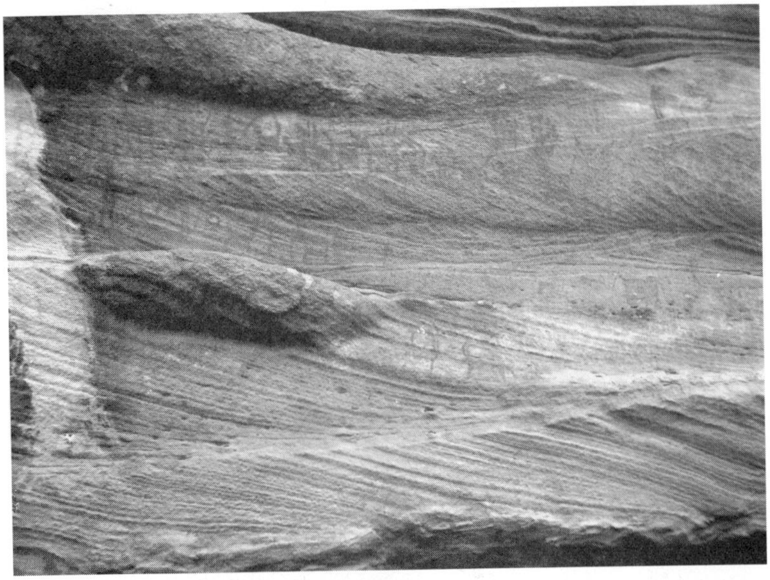

Plate 37.2 : Rock Shalter Kaurihar Khas

Plate 37.3 : Hunter,Animale and Loade Carrier,Ghurahupur

Plate 37.4 : Humped Bull,Ghurahupur

Plate 37.5 : Depications of Budha ,Stupa and female Dancer, Ghurahupur

Plate 37.6 : Painting Belongs to Deference Period,Tanui

Plate 37.7 : A bull shown with roap around in its neck Kharauli

Plate 37.8 : Mesolithic Rock Paintings,Ratanpurawa

फलक 38.1 : त्रिभंग शांतिदेवी, जैन बावनढेरी, चाम्पानेर–पावागढ़, गुजरात

फलक 38.2 : आसनस्थ सरस्वती, जैन बावन ढेरी, चाम्पानेर–पावागढ़, गुजरात

फलक 38.3 : त्रिभंग इन्द्राणी, जैन बावन ढेरी, चाम्पानेर – पावागढ़, गुजरात

Plate 39.1 : Earliest evidence of excavated bronze object from Chechar.
(Photograph courtesy ASI, Patna Circle)

Plate 39.2 : Polychrome Pictographs of human executed on the wall of the shelter very much similar to the bronze image, Chand Block of Kaimur district, Bihar

Plate 39.3 : Pictographs of human holding hammer or stick like object on left hand and rope or symbolic form of an un-iconic form holding on right hand executed on the wall of the cave also very much similar to the bronze image, Chand Block of Kaimur district, Bihar

Plate 45.1 : Rāndala Mātā with Chāyā, a photograph commoly seen during worship in households in the Saurāṣṭra Region

Plate 45.2 : Mānat at Ravi Rāndala Mātā Temple, Daḷavā (Bhavnagar) : For the ailments of the bodyparts devotees offer either small wooden replicas of the whole body or the part(s) which is/are affected; displayed on the left side here are the wooden replicas at a shop for sale. On the right side are the photographs of the new born children being put up after their mānat of childbirth is fullled.

Plate 45.3 : Diaspora of Ravi Rāndala Mātā : Rituals being performed by Non Resident Gujaraties outside a Hindu Temple at Leister in England.

Plate 45.4 : A scene of the celebrations during the inauguration of the International Kite Festival, Ahmedabad.

Plate 45.5 : A large number of domestic as well as foreign kite enthusiasts flying their kites at a venue during the International Kite Festival at Ahmedabad.